THE ROUGH GUIDE TO

Morocco

written and researched by

Hamish Brown, Keith Drew, Mark Ellingham, Daniel Jacobs and Shaun N

with additiona

Thomas Hollo

ROUGH
GUIDES

roughguides.com

Contents

OPPOSITE AÏT BENHADDOU **PREVIOUS PAGE** ROYAL PALACE, RABAT

Introduction to

Morocco

For Westerners, Morocco holds an immediate and enduring fascination. Though just an hour's ride on the ferry from Spain, it seems at once very far from Europe, with a culture – Islamic and deeply traditional – that is almost wholly unfamiliar. Throughout the country, despite the years of French and Spanish colonial rule and the presence of modern and cosmopolitan cities like Rabat and Casablanca, a more distant past constantly makes its presence felt. Fez, perhaps the most beautiful of all Arab cities, maintains a life still rooted in medieval times, when a Moroccan kingdom stretched from Senegal to northern Spain, while in the mountains of the Atlas and the Rif, it's still possible to draw up tribal maps of the Berber population. As a backdrop to all this, the country's physical make-up is extraordinary: from the Mediterranean coast, through four mountain ranges, to the empty sand and scrub of the Sahara.

Across much of the country, the legacy of **colonial occupation** is still felt in many aspects of daily life. The **Spanish zone** contained Tetouan and the Rif, the Mediterranean and the northern Atlantic coasts, Sidi Ifni, the Tarfaya Strip and the Western Sahara; the **French zone** the plains and the main cities (Fez, Marrakesh, Casablanca and Rabat), as well as the Atlas. And while Ceuta and Melilla are still the territory of Spain, it is the French – who ruled their "protectorate" more closely – who had the most lasting effect on Moroccan culture, Europeanizing the cities to a strong degree and firmly imposing their language, which is spoken today by all educated Moroccans (after Moroccan Arabic or one of the three local Berber languages).

This blend of the exotic and the familiar, the diversity of landscapes, the contrasts between Ville Nouvelle and ancient Medina, all add up to make Morocco an intense and rewarding experience, and a country that is ideally suited to independent travel – with enough time, you can cover a whole range of **activities**, from hiking in the Atlas and relaxing at laidback

ABOVE SPICE MARKET, MARRAKESH

Atlantic resorts like Asilah or Essaouira to getting lost in the back alleys of Fez and Marrakesh. It can be hard at times to come to terms with the privilege of your position as a tourist in a country with severe poverty, and there is, too, occasional hassle from unofficial guides, but Morocco is essentially a **safe** and **politically stable** place to visit: the death in 1999 of King Hassan II, the Arab world's longest-serving leader, was followed by an easy transition to his son, Mohammed VI, and the country pretty much carried on as normal while the Arab Spring uprisings toppled governments in nearby Libya, Tunisia and Egypt. Indeed, your enduring impressions are likely to be overwhelmingly positive, shaped by encounters with Morocco's powerful tradition of hospitality, generosity and openness. This is a country people return to again and again.

Where to go

Geographically, the country divides into four basic zones: the coast (Mediterranean and Atlantic); the great cities of the plains; the Rif and Atlas mountains; and the oases and desert of the pre- and fully fledged Sahara. With two or three weeks – even two or three months – you can't expect to cover all of this, though it's easy enough (and highly recommended) to take in something of each aspect.

Broadly speaking, **the coast** is best enjoyed in the north at **Tangier** – still shaped by its old "international" port status despite undergoing considerable recent renovation – **Asilah** and **Larache**, and in the south at **El Jadida**, **Essaouira**, perhaps the most easy-going resort, or remote **Sidi Ifni**. **Agadir**, the main package-tour resort, is less worthwhile – but a functional enough base for exploration.

Inland, where the real interest of Morocco lies, the outstanding cities are **Fez** and **Marrakesh**. The great imperial capitals of the country's various dynasties, they are almost unique in the

FACT FILE

• Morocco's **area** of 446,550 square kilometres (722,550 sq km including the Western Sahara) makes it slightly smaller than France or Spain, slightly larger than California. The population of just over 32 million compares with just eight million at independence in 1956.

• Nearly 99 percent of Moroccans are **Muslim**, with 1 percent **Christian** and a tiny minority (an estimated 6000 people) **Jewish**. The literacy rate is 56.1 percent (68.9 percent for men, 43.9 percent for women).

• The **main languages** are Arabic, Berber (Tarfit, Tamazight and Tashelhaït) and French. English is increasingly spoken by young people, especially in tourist areas.

• Morocco gained **independence** from French and Spanish rule on March 2, 1956. The head of state is **King Mohammed VI**, who succeeded his father Hassan II on July 30, 1999. The government is chosen from an **elected legislature** and is currently run by Prime Minister Abdelilah Benkirane of the moderate Islamist PJD (Party of Justice and Development). The main opposition parties are the Istiqlal (Independence) Party, Morocco's oldest political group, and the RNI (National Rally of Independents).

• Such is the importance of **date palms** in the Moroccan south that oases are traditionally measured by the number of their palms rather than their population, and it was once illegal to sell a date tree, a historically vital source of food.

• Despite the beauty of **zellij** work in *medersas* and fountains across the country, it is thought that there is at least one flaw in every mosaic due to the Islamic belief that only Allah can create perfection.

Canary Islands (Sp.)

ATLANTIC
OCEAN

Tarfaya

Laayoune

Boujdour

Boukra
Smara

Dakhla

Bir Mogrein

S A H A R A

Goulimine

Tan Tan

Border
Closed

Tindouf

MAURITANIA

Nouadibhou

Choum

0   200
kilometres

ATLANTIC

OCEAN

Salé

RABAT

Mohammedia

Casablanca

Azemmour

El Jadida

Berrechid

Settat

Khouribga

Oued
Zem

Oualidia

Safi

Benguerir

Beni Mellal

Kas
Tac

Azilal

Essaouira

Chichaoua

Marrakesh

Demnate

Jebel M'Goun
(4071m)

Oued Tensift

Boumal
du Dad

JEB
N'K

Asni

Jebel
Toubkal
(4167m)

Tizi n'Tichka
(2260m)

Ouarzazate

Oued Dadès

Tin Mal

HIGH

A T L A S

Tizi n'Test
(2092m)

Taroudant

Jebel Sirwa
(3304m)

Tazenakht

Agdz

Agadir

Oued Souss

Taliouine

Zag

Inezgane

Foum Zguid

Tiznit

Tafraoute

Tata

Akka

ALGERIA
(BORDERS
CLOSED)

Sidi
Ifni

A N T I

Bou Izakarn

Foum
el Hassan

Goulimine

Tan Tan & Laayoune   SEE INSET FOR CONTINUATION

Tindouf

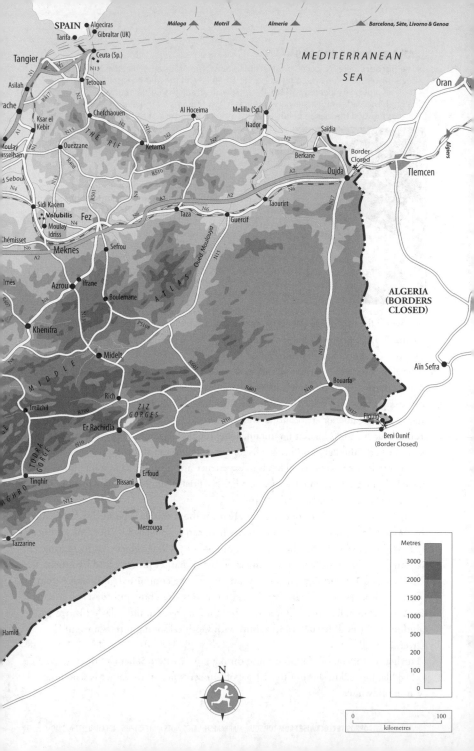

ARABS AND BERBERS

The **Berbers** were Morocco's original inhabitants. The Arabs arrived at the end of the seventh century, after sweeping across North Africa and the Middle East in the name of their revolutionary ideology, **Islam**. Eventually, nearly all the Berbers converted to the new religion and were immediately accepted as fellow Muslims by the Arabs. When Muslim armies invaded the Iberian peninsula from Morocco, the bulk of the troops were Berbers,

and the two ethnic groups pretty much assimilated. Today, most Moroccans can claim both Arab and Berber ancestors, though a few (especially Shereefs, who trace their ancestry back to the Prophet Mohammed, and have the title "Moulay") claim to be "pure" Arabs. In the Rif and Atlas mountains, and in the Souss Valley, though, groups of pure Berbers remain, and retain their **ancient languages** (Tarfit, spoken by about 1.5m people in the Rif; Tamazight, spoken by over 3m people in the Atlas; and Tashelhaït, spoken by around 4m people in the Souss Valley region). Recently, there has been a resurgence in Berber pride (often symbolized by the Berber letter Ж); TV programmes are now broadcast in Berber languages, and they are even taught in schools, but the country's majority language remains Arabic.

Arab world for the chance they offer to witness city life that, in patterns and appearance, remains in large part medieval. For monuments, Fez is the highlight, though Marrakesh is for most visitors the more enjoyable.

Travel in the **south** is, on the whole, easier and more relaxing than in the sometimes frenetic north. This is certainly true of the **mountain ranges**, where the **Rif** can feel disturbingly anarchic, while the southerly **Atlas ranges** (Middle, High and Anti) that cut right across the interior are beautiful and accessible. Hiking in the **High Atlas**, especially around North Africa's highest mountain, **Jebel Toubkal**, is increasingly popular, following old mule paths through mud-brick villages or tackling some of the impressive peaks. Summer treks are possible at all levels of experience and altitude, and despite inroads made by commercialization, the area remains essentially "undiscovered" – like the Alps must have been in the nineteenth century.

Equally exploratory in mood are the great **southern routes** beyond the Atlas, amid the **oases** of the pre-Sahara. Major routes here can be travelled by bus, minor ones by rented car or local taxi, the really remote ones by 4WD vehicles or by getting lifts on local *camions* (lorries), sharing space with market produce and livestock. The oases, around **Tinghir**, **Zagora** and **Erfoud**, or (for the committed) **Tata** and **Figuig**, are classic images of the Arab world, vast palmeries stretching into desert horizons. Equally memorable is the architecture that they share with the Atlas – bizarre and fabulous *pisé* (mud) **kasbahs** and **ksour**, with Gothic-looking turrets and multi-patterned walls.

Further south, you can follow a route through the **Western Sahara** all the way down to Dakhla, just 22km short of the Tropic of Cancer, where the weather is scorching even in midwinter.

OPPOSITE CLOCKWISE FROM TOP SOUK, MARRAKESH; DATES, NUTS AND PASTRIES; SIDI AHMED TIJANI MOSQUE, FEZ

AVERAGE MONTHLY TEMPERATURES AND RAINFALL

	Jan	Feb	Mar	Apr	May	Jun	Jul	Aug	Sep	Oct	Nov	Dec
TANGIER												
Min/max °C	16/7	16/7	18/9	19/11	22/12	26/12	28/18	28/18	26/17	23/14	18/11	16/8
Rain (mm)	103	98	71	62	37	16	2	2	14	65	134	129
FEZ												
Min/max °C	15/4	16/5	18/6	20/8	25/10	28/13	34/17	34/17	30/15	25/11	19/8	16/5
Rain (mm)	72	100	93	87	53	24	3	3	17	62	89	85
MARRAKESH												
Min/max °C	18/4	20/6	23/9	26/11	29/14	33/17	38/19	38/20	33/17	28/14	23/9	19/6
Rain (mm)	25	28	33	31	15	8	3	3	10	23	31	31
LAAYOUNE												
Min/max °C	22/10	23/11	24/12	24/14	26/15	27/17	29/18	30/19	29/18	28/17	25/16	21/10
Rain (mm)	3	2	1	1	0	1	0	0	0	4	7	8

When to go

As far as the **climate** goes, it is better to visit the south – or at least the desert routes – outside midsummer, when for most of the day it's far too hot for casual exploration, especially if you're dependent on public transport. July and August, the hottest months, can be wonderful on the coast, however, while in the mountains there are no set rules.

Spring, which comes late by European standards (around April and May), is perhaps the best overall time, with a summer climate in the south and in the mountains, as well as on the Mediterranean and Atlantic coasts. **Winter** can be perfect by day in the south, though desert nights can get very cold – a major consideration if you're staying in the cheaper hotels, which rarely have heating. If you're planning to **hike in the mountains**, it's best to keep to the months from April to October unless you have some experience of snow conditions.

Weather apart, the **Islamic religious calendar** and its related festivals will have the most seasonal effect on your travel. The most important factor is **Ramadan**, the month of daytime fasting (see p.43); this can be a problem for transport, and especially hiking, though the festive evenings do much to compensate.

Author picks

Our authors have haggled in the souks and camped in the desert, clocked up the kilometres aboard buses and on the back of mules, and generally consumed more mint tea than can possibly be good for them. Here are a few of their favourite things…

Muezzin music One of the most evocative sounds in Morocco, the call to prayer (p.548) is sure to send a tingle down your spine, whether it's sweeping across the rooftops of an imperial city or echoing through a mountain village.

Literary break There's still a hint of Tangier's hipster heyday at the cafés around the Petit Socco, an atmospherically seedy spot once frequented by Burroughs and the Beats (p.76).

A night in Moulay Idriss It's been less than a decade since non-Muslims were first allowed to stay over in the holy town of Moulay Idriss (p.216), and the web of quiet alleyways that shield the mausoleum of Morocco's founder appear unchanged in centuries.

Pastilla Originally made from pigeon but now more often chicken, this crispy filo-pastry pie (p.40) is an unusual combination of savoury and sweet – but boy does it taste good.

Fish supper Tuck into fish fresh off the boat at the busy grills that line Essaouira's port. (p.306).

Middle Earth in the Middle Atlas The charming little town of Bhalil (p.220) is bypassed by most visitors, yet it is one of the most interesting places in the Middle Atlas, its hillsides pocked with cave houses where you can share mint tea and *msammen* pancakes with the Berber families that still call them home.

> Our author recommendations don't end here. We've flagged up our favourite places – a perfectly sited hotel, an atmospheric café, a special restaurant – throughout the guide, highlighted with the ★ symbol.

FROM TOP: KOUTOUBIA, MARRAKESH; PASTILLA; MOULAY IDRISS

things not to miss

It's not possible to see everything that Morocco has to offer in one trip – and we don't suggest you try. What follows is a selective and subjective taste of the country's highlights, in no particular order: fascinating cities, Roman ruins, mountain hikes and stunning buildings. All entries have a page reference to take you straight into the Guide, where you can find out more. Coloured numbers refer to chapters in the Guide section.

1

1 CHEFCHAOUEN
Page 115

Simply the most beautiful small town in Morocco, its blue-washed walls enclosed by mountains.

2 FEZ
Page 162

The most complete medieval city in the Arab world, Fez's labyrinthine streets conceal ancient souks and iconic monuments, none more so than the exquisitely decorated Medersa Bou Inania

3 CAMEL TREKKING
Pages 404, 409 & 439

Venture into the Sahara on an overnight camel trek from Zagora, M'Hamid or Merzouga.

4 ATLAS PASSES
Pages 384 & 393

The nerve-shredding Tizi n'Test and the higher Tizi n'Tichka wend up over the Atlas mountains, providing breathtaking views along the way.

5 CASCADES D'OUZOUD
Page 236
The most dramatic of the country's waterfalls, with overhanging cafés, and inviting pools to plunge into.

6 KOUTOUBIA MOSQUE
Page 320
The symbol of Marrakesh, the Koutoubia's twelfth-century minaret is visible for miles around the city.

7 TIN MAL MOSQUE
Page 382
This great Almohad building stands isolated in an Atlas river valley.

8 CRAFTS
Page 50
From carpets and carpentry to leatherwork and ceramics, Morocco's craft tradition is extraordinarily vibrant, and on magnificent show in its souks.

9 TEA
Page 41
"Whisky Marocain" (mint tea) is the accompaniment to any discussion or transaction.

10 BAB OUDAÏA, RABAT
Page 257
The most beautiful gate of the medieval Moorish world.

11

12

13

14

15

HOTEL DE VILLE

16

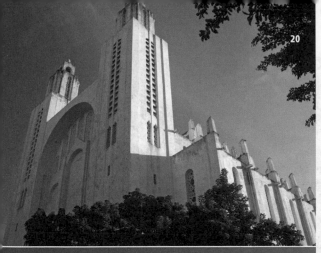

20

17 ESSAOUIRA
Relax by the Atlantic at Morocco's most popular resort, home to a growing windsurfing scene.

18 VOLUBILIS
Volubilis was the chief city of Roman Morocco and is today a beautiful, extensive ruin.

19 TANGIER
The old "International Port", sometime home of Bowles and Burroughs, has a seedy charm of its own.

20 CASABLANCA
Casa's colonial architecture blends traditional Moroccan designs with French Art Deco into a distinctive style known as Mauresque.

21 SKIING AT OUKAÏMEDEN
Not many skiers can list North Africa – but Ouka is a reliable, low-key resort.

22 ROUTE OF A THOUSAND KASBAHS
Morocco's southern oases are dotted with crumbling kasbahs and mud-built villages.

21

22

26

27

Itineraries

The following itineraries will take you right across Morocco, from the Medinas of Marrakesh and Fez to longer trips into the mountains and the desert beyond. With bustling souks and showpiece squares, crumbling kasbahs and dizzy gorges, there is something for everyone, whether you're on an exotic weekend city break, stringing together a hit-list of the country's must-see sights, or looking to get away from it all on the back of a camel.

A SHORT BREAK IN MARRAKESH

DAY ONE

Jemaa el Fna Head straight for the city's famous central square, a feast of visual entertainment. **See p.318**

Dinner Hidden behind clouds of cooking smoke, the Jemaa's food stalls serve up couscous, fried fish and plenty more besides. **See p.345**

DAY TWO

Medersa Ben Youssef A textbook study in zellij, stucco and carved cedarwood. **See p.325**

Souks Shop for rugs and carpets in La Criée Berbère (see p.323), or watch the dyers at work in Souk des Teinturiers (see p.324). **See p.329**

El Badi Palace It may now lay in ruins but this once opulent palace is still a magnificent sight. **See p.329**

Majorelle Garden Head to the Ville Nouvelle for Yves Saint-Laurent's tranquil gardens. **See p.336**

Dinner Book ahead for fine Marrakshi dining at *Le Tobsil*, an intimate palace restaurant on a smaller scale than most. **See p.349**

A SHORT BREAK IN FEZ

DAY ONE

Medersa Bou Inania Arguably the finest building in Morocco, and a dazzling testament to the craftsmen of medieval Fez. **See p.170**

Talâa Kebira Journey through the Medina past *fondouks* and mosques and souks specializing in everything from brass to henna. **See p.172**

Dinner Sample the famous camel burger at hip little *Café Clock*. **See p.191**

DAY TWO

Nejjarine and Seffarine Take in the sights (and smells) of Place en Nejjarine, the carpenter's souk (see p.173), before a spot of people-watching on Place Seffarine (see p.176).

Tanneries A surreal scene: men standing knee-deep in vats of coloured dyes, soaking leather skins red, yellow, blue and black. **See p.178**

Fez el Jedid Home to the synagogues, cemeteries and overhanging houses that make up Morocco's original Jewish district. **See p.180**

Dinner Tuck into pastilla, Fez's signature dish of pigeon pie, amid the palatial surroundings of *Restaurant al Firdaous*. **See p.192**

ABOVE THE ERG CHEBBI DUNES

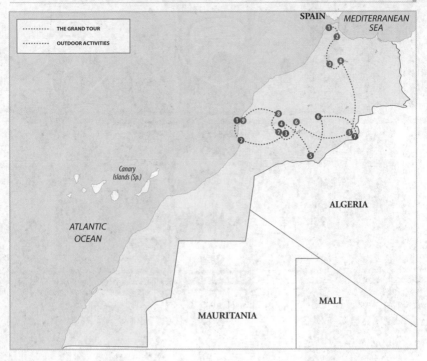

THE GRAND TOUR

❶ **Tangier** Take a breather in one of the Petit Socco's historic cafés. **See p.71**

❷ **Chefchaouen** Laidback and picturesque antidote to Tangier's bustle. **See p.115**

❸ **Meknes** Wander Moulay Ismail's monumental Ville Impériale before exploring the Roman ruins at nearby Volubilis. **See p.197**

❹ **Fez** Getting lost somewhere amid the souks and tanneries of Fez el Bali is a quintessential Moroccan experience. **See p.162**

❺ **Merzouga** The Erg Chebbi dunes make a memorable first sight of the Sahara. **See p.439**

❻ **Aït Benhaddou** There are kasbahs and then there is Aït Benhaddou. **See p.395**

❼ **The High Atlas** The best trekking in the country, along ancient mule tracks and through forgotten Berber villages. **See p.358**

❽ **Marrakesh** Barter for *babouches* and catch the 24hr theatre of the Jemaa el Fna. **See p.312**

❾ **Essaouira** A fish supper is the perfect way to end the day in this artsy coastal town. **See p.298**

OUTDOOR ACTIVITIES

❶ **Kitesurfing in Essaouira** Simply the best place in the country to try your hand at kitesurfing. **See p.298**

❷ **Surfing near Taghazout** Ride Killers, Anchor Point and other challenging breaks at this relaxed surfers' hangout. **See p.466**

❸ **Hiking in the High Atlas** A wealth of scenic routes cut across the Toubkal Massif. **See p.364**

❹ **Skiing at Oukaïmeden** Hitting the slopes at Oukaïmeden is worth it for the novelty value alone. **See p.363**

❺ **Camel trekking in the Erg Chigaga** M'Hamid is the jumping-off point for camel trips into this remote section of the Sahara. **See p.409**

❻ **Climbing in the Todra Gorge** You could spend days scaling the rocky walls of this dramatic mountain gorge. **See p.428**

❼ **Sandboarding in the Erg Chebbi** A surreal contrast to Oukmaïmeden, though carving down the Grand Dune de Merzouga is just as memorable. **See p.439**

BABOUCHES

Basics

Getting there

The simplest way to get to Morocco is, of course, to fly. Alternatively, you could fly to France, Spain or Gibraltar and pick up a ferry there; or, from Britain or Ireland, you could go all the way by land and sea.

Fares usually depend on **season**, the highest being at Christmas and the New Year, and at the peak of summer in July and August, when seats can also be scarce. Flying at weekends may cost more than flying midweek.

You can often cut costs by going through an **online or discount flight agent**. The cheapest tickets will be subject to restrictions such as fixed dates, and some may require advance purchase.

Charter flights are sometimes cheaper than scheduled flights, but departure dates are fixed and withdrawal penalties are high, and it may end up costing less to pick up a **package deal** including accommodation.

Be aware that, on an indirect flight, tight connections make baggage loss more likely, and if your **baggage goes astray** in transit, you cannot have it delivered to your hotel in Morocco, but will have to go back to the airport to pick it up in person when it does arrive.

Flights from the UK and Ireland

Royal Air Maroc (RAM; ⓦ royalairmaroc.com) run **direct scheduled flights** daily from London Heathrow to Casablanca, and twice-weekly flights to Tangier, and British Airways (ⓦ britishairways.com) fly from Heathrow to Casablanca, Marrakesh and Agadir. From Dublin, Aer Lingus (ⓦ aerlingus.com) fly once a week to Agadir, in winter only. In addition to these, there are no-frills flights to Marrakesh with EasyJet (ⓦ easyjet.com) from Gatwick and Manchester, and with Ryanair (ⓦ ryanair.com) from Luton and Stansted. EasyJet also fly from Gatwick to Agadir, Ryanair from Stansted to Fez, and ThomsonFly (ⓦ thomsonfly.com) serve Marrakesh and Agadir from Gatwick and Manchester. Flights typically take around three and a half hours.

In addition to these, there are **charter flights** run by tour operators such as First Choice

(ⓦ firstchoice.co.uk) from Britain or Sunway (ⓦ sunway.ie) from Ireland. Flights are usually from Gatwick, Manchester or Dublin, but occasionally other British and Irish airports, to Agadir and sometimes Marrakesh, although they do not necessarily fly all year and are not especially cheaper than scheduled services; they may also limit you to a two-week stay.

Otherwise, you can get an **indirect flight** to Morocco from most British or Irish airports via London or a European city such as Paris or Amsterdam. From Casablanca, it's possible to take a connecting flight to most other Moroccan airports. The Spanish enclave of Melilla is served by Iberia (ⓦ iberia.com) via Madrid.

A return flight from London to Casablanca with RAM will **cost** £180–260, depending on the specific flights you choose, and how early you book. Fares on flights with the no-frills airlines depend on demand, and can vary from as little as £60 up to £350 for the round trip (the earlier you book, the lower the price will be). A charter flight from Ireland will cost around €200–450 return, while an indirect scheduled flight will set you back €360–800 depending on the time of year and the popularity of the flight (scheduled flights to Marrakesh cost more than to Casablanca).

It is also possible, and often a lot cheaper, to take a **flight to Málaga or Gibraltar**, where you can either get a ferry directly across the Straits, or take a bus to Algeciras for more frequent ferries from there (see p.28). Airlines such as EasyJet and Ryanair run low-cost flights to Málaga from several British and Irish airports. From Gibraltar you'd have to walk across the border to La Linea for the bus. From Málaga airport, there are a two daily direct buses to Algeciras, or else you can change at Marbella (see ⓦ venta.avanzabus.com for details).

Flights from the US and Canada

Royal Air Maroc (RAM; ⓦ royalairmaroc.com) run nonstop flights to Casablanca from New York and Montreal (flight time 7hr 30min). The alternative is to take an **indirect flight** with a European carrier, changing planes at their European hub. Those serving Casablanca include Air France (ⓦ airfrance .com), Alitalia (ⓦ alitalia.com) and Lufthansa

---

ROUGH GUIDES ONLINE

Find everything you need to plan your next trip at ⓦ roughguides.com. Read in-depth information on destinations worldwide, make use of our unique trip-planner, book transport and accommodation, check out other travellers' recommendations and share your own experiences.

A BETTER KIND OF TRAVEL

At Rough Guides we are passionately committed to travel. We believe it helps us understand the world we live in and the people we share it with – and of course tourism is vital to many developing economies. But the scale of modern tourism has also damaged some places irreparably, and climate change is accelerated by most forms of transport, especially flying. All Rough Guides'flights are carbon-offset, and every year we donate money to a variety of environmental charities.

(Ⓦlufthansa.com), while Iberia (Ⓦiberia.com) fly to Casablanca, Marrakesh, Rabat, Tangier and the Spanish enclave of Melilla. If you're flying from elsewhere in North America, you can take a connecting flight to New York or Montreal and continue from there on RAM (Delta codeshare the New York flight, so they should be able to sell you a through ticket without much trouble), or buy a through ticket via Europe with a European airline, or with a North American airline such as Air Canada (Ⓦaircanada.com), American (Ⓦaa.com), Continental (Ⓦcontinental.com), Delta (Ⓦdelta.com) or United (Ⓦunited.com) in conjunction with a European carrier.

From New York, you can expect to pay (including tax) US$1200 in high season, or US$900 in low season for the cheapest flight to Casablanca. From Montreal, the fare will be Can$1300/1200 in high/low season. Getting to Morocco from the west coast will obviously cost more: expect to pay upwards of US$1500/1150 to Casablanca from LA in high/low season, or Can$1965/1425 from Vancouver.

Flights from Australia, New Zealand and South Africa

There are no direct flights from Australia, New Zealand or South Africa to Morocco. **From Australasia**, you will need to change planes in Europe or the Middle East. Emirates (Ⓦemirates.com) or Etihad (Ⓦetihadairways.com) via the UAE are often the most convenient airlines, with Emirates in particular offering a decent choice of Australian and New Zealand airports to depart from. Alternatively, you can also fly with a European airline such as Lufthansa (Ⓦlufthansa.com) or Air France (Ⓦairfrance.com), or buy a through ticket with Qantas (Ⓦqantas.com) or Air New Zealand (Ⓦairnz.co.nz) in conjunction with their partners in Europe, which has the advantage of offering a wider choice of departure airports.

For the cheapest through ticket, you can expect to pay Aus$2250/1800 in high/low season (July/Nov) from Australia, or NZ$2600/2250 from New Zealand. Flying **from South Africa**, you could fly with an

operator such as Emirates (Ⓦemirates.com) via Dubai, Egyptair (Ⓦegyptair.com) via Cairo, or Air France (Ⓦairfrance.com) via Paris. The most direct route, however, is to fly SAA (Ⓦflysaa.com) to Dakar, changing there onto a Royal Air Maroc (Ⓦroyalairmaroc.com) flight to Casablanca. Expect to pay upwards of ZAR5665 from Johannesburg to Casablanca year-round.

By rail from the UK and Ireland

London to Morocco by train and ferry via Paris, Madrid and Algeciras, takes a good two days at full pelt, and will usually cost rather more than a flight. The journey from London to Algeciras costs upwards of £125; details can be found on the Man in Seat 61 website at Ⓦseat61.com/Morocco.htm. Tickets for the London to Paris stage are available online from Eurostar (Ⓦeurostar.com), for Paris–Madrid from Rail Europe (Ⓦraileurope.co.uk), and for Madrid to Algeciras from the Spanish railway company RENFE (Ⓦrenfe.es); be aware that seat reservation is compulsory, so it's advisable to book all your connections in advance, or you may not be able to get on your preferred train.

By bus from the UK and Ireland

There are bus services with Eurolines (Ⓦeurolines.com) from London's Victoria Coach Station to Algeciras for the boat to Tanger-Med, but they aren't an attractive option. It's a gruelling two-day journey, including a change of bus in Paris and another in Spain, and Eurolines won't sell you a single through ticket, so you would need to buy one from London to Paris (£35 if booked seven days ahead), and another from Paris to Algeciras (€120), making sure that both are available before you actually book either one. Connections from elsewhere in Britain and Ireland can involve long stopovers in London.

By car from the UK and Ireland

Driving to Morocco, allow a minimum of four days from London or southern England, and five days from Scotland or Ireland. The most direct **route** is: London–Channel Tunnel–Calais–Paris–Tours–Bordeaux–Bayonne–San Sebastián (Donostia)–Madrid–Granada–Málaga–Algeciras. French and Spanish motorways charge hefty tolls, but routes that avoid them are much slower. From Ireland, you can cut out Britain by taking a ferry to France with Brittany Ferries (W brittany-ferries .co.uk) or Irish Ferries (W irishferries.com). From Britain, you can cut out the French section of the route by taking a direct ferry to northern Spain with Brittany Ferries. Otherwise, you can cut out Spain by taking a ferry to Morocco from Sète in France (see box, pp.28–29).

Entering Morocco by ferry

Leaving Europe for Morocco proper (not Ceuta or Melilla), you have to go through passport control before boarding the ferry. Once on board, you have to obtain a **disembarkation form** from the purser's office, fill it in, and submit it with your passport for stamping to a **Moroccan immigration** official on the boat. Announcements to this effect are not always made in English, but if you don't have a stamp, you'll have to wait until everyone else has cleared frontier and customs controls before being attended to. When disembarking, show your newly acquired stamp to a Moroccan policeman at the exit.

Most ferries to **Tangier** now dock at the new port of Tanger Med (see p.81), 40km east of Tangier itself, although there is a free shuttle bus into town. Only the catamaran from Tarifa (see p.82) drops you at Tangier's old port, from which you can walk straight into town.

Returning from Morocco to Spain, you need to collect an embarkation form and departure card at the ferry port and have these stamped by the port police prior to boarding your ferry.

Vehicle red tape

Taking a vehicle to Morocco you must take out insurance; the best way to do this is to get **Green Card Insurance** (W direct.gov.uk/en/motoring/owningavehicle/motorinsurance) covering Morocco before you leave (it speeds things up on arrival if the reference to Morocco is prominent and in French). Failing that, you can obtain insurance from Assurance Frontière at the border or port of entry (see p.34). You will also need your vehicle registration document – which must be in your name or accompanied by a letter from the registered owner. Trailer caravans, as well as the vehicle itself, need **temporary importation documents (D16TER)**,

which are obtainable at the frontier (or on the ferry, if not travelling to Ceuta or Melilla) for no charge. Information on driving in Morocco can be found under "Getting Around" (see p.32), as can information on legal requirements for driving (see box, p.33).

AGENTS AND OPERATORS

Best of Morocco UK T 0800 171 2151, W morocco-travel.com. Hotels, riads, and upmarket "designer" trekking, culinary tours, birdwatching and other specialist options.

Blue Men of Morocco Spain T 952 463 387, W bluemenofmorocco.com. Málaga-based firm run by a Moroccan–American couple, offering Andalusia/Morocco combination packages as well as tours of Morocco.

Morocco Explored Canada T 1 604 393 3715, W moroccoexplored.com. Specialists in tailor-made tours, including hiking, camel treks and 4WD off-roading.

Naturally Morocco Ltd UK T 0845 345 7195 or T 01239 710814, W naturallymorocco.co.uk. Ecologically oriented tours of Morocco, with vegetarian or vegan food if desired and a variety of special services available, including Arabic and Berber language tuition and even Moroccan cookery lessons.

North South Travel UK T 01245 608291, W northsouthtravel .co.uk. Friendly, competitive travel agency, offering discounted fares worldwide. Profits are used to support projects in the developing world, especially the promotion of sustainable tourism.

STA Travel UK T 0871 230 0040, W statravel.co.uk; US T 1 800 781 4040, W statravel.com; Australia T 134 782, W statravel .com.au; New Zealand T 0800 474400, W statravel.co.nz; South Africa T 0861 781 781, W statravel.co.za. Independent travel specialists, offering good discounts for students and under-26s.

Surf Maroc UK T 01794 322 709, W surfmaroc.co.uk. Surfing holidays based at Taghazout, including lessons for beginners and more advanced surfers.

Trailfinders UK T 020 7408 9000; Ireland T 01 677 7888, W trailfinders.com. One of the best-informed and most efficient agents for independent travellers.

Travel Cuts Canada T 1 800 667 2887, US T 1-800 592 2887, W travelcuts.com. Canadian youth and student travel firm.

USIT Republic of Ireland T 01 602 1906; Northern Ireland T 028 9032 7111, W usit.ie. Ireland's main youth and student travel specialists.

Getting around

Moroccan public transport is, on the whole, pretty good, with a rail network linking the main towns of the north, the coast and Marrakesh, and plenty of buses and collective taxis. Renting a car can open up routes that are time-consuming or difficult on local transport.

FERRY ROUTES

Fares quoted here are the cheapest adult passenger fares (steerage if available, shared cabin if not), the lowest car fares (usually for a vehicle up to 2.5m long), and lowest motorcycle fares (usually up to 250cc), with seasonal variations shown. Children (up to 12 years) normally pay half fare. Most lines offer discounts (usually twenty percent) to holders of youth and student cards, some to senior citizens too. Baleària do not normally charge for bicycles, but Trasmediterranea and FRS may do, though this is inconsistently applied and you can usually avoid the charge if you take your bike apart, pack it up and carry it on as baggage. Certain firms may refuse to take women over six months pregnant. All departures are subject to **weather conditions**. For detailed schedules and prices, contact the operators, or their UK agents: Southern Ferries, 22 Sussex St, London SW1V 4RW ☎0844 815 7785, ⊛southernferries.co.uk are the agents for Trasmediterranea and SNCM; Viamare, Suite 3, 447 Kenton Rd, Harrow, Middlesex, HA3 0XY, ☎020 8206 3420, ⊛viamare.com are the agents for Baleària and GNV.

  Most passenger tickets can be bought at boat stations on departure, but for vehicles, especially at times of high demand, and for departures out of Sète, it is best to book in advance – for vehicles on ferries out of Sète, make that well in advance. Operators and routes change yearly, and sometimes at short notice; the list at ⊛directferries.co.uk/morocco.htm should be up to date, but it's always worth checking by phone before departure.

ALGECIRAS

Tickets can be bought in Algeciras from any travel agent (there are dozens along the seafront and on the approach roads to the town) or at the boat station. Boats regularly depart thirty minutes to an hour late, and the next to leave may not necessarily be the first to arrive, since fast ferries frequently overtake slow boats on the crossing.

Algeciras–Ceuta ferry Acciona Trasmediterranea, Baleària and FRS. 19 crossings daily (30min–1hr). Passenger €31, car €84, motorbike €33, bicycle free.

Algeciras–Tanger-Med ferry Acciona Trasmediterranea, Baleària, FRS and IMTC. Up to 24 crossings daily in summer, depending on demand; 16 daily in winter (2hr). Passenger €20–25, car €79–84, motorbike €24–30, bicycle €10–30.

TARIFA

Tarifa–Tangier catamaran FRS and Comarit (free bus from

Algeciras). 4 daily (35min). Passenger €35, car €86, motorbike €30, bicycle €15.

GIBRALTAR

Gibraltar–Tanger-Med ferry FRS. Weekly (1hr 30min). Passenger £37.50, car £100, motorbike £38, bicycle free.

MÁLAGA

Málaga–Melilla ferry Acciona Trasmediterranea. Daily (7hr 30min–9hr). Passenger €30–38, car €137–140, motorbike €34–38, bicycle free.

ALMERÍA

Almería–Melilla ferry Acciona Trasmediterranea. Daily (6hr–8hr 30min). Passenger €34, car €137.80, motorbike €34.50.

Almería–Nador ferry Acciona Trasmediterranea. Daily (6–8hr). Passenger €62, car €141, motorbike €77.60, bicycle free.

By plane

Royal Air Maroc (RAM; ☎0890 000800, ⊛royalairmaroc.com) operates **domestic flights** from its Casablanca hub to major cities nationwide. You will usually have to change planes at Casablanca in order to travel between any other two points, unless both are stops on a single Casa-bound flight (Dakhla to Laayoune, for example). In general, flying is not really worthwhile except for long-distance routes such as to Laayoune or Dakhla in the Western Sahara, when they can save you a lot of time. A one-way ticket from Casablanca to Laayoune, for example, would set you back 1360dh (£101/$161) and take one hour and forty minutes (plus journey time to the airport, check-in time and delays), compared to nineteen hours by bus. Casa to Dakhla – 1124dh (£84/$133) one-way on RAM – would take you two and a quarter hours by air compared to 28 hours by bus.

Information on Morocco's airports, including daily departure lists for some of them, can be found on the website of the Office National des Aéroports at ⊛onda.ma. You should confirm flights 72 hours before departure. Student and under-26 youth **discounts** of 25 percent are available on RAM domestic flights, but only if the ticket is bought in advance from one of its offices.

By train

Trains cover a limited network of routes, but for travel between the major cities they are easily the best option, comfortable and fairly fast, but sometimes subject to delays.

Almería–Nador ferry Comarit. Daily (summer only; 7hr). Passenger €50, car €189, motorbike €71, bicycle €8.

BARCELONA

Barcelona–Tanger-Med ferry GNV. 2 weekly (26hr). Passenger €72–95, car €133–233, motorbike €16–76, bicycle free.

Barcelona–Tangier ferry Grimaldi. Weekly (36hr). Passenger €80–90, car €140–170, motorbike €65, bicycle free.

SÈTE

Booking well in advance is essential for Sète ferries.

Sète–Tanger-Med ferry GNV. 1 weekly direct (35hr). Passenger €76, car €249, motorbike €58, bicycle free.

FERRY OPERATORS

Acciona Trasmediterranea Ⓦ trasmediterranea.es, telephone enquiries in Spain ☎ 902 454 645; Recinto del Puerto, Algeciras; Estación Marítima, Recinto del Puerto, Local E-1, Málaga; Estación Marítima, Almería; Muelle Cañonero Dato, Ceuta; General Marina 1, Melilla; Av Youssef Ibn Tachfine 5, Tangier ☎ 0539 343980. Algeciras to Ceuta and Tanger-Med; Málaga to Melilla; Almería to Melilla and Nador.

Baleària Ⓦ balearia.com, telephone enquiries in Spain ☎ 902 160 180; Estación Marítima, Locales F-4 & F-23, Algeciras; Estación Marítima, Ceuta; Gare Maritime, Tanger-Med ☎ 0539 934463. Algeciras to Tanger-Med and Ceuta.

Comarit Ⓦ comarit.es; 3 Av Virgen del Carmen, first floor, Algeciras ☎ 956 657 462; Estación Marítima, Tarifa ☎ 956 682 768; Estación Marítima, Almería ☎ 950 620 303; cnr Bd Mohammed V and Av Youssef Ben Tachfine (by Pl des Nations), Tangier ☎ 0539 320032. Algeciras to Tanger-Med; Tarifa to Tangier; Almería to Nador (services suspended at last check).

FRS (Ferrys Rápidos del Sur) Ⓦ frs.es; Estación Marítima, Tarifa ☎ 956 68 18 30; Paseo Marítimo, Algeciras ☎ 956 627 445; c/o Turner & Co, 65–67 Irish Town, Gibraltar ☎ 350 2005

Sète–Tanger-Med ferry GNV. 1 weekly via Barcelona (40hr). Passenger €76, car €249, motorbike €58, bicycle free.

Sète–Nador ferry GNV. 1 weekly (June–Sept). Passenger €75, car €246, motorbike €56, bicycle free.

GENOA

Genoa–Tanger-Med ferry GNV. 3 weekly via Barcelona (48hr). Passenger €83–124, car €203, motorbike €67, bicycle free.

LIVORNO (LEGHORN)

Livorno–Tanger-Med ferry Grimaldi. 1 weekly via Barcelona (61hr). Passenger €140, car €280–330, motorbike €65, bicycle free.

0828, Ⓦ turnershipping.com; 18 Rue Farabi, Tangier ☎ 0539 942612. Tarifa to Tangier, Gibraltar and Algeciras to Tanger-Med; Algeciras to Ceuta.

Grimaldi Lines 13 Via M. Campodisola, Naples ☎ 081 496 444, Ⓦ grimaldi-lines.com; Stazione Marittima Darsena Toscana Ovest, 14G Viale Mogadiscio, Livorno ☎ 0586 426 682; Moll de Barcelona, by Plaça de Carbonera, Barcelona ☎ 93 502 0400; 21 Av Louis Van Beethoven, Tangier ☎ 0531 111111. Livorno via Barcelona to Tanger-Med.

GNV (Grandi Navi Veloci) Ⓦ gnv.it; Via Fieschi 17a, Genoa ☎ 010 550 9705; 1 Moll Sant Bertran, Estació Marítim, Barcelona ☎ 934 437 139; c/o IMTC, Port de Tanger, Tangier ☎ 0538 800020; Port, Beni Enzar ☎ 0536 349121; c/o Atlas Voyages, Av Des FAR 44, Casablanca ☎ 0820 02020. Genoa and Sète via Barcelona to Tanger-Med; Sète direct to Tanger-Med and (summer only) to Nador.

IMTC (International Maritime Transport Corporation) Ⓦ imtc.co.ma; 50 Av Pasteur, Casablanca ☎ 0522 437620; Port, Tanger-Med ☎ 0539 334740; Estación Marítima Algeciras ☎ 956 655 040. Algeciras to Tangier.

There are two main lines: from Tangier in the north down to Marrakesh, and from Oujda in the northeast, also to Marrakesh, joining with the Tangier line at Sidi Kacem. Branch lines serve Nador, El Jadida, Safi, Oued Zem and Casablanca airport. A high-speed line (LGV) from Tangier to Casablanca is scheduled to open in 2015 (for latest news see Ⓦ tgvmaroc.ma), with extensions planned down to Marrakesh and Agadir, as well as eastward all the way (political frictions allowing) through Algeria and Tunisia to Tripoli.

Schedules change very little from year to year, but it's wise to check times in advance at stations. **Timetables** are displayed at major train stations, and any station ticket office will print you off a mini-timetable of services between any two stations. You can also check schedules (*horaires*) and fares (*tarifs*)

on the ONCF website at Ⓦ oncf.ma, though you cannot buy tickets online. Except for sleeper services, tickets do not need to be booked in advance; you can just turn up at the station and buy one. There are two **classes** of tickets – first and second. **Costs** for a second-class ticket are slightly more than what you'd pay for buses; on certain "express" services ("express" refers to the level of comfort rather than the speed), they are around thirty percent higher. In addition, there are **couchettes** (145dh extra) available on the Tangier–Marrakesh and Casablanca–Oujda night trains – worth the money for both the comfort and the security, as couchette passengers are in their own locked carriage with a guard. Most **stations** are located reasonably close to the modern city centres. They do not have **left-luggage** facilities.

By bus

Bus travel is generally only marginally cheaper than taking a shared grand taxi (see opposite), and around thirty percent slower, but also safer and more comfortable, though on some older buses leg room is limited, and for anyone approaching six feet or more in height, long journeys can be rather an endurance test. Many long-distance buses run **at night** when they are both quicker and cooler. Most are fitted with reading lights but they are invariably turned off, so you will not be able to read on buses after dark. Also note that the rate of accidents involving night buses is quite high, especially on busy routes, and most of all on the N8 between Marrakesh and Agadir.

Travelling during the day, especially in summer, it pays to sit on the side away from **the sun**. Travelling from north to south, this means sitting on the right in the morning, on the left in the afternoon, vice versa if going the other way. Travelling from east to west, sit on the right, or on the left if going from west to east. In fact, Moroccan passengers often pull down the blinds and shut the windows, which can block out the scenery and make the journey rather claustrophobic. Note too, especially on rural services, that some passengers may be unused to road travel, resulting in travel sickness and vomiting.

CTM and private lines

Buses run by **CTM** (the national company; ⓦctm .ma) are faster and more reliable than private services, with numbered seats and fixed departure schedules, which can be checked online. CTM services usually have reading lights, though you may have to ask the driver to turn those on. Some of the **larger private company** buses, such as SATAS (which operates widely in the south) and Trans Ghazala (which runs in the north) are of a similar standard, but many other private companies are tiny outfits, with a single bus which leaves only when the driver considers it sufficiently full. On the other hand, such private buses are much more likely to stop for you if you flag them down on the open road, whereas CTM services will only pick up and set down at official stops.

Bus terminals

Most towns have a main **bus station** (gare routière), often on the edge of town. CTM buses usually leave from the company's office, which may be quite a way from the main bus station, though in several places CTM and the private companies share a single terminal, and in some cases the CTM bus will call at the main bus station when departing a city, though not when arriving.

Bus stations usually have a number of ticket windows, one for each of the companies operating out of it. There is occasionally a departures board, but it may be out of date and in Arabic only, so you should always check departure times at the appropriate window. Bus conductors or ticket sellers may be calling out destinations in the bus station in any case, or may greet you as you come in by asking where you want to go. On the more popular trips (and especially with CTM services, which are often just once a day in the south), it's worth trying to buy **tickets in advance**, though this may not always be possible on smaller private-line services.

You may occasionally have problems getting tickets at **small towns** along major routes, where buses can arrive and leave already full. It's sometimes possible to get round this by taking a local bus or a grand taxi for the next section of the trip (until the bus you want empties a little), or by waiting for a bus that actually starts from the town you're in. Overall, the best policy is to arrive at a bus station early in the day (ideally 5.30–6am).

On private-line buses, you generally pay for your **baggage** to be loaded into the hold (or onto the roof). The standard fee is 5dh, but this may be foregone on short hops. Note that you only pay to have your baggage loaded, not to have it unloaded on arrival, whatever anybody may say. On CTM, SATAS and Supratours buses your luggage is weighed and you are issued with a receipt for the

---

FARES

For **comparison**, between Casablanca and Marrakesh, a train will take three and a quarter hours and cost 90dh in second class, 140dh in first. A CTM bus will cost 85dh and take three and a half hours, while an ordinary bus will cost 60dh and take around four hours. A shared grand taxi will cost 120dh and take two and a half hours on ordinary roads, or cost 150dh and take under two hours by motorway (though on most routes in fact the difference between the grand taxi and ordinary bus fare is less). For the forty-minute plane journey, the full economy-class fare is 1700dh, but you can usually get a ticket for 664dh if you book far enough in advance.

POLICE CHECKPOINTS

There are **police checkpoints** on roads throughout the country. European cars, or rental cars, are usually waved through. Buses (other than CTM services) are more likely to be stopped, but usually only briefly. Sometimes the police may ask to check your passport or (if driving) licence, often only because they want to relieve their boredom with a chat. Nonetheless, you should always have your **passport** with you if travelling between towns – even on day-trips.

Checkpoints in the **Western Sahara** are more thorough, and for foreigners they can involve a considerable amount of form-filling and delay (see box, p.512).

In the **Rif mountains**, especially around Ketama, police may stop vehicles to search for cannabis. Buses are usually delayed more than grands taxis at such checkpoints, and passengers may be searched individually. There are also sometimes lengthy checks for duty-free contraband on buses from Nador to Fez.

baggage charge (usually 5–10dh, depending on weight and distance – allow time for this procedure). On arrival, porters with wheeled box-carts (*chariots*) may offer their services, but always agree a price before engaging one.

Supratours buses

An additional service, on certain major routes, is the **Supratours express buses** run as feeder services by the train company, **ONCF**. These are fast and very comfortable, and run from Tetouan, Essaouira, Agadir and the Western Sahara to connect with rail services from Oujda, Tangier and Marrakesh. Timetables and fares for Supratours buses can be found along with those for trains on the ONCF website (Woncf.ma). Supratours services compare, in both time and cost, with CTM buses. They do not use the main bus stations, but depart from outside their own town-centre offices (detailed in the text). Through tickets to and from connecting rail stations are available (Essaouira through to Fez, for example), and travellers with rail tickets for connecting services have priority. It's best to book tickets in advance if possible.

By shared taxi

Shared **grands taxis** are one of the best features of Moroccan transport. They operate on a wide variety of routes, are much quicker than buses (usually quicker than trains, too), and fares vary from slightly more than the bus to around twice as much.

The taxis are usually big Peugeot or Mercedes cars carrying six passengers (Peugeots are less common but have a slightly less cramped seating arrangement). Most business is along specific routes, and the most popular routes have more or less continuous departures throughout the day. You just show up at the terminal (locations are detailed in the guide) and ask for a place to a specific destination. The best time

to arrive is early morning (7–9am), when a lot of people are travelling and taxis fill up quickly; lunchtime, on the other hand, is a bad time to turn up, as fewer people will be travelling, and the taxi will take longer to fill up. As soon as six (or, if you're willing to pay extra, four or five) people are assembled, the taxi sets off. Make sure, when asking about grands taxis, that it is clear you only want a place (*une place* in French, *plassa* in Arabic, or hold up one finger) in a shared taxi (*taxi collectif*), as drivers often "presume" that a tourist will want to charter the whole taxi (see below), which means paying for all six places. Women travelling alone may wish to pay for two places and get the front seat to themselves rather than be squashed up against male passengers.

Picking up a shared taxi on the road is more problematic, as they will only stop if they have a place free (if a passenger has already alighted). To hail a taxi on the open road, hold up one, two or more fingers to indicate how many places you need.

Fares for set routes are fixed, and drivers do not usually try to overcharge tourists for a place (though occasionally they try to charge for baggage, which usually travels free of charge). If you think that you are being overcharged, ask the other passengers, or check the price with your hotel before leaving. Occasionally, five passengers may agree to split the cost of the last place to hasten departure, or one passenger may agree to pay for two places. You pay the full fare for the journey even if travelling only part of the way.

If you want to take a **non-standard route**, or an excursion, or just to have the taxi to yourself, it is possible to charter a whole grand taxi (*une course* in French, *corsa* in Arabic). In theory this should be exactly six times the price of a place in a shared taxi if the route has a set fare, but you'll often have to bargain hard to get that. Hotels can sometimes be useful in helping to charter grands taxis.

Some people consider shared taxis **dangerous**. It is certainly true that they are prone to practices such as speeding, and overtaking on blind curves or the brows of hills, and that they have more than their fair share of accidents. Drivers may work all day and into the night, and it seems a large number of accidents involve them falling asleep at the wheel while driving at night, so you may wish to avoid using them for night-time journeys, especially on busy roads (the N8 between Marrakesh and Agadir is the worst). Note also that with the seating arrangements, it is not usually possible to wear a seat belt, though if you pay for two places, you can get the front seat to yourself and put the belt on.

Trucks and hitching

In the countryside, where buses may be sporadic or even nonexistent, it is standard practice for **vans** and **lorries** (*camions*), **pick-up trucks** (*camionettes*) and **transit-vans** (*transits*) to carry passengers for a charge. You may be asked to pay a little more than the locals, and you may be expected to bargain over the price – but it's straightforward enough.

In parts of the **Atlas**, local people run more or less scheduled truck or transit services, generally to coincide with the pattern of local souks. If you plan on traversing any of the more ambitious Atlas *pistes*, you'll probably be dependent on these vehicles, unless you walk.

Hitching

Hitchhiking is not big in Morocco, but you may resort to it on routes where transport is scarce. Fellow tourists may pick you up, and Moroccans may carry you for free, but usually you pay, around the same as a bus or grand taxi fare. This is especially the case in country areas, where local rides can operate in much the same way as truck taxis. As a rule, however, hitching is not really safe, and it is definitely not advisable for women travelling alone. We have heard of (Moroccan) hitchhikers being robbed on the N12 Tata–Bou Izakarn road, and it probably happens elsewhere too.

By car

There are few real problems driving in Morocco, but **accident rates** are high, largely because motorists routinely ignore traffic regulations and drive aggressively and dangerously (most people pay *baksheesh* for their licence). The N8 between Marrakesh and Agadir is a particular accident blackspot. Do not expect other drivers to indicate or observe lane discipline, beware when coming up to blind curves or hills where vehicles coming in the other direction may be trying to overtake without full view of the road ahead, treat all pedestrians with the suspicion that they will cross in front of you, and all cyclists with the idea that they may well swerve into the middle of the road. All this makes driving a particularly hair-raising experience in towns, and even experienced drivers may find city driving quite stressful. The difficulty of finding places in cities due to lack of street signs adds to the problem. Be particularly wary about driving **after dark**, as it is legal to drive up to 20km/h without lights, which allows all cyclists and mopeds to wander at will; donkeys, goats and sheep do not carry lights, either.

However, with those caveats in mind, daytime and certainly long-distance driving can be as good as anywhere. Good road surfaces, long straight roads, and little traffic between inhabited areas allow for high average speeds. The usual **speed limit** outside towns is 40km/h (25mph) in built-up areas, 100km/h (62mph) on ordinary roads, and 120km/h (75mph) on motorways. There are on-the-spot fines for speeding, and oncoming motorists flashing their headlights at you may well be warning you to slow down for a police check ahead (radar speed traps are common). The French rule of giving priority to traffic from the right is observed at roundabouts and junctions – meaning that cars coming onto a roundabout have priority over those already on it.

By law, drivers and passengers are required to wear **seat belts**. Almost no one does, but if you follow suit and are stopped by the police, you may have a small fine (possibly unofficial) extracted. Given Morocco's high road accident rate, it is foolhardy not to wear a seat belt anyway.

Piste and off-piste driving

On the *pistes* (rough, unpaved tracks in the mountains or desert), there are special problems. Here you do need a good deal of driving and mechanical confidence – and if you don't feel your car is up to it, don't drive on these routes. Obviously, a 4WD vehicle is best suited to the *pistes*, but most *pistes* are passable, with care, in an ordinary small car, though it's worth asking local advice first. On mountain roads, beware of gravel, which can be a real danger on the frequent hairpin bends, and, in spring, flash floods caused by melting snow. The six-volume series, *Pistes du Maroc* (Gandini), are invaluable guides for anyone planning on driving *pistes*; they are available in major Moroccan bookshops or online (Ⓦextrem-sud.com/guides.php).

Driving a 4WD can be an exciting way of exploring the mountains and desert, off-tarmac, or even off-*piste*. Some companies lay on vehicles, driver and mess tent, organize food and cooking and will go wherever requested. For economical and practical reasons groups should number five or eleven, so you'll probably find yourself exploring with strangers. UK-based AMIS (see p.46) specializes in this field.

Car rental

Car rental starts at around 2000dh (£150/$240) per week or 400dh (£30/$47) a day (there's usually a three-day minimum) for a basic car with unlimited mileage and insurance cover. You will be expected to leave credit card details, and fuel prices are high (see below). Having a car pays obvious dividends if you are pushed for time, especially in the **south**, where buses and taxis may be sparse, but chartering a grand taxi and agreeing a daily rate will not cost that much more.

Many visitors rent a car in Casablanca, Marrakesh or Agadir, but it may work out cheaper to **arrange car rental in advance** through the travel company who arranges your flight. With international firms such as Hertz, Budget, Europcar and Avis, you can book from home by phone or online. Local **car rental firms** are listed in city "Arrival and Departure" sections in the guide. Deals to go for are unlimited mileage and daily/weekly rates; paying by the kilometre invariably works out more expensive. Local firms have the advantage that the price is more likely to be negotiable, though the condition of the vehicle should be well checked. Many hotels can arrange car rental at reasonable rates. If you can't or don't want to drive yourself, car rental companies can often arrange a **driver** for around 300dh (£23/$35) a day.

Before setting out, make sure the car comes with spare tyre, toolkit and full documentation – including insurance cover, which is compulsory issue with all rentals. It's a good idea to get full insurance to avoid charges for bumps and scratches. Most car rental agreements prohibit use of the car on unsurfaced roads, and you will be liable for any damage sustained if you do drive off-tarmac.

Equipment

Whether you rent a car or drive your own, always make sure you're carrying a **spare tyre** in good

condition (plus a jack and tools). Flat tyres occur very frequently, even on fairly major roads, and you can often be in for a long wait until someone drives along with a possible replacement. Carrying an **emergency windscreen** is also useful, especially if driving your own car for a long period of time. There are lots of loose stones on the hard shoulders of single-lane roads and they can fly all over the place. If you're not mechanically minded, be sure to bring a car **maintenance manual** – a useful item, too, for anyone planning to rent a vehicle.

Fuel and breakdowns

Filling stations can be few and far between in rural areas: always fill your tank to the limit. Unleaded fuel is available in most places nowadays, but it's always worth filling up when you have the chance as supplies can be sporadic. Fuel prices are generally lower than in Western Europe, at 10.33dh (77p/$1.22) a litre for unleaded (*sans plomb* or *bidoun rasas*), and 7.30dh (55p/86¢) for diesel (*gasoil*, pronounced *"gazwaal"*). In the Saharan provinces (basically the Western Sahara), fuel is subsidized, and costs about a third less. Fuel in the duty-free Spanish enclaves of Ceuta and Melilla is cheaper than it is on the Spanish mainland, but currently costs more than it does in Morocco proper, at around €1.24 for unleaded (*sin plomo*) and €1.14 for diesel (*gasóleo*). As in Morocco proper, unleaded fuel can sometimes be in short supply in the Spanish enclaves.

Moroccan mechanics are usually excellent at coping with breakdowns and all medium-sized towns have garages (most with an extensive range of spare parts for most French cars, and usually for Fiats too). However, if you break down

DISTANCE CHART (KILOMETRES BY ROAD)

	Ag	Al H	Casa	Dakh	Er Rach	Ess	Fez	Figuig
Agadir	–	1037	511	1208	773	173	756	1151
Al Hoceima	1037	–	570	2245	637	940	281	773
Casablanca	511	570	–	1719	557	351	289	935
Dakhla	1208	2245	1719	–	1981	1381	1964	2359
Er Rachidia	773	637	557	1981	–	676	350	378
Essaouira	173	940	351	1381	676	–	640	1054
Fez	756	281	289	1964	350	640	–	706
Figuig	1151	773	935	2359	378	1054	706	–
Laayoune	694	1731	1205	514	1467	867	1450	1845
Marrakesh	273	764	238	1481	500	176	483	878
Meknes	740	341	229	1948	328	580	60	706
Nador	1063	280	596	2271	554	947	307	525
Oujda	1076	397	609	2284	564	960	320	386
Ouarzazate	375	927	442	1483	296	380	646	674
Rabat	602	479	91	1810	466	442	198	1199
Tangier	880	323	341	2088	595	692	303	1457
Tetouan	873	273	362	2081	595	713	276	1478

miles from anywhere you'll probably end up paying a fortune to get a truck to tow you to the nearest town.

If you are driving your own vehicle, there is also the problem of having to re-export any car that you bring into the country (even a wreck). You can't just write off a car: you'll have to take it out of Morocco with you.

Vehicle insurance

Insurance must by law be sold along with all rental agreements. Driving your own vehicle, you should obtain Green Card cover from your insurers. If you don't have it on arrival, you can buy it from Assurance Frontière for 950dh (£77/$113) a month for a car or camper van, at Tangier port, Nador port, or the land frontiers at Ceuta and Melilla; to renew it, the main AF office is at 59 Bd Bordeaux, Casablanca (☎0522 484156 or 7).

Parking

Parking in almost any town, you will find a *gardien de voitures*, usually licensed by local authorities to look after cars, and claiming a couple of dirhams by way of parking fees. Alternatively, most of the larger hotels in the Ville Nouvelle quarters of cities have parking spaces (and occasionally garaging). It's always worth paying for a *gardien* or parking in a garage, as new or well-looked-after cars attract a certain level of vandalism. Red-and-white-striped kerbs mean no parking is allowed.

By motorbike

Morocco has all the major attractions sought by bike enthusiasts, but if you've never taken a bike abroad before, seriously consider going with a group. H-C Travel in the UK (🕸 hctravel.com), Moto Adventures in Andorra (🕸 motoaventures.com) and Wilderness Wheels in Ouarzazate (🕸 wildernesswheels.com) offer off-road and trailbiking packages. Taking your own bike is subject to the same bureaucracy as taking a car (see p.27). One way of avoiding that is to **rent a bike** in Morocco (see p.340 & p.455). So far as road conditions are concerned, our comments on driving (see p.32) also apply to motorbikes.

Taking your own bike

If you take your own motorbike, you will need **special insurance**. Most companies, especially those based outside Europe, will not cover motor-cycling as part of a holiday overseas, particularly when off-road riding is contemplated or inevitable (as it often is in Morocco). You'll have to shop around and remember to take the policy with you, together with your bike registration certificate, biker's licence and International Driving Permit. Even large insurance companies don't give clear answers about "**Green Cards**" for motorcycling in Morocco and do not understand that you may encounter up to a dozen police checks a day.

When **entering Morocco**, try to arrive as early in the day as possible. If you are a lone traveller and speak neither Arabic nor French, you may be left

Laay	Mar	Mek	Nad	Ouj	Ouarz	Rab	Tan	Tet
694	273	740	1063	1076	375	602	880	873
1731	764	341	280	397	927	479	323	273
1205	238	229	596	609	442	91	341	362
514	1481	1948	2271	2284	1483	1810	2088	2081
1467	500	328	554	564	296	466	595	595
867	176	580	947	960	380	442	692	713
1450	483	60	307	320	646	198	303	276
1845	878	706	525	386	674	1199	1457	1478
–	967	1434	1757	1770	1069	1296	1574	1567
967	–	467	790	803	204	321	579	600
1434	467	–	363	380	652	138	267	267
1757	790	363	–	139	840	501	597	547
1770	803	380	139	–	850	518	714	664
1069	204	652	840	850	–	528	783	804
1296	321	138	501	518	528	–	250	271
1574	579	267	597	714	783	250	–	58
1567	600	267	547	664	804	271	58	–

queuing until those without queries have been dealt with. If the office then closes, you may have to return the next morning. In these circumstances, it might be worth investing in a tout who, for a fee, will take your papers to a friendly officer. It's also worth picking up a couple of (free) extra immigration forms for the return journey.

What to take and when to go

If possible, don't take a model of bike likely to be unfamiliar in Morocco. It's worth carrying cables and levers, inner tubes, puncture repair kit, tyre levers, pump, fuses, plugs, chain, washable air filter, cable ties, good tape and a toolkit. For riding off-road, take knobbly tyres and rim locks, brush guards, metal number plate and bashplate. In winter, take tough fabric outer clothing. In summer, carry lighter-weight clothing, woollen jumpers and waterproofs. Drying out leathers takes a long time. In the south, the heat in summer can be overwhelming, making travelling a far from enjoyable experience.

Cycling

Cycling – and particularly **mountain biking** in the Atlas (see box, p.381) and other areas – is becoming an increasingly popular pursuit for Western travellers to Morocco. The country's regular roads are well maintained and by European standards very quiet, while the extensive network of **pistes** – dirt tracks – makes for exciting mountain-bike terrain, leading you into areas otherwise accessible only to trekkers or four-wheel-drive expeditions.

Regular roads are generally surfaced (*goudronné* or *revêtue*) but narrow, and you will often have to get off the tarmac to make way for traffic. Beware also of open land-drains close to the roadsides, and loose gravel on the bends.

Cycling on **pistes**, mountain bikes come into their own with their "tractor" tyres and wide, stabilizing handlebars. There are few *pistes* that could be recommended on a regular tourer. By contrast, some intrepid mountain bikers cover footpaths in the High Atlas, though for the less than super-fit this is extremely heavy going. Better, on the whole, to stick to established *pistes* – many of which are covered by local trucks, which you can pay for a ride in if your legs (or your bike) give out.

Getting your bike to Morocco

Many **airlines** – even charters – carry bikes free of charge, so long as they don't push your baggage allowance over the weight limit, but the no-frills airlines will charge you. When buying a ticket, register your intention of taking your bike and check out the airline's conditions. They will generally require you to invert the handlebars, remove the pedals, and deflate the tyres; some provide or sell a cardboard **box** to enclose the bike, as protection for other passengers' luggage as much as for the bike; you are, however, unlikely to be offered a box for the return journey. A useful alternative, offering little protection but at least ensuring nothing gets lost, is to customize an industrial nylon sack, adding a drawstring at the neck.

If you plan to cross over **by ferry to Morocco**, things couldn't be simpler. You ride on with the motor vehicles (thus avoiding the long queues of foot passengers) and the bike is secured during the voyage. At time of writing, bicycles travel for free on most ferries other than the runs from Tarifa and Algeciras to Tangier or Tanger-Med.

Bicycles and local transport

Cycling around Morocco, you can make use of local transport to supplement your own wheels. **Buses** will generally carry bikes on the roof. CTM usually charges around 10dh per bike – make sure you get a ticket. On other lines it's very much up to you to negotiate with the driver and/or baggage porter (who will probably expect at least 5dh). If you're riding and exhausted, you can usually flag down private-line buses (but not usually CTM services) on the road.

Some **grands taxis** also agree to carry bikes, if they have space on a rack. You may have to pay for this, but of course you can haggle. In mountain or desert areas, you can have your bike carried with you on **truck or transit services** (see p.32). Prices for this are negotiable, but should not exceed your own passenger fare.

Bikes are carried on **trains** for a modest handling fee, though it's not really worth the hassle. They have to be registered in advance as baggage and won't necessarily travel on the same train as you (though they will usually turn up within a day).

Accommodation

Accommodation doesn't present any special problems. The cheaper **hotels** will almost always let you keep your bike in your room – and others will find a disused basement or office for storage. It's almost essential to do this, as much to deter unwelcome tampering as theft, especially if you have a curiosity-inviting mountain bike. At **campsites**, there's usually a *gardien* on hand to keep an eye on your bike, or stow it away in his chalet.

ROUTES

Rewarding areas for biking include:

Tizi n'Test (High Atlas): Asni to Ijoukak, and an excursion to Tin Mal.

Asni to Setti Fatma (High Atlas: Ourika Valley) and beyond if you have a mountain bike.

Northern and Western Middle Atlas (well-watered side).

Jebel Saghro and Jebel Bani: a choice of good east–west Anti-Atlas routes.

Southern oasis routes In summer it wouldn't be a good idea to go much beyond the Atlas, though given cooler winter temperatures, rewarding long routes exist in the southern oasis routes, such as Ouarzazate to Zagora or Ouarzazate to Tinghir, and the desert routes down to Er Rachidia, Erfoud and Rissani.

Repairs

Most towns have **repair shops** in their Medina quarters, used to servicing local bikes and mopeds. They may not have spare parts for your make of bike, but can usually sort out some kind of temporary solution. It is worth bringing **spare spokes** (and tool) with you, plus **brake blocks** and **cable**, as the mountain descents can take it out on a bike. **Tyres** and **tubes** can generally be found for tourers, though if you have anything fancy, best bring at least one spare, too.

Obviously, before setting out, you should make sure that your brakes are in good order, renew bearings, etc, and ensure that you have decent quality (and condition) tyres.

Problems and rewards

All over Morocco, and particularly in rural areas, there are stray, wild and semi-cared-for **dogs**. A cyclist pedalling past with feet and wheels spinning seems to send at least half of them into a frenzied state. Normally, cycling in an equally frenzied state is the best defence, but on steep ascents and off-road this isn't always possible. In these situations, keep the bike between you and the dog, and use your pump or a shower from your water bottle as defence. If you do get bitten, a rabies inoculation is advisable.

Another factor to be prepared for is your susceptibility to the unwanted attentions of local people. Small **children** will often stand in the road to hinder your progress, or even chase after you in gangs and throw stones. Your attitude is important: be friendly, smile, and maintain strong eye contact. On no account attempt to mete out your own discipline: small children always have big brothers.

The heat and the long stretches of dead straight road across arid, featureless plains – the main routes to (or beyond) the mountain ranges – can all too easily drain your energy. Additionally, public **water** is very rare – there are few roadside watering places, and towns and villages can be a long way apart.

Despite all this, cycling in Morocco can be an extremely rewarding experience; as one of our readers put it: "I felt an extra intimacy with the country by staying close to it, rather than viewing it from car or bus windows. And I experienced unrivalled generosity, from cups of tea offered by policemen at roadside checkpoints to a full-blown breakfast banquet from a farming family whose dog had savaged my leg. People went out of their way to give me advice, food, drink and lifts, and not once did I feel seriously threatened. Lastly, the exhilaration I felt on some of the mountain descents, above all the Tizi n'Test in the High Atlas, will remain with me forever. I was not an experienced cycle tourer when I arrived in Morocco, but the grandeur of the scenery helped carry me over the passes."

City transport

You'll spend most time exploring Moroccan cities on foot. The alleys of the old Medina quarters, where the sights and souks are, will rarely accommodate more than a donkey. In the newer quarters, you may want to make use of city taxis and occasionally a bus. Be aware that pedestrian crossings don't count for very much, except perhaps at junctions "controlled" by traffic lights. And even then, bikes and mopeds pay scant attention to traffic lights showing red.

Petits taxis, usually Fiats or Simcas, carry up to three passengers and (unlike grands taxis) can only operate within city limits. All petits taxis should have meters, and you should insist that they use them. Failing that, you will need to bargain for a price – either before you get in (wise to start off with) or by simply presenting the regular fare when you get out. If you are a lone passenger, your taxi driver may pick up one or two additional passengers en route, each of whom will pay the full fare for their journey, as of course will you. This is standard practice.

Don't be afraid to argue with the driver if you feel you're being unreasonably overcharged. During the daytime, you should pay what is on the meter. After 8pm, standard fares rise by fifty percent. Tips are not expected, but of course always appreciated. Taxis from airports usually run at special rates agreed among the drivers, in which case, they will not agree to use the meter.

Accommodation

Hotels in Morocco are cheap, good value, and usually pretty easy to find. There can be a shortage of places in the major cities and resorts (Tangier, Fez, Marrakesh and Agadir) in August, and in Rabat or Casablanca when there's a big conference on. At other times, you should be able to pick from a wide range of accommodation.

In winter, one thing worth checking for in a hotel is **heating** – nights can get cold, even in the south (and especially in the desert), and since bedding is not always adequate, a hotel with heating can be a boon. It's always, in any case, a good idea to ask to see your room before you check in.

Prices quoted for hotels in the guide are for the cheapest double room or dorm bed in high season, and are for the room only, except where we specify BB for bed and breakfast, HB for half-board, or FB for full board. Camping prices are for a pitch and two people.

Unclassified hotels

Unclassified (non-classé) hotels are often in the older parts of cities – the walled Medinas – and are almost always the cheapest accommodation options. They have the additional advantage of being at the heart of things: where you'll want to spend most of your time, and where all the sights and markets are concentrated. The disadvantages are that the Medinas can at first appear daunting – with their mazes of narrow lanes and blind alleys – and that the hotels themselves can be, at worst, dirty flea traps with tiny, windowless cells and half-washed sheets. At their best, if well kept, they're fine, in traditional buildings with white-washed rooms round a central patio.

One other minus point for unclassified Medina hotels is that they sometimes have a problem with **water**. Most of the Medinas remain substantially unmodernized, and some cheap hotels are without hot water, with squat toilets that can be pretty disgusting. On the plus side, there is usually a hammam (Turkish bath; see box, p.38) nearby.

Classified hotels

Classified (classé) hotels are most likely to be found in a town's Ville Nouvelle – the "new" or administrative quarter. They are allowed, regardless of **star-rating**, to set their own prices – and to vary them according to season and demand. Prices should be on display at reception.

For Western-style standards of comfort, you need to look, on the whole, at **four-star hotels**, but even here, you are advised to check what's on offer. The plumbing, heating and lighting are sometimes unreliable; restaurants are often closed and swimming pools empty. Hotels in this price category are particularly likely to offer discounted and promotional rates off-season, and will almost always be cheaper if booked through a travel agent online or abroad than at the "rack rates" offered to travellers who just turn up. One safe but boring option at this level is the Ibis Moussafir chain (ⓦibishotel.com), whose hotels are almost always next to train stations, rather characterless and generally all identical, but comfortable, efficient and good value.

Hotels accorded the **five-star-luxury rating**, can sometimes be very stylish, whether in a historic conversion (most famously the *Hôtel la Mamounia* in Marrakesh and the *Palais Jamaï* in Fez) or in a modern building with a splendid pool and all the international creature comforts, but most Moroccan five-star hotels – particularly those catering for tour groups – are more like four-stars elsewhere; service is frequently amateurish by Western standards, and staff ill-trained and unprofessional.

In the Spanish enclaves of **Ceuta and Melilla**, accommodation at the lower end of the spectrum costs about twice as much as it does in Morocco proper, with a double room in the cheapest *pensiones* at around €25–45. At the top end of the scale, prices tend to be much the same as they are in Morocco, with four-star hotels charging €80–200 for a double room.

Riads

Morocco's trendiest accommodation option is in a **riad** or **maison d'hôte**. Strictly speaking, a riad is a house built around a patio garden – in fact, the word riad correctly refers to the garden rather than the house – while *maison d'hôte* is French for "guest house". The two terms are both used, to some extent interchangeably, for a residential house done up to rent out to tourists, but a riad is generally more stylish and expensive, while a *maison d'hôte* is

---

HAMMAMS

The absence of hot showers in some of the cheapest Medina hotels is not such a disaster. Throughout all the Medina quarters, you'll find local **hammams**. A hammam is a Turkish-style steam bath, with a succession of rooms from cool to hot, and endless supplies of hot and cold water, which you fetch in buckets. The usual procedure is to find a piece of floor space in the hot room, surround it with as many buckets of water as you feel you need, and lie in the heat to sweat out the dirt from your pores before scrubbing it off. A plastic bowl is useful for scooping the water from the buckets to wash with. You can also order a massage, in which you will be allowed to sweat, pulled about a bit to relax your muscles, and then rigorously scrubbed with a rough flannel glove (*kiis*). Alternatively, buy a *kiis* and do it yourself. For many Moroccan women, who would not drink in a café or bar, the hammam is a social gathering place, in which tourists are made very welcome too. Indeed, hammams turn out to be a highlight for many women travellers, and an excellent way to make contact with Moroccan women.

Several hammams are detailed in the text, but the best way of finding one is always to ask at the hotel where you're staying. You will often, in fact, need to be led to a hammam, since they are usually unmarked and can be hard to find. In some towns, you find a separate hammam for women and men; at others the same establishment offers different hours for each sex – usually mornings and evenings for men, afternoons (typically noon to 6pm) for women.

For both sexes, there's more modesty than you might perhaps expect: it's customary for men (always) and women (generally, though bare breasts are acceptable) to bathe in swimming costume (or underwear), and to undress facing the wall. Women may be also surprised to find their Moroccan counterparts completely shaven and may (in good humour) be offered this service; there's no embarrassment in declining.

As part of the Islamic tradition of cleanliness and ablutions, hammams sometimes have a religious element, and non-Muslims may not be welcome (or allowed in) to those built alongside mosques, particularly on Thursday evenings, before the main weekly service on Friday. On the whole, though, there are no restrictions against *Nisara* ("Nazarenes", or Christians).

Finally, don't forget to bring soap and shampoo (though these are sometimes sold at hammams), and a towel (these are sometimes rented, but may not always be as clean as you'd like). Moroccans often bring a plastic mat to sit on, too, as the floors can get a bit clogged. Mats can be bought easily enough in any town. Most Moroccans use a pasty, olive oil-based soap (*sabon bildi*), sold by weight in Medina shops. On sale at the same shops, you'll find *kiis* flannel gloves, a fine mud (*ghasoul*), used by some instead of shampoo, pumice stones (*hazra*) for removing dead skin, and alum (*chebba*), used as an antiperspirant and to stop shaving cuts from bleeding.

likely to be more homely. In a riad, it is often possible to rent the whole house.

The riad craze started in Marrakesh, and quickly spread to Fez and Essaouira. Since then it has gone nationwide and almost every town with tourists now has riads too. Even the Atlas mountains and the southern oases are dotted with them.

Most riads are eighteenth- or nineteenth-century **Medina townhouses** which have been bought and refurbished by Europeans or prosperous Moroccans (often Moroccans who have been living in Europe). Some of them are very stylishly done out, most have roof terraces, some have plunge pools or jacuzzis, pretty much all offer en-suite rooms, and breakfast is usually included in the room price. The best riads have a landlord or landlady who is constantly in attendance and stamps their own individual personality on the place, but many riads nowadays are really just boutique hotels, and can be quite impersonal.

The popularity of riads has also attracted a fair few amateur property developers, some of whom invest minimum money in the hope of maximum returns. Therefore, before you take a riad, even more than with a hotel, it is always best to give it a preliminary once-over. Riads may be more expensive than hotels with a similar level of comfort, but at the top of the market, they can be a lot classier than a run-of-the-mill five-star hotel.

Hostels

Morocco has thirteen *Auberges de Jeunesse* run by its YHA, the Fédération Royale Marocaine des Auberges de Jeunesse (☎0522 470952, ✉frmaj1 @menara.ma). Most are clean and reasonably well run, and charges vary from 30dh (£2.25/$3.60) to 75dh (£5.60/$9) per person per night in a dorm; most have private rooms too. Hostelling International (HI) membership cards are not required but you may have to pay a little extra if you do not have one. The hostels are located at Asni (High Atlas), Azrou (Middle Atlas), Casablanca, Chefchaouen, Fez, Goulmima, Laayoune (Western Sahara; closed at last check), Marrakesh, Meknes, Ouarzazate, Rabat, Rissani and Tinerhir. Most are reviewed in the relevant sections of the guide. Further information on Moroccan youth hostels can be found on the Hostelling International website at ⓦhihostels.com.

Refuges and gîtes d'étape

In the Jebel Toubkal area of the High Atlas mountains, the Club Alpin Français (CAF; 50 Bd Sidi Abderrahmane, Beauséjour, Casablanca ☎0522 990141, ⓦffcam.fr) maintain five huts, or refuges (at Imlil, Oukaïmeden, Tazaghart and Toubkal) equipped for mountaineers and trekkers. These provide bunks or bedshelves for sleeping at 100–180dh per person, with discounts for members of CAF or its affiliates. Some refuges can provide meals and/or cooking facilities.

Also in trekking areas, a number of locals offer rooms in their houses: such places are known as **gîtes d'étape**. Current charges are around 100–150dh per person per night, with meals for around 60–80dh.

Camping

Campsites are to be found at intervals along most of the developed Moroccan coast and in most towns or cities of any size. They vary in price and facilities, with cheap sites charging around 20dh (£1.50/$2.35) per person, plus a similar amount for a tent or camper van; cheap sites often have quite basic washing and toilet facilities, and usually charge 7–10dh for a hot shower. More upmarket places may offer better facilities and even swimming pools, and cost about twice as much, sometimes more. Comprehensive, and often highly critical reviews of Morocco's campsites, in French, can be found in Jacques Gandini's *Campings du Maroc et de Mauritanie: Guide Critique* (Broché, France), which is sometimes available at Moroccan campsites and bookshops.

Campsites don't tend to provide much security, and you should never leave valuables unattended. This obviously applies even more when camping outside official sites; if you want to do this, it's wise to ask at a house if you can pitch your tent alongside – you'll usually get a hospitable response. If you're trekking in the Atlas, it is often possible to pay someone to act as a *gardien* for your tent. In the south especially, and particularly in the winter, campsites are not much used by backpackers with tents, but rather by retired Europeans in camper vans seeking the sun.

If travelling in a camper van, you can often park up somewhere with a *gardien*, who will keep an eye on things for a small tip (usually 20dh per night). Failing that, you may be able to park outside a police station (*commissariat*). In the north of the country, at Larache, Kenitra and Malabata (near Tangier), there are *Aires de Repose*, which are rest areas for tourist coaches, with toilets, showers, a restaurant and *gardien*. There's no fee for parking your camper here or using the facilities, but it is usual to pay a contribution of around 20dh to the *gardien* if you stay overnight.

Food and drink

Basic Moroccan meals may begin with a thick, very filling soup – most often the spicy, bean and pasta *harira*. Alternatively, you might start with a salad (often very finely chopped), or have this as a side dish with your main course, typically a plateful of kebabs – either *brochettes* (small pieces of lamb on a skewer) or *kefta*, (minced lamb). A few hole-in-the wall places specialize in soup, which they sell by the bowlful all day long – such places are usually indicated by a pile of soup bowls at the front. As well as *harira*, and especially for breakfast, some places sell a thick pea soup called *bisara*, topped with olive oil.

Another dish you'll find everywhere is a **tajine**, essentially a stew, steam-cooked slowly in an earthenware dish with a conical earthenware lid. Like "casserole", the term "tajine" actually refers to the dish and lid rather than the food. Classic tajines include lamb or mutton with prunes and almonds, or chicken with olives and lemon. Less often, you may get a fish or vegetable tajine, or a tajine of meatballs topped with eggs.

Kebabs and tajines usually cost little more than 30dh (£2.25/$3.50) at hole-in-the-wall places in the Medina, which typically have just two or three tables. You are not expected to bargain for cooked food, but prices may be higher in such places if you don't ask how much things cost before you order them. There is often no menu – or just a board written in Arabic only.

If you're looking for **breakfast or a snack**, you can buy a half-**baguette** – plus butter and jam, cheese or eggs, if you want – from many bread or grocery stores, and take it into a café to order a coffee. Many cafés, even those which serve no other food, may offer a breakfast of bread, butter and jam (which is also what you'll get in most hotels), or maybe an omelette. Some places also offer soup, such as *harira*, with bread, and others have stalls outside selling by weight traditional griddle breads such as *harsha* (quite heavy with a gritty crust), *melaoui* or *msammen* (sprinkled with oil, rolled out thin, folded over and rolled out again several times, like an Indian *paratha*) and *baghira* (full of holes like a very thin English crumpet). If that is not sufficient, supplementary foods you could buy include dates or olives, yoghurt, or soft white cheese (*ejben*).

Street food includes small kebabs or spicy merguez sausages cooked at roadside stalls (make sure the sausages are well done), peanuts, sunflower seeds or roasted chickpeas sold at peanut stands, and **sfenj** (doughnut-shaped fritters), sold from little shops, particularly in the morning.

Restaurant meals

Restaurants usually offer **fish**, particularly on the coast, lamb (*agneau*) or mutton (*mouton*), usually in a tajine, and **chicken** (*poulet*), either spit-roasted (*rôti*) or in a tajine with lemon and olives (*poulet aux olives et citron*). You will sometimes find **pastilla**, too, a succulent pigeon or chicken pie, prepared with filo pastry dusted with sugar and cinnamon; it is a particular speciality of Fez.

And, of course, there's **couscous**, the most famous Moroccan dish; Berber in origin, it's a huge bowl of steamed semolina piled high with vegetables and mutton, chicken, or occasionally fish. Restaurant couscous can be disappointing as there is no real tradition of going out to eat in Morocco, and this is a dish that's traditionally prepared at home, especially on Friday or for a special occasion.

TAJINES

Like paella or casserole, the word **tajine** strictly refers to a vessel rather than to the food cooked in it. A tajine is a heavy ceramic plate covered with a conical lid of the same material. The prettiest tajines, decorated in all sorts of colours and designs, come from Safi (see p.294), but the best tajines for actual use are plain reddish-brown in colour, and come from Salé (see p.268). The food in a tajine is arranged with the meat in the middle and the vegetables piled up around it. Then the lid is put on, and the tajine is left to cook slowly over a low light, or better still, over a charcoal stove (*kanoun*), usually one made specifically for the tajine and sold with it. The classic tajines combine meat with fruit and spices. Chicken is traditionally cooked in a tajine with green olives and lemons preserved in brine. Lamb or beef are often cooked with prunes and almonds. When eating a tajine, you start on the outside with the vegetables, and work your way to the meat at the heart of the dish, scooping up the food with bread.

At festivals, which are always good for interesting food, and at the most expensive tourist restaurants, you may also come across **mechoui** – roast lamb, which may even take the form of a whole sheep roasted on a spit. In Marrakesh particularly, another speciality is **tanjia**, which is jugged beef or lamb, cooked very slowly in the embers of a hammam furnace.

Dessert may consist of a pastry, or a crème caramel, or possibly yoghurt, which is often – even in cheap places – the restaurant's own. Otherwise you may get fruit, either an orange, or perhaps a fruit salad.

Restaurants are typically open noon to 3pm for lunch, and 7 to 11pm for dinner, though cheaper places may be open in the morning and between times too. Places that don't display prices are likely to overcharge you unless you check the price before ordering.

Eating Moroccan style

Eating in local cafés, or if **invited to a home**, you may find yourself using your hands rather than a knife and fork. Muslims eat only with the **right hand** (the left is used for the toilet), and you should do likewise. Hold the bread between the fingers and use your thumb as a scoop; it's often easier to discard the soft centre of the bread and to use the crust only – as you will see many Moroccans do. Eating from a **communal plate** at someone's home, it is polite to take only what is immediately in front of you, unless specifically offered a piece of meat by the host.

Vegetarian eating

Vegetarianism is met with little comprehension in most of Morocco, though restaurants in some places are becoming aware that tourists may be vegetarian, and many places do now offer a meat-free tajine or couscous. In Marrakesh there is even a vegetarian restaurant (see p.347), and pizzas are usually available in large towns. Otherwise, aside from omelettes and sandwiches, menus don't present very obvious choices. *Bisara* (pea soup), a common breakfast dish, should be meat-free, but *harira* (bean soup) may or may not be made with meat stock, while most foods are cooked in animal fats. It is possible to say "I'm a vegetarian" (*ana nabaati* in Arabic, or *je suis vegetarien/vegetarienne* in French), but you may not be understood; to reinforce the point, you could perhaps add *la akulu lehoum (wala hout)* in Arabic, or *je ne mange aucune sorte de viande (ni poisson)*, both of which mean "I don't eat any kind of meat (or fish)".

If you are a very strict vegetarian or vegan, it may be worth bringing some basic provisions (such as yeast extract, peanut butter and veggie stock cubes) and a small camping gas stove and pan – canisters are cheap though quite hard to find (Carrefour hypermarkets usually have them, as do the DIY chain Mr Bricolage), and some cheap hotels allow guests to cook in their rooms.

The most difficult situations are those in which you are invited to eat at someone's house. You may find people give you meat when you have specifically asked for vegetables because they don't understand that you object to eating meat, and you may decide that it's more important not to offend someone showing you kindness than to be strict about your abstinence. Picking out vegetables from a meat tajine won't offend your hosts, but declining the dish altogether may end up with the mother/sister/wife in the kitchen getting the flak.

Fruit

Morocco is surprisingly rich in seasonal **fruits**. In addition to the various kinds of **dates** – sold all year but at their best fresh from the October harvests – there are grapes, melons, strawberries, peaches and figs, all of which should be washed before eaten. Or for a real thirst-quencher (and a good cure for a bad stomach), you can have quantities of **prickly pear** (cactus fruit), peeled for you in the street for a couple of dirhams in season (winter).

Tea, coffee and soft drinks

The national drink is **mint tea** (*atay deeyal naanaa* in Arabic, *thé à la menthe* in French, "Whisky Marocain" as locals boast), Chinese gunpowder green tea flavoured with sprigs of mint (*naanaa* in Arabic: the gift of Allah) and sweetened with a large amount of sugar, often from a sugar loaf (you can ask for it with little or no sugar – *shweeya soukar* or *ble soukar*). In winter, Moroccans often add wormwood (*chiba* in Arabic, *absinthe* in French) to their tea "to keep out the cold". You can also get black tea (*atai ahmar* in Arabic, *thé rouge* in French, literally meaning "red tea") – inevitably made with the ubiquitous Lipton's tea bags, a brand fondly believed by Moroccans to be typically English. The main **herbal infusion** is verbena (*verveine* or *louiza*).

Also common at cafés and street stalls are a range of wonderful freshly squeezed **juices**: orange juice (*jus d'orange* in French, '*asir burtuqal* in Arabic – if you don't want sugar in it, you'll need to say so say so), almond milk (*jus d'amande* or '*asir louze*), banana "juice", meaning milk shake (*jus des bananes* or *'asir mooz*) and apple milk shake (*jus de pomme* or *'asir tufah*). Also common is *'asir panaché*, a mixed fruit milk shake often featuring raisins. *Leben* – soured milk – is tastier than it sounds, and does wonders for an upset stomach.

Moroccan tap **water** is usually chlorinated and safe to drink, but tourists generally prefer to stick to bottled water. Mineral water is usually referred to by brand name, ubiquitously the still Sidi Harazem or Sidi Ali (some people claim to be able to tell one from the other), or the naturally sparkling Oulmès. The Coca-Cola company markets filtered, processed non-mineral water in bottles under the brand name Ciel. **Coffee** (*café*) is best in French-style cafés – either *noir* (black), *cassé* (with a drop of milk), or *au lait* (with a lot of milk). Instant coffee is known, like teabag tea, after its brand – in this case Nescafé.

Lastly, do not take risks with **milk**: buy it fresh and drink it fresh. If it smells remotely off, don't touch it.

Wine and beer

As an Islamic nation, Morocco gives **drinking alcohol** a low profile, and it is not generally possible to buy alcohol in city Medinas. Ordinary **bars** are very much all-male preserves, in which women may feel uneasy (bartenders may occasionally be female, but female Moroccan customers are likely to be on the game), but upmarket bars – especially in Marrakesh or Casablanca or in tourist hotels – are usually fine. On the drinks front, Moroccan **wines** can be palatable enough, if a little heavy for drinking without a meal. The best is the pinkish red Clairet de Meknès, made purposefully light in French claret style. Beauvallon is another good one, but usually reserved for export. Other varieties worth trying include the strong red Cabernet, and Ksar, Guerrouane and Siraoua, which are also red, the rosé Gris de Boulaoune and the dry white Spécial Coquillages.

Those Moroccans who drink in bars tend to stick to **beer**, usually the local Stork or Flag. Flag from Fez is held by many to be superior to the version brewed in Casablanca (the label will tell you which it is). The most popular foreign brand is Heineken, which is made under licence in Morocco.

The media

British dailies and the *International Herald Tribune* are available at some newsstands in city centres and tourist resorts.

Newspapers and magazines

The **Moroccan press** has a range of papers in French and Arabic, but news coverage, especially of international news, is weak. Of the **French-language** papers, the most accessible is the pro-government daily, *Le Matin* (Ⓦlematin.ma). Others include *L'Opinion* (Istiqlal party; Ⓦlopinion.ma), *Maroc Soir* (pro-government evening daily), *L'Economiste*, (independent; Ⓦleconomiste.com), and *Al Bayane* (communist; Ⓦalbayane.press.ma). Periodicals include *Maroc-Hebdo* (Ⓦmaroc-hebdo.press.ma), *La Vie Eco* (Ⓦlavieeco.com), and the Time/Newsweek-style news magazine *Tel-Quel* (Ⓦtelquel-online.com). There's also an independent online English-language news magazine, Morocco Newsline, at Ⓦmorocco-newsline.com. The most widely read **Arabic** daily newspapers are *Assabah*, the sister paper to *L'Economiste*, and the more sensationalist *Al Ahdath Al Maghribia*, which is independent but left-leaning.

In addition to these, Morocco has a number of football magazines, women's magazines and other publications in French, as well as the excellent Francophone African news magazine, *Jeune Afrique* (Ⓦjeuneafrique.com). Also worth a peruse is the English-language online cultural magazine Tingis (Ⓦtingismagazine.com), billed as "an American-Moroccan magazine of ideas and culture".

Radio

The **BBC** have cut World Service short-wave broadcasts to North Africa, but with a deft twiddle of the dial you may be able to pick up short-wave broadcasts for West Africa, or MW broadcasts to Europe; programme listings can be found online at Ⓦbbc.co.uk/worldservice. You can also pick up **Voice of America**, currently in the afternoon, on 11840 or 13570 KHz and in the evening on 7470 or 9490 KHz, but these sometimes change – see Ⓦvoanews.com/english/programs for up-to-date frequency and programme listings.

Television

Most of the pricier hotels receive **satellite TV** – CNN, the French TV5, and occasionally UK Sky channels. In the north of the country you can also get Spanish TV stations and, in Tangier, English-language **Gibraltar** TV. The independent Qatari news channel Al Jazeera is a major source of news for people in Morocco (many cafés show it), and you may even be able to get it in English if you have access to cable or satellite, but it is unfortunately not obtainable on terrestrial TV.

Morocco's own two TV channels broadcast in Arabic, but include some French programmes – plus news bulletins in Arabic, French, Spanish and, more recently, Berber.

Festivals

Morocco abounds in holidays and festivals, both national and local, and coming across one can be the most enjoyable experience of travel in the country – with the chance to witness music and dance, as well as special regional foods and market souks. Perhaps surprisingly, this includes Ramadan, when practising Muslims, including most Moroccans, fast from sunrise to sunset for a month, but when nights are good times to hear music and share in hospitality.

Ramadan

Ramadan, the ninth month of the Islamic calendar, commemorates the first revelation of the Koran to

Muhammad. Most people observe the fast; indeed Moroccans are forbidden by law from publicly disrespecting it, and a few people are jailed for this each year.

The fast involves abstention from food, drink, smoking and sex during daylight throughout the month. Most local cafés and restaurants close during the day, and many close up altogether and take a month's holiday. Smokers in particular get edgy towards the month's end, and it is in some respects an unsatisfactory time to travel: efficiency drops, drivers fall asleep at the wheel (hence airline pilots are excused fasting), and guides and muleteers are unwilling to go off on treks, and when the fast ends at sunset, almost regardless of what they are doing, everybody stops to eat. The month-long closure of so many eating places can also make life difficult if you are dependent on restaurants.

But there is compensation in witnessing and becoming absorbed into the pattern of the fast. At sunset, signalled by the sounding of a siren, by the lighting of lamps on minarets, and in some places by a cannon shot, an amazing calm and sense of wellbeing fall on the streets. The fast is

RAMADAN AND ISLAMIC HOLIDAYS

Islamic religious holidays are calculated on the **lunar calendar**, so their dates rotate throughout the seasons (as does Ramadan's), losing about eleven days a year against the Western (Gregorian) calendar. Exact dates in the lunar calendar are impossible to predict – they are set by the Islamic authorities in Fez – but approximate dates for the next few years are:

	2013	2014	2015	2016	2017	2018
Mouloud	24 Jan	13 Jan	3 Jan & 23 Dec	12 Dec	1 Dec	20 Nov
1st day of Ramadan	9 July	28 June	18 June	6 June	27 May	16 May
Aïd es Seghir	8 Aug	28 July	17 July	5 July	25 June	15 June
Aïd el Kebir	15 Oct	4 Oct	23 Sept	11 Sept	1 Sept	22 Aug
Moharem	5 Nov	25 Oct	14 Oct	2 Oct	21 Sept	11 Sept

FÊTES NATIONALES

Secular public holidays are tied to Western calendar dates:

January 11	Anniversary of Istiqlal Manifesto (see p.540)
May 1	Labour Day
July 30	Feast of the Throne
August 14	Allegiance Day
August 20	King and People's Revolution Day
August 21	King's Birthday and Youth Day
November 6	Anniversary of the Green March (see p.543)
November 18	Independence Day

Aïd el Kebir and Aïd es Seghir are marked by a two-day **public holiday**, announced or ratified by the king on TV and radio the preceding day. Mouloud is a one-day holiday. On these, and on the secular *fêtes nationales* listed above, all banks, post offices and most shops are closed; transport is reduced, too, but never stops completely. The largest secular holiday is the **Feast of the Throne**, a colourful affair, celebrated throughout Morocco, with fireworks, parades and music over two to three days.

traditionally broken with a bowl of *harira* and some dates, a combination provided by many cafés and restaurants exactly at sunset. You will also see almsgiving (*zakat*) extended to offering *harira* to the poor and homeless.

After breaking their fast, everyone – in the cities at least – gets down to a night of celebration and **entertainment**. This takes different forms. If you can spend some time in Marrakesh during the month, you'll find the Jemaa el Fna square at its most active, with troupes of musicians, dancers and acrobats coming into the city for the occasion. In Rabat and Fez, there seem to be continuous promenades, with cafés and stalls staying open until 3am. Urban cafés provide venues for live music and singing, too, and in the southern towns and Berber villages you will often come across the ritualized *ahouaches* and *haidus* – circular, trance-like dances often involving whole communities.

If you are a **non-Muslim** outsider you are not expected to observe Ramadan, but you should be sensitive about breaking the fast (particularly smoking) in public. In fact, the best way to experience Ramadan – and to benefit from its naturally purifying rhythms – is to enter into it. You may lack the faith to go without an occasional glass of water, and you'll probably have breakfast later than sunrise (it's often wise to buy supplies the night before), but it is worth an attempt.

Other Islamic holidays

Ramadan ends with the feast of **Aïd es Seghir** or **Aïd el Fitr**, a climax to the month's night-time festivities. Even more important is **Aïd el Kebir**, which celebrates the willingness of Abraham to obey God by sacrificing his son (Isaac in the Old Testament, but believed by Muslims to be his older son Ishmael). Aïd el Kebir is followed, about two months later, by **Moharem**, the Muslim new year.

Both *aïds* are traditional family gatherings. At Aïd el Kebir every household that can afford it will slaughter a sheep. You see them tethered everywhere, often on rooftops, for weeks prior to the event; after the feast, their skins can be seen being cured on the streets. On both *aïd* days, shops and restaurants close and buses don't run; on the following day, all transport is packed, as people return to the cities from their family homes.

The fourth main religious holiday is the **Mouloud**, the Prophet's birthday. This is widely observed, with a large number of moussems timed to take place in the weeks around it, and two particularly important moussems at Meknes (see p.206) and Salé (see p.269). There is also a music festival, **Ashorou**, which is held thirty days after Aïd el Kebir, when people gather to play whatever traditional instrument they feel capable of wielding, and the streets are full of music.

Moussems and ammougars

Moussems – or *ammougars* – held in honour of saints or *marabouts*, are local and predominantly rural affairs, and form the main religious and social celebrations of the year for most Moroccans, along with Aïd es Seghir and Aïd el Kebir.

Some of the smaller moussems amount to no more than a market day with religious overtones; others are

MOUSSEM CALENDAR

February	**Tafraoute** Moussem to celebrate the almond harvest (see p.490).
May	**Moulay Bousselham** Moussem of Marabout Moulay Bousselham (see p.100).
	Berkane Harvest moussem for clementines (see p.145).
	El Kelâa M'Gouna Rose festival to celebrate the new crop (see p.414).
June	**Tan Tan** Moussem of Sidi Mohammed Ma el Ainin (see p.511).
July	**Beni Arouss** Moussem of Moulay Abdessalem Ben Mchich (see p.112).
	Sefrou Fête des Cerises (see p.221).
August	**Setti Fatma** Moussem of Setti Fatma (see p.221).
	Sefrou Moussem of Sidi Lahcen el Youssi (see p.221).
	Tiznit Moussem of Sidi Ahmed ou Moussa (see p.484).
	Immouzer des Ida Outanane Honey moussem (see p.467).
September	**Moulay Idriss** Moussem of Moulay Idriss (see p.216).
	Imilchil Marriage moussem (see p.232).
	Fez Moussem of Moulay Idriss II (see p.196).
November	**Erfoud** Festival of Dates (see p.435).
December	**Rafsaï** Olive Festival (see p.149).

essentially harvest festivals, celebrating a pause in agricultural labour after a crop has been successfully brought in, but a number have developed into substantial occasions – akin to Spanish fiestas – and a few have acquired national significance. If you are lucky enough to be here for one of the major events, you'll get the chance to witness Moroccan popular culture at its richest, with horseriding, music, singing and dancing, and of course eating and drinking.

There are enormous numbers of moussems. An idea of quite how many can be gathered from the frequency with which, travelling about the countryside, you see *koubbas* – the square, white-domed buildings covering a saint's tomb. Each of these is a potential focal point of a moussem, and any one region or town may have twenty to thirty separate annual moussems. Establishing when they take place, however, can be difficult for outsiders; most local people find out by word of mouth at the weekly souks. Some moussems are held around religious occasions such as **Mouloud** (see opposite), which change date each year according to the lunar calendar; others follow the solar calendar (see box, p.43).

The **accommodation** situation will depend on whether the moussem is in the town or countryside. In the country, the simplest solution is to take a tent and camp – there is no real objection to anyone camping wherever they please during a moussem.

Aims and functions

The ostensible aim of the moussem is religious: to obtain blessing, or *baraka*, from the saint and/or to thank God for the harvest. But the social and cultural dimensions are equally important. Moussems provide an opportunity for country people to escape the monotony of their hard working lives in several days of festivities, and they may provide the year's single opportunity for friends or families from different villages to meet. Harvest and farming problems are discussed, as well as family matters – marriage in particular – as people get the chance to sing, dance, eat and pray together.

Music and singing are always major components of a moussem, and locals will often bring tape recorders to provide sounds for the rest of the year. Sufi brotherhoods have a big presence, and each bring their own distinct style of music, dancing and dress.

Moussems also operate as **fairs**, or markets, attracting people from a much wider area than the souk and giving a welcome injection of cash into the local economy, with traders and entertainers doing good business, and householders renting out rooms.

At the **spiritual level**, people seek to improve their standing with God through prayer, as well as the less orthodox channels of popular belief. Central to this is *baraka*, good fortune, which can be obtained by intercession of the saint. Financial contributions are made and these are used to buy a gift, or *hedia*, usually a large carpet, which is then taken in procession to the saint's tomb; it is deposited there for the local *shereefian* families, the descendants of the saint, to dispose of as they wish. Country people may seek to obtain *baraka* by attaching a garment or tissue to the saint's tomb and leaving it overnight to take home after the festival.

The procession taking the gift to the tomb is the high point of the more **religious** moussems, such as that of **Moulay Idriss** in Fez, where an enormous carpet is carried above the heads of the Sufi **brotherhoods**, each playing its own hypnotic music. Spectators and participants, giving themselves up to the music, may go into a trance. If you witness such events, it is best to keep a low profile so as not to interfere with people trying to attain a trance-like state, and certainly don't take photographs.

Release through trance probably has a therapeutic aspect, and indeed some moussems are specifically concerned with **cures** of physical and psychiatric disorders. The saint's tomb is usually located near a freshwater spring, and the cure can simply be bathing in and drinking the water. Those suffering from physical ailments may also be treated at the moussem with herbal remedies, or by recitation of verses from the Koran. Koranic verses may also be written and placed in tiny receptacles fastened near the affected parts.

Sports and outdoor activities

Morocco offers magnificent trekking opportunities, impressive golf facilities, a couple of ski resorts (plus some adventurous off-piste skiing) and excellent fishing. The national sporting obsession is football; enthusiasts can join in any number of beach kick-about games, or watch local league and cup matches.

Trekking

Trekking is among the very best things Morocco has to offer. The High Atlas is one of the most rewarding mountain ranges in the world, and one of the least spoilt. A number of **long-distance Atlas routes** can be followed – even a "Grand Traverse" of the full range, but most people stick to **shorter treks** in the **Jebel Toubkal** area (best in spring or autumn; conditions can be treacherous in winter; see p.364). Other promising areas include the **Jebel Sirwa** (see p.475), the **Western High Atlas** (see p.385), and, in winter the **Jebel Saghro (see p.364)** and **Tafraoute** region of the Anti-Atlas (see p.420). The **Middle Atlas** has much attractive walking too, in such places as **Tazzeka** (Taza; see p.491), and around **Azrou** (see p.153).

General **trekking practicalities** are discussed in Chapter Six (see p.223). A good source of trekking information is AMIS (Atlas Mountain Interactive Services; UK ☎01592 873546), a small agency and consultancy. You may be able to acquire specialist trekking maps through AMIS or elsewhere (see pp.370–371).

Skiing

Morocco doesn't immediately spring to mind as a skiing destination, but the High Atlas mountains are reliably snow-covered from late January to early April, with good skiing at **Oukaïmeden** (see p.61)

Off-piste skiing is popular in the High Atlas, particularly in the **Toubkal massif**, where the Toubkal Refuge (see p.463) is often full of groups. Most off-piste activity is ski mountaineering, but skinny skis (*langlauf*) are good in the Middle Atlas if there is snow, in which case the Azilal–Bou Goumez–Ighil Mgoun area is possible. **Snowboarding** is also gaining in popularity at Moroccan resorts. For further information on skiing and mountaineering, contact the Fédération Royale Marocaine du Ski et du Montagnisme (FRMSM; ☎0522 474979, ✉f.rmsn@yahoo.fr).

Riding

The established base for **horseriding holidays** is *Résidence de la Roseraie* at **Ouirgane** (see p.27), which runs trekking tours into the **High Atlas** (bring your own helmet). Another stable offering horseriding is Amodou Cheval near Agadir ⓦamodoucheval.com. A number of operators offer horse and **camel treks**, including Best of Morocco (see p.27).

Fishing

Morocco has an immense Atlantic (and small Mediterranean) **coastline**, with opportunities to arrange boat trips at Safi, Essaouira, Moulay Bousselham (near Asilah), Boujdour, Dakhla and elsewhere.

Inland, the **Middle Atlas** shelters beautiful **lakes** and **rivers**, many of them well stocked with trout. Good bases include Azrou (near the Aghmas lakes), Ifrane (near Zerrrouka), Khenifra (the Oum er Rbia River) and Ouirgane (the Nfis River). Pike are also to be found in some Middle Atlas lakes (such as Aguelmame Azizgza, near Khenifra), and a few of the huge artificial **barrages**, like Bin el Ouidaine (near Beni Mellal), are said to contain enormous bass.

For all fishing in the country, you need to take your own **equipment**. For coarse or fly fishing you need a **permit** from the Administration des Eaux et Fôrets at: 11 Rue Moulay Abdelaziz, Rabat (☎0537 762694); 25 Bd Roudani, Casablanca (☎0522 271598); or any regional office. For trout fishing, you are limited to the hours between 6am and noon; the season varies slightly from year to year, but usually runs April–September.

Watersports and swimming

Agadir offers opportunities for **sailing**, **yachting**, **windsurfing** and **diving**, while Taghazout, just to its

---

ANIMAL WELFARE

Animals – and especially pack animals – have a tough life in Morocco. The **Society for the Protection of Animals Abroad** (SPANA; ⓦspana.org and ⓦspana.org.ma), works throughout North Africa to improve conditions for working donkeys and horses, replacing painful, old-style bits, employing local vets and technicians and running animal clinics. There are SPANA centres in Tangier, Rabat, Casablanca, Marrakesh (see p.355), Khémisset, Khenifra, Midelt, Had Ouled Frej (near El Jadida) and Chémaia (near Marrakesh); they also manage the birdwatching reserve at Sidi Bourhaba near Kenitra. All of these can be contacted or visited if you are interested or are concerned about animals you come across. The best initial contact address in Morocco is SPANA's administrative office in Harhoura (☎0537 747209), 14km south of Rabat.

north, has become something of a **surfing** village, with board rental and board repair shops and some great surfing sites (see p.466). There are lesser surfing centres at Sidi Ifni, Mirhleft, Kenitra, Bouznika Plage (between Rabat and Casablanca), El Jadida, Safi, and even Rabat. With your own transport, you could scout out remote places all the way down the coast. When they're working, all breaks can be busy in peak season (Oct–Feb), when deep lows come barrelling east across the mid-Atlantic. Wet suit-wise, a good 3mm will cover winter months (although a thermal rash vest keeps things snug in Jan) and it's also worth bringing booties, unless you enjoy digging urchin spines out of your feet.

For **windsurfing**, the prime destination is Essaouira, which draws devotees year-round. Online **weather information** for surfers and windsurfers can be found at ⓦwindguru.com/int.

The Atlantic can be very exposed, with crashing waves, and surfers, windsurfers and **swimmers** alike should beware of strong undertows. Inland, most towns of any size have a municipal **swimming pool**, but women especially should note that they tend to be the preserve of teenage boys. In the south, you'll be dependent on campsite pools or on those at the luxury hotels (which often allow outsiders to swim, either for a fee or if you buy drinks or a meal).

The High and Middle Atlas have also become a popular destination for **whitewater rafting** and **kayaking** enthusiasts. One holiday firm specializing in these sports is Water by Nature (ⓦwaterbynature .com).

Golf

The British opened a **golf course** in Tangier as far back as 1917. Today the country has an international-level course at Rabat (see p.267), eighteen-hole courses at Mohammedia (see p.273), Marrakesh (see p.354), Tangier (see p.88), Cabo Negro (see p.114), Saïdia (see p.143), Larache (see p.97), El Jadida (see p.293), Essaouira (see p.307), Agadir (see p.460), Fez (p.197) and Ben Slimane (Royal Golf, Av des FAR, BP 83, Ben Slimane ☎0523 297225), and nine-hole courses at Meknes (see p.211), Ouarzazate (see p.402) and Bouznika (near Mohammedia, Route Secondaire de Bouznika Plage, km22, ☎0537 625371). Further information on courses can be found online at ⓦgolftoday. co.uk/clubhouse/coursedir/world/morocco and ⓦmoroccangreens.com. Several tour operators (including Best of Morocco; see p.27) offer Moroccan golfing holidays.

Football (soccer)

Football is important in Morocco and the country is a growing force in international football. The national side has made the World Cup finals on four occasions, and was the first African team to reach the finals (in 1970), and the first to progress beyond the group stage (in 1986). Morocco has won the African Nations Cup only once (in 1976), but reached the final in 2004, and will host the tournament in 2015. Moroccan teams have been very successful in African club competitions in the past, though the last Moroccan side to win the African Champions League was Raja Casablanca, back in 1999, though Wydad Casablanca reached the final in 2011. Moroccan clubs have done better in recent years in the Confederation Cup (equivalent to Europe's UEFA Cup), which was won by FAR Rabat in 2005, FUS Rabat in 2010, and MAS Fez in 2011.

Moroccan clubs compete in an annual **league** and the (knockout) **Throne Cup**. For a long time there was just one full-time professional team, **FAR** (the army), but the 1990s saw the introduction of sponsorship and a number of semi-professional sides, whose big names include **Wydad** (WAC) and **Raja**, the two big Casablanca teams, plus **FUS** from Rabat, **MAS** from Fez and **Hassania** from Agadir. The result is a fairly high standard of skill in the Moroccan league, but unfortunately Moroccan clubs are unable to afford the money commanded by top players in Europe, with the result that the best Moroccan players end up in European clubs.

Other sports

Morocco has two **marathons**: the Marrakesh Marathon (see p.354) and the even more gruelling Marathon des Sables (see p.411).

Most four-star and five-star hotels (especially in Agadir and Marrakesh) have **tennis** courts, though equipment, if available, is not often up to much, so you're advised to bring your own racket and balls.

Paragliding is increasingly popular in the south of Morocco, around Tafraoute and Mirhleft in particular, where there are thermals even during winter. Paragliding, hang-gliding and paramotoring trips, with instructors, are offered by Paraglide Morocco (ⓦparaglidemorocco.com) and Passion Paragliding (ⓦpassionparagliding.com).

Also popular in the south is **rock climbing**, particularly in the region around Tafraoute, and at Todra Gorge, where Rock & Sun (ⓦrockandsun .com) offer package tours for experienced climbers. Claude Davies's comprehensive *Climbing in the Moroccan Anti-Atlas: Tafroute and Jebel El Kest* (Cicerone Press, UK) has marked-up photos and detailed descriptions of Anti-Atlas ascents.

Culture and etiquette

Moroccans are extremely hospitable and very tolerant. Though most people are religious, they are generally easy-going, and most young Moroccan women don't wear a veil, though they may well wear a headscarf. Nonetheless, you should try not to affront people's religious beliefs, especially those of older, more conservative people, by, for example, wearing skimpy clothes, kissing and cuddling in public, or eating or smoking in the street during Ramadan.

Clothes are particularly important: many Moroccans, especially in rural areas, may be offended by clothes that do not fully cover parts of the body considered "private", including both legs and shoulders, especially for women. It is true that in cities Moroccan women wear short-sleeved tops and knee-length skirts (and may suffer more harassment as a result), and men may wear sleeveless T-shirts and above-the-knee shorts. However, the Muslim idea of "modest dress" (such as would be acceptable in a mosque, for example) requires women to be covered from wrist to ankle, and men from over the shoulder to below the knee. In rural areas at least, it is a good idea to follow these codes, and definitely a bad idea for women to wear shorts or skirts above the knee, or for members of either sex to wear sleeveless T-shirts or very short shorts. Even ordinary T-shirts may be regarded as underwear, particularly in rural mountain areas. The best guide is to note how Moroccans dress locally.

When **invited to a home**, you normally take your shoes off before entering the reception rooms – follow your host's lead. It is customary to take a gift: sweet pastries or tea and sugar are always acceptable, and you might even take meat (by arrangement – a chicken from the countryside for example, still alive of course) to a poorer home.

Tipping

You're expected to **tip** – among others – waiters in cafés (1dh per person) and restaurants (5dh or so in moderate places, 10–15 percent in upmarket places); museum and monument curators (3–5dh); *gardiens de voitures* (5dh; see p.34); filling station attendants (3–5dh); and porters who load your baggage onto buses (5dh). Taxi drivers do not expect a tip, but always appreciate one.

Mosques

Without a doubt, one of the major disappointments of travelling in Morocco if you are not Muslim is not being allowed into its mosques. The only exceptions are the partially restored Almohad structure of Tin Mal in the High Atlas (see p.382), the similarly disused Great Mosque at Smara in the Western Sahara (see p.512), the courtyard of the sanctuary-mosque of Moulay Ismail in Meknes (see p.200) and the Hassan II Mosque in Casablanca (see p.279). Elsewhere, if you are not a believer, you'll have to be content with an occasional glimpse through open doors, and even in this you should be sensitive: people don't seem to mind tourists peering into the Kairaouine Mosque in Fez (the country's most important religious building), but in the country you should never approach a shrine too closely.

This rule applies equally to the numerous white-washed **koubbas** – the tombs of *marabouts*, or local saints (usually domed: *koubba* actually means "dome") – and the "monastic" **zaouias** of the various Sufi brotherhoods. It is a good idea, too, to avoid walking through **graveyards**, as these also are regarded as sacred places.

Women in Morocco

There is no doubt that, for **women** especially, travelling in Morocco is a very different experience from travelling in a Western country. One of the reasons for this is that the separate roles of the sexes are much more defined than they are in the West, and sexual mores much stricter. In villages and small towns, and even in the Medinas of large cities, many women still wear the veil and the street is strictly the man's domain. Most Moroccan men still expect to marry a virgin, and most women would never smoke a cigarette or drink in a bar, the general presumption being that only prostitutes do such things.

It should be said, however, that such ideas are gradually disappearing among the urban youth, and you will nowadays find some Moroccan women drinking in the more sophisticated bars, and even more often in cafés, which were, until quite recently, an all-male preserve. In the Villes Nouvelles of large cities, and especially in the Casa–Rabat–El Jadida area, and in Marrakesh, you'll see most women without a veil or even a headscarf. You'll also see young people of both sexes hanging out together, though you can be sure that opportunities for premarital sex are kept to a minimum. Even in traditional Moroccan societies, mountain Berber women, who do most of the hard work, play a much more open role in society, and rarely use a veil.

Sexual harassment

Different women seem to have vastly different experiences of **sexual harassment** in Morocco. Some travellers find it persistent and bothersome, while others have little or no trouble with it at all. Many women compare Morocco favourably with Spain and other parts of southern Europe, but there is no doubt that, in general, harassment of tourists here is more persistent than it is in northern Europe or the English-speaking world.

Harassment will usually consist of men trying to chat you up or even asking directly for sex, and it can be constant and sometimes intimidating. In part this is to do with Moroccan men's misunderstanding of Western culture and sexual attitudes, and the fact that some think they can get away with taking liberties with tourists that no Moroccan woman would tolerate.

The obvious **strategies** for getting rid of unwanted attention are the same ones that you would use at home: appear confident and assured and you will avoid a lot of trouble. Making it clear that you have the same standards as your Moroccan counterparts will usually deter all but the most insistent of men. No Moroccan woman would tolerate being groped in the street for example, though they may often have to put up with catcalls and unwanted comments. Traditionally, Moroccan women are coy and aloof, and uninhibited friendliness – especially any kind of physical contact between sexes – may be seen as a come-on, so being polite but formal when talking to men will diminish the chances of misinterpretation. The negative side to this approach is that it can also make it harder for you to get to know people, but after you've been in the country for a while, you will probably develop a feel for the sort of men with whom this tactic is necessary. It is also wise not to **smoke** in public, as some men still seem to think this indicates that you are available for sex.

How you **dress** is another thing that may reduce harassment. Wearing "modest" clothes (long sleeves, long skirts, baggy rather than tight clothes) will give an impression of respectability. Wearing a headscarf to cover your hair and ears will give this impression even more. One reader told us she felt a headscarf was "the single most important item of dress", adding that you can pull it over your face as a veil if unwanted male attention makes you feel uncomfortable. Indeed, Western liberals often forget that the purpose of wearing a veil is to protect women rather than to oppress them. However, you will notice that many Moroccan women totally ignore the traditional dress code, and do not suffer excessive harassment as a result. As for immodestly dressed women being taken for prostitutes, the fact is that actual sex workers in Morocco are often veiled from head to foot, as much to disguise their identities as anything else.

Other strategies to steer clear of trouble include avoiding eye contact, mentioning a husband who is nearby, and, if travelling with a boyfriend or just with a male friend, giving the impression that he is your husband. You should also avoid physical contact with Moroccan men, even in a manner that would not be considered sexual at home, since it could easily be misunderstood. If a Moroccan man touches *you*, on the other hand, he has definitely crossed the line, and you should not be afraid to **make a scene**. Shouting *"Shooma!"* ("Shame on you!") is likely to result in bystanders intervening on your behalf, and a very uncomfortable situation for your assailant.

It is often said that women are second-class citizens in Islamic countries, though educated Muslim women are usually keen to point out that this is a misinterpretation of Islam. While sex equality has a long way to go in Morocco, in some ways, at least in theory, the sexes are not as unequal as they seem. Men traditionally rule in the street, which is their domain, the woman's being the home. One result is that Moroccan women will receive their friends at home rather than meet them in, say, a café (although this is slowly changing) and this can make it difficult for you to get to know Moroccan women. One place where you *can* meet up with them is the hammam (see p.38). It may also be that if you are travelling with a man, Moroccan men will address him rather than you – but this is in fact out of respect for you, not disrespect, and you will not be ignored if you join in the conversation. In any case, however interpreted, Islam most certainly does not condone sexual harassment, and nor do any respectable Moroccans. Being aware of that fact will make it seem a lot less threatening.

Shopping

Souks (markets) are a major feature of Moroccan life, and among the country's greatest attractions. They are found everywhere: every town has a souk area, large cities like Fez and Marrakesh have labyrinths of individual souks (each filling a street or square and devoted to one particular craft), and in the country-side there are hundreds of weekly souks, on a different day in each village of the region.

When buying souvenirs in Morocco, it's worth considering how you are going to get them home, and you shouldn't take too literally the claims of shopkeepers about their goods, especially if they tell you that something is "very old" – *trafika* (phoney merchandise) abounds, and there are all sorts of imitation fossils and antiques about.

Souk days

Some villages are named after **their market days**, so it's easy to see when they're held.

The souk days are:

Souk el Had – Sunday (literally, "first market")
Souk el Tnine – Monday market
Souk el Tleta – Tuesday market
Souk el Arba – Wednesday market
Souk el Khamees – Thursday market
Souk es Sebt – Saturday market

There are very few village markets on **Friday** (el Jemaa – the "assembly", when the main prayers are held in the mosques), and even in the cities, souks are largely closed on Friday mornings and very subdued for the rest of the day.

Village souks usually begin on the afternoon preceding the souk day, as people travel from across the region; those who live nearer set out early in the morning of the souk day, but the souk itself is often over by noon and people disperse in the afternoon. You should therefore arrange to arrive by mid-morning at the latest.

Craft traditions

Moroccan **craft** traditions are very much alive, but finding pieces of real quality is not that easy. For a good price, it's always worth getting as close to the source of the goods as possible, and steering clear of tourist centres. **Tangier**, **Casablanca** and **Agadir**, with no workshops of their own, are

generally poor bets, for example, while **Fez** and **Marrakesh** have a good range but high prices. In places like Fez and Marrakesh, different parts of the Medina produce specific goods, from furniture to ironwork to sandals to musical instruments. Jewellery and carpets tend to come in from the countryside, where each region – each village even – has its own style and its own techniques. Shopping in a big city, you'll have a wide range to choose from, but there's a very special pleasure in tracking the souvenir you want down to the place where it's made, and even seeing the artisans at work making it. A good way to get an idea of standards and quality is to visit **craft museums**: there are useful ones in Fez, Meknes, Tangier, Rabat and Marrakesh.

Carpets, rugs and blankets

Morocco produces some lovely carpets in wonderful warm colours – saffron yellow, cochineal red, antimony black – that look great in any living space. Nowadays most carpets are coloured with synthetic dyes, but their inspiration remains the natural dyes with which they were traditionally made. The most expensive carpets are hand-knotted, but there are also kilims (woven rugs).

Knotted carpets are not cheap – you can pay €1500 and more for the finer Arab designs in Fez or Rabat – but rugs and kilims come in at more reasonable prices, and you can buy a range of strong, well-designed weaves for €50–70. Most of these kilims will be of Berber origin and the most interesting ones usually come from the High and Middle Atlas. You'll find a big selection in Marrakesh, but if you're looking seriously, try to get to the town souk in Midelt or the weekly markets in Azrou and other villages in the region. The chain of Maison Berbère shops in Ouarzazate, Tinerhir and Rissani are good hunting grounds too, but one of the best ways to find carpets is to wander around villages or parts of town where they are made, listen for the telltale sound of the loom in use, and ask at the weavers' homes if they have any carpets for sale.

On a simpler and cheaper level, the Berber blankets (*foutahs*, or *couvertures*) are imaginative, and often very striking with bands of reds and blacks; for these, Tetouan and Chefchaouen, on the edge of the Rif, are promising.

Ceramics

Pottery is colourful if fairly crudely made on the whole, though the blue-and-white designs of Fez and the multicoloured pots of Chefchaouen (both produced largely for the tourist trade) are highly attractive. The essentially domestic pottery of Safi – Morocco's major pottery centre – is worth a look, too, with its colourful plates, tajines and garden pots. Safi tajines are nice to look at, but for practical use, the best are those produced by the Oulja pottery at Salé, near Rabat, in plain red-brown earthenware.

Jewellery

Arabic-style gold jewellery tends to be a bit fussy for Western tastes, but silver is another story. In the south particularly, you can pick up some fabulous Berber necklaces and bracelets, always very chunky, and characterized by bold combinations of semiprecious (and sometimes plastic) stones and beads. Women in the Atlas and the Souss Valley regions in particular often wear chunky silver bracelets, belts embellished with old silver coins, or heavy necklaces with big beads of amber, coral and carnelian. Silver brooches are used to fasten garments, and many of the symbols found in Moroccan jewellery, such as the "hand of Fatima" and the five-pointed star, are there to guard against the evil eye. Essaouira, Marrakesh and Tiznit have particularly good jewellery souks.

Wood

Marquetry is one of the few crafts where you'll see genuinely old pieces – inlaid tables and shelves – though the most easily exportable objects are boxes. The big centre for marquetry is Essaouira, where cedar or thuya wood is beautifully inlaid with orange-tree wood and other light-coloured woods to make trays, chess and backgammon sets, even plates and bowls, and you can visit the workshops where they are made.

Fez, Meknes, Tetouan and Marrakesh also have souks specializing in carpentry, which produce not only furniture, but also chests, sculptures, and kitchen utensils such as the little ladles made from citrus wood that are used to eat *harira* soup.

Clothes

Moroccan clothes are easy to purchase, and though Westerners – men at least – who try to imitate Moroccan styles by wearing the cotton or wool *jellaba* (a kind of outer garment) tend to look a little silly in the street, they do make good nightgowns. Some of the cloth on sale is exquisite in itself, and walking through the dyers' souks is an inspiration. Women will find some sumptuous gowns if they look in the right places – Marrakesh in particular has shops selling beautiful dresses, kaftans, *gandoras* (sleeveless kaftans) and tunics.

Brightly coloured knitted caps are more likely to appeal to men, and there are plenty of inexpensive multicoloured silk scarves on offer too. Even ordinary jackets and trousers are often on sale in the souks at bargain prices.

Leatherware

Morocco leather is famously soft and luxurious. In towns like Fes, Marrakesh and Taroudant you can even visit the tanneries to see it being cured. It comes in a myriad of forms from belts, bags and clothing to pouffes and even book covers, but Morocco's best-known leather item is the *babouche*, or slipper. Classic Moroccan *babouches*, open at the heel, are immensely comfortable, and produced in yellow (the usual colour), white, red (for women) and occasionally grey or black; a good pair – and quality varies enormously – can cost anything between €5 and €25. Marrakesh and Tafraoute are especially good for *babouches*.

Minerals and fossils

You'll see a variety of semiprecious stones on sale throughout Morocco, and in the High Atlas they are often aggressively hawked on the roadsides. If you're lucky enough to be offered genuine amethyst or quartz, prices can be bargained to very tempting levels. Be warned, however, that all that glitters is not necessarily the real thing. Too often, if you wet the stone and rub, you'll find traces of dye on your fingers.

Fossils too (see p.442) are widely sold in Morocco, and can be as beautiful as they are fascinating. The fossil-rich black marble of the Erfoud region, for example, is sold in the form of anything from ashtrays to table tops. But again, things aren't always what they seem, and a lot of fossils are in fact fakes, made out of cement. This is particularly true of trilobites, or any black fossil on a grey background.

Foodstuffs

Some Moroccan **food products** would be hard to find at home, and make excellent and inexpensive gifts or souvenirs (assuming your country's customs allow their importation). Locally produced **olive oil** can be excellent, with a distinctive strong flavour, and in the Souss Valley there's delicious sweet **argan oil** too (see p.474). Olives themselves come in numerous varieties, and there are also almonds, walnuts and spices available, notably **saffron** from Taliouine, and the spice mix known as Ras el Hanout. A jar of lemons preserved in brine is useful if you want to try your hand at making a tajine back home.

Bargaining

Whatever you buy, other than groceries, you will be expected to **bargain**. There are no hard and fast rules – it is really a question of paying what something is worth to you – but there are a few general points to keep in mind.

First, don't worry about **initial prices**. These are simply a device to test your limits. Don't think that you need to pay a specific fraction of the first asking price: some sellers start near their lowest price, while others will make a deal for as little as a tenth of the initial price.

Second, have in mind a figure that you want to pay, and a maximum above which you will not go. If your maximum and the shopkeeper's minimum don't meet, then you don't have a deal, but it's no problem.

Third, **don't ever let a figure pass your lips** that you aren't prepared to pay – nor start bargaining for something you have absolutely no intention of buying – there's no better way to create bad feelings.

Fourth, **take your time**. If the deal is a serious one (for a rug, say), you'll probably want to sit down over tea with the vendor, and for two cups you'll talk about anything but the rug and the price. If negotiations do not seem to be going well, it often helps to have a friend on hand who seems – and may well be – less interested in the purchase than you and can assist in extricating you from a particularly hard sell.

Fifth, remember that even if you're **paying more than local people**, it doesn't necessarily mean you're being "ripped off". As a Westerner, your earning power is well above that of most Moroccans and it's rather mean to force traders down to their lowest possible price just for the sake of it.

The final and most golden rule of all is never to go shopping with a **guide** or a hustler. Any shop that a guide steers you into will pay them a commission, added to your bill of course, while hustlers often pick up tourists with the specific aim of leading you to places that (even if you've agreed to go in "just to look") will subject you to a lengthy high-pressure hard-sell.

An approximate idea of what you should be paying for handicrafts can be gained from checking the **fixed prices** in the state- or cooperative-run Ensembles Artisanals, which are slightly higher than could be bargained for elsewhere.

Travelling with children

Travelling with small children, you may well find that people will frequently come up to admire them, to compliment you on them and to caress them, which may be uncomfortable for shyer offspring. In Moroccan families, children stay up late until they fall asleep and are spoiled rotten by older family members. The streets are pretty safe and even quite small children walk to school unaccompanied or play in the street unsupervised.

As a parent, however, you will encounter one or two difficulties. For example, you won't find baby changing rooms in airports, hotels or restaurants, and will have to be discreet if breastfeeding – find a quiet corner and shield infant and breast from view with a light cloth over your shoulder. Beach resort and package tour hotels may have facilities such as playgrounds, children's pools and a babysitting service, but mid-range city hotels are far less likely to cater for children, though many allow children to share their parents' room for free.

You may want to try a holiday with Club Med (Ⓦ clubmed.com), whose purpose-built holiday resorts at Agadir and Marrakesh feature kids' club, entertainment and sports facilities on site. Attractions that should appeal to small people include Magic Park in Salé (see p.267), Oasiria in Marrakesh (see p.354), and the tourist train in Agadir (see p.451).

Disposable nappies (diapers) are available at larger supermarkets, and sometimes city pharmacies, at prices similar to what you pay at home, but off the beaten track, you may need to stock up, or take washables. You may also want to take along some dried baby food; any café can supply hot water.

On buses and grands taxis, children small enough to share your seat will usually travel free, but older kids pay the full adult fare. On trains, travel is free for under-fours, and half price for four-to eleven-year-olds.

Among hazards that you'll need to bear in mind are traffic and stray animals. Dogs can be fierce in Morocco, and can also carry rabies, and there are a lot of feral cats and dogs about. Children (especially young ones) are also more susceptible than adults to heatstroke and dehydration, and should always wear a sunhat, and have high-factor sunscreen applied to exposed skin. If swimming at a beach resort, they should do so in a T-shirt, certainly for the first few days. The other thing that children are very susceptible to is an

> **CHILDREN ON PARENTS' PASSPORTS**
>
> If travelling as a family, note that **children travelling on their parents' passports** must have their photographs affixed to the passport. If this is not done, it is possible that you will be refused entry to Morocco. This is not just a piece of paper bureaucracy: families are sometimes refused entry for failing to comply.

upset tummy. Bear in mind that antidiarrhoeal drugs should generally not be given to young children; read the literature provided with the medication or consult a doctor for guidance on child dosages. For more tips, see *The Rough Guide to Travel with Babies & Young Children*.

Travel essentials

Costs

Costs for food, accommodation and travel in Morocco are low by European or North American standards. If you stay in the cheaper hotels (or camp out), eat local food, and share expenses and rooms with another person, £150/$250 each a week would be enough to survive on. On £300/$500 each you could live pretty well, while with £700–1000/$1000–1500 a week between two people you would be approaching luxury.

Accommodation costs range from £10/$15 a night – sometimes even less – for a double room in a basic hotel to as much as £300/$450 a night in a top luxury hotel or riad. The price of a **meal** reflects a similar span, ranging from £4/$6 to around £25/$35 a meal. **Alcohol** is really the only thing that compares unfavourably with Western prices: a bottle of cheap Moroccan wine costs £3.50/$5, a can of local beer about £1/$1.50 in the shops, £2.50/$4 in a normal bar, or £5/$7.50 in clubs.

Inevitably, **resorts** and larger **cities** (Marrakesh especially) are more expensive than small towns with few tourists, but in **remote parts** of the country (including trekking regions in the High Atlas), where goods have to be brought in from some distance, prices for provisions can be high.

Beyond accommodation and food, your major outlay will be for **transport** – expensive if you're renting a car (prices start at around £200/$300 a week plus fuel), but very reasonable if you use the local trains, buses and shared taxis (see box, p.30).

Youth/student ID cards can save you a small amount of money, entitling you to cheaper entry at some museums and other sights, and a small discount on some ferry tickets and domestic airfares.

They're not worth going out of your way to get, but if you have one you may as well bring it along.

In the Spanish enclaves of Ceuta and Melilla, prices for most things are the same as they are in mainland Spain (except that there is no duty on alcohol, tobacco and electronic goods), and around twice as expensive as in Morocco proper.

Hidden costs

You'll probably end up buying a few **souvenirs**. Rugs, carpets, leather, woodwork, pottery and jewellery are all outstanding – and few travellers leave without something.

Harder to come to terms with is the fact that you'll be confronting real **poverty**. As a tourist, you're not going to solve any problems, but with a labourer's wages often little more than 5dh (40p/60¢) an hour, even small **tips** can make a lot of difference to people. For Moroccans, giving alms to **beggars** is natural, and a requirement of Islam, especially since there is no social security here, so for tourists, rich by definition, local poverty demands at least some response. Do not, however, dispense money indiscriminately to **children**, which encourages pestering and promotes a dependence on begging.

Crime and personal safety

Keep your luggage and money secure. Morocco does not have a high crime rate, but it is obviously unwise to carry large sums of cash or valuables on your person – especially in Casablanca and Tangier, and to a lesser extent Fez and Marrakesh. Mugging as such is pretty rare – those who fall victim to theft usually have things taken by stealth, or are subject to some kind of scam (see box, pp.54–55). Be especially vigilant at transport stations (new arrivals are favourite targets, and just before departure is a favourite time to strike) and in crowd situations where pickpockets may operate. Credit card fraud is also relatively common, so don't let the plastic out of your sight while using it, and keep an eye out when withdrawing money from ATMs.

Hotels, generally, are secure and useful for depositing money before setting out to explore; larger ones will keep valuables at reception and some will have safes. **Campsites** are considerably less secure, and many campers advise using a **money belt** – to be worn even while sleeping. If you do decide on a money belt (and many people spend time quite happily without), leather or cotton materials are preferable to nylon, which can irritate in the heat.

The police

There are two main types of Moroccan **police**: the *Gendarmerie* (who wear grey uniforms and man the checkpoints on main roads, at junctions and the entry to towns), and the Police (*Sûreté*), who wear navy blue uniforms or plain clothes. Either may demand to see your passport (and/or driving papers). It is obligatory to carry official ID (in practice a passport), though you should not have any problems if you leave yours in a hotel safe while wandering around town, especially if you carry a photocopy of the important pages. You are unlikely to have any contact with the green-uniformed *Force Auxiliaire*, a backup force who wear berets and look more like the army.

The *gendarmes* have jurisdiction outside built-up areas, the police, within towns. Both are usually polite and helpful to visitors, and there is a *Brigade Touristique* in cities such as Marrakesh and Fez, specifically set up to protect tourists.

If you do need to **report a theft**, try to take along a fluent French- or Arabic-speaker if your own French and Arabic are not too hot. You may only be given a scrap of paper with an official stamp to show your insurance company, who then have to apply themselves to a particular police station for a report (in Arabic). If you cannot prove that a theft has taken place, the police may decline to make any report, especially if the theft is of money only. They will always give you a report, however, if you have lost any official document (passport, driving licence, etc).

GUIDES, HUSTLERS, CONMEN AND KIDS

Armed with this book, you shouldn't need a guide, but some people like to hire one to negotiate the Medinas of larger cities. **Official guides**, identified by a large, brass "sheriff's badge", can be engaged through tourist offices or large hotels. They charge around 150–200dh for half a day, twice that for a full day, plus sustenance. The rate is for the guide's time, and can be shared by a group (though you'd then be expected to give a good tip).

Young Moroccans may also offer their services as **unofficial guides**, which is illegal, and subject to occasional police clampdowns. Be very careful in making use of unofficial guides. Some are indeed genuine, usually unemployed youths hoping to make a few dirhams by showing tourists around, and they should be cheaper than official guides, less formal, offer a more street-level view, and perhaps show you things that official guides would not – indeed, many tourists end up making lasting friendships with people who've approached them as unofficial guides – but some will be aiming only to get you into shops or hotels which pay them commission, or they may be confidence tricksters. If you do decide to hire an unofficial guide, be sure to **fix the rate** in advance (make it clear that you know the official rates), as well as the **itinerary** (so that it does not include shops, for example – this also applies to official guides). In general, never agree to a guide showing you to a **hotel**, and never go **shopping** with a guide, official or otherwise, as they will only take you to places which pay them a commission, meaning a higher bill for you – often as much as fifty percent higher. Hotels that pay commission to guides for bringing tourists to them are also likely to be dubious in other ways. On the other hand, letting someone guide you to a **café** or **restaurant** won't increase the price of a meal (although waiters will generally make a small tip to the guide).

CONMEN AND SCAMS

Hustlers and conmen have been largely cleaned off the streets, and those who remain are less persistent, but tourists are the obvious target for them. However, it's important not to treat every Moroccan who approaches you as a hustler – many (though not usually in tourist hot spots) are just trying to be friendly. However, forewarned is forearmed, so a few notes on the **most common scams** follow:

• Most hustlers (and guides, official or not) hope to earn money by steering you, sometimes with the most amazing deviousness, into shops that will pay them a commission, most commonly carpet shops where you will be subjected to hours of hard-sell. Never be afraid to walk away from such as situation, even if (as is quite likely) you are then subjected to abuse, and never buy anything from a shop that you are taken to by a guide or hustler.

Kif and hashish

The smoking of **kif** (marijuana) and hashish (cannabis resin) has long been a regular pastime of Moroccans and tourists alike, but it is nonetheless illegal, and large fines (plus prison sentences for substantial amounts) do get levied for possession. If you are arrested for cannabis, the police may expect to be paid off, and this should be done as quickly as possible while the minimum number of officers are involved (but offer it discreetly, and never refer to it as a bribe or even a *cadeau*). Consulates are notoriously unsympathetic to drug offenders, but they can help with technical problems and find you legal representation.

Obviously, the best way to avoid trouble is to keep well clear – above all, of the *kif*-growing region of **Ketama** in the Rif mountains (see box, p.131) – and always reply to hustlers by saying you don't smoke. If you are going to indulge, be very careful who you buy it from (definitely do not buy it from touts or hustlers), and above all do not try to take any out of the country, even to Spain, where attitudes to possession are relaxed but much harsher for importing. Searches at Algeciras and Málaga can be very thorough, with sniffer dogs, which also operate at Moroccan ports and airports, and you'll get sometimes as many as four checks if travelling through Ceuta or Melilla.

Electricity

The supply is 220v 50Hz. Sockets have two round pins, as in Europe. You should be able to find adaptors in Morocco that will take North American plugs (but North American appliances may need a transformer, unless multi-voltage). Adaptors for British and Australasian plugs will need to be brought from home.

- If a hustler guides you into the Medina till you have no idea where you are, and then demands a large fee to take you back out, don't be afraid to appeal to people in the street, and if you feel genuinely menaced or harassed, threaten to go to the police: hustlers tend to vanish fast at the prospect of police involvement.
- Hustlers may attach themselves to you using the excuse of a letter ("Could you help translate or write one?"), or by pretending to be someone you have met but forgotten – so if someone you don't remember says, "Hey, remember me?" it's probably a hustler trying to practise some scam on you. Another trick is to tell you that a site that you are on your way to visit is closed and that they can show you something else instead, or they may tell you that there is a Berber market taking place and this is the only day of the week to see it. If you ignore these people or turn them down, they may accuse you of being paranoid, angry or racist – and such an accusation is a sure sign that you were right.
- Con merchants, working alone or in couples, may befriend tourists, and then, after a day or two, tell some sad tale about needing money to get a passport or for a sick relative, or some such.
- On trains, especially at Tangier, hustlers sometimes pose as porters or railway staff, demanding an extortionate fee for carrying baggage or payment of supplements. Genuine rail staff wear beige overalls and have ID cards, which, if suspicious, you should ask to see.
- Drivers should beware of hitchhiking hustlers, who spend all day hitching between a pair of towns and can get highly obnoxious in their demands for money when you approach one or other destination. Alternatively, they may wish to thank you for the lift by taking you home for a cup of tea – except that "home" turns out to be a carpet shop, where you are then subjected to hours of hard-sell. A variation on this is the fake breakdown, where people on the road flag down passing tourists and ask them to take a note to a "mechanic", who turns out to be a carpet salesman. This one is particularly common on the N9 between Marrakesh, Ouarzazate and Zagora, and the N10 between Ouarzazate and Tinerhir.

DEALING WITH CHILDREN

In the countryside especially, children may demand a dirham, *un cadeau* (present) or *un stylo* (a pen/pencil). Working out your own strategy is all part of the game, but be sure to keep good humour: smile and laugh, or kids can make a serious nuisance of themselves. Faced with **begging from children**, we recommend not obliging, as this ties them to a begging mentality, and encourages them to harass other visitors.

Entry requirements

If you hold a full passport from the UK, Ireland, the US, Canada, Australia, New Zealand or any EU country, you don't need a visa to enter Morocco as a tourist for up to ninety days. However, your passport must be valid for at least six months beyond your date of entry, and always double check your visa requirements before departure as the situation can change. South African citizens are among those who need a visa; applications should be made to the Moroccan embassy or consulate in your country of residence (South Africans should be able to get one in London), with three passport photos, and a form that you can download from the websites of some Moroccan consulates (for example, London's at Ⓦmoroccanembassylondon .org.uk/Docs/VisaForm.pdf).

Entry formalities are fairly straightforward, though you will have to fill in a form stating personal details, purpose of visit and your **profession**. In the past, Moroccan authorities have shown an occasional reluctance to allow in those who categorize themselves as "journalist"; an alternative profession on the form might be wise.

Customs regulations

You can bring in, without charge: one litre of spirits, or two litres of wine; 200 cigarettes, 50 cigars or 400g of tobacco; 150ml of perfume or 250ml of eau de toilette; jewellery; a camera and a laptop for personal use; gifts worth up to 2000dh (£150/$240). Prohibited goods include arms and ammunition (except for hunting), controlled drugs, and "books, printed matter, audio and video cassettes and any immoral items liable to cause a breach of the peace".

Items such as **electronic equipment and video cameras** may occasionally be entered on your passport. If you lose them during your visit, they will be assumed "sold" when you come to leave and (unless you have police documentation of theft) you will have to pay one hundred percent duty. All goods entered on your passport should be "cleared" when leaving to prevent problems on future trips. Vehicles need a Green Card (see p.27).

Carrying ID

It is in theory obligatory in Morocco to carry official ID at all times. In practice, a photocopy of the important pages of your passport will do, so long as the real thing is in your hotel in the same town. When travelling between towns, you should always have your passport on you.

Visa extensions

To **extend your stay** in Morocco you should – officially – apply to the Bureau des Étrangers in the nearest main town for a residence permit (see below). This is, however, a very complicated procedure and it is usually possible to get round the bureaucracy by simply leaving the country for a brief time when your three months are up. If you decide to do this – and it is not foolproof – it is best to make a trip of at least a few days outside Morocco. Spain is the obvious choice and some people just go to Ceuta; the more cautious re-enter the country at a different post. If you are unlucky, you may be turned back and asked to get a **re-entry visa**. These can be obtained from any Moroccan consulate abroad (see opposite).

Extending a stay officially involves opening a bank account in Morocco (a couple of days' procedure in itself) and obtaining an *Attestation de Résidence* from your hotel, campsite or landlord. You will need a minimum of 20,000dh (£1500/$2400) in your account.

You then need to go to the **Bureau des Étrangers** in the central police station of a large town at least fifteen days before your time is up, equipped with: your passport and a photocopy of its main pages; four passport photos; two copies of the *Attestation de Résidence*; and two copies of your bank statement (*Compte de Banque*). If the police are not too busy they'll give you a form to fill out in duplicate and, some weeks later, you should receive a plastic-coated permit with your photo laminated in.

Foreign embassies and consulates in Morocco

Foreign embassies and consulates in Morocco are detailed in the "Directory" sections for Rabat (see p.267), Casablanca (see p.286), Tangier (see p.88), Marrakesh (see 354) and Agadir (see p.459). Foreign representation in Morocco is detailed on the Moroccan Foreign Ministry's website at Ⓦdiplomatie.ma (in "Corps diplomatique et consulaire au Maroc" under "Les Ambassades").

Ireland has honorary consuls in Casablanca (see p.286) and Agadir (see p.459), but no embassy (the nearest is in Lisbon, ☎00 351 1 396 9440). New Zealanders are covered by their embassy in Madrid (☎00 34 915 230 226), but can use UK consular facilities in Morocco. Australians are covered by their embassy in Paris (☎00 33 1 4059 3300), but can use Canadian consular facilities in Morocco.

MOROCCAN EMBASSIES AND CONSULATES ABROAD

A complete up-to-date list of Moroccan diplomatic missions around the world can be found on the Moroccan Foreign Ministry's website at ⓦ diplomatie.ma (in "Missions diplomatiques et consulaires du Maroc" under "Les Ambassades").

Algeria 12 Rue Branly, al-Mouradia, 12070 Algiers (☎ 021 697094, Ⓔ ambmaroc-alg@maec.gov.ma); 26 Av Cheikh Larbi Tebessi, 31000 Oran (☎ 041 411627, Ⓔ consulatmaroc.oran@assila.net); 5 Av De l'ANP, Sidi Bel Abbes (☎ 048/543470, Ⓔ cgsba@live.fr).

Australia 17 Terrigal Crescent, O'Malley, Canberra, ACT 2606 (☎ 02 6290 0755, Ⓔ sifmacan@moroccoembassy.org.au).

Canada 38 Range Rd, Suite 1510, Ottawa, ON K1N 8J4 (☎ 1 613 236 7391, Ⓔ sifamaot@bellnet.ca); 2192, Bd Lévesque Ouest, Montreal, PQ H3H 1R6 (☎ 1 514 288 8750, ⓦ www.consulatdumaroc.ca).

Ireland (Chargé d'Affaires) 39 Raglan Rd, Ballsbridge, Dublin 4 (☎ 01 660 9449, Ⓔ sifamdub@indigo.ie).

Mauritania Av Général de Gaulle, Tevragh Zeina 634, BP621, Nouakchott (☎ 525 1411, Ⓔ sifmanktt@gmail.com); Av Maritime, Nouadhibou BP233 (☎ 574 5084, Ⓔ cons.ndb@maec.gov.ma); formalities for entering Morocco (by car, for example) can only be completed in Nouakchott, not Nouadhibou.

Spain c/Serrano 179, 28002 Madrid (☎ 915 631 090, ⓦ embajada-marruecos.es); c/Teniente Maroto 2, first floor, 11201 Algeciras (☎ 956 661 803, Ⓔ cg.algesiras@hotmail.com); Palmera Bldg, Suite 178, 3rd floor, Av del Mediterraneo (corner Sierra Alhamilla), 04007 Almería (☎ 95 020 6179, Ⓔ cgalmeria@hotmail .com); also in Seville, Barcelona, Tarragona, Valencia, Bilbao, Burgos and Las Palmas.

South Africa 799 Schoemaan St (corner Farenden), Arcadia, Pretoria 001 (☎ 012 343 0230, Ⓔ sifmapre@mwebbiz.co.za).

UK Diamond House, 97–99 Praed St, London W2 1NT (☎ 020 7724 0719, ⓦ www.moroccanembassylondon.org.uk).

US 1601 21st St NW, Washington DC 20009 (☎ 1 202 462 7979, Ⓔ embassy@moroccous.com); 10 E 40th St, 24th Floor, New York, NY 10016 (☎ 1 212 758 2625, ⓦ moroccanconsulate.com).

Gay and lesbian travellers

As a result of sexual segregation, **male homosexuality** is relatively common in Morocco, although attitudes towards it are a little schizophrenic. Few Moroccans will declare themselves gay – which has connotations of femininity and weakness; the idea of being a passive partner is virtually taboo, while a dominant partner may well not consider himself to be indulging in a homosexual act. Private realities, however, are rather different from public show (on which subject, note that Moroccan men of all ages often walk hand in hand in public – a habit that has nothing to do with homosexuality and is simply a sign of friendship).

Gay sex between men is **illegal** under Moroccan law. Article 489 of the Moroccan penal code prohibits any "shameless or unnatural act" with a person of the same sex and allows for imprisonment of six months to three years, plus a fine. There are also various provisions in the penal code for more serious offences, with correspondingly higher penalties in cases involving, for example, corruption of minors (under-18s). Despite this, a gay rights association called Kif-Kif has now been formed, and there's even a gay magazine, (ⓦ mithly.net, in Arabic only). The Behind the Mask at website (ⓦ mask.org.za) posts information and news on gay rights in Morocco.

A certain amount of information on the male gay scene in Morocco (gay bars, meeting places and cruising spots) can be found in the annual *Spartacus Gay Guide* (ⓦ spartacusworld.com). Tangier's days as a gay resort are long gone but a tourist-oriented gay scene does seem to be emerging, very discreetly, in Marrakesh (see p.352), and to a lesser extent Agadir, though pressure from religious fundamentalists makes it difficult for the authorities to ease up, even if they wanted to, and arrests of tourists for having gay sex are not unknown.

There is no public perception of **lesbianism** in Morocco, and as a Western visitor, your chances of making contact with any Moroccan lesbians are very small indeed. Moroccan women are under extreme pressure to marry and bear children, and anyone resisting such pressure is likely to have a very hard time of it.

Health

For minor health complaints, a visit to a **pharmacy** is likely to be sufficient. Moroccan pharmacists are well trained and dispense a wide range of drugs, including many available only on prescription in the West. If pharmacists feel you need a full diagnosis, they can recommend a doctor – sometimes working on the premises. Addresses of English- and French-speaking doctors can also be obtained from consulates and large hotels.

If you need **hospital treatment**, contact your consulate at once and follow its advice. If you are near a major city, reasonable treatment may be available locally. State hospitals are usually OK for minor injuries, but for anything serious, a private clinic is generally preferable. Depending on your condition, repatriation may be the best course of action.

The latest advice on health in Morocco can be found on the US government's travel health website at ⓦ cdc.gov/travel.

Inoculations

No **inoculations** are required but you should always be up to date with polio and tetanus. Those intending to stay a long time in the country, especially if working with animals or in the health-care field, are also advised to consider vaccinations against typhoid, TB, hepatitis A and B, diphtheria and rabies, though these are not worth your while if just going on holiday.

A very low level of **malaria** does exist in the form of occasional cases between May and October in the region to the north of Beni Mellal and Khenifra, between Chefchaouen and Larache, and in the province of Taza, but local strains are not life-threatening and malaria pills are not normally considered necessary unless you actually fall ill with it (in which case they are easy enough to get at any pharmacy). More importantly, avoid bites; use mosquito repellent on all exposed areas of skin, especially feet, and particularly around dusk. Repellents containing DEET are usually recommended for adults.

Water and health hazards

Tap water in most of Morocco is generally safe to drink, though in the far south and Western Sahara it's best to stick to bottled mineral water.

A more serious problem in the south is that many of the **river valleys and oases** are infected with **bilharzia**, also known as **schistosomiasis**, caused by a tiny fluke worm that lives part of its life cycle in a freshwater snail, and the other part in the blood and internal organs of a human or other mammal which bathes in or drinks the water. The snails only live in stagnant water, but the flukes may be swept downstream. Staying clear of slow-flowing rivers and oasis water is the best way to avoid it. If infected while bathing, you'll probably get a slightly itchy rash an hour or two later where the flukes have entered the skin. Later symptoms may take several months to appear, and are typified by abdominal pains, and blood in faeces or even urine. If you suspect that you might have it, seek medical help. Bilharzia is easily cured, but can cause permanent intestinal damage if untreated. Care should be taken, too, in drinking water from **mountain streams**. In areas where there is livestock upstream **giardiasis** may be prevalent and is a common cause of travellers' diarrhoea. Other symptoms include nausea, weight loss and fatigue which usually last no more than two weeks and settle without treatment. If they continue for longer, then a course of **metronidazole** (Flagyl) generally leads to effective eradication, but always finish the course, even after symptoms have gone, and even though this antibiotic will probably make you feel nauseous and precludes consumption of alcohol. Using iodine water purification tablets, or boiling any drinking or cooking water (remember that you'll have to boil it for longer at high altitudes, where the boiling point is lower) is the simplest way to avoid putting yourself at risk from either of these illnesses.

Diarrhoea

At some stage in your Moroccan travels, it is likely that you will get **diarrhoea**. As a first stage of treatment it's best simply to adapt your diet. Plain boiled rice is your safest bet, while yoghurt is an effective stomach settler and prickly pears (widely available in summer) are good too, as are bananas, but other fruit is best avoided, along with greasy food, dairy products (except yoghurt), caffeine and alcohol. If you have diarrhoea, it's important to replace the body fluids and salts lost through dehydration (this is especially the case with children); dissolving **oral rehydration salts** (*sels de réhydratation orale* in French) in water will help. These are available at any pharmacy, but if you can't get any, a teaspoon of salt plus eight of sugar per litre of water makes a reasonable substitute. Water (at least two litres per adult daily) should be drunk constantly throughout the day, rather than all in one go.

If symptoms persist for several days – especially if you get painful cramps, or if blood or mucus appear in your stools – you could have something more serious (see above) and should seek medical advice.

Other hazards

There are few natural hazards in northern Morocco, where wildlife is not very different from that of Mediterranean Europe. If you venture into the Sahara, however, be aware of the very real dangers of a bite from a **snake** or **scorpion**. Several of the Saharan snakes are deadly. Bites should be treated as medical emergencies.

Certain scorpions are very dangerous; their sting can be fatal if not treated. Avoid going barefoot or in flip-flops (thongs) in the bush, or turning over stones. In the desert, shake out your shoes before putting them on in the morning. All scorpions sting, which can be extremely painful, especially if you are allergic, but not many are life-threatening. Most snakes are non-venomous and, again, few are life-threatening, but one or two species can be dangerous, most notably the horned viper.

If you do get bitten by a snake or stung by a scorpion, don't panic – even in the case of life-threatening species, actual fatalities are rare, and you should be in no danger if treated in a reasonable time. Sucking out the poison only works in movies, and tourniquets are dangerous and ill-advised. The important thing is to relax, try not to move the affected part of your body, and seek medical help as quickly as possible. Try to remember what the creature looked like, and if it's possible to kill or catch it without danger, then do so, so that you can show it to doctors or paramedics.

Never underestimate Morocco's **heat**, especially in the south. A hat – preferably light in both weight and colour – is an essential precaution and, especially if you have very fair skin, you should also take sunblock cream with a very high screening factor, as the sun really is higher (and therefore stronger) in Morocco than in northern latitudes. Resulting problems include **dehydration** – make sure that you're drinking enough (irregular urination such as only once a day is a danger sign) – and **heatstroke**, which is potentially fatal. Signs of heatstroke are a very high body temperature without a feeling of fever, but accompanied by headaches, nausea and/or disorientation. Lowering body temperature, with a tepid shower or bath, for example, is the first step in treatment, after which medical help should be sought.

Contraceptives and tampons

Poor quality and rather unreliable condoms (*préservatifs*) can be bought in most pharmacies, and so can the pill (officially by prescription, but this isn't essential).

Tampons can be bought at general stores, not pharmacies, in most Moroccan cities. Don't expect to find them in country or mountain areas.

Insurance

It's frankly reckless to travel without insurance cover. Home insurance policies occasionally cover your possessions when overseas, and some private medical schemes include cover when abroad. Bank and credit cards often have certain levels of medical or other insurance included and you may automatically get travel insurance if you use a major credit card to pay for your trip. Otherwise, you should contact a specialist travel insurance company. A typical travel insurance policy usually provides cover for the loss of baggage, tickets and – up to a certain limit – cash or cheques, as well as cancellation or curtailment of your journey. Most of them exclude so-called dangerous sports unless an extra premium is paid: in Morocco this could include mountaineering, skiing, water rafting or paragliding. Read the small print and benefits tables of prospective policies carefully; coverage can vary wildly for roughly similar premiums. Many policies can be chopped and changed to exclude coverage you don't need. For medical coverage, check whether benefits will be paid as treatment proceeds or only after returning home, and whether there is a 24-hour medical emergency number. When securing baggage cover, make sure that the per-article limit – typically under £500/$1000 – will cover your most valuable possession. If you need to make a claim, you should keep receipts for medicines and medical treatment, and in the event you have anything stolen, you must obtain an official statement from the police (called a *papier de déclaration*).

Internet

Cybercafés (*cybers*, pronounced "sea-bear", with a little French gargle at the end) are widespread, and usually charge around 5dh per hour, though some places charge double that, and hotels with internet services often charge even more; conversely, some places in small towns in the south charge as little as 3dh per hour. Note that Moroccan cybercafés are rife with malware, so think twice before sticking your USB stick into one of their machines, and always scan it with a good anti-virus and anti-malware program afterwards.

ROUGH GUIDES TRAVEL INSURANCE

Rough Guides has teamed up with WorldNomads.com to offer great **travel insurance** deals. Policies are available to residents of over 150 countries, with cover for a wide range of **adventure sports**, 24-hour emergency assistance, high levels of medical and evacuation cover and a stream of **travel safety information**. Roughguides.com users can take advantage of their policies online 24/7, from anywhere in the world – even if you're already travelling. And since plans often change when you're on the road, you can extend your policy and even claim online. Roughguides.com users who buy travel insurance with WorldNomads.com can also leave a positive footprint and donate to a community development project. For more information go to ⓦ**roughguides.com/shop**.

Laundry

In the larger towns, laundries will take in clothes and wash them overnight, but you'll usually find it easier to ask at hotels – even in cheap hotels without an official laundry service, the cleaning lady will almost certainly be glad to make a few extra dirhams by taking in a bit of washing.

Left luggage

You can deposit baggage at most train stations, but it will have to be locked or padlocked (unlockable rucksacks will not be accepted); if you are catching a late train, make sure that the office will be open on your return. There are similar facilities at the main bus stations, CTM offices and ferry stations. Where no left- luggage facilities are available, café proprietors may agree to look after baggage for you, sometimes for a small fee, more often for free in out-of-the-way places.

Living in Morocco

Your best chance of paid work in Morocco is **teaching English**. The schools listed here will require reasonable spoken French and an EFL qualification, and usually do their recruiting at home, but they sometimes advertise jobs online, and they may be able to direct you to smaller schools in Casablanca, Rabat and other Moroccan towns.

It is also possible to **volunteer** for a **work camp**. Most are open to anyone over eighteen. You pay travel costs but generally receive free accommodation (take a sleeping bag) and meals.

ENGLISH SCHOOLS

American Language Center 1 Pl de la Fraternité, Casablanca ☎ 0522 277765, Ⓦ casablanca.aca.org.ma. Also in Agadir, Fez, Kenitra, Marrakesh, Meknes, Mohammedia, Oujda, Rabat, Tangier and Tetouan – for contact details see Ⓦ aca.org.ma/contact.
British Council 11 Av Allal Ben Abdellah, Rabat ☎ 0537 218130; 87 Bd, Nador, Polo, Casablanca ☎ 0522 529360, Ⓦ britishcouncil.org/morocco.
The American School 1 bis Rue el Amir Abdelkader, Agdal, Rabat ☎ 0537 671476, Ⓦ ras.ma; Route de la Mecque, Lotissement Ougoug, Quartier Californie, Casablanca ☎ 0522 214115, Ⓦ cas.ac.ma; BP 6195, Km9, Route de Ouarzazate, Marrakesh ☎ 0524 329860, Ⓦ asm.ac.ma; 149 Rue Christophe Colombe, Tangier ☎ 0539 939827, Ⓦ ast.ma.

WORK CAMPS

Amis des Chantiers Internationaux de Meknès (ACIM) BP 8, 50001 Meknes ☎ 0535 511829, Ⓔ boubou_b@live.fr. Projects

generally involve agricultural or construction work around Meknes – three weeks in July and August, accommodation and food provided.
Association Chantiers de Jeunesse (ACJ) BP 171, CCP 4469 H, 11000 Salé ☎ 0537 855350, Ⓔ acj_ong@yahoo.com.
Chantiers Jeunesse Maroc (CJM) BP 1351, 10001 Rabat ☎ 0537 722140, Ⓔ cjm@mtds.com.
Chantiers des Jeunes Volontaires (CJV) BP 558, Batha, 30200 Fez ☎ 0535 700258, Ⓔ cjv1962@yahoo.fr
Chantiers Sociaux Marocains (CSM) BP 456, 10001 Rabat ☎ 0537 297184, Ⓔ csm@planete.co.ma.
SCI/IVS Ⓦ sciint.org; US ☎ 1 434 336 3545, Ⓦ sci-ivs.org; Canada ☎ 1 571 319 1563, Ⓦ ivscanada.org; Great Britain ☎ 0131 243 2745 Ⓦ ivsgb.org; Ireland (Republic and North) ☎ 01 855 1011, Ⓦ vsi.ie; Australia ☎ 02 9699 1129, Ⓦ ivp.org.au. Recruits workcamp volunteers.
Volunteers for Peace 7 Kilburn St, Suite 316, Burlington, VT 05401 ☎ 1 802 540 3060, Ⓦ vfp.org. Recruits volunteers for projects detailed on the website.

Mail

Letters between Morocco and Western Europe generally take around a week to ten days, around two weeks for North America or Australasia. There are postboxes at every post office (*La Poste*) and on the wayside; they seem to get emptied fairly efficiently, even in out-of-the-way places.

Stamps can sometimes be bought alongside postcards, or from some *tabacs* as well as at the post office, where there is often a dedicated counter (labelled *timbres*), and where stamps may also be sold in the phone section, if there is one. At major post offices, there is a separate window for **parcels**, where the officials will want to examine the goods you are sending. Always take them unwrapped; there is usually someone to supply wrapping paper, string and tape.

Post office hours are typically Monday to Friday 8am–4.15pm; larger offices may stay open until 6pm, and may also open Saturday 8am–noon, for stamps, money changing and money transfer, but not for parcels or poste restante. During Ramadan, offices open Monday to Friday 9am–3pm, larger ones also Saturday 9am to noon.

Poste restante

Receiving letters **poste restante** (general delivery) can be a bit of a lottery, as Moroccan post office workers don't always file letters under the name you might expect. Ask for all your initials to be checked (including *M* for Mr or Ms, etc) and, if you're half-expecting anything, suggest other letters as well. To pick up your mail you need your passport. To have mail sent to you, it should be addressed (preferably with your surname underlined) to Poste Restante at the central post office of any major city.

Maps

The **maps of Moroccan towns** in this book should be sufficient for most needs, though commercial plans of greater Rabat or Casablanca may be useful if you need to visit the suburbs, and detailed maps of the Medinas in Marrakesh and Fez may help to navigate tortuous Medina alleyways.

Reasonable **road maps** are sometimes available at ONMT tourist offices, and these are adequate if you are not driving or going far off the beaten track. The best is the Rough Guide Map, on a scale of 1:1,000,000 (1cm to 1km). Among the alternatives, a good choice is GeoCenter or IGN's 1:800,000 map, with the Western Sahara on a 1:2,500,000 inset. Also good are the Bay-Foldex Morocco map, on a scale of 1:800,000, with the Western Sahara on a 1:5,000,000 inset, and Michelin's Morocco map (#959), on a scale of 1:1,000,000. Maps (or guidebooks) which do not show the Western Sahara as part of Morocco are banned and liable to confiscation.

Trekking maps and guides

Topographical maps used by trekkers, climbers, skiers, etc (1:50,000 and 1:100,000) are difficult to find in Morocco. You may have to go in person to the Division de la Cartographie, Avenue Hassan II, Km4, Rabat ☎0660 102715 (near the *gare routière* bus station, ask for *Résidence Oum Kaltoum*); for some maps, you have to show your passport and submit an order which *may* then be available for collection two working days later – if the request is approved, which is far from certain, although maps of Toubkal and some others will be served over the counter. Trekking maps are also sporadically available at the *Hôtel Ali*, Marrakesh, or in Imlil, the trailhead for treks in the area. However, if you are planning to go trekking, it is best to try and get maps through a **specialist map outlet** before you leave home. Look for 1:100,000 (and if you're lucky 1:50,000) maps of the Atlas and other mountain areas. Stanfords in London (online orders worldwide at ⊛stanfords.co.uk) has several trekking maps covering the High Atlas and in particular the Jebel Toubkal area.

AMIS (see p.46) produces brief **map-guides** to the Asni-Toubkal, Western High Atlas (Taroudant) and Sirwa (Taliouine), Anti-Atlas (Tafraoute), Aklim (Igherm) and Jebel Bou Iblane/Bou Naceur (Middle Atlas) areas, which are useful complements to the coverage in this guide. AMIS offer mail order

worldwide, and are definitely the best place to try for Moroccan maps that are unobtainable elsewhere.

More **detailed trekking guidebooks** are also available in both English and French. The most useful are Hamish Brown's *The High Atlas: Treks and Climbs on Morocco's Biggest and Best Mountains* (Cicerone Press, 2012), and – though now dated – Robin Collomb's *Atlas Mountains* (West Col, 1980), Michael Peyron's *Grand Atlas Traverse* (2 vols, West Col, 1990), Karl Smith's *Atlas Mountains: A Walker's Guide* (Cicerone Press, 1998), and Richard Knight's *Trekking in the Moroccan Atlas* (Trailblazer Publications, 2000). Also useful if you can find it is West Col's map guide to the Mgoun Massif at 1:100,000, which covers a wide region, second only to Toubkal in popularity. For climbing, a modern reproduction of the 1942 Dresch–Lépiney *Le Massif du Toubkal*, available at some bookshops, is useful. These can sometimes be found in Marrakesh's Librairie Chatr (see p.353).

Money

Though the easiest way to carry your money is in the form of plastic, it is a good idea to also carry at least a couple of days' survival money in cash, and maybe some travellers' cheques as an emergency backup.

Morocco's basic unit of **currency** is the **dirham** (dh). The dirham is not quoted on international money markets, a rate being set instead by the Moroccan government. The present rates are approximately 14dh to £1, 8.80dh to US$1, 11dh to €1. As with all currencies there are fluctuations, but the dirham has roughly held its own against Western currencies over the last few years. A dirham is divided into 100 **centimes**, and you may find prices written or expressed in centimes rather than dirhams. Confusingly, centimes may also be referred to as **francs** or, in former Spanish zones of the country, as **pesetas**. You may also hear prices quoted in **rials**, or *reales*. In most parts of the country a dirham is considered to be twenty rials, though in Tangier and the Rif there are just two rials to the dirham. Coins of 10, 20 and 50 centimes, and 1, 5 and 10 dirhams are in circulation, along with notes of 20, 50, 100 and 200 dirhams.

In Algeciras, you can buy dirhams at poor rates from travel agents opposite the port entrance, and at slightly better rates from those inside the ferry terminal. You can also buy dirhams at similar rates from agents near the ferry terminals in Ceuta and Melilla. In Gibraltar, moneychangers will usually give you a very slightly better rate than in Morocco itself. When you're nearing the end of your stay, it's best to get down to as little Moroccan money as possible.

You can change back dirhams at the airport on departure (you can't use them in duty-free shops), but you may be asked to produce bank exchange receipts – and you can change back only fifty percent of sums detailed on these. You'll probably be offered re-exchange into euros only. You can also change dirhams (at bad rates) into euros in Ceuta, Melilla and Algeciras, and into sterling in Gibraltar. It is illegal to import or export more than 1000dh.

Banks and exchange

English pounds and US and Canadian dollars can all be changed at banks, large hotels and some travel agents and tourist shops, but by far the most widely accepted foreign currency is the **euro**, which many people will accept in lieu of dirhams, at time of writing for the (bad) rate of €1 to 10dh. Gibraltarian banknotes are accepted for exchange at a very slightly lower rate than English ones, but Scottish and Northern Irish notes are not negotiable in Morocco, and nor are Australian and New Zealand dollars, South African rand, Algerian dinars or Mauritanian ouguiya, though you should be able to change CFAs. Moroccan bank clerks may balk at changing banknotes with numbers scrawled on them by their counterparts abroad, so change any such notes for clean ones before leaving home.

BMCE tends to be the best bank for money changing. Usually at banks, you fill in forms at one desk, then join a second queue for the cashier, and you'll usually need to show your passport as proof of identity. Standard **banking hours** for most of the year are Monday to Friday 8.15am to 3.45pm. During Ramadan (see p.43), banks typically open 9.30am to 2pm. BMCE and Attijariwafa Bank sometimes have a separate bureau de change open longer hours and at weekends, and there are now private foreign exchange bureaux in most major cities and tourist destinations, which open longer hours, often on Sundays too, change money with no fuss or bureaucracy, and don't usually charge commission. Many post offices will also change cash, and large hotels may change money out of banking hours, though their rates may not be good.

There is a **small currency black market** but you are recommended not to use it: changing money on the street is illegal and subject to all the usual scams, and the rate is not particularly preferential.

Credit and debit cards

Credit and debit cards on the Visa, Mastercard, Cirrus and Plus networks can be used to withdraw cash from **ATMs** at many banks, but not the ones outside post offices. Otherwise, banks may advance cash against Visa or Mastercard. By using ATMs, you get trade exchange rates, which are better than those charged by banks for changing cash, but your card issuer may add a transaction fee, sometimes hefty. There is a daily limit on ATM cash withdrawals, usually 3000dh.

You can pay directly with plastic (usually with Mastercard, Visa or American Express, though the latter cannot be used in ATMs) in upmarket hotels, restaurants and tourist shops.

Travellers' cheques and prepaid cards

Travellers' cheques are as secure as plastic but nothing like as convenient. Some banks won't change them, and staff often find spurious reasons not to do so: they may demand to see the original receipt for the cheques, though of course you are not supposed to carry that and the cheques together (if you do show it, don't let the bank keep it). Travellers' cheques have now generally been superseded by **prepaid cards**, such as those issued by Visa, which you can load up with credit before you leave home and use in ATMs like a debit card.

American Express and wiring money

American Express is represented by S'Tours at 2 Av Hassan Souktani, 4th floor, apt 10, Casablanca (☎0522 203552), and at Residence Nadia, 22 Rue Moulay Ali Cherif, Guéliz, Marrakesh (☎0524 437469), but these are only agents: they can issue Amex travellers' cheques, but they cannot receive mail or wired money, nor cash personal cheques.

For wiring money, **Western Union** is represented at every post office. MoneyGram's local agents include branches of Crédit du Maroc and Banque Centrale Populaire.

Opening hours

Opening hours follow a reasonably consistent pattern: banks (Mon–Fri 8.15am–3.45pm); museums (daily except Tues 9am–noon & 3–6pm); offices (Mon–Thurs 8.30am–noon & 2.30–6.30pm; Fri 8.30–11.30am & 3–6.30pm); Ville Nouvelle shops (Mon–Sat 8.30am–noon & 2–6.30pm); Medina shops (Sat–Thurs 9am–6pm, Fri 9am–1pm). These hours will vary during Ramadan (see p.43), when banks, for example, open 9.30am to 2pm, and everything will close before nightfall, when those observing the fast – which is to say, nearly everybody – have to stop and eat.

Phones

The easiest way to call within Morocco or abroad is to use a public phone booth (*cabine*), which takes a **phonecard** (*télécarte*) issued by Maroc Télécom. The cards are available from some newsagents and *tabacs*, and from post offices, and come in denominations of 10dh, 20dh, 50dh and 100dh. Cardphones are widespread, and you can usually find a number of them by a town's main post office if nowhere else. Unfortunately, they are not very well maintained, and often don't work. Not infrequently, they dock a unit from your card and fail to connect you, but they are still the best and most convenient way to make calls.

An alternative is to use a **téléboutique**, common everywhere. Some use coins – 5dh and 10dh coins are best for foreign calls (you'll probably need at least 20dh) – others give you a card and charge you for the units used. International calls from a hotel are pricey and may be charged in three-minute increments, so that if you go one second over, you're charged for the next period.

Morocco now has about ninety percent **mobile** coverage. Calls are expensive if using your own SIM card from home, and you pay to receive as well as make them; in addition, you can't top up in Morocco, so bring enough credit with you. Depending on how long you are spending in Morocco, it may be worth signing up with Maroc Télécom or Meditel, using their SIM card and getting a Moroccan number.

Instead of a dialling tone, Moroccan phones have a voice telling you in French and Arabic to dial the number. When calling a Moroccan number, the **ringing tone** consists of one-and-a-half-second bursts of tone, separated by a three-and-a-half-second silence. The **engaged tone** is a series of short tones (pip-pip-pip-pip), as in most

other parts of the world. A short series of very rapid pips may also indicate that your call is being connected.

Phone numbers

Maroc Télécom seem to change all their numbers every couple of years. Moroccan numbers are now ten-digit, and all ten digits must be dialled, even locally. All mobile numbers now begin with 06, all ordinary landline numbers with 05. If the number you have doesn't start with either of these, you'll need to convert it (see box below).

The Spanish enclaves of **Ceuta and Melilla** have nine-digit numbers, incorporating the former area codes (956 for Ceuta, 952 for Melilla), and all nine digits must be dialled, even locally. To call from mainland Spain, you will only need to dial the nine-digit number. Calling Ceuta or Melilla from abroad, or from Morocco proper, dial the international access code (00 from Morocco), then 34, then the whole nine-digit number. To call Morocco from Ceuta or Melilla, dial 00 212, then the last nine digits of the number, omitting the initial zero.

International calls

To **call Morocco from abroad**, you dial the international access code (00 from Britain, Ireland, Spain, the Netherlands and New Zealand; 0011 from Australia; 011 from the US and most of Canada), then the country code (212), then the last nine digits of the number, omitting the initial

EMERGENCY NUMBERS

Fire ☎ 15
Police (in towns) ☎ 19
Gendarmes (police force with jurisdiction outside towns) ☎ 177

CONVERTING PHONE NUMBERS

	pre-2002	2002	2006	since 2009
Casablanca region	☎ 02/xxxxxx	☎ 022 xxxxxx	☎ 022 xxxxxx	☎ 0522 xxxxx
El Jadida region	☎ 03/xxxxxx	☎ 023 xxxxxx	☎ 023 xxxxxx	☎ 0523 xxxxx
Marrakesh region	☎ 04/xxxxxx	☎ 044 xxxxxx	☎ 024 xxxxxx	☎ 0524 xxxxx
Fez/Meknes region	☎ 05/xxxxxx	☎ 055 xxxxxx	☎ 035 xxxxxx	☎ 0535 xxxxx
Oujda region	☎ 06/xxxxxx	☎ 056 xxxxxx	☎ 036 xxxxxx	☎ 0536 xxxxx
Rabat region	☎ 07/xxxxxx	☎ 037 xxxxxx	☎ 037 xxxxxx	☎ 0537 xxxxx
Agadir region	☎ 08/xxxxxx	☎ 048 xxxxxx	☎ 028 xxxxxx	☎ 0528 xxxxx
Tangier region	☎ 09/xxxxxx	☎ 039 xxxxxx	☎ 039 xxxxxx	☎ 0539 xxxxx
old mobiles	☎ 01/xxxxxx	☎ 061 xxxxxx	☎ 061 xxxxxx	☎ 0661 xxxxxx
newer mobiles			☎ 0xx xxxxxx	☎ 06xx xxxxxx

INTERNATIONAL DIALLING CODES

	From Morocco, Ceuta or Melilla	To Morocco	To Ceuta or Melilla
UK	☎ 00 44	☎ 00 212	☎ 00 34
Ireland	☎ 00 353	☎ 00 212	☎ 00 34
US and Canada	☎ 001	☎ 011 212	☎ 011 34
Australia	☎ 00 61	☎ 0011 212	☎ 0011 34
New Zealand	☎ 00 64	☎ 00 212	☎ 00 34
South Africa	☎ 00 27	☎ 09 212	☎ 09 34

zero. To **call Ceuta or Melilla**, dial the international access code, then 34, then all nine digits of the number, beginning with 956 for Ceuta, 952 for Melilla.

For an **international call** from Morocco, Ceuta or Melilla, dial 00, followed by the country code (1 for North America, 44 for the UK, etc), the area code (omitting the initial zero which prefixes area codes in most countries outside North America) and the subscriber number.

To reverse call charges, a good policy is to phone someone briefly and get them to ring you back, as collect (reverse charge) calls are hard to arrange.

Photography

Photography needs to be undertaken with care. If you are obviously taking a photograph of someone, ask their permission – especially in the more remote, rural regions where you can cause genuine offence. In Marrakesh's Jemaa el Fna, taking even quite general shots of the scene may cause somebody in the shot to demand money from you, sometimes quite aggressively. Also note that it is illegal to take photographs of anything considered strategic, such as an airport or a police station, so be careful where you point your camera – if in doubt, ask. On a more positive front, taking a photograph of someone you've struck up a friendship with and sending it on to them, or exchanging photographs, is often greatly appreciated.

Time

Morocco is on Greenwich Mean Time, with daylight saving (GMT+1) from the beginning of June to the end of September. Ceuta and Melilla keep Spanish time, which is GMT+1 in winter and GMT+2 in summer. The difference should be borne in mind if you're coming from Morocco to catch ferries out of Ceuta or Melilla, or trains out of Algeciras, especially when Spain is on summer time but Morocco isn't,

as there's then a two-hour time difference.

Tourist information

Morocco's national tourist board, the **Office National Marocain de Tourisme** (ONMT; ⓦ visitmorocco.com) maintains general information offices in several Western capitals, where you can pick up pamphlets on the main Moroccan cities and resorts, and a few items on cultural themes.

In Morocco itself, you'll find an **ONMT** office (*délégation de tourisme*) or a locally run office called a **Syndicat d'Initiative** bureau in all towns of any size or interest – often both (addresses detailed in the guide). They can of course answer queries, though the *délégation*'s main function is promoting tourism and gathering statistics. Both offices should also be able to put you in touch with an officially recognized guide.

In addition, there is quite a bit of information available online, and plenty of books on Morocco (see p.568). The Maghreb Society, based in the UK at the Maghreb Bookshop, 45 Burton St, London WC1H 9AL (☎ 020 7388 1840, ⓦ maghrebreview.com), publishes the *Maghreb Review*, the most important English-language journal on the Maghrebian countries.

ONMT OFFICES ABROAD

Canada PI Montréal Trust, 1800 Rue McGill College, Suite 2450, Montreal, PQ H3A 3J6 ☎ 1 514 842 8111, ✉ onmt@qc.aira.com.

Spain c/Ventura Rodriguez 24, first floor, left, 28008 Madrid ☎ 91 542 7431, ✉ informacion@turismomarruecos.com.

UK 205 Regent St, London W1B 4HB ☎ 020 7437 0073, ✉ mnto@morocco-tourism.org.uk.

US 104 W 40th St, Suite 1820, New York, NY 10018 ☎ 1 212 221 1583, ✉ info@mnto-usa.org.

TRAVEL ADVICE

Australian Department of Foreign Affairs ⓦ smartraveller .gov.au.

British Foreign & Commonwealth Office ⓦ fco.gov.uk.

Canadian Department of Foreign Affairs ⓦ voyage.gc.ca.

US State Department ⓦ travel.state.gov.

Travellers with disabilities

Facilities for people with disabilities are little developed in Morocco, and, although families are usually very supportive, many disabled Moroccans are reduced to begging. Despite this, able-bodied Moroccans are, in general, far more used to mixing with disabled people than their Western counterparts, and are much more likely to offer help without embarrassment if you need it.

Blindness is more common than in the West, and sighted Moroccans are generally used to helping blind and visually impaired people find their way around and get on and off public transport at the right stop.

There is little in the way of **wheelchair access** to most premises. In the street, the Ville Nouvelle districts are generally easier to negotiate than the often crowded Medinas, but don't expect kerb ramps at road crossings or other such concessions to wheelchair users. Medina areas in cities like Rabat and even Marrakesh should not be too hard to negotiate at quiet times of day, but in Fez and Tangier, where the streets are steep and interspersed with steps, you would need at least one helper and a well-planned route to get around.

Bus and train **travel** will be difficult because of the steps that have to be negotiated, but grands taxis are a more feasible mode of transport if you can stake a claim on the front seat (maybe paying for two places to get the whole of it) – if you don't have a helper travelling with you, and you require assistance, the driver or other passengers will almost certainly be happy to help you get in and out.

Accommodation at the lower end of the market is unlikely to be very accessible. Cheap city hotels tend to have small doorways and steep, narrow staircases, and often no elevator, though many will have ground-floor rooms. Beach hotels are more able to cater for visitors with mobility difficulties. Some package hotels, especially in Agadir, make an attempt to cater for wheelchair-users, with ramps, for example, but no accessible toilets. It is at the very top end of the market, however, that real changes are being made: new five-star hotels usually have a couple of rooms specifically adapted for wheelchairs. Obviously these need to be booked well in advance, and this also confines you to very expensive places, but it is at least a start.

You'll probably find a **package tour** much easier than fully independent travel, but contact any tour operator to check they can meet your exact needs before making a booking. It's also important to ensure you are covered by any **insurance** policy you take out (see p.59).

Hotels with rooms specially adapted for wheelchair users include the *Mövenpick* in Tangier (see p.84), the *Tryp* in Melilla (see p.141) the *Palais Jamaï* in Fez (see p.188), the *Sofitel* in Rabat (see p.265), the *Sheraton* and *Hyatt Regency* in Casablanca (see p.283 & p.282), the *Médina* in Essaouira (see p.305), and the *Atlas Medina* and *Ryad Mogador Menara* among other Hivernage hotels in Marrakesh (see p.345). The Ibis Moussafir chain (Ⓦ ibishotel.com) has adapted rooms at several of its hotels, including those in Tangier, Fnideq, Meknes, Casablanca, El Jadida, Essaouira and Ouarzazate. *Auberge Camping Toubkal* in Talioune (see p.475) also has rooms adapted for wheelchair users. Other hotels, such as the *Agadir Beach Club* and *Royal Atlas* in Agadir (see p.457), claim to be accessible, and to cater for wheelchair users, but do not have specially adapted rooms. Obviously, you should always call ahead to check whether any particular hotel can meet your specific needs.

Tangier,
Tetouan
and the
northwest

VIEW OVER TANGIER

1

Tangier, Tetouan and the northwest

At first glance, it would appear that Morocco's northwest corner has everything a traveller could want. Bordered on one side by sweeping expanses of near-deserted coastline washed by both Atlantic and Mediterranean waters, and on the other by the wild, rugged Rif mountain range that defines the physical boundary between Europe and Africa, this part of the country is home to a number of ancient, walled Medinas that remain mainly non-touristed and begging to be explored. As idyllic as it may sound, in reality the region has often been the country's ugly duckling and, especially in the latter half of the twentieth century, was virtually ignored by both king and state.

The reasons for this cold shoulder were historical and twofold – Tangier's reputation for European-influenced vice and extravagance, and two assassination attempts on the king (Hassan II, the current king's late father) that were widely believed to have emanated from within the largely lawless interior of the Rif mountains. This is all firmly in the past now, however. As a young prince, King Mohammed VI enjoyed many a summer holiday here jetskiing and hiking, and since the death of his father in 1999 he has steadily opened the country's (and foreign investors') eyes to the northwest's obvious charm and attraction, both in its natural beauty and close proximity to Europe.

Nowhere is this progress more visible than in **Tangier**. Once seedy from its days as a centre of international espionage and haven for gay Europeans and dodgy banks, the city has reinvented itself over the past decade as a vibrant, accessible and modern Mediterranean beach resort. South of Tangier along the Atlantic coast are the seaside resorts of Asilah and Larache, both of which offer wonderful, aimless meanderings within their compact whitewashed Medinas. **Asilah** is a relaxed and low-key town, well known for its International Arts festival, while **Larache** is similarly attractive, and close to the ancient Carthaginian-Roman site of **Lixus**. A more distinctively Moroccan resort is **Moulay Bousselham**, south of Larache, with its windswept Atlantic beach and abundance of birdlife.

The Spanish enclave of **Ceuta** was a possession too valuable for the Spanish to hand back to Morocco upon the latter's independence in 1956, and makes a pleasant change of pace when coming from the relatively haphazard and chaotic Moroccan side of the border. In the shadow of the Rif mountains, **Tetouan** has a proud Andalusian-Moroccan heritage and offers up yet another fascinating, authentic Medina while its nearby beaches are popular with both locals and visitors. South of Tetouan is the mountain town of **Chefchaouen** – a small-scale and enjoyably laidback place with perhaps the most photographed Medina of them all.

ANCIENT LIXUS

Highlights

❶ Tangier's café squares Sit with the ghosts of French spies and British secret agents as you while away the hours over a mint tea or espresso. **See p.76 & p.78**

❷ The Caves of Hercules Look out to sea from this grotto in the cliffs, through a cave window shaped like Africa. **See p.90**

❸ Asilah A laidback beach resort with an intimate pastel-washed Medina, an international arts festival, and the palace of an old bandit chief. **See p.91**

❹ Ancient Lixus Extensive Roman ruins in a fine setting, which you'll have pretty much to yourself to explore. **See p.98**

❺ Moulay Bousselham Wander the expansive windswept Atlantic beach and take a boat ride on the nearby lagoon, home to diverse birdlife and pink flamingos. **See p.99**

❻ Ceuta A Spanish enclave with a couple of forts and no less than three army museums – not to mention good beer, tapas and shops full of duty-free booze. **See p.101**

❼ Chefchaouen One of the prettiest and friendliest towns in Morocco, up in the Rif mountains, with a Medina full of pastel-blue houses. **See p.115**

HIGHLIGHTS ARE MARKED ON THE MAP ON P.70

Northern Morocco has an especially quirky **colonial history**, having been divided into three separate zones. Tetouan was the administrative capital of the Spanish zone; the French zone began at Souk el Arba du Rharb, the edge of rich agricultural plains sprawling southward; while Tangier experienced International Rule under a group of foreign legations. Subsequently, although French is the official second language (after Arabic) throughout Morocco, older people in much of the northwest are equally, or more, fluent in Spanish – a basic knowledge of which can prove useful.

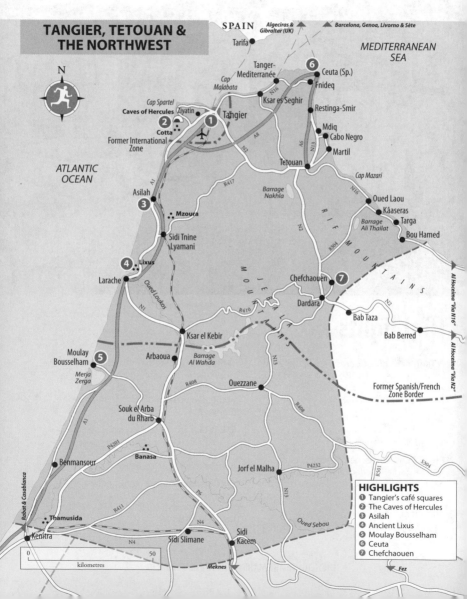

TANGIER, TETOUAN & THE NORTHWEST

HIGHLIGHTS

1 Tangier's café squares
2 The Caves of Hercules
3 Asilah
4 Ancient Lixus
5 Moulay Bousselham
6 Ceuta
7 Chefchaouen

Tangier

At the meeting point of two seas as well as two continents, **TANGIER**'s strategic location has made it a highly sought-after locale since ancient times. Founded by Mediterranean trading nations, ruled by empirical Romans, and squabbled over by European powers before finally returning to the Moroccan nation in 1956, it's perhaps no surprise that the city defies comparison with any other in Morocco.

For the first half of the twentieth century, Tangier was an international city with its own laws and administration, plus an eclectic community of exiles, expatriates and refugees. It was home, at various times, to Spanish and Central European refugees, Moroccan nationalists and – drawn by loose tax laws and free-port status – to over seventy banks and four thousand companies, many of them dealing in currency transactions forbidden in their own countries. Writers were also attracted to the city, including the American novelist **Paul Bowles**, who called it his "dream city", and **William Burroughs**, in whose books Tangier appears as "Interzone", spent most of the 1950s here. Tangier was also the world's first and most famous **gay resort**, favoured by the likes of Tennessee Williams, Joe Orton and Kenneth Williams.

Rooted in an enduring eccentricity, Tangier's charm is undeniable. Until fairly recently, the city's tourism future didn't look too rosy, having, over the years, gained a reputation as somewhere to avoid due to continuing reports of a large population of hustlers and unsavoury characters known to prey on foreign arrivals. King Mohammed VI, however, has provided much of the impetus for Tangier to re-invent itself under a flurry of renovation and building projects that will culminate in 2016 with the completion of a remodelled port and marina that aims to compete with better-known holiday ports along the Mediterranean.

Brief history

Tingis is Amazigh (Berber) for a marsh, revealing the site's Berber origins, though it was colonized around the seventh century BC by the **Phoenicians**, a seafaring people from what is now Lebanon. In 42 AD, the **Romans** made Tingis the capital of their newly created province of Mauretania Tingitania (roughly the north of modern Morocco). In 429 AD, with the collapse of the Roman Empire's western half, Tangier was taken by the Vandals, after which point things become a bit hazy. It seems to have

---

TANGIER'S HUSTLERS

Faux guides ("false guides") are petty crooks who attach themselves to new-in-town tourists, usually claiming to be "guiding" you and therefore due payment, or just steering you into hotels or shops where they receive a commission (added to your bill, naturally). At one time, Tangier's *faux guides* were particularly heavy; nowadays they have largely been cleaned out of town thanks to a nationwide police crackdown. Generally speaking, *faux guides* now limit their activities to encouraging you to visit the shops that employ them – though if they can hustle you into a hotel that will pay them commission, they will do that too. Some may also try to sell you *kif* (cannabis).

Faux guides have a number of approaches you will soon learn to recognize: a favourite is trying to guess your nationality, or asking "Are you lost?" or "What are you looking for?" If you ignore them or turn down their advances, they will sometimes accuse you of being angry or "paranoid". The best way to get rid of them is to ignore them completely, or explain politely (while never slackening your pace) that you are all right and don't need any help. As a last resort – and it should not come to this – you can dive into a café or even threaten to go to the police if necessary (the Brigade Touristique are based in the former Gare de Ville train station by the port, and there is also a police post in the kasbah). Bear in mind that local residents, as well as the law, are on your side.

1

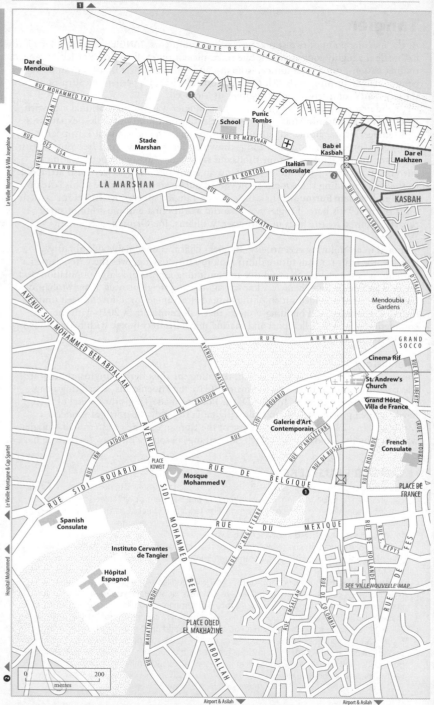

ROUTE DE LA PLAGE MERCALA

Dar el Mendoub

RUE MOHAMMED TAZI

School

Punic Tombs

RUE DE MARSHAN

Stade Marshan

Bab el Kasbah

Dar el Makhzen

Italian Consulate

KASBAH

AVENUE F. ROOSEVELT

RUE DES USA

AVENUE HASSAN II

RUE

RUE AL KORTOBI

LA MARSHAN

RUE DU DR CENATRO

RUE DE LA KASBAH

RUE OTTAILE

Mendoubia Gardens

RUE HASSAN I

Le Vielle Montagne & Villa Josephine

AVENUE SIDI MOHAMMED BEN ABDALLAH

RUE ARRAKIA

GRAND SOCCO

Cinema Rif

AVENUE HASSAN II

SIDI BOUABID

St. Andrew's Church

Grand Hôtel Villa de France

RUE DE LA LIBERTE

RUE IBN ZAIDOUN

RUE

Galerie d'Art Contemporain

RUE D'ANGLETERRE

RUE EL HOURIAT

French Consulate

RUE SIDI BOUABID

RUE IBN ZAIDOUN

AVENUE SIDI

PLACE KOWEIT

Mosque Mohammed V

RUE DE BELGIQUE

RUE DE RUSSIE

RUE DE HOLLANDE

Le Vielle Montagne & Cap Spartel

PLACE DE FRANCE

Spanish Consulate

SIDI MOHAMMED BEN

RUE DU MEXIQUE

RUE DE HOLLANDE

RUE DE PEPYS

RUE DES FES

Instituto Cervantes de Tangier

RUE D'ANGLETERRE

Hôpital Espagnol

Hospital Mohammed

RUE MAHATMA GANDHI

SEE 'VILLENOUVELLE' MAP

RUE DE GOUMBIA

PLACE OUED EL MAKHAZINE

ABDALLAH

RUE EMSALLAH

0   200
metres

Airport & Asilah   Airport & Asilah

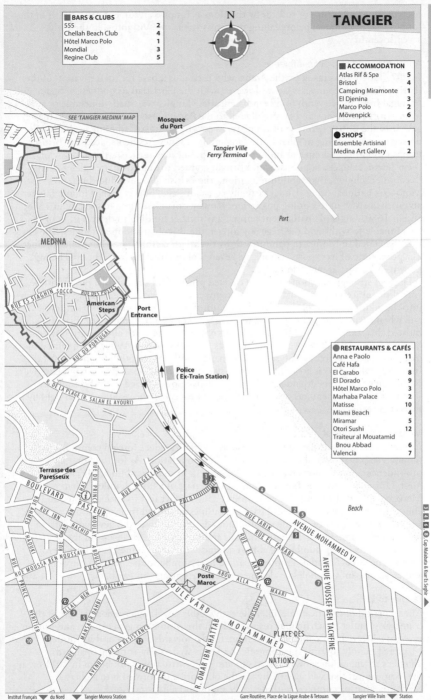

TANGIER

BARS & CLUBS
555	2
Chellah Beach Club	4
Hôtel Marco Polo	1
Mondial	3
Regine Club	5

N

ACCOMMODATION
Atlas Rif & Spa	5
Bristol	4
Camping Miramonte	1
El Djenina	3
Marco Polo	2
Mövenpick	6

SHOPS
Ensemble Artisinal	1
Medina Art Gallery	2

RESTAURANTS & CAFÉS
Anna e Paolo	11
Café Hafa	1
El Carabo	8
El Dorado	9
Hôtel Marco Polo	3
Marhaba Palace	2
Matisse	10
Miami Beach	4
Miramar	5
Otori Sushi	12
Traiteur al Mouatamid	
Bnou Abbad	6
Valencia	7

SEE 'TANGIER MEDINA' MAP

Mosquee du Port

Tangier Ville Ferry Terminal

Port

MEDINA

PETIT SOCCO

RUE DES POSTES

RUE ES SIAGHIN

American Steps

Port Entrance

RUE DU PORTUGAL

RUE DE LA PLAGE (R. SALAH EL AYOURI)

Police (Ex-Train Station)

Terrasse des Paresseux

BOULEVARD PASTEUR

RUE DU PRINCE MOULAY

RUE IBN RACHID

RUE OMAR IBN

RUE AHMED CHAOUKI

BOULEVARD ABOULLAH

RUE IBN

RUE MOUSSA BEN NOUSSAIR

RUE PRINCE HERITIER

RUE ALLAL BEN ABDALLAH

RUE MANSOUR DAHBI

RUE EL

RUE DE LA RESISTANCE

AVENUE

RUE LAFAYETTE

RUE MAGELLAN

RUE MARCO POLO

RUE TARIK

RUE EL FARABI

RUE ABOU ALLA EL MAARI

RUE EL ANTAKI

Poste Maroc

BOULEVARD MOHAMMED

PLACE DES NATIONS

AVENUE MOHAMMED VI

AVENUE YOUSSEF BEN TACHFINE

Beach

V

Cap Malabata & Ksar Es Seghir

3 4 6

1

been regained a century or so later by the Roman Empire's resurgent eastern half in the form of the **Byzantines**, before falling to Spain's rulers, the **Visigoths**, in the early seventh century.

Andalusian and European Influence

In 707, Tangier was taken by the **Arabs**, who used it as a base for their invasion of the Iberian Peninsula four years later. However, with the Christian reconquest of Spain and Portugal from the eleventh to fifteenth centuries, Tangier was itself vulnerable to attack from across the Straits, and eventually fell to the **Portuguese** in 1471. In 1661, they gave it to the **British** (along with Bombay) as part of Princess Catherine of Braganza's dowry on her wedding to Charles II. Tangier's Portuguese residents, accusing British troops of looting and rape, abandoned the town, but new settlers arrived, many of them Jewish refugees from Spain, and Britain granted the city a charter guaranteeing freedom of religion, trade and immigration. The British also introduced tea, now Morocco's national drink. Under virtually constant siege, however, they found Tangier an expensive and unrewarding possession. **Moulay Ismail** laid siege to the city in 1678, and in 1680, England's parliament refused any further funding to defend it. Four years later, unable to withstand the siege any longer, the British abandoned Tangier. The city then remained in Moroccan hands until the twentieth century, growing in importance as a port – one of its exports, mandarins, even took their name from the city, being known in Europe as **tangerines**.

Tangier's strategic position made it a coveted prize for all the colonial powers at the end of the nineteenth century. European representatives started insinuating themselves into the administration of the city, taking control of vital parts of the infrastructure, and when France and Spain decided to carve up Morocco between them, Britain insisted that Tangier should become an **International Zone**, with all Western powers having an equal measure of control. This was agreed as early as 1905, and finalized by treaty in 1923. An area of 380 square kilometres, with some 150,000 inhabitants, the International Zone was governed by a Legislative Assembly headed by a representative of the sultan called the Mendoub. While legislative power rested with the assembly – consisting of 27 members of whom 18 were European – the real power was held by a French governor.

Morocco takes control

At the International Zone's peak in the early 1950s, Tangier's foreign communities numbered sixty thousand – then nearly half the population. As for the other half, pro-independence demonstrations in 1952 and 1953 made it abundantly clear that most Tanjawis (natives of Tangier) wanted to be part of a united, independent Morocco. When they gained their wish in 1956, Tangier lost its special status, and almost overnight, the finance and banking businesses shifted their operations to Spain and Switzerland. The expatriate communities dwindled too as the new national government imposed bureaucratic controls and instituted a "clean-up" of the city. Brothels – previously numbering almost a hundred – were banned, and in the early 1960s "**The Great Scandal**" erupted, sparked by a number of paedophile convictions and escalating into a wholesale closure of the once outrageous gay bars.

Tangier today

After a period of significant decline, the early 2000s saw Tangier reborn as one of the country's premier **beach holiday resorts** as both the Moroccan government and foreign investors directed more interest (and more funds) towards the city and its future. Marketed mainly towards the domestic market as well as day-tripping Spaniards, Tangier's regeneration shows no sign of fading. Construction work began in 2011 on a five-year project that will eventually see the old port transformed into a glitzy residential marina complete with designer shops and a five-star hotel.

The Medina

The layout within Tangier's **Medina**, like most throughout Morocco, was never planned in advance. As the need arose, a labyrinth of streets and small squares emerged that eventually became the various quarters there today.

GETTING THERE

Approaches to the Medina The Grand Socco offers the most straightforward approach to the Medina. The arch at the northern corner of the square opens onto Rue d'Italie, which becomes Rue de la Kasbah, the northern entrance to the kasbah quarter. Through an opening on the right-hand side of the square is Rue es Siaghin, off which are most of the souks and at the end of which is the Petit Socco (see p.76), the Medina's main square. An alternative approach to the Medina is from the seafront: follow the American steps, west of the port, up from Av Mohammed VI, walk round by the Grand Mosque, and Rue des Postes (Rue Mokhtar Ahardane) will lead you into the Petit Socco.

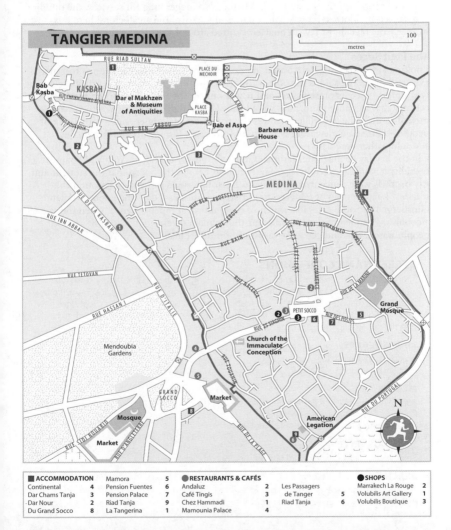

■ ACCOMMODATION			● RESTAURANTS & CAFÉS				● SHOPS	
Continental	4	Mamora	5	Andaluz	2	Les Passagers		Marrakech La Rouge	2
Dar Chams Tanja	3	Pension Fuentes	6	Café Tingis	3	de Tanger	5	Volubilis Art Gallery	1
Dar Nour	2	Pension Palace	7	Chez Hammadi	1	Riad Tanja	6	Volubilis Boutique	3
Du Grand Socco	8	Riad Tanja	9	Mamounia Palace	4				
		La Tangerina	1						

1

Rue es Siaghin

Rue es Siaghin – Silversmiths' Street – connects Grand Socco with the smaller Petit Socco, and was Tangier's main thoroughfare into the 1930s. Many of the buildings along here were constructed by Europeans in the late 1800s, with windows and balconies looking out onto the street rather than the traditional inward-looking Medina architecture. Most of the silversmiths have since been replaced by bureaux de change and souvenir shops, but it's a pleasant enough thoroughfare and isn't too challenging for first-time Medina navigators.

Church of the Immaculate Conception

Rue es Siaghin

The **Church of the Immaculate Conception**, halfway along Rue es Siaghin, was built in 1880 by a Franciscan missionary, Father José Lerchundi and is the only church in Morocco found within the walls of a Medina. No longer used for services, the building is occupied by Mother Teresa's Missionaries of Charity. The area behind here was formerly the **Mellah**, or Jewish quarter, centred around Rue des Synagogues.

The Petit Socco

Looking at it today, the **Petit Socco**, or Zoco Chico (Little Market), seems too small ever to have served such a purpose, though up until the nineteenth century the square was almost twice its present size, and it was only at the beginning of the twentieth century that the hotels and cafés were built. Up until the 1930s, when the focus moved to the Ville Nouvelle, this was the true heart of Tangier, and a broad mix of people – Christians, Jews and Muslims, Moroccans, Europeans and Americans – would gather here daily.

In the heyday of the "International City", with easily exploited Arab and Spanish sexuality a major attraction, it was in the alleys behind the Socco that the straight and gay brothels were concentrated. William Burroughs used to hang out around the square: "I get averages of ten very attractive propositions a day", he wrote to Allen Ginsberg. The Socco cafés lost much of their appeal at independence, when the sale of alcohol was banned in the Medina, but they remain diverting places to sit around, people-watch, talk and get some measure of the Medina.

STREET NAME CONFUSIONS

Spanish and French colonial names are still in use alongside their Arabicized successors. In addition, both *Rue* and *Calle* are sometimes replaced by *Zankat*, and *Avenue* and *Boulevard* by *Charih*. Local maps tend to use the new Arabic versions, though not all of the street signs have been changed. In the text and maps of this guide, we have used new names only when firmly established. Among the main street-name changes, note:

MAIN SQUARES

Grand Socco – Place du 9 Avril 1947
Petit Socco – Place Souk Dakhil

MEDINA

Rue des Chrétiens – Rue des Almouahidines
Rue de la Marine – Rue Djemaa Kebir
Rue des Postes – Rue Mokhtar Ahardane

VILLE NOUVELLE

Boulevard de Paris – Avenue Sidi Mohammed Ben Abdallah

BEACH

Avenue d'Espagne – Avenue Mohammed VI
Avenue des FAR – Avenue Mohammed VI

The American Legation (TALIM)

8 Rue d'Amérique • Mon–Thurs 10am–1pm & 3–5pm, Fri 10am–noon & 3–5pm, other times by appointment • Free • ☎ 0539 935317, Ⓦ legation.org

A former palace given to the US government by the sultan Moulay Slimane, the **American Legation**, tucked away in the southern corner of the Medina, is America's only National Historic Landmark located abroad. Morocco was the first overseas power to recognize an independent United States and this was the first American ambassadorial residence, established in 1777. A fascinating three-storey palace, bridging an alleyway (the Rue d'Amérique) below, it houses excellent exhibits on the city's history – including the correspondence between Sultan Moulay Ben Abdallah and George Washington – and has displays of paintings by, mainly, Moroccan-resident American artists. Malcolm Forbes's military miniatures of the Battle of Songhai and the Battle of Three Kings are also on display having been donated by the Forbes family when the Forbes Museum was closed (see box, p.80). Downstairs, by the library, a room dedicated to Paul Bowles features photographs of Bowles and his contemporaries, including a shot of him by Beat poet Allen Ginsberg. Separate from the downstairs library, there is a research library containing an interesting selection of books on Moroccan history and archeology which you can peruse if you call ahead and book an appointment.

The kasbah

The **kasbah**, walled off from the Medina on the highest rise of the coast, has been the city's palace and administrative quarter since Roman times. It was the Brits who destroyed the city's medieval fortifications, including a great upper castle which covered the entire site of the present-day kasbah. It is a strange, somewhat sparse area of walled compounds, occasional colonnades, and a number of luxurious villas built in the 1920s, when this became one of the Mediterranean's choicest residential sites.

The eccentric Woolworths heiress, Barbara Hutton, moved here in 1947, reputedly outbidding General Franco for her mini palace, Sidi Hosni. Her parties were legendary – including a ball where thirty Reguibat racing camels and their drivers were brought 1000 miles from the Sahara to form a guard of honour.

The main gateway from the Medina to the kasbah is **Bab el Assa**, featured in the 1912 painting *La porte de la Kasbah* by the French artist, Henri Matisse. Just inside the gate is the Seqaya Bab el Assa, one of the largest and most beautiful fountains of the Medina featuring exquisite zellij mosaic tiling and an ornamental wooden roof. The kasbah's main point of interest is the former **Dar el Makhzen**, or Sultanate Palace (see below). It stands to the rear of a formal court, or *mechouar*, where the town's pashas held public audience and gave judgment well into the twentieth century. Just before the entrance to the palace, you pass (on your left) the ramshackle clubhouse of the **Orquesta Andalusi de Tanger**, a fine group of musicians who play Andalous music with a lot of swing (see box, p.112). If they're around practising, they may well invite you in to watch them play.

Museum of Antiquities

Dar el Makhzen, Place Kasba • Daily except Tues 9–11.30am, 1.30–4pm • 10dh • ☎ 0539 932097, Ⓦ maroc.net/museums

The **Dar el Makhzen** – built, like the Grand Mosque, by Moulay Ismail – last saw royal use in 1912, as the residence of the sultan Moulay Hafid and his entourage of 168, who was exiled to Tangier after his forced abdication by the French. The ground floor of the otherwise off-limits palace is home to the **Museum of Antiquities**, centred on two interior courtyards, each with rich arabesques, painted wooden ceilings and marble fountains. Some of the flanking columns are of Roman origin, particularly well suited to the small display of mosaics and finds from Volubilis (see p.211). Within other rooms are well-presented artefacts discovered in and around Tangier, with origins dating from the Palaeolithic era up until Portuguese occupation. Other exhibits include

1

a map depicting international trade routes, a section dedicated to the Islamization of Tangier, and an interesting room concerned with Roman religion and funeral rites.

Opposite the museum's entrance, and off the main interior courtyard, are the herb- and shrub-lined palace **gardens**, shaded by jacaranda trees.

The Ville Nouvelle

Sprawling westwards and southwards from the ancient Medina is the European-built Ville Nouvelle. Much of its architecture and layout, especially immediately outside the Medina, is of Spanish origin, reflecting the influence of the city's large Spanish population during the nineteenth and early twentieth centuries.

The Grand Socco

The **Grand Socco** is the obvious place to start a ramble around the town. Its name, like so many in Tangier, is a French–Spanish hybrid, proclaiming its origins as the main

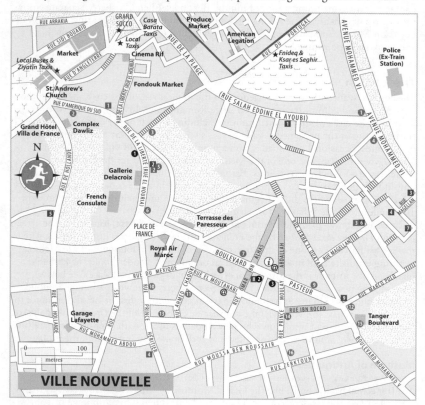

■ ACCOMMODATION		● RESTAURANTS & CAFÉS				■ BARS & CLUBS		● SHOPS	
Biarritz	3	Africa	1	L'Marsa	4	Atlas Bar	4	Bazaar Tindouf	1
Exclesior	4	Agadir	10	Number One	12	Caid's Bar	2	Blanco y Negro	2
Hollanda	5	Café Metropole	7	Pagode	13	Dean's Bar	1	Librairie des	
El Minzah	2	Café de Paris	6	Populaire Saveur		Tanger Inn	3	Colonnes	3
El Muniria	6	Café Porte	14	de Poisson	3				
Nabil	7	Dolcy's	9	Rahmouni	16				
De Paris	8	Eric's Hamburger		Relais de Paris	2				
Pension Miami	1	Shop	8	San Remo	11				
Rembrandt	9	El Korsan	5	Terrasse Boulevard	15				

market square. The markets have since long gone, but the square remains a meeting place and its cafés make good spots to soak up the city's life. The Grand Socco's official but little-used name, **Place du 9 Avril 1947**, commemorates the visit of Sultan Mohammed V to the city on that date – an occasion when, for the first time and at some personal risk, he identified himself with the struggle for Moroccan independence.

A memorial to this event (in Arabic) is to be found amid the **Mendoubia gardens**, flanking the square, which enclose the former offices of the Mendoub – the sultan's representative during the international years – and now home to the local Chamber of Commerce. Here there's also a spectacular banyan tree, said to be over 800 years old. Essentially now an open grassed area, the gardens are popular with local families who enjoy the small playground.

Place de France

In **Place de France**, south and uphill of the Grand Socco, the cafés are the main attraction – and at their best in the late afternoon and early evening, when an interesting mix of local and expatriate regulars turn out to watch and be watched. The seats to choose are outside the 1920s *Café de Paris*, a legendary rendezvous throughout the years of the International Zone. During World War II, this was notorious as a centre of deal making and intrigue between agents from Britain, America, Germany, Italy and Japan. Later the emphasis shifted to Morocco's own politics: the first nationalist paper, *La Voix du Maroc*, surfaced at the café, and the nationalist leader Allal el Fassi, exiled in Tangier from the French-occupied zone, set up his Istiqlal party headquarters nearby.

Terrasse des Paresseux

Just to the east of Place de France is a wide terrace-belvedere looking out over the Straits to Spain. Officially titled Place de Faro but known as **Terrasse des Paresseux** ("terrace of the lazy"), it's a great spot for people-watching, and on a clear day the pay-for-use telescopes (1dh) afford a good view of the Spanish port of Tarifa.

St Andrew's Church
Rue d'Angleterre

The nineteenth-century Anglican **Church of St Andrew** is one of the city's odder sights in its fusion of Moorish decoration, English country churchyard and flapping Scottish flag – the cross of St Andrew, to whom the church is dedicated (though, being an English church, they sometimes fly the cross of St George instead). The regular congregation has fallen considerably but the church is still used for a Sunday morning service (11am), when the numbers are swollen by worshippers from West African countries en route (hopefully) to a better life in Europe.

In the strangely serene graveyard, among the laments of early deaths from malaria, you come upon the tomb of **Walter Harris** (see p.568), the most brilliant of the chroniclers of "Old Morocco" in the closing decades of the nineteenth century and the beginning of the twentieth. Also buried here is **Dean** of *Dean's Bar* ("Missed by all and sundry"), a former London cocaine dealer (real name Don Kimfull) who tended the bar in the *El Minzah* hotel, before opening his own place in 1937, and worked as a spy for British intelligence in Tangier during World War II; and **Caid Sir Harry Maclean**, the Scottish military adviser to Sultan Moulay Abd el Aziz at the turn of the twentieth century. Inside the church another Briton, **Emily Keane**, is commemorated. A contemporary of Harris, she lived a very different life, marrying in 1877 the Shereef of Ouezzane – at the time one of the most holy towns of the country (see p.122).

Le Grand Hôtel Villa de France
Corner of Rue de Hollande and Rue d'Angleterre

The restoration of the long-derelict **Grand Hôtel Villa de France** is proof of Tangier's urban renewal. Severely neglected after it closed in 1992, restoration started in 2006

1

MALCOLM FORBES: TANGIER'S LAST TYCOON

The American publishing tycoon **Malcolm Forbes** bought the **Dar el Mendoub**, Rue Mohammed Tazi, in 1970. His reason, ostensibly at least, was the acquisition of a base for launching and publishing an Arab-language version of *Forbes Magazine* – the "millionaires' journal". For the next two decades, until his death in 1990, he was a regular visitor to the city, and it was at Dar el Mendoub that he decided to host his last great extravagance, his **seventieth birthday party**, in 1989.

This was the grandest social occasion Tangier had seen since the days of Woolworths heiress Barbara Hutton (see p.77), whose scale and spectacle Forbes presumably intended to emulate and exceed. Spending an estimated $2.5m, he brought in his friend Elizabeth Taylor as co-host and chartered a 747, a DC-8 and Concorde to fly in eight hundred of the world's rich and famous from New York and London. The party entertainment was on an equally imperial scale, including six hundred drummers, acrobats and dancers, and a *fantasia* – a cavalry charge which ends with the firing of muskets into the air – by three hundred Berber horsemen.

Forbes's party was a mixed public relations exercise, with even the gossip press feeling qualms about such a display of American affluence in a country like Morocco. However, Forbes most likely considered the party a success, for his guests included not just the celebrity rich – Gianni Agnelli, Robert Maxwell, Barbara Walters, Henry Kissinger – but half a dozen US state governors and the chief executives or presidents of scores of multinational corporations likely to advertise in his magazine. And, of course, it was tax deductible.

After Forbes's death, Dar el Mendoub passed into the hands of the state and was used to house personal guests of King Hassan II, before being converted into a museum. It has now reverted back to being a VIP residence for royal and state guests.

---

and was finally nearing completion at the time of research. The hotel looks out over St Andrew's Church and beyond the Medina to the Mediterranean; this was the view from room 35, where French impressionist Henri Matisse painted his famous *Vue de la fenêtre à Tanger* (View from a Window in Tangier) in 1912.

La Marshan

To the west of the kasbah is **La Marshan**, an upmarket 1840s residential district that offers a pleasant meander through its rich spread of villas, consulates and royal properties. Here you'll also find *Café Hafa* (see p.86).

The beach

Tangier's beach is a pleasant place to escape the city streets. It's especially good for a daytime stroll, either on the beach itself or along the 3km-long promenade that runs between the sand and Avenue Mohammed VI. Adjoining the promenade is a string of **beach bars** (see p.86), some of which offer a place to change into/out of your beach wear as well as showers, deckchairs, food and drink. *The Sun Beach* (99 Av Mohammed VI) is where Tennessee Williams wrote a first draft of *Cat on a Hot Tin Roof*, though renovations have stripped it of its original character. The promenade is quite safe at night, but it's advisable to avoid walking on the beach in the evenings.

ARRIVAL AND DEPARTURE   **TANGIER**

Tangier is one of the major transport hubs in Morocco. Travelling on into Morocco from Tangier is simplest either by train (the lines run to Meknes–Fez–Oujda or to Rabat–Casablanca–Marrakesh; all trains stop at Asilah en route), or, if you are heading east to Tetouan, by bus or shared grand taxi.

BY PLANE

Tangier's airport, Ibn Batouta International (☎ 0539 393720) is 15km west of the city and is served by flights from Casablanca (1–2 daily; 1hr) by RAM. There are three bureaux de change that are usually open to meet incoming flights, as well as a couple of ATMs, cafés and shop. Car rental is also available here (see p.82). Cream/beige grands taxis line up outside the terminal; there is a notice board listing prices at the terminal's exit and another at the taxi rank itself. Fares differ between daytime (5.30am–10.30pm) and night time (10.30pm–5.30am), with current daytime fares 100dh (Tangier city centre), 120dh (Tanger Ville train station), 150dh (beach hotels), 200dh (Asilah), 300dh (Tanger Port Med), and 350dh (Larache or Tetouan). These costs are per vehicle, seating a maximum of six passengers. Other than pre-organizing a private transfer with your Tangier accommodation, the only other transport option from the airport is to walk 2km to the main road, where you can pick up bus #9, which goes to Rue de Fez in town. To get to the airport from Tangier, most hotels will be able to organize a transfer for you, or you can rent a grand taxi from the Grand Socco (120dh is the standard rate, though you may need to bargain hard to get it). Royal Air Maroc have an office at 1 Pl de France (☎ 0539 379507 or ☎ 0900 00800).

BY TRAIN

Tangier's main train station, Tanger Ville, is 2km east of town on the continuation of Bd Mohammed V, and only 300m or so off the eastern end of the beach. The station has a branch of CIH bank (Mon 12.15–3.45pm, Tues–Fri 8.18am–3.45pm, Sat 9.15am–12.45pm) with an ATM, plus a Budget car rental desk (☎ 0675 386167). The best way to reach the staion is by petit taxi (15dh or so); it is also served by bus #16 from the bus station but not by any buses from the city centre. A convenient service from Tangier is the night train to Marrakesh, departing at 9.35pm and arriving the following morning at 8.05am; it's regularly full, so book ahead at any train station or Supratours office if possible.

Destinations Asilah (10 daily; 40min); Casablanca Voyageurs (8 direct & 1 connecting daily; 4hr 45min–6hr 5min); Fez (2 direct & 3 connecting daily; 4hr 30min–5hr 10min); Marrakesh (1 direct & 7 connecting daily; 8hr 30min–10hr 30min); Meknes (2 direct & 3 connecting daily; 4hr–4hr 15min); Oujda (1 direct & 1 connecting daily; 10hr 20min–10hr 30min); Rabat (8 direct & 1 connecting daily; 3hr 35min– 5hr); Souk el Arba du Rharb (9 daily; 2hr); Taza (1 direct & 1 connecting daily; 6hr 50min–7hr 5min).

BY BUS

The *gareroutière* is 2km south of the Ville Nouvelle on Pl Jamia al Arabia (☎ 0539 946928). All long-distance buses operate from here, including CTM, who no longer have a ticket office nor stop at the port entrance. There's a handy *consigne* (left luggage) counter here (daily 5am–1am; 5–7dh). The *gare routière* is a fifteen-minute walk from the centre of town; a petit taxi costs around 10dh.

Destinations Agadir (1 CTM & 1 other daily; 14hr); Al Hoceima (1 CTM & 7 others daily; 6hr); Asilah (No CTM services; 22

others daily; 40min); Casablanca (5 CTM & 12 others daily; 6hr); Chefchaouen (3 CTM & 9 others daily, ask for a direct *sans détour* service; 4hr); Fez (6 CTM & 9 others daily; 7hr); Fnideq (for Ceuta; no CTM services; 8 others daily; 1hr); Larache (5 CTM & 22 others daily; 1hr 30min); Marrakesh (1 CTM & 6 others daily; 10hr); Meknes (4 CTM & 9 others daily; 5hr); Nador (2 CTM & 6 daily; 12hr); Rabat (5 CTM and 22 others daily; 5hr); Tetouan (3 CTM and over 20 others daily; 1hr 30min).

BY GRAND TAXI

Grands taxis mostly operate from the *gare routière* and its immediate surrounds. From the rank in the *gare routière*, grands taxis run to/from Chefchaouen, Tetouan and Fnideq. Occasionally you may find a taxi direct to the Ceuta border, 2km beyond Fnideq. Grands taxis running to the Malabata beaches and Ksar es Seghir are parked along Av Moulay Idriss I, opposite the main bus exit. It's also possible to pick up grands taxis to Fnideq and Ksar es Seghir from Rue du Portugal, off Rue de la Plage at the southernmost corner of the Medina. For destinations in the immediate vicinity of Tangier, you may need to charter a grand taxi at the rank on the Grand Socco, though it's possible to get to places like the Caves of Hercules or Cap Malabata by shared grand taxi or city bus (see p.82).

Destinations Asilah (40min); Chefchaouen (2hr); Fnideq (for Ceuta; 1hr); Ksar es Seghir (30min); Tetouan (1hr).

BY FERRY

Fast hydrofoils for Tarifa in Spain arrive and depart from the old port, Tanger Ville. All other ferries run to and from the new port, Tanger Med. Reservations are essential at the end of the Easter week and during the last week of August. Full details of routes and immigration formalities can be found in "Basics" (see p.27 & box on pp.28–29); be aware, too, that immigration formalities take place as you are sailing to Morocco (see p.56). Departing Morocco, each passenger needs an embarkation form and departure card, which must be stamped by the port police prior to boarding. At both ports, all passengers must clear a security check, so allow plenty of time for this. Tickets and timetables can be obtained from any travel agent in Tangier or from the ferry companies themselves (see box, pp.28–29).

Tanger Med (Gare Maritime de Tanger Mediterranée) Ticket booths for all the ferry companies (see box, pp.28–29), plus bureaux de changes, ATMs, and Budget and Europcar offices, are on the ground floor of the port terminal building. Tangier's public bus operator AUTASA operates a free shuttle bus (hourly: 6am–10pm from Tangier city; 7am–11pm from Tanger Med; 45–60min; ☎ 0539 351010) between the port terminal and the *gare routière* for foot passengers, regardless of ferry company. To find the shuttle bus, exit the terminal and bear immediately right for 30m, towards a car park – unfortunately the bus

1

isn't clearly signposted, so look for an all-white bus or passengers waiting for its arrival. Heading back to the port, the bus picks up from Pl Jamia al Arabia, opposite the *gare routière* between the Total petrol station and the mosque. Destinations Algeciras (16–22 daily; 1hr 30min–2hr); Barcelona (4 weekly; 24hr); Genoa (3 weekly; 48hr); Gibraltar (weekly, 2hr); Livorno (weekly, 48hr); Sète (4 weekly; 36hr).

Tanger Ville (Gare Maritime du Tanger Ouest) All hydrofoil "fast" ferries to/from Tarifa (7–10 daily; 35min),

as well as an increasing number of cruise liners, operate from the old port. There are bureaux de change and ATMs here, and left luggage (daily 7am–9pm; from 10dh) just outside the arches of the port entrance, about 20m up Rue du Portugal towards the Medina Steps. It's a relatively short – though at times uphill – 20min walk into the centre from the port or a short ride by petit taxi (around 10dh on the meter; you may need to insist that it's used). The ticket offices are located opposite the bureaux de change in the port terminal building.

GETTING AROUND

By bus City buses are not much use to tourists. The most useful route is #2, which runs from St Andrew's Church in the Grand Socco to Ziyatin and on to the village of Jabila, not far from the Caves of Hercules. Route #9 goes from Rue de Fez along the Rabat road to the airport turn-off, some 2km from the airport itself. Route #16 connects the train station and the bus station, and runs on to Cape Malabata, but does not serve the city centre. Fares are never more than 8dh.

By grand taxi Grands taxis (large cream/beige Mercedes) are permitted to carry up to six passengers. The price for a ride should be fixed in advance – 15–20dh per person is standard for any trip within the city, including tip.

By petit taxi Small blue/green petits taxis (which carry just three passengers) can be flagged down around the

town. Most of these are metered – a typical rate for a city trip is 10dh per person – make sure the driver starts his meter from zero.

By car While Tangier's traffic is rarely gridlocked and a car can be handy for day-trips within the region, the city itself is small enough to explore on foot. There are a number of car rental agencies around town, including Amine Car, 43 Bd Mohammed V (☏ 0539 944050); Avis, 54 Bd Pasteur (☏ 0539 934646) and at the airport (☏ 0539 393033); Europcar, 87 Bd Mohammed V (☏ 0539 393273) and at the airport (☏ 0539 941938); Hertz, 36 Bd Mohammed V (☏ 0539 322165 or ☏ 0663 614211) and at the airport (☏ 0539 934179). Most car repairs can be undertaken – or arranged – by Garage Lafayette, 27 Rue Mohammed Abdou (☏ 0539 932887).

INFORMATION

Tourist information ONMT Délégation de Tourisme, 29 Bd Pasteur (Mon–Fri 8.30am–4.30pm; ☏ 0539 948050);

official guides can be hired here.

ACCOMMODATION

Tangier has dozens of hotels and *pensions*, and finding a room is rarely much of a problem. The city does, however, get crowded during July and August, when many Moroccan families holiday here. Cheaper hotels and *pensions* hike up their prices at this time of year, and you'll often get a better deal at one of the mid-range hotels.

MEDINA

In the Medina you have a choice between basic *pensions* and pricey *maisons d'hôtes*.

Continental 36 Rue Dar el Baroud ☏ 0539 931024, ☹ continental-tanger.com; map p.75. Commanding a great view over the port and Straits, the *Continental* opened in 1870, with Queen Victoria's son Alfred its first official guest; other notable visitors have included Degas and Churchill. Today, the hotel has a somewhat stilted feel despite recent renovations, but it's still comfortable enough and the service is usually pretty good. The quality of the artisanship within the hotel's public salons is worth a look. Free wi-fi throughout. BB <u>704dh</u>

Dar Chams Tanja 2–4 Rue Jnan Kabtan, Bab el Assa ☏ 0539 332323, ☹ darchamstanja.com; map p.75. One of the best *maisons d'hôtes* in the Medina. Surprisingly spacious inside, the large uncluttered rooms all have a/c

and satellite TV, and some enjoy glorious port and bay views. There's a floor dedicated to wellness, offering a hammam, separate massage room, and a chill-out room to saviour the experience. Meals can be taken formally in the dining room or casually up on the roof terrace. BB <u>1490dh</u>

★ **Dar Nour** 20 Rue Gourna, in the kasbah, off Rue Sidi Ahmed Boukouja ☏ 0662 112724, ☹ darnour.com; map p.75. One of Tangier's first top-end guesthouses, run by a French trio who have created ten individually styled rooms and suites in what was once five small houses. There are a number of communal areas, including little nooks and crannies perfect for a spot of quiet reading, interesting objets d'art throughout, and a well-stocked library. Literally topping it all off are three terraces with sweeping views of the Medina and Straits. BB <u>766dh</u>

Du Grand Socco (aka *Hôtel Taïef*) Grand Socco, entrance round the back on Rue Imam Layti; map p.75.

The oldest hotel in Tangier has seen better days, but the large rooms are reasonable value if shared, and the café has a great vista over the Grand Socco. No showers, but there are public ones ("Douche Laayoune") less than 50m away. **140dh**

Mamora 19 Rue des Postes ☏ 0539 934105; map p.75. Centrally located in the heart of the Medina, with clean, pleasant rooms, all with showers – though there's only hot water in the mornings. It's a little bit sterile but pretty good value for the location. **340dh**

Pension Fuentes 9 Petit Socco, at the heart of the Medina ☏ 0539 934669; map p.75. One of the first hotels in Tangier and still a friendly and atmospheric dive. Twin marbled staircases either side of the noisy café below lead up to two levels of basic rooms. Showers with hot water are shared. **100dh**

Pension Palace 2 Rue des Postes ☏ 0539 936128; map p.75. A touch of past splendours – balconies and a central court with fountain – led Bertolucci to shoot part of *The Sheltering Sky* here. Many rooms have a rugged charm and there are a few with en suites. **200dh**

Riad Tanja 2 Rue Amar Alilech, turn off Rue de Portugal near the American Legation ☏ 0539 333538, ⓦ riadtanja.com; map p.75. One of the more easily accessed of the Medina's riads, *Riad Tanja* is known for exemplary service and a warm, understated character. Beyond the riad's popular restaurant are five rooms decorated with zellij tiling, some with their own sitting room. Parking is available near the American Steps. BB **1462dh**

La Tangerina 19 Riad Sultan, in the kasbah ☏ 0539 947731, ⓦ latangerina.com; map p.75. Pared-down Mediterranean elegance, stylishly composed interiors, an ambience of simple luxury and an outstanding terrace overlooking the Straits have quickly established this well-run guesthouse as one of Tangiers' best. BB **891dh**

VILLE NOUVELLE

Most of these recommendations are within a few blocks of Pl de France and the central Bd Pasteur; it's a steep climb from the port or bus station, so a taxi can be useful if you've got a lot of luggage.

Camping Miramonte Marshan ☏ 0539 423322 or ☏ 0672 207055, ⓦ campingmiramonte.com; map pp.72–73. This is one of the best campsites on the Atlantic Coast, but unfortunately access for camper vans is a little difficult. There are well-maintained grounds that include electrified sites, ablutions with hot water, self-contained bungalows, two restaurants, two swimming pools and a bar. Gets pretty busy and noisy in August. It's best accessed by a new oceanside road that links the port with the city's Marshan neighbourhood (see p.80). Camping **75dh**, bungalow **1000dh**

Hollanda 139 Rue de Hollande ☏ 0539 937838, ⓦ hotelhollanda.com; map p.78. Behind the French Consulate, this large, airy former maternity hospital, shaded by trees, offers simple, but good-value rooms and convenient off-road parking. Free wi-fi throughout. **350dh**

El Minzah 85 Rue el Houria (Rue de la Liberté) ☏ 0539 333444, ⓦ elminzah.com; map p.78. Built in 1931, this remains one of Morocco's most prestigious hotels, with a wonderful garden, a pool overlooking the sea and town, an elegant (if pricey) bar, and a new wellness centre with hammam. There's a range of rooms and suites of slightly faded grandeur that are still worth the price for soaking up the hotel's nostalgic ambience. Free wi-fi throughout. BB **2434dh**

De Paris 42 Bd Pasteur ☏ 0539 931877, ☏ 0539 938126; map p.78. Central hotel with spacious and spotless rooms, good breakfasts, a few Art Deco touches in the public areas, some interesting old photos in the lobby and very helpful staff. **552dh**

Rembrandt Corner of bds Pasteur and Mohammed V ☏ 0539 937870, ⓦ hotel-rembrandt.com; map p.78. Recently renovated, this is now one of the city's better hotels. The modern, tiled rooms come with all the mod cons, while downstairs there's a restaurant with sea views, a shaded poolside café and a sultry, purple-blue lounge bar. Free parking. BB **836dh**

SEAFRONT

Several hotels are on Rue Magellan, which is easy to miss: it zigzags up from the seafront alongside the *Hôtel Biarritz* towards Bd Pasteur in the Ville Nouvelle. A number of others are on Rue de la Plage, which runs uphill from the port to the Grand Socco and is lined with small *pensions*.

Atlas Rif & Spa Hôtel 152 Av Mohammed VI ☏ 0539 349300, ⓦ hotelsatlas.com; map pp.72–73. Known as the *Hôtel Rif* in the days when Churchill and Elizabeth Taylor were guests, this luxury four-star overlooks the beach and is the best-value pick of the upmarket seafront hotels. Thick Berber carpets lie over shiny marble floors in the large, modern rooms and suites, and the hotel has two restaurants, a swimming pool, fitness centre and an atmospheric lounge bar. Free wi-fi in public areas. **1734dh**

Biarritz 104 Av Mohammed VI ☏ 0539 932473; map p.78. An old hotel with comfortable en-suite rooms and a fair bit of old-fashioned charm. Ask for a room away from the busy road. Reductions available for long stays. **320dh**

Bristol 14 Rue el Antaki ☏ 0539 942914; map pp.72–73. Situated 100m uphill from the beach, this is a good bet, with large brightly coloured rooms with TVs. Rooms on the upper floors miss most of the noise from the street-level bar. **300dh**

El Djenina 8 Rue el Antaki ☏ 0539 942244, ⓔ eldjenina@menara.ma; map pp.72–73. Though the bland but modern rooms are a little on the small side, they are all en suite with TV and always sparkling clean.

1

It's well managed and a good choice. Free wi-fi throughout. **490dh**

Exclesior 17 Rue Magellan, straight up from Hôtel Biarritz ☎0534 436987; map p.78. This 23-roomed hotel has seen better days but is good value for the price. A stately marbled staircase leads up to large, airy rooms, some with small balconies and views. Shared bathrooms; hot showers 10dh. **190dh**

Marco Polo 2 Rue el Antaki ☎0539 941193, ✉0539 941508; map pp.72–73. A very efficiently run hotel, with 33 modern and comfortable rooms set away from the busy road. There's also a popular restaurant, lively bar (both open to non-residents), and small hammam. **648dh**

Mövenpick Route de Malabata ☎0539 329300, ⬤moevenpick-hotels.com; map pp.72–73. One of Tangier's most deluxe hotels, 3km east of town on the road to Malabata, with all the facilities you'd expect from this Swiss chain – three restaurants, a pool, health club, sauna and casino. It's close to the train station but a long way from the Medina, and perhaps not quite worth the splurge. Two rooms have been adapted for wheelchair users. Free wi-fi throughout. **2836dh**

El Muniria 1 Rue Magellan ☎0539 935337 or ☎0510 047227; map p.78. This is where William Burroughs wrote *The Naked Lunch* (in room 9, no longer available), and Jack Kerouac and Allen Ginsberg also stayed here when they came to visit him. Nowadays it's a clean and quiet

family-run *pension* – the main remnant of its Beat history being the adjoining *Tanger Inn* (see p.87). Hot water mornings and evenings only. **250dh**

Nabil 11 Rue Magellan ☎0539 375407; map p.78. A refurbished warehouse converted into a friendly lower-end hotel. All 44 rooms are en suite, and there are stunning views from the front top-floor rooms. Parking garage for residents. **255dh**

Pension Miami 126 Rue de la Plage ☎0539 932900; map p.78. Beautifully tiled old Spanish townhouse said to be over a hundred years old. Pleasant rooms, and bathrooms on each corridor. **180dh**

OUT OF TOWN

Villa Josephine 231 Rue de la Montagne, Sidi Masmoudi ☎0539 334535, ⬤villajosephine-tanger .com; map pp.72–73. Resplendent in antiques, oak panelling and Moroccan carpets, the villa has ten opulent suites – five with private balconies or terraces overlooking the sea. Built in the 1920s by Walter Harris (see p.568) and a former summer residence of Pasha el Glaoui (see p.327) the estate is in impeccable condition. There's also a colonial-esque bar and a very good restaurant (non-guests welcome) offering daytime snacks and a French-inspired dinner menu (mains 75–165dh), served either inside the classy restaurant or on the outdoor poolside terrace with fantastic Straits views. **2562dh**

EATING AND DRINKING

Tangier is certainly no culinary hot spot nor does it offer any must-visit drinking establishments, but the city's continuing rejuvenation has encouraged a general rise in the standard and variety of what is available. Most top-end restaurants serve alcohol with their meals.

RESTAURANTS
VILLE NOUVELLE

Africa 83 Rue de la Plage at the bottom of the hill ☎0539 935436; map p.78. A simply decorated and peaceful dining room known for its excellent-value four-course set menu (55dh). There's also a la carte standards such as lamb tajine and beef couscous (45–65dh). Daily 11am–10pm.

Agadir 21 Rue Prince Héritier, off Pl de France, ☎0668 827696; map p.78. This small and friendly restaurant, run by a Tafraouti, with accomplished Mediterranean and Moroccan offerings (35–75dh), is a popular traveller's favourite. Daily except Wed 1–3pm & 7–11pm.

Anna e Paolo 77 Av Prince Héritier, ☎0539 944617; map pp.72–73. Quite simply the best Italian food in Tangier. The dark interior is decorated with pictures of old Italy and the menu bows to tradition with a host of authentic pizza, pasta meat and seafood dishes (55–125dh). Mon–Sat noon–3pm & 7.30–11pm.

El Dorado 21 Rue Allal Ben Abdallah, near the Hôtel Chellah; map pp.72–73. A stalwart of Tangier's dining

restaurant scene with a dependable Moroccan-Spanish menu that also includes a good selection of seafood dishes. Try their couscous on Fridays or the good-value paella on Sundays (mains 50–140dh). Daily noon–3pm & 7.30–11pm.

El Korsan Hôtel el Minzah, 85 Rue de la Liberté ☎0539 935885; map p.78. The hotel's Moroccan restaurant has a reputation as one of the country's best, serving authentic and traditional specialities (130–260dh). The split-level salon has fantastic uninterrupted views of the Straits from its low-lying tables. Andalous musicians and (uninspiring) belly dancing accompany dinner. Daily 8–11pm.

Eric's Hamburger Shop Arcade Mentoubi, between Bd Pasteur and Rue el Moutanabi; map p.78. It doesn't get much simpler than this; *Eric's* has been open 24/7 since 1968 and succeeds because it doesn't claim to be anything other than a cheap diner. There's a row of wooden stools lined up against the stainless steel counter, and the menu consists of four hamburgers and four hot dogs. Close to some of the city's more seedier nightclubs, it's immensely more attractive at midnight than midday. No alcohol. Mains 16–20dh. Daily 24hr.

Number One 1 Bd Mohammed V, across the side street from the Rembrandt Hôtel ✆ 0539 941674; map p.78. A long-time, well-managed resident of the local restaurant scene, with an extensive French–Moroccan menu (75–150dh) that attracts a lunchtime business crowd. It tends to be fairly quiet in the evenings, when the pace slows down with some smooth background jazz. Daily noon–3pm & 7–11pm.

Otori Sushi 41 Av de la Résistance ✆ 0539 325533, ⓦ otorisushi.com; map pp.72–73. Though lacking atmosphere, sushi lovers will be pleased to find Tangier's international reputation manifest in quality maki rolls and by-the-piece sushi (45–100dh). Fresh fish arrives daily from the nearby port. No alcohol. Mon–Sat noon–3pm & 7.30–11.15pm, Sun 12.30–3.15pm & 8–11.15pm.

Pagode Rue el Boussiri, just off Rue Prince Héritier ✆ 0539 938086; map p.78. The Viet-Chinese menu here is a winner, including specialities like *poisson à la sauce Pékinoise* (grilled fish in a ginger sauce) and *bouef à la citronelle* (stir-fried beef with lemongrass). The service is dependable, if not fantastic. Mains 85–100dh. Tues–Sun noon–2pm & 7.30–11pm.

★ **Populaire Saveur de Poisson** 2 Escalier Waller, on the steps leading down from Rue de la Liberté to the Fondouk Market ✆ 0539 336326; map p.78. This family-run seafood restaurant is as friendly (and good) as they come. Just one room, cluttered with paintings, and an adjoining kitchen, it's often packed with in-the-know locals. There's no choices as such, just a single *menu du jour* that changes daily (200dh). Count on dishes like brochettes of char-grilled sole or *merlan* (whiting) pan-fried in butter with garlic, onions and spinach. Their in-house fruit punch is brewed daily in a big vat in the kitchen. No alcohol. Daily except Fri 1–5pm & 8–11pm, closed during Ramadan.

Relais de Paris Complex Dawliz, 42 Rue de Hollande ✆ 0539 331819 or ✆ 0539 334848; map ; map p.78. Popular with the chichi French expat crowd, with a reputation for fine French cuisine (140–180dh), including succulent grills and a set menu for 150dh. There's also lighter dishes such as a quiche of the day. Daily noon–4pm & 8pm–11pm.

San Remo 15 Rue Ahmed Chaouki, a side street opposite Terrasse des Paresseux on Bd Pasteur ✆ 0539 938451; map p.78. This popular restaurant serves up credible, good-value Mediterranean cooking, including a dependable selection of seafood and meat grills (mains 60–180dh). There's also a good choice of pizzas, available either in-house or from their cheaper pizzeria across the road. Daily noon–3 & 7–11pm.

MEDINA

Andaluz 7 Rue du Commerce; the first alley to the left off Rue de la Marine; map p.75. With a trio of tables, this is about as simple as it's possible to be – and excellent, serving impeccably fried swordfish steaks and grilled brochettes (25–65dh). No alcohol. Daily 11am–late.

Chez Hammadi 2 Rue de la Kasbah ✆ 0539 934514; map p.75. Just outside the west wall of the Medina, this is a rather kitsch salon, where traditional Moroccan dishes (55–95dh) – and good pastilla – are served to entertainment from a worthwhile band of Andalous musicians. No alcohol. Daily noon–3pm & 7.30–11pm.

Mamounia Palace 4 Rue es Siaghin ✆ 0539 935099; map p.75. A nicely done-out place, not quite achieving the palatial style it aspires to, but laidback, with comfortable seating, unobtrusive musicians and good Moroccan food. It's often overrun with day-tripping tour groups. The only options are two set menus, at 115dh each. Daily noon–11pm.

Marhaba Palace 26 Palais Ahannar, off Rue de la Kasbah at no. 67, just outside the Medina ✆ 0539 937927; map pp.72–73. A splendid old palace, stacked with antiques, and with music and good food. Set menus for 170dh and 240dh. Daily noon–3pm & 7.30–11pm.

Les Passagers de Tanger Grand Socco ✆ 0619 000250 or ✆ 0539 371251; map p.75. A rooftop brasserie overlooking the square, run by a French couple, popular with an affluent expat crowd and known for delicious *tartines* (open sandwiches) and indulgent desserts. There's also a daily blackboard menu. Service can be a bit up and down. Mains 110–170dh. Mon–Sat noon–midnight.

★ **Riad Tanja** 2 Rue Amar Alilech, turn off Rue de Portugal near the American Legation ✆ 0539 333538, ⓦ riadtanja.com; map p.75. A small and intimate restaurant, stylishly and simply decorated, whose signature *nouvelle cuisine Marocaine* includes light vegetable salads, fish tajines and caramelized fruit desserts. Set menu 350dh. Reservations recommended. Tues–Sun noon–3pm & 7.30–11pm.

SEAFRONT

El Carabo Chellah Beach Club, Av Mohammed VI, opposite Av Louis van Beethoven ✆ 0539 325068; map pp.72–73. Located within the popular beachside *Chellah Beach Club*, *El Carabo* offers Moroccan and Mediterranean standards such as brochettes and *grillés*, along with a few seafood dishes (mains 55–125dh). It's a lively place in the evening. Daily noon–10pm.

L'Marsa Hôtel L'Marsa, 92 Av Mohammed VI; map p.78. Superb pizzas and spaghetti, with home-made ice cream to follow, served (slowly) on the roof terrace, patio or inside. Mains 45–95dh, and there's an 80dh set menu. No alcohol. Daily noon–10pm.

1

TANGIER'S PATISSERIES

Tangier has a wealth of attractive **cafés** and some excellent **patisseries**, among which three in particular are rated by the cognoscenti: *Matisse*, 53 Rue Allal Ben Abdallah (see map pp.72–73), which is the poshest; *Rahmouni*, 35 Rue du Prince Moulay Abdallah (see map, p.78), which is the oldest; and the upstart *Traiteur al Mouatamid Bnou Abbad*, 16 Rue al Mouatamid Ibn Abadd (see map, p.72–73).

Miami Beach 3 Av Mohammed VI ☎ 0539 322463; map pp.72–73. This beachside restaurant is managing to continue its high standards and excellent menu despite the ongoing port renovation going on just outside. The menu offers mainly seafood with French influences (mains 100–165dh), accompanied by an impressive wine list. Daily noon–4pm & 7–11pm.

Miramar Av Mohammed VI, opposite the Hôtel Rif ☎ 0539 944033; map pp.72–73. A beach restaurant with a varied menu of Moroccan, Spanish and seafood dishes (55–120dh) – their steaks are recommended, especially the *escalope avec sauce poivron*. There's a separate lively tapas bar at the rear. Daily noon–11pm.

Valencia 6 Av Youssef Ben Tachfine ☎ 0539 945146; map pp.72–73. A simply furnished fish restaurant, very popular with both locals and tourists. The straightforward menu includes a variety of *friture* (fried) or *grillé* (grilled) dishes, with *calamars* (calamari), *merlan* (whiting) and sole the most prevalent (mains 35–70dh). No alcohol. Daily except Tues 11am–10pm.

CAFÉS

★ **Café de Paris** Pl de France; map p.78. Tangier's most famous café from its conspiratorial past. There's two levels of seating inside, including the original 1920s section with studded leather seats. Outside there's the standard line of chairs for people-watching. It's still a staple meeting place for expats and usually a good place to track down English newspapers in the morning. Coffee & pastry 15dh. Daily 7am–11pm.

Café Hafa La Marshan; map pp.72–73. A ramshackle affair and popular locals' café, with steep terraces looking directly out to the Straits. While the service can be overly casual, the mint tea (8dh) is good and the views sublime.

Daily 10am–7pm.

Café Metropole 27 Bd Pasteur, next to the synagogue; map p.78. The *Metropole* serves one of the best *café au laits* (8dh) in town; pastries can be bought across the road at *Pâtisserie Le Petit Prince* and consumed at your table. Daily 7am–11pm.

Café Porte Cnr Rue Prince Moulay Abdellah and Rue Ibn Rochd ☎ 0661 163644; map p.78. A 1950s café that was modernized in 2011, the *Porte* is popular with a young crowd who come for the ice-cream selection and free wi-fi. There's also a decent menu offering breakfast and light meals (20–55dh). Daily 7am–10pm.

Café Tingis Petit Socco; map p.75. A favourite haunt of Tennessee Williams and Paul Bowles, this traditional café remains full of charm and character. A raised terrace looks down upon the Petit Socco and is the best spot in the Medina for people-watching. Within its high-ceilinged interior is the Tingis' sole concession to the 21st century, a flat-screen TV showing football matches. Mint tea 5dh. Daily 7am –10pm.

Dolcy's On the eastern end of Bd Pasteur; map p.78. Central and friendly, this is a great spot for breakfast, offering eggs, toasted sandwiches and fresh juices. With an extra-long line of outdoor seats facing the busy footpath, it's a prime spot for people-watching at any time of the day. Daily 7am–11pm.

Terrasse Boulevard Tanger Boulevard Complex, 23 Bd Mohammed V ☎ 0553 036848; map p.78. This new café has magical views of the port and Straits, and is comfortable at any time of the year thanks to ceiling-high glass windbreakers and a covered roof. If you want more than a coffee, they have a pretty good menu of light meals, as well as milk shakes and fresh juices. Daily 7am–11pm.

NIGHTLIFE AND ENTERTAINMENT

The city's possibilities for films, theatre, the occasional concert and, at the right time of year, festivals are refreshingly varied nowadays. Unfortunately the same can't really be said for most of the **bars** and **clubs**, which seem to be either stuck in a time warp or grossly expensive.

BARS

A decadent past has taken its toll on Tangier's bars and most of those that have survived have fallen into a rather bland seediness and are the domain of hard drinking,

heavy smoking Moroccan men. The better options are in or alongside the older hotels, supplemented by the beach bars, which stay open till 1am or so (though take care in this area after dark).

Atlas Bar 30 Rue Prince Héritier, across the road from the Hôtel Atlas; map p.78. Small, friendly tapas pub open nightly. Proudly in business since 1928 and has barely changed since – the intimate dive-bar atmosphere is still fully intact. Beer 15dh. Daily 8pm–1am.

Caid's Bar Hôtel el Minzah, 85 Rue de la Liberté; map p.78. Classy establishment that oozes nostalgia for Tangier's International Zone days. There's a pianist tinkling away most nights, while over the bar is the centrepiece of the ritzy decor, a grand painting of Caid Sir Harry Maclean, former commander in chief of the sultan's army (see p.79). Cocktails 85dh. Daily 10am–midnight.

★ **Chellah Beach Club** Av Mohammed VI, opposite Av Louis van Beethoven ☎0539 325068; pp.72–73. This beachside bar has been around for ages and remains popular thanks to its fun atmosphere and a lack of pretension. The music, both live and deejayed, ranges from jazz and flamenco, to Moroccan gnaoua. Draught beer 25dh. Daily 7pm–midnight.

Dean's Bar 2 Rue d'Amérique du Sud; map p.78. This tiny and smoky establishment was once the haunt of Tennessee Williams, Francis Bacon and Ian Fleming. It is now frequented more or less exclusively by Moroccans although tourists are welcomed. Beer 12dh. Daily noon till late.

Marco Polo Av Mohammed VI; map pp.72–73. This dark, streetfront hotel bar is popular with locals and gets pretty lively most nights. There's an adjacent, shaded courtyard with tables and chairs that makes an appealing place for a quiet drink. Glass of wine 22dh. Daily 11am till late.

Tanger Inn 16 Rue Magellan, below the Hôtel el Muniria; map p.78. One of Tangier's last surviving International Zone relics, the *Tanger Inn* is a good spot for a quiet drink. There's a grand piano in the corner and photos on the wall of Burroughs, Ginsberg and Kerouac while they were staying at the hotel above. Beer 18dh. Daily 9pm–2am.

CLUBS

The principal areas for clubs are the grid of streets south of Pl de France and Bd Pasteur, and along the beach promenade. Admission can be as high as 100dh and drinks are two or three times regular bar prices. Be careful leaving late at night as the streets can be none too safe; the best idea is to tip the doorman 5dh to call a taxi.

555 Av Mohammed VI, opposite the Atlas Rif & Spa ☎0678 181085, ⓦbeachclub555.com. By day, this is a classy beach bar & restaurant, by night, resident and guest DJs (like David Vendetta) serve up body-thumping dance mixes. Both the entrance fee (150dh) and the drinks (beer 75dh, spirits 85dh) are expensive, and things don't really get going until midnight. Daily 8pm–4am.

Mondial 52 Av Mohammed VI; map pp.72–73. Catering to a crowd of twenty-something Moroccans and weekender Europeans, with two resident DJs and regular guest DJs. There's also a separate cabaret lounge where synthesized Arabic music is performed, as well as a female-friendly tapas bar. Club entrance 50dh. Daily 11pm–5am.

Regine Club 8 Rue el Mansour Dahbi (opposite the Roxy Cinema); map, pp.72–73. Mainstream club firmly stuck in the 1980s. It's larger and a little cheaper than most, and can offer a fun night, especially after midnight. Free admission. Mon–Sat 10pm–3am.

ENTERTAINMENT AND FESTIVALS

Up-to-date information on local events can be found in the monthly brochure, *Tanger Pocket* (in French), available at most hotel receptions and in some bureaux de change, or online at ⓦtangerpocket.com.

American Legation (TALIM) 8 Rue d'Amérique, Medina ☎0539 935317, ⓦlegation.org. The American Legation (see p.77) often hosts free cultural events such as live performances, book launches and discussions on a range of themes, such as North African art, military history and languages.

Cinema Rif Grand Socco ☎0539 934683, ⓦcinemathequedetanger.com. Renovated in 2006, this 1930s Art Deco landmark has nightly showings of new releases, documentaries and classics, plus regular week-long film festivals, including the Mediterranean Short Film Festival of Tangier (ⓦccm.ma). Check beforehand if the film is dubbed into Arabic.

Institut Français du Nord 1 Rue Hassan Ibn Ouazzane, Ville Nouvelle ☎0539 942589, ⓦiftanger-tetouan.org. The cultural arm of the French government presents a weekly programme of events that includes art & literary functions, as well as films and live performances from its 170-seater theatre.

Instituto Cervantes de Tanger 99 Av Sidi Mohammed Ben Abdallah, Ville Nouvelle ☎0539 932001, ⓦtanger.cervantes.es. Like its French counterpart, this branch of Spain's cultural arm is enthusiastically involved in Tangier's social scene, providing a weekly programme of film screenings, discussions, concerts and general cultural exchange.

TanJazz ⓦtanjazz.org. Highly regarded jazz festival, attracting artists from both North America and Europe, which takes place over four days in September.

GALLERIES AND CRAFTS

There's a vibrant art scene in Tangier, with at least two to three exhibitions on at any given time. With regards to craftwork, many of the city's **market stalls and stores** are eminently avoidable, geared to selling tourist goods that wouldn't pass muster elsewhere.

1

GALLERIES

Up-to-date listings and information on various other small galleries can be found in the window of Bab el Fen, a well-stocked art supply shop at 25 Rue Ibn Rochd across from the *Rembrandt Hôtel*.

Galerie d'Art Contemporain Mohamed Drissi 52 Rue d'Angleterre, Ville Nouvelle ☎ 0539 936073. Located in the former British Consulate, with a number of rooms hosting contemporary works by mainly Moroccan and European artists. Admission 10dh. Daily except Tues 9–11.30am & 3–6pm.

Galerie Delacroix 86 Rue de la Liberté, Ville Nouvelle ☎ 0539 932134, ⊛ iftanger-tetouan.org/fr/galerie-delacroix. The gallery for Tangier's Institut Français du Nord, with regular exhibitions by Moroccan artists, and sometimes non-Moroccans residing in Tangier. Tues–Sun 10am–1pm & 4–8pm,

★ **Medina Art Gallery** 30 Av Abou Chouaib Doukali, Ville Nouvelle ☎ 0539 372644, ⊛ medinagallery.com; map p.72–73 Founded in 1999 by local artists Saïd Kadiri and Omar Salhi, this gallery aims to discover new local talent and refocus attention on some of the past Moroccan masters, such as Mohamed Hamri. Mon–Sat 10am–1pm, 4–8pm.

Volubilis Art Gallery 6 Sidi Boukouja, Kasbah ☎ 0539 333875, ⊛ volubilisartgallery.com; map p.75 This little gallery has regular exhibitions of mainly Moroccan artists. Tues–Sun 10.30am–1pm & 3.30–7pm.

CRAFTS AND SOUVENIRS

★ **Bazaar Tindouf** 64 Rue de la Liberté, opposite the Hôtel el Minzah ☎ 0539 931525; map p.75. One of the better-quality junk/antique shops, with a good array of cushions, carpets, Moroccan lamps and ceramics from both Fez and Salé. Daily 9am–7pm.

Blanco y Negro 40 Bd Pasteur, next door to Hôtel de Paris ☎ 0671 273636; map p.78. This small music shop has a pretty good selection of CDs by Moroccan artists, as well as music from North Africa and the Middle East. Daily 9am–9pm.

Ensemble Artisanal Cnr Rue Belgique & Rue M'sallah (left-hand side, going west from the Pl de France) ☎ 0661 924952; map p.72–73. A government-run centre that both produces and sells Moroccan crafts, such as *zellij* (mosaics), woodwork and book binding. There's virtually no haggling which often relates to higher prices than what you might get elsewhere, but without the stress. It's currently receiving a major refurbishment; the artisans are being temporarily housed around the corner in the Nil Boutique, opposite the M'sallah post office. Daily except Wed 9am–1pm & 3–7pm.

Marrakech la Rouge 50 Rue Siaghin, Medina ☎ 0539 931117; map p.75. Large and not-too-pushy bazaar selling rugs, jewellery, pottery, antique weaponry and leather, wood and metal crafts. Daily 9am–7pm.

Volubilis Boutique 15 Pl Petit Socco, Medina ☎ 0539 931362 or ☎ 0668 373340; map p.75. Shop for the artist and designer Mohamed Raiss el Fenni, with an interesting mix of traditional Moroccan and Western clothing and accessories on offer, as well as paintings. Daily with irregular opening hours between10am–8pm.

DIRECTORY

Banks and exchange Most banks, as well as a number of private bureaux de change, are grouped along Bd Pasteur and Bd Mohammed V. BMCE has branches at 21 Bd Pasteur and in the Grand Socco, both with ATMs, and SGMB also has a Grand Socco branch with ATM. EuroSol Bureau de Change (☎ 0539 334901) at 47 Bd Pasteur opens from 9am–9pm every day, as does Société Minzah Exchange (☎ 0539 933152) at 68 Rue Siaghine in the Medina. Most banks in Tangier will cash travellers' cheques, a service not widely offered in many other parts of the country.

Books Librairie des Colonnes, 54 Bd Pasteur (Mon–Sat 9.30am–1pm & 4.30–7pm; ☎ 0539 936955) (see map p.78).

Consulates UK, Trafalgar House, 9 Rue Amérique du Sud (Mon–Fri 8am–noon; ☎ 0539 936939 or ☎ 0661 093411). Closed at the time of writing, with all enquiries directed to the embassy in Rabat.

Golf Tangier Royal Golf Club, Route de Boubana (18 holes; ☎ 0539 938925).

Hammam The *Hôtel el Minzah's* Wellness Centre (150dh; daily 7am–10pm; ☎ 0539 333311, ⊛ elminzah.com) is open to non-residents.

Hospitals Clinique Assalam, 10 Av de la Paix, off Av Moulay Youssef to the west of the *gare routière* (☎ 0539 322558), is regarded as the best private clinic in Tangier for medical emergencies. Closer to the city centre is Hôpital Espagnol ☎ 0539 931018 on Rue de l'Hôpital Espagnol near Pl Oued El Makhazine. For a private ambulance, call ☎ 0539 954040 or ☎ 0539 946976.

Internet access Most cybercafés in the city are open daily from around 9am–10pm. Cybercafé Juliana, cnr Rue el Antaki & Rue Abou Alaa al Maari; Euronet, 5 Rue Ahmed Chaouki (off Bd Pasteur); Club Internet 3000, 27 Rue el Antaki (also sells computer accessories).

Pharmacies There are several English-speaking pharmacies on Pl de France and along Bd Pasteur. A roster of all-night and weekend pharmacies is displayed in every *pharmacie* window. Pharmacists can also recommend local doctors.

Police The Brigade Touristique has its HQ at the former train station by the port (☎ 0539 931129). There are smaller police posts on the Grand Socco and in the kasbah. Emergency ☎ 19.

FROM TOP GRAND SOCCO, TANGIER (P.78); MARKET, TANGIER >

1

Post office The main Poste Maroc office is at 33 Bd Mohammed V and has a poste restante service (Mon–Fri 8am–6pm & Sat 8am–noon).

Travel agencies Koutoubia, 112 bis Av Mohammed VI (☏ 0539 935540); Voyages Marco Polo, 72 Av Mohammed VI (☏ 0539 934345).

The Caves of Hercules

5km south of Cap Spartel · Daily 9am–sunset · 5dh

The **Caves of Hercules** (Les Grottes d'Hercule) are something of a symbol for Tangier, with their strange sea window, shaped like a map of Africa. The name, like Hercules' legendary founding of Tangier, is purely fanciful, but the caves, 16km outside the city and above the Atlantic beach, make an attractive excursion. If you feel like staying for a few days by the sea, the beach can be a pleasant base, too; outside of July and August only stray groups of visitors share the long surf beaches. Take care with currents, however, which can be very dangerous even near the shore.

Africa's most northwesterly promontory, **Cap Spartel**, is a dramatic and fertile point, and was known to the Greeks and Romans as the "Cape of the Vines". You can visit the lighthouse and sometimes, if the keeper is around, enter and climb it.

To the south of Cap Spartel begins the vast and wild Atlantic, known locally as **Robinson Plage**. It is broken only by a rocky spit, 5km from the Cape, which is home to the Caves of Hercules. Natural formations, which were occupied in prehistoric times, the caves are most striking for a man-made addition – thousands of disc-shaped erosions created by centuries of quarrying for millstones. There were still people cutting stones here for a living until the 1920s, but by that time their place was beginning to be taken by professional guides and discreet sex hustlers; it must have made an exotic brothel.

ARRIVAL AND DEPARTURE

CAVES OF HERCULES

By bus On summer weekends, the #2 bus runs here from St Andrew's Church by the Grand Socco in Tangier; at other times it runs to the nearby village of Jabila, a long walk from the caves –you're better off alighting before then, at Ziyatin on the old airport road, from where there are connecting taxis to the caves. The bus operates three times daily, departing the Grand Socco at around 9am, 11am & 4pm, and takes around 45 minutes.

By grand taxi Chartering a grand taxi from the Grand

Socco should cost you around 100dh including waiting time. You can also get to Ziyatin in shared grands taxis from St Andrew's Church.

By car The caves are a 15-minute drive from Tangier, travelling west of the city via the plush residential quarter of La Vieille Montagne and Cap Spartel. If you don't feel like backtracking, make a round trip by continuing along the coast road, then take either the minor road through Jabila or the faster main road (N1), back to Tangier.

ACCOMMODATION AND EATING

Camping Ashakar Caves of Hercules ☏ 0674 719419. Across from *Le Mirage*, this is a pleasant, well-wooded campsite with grass pitches and thirteen small bungalows. Showers are clean but usually cold, and there's a café, restaurant and small shop. Camping **45dh**, bungalow **250dh**

Le Mirage Caves of Hercules ☏ 0539 333332,

☏ lemirage-tanger.com. Close to the caves, this upmarket clifftop complex of bungalows has full facilities including a swimming pool. The restaurant and piano bar are open to non-residents and make a very pleasant, albeit expensive, lunch stop if you are on a day's outing from Tangier. BB **2476dh**

East of Tangier

The best beaches in the immediate vicinity of Tangier are to be found at **Cap Malabata**, where much wealthy villa development has been taking place, but long open swathes of sandy beach can still be found. Beyond here, **Ksar es Seghir** offers a pleasant day by the sea, or a stop on the coast road to Ceuta.

The ongoing expansion of the new Tanger Méditerranée port near the village of Dalia, 20km from Ceuta has, together with a new road and rail network, transformed the rugged coastline into a busy trade hub.

Cap Malabata

The bay east of Tangier is flanked by long stretches of beach and a chain of elderly villas and newer apartment blocks until you reach **Cap Malabata**, which has a couple of intermittently open hotels and some attractive stretches of beach. Further on, an old Portuguese fort on an outcrop makes a good destination for coastal walks.

ARRIVAL AND DEPARTURE **CAP MALABATA**

From Tangier, you can get to Cap Malabata on bus #15 or #16 from the Grand Socco, or by petit taxi.

Ksar es Seghir

The formerly picturesque little fishing port of **KSAR ES SEGHIR** has grown a little ugly in recent years, with a new breakwater constructed at its western entrance and the autoroute from Tanger Med Port towering over the village to its south. Although it continues to attract a fair number of Moroccan beach campers in summer, it now sees few European visitors. Just across the river from the town centre lie the remains of a medieval Islamic town and Portuguese fortress (there's a plan of the site posted up by the west side of the bridge). Ksar es Seghir has been of specific interest to archeologists, being positioned at the meeting point of three distinct terrains: the Habt (Atlantic lowlands), Jabala (sandstone hills), and the Rif mountains.

ARRIVAL AND DEPARTURE **KSAR ES SEGHIR**

By bus Buses travelling between Tangier and Fnideq stop at the junction in the centre of town.

By grand taxi Shared grands taxis from Rue de Portugal in Tangier will drop you at the junction in the centre of town.

ACCOMMODATION AND EATING

Diamant Bleu At the western entrance to the town. This restaurant has a nice view of the coast and offers a Moroccan and Mediterranean menu, specializing in seafood (mains 35–90dh). Daily 10am–9pm; often Nov–Feb.

Ksar al Maja N16 highway, 3km from Tanger Med Port ☎0539 593647. New block-type hotel built to take advantage of passing trade from the new port. Lacking any real character, the modern rooms are nonetheless comfortable and good value. There are a number of café-restaurants close by. <u>248dh</u>

Tarifa On the old, coastal road from Tangier, 12km before the town ☎0539 561849. A pleasant place with comfortable en-suite rooms overlooking the sea, and a restaurant serving Moroccan staples and seafood. <u>396dh</u>

Asilah

The first town south of Tangier – and first stop on the train line – **ASILAH** is one of the most elegant of the old Portuguese Atlantic ports, small, easy to manage, and exceptionally clean. First impressions are of wonderful square stone ramparts, flanked by palms, and an outstanding beach – an immense sweep of sand stretching to the north halfway to Tangier. The town's Medina is one of the most attractive in the country, colourwashed in pastel shades, and with a series of murals painted for the town's **International Cultural Festival** (3–4 weeks in Aug; ⓦc-assilah.com), which attracts performers from around the world with a programme of art, dance, film, music and poetry.

Before the tourists and the International Festival, Asilah was just a small fishing port, quietly stagnating after the indifference of Spanish colonial administration. Whitewashed and cleaned up, it now has a prosperous feeling to it: the Grand Mosque, for example, has been rebuilt and doubled in size, there's a wide paved seaside promenade and property developments, including a marina and golf course estate, are popping up either side of the town. As with Tangier, the **beach** is the main focus of life in summer. The most popular stretches are to the north of the town, out towards the train station. For more isolated strands, walk south, past the Medina ramparts.

1

The ramparts and Medina

The Medina's circuit of **towers and ramparts** – built by the Portuguese military architect Botacca in the sixteenth century – are pleasant to wander around. They include two main gates: **Bab el Homar**, on Avenue Hassan II, and **Bab el Kasba**. If you enter by the latter, you pass the **Grand Mosque** and the **Centre Hassan II des Rencontres Internationales**, formerly a Spanish army barracks and now an arts venue and accommodation centre for the festival, with a cool open courtyard.

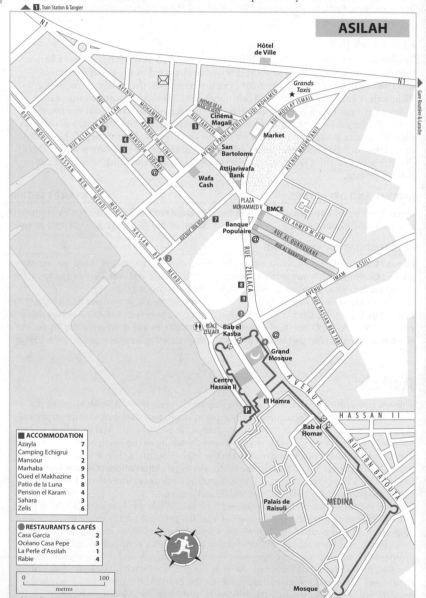

ASILAH

■ ACCOMMODATION	
Azayla	7
Camping Echigrui	1
Mansour	2
Marhaba	9
Oued el Makhazine	5
Patio de la Luna	8
Pension el Karam	4
Sahara	3
Zelis	6

● RESTAURANTS & CAFÉS	
Casa Garcia	2
Océano Casa Pepe	3
La Perle d'Assilah	1
Rabie	4

0 — 100
metres

Further on is a small square overlooked by the "red tower", **El Hamra**. This is used for exhibitions, particularly during the festival. Turn right past here, along a tiny network of streets, and down towards the platform overlooking the sea, and you'll come upon at least a half-dozen **murals** painted (and subsequently repainted) during the festival; they form an intriguing mix of fantasy-representational art and geometric designs. Keep an eye out for the small art galleries of local artists which are scattered around the Medina.

Palais de Raisuli

Rue Sidi Ahmed Ben Mansour

The town's focal sight – stretching over the sea at the heart of the Medina – is the **Palais de Raisuli**, built in 1909 with forced tribal labour by Moulay Ahmed er Raisuli, a local bandit. One of the strangest figures to emerge from what was a bizarre period of Moroccan government, he began his career as a cattle rustler, achieved notoriety with a series of kidnappings and ransoms (including the British writer Walter Harris and a Greek-American millionaire, Perdicaris, who was bailed out by Teddy Roosevelt), and was eventually appointed governor over practically all the tribes of northwest Morocco. Harris described his captivity in *Morocco That Was* as an "anxious time", made more so by being confined in a small room with a headless corpse. Despite this, captor and captive formed a friendship, Harris finding Raisuli a "mysterious personage, half-saint, half-blackguard", and often entertaining him later in Tangier.

Another British writer, Rosita Forbes, visited Raisuli in his palace in 1924. Raisuli told Forbes that he made murderers walk to their death from the palace windows – a 27-metre drop to the rocks. One man, he said, had turned back to him, saying, "Thy justice is great, Sidi, but these stones are more merciful".

The palace overhangs the sea ramparts towards the far end of the Medina (away from the beach). Other than at times during the International Cultural Festival, it's not officially open to visitors but if you're interested – the interior is worth seeing – knock or enlist the help of a local and you may strike lucky with the caretaker.

Church of San Bartolome

Junction of Avenue Mohammed V and Avenue Prince Héritier Sidi Mohamed • Visitors are welcome at any time – ring the bell by the door alongside the church

The **Church of San Bartolome** was built in 1925 by Franciscan priests from Galicia, in northwest Spain. The cool and airy colonial-Spanish-style interior is complemented by the nuns' own small chapel in Moorish style, with prayers common to Islam and Christianity carved in Arabic. One of the few church bells allowed to be used in Morocco is rung for Mass at 11am on Sundays and the sisters, from a teaching order founded by Mary Ward in Yorkshire in 1585, train local girls in dressmaking, embroidery and literacy.

ARRIVAL AND DEPARTURE
ASILAH

By train The train station is inconveniently located 2km north of the town; there is occasionally a taxi to meet arrivals but don't count on it. It's a straightforward 15min walk into town. Book ahead if you're planning on catching the overnight couchette service to Marrakesh, which calls in at Asilah at about 11pm.

Destinations Casablanca Voyageurs (8 direct & 1 connecting daily; 4hr–5hr 30min); Fez (2 direct & 3 connecting daily; 4hr–4hr 45min); Marrakesh (1 direct & 6 connecting daily; 8hr–9hr 30min); Meknes (2 direct & 3 connecting daily; 3hr 15min–3hr 30min); Oujda (1 direct & 1 connecting daily; 9hr 45min); Rabat (8 direct & 1

connecting daily; 3hr–4hr 30min); Souk el Arba du Rharb (9 direct daily; 1hr 10min); Tangier (10 direct daily; 45min); Taza (1 direct & 1 connecting daily; 6hr 10min).

By bus Buses arrive at the *gare routière* on the Tangier–Larache (N1) road. From here it's a short walk across the N1 and down Av Moulay Ismail to the central Plaza Mohammed V. Note that CTM no longer stops at Asilah.

Destinations Larache (25 daily; 1hr); Tangier (25 daily; 40min).

By grand taxi Grand taxis park just north of Plaza Mohammed V on Av Moulay Ismail.

Destinations Larache (40min); Tangier (40min).

1

ACCOMMODATION

Asilah can be packed during its festival but at other times, even high season, there's usually space in the dozen or so *pensions* and hotels. Camper vans are usually allowed to park for the night in an open parking area just outside the Medina wall at the end of Rue Moulay Hassan Ben Mehdi – tip the *gardien* 10dh.

★ **Azayla** 20 Av Ibn Rochd ☎0539 416717. Good-value bright and clean rooms with a/c; some extra-large rooms benefit from a sitting area. Good location just a short stroll from the Medina and the beach. Free wi-fi in reception. BB **386dh**

Camping Echrigui Av Mohammed V, 500m north of town ☎0539 417182. Marginally the better of two campsites on this road, offering hot showers (10dh) and electricity (20dh). Somewhat tatty and overgrown, they usually clean it up for the summer season, when there's mosquitoes to contend with. **30dh**

Mansour 49 Av Mohammed V ☎0539 417390. This has long been one of the better mid-range hotels in town, though the rooms are beginning to look a little tired. The staff are friendly and the English-speaking owner also runs a handy travel agency. BB **350dh**

Marhaba 9 Rue Zellaca ☎0539 417144. A friendly place, close to the Medina, with small, simple rooms and ancient, shared bathrooms. Good value for money, though prices increase in summer. **150dh**

Oued el Makhazine Av Melilla ☎0539 417090, ☎0394 17500. A pleasant and comfortable hotel, tiled throughout, and with some suites that can comfortably sleep four. A rooftop terrace gives a nice view of the harbour and across to the northern beaches. **450dh**

Patio de la Luna 12 Rue Zellaca ☎0539 416074, ⊕patiodelaluna.com. A small house, beautifully converted into a tastefully decorated guesthouse, with simple, rustic rooms overlooking a peaceful patio-garden. There's also a sunny rooftop terrace and friendly management. **500dh**

Pension el Karam 40 Rue Mansour Eddahbi ☎0539 417626. A small, homely *pension* close to the seafront but a little way from the Medina. Rooms are all ground level, opening onto a pleasant, open courtyard. Shared bathrooms. **300dh**

Sahara 9 Rue Tarfaya ☎0539 417185. A little away from the action, behind the Cinéma Magali, but it's quiet, clean, comfortable and great value. Rooms look onto a central courtyard, some are without external windows, and all have shared showers (5dh extra). **150dh**

Zelis 10 Rue Mansour Eddahbi ☎0539 417029, ☎0539 417098. Still one of the better hotels in town but not especially attractive. Bright, airy rooms, some of which have ocean views, and there's a swimming pool and café. The restaurant, however, is not recommended. BB **604dh**

EATING, DRINKING AND NIGHTLIFE

Casa Garcia 51 Rue Moulay Hassan Ben Mehdi ☎0539 417465. Popular restaurant across the road from the promenade, with tables inside and out. Regulars compliment the consistently high standard of the dishes, such as a delicious seafood tajine, prawn tagliatelle and a *kefta* lasagne (mains 80–200dh). It can get pretty busy at times (book on Sundays). Daily noon–4pm & 8–11.30pm.

Océano Casa Pepe 22 Pl Zellaca (opposite Bab Kasbah) ☎0539 417395. An Asilah institution, this is one of the more formal dining options in town. Seafood dishes dominate the menu, including the Asilah speciality of marinated white anchovies (mains 70–200dh). There's seating inside and out, black-tied waiters and a wine list dominated by Spanish vineyards. Daily noon–4pm & 8–11.30pm.

★ **La Perle d'Assilah** Cnr Rue Allal Ben Abdallah and Av Melilla ☎0539 418758. This classy, friendly restaurant is owner-managed by Moroccan-Irish couple Lahcen and Helen Iouani, Lahcen doubling as head chef. Outdoor tables are shielded by glass windbreakers, while the wood-panelled and spacious interior creates an intimate dining area. The menu includes a good variety of seafood, meat and vegetarian choices (90–250dh), as well as good-value set menus (160–190dh). Daily noon–3pm & 7–10.30pm.

Rabie Av Hassan II. One of a number of alfresco places to eat on this street. Shaded under tall eucalyptus trees with plastic tables and chairs, the menu includes tajines, brochettes and pasta dishes, along with plenty of seafood options (mains 25–75dh). No alcohol. Daily 11am–11pm.

DIRECTORY

Banks Banque Populaire, BMCE, Crédit Agricole and Attijariwafa Bank all have branches with ATMs on Plaza Mohammed V. There's a Wafa Cash bureau de change on Av Prince Héritier Sidi Mohamed (Mon–Fri 8am–8pm, Sat 9am–1pm).

Internet Cyber World.net, Rue Mansour Eddahbi, opposite *Hôtel Zelis*, and Internet al Ahram, Rue al Banafsaje (b).

Market There's a villagers' market, at its liveliest on Thursday and Sunday held on Av Moulay Ismail below the grand taxi stand.

1

MZOURA

If you have an interest in ancient sites, you might devote a half-day to explore the prehistoric **stone circle of Mzoura**, south of Asilah. The desolate, unfenced site, whose name means "Holy Place" in Arabic, originally comprised a tumulus, assumed to be the tomb of some early Mauritanian king, enclosed by an elliptical circle of some 167 standing stones, mostly around 1.5 metres in height but some up to 5 metres. It was excavated in 1935 and the mound is now reduced to a series of watery hollows. There are photographs of Mzoura, pre-excavation, in the archeological museum in Tetouan (see p.110).

   To reach Mzoura, follow the N1 south of Asilah for 16km, then turn left along the R417 towards Tetouan. After crossing the railway line, and 4km from the junction with the N1, turn left by the Somepi petrol station and onto a side road signposted El Yamini (Tnine Sidi Lyamani). From here the site is 5km northeast, across a confusing network of sandy tracks; it's a good idea to enlist a guide at El Yamini for around 50dh.

Larache

LARACHE is a relaxed, easy-going town, its summer visitors primarily Moroccan tourists who come to enjoy the beaches to the north of the estuary of the River Loukos. You'll see as many women around as men – a reassuring feeling for women travellers looking for a low-key spot to bathe. Nearby, and accessible, are the ruins of **ancient Lixus**, legendary site of the Gardens of the Hesperides.

   Larache was the main port of the northern Spanish zone and still bears much of its former stamp. There are faded old Spanish hotels, Spanish-run restaurants and Spanish bars, even an active Spanish cathedral for the small colony who still work at the docks. In its heyday it was quite a metropolis, publishing its own Spanish newspaper and journal, and drawing a cosmopolitan population that included the French writer Jean Genet, who spent the last decade of his life here and is buried in the old Spanish cemetery found to the southwest of town.

   Before its colonization in 1911, Larache was a small trading port. Its activities limited by dangerous offshore sand bars, the port-town eked out a living by building pirate ships made of wood from the nearby Forest of Mamora for the "Barbary Corsairs" of Salé and Rabat.

   Downtown Larache remains delightfully compact and relaxed, largely bereft of any hustle or hassle, despite the ongoing construction of a golf and marina resort to the north of the estuary. A true hybrid of its Andalusian-Arabic heritage, this is a town where paella is served alongside tajine, and where the evening *paseo* (promenade) is interrupted by the call to prayer.

Place de la Libération

The town's circular main square, **Place de la Libération**, is still often identified by its original name, Plaza de España. Set just back from the sea and centred around a fountain within well-kept gardens and impressive palm trees, the plaza is encircled by many striking examples of Spanish colonial architecture, best appreciated by one of the cheap and cheerful cafés underneath the section known simply as "the Arches".

The cathedral

Avenue Mohamed V • Mass Sun 11am

Built in the 1920s and designed by Spanish architects, the **Iglesia de Nuestra Señora del Pilar** (Our Lady of the Pillar) cathedral is another architectural reminder of Larache's Andalusian relationship. Its exterior is not unlike a mosque, while the interior is very much that of a traditional Catholic cathedral. Mass is still given every Sunday at 11am.

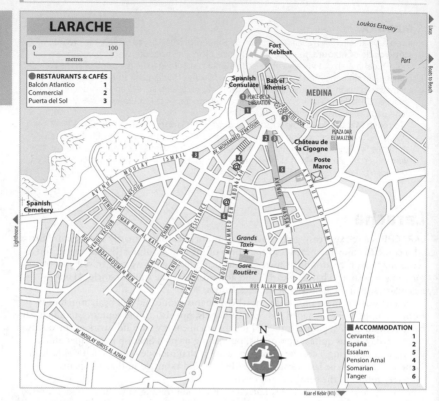

LARACHE

Loukos Estuary

Lixus

Boats to Beach

0 — 100
metres

Fort Kebibat

Port

RESTAURANTS & CAFÉS
Balcón Atlantico   1
Commercial   2
Puerta del Sol   3

Spanish Consulate

Bab el Khemis

MEDINA

PLACE DE LA LIBÉRATION

ZOCO PETIT SOUK

PLAZA DAR EL MAJZEN

AV. MOHAMMED ZERKTOUNI

Château de la Cigogne

Poste Maroc

MOULAY ISMAIL

AVENUE AL MANSOUR

AVENUE AL ABDALLAH

AVENUE HASSAN

Spanish Cemetery

Lighthouse

RUE YACOUB OMAR BEN AL KATTABI

AV. ABI AL MOUMEN BEN ALI

CARM

AVENUE DE LA RESISTANCE

SIDI AL

MOULAY MOHAMMED BEN ABDALLAH

AVENUE

RUE D'ALGÉRIE

AVENUE MOHAMMED V

@

@

Grands Taxis ★

Gare Routière

RUE ALLAH BEN ABDALLAH

AV. MOULAY IDRISS AL AZHAR

N

Ksar el Kebir (H1)

■ **ACCOMMODATION**
Cervantes   1
España   2
Essalam   5
Pension Amal   4
Somarian   3
Tanger   6

The Medina

A high Hispano-Moorish archway on Place de la Libération, **Bab el Khemis**, leads into the **Medina**, a surprisingly compact wedge of alleys and stairways leading down towards the port and up to Plaza Dar el Majzen. The colonnaded market square, Zoco de la Alcaiceria, just inside the archway, was built by the Spanish in the seventeenth century.

Though lacking in actual sights, wandering through the Medina's blue- and whitewashed streets is a wonderful opportunity to absorb and view everyday Medina life without the niggling concern of getting lost or being pressured to buy something. At the high, eastern edge of the Medina are the the small twin plazas of **al Anuar** and **Dar el Majzen**. Separated by a small archway and mosque that defines the Medina's outer wall, this is a great spot to view midday prayers, especially on a Friday, when worshippers spill out onto a shaded, matted area on Plaza al Anuar. On Plaza Dar el Majzen is the **Château de la Cigogne** (House of the Stork), a grand two-storey colonial mansion that has been renovated and now houses a music school. Standing guard over the plaza, is a hulking, three-sided fortress, the **Kasbah de la Cigogne**, dating back to the original Spanish occupation in the seventeenth century.

The beach

The shore below Avenue Moulay Ismail is wild and rocky; cross the estuary of the Oued Loukos, however, and you'll find a popular sandy **beach** sheltered by trees and flanked by a handful of café-restaurants during summer. You can get there by bus (#4 from the port, June–Aug only, every 20min – some buses start from Plaza Dar el Majzen) or grand taxi. But the most enjoyable way is to take one of the **fishing boat s** (5–15dh), which shuttle across to the opposite bank, from where it's a short but hot walk over to the beach.

ARRIVAL AND DEPARTURE LARACHE

By bus Long-distance buses, including CTM, use the town bus station (*estación de autobús*) just off Rue Moulay Mohammed Ben Abdullah. The bus station is a straight-forward 400m walk from Place de la Libération, down Rue Moulay Mohammed Ben Abdallah.

Destinations Asilah (20 daily; 1hr); Casablanca (4 CTM & 5 others daily; 4hr); Fez (4 CTM and 4 others daily; 4hr 30min); Ksar el Kebir (8 daily; 40min); Meknes (2 daily; 5hr 30min); Rabat (20 daily; 3hr 30min); Souk el Arba (8 daily; 1hr); Tangier (5 CTM and 20 others daily; 1hr 30min).

By grand taxi Grand taxis operate from outside the bus station.

Destinations Asilah (40min); Ksar el Kebir (30min); Souk el Arba du Rharb (45min).

ACCOMMODATION

Larache has some decent accommodation and it's a good idea to book ahead in summer.

Cervantes 3 Rue Tarik Ibnou Ziad, off Pl de la Libération ☎0539 910874. Don't be put off by the unappealing paintwork – this is a friendly little place, with comfortable enough rooms and shared hot showers. **140dh**

España Pl de la Libération/entrance at 6 Av Hassan II ☎0539 913195, ⓦhotelespanalarache.com. This was the *Grand Hôtel* in Spanish days, and there's still a touch of elegance about the place today. An ornate, carpeted staircase leads from an impressive reception area to a range of large rooms that are all en suite with a/c and TV. **340dh**

★ **Essalam** 9 Av Hassan II ☎0539 916822, ☎0539 916822. One of our readers described this place as "the best budget hotel in Morocco", and we'd be hard-pressed to disagree: the rooms, some of which are en suite, are spacious and immaculate, with constant hot water and even a TV. **160dh**

Pension Amal 10 Rue Abdallah Ben Yasin, off Rue Moulay Mohammed Ben Abdallah ☎0539 912788. Very basic, cheap and cheerful place, with simple but decent rooms. Hot showers (10dh) and toilets are in the hallways. **100dh**

Somarian 68 Av Mohammed Zerktouni ☎0539 910116. Ignoring the slightly bizarre decor in the lobby, this business-class hotel offers large attractive rooms with a/c and TV. Noise from the local market across the road usually isn't a problem. **400dh**

Tanger Cnr Rue Moulay Mohammed Ben Abdallah and Rue Tanger ☎0539 916814, ☎0539 916759. Opened in 2012, this newcomer has large, bright roomś, some en suite though those with shared facilities are particularly good value. Spread over a number of floors, there's no lift but the friendly management are on hand to assist with luggage. It's very well located, only a 10min walk from the bus station and Pl de la Libération. **140dh**

EATING AND DRINKING

Balcón Atlantico Rue de Casablanca ☎0539 910110. One of the nicest locations in town, overlooking a popular promenade with great views out to the Atlantic. They offer some good breakfast menus, as well as light meals like pizza, panini and savoury crêpes (mains 30–45dh). Daily 8am–10pm.

Commercial Pl de la libération. This old restaurant is pretty basic inside but has a good location on the main square. It's popular with the locals, who come for its simple and cheap dishes such as paella and fried fish. Mains 25dh Daily noon–1pm.

Puerta del Sol (aka Porte du Soleil) Rue de Salé, off Av Hassan II ☎0539 913641. This small setup offers up the usual Mediterranean-Moroccan standards. Choose a combination of both by ordering their seafood tajine, or simply choose a fillet of line fish from their refrigerated display and have it fried or grilled just the way you like (mains 25–40dh). Daily noon–10pm.

DIRECTORY

Banks and exchange Banque Populaire, Crédit Agricole and Crédit Immobilier et Hôtelier (CIH) are all on Av Mohammed V, just south of Pl de la Libération. Larache Oscar Currency Exchange Point, Pl de la Libération (daily 9am–9pm).

Consulate Spain, 1 Rue de Casablanca ☎0539 913302.
Golf Port Lixus Resort Golf Club, north of Oued Loukkos, turn off at Lixus Ruins (18 holes; ☎0539 500782).
Internet Marnet Cyber, cnr Av Moulay Mohammed Ben Abdallah and Rue Mouatamid Ben Abad (Mon–Sat 10am–11pm).

1 Ancient Lixus

Ancient Lixus is one of the oldest – and most continuously – inhabited sites in Morocco. It had been settled in prehistoric times, long before the arrival of Phoenician colonists around 1000 BC, under whom it is thought to have become the first trading post of North Africa. Later, it was in turn an important Carthaginian and Roman city, and was deserted only in the fifth century AD, two hundred years after Diocletian had withdrawn the empire's patronage. There are remains of a church from this period, and Arabic coins have also been found.

As an archeological site, then, Lixus is certainly significant, and its legendary associations with Hercules (see box below) add an element of mythic allure. The ruins lie upon and below the summit of a low hill on the far side of the Oued Loukos estuary, at the crossroads of the main Larache–Tangier road and the narrow lane to Larache beach. A track, worth climbing for the panoramic view alone, wends up to the amphitheatre area, where there are mosaics. The ruins are interesting rather than impressive, and only around a quarter of the site has been excavated.

The site

A visitor's centre was being constructed at the time of writing but currently the site is not effectively enclosed and therefore always open and accessible. A notice by the roadside at the entrance explains the site with a useful map board. The Lower Town, spreading back from the modern road, consists largely of the ruins of factories for the production of salt – still being panned nearby – and *garum* fish sauce. The factories seem to have been developed in the early years of the first century AD and they remained in operation until the Roman withdrawal.

A track, some 100m down the road to Tangier, leads up to the Acropolis (upper town), passing on its way eight rows of the Roman **theatre** and **amphitheatre**, unusually combined into a single structure. Its deep, circular arena was adapted for circus games and the gladiatorial slaughter of animals. Morocco, which Herodotus knew as "the wild-beast country", was the major source for these Roman *venations* (controlled hunts), and local colonists must have grown rich from the trade. Until 1998, the **baths** built into the side of the theatre featured a remarkable **mosaic** depicting Neptune's head on the body of a lobster; unfortunately, the mosaic was irreparably damaged when the *gardien*'s son tried to dig it up to sell, and just about a third of it remains.

Climbing above the baths and theatre, you pass through ramparts to the main fortifications of the **Acropolis** – a somewhat confused network of walls and foundations – and **temple sanctuaries**, including an early **Christian basilica** and a number of **pre-Roman buildings**. The most considerable of the sanctuaries, with their underground cisterns and porticoed priests' quarters, were apparently rebuilt in the first century AD, but even then retained Phoenician elements in their design.

LIXUS AND HERCULES

The legendary associations of Lixus – and the site's mystique – centre on the **Labours of Hercules**. For here, on an island in the estuary, Pliny and Strabo record reports of the palace of the "Libyan" (by which they meant African) King Antaeus. Behind the palace stretched the Garden of the Hesperides, to which Hercules, as his penultimate labour, was dispatched. In the object of Hercules' quest – the Golden Apples – it is not difficult to imagine the tangerines of northern Morocco, raised to legendary status by travellers' tales. The site, too, seems to offer reinforcement to conjectures of a mythic pre-Phoenician past. **Megalithic stones** have been found on the Acropolis – they may have been linked astronomically with those of Mzoura (see box, p.95) – and the site was known to the Phoenicians as Makom Shemesh (City of the Sun).

ARRIVAL AND DEPARTURE

It's a four- to five-kilometre walk to the ruins from both Larache beach or town. Currently lacking any great signage, the entrance to the site is on the corner of the Larache–Asilah road and a minor road signposted as "Plage Ras Rmel".

By bus and grand taxi From Larache port, bus #4 (June–Aug only, every 20 min) and bus #5 (five times daily) will both drop off at the ruins; bus #4 continues on to the beach; alternatively, charter a grand taxi (around 100dh) but be sure to agree on a collection time from the ruins and only pay once you're back in town.

Ksar el Kebir

As its name – in Arabic, "the Great Enclosure" – suggests, **KSAR EL KEBIR**, an eleventh-century Arab power base 36km southeast of Larache, was once a place of some importance. It was 12km north of here where, in August 1578, the Portuguese fought the disastrous **Battle of the Three Kings**, the most dramatic and devastating in their nation's history – a power struggle disguised as a crusade, which saw the death or capture of virtually the entire nobility and which ultimately resulted in 62 years of Spanish rule.

The town fell into decline in the seventeenth century, after a local chief incurred the wrath of Moulay Ismail, though its fortunes were revived to some extent under the Spanish protectorate, when it served as a major barracks.

The **Sunday souk** is held right by the *gare routière* and Moulay el Mehdi station. On any morning of the week, however, there are lively **souks** around the main **kissaria** (covered market) of the old town – in the quarter known as Bab el Oued (Gate of the River). Beyond Ksar el Kebir, a decaying customs post at **Arbaoua** marks the old colonial frontier between the Spanish and French zones.

ARRIVAL AND DEPARTURE   KSAR EL KEBIR

By train The easiest way to get to Ksar el Kebir is by train. Ksar el Kebir station is way out on the northern edge of town; for the town centre, get off at Moulay el Mehdi station, one stop south.
Destinations Asilah (10 daily; 45min); Casablanca Voyageurs (8 direct & 1 connecting daily; 3hr 30min–5hr); Fez (2 direct & 3 connecting daily; 3hr); Marrakesh (1 direct & 6 connecting daily; 7hr 10min–9hr); Meknes (2 direct & 3 connecting daily; 2hr 30min); Oujda (1 direct & 1 connecting daily; 9hr); Rabat (8 direct & 1 connecting daily; 2hr 20min–3hr 45min); Tangier (10 direct daily; 1hr 40min); Taza (1 direct & 1 connecting daily; 5hr 30min).

By bus The *gare routière* is next to Moulay el Mehdi station, however, as the motorway bypasses the town, few long-distance buses come here.
Destinations Moulay Bousselham (5 daily; 35min); Ouezzane (3 daily; 1hr 30min).
By grand taxi Grands taxis from Larache operate to and from a station just across the tracks from the *gare routière*, and those from Ouezzane and Souk el Arba du Rharb operate from one 500m further south.
Destinations Larache (30min); Moulay Bousselham (30min); Ouezzane (1hr); Souk el Arba du Rharb (30min).

ACCOMMODATION AND EATING

There are a number of hotels and basic places to eat located on or near the town square; head south from the Moulay el Mehdi station and turn right after 300m.

Ksar al Yamama 8 Bd Hassan II ☎ 0539 907960, ☎ 0539 903838. A good-value place, with nice, large, airy rooms, some en suite with a bathtub, and some with balconies overlooking the town square. **250dh**

Moulay Bousselham

MOULAY BOUSSELHAM, 55km from Ksar el Kebir, is a very low-key resort, popular almost exclusively with Moroccans. It comprises little more than a single street, crowded with grill-cafés and sloping down to the sea at the side of a broad lagoon and

1

WETLAND WILDLIFE

Adjoining the Moulay Bousselham lagoon is a large wetland area known as **Merja Zerga** ("Blue Lake"). The lagoon's periphery is used for grazing by nomadic herds of sheep, cattle and goats, and the lagoon itself is a Ramsar-listed Wetland of International Importance, and is one of the largest of its kind in Morocco.

The huge extent of the site ensures rewarding **birdwatching** at all times of the year. There are large numbers of waders, including a large colony of flamingos, plus little-ringed plovers, black-winged stilts and black-tailed godwits.

For serious birdwatchers, it is the **gulls and terns** that roost on the central islands which are worthy of the closest inspection, as, among the flocks of lesser black-backed gull and black tern, it is possible to find rarer species such as **Caspian tern**. The adjacent grassland is probably the best place in Morocco to see pairs of North African **marsh owl**, which usually appear hunting above the tall grasses shortly after sunset. Marsh harrier and osprey can also sometimes be spotted. One bird you'll certainly see wintering here, usually around cattle (and sometimes sitting on their backs), is the **cattle egret**. For rarity-spotters, the current grail is the lesser crested tern and its cousin the royal tern, both immigrants from Mauretania during spring and summer.

English-speaking local ornithologist Hassan Dalil (☎0668 434110) is easily the best guide in the region, and can be contacted directly or via the *Café Milano* in Moulay Bousselham, which also keeps a **bird log**. Hassan charges 100dh per hour for a tour around Merja Zerga by boat and his expertise is immediately evident. These tours are best taken in early morning or at dusk, depending on the tides; the boat isn't shaded so bring along a hat, protective clothing, sunscreen and water.

wetland area, known as **Merja Zerga**. This is one of northern Morocco's prime **birdwatching** locations (see box above), and avid bird watchers from all over the world come here to see the lagoon's flamingo and other bird colonies.

The **beach** itself is sheltered by cliffs – rare along the Atlantic – and has an abrupt drop-off, which creates a continual crash of breaking waves. While a lot of fun for swimming as well as beginner surfers, the currents can at times be quite strong and only the most confident of swimmers should venture out past the breakers. In summer, a section of the beach is patrolled by lifeguards.

For Moroccans, the village is part summer resort, part pilgrimage centre. The saint from whom the village takes its name, the **Marabout Moulay Bousselham**, was a tenth-century Egyptian, whose remains are housed in a *koubba* prominently positioned above the settlement. In July this sees one of the largest **moussems** in the region.

ARRIVAL AND DEPARTURE   MOULAY BOUSSELHAM

By bus Buses stop at a car park at the entrance to the village. From here it's a short, slightly uphill walk to the village centre or a similar distance but slightly downhill to the two camping sites.
Destinations Ksar el Kebir (5 daily; 35min); Souk el Arba du Rharb (4 daily; 40min).
By grand taxi Grands taxis stop at the same spot as the

buses, though it's worth asking the driver to drop you off in the village centre or even at your accommodation. The frequency of services increases greatly during the summer holiday season.
Destinations Ksar el Kebir (5–10 daily; 20min); Larache (5–10 daily; 1hr); Souk el Arba du Rharb (5–10 daily; 30min).

ACCOMMODATION AND EATING

During the summer, accommodation should be booked in advance. In the village centre is a line of **grill-cafés**; indistinguishable from each other, they will all fix you a large mixed platter of freshly fried fish for around 60dh.

Camping Caravanning International 500m east of town on the lagoon ☎0537 432477. This large, grassy, shaded but ageing campsite remains ever popular due to its

lagoon-side location. It can get very busy during summer, when both the ablutions and mosquitoes are a worry. A restaurant is conveniently located across the road. 70dh

Flamants Loisirs Camping 1km east of town, signposted opposite the post office ☎0537 432539 or ☎0661 892214, ✆flamants-loisirs.fr. The "leisurely flamingos" is set away from the village in a relatively secure lot overlooking the lagoon from up high. There's lots of shady sites and basic ablutions with hot water, as well as an on-site restaurant and swimming pool (summer only). A number of stuffy four-person bungalows are also available. Camping **140dh**, bungalow **400dh**

Le Lagon Main road, village centre ☎0537 432650, ☎0537 432649. An ageing, crumbling, overpriced 80s-era hotel with fantastic views over the lagoon – its one and only attribute. Rooms are en suite, some also have TV. **300dh**

La Maison des Oiseaux About 2km east of town, phone ahead for directions ☎0537 432543 or ☎0661 301067, ✆moulay.bousselham.free.fr. The "house of the birds", down by the lagoon, is a whitewashed villa with a pleasant garden and a homely atmosphere. There's a variety of rooms, including some family suites that sleep up to four adults. Themed courses such as cooking and yoga can also be arranged. HB **750dh**

★ **Villa Nora** At the far northern end of town, about 1.5km from the centre ☎0537 432071. This British-owned, friendly guesthouse overlooks the beach and the Atlantic rollers, and is easily the village's best accommodation. Rooms are small but comfortable, with a shared bathroom, and meals can be arranged. BB **500dh**

DIRECTORY

Banks Attijariwafa, Banque Populaire and Crédit Agricole are all located at the entrance to the village; all have ATMs.

Festival The Moussem of Moulay Bousselham is held in mid-July every year. The village, already bursting at the seams at this time of the year, overflows with pilgrims dressed in white who come to pay homage to the saint by visiting the *koubba*.

Post office At the entrance to the village, close to the banks.

Ceuta

A Spanish enclave since the sixteenth century, **CEUTA** (Sebta in Arabic) is a curious political anomaly. Along with Melilla, east along the coast, it was retained by Spain after Moroccan independence in 1956 and today functions largely as a military base, its economy bolstered by a limited duty-free status. It has been an autonomous city, with a large measure of internal self-government for its 80,000 inhabitants, since 1995. The city makes for an attractive stop when en route either to or from Morocco with its relaxed European atmosphere, pristine squares, tapas bars, coastal walks and pleasant accommodation options.

Plaza de Nuestra Señora de Africa

The most attractive part of Ceuta is within several hundred metres of the ferry terminal, where the **Plaza Nuestra Señora de Africa** is flanked by a pair of Baroque churches, **Nuestra Señora de Africa** (Our Lady of Africa – open most days) and the **cathedral** (usually locked). Bordering the square, to the west, are the most impressive remainders of the city walls – the walled moat of **Foso de San Felipe** and the adjacent **Muralla Real** (Royal Walls; daily 10am–2pm & 4–8pm; free). The oldest sections of the fortifications were built by the Byzantines.

Museo de Ceuta

30 Paseo del Revellín • June–Aug Mon–Sat 10am–2pm & 7–9pm, Sun 10am–2pm; Sept–May Mon–Sat 10am–2pm & 5–8pm, Sun 10am–2pm • Free

To the east of Plaza de la Constitución, an oldish quarter rambles up from the bottom of the long **Paseo del Revellín**. There's an interesting little municipal museum here, the **Museo de Ceuta**, displaying archeological finds from Stone Age and Roman times through to the Islamic era, well laid out and with good explanations, but in Spanish only. There is also a section dedicated to contemporary art exhibitions on the ground floor.

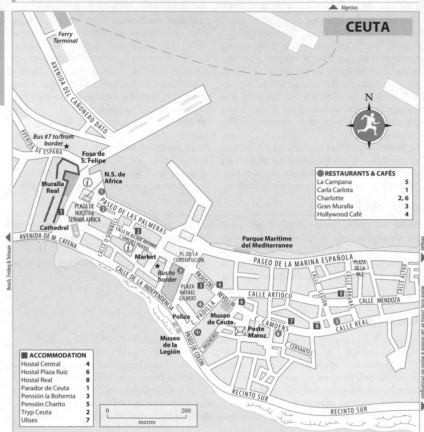

Museo de la Legión

1 Paseo de Colón • Mon–Fri 10am–1.30pm, Sat 10am–1.30pm, 4–6pm • Free

On the southern flank of the city centre, the **Museo de la Legión** offers an interesting glimpse of Spanish–African military history. Relatively small in size, its four exhibition rooms are crammed with uniforms, weapons and paraphernalia of the infamous Spanish Foreign Legion. Opposite the museum is a statue of a *legionario* accompanied by a Barbary sheep, just one of many mascots that the Ceuta regiment has had over the years.

The peninsula

A round circuit of the peninsula makes for a pleasant day-trip if the weather is fine. Start by heading east (and uphill) on Recinto Sur; as the buildings gradually disappear from view, the land swells into a rounded, pine-covered slope offering fine views out to the Rock of Gibraltar. Known as **Monte Acho**, the summit is crowned by a Byzantine-era fort that is still an active military setup, and therefore off-limits. Around midway, signs direct you to the **Ermita de San Antonio**, an old convent rebuilt during the 1960s and dominated by a monument to Franco. At the very eastern end of the peninsula is another military museum, the **Museo del Desnarigado**, (Sat & Sun 11am–2pm &

BORDER TRADE: PEOPLE AND DRUGS

Over the last few decades, the economies on both sides of the border seemed to benefit from the enclave, spurred on by Ceuta's duty-free status. However, the border is also the frontier between Africa and Europe and inevitably the EU became increasingly concerned about traffic in drugs and illegal immigrants, financing in 2005 a £15m ($22m) hi-tech "wall" with closed-circuit TV and sensors along the eight-kilometre boundary.

The money to be made from outflanking these defences has attracted equally hi-tech smugglers, trading in hash, hard drugs, disadvantaged Moroccans, and refugees from as far south as Liberia and Rwanda. More affluent refugees have been sent over to Spain by night, often in small boats unsuited to the short but difficult crossing. The more desperate try to swim across to Ceuta from Fnideq's beach or scale the six-metre-high border fence. Most recently, there has been growing dissent in the impoverished residential areas of Ceuta where Moroccan residents have come into conflict with the Spanish authorities over a severe lack of employment and poor living conditions.

4–6pm; free), housed in a fort that is mainly nineteenth-century though with remnants from the sixteenth and seventeenth centuries. Below the lighthouse here is a secluded beach – Playa Torrecilla.

Parque Maritime del **Mediterráneo**
Paseo de la Marina Española • Daily 11am–8pm; closed Thurs Oct–April; pools April–Sept • €5

This seafront leisure and amusement complex is very popular in summer, with hordes of families and young people enjoying three large saltwater pools set among waterfalls and sculptures. A replica *Muralla Real* houses several restaurants, as well as a disco and casino (daily 10pm–3am).

ARRIVAL AND DEPARTURE

CEUTA

By bus & taxi Running between Ceuta's Plaza de la Consitutíon and the border (see box, p.104) are local bus #7 and metered taxis. Taxis can also be usually found waiting outside Ceuta's ferry terminal, while the closest bus stop is opposite the *Real Murilla* (Royal Walls) on Avda de España.

By ferry The ferry terminal is a short walk northwest of the town centre. Aside from Semana Santa and the last week in Aug, it's usually possible to board a ferry for Algeciras (12–30 daily; 45min–1hr 30min) within a couple of hours of arriving at the port. For hydrofoil services, it's best to book the previous day. Ticketing offices for Acciona Trasmediterránea (☎956 522215),

Balearia Nautus.(☎956 205190) and FRS (☎956 629620) are inside the terminal, and there are ticket agencies along Avda del Cañonero Dato.

By helicopter It's possible to travel by helicopter between Ceuta and Algeciras (€120 one-way) or Málaga (€150 one-way), with Inaer (Málaga ☎952 048700, Ceuta ☎956 504974, ⓦinaer.com); note that at the time of writing, Cat Helicopters (Barcelona ☎932 240710, ⓦcathelicopters .com) looked set to take over and add another service from Ceuta to Tangier.

Destinations Algeciras (2–4 daily; 7min); Málaga (2–4 daily, 30min).

INFORMATION

Tourist information Under the traffic flyover at the western end of Paseo de las Palmeras (Mon–Fri

8.30am–8.30pm, Sat & Sun 9am–8pm; ☎856 200560 or ☎956 506275).

ACCOMMODATION

It's advisable to book ahead throughout the year, but especially during the main festivals: Carnival (Feb), Holy Week (Easter), the Fiesta de Nuestra Señora de Monte Carmel (July 16), and the Fiesta de Nuestra Señora de Africa (Aug 5).

Hostal Central 15 Paseo del Revellín ☎&☎956 516716, ⓦhostalsceuta.com. One of the cleaner and more modern of the city's cheap hotels, in a good, central location, and offering small but comfortable rooms with own bathroom, TV and fridge; single rooms available (€45). **€66**

★ **Hostal Plaza Ruiz** 3 Plaza Teniente Ruiz ☎956 516733, ⓦhostalsceuta.com. Offers slightly larger rooms than its sister hotel down the road, *Hostal Central*, some of which benefit from wrought-iron balconies overlooking the plaza below. **€66**

1

CROSSING THE BORDER AT CEUTA

Since the Algeciras–Ceuta ferries and hydrofoils are quicker than those to Tangier (and the ferries significantly cheaper for cars or motorbikes), Ceuta is a popular **point of entry and exit** to Morocco. There is no customs/passport check at the port as the *frontera* (border; open 24hr) is 3km out of town and a further 2km from the Moroccan town of Fnideq (see p.112).

At the border, which is well signposted from the port and vice versa, formalities for entering and leaving Spain are brief. On the **Moroccan side**, the procedure can be time-consuming, especially for drivers. Each passport holder needs an immigration form (yellow or photocopied white) and, if you have a car, an additional green form; these are available – though you have to ask for them – from the officials sitting inside the small immigration posts. The car form requires inconvenient details such as chassis number and date of registration. If you despair of getting a form and having it processed, you can always enlist one of the innumerable touts for a 10–20dh tip; ignore their standard scam of trying to charge you for immigration forms, (which are free). The whole business can take ten minutes on a good day, an hour or two on a bad one, and the noise and chaos can be a bit unsettling. Just try to keep a steady head and if you are in doubt as to where and what you should do, ask one of the (sometimes over-stressed) officials for assistance or directions.

Coming from Ceuta into Morocco, try to arrive early in the day so that you have plenty of time to move on to Tetouan or Tangier – and possibly beyond. Once across and into Morocco proper, you can take a shared **grand taxi** to Fnideq (see p.112), 2km away (3dh; 5dh after 9pm), where you'll find connecting bus and taxi services to **Tetouan** (15dh; 20dh after 9pm) or **Tangier** (25dh; 30dh after 9pm) To charter your own grand taxi from the border to Tangier will set you back €50. On the Moroccan side of the border is an Attijariwafa bureau de change (Mon 12.15–3.45pm, Tue–Fri 8.15am–3.45pm, Sat 9.15am–12.15pm), and on the Spanish side there are a couple of travel agencies that will change Moroccan dirhams into Euros.

Hostal Real Calle Real 1, third floor ☎&☏ 956 511449. A cut above the average, this is a pleasant, comfortable little *pensión*, though most rooms lack outside windows and can get a little stuffy. Free laundry facilties available. Good-value triples (€50) and quads (€65). **€40**

Parador de Ceuta Pl Nuestra Señora de África 15 ☎ 956 514940, ⓦ parador.es. Formerly the *Gran Hôtel La Muralla* and set into the *Muralla Real*, Ceuta's grand old dame retains a certain colonial charm. Rooms, some with balcony, are looking a little tired but offer great views of the verdant garden and swimming pool or across a car park to the Mediterranean. BB **€100**

Pensión la Bohemia Paseo del Revellín 12, first floor ☎ 956 510615. Best deal among the cheapies, this clean and comfortable *pensión* is centred around a pleasant interior courtyard. Most of the rooms lack outside windows but all come with a fan; bathrooms, with hot water, are shared. Can be difficult to locate as trees sometimes obscure the *pensión's* blue sign. **€35**

Pensión Charito Calle de Teniente Arrabal 5, first floor ☎ 956 513982. Despite looking a little tired, this is still one of the best and most welcoming places among a number of small, cheap lodgings in this area. Bathrooms with hot water are shared, and there's a small kitchen. Look for the small "CH" sign located on the second floor of an unmarked building, one door down the hill from the (currently) cream and green *Limité* bar. **€25**

Tryp Ceuta Calle de Alcalde Antonio L. Sánchez Prados ☎ 956 511200, ⓦ melia.com. Modern, large three-star chain hotel centred around a gleaming white atrium. The breakfast buffet is extensive but the in-house restaurant isn't so great. **€120**

Ulises Calle Camoens 5 ☎ 956 514540, ⓦ hotelceuta .com. After many years of severe neglect, a major refurbishment has made the *Ulises* one of the best hotels in town. All 124 rooms sport a contemporary look with wood-panelled floors and works of art adorning the walls. BB **€80**

EATING AND DRINKING

Ceuta's main concentration of restaurants is around the Plaza de la Constitución. For tapas bars, check the smaller streets off Calle Camoens.

La Campana Calle Real 13. A smoke-filled bar-café with a reasonable €6 set menu (though no choice for non-pork eaters), plus tapas, spaghetti, sandwiches, beer and wine from the barrel. The hilariously grumpy service alone makes it worth the visit. Mon–Sat 9am–3pm & 5–10pm, Sun 10am–3pm.

Charlotte Plaza de los Reyes, Calle de Beatriz de Silva (opposite the Cathedral of San Francisco). This popular and inviting café-tapas bar overlooks a busy plaza and offers a varied menu of light dishes. There's also plenty of beers, wine and cocktails to choose from, and a great range of leaf teas served in heavy clay teapots. A second café is located down at Paseo de las Palmeras 10, and attracts more of a drinking crowd. Mains €1–8. Daily 9am–midnight.

★ **Carla Carlota** Club Nautico, Calle Edrissis ☎ 956 514400. This small fish restaurant, with both indoor and outdoor seating, overlooks the yacht harbour and serves some of Ceuta's best seafood dishes (mains €5–10). There's also a good-value *menú del día* (daily set menu;

€7). Mon–Sat 9am–3pm & 5pm–midnight, Sun 10am–3pm.

Gran Muralla Plaza de la Constitución 4 ☎ 956 517625. A popular, long-established Chinese restaurant with sweeping views over the harbour. The extensive menu offers the usual standard dishes, including some good seafood choices (€4.50–11). Mon–Sat noon–4pm, 7–11pm.

Hollywood Café Calle Padilla 4. Very friendly, family-run café with toasted *bocadillos* (sandwiches), paella and other Spanish dishes (€1.50–4), and both indoor and covered outdoor seating. Mon–Fri 9am–4pm, 7–11pm.

DIRECTORY

Currency Only the Euro is used in Ceuta. Currency exchange is available on the Spanish side of the border and at most banks on Paseo Del Revellin. There is a *telebanco* (ATM) on the ground floor of the ferry terminal.

Internet Cyber Ceuta, Paseo Colón (Mon–Sat 11am–2pm, 5pm–10pm; Sun 5pm–10pm).

Police Paseo de Colón, next door to the Museo de la Legión.

Time Ceuta works to Spanish time, an hour ahead of

Morocco (two hours ahead between the times when Europe and Morocco change to daylight saving).

Telephone When phoning Ceuta from Morocco (or anywhere else outside Spain), you must prefix phone numbers with the international code (☎ 00 34). Dialling numbers within Ceuta you must include the old local code (☎ 956) as part of the nine-digit number. To phone Morocco from Ceuta, you need to dial ☎ 00 212, followed by the local code (minus the initial zero) and number.

Tetouan

Approaching Tetouan from the landward side it looks strikingly beautiful, poised atop the slope of an enormous valley against a dark mass of rock. Its name (pronounced Tet-tá-wan) means "open your eyes" in Berber, an apparent reference to the town's hasty construction by Andalusian refugees in the fifteenth century.

During the 1990s and early 2000s, the city had a bad reputation for conmen and hustlers, which, combined with a neglected Spanish quarter and a Medina that was considered tourist unfriendly, meant it was bypassed by most travellers. Times have changed, however, and, thanks to both Moroccan and Euoprean investment, the past few years have seen Tetouan almost reborn again – in particular, the Medina is now looked upon affectionately as one of the most "untouched" in the country. Tetouan has remained a popular Moroccan resort that attracts huge numbers of Moroccan families during the summer holiday season, who flock to the city's nearby beaches in the summer to escape the heat.

Brief history

Two cities rose and fell in the vicinity of Tetouan before the present-day city was built. Tamuda, the scant ruins of which can still be seen on the south side of Oued Martil, 4km southeast of town, was founded by the Berber Mauritanians in the third century BC, and razed by the Romans in 42 AD; and the original Tetouan, built by the Merenids in 1307, on the same site as today's Medina, destroyed by a Castilian raiding party in 1399. The present town was established in 1484 by Muslims and Jews fleeing the Christian reconquest of Andalusia in southern Spain. Jewish merchants – able to pass relatively freely between Muslim North Africa and Christian Europe – brought prosperity to the city, and ramparts were put up in the seventeenth century under Moulay Ismail.

Tetouan has since been occupied twice by the Spanish. It was seized briefly, as a supposed threat to Ceuta, from 1859 to 1862, a period which saw the **Medina** converted

1

to a town of almost European appearance, complete with street lighting. Then, in 1913 a more serious, colonial occupation began. Tetouan served first as a military garrison for the subjugation of the Rif, later as the capital of the **Spanish Protectorate Zone**. As such it almost doubled in size to handle the region's trade and administration, and it was here in 1936 that **General Franco** declared his military coup against Spain's elected Liberal–Socialist coalition government, thus igniting the Spanish Civil War.

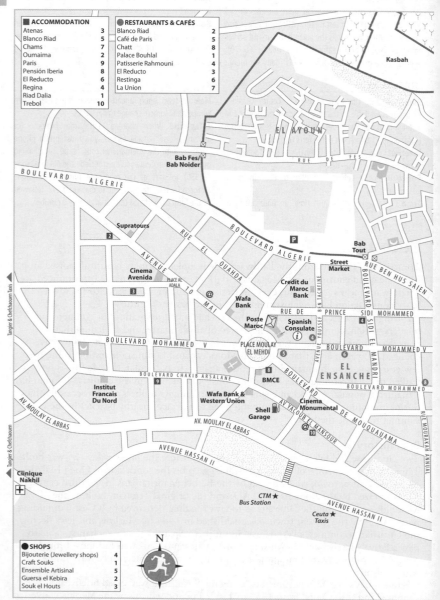

■ ACCOMMODATION	
Atenas	3
Blanco Riad	5
Chams	7
Oumaima	2
Paris	9
Pensión Iberia	8
El Reducto	6
Regina	4
Riad Dalia	1
Trebol	10

● RESTAURANTS & CAFÉS	
Blanco Riad	2
Café de Paris	5
Chatt	8
Palace Bouhlal	1
Patisserie Rahmouni	4
El Reducto	3
Restinga	6
La Union	7

● SHOPS	
Bijouterie (Jewellery shops)	4
Craft Souks	1
Ensemble Artisinal	5
Guersa el Kebira	2
Souk el Houts	3

For Tetouan's Moroccan population, there was little progress during the colonial period. Spanish administration retained a purely military character and only a handful of schools were opened throughout the entire zone. This legacy had effects well beyond independence in 1956, and the town, alongside its Rif hinterland, adapted with difficulty to the new nation and was at the centre of anti-government rioting as recently as 1984. Aware of this undercurrent, the new king, **Mohammed VI**, made it his business

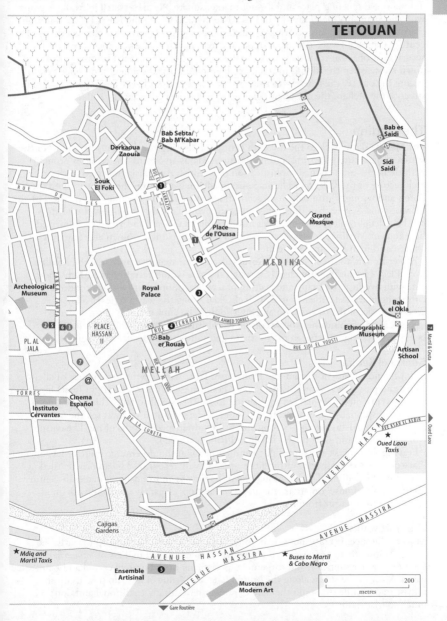

TETOUAN

1

to visit the former Spanish protectorate almost as soon as he ascended the throne in 1999, a gesture that helped to give Tetouan and its region a much stronger sense of nationhood than it had under the previous monarch.

Place Hassan II

Tetouan's old meeting place and former market square, **Place Hassan II** joins the Medina with the Spanish Ville Nouvelle, El Ensanche. It's also where the Royal Palace (built on the site of the old Spanish consulate) stands, incorporating parts of a nineteenth-century Caliphal Palace that once stood beside it. Much of the square is roped off for security reasons, but it's usually OK to take a picture of the palace from the perimeter. You'll know when the king is in residence by the number of soldiers and police here. Facing the palace, the laneway to the right off Place Hassan II is Rue al Qods, the main street of the **Mellah**, the old Jewish quarter that was created as late as 1807.

The Medina

The **Medina** dates back to the fifteenth century, following the mass migration to North Africa of persecuted Muslims and Jews from Andalusian Spain. The refugees brought with them the most refined sophistication of Moorish Andalusia, reflected in the architecture of the UNESCO heritage-listed Medina, and even their houses, with tiled lintels and wrought-iron balconies, seem much more akin to the old Arab quarters of Cordoba and Seville than those of Moroccan towns. Largely hassle-free, the Medina can be a delight to explore; meander into the Medina's heart and you'll be immersed into ancient Medina life – no traffic, children playing games, women chatting over chores, and men chatting over coffee.

Bab er Rouah, to the right of the Royal Palace, is the main gateway into the Medina from Place Hassan II. Immediately through the gate is Rue Terrafin, a relatively wide lane with overhead terracing and a string of jewellery shops that (with its continuations) cuts straight across to the east gate, Bab el Okla. Along the way a series of alleys give access to most of the town's food and craft souks. The **Souk el Houts**, a small shaded square directly behind the grounds of the Royal Palace is a good point of reference, being a central point between the northern and southern halves of the Medina.

Guersa el Kebira

From the north side of the Souk el Houts, two lanes wind up through a mass of alleys, souks and passageways towards Bab Sebta. Following the one on the right (east) for about twenty metres, you'll see an opening to another small square. This is the **Guersa el Kebira**, essentially a cloth and textile souk, where a number of stalls sell the town's highly characteristic *foutahs* – strong and brilliantly striped lengths of rug-like cotton, worn as a cloak and skirt by the Jebali and Riffian women.

Leaving the Guersa at its top right-hand corner, you should emerge more or less on **Place de l'Oussa**, another beautiful little square, easily recognized by an ornate, tiled fountain and trellises of vines. Along one of its sides is an imposing nineteenth-century **Xharia**, or almshouse; on another is an artisania shop, elegantly tiled and with good views over the quarter from its roof.

The craft souks

Most of the specific **craft souks** lie beyond Place de l'Oussa, heading up towards Bab Sebta. Among them are copper and brass workers, renowned makers of *babouches* (pointed leather slippers), and carpenters specializing in elaborately carved and painted wood. Most of the shops along the central lane here – **Rue el Jarrazin** – focus on the tourist trade, while the souks themselves remain refreshingly traditional and don't see much tourist traffic.

Ethnographic Museum

Bab el Okla, Medina • Mon–Thu 9am–11:30am, 3–6pm, Fri 9–11am, 3–6.30pm •10dh • ☎ 0539 970505, ⓦ maroc.net/museums

The **Ethnographic Museum** is housed in a former arms bastion of the nineteenth-century Alaouite sultan Moulay Abderrahman. Themed around the everyday but staunchly private elements of Moroccan life, the museum's exhibits include exquisitely detailed traditional costumes (wedding gowns, for example) as well as a decorative funeral coffin. There's also a great view of the surrounding countryside from the roof terrace.

Artisan School

Opposite Bab el Okla, outside Medina • Mon–Thurs & Sun 8am–4.30pm • 10dh

At the **Artisan School** (École des Métiers) you can see master craftsmen (*maâlem*) watch over apprentices working at new designs in the old ways, essentially unmodified since the fourteenth century. Ranging in trades from metalwork and wood turning to embroidery, many of the workshops have items for sale. Perhaps owing to its Andalusian heritage, Tetouan actually has a slightly different zellij (enamelled tile mosaics) technique to other Moroccan cities – the tiles are cut before rather than after being fired. A slightly easier process, it is frowned upon by the craftsmen of Fez, whose own pieces are more brittle, but brighter in colour and closer fitting.

Museum of Modern Art

Junction of Avenue Hassan II and Avenue Massira • Daily 9am–7pm • ☎ 0666 046081

Tetouan's **Museum of Modern Art** (Centro de Arte Moderno de Tetuán) finally opened in 2012 after a laborious five-year renovation. Located in the city's old train station, the green and white building looks half castle, half mosque but is all sleek and modern inside. The main entrance is from the rear of the building, and visitors are welcomed to a large sunlit space with welded figurative sculptures, while to the right is a colonnaded gallery currently displaying traditional classics from painters such as Mohamed Serguini and others. A second, larger ground-floor gallery is dedicated to contemporary works from a number of leading Moroccan artists, including Tetouan-based Hassan Echair and Safaa Erruas. The upstairs gallery exhibits a wide range of works – abstract, impressionist and contemporary – by Moroccan artists.

Ensemble Artisanal

Avenue Hassan II • Mon–Sat 9.30am–1pm & 3.30–7pm • ☎ 0539 994112

The **Ensemble Artisanal** on the main road below the town has a wide range of handicrafts for sale on the ground floor, which are worth a look if you're planning to make purchases in the souks and want to assess prices and quality first. However, the main points of interest are upstairs, where you will find a fascinating array of carpet and embroidery workshops, and outside the building, where there are metalwork, basketry and musical instrument artisans at work. This is a unique opportunity to get up close to the craftsmen and-women and their work without feeling pressured into buying anything.

El Ensanche

The Spaniards left an attractive architectural legacy behind in Tetouan, largely in the Spanish quarter, **El Ensanche** ("the widening"). Directly west of the Medina's walls, this neighbourhood of wide *avenidas* and tall colonial buildings was the Spanish version of the French Ville Nouvelle. Upon independence, however, El Ensanche faded into a derelict obscurity following decades of little development or investment by the state. In

1

recent years, however, the quarter has benefited greatly from the renewed interest and investment in Tetouan. El Ensanche is once again looking proud and grand, with renovations, roadworks and paint jobs the order of the day. A meander along Boulevard Mohammed V between Place Moulay el Mehdi and Place al Jala is a pleasant one, with some interesting examples of Spanish colonial and 1920s Art Deco architecture.

Archeological Museum

2 Rue Ben Hussaien, off Place al Jala • Mon–Sat 10am–6pm • 10dh • ☎ 0539 932097, ⓦ maroc.net/museums

The **Archeological Museum** was founded during the Spanish protectorate and, unsurprisingly, features exhibits from throughout their zone, including rock carvings from the Western Sahara. Highlights, as so often in North Africa, are the Roman mosaics, mostly gathered from Lixus and the oft-plundered Volubilis. Other than these, the most interesting exhibits are concerned with the stone circle at Mzoura (see box, p.95), including a model and aerial photographs.

ARRIVAL AND DEPARTURE TETOUAN

By bus Besides CTM, all buses serve Tetouan's *gare routière*, 1km south of the city; petits taxis are usually parked out the front of the building (around 10dh to Pl Hassan II). Ticket booths are on the ground floor, and Supratours also have an office in the Ville Nouvelle, on Bd 10 Mai. CTM (☎0539 711654) buses use their own separate station, more conveniently located just below the Medina on Av Hassan II. Destinations Agadir (1 CTM bus daily; 15hr); Al Hoceima (2 CTM and 9 others daily; 8hr); Casablanca (5 CTM & 20 others daily; 7hr); Chefchaouen (6 CTM & 20 others daily; 1hr 30min); Fez (5 CTM & 10 others daily; 6hr); Fnideq (for Ceuta; 1 CTM & 10 daily; 1hr); Larache (4 CTM & 6 daily; 2hr); Marrakesh (1 CTM & 7 others daily; 11hr 30min); Meknes (1 CTM & 5 others daily; 6hr); Nador (2 CTM & 7 others daily; 11hr); Oued Laou (5 daily; 1hr 30min); Rabat (5 CTM & 20 others daily; 5–6hr); Tangier (4 CTM & 50 others daily; 1hr 30min).

By grand taxi Collective grands taxis for Tangier and Chefchaouen arrive and depart from Av Khaled Ibnou el Oualid, west of town, a 20min walk or 15dh petit taxi ride. Grands taxis to Fnideq (Ceuta border), Mdiq, Martil and Cabo Negro leave from Av Hassan II; those for Oued Laou leave from the beginning of Av Ksar el Kebir, which is the Oued Laou turn-off from Av Hassan II, not far from Bab el Okla.

Destinations Chefchaouen (1hr); Fnideq (for Ceuta; 20min); Martil (15min); Mdiq (20min); Oued Laou (1hr); Tangier (1hr).

INFORMATION

Tourist information 30 Bd Mohammed V (Mon–Thurs 8.30am–4.30pm, Fri 8.30–11.30am & 2–4.30pm; ☎0539 961915, ☎0539 961402); official guides can be enlisted here.

ACCOMMODATION

Other than at the height of the holiday season in August, it's generally pretty easy to find a bed in Tetouan.

MEDINA

Blanco Riad 25 Rue Zawya Kadiriya, in an arched lane off Bd Mohammed V ☎0539 704202, ⓦblancoriad .com. This former Spanish Consulate is surprisingly spacious with a central courtyard and a separate outdoor paved garden area. The seven rooms and one suite range in style from small and minimalistic to grand and exquisitely Andalusian. There's also an in-house hammam and a small library. BB 1026dh.

★ **El Reducto** 38 Rue Zawya Kadiriya, in an arched lane off Bd Mohammed V ☎0539 968120, ⓦriadtetouan.com. Tetouan's most upmarket accommodation, this small riad was the home of the city's Grand Vizier in the 1940s, and was lovingly brought back to life in 2006 by the current owner. Five suites, each individually furnished in the Andalusian style, overlook a central courtyard and an excellent restaurant. Book ahead. BB 861dh

Riad Dalia 25 Pl el Ouessaa ☎0539 964318, ⓦriad-dalia.com. This older riad once housed the Dutch Consul-General. A quirky combination of palatial and antique (though they're in danger of becoming tired), the seven rooms range from a very large and luxurious suite to rooms with a shared bathroom. There's a great roof terrace and an in-house restaurant. BB 476dh

EL ENSANCHE

Atenas 7 Bd Allal ben Abdallah ☎0539 700065 ⓦhotelatenas.amawebs.com. This new hotel is a class above anything else in this part of town, with eighty large rooms over four floors, all en suite with satellite TV and free wi-fi throughout. **626dh**

Oumaima Av 10 Mai ☎ 0539 963473. This ageing hotel is central and functional but a little soulless. The rooms are on the small side but are all en suite with TV. The ground-floor café does a nice breakfast. **295dh**

Paris 31 Rue Chkil Arssalane ☎ 0539 966750, ☎ 0539 712654. Stock-standard two-star hotel with uninspiring but adequate en-suite rooms; those at the back are the quietest. The restaurant is open in summer only. **318dh**

Pensión Iberia 5 Pl Moulay el Mehdi, third floor ☎ 0539 963679. Above the BMCE bank, this old dame is central, clean, and excellent value for money. Some of the classic high-ceilinged rooms have shuttered balconies overlooking busy Pl Moulay el Mehdi. Shared bathrooms with hot showers (10dh). **108dh**

Regina 8 Rue Sidi Mandri ☎ 0539 962113. This ageing, budget hotel still offers very good value for money. The

large, bright rooms have colourful, Riffian fabrics on the beds and clean, though tired, bathrooms with constant hot water. A ground-floor café serves breakfast. **200dh**

Trebol 3 Av Yacoub el Mansour ☎ 0539 962093. Popular with budget travellers, this very cheap hotel has clean, high-ceilinged rooms that come with a hand basin, though there is only intermittent running water; toilets are shared and there's no showers. Good-value singles (50dh). **70dh**

OUT OF TOWN

Chams Rue Abdelkhaleq Torres ☎ 0539 990901, ☎ 0539 990907. This three-storey, modern hotel is 3km out of town and perhaps only worth it if you have your own transport. The en-suite rooms are all very comfortable with a/c and satellite TV, and there's a good-sized swimming pool and in-house restaurant. Large discounts out of high season. **1058dh**

EATING AND DRINKING

RESTAURANTS

★ **Blanco Riad** 25 Rue Zawya Kadiriya, in an arched lane off Bd Mohammed V ☎ 0539 704202, ⓦ blancoriad.com. Serving the best cuisine in the city, this riad's restaurant offers tables inside a traditional indoor courtyard of whitewashed walls studded with exquisite zellij tiling, or in a peaceful, sunny stone-paved outdoor garden. The menu – traditional Moroccan with a contemporary Mediterranean twist – is incredibly inventive; think pastilla of pigeon and foie gras, and an tail *kefta* and quince tajine (mains 90–145dh). Daily noon–11pm.

El Reducto 38 Rue Zawya Kadiriya, in an arched lane off Bd Mohammed V ☎ 0539 968120, ⓦ riadtetouan .com. The menu (in Spanish, ask for a translation) at this stylish riad restaurant takes inspiration from Tetouan's Spanish and Moroccan heritage; try their signature dolmas or *kefta* tajine. Choose to dine on the cosy, traditionally decorated ground-floor courtyard or flop back on lounges under a rooftop tent (mains 65–80dh). Daily noon–10pm.

Palace Bouhlal 48 Jamaa el-Kebir, a lane north of the Grand Mosque ☎ 0539 998797. A palace restaurant with a richly decorated interior, serving indulgent Moroccan four-course meals (set menu 130dh) accompanied by traditional musicians and dancers. Popular with tour groups. Daily noon–4pm.

Restinga 21 Bd Mohammed V ☎ 0539 963576. Eat indoors or in the courtyard at this very pleasant restaurant that's been serving tajine, couscous and fried

fish every day since 1968 (mains 35–70dh). Daily 11:30am–11pm.

La Union 1 Pasaje Achaach, off Bd Mohammed Torres – to find it, go through the arcades opposite Cinema Español. Popular with locals, this budget place serves up standard Moroccan fare, including *harira*, brochettes and a reasonable meat tajine (mains 25–40dh). No alcohol. Daily noon–9.30pm.

CAFÉS

Café de Paris Place Moulay el Mehdi. A large café on the main square, which has become quite a fashionable and relatively female-friendly hangout. Besides great coffee and mint tea (8–15dh), there's also fresh pastries and some delicious gateaux (5–18dh) on offer. Daily 9am–11pm.

Chatt Rue Mourakah Annual. A small and popular diner that's been serving up fast (and cheap) snack food for years. The wall-mounted menu offers pretty much everything you'd need for breakfast (pastries 4dh, fresh orange juice 3dh), plus tea, coffee, burgers, omelettes and snacks (mains 9–23dh). Daily 7am–midnight.

Patisserie Rahmouni Bd Youssef ben Tachfine. Clean, modern café-patisserie with a good selection of breakfast and tea delights, such as chocolate dougnuts, croissants, *baghrir* (Moroccan crumpet), and plenty of cakes and biscuits, purchased by weight (8dh/100g). There's also ice cream, coffee and tea, and tables with waiter service. Daily 8am–1pm, 4–10pm.

ENTERTAINMENT

Tetouanis largely restrict their evening pursuits to the standard Moroccan café session or a walk along the riverside promenade on the city's southern edge.

THE ORQUESTA ANDALUSI DE TETOUAN

The **Orquesta Andalusi de Tetouan** is one of the best-known groups playing Moroccan-Andalous music, a seductive style awash with Oriental strings. It was founded, and is still conducted, by Abdessadaq Chekana, and his brother Abdellah leads on lute. The orchestra has recorded with Spanish flamenco singer Juan Peña Lebrijano and has toured with British composer Michael Nyman (best known for his soundtracks for Peter Greenaway's films – and for *The Piano*), from which came the 1994 album "Michael Nyman - Live". Despite such collaborations, none of them reads music; everything is committed to memory. They often play in Tetouan and you may be able to catch them locally at an official reception, or at a wedding or festival; ask at the tourist office, where staff may be able to help.

Cinema Avenida Pl al Adala ☎0539 965611. Shows current release movies, including the odd Hollywood flick though it will always be dubbed.

Cinema Español Bd Mohammed Torres ☎0539 964329. Mainly shows "*L'histoire et la géographie*" (a double bill of Bollywood and kung fu).

Institut Français du Nord 13 Bd Chakib Arsalane, opposite Bd Moulay Abdesalam, Ville Nouvelle ☎0539 961212, ⓦiftanger-tetouan.org. The cultural arm of the

French government, the Tetouan branch is quite active and often presents cultural events such as exhibitions, films and live performances.

Instituto Cervantes 93 Bd Mohammed Torres, Ville Nouvelle ☎0539 967056, ⓦtetuan.cervantes.es. Like its French counterpart, this branch of Spain's cultural organization provides a weekly programme of film screenings, discussions, concerts and general cultural exchange.

DIRECTORY

Banks and exchange Attijariwafa Bank, BMCI and Société Général Bank are all on Bd Sidi el Manri, as is Cabana Bureau de Change (daily 9am–8pm; ☎0539 702892).

Festivals Tetouan's International Mediterranean Film Festival (Festival International du Cinéma Méditerranéen; ⓦfestivaltetouan.org), takes place around the end of March each year. The moussem of Moulay Abdessalem Ben Mchich is a very religious, traditional occasion with a large number of Riffian tribesmen in attendance. It's usually held on 1 July at the saint's *marabout*, or tomb on a flat mountain top near the village of Beni Arouss, about

half-way between Tetouan and Chefchaouen off the N2. Contact the Tourist Information Office in Tetouan (see p.110) for more information.

Hospitals Clinique Nakhil, 72 Av Hassan II (☎0539 962600, ⓦcliniquenakhil.com); Hôpital Principal, Route de Martil (about 2km from the city centre; ☎0539 972430).

Internet Cyber al Mechoir es Said, 1st floor, cnr Bd Mohammed Torres and Rue de la Luneta on the southern end of Pl Hassan II; Tetouan Web, Bd Yacoub Mansour, close to *Hôtel Trebol*. Both open daily 9am–11pm.

The Tetouan coast: Fnideq to Oued Laou

Despite the numbers of tourists passing through, Tetouan is above all a resort for Moroccans, rich and poor alike – a character very much in evidence on the extensive beaches to the east of the town. Throughout the summer whole villages of family tents appear at **Martil**, **Mdiq** and, particularly, around **Restinga-Smir** and **Fnideq**, further north. **Oued Laou**, 40km southeast of Tetouan, is the destination of a younger, more alternative crowd. The general increase of investment in the region has encompassed this section of the coast, with the appearance of beachside promenades (*corniches*) as well as new hotels and all-inclusive resorts with private mini-marinas.

Fnideq

Fnideq, sometimes called by its Spanish name Castillejos, has little to recommend it, especially compared with Mdiq and Martil further along the coast. However, it has seen some development of late, including a new beachside promenade between here and the beach at Restinga-Smir, and there's a couple of good hotels; if you're arriving late in the day on your way to or from Ceuta, it makes a decent stopover.

ARRIVAL AND DEPARTURE FNIDEQ

By bus Fnideq's *gare routière* is in the centre of the town, set a couple of blocks back from the seafront highway. Grands taxis ply the route from the station to the Ceuta border, about 3km away (5dh).

Destinations Casablanca (1 CTM & 2 others daily; 6hr 30min); Martil (6–10 daily; 30min); Mdiq (6–10 daily; 20 min); Rabat (1 CTM & 2 others daily; 5hr); Tangier (1 CTM & 15 others daily; 1hr); Tetouan (20 daily; 45min).

By grand taxi Grands taxis gather at both the bus station and a separate taxi rank at the northern (Ceuta) end of town. They depart for the Ceuta border (5min; see box, p.104) throughout the day, though the wait is a little longer during the night, and similarly for Tetouan (35min) via Restinga-Smir, Mdiq (15min) and Martil (25min). There are also irregular runs to Tangier (1hr), travelling directly past the Tanger Med port.

ACCOMMODATION AND EATING

There are a few decent hotels and restaurants dotted along Fnideq's sea-facing main road, Av Hassan II, and the parallel Av Mohammed V. Out of the summer season, ask for discounts at the hotels.

La Corniche Av Hassan II, southern end of town towards Restinga-Smir ☎0539 976163, ⓦla-corniche-hotel.com. The best of Fnideq's hotels, with modern, comfortable rooms, some with sea views and balconies. There's also a classy sea-facing café-restaurant, which offers light meals like omelettes, pizzas and salads (20–55dh). 623dh

Dreamland Av Hassan II ☎0539 976357. Surprisingly

modern and clean hotel in the middle of town; rooms are en suite, though note that those facing the sea also face the busy road. Guest parking out the front. 258dh

Tarik Bd Mohammed V ☎0539 976421, ⓦla-corniche-hotel.com. Sister hotel to the more upmarket *La Corniche*, located a couple of blocks back from the seafront. Bright, tiled rooms with TV, and an in-house restaurant that serves a pastry and coffee breakfast. 323dh

Mdiq

Mdiq is a lovely coastal town and semi-active fishing port. A popular promenade overlooks the town beach (which gets better the further north and away from the redeveloping port you venture) while a vibrant café-restaurant quarter lies one block back. The small port is undergoing a major facelift that will turn it into a compact, upmarket marina and there are a handful of nice places to stay nearby, which only adds weight to the town's honest claim of being the best of Morocco's northwestern coastal resorts.

ARRIVAL AND DEPARTURE MDIQ

By bus and grand taxi Mdiq is on the bus and grand taxi route between Fnideq and Tetouan, with the frequency of services increasing between July and August. Buses and grands taxis both operate from a large open stand at the northern entrance to the town, only a 5- to 10-minute walk

from the hotels, restaurants and beach.
Destinations Fnideq (for Ceuta; 15–20min); Martil (10–15min); Tangier (via Fnideq or Tetouan; 1hr 30min to 2hr); Tetouan (15–25min).

ACCOMMODATION

Besides the eating options listed below, there's a bevy of cafés and cheap restaurants gathered along a couple of pedestrianized streets just one block back from the beach. During the season, this area has a great atmosphere throughout the day and into the night.

Badis Cnr Av Lalla Nezha and Av Casablanca, northern end of town ☎0539 663030, ☎0539 663030. Opened in 2011, *Hôtel Badis* offers three floors of modern rooms, some sleeping up to four comfortably and others with sea views. A ground-floor café (daily 7am–10pm) serves a decent pastry and egg breakfast and offers free wi-fi. BB 800dh

Golden Beach Av Lalla Nehza, on the beachside corniche at the northern entrance to town

☎0539 975077, ⓦgolden-beachotel.com. This large resort -style hotel has long been one of the best along this coast. The sea is so close that rooms with a sea view feel like they're literally in the water. Besides a very decent restaurant, there's a large swimming pool, a bar (daily 10am–11pm) and a nightclub (daily 10pm–3am in season) which can get pretty loud during the summer holidays; request a room away from it during this time. 750dh

1

Narjiss Av Lalla Nezha, at the southern (Cabo Negro) entrance to town ☎0539 663770. The town's best budget option, a short uphill walk from the corniche. The bland, modern rooms have tiled floors, satellite TV and spotless bathrooms, and there's a handy streetside café serving pastry and coffee breakfasts. 250dh

Playa Av Lalla Nezha, centre of town ☎0539 975166. This modern and comfortable hotel is directly across the road from the beach, with four floors of bright and airy en suites, the majority of which have uninterrupted sea views. There is also a bar and restaurant on the ground floor. 450dh

EATING

Las Olas Corniche car park, Av Lalla Nezha ☎0539 664433. This beachfront landmark, resembling a lighthouse, offers fantastic views as well as a decent menu. More of a café downstairs and restaurant upstairs, the a la carte menu offers good variety, with some Italian and Moroccan standards accompanying the seafood. Mains 40–130dh. Daily: café 9am–11pm; restaurant noon–10pm.

La Vie en Rose Golden Beach Hotel, Av Lalla Nehza

☎0539 975077, ⓦgolden-beachotel.com. This hotel restaurant is a cut above the usual and is very popular during the summer season. Overlooking the beach, it offers an impressive and reasonably priced a la carte menu (mains 60–120dh), as well as a three-course *menu du jour* (160dh) for both lunch and dinner. As you would expect, seafood is a speciality. Daily 7am–10.30am, noon–2.30pm & 7–11pm.

DIRECTORY

Banks Attijariwafa Bank, Banque Populaire BMCE and Crédit Agricole (all with ATMs) are all on Av Lalla Nehza.
Golf Cabo Negro Royal Golf Club, Route de Martil, located

between Martil and Mdiq, (18 holes; ☎0539 978141).
Post office Poste Maroc is on Av Abdelkarim el Khatabi, opposite the bus and grand taxi stand.

Martil

Martil, only 10km from the centre of Tetouan and essentially the city's beach, was its port as well until the river between the two silted up. Today it is a modern seaside town which takes on a resort-like feel in summer when Moroccan families flood the beach to escape the heat. The beach, stretching all the way around to the headland of Cabo Negro, is superb – an eight-kilometre stretch of fine, yellow sand that is long enough to remain uncrowded, despite its summer popularity and colonization by Club Med and other tourist complexes.

ARRIVAL AND DEPARTURE

By bus and grand taxi Martil is on the bus and grand taxi route between Fnideq and Tetouan, with the frequency of services increasing between July and August. Buses operate from a large water tower located five streets back from the southern end of the beachside corniche, while grands taxis

can be found opposite the Mohammed V Mosque off Av Moulay el Hassan II (the N16 highway to Tetouan).
Destinations Fnideq (for Ceuta; 25–35min); Mdiq (10–15min); Tangier (via Fnideq or Tetouan; 1hr 40min to 2hr 15min); Tetouan (10–15min).

ACCOMMODATION AND EATING

Besides the restaurants within the hotels mentioned below, there's a string of café-restaurants on the land side of the beachside promenade.

Camping al Boustane Av el Hamra, between N16 highway and beachfront corniche ☎0539 688822. At the northern end of the town, this well-established campsite offers plenty of shade but is in need of maintenance, with ageing ablution and drainage facilities. Both a restaurant and pool open up for summer. 95dh

Etoile de la Mer (aka Nejma el Bahr) Av Moulay el Hassan II, southern end of the beachfront ☎0539 979058, ☎0539 979276. One block from the beach and

close to the grand taxi rank, with clean and colourful rooms, some with sea views. The in-house restaurant (open to non-guests) is licensed and serves up a good selection of fresh seafood dishes. BB 268dh

Residence L'Hacienda Route de Cabo Negro ☎0539 688668, ⓦhaciendamartil.com. This sprawling, friendly hacienda offers a surprising number of spacious, though slightly dated rooms (some sleep four comfortably), as well as large bungalows with equipped kitchen and living room. There's a lovely swimming pool surrounded by a leafy, healthy garden, and a good in-house restaurant (licensed, open to non-guests). BB <u>600dh</u>

Suites Hôtel Omeya Av Lalla Hasna Corniche ☎0539 688888, ☎0539 979779. Easily the best hotel in town with a range of modern rooms and suites, some with a sizeable balcony and great sea views. The in-house restaurant specializes in seafood and Moroccan standards, while a streetfront café is a good spot for a quick breakfast or pizza. There's also a piano-lounge-cum-bar with live music most weekends. <u>1080dh</u>

Oued Laou

Travelling southeast from Tetouan, the coastline almost immediately changes and you come under the shadow of the **Rif**. The road (N16, formerly S608) continues to follow the coast while also hugging the foothills of the Rif; it's a stunning drive made all the more pleasurable by recent roadworks

Quieter than the more popular beach towns closer to Tetouan, **Oued Laou** is named after the River Laou that reaches the ocean here from its source in the Rif mountains near Chefchaouen. It's not an especially pretty place – Riffian villages tend to look spread out and lack any core – but it has a near-deserted beach, which extends for miles on each side, particularly to the southeast, where the river has created a wide, fertile bay down to Kâaseras, 8km distant. There's not much to do other than relax, read, watch the fishermen hauling in their nets, and swim – not an altogether terrible itinerary. On Saturdays, there is a **souk**, held 3km inland from Oued Laou, which draws villagers from all over the valley.

ARRIVAL AND DEPARTURE   OUED LAOU

By bus and grand taxi Buses and grands taxis operate from the old village square, one block back from the beach, opposite the mosque.

Destinations (bus) Chefchaouen (daily; 1hr 30min); El

Jebha via Kâaseras (daily; 5hr); Tetouan (3 daily; 2hr).
Detsinations (grand taxi) Dar Ackoubaa (for connecting taxis to Chefchaouen and Tetouan; 20min); Kâaseras (20min).

ACCOMMODATION

Camping Oued Laou Av Hassan II (N16 highway) ☎0539 670895. A secure site, shaded by olive trees, with hot showers and washing facilities, a small shop and a café. Camping fees are reasonable and there are three two-bedroom bungalows that will comfortably house four adults or a family. Gets very busy in summer. Camping <u>88dh</u>, bungalow <u>300dh</u>

Mare Norstrum 4km north of Oued Laou, signposted off the N16 ☎0664 376056, ⓦmarenostrumhotel.net. The Tetouan coast's one true luxury option, situated on a

cliff overlooking a secluded bay. The twelve large rooms with four-poster beds all offer sea views from good-sized balconies, and there's a good restaurant and a large swimming pool; however, it's a bit of a trek down to the beach and back up. BB <u>1500dh</u>

Oued Laou 8 Bd Massira ☎0648 064435. This basic but friendly hotel is one block from the beach in a cul-de-sac bordering the village's new square and corniche. It is open all year round and has simple yet clean and sunny rooms, with shared toilets and bathrooms. <u>150dh</u>

EATING AND DRINKING

Aramar 2 Bd Massira ☎0539 569854. The best of a number of beachfront restaurants. While fresh fish is the house speciality (the fishing boats are right out front), there's also a pretty good menu offering Moroccan standards such as tajines, brochettes and *harira* soup (35–80dh). Daily 8am–10pm.

Café Picasso Picasso beach, 3km north of village centre ☎0661 459865. Built into the rock and made from driftwood and reeds, *Café Picasso* is like something out of *Robinson Crusoe*. This is a great place to relax – the owner has been cooking up tajines on the beach for over a decade, and they serve (usually warm) beer. Daily 10am–8pm.

Chefchaouen

An isolated refuge for over 400 years before absorption in the 1920s into the Spanish Protectorate, **CHEFCHAOUEN** (pronounced "shef-*sha*-wen", sometimes abbreviated to Chaouen) remains today somewhat aloof from the goings-on in the rest of the country.

1

Visiting Chefchaouen requires venturing into the rugged Rif mountains and it almost feels by chance that one comes upon the town, still hidden beneath the towering peaks from which it takes its name. The setting, like much of the Rif, is largely rural and the bright lights and bustling noise of cities less than half a day's drive away are soon forgotten. That's not to say that Chefchaouen is completely isolated, for the town has long been a stop on the intrepid backpacker circuit – thanks in part to the easy availability of the Rif's *kif* – and has also gradually become popular with mainstream tourists, who are arriving in increasing numbers to wander the town's blue-washed Medina, surely the prettiest in the country.

While the increase in visitors has inevitably led to a slight rise in hassle, local attitudes are still very relaxed, and the Medina *pensions* are among the friendliest and cheapest around.

Brief history

Chefchaouen translates to "two horns" in Arabic, in reference to the mountain that is split in two by the slope on which the town lies. The region hereabouts has forever been sacred to Muslims due to the presence of the tomb of **Moulay Abdessalam Ben Mchich** – patron saint of the Jebali Riffian tribesmen and one of the "four poles of Islam" – and over the centuries has acquired a considerable reputation for pilgrimage and *marabouts* – "saints", believed to hold supernatural powers. An isolated location, it was the perfect base in 1471 for one of Moulay Abdessalam's *shereefian* (descendant of the Prophet) followers, Hassan Ben Mohamed el Alami, known as Abu Youma, to launch secret attacks on the Portuguese in their coastal enclaves of Asilah, Tangier, Ceuta and Ksar es Seghir. Abu Youma perished in one of these raids and his cousin, Ali Ben Rachid moved the settlement to its current site on the other side of the river.

In the ensuing decades, as the population was boosted by Muslim and Jewish refugees from Spain, Chefchaouen grew increasingly anti-Christian and autonomous. For a time, it was the centre of a semi-independent emirate, exerting control over much of the northwest, in alliance with the Wattasid sultans of Fez. Later, however, it became an almost completely isolated backwater. When the Spanish arrived in 1920, they were astonished to find the Jews here speaking medieval Castilian, a language that hadn't been heard on the Iberian peninsula for 400 years. In 1924 the Spanish were repelled back to the coast by the Riffian rebel leader Abd el Krim el Khattabi (see box, p.130), but two years later they retook Chefchaouen and held it until the end of the Protectorate in 1956.

The Medina

Chefchaouen's Medina is small when compared to others in Morocco, and it is undoubtedly a place to enjoy exploring at random. The architecture has a strong Andalusian character, reflecting the city's history: Sultan Mohammed Ben Abdallah (Mohammed III) ordered the Jewish families to move into the Medina around 1760, their Mellah taking in the area that today encompasses the southern quarter between the kasbah and Bab el Aïn. Here they built their whitewashed ochre houses with small balconies, tiled roofs and Andalusian-style courtyards. It's from this time that Chefchaouen's famous shades of blue arose, the Jews adding indigo into the whitewash to contrast the Mellah against the traditional green of Islam.

The main gateway to the Medina is Bab el Aïn, a tiny arched entrance at the junction of Avenue Hassan II with Rue Moulay Ali Ben Rachid. Through the gate a clearly dominant lane winds up through the Medina to the main square, **Plaza Outa el Hammam** and beyond to a second, smaller square, **Plaza el Makhzen**.

Plaza Outa el Hammam

Considering the compact layout of the Medina, **Plaza Outa el Hammam** is surprisingly large. It takes its name from the number of public hammams that used

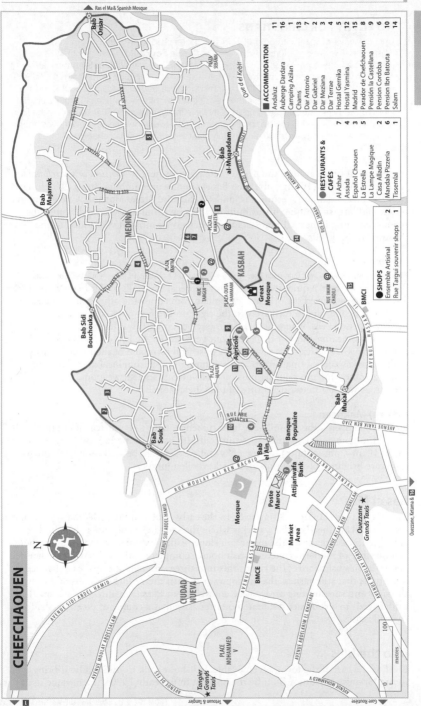

CHEFCHAOUEN

N

ACCOMMODATION
Andaluz	11
Auberge Dardara	16
Camping Azilan	1
Chams	13
Dar Antonio	7
Dar Gabriel	2
Dar Meziana	3
Dar Terrae	4
Hostal Gernika	5
Hostal Yasmina	12
Madrid	15
Parador de Chefchaouen	8
Pensión la Castellana	9
Pension Cordoba	6
Pension Ibn Batouta	10
Salam	14

● RESTAURANTS & CAFÉS
Al Azhar	7
Assada	4
Español Chaouen	5
La Estrella	3
La Lampe Magique	2
Casa Alladin	6
Mandala Pizzeria	1

Tissemlal

● SHOPS
Ensemble Artisinal	2
Rue Targui souvenir shops	1

1

NO ENTRY FOR CHRISTIANS

Until the arrival of Spanish troops in 1920, Chefchaouen had been visited by just three Westerners. Two were missionary explorers: **Charles de Foucauld**, a Frenchman who spent just an hour in the town in 1883, disguised as a Jewish rabbi, and **William Summers**, an American who was poisoned by the townsfolk here in 1892. The third, in 1889, was the British journalist **Walter Harris** (see p.568), whose main impulse, as described in his book, *Land of an African Sultan*, was "the very fact that there existed within thirty hours' ride of Tangier a city in which it was considered an utter impossibility for a Christian to enter". Thankfully, Chefchaouen today is more welcoming towards outsiders, and a number of the Medina's newer guesthouses now include owners hailing from Britain, Italy and the former Christian enemy, Spain.

to be located on or around the plaza – one remains next to *Pension la Castellana* and it's tourist-friendly (10dh; daily: men 8am–noon, women noon–8pm). Watching over the plaza's daily proceedings is Jamae Kebir, the **Grand Mosque**. Chefchaouen's oldest and largest mosque, it was built in 1560 by Moulay Mohamed, son of the town's founding father Ali Ben Rachid; its octagonal minaret was added to the mosque in the 1700s.

The kasbah

Plaza Outa el Hammam • Mon, Wed, Thurs & Sun 10am–2pm & 4–7.30pm, Tues 4–7.30pm, Fri 10am–1pm & 4–7.30pm • 10dh

The town's **kasbah**, a quiet ruin with shady gardens, was built by Ali Ben Rachid in 1471, when he moved the original settlement from across the other side of the Ras el Ma River. Inside, and immediately to the right, in the first of its compounds, are the old town prison cells, where Abd el Krim (see box, p.130) was imprisoned after his surrender in nearby Targuist in 1926. Four years earlier, he had driven the Spanish from the town, a retreat that saw the loss of several thousand of their troops. Also within the kasbah is a small art gallery exhibiting works from local artists, and an Ethnographic Museum housing musical instruments, ancient weapons, tapestries and carpets, as well as interesting photos of old Chefchaouen.

Plaza el Makhzen

Plaza el Makhzen – the colonial-era "government square" – is an elegant clearing with an old fountain and flanked by souvenir stalls. It's home to the Ensemble Artisanal (daily 10am–2pm, 4–6pm), where a few craftworkers can be seen producing the town's signature brightly coloured rugs and thick woollen jumpers.

Ras el Ma

Just outside Bab Onsar – dating back to the early 1500s and the Medina's easternmost exit – **Ras el Ma** (head of the water) is where the Oued el Kebir bursts from a sheer cliff-face to cascade down the mountain slope. Riffian women do their laundry here, at a number of modern, concrete wash houses complete with diverted water channels and built-in washboards. The river splits into three different streams, each flanked by flour mills that still harness the hydropower to turn their millstones. A good view of the river and surrounding area can be enjoyed from Plaza Sebanin, where a small bridge leads to a compact residential quarter as well as a couple of pleasant, shaded riverside cafés.

Into the hills

Over to the east of the town, an enjoyable, half-hour walk from Bab Onsar brings you to the "**Spanish Mosque**". Built by the Spanish in the early 1920s, the mosque itself has

1

never been used and was derelict up until 2010, when it was restored, again by the Spanish. It is set on a hilltop, with exterior patterned brickwork and an interior giving a good sense of the layout of a mosque – normally off-limits in Morocco.

Alongside the path to the Spanish Mosque are some spectacular rock-climbing pitches, frequented by European climbers (ask at *Dar Antonio* or *Camping Azilan* for trekking and climbing information); and in the limestone hills behind there are active cave systems – the source of local springs.

Further afield, a good **day's hike** is to head east, up over the mountains behind Chefchaouen. As you look at the "two horns" from town, there is a path winding along the side of the mountain on your left. A four-hour (or more) hike will take you up to the other side, where a vast valley opens up, and if you walk further, you'll see the sea. The valley, as even casual exploration will show, is full of small farms cultivating *kif* – as they have done for years. Walking here, you may occasionally be stopped by the military, who are cracking down on foreign involvement in the crop. For more ambitious hikes – and there are some wonderful paths in the area – ask at the *pensions* (or *Camping Azilan*; see opposite) about hiring a **guide**. Someone knowledgeable can usually be found to accompany you, for around 150dh a day; the harder the climb, the more it costs.

ARRIVAL AND DEPARTURE
CHEFCHAOUEN

By bus The *gare routière* is 1.5km southwest from the town centre – about a 15min walk. Alternatively catch a petit taxi (unmetered) to/from Bab el Aïn (around 10dh). CTM and most other companies start their Chefchaouen routes elsewhere so buses can arrive full, with no space. It's best to book a ticket in advance, or at least arrive at the station early.

Destinations Al Hoceïma (daily; 4hr 30min); Casablanca (1 CTM & 1 other daily; 6hr 30min); Fez (4 CTM and 8 others daily; 4hr); Fnideq (4 daily; 2hr 30min); Jorf el Malha (4 CTM and 6 others daily; 2hr 30min); Meknes (4 daily; 5hr 30min); Oued Laou (daily; 1hr 30min); Ouezzane (5 CTM and 10 others daily; 1hr 15min); Rabat (1 CTM & 2 daily; 5hr); Tangier (2 CTM and 9 others daily; 3hr); Tetouan (4 CTM daily

& others at least hourly 6am–6pm; 1hr 30min).

By grand taxi Grands taxis for Ouezzane and Bab Berred (connecting there for Issaguen and points east) operate from around the junction of Av Allal Ben Abdallah and Av Zerktouni. Tangier and Tetouan services operate from Av Jamal Dine el Afghani, off the west side of Pl Mohammed V. To reach Fez or Meknes, you can change vehicles at Ouezzane and again at Jorf el Malha (where grands taxis to Fez and Meknes are sparse, and you'll probably end up having to wait for a bus) or charter a grand taxi – you'll need to bargain hard, but the trip should cost around 450dh for up to six passengers.

Destinations Bab Berred (50min); Ouezzane (1hr 15min); Tangier (2hr); Tetouan (1hr).

ACCOMMODATION

Chefchaouen can get bitterly cold during winter and all of those listed proclaim to have hot water, though few will have any room heating other than plenty of blankets; it's also worth asking for a discount.

THE MEDINA

Andaluz 1 Rue Sidi Salem ☎ 0539 986034. Small, functional *pension* with friendly management, signposted off to the left at the near end of Pl Outa el Hammam. Rooms face an inner courtyard and have shared showers; there's a kitchen, and a nice rooftop terrace, with a handy tub for doing your laundry. 120dh

Chams 22 Rue Lalla el Hora, Quartier Kharazine ☎ 0539 987784. A good compromise between *pension* price and hotel comfort, this centrally located place has large, modern rooms, a dining area and a very pleasant terrace. 240dh

★ **Dar Antonio** 36 Calle Garmata ☎ 0539 989997, ☜ darantonio.com. This cosy guesthouse was personally

---

THE R410

If you have your own transport and wish to head towards the west coast from Chefchaouen, the **R410 to Ksar el Kebir** is a highly recommended scenic route and shortcut. The road is signed off the N13 to Ouezzane on your right coming from Chefchaouen. The route wends its way through wooded high country following the Oued Loukos to the Barrage Oued el Makhazine, where there are magnificent vistas, and on to Ksar el Kebir.

restored and imaginitively decorated by owner-manager Hicham. Each room is unique, colourful and warm, and there's even one with a working fireplace. Guests have access to a kitchen and the shared showers are in a cave-like grotto. 350dh

Dar Gabriel Derb Cadi Ben Maimoun, off Av Hassan I, Bab Souk ☎0539 989244, ✆dargabriel.com. British-owned and Moroccan-managed, this is one of the better guesthouses in the Medina. The compact (though not poky) rooms are all simply but thoughtfully furnished, while the common areas include a dining room with fireplace, and a three-tiered rooftop terrace. BB 550dh

Dar Meziana Rue Zagdud, off Av Hassan I, Bab Souk ☎0539 987806, ✆darmezianahotel.com. One of the Medina's most luxurious guesthouses, with tastefully decorated en-suite rooms and suites overlooking an open-plan courtyard and kitchen. There's plenty of light and some comfortable common areas, as well as great panoramic views from the terrace, and a hammam to top it off. HB 950dh

Dar Terrae Av Hassan I ☎0539 987598, ✆darterrae .com. One of Chefchaouen's earliest Medina riads, this charming old Andalusian-style house has a great homely atmosphere. The six cheerful rooms are all tastefully furnished, reflecting the Italian's owner's taste, and though not all are en suite each has its own terrace. BB 438dh

Hostal Gernika 49 Rue Onsar ☎0539 987434. This old house, in the higher quarter of the Medina, towards Bab Onsar, has been superbly converted by its Basque owner. Life here revolves around the central fireplace and small library in winter, and the rooftop terrace in summer. Some rooms are en suite, ask for a "mountain (and sun) view" during the colder months. 250dh

Hostal Yasmina 12 Rue Lalla el Hora ☎0539 883118. Small, bright and clean with just six modern rooms, the back four facing inward with no outside windows. It's very conveniently located, just off Plaza Outa el Hammam, and a very pleasant little place to stay. Hot (shared) showers 10dh. Book ahead in summer. 150dh

Pension la Castellana 4 Rue Bouhali ☎0539 986295. Just to the left at the near end of Plaza Outa el Hammam – follow the signs. Aficionados return loyally to the *Castellana* each year, creating a distinctly laidback and youthful atmosphere; others take one look at the poky (yet clean) rooms and leave. The key is the manager, Mohammed Nebrhout, who arranges communal meals and excursions on request. There are bathrooms and separate toilets on each floor, and there's a hammam right next door. 150dh

Pension Cordoba Rue Garnata ☎0539 989969 or ☎0664 430044. Lovely rooms and tasteful decor in a charming old Andalusian-style house, which has been

beautifully restored. The rooms all look inwards to a central courtyard and bathrooms are shared. Not quite a riad, but a lot cheaper than one. BB 200dh

Pension Ibn Batouta 31 Rue Abie Khancha ☎0539 986044. One of the quietest of the *pensions*, with less of a "travellers' hangout" feel; located in an alley, about 70m along from Bab el Ain, beyond the *Restaurant Assada*. Rooms open onto a central courtyard of potted plants, and are very cheap if a little dingy; bathrooms are shared (hot showers 5dh). 80dh

CIUDAD NUEVA (NEW TOWN)

Camping Azilan Located on a hill above the Medina, follow signs for the Atlas Riad Chaouen Hotel ☎0539 986979, ✆campingchefchaouen.com. Shaded and inexpensive, with plenty of sites with electricity and a few bungalows, plus a café, small shop, and internet café, but it can be crowded in summer. A good place to enquire about mountain treks. Camping 95dh, bungalow 150dh

Madrid Av Hassan II, 200m downhill from Pl el Makhzen ☎0539 987496, ✆moroccanhousehotels .com. An ageing but well-managed and popular hotel. Rooms are clean if slightly garish, and the large ground-floor reception area hosts a buffet breakfast. BB 428dh

Parador de Chefchaouen Pl el Makhzen ☎0539 986136, ✆hotel-parador.com. This former Spanish "grand hotel" is in a great location on the edge of the Medina. Popular with both independent travellers and tour groups, there are stunning mountain views from a poolside terrace and bar. While the carpeted rooms are definitely ageing, they are nonetheless comfortable and heated in winter, 536dh

Salam 39 Av Hassan II, 100m downhill from Pl el Makhzen ☎0539 986239. A cheap, friendly place and a favourite with backpackers who don't want to be in the Medina. The high-ceilinged rooms are basic, and bathrooms are shared. The back rooms as well as a shady roof terrace overlook the valley. BB 120dh

OUT OF TOWN

Auberge Dardara 11km from Chefchaouen at the junction of the N2 to Al Hoceima and the P28 to Ouezzane ☎0539 707007, ✆dardara.chez.com. Guests, which have included King Mohammed VI when he was prince, come here to experience a unique blend of rustic getaway and agri-tourism. The brainchild of local man El Hababi Jaber ("Jabba"), the *auberge* has twelve comfortably furnished rooms – each named after an influential woman in Jabba's life – and focuses on environmentally friendly practices and community involvement. The restaurant serves fresh, hearty food. HB 826dh

1

EATING

While not offering any great culinary experience, Plaza Outa el Hammam is Chefchaouen's prime spot for a meal at any time of the day or night. There are about a dozen restaurants on the plaza, all of them facing outwards for prime people-watching.

MEDINA

Assada On a nameless lane just north of Bab el Aïn, opposite the Hôtel Bab el Aïn. This has long been a favourite of locals and travellers alike, and extends across the lane and above to an open rooftop terrace. Very friendly, and serves food all day from breakfast (menus 18–25dh) through to tajine or couscous (mains 19–38dh) at dinner. Daily 9am–9pm.

Español Chaouen Plaza Outa el Hammam, at the far western entrance. This small restaurant serves up a pretty decent menu of couscous, tajines, brochettes and salads as well as pizzas and steak (mains 35–120dh). There's a few choice tables downstairs, as well as a small salon upstairs and a rooftop terrace with a great view of the plaza's mosque. Wi-fi available. Daily 9am–11pm.

La Estrella Plaza Outa el Hammam. Atmospheric restaurant decked in natural Riffian fibres with lounges and low tables, dim lighting at night and world music playing in the background. The lounges are the best place on the plaza for a long, casual meal. The menu is pretty standard, with grilled fish a speciality (mains 30–100dh). Daily 10am–10pm.

La Lampe Magique Casa Alladin Rue Targui, off northern end of Plaza Outa el Hammam. Two floors and a terrace, beautifully done out in Arabian Nights style, as its name suggests, serving great tajines, couscous (including vegetarian) and other staple fare (mains 45–85dh, set

menu 75dh). Daily 11am–11pm.

Tissemlal Casa Hassan, 22 Rue Targui, off northern end of Plaza Outa el Hammam ☎0539 986153. A long-standing and popular restaurant, with a choice between tables on the ground floor with a fireplace and an upstairs roof terrace. Serving a set menu only (85dh), a small selection of starters is followed by a good choice of mains that include a few tajines, *grillés*, fish and couscous dishes. The atmosphere is nice here and the standard is a step up from what's available on the nearby plaza. Daily noon–3pm & 7–11pm.

CIUDAD NUEVA (NEW TOWN)

Al Azhar At the bottom of the steps on Av Moulay Idriss. Popular local snack restaurant with good food and service. Fast and cheap, with a choice of brochettes, tajines, grilled chicken, sandwiches and omelettes (mains 20–50dh). Daily 10am–10pm.

★ **Mandala Pizzeria** Cnr Av Hassan II and Rue Sidi Ahmed el Ouafi ☎0539 882808. This intimate Italian restaurant is popular with young locals and travellers alike. The English-speaking Moroccan owner runs a tight ship and the kitchen is open for all to see. As well as pizzas, the menu offers numerous pasta and meat dishes, as well as some great salads, desserts and ice cream (mains 35–75dh). Takeaway & delivery available. Daily noon–11pm.

DIRECTORY

Banks and exchange Banque Populaire and Attijariwafa Bank (with ATMs) are both on Av Hassan II, opposite Bab el Aïn. A BMCI bureau de change (with ATM) is on Av Hassan II, close to *Hôtel Madrid* (daily 9.45am–5.30pm). Crédit Agricole, with a bureau de change is on Plaza Outa el

Hammam.
Internet Cyber Andalucia, Rue Moulay Ali ben Rachid; Téléboutique Cyber Samir, Av Hassan II; Internet Kasbah, Plaza el Makhzen (all daily 10am–11pm).
Post office Av Hassan II, opposite the mosque.

Ouezzane

Situated at the edge of the Rif, **OUEZZANE** traditionally formed the border between the Bled es-Makhzen (the governed territories) and the Bled es-Siba (those of the lawless tribes). As such, the town was an important power base, and particularly so under the last nineteenth-century sultans, when its local sheikhs became among the most powerful in Morocco.

Ouezzane is also a place of pilgrimage for Moroccan Jews, who come here twice a year (April & Sept) to visit the tomb of Rabbi Amrane Ben Diwane, an eighteenth-century Jewish *marabout* buried in a Jewish cemetery north of town.

Brief history

Ouezzane's sheikhs – the Ouezzani – were the spiritual leaders of the influential **Tabiya brotherhood**. They were *shereefs* (descendants of the Prophet) and came in a direct line from the Idrissids, the first and founding dynasty of Morocco. This however, seems to have given them little significance. In the eighteenth century, Moulay Abdallah es-Shereef established a *zaouia* at Ouezzane, which became a great place of pilgrimage.

Until the beginning of the twentieth century Jews and Christians were allowed to take only temporary residence in the town. However, in 1877, an Englishwoman, **Emily Keane**, married the principal *shereef*, Si Abdesslem. The marriage was, of course, controversial. For several decades she lived openly as a Christian in the town, and is credited with introducing vaccinations to Morocco. Her *Life Story*, published in 1911 after her husband's death, ends with the balanced summing up: "I do not advise anyone to follow in my footsteps, at the same time I have not a single regret." She is commemorated in St Andrew's Church in Tangier (see p.79).

The souks

The main **souks** climb up from an archway on the main square, Place de l'Indépendance, by the optimistically named *Grand Hôtel*. Ouezzane has a local reputation for its woollen rugs – most evident in the weavers' souk, around Place Rouida near the top end of the town. Also rewarding is the metalworkers' souk, a covered lane under the Mosque of Moulay es-Abdallah Shereef; to find it, ask directions for the pleasant (and adjacent) *Café Bellevue*.

ARRIVAL AND DEPARTURE · OUEZZANE

Ouezzane provides a useful link if you're travelling by **public transport** (bus or grand taxi) between Chefchaouen and the Atlantic coast.

By bus The bus terminal is about 50m below the Pl de l'Indépendance. Buy onward tickets in advance as it's not unusual for buses to arrive and leave full.
Destinations Casablanca (1 CTM daily; 5hr 15min); Chefchaouen (3 CTM and 10 others daily; 1hr 15min); Fez (4 CTM and 3 others daily; 3hr); Jorf el Malha (4 CTM and 10 others daily; 1hr); Meknes (2 daily; 3hr); Rabat (1 CTM daily & 1 other daily, 4hr); Souk el Arba (1 CTM and 5 others daily; 1hr); Tangier (1 CTM and 1 daily; 4hr).

By grand taxi The grand taxi terminal is about 50m below the Pl de l'Indépendance. Grands taxis occasionally run direct to Fez, but usually you have to take one to the truck-stop village of Jorf el Malha and pick up onward transport there.
Destinations Chefchaouen (1hr 15min); Jorf el Malha (for Fez; 45min); Ksar el Kebir (1hr); Souk el Arba (1hr).

ACCOMMODATION AND EATING

Bouhlal Rue 1, Hay el-Haddadine Echaouen, signposted off the main road (N13) ☎ 0537 907154. A family home with a few rooms, this is currently the town's most comfortable option, despite its location in a dusty side street. The rooms have optional a/c (40dh extra), and the bathrooms (with hot water) are shared. **120dh**

Motel Rif 2km out on the Fez road ☎ 0537 907172, ⓦ motel-rif.ma. This sprawling motel-like complex offers functional rooms with a/c and with or without en suite, as well as some self-catering two-bedroomed apartments. There's also sites with electricity for campers, as well as a decent-sized swimming pool and a large restaurant that serves up the usual Moroccan standards, sourced from the adjoining farm. Camping **30dh**, double **268dh**, apartment **700dh**

The Mediterranean coast and the Rif

MELILLA PORT

The Mediterranean coast and the Rif

Morocco's Mediterranean coast extends for nearly 500km, from the Spanish enclave of Ceuta east to Saïdia on the Algerian border. Much of it lies in the shadow of the Rif mountains, which restrict access to the sea to a very few points. Despite a rash of stalled tourism developments dotted along the coast, such beaches as there are here remain mostly low-key and charming; for a seaside stop head for the fishing harbour and holiday resort of Al Hoceima, or to the lively summer resort of Saïdia on the country's (closed) border with Algeria. To the east of the Rif is Oujda, a pleasant, relaxed city within a day's travel from the scenic Zegzel Gorge, and there are further gorges cutting into the Middle Atlas, near the once important trading centre of Taza. Between Al Hoceima and Oujda is the Spanish enclave of Melilla, an attractive town offering an authentic slice of Spanish life; the dunes and lagoons spreading around nearby Nador are among the richest birdwatching sites in Morocco.

The **Rif mountains** themselves are even less on the tourist trail than the coast – and with some reason. A vast, limestone mass, over 300km long, up to 2500m in height, and with forests of towering oak and cedar, the Rif is the natural boundary between Europe and Africa. Traditionally isolated from central government and the authorities, and with an infamous economy based almost solely on the cultivation of cannabis, or *kif* (see box, p.131), the Rif is also considered the most wild and remote of Morocco's mountain ranges. For some dramatic Riffian scenery, travel between Chefchaouen and Fez, via Issaguen (Ketama) or between Al Hoceima/Nador and Taza, via Aknoul.

Chefchaouen to Al Hoceima

One of Morocco's most memorable journeys is the 210-kilometre mountain road from **Chefchaouen** (see p.115) to **Al Hoceima** which weaves along high on the crests of the Rif mountains. Snow may occasionally block the road in winter but snowploughs soon restore the flow of traffic. The views for most of the year, however, are spectacular. Paul Bowles describes the route well in "The Rif, to Music" chapter of *Their Heads Are Green* – "mountains covered with olive trees, with oak trees, with bushes, and finally with giant cedars".

The road from Chefchaouen sweeps steadily upwards through attractive countryside with olive farms, cork oaks and flowery hedgerows to reach the village of **Bab Taza**, where, suddenly, the feeling of being at altitude kicks in. Beyond **Khamis Medik**, the road runs through woods of various oak species with the richest cultivation in the Rif on the impressively deep slopes below, dotted with farms and the expensive and isolated villas that are testimony to the wealth generated by the cannabis trade. The

THE BEACH AT SAÏDIA

Highlights

❶ Chefchaouen to Al Hoceima The scenic and sometimes vertiginous drive along the northern slopes of the Rif is simply spectacular. **See p.126**

❷ The coast road Recently upgraded all the way from Tetouan's coast to the Algerian border, with deserted coves, rich pickings for birdwatchers among the dunes, and a few easy-going resorts. **See p.130**

❸ Melilla This sophisticated Spanish enclave boasts a wealth of Art Nouveau buildings and an imposing fortress-like Medina, perfect for touring after tapas. **See p.137**

❹ Saïdia Close to the Algerian border, this enjoyable beach resort comes alive in summer, hosting a *raï* music and popular arts festival in May. **See p.143**

❺ Zegzel Gorge Fantastic hiking through dramatic limestone cliffs, terraced fruit groves and magnificent cedar and oak forests. **See p.148**

❻ Cirque du Jebel Tazzeka This classic car-driver's route offers stupendous views of both the Rif and Atlas ranges and passes by the massive Friouato Caves. **See p.153**

HIGHLIGHTS ARE MARKED ON THE MAP ON PP.128–129

road reaches its highest level at **Bab Besen** (1600m) where the landscape is covered in magnificent cedar forests.

Issaguen (Ketama)

Issaguen (usually marked on maps simply as "Ketama", though that is the name of the region, not the village) sits at the heart of *kif* country, and although hassle has toned down somewhat in recent years, it still has a somewhat lawless and menacing edge; if you choose to stop in or around the town your presence may gain the attention of the local *kif* sellers.

Issaguen itself is not much of a place and is only worth stopping at if you have to change grands taxis or want to check out the Thursday souk. **Driving** through in and around Issaguen (Ketama) is perfectly possible and immensely picturesque and enjoyable. However, common sense applies; drive only in daylight, don't stop for hitchhikers or people who appear to be asking for help, and never stop if a car pulls over to the side of your vehicle – local sellers sometimes try to pressurize drivers into buying low-grade hash.

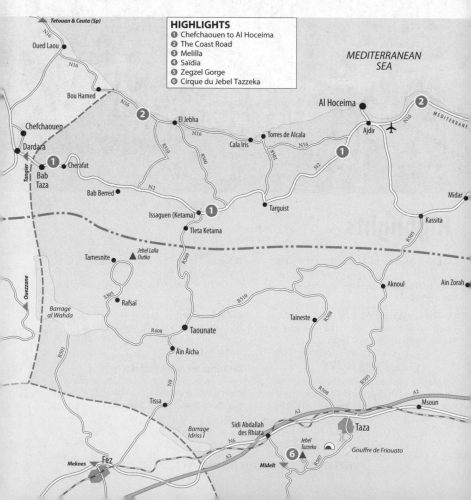

HIGHLIGHTS
1 Chefchaouen to Al Hoceima
2 The Coast Road
3 Melilla
4 Saïdia
5 Zegzel Gorge
6 Cirque du Jebel Tazzeka

ARRIVAL AND DEPARTURE

By grand taxi Grands taxis congregate on the main road. Services operate throughout the day, and increase in frequency during the kif harvest season (July and August).

ISSAGUEN(KETAMA)

Destinations Al Hoceima (2hr 30min); Bab Berred (45min); Chefchaouen (2hr); Taounate (1hr 20min); Targuist (45min).

ACCOMMODATION AND EATING

With a reputation that certainly precedes itself, Issaguen (Ketama) sees little tourist traffic. Other than the hotel below, there are a few scruffy hotels and café-restaurants lining the main road through town.

Tidghine ☎ 0539 813132, ⓦ hoteltidghine.com. An old Spanish *parador* just south of the junction and a surprisingly good hotel despite the lack of any recent investment. Rooms are all en suite with TV, and heating in winter, and there's an in-house restaurant and bar, as well as a swimming pool. **420dh**

Targuist

Continuing east from Issaguen-Ketama the cedar forests give way to a more barren, stony landscape. The road continues to wend down the southern flank of the hills then

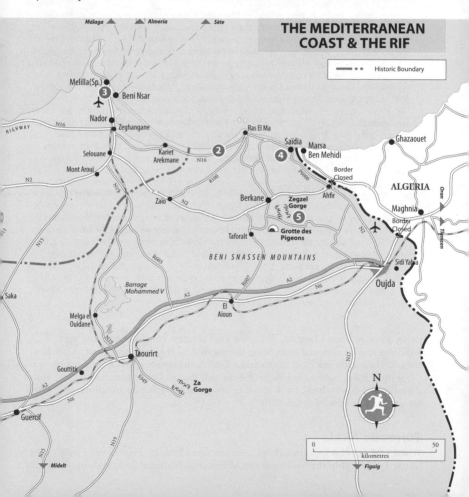

2

ABD EL KRIM AND THE REPUBLIC OF THE RIF

Until the establishment of the Spanish Protectorate in 1912, the **tribes of the Rif** existed outside government control. They were subdued temporarily by *harkas*, the burning raids with which sultans asserted their authority, and for a longer period under Moulay Ismail; but for the most part, bore out their own name of *Imazighen*, or "Free Ones".

Closed to outside influence, the tribes developed an isolated and self-contained way of life. The Riffian soil, stony and infertile, produced constant problems with food supplies, and it was only through a complex system of alliances (*liffs*) that outright wars were avoided. Unique in Morocco, the Riffian villages are scattered communities, their houses hedged and set apart, and where each family maintained a pillbox tower to spy on and fight off enemies. They were different, too, in their religion: the *salat*, the prayers said five times daily – one of the central tenets of Islam – was not observed. *Djinns*, supernatural fire spirits, were widely accredited, and great reliance was placed on the intercession of local *marabouts*.

It was an unlikely ground for significant and organized rebellion, yet for over five years (1921–27) the tribes forced the Spanish to withdraw from the mountains. Several times they defeated whole Spanish armies; first and most memorably at **Annoual** in 1921 (see p.539). It was only through the intervention of France, and the joint commitment of nearly half a million troops, that the Europeans won eventual victory.

In the intervening years, **Abd el Krim el Khattabi**, the leader of the revolt, was able to declare a **Republic of the Rif** and to establish much of the apparatus of a modern state. Well educated, and confident of the Rif's mineral reserves, he and his brother, Mohammed, manipulated the *liff* system to forge an extraordinary unity among the tribes. Impressively, the brothers managed to impose a series of social reforms – including the destruction of family pillboxes and the banning of *kif* – which allowed the operation of a fairly broad administrative system. It was the first nationalist movement in colonial North Africa, and although the Spanish were ready to quit the zone in 1925, it was politically impossible for the French to allow that. Defeat for the Riffians – and the capture of Abd el Krim at Targuist – brought a virtual halt to social progress and reform. The **Spanish** took over the administration en bloc but there was no road-building programme nor any of the other "civilizing benefits" introduced in the French zone. Many of the Riffian warriors were recruited into Spain's own armies, allowing General Franco to build up a power base in Morocco. It was with **Riffian troops** that he invaded Andalusia in 1936, and it was probably their contribution that ensured the Fascist victory in the Spanish Civil War.

When, in April 1957, the Spanish finally surrendered their protectorate, the Berbers of the former Spanish zone found themselves largely excluded from government. Administrators were imposed on them from Fez and Casablanca, and in October 1958, the Rif's most important tribe, the Beni Urriaguel, rose in open **rebellion**. The mutiny was soon put down, but necessitated the landing at Al Hoceima of then Crown Prince Hassan and some two-thirds of the Moroccan army.

The Rif is still perhaps the most unstable part of Morocco, remaining conscious of its under-representation in government and its historical underdevelopment. However, King Mohammed VI seems sympathetic to this situation and over the past decade the region has witnessed substantial school-building programmes, improved road, air and ferry accessibility, large agricultural projects in the plains south of Nador and Al Hoceima, and continues to see an increase in tourism development along its coast.

twists down to bypass **Targuist**. The town itself is a new conglomeration of ugly buildings and far removed from being the site of Abd el Krim's headquarters (see box above). There are a few basic hotels and a lively Saturday souk, but no real reason to stay.

It is only 46km before the village of Ajdir that the sea finally comes into view, and that distance descends the flank of a single long ridge; rather an anticlimax if it wasn't for the payoff of reaching the coast.

Torres de Alcala

TORRES DE ALCALA remains a simple, whitewashed hamlet, 250m from a small, pebbly beach. Lying within the borders of the Al Hoceima National Park, and thus hopefully safe from rampant development, its beach is framed by cliffs, and on the western headland is a deserted fort, probably Spanish, with stunning views along the Mediterranean coast. There's just a bakery, the smallest of shops and a tiny café on the beach – it's still about as laidback as you can get. There are currently no hotels or campsites, though somebody will offer you a room if you ask around.

Along a rocky cliff-path, 5km to the west, are the **ruins of Badis**, which from the fourteenth to the early sixteenth century was the main port of Fez, and used for trade with the western Mediterranean states, in particular Venice. A once-considerable caravan route ran across the Rif, following the course of the modern R509 road, the so-called Route de l'Unité (see p.148).

2

Cala Iris

At **CALA IRIS**, 4km west of Torres de Alcala along a paved road, there's a longer beach, with a natural breakwater, formed by a sandspit that runs out to one of two islets in the bay. A massive tourism development, which will eventually accommodate up to eleven thousand tourists in half a dozen luxury hotels, is earmarked for the town; however, much of the construction work is currently stalled, leaving the village somewhere not quite undiscovered, but not quite developed. Despite this, the village still manages to offer a little charm, with a couple of sleepy cafés by the small fishing harbour at the western end of the beach.

KIF IN MOROCCO

Although many of the Riffian tribes in the **mountains** had always smoked *kif*, it was the Spanish who really encouraged its cultivation – probably as an effort to keep the peace. This situation was apparently accepted when Mohammed V came to power, though the reasons for his acceptance of the status quo aren't obvious. There is a story, probably apocryphal, that when he visited Ketama in 1957, he accepted a bouquet of cannabis as a symbolic gift.

In the early 1970s the Rif became the centre of a significant drug industry, exporting to Europe and America. This sudden growth was accounted for by the introduction, by an American dealer, of techniques for producing hash resin. Overnight, the Riffians had access to a compact and easily exportable product, as well as a burgeoning world market for dope. Inevitably, big business was quick to follow and to this day Morocco is reckoned to be the world's leading producer of cannabis, supplying the vast majority of Europe's demand, and with well over a million people said to depend on the crop for their existence, providing the economic base for much of the country's north. The government, with help from EU and US grants, has tried to reduce cultivation – a project near Rafsaï has replaced cannabis with 600,000 olive trees, for example – and the authorities claim that cultivation has decreased by almost thirty percent over the past decade. However, these figures are estimations gleaned from satellite photographs and are reckoned by European experts to be highly dubious. While the government's stated aim to eradicate cannabis cultivation by 2008 clearly failed, there has recently been a steady increase in the number of police-supervised clearing of crops, many of them well publicized to no doubt please Morocco's European neighbours. The bare fact remains, however, that farmers earn immeasurably more from cannabis than they would from growing legal crops.

Some (non-government) experts are saying that the eradication cause is a lost one, and believe it's better to encourage farmers to rotate cannabis with other crops to avoid ruining their land with overuse of chemical fertilizers – whatever European hippies might like to think, cannabis grown in the Rif is anything but "organic" – rather than waste resources on trying to stop the industry altogether.

It's worth noting here that Moroccan law forbids the sale, purchase and possession of cannabis (see p.55). These laws are enforced on occasion with some vigour, so don't be seduced by the locals: police roadblocks are frequent, informers common. Cannabis in the Rif is obviously big business and potentially dangerous for casual visitors to get mixed up in.

Al Hoceima

Coming from the Rif, **AL HOCEIMA** can be a bit of a shock. It may not be quite the "exclusive international resort" the tourist board claims, but it is truly Mediterranean and has developed enough to have little in common with the farming hamlets and tribal markets of the surrounding mountains. Relaxed and friendly throughout the year, Al Hoceima is at its best in late spring or September, when the beaches are quiet and not so crowded under the midsummer weight of Moroccan families and French and German tourists.

Al Hoceima was developed by the Spanish after their counteroffensive in the Rif in 1925 (see p.130), and was known by them as **Villa Sanjuro**. The name commemorated the Spanish general José Sanjuro, who landed in the bay, under the cover of Spanish and French warships, with an expeditionary force. Coincidentally, it was at Al Hoceima, too, that then Crown Prince Hassan led Moroccan forces to quell the Riffians' revolt in 1958, following independence.

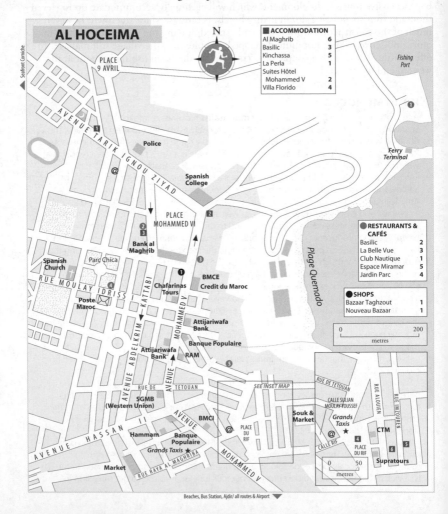

AL HOCEIMA

ACCOMMODATION	
Al Maghrib	6
Basilic	3
Kinchassa	5
La Perla	1
Suites Hôtel Mohammed V	2
Villa Florido	4

RESTAURANTS & CAFÉS	
Basilic	2
La Belle Vue	3
Club Nautique	1
Espace Miramar	5
Jardin Parc	4

SHOPS	
Bazaar Taghzout	1
Nouveau Bazaar	1

Al Hoceima's compact size is one of its charms. Until the 1950s, it consisted of just a small fishing port to the north of the bay, and a fringe of white houses atop the barren cliffs to the south. At the heart of this older quarter is the atmospheric **Place du Rif**, enclosed by café-restaurants and *pensions*.

Spanish College

Pl Mohammed VI

Names aside, the Spanish left little to distinguish their occupation. The only notable architectural feature is the attractive **Spanish College** (Colegio Español de Alhucema), overlooking Place Mohammed VI, which, until 1956, was the provincial headquarters of the Misión Cultural Española in Morocco. An attractive colonial villa, it is distinguishable by its exterior blue and white *azulejo* tiles, common throughout parts of the Iberian peninsula. In addition to offering Spanish Baccalaureate-level education, the college sometimes hosts live cultural events as well as art and craft exhibitions.

Peñon de Alhucemas

From some vantage points just south of the city centre, such as the beaches Calla Bonita and Plage Izly, you get a view of the **Peñon de Alhucemas**, another of the Spanish-owned islands off this coast (and a former penitentiary). Housing a garrison of sixty soldiers and off-limits to visitors, the rocky outcrop is topped with sugar-white houses, a church and tower. The Spanish took it in 1673 and have held it ever since – a perennial source of dispute between Morocco and Spain.

Beaches

For many visitors, Al Hoceima's beaches are its main drawcard; unfortunately, rubbish can be a problem throughout the year. The most central, Plage Quemado, set in a protected bay and a bit of a downhill hike from the town centre, has a stunning setting, despite the two towering hotels currently being constructed right on the beach. There are also some nice beaches to the southeast; **Cala Bonita** is the first, down an unmarked road 1km out of town, with pedaloes and a couple of cafés. Three kilometres from town is **Plage Izly**, a long shingle beach, and another 2km will bring you to **Souani**, a long sandy beach with cafés and good sun loungers, though it's earmarked for major development.

ARRIVAL AND DEPARTURE   AL HOCEIMA

By plane Al Charif al Idrissi Airport (☎ 0539 982560) is 17km southeast of Al Hoceima, just before the village of Imzouren. The airport currently caters solely for flights from Amsterdam and Brussels, plus charter flights from Paris and Madrid during summer. Grands taxis are found directly outside the terminal building, charging 175dh/vehicle (1–6 passengers) for the 15min drive into Al Hoceima. Royal Air Maroc have an office on the corner of Av Hassan II and Av Mohammed V (Mon–Fri 8.30am–12.15pm, 2.20–7pm; Sat 9am–noon, 3–6pm).
By bus The bus station is 2km south of the city centre; all of the bus companies have ticket booths here. Blue and yellow petit taxis are sometimes waiting outside the station, otherwise just hail one from the busy main road opposite; it's around 10dh into town. CTM and Supratours also have offices on Place du Rif, although their buses no longer call here.

Destinations Aknoul (daily; 1hr 30min); Bab Berred (2 CTM & 3 others daily; 4hr 30min); Casablanca (1 CTM daily; 10hr); Chefchaouen (2 CTM & 4 others daily; 6hr 30min); Fez (1 CTM daily; 5hr 15min); Issaguen-Ketama (2 CTM & 5 others daily; 3hr 30min); Meknes (1 CTM daily; 6hr); Nador (2 CTM & 10 others daily; 3hr 15min); Oujda (daily; 4hr 30min); Rabat (1 CTM daily; 8hr 15min); Tangier (1 CTM & 3 others daily; 10hr); Taza (1 CTM daily; 3hr); Tetouan (2 CTM & 8 others daily; 7hr 30min).
By grand taxi Most grands taxis gather in and around Pl du Rif, other than those from Imzouren and Cala Iris, which congregate west of Av Mohammed V on Rue Raya al Maghriba.
Destinations Cala Iris (45min); Issaguen (Ketama; 2hr); Kassita (1hr); Nador (2hr 15min–3hr); Oujda (5hr 30min).

2

Occasionally direct to Fez (4hr); Targuist (1hr 30min); Taza (4hr 30min).

By ferry The small ferry terminal is between Plage Quemado and the fishing harbour. At the time of writing, the twice-daily crossings to Almería (late June to early Sept) had been stopped by operator Acciona Trasmediterránea (ⓦtrasmediterranea.com). The nearest regular ferries depart from Nador (see p.136).

INFORMATION

Tourist information ONMT, Bd al Hamra, Cala Bonita (1km south of the town centre; ☎0539 981185).

Tour operator Chafarinas Tours, 109 Bd Mohammed V (☎0539 840202, ⓦrifitours.tripod.com), can help with travel information, and also organize walking tours and pony trekking in the Rif mountains.

ACCOMMODATION

Outside of the summer months (June–Aug), most places will offer sizeable discounts; during the summer months, it's advisable to book ahead.

Al Maghrib 23 Rue Imzouren ☎0612 245699. This clean and friendly cheapie is located on a busy side street off Pl du Rif, surrounded by plenty of cafés offering cheap breakfasts. Spread out over a number of floors accessed by a narrow staircase, the large, tiled rooms (no heating in winter) come with comfortable beds, hand basins and balconies. The spotless bathrooms are shared and have hot water. 160dh

Basilic 131 Av Abdelkrim Kattabi ☎0539 980083, ☎0539 980087. Opened in 2012, this stylish hotel has a touch of luxury about it. The large, chocolate-beige rooms are carpeted throughout and include a separate sitting area and modern bathrooms, and some have sea-view balconies – though the accompanying street noise can be a negative. 1200dh

Kinchassa 35 Rue Imzouren ☎0670 786978. One of a number of cheapies on a busy side street off Pl du Rif, the *Kinchassa* is well managed and fills up early in the day during summer. While the corridors are a bit dark and poky, the small rooms all have outside-facing windows and are bright and clean, as are the shared toilets and showers. 120dh

La Perla Av Tarik Ibnou Ziyad ☎0539 984513, ⓦhotelperlamorocco.com. Friendly mid-range hotel offering rather bland en-suite rooms. Overlooking a busy street and with a popular ground-floor café, it's best to request a room at the back of the hotel. BB 850dh

Suite Hotel Mohammed V Pl Mohammed VI ☎0539 982233 or 34, ⓦhotelsuitesmohammedv.com. Reopened in 2011 after a major refurbishment, all rooms are now contemporary-styled suites with a tasteful combination of marble and wood throughout. More spacious than average, the suites come with a sitting area and large, modern bathroom, and plenty of light from a balcony with impressive views over Plage Quemado. BB 930dh

★ **Villa Florido** 40 Pl du Rif ☎0539 840847, ⓦflorido .alhoceima.com. This 1929 Art Deco dame received a major facelift in 2010 and is easily the city's best value accommodation. While slightly garish in decor, the rooms – most with balcony – are all spacious and sport shiny, modern bathrooms; the corner rooms sleep three adults comfortably. Single (258dh) and triple (424dh) rooms available. 316dh

EATING AND DRINKING

Al Hoceima has quite a lot of good, cheap **places to eat**, though nothing very upmarket, nor much in the way of nightlife. All the restaurants listed below are unlicensed unless mentioned.

Basilic 131 Av Abdelkrim Kattabi ☎0539 980083. Popular and friendly, with plenty of chairs and tables both streetside (with glass windbreakers) and inside on two a/c levels, through the ground level can get a bit smoky. The varied menu, offers a dozen breakfast set menus, a wide range of light dishes, including savoury crêpes, as well as more substantial meat and seafood dishes. For simple tea/coffee and pastry, first visit their patisserie annexe next door. Breakfast menus 23–30dh, mains 40–120dh. Daily 7am–10pm.

La Belle Vue Av Mohammed V by Pl Mohammed VI. One of a number of local cafés sitting side by side here, this one offers a "belle vue" indeed of the beach below from a pleasant open-sided terrace. Not renowned for its cuisine and more a place to have a coffee and write postcards, there is nonetheless a cheap menu of fish and Moroccan standards during the summer months (mains 25–50dh). Daily 6am–midnight.

★ **Club Nautique** Inside the fishing port (gate 2) ☎0539 981641. Overlooking the port, this restaurant is renowned for huge plates of fresh fish, unloaded daily from the fishing boats just metres away and grilled or fried to your liking. Upstairs is slightly more formal than downstairs, where the bar can get lively with local drinkers. Mains 60–120dh. Daily 2pm–1am.

Espace Miramar Rue Moulay Ismail. This popular place sprawls over four terraces that accommodate an indoor-outdoor restaurant, separate pizzeria, small

AL HOCEIMA NATIONAL PARK

The **Al Hoceima National Park**, the entrance to which is on the N16 about 20km east of Al Hoceima, is a fantastic spot for **walking** and **mountain biking**. Covering 285 square kilometres, the park's majestic rocky canyons and pine forests harbour several rare species of birds and reptiles as well as jackals and wild boar. As well as three accessible bird hides, 30km of well-marked tracks crisscross the park, most negotiable by a tourist vehicle, and you can also scramble down to a few isolated beaches where you may be lucky enough to spot dolphins. A few Berber settlements are dotted around the park, where you can see traditional crafts such as pottery and basket weaving in action. Accommodation is offered in four attractive *gîtes* (houses), sleeping between two and twelve people and with a kitchen and hot water (200–400dh), which can be organized by the very helpful Anissa el Khattabi (☎0662 101279) who can also arrange guides and suggest itineraries. Without your own transport, you'll have to take a grand taxi from Al Hoceima (about 150dh). For more on the park, see ⓦrodpal.org.

2

children's play area and plenty of tables on grassed, shaded spots. The menu ranges from soups, salads and omelette, to pizzas, hamburgers and heavier meat and seafood dishes (25–90dh). Daily 9am–late.

Jardin Parc Parc Chita, Rue Moulay Idriss I (opposite Poste Maroc). Relaxing spot on the southeast corner of the square with outdoor tables, serving basic but well-cooked tajine and chicken dishes (25–55dh). Daily 7.30am–midnight.

DIRECTORY

Banks & exchange There are many banks on Av Mohammed V; Wafacash bureau de change is on (Mon–Fri 8am–8pm, Sat 9am–7pm).

Festival Taking place in mid-May each year since the inaugural event in 2009, Festival Nekor (ⓦagraw.com) incorporates three days of theatre and music, often with discussions and conferences on the side. Productions take place at the Maison de la Culture Moulay el Hassan, off Rue Moulay Idriss I.

Hammam 12 Rue Azzalaga, parallel with Av Hassan II behind the Banque Populaire (women daily 9am–6pm, men daily 6–9pm & Sat 5–9am) – a picture hung outside tells you which sex is in occupation.

Internet Cyber al Ahram, 33 Rue Imzouren (next to *Hôtel Kinchassa*); Cyber Surfnet, off Av Tarik Ibnou Ziyad; Cyber Safir Chamal, Calle Rif, Pl du Rif; Cyber Café, Calle Sultan Moulay Youssef (all daily 9am–10pm).

Post office Rue Moulay Idriss I, opposite Parc Chica.

Souvenirs Bazaar Taghzout and Nouveau Bazaar sit side by side at 145–147 Av Mohammed V, opposite *Café Nejma* (daily 9am–7pm).

Nador

Upon independence in 1956, **Nador** was just an ordinary Riffian village, given work and some impetus by the port of the nearby Spanish enclave of Melilla. Its later designation as a provincial capital led to extensive growth based on the cement industry and the legal and illegal traffic passing through its own busy port at Beni Nsar. It has steadily grown into an ugly, sprawling town and until recently the future looked grim. However, swept up in the country's ambitious tourism vision, there are lofty plans (endorsed by King Mohammed VI himself) in the pipeline to develop Mar Chica Lagoon, beside which the city lies, and its outerlying spit into one of the world's cutting-edge environmental, residential and tourism developments. For the time being, Nador is primarily a transport hub with little to offer other than a pleasant lagoon-side promenade and some birdwatching in the marshes and dunes east of the town, (see box, p.143).

ARRIVAL AND DEPARTURE
NADOR

As Nador is a duty-free port, roads between here and Fez are invariably used for smuggling and therefore subject to numerous police and even customs checks and subsequent delays; the best ground transport option is rail.

2

NADOR

■ ACCOMMODATION
Al Habib	3
Geranio	4
Mediterranée	2
Ryad	1

● RESTAURANTS & CAFÉS
Café Mar Chica	1
Marhaba	2
Romero	3

By plane Nador-Laroui Airport (☎0536 361075) is located 23km south of the city; there are daily flights to Casablanca (1hr 35min).

By train Nador has two train stations, Nador Sud (South) and Nador Ville; the latter is only 500m north of the city centre. Red petits taxis are sometimes waiting in the station car park, otherwise it's usually pretty easy to hail one from the adjoining main road; a fare into town will cost no more than 8dh.

Destinations Beni Nsar Port (4 daily; 20min); Beni Nsar Ville/Melilla border (4 daily; 11min); Casablanca Voyageurs (1 direct & 2 connecting daily; 10hr 30min); Fez (2 direct & 1 connecting daily; 6hr); Meknes (1 direct & 2 connecting daily; 7hr); Oujda (1 connecting daily; 4hr 15min); Rabat (1 direct & 2 connecting daily; 11hr); Taourirt (3 direct daily; 2hr).

By bus The main bus station lies southeast of the city centre, at the southern end of Av des FAR. CTM and a number of long-distance private companies operate from another bus rank at the junction of Av Mohammed V and Rue Général Meziane.

Destinations Aknoul (daily; 3hr 30min); Al Hoceima (2 CTM & 10 others daily; 3hr 15min); Bab Berred (2 CTM & 10 others daily; 7hr); Beni Nsar (at least hourly; 25min); Berkane (over 10 daily; 1hr 30min); Casablanca (3 CTM & 10 others daily; 11hr); Chefchaouen (2 CTM & 4 others daily; 6hr); Fez (4 CTM & at least 10 others daily; 5hr 30min); Guercif (at least hourly; 3hr); Imzouren (2 CTM & 8 others daily; 2hr); Issaguen-Ketama (2 CTM & 10 others daily; 6hr); Meknes (3 CTM & 5 others daily; 6hr 45min); Oujda (at least 15 daily; 2hr 30min); Rabat (3 CTM & 10 others daily; 9hr); Saïdia (1 CTM & 4 others daily; 2hr); Tangier (2 CTM & 6 daily; 12hr); Taza (at least hourly; 2hr 30min); Tetouan (2 CTM & 7 others daily; 11hr).

By grand taxi The sprawling grand taxi rank is opposite the main bus station at the southern end of Av des FAR.

Destinations Al Hoceima (2hr 15min–3hr); Beni Nsar (15min); Berkane (1hr 30min); Oujda (3hr); Taza (2hr).

By ferry Ferries operate from the Gare Maritime Beni Nsar, 8km north of Nador. Shared grands taxis constantly ply the route to/from Nador (5dh), arriving and departing from the busy roundabout 300m west of the ferry terminal.

Destinations Almería (June–Sept 2 daily; 6hr); Sète (June–Sept Wed; 29hr).

INFORMATION

Tourist information ONMT tourist office, 88 Bd Ibn Rochid (Mon–Fri 8.30am–4.30pm; ☎ 0536 330348).

ACCOMMODATION

Al Habib 17 Bd Sakia el Hamra, Hay el Khattabi ☎ 0536 332924. This popular hotel is often full; a grand marble staircase leads to upper floors, each with a small lounge/reading area and airy, light en-suite rooms. 184dh

Geranio 16 Rue 20, Hay el Khattabi ☎ 0536 602828, ☏ 0536 604155. Definitely cheap and cheerful, offering clean rooms with small bathrooms and plenty of hot water, though ask for a room away from the often noisy street. There's also a decent ground-floor café. 188dh.

Mediterranée 2–4 Av Youssef Ibn Tachfine ☎ 0536 606495. The best mid-range option in town, just one street from the lagoon promenade. A multistorey block-type hotel, the rooms are pretty bland and functional; those on the lower floors have a/c and wi-fi. A ground-floor restaurant serves breakfast plus there's a café next door. Singles and triples available. 572dh

Ryad Av Mohammed V ☎ 0536 607717, ☏ 0536 607719. A once shiny and spectacular wedding cake of a hotel, now looking tarnished and drab. The rooms on the top floor are quieter and have lagoon views. Not really worth the splurge, though it does have a restaurant, a bar and a nightclub. BB 986dh

EATING & DRINKING

For an alcoholic drink, head to *Hôtel Ryad*.

Café Mar Chica Bd Mohammed Ezzeraktouni. Jutting into Mar Chica Lagoon, this dark but cosy café has seashell-embedded walls and is decorated wth anchors, antique gas lamps and other paraphernalia. There are plenty of tables outside, with stunning lagoon and promenade views. Besides a pastry and tea/coffee breakfast, the kitchen offers a small menu of unmemorable Moroccan standards (40dh). Daily 8am–10pm.

★ **Marhaba** Av Ibn Rochd ☎ 0536 603311. By far the best restaurant in town, specializing in seafood but with plenty of other offerings, including good-value couscous (Fri, Sat, Sun & public holidays only; 50dh) and a variety of tajines, including rabbit. The sparkling kitchen is open for all to see, and the service is professional and friendly. Choose between a table in the large marble and stucco interior or under a smaller shaded outdoor patio. Daily noon–11pm.

Romero Cnr Av Youssef Ibn Tachfine & Av Hassan II. This stalwart has been around for years and serves up a decent offering of fish and seafood dishes (mains 45–90dh). Located on a busy corner, seating is mostly inside where it's air-conditioned and quieter. Noon–10pm.

Melilla

Spanish-occupied **MELILLA** (Mlilya) is a friendly little place, with a pride in its mix of cultures and an interesting selection of early twentieth-century modernist architecture. Pleasures are to be found, too, in an exploration of the walled old town, **Medina Sidonia**, with its stunning views out across the Mediterranean. It's a popular weekend destination for those living in Morocco, and if you're here in August, there's the marvellous, if misleadingly titled **Semana Naútica**, when the port fills with sailing boats from mainland Spain and further afield for a fortnight (*semana* means one week) of maritime extravaganzas and regattas.

Melilla centres on **Plaza de España**, overlooking the port, and **Avenida Juan Carlos I Rey**, leading inland off it. This is the most animated part of town, especially during the evening *paseo*, when everyone promenades up and down, or strolls through the neighbouring **Parque Hernandez**. To the northeast, Medina Sidonia rises up from a promontory, to watch over the town centre and marina.

Brief history

Together with Ceuta, Melilla is the last of Spain's Moroccan enclaves – a former penal colony that saw its most prosperous days under the Protectorate until 1956, when it was the main port for the Riffian mining industry. Between1956 and 2000, the city's population halved to a little over 65,000, split roughly two to one between Christians and Muslims (mostly Berber), along with minor populations of Jews and Indian

Hindus. Since 2000, however, immigration from the European mainland has risen, due largely to attractive tax laws and the city's duty-free status. The enclave's various religious and ethnic communities get along reasonably well, despite an episode of rioting in 1986, after the enactment of Spain's first real "Aliens Law" threatened to deprive certain Muslim families of their residence rights. There were further riots in 1996, when four hundred Spanish Foreign Legionnaires, a tough bunch posted here by the Madrid authorities out of harm's way, went on the rampage after one of their number had been killed in a bar brawl.

Along with Ceuta, Melilla achieved autonomous status in 1995 after years of shilly shallying on the issue by Madrid for fear of offending Morocco. The enclave is still staunchly Spanish, however, highlighted by a 2007 visit by King Juan Carlos and Queen Sofia – the first royal visit in 80 years – seen by some to be almost an act of defiance towards persistent Moroccan calls for re-integration.

Medina Sidonia

Until the beginning of the twentieth century, the walled "Old Town" of **Medina Sidonia**, wedged in above the port, was all there was of Melilla. This was the site of the original Phoenician colony of Rusadir around the tenth century BC, which the Spanish took in 1497, a kind of epilogue to the expulsion of the Moors from Spain after the fall of Granada in 1492. As an enclave, its security was always vulnerable, and at various periods of expansionist Moroccan rule – it was blockaded throughout the reign of Moulay Ismail – the Spanish population was limited to their fortress promontory and its sea approaches. The quarter's streets were laid out along the lines of a Castilian fort, following a major earthquake in the sixteenth century.

Steps near the fishing port lead up to the quarter's main square, **Plaza Maestranza**, entered by the Gothic **Puerta de Santiago**, a gate flanked by a chapel to St James the Apostle – known to Spaniards as *Matamoros*, "the Moor-Slayer". Beyond the square you come to an old barracks and armoury, and, if you follow the fortifications round from here, a small fort, below which is the church of **La Concepción**, crowded with Baroque decoration, including a revered statue of Nuestra Señora de Victoria (**Our Lady of Victory**), the city's patroness. Back on Plaza Maestranza is the **Museo Municipal** (Museo de la Ciudad Autonoma de la Melilla; Tues–Sat 10am–2pm & 4–8.30pm winter; 10am–1.30pm & 5–9.30pm summer; Sun 10am–2pm; free), which houses a miscellany of historical documents, coins and ceramics. Also interesting is the nearby **Rumbo Melilla** museum (same hours as above; free), which shows a fifteen-minute audiovisual projection on the history of the various peoples to have occupied and influenced the town.

The New Town

In the new town, many of the buildings around **Plaza de España** were designed by **Enrique Nieto**, a *modernista* (Art Nouveau) disciple of the renowned Catalan architect, Antoni Gaudí. Nieto arrived in 1909 at the age of 23 and, over the next four decades, transformed Melilla's architecture. The tile and stucco facades left by Nieto and his imitators – in a style more flowery than Gaudí's – are a quiet delight of the New Town if you cast your eyes above the shops.

A short, circular **walk** taking in these delights starts in Plaza de España with Melilla's most famous Art Deco building, the town hall, a Nieto building of 1947. Avenida Juan Carlos I Rey, leading away from the Plaza de España, begins with the 1917 Trasmediterránea building on the left, followed by another fine piece of Art Nouveau at no. 9, built in 1915. From here head for Calle Ejército Español to have a look at no.16 and continue up Calle Lopez Moreno, checking out the *modernista* buildings on the right-hand side, among them Nieto's **Or Zoruah (Holy Light) Synagogue**, built in 1924,

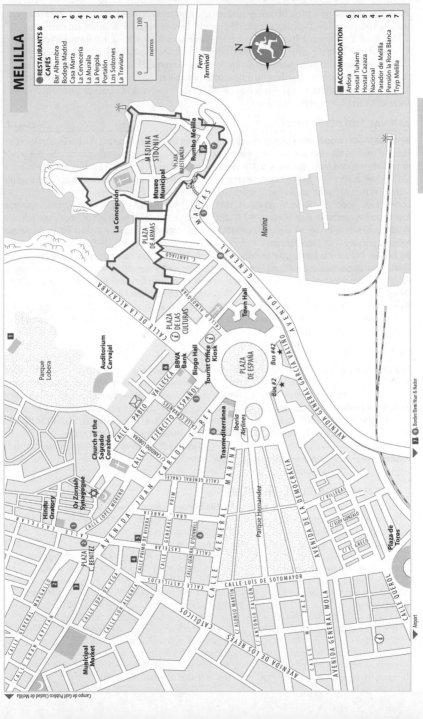

MELILLA

● RESTAURANTS & CAFÉS
Bar Alhambra 2
Bodega Madrid 1
Casa Marta 6
La Cervecería 4
La Muralla 7
La Pérgola 5
Los Solzones 8
Portalón 9
La Traviata 3

■ ACCOMMODATION
Anfora 6
Hostal Tuhami 2
Hostal Cazaza 5
Nacional 4
Parador de Melilla 1
Pensión la Rosa Blanca 3
Tryp Melilla 7

0   100
metres

N

2

the ground floor of which bizarrely houses a cheap trinket shop. Visits can be arranged via the tourist office. Opposite is the Polygon Mosque, also by Nieto, and dating to 1945. Back on Avenida Juan Carlos I Rey, there is quite a selection around Plaza Comandante Benitez and, just down Calle Reyes Catolicos, check out those on Calle Sor Alegría, before heading along Avenida General Prim to see the building on the corner of Castelar. The last building, the **bingo hall** on the corner of Comandante Emperador and Ejército Español, just off Plaza de España, has another fine stucco facade, in Art Deco style this time.

ARRIVAL AND DEPARTURE   MELILLA

By plane Melilla's airport (☎952 698614, ⓦ aena.es) is 3km southwest of the town and services a number of routes from mainland Spain. Rent-a-Car Melilla (☎952 686122) have an office here. Metered taxis from here cost about €7 to Plaza de España, and another €1 to Beni Nsar border post. Both Air Nostrum (☎952 673800, ⓦ airnostrum.es) and Helitt Líneas Aéreas (☎902 223020, ⓦ helitt.com) have offices at the airport; Iberia Airlines have an agency at 20 Calle Generál Marina.

By bus Bus #43 operates between the border post and Melilla's main square, Plaza de España, and costs €0.80. On the Moroccan side of the border, bus #19 operates between Beni Nsar and Nador.

By grand taxi Grands taxis from Nador drop you at the border post of Beni Nsar. Metered taxis are available on the Spanish side, and it costs around €7 (1–4 passengers) to get to/from the border and Plaza de España. Travelling into Morocco, you can usually pick up collective grands taxis for Nador just over the border, or at the informal rank just to the west of the roundabout (100m from the border).

By ferry Melilla's ferry terminal (*estacíon maritima*; ☎956 686613) is at the far end of Avda Generál Macías, a short walk from Plaza de España. Offices for Acciona Trasmediterránea (☎952 690902) and Naviera Armas (☎902 456400) are in the terminal, and there are a couple of travel agencies just outside. Advance bookings are essential in August and at the end of Easter week. Full details on ferries can be found in "Basics" (see box, pp.28–29).

Destinations Almería (1–2 daily; 3–7hr); Málaga (1–2 daily; 3hr 30min–9hr); Motril-Granada (6–7 weekly May–Oct only; 3hr 30min).

INFORMATION

Tourist information Plaza de las Culturas (Mon–Sat 10am–2pm & 4.30–8.30pm; ☎952 976190, ⓦ melillaturismo.com). There's also a kiosk by the town hall on Plaza de España (Mon–Fri 10am–2pm & 4–8pm).

Travel agent Viajes Mariaire, Avda Juan Carlos I Rey 30 (Mon–Fri 9am–1pm & 4.30–8pm; ☎952 681017, ☎952 690023).

Phones When phoning Melilla from Morocco (or anywhere else outside Spain), you must prefix numbers with the international code (☎00 34). Dialling numbers within Melilla you must include the old local code (☎952) as part of the new nine-digit number. To phone Morocco from Melilla, you need to dial ☎00 212, followed by the local code (minus the initial zero) and number.

Time Melilla works to Spanish time, an hour ahead of Morocco.

THE NADOR–MELILLA BORDER

On a good day you can cross the **Nador–Melilla border** in ten or fifteen minutes. At other times, you may need considerable time and patience. During the summer it's often extremely crowded, with Moroccans returning from (or going to) jobs in Europe, as well as travellers off the ferry. If you want to avoid the queues, it is a good idea to spend a couple of hours in Melilla after arriving off a ferry, to let the main traffic get through. Early mornings are very busy on both sides of the border.

If you are **driving**, be aware that smuggling goes on at the border, with periodic police crackdowns; in recent years, trading has included both drugs and people, with Moroccans (and sub-Saharan Africans) attempting to cross illegally into mainland Spain. Driving at night, keep an eye out for road checks – not always well lit but usually accompanied by tyre-puncturing blockades. If you've rented a car in Morocco, you can usually take it into Melilla but not into mainland Spain. The 200m that separate the Moroccan and the Spanish sides of the border are much more than just a geopolitical anomaly. They are a no-man's-land isolating a prosperous European town from an unemployment-ridden Moroccan one, and the sharp contrast between the two illustrates why so many Moroccans risk – and lose – their lives trying to reach the Spanish coast on makeshift rafts in search of better prospects.

ACCOMMODATION

Rooms tend to be in short supply in Melilla, and are expensive by Moroccan standards. If you have problems, the tourist offices (see opposite) might be able to help.

Anfora Calle Pablo Vallesca 16 ☎952 683340, ⓦ hotelanfora.net. This functional mid-range option is in a great location, with stunning views from the rooftop terrace. The softly coloured rooms are a good size with modern bathrooms and private balconies; the breakfast buffet is unfortunately very poor. BB €80

Hostal Cazaza Calle Primo de Rivera 6 ☎952 684648. The rooms are a little scruffy, but it's a friendly, well-maintained place. All rooms have TV and a large bathroom, and there's a small café on the ground floor for breakfast. €38

★ **Hostal Tuhami** Calle General García Margallo 13 ☎952 686045, ⓔ hostaltuhami@hotmail.com.es. Within strolling distance to everything, the friendly staff and good-value rooms makes this one of the town's best choices. The tiled rooms all have a/c and satellite TV, but the bathrooms are a bit on the small side €45

Nacional Calle José A. Primo de Rivera 10 ☎952 684540, ☎952 684481. This quaint and friendly hotel has small but comfortable rooms with modern bathrooms; those facing outwards are brighter and fresher. There's also

a quiet street-level restaurant, and car rental is available for day-trips to Morocco. €58

Tryp Melilla Puerto Esplanada de San Lorenzo ☎952 695525, ⓦ melia.com. Once renowned for inefficiency and lacklustre service, this hotel has pulled up its socks and is now delivering the goods. The rooms (including one adapted for wheelchair users) are a bit sparse but spacious, but the beachfront location is very appealing, only a short stroll from the town centre. There's a decent in-house restaurant and separate café, a small gym and guest parking. €198.

Parador de Melilla Avda de Cándido Lobera – overlooking the Parque Lobera ☎952 684940, ⓦ parador.es. Rather dated but with large rooms and balconies providing fine views over the town, plus a swimming pool (June–Oct), though unfortunately both food and service often leave something to be desired. Its elevated location can challenge tired legs at the end of the day. €128

Pensión la Rosa Blanca Calle Gran Capitán 7 ☎952 682738. A charming, quiet little *pension* with large, clean rooms (shared bathrooms) ; some have balconies but others are beginning to age badly. Good-value singles (€23). €35

EATING AND DRINKING

Melilla has some great **tapas bars**, but not much in the way of **restaurants**; the main concentration lies in the area east of Avenida Juan Carlos I Rey, between the Plaza de España and the Municipal Market. There is also a cluster of cafés and restaurants in the new marina to the south of the fishing port. Coming from Morocco, the easy availability of alcohol and open drinking culture are refreshing in more ways than one.

Bar Alhambra Calle Castelar 3. A large, local bar that is quite relaxed but can get very busy around midday. Tapas offerings (€2–8) are varied, and include mini sandwiches *(bocadillos)*, bacon-wrapped shrimp and a delicious paella. The sangria and beer are both cold and served quickly. Daily except Sun 10.30am–3pm & 8.30–11pm.

Bodega Madrid Calle Castelar 8. One of a number of tapas bars in this neighbourhood, the *Madrid* is more old school than most, with aproned barmen, plenty of standing room, bright lights and big beers. The tapas includes huge rations of freshly cooked fish and seafood (€3–10). Daily 11.15am–3pm & 8.30–10.45pm.

Casa Marta Calle Justo Sancho Miñano 4. Great little tapas bar-restaurant in the main shopping quarter, with shaded tables on the pavement and barrels to stand at inside. The grilled shrimp is delicious (€9), as are the large (and free) tapas that accompany each beer. Daily noon–

5pm & 8pm–2am.

La Cervecería Calle General O'Donnell 23. Popular tapas bar with whacky all-green *modernista* decor, good food (tapas €1.50) and decent wines available by the glass. Service is very friendly, too. Daily 12.30–4pm & 8.30–midnight.

La Muralla Calle Mirador de Florentina, near the southeast corner of Medina Sidonia ☎952 681035, ⓦ restaurantelamuralla.net. This century-old restaurant is built into the Medina wall and oozes history, with many artefacts adorning the walls, while a small outdoor section has fantastic views over the port. While specializing in meat dishes, there are also plenty of seafood options, though not much for vegetarians (mains €9–22). Thurs–Sat 9pm–1am.

La Pérgola Avda General Macías ☎952 685628. Enjoy coffee or cocktails on the waterside terrace then tackle the huge restaurant menu, which includes plenty of fish (mains €3–8) and a good-value *prix-fixe* menu (€10). Packed at weekends. Daily noon–midnight.

La Traviata Calle Ejército Español 5 ☎952 681925. Well-run and popular bar-restaurant serving modern gourmet Spanish food at top-end prices (mains €15–22). The portions are huge, and try to leave space for dessert. Daily 12.30–3pm & 8pm–1am.

Los Salazones Calle Conde de Alcaudete 15 ☎952 673652. Established in 1967 and still going strong,

this large tapas bar-restaurant serves traditional Spanish fare with great aplomb (mains €12–18). Tues–Sun 12.30–3pm & 8pm–midnight.
Portalón Avda General Macías 9. Popular café-

restaurant across from the fishing port serving tapas, pizza, and average seafood (mains €2.50–8). Good coffee though. Daily 8–10.30am, 12.30–3pm & 8pm–midnight.

DIRECTORY

Banks & exchange There are a number of banks on or near Avda Juan Carlos I Rey, all of which have ATMs and will change cheques, sterling, dollars or dirhams. It's worth shopping around to get the best exchange rates. Bear in mind that, as part of Spain, Melilla uses euros.
Golf Campo de Golf Público Ciudad de Melilla, Calle de Chile (18 holes; ☎ 952 116102, ✆ golfmelilla.com).

Hospitals Hospital Comarcal, Calle Remonta 2 (☎ 952 670000); Hospital Militar, Calle General Polavieja s/n (☎ 952 674743).
Post office Calle Pablo Vallescá (Mon–Fri 8.30am–8.30pm, Sat 9.30am–1pm).

The far east coast

The Mediterranean coastline stretches east from Nador all the way to the Algerian border. Until recently it was relatively undisturbed, with just a few small villages that burst at the seams in summer but counted more birds than people for the rest of the year. Change has come, however, and the wave of development that continues to wash over much of Morocco has found its way to these shores. Beachfront promenades have been laid, and concrete apartment blocks are inevitably following. Just west of the pleasant seaside resort of **Saïdia** is perhaps the country's most ambitious tourism development of all Saïdia Mediterrania, a designated tourist zone complete with mega-resorts, an 18-hole golf course, 700-berth marina and even a *faux* Medina. The atmosphere along this coast during summer is infectious and it's a great time to experience modern Morocco, where families play in the shallows and Arabic pop music blares out from mobile phones. Unfortunately, this development comes at an inevitable cost, and the coastline's remarkable ecosystem appears to be under siege from the increase in development and the resultant waste issues.

Kariet Arekmane

The village of **Kariet Arekmane**, 30km from Nador, gives access to the eastern fringe of Mar Chica Lagoon. This is a desolate area but picturesque in its own way, with salt marshes that provide manifold attractions for birdwatchers. From the village, a recently tarred road rudely cuts across the marshes to a sandy beach – a popular weekend spot with Spaniards from Melilla. The inevitable promenade has recently been completed and a few semi-permanent restaurants have sprung up, though there's still no accommodation as yet, just expensive holiday homes. During summer, the beach comes to life with umbrellas for rent, jetskis zipping across the flat waters, and even lifeguards on duty.

Ras el Ma

Also known as Cap de l'Eau and Ras Kebdana, **Ras el Ma** is a pleasant, if at times scruffy, fishing village, facing another of Spain's offshore island possessions on this coast, the three tiny **Islas Chafarinas**. The village has a brown sandy **beach**, a smattering of decent cafés and restaurants and a little harbour where you can watch the daily catch come in. Be here on a summer Sunday and you'll find the beach packed with people, many of them bussed in from inland villages. Often strewn with rubbish. the condition of the beach gets better the further east (away from the port) you walk.

BIRDS AND DUNES

The coast east of Nador offers compelling sites for **birdwatching** – and plant wildlife – with a series of highly frequented freshwater and saline sites.

At **Kariet Arekmane** a path leads out, opposite the village mosque, past salt pans and a pumping station (right-hand side) to an extensive area of **salt marsh**. This is covered by the fleshy-stemmed marsh glasswort or *salicornia*: a characteristic "salt plant" or *halophyte*, it can survive the saline conditions through the use of glands which excrete the salt. The **insect life** of the salt marsh is abundant, including damselflies, brightly coloured grasshoppers and various ants and sand spiders. The **birds** are even more impressive, with black-winged stilt, greater flamingo, coot, great-crested grebe, and various gulls and terns wheeling overhead.

Further along the coast, a walk east of the resort of **Ras el Ma** demonstrates the means by which plants invade **sand dunes**: a sequential colonization is known as "succession", where one plant community gradually cedes to the next as a result of its own alteration of the environment. Typical early colonizers are marram grass and sea couch, which are eventually ousted by sea holly and sea spurge and finally by large, "woodier" species such as pistacihu, juniper and cistus species. Whole sequences can be seen occurring over time along the beach. The area attracts a variety of interesting **sea birds** as well, including the internationally rare slender-billed curlew and **Audouin's gull** (thought to breed on the adjacent offshore Chafarinas Islands; see below). Other more familiar birds include dunlin, Kentish plover and oystercatcher.

Even further along the coast is the freshwater lagoon system that marks the mouth of the **Oued Moulouya**. The lagoons here are separated from the sea by a remarkable series of sand spits, no more than fifty metres across, and the **birdlife** is outstanding. Secluded among the reedbeds, it is possible to locate grey heron, white stork and little egret while the water's surface is constantly patrolled by the ever-alert black terns and kingfishers. Other varieties that you should manage to spot, wading in the shallows, are redshank, spotted redshank (in summer) and black-tailed godwit. The mouth and adjacent wetlands are, however, under serious threat from tourism development. In response to local and international pressure, a small parcel of wetland encompassing the mouth has been declared a protected area funded by, among others, the Global Environmental Fund and UNDP. Bird hides and information signboards have been erected along a marked walking path.

The Spanish-owned **Islas Chafarinas**, incidentally, are another important wildlife site, which has been declared a nature reserve. The three small islets support the Mediterranean's largest sea-bird colonies; sadly, the endangered monk seals disappeared from the islands in the 1990s and haven't been seen since.

ARRIVAL AND INFORMATION   RAS EL MA

By bus There's a daily bus from Nador to Kariet Arekmane and Ras el Ma. It turns around on arrival at Ras el Ma and heads back to Nador, so you'll have to sleep over if you want to spend any time here.

By grand taxi During summer, you'll usually find a few grands taxis in Nador departing in the morning for Kariet Arekmane and returning in the late afternoon. There's also the option of chartering a grand taxi in Nador (around 250dh for the day).

Banks Attijariwafa Bank and Banque Populaire, both with ATMs, are located just before Ras el Ma's port, opposite the Gendarmerie Royale.

ACCOMMODATION AND EATING

Auberge de Cap de L'eau Ras el Ma (on the road to Saïdia) ☎0536 640264. Spacious en-suite rooms that sleep up to four people, and there's also a large restaurant serving both Moroccan staples and plenty of fish. **350dh**

Capado Ras el Ma (next to port) ☎0536 893548.

Specializes in fresh fish, offering some dishes by the kilo, and also serves wood-fired pizza (mains 20–120dh). A shaded rooftop terrace provides a sweeping coastal panorama and there's also a little playground for toddlers. Daily 11am–10pm.

Saïdia

Only a few years ago, **SAÏDIA** was a low-key holiday town, rambling back from the sea in the shadow of a still-occupied nineteenth-century kasbah, and fronted by one of the best beaches on the Mediterranean. Recent years, however, have seen massive development along the coast to the west of town. Officially named "Saïdia Mediterrania" though signposted along the coast simply as Station Balnéaire ("seaside resort"), the new development functions as a separate resort from Saïdia itself, even though the two almost meet. The growth has been enormous to say the least, with hundreds of apartment blocks, many of them half-finished and already looking tired, stretching along the beach and for a few hundred metres inland. In addition, the resort is home to one of the country's largest marinas, an adjacent outdoor shopping complex, four sprawling five-star resorts, and an eighteen-hole golf course (with another two in the pipeline).

If you prefer birds to beaches, there are rewarding birdwatching sites in the marshes and woodland stretching behind the beach towards the Oued Moulouya (see box, p.143), although in high season you'll have to pick your way through the rubbish. Each year, Saïdia hosts the annual two-week Festival Saïdia Raggada (May). It's a great opportunity to listen to some indigenous *chaabi*, *raï* and *amazigh* music, and see *raggada* and *laäoui* folk-dancing ensembles.

ARRIVAL AND DEPARTURE   SAÏDIA

By bus A new bus station is nearing completion right next to the old one, just north of the kasbah and market. It's a five-minute walk from here to the beach.
Destinations Afhir (over 10 daily; 45min); Berkane (5 daily; 45min); Nador (3 daily; 2hr); Oujda (7 daily; 1hr 30min).

By grand taxi Grands taxis currently operate from the eastern edge of the market, though they may move to within the car park lot of the adjacent new bus station.
Destinations Ahfir (30min); Berkane (30min); Oujda (1hr).

ACCOMMODATION

★ **Atlal** 44 Bd Hassan II ☎0536 625021, ✉atlalben@ menara.ma. One of the town's better all-round packages, combining genuine friendly service with a good restaurant, a separate bar, and bright, modern rooms. BB 510dh

Be Live Grand Saïdia Saïdia Mediterrania ☎0536 633366, ⌨belivehotels.com. The closest to town, and perhaps the best, of the mega resorts. The attractive rooms are quite large and have all the mod cons you'd expect. There's a number of swimming pools and in-house restaurants, as well as a private beach area which can become not-so-private in summer when musicians, souvenir hawkers and camel rides throng the sand.€266

Hannour Pl du 20 Août ☎0536 625115, ✉0536 624343. A well-established mid-range establishment set one block back from the beach, with simply furnished rooms with fans. It can get a bit noisy here during summer, thanks to the popular ground-floor café. 400dh

Iberostar Saïdia Saïdia Mediterrania ☎0536 630010, ⌨iberostar.com. Decked out in Mediterranean blue and white, this beachfront chain resort offers almost six hundred large rooms with all the mod cons. There are also three restaurants, four swimming pools and a lobby bar. €250

Manhattan Cnr Rue Zerktouni & Av Mohammed V ☎0536 624243. This seafront hotel is located above its own popular café-restaurant. The sparsely furnished rooms, some with sea-facing balconies, are quite large, airy and tiled throughout – the reverse a/c helps to warm them up in winter. 550dh

Paco Bd Hassan II opposite the Atlal ☎0536 625110. Although a rather spartan hotel, this is still the town's best budget option. Rooms are en suite with hot water, and there's a slightly seedy, though friendly ground-floor bar. 200dh

Titanic Cnr Av Mohammed V & Place du 20 Août ☎&✉0536 624071. Modern, airy rooms lead onto good-sized balconies offering unbeatable sea views; there are a few larger suites that will sleep three adults comfortably. The popular downstairs café does a good juice and pastry breakfast. 350dh.

EATING & DRINKING

Hôtel Atlal 44 Bd Hassan II ☎0536 625021. The best restaurant in town, with a cosy dining room and pretty terrace; serving fresh fish and hearty tajines (45–120dh), and a good selection of Moroccan wines. Daily 11am–11pm.

La Corniche Av Mohammed V, opposite Pl du 20 Août ☎0536 625051 or ☎0660 358944. This popular restaurant offers plenty of tables both inside and under a covered, wooden-decked terrace, overlooking the beach. The menu offers decent light options, such as shawarmas,

paninis and pizza, as well as delicious savoury crêpes and a few pasta dishes (20–65dh). The service can be a bit up and down, but the views make up for it. Daily 8am–11pm.

De la Paix Bd Hassan II, opposite Pl du 20 Août ☎0536 625411. This small, well-established restaurant serves up a decent selection of seafood specialities as well as Moroccan staples (25–80dh). The service is usually prompt and cheerful, and there's seating both inside and on the pavement overlooking the square. Daily 11am–11pm.

Paloma Blanca Av Mohammed V ☎0664 758454. Slightly more formal than the other beachfront restaurants, with a menu that focuses on seafood, with other choices restricted mainly to tajines and pizzas (mains 35–90dh). Daily 11am–11pm.

Berkane and the Zegzel Gorge

The route east from Nador to Oujda along the N2 is well served by buses and grands taxis. It holds little of interest along the way, but if you've got the time (and ideally a car), there's a pleasant detour around Berkane into the **Zegzel Gorge**, a dark limestone fault in the Beni Snassen mountains – the last outcrops of the Rif.

Berkane

BERKANE is a strategic market town, French-built and prosperous, set amid an extensive region of orchards and vineyards. If you stay, you're likely to be the only tourist in the town – so there aren't any hustlers. Berkane is surrounded by vast orchards, most of them growing clementines. Many of the town's buildings are painted in shades of orange, and a **festival** is held each May to commemorate the harvest.

Berkane's main square, Place Mohammed V is at the western end of town on the N2 road (Boulevard Mohammed V), next to the bridge over the Oued Cherrâa. About 1km further along Boulevard Mohammed V is the main roundabout junction of the Nador–Oujda N2 highway, as well as the offshoot highway to Saïdia and the coast. Almost everything you'll need in Berkane lies between the roundabout and Place Mohammed V.

There isn't much to see in Berkane, but worth a glance is the 1909 **French Church**, on Rue Moulay Abdellah, 100m east of Place Mohammed V. Painted in red ochre, with a row of strange grimacing faces picked out in yellow along the top of its facade, the church is no longer in use as a house of prayer, and is now the base for the Association Homme et Environnement (☎0536 610289, ⓦee.ouvaton.org). A lone voice highlighting both regional and world environmental issues, their staff members can also show you the church's interior.

ARRIVAL AND DEPARTURE   BERKANE

Berkane is a handy transport hub for the far east of the country. Drivers should be wary of buying plastic bottles of cheap petrol from roadside stalls; it's often watered down.

By bus CTM operates from a bus rank on Pl Annasr, Bd Mohammed V, opposite *Hôtel Rosalina*. Other bus companies, as well as most grands taxis, operate also from Pl Annasr or the adjoining streets.
Destinations Casablanca (CTM daily; 11hr); Fez (CTM daily; 6hr); Meknes (CTM daily; 7hr); Nador (over 10 daily; 1hr 30min); Oujda (over 10 daily; 1hr 30min); Rabat (CTM daily; 9hr); Saïdia (5 daily; 45min); Taforalt (2 daily; 30min).

By grand taxi Grands taxis for Nador can be found at the top end of Bd Mohammed V, just before the bridge over the Oued Cherâa. Those for Saïdia leave from just north of the main Nador–Oujda roundabout on Bd Mohammed V, while those for Oujda and Taforalt gather on Pl Annasr.
Destinations Nador (1hr 30min); Oujda (45min); Saïdia (30min); Taforalt (45min).

ACCOMMODATION AND EATING

Café Le Prince d'Or Cnr Bd Mohammed V and Rue Moulay Abdellah, 100m east of Pl Mohammed V. This modern café is popular with a young crowd, offering a menu of light meals, including pizzas and paninis (20–35dh). Daily 8am–10pm.

Rosalina 82 Bd Mohammed V, 500m west of the main roundabout ☎0536 618992, ⓦrosalina-hotel.com. The town's newest and best hotel, with modern but slightly garish rooms & suites. There's a lift and private parking, as well as a lively ground-floor café. **450dh**

Zaki 27 Bd Mohammed V, 400m east of the main roundabout ☎0536 613743, ☎0536 619900. Looking slightly tired nowadays, this mainstay of the Berkane hotel scene still offers decent, individually decorated rooms. The in-house restaurant serves up a decent tajine as well as pizzas and paninis. BB **420dh**

2

A NOTE ON ALGERIA

Throughout the 1990s and into the early 2000s **Algeria** was effectively off-limits to all foreign visitors. During the civil war between 1992 and 1998, over 150,000 people were killed in attacks and reprisals by Islamic fundamentalists and the army; foreigners, as well as Algerian intellectuals, journalists and musicians, were particular targets. After elections in 1999 the situation improved somewhat, although there were still occasional skirmishes with militant Islamic extremists. 2007 saw a worrying resurgence of violence, with Al-Qaeda in the Islamic Maghreb (AQIM) implicated in attacks in Algeria and Morocco that left many dead. The kidnapping of Westerners in southern Algeria, again said to be the work of AQIM, is also on the increase. Three aid workers (two Spaniards and one Italian) were abducted in 2011, from a refugee camp near the border with Morocco's disputed Western Sahara region. A year later, the two Spaniards were still being held captive.

Algeria and Morocco have disputed their borders since Algerian independence in 1963. The border was closed in 1975 following Morocco's "Green March" into Spain's former colony of Western Sahara – the Algerians supported Polisario, the Saharan independence movement. The border reopened some years later but was closed again in 1994 when Morocco imposed strict visa restrictions on Algerians following a terrorist attack in Marrakesh.

In 2004, in an attempt to improve relations, Morocco lifted all visa entry requirements for Algerians, a move the Algerians then reciprocated, but the borders remained closed. In 2008, Morocco, citing their "common past and shared destiny", called on Algeria to normalize relations and reopen the border – it is estimated that the border closure costs Morocco $1bn a year in lost trade and tourist revenues. There was then a brief breakthrough in the impasse in February 2009 when the border was opened to allow the passage of an aid convoy heading for the Gaza Strip, and in 2012 both countries' foreign ministers stated a desire to open the border amid a greater post-Arab Spring plan to revitalize the Arab Maghreb Union (comprising Algeria, Libya, Mauritania, Morocco and Tunisia). However, most political commentators believe that the Western Sahara issue will need to be resolved to Algeria's satisfaction before the border gates open again. It's possible for non-Moroccans to obtain entry visas for Algeria at the embassy in Rabat, but as the situation currently stands, entry to Algeria from Morocco is still only possible by air, flying out of Casablanca.

Taforalt

TAFORALT (Tafoughalt) is a quiet mountain village, 20km southwest of Berkane, active only for the **Wednesday souk**, but serves as a good base for hikers or birdwatchers interested in exploring the gorges and peaks of the nearby Beni Snassen mountains.

Grottes des Pigeons and Grotte du Chameau

Grottes des Pigeons 2km from Taforalt • Grotte du Chameau 10km from Taforalt • Both caves are signed off the Zegzel Gorge road, which is signed off the N2 10km southwest of Berkane

The **Grottes des Pigeons** is a complex of *grottes* (caves) currently being excavated by a team from Oxford University; some of the earliest human remains in the world have been found here, as well as jewellery – pierced shells which date back a staggering 90,000 years. Information is displayed on a board in the picnic area below the caves, from where a short path brings you to the caves' entrance. While the caves themselves are off-limits, visitors can get quite close to the excavation digs.

A further 8km on is the **Grotte du Chameau**, a cavern of vast stalactites, one of which is remarkably camel-like in shape. This has been closed to visitors for years and now houses a herd of goats. Local boys stationed just before the cave will charge 5dh per vehicle for the use of the car park at the end of the road where you can enjoy the picnic area underneath towering limestone buttresses and dense cedar trees.

RIGHT ZEGZEL GORGE (P.148) >

Zegzel Gorge

11km from Tarforalt

The **Zegzel Gorge** is actually a series of gorges 10km long, that dramatically define the eastern edge of the Rif mountain range. The gorges offer wonderful hiking following the seasonal riverbed of the Oued Zegzel, terraced and cultivated at its wider points with citrus and fruit trees. 3km south from the Grotte du Chameau, a rough track branches off the main dirt road, only suitable for hiking and sturdy 4WD vehicles and perennially subject to rock avalanches and flash-floods. As the track criss crosses the riverbed, the gorges progressively narrow, drawing your eye to the cedars and dwarf oaks at the summit, until you eventually emerge (22km from Taforalt) onto the Berkane plain.

ARRIVAL AND DEPARTURE

TAFORALT

By bus and grand taxi Two buses daily operate between Berkane and Taforalt, while grands taxis ply the route throughout the day, more frequently on souk days (Wed & Sun). A limited number of grands taxis offer services along the circular gorge route, depending on the condition of the road.

ACCOMMODATION AND EATING

★ **Auberge de Taforalt** ☎ 0662 045119, ⓦ taforaltclub.com. Among a smattering of roadside cafés at the northern entrance to town, this very good hotel has quirky rooms, Berber tents on the roof (BB 250dh) and kitchens, if you want to self-cater. They also run *Club Taforalt*, across the street, with a pool, bar and restaurant. BB. Berber tent 250dh, room 350dh

The Route de L'Unité: Ketama to Fez

At the end of the Spanish Protectorate in 1957, there was no north–south route across the Rif, a marked symbol both of its isolation and of the separateness of the old French and Spanish zones. The Route de l'Unité, a road cutting right across the range from Ketama to Fez, was planned to provide working contact between the Riffian tribes and the French-colonized Moroccans.

The Route (more prosaically known as the R509), completed in 1963, was built with volunteer labour from all over the country – Hassan II himself worked on it at the outset. It was the brainchild of Mehdi Ben Barka, first president of the National Assembly and the most outstanding figure of the nationalist Left before his exile and subsequent "disappearance" in Paris in 1965. Ben Barka's volunteers, fifteen-thousand-strong for much of the project, formed a kind of labour university, working through the mornings and attending lectures in the afternoons.

Today the Route de l'Unité sees relatively little traffic – travelling from Fez to Al Hoceima, it's quicker to go via Taza and the R505; from Fez to Tetouan, via Ouezzane. Nevertheless, it's an impressive and very beautiful road, certainly as dramatic an approach to Fez as you could hope for. However, see the **warning** about driving through here on p.140.

Taounate

TAOUNATE is a pleasantly bustling little town with sweeping views over the plains to the south. If you can make it for the huge **Friday market**, you should be able to organize a lift out to any number of villages in the region. Numerous cafés and banks, a petrol station and a good daily market line Avenue Mohammed V, the main road through the town.

ARRIVAL AND DEPARTURE

TAOUNATE

By grand taxi Grands taxis operate all day between the two major transport hubs of Fez and Issaguen-Ketama. They congregate near the Ziz petrol station on Av Mohammed V. Destinations Fez (1hr 30min); Issaguen-Ketama (1hr 20min).

ACCOMMODATION AND EATING

Du Lac 27 Av Mohammed V ☏0535 689367. In the middle of town, up an alley opposite the market entrance, this is a surprisingly good hotel, offering comfortable rooms with a/c. There's also a decent restaurant offering the usual Moroccan standards and a pastry breakfast. <u>**296dh**</u>

Tissa

The region around the village of **Tissa** is known for its thoroughbred Hayani horses. Here, in late September/early October, horses and riders from the region gather to compete at the annual **horsefair**. The climax are the competitive **fantasias** judged on speed, discipline and dress. Elsewhere, *fantasias* – traditional cavalry charges culminating in firing of muskets in the air – are put on largely for tourists, but these are the real thing, for aficionados.

Rafsaï

RAFSAÏ, to the west of Taounate, was the last village of the Rif to be overrun by the Spanish. Vast hectares of olive groves surround the village, many of them recently planted thanks to government grants in a bid to offer an alternative to growing *kif* (see p.131). A lively festival takes place here every December to celebrate the olive harvest. If you are into scenic roads and have transport, you might consider taking a forty-kilometre dirt road out from Rafsaï to the peak, **Jebel Lalla Outka**, offering a sweeping view of the whole Rif range. The road is reasonable as far as the village of Tamesnite, but thereafter is very rough *piste* – accessible only in summer.

Taza

TAZA was once a place of great importance: the capital of Morocco for periods of the Almohad, Merenid and Alaouite dynasties, and controlling the Taza Gap, the only practicable pass from the east. It forms a wide passage between the Rif and Middle Atlas and was the route to central power taken by Moulay Idriss and the first Moroccan Arabs, as well as the Almohads and Merenids, both of whom successfully invaded Fez from Taza. However, the local Zenatta tribe were always willing to join an attack by outsiders and in the nineteenth century, managed to overrun Taza completely, with centralized control returning only with the French occupation of 1914. Following occupation, Taza was an important centre of the resistance movement; troops fought long and hard in the Rif mountains in skirmishes which occurred sporadically right up to independence.

Modern Taza seems little haunted by this past, its monuments sparse and mostly inaccessible to non-Muslims. The town splits into two parts, the **Medina** and the French-built **Ville Nouvelle**, distinct quarters separated by 2km of road. The Ville Nouvelle is of little interest, though it has the usual facilities, but the Medina, with its magnificent hilltop site, is steeped in history and has a quiet charm.

Aside from offering a pleasant day or two exploring the Medina, Taza is also a good base from which to explore the national park of **Jebel Tazzeka**, a treat for drivers and hikers alike (see p.153).

The Medina

The **Medina** is easy enough to navigate, though you may need to ask directions for the few scattered sites. You can get a taste of the town's more recent history at the museum on the Mechouar (daily 10am–5pm; free), which houses a small but poignant collection of photos, newspaper cuttings and artefacts.

2

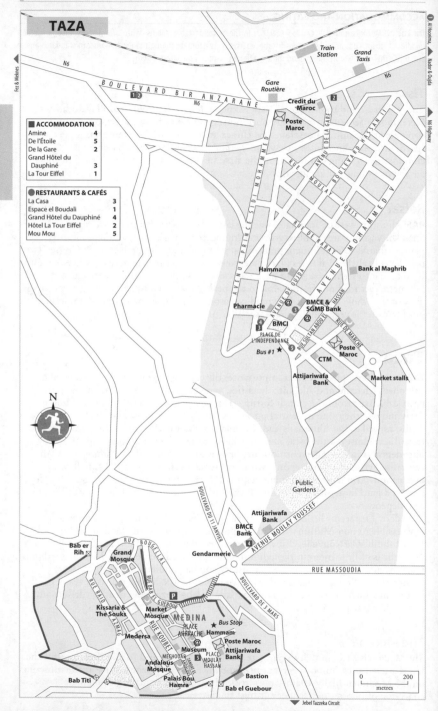

TAZA

Fez & Meknes

Al Hoceima · Nador & Oujda · N6 Highway

N6

BOULEVARD BIR ANZARANE

N6

Train Station

Grand Taxis

Gare Routière

Crédit du Maroc

Poste Maroc

AVENUE DE LA GARE

RUE MOULAY IDRIS

BOULEVARD HASSAN II

AVENUE PRINCE SIDI MOHAMMED

RUE DE RABAT

AVENUE MOHAMMED V

ACCOMMODATION
Amine	4
De l'Étoile	5
De la Gare	2
Grand Hôtel du Dauphiné	3
La Tour Eiffel	1

RESTAURANTS & CAFÉS
La Casa	3
Espace el Boudali	1
Grand Hôtel du Dauphiné	4
Hôtel La Tour Eiffel	2
Mou Mou	5

Hammam

Bank al Maghrib

Pharmacie

AVENUE DE OUJDA

AVENUE HASSAN

BMCE & SGMB Bank

BMCI

RUE SULTAN ABDOUL

RUE DE MARCHE

PLACE DE L'INDÉPENDANCE

Bus #1 ★

Poste Maroc

CTM

Attijariwafa Bank

Market stalls

N

Public Gardens

BOULEVARD DU 11 JANVIER

Attijariwafa Bank

BMCE Bank

AVENUE MOULAY YOUSSEF

Gendarmerie

RUE MASSOUDIA

Bab er Rih

RUE BOUGELLAL

RUE RAID R'MIG

RUE BAB EL GUEBOUR

Grand Mosque

Kissaria & The Souks

Market Mosque

RUE KOUBET

P

MEDINA

PLACE AHRRACHE

Bus Stop ★

Hammam

BOULEVARD DE 3 MARS

Medersa

Museum

MECHOUAR

PLACE MOULAY HASSAN

Poste Maroc

Attijariwafa Bank

Andalous Mosque

Bab Titi

Palais Bou Hamra

Bastion

Bab el Guebour

0 ——— 200
metres

Jebel Tazzeka Circuit

The Andalous Mosque
Zanqat el Andalous

The twelfth-century **Andalous Mosque** is the largest building in the southern section of the Medina – though its courtyards are characteristically well concealed from outside view. The minaret is best viewed from the Mechouar.

Palais Bou Hamra
Zanqat el Andalous

The **Palais Bou Hamra**, to the rear of the Andalous Mosque, is the largely ruined and off-limits residence of Bou Hamra, the *Rogui* or pretender to the throne in the early years of the twentieth century. Like most protagonists of the immediate pre-colonial period, Bou Hamra was an extraordinary figure, a former forger, conjurer and saint, who claimed to be the legitimate Shereefian heir and had himself proclaimed Sultan at Taza in 1902.

The name Bou Hamra – "man on the she-donkey" – recalled his means of travel round the countryside, where he won his followers by performing "miracles". One of these involved talking to the dead, which he perfected by the timely burying of a disciple, who would then communicate through a concealed straw; the pronouncements over, Bou Hamra flattened the straw with his foot (presumably not part of the original deal) and allowed the amazed villagers to dig up the by-then-dead witness.

Bou Hamra's own death – after his capture by Sultan Moulay Hafid – was no less melodramatic. He was brought to Fez in a small cage on the back of a camel, fed to the court lions (who refused to eat him), and was eventually shot and burned. Both Walter Harris and Gavin Maxwell give graphic accounts (see p.568 & p.569).

The souks

Taza's **souks** branch off to either side of Rue Koubet, midway between the Andalous and Grand Mosque. Since there are few tourists, these are very much working markets, free of the artificial "craft" goods so often found. The **granary** and the covered stalls of the **kissaria** are also worth a look, in the shadow of the **Market Mosque** (Djemaa es Souk).

Grand Mosque
Rue Koubet

Taza's **Grand Mosque** is historically one of the most interesting buildings in the country, though, like the Andalous, it is so discreetly screened that it's difficult for non-Muslims to gain any glimpse of the interior. Founded in the twelfth century by the Almohad sultan Abd el Moumen, it is probably the oldest Almohad structure in existence, predating even the partially ruined mosque at Tin Mal (see p.382), with which it shares most stylistic features.

Bab er Rih and the bastions

Above the Medina, at **Bab er Rih** (Gate of the Winds), it is possible to get some feeling for Taza's historic and strategic significance. You can see up the valley towards the Taza Gap: the Jebel Tazzeka and the Middle Atlas on one side, and the reddish earth of the Rif behind on the other.

The actual gate now leads nowhere and looks somewhat lost below the road, but it is Almohad in origin and design. So, too, is most of the circuit of walls, which you can follow round by way of a **bastion** (added by Moulay Ismail, in Spanish style) back to Place Moulay Hassan.

ARRIVAL AND DEPARTURE   **TAZA**

Most of the transport options are conveniently located close to each other to the north of the Ville Nouvelle, though it's a steep 20-minute uphill walk from here to Pl de l'Indépendance. Petits taxis constantly ply the route between the train and bus stations, Pl de l'Indépendance, and the Medina; local bus #1 travels between the latter two.

2

By train The train station (Le Gare Taza) is at the north end of the Ville Nouvelle, 1km from Pl de l'Indépendance.

Destinations Casablanca (3 direct & 4 connecting daily; 6hr 30min); Fez (7 daily; 2hr); Guercif (6 daily; 1hr); Marrakesh (4 connecting daily; 9hr 30min); Meknes (5 direct & 3 connecting daily; 3hr); Nador (2 direct & 2 connecting daily; 4hr); Rabat (3 direct & 4 connecting daily; 6hr); Tangier (2 direct & 1 connecting daily; 8hr).

By bus CTM operates from just off Pl de l'Indépendance, while all other companies operate from a chaotic open rank on Bd Bir Anzarane, about 300m west of the train station. Very few routes originate in Taza, so book ahead or arrive early. Most direct services to the coast leave very early in the morning.

Destinations Aknoul (3 daily; 1hr 30min); Al Hoceima (2 CTM & 4 other daily; 3hr 30min); Berkane (1 CTM & 2 others daily; 4hr 15min); Casablanca (6 CTM & 9 others daily; 7hr 30min); Fez (9 CTM daily & others roughly hourly; 2hr 30min); Guercif (1 CTM daily & others roughly hourly; 1hr); Meknes (5 CTM & 4 others daily; 3hr 15min); Nador (4 CTM & over 10 others daily; 2hr 30min); Oujda (4 CTM daily & others roughly hourly; 3hr); Rabat (6 CTM & 9 others daily; 6hr); Tangier (3 CTM daily; 8hr); Taourirt (1 CTM daily & others roughly hourly; 2hr).

By grand taxi Grands taxis operate from their own, almost hidden, rank 300m east of the train station. Those heading for Fez run throughout the day. For Al Hoceima and Nador, you may first have to catch a grand taxi to Aknoul and/or Kassita. From Aknoul you can also catch sporadic grands taxis across the southern slopes of the Rif to Taounate on the Route de l'Unité.

Destinations Aknoul (1hr); Fez (1hr 30min); Guercif (45min); Kassita (2hr); Oujda (3hr). Occasionally direct to Al Hoceima (2hr 45min).

ACCOMMODATION

Taza doesn't have a great choice of accommodation but you should find a room any time of year. Don't be shy to ask for a discount during the colder months or for more than one night.

★ **Amine 3** Av Moulay Youssef ☎0535 672921, ⓦhotelamine-taza.com. Slightly garish, tiled rooms, plus an in-house restaurant that provides the usual bread and pastry breakfast. A possible drawback is its location, neither in the Medina nor the Ville Nouvelle nor near any public transport options. BB **368dh**

De l'Étoile Pl Moulay Hassan, the southern extension of Pl Ahrrache ☎0535 270179. This is a bargain cheapie and the only accommodation within the Medina. A friendly, family-run place with twelve decent rooms off a tiled courtyard, all with shared squat toilets. The nearby hammam compensates for the absence of showers. There's not much in the way of places to eat round here but there are kitchen facilities for self-catering. **50dh**

De la Gare Corner of Bd bir Anzarane & Av de la Gare, opposite the train station ☎0535 672448, ☎0535 670844. The best option in the Ville Nouvelle and handy for transport, though a long haul from the Medina. Rooms are off a small shaded courtyard, and many have showers and toilets, and hot water mornings and evenings. There's a popular café next door. Good-value singles (65–100dh). **150dh**

Grand Hôtel du Dauphiné Pl de l'Indépendance ☎0535 673567. Not so grand anymore, this old Art Deco hotel nonetheless offers decent-sized rooms. In the lobby are some interesting photos of French explorers visiting the Friouato caves back in 1951. There's also a ground floor café-restaurant, only good for a pastry breakfast. **280dh**

La Tour Eiffel Bd bir Anzarane ☎0535 671562, ☎0535 671563. A slightly overpriced three-star hotel, with a scale model of the Parisian icon above the front door, located a petit taxi ride from Pl de l'Indépendance. Though lacking any great character, the good-sized carpeted rooms boast all mod cons – ask for a mountain view. There's also a handy lift, and a decent ground floor restaurant. **385dh**

EATING AND DRINKING

Good street food, such as brochettes, sandwiches and *harira* soup can be had from stalls in the Medina, as well as the market on Rue de Marché.

★ **La Casa** 4–6 Av Mohammed V ☎0535 670101. Taza's best dining option, offering all-day breakfasts and mains (20–75dh) that encompass pasta, seafood paella, shawarmas and made-to-order couscous and pastilla – but leave room for the chocolate mousse. The pleasant a/c interior is complemented by a welcome non-smoking policy. Daily 6am–10pm.

Espace el Boudali N6 Highway, 2km east of town ☎0535 212227. On the edge of town, this large roadside complex includes a restaurant offering the usual Moroccan standards, as well as pizzas (mains 30–75dh), a separate *salon de thé* and a toddlers' playground. Daily 8am–10pm.

Mou Mou Av Moulay Youssef, off Pl de L'Indépendance. A popular, compact restaurant, with tables both inside and out, and young, friendly staff. The menu offers a good variety of light meals, including panini, tacos and shawarmas, as well as a few heartier tajines (mains 20–55dh). Daily 10am–10pm.

La Tour Eiffel Bd bir Anzarane ☎0535 671562, ☎0535 671563. This hotel restaurant is worth a try, serving a good selection of fish specialities, including a meze-like selection of fried fish (mains 25dh–85dh). There's also a good

selection of fresh juices, salads and light meals. Daily 7–10.30am, noon–3pm & 7–10pm.

DIRECTORY

Banks Attijariwafa Bank and BMCE are on Av Moulay Youssef and on Pl Moulay Hassan, in the Medina; Crédit du Maroc is on Av de la Gare.

Hammams 34 Av d'Oujda, Ville Nouvelle, and Rue Bab el Guebour, just off Pl Ahrrache, Medina.

Internet Cyber le Bon Coin, Av Mohammed V; Cyber Friwato, Av de Oujda; Cyber Taza Net, Pl Ahrrache (all daily from 8am–11pm).

Post office Rue de Marché, Ville Nouvelle; Pl Moulay Hassan, Medina.

The Cirque du Jebel Tazzeka

A loop of some 123km around Taza, the **Cirque du Jebel Tazzeka** is a scenic, serpentine circuit through forests of cork, oak and cedar, with sweeping vistas over both the Rif and Middle Atlas ranges. Along the way is the immense **Gouffre du Friouato** (Friouato Caves) and the whole route is fertile ground for birdwatching and other wildlife (see box, p.154). If you don't have transport, grand taxi circuits can be arranged from most accommodation in Taza, starting at 250dh for the day.

Heading in an east–west direction from Taza, the **road** starts out curling around below the Medina before climbing to a narrow valley of almond and cherry orchards. Twelve kilometres out of Taza, the *Café Ras el Ma* is worth a pit stop for the aerial views of the village afforded by its shaded terrace. Beyond here, the road, prone to rock avalanches but generally in good condition, loops towards the first pass (at 1198m), passing some great picnic spots and eventually emerging onto the Chiker Plateau. Here, in exceptionally wet years, the **Dayat Chiker** appears as a broad, shallow lake. More often than not, though, it is just a fertile saucer, planted with cereals; geographers will recognize its formation as a classic limestone polje.

Gouffre du Friouato

22km from Taza • Daily 8am–6pm • 3dh

The **Gouffre du Friouato** cave complex, starting 300m below ground level, is said to be the deepest in North Africa – and it feels it, entered by descending into a huge naturally lit "pot", over 30m wide, with over five hundred wall-clinging steps down to a scree-filled base. The sense of descending into the entrails of the earth is exhilarating. The entrance fee will get you as far as the base of the steps – essentially the mouth of the cave – but a more exploratory trip, which takes you 2km into the cave, is available with the charming Youness Kassimi (☎0613 267185; 200dh for up to five; torches and waterproofs available for rent), who is usually found hanging around near the cave's entrance. Warm clothing is essential, and allow around three hours in total.

Jebel Tazzeka National Park

The **Jebel Tazzeka National Park**, formed in 1950 and covering some 120 square kilometres, contains some of the most pristine forest remaining in North Africa, and is considered one of the best managed parks in Morocco. Sitting within the park is the 1980m-high Jebel Tazzeka, whose cedar-topped peak can be accessed by driving 9km up a *piste* that turns off 15km west of Bab Bou Idir, as well as a picnic site, Vallée des Cerfs (Valley of the Stags), set in among moss-covered cork trees and resembling something out of Tolkein's Middle Earth. **Bab Bou Idir** is a low-key *éstivage* (summer resort), 8.5km west of the Gouffre du Friouato; here you'll find an office, café and campsite (open July & Aug), and several good walks, ranging from twenty-minute rambles to eight-hour hikes.

2

WILDLIFE IN THE JEBEL TAZZEKA

The **Jebel Tazzeka National Park** is one of northern Morocco's most rewarding wildlife sites, positioned, as it is, at the point where the Rif merges with the Middle Atlas. The range's lower slopes are covered in cork oak, the prime commercial crop of this area, and interspersed with areas of mixed woodland containing holm oak, the pink-flowered cistus and the more familiar bracken.

These woodland glades are frequented by a myriad of **butterflies** from late May onwards; common varieties include knapweed, ark green fritillaries and Barbary skippers. The forest floor also provides an ideal habitat for **birds** such as the multicoloured hoopoe, with its identifying crest, and the trees abound with the calls of wood pigeon, nuthatch, short-toed treecreeper and various titmice. The roadside telegraph lines also provide attractive hunting perches for such brightly coloured inhabitants as rollers and shrikes, both woodchat and great grey, who swoop on passing insects and lizards with almost gluttonous frequency.

Taza to Oujda

The route from **Taza to Oujda** is as bare as it looks on the map: a semi-desert plain, broken by little more than the odd roadside town. Nonetheless, if you've got time to spare, and transport, there are a couple of recommendable detours.

Msoun

The village of **MSOUN**, 29km east of Taza, just north of the N6 highway sits within a **kasbah** that dates to the reign of Moulay Ismail (1672–1727). Inhabited by a hundred or so members of the semi-nomadic Haoura tribe, the kasbah is still turreted and complete on three sides. You can view its original rainwater cistern and grain silos, alongside the settlement's shop, post office and mosque.

Taourirt

TAOURIRT, the largest town between Taza and Oujda, was the crossroads between the old north–south caravan route linking Melilla and the ancient kingdom of Sijilmassa (see box, p.438), and the Taza corridor between Morocco and Algeria. Taourirt itself is of little interest, save for its large **Sunday souk**, but the peaceful Za Gorges, through which the usually running Oued Za meanders, make a good side trip. Situated about 6km southeast of Taorirt, the road to the gorges unfortunately isn't signposted – it's best to ask for directions at the *Café Sabrin* located on the town's main roundabout.

ARRIVAL AND DEPARTURE   TAZA TO OUJDA

MSOUN

Grands taxis and buses travelling on the N6 highway (rather than the A2 autoroute) can stop at *Motel La Kasbah*, from where the Msoun kasbah is visible 500m north. Services are more frequent (1–2 hourly) during the day. It's also possible to hitch-hike along the N6.

TAOURIRT

Taourirt is a useful transport junction, with trains north to Nador connecting reasonably well with arrivals from

Oujda or Fez.

By train The train station is about 1km south of the town's main roundabout.

Destinations Fez (4 daily; 3hr 40min); Nador (4 daily; 2hr); Oujda (4 daily; 1hr 45min); Taza (4 daily; 1hr 30min).

By bus Buses operate from the *gare routière* on the western edge of town, on the N6.

Destinations Oujda (1 CTM and over 10 others daily; 1hr 20min); Fez (1 CTM and over 10 others daily; 4hr); Taza (1 CTM daily & others roughly hourly; 2hr).

ACCOMMODATION AND EATING

MSOUN

Motel La Kasbah On the N6, about 100m west of the Msoun turnoff ☎ 0535 674651. A friendly place for a

meal or overnight stop, with basic rooms and a café-restaurant serving tajines and *grillés*. There's also a dusty children's playground. **120dh**

TAOURIRT

Mansour N19 Highway south (Debdou direction), 300m south of the main roundabout ☎ 0536 694003. A friendly cheapie in a good location close to the main roundabout. The large rooms are a bit sparse but more than adequate for a night's stopover, with clean tiled floors, comfortable beds and big windows, the street noise usually recedes by 10pm. Bathrooms are shared and clean, with constant hot water. 190dh

Oujda

2

Open and easy-going, with a large and active university, **OUJDA** has that rare quality in Moroccan cities – nobody makes demands on your instinct for self-preservation. Coming from the Rif, it is a surprise to see women in public again, and to re-enter a Gallic atmosphere, as you move out of what used to be Spanish Morocco into the old French Protectorate zone. Morocco's easternmost town, Oujda was the capital of French Maroc Orient and an important trading centre.

Brief history

With its strategic location at the crossroads of eastern and southern routes across Morocco and Algeria, Oujda, like Taza, was always vulnerable to invasion and has frequently been the focus of territorial claims. Founded in the tenth century by Berber chieftain Ziri Ben Attia, it was occupied for parts of the thirteenth and fourteenth centuries by the Ziyanids, whose capital at Tlemcen is today just across the Algerian border. From 1727 until the early nineteenth century Oujda was under Turkish rule – the only town in present-day Morocco to have been part of the Ottoman Empire. Following the French defeat of the Ottomans in Algeria, France twice occupied the town prior to its incorporation within the Moroccan Protectorate in 1912, an early and prolonged association that remains tangible in the city's streets and the locals' attitudes.

In more recent years, Oujda's proximity to the Algerian border and distance from the government in Rabat led to a reputation for dissidence and unrest. This was particularly evident during the Algerian border war in the early 1960s, and again, in the 1980s, in a series of student strikes. Following the restoration of Moroccan–Algerian relations in 1988 the city became truly pan-Maghrebi, with Algerians coming in to shop, and Moroccans sharing in some of the cultural dynamism of western Algeria, particularly Oran, the home of *raï* music. Alas, this is all in the past since the closure of the border in 1994 (see box, p.146), after which Oujda lost most of its passing trade, including a steady flow of tourists. However, Oujda still holds a big *raï* festival each July and this is the time to see the city at its best.

The medina and around

The **Medina**, walled on three sides, lies right in the heart of Oujda and is largely a French reconstruction – obvious by the ease with which you can find your way around. It has an enjoyably active air, with **Place du 16 Août**, the city's main square, at its northwest corner.

Entering from **Bab el Ouahab**, the principal gate, you'll be struck by the amazing variety of food – on both café and market stalls. Olives are Oujda specialities, and especially wonderful if you're about after the September harvest. In the old days, more or less up until the French occupation, it was the heads of criminals, rather than olives, that were displayed here. From the gate, the main street leads to **Place el Attarin**, flanked by a *kissaria* (covered market) and a grand *fondouk*. To the northwest of the *kissaria* is **Souk el Ma**, the irrigation souk. This is where the supply of water used to be regulated and sold by the hour. While no longer in use, some of the old irrigation channels can still be seen here.

Running along the outside of the Medina walls, the **Parc Lalla Aïsha** is a pleasant area to seek midday shade. Following it round to the west takes you to the Bab el Gharbi from which Rue el Ouahda runs north to the old French **Cathédrale Saint**

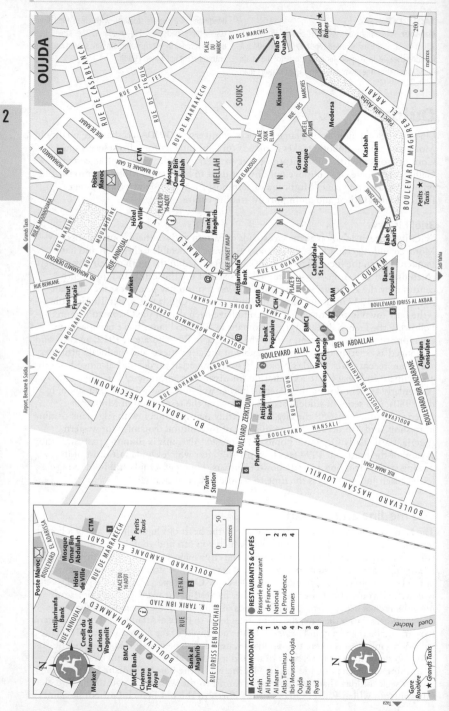

OUJDA

RESTAURANTS & CAFÉS
Brasserie Restaurant de France	1
National	3
Le Providence	2
Ramses	4

ACCOMMODATION
Afrah	2
Al Hanna	5
Al Manar	1
Atlas Terminus	6
Ibis Moussafir Oujda	4
Oujda	7
Raiss	3
Ryad	8

Louis (Mass Sat 6.30pm & Sun 9am). The fonts are dry, and the statue niches empty, but there is a beautiful chapel; for admission, ring at the door of the presbytery at the back, on Rue d'Azila.

Sidi Yahia

SIDI YAHIA, 6km east of Oujda, is a rather unimpressive little oasis for most of the year, with only a run-down park area and a few cafés. However, it's a place of some veneration, purportedly housing the tomb of John the Baptist. There are spectacular **moussems** held here in August and September when almost every shrub and tree in the oasis is festooned with little pieces of cloth, a ritual as lavish and extraordinary as anything in the Catholic Church. There are no regular bus services here; take a grand taxi and haggle over the price depending on how long you want to stay.

ARRIVAL AND DEPARTURE   OUJDA

By plane Oujda–Angad Airport (☎0536 683636) is 12km north of Oujda, and is served by daily flights to Casablanca (1–2 daily; 1hr 10min). Inside the terminal you will find bureaux de change, an ATM, and a number of car rental desks, including Avis (☎0536 701616 or ☎0661 289826), Europcar (☎0536 704416 or ☎0661 171461), and local company Anyway Car (☎0536 708060 or ☎0661 147680). Grands taxis are usually waiting outside to meet all arrivals and charge around 150dh to take up to six people into the city; other destinations are also possible, including Berkane (300dh), Nador (600dh) and Saïdia (300dh). Royal Air Maroc have an office on Bd Mohammed V (☎0536 683909).

By train Oujda is the end (or beginning) of the east–west route that connects in Fez to the remainder of the national rail network. Directly outside the station building are offices for Budget (☎0660 174120) and Supratours (☎0566 89673 or ☎0662 624567). The city centre is an easy 15min walk straight down Bd Zerktouni, or you can flag down a red petit taxi from the junction 75m east of the station.

Destinations Casablanca (2 direct & 1 connecting daily; 10hr); Fez (4 direct daily; 5hr 30min); Guercif (4 direct daily; 2hr 30min); Marrakesh (2 connecting daily; 14hr); Meknes (3 direct daily; 7hr); Nador (1 connecting daily; 4hr); Rabat (2 direct & 1 connecting daily; 9hr); Tangier (2 direct & 1 connecting daily; 10hr); Taourirt (4 direct daily; 1hr 45min); Taza (4 direct daily; 3hr 30min).

By bus The bus station is 500m southwest of the train station at the junction of the N2, N6 (to Taza) and N17 (to

Figuig) highways; it's not very well signposted, look for the large Mohammed VI Mosque next door. Petits taxis congregate outside the station and cost around 6dh to the city centre and Medina. Destinations serviced daily from the main bus station include Al Hoceima, Fez, Figuig (via Bouarfa), Meknes, Nador, Saïdia, Taza and even Tangier (via Tetouan). CTM operate separately from their office on Bd Ramdane el Gadi, just off Pl du 16 Août on the edge of the Medina, as does one of the main long-haul private bus companies, Trans Ghazala.

Destinations Al Hoceima (3 daily; 8hr); Berkane (5 daily; 1hr); Bouarfa/Figuig (1 CTM & 2 others daily; 4hr/6hr); Casablanca (2 CTM & over 5 others daily; 10hr); Fez (4 CTM & over 10 others daily; 6hr); Guercif (1 CTM & 3 others daily; 3hr); Meknes (2 CTM & over 10 others daily; 7hr); Nador (over 10 daily; 2hr 30min); Rabat (2 CTM & over 5 others daily; 8hr 30min); Saïdia (3 daily; 1hr 30min); Tangier (2 CTM and 2 others daily; 11hr); Taza (4 CTM & over 10 others daily; 3hr).

By grand taxi Grands taxis for the airport, Ahfir, Al Hoceima, Berkane, Nador, and Saïdia leave from north of the city centre, at the junction of Bd Mohammed Derfouti and Rue Ibn Abdelmalek; those for Taourirt and Taza leave by the main bus station – you'll have to change at Taza for Fez, and there for most points beyond.

Destinations Ahfir (45min); Berkane (50min); Saïdia (1hr); Taza (3hr). Occasionally direct to Al Hoceima (5hr 30min) & Nador (2hr), more frequently during summer.

INFORMATION

Tourist information Pl du 16 Août (Mon–Fri 8.30am–5.30pm; ☎0536 682036).

Travel agency Carlson Wagonlit, Pl du 16 Août

(☎0536 682520, ⓦcarlsonwagonlit.com); agent for Europcar, Royal Air Maroc and Air France as well as dealing with general travel arrangements.

ACCOMMODATION

Afrah 15 Rue Tafna ☎0536 686533. Located on a busy pedestrianized street, offering comfortable rooms with plenty of hot water all day, and great views across the Medina from its rooftop terrace. Good-value singles (80dh). **120dh**

★ **Al Hanna** 132 Rue de Marrakech ☎&ⓕ0536 686003. The best budget option in town, offering neat and clean rooms, some of them with balconies and some en suite. The vast terrace overlooks Pl du 20 Août and the

2

minaret of the Omar Bin Abdullah mosque. <u>120dh</u>

Al Manar 50 Bd Zerktouni ☎ 0536 688855. Functional mid-range hotel with comfortable rooms, all en suite with a/c and satellite TV. A simple pastry breakfast is served to one side of the hotel's large reception, and there's a separate café & fast food restaurant next door. <u>420dh</u>

Atlas Terminus Pl de la Gare ☎ 0536 711010, ⓦ hotelsatlas.com. Very conveniently located for the train station, this top-notch five-star hotel has all the facilities you'd expect for the price, including a spa, pool and small gym. The large rooms have all the mod cons, and there's three restaurants and a nightclub. Request an inward-facing room, away from the street and club noise. <u>1900dh</u>

Ibis Moussafir Oujda Pl de la Gare ☎ 0536 688202, ⓦ ibishotel.com. This reliable chain hotel right next to the train station delivers the usual characterless rooms; a few have balconies that overlook the busy Bd Abdallah Chefchaouni. A bar and in-house restaurant look out onto pleasant gardens surrounding the swimming pool. <u>550dh</u>

Oujda Bd Mohammed V ☎ 0536 684482, ℗ 0536 685064. While in need of a facelift, the decor in the public spaces of this multistorey 1970s hotel still manages to look quite funky. Rooms are a bit shabby but have satellite TVs, a/c and baths, and the staff are generally friendly. The in-house restaurant is good for breakfast and the rooftop bar has great views over Pl 9 Juillet and the Cathédrale Saint Louis. <u>420dh</u>

Raiss Bd Mohammed V ☎ 0536 703058, ℗ 0536 688008. A friendly, business-class-style hotel with modern, clean rooms that are a touch on the small side but still comfortable and good value– those at the back are quietest. There's a handy lift, a ground-floor café, and parking available. <u>370dh</u>

Ryad Bd Idriss al Akbar ☎ 0536 688353. An ageing but friendly block-type hotel. The rooms are a good size, clean and reasonable for the price, with a few mod cons and bath/shower combos. There's also an average restaurant, as well as a piano bar and nightclub, all open to non-residents but all ageing as well. <u>510dh</u>

EATING AND DRINKING

Oujda has a strong cultural life and is one of the most enjoyable Moroccan cities in which to while away an evening. The focus of much evening activity is Bab el Ouahab, around which you can get all kinds of grilled food as well as *harira* and boiled snails from stalls. On the other side of the Medina there are plenty of eating places on, or just off, Bd Mohammed V and Bd Zerktouni. Those listed here are unlicensed unless mentioned.

Brasserie Restaurant de France Bd Mohammed V ☎ 0536 685987. One of the fancier places in town, offering a selection of mostly French fish and meat dishes (45–120dh). It's located upstairs from a café-patisserie, with a nightclub attached. Licensed. Daily 6–11pm.

★ **Le Providence** Bd Mohammed V. This popular café enjoys a great street-side location opposite Pl 9 Juillet. Besides serving possibly the best espresso in town, there's also a great selection of pastries and cakes, as well as more substantial offerings like pizza, panini and omelettes (20–35dh). Daily 7am–10pm.

National Bd Zerktouni, corner of Bd Allal Ben Abdallah. Popular and long-time stalwart of the city's restaurants,

with an impressive facade and a spiral staircase of black marble that leads up to an often full and slightly stuffy mezzanine level of tables. An old-fashioned *boucherie* restaurant, you can order your meat by the piece or kilo, and then watch it cooked brochette style or in a tajine (30–35dh). Daily 7am–11pm.

Ramses 2 Bd Mohammed V. The downstairs restaurant (daily noon–11pm) serves mainly pizza and panini (mains 15–35dh) whilst the upstairs café and patisserie (daily 5am–11pm) has a great breakfast menu (15–22dh) and fresh juices. Daily: café 5am–11pm; restaurant noon–11pm.

DIRECTORY

Banks & exchange Banque Populaire, Bd Idriss al Akbar; Attijariwafa Bank, Bd Zerktouni; Wafacash bureau de change, Bd Mohammed V (Mon–Fri 8am–8pm, Sat 8am–noon).

Festivals The Festival Internationale du Rai (ⓦ festivalraioujda.com) is a week-long music festival

that takes place each July at various venues around the city.

Internet Cyber Ami Net, Bd Mohammed Derfoufi; Téléboutique, 69 Bd Mohammed V (both daily 9am–11pm).

Post office Bd Mohammed V, north of Pl du 16 Août.

South to Figuig

In past years, before the eruption of civil war in Algeria, there was a well-established travel route from Oujda, south to the ancient date palm oasis of **Figuig**, and across from there into the Algerian Sahara. While the latter is no longer a possibility, those into isolated journeys might still want to consider the route from **Oujda** to **Figuig** – and on from here to the southern Moroccan oasis town of **Er Rachidia** (see p.431).

If you're up for the trip, be warned it's a long, hot haul: 369km from Oujda to Figuig, and a further 393km to Er Rachidia. You can travel by bus or, if you have transport, you can drive: the road is sealed all the way. Whichever way you travel, expect to explain yourself at a number of military checkpoints: this is a sensitive border area (see box, p.31).

The route

En route between Oujda and Figuig there are just a few roadside settlements and mining towns – for coal, copper, manganese and zinc. If you are driving, **Aïn Benimathar**, 83km from Oujda, is a good point to break the journey: the village has a group of kasbahs, an important (and ancient) **Monday souk**, and some grill-cafés. About 4km to its west is a small oasis, **Ras el Aïn**, with a highly seasonal waterfall.

Another possible stop is **Tendrara**, 198km from Oujda, a larger settlement with an important **Thursday souk**; it has a traditional marketplace in the centre and sheep and goats corralled on the outskirts.

At 241km, you reach **Bouarfa**, the region's administrative centre and transport hub, with buses to Er Rachidia (as well as Figuig and Oujda).

2

Fez, Meknes and the Middle Atlas

CARPETS FOR SALE IN FEZ

Fez, Meknes and the Middle Atlas

The undoubted highlight of this region is Fez, the city that has for the past ten centuries stood at the heart of Moroccan history as both an imperial capital and an intellectual as well as spiritual centre. Unique in the Arab world, Fez boasts as many monuments as Morocco's other imperial capitals put together, while the latticework of souks, extending for over a mile, maintain the whole tradition of urban crafts.

Neighbouring **Meknes** has an allure of its own, found throughout the city's pleasant souks and the architecturally rich streets of its sprawling imperial district, a vast system of fortified walls and gates that was largely the creation of Moulay Ismail, the most tyrannical of all Moroccan sultans. Just north of Meknes, the holy mountain town of **Moulay Idriss** and the impressive Roman ruins of **Volubilis** make for a rewarding day-trip.

Though many people heading south from Fez take a bus straight to either Marrakesh or Er Rachidia, it is worth stopping off en route to explore the cedar-covered slopes and remote hinterlands of the **Middle Atlas**. The most popular route passes through the Berber market town of **Azrou** to emerge, via Beni Mellal and the dramatic **Cascades d'Ouzoud**, at Marrakesh. Alterntaively, you could cut southeast from Azrou towards **Midelt** before descending through the Ziz Gorges to Er Rachidia and the vast date-palm oases of the Tafilalt. In between Beni Mellal and Midelt, and accessible from both, lies **Imilchil**, home to Morocco's most famous festival and the midway point along a tortuous route across the High Atlas to the Todra Gorge and Tinghir.

Fez

The history of Fez is composed of wars and murders, triumphs of arts and sciences, and a good deal of imagination.
The Land of an African Sultan, Walter Harris

The oldest of Morocco's four imperial capitals and the most complete medieval city of the Arab world, **FEZ** stimulates all the senses: a barrage of haunting and beautiful

CASCADES D'OUZOUD

Highlights

① Borj Nord and the Merenid tombs The fabled panorama of Fez Medina is pure magic at sunset, accompanied by the call of muezzins. **See p.167 & p.179**

② Medersa Bou Inania, Fez Delicate zellij, intricate stucco and finely carved cedarwood combine to make this the finest Merenid Islamic college in the country. **See p.170**

③ The tanneries Chouwara The hypnotic view of these leather-tanning vats can have barely changed since medieval times. **See p.178**

④ Ville Impériale, Meknes Moulay Ismail's immense walled complex contains ceremonial gateways, vast granaries and the venerated mausoleum of the man himself. **See p.198**

⑤ Volubilis and Moulay Idriss Remarkable Roman and Islamic sites that can be combined on an easy day-trip from Meknes. **See p.211 & p.216**

⑥ Cascades d'Ouzoud If you visit only one waterfall in Morocco, make it these spectacular falls. **See p.236**

⑦ Aït Bouguemez While the hordes flock to Toubkal, trekkers in the know hit the peaceful trails of this glorious High Atlas valley. **See p.237**

⑧ Cirque de Jaffar Exciting *piste* circuit that cuts through foreboding badlands scenery, offering standout views of the mountains to the south. **See p.242**

HIGHLIGHTS ARE MARKED ON THE MAP ON P.164

sounds, infinite visual details and unfiltered odours. It has the French-built **Ville Nouvelle** of other Moroccan cities – familiar and contemporary in looks and urban life – but a quarter or so of Fez's one-million-plus inhabitants continue to live in the extraordinary Medina-city of **Fez el Bali**, which owes little to the West besides electricity and tourists. More than any other city in Morocco, the old town seems suspended in time somewhere between the Middle Ages and the modern world.

Like much of "traditional" Morocco, Fez was "saved" then recreated by the French, under the auspices of **General Lyautey**, the Protectorate's first Resident-General. Lyautey took the philanthropic and startling move of declaring the city a historical monument; philanthropic because he certainly saved Fez el Bali from destruction (albeit from less benevolent Frenchmen), and startling because until then Moroccans

FEZ, MEKNES & THE MIDDLE ATLAS

HIGHLIGHTS
❶ Borj Nord and the Merenid tombs
❷ Medersa Bou Inania, Fez
❸ The tanneries Chouwara
❹ Ville Impériale, Meknes
❺ Volubilis and Moulay Idriss
❻ Cascades d'Ouzoud
❼ Aït Bouguemez
❽ Cirque de Jaffar

were under the impression that Fez was still a living city – the imperial capital of the Moroccan empire rather than a preservable part of the nation's heritage. More conveniently for the French, this paternalistic protection helped to disguise the dismantling of the old culture. By building a new European city nearby – the Ville Nouvelle, now the city's business and commercial centre – then transferring Fez's economic and political functions to Rabat and the west coast, Lyautey ensured the city's eclipse along with its protection.

To appreciate the significance of this demise, you only have to look at the Arab chronicles or old histories of Morocco – in every one, Fez takes centre stage. The city had dominated Moroccan trade, culture and religious life – and usually its politics, too – since the end of the tenth century. It was closely and symbolically linked with the birth of an "Arabic" Moroccan state due to their mutual foundation by **Moulay Idriss I**, and was regarded as one of the holiest cities of the Islamic world after Mecca and Medina. Medieval European travellers described it with a mixture of awe and respect, as a "citadel of fanaticism" yet the most advanced seat of learning in mathematics, philosophy and medicine.

The decline of the city's political position notwithstanding, **Fassis** – the people of Fez – continue to head most government ministries and have a reputation throughout Morocco as successful and sophisticated. What is undeniable is that they have the most developed Moroccan city culture, with an intellectual tradition and their own cuisine, dress and way of life.

Brief history

When the city's founder, Moulay Idriss I, died in 791 AD, Fez was little more than a village on the east bank of the Oued Boukhrareb. It was his son, **Idriss II**, who really began the city's development, at the beginning of the ninth century, by making it his capital and allowing in refugees from Andalusian Cordoba and from Kairouan in Tunisia – at the time, the two most important cities of western Islam. The impact of these refugees on Fez was immediate and lasting: they established separate, walled towns on either riverbank (still distinct quarters today), and provided the superior craftsmanship and mercantile experience for Fez's industrial and commercial growth. It was at this time, too, that the city gained its intellectual reputation – the tenth-century Pope Sylvester II studied here at the **Kairaouine University**, technically the world's first, where he is said to have learned the Arabic mathematics that he introduced to Europe.

The seat of government – and impetus of patronage – shifted south to Marrakesh under the Berber dynasties of the **Almoravids** (1062–1145) and **Almohads** (1145–1248). But with the conquest of Fez by the **Merenids** in 1248, and their subsequent consolidation of power across Morocco, the city regained its pre-eminence and moved

FEZ ORIENTATION

Even if you felt you were getting to grips with Moroccan cities, Fez – with a population of just over a million – is bewildering. The basic layout is simple enough, with a Medina and a French-built **Ville Nouvelle** to its southwest, but here the **Medina** comprises two separate cities: Fez el Bali (Old Fez), in the pear-shaped bowl of the Sebou valley, and Fez el Jedid (New Fez), established on the western edge of the valley during the thirteenth century. **Fez el Jedid**, dominated by a vast enclosure of royal palaces and gardens, is relatively straightforward. But **Fez el Bali**, where you'll want to spend most of your time, is an incredibly intricate web of lanes, blind alleys and souks – it takes two or three days before you even start to feel confident of where you're going. The Medina is vast, and you'll probably find yourself returning from the more far-flung sights in one of the petits taxis stationed by the main gates into Fez el Bali (see p.167); while it's easy enough to walk between Fez el Bali and Fez el Jedid, you're better off taking a taxi between the Medina and the Ville Nouvelle (see box, p.186).

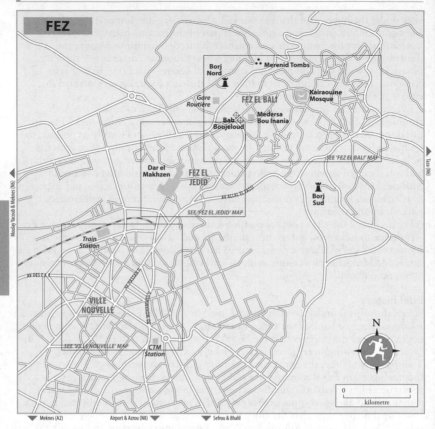

into something of a "golden age". Alongside the old Medina, the Merenids built a massive royal city – **Fez el Jedid** or New Fez – which reflected both the wealth and confidence of their rule. Continued expansion, once again facilitated by an influx of refugees, this time from the Spanish reconquest of Andalusia, helped to establish the city's reputation as "the Baghdad of the West".

After the fall of the Merenids, Fez became more isolated under the **Saadians** and **Alaouites**, and French colonial rule allowed the city little more than a provincial existence. Despite the crucial role the Fassis played in the struggle for **independence** (a time brought to life in Paul Bowles' novel *The Spider's House*), Mohammed V retained the French capital of Rabat, condemning the city to further decline. If **UNESCO** had not inscribed it onto their World Heritage list in 1981, it seems likely that much of the old city would have been threatened by extensive physical collapse.

Fez el Bali

With its mosques, medersas and *fondouks*, back alleys crammed with goods-laden donkeys, and a mile-long labyrinth of souks, there are enough sights in **Fez el Bali** (Old Fez) to fill three or four days just trying to locate them. In this – the apparently wilful secretiveness – lies part of Fez's fascination, and there is much to be said for Paul Bowles' somewhat lofty advice to "lose oneself in the crowd – to be pulled along by it – not knowing where to and for how long…to see beauty where it is least likely to appear". Do the same and you must be prepared to get really lost, but then that is half the fun – and it is all the more uplifting to stumble across the magnificent **Medersa Bou Inania**, or to unexpectedly find yourself on Rue Boutouail and realize that the courtyard you are peering into is that of the **Kairaouine Mosque**, the epicentre of religious life in Morocco.

ESSENTIALS

If you want to avoid coinciding with tour groups, especially in summer, try visiting the main sights in Fez el Bali between noon and 2pm, when the groups stop for lunch. The flow of life eases considerably on Friday, when much of the Medina takes the day off and crowds thin.

ACCESS
There are four principal entrances and exits to Fez el Bali:
Bab Boujeloud The western gate, easily identified by its bright polychrome decoration and the hotels and cafés grouped on either side. Bus #12 runs between Bab Boujeloud and Bab Ftouh, bus #47 between Boujeloud and the train station. See below.
Bab er R'cif A central gate by the square and mosque of the same name, and a convenient entrance, just a few blocks below the Kairaouine Mosque. Buses #19 and #29 run between the square and Bd Mohammed V in the Ville Nouvelle, #19 continuing to the train station, #29 to Pl de l'Atlas; Pl er R'cif is also home to a petit taxi rank. See p.178.
Bab Ftouh The southeast gate at the top of El Andalous.

Bus #10 runs between here and the bus and train stations, #12 to and from Bab Boujeloud; there is also a petit taxi rank here. See p.180.
Bab Guissa The north gate, up at the top of the city by the *Palais Jamaï*, and a convenient point for the Merenid tombs; petits taxis are available by the gate. See p.178.

GETTING AROUND
Routes To help visitors find their way around the Medina, tourism masterminds have scattered star-shaped signs throughout Fez el Bali; the directional markers, positioned at door-top height, correspond with the six colour-coordinated routes in the map produced by the tourist board (see p.187).

Bab Boujeloud and around

Most people begin their exploration of Fez el Bali at **Bab Boujeloud**, a meeting place with a great concentration of cafés and stalls, and where people come to talk and stare. With its polychrome-tiled facades – blue (the traditional colour of Fez) on the outside, facing the ramparts, and green (the colour of Islam) on the interior, facing into the Medina – it's a pretty unmistakeable landmark.

From the square just inside the gate, lanes lead down into the Medina: straight ahead for the craft shops of the **Kissaria Serrajine** and for **Talâa Kebira**, the major artery of Fez el Bali (see p.172); or right, via a handful of patisserie stalls, for **Talâa Seghira**, a lane that runs parallel to Kebira for much of its length and where, in the **Palais M'nebhi**, about halfway down, the agreement for the France-Morocco Protectorate was signed in 1912.

THE BORJ NORD

Like its southern counterpart across the valley, the fortress of **Borj Nord**, perched on the hillside overlooking Bab Boujeloud, was built in the late sixteenth century by the Saadians to *control* the Fassis rather than to defend them. Carefully maintained, the *borj* now houses the country's **arms museum** (daily except Tues 8.30am–noon & 2.30–6.30pm; 10dh; ☎0535 645241), full off daggers encrusted with stones and an interminable display of row upon row of muskets, most of them confiscated from the Riffians in the 1958 rebellion. The pride of place is a cannon 5m long and weighing twelve tonnes, said to be used during the Battle of the Three Kings (see p.535). The main reason for coming up here, though, is for the commanding **views** across the Medina: a spectacular sweep of daily life that, together with the views from the Merenid tombs (a 500m walk round the hillside, along Avenue des Merenides; see box, p.179), constitute the best panorama of the city.

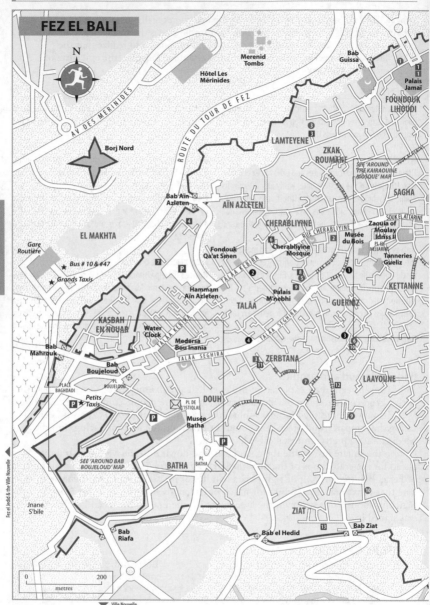

FEZ EL BALI

Musée Batha

Place de l'Istiqlal; entrance on Mahaj el Methab • Daily except Tues 9am–5pm • 10dh

Housed in a late nineteenth-century palace built by Hassan I, the **Musée Batha**
is worth a visit just for its courtyards and gardens, whose cypresses and
myrtle trees provide a respite from the exhausting pace of the Medina. The art and
crafts collections concentrate on local artisan traditions, with displays of carved

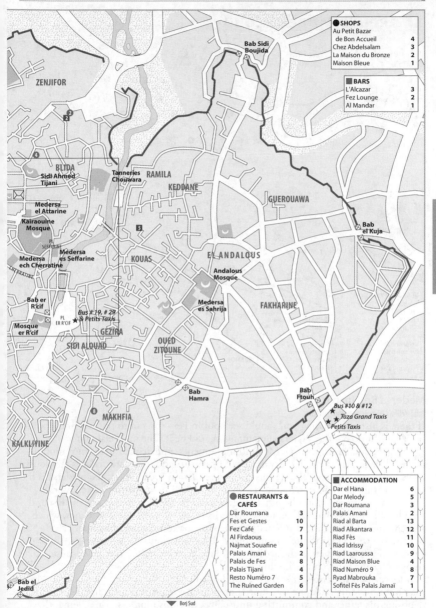

● SHOPS

Au Petit Bazar de Bon Accueil	4
Chez Abdelsalam	3
La Maison du Bronze	2
Maison Bleue	1

■ BARS

L'Alcazar	3
Fez Lounge	2
Al Mandar	1

● RESTAURANTS & CAFÉS

Dar Roumana	3
Fes et Gestes	10
Fez Café	7
Al Firdaous	1
Najmat Souafine	9
Palais Amani	2
Palais de Fes	8
Palais Tijani	4
Resto Numéro 7	5
The Ruined Garden	6

■ ACCOMMODATION

Dar el Hana	6
Dar Melody	5
Dar Roumana	3
Palais Amani	2
Riad al Barta	13
Riad Alkantara	12
Riad Fès	11
Riad Idrissy	10
Riad Laaroussa	9
Riad Maison Blue	4
Riad Numéro 9	8
Ryad Mabrouka	7
Sofitel Fès Palais Jamaï	1

Borj Sud

wood, much of it rescued from the Misbahiya and other medersas (look out for the tenth-century *minbar* recovered from the Andalous Mosque), and examples of calligraphy and local embroidery. Above all, though, it is the pottery from Fez that stands out. The beautiful pieces, dating from the sixteenth century to the 1930s, stress the preservation of age-old techniques rather than innovation.

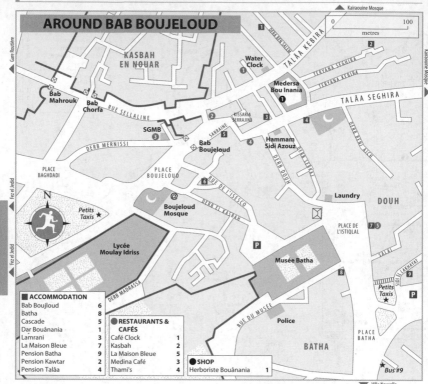

AROUND BAB BOUJELOUD

ACCOMMODATION

Bab Boujloud	6
Batha	8
Cascade	5
Dar Bouânania	1
Lamrani	3
La Maison Bleue	7
Pension Batha	9
Pension Kawtar	2
Pension Talâa	4

RESTAURANTS & CAFÉS

Café Clock	1
Kasbah	2
La Maison Bleue	5
Medina Café	3
Thami's	4

SHOP

Herboriste Bouânania	1

Medersa Bou Inania

Talâa Kebira • Daily 9am–5.30pm • 10dh

If there is just one building you should seek out in Fez – or, not to put too fine a point on it, in Morocco – the **Medersa Bou Inania** should be it. The most elaborate, extravagant and beautiful of all Merenid monuments, immaculate after renovation, it comes close to perfection in every aspect of its construction: its dark cedar is fabulously carved, the zellij tilework classic, the stucco a revelation. In addition, the medersa is the city's only building still in religious use that non-Muslims are permitted to enter.

Set somewhat apart from the other medersas of Fez, the Bou Inania was the last and grandest built by a Merenid sultan. It shares its name with the one in Meknes, which was completed (though not initiated) by the same patron, **Sultan Abou Inan** (1351–58), but the Fez version is infinitely more splendid. Its cost alone was legendary – Abou Inan is said to have thrown the accounts into the river on its completion because "a thing of beauty is beyond reckoning".

At first, Abou Inan doesn't seem the kind of sultan to have wanted a medersa – his mania for building aside, he was more noted for having 325 sons in ten years, deposing his father and committing unusually atrocious murders. The Ulema, the religious leaders of the Kairaouine Mosque, certainly thought him an unlikely candidate and advised him to build his medersa on the city's rubbish dump, on the basis that piety and good works can cure anything. Whether it was this or merely the desire for a lasting monument that inspired him, he set up the medersa as a **rival to the Kairaouine** itself and for a while it was the most important religious building in the city. A long campaign to have the announcement of the time of prayer transferred here failed in the face of the Kairaouine's powerful opposition, but the medersa was granted the status of a **Grand Mosque** – unique in Morocco – and retains the right to say the Friday *khotbeh* prayer.

The interior

The basic **layout** of the medersa is quite simple – a single large courtyard flanked by two sizeable halls (*iwan*) and opening onto an oratory – and is essentially the same design as that of the wealthier Fassi mansions. For its effect it relies on the mass of decoration and the light and space held within. You enter the exquisite marble **courtyard**, the medersa's outstanding feature, through a stalactite-domed entrance chamber, a characteristic adapted from Andalusian architecture. From here, you can gaze across to the **prayer hall** (off-limits to non-believers), which is divided from the main body of the medersa by a small canal. Off to each side of the courtyard are stairs to the upper storey (closed to the public), which is lined by **student cells**.

In the courtyard, the **decoration** – startlingly well preserved – covers every possible surface. Perhaps most striking in terms of craftsmanship are the woodcarving and joinery, an unrivalled example of the Moorish art of *laceria*, "the carpentry of knots". Cedar beams ring three sides of the courtyard and a sash of elegant black Kufic script wraps around four sides, dividing the zellij from the stucco, thus adding a further dimension; unusually, it is largely a list of the properties whose incomes were given as an endowment, rather than the standard Koranic inscriptions. Abou Inan is bountifully praised amid the inscriptions and is credited with the title *caliph* on the foundation stone, a vainglorious claim to leadership of the Islamic world pursued by none of his successors.

The water clock

More or less opposite the medersa entrance, just across Talâa Kebira, Bou Inania's property continues with an extraordinary **water clock** (*magana*), built above the stalls in the road. This was removed around a decade ago for research and possible restoration; the woodwork has now been restored, but the metal parts have yet to be replaced. An enduring curiosity, it consisted of a row of thirteen windows and platforms, seven of which retained their original brass bowls. Nobody has yet been able to discover exactly how it functioned, though a contemporary account detailed how at every hour one of its windows would open, dropping a weight down into the respective bowl.

THE FUNCTION OF MEDERSAS

Medersas – student colleges and residence halls – were by no means unique to Fez. Indeed, they originated in Khorasan in northeastern Iran and gradually spread west through Baghdad and Cairo, where the Medersa al Azhar was founded in 972 AD and became the most important teaching institution in the Muslim world. They seem to have reached Morocco under the Almohads, although the earliest ones still surviving in Fez are Merenid, dating from the late thirteenth century.

The word medersa means "**place of study**", and there may have been lectures delivered in some of the prayer halls. However, most medersas served as little more than **dormitories**, providing room and board to poor (male) students from the countryside, so that they could attend lessons at the mosques. In Fez, where students might attend the Kairaouine University for ten years or more, rooms were always in great demand and "key money" was often paid by the new occupant. Although medersas had largely disappeared from most of the Islamic world by the late Middle Ages, the majority of those in Fez remained in use right up into the 1950s. Non-Muslims were not allowed into the medersas until the French undertook their repair at the beginning of the Protectorate, and were banned again (this time by the colonial authorities) when the Kairaouine students became active in the struggle for independence.

Since then, **restoration** work, partly funded by UNESCO, has made medersas more accessible, although it will still be some while before all the work is complete – at the time of writing, for example, the Medersa es Seffarine and the Medersa es Sahrija were both closed for renovation. As restoration across the city continues, accessibility is impossible to predict.

Clocks had great **religious significance** during the Middle Ages in establishing the time of prayer, and it seems probable that this one was bought by Abou Inan as part of his campaign to assert the medersa's pre-eminence. Fassi conspiracy theories are told to account for its destruction, most revolving around the miscarriage of a Jewish woman passing below at the time of its striking and a Jewish sorcerer casting the evil eye on the whole device – the building to which the clock is fixed, once owned by a rabbi, is popularly known as "The House of the Magician".

Talâa Kebira

Cutting through Fez el Bali and running all the way down to the Kairaouine Mosque (albeit under different names), **Talâa Kebira** is the Medina's principal thoroughfare, a shop-laden route that's interesting less for specific sights than the accumulation of stimuli that barrage the senses along the way: camel heads advertising the location of the local butchers; vendors bartering in the spice and slipper souks; and donkeys, seemingly everywhere, hauling their heavy loads up and down the rutted lanes.

3

The fondouks

Along Talâa Kebira's first main stretch, heading down from the Medersa Bou Inania, you pass a number of old **fondouks**. Before the advent of French-style cafés in Morocco at the beginning of the twentieth century, the *fondouks* – or caravanserais as they were called in the East – formed the heart of social life outside the home. They provided rooms for traders and richer students, and frequently became centres of vice, intrigue and entertainment. There were once around two hundred in Fez el Bali, and many of those that survive now serve as small factories or warehouses, often graced with beautiful fourteenth- and fifteenth-century decorations. The most interesting of the five or so in the area is **fondouk Qa'at Smen**, at no. 89, which was originally a Merenid prison, fitted out with solid colonnades and arches. It's still is use, as a place to buy salted butter (*smen*), olive oil and a dozen types of honey, though the traditional *jubbana* (lidded jars) that once held the goods were replaced by plastic barrels a long time ago.

Rue Cherabliyine

As Talâa Kebira becomes **Rue Cherabliyine**, so, too, the surroundings change. A district of leather stalls and cobblers, the aptly named "Road of the Slippermakers" is one of the best areas for buying handmade traditional **babouches** (leather slippers). Keep an eye out for the sophisticated-looking grey and black pairs that are unique to Fez; prices vary depending on the quality of the leather (the best type is *ziouani*, or goat skin) and stitching.

Like all neighbourhoods in Fez, Cherabliyine has its focal **mosque** – a fourteenth-century structure with an attractive minaret – but more interesting is the mosque's **washroom**, on the opposite side of the street, open to the elements and clearly neglected but still in its original state, with a horseshoe of toilets surrounding a central ablutions area.

Souk el Attarine

The sweet smell of cinnamon, cumin and cloves wafting around the arched gateway at the end of Rue Tarafine (Talâa Kebira) denotes your entry into the covered **Souk el Attarine**, or "Souk of the Spice Vendors", once the formal heart of the old city and its richest and most sophisticated shopping district. It was traditionally around the grand mosque of a city that the most expensive commodities were sold and kept, a pattern more or less maintained as you approach the Kairaouine, as the spices give way to silk traders and shops selling finely embroidered *takchitas* (two-piece wedding garments).

Souk el Henna

Just off Souk el Attarine; accessed through an arch opposite the *Dar Saada* restaurant, or from Derb Fakharine

A quiet, tree-shaded square **Souk el Henna** adjoins what was once the largest madhouse in the Merenid empire, said to be the first asylum in the world to implement musical therapy as a method for treating patients. Stalls here continue to sell **henna** and other traditional cosmetics such as *kohl* eyeliner (historically antimony but usually now lead sulphide, which is cheaper but also toxic), and lip reddener made from crushed poppy petals; on the southern side of the square there is a huge pair of scales used for weighing the larger deliveries. In addition, several outlets here offer the more esoteric ingredients required for medical cures, aphrodisiacs and the odd magical spell.

That said, these are gradually becoming outnumbered, as **pottery stalls** encroach on this traditional pharmacological business. Cheap but often striking in design, the pieces include Fassi pots, which are usually blue and white or simple black on earthenware; those from Safi, the pottery most commonly exported from Morocco and distinguished by its heavy green or blue glazes; and from Salé, often elaborate modern designs on a white glaze.

Place en Nejjarine and around

Accessed off Souk el Attarine, along Derb Fakharine; or from Derb Dermami, down the steps near the end of Zkak Lahjar (Talâa Seghira)

The beautiful canopied Nejjarine fountain, the best known of several mosaic fountains in the Medina, is the focal point of picturesque **Place en Nejjarine**. The square is surrounded by a tangle of workshops making mule saddles and stirrups or huge, gaudy silver wedding chairs, and souks filled with the sound and smell (one of Morocco's finest) of carpenters (the *nejjarine*) chiselling away at sweet cedarwood.

Faux guides may try and lead you to the **tanneries** here, but note that these are the smaller tanneries Guéliz and not the more famous tanneries Chouwara, near Place Seffarine (see p.178).

Musée du Bois

Place en Nejjarine • Daily 10am–5pm • 20dh; 10dh for a drink on the terrace

Still used until a few years ago as a hostel for students at the nearby Kairaouine University, the imposing eighteenth-century Nejjarine *fondouk* now houses the delightful **Musée du Bois**. Of particular interest are the fourteenth- to eighteenth-century cedarwood friezes exhibited on the first floor, and, on the floor above, a much more modern *rabab* (string instrument) beautifully inlaid with mother-of-pearl. However, it is the interior of the building itself that is worth the entrance fee, wonderfully restored after six years of work – a small exhibit on the roof terrace covers the renovation, where there's also a **café** offering views over the Medina.

Musée Ryad Belghazi

16 Derb el Ghorba, signed from Place en Nejjarine, the Karaouine Mosque and Talâa Seghira • Daily 9.30am–5.45pm • 40dh • ☎ 0535 741178

Tucked away in a maze of narrow lanes south of Place en Nejjarine, the **Musée Ryad Belghazi** is housed in a traditonal riad built in the seventeenth century and now owned by the family of the same name. The museum explains the basic layout and features of this type of architecture, and gives you an insight into how a Fassi merchant's house might have looked in the 1800s, with displays of carpets, kaftans, jewellery and furniture.

Zaouia of Moulay Idriss II and around

Accessed from Place en Nejjarine, along Derb Bab Moulay Ismail; or through the first archway on the right on Souk el Attarine • Closed to non-Muslims

The major landmark south of Souk el Attarine is the **Zaouia Moulay Idriss II**, one of the holiest buildings in Fez. The shrine has dominated this part of the Medina for over five

THE CULT OF MOULAY IDRISS

There is no particular evidence that **Moulay Idriss II** was a very saintly *marabout*, but as the effective founder of Fez and son of the founder of the Moroccan state he has considerable **baraka**, the magical blessing that Moroccans invoke, and his moussem (see box, p.196) brings the city to a standstill. Originally, it was assumed that Idriss had been buried near Volubilis, like his father, but in 1308 an uncorrupted body was found on the spot where his *zaouia* now stands and the cult was launched. Presumably, it was an immediate success, since in addition to his role as the city's patron saint, Idriss has an impressive roster of **supplicants**: this is the place to visit for poor strangers arriving in the city, for boys before being circumcised and for women wanting to facilitate childbirth – and for some long-forgotten reason, Idriss is also the protector of Morocco's sweetmeat vendors.

hundred years, but was rebuilt in the eighteenth century by Sultan Moulay Ismail – his only act of pious endowment in the city. The wooden bar that breaches the foot of Derb Bab Moulay Ismail, the lane running off the southeast corner of Place en Nejjarine, marks the beginning of the shrine's *horm*, or **sanctuary precinct**. Until the French occupation of the city in 1911, this was as far as Christians, Jews or mules could go, and any Muslim who went beyond it had the right to claim asylum from prosecution or arrest. These days, non-Muslims are allowed to walk around the outside of the *zaouia*, and although they are not permitted to enter, it is possible to glimpse discreetly inside the shrine and even see the saint's tomb.

Ducking under the bar, head up Derb Bab Moulay Ismail – full of stalls selling silverware and other devotional offerings – to the women's entrance, where you can look in from the doorway; the fifteenth-century **tomb of Moulay Idriss II** is on the left amid a scene of intense and apparently High Baroque devotion all around. Women, Idriss's principal devotees, burn candles and incense here, then proceed around the corner of the precinct to touch or make offerings at a brass grille that opens directly onto the tomb. A curious feature, common to many *zaouias* but rarely visible from the outside, are the numerous European clocks – prestigious gifts and very popular in the nineteenth century, when they were shipped from Manchester by Fassi merchant families (their main export base for the cotton trade).

The kissaria

From the end of Derb Bab Moulay Ismail, you can make your way round to the other side of the *zaouia*, along the way passing through a tight network of lanes, the **kissaria, or covered market**, which are full of clothes stalls selling *jellabas* and *hendiras* (embroidered wedding shawls). If you want a **fez hat**, this is the place to come – the best shop is a small, plain-looking stall at the southeast corner of the *zaouia* (daily 9am–8pm), where you can pick up a stylish headpiece for around 150dh.

Medersa el Attarine

Entrance at the eastern end of Souk el Attarine • Daily 9am–5pm • 10dh

After the Bou Inania, the **Medersa el Attarine** is the finest of the city's medieval colleges, graced by an incredible profusion and variety of patterning. For all the startling richness of its zellij, wood and stucco, the decoration retains an air of ease, and the building's elegant proportions are never threatened with being overwhelmed. The medersa was completed in 1325 by the Merenid sultan, Abou Said Othman, and is thus one of the earliest in Fez. Its general lightness of feel is achieved by the simple device of using pairs of symmetrical arches to join the pillars to a single weight-bearing lintel.

On your way in, stop awhile in the **entrance hall**, whose zellij decoration is perhaps the most complex in the city. Its circular pattern, based on an interlace of pentagons and five-pointed stars, perfectly demonstrates the intricate science (and philosophy)

THE FEZ

The red cylindrical hat with its black tassel, more correctly known as a Fassi *tarbouche*, is not only worn and manufactured in Fez but as far afield as Egypt and Syria. In the eighteenth and nineteenth centuries, **the fez** became associated with the Ottoman Empire and in some places it was donned as a mark of support, a gesture that led to it being banned by Kemal Atatürk when he took power in Turkey and abolished the empire. The fez is also going out of fashion in its home town, and tends to be worn only by older men – most young men now prefer the Tunisian *chechia* or baseball caps.

employed by the craftsmen, the patterns radiating – as Titus Burckhardt notes in *Moorish Art in Spain* – from "a single point as a pure simile for the belief in the oneness of God, manifested as the centre of every form or being".

Around the first floor, out of bounds to visitors while it's being renovated, are **cells** for over sixty students, which operated as an annexe to the Kairaouine University until the 1950s. If you can get onto it, the medersa's roof affords one of the most complete possible **views of the Kairaouine Mosque**.

Kairaouine Mosque
Closed to non-Muslims

The **Kairaouine Mosque** was the largest mosque in Morocco until the construction of the new Hassan II Mosque in Casablanca – and vies with Cairo's Al-Azhar for the title of the world's oldest university. It remains today the fountainhead of the country's religious life, governing, for example, the timings of Ramadan and the other Islamic festivals. An old Fassi saying goes that all roads in Fez lead to the Kairaouine, a claim that retains some truth.

The mosque was founded in 859 AD by the daughter of a wealthy refugee from the city of Kairouan in Tunisia, but its present **dimensions**, with sixteen aisles and room for twenty thousand worshippers, are essentially the product of tenth- and twelfth-century reconstructions: first by the great Caliph of Córdoba, Abd er Rahman III, and later under the Almoravids.

For non-Muslims, who cannot enter the mosque's courts and prayer halls, the Kairaouine is a rather elusive sight. The building is so thoroughly enmeshed into the surrounding houses and shops that it is impossible to get any clear sense of its shape, and at most you can get only partial views of it from the adjoining rooftops or through the four great **entrances** to its main courtyard – the door just past *Café Boutouail* (see p.191) is usually open, while following **Smat el Adoul**, the first lane to the right after this, lets you peek through a number of gates into the mosque's rush-matted and round-arched interior as you loop back to the Medersa el Attarine.

Nobody seems to object to tourists gaping through the gates, though inevitably the centrepieces that would give order to all the separate parts – the main aisle and the main *mihrab* – remain hidden from view. The overall **layout** was inspired by the Mezquita in Córdoba: the courtyard is open to the sky, with a large fountain at its centre and two smaller ones under porticoes at each side, added in the seventeenth century and based on originals in the Alhambra in Granada.

Place Seffarine and around

A wedge-shaped square on the southeastern side of the Kairaouine Mosque, **Place Seffarine** is almost wilfully picturesque, with its metalworkers hammering away at immense iron and copper cauldrons, and a gnarled old tree at its centre. A chance for a breather after the intensity of the central Medina, the square is a good place to stop for a drink (see p.191) and to get your bearings before taking one of a number of onward routes; the lanes off the southern end of Place Seffarine are filled with **souks** specializing in gold and silver jewellery and used metal goods, especially ornate pewter teapots.

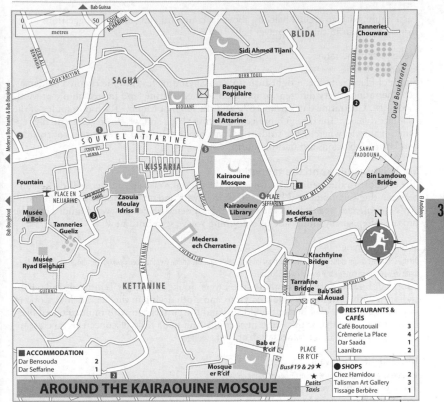

AROUND THE KAIRAOUINE MOSQUE

Kairaouine Library

On the western side of Place Seffarine • Closed to the public

Established by the Kairouan refugees in the ninth century, then stocked by virtually the entire contents of Córdoba's medieval library, the **Kairaouine Library** once held the greatest collection of Islamic, mathematical and scholarly books outside Baghdad. That much of the library was lost or dissipated in the seventeenth century is a pointed marker of Fez's decline. Restored and in use once more by scholars hunched over texts in the large study hall, it is again one of the most important in the Arab world.

Despite the studious atmosphere of the library, the **university** here has been largely usurped by modern departments around Fez el Jedid and the Ville Nouvelle, and dispersed throughout Morocco. Until recent decades, though, it was the only source of Moroccan higher education. Entirely traditional in character, studies comprised courses on Koranic law, astrology, mathematics, logic, rhetoric and poetry – very much as at the medieval universities of Europe. Study, of course, was an entirely male preserve.

Medersa es Seffarine

Place Seffarine, opposite the Kairaouine Library • Closed for renovation at the time of writing

The earliest of the Fez colleges, the **Medersa es Seffarine** was, before renovation began, the only one still used as a hostel for students studying at the Kairaouine. Built around 1270 – 35 years before the Attarine, and over eighty before the Bou Inania – the Seffarine is unlike all the other medersas in that it takes the exact form of a traditional

Fassi house, with an arched balcony above its courtyard and still with suggestions of former grandeur in the lofty prayer hall.

Medersa ech Cherratine

Rue Cherratine • Daily 9am–4pm • 10dh

South of Place Seffarine, a right turn up Rue Cherratine leads to the restored **Medersa ech Cherratine**, a very different proposition to the Seffarine (and indeed all the previous medersas). Cherratine dates from 1670 and the reign of Moulay Rachid, founder of the Alaouite dynasty. The design represents a shift in scope and wealth to an essentially functional style, whereby the student cells are grouped around three corner courtyards and latrines/ablutions around the fourth.

Souk Sabbaghine and the tanneries

The antidote to the medieval prettiness of the central souks and medersas is the region between the Kairaouine and El Andalous: the **dyers' and tanners' souks** on which the city's commercial wealth from the tenth to the nineteenth century was founded and the prosaic, often smelly, underside of everything you've seen until now.

Souk Sabbaghine

Off the southeast corner of Place Seffarine, then right immediately before the bridge over the Oued Boukhrareb; also accessible from the south by bus or petit taxi to Place er R'cif (see opposite)

Short but bizarre, **Souk Sabbaghine** (the Dyers' Souk, or Rue des Teinturiers in French) is draped with fantastically coloured yarns and cloth drying in the heat. Below, workers in grey overalls toil over ancient cauldrons and the gutters run with multicoloured dyes in an atmosphere that is thick and mysterious, and not a little disconcerting so close to one of the city's main entrances, **Bab er R'cif**.

The tanneries Chouwara

Rue Chouwara • Small fee (10dh is usual) requested by the *gardiens*

There is a compulsive fascination about the **tanneries Chouwara**, the biggest in Fez and the most striking sight in the Medina. Every morning, when the tanneries are at their most active, cascades of water pour through holes that were once the windows of houses, hundreds of skins lie spread out on the rooftops to dry, while amid the vats of dye and pigeon dung (the white vats at the back), an unbelievably Gothic fantasy is enacted as tanners treat the hides. The rotation of colours in the honeycombed **vats** follows a traditional sequence – yellow (supposedly "saffron", in fact turmeric), red (poppy), blue (indigo), green (mint) and black (antimony) – although vegetable dyes have largely been replaced by chemicals, to the detriment of workers' health.

This "innovation" and the occasional rinsing machine aside, there can have been little change here since the sixteenth century, when Fez replaced Córdoba as the pre-eminent city of **leather production**. As befits such an ancient system, the ownership is also intricately feudal: the foremen run a hereditary guild and the workers pass down their specific jobs from generation to generation.

For all the stench and voyeurism involved, there is a kind of sensuous beauty about the tanneries. However, it is a guilty pleasure, as one glance across at the gallery of camera-touting foreigners snapping away will testify.

North to Bab Guissa

From Rue Hormis, the first lane on the left just inside the entrance to Souk el Attarine, a network of alleys wend their way northwards through a series of produce markets before emerging at **Bab Guissa**. The sights en route are more curiosities than monuments, and are troubled by few tourists – which, of course, is part of the area's appeal. About halfway between Souk el Attarine and the gate, the route passes the western end of **Souk Achebine**, whose historical function as a traditional-medicine souk

A TOMB WITH A VIEW

Up above Bab Guissa, the crumbling remnants of the **Merenid tombs** stand vigil over the sprawling Medina, a particularly atmospheric place at dawn or dusk, when the call to prayer sweeps across Fez el Bali. From this superb vantage point you can delineate the more prominent of Fez's reputed 365 mosque minarets. At sunset, the sky swarms with a frenzy of starlings, egrets and alpine swifts adding further spectacle to the scene. All around you are spread the Muslim cemeteries that flank the hills on each side of Fez, while below, the city's major **monuments** protrude from the hubbub of rooftops. The pyramid-shaped roof of the Zaouia of Moulay Idriss II is easily defined. To its left are the two minarets of the Kairaouine Mosque: Burj en Naffara or the Trumpeter's Tower (the shorter of the two) and the original minaret. The latter, slightly thinner in its silhouette than usual and with an unusual whitewashed dome, is the oldest Islamic monument in the city, built in 956 AD.

The sounds of the city, the stillness and the contained disorder below all seem to make manifest the mystical significance that Islam places on urban life as the most perfect expression of culture and society.

3

survives in the shop on the left-hand side that still sells snakeskins, chameleons and other supposed "cures".

Up towards the northern walls, a right turn before the gate leads to the *Palais Jamaï*, whose luxury comes as quite a shock to the Medina below; the view from the bar terrace merits the drink prices if you fancy a splurge (see p.194). From Bab Guissa, you can take a petit taxi to Bab Boujeloud or the Ville Nouvelle, or head up the hill behind the gate to the **Merenid tombs**, an astounding spot to watch dusk descend over the Medina (see box above); the route to and from the tombs can lead through some unsavoury areas, so it's best to catch a petit taxi (5dh).

El Andalous

The eastern quarter of Fez el Bali, across the Oued Boukhrareb from the Kairaouine, is known as **El Andalous**, after the Arab imigrants who settled here after fleeing Córdoba in the early ninth century. For the first three centuries of their existence, El Andalous and the Kairaouine (settled just seven years later) were separate walled cities – the name for the most northerly bridge across the river, Bin Lamdoun, translates as "The Bridge Between the Cities" – and the intense rivalry between them often erupted as factional strife. It still lingers enough to give each area a distinct identity, although since the thirteenth century this has been a somewhat one-sided affair: according to Fassis, the Andalousis had more beautiful women and braver soldiers, but the Kairaouinis have always had the money.

Whatever the truth of the tale, nearly all of the most famous Andalusian scholars and craftsmen lived and worked on the other side of the river, and as a result the atmosphere in the quarter has a somewhat provincial character. Monuments are few and far between – and with the closure of the Medersa es Sahrija due to ongoing restoration, off-limits to visitors – and the streets are quieter and predominantly residential. As such, it can be a pleasant quarter to spend the early evening and get caught up in the rhythms of daily life in Fez el Bali: most street trading here revolves around daily necessities, providing a link between the "medieval" town and continuing urban life, and your relationship with the city changes accordingly as you cease to be a consuming tourist – there is a near-total absence of "guides" and hustlers.

GETTING TO EL ANDALOUS

From the Kairaouine Three bridges connect the Kairaouine Mosque and the tanneries quarter with El Andalous: the Bin Lamdoun, reached down the right-hand branch of Rue Mechattine; humpbacked Krachfiyine, at the bottom of the Dyers' Souk; and the Tarrafine, north of Pl er R'cif.

From Pl er R'cif The Tarrafine is the closest bridge to Pl er R'cif, which is served by buses #19 and #29 from the

Ville Nouvelle as well as petits taxis from across the city. **From Bab Ftouh** You can also begin your exploration at Bab Ftouh, at the top of El Andalous, a stop for buses #10 from the Ville Nouvelle and #12 from Bab Boujeloud; there's also a petit taxi rank here.

Medersa es Sahrija

Derb Yasmina • Closed for renovation at the time of writing

The quarter's most interesting monument, the **Medersa es Sahrija** is generally rated the third finest medersa in the city after the Attarine and Bou Inania. Anywhere else but Fez it would be a major sight, but such is the brilliance of the more accessible monuments, it rarely receives the attention it deserves. What makes it worth the visit (aside from the unusual, large pool in the courtyard that gives the medersa its name) is the considerable range and variety of the original decoration: the zellij is among the oldest in the country, and the palmettes and pine cones of the cedarwood carving hark back to Almohad and Almoravid motifs – and it should be looking even better than ever once the current restoration programme is complete. Built around 1321 by Sultan Abou el Hassan, the Sahrija is more or less contemporary with the Attarine and a slightly earlier version of his medersa in Meknes (see p.205), which it resembles in many ways.

Andalous Mosque

Derb Andalous • Closed to non-Muslims

Fronting the square just along the lane from the Medersa es Sahrija and built at the highest point of the valley, the **Andalous Mosque** was founded in the late ninth century (allegedly by the sister of the woman who founded the Kairaouine Mosque) and saw considerable enlargements under the Almoravids and Merenids. There's little to be seen other than the monumental entrance gates, a thirteenth-century Almohad addition designed by artisans from Granada and most notable for their beautifully carved wooden awning.

Bab Ftouh and around

A strange no-man's-land of run-down houses, the region south of the Andalous Mosque and extending beyond **Bab Ftouh** was once a leper colony and is traditionally known as a quarter of necromancers, thieves, madmen and saints. The **cemetery** that covers the hills just outside the gate, the largest in Fez, is home to the whitewashed **koubba of Sidi Ali Ben Harazem**, a twelfth-century mystic who has been adopted as the patron saint of students and the mentally ill; Harazem's *koubba* is the squat, green-roofed building that dominates the skyline. The saint's moussem, held in the spring, is one of the city's most colourful; in past centuries, it was often the cue for riots and popular insurrections.

Fez el Jedid

Unlike Fez el Bali, whose development and growth seems to have been almost organic, **Fez el Jedid** ("New Fez") was a planned city, built by the Merenids at the beginning of their rule, under Sultan Abou Youssef in 1276, as a practical and symbolic seat of government.

The chronicles present the Merenids' decision to site their city some distance from Fez el Bali as a defence strategy, though this would seem less against marauders than to safeguard the new dynasty against the Fassis themselves – and it was only in the nineteenth century that the walls between the old and new cities were finally joined. It was not an extension for the people in any real sense, being occupied largely by the vast royal palace of **Dar el Makhzen** and a series of garrisons. This process continued with the addition of the **Mellah** – the Jewish ghetto – at the beginning of the fourteenth century; forced out of Fez el Bali after one of the periodic pogroms,

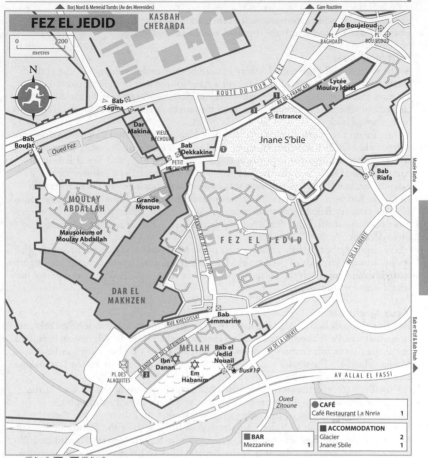

the Jews provided an extra barrier (and scapegoat) between the sultan and his Muslim faithful, not to mention a source of ready income conveniently located by the palace gates.

GETTING TO FEZ EL JEDID

On foot Fez el Jedid can be reached on a 10min walk from Bab Boujeloud, via the Jnane S'bile; locals advise against walking from the Ville Nouvelle on your own (see box, p.186). **By bus** Bus #19 runs from the Ville Nouvelle to Pl er R'cif in Fez el Bali, stopping at Bab el Jedid Nouail, the southern entrance to the Mellah from Rue de la Liberté. **By petit taxi** There's a petit taxi rank at Pl des Alaouites, near the Dar el Makhzen, at the southern tip of Fez el Jedid.

Jnane S'bile

Entrances along Avenue des Français (Av Moulay Hassan) • Tues–Sun 10am–5pm

The scale shifts as you walk to Fez el Jedid from Bab Boujeloud, the labyrinthine alleyways and souks of the Medina giving way to a stretch of massive walls. Within them spread the public gardens of **Jnane S'bile** (sometimes called the Jardins de Boujeloud), its pools diverted from the Oued Fez. The latter are a vital lung for the old city – if everything gets too much, wander in, lounge on the grass and spend an hour or two at the tranquil café-restaurant at their southwestern corner (see p.191), adjacent to an old water wheel that once supplied water to the gardens.

Petit Mechouar

At the western end of Avenue Moulay Hassan lies the enclosed sqaure of the **Petit Mechouar**, once the focus of city life and a stage for the sort of snake charmers, acrobats and storytellers that are still found in Marrakesh's Jemaa el Fna; they were cleared out when the *mechouar* was closed for repairs in the mid-1970s and have never been allowed back.

The gate on the northern side of the square is the monumental **Bab Dekkakine**, more correctly known as **Bab Sebâa** (Gate of the Lions), a thirteenth-century Merenid structure that was the main approach to the Dar el Makhzen and Fez el Bali until King Hassan II realigned the site in 1967–71. It also served as a gallows for the Infante Ferdinand of Portugal, who was hanged here, head down, for four days in 1443. He had been captured during an unsuccessful raid on Tangier and was doomed after his country failed to raise the ransom. As a further, salutary warning, his corpse was cut down, stuffed and displayed beside the gate, where it remained for the next three decades.

Less imposing but equally as important is **Bab Mechouar**, the gate to the south, which opens onto the grounds of the Dar el Makhzen. It was through this gate that ordinary citizens would approach the palace to petition the king – the *mechouar* was where they would wait for admission.

Vieux Mechouar

Heading through Bab Dekkakine leads into the **Vieux Mechouar**, understandably much larger then the Petit Mechouar but surprisingly nowhere near as old, having been laid out at the nineteenth century by Sultan Moulay Hassan (it is also known as Place Moulay Hassan). The square is flanked along the whole of one side by the **Dar Makina**, an arms factory built by Italians in 1886.

A smaller gate, the nineteenth-century **Bab Sagma**, stands at the far end of the court, forcing you into an immediate turn as you leave the city through the Merenid outer gateway, whose twin octagonal towers slightly resemble the contemporary Chellah in Rabat. The huge complex abutting the Route du Tour de Fez opposite is the **Kasbah Cherarda**, a fort built by Sultan Moulay Rachid in 1670 to house – and keep at a distance – the Berber tribes of his garrison. The partially walled compound is now the site of a hospital, a school and an annexe of the Kairaouine University.

Moulay Abdallah

At the southwest corner of the Petit Mechouar, Bab Moulay Abdallah leads to the eponymous **Moulay Abdallah** district, an old *quartier réservé* that was once home to cafés, dance halls and brothels – a red-light district established by the French Protectorate. The prostitutes were mostly young Berber girls, lured by the chance of a quick buck; most returned to their villages after they had earned enough to marry or to keep their families. The quarter – focused around a main street that twists to Fez el Jedid's 1276 **Grand Mosque** – has a slightly forlorn feel about it today. West of the mosque, on the way to Bab Boujat, is the **Moulay Abdallah Mausoleum** (closed to non-Muslims), a mosque and medersa complex that also contains the tombs of four sultans of the current Alaouite dynasty, from the eighteenth and twentieth centuries; to get here from the Grand Mosque, follow the street to the west for 50m onto a small square and take the right fork at the far end. You will see the minaret of the mausoleum shortly after, from which you can reach **Bab Boujat** by heading northwest (up the lane on the right just before the minaret).

The Mellah

South of the Petit Mechouar, beyond the double archway of Bab Baghdadi, souk-speckled Grand Rue de Fez el Jedid leads down to the **Mellah**, once home to the city's Jewish families but now largely resettled by poor Muslim emigrants from the countryside. Although the quarter's name came to be used for Jewish ghettos throughout Morocco, it originally applied only to this one in Fez, christened from the Arabic word for "salt" (*mellah*), perhaps in reference to the Fassi Jews' job of salting the heads of criminals before they were hung on the gates.

In the immediate aftermath of independence in 1956, the Mellah's seventeen-thousand-strong **Jewish population** left for Casablanca, Paris and Israel virtually en masse. Today, just a handful of Jewish families live here and in the Ville Nouvelle, and all that remains of their presence are their eighteenth- and nineteenth-century **houses**, conspicuously un-Arabic, with their tiny shuttered windows and elaborate ironwork balconies that overhang busy Grand Rue des Merenides; cramped even closer together than the houses in Fez el Bali, they are interestingly designed and worth a peek if you are offered a look inside.

3

Jewish cemetery

Next to the garage behind the car park just east of Place des Alaouites • Mon–Fri & Sun 8am–sunset, closes slightly earlier on Fri for Jewish Sabbath • Free; donation expected for the Em Habanim Synagogue

On the southern edge of the Mellah, the white, rounded gravestones of the **Jewish cemetery** seem to extend for as far as the eye can see; twelve thousand have names, around six hundred are anonymous, mostly victims of a typhus epidemic in 1924, and none are more pitiful than the tiny tombs of children. Visitors leave a pebble on the gravestone to mark their visit or burn a candle in the recess provided. The most visited tombs are those of former chief rabbis, notably that of eighteenth-century **Rabbi Yehuda Ben Attar**, which is covered in green and black mosaic tiles, and that of **Lalla Solika Hatchouel**, topped by three vase-like turrets. Hatchouel caught the eye of Prince Moulay Abderrahman, who asked her to convert to Islam, so he could marry her; she refused and was promptly imprisoned and executed for the affront, and has since been venerated as a martyr.

Built in 1928 and until fairly recently in regular use for services and as a religious school, the restored **Em Habanim Synagogue** now serves as a museum, containing a clutter of bric-a-brac, much of it only tangentially related to Fez's Jewish community. The *gardien* of the cemetery can also direct you to other synagogues on or just off the Grande Rue des Merenides, including the seventeenth-century **Ibn Danan Synagogue**.

Dar el Makhzen

Lording it over Place de Alaouites at the bottom of Grand Rue des Merenides, the **Dar el Makhzen**, or Royal Palace, is one of the most sumptuous complexes in Morocco. Set

---

THE JEWS OF FEZ

The enclosed and partly protected position of the Mellah fairly accurately represents the historically ambivalent position of **Moroccan Jews**. Arriving for the most part with compatriot Muslim refugees from Spain and Portugal, they were never fully accepted into the nation's life. Yet nor were they quite rejected as in other Arab countries. Inside the Mellah, they were under the direct protection of the sultan (or the local *caïd*) and maintained their own laws and governors.

Whether the creation of a ghetto ensured the actual need for one is debatable. Certainly, it greatly benefited the reigning sultan, who could depend on Jewish loyalties and also manipulate the international trade and finance that they came to dominate in the nineteenth century. But despite their value to the sultan, even the richest Jews led extremely circumscribed lives. In Fez before the French Protectorate, no Jew was allowed to ride or even to wear shoes outside the Mellah, and they were severely restricted in their travels elsewhere.

TAKING THE WATERS OF MOULAY YACOUB

A pleasant day-trip for a swim and a hot bath, the spa village of **Moulay Yacoub**, 21km northwest of Fez, has been offering cures for the afflicted for centuries. Legend relates that the village was named either after Sultan Moulay Yacoub Ben Mansour – cured after his first bath, they say – or from the corruption of Aquae Juba, the spring of a local Berber king, Juba, who was envious of Roman hot baths. Either way, the hillside village's fame is founded on its sulphur-rich spa waters, which are pumped from some 1500m below ground and reach temperatures of around 54°C. Cars and taxis park at the top of the village, leaving you to descend flights of steps past stalls whose bathing goods add a chirpy resort atmosphere; the **swimming pool** (daily 6am–10pm; separate areas for men and women; 8dh) is near a square halfway down the hill.

Buses run hourly from the main bus station in Fez (30min); alternatively, a *place* in a grand taxi from the *gare routière* costs 10dh.

OLD THERMAL BATHS

Mon 6am–6pm, Tues–Sun 6am–10pm • Hot bath and massage 45dh

The old **thermal baths** (*baignoires* or *anciennes thermes*) are a short walk beyond the swimming pool, and have a more medicinal purpose – albeit fairly basic to Western eyes. They're usually busy, but you can enjoy a hot bath on your own (*baignoire individuelle*) or with a friend. Massage and jacuzzi are also available, while the masseurs in the thermal baths can put you through your paces with a hammam-style scrub. Beware that both facilities – baths and pool – are only cleaned once a week on Monday evening, so you're probably best not swimming that afternoon.

THERMES DE MOULAY YACOUB

☎ 0535 694064, ⌨ moulayyacoub.com • Hot bath 120dh for 15min; massages, manicures, pedicures and facials cost between 130dh for a manicure and 240dh for a basic massage

Much more upmarket than the old thermal baths, the **Thermes de Moulay Yacoub** is a spa for serious medical treatment – mostly rheumatism and respiratory problems – and serious self-indulgence that is as exclusive as it gets in Morocco. Not surprisingly, prices rise accordingly, though they do include a bathrobe and towel. The main reason to come, however, is that the main pool is mixed – a rare chance for couples to bathe together.

amid vast gardens, it has constantly been rebuilt and expanded over the centuries, and while the numerous pavilions and guest wings that make up the current complex are strictly off-limits to the public, you can still admire the fabulous ceremonial **gateway** that fronts the square, with its different-sized doors each adorned with enormous brass knockers and surrounded by dizzying zellij tilework.

ARRIVAL AND DEPARTURE   FEZ

BY PLANE

Fes-Saïs Airport is 15km south of Fez, off the N8 to Azrou (☎ 0535 624800). There are branches of Banque Populaire and BCME in Arrivals, offering decent exchange rates. Grands taxis to the town centre cost a fixed 120dh, whether you're on your own or in a group of up to six people; alternatively, bus 16 to the train station leaves the airport at least every hour. In Fez, the offices of Royal Air Maroc are at 54 Av Hassan II (☎ 0535 948551).

Destinations Casablanca (RAM daily; 1hr).

BY TRAIN

Fez train station is off Av des Almohades in the Ville Nouvelle (☎ 0535 930333), a 10min walk from the

concentration of hotels around Pl Mohammed V; from the station, the #16 bus runs to the airport roughly every hour.

TRANSPORT INTO TOWN

Buses Bus #10 passes the *gare routière* on its way to Bab Ftouh, while the #47 runs to Bab Boujeloud, both in Fez el Bali; if you walk to Av Hassan II, you can pick up the #9 bus to nearby Pl Batha (pronounced *baat-ha*).

Petits taxis Beware of unofficial taxi drivers (official petits taxis in Fez are metered), who charge very unofficial rates for the trip into town; the fare to Bab Boujeloud is around 10dh.

Destinations Asilah (5 daily; 4hr–4hr 45min); Casablanca (20 daily; 3hr 20min–4hr 20min); Kenitra (20 daily; 1hr 55min–2hr 25min); Marrakesh (8 daily; 7hr 15min); Meknes

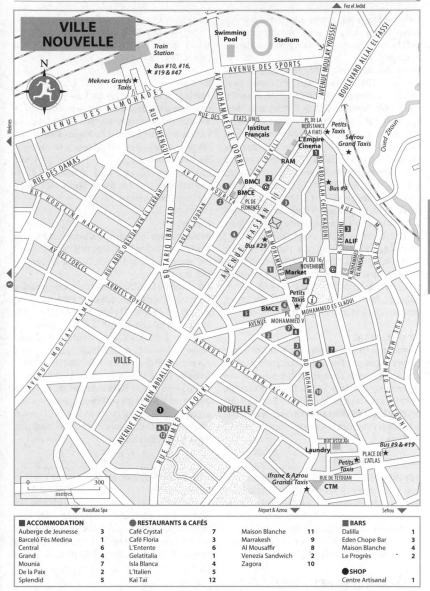

■ ACCOMMODATION		● RESTAURANTS & CAFÉS				■ BARS	
Auberge de Jeunesse	3	Café Crystal	7	Maison Blanche	11	Dalilla	1
Barceló Fès Medina	1	Café Floria	3	Marrakesh	9	Eden Chope Bar	3
Central	6	L'Entente	6	Al Mousaffir	8	Maison Blanche	4
Grand	4	Gelatitalia	1	Venezia Sandwich	2	Le Progrès	2
Mounia	7	Isla Blanca	4	Zagora	10		
De la Paix	2	L'Italien	5			● SHOP	
Splendid	5	Kaï Taï	12			Centre Artisanal	1

(24 daily; 30min); Nador (2 daily; 6hr); Oujda (5 daily; 5hr 20min–5hr 50min); Rabat (20 daily; 2hr 20min–3hr 10min); Tangier (4 daily; 4hr 30min–5hr 10min); Taza (7 daily; 2hr).

BY BUS

Stations The *gare routière* (☎ 0535 732992) is just north of Bab Mahrouk, on the western edge of Fez el Bali, though

there are also terminals in the Ville Nouvelle (the one for Sefrou, for example, is on Pl de la Résistance) and by the various gates to the Medina; if you're coming from Taza and the east, buses stop at Bab Ftouh, before continuing to the *gare routière*. CTM has an office in the *gare routière*, though its own principal station is on the corner of Rue Tetouan and Bd Mohammed V in the Ville Nouvelle (☎ 0535 732992);

buses call here before continuing on to the main bus station. Leaving Fez for the south, note that convenient night buses cover most routes – to Marrakesh and Rissani, for example.

Destinations Agadir (3 CTM & 5 others daily; 12hr); Al Hoceima (1 CTM & 2 others daily; 5hr 15min); Azrou (2 CTM, 2 Supratours & 10 others daily; 1hr 30min–2hr 30min); Beni Mellal (2 CTM & 8 others daily; 6hr); Casablanca (10 CTM & 18 others daily; 5hr 30min); Chefchaouen (4 CTM and 8 others daily; 4hr); Er Rachidia (1 CTM, 1 Supratours & 7 others daily; 7hr 45min–8hr 30min); Erfoud (1 Supratours daily; 9hr 45min); Ifrane (2 CTM & 10 others daily; 45min); Larache (4 CTM and 4 others daily; 4hr 30min); Marrakesh (4 CTM & 9 others daily; 8hr 30min–10hr); Meknes (11 CTM & 12 others daily; 1hr); Midelt (1 CTM, 1 Supratours & 9 others daily; 5hr 40min–6hr 30min); Moulay Yacoub (roughly hourly; 30min); Nador (4 CTM & 12 others daily; 5hr 30min); Oujda (4 CTM & 12 others daily; 6hr); Rabat (13 CTM & 15 others daily; 3hr 30min); Rich (1 CTM & 1 Supratours daily; 6–7hr); Rissani (1 CTM, 1 Supratours & 3 others daily; 9hr 15min–10hr); Sefrou (roughly hourly; 1hr); Tangier (6 CTM & 9 others daily; 7hr); Taza (9 CTM & 13 others daily; 2hr 30min); Tetouan (5 CTM & 10 others daily; 6hr).

BY GRAND TAXI

Ranks Grands taxis mostly operate from the rank outside the *gare routière* near Bab Mahrouk. Exceptions are those from Meknes, which arrive and depart from the train station; Ifrane and Azrou (and sometimes Marrakesh); which use a rank opposite the CTM office, 100m west of Pl de l'Atlas; Sefrou, which use a rank 100m southeast of Pl de la Résistance (also called La Fiat); and Taza, which arrive at Bab Ftouh.

GETTING AROUND

By petit taxi Petits taxis in Fez use their meters, so offer good value (note that prices increase by fifty percent after 8pm). Useful petit-taxi ranks include: Pl de l'Istiqlal, southeast of Bab Boujeloud; Pl Baghdadi, southwest of Bab Boujeloud; Bab Guissa, by the *Palais Jamaï*; Pl er R'cif, south of the Kairaouine Mosque; Bab Ftouh, at the top of the El Andalous quarter (all Fez el Bali); Pl des Alaouites (Fez el

Destinations Azrou (1hr); Casablanca (3hr 30min); Ifrane (30min); Marrakesh (8hr); Meknes (45min); Midelt (3hr); Moulay Yacoub (30min); Rabat (2hr 30min); Sefrou (30min); Taza (1hr 15min).

BY CAR

Parking For Fez el Bali, you can leave your car in car parks around Bab Boujeloud (southwest of the gate, on the wasteground opposite the Lycée Moulay Idriss; or south by the Musée Batha); in Aïn Azleten, north of Talâa Kebira; or by Bab Guissa. Central options for parking in the Ville Nouvelle include Pl de Florence; the square backed by *Hôtel Sofia* one block south; and Pl du 16 Novembre. Expect to pay the *gardien* at each around 10dh/day, 20dh overnight.

MOVING ON

Petrol stations There are several petrol stations in the Ville Nouvelle: around Pl de l'Atlas, near the beginning of the road to Sefrou and Midelt; and off Bd Abdallah Chefchaouni.

Car rental Fez has quite a number of rental companies. The following allow return delivery to a different centre: Avis, 50 Bd Abdallah Chefchaouni (☎0535 626969); Budget, 6 Av Lalla Asmae (☎0535 940092); Europcar, 45 Av Hassan II (☎0535 626545); First Car, *Hôtel Royal Mirage*, Av des FAR (☎0359 30909); Hertz, Bd Lalla Maryem, 1 Kissariat de la Foire (☎0535 622812); Tourvilles, 13 Rue Mokhtar Soussi, off Bd Mohammed V (☎0535 626635). Avis, Europcar, Budget and Hertz have desks at the airport. You'll get a cheaper deal with a local company such as Maribel Car, Av Abdelali Ben Chakroun (☎0535 930712, ⌨maribelcar.com), with small cars available from 250dh a day.

Jedid); Pl de la Résistance; and Pl Mohammed V (both in the Ville Nouvelle).

By bus You're unlikely to need city buses, which are less convenient but hardly any cheaper than petits taxis, though the following can be useful (note that the numbers to look for are marked on the sides of the buses; those on the back are completely different): #9 (Pl de l'Atlas to Pl

---

SECURITY IN FEZ

Despite what some *faux guides* may say, the **Medina** is not a dangerous place, though it's better to avoid walking around the quieter areas before 8am if you can help it; and note that there have been several reports of daytime muggings by people walking to and from the Merenid tombs, north of Bab Guissa. In the **Ville Nouvelle**, locals warn that robbery is a problem at night on Avenue Allal Fassi, the isolated main road between Place de la Résistance and the Musée Batha; if you must walk it, do so only in groups of at least three people. Avoid, also, the overgrown hillside east of Place de la Résistance, between *McDonald's* and the train track, where muggings have occurred even during the day.

Batha, via Bd Abdallah Chefchaouni); #10 (train station to Bab Ftouh, via the *gare routière*); #12 (Bab Boujeloud to Bab Ftouh); #16 (train station to the airport); #19 (train station to Pl er R'cif, via Bab el Jedid Nouail on Rue de la Liberté); #29 (Pl de l'Atlas to Pl er R'cif, via Bd Mohammed V); #47 (train station to Bab Boujeloud).

INFORMATION

Tourist office The Syndicat d'Initiative is on the east side of Pl Mohammed V (Mon–Fri 8.30am–noon & 2.30–6.30pm; ☎0535 624769), though it isn't particularly helpful.

Useful wesbites The best blog on Fez is the well-respected and up-to-date Ⓦ theviewfromfes, written by expats living in the city and full of interesting articles and wide-ranging news. For a good cultural calendar, with the latest on arts and music events, it's worth checking out Ⓦ culturevulturesfez.org.

MAPS

More than any other Medina in Morocco, Fez el Bali is composed of an impenetrable maze of lanes and blind alleys whose precise orientation and localized names do not exactly lend themselves to cartography; there are, however, a couple of maps of the Medina for sale that are worth noting:

Fès: The Thematic Tourist Circuits Includes a large fold-out map of the Medina and provides information on half a dozen themed itineraries using colour-coded routes that correspond with the star-shaped tourist signs scattered throughout the Medina (see p.167). Available from most newsstands and *bureaux de tabac* (100dh) – check those across from the Museé Batha.

Plan de Fès Simple but useful plan detailing both the Medina and the Ville Nouvelle, with a smaller insert of Fez el Jedid, though unfortunately the current edition is marred by badly placed photographs of monuments. Free from the tourist office, or 20dh from most newsstands.

3

GUIDES AND TOURS

A tour is a useful introduction to Fez el Bali, but the normal rules apply (see box, pp.54–55), so whether you get an official or unofficial **guide**, or even one from your hotel or riad, it's essential to work out in advance the main points you want to see and – as elsewhere in Morocco – make it absolutely clear if you are not interested in shopping. Note that most **organized tours** don't run on Fridays.

GUIDES

Official guides Legitimate guides identify themselves by laminated identity cards around their necks and can be engaged at the tourist offices in the Ville Nouvelle or through the more upmarket hotels in the Medina. No matter how many people are in your group, the fee is 150dh for a half-day and 250dh for a whole day, although it is always a good idea to clarify in advance exactly what is meant by a "full" day.

Unofficial guides Guides who tout their services are likely to be unofficial and technically illegal. This doesn't necessarily mean they're to be avoided – some who are genuine students (as most claim to be) can be excellent – but you have to choose carefully, ideally drinking a tea together before settling a rate or declaring interest. Reckon on around 100dh for an hour. One of the downsides of hiring an unofficial guide is that in order not to be spotted by their official counterparts, they sometimes follow convoluted and ill-frequented routes around the Medina, or call out directions from a few metres in front of or behind you, so they don't look like they are at your service – not a good way to gain information about the places you are walking by.

TOUR COMPANIES

Culture Vultures ☎ 0645 223203, Ⓦ culturevulturesfez .org/artisanal-affairs. Unusual half- and full-day small-group tours (max 4 people) that explore the city's rich tradition of commerical crafts, visiting the workshops of tanners, potters, slippermakers and zellij *maalem* (master craftsmen) along the way.

Plan-it Fez ☎ 0535 638708, Ⓦ plan-it-fez.com. Organizes a range of interesting activities, from night-time walks in Fez el Jedid and picnic dinners on nearby Mount Zalagh to food-tasting tours of the Medina.

ACCOMMODATION

Staying in Fez used to mean either comfort (and a reliable water supply) in modern **Ville Nouvelle** hotels or roughing it in the Medina hotels of Fez el Bali and Fez el Jedid. No longer. While the majority of hotels in **Fez el Bali** are still basic pensions, most of which could do with a makeover and better plumbing, the rise and rise of Fez's **riad** scene means that there is plenty of class and character in renovated old-city palaces, if you are prepared to pay for it – though most riads have one smaller room available to suit restricted budgets. The group of backpacker hostels around **Bab Boujeloud**, though, remain an ideal launchpad from which to explore the old city's sights and souks. As an alternative, the places in **Fez el Jedid** are within a 15min walk of Fez el Bali and less frequented by tourists (and hustlers). Space is at a premium in all categories, so be prepared for higher prices than usual and reserve in advance if possible.

3

FEZ EL BALI
HOTELS

Bab Boujloud 49 Pl Iscesco ☎0535 633118, ⓦhotelbabboujloud.com; map p.170. One of the few mid-range options around Bab Boujeloud. Most rooms are en suite with a/c and offer comfort at the expense of character – many have "views" of adjoining buildings, though the incredible Medina panorama from the large terrace makes up for that. 350dh

Batha Pl de l'Istiqlal ☎0535 634824, ⓔhotelbatha @menara.ma; map p.170. A tour-group favourite next to the Musée Batha, this three-star is comfy if a little bland, its character concealed in the bar of the older block behind, formerly the British consulate. Also has a small swimming pool. BB 600dh

Cascade 26 Rue Sarrajine ☎0535 638442; map p.170. Usually full by midday during high season, a busy Boujeloud favourite frequented by a young international crowd. Offers small, simple rooms, a few with tiny windows, hot showers and the best terrace in Bab Boujeloud (where you can also bed down for the night). Terrace 40dh, double 150dh

Dar Bouânania 21 Derb Ben Salem, off Talâa Kebira ☎0535 637282, ⓔdarbouanania@gmail.com; map p.170. Simple, fairly minimalist rooms (two en suite; 100dh extra) arranged around an intimate courtyard of painted woodwork and zellij that hints at riad charm at a fraction of the price. 300dh

★ **Dar Melody** 18 Rue Laalouj Kebira ☎0535 711343, ⓦdarmelody.fr; map pp.168–169. In the quieter El Andalous quarter, just across the Oued Boukhrareb from the tanneries, this beautifully renovated old merchant's house has just three (spacious) rooms. All are charmingly designed – and the top-floor room has its own tremendous terrace – but it is the incredibly helpful hosts that set this place apart and ensures that wannabe guests will need to book well in advance. That and the great breakfasts. BB 550dh

Lamrani 3 Talâa Seghira, opposite the Hammam Sidi Azouz ☎0535 634411; map p.170. A friendly place in a very central location, with small but clean rooms, most with double beds. Shared bathrooms, with hot showers available (10dh). 150dh

Palais Amani 12 Derb el Miter ☎0535 633209, ⓦpalaisamani.com; map pp.168–169. Expansive palace bearing the Art Deco hallmarks of its 1930s refurb, with five rooms and nine suites (all crisply modern, with iPods and flat-screen TVs) set around a courtyard garden. Standard rooms are quite subdued, so it's worth paying a few hundred extra dirhams for a bit more character. You can eat here in one of the best hotel restaurants in the city (see p.192), while the on-site spa has its own hammam. BB 1500dh

Pension Batha 8 Sidi Lakhayat ☎0535 741150; map p.170. Away from the hustle around Bab Boujeloud, this airy *pension* – difficult to miss thanks to its bright pink shutters – has half a dozen pleasant, old-fashioned rooms (rooms 4 and 5 feature nice stuccowork on the ceiling), with hot showers and a terrace overlooking Pl Batha. BB 250dh

Pension Kawtar 25 Derb Tarjana, signposted off Talâa Seghira ☎0535 740172, ⓔpension_kaw@yahoo.fr; map p.170. Brightly decorated, family-owned Moroccan townhouse with various-sized (but rather cramped) rooms, scattered over two floors, some with shower units shoehorned into the corner. BB 250dh

Pension Talâa 14 Talâa Seghira, opposite the Medersa Bou Inania ☎0535 633359; map p.170. A mellower alternative to the *Cascade*, this well-maintained and well-located *pension* offers a strip of pleasant doubles, though singles are rather hutch-like. Shared hot showers. 150dh

Sofitel Fès Palais Jamaï Bab Guissa ☎0535 634331, ⓦsofitel.com; map pp.168–169. Along with Marrakesh's *Mamounia* (see p.321) this is the most famous and historic hotel in Morocco, a five-star number founded on a nineteenth-century vizier's palace that also served as a principal setting for Paul Bowles' novel *The Spider's House* (see p.571). Unless you pay upwards of 4450dh for a prestige suite, though, you're in the modern block behind; the best of the smallish rooms, refurbished in 2010, offer excellent views of the Medina. There are three restaurants, a terrace bar (see p.194), two spas and a large pool. 1950dh

RIADS

Dar Bensouda 14 Zkak el Bghel ☎0535 638949, ⓦriaddarbensouda.com; map p.177. Hidden down a quiet alleyway south of Pl en Nejjarine, this attractive *dar* makes a big first impression, with its striking central courtyard and tremendous roof terrace; rooms are (stylishly) pared-back in comparison to the lavish zellij and decoration of the house itself. Most rooms are around the 1250dh mark, though a simpler one is available for a good deal less. 760dh

Dar el Hana 22 Rue Ferrane Couicha ☎0535 635854, ⓦdarelhana.com; map pp.168–169. Tastefully renovated by the same minds behind *Dar Seffarine*, this intimate guesthouse offers three comfortable rooms (one a twin) and an instantly homely, sociable atmosphere. Home-cooked meals are served in the snug courtyard or on the terrace. BB 720dh

★ **Dar Roumana** 30 Derb el Amer ☎0535 741637, ⓦdarroumana.com; map pp.168–169. Very stylish riad in the north of the Medina. The five suites (three with lovely baths) are all nicely done, and those on the ground floor are particularly spacious, but if you can push the boat out a bit the four-poster Yasmina Suite is a real beauty, with its very own balcony (1450dh). The split-level terrace boasts one of the best views in Fez, and there's a superb on-site restaurant as well (see p.191). BB 850dh

HAMMAM A GOOD TIME

With a reputed 250 **hammams** sprinkled across the city, Fez is one of the best places in Morocco to join the locals in a long, relaxing hot bath, with a rigorous scrub-down thrown in for good measure. If you're unfamiliar with the routine (see box, p.38), it is best, especially for women, to ask someone at your hotel to escort you. Don't forget to take your towel, soap, shampoo (or *ghasoul*, the fine-mud alternative) and swimsuit (or change of underwear). Several upscale **riads** have their own hammams and spas, which are more luxurious and less daunting, but also much pricer and, at the end of the day, not quite the same experience.

HAMMAMS

Hammam Aïn Azleten Talâa Kebira; map pp.168–169. In a convenient location between the Medersa Bou Inania and the *fondouks* on Talâa Kebira, Ain Azleten is one of the cleanest hammams in Fez; a scrub costs just 15dh. Men 6am–12.30pm & 9pm–midnight, women 12.30pm–midnight.

Hammam Sidi Azouz Talâa Seghira, opposite Hôtel Lamrani; map pp.168–169. Open later than most of the hammams In the Medina, and charging just 10dh (30dh for a massage). Men 6am–1pm & 10pm–2am, women 1–10pm.

SPAS

Maison Bleue Spa and Hammam Riad Maison Bleue, 33 Derb el Miter, across the Aïn Azleten car park north of Talâa Kebira ☎0535 741873, ⓦmaisonbleue.com; map p.168–169. You know you're in for a treat when the list of therapies includes a "Thousand Senses" steam bath and an orange-blossom massage. Hammam 400dh, treatments from 800dh.

Nausikaa Spa Av Bahnini, Route Aïn Smen ☎0535 610006, ⓦnausikaaspa.com; map p.185. Marble-clad modern spa in the southern Ville Nouvelle, centred round a hammam, steam rooms and sauna, and offering massages, reflexology and various other treatments.

Spa Laaroussa Fes Riad Laaroussa, 3 Derb Bechara, off Talâa Seghira ☎0674 187639, ⓦspalaaroussafez .com; map p.168–169. Detox amid the sublime surroundings of a sympathetically restored seventeenth-century bathhouse. Try a hammam and aromatic body scrub followed by a massage with essential oils (both 45min; 330dh).

★ **Dar Seffarine** 14 Derb Sbaa Louyate, 20m north of Pl Seffarine ☎0671 113528, ⓦdarseffarine.com; map p.177. Slap-bang in the heart of Fez el Bali, with some of the oldest zellij and stucco of the city's riads, and rooms styled in a sort of Moroccan minimalism by its designer-architect owners; the Kobbe suite is a knockout (1200dh). Add in a community spirit that sees guests breakfast together and you have one of the most appealing – and well-priced – options in the Medina. BB 700dh

La Maison Bleue 2 Pl de l'Istiqlal ☎0535 741843, ⓦmaisonbleue.com; map p.170. The first riad in Fez and still one of the best, an intimate world of luxury opposite the Musée Batha, where rooms, some with a private terrace, are named after female members of the family who built and still own it; the library once belonged to a professor at the Kairaouine. Style is a mix of Moroccan and classy European pieces, and there's excellent traditional dining in its restaurant (see p.191). Its sister establishment, *Riad Maison Bleue*, across the Aïn Azleten car park north of Talâa Kebira (see map, pp.168–169), has the added appeal of a garden and a swimming pool in the courtyard, plus a hammam hidden away among its many levels (see box above). Both BB 1990dh

Riad al Bartal 21 Rue Sournas ☎0535 637053, ⓦriadalbartal.com; map pp.168–169. Just inside the Medina's southernmost gate, but an attractive and welcoming choice – the light touch of its owners abounds, from the arty, pared-down decor in a plant-filled courtyard to individually styled rooms with painted ceilings and *tadelakht* walls. If you can afford it, suites are worth the extra 250dh. 850dh

★ **Riad Alkantara** 24 Oued Souaffine ☎0535 740292, ⓦriadalkantara.com; map pp.168–169. Stunning complex of riads set around lush gardens roamed by tortoises and plenty of cats, and boasting a lovely (and large) swimming area. The five rooms occupy an immaculately refurbished palatial building – more are being developed in the other riads – with two huge ground-floor rooms opening onto a towering atrium and a snug reading area. There's an a la carte restaurant and a lounge bar. BB 1500dh

Riad Fès 5 Derb Ben Slimane ☎0535 947610, ⓦriadfes.com; map pp.168–169. Less a *maison d'hôte* than a boutique hotel – architecturally one of the grandest in Fez – this Relais & Châteaux property gives guests the option of staying in Baroque, traditional or modern themed accommodation. Public areas are sumptuous, there's a plunge pool in the garden, a stylish bar (see p.194) and immaculate service throughout. 1920dh

★ **Riad Idrissy** 13 Derb Idrissy, opposite Sidi Ahmed Chaoui ☎0535 633066, ⓦriadidrissy.com; map pp.168–169. Beautifully renovated riad full of set-piece

3

furnishings, such as the wooden *makarba* adorning the wall of one suite, and thoughtful styling throughout; the suite on the top floor (there are only four, though they are all a good size) has its own terrace. The charming host is full of tips about life in Fez, though perhaps the best advice he could give is to lunch one day in the riad's "ruined garden" (see p.192). BB 1400dh

Riad Laaroussa 3 Derb Bechara, off Talâa Seghira ☎0674 187639, ⚲riad-laaroussa.com; map pp.168–169. Housed in a seventeenth-century palace, *Laaroussa* is a popular contender with a modern twist on traditional decor. Rooms enjoy deliciously smooth *tadelakht* bathrooms (coloured depending on their name); large suites come with open fireplaces and beautiful painted wooden ceilings. The grassy courtyard and spacious furnishings provide a calming retreat from the commotion of the Medina, and there's also a stylish hammam and spa (see box, p.189). BB 1100dh

★ **Riad Numéro 9** 9 Derb el Masid ☎0535 634045, ⚲riad9.com; map pp.168–169. Beautiful riad, lavishly renovated with real attention to detail and bearing the sophisticated touch of an interior designer throughout. The accommodating host and his equally helpful staff show a genuine concern for your enjoyment, while meals are of a consistently high standard – so much so that they have recently opened their own restaurant nearby (see p.192). BB 1000dh

Ryad Mabrouka 25 Derb el Miter ☎0535 636345, ⚲ryadmabrouka.com; map pp.168–169. Through a door in an unassuming dead-end alley, Moroccan style is paired with French antiques and European paintings, a reflection of the eclectic tastes of its friendly owners. There's also a plunge pool in an idyllic garden, and great views of the Medina from the terrace to boot. BB 1495dh

FEZ EL JEDID

Glacier 9 Derb Jedid, near Pl des Alaouites ☎0535 626261; map p.181. Located at the bottom of an alleyway off Rue des Merenides and run by two friendly women, this brightly painted hotel is the best budget choice in this part of town. Basic but tidy rooms with shared hot-water showers (10dh) are arranged around an interior courtyard, some overlooking the Jewish cemetery. 150dh

Jnane Sbile 22 Kasbat Chems, opposite the gardens of the same name ☎0535 638635, ⚲hoteljnanesbile.com; map p.181. Two-star with a glitzy salon and offering comfortable and cosy, if slightly poky, mod con rooms and nice views from the terrace over the gardens across the road. A good option for those looking for proximity to the Medina without the noise. 330dh

VILLE NOUVELLE

★ **Auberge de Jeunesse** 18 Rue Abdeslam Seghrini ☎0535 624085; map p.185. Set in a small garden in a quiet backwater, this is one of the best youth hostels in Morocco: easy-going, friendly and with spotless dorms and doubles. There are free hot showers in the morning, and the nearby *Hôtel Menzah Zalagh* usually allows guests to swim in its pool for a reduced fee. The enthusiastic Fassi manager is also a mine of local information. Doors close at 10pm. BB dorm 75dh, double 170dh

Barceló Fès Medina 53 Av Hassan II ☎0535 948800, ⚲barcelo.com; map p.185. Dominating the northern end of Av Hassan II, this huge white curve of a building does a lot of things right, despite the confusing name – this being the Ville Nouvelle and all, and some way from the actual Medina. Rooms are surprisingly perfunctory, though, and the suites, particularly, are rather bare for the price (2100dh), but you're paying for service and facilities, which include a swimming pool, gym and spa with hammam, plus a sleek restaurant and an equally modern café overlooking La Fiat. BB 1100dh

Central 50 Rue Brahim Roudani ☎00535 622333; map p.185. Good-value, popular one-star that's often full thanks to its clean and bright rooms – some with small en-suite shower cubicles – that are heated in winter. 200dh

Grand Bd Abdallah Chefchaouni ☎0535 932026, ✉grand2008hotel@yahoo.fr; map p.185. An old colonial hotel with an Art Deco facade and similarly impressive proportions in refurbished rooms, somewhat spartan though all with a/c, heating and private bathrooms (many have a bath). Facilities include a bar, restaurant, nightclub and garage. 430dh

Mounia 60 Bd Zerktouny ☎0535 624838, ⚲hotelmouniafes.ma; map p.185. This friendly, modern hotel is one of the best mid-range choices in the Ville Nouvelle. Attractive public areas are decorated with zellij, and the smart rooms all come with central heating, a/c and satellite TV. 600dh

De la Paix 44 Av Hassan II ☎0535 625072, ⚲hoteldelapaixfez.com; map p.185. A long-established tour-group hotel, with red-carpeted corridors leading to modern(ish) spotless rooms enjoying full bathroom suites, TV, a/c and heating. The hotel's predominantly seafood restaurant, *Le Nautilus*, is open to non-residents, and there's quite a cool little downstairs bar. 310dh

Splendid 9 Rue Abdelkrim el Khattabi ☎0535 622148; map p.185. An efficient modern hotel, with pleasant en-suite rooms, a good restaurant, bar and small swimming pool, though staff sometimes seem a little cold. One of the best-value options in the Ville Nouvelle when not booked out by tour groups. 500dh

EATING

Fez is the culinary capital of Morocco, and you should try pastilla, the great Fassi delicacy of pigeon pie, at least once during your stay. Eating options in **Fez el Bali** and **Fez el Jedid** have improved greatly in recent years, though outside the riads and the smarter palace-restaurants, they are generally on the basic side; this is a good place, though, to try street-stall snacks such as *bisara* soup (see box below), while the colourful fruit and veg market near Bab er R'cif (9am–1pm & 2–7pm; closed Fri) is worth a visit for its mounds of olives, dates and other nibbles. The **Ville Nouvelle** is home to most of Fez's patisseries and modern (licensed) restaurants, and if you want to talk with Fassis on any basis other than guide or tout to tourist, your best chance will be in its numerous modern cafés – as the home of the city's university, it's also more likely that the students you meet here will be exactly that.

FEZ EL BALI AND FEZ EL JEDID

CAFÉS
Café Boutouail Rue Boutouail, opposite Medersa el Attarine; map p.177. At the very heart of the old city, *Café Boutouail* does a good line in coffee and pastries – extra seating is hidden away upstairs – but its speciality is *panachi*, a mixture of milk, almond milk and raisins, with a blob of ice cream on top for good measure (a bargain 5dh). Daily 8.30am–9pm.

★ **Café Clock** 7 Derb el Magana, signposted off Talâa Kebira near the water clock ☎0535 637855, ☺cafeclock.com; map p.170. This café-restaurant cum cultural centre housed in a restored *dar* is a popular hangout for students and tourists alike. The food is inventive and delicious, ranging from pumpkin *bisara* (40dh) to *maakouda* (potato cakes) with warm tomato salad (95dh) – though few people can resist the camel burger, fresh off the dromedary stall outside. Check the website for weekly schedules that include yoga and music nights and courses in Arabic and cooking (see box, p.193). Daily 9am–10pm.

Café Restaurant La Noria By the water wheel behind the Jnane S'bile, off Av Moulay Hassan ☎0535 654 255; map p.181. A quiet spot for breakfast (until 11am) or a bargain cup of a coffee, though you can also grab *harira* soup (25dh) or a Berber omlette (40dh), or tuck into a range of menus that are big enough to share (from 80dh). Daily 7am–10.30pm.

★ **Crèmerie La Place** Pl Seffarine; map p.177. Relax over an orange juice or a mint tea accompanied by the sound of metalworkers on one of the most attractive squares in Fez el Bali. Daily 7am–7pm.

Fes et Gestes 39 Arsat el Hamoumi ☎0535 638532, ☺fes-et-gestes.ma; map pp.168–169. Charming French colonial house that's a great spot for a herbal tea, whether in the lush garden full of citrus trees or in billowing armchairs in the library indoors. Hosts regular events such as Moroccan storytelling and painting exhibitions. Daily except Wed noon–9.30pm.

RESTAURANTS
★ **Dar Roumana** 30 Derb el Amer ☎0535 741637, ☺darroumana.com; map pp.168–169. One of the best riad restaurants in the Medina, where creative two- and three-course menus (250/350dh) are served in a pretty candlelit courtyard. Food varies with the season, taking in roasted fig and goat's cheese salad, seafood risotto, and charcoal-cooked quail with date molasses and pomegranate seeds – a signature dish of sorts (*roumana* means "pomegranate"). Book in advance. Tues–Sat 7.30–9pm.

Dar Saada 21 Rue el Attarine ☎0535 637370, ☺restaurantdarsaada.com; map p.177. Tasty Moroccan dishes (tajines around 80dh) all in vast portions – two people could order one main dish and a plate of vegetables – in another century-old palace whose fine carving was renewed after a fire in 1972. Also open for breakfast (30dh). Daily 8–10.30am & noon–8.30pm.

Fez Café Le Jardin des Biehn, 13 Akbat Sbaa ☎0535 638690, ☺jardindesbiehn.com; map pp.168–169. The laidback restaurant of the attached *maison d'hôte* has a pricey and limited menu (there's just three daily dishes to choose from), but it's a very tranquil spot, on a veranda overlooking a cactus garden, and the quality food – along the lines of liver salad (105dh) and a trio of brochettes with roast veg (140dh) – often brings a slight twist to the usual Moroccan fare. Daily noon–3pm & 7pm–midnight.

Kasbah Bab Boujeloud, opposite Hôtel Cascade; map p.170. One of the most appealing options in Bab Boujeloud due to two terraces with views and zellij-covered walls. A la carte brochettes, *kefta* and sausages (40dh) are a better bet than the fairly uninspiring set menu. Daily 9am–midnight.

La Maison Bleue 2 Pl de l'Istiqlal ☎0535 741843, ☺maisonbleue.com; map p.170. This beautiful riad

3

STREET EATS
Wandering the lanes of Fez el Bali, you'll notice whisps of steam swirling around metal cauldrons and carrying with them the tempting aroma of **bisara**, a thick fava-bean soup; vendors (try those near the start of Talâa Kebira) usually top it with a glug of local olive oil and a sprinkle of cumin. Braver souls may like to tackle the **snail stands** on the corner of Talâa Seghira and Derb el Horra, where safety pins constitute the cutlery – they're used for plucking the little critters out of their softened shells. Another street snack worth trying is *jben*, an acidic white **goat's cheese** that's only vaguely removed from yoghurt; the stall on the corner of Talâa Seghira and Sidi Mohammed Belhaj proudly displays theirs stacked on dark green leaves.

3

FOOD FIT FOR A KING?

Several of Fez's finest old mansions have been converted into **palace restaurants**, popular places, particularly with tour groups, for sampling (relatively) traditional cuisine in sublime surroundings. Some really do provide a Fassi banquet, but you'll need to choose your "palace" carefully – the more elaborate the decor, the less, it seems, the need to worry about the quality of the cooking, and some menus are positively bland in comparison. The belly-dancing floor shows, musicians and, on occasion, staged "marriages" aren't to everyone's taste, especially when you're paying a substantial surcharge for the privilege, but the whole package (usually around 300dh per person) can make for an entertaining evening.

Al Firdaous 10 Derb Zenjifor, near Bab Guissa ☎0535 634343; map pp.168–169. A rich merchant's house of the 1920s is the setting for darkly atmospheric meals – there's a choice of several five-course set menus, including pastilla made the original Fassi way, with pigeon (from 310dh, though the pastilla option will set you back 540dh) – and music and a floorshow (featuring mock weddings, fire dancing and belly-dancing) in the evenings. Daily noon–3.30pm & 8–11.30pm.

Laanibra 61 Aïn Lakhail, signed off Zkak Rouah ☎0535 741009; map p.177. A wonderful seventeenth-century palace that's home to a friendly restaurant, serving a la carte dishes and a choice of menus (from 250dh). More intimate than the grander *Palais des Merinides* nearby, whose beautifully restored palatial interior is let done by the food on offer. Daily noon–4pm.

Palais Tijani 51–53 Derb Ben Chekroune, east of the Sidi Ahmed Tijani mosque ☎0535 741071, ✉tijanifes@gmail.com; map pp.168–169. Less grandiose than the other palace-style eateries and without the floor show, but better value for money – the range of ten set menus starts at 130dh. The emphasis here is on the food ("Fez seen through its cuisine"), and the diners are as likely to be Moroccan as foreign. Daily noon–4pm.

makes a romantic setting for generous three- and four-course menus served by attentive slipper-wearing waiters. The former features *seffa medfouna*, fluffy couscous cooked to a thirteenth-century recipe (350dh), the latter pastilla (550dh with wine); both start with a mouthwatering array of eight cooked salads, a meal in itself. An *oued* player and Gnaoua musicians add to the ambience. Daily 1–3pm & 7–10.30pm.

Najmat Souafine 9 Oued Souaffine ☎0535 633149, ✉najmatsouafine@gmail.com; map pp.168–169. Housed in an old water mill in the low-key Ziat district, some way off the tourist-trodden path – and all the better for it. Good-value dishes range from sardines and brochettes (30dh) to Thai chicken curry (80dh), and are best enjoyed on the romantic backyard terrace. Daily 10am–8.30pm.

Palais Amani 12 Derb el Miter, off Rue Oued Zhoune ☎0535 633209, ⓦpalaisamani.com; map pp.168–169. This former palace north of the tanneries makes a swish setting for delicate French/Moroccan cuisine, with a daily-changing three-course menu (395dh) that may include cauliflower purée, delicately stacked beef tajine and (hopefully) their sinfully soft home-made lemon mousse. Finish with a nightcap on the terrace bar (open til midnight). Daily noon–9.30pm.

Palais de Fes 15 Derb Makhfia ☎0535 761590; map pp.168–169. Delicious pastilla and fine Medina views are the specialities of this highly regarded restaurant and *maison d'hôte* (also known as *Dar Tazi*), both served up on one of the best terraces in town. There's a choice of set menus (around 350dh), and reservations are recommended, if only to request a free car to pick you up from your hotel. Daily 10am–midnight.

★ **Resto Número 7** 7 Zkak Rouah ☎0535 638924 ⓦrestaurantnumero7.com; map pp.168–169. This über-stylish eatery was one of the most eagerly awaited restaurant openings in Fez el Bali when it first started serving market-fresh meals in late 2012. As with their nearby *Riad Número 9* (see p.190), the owners have brought something different to their restaurant offering: decor is starkly black and white, even the intricate zellij, and the daily changing menu feels excitingly unusual – think salad of baby squid and poached pear (60dh) and chicken *m'hammer* (first sautéed, then roasted), with honeyed courgette puree and okra (120dh). The tarts, pies, crumbles and other mouthwatering desserts are decent value at 30dh. Reserve in advance, before 11am on the day of the booking. Daily except Wed 7–10pm.

★ **The Ruined Garden** Riad Idrissy, 13 Derb Idrissy, opposite Sidi Ahmed Chaoui ☎0535 633066, ⓦruinedgarden.com; map pp.168–169. A cracking concept, this novel setup south of Talâa Seghira specializes in relaxed lunches of tasty Moroccan street food (fried sardines, salads, smoky *zaalouk* and the like; 40dh/plate) in a sunken garden that was only discovered while renovating the attached riad (see p.189). Dinner (by prior reservation) is a *mechoui* feast (500dh/person), though you can also drop by for afternoon tea (from 3pm), a nod to the charming owner's past life as *maître d'hôte* of The Ivy in London. Daily noon–2.30pm & 3–5pm.

★ **Thami's** 50 Serrajine, Bab Boujeloud ☎070 640130; map p.170. An unbeatable location at the top of Talâa Seghira, where you can people-watch to your heart's content over simple but satisfying food, great value at around 40dh for dishes such as egg-topped *kefta* tajine. Daily 8.30am–11pm.

VILLE NOUVELLE

CAFÉS AND SNACK BARS

Café Crystal Pl Mohammed; map p.185. A good central spot for a quiet drink (including beer), its split-level interior ruled by uniformed waiters who help enthuse the place with a vintage 1960s vibe. Daily 5.30am–midnight.

Café Floria Av Hassan II, a block north of the main post office; map p.185. A great place for people-watching on Av Hassan II, boasting excellent croissants (breakfast is just 4dh) and – almost as important – very clean toilets. Daily 6am–9pm.

★ **L'Entente** 83 Bd Mohammed V; map p.185. Tiny patisserie selling excellent bread but also lovely cakes, pastries and a range of sticky treats, such as macaroons, almond biscuits and gazelle horns; you can order a box to go (around 100dh) or enjoy them in the on-site café. Daily 7am–8.30pm.

Gelatitalia 3 Rue Libya, just off Av el Houria, near Pl de Florence; map p.185. You wouldn't make the trip especially, but it's worth popping in if you're passing for a bargain scoop (8dh) of ice cream, especially the pistachio, before heading to Av Hassan II for an early evening stroll. Daily 9am–10pm.

Venezia Sandwich 7 Av el Houria (formerly Av de France); map p.185. A superior fast-food joint with grilled sausages, fish and *kefta*, plus a range of cheap panini (around 20dh). Daily noon–1.30am.

RESTAURANTS

Isla Blanca 32 Av Hassan II ☎0535 930357, ✉isla_restaurant@hotmail.fr; map p.185. Predominantly Italian dishes, with tagliatelle and upmarket pizzas (80dh) on the menu, plus Mediterranean dishes such as grilled swordfish. Daily noon–3pm & 6.30pm–1am.

L'Italien Av Omar Ibn Khattab ☎0535 940685, ⓦrestaurantitalien.ma; map p.185. Well-produced classics such as carpaccio, escalope Milanaise and a dozen or so pastas (from 60dh), but pizza is the speciality at this slick Italian dinner near the train station: stylishly presented thin-crust beauties, from margharitas (60dh) to the signature truffle-oil-laced L'Italien (100dh). There's a select list of Moroccan wines to wash them down with. Daily noon–11pm.

Kaï Taï 12 Rue Ahmed Chaouki ☎0535 651700, ⓦkaitaifes.com; map p.185. Hip little Japanese/Thai restaurant, with a very feng-shui interior and two chefs serving a fairly short but refreshing menu of surimi California rolls, mixed sashimi, pad thai and the like (mains around 135dh). Daily noon–3pm & 7–11pm.

★ **Maison Blanche** 12 Rue Ahmed Chaouki ☎0535 622727, ⓦfesrestaurant.com; map p.185. Ultra-trendy restaurant whose clean-lined interior of granite walls, smoked mirrors and designer Italian furniture sets the scene for French-Moroccan fusion food, beautifully presented by the chef behind the *Café Faubourg* in Paris. Mains from 150dh. Daily noon–3pm & 6pm–1am.

Marrakesh 11 Rue Omar El Mokhtar, between Av Mohammed V and Hôtel Mounia ☎0535 930876; map p.185. Small but cute, with a fairly limited menu, though the food (tajines, couscous and the like; from 70dh) is well cooked and tasty. Daily noon–3pm & 6–10pm.

Al Mousaffir 47 Bd Mohammed V ☎0535 620019; map p.185. This delicately tiled establishment, which

FASSI EATERS

It's never going to be easy to replicate the rich and resounding flavours of **Fassi cuisine** in your kitchen back home, but knowing the right blend of spices to put into your tajine will make a real difference to your cooking, while whipping up a sweet pastilla pie should wow even the most discerning of dinner-party guests. Most **cookery classes** focus on a three-course menu and start with a visit to one of the Medina souks to pick up the necessary (fresh) ingredients. Some, such as Plan-It Fez, also include bread-making and the opportunity to bake your creation in a local *farine* (oven). Full-day cookery classes cost around 500dh to 600dh.

Clock Kitchen ☎0535 637855, ⓦcafeclock.com/ clock-kitchen. The cookery school from the team at *Café Clock* (see p.191). Learn how to make the classics in their cookery workshop, brush up your pastry skills on a patisserie day course or have a go at making and baking traditional bread.

Lahcen Beqqi ☎0615 866144, ⓦfescooking.com. Fez's original cookery school, run by the amicable Lahcen, a former restaurant chef with intimate

knowledge of Berber cooking and Fassi cuisine. Whip up a tajine using produce from your visit to the souks, or head into the Middle Atlas to try your hand at a *mechoui* BBQ in the cedar forests around Azrou.

Plan-It Fez ☎0535 638708, ⓦplan-it-fez.com. Moroccan cookery classes with a twist, held in a Fassi home where you can discover the secrets of a good marinade and learn to cook traditional tajines before tucking in with your hosts.

prides itself on not depending on tour groups and agencies for its survival, offers a wide selection of well-cooked meat and fish dishes (from 90dh), as well as local wines and beer brewed in Fez. Daily 11am–3pm & 6pm–midnight.

Zagora 5 Bd Mohammed V ☎ 0535 940686; map p.185. In a shopping mall off the main street, this classy place serves French dishes a la carte or a set menu of Moroccan cuisine (from 110dh); service is immaculate and helpful. Daily noon–3.30pm & 7–11pm.

DRINKING

As with Medina quarters throughout Morocco, drinking in **Fez el Bali** and **Fez el Jedid** is mostly restricted to hotels and riads; consequently, the area is much quieter at night, except during Ramadan, when shops and stalls stay open until 2 or 3am. The **Ville Nouvelle** has a slightly wider range of bars, though note that of the places listed below, only *Maison Blanche* will feel comfortable for women; other options include the bars in *Hôtel Mounia*, *Grand Hôtel* and *Hôtel de la Paix*.

FEZ EL BALI AND FEZ EL JEDID

L'Alcazar Riad Fès, Derb Ben Slimane ☎ 0535 947610, ⊕ riadfes.com; map pp.168–169. Contemporarily cool bar, where you relax poolside with a range of cocktails and some two hundred varieties of wine, including several from the vineyards of Morocco. Daily 8–11pm.

Fez Lounge 95 Zkak Rouah ☎ 0535 633097, ⊕ fezlounge.com; map pp.168–169. This trendy lounge bar – all smooth, bare walls and dotted with cubed pouffes – is a rare find in the Medina, a chance to relax over a drink outside of a hotel or riad. Food is available but is all too often underwhelming and expensive. Discounted drinks from 6pm on Fri, plus occasional events. Daily 11am–10pm.

Al Mandar Sofitel Fès Palais Jamaï, Bab Guissa ☎ 0535 634331, ⊕ sofitel.com; map pp.168–169. The house cocktails and fine wines don't come cheap, but it's difficult to put a price on the superlative views from this hotel terrace bar at the foot of the Merenid tombs, particularly at dusk, when lights start flickering across the Medina. Daily 10am–1am.

★ **Mezzanine** 17 Kasbat Chams, across from the Jnane S'bile ☎ 0535 638668, ⊕ restaurantfez.com; map p.181. Super-chic joint that works just as well in the early evening as it does in the early hours. Pull up a glitzy golden chair and quaff mojitos and vintage champagne; Mediterranean tapas platters (from 100dh) are served as an accompaniment. Daily 11am–1am, happy hour 6–7pm.

VILLE NOUVELLE

Dalila 17 Bd Mohammed V; map p.185. Seedy but cheap, where pushing through the beaded "door" reveals an interesting interior of futuristic metal panels set off by ultraviolet lighting. The upstairs bar is a place for *serious* drinking. Daily 8am–10pm.

Eden Chope Bar Bd Mohammed V; map p.185. Dark, despite the neon-illuminated interior, and with a motley gang of regulars camped around the U-shaped bar and making the most of the "2 for 25dh" deal that runs between 11am and 5pm. Daily 11am–11pm.

Maison Blanche 12 Rue Ahmed Chaouki ☎ 0535 622727, ⊕ fesrestaurant.com; map p.185. The mezzanine lounge bar at this swanky restaurant (see p.193) makes a stylish late-night destination for cocktails and cognacs. Daily noon–3pm & 6pm–1am.

Le Progrès 21 Av Mohammed es Slaoui; map p.185. With a pool table and a crowd of regulars, this is a dark, boozy place that seems permanently stuck in the twilight hours. Daily 8.30am–midnight.

ENTERTAINMENT

As the country's cultural capital, there is normally something going on in Fez, whether it's Moroccan storytelling at *Fes et Gestes* (see p.191), a photography show at the Institut Français or an evening of Gnaoua music at *Café Clock* (see p.191).

L'Empire Cinema Av Hassan II, near Pl de la Résistance; map p.185. One of several in the Ville Nouvelle screening foreign films, mainly dubbed into French; there are four showings daily, from 2.15pm (30dh).

Institut Français 33 Rue Ahmed Loukili ☎ 0535 623921, ⊕ institutfrancaisfes.com; map p.185. The institute's gallery in the Ville Nouvelle holds art exhibitions and talks, and there are regular traditional-music concerts in the Musée Batha. Tues–Sat 10am–12.15pm & 2.30–6.30pm; closed Thurs afternoon.

SHOPPING

Fez has a rightful reputation as the centre of Moroccan traditional crafts, but bear in mind that it also sees more tourists than almost anywhere bar Marrakesh. However much you bargain, **rugs** and **carpets** will probably be cheaper in Meknes, Azrou or Midelt, and although the **brass, leather and cloth** here are the best you'll find, you will need plenty of energy, a good sense of humour and a lot of patience to get them at a reasonable price. Fassi dealers are expert hagglers – making

CLOCKWISE FROM TOP: CAFÉ CLOCK (P.191); DAR SEFFARINE (P.189); RIAD NÚMERO 9 (P.190) >

you feel like an idiot for suggesting a ludicrously low price, jumping up out of their seats as if to push you out of the shop, or lulling you with mint tea and elaborate displays.

Au Petit Bazar de Bon Accueil 35 Talâa Seghira; map pp.168–169. Fifth-generation Fassi dealers, specializing in antiques and Berber jewellery – the older, more interesting stuff is in the room upstairs. Mon–Thurs, Sat & Sun 9am–1pm & 2.30–8pm.

Centre Artisanal Av Allal Ben Abdallah ☎0535 621007; map p.185. It's not the best in the country, but the government-run Centre Artisanal is a good place to visit for an idea of prices (theirs are all strictly fixed), and, for better or for worse, you won't get the strong-arm tactics of the more atmospheric stalls within the souks. Daily 9am–12.30pm & 2.30–6.30pm.

Chez Abdelsalam Sidi Mohammed Belhaj, off Derb er Rom; map pp.168–169. Lovely hand-painted wooden pieces, including *mashrabiyas* (latticework windows), from a craftsman who worked on objects in the Musée du Bois. 9am–6.30pm, closed Fri.

★ **Chez Hamidou** 14 Derb Chouwara, near the main entrance to the tanneries; map p.177. Surprisingly overlooked by tour groups, Hamidou's little enterprise consists of no more than a hole in the wall stacked with cushion covers, the speciality of the shop and reputedly the best in the Medina. Mon–Thurs, Sat & Sun 8.30am–6pm.

Herboriste Bouânania Derb Lamz Daatahti; map p.170. Smart, tidy little shop selling a range of hammam essentials (argan soap and *ghassoul* clay amog other things) and various medicinal herbs. Daily 10am–7pm.

Maison Bleue 68 Talâa Seghira; map pp.168–169. Three rooms crammed with traditional ceramics and pottery from Fez (the distinctive blue-and-white pieces) and Safi (dark green). Daily 9am–7.30pm.

La Maison du Bronze 3 Derb el Horra; map pp.168–169. Large selection of gleaming brasswork and items of silver jewellery, old and new and in all shapes and sizes, from door knockers and plates to mirrors and chandeliers. Mon–Thurs, Sat & Sun 9am–7pm, Fri 9am–12.30pm.

Talisman Art Gallery 155 Sidi Moussa ☎0535 636960, ⓦtalismanfesgallery.com; map.177. Well worth a browse for the gorgeous surroundings – intricate zellij floors and carved cedar doors – even if you can't afford the beautifully presented but (generally) pricey goods on offer. Mon–Thurs, Sat & Sun 9am–6.30pm.

Tissage Berbère 4 Derb Taouil, signed off Derb Chouwara near the main entrance to the tanneries; map p.177. Reasonable carpet prices, despite its location on a well-trodden route, and bartering with the informative owner over his silk and woolen kilims is enjoyable. Mon–Thurs, Sat & Sun 9am–6pm.

PUTTING THE FEZ IN FESTIVALS

Fez is home to several important **festivals** and **moussems**, ranging from annual pilgrimages to week-long celebrations of Fassi cuisine. The focal point of the cultural calendar, though, is the nine-day-long Festival of World Sacred Music, a highly regarded gathering of global musicians that has produced spin-offs in the UK and North America.

FESTIVAL OF WORLD SACRED MUSIC

Since 1994, Fez has hosted the **Festival of World Sacred Music** (☎0535 740535, ⓦfesfestival .com) each June, which has developed into the country's most interesting and inspiring cultural festival. Recent years have seen Sufi chanters from Azerbaijan, *kathak* dancers from India, a Javanese gamelan and a Byzantine choir from Greece. Concerts take place throughout the Medina and in the Ville Nouvelle: at the Musée Batha; by Bab Boujeloud and Bab Makina; at the Institut Français; and sometimes further afield, such as amid the ruins of Volubilis.

FEZ FESTIVAL OF SUFI CULTURE

The **Fez Festival of Sufi Culture** (ⓦfestivalculturesoufie.com) is usually held over a week in April and comprises a number of performances that take place each night in the courtyard of the Musée Batha (organized discussions are held during the day); it's a rare opportunity to experience the music of the world's most renowned Sufi musicians and vocalists.

MOUSSEM OF MOULAY IDRISS II

The largest moussem held inside a major city, the **Moussem of Moulay Idriss II** takes place in Fez each September and involves a long procession to the saint's tomb. The Medina is packed out, however, and you will have a better view from Place Batha or Place Boujeloud, before the procession enters the Medina proper.

DIRECTORY

Banks and exchange Most banks are grouped along Bd Mohammed V. As always, the BMCE (branches at Pl Mohammed V, Pl Florence and Pl de l'Atlas) is best for exchange and handles Visa/Mastercard transactions, as well as travellers' cheques; there's also a BMCI office just a few metres beyond the BMCE on Pl Florence. Banque Populaire has three branches in Fez el Bali: halfway down Talâa Seghira; north of the Medersa el Attarine, by the Sidi Tijani mosque; and on Derb Kaid el Khammar, by Bab Ftouh. Others elsewhere include: Banque Populaire on Bd Mohammed V, with quick service for currency and travellers' cheques, and opposite the Dar el Makhzen at the bottom of Rue Bou Khessissat in Fez el Jedid, with change facilities and cashpoint; Crédit du Maroc on Bd Mohammed V; and SGMB by Bab Boujeloud.

Golf The Fes Royal Golf Club, 17km from Fez on the Route d'Ifrane (T0535 665210), was designed by Cabell B Robinson and has an 18-hole, par 72 course.

Internet access The best option in Fez el Bali is Cyber Café Bab Boujeloud, tucked in the corner just east of the Boujeloud Mosque (daily 9am–10pm). In the Ville Nouvelle, try Cyber above the téléboutique a few doors down from *Hôtel de la Paix* on Av Hassan II (daily 9am–11pm).

Laundry There's a laundry near Bab Boujeloud at the northern end of Pl de l'Istiqlal, facing the local post office; in the Ville Nouvelle, try Pressing Dallas, 44 Rue Assilah.

Language courses The Arabic Language Institute in Fez (ALIF), 2 Rue Ahmed Hiba (☏ 0535 624850, ✍ alif-fes.com) is an American initiative offering a range of courses plus private lessons. There are three-week (6000dh) and six-week (10,400dh) courses in Modern Standard Arabic or Colloquial Moroccan Arabic at all levels. ALIF also has its own residence for students, or the option of a homestay with a Moroccan family.

Left luggage/baggage Deposits are available at the bus and train stations.

Pharmacies There are pharmacies opposite the SGMB bank by Bab Boujeloud, at the northern end of Pl de l'Istiqlal and on the Grande Rue des Merenides in the Mellah, plus numerous ones throughout the Ville Nouvelle. The Pharmacie du Municipalité, just up from Pl de la Résistance, on Av Moulay Youssef, is open 24hr.

Police There are *commissariats* at the Préfecture de Medina, just up from the Musée Batha, and by the post office on Bd Mohammed V. The police emergency number is ☏ 19.

Post office The main post office is on the corner of Bd Mohammed V and Av Hassan II in the Ville Nouvelle (Mon–Fri 8am–4.30pm, Sat 8.30am–noon); the poste restante section has a separate side entry to the right of the main building (same hours). There's also a post office on Pl de l'Istiqlal, and branch offices just north of the Medersa el Attarine and on Pl des Alouites, on the edge of the Mellah.

Swimming The municipal pool is at Av des Sports, just west of the train station (closed mid-Sept to mid-June).

Meknes and around

Cut in two by the wide river valley of the Oued Boufekrane, **MEKNES** is a prosperous city with a notably relaxed and friendly atmosphere, due in part to a large student population. Monuments from its past, particularly the extraordinary creations of Moulay Ismail, justify a day or two's rambling exploration, as do the varied and busy souks of its Medina – a uniquely well-preserved combination that have earned the entire city a place on UNESCO's World Heritage list. Visitors en route to Fez will find Meknes a good introduction to the drama of its illustrious neighbour, while those arriving from Fez are sure to enjoy the reduced tempo.

An easy excursion from Meknes, **Volubilis** and **Moulay Idriss** embody much of Morocco's early history: Volubilis as its Roman provincial capital, Moulay Idriss in the creation of the country's first Arab dynasty. Their sites stand 4km apart, at either side of a deep and very fertile valley, about 25km north of the city.

MEKNES ORIENTATION

Meknes is simpler than it looks on the map. Its **Ville Nouvelle** (the modern district constructed by the French) stretches along a slope above the east bank of the river, radiating from the impressive **Place Administrative**. The **Medina** and its neighbouring **Mellah** (the old Jewish quarter) occupy the west bank, with the walls of Moulay Ismail's **Ville Impériale** edging away, seemingly forever, to their south; marking the transition between the Medina and the Ville Impériale – and a focal point for both – is **Place el Hedim**, a good place to fix your bearings.

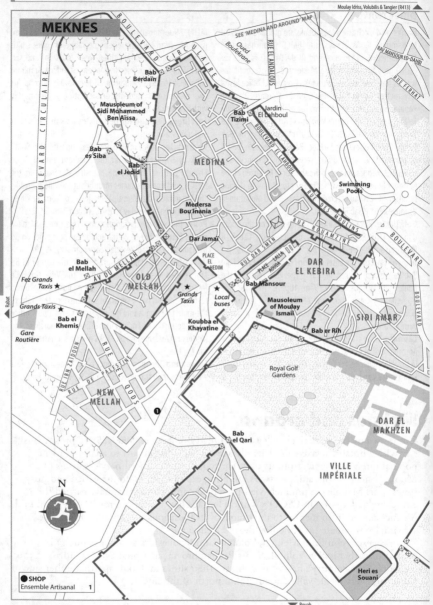

SHOP
Ensemble Artisanal   1

Ville Impériale

More than any other town in Morocco, Meknes is associated with a single figure, **Sultan Moulay Ismail** (see box, p.201). During his 55-year reign, the city was tranformed from a forgettable provincial centre into a spectacular capital with twenty gates and over fifty palaces enclosed within 45km of exterior walls. The principal remains of Ismail's creation – the **Ville Impériale** of palaces and gardens, barracks,

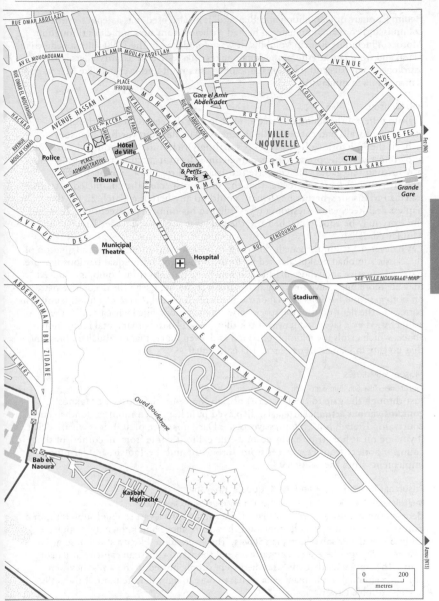

3

granaries and stables – sprawl below the Medina amid a confusing array of walled enclosures, and it's a long morning's walk to take in everything.

Place el Hedim and around

Seeking a grand approach to his palace quarter, the Dar el Kebira, Moulay Ismail demolished the houses that formed the western corner of the Medina to create **Place el**

Hedim ("Square of Demolition and Renewal"); he also used it as a depot for marble columns and construction material he had gathered from sites and cities throughout Morocco, including Roman Volubilis. It was remodelled in the 1990s into a pedestrian plaza, and from late afternoon the square takes on a festive air as storytellers and astrologers, acrobats and traditional doctors gather until mid-evening, like Marrakesh's Jemaa el Fna in miniature.

Bab Mansour

Framing the southern end of Place el Hedim and the centrepiece of the city's ensemble of walls and gateways, the immense **Bab Mansour** (or Bab Mansour Laheej, the "Victorious Renegade") is startlingly rich in its ceremonial decoration and almost perfectly preserved. Its name comes from its architect, one of a number of Christian renegades who converted to Islam and rose to a high position at Ismail's court. A local tale relates that the sultan inspected the completed gate, then asked El Mansour whether he (Ismail) could do any better, a Catch 22 for the hapless architect, whose response ("yes") led to his immediate execution. That said, the story may be apocryphal because the gate was completed under Ismail's son, Moulay Abdallah.

Whatever the truth, the gate is the finest in Meknes and an interesting adaptation of the classic Almohad **design**, flanked by unusual inset and fairly squat bastions that are purely decorative and whose marble columns were brought from Volubilis – indeed, they are more impressive than any that remain at the site itself. The decorative patterns on both gate and bastions are elaborations of the Almohad *darj w ktaf* motif (similar in pattern to the fleur-de-lys), the space between each motif filled with a brilliant array of zellij created by a layer of cutaway black tiles – just like the ornamental inscription above, which extols the triumph of Ismail and, even more, that of Abdallah, bragging that no gate in Damascus or Alexandria is its equal.

Musée de Meknès

Rue Dar Smen • Tues–Sun 10am–5pm • 10dh

Just through the gate to the left (east) of Bab Mansour, the **Musée de Meknès** contains various artisanal artefacts, displayed in half a dozen rooms around a central courtyard. Though not as impressive as the Dar Jamaï (see p.203), it is worth a visit if you are on a short trip to Morocco, as the exhibits come from all corners of the country: pottery from Fez, pieces from Taroudant and the Tafilalt, and farming implements from the south.

Prison of Christian Slaves and the Koubba el Khayatine

Place Lalla Aouda • Daily: July to mid-Sept 9am–6.30pm; mid-Sept to June 9am–5.30pm • 10dh

Beneath the southwest corner of Place Lalla Aouda runs a vast series of subterranean vaults, lit only by the skyholes that stud the square above and known, by popular tradition, as the **Prison of Christian Slaves**. They were more likely a storehouse or granary, although there were certainly several thousand Christian captives at Ismail's court. The story goes that any who died were simply buried in the walls they were building, although no human remains have come to light despite most of the walls having crumbled away.

The green-tiled building to the left of the prison's entrance is the seventeenth-century **Koubba el Khayatine** (same ticket), an anonymous zellij-covered reception hall for ambassadors to the imperial court.

Mausoleum of Moulay Ismail

Daily 9am–noon & 2.30–6pm, closed Fri morning; tomb open to Muslims only • Free • Modest dress, for both women and men, required

Together with the tomb of Mohammed V in Rabat, and the Medersa Bou Inania in Fez, the **Mausoleum of Moulay Ismail** is the only active Moroccan shrine that

SULTAN MOULAY ISMAIL (1672–1727)

"The **Sultan Moulay Ismail**," wrote his chronicler, Ezziani, "loved Mequinez, and he would have liked never to leave it." But leave it he did, ceaselessly campaigning against the rebel Berber chiefs of the south, and the Europeans entrenched in Tangier, Asilah and Larache, until the entire country lay completely under government control for the first time in five centuries. His reign saw the creation of Morocco's strongest ever – and most coherent – army, which included the Black Guard, a regiment of sub-Saharan "slave soldiers", and, it is reckoned, a garrison force of one in twenty of the male population. The period was Morocco's last golden age, though the ruthless centralization of all decisions, and the fear with which the sultan reigned, led to a slide into anarchy and weak, inward-looking rule.

Ismail's achievements were matched by his **tyrannies**, which were judged extreme even by the standards of the time – and contemporary Europeans were burning their enemies and torturing them on the rack. His reign began with the display of four hundred heads at Fez, most of them of captured chiefs, and over the next five decades it is estimated that he was responsible for over thirty thousand deaths, not including those killed in battle. Many of these deaths were quite arbitrary. Mounting a horse, Ismail might slash the head off the eunuch holding his stirrup; inspecting the work on his buildings, he would carry a weighted lance, with which to batter skulls in order to "encourage" the others. "My subjects are like rats in a basket," he used to say, "and if I do not keep shaking the basket they will gnaw their way through."

Yet the sultan was a tireless **builder** throughout Morocco, constructing towns and ports, and a multitude of defensive kasbahs, palaces and bridges. By far his greatest efforts were focused on Meknes, where he sustained an obsessive building programme, often acting as architect and sometimes even working alongside the slaves and labourers. Ironically, time has not been kind to his constructions in his favoured home town. Built mainly of *tabia*, a mixture of earth and lime, they were severely damaged by a hurricane even in his lifetime, and were left to decay thereafter, as subsequent Alaouite sultans shifted their capitals back to Fez and Marrakesh. Walter Harris, writing only 150 years after Ismail's death, found Meknes "a city of the dead…strewn with marble columns and surrounded by great masses of ruin". Thankfully, more recent city authorities have tackled the restoration of the main monuments with more energy.

3

non-Muslims may visit. The mausoleum has been a point of reverence since Ismail's death (it was constructed in his own lifetime) and is still held in high esteem. Given tales of the ruler's excesses, this might seem puzzling to Westerners, but Ismail is remembered in his homeland for his achievements: bringing peace and prosperity after a period of anarchy, and driving out the Spanish from Larache and the British from Tangier. His extreme observance of orthodox Islamic form and ritual also conferred a kind of magic on him, as, of course, does his part in establishing the ruling Alaouite dynasty – although, technically, the dynasty began with his brother, Moulay Rachid, Ismail is generally honoured as the founder.

You are allowed to approach the **sanctuary** in which the sultan is buried, but cannot go beyond the annexe, though this still gives you a good idea of the reverence with which the shrine is treated – you will almost invariably see villagers here, especially women seeking *baraka* (charismatic blessing) and intercession from the saintly sultan's remains.

Dar el Kebira

The dilapidated quarter of **Dar el Kebira**, accessed through a gate on the left beyond the Mausoleum of Moulay Ismail, was the sultan's great palace complex, and you can still make out the imperial structures – there were originally twelve pavilions within the complex – above and between the houses here: ogre-like creations of massive scale compared with the modest dwellings. They were completed in 1677 and dedicated at a midnight celebration, when the sultan personally slaughtered a wolf so its head could be displayed at the centre of the gateway.

Some later commentators saw a conscious echo of Versailles – its contemporary rival – in the grandeur of Ismail's plan, though it would be another decade until the first reports of Louis XIV's palace reached the imperial court. When they did, however, Ismail's interest was pricked, and in 1699 he sent an ambassador to Paris to negotiate the addition of Louis' daughter, Princess Conti, to his harem. The ambassador returned without the girl but bearing some magnificent grandfather clocks, offered as a conciliatory gesture by the Sun King and now on display in the mausoleum.

Dar el Makhzen

The buildings that make up Ismail's last and finest palace, the **Dar el Makhzen**, lie partially hidden behind the mile-long corridor running beyond Bab er Rih. The most you can get to see are a few brief glimpses over the heads of the guards posted by occasional gates in the crumbling 20ft walls. The corridor itself was a favourite drive of the sultan – according to several sources, he was driven around in a bizarre chariot drawn by his women or eunuchs. The palace backs onto the landscaped grounds of the **Royal Golf Gardens**, once the sultan's sunken garden but now private and strictly *interdit* unless you play a round on one dedicated section (see p.211).

Unlike the Dar el Kebira, which was destroyed by the great earthquake of 1755, the Makhzen is still a minor royal residence, though Mohammed VI rarely visits Meknes – and prefers to stay with his aunt in Lahboul on the few occasions that he does.

Heri es Souani

Daily 9am–noon & 3–6.30pm • 10dh

Following the corridor that runs behind the Dar el Makhzen will eventually bring you out by the **Heri es Souani** (or Dar el Ma), the chief sight of the Ville Impériale. Often introduced by local guides as "Ismail's stables" (the stables are in fact further south; see below), the startling series of high-vaulted chambers here were actually storerooms and granaries, filled with provisions for siege or drought. Each of Moulay Ismail's palaces had underground plumbing (well in advance of Europe), and here you can see a remarkable system of chain-bucket wells built between each of the storerooms – one on the right, near the back, has been restored – giving a powerful impression of the complexity of seventeenth-century Moroccan engineering.

Just as worthwhile is the **view from the roof**, which is accessed through the second entrance on the right (though it's frequently closed to visitors). From its **garden**, you can gaze out over the Dar el Makhzen and the placid waters of the Agdal Basin, built as an irrigation reservoir and pleasure lake, where families picnic in summer.

The Rouah

Follow the road diagonally behind the Heri es Souani for 500m, then turn right at the first junction; the Rouah is southeast of the large mosque ahead (30min total) • The *gardien* will usually let you have a quick look for a small tip

The ramshackle ruins of Moulay Ismail's stables, the **Rouah** are officially closed to visitors and not really worth the walk from the Heri es Souani unless you have a serious interest in archeology. It is a massive complex, perhaps twice as large as the Heri es Souani, and in contemporary accounts is often singled out as the greatest feature of all Ismail's building projects: some three miles in length, traversed by a long canal, with flooring built over vaults used for storing grain, and space for over twelve thousand horses. More than anything else in Meknes, it recalls the scale and madness of Moulay Ismail's vision.

The Medina

Although taking much of its present form and size under Moulay Ismail, the Medina bears far less of his stamp, having grown organically since the time of the Almoravids and been far too congested to accommodate any of his grandiose plans. Its main sights, in addition to the extensive **souks**, are the delicately decorated **Medersa Bou Inania** and the **Dar Jamaï**, a rewarding palace museum on the southern fringes.

Dar Jamaï

Rue Sekkakine, off the northern end of Place el Hedim • Daily except Tues 9am–5pm • 10dh

One of the finest examples of a late nineteenth-century Moroccan palace, the **Dar Jamaï** was built in 1882 by the same family of viziers (high government officials) who

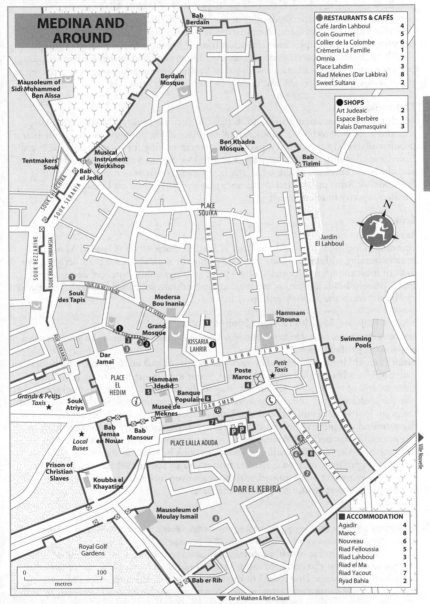

● RESTAURANTS & CAFÉS

Café Jardin Lahboul	4
Coin Gourmet	5
Collier de la Colombe	6
Crèmería La Famille	1
Omnia	7
Place Lahdim	3
Riad Meknes (Dar Lakbira)	8
Sweet Sultana	2

● SHOPS

Art Judeaic	2
Espace Berbère	1
Palais Damasquini	3

■ ACCOMMODATION

Agadir	4
Maroc	8
Nouveau	6
Riad Felloussia	5
Riad Lahboul	3
Riad el Ma	1
Riad Yacout	7
Ryad Bahia	2

erected the Palais Jamaï in Fez. After 1912, it was used as a military hospital, becoming the Museum of Moroccan Art in 1920. Today, it houses one of the best museums in Morocco.

Its exhibits, some organized to recreate the gloriously cluttered reception rooms of nobility in the late 1800s, are predominantly of the same age as the palace, though several pieces of **Meknes pottery** date back to around Ismail's reign, and some of the beautiful cedarwood doors were carved in the fourteenth century. A display of Berber jewellery also catches the eye, though the best is that of **Middle Atlas carpets**, in particular the bold geometric designs of the Beni M'Guild tribe.

Artefacts and antiques aside, the museum is worth a visit as much for the building, boasting a gorgeous upper-floor reception room – arguably the museum's highlight – with intricate woodcarvings on the ceiling. The viziers' **Andalusian Garden** has also been preserved, a lush courtyard with palm, banana, lemon and orange trees, as well as papyrus, roses and cypresses, and usually twittering with birds.

The souks

Much more compact than their counterparts in Fez, the **souks** of Meknes are hassle-free and a pleasure to browse. **Souk Atriya**, on Place el Hedim itself, is one of the best produce markets in the country, particularly worth visiting for its spice and sweet stalls; from here, dive into the Medina proper and follow the lanes around **Souk en Nejjarine** and along the city walls to the west. The best times to visit are early in the morning (around 7 or 8am) or late afternoon; note that the shops close on Friday, when the Medina is pretty much deserted.

Souk Atriya
Place el Hedim

Running along the western side of Place el Hedim, **Souk Atriya** (Covered Market) is usually buzzing with locals doing their shopping for the day. Pick a path between the rows of multicoloured spice stalls, olives piled into pyramids, butchers doing a brisk trade in sheep heads and fat ox tongues, and sweet stalls so loaded with cakes that you can hardly reach the stallholder to pay.

Souk en Nejjarine, Souk des Tapis and Souk es Sebbat
Head through the archway to the left of the Dar Jamaï, and follow the lane (Rue Tiberbarine) north, forking left at the mosque – you've gone too far if you get to Espace Berbère

From Place el Hedim, twisting alleyways lead north to **Souk en Nejjarine**, which together with Souk es Sebbat makes up the Medina's major market street. Turning left, you'll enter an area of textile stalls, which give way to the carpenters (*nejjarine*) workshops that give the souk its name. The passageways on the left along here lead into a parallel arcade, the Souk Joutiya es Zerabi, or **Souk des Tapis** (carpet market), where Berber traders from the surrounding countryside proudly display their wares. Quality can be very high, as can prices, though because Meknes lacks the constant stream of tourists of Fez or Marrakesh, dealers are more willing to bargain; don't be afraid to start low.

Turning right onto Souk en Nejjarine brings you to **Souk es Sebbat** and a classier section of the market – starting off with *babouche* vendors and moving on to the fancier goods aimed at tourists near the medersa.

Kissaria Lahrir
At the eastern end of Souk es Sebbat; keeping the Grand Mosque on your right, follow the lane as it curves round and you'll see the entrance to the *kissaria* opposite one of the doorways (marked no. 20) to the mosque

Most of the work in the **Kissaria Lahrir** is dedicated to textiles, with a throng of bobbin-makers near the entrance using battered old bicycle wheels to spin their threads. But follow the lane round to the far northeast corner and you will find traditional **silver damascene** being made, a craft brought here from Damascus by

Jewish settlers in the late fifteenth century – the hair-thin silver thread is slowly engraved in steel from memory, and the ceramic then burnt in a kiln to produce the striking black colouring. At the Palais Damasquini (see p.211), the family of Essaidi M'Barek has passed on the skills for such delicate work from one generation to the next; his English-speaking son, Saidi, will explain the process if you're interested.

Souk Bezzarine

Running on either side of the city wall, just outside of the tangled alleyways of the Medina proper, **Souk Bezzarine** looks unpromising and run-down at first, but things get more interesting if you follow the inner side of the wall to an assortment of **craftsworkers**, grouped in trade guilds. There are basketmakers, ironsmiths and saddlers, charcoal-sellers and men chipping away at rocks of salt, and at the top, around **Bab el Jedid**, you'll find **musical-instrument workshops** and a side street that's the domain of **tent-makers** – although they rarely sew any traditional tents these days. North of the gate, a **meat market** takes over, dotted with pens of chickens nervously awaiting their fate, before giving way to **fruit and veg stalls** as the road nears Bab Berdaïn.

Medersa Bou Inania

Daily 9am–5pm • 10dh

Built around 1358, so more or less contemporary with the great medersas of Fez, the **Medersa Bou Inania** would be virtually hidden amid the souks were it not for its imposing portal. It takes its name from the notorious Sultan Abou Inan, though it was founded by his predecessor, Abou el Hassan, the great Merenid builder behind the Chellah in Rabat and Salé's eponymous medersa. A modest and functional building, the medersa, or Islamic college (see box, p.171), follows the plan of Hassan's other principal works in that it has a single **courtyard** opening onto a narrow **prayer hall**, and is encircled on both floors by students' **cells**, with exquisitely carved cedar screens. It has a much lighter feel to it than the Salé medersa, and in its balance of wood, stucco and zellij achieves a remarkable combination of intricacy – no area is left uncovered – and restraint. Architecturally, the most unusual feature is a ribbed dome over the **entrance hall**, an impressive piece of craftsmanship that extends right out into the souk.

From the **roof**, generally open to visitors, you can gaze across to the tiled pyramids of the **Grand Mosque** (you can just catch a glimpse of the interior) and its towering minaret, inlaid with bands of green tiles. Its simple decoration is echoed in the minarets beyond, a design that's unique to Meknes – those of Fez or Marrakesh tend to be more elaborate and multicoloured.

The northern Medina

Beyond the Bou Inania Medersa, the Medina is largely residential, dotted with the occasional fruit and vegetable market, and the lone **Ben Khadra Mosque**, which has beautiful polychrome doors and some exquisite coloured stucco. Continuing north along Rue Karmouni, you'll pass the **Berdaïn Mosque**, still being reconstructed after its minaret tragically collapsed in February 2010 (during Friday prayers, the busiest time of the week), killing over forty worshippers. Just beyond here, the narrow lanes end and you emerge into a long, open square, at the far end of which stands the monumental **Bab Berdaïn** (Gate of the Saddlers), another of Ismail's creations; a rugged, genuinely defensive structure, it looks like a more muscular version of the central section of Bab Mansour.

Mausoleum of Sidi Mohammed Ben Aïssa

Closed to non-Muslims

Follow the city walls that extend along the main road west of the Medina and you will catch occasional glimpses on your right of an enormous **cemetery** – almost half the size of the Medina in extent. Non-Muslims are not permitted to enter the enclosure near

3

MOUSSEM OF SIDI MOHAMMED BEN AÏSSA

The **Moussem of Sidi Mohammed Ben Aïssa**, or Moussem Cheikh al Kamel, held on the eve of Mouloud (see p.44), was once one of the most outrageous spectacles in Morocco. The moussem was the principal gathering of the **Aissaoua** brotherhood, an occasion for them to display their powers of endurance under trance, piercing their tongues and cheeks with daggers, eating serpents and scorpions and devouring live sheep and goats.

While their activities today are more subdued, the event is still a dramatic sight. With enormous conical tents popping up around the *marabout* tomb of Sidi Mohammed Ben Aïssa, and crowds of country people in white *jellabas* gathering beneath the city walls, the modern moussem has the appearance of a medieval tournament, never more so than during the spectacular focal **fantasia** (a charge of horses with riders firing guns at full gallop) that takes place near Place el Hedim.

the centre, home to the mausoleum of one of the country's most famous and curious saints, **Sidi Mohammed Ben Aïssa**. Reputedly a contemporary of Moulay Ismail, Ben Aïssa conferred on his followers the power to eat anything, even poison or broken glass, without suffering any ill effects. His cult, the Aissaoua, became one of the most important in Morocco, and certainly the most violent and fanatical. Until prohibited by the French, some fifty thousand devotees regularly attended the saint's annual **moussem** (see box above).

ARRIVAL AND DEPARTURE

By train The town's two train stations are both in the Ville Nouvelle: the main station, the Grande Gare, is 1km east of the centre; the smaller, more convenient Gare el Amir Abdelkader is a couple of blocks away (behind the *Hôtel Majestic*), though not all trains stop here.

Destinations Asilah (5 daily; 3hr 15min); Casablanca (19 daily; 3hr 20min); Fez (23 daily; 35min); Kenitra (19 daily; 2hr); Marrakesh (8 daily; 7hr); Nador (3 daily; 7hr); Oujda (4 daily; 6hr 30min); Rabat (19 daily; 1hr 50min); Tangier (6 daily; 3hr 45min); Taza (9 daily; 3hr).

By bus The main bus station (also known as the Gare Routière Sidi Said) is on the north side of the New Mellah, just outside Bab el Khemis (☎0535 532649). Arriving by CTM, you'll be dropped at the station just off Av de Fes, at the eastern end of the Ville Nouvelle (☎0535 514618); there's a handy central CTM ticket office in a *téléboutique* at 15 Rue Rouamazine.

Destinations Agadir (2 CTM & 5 others daily; 11hr); Al Hoceima (1 CTM daily; 6hr 20min); Azrou (4 CTM & 12 others daily; 2hr); Beni Mellal (6 daily; 6hr); Casablanca (7 CTM & 11 others daily; 3hr 30min); Chefchaouen (4 daily; 5hr 30min); Er Rachidia (3 CTM & 5 others daily; 5hr 30min); Fez (11 CTM & 12 others daily; 1hr); Ifrane (2 CTM & 12 others daily; 1hr 10min–2hr); Larache (5 CTM

MEKNES

& 2 others daily; 3hr 30min–5hr 30min); Marrakesh (2 CTM & 7 others daily; 7–9hr); Midelt (3 CTM & 12 others daily; 4hr 40min); Moulay Idriss (11 daily; 35min); Nador (3 CTM & 5 others daily; 3hr 45min–6hr 45min); Ouezzane, for Volubilis (2 daily; 35min to the turn-off to the ruins); Oujda (2 CTM & 20 others daily; 5hr 40min–7hr); Rabat (8 CTM & 10 others daily; 2hr–2hr 30min); Rissani (1 CTM & 1 other daily; 8hr 45min); Tangier (5 CTM & 9 others daily; 4hr 45min); Taza (7 CTM & 4 others daily; 2hr 45min–3hr 15min); Tetouan (1 CTM & 5 others daily; 5hr 45min).

By grand taxi Most services, including those to Fez and Oujda, use a yard alongside the *gare routière*, though there are also ranks next to the CTM bus station and at the junction of Av des FAR and Av Mohammed V. Grands taxis for Moulay Idriss leave from near the Institut Français just off Pl Ferhat Hachad in the Ville Nouvelle.

Destinations Azrou (1hr); Fez (45min); Ifrane (1hr); Kenitra (1hr 30min); Midelt (3hr 30min); Moulay Idriss (25min); Oujda (4hr); Rabat (1hr 50min).

By car If you're driving in the Ville Nouvelle, it's worth noting that traffic on Av Mohammed V and Av Allal Ben Abdallah is one-way, circulating anticlockwise; parking near the Medina is available on Pl Lalla Alouda.

GETTING AROUND

As an idea of **distances** within Meknes, the walk between Pl Administrative in the Ville Nouvelle and Pl el Hedim in the Medina takes around 20min. There are a few useful **local bus** services, but on the whole it's much more convenient to jump in a **petit taxi**, with fares from the Medina to the Ville Nouvelle costing around 10dh. Further afield, buses run to **Moulay Idriss** (see p.216) and drop off passengers at a junction near **Volubilis** (see p.211); while grands taxis run to both the town and the ruins.

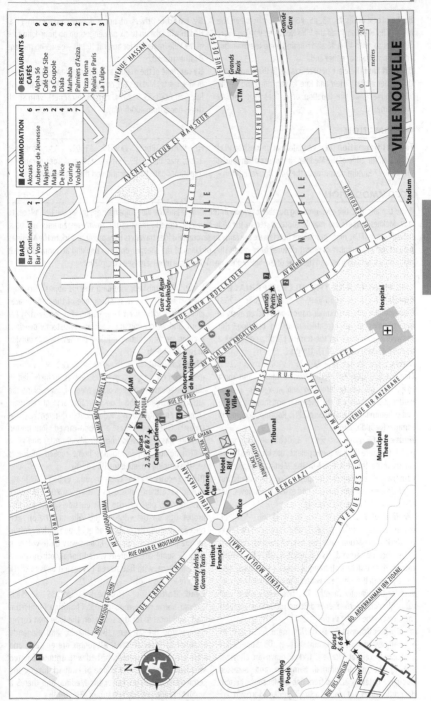

VILLE NOUVELLE

■ ACCOMMODATION 6
Akouas ... 6
Auberge de Jeunesse ... 1
Majestic ... 3
Malta ... 2
De Nice ... 4
Touring ... 5
Volubilis ... 7

■ BARS
Bar Continental ... 2
Bar Vox ... 1

● RESTAURANTS & CAFÉS
Alpha 56 ... 9
Café Obir Sibe ... 6
La Coupole ... 5
Diafa ... 4
Marhaba ... 8
Palmiers d'Aziza ... 2
Pizza Roma ... 7
Relais de Paris ... 1
La Tulipe ... 3

3

By bus Local buses #2, #3, #5, #6 & #7 run between the Medina (Pl el Hedim) and the Ville Nouvelle, leaving every 30min or so, with #5 & #6 also running on to the main bus and train stations at either end.

By petit taxi There are petit taxi ranks in the Medina, on the corner of Dar Smen and Rue Rouamzine, and in the Ville Nouvelle, at the junction of Av des FAR and Av Mohammed V.

By calèche Drivers of horse-drawn carriages in Pl el Hedim will take up to six passengers on an hour-long tour of the Ville Impériale for around 100dh – easier on the legs if rather rushed.

By car None of the major car rental companies have offices in Meknes: try Meknes Car, on the corner of Av Hassan II and Rue Safi (☏ 0535 512074, ⊕ meknescar.net), with small three-doors from 400dh/day.

INFORMATION

Tourist information There's an information kiosk on Pl el Hedim, on the edge of the Medina. The town's main tourist office, at 27 Pl Administrative in the Ville Nouvelle (Mon–Fri 9am–4.30pm; ☏ 0535 516022, ⊕ meknes-net .com), has unusually helpful staff and considerable, if sometimes dated, information on the notice board.

ACCOMMODATION

If you can afford it, the ever-growing number of **riads** in the Medina and the Ville Impériale are by far the best places to stay. Meknes' **hotels** are mainly concentrated in the Ville Nouvelle, close to most of the town's restaurants and bars, though some of the more prominent hotels here are fairly unsavoury. Budget travellers may prefer to stick to the Medina's **pensions**, as a number of recent closures have made slim pickings of the cheaper options. Booking accommodation is really only a necessity around the time of the Sidi Mohammed Ben Aïssa moussem (see box, p.206).

THE MEDINA AND THE VILLE IMPÉRIALE

Agadir 9 Rue Dar Smen ☏ 0535 530141; map p.203. Clean and friendly, with small, basic rooms tucked away in odd crannies of an eccentric, rambling building. Hot showers are available on the terrace (7dh), and there's a hammam nearby (see p.211). 100dh

Maroc 7 Rue Rouamzine ☏ 0535 530075; map p.203. Cleanest and quietest of the Medina hotels, and most rooms are pleasantly furnished and look onto a patio garden full of orange trees. There are hot showers (10dh) and a hammam nearby (see p.211). Rooftop sleeping in summer for 50dh. 200dh

Nouveau 65 Rue Dar Smen ☏ 0667 309317; map p.203. Opposite the Banque Populaire, this blue-tiled place claims to be the first hotel in the Medina (despite the name) and is certainly the cheapest. It's cool and shady, but facilities are basic and there are no external windows. Hot showers available for 5dh. 120dh

★ **Riad el Ma** 4 Derb Sidi Besri ☏ 0661 514824, ⊕ riad-el-ma.com; map p.203. This cute little riad – in the thick of the action, on a lane behind the Kissaria Lahrir – is focused around its atmospherically lit central courtyard, complete with tranquil tinkling fountain. There are log fires in the lounge in winter and a small roof-terrace pool for the warmer months. The two suites are decent value, though the cheaper Red Room (600dh) is arguably the nicest in the riad. 500dh

★ **Riad Felloussia** 23 Derb Hammam Jedid ☏ 0535 530840, ⊕ riadfelloussia.com; map p.203. Superb riad in a handy central location, tucked down an alleyway beyond the neighbourhood hammam and accessed through a gateway just up from Bab el Mansour. The four delightful suites, set around a small garden courtyard, are beautifully furnished, including various objets d'art from the owner's time in West Africa; one of the two terraces enjoys good views over Pl el Hedim. The kindly staff are warm and welcoming and cook up consistently delicious evening meals, including arguably the best pastilla outside of Fez. BB 800dh

Riad Lahboul 6 Derb Ain Sefli ☏ 0535 559878, ⊕ riadlahboul.com; map p.203. Sweet, homely riad in the quieter eastern fringes of the Medina, overlooking the attractive Jardin Lahboul on the other side of the road. Compact en-suite rooms are done out in different regional styles ("Chleuhowi" has a wood-carved four-poster, "Berber" has bed covers from the Middle Atlas and kilim wall hangings), while Mouna's home-cooked cuisine is worth skimping on lunch for. BB 705dh

Riad Yacout 22 Pl Lalla Aouda ☏ 0535 533110, ⊕ riad-yacout-meknes.com; map p.203. A slick upscale riad, perhaps the best outside of the Medina proper (it's on the edge of the Ville Impériale), well priced, tastefully decorated and equipped with a rooftop plunge pool and restaurant. Rooms vary quite wildly in style – some are opulently traditional, others much more modern, with flat-screen TVs – so it pays to check out a few. BB 595dh

Ryad Bahia Rue Tiberbarine ☏ 0535 554541, ⊕ ryad-bahia.com; map p.203. Charming family-run riad, well located for the souks, on the lane that curves up towards the Medersa Bou Inania and elegantly restored by local artisans. All rooms are en suite and have a/c, and many are furnished with antique painted woodwork, yet the vibe is one of laidback luxury. The terrace has good views over the Medina, and there's a small but high-quality restaurant. BB 600dh

VILLE NOUVELLE

Akouas 27 Rue Amir Abdelkader ☎ 0535 515967, ⓦ hotelakouas.com; map p.207. All the mod cons – double-glazing, a/c, heating, satellite TV – in an international-standard business hotel near the CTM station. There's a small indoor pool and a decent restaurant, *El Menzeh*, open to non-residents; the *Akouas* also has its own nightclub (daily 11pm–2am). **420dh**

Auberge de Jeunesse Rue Okba Ben Nafia ☎ 0535 524698, ⓔ aubergejeune-meknes.com; map p.207. Well-maintained hostel set around a garden courtyard, with single beds shoehorned into dorm rooms, plus functional doubles, triples and four-bed rooms; hot showers cost an extra 7dh. Organizes good-value trips to Volubilis and Moulay Idriss (175dh). Open 8am–10pm (till midnight in summer; closed Sun 10am–6pm). Dorm **60dh**, double **75dh**

★ **Majestic** 19 Av Mohammed V ☎ 0535 522035, ⓕ 0535 527427; map p.207. This 1930s hotel marries vintage charm with comfortable, clean rooms (most en suite) offering heating and – in some cases – balconies. Add in friendly management and a large roof terrace and you've got what is probably the best mid-priced choice in the Ville Nouvelle. BB **340dh**

Malta 3 Rue Charif el Idrissi ☎ 0535 515020, ⓦ hotel-malta.ma; map p.207. A spacious and friendly addition to Meknes's upmarket hotel scene, with four-star facilities in its en-suite rooms (including satellite TV and wi-fi), plus its own restaurant, two bars and the intriguingly named *Cow Palace* nightclub (daily midnight–3.30am). **850dh**

De Nice Cnr Rue Accra (also known as Rue Omar Ben Chemssi) and Rue Antsirabé ☎ 0535 520318, ⓔ nice_hotel@menara.ma; map p.207. Friendly place whose good-value rooms on the fourth and fifth floors provide bright modern en suites with three-star facilities, including a/c. The two low-key bars aren't a bad place to wind down at the end of an evening. **530dh**

Touring 34 Av Allal Ben Abdallah ☎ 0535 522351; map p.207. Central cheapie with pretty average facilities – functional at best, and a little threadbare in places. Some rooms are en suite, though there are hot showers throughout. **110dh**

Volubilis 45 Av des FAR ☎ 0535 525082; map p.207. A bit of faded grandeur from the 1930s, complete with a (dark) Art Deco lobby and facade. One of the oldest hotels in the quarter, and still decent, but located at a noisy road junction. **290dh**

EATING AND DRINKING

The **Ville Nouvelle** is home to the city's finest patisseries, the classiest clustered near Pl Ifriquia, as well as a dozen or so decent restaurants, most serving a daily three-course menu. Eating in the **Medina** is largely at basic café-grills – as well as those listed here, cheap hole-in-the-wall joints doing fried fish and brochettes line Rue Rouamazine – or traditional houses such as *Restaurant Omnia* and *Riad Meknes*, where you can tuck into excellent food at a fraction of the price you'd pay in the touristy equivalents in Fez. All smarter options, and a few of the moderates, are licensed to serve alcohol.

MEDINA

CAFÉS AND PATISSERIES

Café Jardin Lahboul Bd el Lahboul, outside the Medina walls; map p.203. Pleasant café on the river's edge, shaded by trees and with views across to the Ville Nouvelle. It's near the main swimming pools, so is popular with families, who get their own separate seating area. Daily 8am–11.30pm.

Crèmería La Famille Souk en Nejjarine; map p.203. Friendly fruit-juice place where you can mix and match your own combinations (from 7dh) – anything with pistachio is generally delicious – and take a well-earned breather at the upstairs tables. Simple food also served (meals from 20dh). Daily 8am–9pm.

RESTAURANTS

Coin Gourmet Rue Rouamazine ☎ 0535 535454; map p.203. Clean, modern diner doing its best to look like a Western fast-food branch, with uniformed staff turning around pizzas, burgers, panini and schwarma (from 20dh). Daily 9am–11pm.

Collier de la Colombe 67 Rue Driba ☎ 0535 55 5041; map p.203. This smart restaurant, in the ornate mansion of "Sultan" Lakhal (a non-Alaouite pretender to the throne on the death of Moulay Youssef in 1927), serves pretty average dishes (mains from around 90dh), so many people just come here for a drink – night and day, the views across the valley to the Ville Nouvelle are stunning, especially from the roof terrace. Daily 11.30am–3.30pm & 6.30–11pm.

Omnia 8 Derb Aïn el Fouki, signed from Rue Rouamzine ☎ 0535 533938; map p.203. Cosy Medina home where you dine in a couple of beautifully decorated alcoves while the family seemingly go about their business. The menu is succinct, but what is on there – smokey aubergine *zaalouk* and lamb *mrouzia* (honey-sweetened tajine) among others – is unfailingly tasty. Dishes from around 80dh. Daily 8–11pm.

Place Lahdim Pl el Hedim; map p.203. A pleasant spot for lunch, with tajines (from 50dh) and brochettes served on multi-level terraces. The aerial view of Pl el Hedim is great for people-watching, especially at sunset (drinking on the terrace costs 10dh extra). Daily 8.30am–11pm.

★ **Riad Meknes (Dar Lakbira)** 79 Ksar Chaacha, Dar el Kebira; follow signs from Bab er Rih ☎ 0535 530542, ⓦ riadmeknes.com; map p.203. A lovely little place snug in the last of Moulay Ismail's original twelve pavilions, the only one to have survived the 1755 earthquake. It's quite

3

tricky to find, but well worth the effort to sample refined traditional cuisine (including pastilla and *mechoui*) in beautifully restored salons or in the patio cactus garden that's magical in the evening. As well as very reasonable a la carte eating, there are set menus starting from 130dh. Daily 7–9.30pm.

Sweet Sultana 4 Derb Sekkaya, Rue Tiberbarine ☎ 0535 535720, ⊛ dar-sultana.com; map p.203. One of the better traditional restaurants in the Medina, set in a nicely refurbished riad, with tables squeezed into a light, bright central courtyard. Friendly staff serve up a variety of Moroccan salads (35dh) and good-value pastilla (50dh) on a fairly short but appetizing menu. Daily noon–2pm & 7–11pm.

VILLE NOUVELLE

CAFÉS AND PATISSERIES

Alpha 56 16 Av Mohammed V; map p.207. A heavenly *tarte tatin* and butter-soft profiteroles make this patisserie a favourite haunt in Meknes. Scrumptious, although at prices to match (110dh/kg). Daily 6.30am–9pm.

Café Obir Sibe 1 Rue Antisarpe; map p.207. The leafy frontage conceals a chilled little café, with a spacious main salon and a couple of side rooms, all brightly decorated and populated with locals sipping lattes, reading papers or chewing the fat. Daily 8am–9pm.

Palmiers d'Aziza 9 Rue de Tarfaya, near Pl Ifriquia; map p.207. The chicest option of Meknes's café scene, with a choice of terraces, all ruled by waiters in black and white and frequented by a trendy clientele. The palm tree shading the main terrace is a nod to the owner's home town of Figuig, in southern Morocco. Daily 7am–10pm.

La Tulipe Pl Maarakat Lahri ☎ 0535 511094; map p.207. A semi-smart place to indulge yourself with expensive ice cream or sticky patisserie, which you can eat

in a fondant-hued interior or on a quiet terrace overlooking a car-filled little square – or take away for later. Daily 7.30am–9.30pm.

RESTAURANTS

La Coupole Corner of Av Hassan II and Rue du Ghana ☎ 0535 522196; map p.207. Popular with locals for an extensive range of reasonably priced Moroccan and European dishes, including pizzas (mains from around 55dh); grilled meats are the house special. There's also a bar and a noisy nightclub. Daily noon–3pm & 7pm–3am.

Diafa 12 Rue Badr el Kobra ☎ 0535 528302; map p.207. What looks like a private house has extremely good and reasonably priced cooking, though there's just one set menu (150dh) and not a vast choice of dishes. Daily noon–3pm & 7–10pm.

Marhaba 23 Av Mohammed V ☎ 0535 521632; map p.207. A no-nonsense eating spot, set off Av Mohammed and popular with locals for a budget serving of thick *harira* soup (from 5dh), brochettes and rotisserie chicken (20dh). Daily noon–9pm.

Pizza Roma 8 Rue Accra, alongside the Hôtel de Nice; map p.207. Limited menu beyond the pizzas, but good value (a margherita is yours for just 20dh), and handy for out-of-hours snacks such as omlettes – even cheaper at 10dh. Daily 24hr.

Relais de Paris 46 Rue Okba Ben Nafia, across from the Auberge de Jeunesse ☎ 0665 186818; map p.207. Sister operation of its successful counterpart in Tangier, serving delicious French cuisine, from foie gras (140dh) to *papillote des poissons* (fish cooked in a paper parcel; 180dh), accompanied by an extensive wine list. The terrace enjoys superb views over the Medina, and there's also a trendy lounge bar downstairs. Daily: restaurant 11am–3pm & 8pm–midnight; lounge-bar 5pm–2am.

DRINKING AND NIGHTLIFE

Many of the **Ville Nouvelle** hotels have bars and nightclubs, often quite lively in the evenings. The lounge bar of the *Relais de Paris* (see above) is your best bet for a mellow drink, especially recommended for Medina views at sunset; or the nightclub of the *Hôtel Rif*, on Rue Accra, is a mite more lively. The bars below are more boisterous, and although some have female staff, women may find the raucous, all-male clientele intimidating.

Bar Continental Cnr of Av des FAR and Av Nehru; map p.207. A rather seedy dive, but kind of fun if you're in the mood for a no-nonsense boozey vibe. Outside tables are blighted by traffic, so go inside. Daily 6am–10.30pm.

Bar Vox Av Hassan II, next to the Camera Cinema; map p.207. A straightforward drinker, veering on contemporary and considerably less intimidating than most, with a varied clientele – if you can make them out through the clinging smoke. Daily 8am–3am.

ENTERTAINMENT

The Camera Pl Ifriquia; map p.207. Cinema showing a varied programme of Bollywood, American and French movies, with daily screenings at 2.45pm and 9pm, the afternoon screening offering a double-bill for the price of a single ticket (15dh).

Conservatoire de Musique Between avs Mohammed V and Allal Ben Adallah, behind Bank Al-Maghreb ☎ 0534 530065; map p.207. Students study classical Arab-Andalous music at this impressive French-style building near Pl Ifriquia, together with

milhûn and, less so, *gharnati*, and the conservatoire gives occasional concerts.
Institut Français Rue Ferhat Hachad ☎ 0535 516500; map p.207. Comprehensive programme of well-priced

hip-hop (H-Kayne, Morocco's most famous hip-hop group, are from Meknes), theatre, dance, cinema and literature events, plus a popular student café.

SHOPPING

Art Judeaic Chez Sidi Mohammed, Rue Tiberbarine; map p.203. This incredible collection of Jeiwsh art and trinkets – *menoras*, ancient *mezuzahs* and the like – has been painstakingly assembled by the friendly proprietor. You're unlikely to find a bargain, but it's great fun browsing and listening to his passionate patter. Daily 10am–5pm.

Ensemble Artisanal Above the local bus station on Av Zine el Abidine Riad; map pp.198–199. This large place trains apprentices, and while there's little to actually buy here there, is a lot to be seen, including the work of young craftsmen making zellij tiles. The building also houses several

active cooperatives. Mon–Sat 9am–1pm & 3–7pm.
Espace Berbère 32 Rue Tiberbarine; map p.203. An interesting and eclectic collection of craft items including lamps, silver tables and, of course, Berber carpets, on the road that leads up from Dar Jamaï and into the Medina. Daily 9am–6pm.
★ **Palais Damasquini** Kissaria Lahrir; map p.203. The oldest establishment in Meknes still working with silver damascene, and something of an institution in these parts – King Mohammed V shops here when he's in town – this little workshop turns out exquisite plates (from 150dh), jugs and other items. Daily 7am–dusk.

ACTIVITIES

Golf The Meknes Royal Golf Club at Bab Belkari (☎ 0535 530753, ☎ 0535 557934) has a nine-hole, par-36 course in the landscaped grounds of the Royal Golf Gardens.
Hammams Hammam Zitouna, opposite the mosque, is allegedly the oldest – and many say the nicest – hammam in Meknes (daily: men 6am–noon & 9pm–midnight; women 1–9pm; 10dh, massage 30dh). Hammam Jedid, down an alley off the lane that runs from Rue Dar Smen to the Bou Inania Medersa (follow signs for *Riad Felloussia*), is

an atmospheric traditional neighbourhood hammam, offering *gh assoul* (clay) scrubs and massages (same hours and prices as Hammam Zitouna).
Swimming pools There are two public pools down by the Oued Boufekrane, reached along a lane from Bd el Lahboul or from the intersection of avenues Hassan II and Moulay Ismail, both open May–Sept only. The first is very cheap at 5dh; just to its north is CODM Natation – classier, less crowded, and eight times the price.

DIRECTORY

Banks and exchange Several in the Ville Nouvelle, concentrated around Pl Administrative, and along Av Mohammed V and Av des FAR. In the Medina, the Banque Populaire is on Rue Dar Smen, near Bab Mansour, and the BMCE is on Rue Rouamazine and have ATMs; the former also has exchange facilities. The BMCI near the Dar Jamaï off Pl el Hedim has a bureau de change (Mon–Fri 8.15am–4pm), while the *Hôtel Rif* on Rue Accra will exchange cash round the clock.
Internet Counter Strike, 86 Rue Dar Smen (daily 10am–9pm).

Medical care Hôpital Moulay Ismail (☎ 0535 524921). English-speaking doctors include Dr Mohammed Dbab at 4 Rue Accra in the Ville Nouvelle (☎ 0535 521087).
Pharmacy The emergency night pharmacy in the Hôtel de Ville on Pl Administrative is open throughout the night (daily 8.30pm–8.30am).
Police The local HQ is on Pl Ferhat Hachad, at the western end of Av Hassan II (☎ 19). There's a smaller station next to Bab Jemaa en Nouar in the southwest corner of Pl el Hedim.
Post office The main post office is on the northeast corner of Pl Administrative (Mon–Fri 8am–7pm & Sat 8.30am–noon).

Volubilis

A striking sight, visible for miles on the bends of the approach roads, the Roman ruins of **VOLUBILIS** occupy the ledge of a long, high plateau, 25km north of Meknes. Below their walls, towards Moulay Idriss, stretches a rich river valley; beyond lie the dark, outlying ridges of the Zerhoun mountains. The drama of this scene – and the scope of the ruins themselves – are undeniably impressive, so much so that the site was a key location for Martin Scorsese's film *The Last Temptation of Christ*.

Brief history

Except for a small trading post on an island off Essaouira, Volubilis was the Roman

Empire's most remote and far-flung base. It represented – and was, literally – the end of the imperial road, having reached across France and Spain and then down from Tangier, and despite successive emperors' dreams of "penetrating the Atlas", the southern Berber tribes were never effectively subdued.

In fact, direct **Roman rule** here lasted little over two centuries – the garrison withdrew early, in 285 AD, to ease pressure elsewhere. But the town must have taken much of its present form well before the official annexation of the Kingdom of Mauretania by Emperor Claudius in 40 AD. Tablets found on the site, inscribed in Punic, show a significant **Carthaginian trading presence** in the third century BC, and prior to colonization it was the western capital of a heavily Romanized, but semi-autonomous, **Berber kingdom** that reached into northern Algeria and Tunisia. After the Romans left,

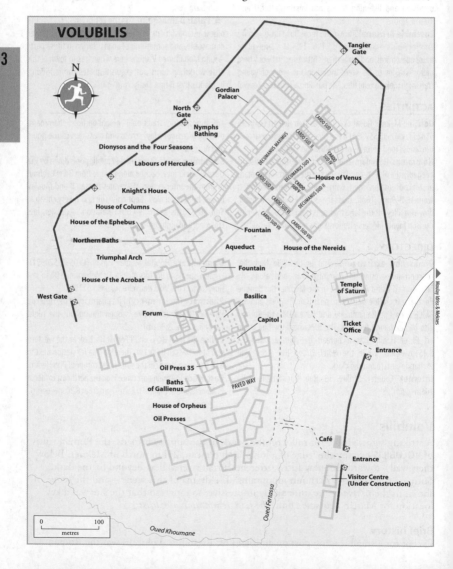

3

VOLUBILIS

N

Tangier Gate

Gordian Palace

North Gate

Nymphs Bathing

Dionysos and the Four Seasons

Labours of Hercules

DECUMANUS MAXIMUS

CARDO SUD I

CARDO SUD II

CARDO SUD III

CARDO SUD IV

CARDO SUD V

CARDO SUD VI

DECUMANUS SUD I

House of Venus

Knight's House

House of Columns

House of the Ephebus

Northern Baths

Triumphal Arch

House of the Acrobat

West Gate

CARDO SUD VII

CARDO SUD VIII

Fountain

Aqueduct

House of the Nereids

Fountain

Basilica

Forum

Capitol

Temple of Saturn

Ticket Office

Entrance

Oil Press 35

Baths of Gallienus

PAVED WAY

House of Orpheus

Oil Presses

Café

Entrance

Visitor Centre (Under Construction)

Oued Fertassa

Mouley Idriss & Meknes

0   100
metres

Oued Khoumane

Volubilis experienced very gradual change. Latin was still spoken in the seventh century by the local population of Berbers, Greeks, Syrians and Jews; Christian churches survived until the coming of Islam; and the city itself remained active well into the seventeenth century, when its marble was carried away by slaves for the building of Moulay Ismail's Meknes.

What you see today, well excavated and maintained, are largely the ruins of second- and third-century AD buildings – impressive and affluent creations from its period as a **colonial provincial capital**. The land around here is some of the most fertile in North Africa, and the city exported wheat and olives in considerable quantities to Rome, as it did wild animals from the surrounding hills. Roman games, memorable for the sheer scale of their slaughter (nine thousand beasts were killed for the dedication of Rome's Colosseum alone), could not have happened without the African provinces, and Volubilis was a chief source of their lions – within just two hundred years, along with Barbary bears and elephants, they became extinct.

The site

Daily 8am– sunset, though in practice the site closes at around 6.30pm • 10dh; guides cost 150dh per hour, though most showpiece buildings are demarcated with a plaque • At the time of writing, the archeological museum that has slowly been taking shape near the entrance was still under construction

The **entrance to the site** is through a minor gate in the city wall – or through a break in the wall further down, depending on construction work – built along with a number of outer camps in 168 AD, following a prolonged series of Berber insurrections. The best of the finds, which include a superb collection of bronzes, have been taken to the Archeological Mueseum in Rabat (see p.260), though Volubilis has retained *in situ* the great majority of its **mosaics**, some thirty or so, which are starting to show the effects of being exposed to the elements. The finest mosaics line the **Decumanus Maximus**, the main thoroughfare through Volubilis, but aside from those subjected to heavy-handed restoration, the once brightly coloured tiles have faded to a subtle palette of ochres and greys. Similarly, the site requires a bit of imagination to reconstruct a town (or, at least, half a town, for the original settlement was twice the size of what remains today) from the jumble of low walls and stumpy columns. Nevertheless, you leave with a real sense of Roman city life and its provincial prosperity, while it is not hard to recognize the essentials of a medieval Arab town in the layout.

House of Orpheus

Starting at the southern end of the site, in what was effectively a suburban quarter, the **House of Orpheus** is an enormous complex of rooms just beside the beginning of a paved way. Although substantially in ruins, it offers a strong impression of its former luxury – an opulent mansion, perhaps for one of the town's richest merchants. Its two main sections – public and private – each have their own separate entrance and interior court. The private rooms, which you come to first, are grouped around a small patio, which is decorated with a more or less intact **dolphin mosaic** (in the southwest corner). You can also make out the furnace and heating system (just to the right of the entrance), the kitchen and the **baths**, an extensive system of hot, cold and steam rooms.

A little further inside, the house's public apartments are dominated by a large atrium – half reception hall, half central court, and again preserving a very fine mosaic, **The Chariot of Amphitrite Drawn by a Seahorse**. The best mosaic here, however, from which the house takes its name, is that of the **Orpheus Myth**, located just behind this in a room that was probably the *tablinium*, or archives.

Oil presses and the Baths of Gallienus

South of the House of Orpheus is a mixed area of housing and industry, each of its buildings containing the remains of at least one **olive press**. The extent and number of these presses, built into even the grandest mansions, reflect the olive's central importance to the city and indicate perhaps why Volubilis remained unchanged for so long after the Romans' departure. A significant proportion of its twenty thousand population must have been involved in some capacity in the oil's production and export.

Heading north from the House of Orpheus, you pass first through the remains of the city's main **public baths**, restored by the Emperor Gallienus in the third century AD and clearly monumental in their intent (though sadly the mosaics are only fragmentary), and then alongside **Oil Press 35**, repaired in 1990 and featuring a reconstruction of the grinding mechanism, including both grinding stones.

The Forum, Capitol and Basilica

Above the House of Orpheus, a broad, paved street leads up towards the **Forum**, the arrangement of which is typical of a major Roman town: built on the highest rise of the city and flanked by a triumphal arch, a market, and a capitol and basilica, the sand-coloured ruins of which dominate the site.

Inscriptions date the **Capitol**, the smaller and lower of the two main buildings, to 217 AD, when this public nucleus seems to have been rebuilt by the African-born Severian emperors. Adjoined by small forum **baths**, it is a simple building with a porticoed court that leads on to a small temple and altar dedicated to the official state cult of Capitoline Jupiter, Juno and Minerva. The large five-aisled **Basilica** to its side served as the courthouse, while immediately across the Forum were the small court and stalls of the **central market**. Storks have colonized some columns of the Capitol and Basilica; on a quiet day, you can hear their clacking noises and will almost certainly see a few circling above or standing sentinel over their nests.

The Triumphal Arch and around

The **Triumphal Arch**, right in the middle of the town, had no purpose other than to create a ceremonial proscenium for the principal street, the **Decumanus Maximus**, which was fronted in traditional Roman and Italian fashion by shops built in the tiny cubicles. It was erected to honour the Severian emperor Caracalla and was once topped with a bronze chariot, according to a weathered inscription. The heavily eroded medallions on either side presumably depict Caracalla and his mother, Julia Domna, who is also named in the inscription. The aqueduct and fountains across from the arch once supplied yet another complex of public baths, the **Northern Baths**. Opposite them is the **House of the Acrobat** (also called House of the Athlete), which retains an impressive **Mosaic of an Acrobat** or "chariot jumper" – depicted receiving the winner's cup for a desultor race, a display of great skill that entailed leaping on and off a horse in full gallop.

House of the Ephebus

The first of the great Decumanus Maximus mansions, the **House of the Ephebus** takes its name from the bronze of a youth found in its ruins (and today displayed in Rabat). In general plan, it is very similar to the House of Orpheus, once again containing an olive press in its rear section, though this building is on a far grander scale – almost twice the size of the other – with pictorial mosaics in most of its public rooms and an ornamental pool in its central court. Finest of the mosaics is a representation of **Bacchus Being Drawn in a Chariot by Panthers** – a suitable scene for the *cenacula*, or banqueting hall, in which it is placed.

The House of Columns to the House of the Nymphs Bathing

Separated from the House of the Ephebus by a narrow lane is a mosaic-less mansion, known after its facade as the **House of Columns**, and adjoining this, the **Knight's House** with an incomplete mosaic of **Dionysos Discovering Ariadne** asleep on the beach at Naxos; both houses are largely ruins. More illuminating is the large mansion that begins the next block, similar in plan but with a very complete mosaic of the **Labours of Hercules**; almost comic caricatures, these give a good idea of typical provincial Roman mosaics. The next house along, the **House of Dionysos**, holds the site's best-preserved mosaic, **Dionysos and the Four Seasons**, which still hints at the exuberant original colours. In the neighbouring house, the mosaic of the **Nymphs Bathing** is severely deteriorated around its central area.

Gordian Palace

North of the House of Dionysos, approaching the partially reconstructed **Tangier Gate**, stands the **Gordian Palace**, former residence of the procurators who administered both the city and the province. Despite its size, however, and even with evidence of a huge **bathhouse** and pooled courtyards, it is unmemorable, stripped of its columns and lacking any mosaics. Its grandeur may have made it a target for Ismail's building mania. Indeed, how much of Volubilis remained standing before his reign is an open question – Walter Harris, writing at the turn of the twentieth century, found the road between here and Meknes littered with ancient marbles, left as they fell following the announcement of the sultan's death.

House of Venus

On the road running parallel to the Decumanus Maximus, the **House of Venus** features the most exceptional ensemble of mosaics in Volubilis. You cannot enter the house itself, but most of the fine tiling can be seen by walking round the outside of the ruins. Around the central court is a small group of mosaics, including an odd, very worn representation of a **Chariot Race** – with birds instead of horses. The villa's most outstanding mosaics lie beyond, in the "public" sections: on the left, in the corner, is a geometrical design, with medallions of **Bacchus Surrounded by the Four Seasons**; straight ahead is the **Cortege of Venus**, in which the Three Graces are depicted rowing the goddess to shore accompanied by a retinue of Nereids and Tritons; and off to the far right are **Diana Bathing** (and surprised by the huntsman Acteon) and the **Abduction of Hylas by Nymphs**. Each of these scenes – especially the last two – is superbly handled in stylized, fluid animation. They date – like that of the mosaic in the **House of the Nereids** (two houses further down, on the opposite side of the road) – from the late second or early third century AD, and were a serious commission. It is not known who commissioned the house itself, but its owner must have been among the city's most successful patrons – magnificent bronze busts of Cato the Younger and Juba II were also found here and now form the centrepiece of Rabat's Archeological Museum (see p.260).

Temple of Saturn

Leaving the site by the path below the Forum, you pass close by the ruins of a **temple** on the opposite side of the stream. The Romans dedicated it to Saturn, but it seems to have previously been used for the worship of a Carthaginian god; several hundred votive offerings were discovered during its excavation.

ARRIVAL AND DEPARTURE   VOLUBILIS

By bus You can take an Ouezzane bus from Meknes (2 daily) and ask to be set down by the turn-off to the site (35min); the ruins are a 500m walk downhill from the N13.

By grand taxi Taxis run to the ruins from Meknes (60dh for the whole taxi, though drivers are likely to try and charge more); if you pay more, the driver will wait at

Volubilis and take you on to Moulay Idriss, where you can look round at leisure and then get a regular *place* in a grand taxi back to Meknes. You could also charter a private taxi for a half-day excursion (with 3hr or so at the site) for around 400dh.

By car If you're driving to Volubilis from the north, note that after you've turned east after Sidi Kacem the route might be signposted only to Oualili, the Arabic for "Volubilis" (a corruption of *oualili*, meaning oleander).

On a tour Most of the riads and hotels in Meknes can organize a car and driver for the trip to both Volubilis and Moulay Idriss (around 350dh), or you can join a cheaper guided tour with the *Auberge de Jeunesse* (see p.209).

On foot You can walk between Moulay Idriss and Volubilis, a scenic and safe 4km stroll, particularly enjoyable in the early morning when locals will join you on their way to the olive groves.

ACCOMMODATION

Volubilis Inn 1km north of the site ☏ 0535 544405, ⓦ hotelvolubilisinn. Modern four-star with a colonnaded theme running throughout the public areas, and smart rooms that have a touch of the Mediterranean about them, with tiled floors and either a balcony or terrace offering astounding views over the ruins; the Triumphal Arch makes an impressive distant backdrop to a dip in the pool. It's geared more towards tour groups, though, who perhaps unknowingly absorb the high price in part of a longer itinerary. **1050dh**

Moulay Idriss

The holy town of **MOULAY IDRISS**, spread across the foothills of Jebel Zerhoune, 25km north of Meknes and 4km from Volubilis, takes its name from its founder, Morocco's most venerated saint and the creator of its first Arab dynasty. His mausoleum, the reason for its sacred status, is the object of constant pilgrimage, not to mention an important summer **moussem** – a trip to which is worth a fifth of the *hajj* to Mecca. For most Western tourists, there is little specific to see and certainly nothing that may be visited – non-Muslims are barred from the shrine – but you could easily lose a happy half-day exploring the tangled lanes that shimmy between the sugar-cube houses scattered over the hills, enjoying delightful window-views or just absorbing the laidback atmosphere. Few tourists bother to stay overnight, another reason to linger.

Mausoleum of Moulay Idriss

Closed to non-Muslims • From the main square, head north through the archway and the mausoleum is directly ahead • For the best viewpoint, take the passageway on your left (facing the shrine) and climb the steps towards a fountain, 50m beyond, where the lane splits in two; take the right fork and after another 30m or so, turn left up another flight of steps (all 150 of them), following the signs for Sidi Abdallah el Hajjam

Rebuilt by Moulay Ismail, the green-tiled pyramids of Moulay Idriss's **mausoleum** lie right at the heart of town, flanked on either side by the hillside residential quarters of Khiber and Tasga. The shrine itself is cordoned off from the street by a low, wooden bar, to keep out Christians and beasts of burden, and while you can get an idea of its

MOULAY IDRISS AND THE FOUNDATION OF MOROCCO

Moulay Idriss el Akhbar (The Great) was a great-grandson of the Prophet Mohammed; his grandparents were Mohammed's daughter Fatima, and his cousin and first follower, Ali. Heir to the Caliphate in Damascus, he fled to Morocco around 787 AD, following the Ummayad victory in the great civil war that split the Muslim world into Shia and Sunni sects.

In Volubilis, then still the main centre of the north, Idriss seems to have been welcomed as an *imam* (a spiritual and political leader), and within a few years had succeeded in carving out a considerable kingdom. At this new town site, more easily defended than Volubilis, he built his capital, and he also began the construction of Fez, continued and considerably extended by his son, Moulay Idriss II, that city's patron saint. News of his growing power filtered back to the East, however, and in 791 the Ummayads had Idriss poisoned, doubtless assuming that his kingdom would crumble.

They were mistaken. Alongside the faith of Islam, Idriss had instilled a sense of unity among the region's previously pagan (and sometimes Christian or Jewish) Berber tribes, which had been joined in this prototypical Moroccan state by increasing numbers of Arab Shiites loyal to the succession of his *Alid* line. After his assassination, Rashid, the servant who had travelled with Moulay Idriss to Morocco, took over as regent until 805, when the founder's son was old enough to assume the throne of what was Morocco's first independent kingdom.

grandeur on the ground, you'll have to climb up towards one of the vantage points near the pinnacle of each quarter for a true sense of its scale – aim for the terrace near **Sidi Abdallah el Hajjam**, above Khiber (the taller hill), where you'll also find souks selling a variety of religious artefacts for Muslim visitors, especially plain white candles for use in the mausoleum.

Merdersa Idriss

On your way up into the Khiber quarter, aim for the unusual minaret of the **Medersa Idriss**, now a Koranic school. The medersa was constructed with materials taken from Volubilis, and the cylindrical minaret – the only one of its kind in Morocco – was built in 1939 by a *hadji* who had been inspired by those he had seen in Mecca. A *surah* (chapter) from the Koran is inscribed in Kufic script around it, made out of green mosaics.

ARRIVAL AND INFORMATION   MOULAY IDRISS

By bus Buses from Meknes (11 daily; 35min) drop you at the very base of the town, from where it's a short but steep walk up the stall-lined road to the main square.

By grand taxi Grands taxis make regular runs from Meknes (25min), leaving from near the Institut Français just off Pl Ferhat Hachad in the Ville Nouvelle. You could charter a private taxi for a half-day tour, taking in both

Moulay Idriss and Volubilis for around 400dh, though it's actually cheaper to take a tour (see opposite).

Guides It's not easy to find your way up through the winding streets (most end in abrupt blind alleys), particularly around the Khiber quarter, but unofficial guides can be enlisted for around 50dh. Alternatively, most guesthouses can provide half-day tours of Moulay Idriss for 150dh or so.

ACCOMMODATION

Until recently, non-Muslims were not permitted to stay overnight in Moulay Idriss – the last place in Morocco to keep this religious prohibition – but after the king decreed this unfair following a visit in 2005, a number of family-run *maisons d'hôte* have appeared. As well as the below, more upscale accommodation can be found at the *Volubilis Inn*, 3km from Moulay Idriss (see opposite).

La Colombe Blanche 21 Derb Zouak, Tasga; turn right at the mausoleum, left at the fountain and then follow the green signs ☎ 0535 544596, ⓦ maisondhote-zerhoune.ma. Well-established *maison d'hôte* in an intimate family home, with eight missmatched rooms spread around the first floor and the terrace. Home-cooked menus in the tiled salon are good value at 85dh. Tour groups sometimes stay here at the weekend, so book ahead. BB **300dh**

Dar Al Andaloussiya Diyafa 169 Derb Zouak, Tasga; turn right at the mausoleum, left at the fountain and then follow the red signs ☎ 0535 544749, ⓦ maisondhote-volubilis.com. Popular *maison d'hôte*, with four sizeable a/c rooms, some more traditional than

others, and a flat-screen satellite TV in the lounge – you can even bed down for the night in one of the beautifully decorated salons. While the staff are perfectly courteous, it does seem to lack the personal touch of *La Colombe Blanche*. BB salon **100dh**, double **400dh**

Dar Zerhoune 42 Derb Zouak, Tasga; turn right at the mausoleum, left at the fountain and then follow the green signs ☎ 0535 544371, ⓦ buttonsinn.com. Modest house with some nice traditional touches (including keyhole doors throughout), excellent meals and great views of Jebel Zerhoune from the cushion-strewn roof terrace – though noise can be a problem. Bikes are available for the short ride to Volubilis. BB dorm **200dh**, double **500dh**

EATING

Restaurants are pretty scarce, as the majority of the town's *maisons d'hôte* cook up evening meals for guests, though the climb up to *Scorpion House* is certainly worth it. For a quick bite, your best bet is the grill cafés on the square by the mausoleum, followed by some excellent local nougat from the Khiber souks.

Al Baraka 22 Aïn Smen ☎ 0535 544184. Pleasant panoramic restaurant on the road that winds out of town above Khiber, serving tasty tajines sprinkled with local olives, accompanied by tremendous views from the terrace. Daily 11.30am–3pm.

Diyar Timnay 7 Rue Aïn Rjal, below the grand taxi rank ☎ 0535 544400, ⓦ diyar-timnay.com. This pleasant guesthouse restaurant is a good option for tajines (70dh) and brochettes (80dh), and enjoys a fine panorama across the whitewashed rooftops and beyond. Daily 8am–11pm.

3

Scorpion House (Dar Akrab) 54 Drouj el Hafa, Khiber; turn left at the mausoleum and follow the green signs ☎0655 210172, ⓦscorpionhouse.com. The latest venture from the team behind Fez's *Café Clock* (see p.191) is a magical spot, sitting high up on the Khiber hill and looking directly over the mausoleum. It's all very chic, and the food, be it *maakouda* (spicy potato cakes) or *kefta* kebab, is top-notch, though it is so exclusive that it opens by prior reservation only (3000dh for 1–4 people, 500dh per person beyond that – which effectively gets you your very own restaurant for a couple of hours). Open for breakfast, lunch or dinner.

The Middle Atlas

Covered in forests of oak, cork and giant cedar, the **Middle Atlas** is a beautiful and relatively little-visited region. The dark brown tents of nomadic Berber encampments immediately establish a cultural shift away from the European north; the plateaux are pockmarked by dark volcanic lakes; and the towns initially feel different, too, their flat, gabled houses lending an Alpine-resort feel, particularly at the "hill station" resort of **Ifrane**, where the king has a summer palace. If you just want a day-trip from Fez, the Middle Atlas is most easily accessible at **Sefrou**, a relaxed market town 28km southeast of the city, though **Azrou** should be on most itineraries as well, an interesting Berber settlement with an excellent and authentic souk, and ideally located for forays into the surrounding cedar forests.

At Azrou, the road forks and you can take one of two routes. The N13 heads southeast to the former mining town of **Midelt** and on to Er Rachidia, a journey that traces the old **Trek es Sultan**, or Royal Road, an ancient trading route that once carried salt, slaves and other commodities with caravans of camels across the desert from West Africa. Heading southwest, the N8, the main route to Marrakesh, skirts well clear of the Atlas ranges, and is lined with dusty, functional market centres, though **Beni Mellal** is something of a transport hub along the way. From here you can cut south to **Azilal**, jumping-off point for the magnificent **Cascades d'Ozoud** and the stunning High Atlas valley of **Aït Bouguemez**, or strike out for **Imilchil** and the epic mountain roads that lie beyond.

GETTING AROUND THE MIDDLE ATLAS

By public transport Buses are plentiful on the stretch between Fez and Er Rachidia, but travellers may find a few problems stopping en route between Fez and Marrakesh, where buses are often full when they pull into towns and few people alight along the way. The solution is flexibility: take the occasional grand taxi or stop for a night to catch an early bus, and you won't be stuck for long.

By car You'll be able to properly explore the Middle Atlas if you've got your own wheels, enabling you to venture deeper into the cedar forests around Azrou and up (and down) surfaced mountain roads, to Imilchil and the Aït Bouguemez. A 4WD opens up the network of *pistes* in the southern half of the range, and allows for some pretty adventurous journeys in the High Atlas, particularly in the eastern areas of the Aït Bouguemez.

Sefrou and around

The fate of **SEFROU** is to be just 28km south of Fez. Anywhere else in Morocco, this ancient walled town in the foothills of the Middle Atlas would receive a steady flow of visitors, just as it did when it served as the first stop on the caravan routes to the Tafilalt; until the Protectorate, it marked the mountain limits of the **Bled el Makhzen** – the Governed Lands. Instead, the pull of the larger city leaves Sefrou, once known as the Jardin du Maroc, virtually ignored by most tourists, a source of some local resentment and the reason, perhaps, for the extreme persistence of the few hustlers here.

To add insult to injury, Sefrou actually predates Fez as a city, but while Fez became a playground for the finest medieval crafstmen Morocco had to offer, Sefrou ended up with just a couple of **mosques** to its name. Indeed, there are few sights per se, and nothing that you can actually visit, though a trip here is more about wandering the compact **Medina** and the adjacent **Mellah**, heading off on **walks** into the surrounding hills or to the unusual cave houses in nearby **Bhalil**.

The Medina

In comparison with Fez, the **Medina** of Sefrou inevitably feels rather low-key. However, it is equally well preserved on its modest scale – a pocket-size version of Fez el Bali that is far less intimidating for many visitors – and the untouristy atmosphere makes it a pleasant place to explore by instinct. The **Thursday souk**, in particular, remains a largely local affair, drawing Berbers from neighbouring villages to sell garden produce and buy basic goods.

The main entrance into the Medina is through **Bab M'kam**, set into the nineteenth-century ramparts on the eastern side of Place Moulay Hassan. Beyond here, the main street of the old Arab town winds down to the rubbish-strewn **Oued Aggaï**, where it follows the river past the **Adloun Mosque** and the **Grand Mosque**, with its domed minaret; both are closed to non-Muslims. Turning left here leads into an area of covered **souks**, where traders set up shop behind uniformly mint-green doorways and chickens amble about among them.

Walking back to the bridge by the Grand Mosque, you can cross the river and head right (southwest) for **Bab Merba** (and the covered market) or left (southeast) to come out of the Medina via **Bab Mejles**.

The Mellah

A dark, cramped conglomeration of tall, shuttered houses and tunnel-like streets, Sefrou's **Mellah** is one of the oldest in Morocco. There seems to have been a Jewish-Berber population here long before the coming of Islam and, although most converted, a large number of Jews from the south settled again in the town under the Merenids. As late as the 1950s, at least a third of the population were Jews, and while only a handful remain – most having left for Casablanca, Israel or Paris – the district still seems distinct.

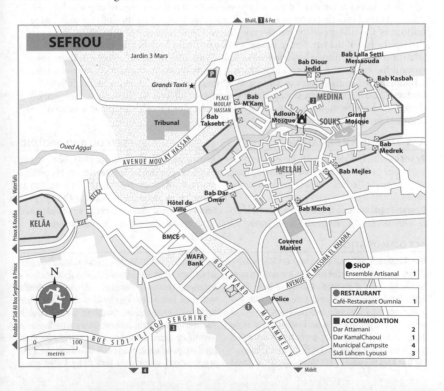

WALKS AROUND SEFROU

High enough into the Middle Atlas to avoid the suffocating dry heat of summer, Sefrou is a good base for some modest **walking**. Dozens of **springs** emerge in the hills above the town and a few waterfalls are active for part of the year.

KOUBBA OF SIDI ALI BOU SERGHINE

For a relatively easy target, take the road up behind the Ville Nouvelle post office on Boulevard Mohammed V (Rue Sidi Ali Bou Serghine), which divides into a fork after about a kilometre. The right-hand branch leads to a small, deserted French fort, known as the **Prioux**, and to the **koubba** of one Sidi Ali Bou Serghine. The views from around here are thrilling: in winter, the snowcapped Mischliffen; in summer, the cedars and holm oaks cresting the ridges to infinity. You can also reach the *koubba* (and fort) by taking the left fork in the road that splits in front of **El Kelâa**, a *ksar* (fortified settlement) that's quite interesting in itself and reached on Rue de la Kelâa, west of the sharp bend in the main road across the Oued Aggaï.

THE WATERFALLS

Heading up Rue de la Kelâa from the main road and taking the right-hand fork in front of El Kelâa leads to a junction signposted "*Cascades*", from where a single-lane tarmac road follows the river to a small hydroelectric power station; 250m beyond this, below imposing rocky outcrops, are the **waterfalls**, at their best in spring. Flash floods regularly wash away the path here, so repair work may bar your access to a pool beneath for a paddle.

Bhalil

Tumbling down a hillside 6km northwest of Sefrou, the extraordinary village of **Bhalil** is laid out over a honeycomb of caves, many of which are still in use as troglodyte dwellings. The **cave houses** are in the old part of the village, a charming network of pink- and yellow-painted buildings connected by innumerable bridges; go through the arch at the bottom of the village (where grands taxis drop off) and take any of the narrow lanes that run up the hill to the left. You're unlikely to be in Bhalil long before attracting the attention of the amicable Mohammed Chraibi, the "official guide", who will show you around the village and take you to his own (cramped) cave home (100dh for the tour).

Bhalil's other quirky claim to fame is as Morocco's "centre" for producing **jelleba buttons**. You'll see women sitting along the edge of alleyways, chatting as they work their way through mounds of thread – a long job, given that there are at least two hundred buttons on every *jelleba*.

ARRIVAL AND INFORMATION

By bus Buses from Fez (roughly hourly; 1hr) leave from Pl de la Résistance (La Fiat) in the Ville Nouvelle, usually dropping off passengers at "Le Jardin", the area around Pl Moulay Hassan.

By grand taxi From Fez, grands taxis run from just below Pl de la Résistance to Pl Moulay Hassan (30min). Grands taxis regularly shuttle between here and Bhalil (5min). Moving on, you can cross onto the Fez–Marrakesh road by getting a grand taxi to Immouzer du Kandar (30min) and picking up another taxi from there to Ifrane (30min) or Azrou (45min).

Services The post office and banks are on Bd Mohammed V, the principal street of the modest Ville Nouvelle.

ACCOMMODATION

Dar Attamani 414 Bastna, Sefrou ☎0535 969174, ⓦdarattamani.com. At the end of an impossibly narrow lane in the heart of the Medina, *Attamani* is the finest option in Sefrou, a thoughtful little place with five immaculate but minimimally decorated rooms and a small terrace (also an option for summer sleeping). It's all nicely done, down to the peppermint-green shutters that reflect the streets outside. BB terrace 110dh, doubles 330dh

★ **Dar KamalChaoui** 60 Kaf Rhouni, Bhalil (call ahead for directions) ☎0535 969174, ⓦkamalchaoui.com. The family home of Kamal and Beatrice Chaoui is a real gem: lovely bedrooms, sensitively furnished and with *tadelakht* bathrooms; friendly hosts who are full of advice; and simple but successful little touches throughout, like the candlelit stairwell. It's even warm in winter, thanks to the ingenious home-made underfloor heating. Kamal is passionate about Bhalil and guides guests on an excellent (and free) tour of the neighbourhood, where you're likely to get invited into a

---

FESTIVALS IN SEFROU

Sefrou hosts the **Moussem of Sidi Lahcen el Youssi**, a seventeenth-century saint, in August or September each year (exact date varies depending on the Islamic calendar), but it is the **Fête des Cerises** (W festivalcerises-sefrou.com), the annual cherry festival held a couple of months earlier, that is the big do around these parts, drawing sizeable crowds for its music, folklore and sports events – it usually takes place over the last weekend in June, climaxing with the crowning of the Cherry Queen on the Saturday evening.

Berber cave house to share mint tea and pancakes. Beatrice cooks tasty Moroccan meals (with a French dessert) for 180dh per person. BB **500dh**

Sidi Lahcen Lyoussi Rue Sidi Ali Bou Serghine, Sefrou T 0535 683428. Sefrou's longest running accommodation option, an Alpine-esque building on the south side of town, is showing its age: en-suite rooms have balconies but pretty grubby bathrooms and the restaurant is erratic. There's a popular cellar bar, though, and a swimming pool – sometimes even full of water in summer (20dh non-residents). **320dh**

CAMPING

Municipal campsite 2km west of Sefrou (no phone). Well maintained, with plenty of shade and stunning views. Staff are friendly, and there's a little on-site café to save the walk into town. Gates are open until 8pm. **60dh**

EATING

Café-Restaurant Oumnia Bd Mohammed V, Sefrou. Cheap but perfectly friendly place, whose dark split-level dining room is beyond a smoky café. Brave the fumes for simple omelettes or a 65dh menu that includes *kefta*, tajines and the like. Daily 11am–9pm.

SHOPPING

Ensemble Artisanal Just up from Bab M'kam on Pl Moulay Hassan, Sefrou. With just a handful of shops that open in rotation, Sefrou's tiny Ensemble Artisanal is small beer compared with those in Fez or Marrakesh but still worth a visit – you can usually see woodcarvings, metalwork and *jellebas* being created by hand. Mon–Fri 8am–7pm.

Dayet Aaoua and the Route des Lacs

The gorgeous freshwater lake of **Dayet Aaoua**, 45km south of Fez, makes a good place to break the journey to Ifrane or Azrou, and marks the start of a circuit that runs around a couple of other attractive lakes in the area. Like these, Aaoua can often be dry beyond early spring, but when full its mosaic of habitats supports a wide variety of animals, particularly birds (see box, p.222). Green frogs take refuge from the summer drought within the lake's protective shallows, and a multitude of dragonflies and damselflies of shimmering reds, blues and greens patrol the water's surface.

You can follow the road all the way around Dayet Aaoua, or take the left-hand fork at its northeastern edge to pick up the P5016 and complete the rest of the so-called **Route des Lacs**. This *piste* connects with the P7237 to loop south past **Dayet Ifrah**, one of the largest lakes in the area, before fringing the drought-ridden lake of **Dayet Hachlaf** on its way back up to Aaoua. If you're heading on to Ifrane, 16km to the south, you can take the S309 en route (on your left) and rejoin the N8 closer to town.

ACCOMMODATION   **DAYET AAOUA**

Le Gîte Dayet Aoua Take the left fork at the northeastern end of the lake; it's on the left after 200m T 0535 610575, W gite-dayetaoua.com. An inviting chalet-style house at the far end of the lake, with wood-panelled rooms, a library and a cosy licensed restaurant, plus a good-sized pool for summer. Treks and horseriding excursions can be arranged and there are mountain bikes for rent from 100dh/day. BB **300dh**

Gîte de la Montagne Signposted off the southern side of the lake, 3km up a winding track T 0662 586472. Tucked away in the hills above the lake and accessible only with your own transport, this secluded compound offers basic but comfortable (and heated) rooms, home-cooked meals and refreshing walks. BB **300dh**

BIRDLIFE ON THE DAYET AAOUA

When the waters of Dayet Aaoua are full, the lake attracts all kinds of waders and wildfowl, and over forty different species winter on the lake, including **cranes** and **flamingos**. Waders include **black-winged stilt**, **green sandpiper** and **avocet** (one of Morocco's most elegant birds), and the deeper waters provide food for flocks of **grebes** (great-crested, black-necked and little varieties) and, in spring, the magnificent **crested coot** (which has spectacular bright red knobs on either side of its white facial shield, when in breeding condition). The reedbeds shelter **grey heron** and **cattle egret** and ring with the songs of well-hidden **reed-** and **fan-tailed warbler**.

The abundance of summer migrators, sand martins especially, proves an irresistible draw for resident and migrant **birds of prey** – there are regular sightings of the acrobatic **red kite** here, and you may also see **Montagu's harrier**, quartering overhead and ever alert for any unsuspecting duck on the lake below.

Ifrane

3

With its manicured parks, ornamental lakes, and pseudo-Alpine villas set along broad leafy streets, **IFRANE** is something of an anomaly among Moroccan towns: a little prim, even perhaps a little smug. Although the name reveals the site has long been inhabited – "*yfran*" are the "caves" in which local Berbers once lived – the modern town was created by the Protectorate in 1929 as a self-conscious "*poche de France*" (pocket of France), then adopted enthusiastically after independence by Moroccan government ministries and the wealthier bourgeoisie, who own the gleaming top-of-the-range motors parked throughout town during summer. In recent times, Ifrane has won extra prestige with the addition of a **Royal Palace**, whose characteristic green tiles (a royal prerogative) can be glimpsed through the trees on the descent into the valley.

The stone lion and around

While Ifrane retains an easy-going, affluent air, it rather lacks the human touch of older settlements, and most visitors content themselves with a walk by the **Oued Tizguit**, below the Royal Palace, or maybe a stroll around the **university** (see box opposite), before heading further into the Middle Atlas. One "sight" on everyone's itinerary, though, is Ifrane's landmark **stone lion**, located in a copse fronting *Hôtel Chamonix* just south of the town's squeaky-clean Alpine resort-style centre; a reminder of the lions that once roamed the Atlas, it was allegedly carved by an Italian prisoner of war (in summer, a policeman is posted to stop anyone clambering onto its back).

You can also take a dip in the excellent municipal **swimming pool** (summer only) signposted off the main road 400m north of the turning for the *Mischliffen Suites & Spa*.

ARRIVAL AND DEPARTURE   IFRANE

By bus The new bus station is just north of the municipal market, 750m west of the town centre.
Destinations Azrou (3 CTM & 10 others daily; 20min); Fez (2 CTM & 10 others daily; 45min); Marrakesh (2 CTM daily; 8hr 45min); Meknes (2 CTM & 12 others daily; 1hr 10min–2hr).
By grand taxi Grands taxis gather just beside the bus station, plying routes to Fez (30min) and Azrou (15min) on a regular basis, and, less frequently, Meknes (1hr).

INFORMATION

Tourist information The regional Délégation du Tourisme office is on Pl du Syndicat, on the corner of Av Mohammed V and Av Prince Moulay Abdallah (☎0535 566821, ✉dtifrane@menara.com; Mon–Fri 8am–4.30pm), and can provide you with maps of the area.
Services There's a BCME bank and a post office on the main central square, behind the *Hôtel Chamonix*.

ACCOMMODATION

To help maintain its air of exclusivity, Ifrane doesn't do cheap **accommodation**, nor is it always easy to find a place in summer, when reservations are recommended. That said, you're unlikely to need to stay over, particularly given the proximity of the more interesting town of Azrou (see opposite), and its greater range of options.

BY ROYAL DEGREE

On January 16, 1995, King Hassan II inaugurated the **Al Akhawayn University** (⋓ aui.ma) on the northern edge of Ifrane, its chalet-style buildings, cream walls and russet-tiled roofs the design of Michel Pinseau, the architect behind the king's showpiece Hassan II Mosque in Casablanca (see p.279). The name Al Akhawayn ("Brothers" in Arabic) denotes it as the brainchild (and beneficiary) of the Moroccan king and his "brother", King Abdullah Bin Abdulaziz of Saudi Arabia; it has also been funded by the United States and, to a lesser extent, the British Council. The undergraduate and postgraduate curricula are modelled on the American system of higher education, and English is used for lectures.

King Hassan was keen to underpin his creation with the religious and cultural values of **Christianity** and **Judaism** as well as of **Islam**. The university is dedicated to "practical tolerance between faiths" and a mosque, church and synagogue are on campus to provide, as the king put it, "a meeting place for the sons of Abraham", a concept endorsed by the Prince of Wales when he visited Ifrane in 1996.

You can arrange **to visit the campus** by contacting the Office of Admissions in advance (☎ 0535 862086 or ✉ admissions@aui.ma); try to go on a weekday afternoon when the students are about.

3

Chamonix Av de la Marche Verte ☎ 0535 566028. Comparatively good-value hotel, whose light, spotless rooms come with heating, a/c and TV. It's a short walk from the restaurants grouped around the town centre –though it also has a reasonable enough one of its own (see below). **580dh**

Mischliffen Ifrane Suites & Spa Av Hassan II ☎ 0535 864000, ⋓ michlifenifrane.com. Exclusive destination hotel that sits somewhere between luxury Alpine chalet and Scottish hunting lodge. "Deluxe" rooms are certainly nice enough, and come with all the mod cons you'd expect in this category, but lack the cosy wood-panelled decor (and space) of the much more expensive suites – though

incredibly, given the price of both, you'll still have to fork out extra for breakfast. Two pools, an ultra-chic spa, three restaurants (see below) and a sports complex complete the picture. Booking online in advance can knock around 15 percent off the rack rate of the cheapest rooms, and around 35 percent off the suites. **3100dh**

CAMPING

Municipal campsite Bd Mohammed V ☎ 0535 566025. Coveniently located just to the west of the bus station and the market, the town campsite is refreshingly verdant for Morocco – hardly surprising, though, given the surroundings – and has a little shop that's open in summer. **40dh**

EATING

Forest Hay Riad ☎ 0535 566544. Stylish patisserie occupying a chalet-style building in the heart of the pedestrianized town centre, serving equally stylish and intricately crafted gateaux, plus more substantial snacks such as cheeseburgers (39dh). Daily 8am–midnight.

Mischliffen Ifrane Suites & Spa Av Hassan II ☎ 0535 864000, ⋓ michlifenifrane.com. Fine dining with a heavy French accent in the Art Deco *Le Grande Carte* (reservations recommended), where roasted lamb with pepper and honey ice cream (240dh) is symbolic of the menu; slightly cheaper traditonal meals such as *tanjia* and calves' feet with chickpeas (180dh) in *Le Marocain*; and lunchtime tagliatelle carbonara and other pasta dishes (120dh) in the more relaxed *La*

Brasserie. Daily: La Grande Carte & Le Marocain 7.30–11pm, La Brasserie 7am–4pm.

La Paix Av de la Marche Verte ☎ 0535 566675, ⋓ lapaixifrane.com. Upmarket, modern place, where a la carte meals in the restaurant start at 75dh for *merguez* or rabbit tajine. The attached café-cum-patisserie provides cheaper sandwiches and pizzas. Daily 11am–2pm & 7–11.30pm.

La Perle de l'Atlas Hôtel Chamonix, Av de la Marche Verte ☎ 0535 566028. Decent hotel restaurant, nothing too flash, offering a variety of meals from pizzas (60dh) to Atlas trout *à la meunière* (80dh). There's also a simpler café and bar. Daily noon–3pm & 7–11pm.

Azrou and around

The first real town of the Middle Atlas, **AZROU** makes an attractive "introduction" to the region, an important but welcoming Berber market centre enclosed by wooded slopes on three sides. The town grew at the crossroads of two major routes – north to Meknes and Fez, south to Khenifra and Midelt – and long held a strategic role in controlling the mountain Berbers. Moulay Ismail built a **kasbah**

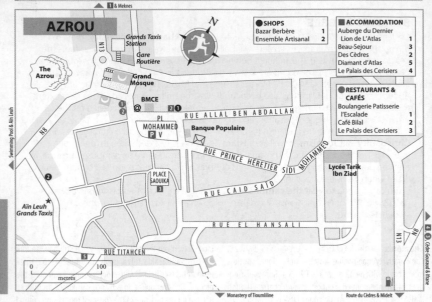

here, the remains of which survive, while more recently the French established the prestigious **Collège Berbère** – one plank in their policy to split the country's Berbers from the urban Arabs.

South of Azrou lies some of the most remote and beautiful country of the Middle Atlas: a region of dense **cedar forests**, limestone plateaus and polje lakes that is home to some superb wildlife, including Barbary apes. At its heart, and an obvious focus for a trip, are the waterfalls of **Oum er Rbia**, the source of Morocco's largest river.

The azrou

Azrou's defining feature is the massive knobble of rock on its western edge – the **azrou** ("rock" in Berber) after which it is named. Villagers allegedly used to gather at the rock to trade goods (there's been a Berber market here since the 1840s), though the bigger outcrop to the northeast has a more justifiable claim. Locals clamber to the top of the *azrou*, but you can get just as good a view of the plains that run southwest of town from the **lookout** opposite the impressive Grand Mosque that adjoins the main square, Place Mohammed V.

The souk

One of the most compelling reasons to visit Azrou is its Tuesday **souk**, which is held above the main part of town (just follow the crowds up to the quarter across the valley) and draws Berbers from the surrounding mountain villages. At first it appears to offer little more than fruit and vegetable stalls, but keep going and you'll see a stretch of wasteland where locals strike deals over donkeys, sheep and goats and there are often a few musicians and storytellers performing; beyond this is a smaller section for high-quality **carpets** and textiles.

Lycée Tarik Ibn Ziad

One of the most dominant buildings in town, the **Lycée Tarik Ibn Ziad** is the former home of the **Collège Berbère**, which provided many of the Protectorate's interpreters, local administrators and military officers. In spite of its ban on using

Arabic and any manifestation of Islam, the policy was a failure, and Azrou graduates played a significant role in the nationalist movement – and were uniquely placed to do so, as a new French-created elite. Since independence, however, their influence has been minor outside of the army, in part because many Berber student activists of the 1950s and 60s pledged allegiance to Mehdi Ben Barka's ill-fated socialist UNFP party (see p.541).

Benedictine Monastery of Tioumliline

One of several good walks to be had in the surrounding hills – lush when watered by seasonal springs and home to Barbary apes – is the pleasant afternoon stroll to the derelict twentieth-century **Benedictine Monastery of Tioumliline** (see box below), 3km away in the hills above Azrou (and also reached along the back road to Aïn Leuh, which branches off the N13 to Midelt). On your way back to town, you can cut across the hills south of the monastery on any of the footpaths that crisscross the area.

3

ARRIVAL AND DEPARTURE   AZROU AND AROUND

Azrou is something of a transport hub, located at the apex of roads heading north **to Fez and Meknes** and at the point where the route south forks: **to Marrakesh** (the N8) or **to Midelt and Er Rachidia** (N13). As most bus services are just passing through, tickets sometimes only go on sale when the bus arrives and the conductor tells the people in the ticket office how many places are available – cue a mad scramble if seats are scarce. Arrive early and set up a place by the ticket window, and you'll be at the front of the queue if that happens.

By bus The bus station is just north of the central Grand Mosque; the CTM office is on Bd Hassan II (☎ 0555 560635). Destinations Aïn Leuh (daily; 40min); Beni Mellal (2 CTM, 1 Supratours & 7 others daily; 3hr 15min–3hr 50min); Casablanca (3 CTM & 5 others daily; 6hr); Er Rachidia (4 CTM, 1 Supratours & 5 others daily; 3hr 40min–6hr 15min); Fez (2 CTM, 2 Supratours & 10 others daily; 1hr 30min–2hr 30min); Ifrane (3 CTM & 10 others daily; 20min); Marrakesh (2 CTM & 7 others daily; 6hr 50min–7hr 30min); Meknes (4 CTM & 12 others daily; 1hr 50min–2hr 30min); Midelt (3 CTM & 1 Supratours daily, others every 30min; 1hr 45min–3hr 30min); Rabat (3 CTM & 7 others daily; 4hr 15min–5hr 15min); Rissani (1 CTM, 1 Supratours & 4 others daily; 6hr 30min–8hr).

By grand taxi The main grand taxi rank is just behind the bus station, from where taxis run regularly to Ifrane (25min), Fez (1hr), Meknes (1hr) and Midelt (2hr), and occasionally to Beni Mellal (3hr 30min). Grands taxis for Aïn Leuh (30min) have their own stop just south of the Ensemble Artisanal.

THE MONKS OF TIOUMLILINE

The functional **monastery of Tioumliline** was built in 1926 by French Benedictines, and until the late 1960s played an important role in the life of the local Berber community. The focus of the monastery's life was its *dispensaire* or clinic, outside the walls of the complex and by the road to Aïn Leuh. The clinic offered free medical treatment and medicines to any passer-by; Berber families in isolated mountain villages used to bring their sick relatives to be treated and looked after by the monks. As well as free medical care, the monastery supplied the poorest Berber families – and generally anyone whose harvests failed – with basic foodstuffs.

The Istiqlal Party closed the monastery down in 1968, believing that the monks were trying to convert the locals. Most of the Benedictines were relocated to the Abbey of Calcat in France, while their superior, Father Gilbert, went to the Abbey of Saint Benoît de Koubiri, near Ouagadougou in Burkina Faso. Since then, the monastery has slowly fallen into disrepair, though it did receive a touch of TLC in 2010 when it served as the setting for Xavier Beavouis's French film *Of God and Men*, based on the kidnapping and murder of monks in Algeria in 1996; one of the two survivors of that massacre has since taken up residency at the monastery of Nôtre Dame de l'Atlas near Midelt (see p.242). The monks themselves may have long gone, but they are still affectionately remembered by many of the locals, including Boujemâa Boudaoud, who lives with his family in the former dispensary; Monsieur Boudaoud, now a mountain guide (see p.226), can tell you stories about the monastery and show you around the ruins.

INFORMATION

Guides To explore the extensive cedar forests south of Azrou (see opposite), contact Moulay Abdellah Lahrizi (☎0662 190889, ✉lahrizi37@yahoo.co.uk), president of the local branch of the Association of Mountain Guides (☏tourisme-vert-ifrane.com), or Boujemâa and Saleh Boudaoud (☎0663 760825 or ☎0614 840967, ✉boujemaa_boudaoud@yahoo.com), knowledgeable guides who live with their families in the monastery of Tioumliline's old dispensary. All speak good English, and charge around 200dh for half-day trips, 300dh for the full day (Moulay Abdellah also runs mountain-bike day-trips for 600dh, including bike rental and guide); for multi-day tours of the Middle Atlas expect to pay around 500dh/day, 700dh if mountain biking.

ACCOMMODATION

Azrou's position at a major road junction means that there are plenty of hotels in town; bear in mind that the nights are cold, particularly in winter, and central heating is only provided in dearer (and more distant) places.

Auberge du Dernier Lion de L'Atlas 16 Bd Hassan II ☎0535 561868, ☏dernierlionatlas.ma. Super-friendly place, and owner Aziz is a wealth of information on the region, promoting cultural awareness from his auberge-cum-cultural centre. Most of the twenty mix-and-match but comfortable rooms are en suite, and meals can be arranged in the cafeteria. **300dh**

Beau-Sejour 45 Pl Saouika ☎0535 560692. Rooms are boxy (particularly the triples) but clean and some come with balconies overlooking the square; all have shared bathrooms (hot showers 10dh). The terrace enjoys 360-degree views of the surrounding hills; beds are available up here in the summer. Terrace **50dh**, double **120dh**

Des Cèdres Pl Mohammed V ☎0535 562326, ☏hoteldescedres.ma. Very dark and in need of some TLC, but perhaps the best value in central Azrou. Spacious, comfortable rooms (en suites cost 55dh extra) are enjoyably old-fashioned, all with high ceilings and washbasins; a shared balcony overlooks the square. **105dh**

★ **Diamant d'Atlas** Rue Titahcen ☎0535 564354, ☏hotel-diamant-atlas.com. While the rooms might not offer much more in the way of furnishings than a blanket on the comfy bed and a rug on the polished floor, they are clean, spacious and terrific value (10dh extra for a room with satellite TV). Each has a corner sink, and they share bathrooms. Guests can make use of the kitchen, and there's also a washing machine available. BB **100dh**

Le Palais des Cerisiers Route du Cèdre Gouraud, signed off the N8 6km northeast of Azrou ☎0535 563830, ☏lespalaisdeceresiers.com. The tone at this Alpine-esque lodge is set by the very grand wooden staircase and continues in the large comfortable bedrooms, some with balconies looking out across the surrounding cherry-blossom trees (hence the name) to the hills beyond. Half-board rates include very good food at the refined resturant (see below). There's a swimming pool and spa, and mountain bikes for exploring the cedar forest – the Cèdre Gouraud (see box opposite) is 7km away. HB **1500dh**

EATING AND DRINKING

Basic grills line the roads around the Grand Mosque and prepare the usual brochettes and spit-roast chicken – the stalls towards the *azrou* tend to be better than those towards the bus station, but as ever, double check that the birds were not left on the spit overnight if you choose chicken for lunch.

Boulangerie Patisserie l'Escalade Off the northwest corner of Pl Mohammed V. Classy patisserie, perhaps the best of several clustered around Pl Mohammed V, selling a variety of fresh French bread as well as tasty cakes and pastries, some of them savoury. Daily 6am–9pm.

Café Bilal Bd Mohammed V. Café-cum-restaurant doing a range of meals, from simple sandwiches (15dh) to chicken pastilla (60dh), served either at the sitting area inside or on the small terrace by the road. Daily: July & Aug 24hr; Sept–June 10am–11pm.

★ **Le Palais des Cerisiers** Route du Cèdre Gouraud, signed off the N8 6km northeast of Azrou ☎0535 563830, ☏lespalaisdeceresiers.com. The attentive staff at this silver-service restaurant proudly serve excellent food that includes warm goat's cheese salad, *entrecôte* with Roquefort sauce, grilled Atlas trout with almonds (a speciality) and chocolate fondant (195dh menu). There's usually a roaring log fire in the wood-panelled *British Bar*, plus sink-worthy Chesterfields and a good selection of wines (especially reds) and spirits. Restaurant daily noon–3.30pm & 7.30–11pm; bar Mon–Fri 11am–11pm, Sat & Sun 11am–midnight.

SHOPPING

In addition to the Tuesday souk, the craft stalls in the old quarter of town around Pl Saouika (Pl Moulay Hachem Ben Salah) and Pl Mohammed V can turn up some beautiful items, fairly priced if not exactly bargains.

Bazar Berbère 7 Pl Mohammed V. There's less hard sell at this carpet and cedar-carving shop, which has a comprehensive selection of rugs from the various Beni M'Guild tribes of the Middle Atlas, most with bright, geometric designs based on traditional tribal patterns. The affable owner is a knowledgeable *chasseur des tapis* (carpet hunter), as he calls himself, who will explain the difference between good Berber carpets and mere souvenirs if you show enough interest. Daily 8.30am–6.30pm

Ensemble Artisanale On the Khenifra road. It may have seen better days and feel a bit sleepy compared with other cooperatives, but this small collection of craft shops still produces some decent modern rugs, plus stone and cedar carvings. Mon, Tues, Thurs & Fri 9–11am & 3–6pm, Wed & Sat 8.30am–6pm.

DIRECTORY

Banks and exchange The BMCE and Banque Populaire on Pl Mohammed V have ATMs and change facilities for travellers' cheques.

Internet access Available at ABRIDNet, on the first floor of the mini mall to the left of the BMCE (daily 9am–midnight).

Post office The post office is just east of the square, behind the Banque Populaire.

Swimming In summer, Azrou's public swimming pool, signposted 300m along the Route du Khenifra, is almost reason enough to stop.

Route des Cèdres

The **cedar forests** that lie to the south of Azrou are a unique habitat in Morocco, their verdant, soaring treetops contrasting starkly with the surrounding aridity and barrenness of the Middle Atlas range and providing dense cover for troupes of **Barbary apes** (see box below). You can best appreciate this on the signed, 35km-long **Route des Cèdres**, which dissects large swathes of forest (holm oak as well as cedar) as it wends its way from a junction on the N13 (known locally as the "Moudmane junction"), 8km south of Azrou, towards Aïn Leuh.

If you're not going all the way to Aïn Leuh, then reaching the roadside **picnic spot** around 10km in is a satisfactory second best, cutting through enough of the forest to give you a good impression of its splendour. With more time it's worth continuing 11km beyond this to **Lac Afenourir**, the largest lake in the Middle Atlas and home to wigeon, black-necked grebe and significant numbers of regionally rare ruddy shelduck and crested coot.

Cèdre Gouraud

Turning left instead of right at the Moudmane junction leads to more mighty cedars, among them the 130ft-high **Cèdre Gouraud**, singled out by a makeshift sign nailed to the tree – and the fact that, after a life allegedly spanning nine centuries, it is now well and truly dead. The history of its name is a mystery – Colonel Gouraud was General Lyautey's second in command from 1912 to 1914, but why a soldier should lend his name to a tree is not clear, the confusion only confounded by a recent authority that claimed Gouraud's cedar was actually felled at the turn of the century.

BARBARY APES

The cedar forests around Azrou shelter several troupes of **Barbary apes** (*singe margot*), a glimpse of which is one of the wildlife highlights of a visit to Morocco. Despite the name, they are actually members of the **macaque** family (they picked up the "ape" moniker due to their lack of a tail) and roam the forests in troupes of up to a hundred monkeys. The Middle Atlas is home to three-quarters of the world population, though numbers are severely in decline due to a combination of habitat destruction and illegal pet trading, and in 2009 the International Union for Conservation of Nature (IUCN) added them to their Red List of **endangered** species.

Barbary apes can be found throughout the region, feeding along the forest margins, though you are virtually guaranteed to see them around the **Cèdre Gouraud** and at the **Moudmane junction** (on the N13, 8km southeast of Azrou), where they laze around the picnic area in search of food. Be warned that they are *very* accustomed to humans due to the unfortunate local habit of feeding them for camera-toting tourists.

Aïn Leuh

The large Berber village of **AÏN LEUH**, 30km from Azrou, is typical of the Middle Atlas, with its flat-roofed houses tiered above the valley. As at Azrou, there are ruins of a kasbah built by Moulay Ismail, and in the hills behind the town there are **springs** and a more or less year-round waterfall – the main reason, for those without their own wheels, for coming here, as the Sources de l'Oum er Rbia, a further 35km along the S303, are inaccessible on public transport.

Aïn Leuh's **souk** is held on Wednesday (though it can extend a day in either direction), and serves as the weekly gathering of the Beni M'Guild tribes, still semi-nomadic in this region – you may see them camping out with their flocks in heavy, dark tents. As a colonial *zone d'insécurité*, this part of the Atlas was relatively undisturbed by French settlers, and the traditional balance between pasture and forest has remained largely intact.

ARRIVAL AND DEPARTURE   AÏN LEUH

By public transport One bus a day runs from Azrou (40min), though grands taxis make the journey (30min) on a more regular basis.
By car The most direct route from Azrou is south along the N8, turning left (after 17km) on to the S303 and following it into Aïn Leuh, though the cross-country Route des Cèdres (which emerges on the N8 just south of Aïn Leuh) is the more scenic option.

ACCOMMODATION

Auberge Le Magot de L'Atlas Route Tagounit, signposted just before Aïn Leuh on a back road to Azrou ☎0535 569517, ✉aubergelemagot@hotmail.com. A dozen neat little rooms in a rambling country house, with an enclosed camping area and a restaurant that serves humble tajines as well as a variety of grills. Organizes trout-fishing trips to the area's many lakes and rivers. Camping 70dh, double 200dh

Sources de l'Oum er Rbia

From Aïn Leuh, follow signposts to "Aguelmane Azigza/Khenifra"; though completely paved, the road to the falls is quite potholed in parts and can become waterlogged and impassable in winter, when you should ask about conditions in Azrou (or, if coming from the south, Khenifra) before you set out • Parking is by the concrete bridge over the Rbia, from where it's a 10–15min walk to the falls

Bubbling along the bottom of a twisting valley, the **Sources de l'Oum er Rbia** are a popular pilgrimage for Moroccans, marking the starting point of the country's longest river – though the back route there from Azrou is equally as interesting, a 35km drive through mountain forest (where you're almost certain to come across apes) and open country dotted with grazing sheep and odd pitched-roof farmsteads.

Guides may offer to walk you to the falls, although this is entirely unnecessary given the very clear path that leads up to the gorge. Along the river's edge, the water comes out in forty or more **springs** (*sources*), many of them marked with café-shelters that are tightly wedged along the banks – a great spot to kick back with a sugary mint tea. You may see locals taking a dip further up the gorge, by a small waterfall, but swimming is not advisable as the currents are extremely strong.

Aguelmane Azigza

Beyond the springs at Oum er Rbia, the main road heads off to the west, crossed by a confusing array of *pistes*. After 18km, a turn-off on the left leads 3.5km to the **Aguelmane Azigza**, a dark and deep lake, secluded among the cedar trees. You can camp and swim here, as many Moroccans do, and the area is home to some terrific **wildlife**: the wooded slopes of the lake throng with insects, including the brilliant red and black grasshopper and the small Amanda's blue butterfly, while the forest provides nesting and feeding areas for woodland finches and titmice, including the elusive hawfinch, identified by its heavy bill. There's more birdlife in the waters, too, notably diving duck (mainly grebes and coot), and marbled teal in autumn and winter.

Kasba Tadla

The strongest argument for visiting **KASBA TADLA** is that nobody else does. The only "sight", such as it is, is a walled **kasbah** at the southern end of the main street, Avenue Mohammed V, featuring an impressive derelict Grand Mosque with a crumbling brick minaret, and an interesting smaller mosque, whose minaret has the same protruding perches as that of the Great Mosque in Tiznit.

Kasba Tadla takes its name from a fortress Moulay Ismail built here, strategically positioned beside the Oum er Rbia River, and remains a military town, not that you'd know it, in a surprisingly sleepy centre. As you enter town, keep an eye out for four tall, square pillars near the turn-off on the N8 (about 1km from the town centre), a **memorial** to the French soldiers killed hereabouts between 1912 and 1933; it affords a fine view of the *bidonville* by the river and the town beyond. The town's other main feature is a sizeable **souk** held on Mondays.

ARRIVAL AND DEPARTURE   KASBA TADLA

By bus Buses plying the N8 from Fez and Marrakesh pull into the station 500m north of the centre. There are fairly frequent services to Beni Mellal (45min), but none, surprisingly, to nearby El Ksiba (for the journey south across the Atlas).

By grand taxi The taxi rank is diagonally opposite the bus station, serving El Ksiba (30min), Beni Mellal (30min) and Marrakesh (3hr 30min).

ACCOMMODATION AND EATING

Des Alliés 38 Av Mohammed V, a few blocks north of the kasbah ☎0523 418587. Ramshackle place with cold showers but still the better of the town's two hotels (you're really down on your luck if you end up staying at the *Atlas*, the other option just round the corner). *Alliés* features iron bedsteads in blue-washed rooms and a barn-like bar that could have been transported from 1930s pastoral France –

minus the alcohol. 80dh
Pizza Bella Roma Rue el Mejjati Obad, the street just down from the *Alliés* ☎0662 260102. One of very few options in Kasba Tadla, this little takeaway place does over a dozen varieties of pizza, from a bargain 20dh for a small margherita (45dh to upgrade to a large). Daily 10am–10pm.

El Ksiba, Imilchil and across the Atlas

Enclosed by apricot, olive and orange groves, the dusty Berber village of **EL KSIBA**, 4km from the N8, serves primarily as a jumping-off point for the journey to Imilchil and across the High Atlas, a dizzying trip that eventually wends its way through the Todra Gorge to Tinghir, at the heart of the great southern oases routes.

Aghbala, Ikassene and the Plateau des Lacs

South of El Ksiba, the **R317** (also known here as the Trans-Atlas road) twists through varied forest to cross the Tizi n'Isli pass. At the junction just beyond this, an unnamed road branches eastward to **Aghbala** (65km from El Ksiba), a busy market town with a Wednesday souk, before eventually connecting with the R503 Beni Mellal–Midelt road – an attractive circuit, surfaced but in a poor state. Staying on the R317, the route south to Imilchil provides a spectacular itinerary, with steep drops off the roadside and constant hairpin climbs and descents. Beyond **Ikassene**, something of a staging post on this route, the road improves as it hauls upwards past Tassent (periodic landslides may block it) to a high valley and a *col*, giving views of the the **Plateau des Lacs** – the twin mountain lakes of **Tislit** (near the road) and **Isli** (pristine and much larger, but a 10km walk away), named after a thwarted couple from Berber folklore, whose tears fell to form the two lakes.

Imilchil and beyond

Despite losing some of its striking old buildings, there's still a certain beauty about **IMILCHIL** (115km from El Ksiba), the main draw of the central High Atlas and the destination for many trans-Atlas travellers. The village serves as the regular souk

3

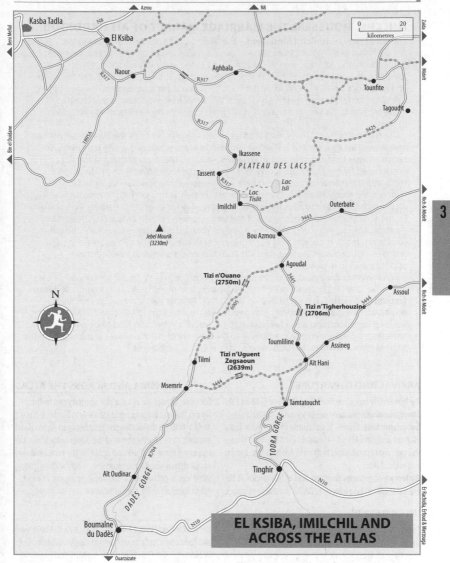

EL KSIBA, IMILCHIL AND
ACROSS THE ATLAS

(Friday) for the whole region but is more famous for its September moussem, the so-called **Marriage Market of Aït Haddidou** (see box, p.232), which attracts streams of tourist traffic up the surfaced road from Rich.

Beyond Imilchil, the R317 runs through fertile land to Bou Azmou, where it heads east to Rich on the Midelt–Er Rachidia road. To fully cross the Atlas, you'll need to press on south to the friendly village of **Agoudal**, at which point the road splits: southwest for the fairly tortuous 6905 *piste* via the Tizi n'Ouano (2750m) to Msemrir and the **Dàdes Gorge**; southeast for the recently paved route via the Tizi n' Tigherhouzine (2706m) to Aït Hani, Tamtatoucht and the **Todra Gorge**.

IMILCHIL MOUSSEM: THE MARRIAGE MARKET OF AÏT HADDIDOU

The world-famous **Imilchil Moussem** – the "Fête des Fiancés" or "Marriage Market" – is the mother of all Moroccan mountain souks, a gathering of thirty thousand or more Berbers from the Aït Haddidou, Aït Morghad, Aït Izdeg and Aït Yahia tribes. Over the three days of the September fair (Friday to Sunday), animals are traded; clothes, tools and provisions bought and sold; and distant friends and family members reunited before the first snowfalls isolate their high villages. What makes it especially highly charged, however, is that it is here the region's youngsters come to decide whom they're going to marry.

The tradition derives from colonial times, when the officials from the Bureau des Affaires Indigènes used to insist the Berbers assembled in Agdoul, site of a yearly transhumance fair, to register births, deaths and **marriages**. After independence, the custom was encouraged by the Moroccan tourist office, which the locals blame for propagating the myth that the marriages contracted here were entered into spontaneously. In fact, the matches are nearly all arranged in advance and merely formalized at the moussem. All the same, the fair provides the perfect opportunity for unmarried Berbers – particularly women trapped at altitude for most of the year – to survey their prospects. Dressed in traditional finery, with hefty jewellery and eyes rimmed with heavy black *kohl*, the girls parade around in groups, flirting outrageously while the boys as eagle-eyed elder relatives look on. Later, singing, dancing and drumming give both sexes further opportunities to mingle.

Unfortunately, the influx of tourism has seriously compromised the authenticity of the event, and while local life continues with its serious market and marriage elements, a pure **folklore festival** for tourists has been shifted up to Lac Tislit. Neither part is actually at Imilchil, of course, and the date is not always easy to discover – contact the ONMT (see p.64) for details. Rates for beds, food and water (which has to be brought in by lorry) tend to be greatly inflated, so fix prices in advance; it's also advisable to bring plenty of warm clothing as the nights at this altitude (over 2000m) can get bitterly cold by the end of September.

ARRIVAL AND DEPARTURE

By bus Hourly buses run from Beni Mellal to El Ksiba (1hr 30min), from where a daily bus heads on to Aghbala (2hr).
By grand taxi Grands taxis shuttle from Kasba Tadla (30min) and Beni Mellal (45min) to El Ksiba, from where you can connect with other taxis on to Aghbala (1hr 30min) and Imilchil (4hr).
By lorry Berber lorries provide a kind of bus service at the weekend, covering the journey to Tinghir in a couple of stages;

EL KSIBA AND ACROSS THE ATLAS

from Bou Azmou, you can also pick up a lorry east to Rich.
By car The road is now paved all the way to Tinghir, but you'll need a 4WD for the challenging *piste* between Agoudal and Msemrir, at the northern end of the Dàdes Gorges, plus the proper equipment: a pick and spade for the occasional very rough detour (beware of scorpions when shifting rocks), some warm clothes and a tent for sleeping out at night – Atlas nights are chilly, even in summer.

INFORMATION

Services El Ksiba has a bank and a post office (next door to the *Henry IV* hotel), while Imilchil also has a post office in the village centre.
Guides Among the resident guides in Imilchil, the reliable

Bessou Chabou (☎0523 442402 or ☎0672 521389), who also runs a *pension* in town (see opposite), is qualified both in Morocco and France and can organize local treks and longer trips further afield.

ACCOMMODATION AND EATING

Travelling across the Atlas from El Ksiba can be a time-consuming affair; without your own wheels, you'll probably need to stop for a night along the way. In addition to the hotels listed below, there are **rooms** to rent in Ikassene and Agoudal, both of which also have a few **cafés** providing simple meals.

EL KSIBA

Henri IV In the Quartier Administratif; from opposite the central petrol station, head uphill and bear left after about 300m; if coming by car from the N8, take the left

before you enter El Ksiba ☎0523 415002. One of the few options in El Ksiba, this small hotel makes a passable place to bed down if you need to stop en route, in attractive surroundings and with plenty of scope for day walks. **200dh**

LAC TISLIT

Tislit On the west side of Lac Tislit ☎ 0535 524874. This kasbah-style place is a marvellously atmospheric spot, with basic rooms, shared showers and excellent home-cooked meals – or you can sleep in Berber tents by the lake. Tent 50dh, double 150dh

IMILCHIL

Chez Bassou In the centre of the village ☎ 0523 442402, ⓦ chezbassou.com. Budget minimalism in a new *pension*, the simple but spotless bedrooms (most en suite) given just a blanket on the bed by way of decor. Traditional Berber cuisine is served in the very sparse restaurant. Bassou himself is a qualified mountain guide, and can organize treks in the area (see opposite). HB 450dh

Islane In the centre of the village ☎ 0524 442806. Cheerily decorated little place, with (sporadic) hot showers and a terrace with fine mountain views. The friendly staff can arrange guides and mules for regional treks. 80dh

Beni Mellal

Conveniently located between Marrakesh and Fez, and on the main routes to Casablanca and Rabat, **BENI MELLAL** is one of Morocco's fastest-growing towns, its haphazardly planned new suburbs nibbling deeper into the surrounding olive groves with every year. A largely modern town, it has few specific sights – and even fewer tourists – but is a useful **transit point** for Azilal (for the Cascades d'Ouzoud and the Aït Bouguemez valley) and El Ksiba (for Imilchil and the road across the Atlas).

Serving as a market centre for the broad, prosperous flatlands to the north, Beni Mellal hosts a large Tuesday **souk**, which is good for olives, oranges and woollen blankets that feature unusual Berber designs. If you're in town on a Saturday, it's also worth a side trip to what is traditionally the Middle Atlas's largest weekly **market**, held 35km to the southwest at **Souk Sebt des Oulad Nemâa**.

Aïn Asserdoune and Kasbah Ras el Aïn

Around 3km south of the town centre • Catch bus #3 (summer only) or take a petit taxi (10dh) from the Medina to Aïn Asserdoune, from where it's a 15min walk to Kasbah Ras el Aïn up the footpath behind the car park – start from the steps at the far left

The spring of **Aïn Asserdoune**, just to the south of town, feeds a series of artificial falls amid well-tended gardens and makes a pleasant spot for an afternoon stroll, particularly if you combine a trip here with a walk up to nearby **Kasbah Ras el Aïn**. The kasbah, actually a stone *borj* (fort), is one of Beni Mellal's few remaining historical sights – Moulay Ismail's kasbah in the old Medina has been restored to the point of no interest – and affords fine views across the surrounding plains and orange groves and over Beni Mellal.

ARRIVAL AND DEPARTURE	BENI MELLAL

By bus The *gare routière* is on the main road from Fez to Marrakesh (here called the N8a), a 20min walk north of the centre; a petit taxi into town will cost around 7dh.

Destinations Agadir (1 CTM & 3 others daily; 8hr); Azilal (5 daily; 2hr 30min); Azrou (2 CTM & 8 others daily; 4hr 45min); Casablanca (3 CTM daily & others every 30min; 4hr); Demnate (6 daily; 3hr); El Ksiba (hourly; 1hr 30min); Fez (2 CTM & 8 others daily; 6hr); Marrakesh (2 CTM & 13 others daily; 3hr 30min–4hr); Meknes (6 daily; 6hr); Midelt (3 daily; 4hr 30min); Souk Sebt des Oulad Nemâa (frequent; 45min).

By grands taxis Grands taxis to Fez (4hr 30min) and Azrou (3hr 30min) leave from the esplanade opposite the CTM office; those to Marrakesh (3hr), Azilal (2hr), the Cascades d'Ouzoud (2hr 30min) and Demnate (1hr), as well as Kasba Tadla (30min) and El Ksiba (45min), leave from a parking area behind the bus station.

ACCOMMODATION	

Aïn Asserdoun Av des FAR ☎ 0523 483493, ⓦ hotelainasserdoune.com. A friendly block in the centre of town, just south of the bus station, whose comfortable en-suite accommodation is popular with Moroccans passing through. There's also a small restaurant. 140dh

Chems ☎ 0523 483460, ⓦ hotelchems.com. One of two garden hotels on the original Marrakesh road – and so a good couple of kilometres from the town centre – this is less flash than the nearby *Hôtel Ouzoud* but also more friendly. The functional, modern accommodation

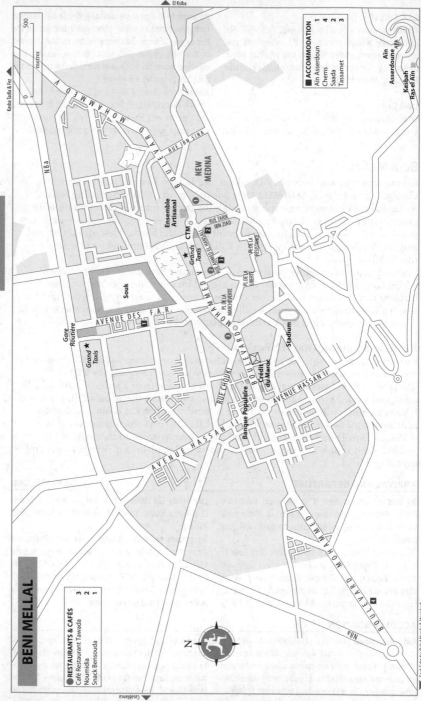

BENI MELLAL

● RESTAURANTS & CAFÉS
Café Restaurant Tawada 3
Noumidia 2
Snack Bensouda 1

■ ACCOMMODATION
Ain Asserdoun 1
Chems 4
Saada 2
Tassamet 3

El Ksiba

NEW MEDINA

Ensemble Artisanal

RUE IBN SINA

BOULEVARD MOHAMMED V

N8a

Kasba Tadla & Fez

Souk

AVENUE DES F.A.R.

Gare Routière

Grand Taxis

Grands Taxis

CTM

RUE TARIK IBN ZIAD

RUE AHMED EL HANSALI

PL DE LA RÉSISTANCE

PL DE LA LIBERTÉ

PL DE LA MARCHEVERTE

BOULEVARD MOHAMMED V

RUE CHOUKI

Banque Populaire

Crédit du Maroc

Stadium

AVENUE HASSAN II

AVENUE HASSAN II

BOULEVARD MOHAMMED V

N8a

N

Ain Asserdoune

Kasbah Ras-el-Ain

Casablanca

Souk Sebt des Oulad Nemâa & Marrakech

could do with a bit of TLC but is popular with tour groups, while facilities include a pool, tennis courts and a nightclub. BB <u>675dh</u>

Es Saada 129 Rue Tarik Ibn Ziad ☎0523 482991. The cheapest option in town, closer to a borstal than a hotel, with cleanish but very spartan rooms, some windowless. Hot showers (10dh) are available next door. <u>80dh</u>

Tassamet 186 Rue Ahmed el Hansali (actually down a side street) ☎0523 421313. The area directly outside the *Tassamet* isn't the most salubrious, but the place itself is a cut above the usual Medina cheapies: clean and welcoming, with en-suite rooms and constant hot water. There are good views from front-facing rooms – ask for a balcony – and the roof terrace. <u>150dh</u>

EATING

Café Restaurant Tawada Next to the Total garage on Bd Mohammed V. On a busy roundabout slap-bang in the middle of town and rustling up tasty food at lower-than-usual prices – the rabbit tajine with raisins and cinnamon (35dh) takes some beating. Daily 5am–10pm.

Noumidia 141 Rue Ahmed el Hansali. The best of a trio of popular restaurants in this patch of the Medina, this unsigned joint is dark, and perhaps a bit of a gamble if

you're not blessed with a cast-iron stomach, but it does cheap roast chicken (22dh), brochettes and *kefta* kebabs. Daily 8am–8pm.

Snack Bensouda 136 Bd Mohammed V. Popular, unpretentious place, offering exotic (but cheap) dishes such as liver and brain kebabs alongside the usuals, although outside tables are blighted by traffic fumes. Daily noon–midnight.

Azilal and around

The perfunctory town of **AZILAL**, 27km southwest of Beni Mellal, feels more of an oversized village than provincial capital, yet its loose affiliation of streets have a garrison, banks and hotels, and a Thursday souk. It's a fairly low-key place, and unlikely to feature on anyone's radar were it not conveniently placed for the Cascades d'Ouzoud and the High Atlas villages of the beautiful Aït Bouguemez; in addition, the road from Marrakesh to Beni Mellal that runs via Azilal is surfaced all the way and makes a far more interesting route north than the N8 across the Tadla plain.

The quickest route from Beni Mellal to Azilal heads off 20km along the N8 through the village of Afourer and hauls uphill – providing a vast panorama of the huge plain that sweeps west into the distance – before cresting a pass to zigzag down through the hills to the **Bin el Ouidane** reservoir. This was one of the earliest (1948–55) and most ambitious of the country's irrigation schemes and has changed much of the land hereabouts – formerly as dry and barren as the phosphate plains to the northwest. Over the last few years, several hotels have cropped up on the lake's shores, offering a scenic chance to get away from it all for a couple of days (see p.236).

ARRIVAL AND INFORMATION

AZILAL AND AROUND

AZILAL

By bus Buses drop off at a patch of wasteground behind the main square (backed by a large mosque) near the budget hotels on Av Hassan II.
Destinations Beni Mellal (5 daily; 2hr 30min); Demnate (2 daily; 1hr); Marrakesh (4 daily; 3hr 30min).
By grand taxi Taxis from a rank beside the bus yard mostly serve Beni Mellal (2hr) and Demnate (1hr), but they

also run to the Cascades d'Ouzoud (30min) and Agouti (2hr) in the Aït Bouguemez.

Services The Banque Populaire opposite Azilal's main square has an ATM, and there's a Crédit Agricole 200m to the east. Internet access is widely available on the main drag (Av Hassan II); try Cyber Espace Bleu beside *Hôtel Assounfou*. There's a post office next to *Hôtel Dades*.

ACCOMMODATION AND EATING

Azilal has a couple of decent cheapies, if you need to stop over. With your own wheels (and a bigger budget), the lakeside hotels at **Bin el Ouidane** are an attractive alternative, providing great views of the deep-blue waters.

AZILAL

Assounfou Av Hassan II, 250m east of the town square ☎0523 459220. Probably the smartest option in town –

the rooms even have carpets and are heated in winter – though still rather shabby. <u>180dh</u>

Dades Av Hassan II, 300m west (left) of the bus station

☎ 0523 458245, ✉ hoteldades1@yahoo.fr. The best of Azilal's budget places, friendly and with a dozen colourful rooms set above a café – though the decor and style in some, particularly the twins, is more hospital-like than hotel. **70dh**

Ibnou Ziad Restaurant Av Hassan II, 50m west of the town square. One of the (few) simple café-restaurants that are the only places to eat in Azilal, this down-to-earth spot is fronted by a line of bubbling tajines that are sold by the weight (250g for 40dh, 2kg for 220dh). Daily 7am–9pm.

BIN EL OUIDANE

Bin el Ouidane Route de Ouaouizaght ☎ 0523 442600, ⓦ hotelbinelouidane.com. Comfortable, fashionably rustic lodge whose rooms enjoy lovely views over the reservoir. There's a surprisingly lush little garden with a kidney-shaped pool and a kids' play area. Activities include

recommended boat safaris on the Oued Ahansal. BB **680dh**

L'Eau Vive Route de Ouaouizaght ☎ 0523 442931, ⓦ dar-eauvive.com. Modest campsite with homely rooms (some en suite) and pitches on a beautiful grassy terrace overlooking the river downstream of the dam – an idyllic place to stop for a coffee or lunch. Restaurant daily 8am–11pm. Camping **80dh**, double **300dh**

Widiane Suites & Spa Route de Ouaouizaght ☎ 0523 442776, ⓦ widiane.net. Swish but pricey new complex running down the hillside on the reservoir's northern shore. Both the traditional and more modern suites are very spacious; some come with private terraces, all have superb views over Bin el Ouidane. There are two restaurants and a bar, a couple of infinity pools and a plush spa offering Thai and Balinese treatments. The very friendly management can help you organize lots of activities on the *barrage*, from kayaking to jetskiing. BB **2700dh**

Cascades d'Ouzoud

The **Cascades d'Ouzoud** are the most spectacular in Morocco, their ampitheatre of waterfalls falling into pools in a lush valley that remains invisible till the last moment. The wide spread of cataracts at the top isn't entirely natural – water from the river is funnelled through a variety of irrigation channels towards the rim of the falls – but the result is an image that is not too far removed from the Muslim idea of Paradise depicted on gaudy prints throughout the nation. Nor has the site been overcommercialized – despite the cascades appearing in every national tourism brochure, the atmosphere remains laidback and relaxing. That there are pleasant walks in the locale is just another reason to stay overnight: to swim in pools below the cascades by moonlight (technically forbidden) is something special, and in late afternoon, arching rainbows appear in the mist around the falls.

The falls

The path to the base of the falls starts from the top of Ouzoud, to the left of the *Dar Essalam*, then zigzags past cafés and souvenir stalls to the great basins below the cascades, where boatmen in rickety rafts row visitors to the **main pool**; the first viewpoint, halfway down the path, is the best place to see the largest rainbows and is close enough to feel the spray on your face. Before you descend, however, take a look at the **lip of the falls** just past the *Riad Cascades d'Ouzoud* at the top of the village. The little concrete huts here shelter small **watermills**, some still grinding wheat into flour as the river is diverted through the wheels before it plunges over the edge. Although strictly speaking it's not permitted, you can swim in one of the **lower pools** – currents are dangerous in the main pool beneath the falls – and you might spot the occasional Barbary ape under the oak and pomegranate trees; your best chance is at daybreak or an hour or so before dusk, when they come to drink in the river.

Hikes around the falls

For a memorable short hike (3hr round-trip), head beyond the lower pools to **Tanaghmelt**, the so-called Mexican village (though some guides prefer "Berber village"), a fascinating place connected by semi-underground passages. To get there, follow the path that runs past the lower pools and up to the left, past a farmhouse and on up to the top of the plain; the village is sited on the slopes of the wooded hills to the west, about 1km along the path, which drops to a stream before climbing up towards the houses.

Another path follows the river valley beyond the falls for 3.5km to the **Gramâa Nakrouine**, a series of caves located near the point where the river drops into a tributary flowing from Bin el Ouidane (2hr). Following the path for a further 3.5km leads to the **Gorges de l'Ouzoud el Abid**, where the valley is at its narrowest and most impressive (5hr round-trip from the caves). With your own transport, you could also see this on the road north towards the N8 (a guide can join you for around 150dh).

ARRIVAL AND DEPARTURE   CASCADES D'OUZOUD

By bus From Marrakesh, you'll need to get a bus for Azilal and get off at the turning for Ouzoud (3 daily; 3hr to the turn-off), from where it's a 15min grand taxi ride. Heading in the other direction, it's easiest to backtrack to Azilal, picking up a bus there to Beni Mellal or (if you time it right) direct to Marrakesh.

By grand taxi There are regular taxis to and from the falls from Azilal (30min) and, less so, Beni Mellal (2hr 30min).

By car Ouzoud lies 16km down a surfaced road off the R304, a turning 21km northwest of Azilal. Going to and from Marrakesh, it's quickest to travel along the P3105 via Khemis des Oulad on the N8 – 51km of tarred road – though the R304 via Demnate (see p.240) is the more interesting route.

On a tour Agencies in Marrakesh offer day-long tours of the falls.

INFORMATION

When to visit The falls are at their best from March until mid-June (the paths get busy in high summer); they're shrouded in darkness for much of the morning and early afternoon, so aim to visit mid- to late afternoon.

Guides Most of the hotels can organize hikes to Tanaghmelt and the Gorges de l'Ouzoud el Abid (150–200dh), or you can ask at the café at the top of the village, by the turn-off to the *Hôtel Restaurant de France*.

ACCOMMODATION AND EATING

Camping at Ouzoud can be great in spring and early summer: several **campsites** lie at the top of the village, all fairly basic but offering shady spots for tents and motorhomes, while cafés on the path downhill have spaces where you can camp for a small fee (10–15dh). On the other side of the falls, there are a number of pleasant sites attracting a young backpacking clientele.

Chellal d'Ouzoud 100m down the path to the falls ☎ 0523 429180, ⊛ hotelchellaldouzoud.com. Nicely renovated, with bright, comfortable rooms and chilled communal salons, plus a friendly proprietor who can do the plummiest British accent this side of Eton. The restaurant offers a menu of Moroccan staples from 85dh. Terrace **40dh**, double **350dh**

Dar Essalam On the northwest corner of the square at the bottom of the village (no phone). Friendly place renting cold, bare rooms around a wide central courtyard – fine in late spring or summer – or sleeping space on the roof. Terrace **40dh**, double **100dh**

De France 500m from the top of the village, on the other side of the river ☎ 0523 429176, ⊛ hotelfrance-ouzoud.com. Set among olive groves on the opposite side of the river and offering something more tranquil, the *Hôtel de France* has bright rooms, some en suite, and a pleasant garden with a child-friendly swimming pool. **200dh**

★ **Riad Cascades d'Ouzoud** On the northeast corner of the square at the bottom of the village ☎ 0523 429173, ⊛ ouzoud.com. The only upmarket choice in the village, a beautifully restored *pisé* house whose rustic chic sits comfortably alongside traditional features. Berber rugs and lovely *tadalekht* bathrooms set off the rooms, which have open fires in the winter. The restaurant (120dh menu) and reading area are just as cosy. BB **710dh**

Aït Bouguemez

The remote and breathtaking **Aït Bouguemez** is second only to Jebel Toubkal in popularity among mountain-lovers, not only for its own unique beauty but also as a base for ascending **Jebel M'Goun**, one of Morocco's highest summits (see box, p.239). Sometimes referred to as the *Vallée Heureuse* or Happy Valley, this flat, fertile stretch is memorably picturesque, its patchwork of cultivated barley fields spread beneath soaring peaks. Mud-brick villages cling to the lower slopes, which are barren for the best part of the year bar spring, when they are carpeted in wild flowers.

A world away from the well-trodden routes around Jebel Toubkal, the valley has until recently existed in relative isolation – the road in here was only built at the turn of the millennium. This arduous way of life has fostered a remarkable community spirit among the valley's villages and led to the creation of a considerable number of self-help initiatives (see box below).

Around the valley

Despite the variety of mountainous day-hikes on offer, one of the best walks is the simple ramble along the valley floor, dropping in on a few of the villages that dot the landscape between **Agouti**, the westernmost settlement in the valley, and **Tabant**, an administrative centre that's home to the regional Sunday souk.

A track up behind **Timit**, around 5km east of Agouti, leads to the fortified hilltop granary of **Sidi Moussa**, a squat, circular building that doubles as a shrine. Women villagers head up here to receive *baraka* at the tomb of the *marabout* Sidi Moussa, a holy man said to help with infertility – though the twenty-minute climb is equally worth it for the spectacular views over the entire valley.

In nearby **Aguerd n'Ouzrou**, faint **dinosaur footprints** can just about be made out on the rocks at the bottom of the slope behind *La Kasbah du M'Goun*, the fossilized footfall of 15m-long *Atlasaurus imelakei* (from *imelake*, Arabic for "giant"), which roamed the Aït Bouguemez over 165 million years ago.

Heading along the *piste* that runs past **Imelghas**, the tiny settlement that lies just beyond the turning to Tabant, a side track at Ifrane leads to **Zaouia Oulemsi**, which essentially defines the eastern or upper end of the valley. From here, you can hike down to the seasonal **Lac Izoughar**, dominated by **Jebel Azourki** (3677m) and other big hills, and a favoured pasture for nomads tending their flocks.

Zaouia Ahansal and beyond

Beyond the village of Ifrane, the eastbound *piste* climbs over the **Tizi n'Tirghist** (2629m) to meet up with the back road from Aït Mohammed (see opposite) before climbing yet again, over the **Tizi n'Tselli** (2603m), to descend down to **Zaouia Ahansal**. The village was founded in the twelfth century by Sidi Said Ahansal and is home to the *marabout*'s

---

HELPING HANDS IN THE HAPPY VALLEY

There are over thirty **associations** and **cooperatives** in the Aït Bouguemez, more than one for every village in the valley, and each is committed to aiding and enhancing their community, developing the right kind of tourism and maintaining the skills needed to produce traditional crafts. You can visit several of these, as well as a couple of forward-thinking schools, for an insight into valley life that is difficult to otherwise obtain, and the chance to give something directly back to the local communities.

Association Ighrem Agouti ☎0673 753163. Principally home to the Atelier de Sculpteur and their beautifully carved boxwood bowls, this very active association is also currently developing a women's carpet cooperative. Past initiatives include free eye tests for the valley's villagers. Daily 8am–6pm.
Atelier Feminin Tissage Imelghas ☎0651 540831. Run by local teacher Fatima Ouakhoum, this workshop shed on the hillside in Imelghas is a hive of activity, with local women weaving traditional Berber rugs using natural vegetable dyes – it's quite hard to find, so you may need

to ask for directions at *Dar Itrane* (see p.240). Mon–Sat 10am–noon & 2–6pm.
Coopérative Tikniouine Timit ☎0668 909308. Small artisan food shop signed down the bottom of a rutted path in Timit, selling locally produced walnut oil, apple jam, honey and cheese. Daily 8am–1pm.
École Vivante On the road between Timit and the turning to Tabant. Since 2010, this primary school has been providing much-needed formal education for the valley's dispersed villages; you can visit (and help out) at around 11am, or ring Stefanie in advance (☎0672 267688). Donations appreciated. Closed July & Aug.

CLIMBING JEBEL M'GOUN

Snowcapped **Jebel M'Goun** (4068m) is Morocco's only summit above 4000m outside the Toubkal massif, and a popular target for trekkers, giving an easy but long ascent from the Tarkeddid plateau, directly south of Agouti. Most guides (see below) follow the *piste* southwest out of Tabant, tracing the Oued Arous via the village of Aït Sayd to the shepherd's pastures around **Azib Ikkis** (2hr 30min). The path then climbs up over the **Tizi n'Tarkeddit** (a further 3hr 30min or so), before descending to the refuge at **Tarkeddit** (☎02165 1073576; 130dh), reached after another 1hr 30min. An early start the next day leads southeast to the pyramid peak of **M'Goun West** (3978m) before curving northeast around the ridge to **Jebel M'Goun** itself (8–10hr return from the refuge).

shrine, but its spectacular surrounding landscapes are the real draw: the remarkable tower architecture of **Agoudim**, a village just off the main *piste* to the southeast, is unique north of the Atlas, while **Taghia**, a dozen or so kilometres further south, faces some of the finest gorge and cliff scenery in the country, a rock climber's playground of Dolomitic scope.

The *piste* makes a sharp descent from Zaouia Ahansal to Tamga and the towering limestone walls of **La Cathédrale**, a striking rock formation surrounded by Aleppo pines that wouldn't look out of place in Yosemite National Park – a spectacular goat path actually leads to the summit dome. From here, the *piste* continues north to **Tillouguite** (Saturday souk) and ultimately **Ouaouizaght** (100km from Zaouia Ahansal), at the far northeastern end of Bin el Ouidane (see p.235).

ARRIVAL AND DEPARTURE   AÏT BOUGUEMEZ

BY CAR

By 2WD Until the new road from Demnate is built, there's only one way into the Aït Bouguemez. Agouti, the first village in the valley (at its western end), is 69km from Azilal (2hr or so, depending on your vehicle). Just before the village of Aït Mohammed (50km from Azilal), turn right onto a highly spectacular road that wends its way down to the lower end of the valley; the route is usually passable in a normal saloon car, but it's worth ringing your accommodation in advance to check in early spring or after rain, as "dry" riverbeds cross the road at various parts. You can get as far as Imelghas and Tabant, 8km beyond Agouti, but will need a 4WD to get any further (though note that the passes east of Tabant are often snowbound in winter).

By 4WD With a 4WD, you can continue through Aït Mohammed and follow the (decent) *piste* that drops down to the eastern end of the Aït Bouguemez, turning right for Ifrane (for Lac Izoughar) and Tabant or left for Zaouia Ahansal (85km from Aït Mohammed) and La Cathédrale; Zaouia Ahansal can also be reached on a *piste* southeast of Bin el Ouidane via Ouaouizaght and Tillouguite. Alternatively, a fairly well-maintained *piste* from Demnate accesses the Aït Bouguemez via Imi n'Ifri and the Aït Bou Oulli.

BY PUBLIC TRANSPORT

By bus A daily minibus service runs from near the mosque in the centre of Azilal to Tabant (3hr).

By grand taxi Taxis from Azilal serve most villages in the western Aït Bouguemez, taking around 2hr to get to Agouti.

INFORMATION AND GUIDES

Guides Most of the accommodation in the valley can provide guides for treks that range from a ninety-minute walk around the valley's villages to a multi-day ascent of Jebel M'Goun (see box above), or you can hire one at the Bureau des Guides in Tabant (Mohammed Achari is particularly recommended; ☎0523 459327) or via the Association Ighrem in Agouti (see box opposite); expect to pay around 300–350dh/day (whether you're on your own or trekking in a group) and a further 120–150dh for a mule (available to rent in Agouti, Tabant and other villages; your accommodation can normally help sort this out). Trekking here can be a serious undertaking, so make sure you are properly equipped (see box, pp.370–371).

Guidebooks The best guides to the region (in English) are Des Clark's *Mountaineering in the Moroccan High Atlas* and Michael Peyron's *Grand Atlas Traverse*. While useful, the gorge explorations mentioned in *Randonnées Pédestres dans le Massif du Mgoun*, a topographical guide published in Morocco (and unobtainable anywhere else), are highly dangerous scrambles rather than sedate walks, and the text should be treated with caution.

Maps West Col's 1:100,000 *Mgoun Massif* ridge map and EWP's 1:160,000 *Azilal - M'Goun* cover the Aït Bouguemez and Jebel M'Goun and are available in the UK.

ACCOMMODATION AND EATING

There are several surprisingly chic places to stay in and around the Aït Bouguemez, and those on cheaper budgets will find dozens of simple *gîtes* spread among the villages, including *Gîte Flilou*, on the left shortly after you enter Agouti coming from Azilal (☎0524 343798, ✉tamsilt@menara.ma), and *Gîte Amezraï* (☎0523 458928), by the perched *ighrem* 1km north of Agoudim.

La Casbah du M'Goun Aguerd n'Ouzrou ☎0662 778148, ⓦhotel-ait-bouguemez.com. Set back from the road on a little hillock above the rest of this tiny village and offering traditional rooms with rug-strewn floors and four- to six-bed dorms (available to groups of four or more). The owner, a qualified mountain guide, organizes hikes around the valley and ascents of Jebel M'Goun. Dorm <u>100dh</u>, double <u>150dh</u>

Dar Ahansal Amazraï, on the roadside in the upper part of the village; 1km north of Agoudim ☎0523 310585, ⓦdarahansal.net. Very comfortable accommodation, particularly given the remote location, in a modern stone-built house set on a lip overlooking the Ahansal valley. Dinners of soups, tajines and the like use garden-fresh produce. Discounts for stays of two nights or longer. Full-board rates also available. HB <u>500dh</u>

Dar Itrane Imelghas, 400m along a piste from the turning to Tabant ☎0523 459312, ⓦorigins-lodge .com. Sensitively constructed hotel that blends into the village of Imelghas. Smartly simple, comfortable rooms have duvet-topped beds and heaters in winter – the valley can get *very* cold – while wholesome dinners are served gathered around the log fire in the main salon. The terrace enjoys superb panoramic views of snowcapped mountains by day and a star-studded sky at night. There's also a library and a wood-fired hammam. *Dar Itrane* is involved in several local projects and contributes a percentage of its profits to the local community. HB <u>800dh</u>

Demnate

You may have to change buses along the way to Marrakesh at **DEMNATE**, a walled market town 65km or so from Ouzoud and Azilal and 93km from Marrakesh, but there is little incentive to stop unless you can time your visit for the interesting Sunday **souk**, by far the largest in the region, which is held 2km out of town on the Sidi Rahal road. There is also a small daily souk just outside the ramparts, as well as a central market with butchers and bakers, and fruit and vegetable stalls (the surrounding area is renowned for its olives), though you could also while away the time between connections poking around the Glaoui-era **kasbah** or the old **Mellah** (until the 1950s, half the population were Jews).

Imi n'Ifri

Around 6.5km southeast of Demnate • Take a grand taxi from the square 300m beyond Bab el Arabi

The impressive natural bridge of **Imi n'Ifri** spans a yawning gorge, the result of the partial collapse of an underground cave system, and is guaranteed to unnerve anyone of a vertiginous disposition. It's a quiet, untouristed spot, with a seasonal restaurant to sit in and little to do but watch the aerobatic displays of choughs and swifts, with their white rumps and square tails, or the *sibsib* (ground squirrels) on roadside walls.

ARRIVAL AND INFORMATION   DEMNATE

By bus Buses to and from Marrakesh (12 daily; 1hr 30min), Beni Mellal (6 daily; 3hr) and Azilal (2 daily; 1hr) drop you at a stop 400m to the right of the old town gate, Bab el Arabi.

By grand taxi Grands taxis to and from Azilal (1hr), Marrakesh (1hr 15min) and Beni Mellal (2hr) run from just outside Bab el Arabi.

By car From the Imi n'Ifri bridge, southeast of town, the R307 (the right-hand fork) sets off over the Atlas, emerging eventually on the plains between Ouarzazate and Skoura (see box, p.413).

Services The post office just inside the gate has an ATM, and there's a Banque Populaire 100m further up Bd Mohammed V.

ACCOMMODATION

★ **Kasbah Timdaf** On the El Attaouia road, 6.5km north of Demnate ☎0523 507178, ⓦkasbah-timdaf .com. Surrounded by poppy fields, this delightful ecolodge and working farm is far superior to anything in town, an aesthetic blend of stonework and wood ceilings, its spacious, warmly decorated rooms kitted out with Berber blankets and bright wardrobes daubed with Amazigh symbols. The tranquil garden is planted with jasmine and papyrus, and there's a pool and traditional *beldi* hammam. Village walks, bike rides and cooking lessons are available. **725dh**

Marrakesh Av Bab el Had ☎0523 506996. By far the best option in town itself, the *Marrakesh* has clean, good-value standard rooms, with blanket-clad beds and Western toilets – fairly unusual for Demnate in this price category. **100dh**

Midelt and around

At **MIDELT**, reached through a bleak plain of scrub and desert, you have essentially left behind the Middle Atlas. As you approach from the north, the greater peaks of the High Atlas appear suddenly through the haze, rising behind the town to a massive range, the **Jebel Ayachi**, at over 3700m. The sheer drama of the site – tremendous in the clear, cool evenings – is one of the most compelling reasons to stop over. Though the town is comprised of little more than a street with a few cafés and hotels and a small souk, it's a pleasant place to break a journey, partly because so few people do and partly because of its easy-going (and predominantly Berber) atmosphere. Indeed, there is a hint of the frontier town about Midelt, a sense reinforced by the deserted mining settlements at **Mibladene** and **El Ahouli**, 22km to the northeast.

Midelt is so far inland that it has a microclimate of extremes: bitterly cold in winter and oppressively hot in summer. Consequently, one of the best times to visit is autumn, particularly at the start of October, when the town hosts a modest **apple festival**. Year-round, try to arrive for the huge **Sunday souk**, which spreads back along the road towards Azrou and is a fruitful hunting ground for quality carpets.

Souk el Jedid and Souk Tapis

The most interesting section of town is the area around **Souk el Jedid**, a daily fruit and vegetable market located behind the stalls facing the bus station. Just to the south of

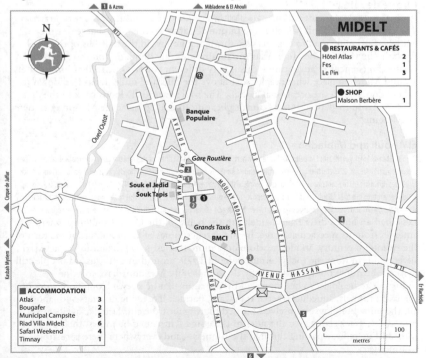

the main souk is the arcaded **Souk Tapis**, or carpet souk, a relaxed place to shop for (superb) rugs – mostly local, geometric designs from tribes of the Middle Atlas. Ask to see the "antique" ones, few of which are actually more than ten or twenty years old but which are usually the most idiosyncratic and inventive.

Kasbah Myriem
1.5km southwest of Midelt, on the road to Tattiouine • Mon–Fri 8am–noon & 2–5.30pm • ☎ 0664 447375

Housed in a former convent building, the *atelier* (workshop) of **Kasbah Myriem** is run by six Franciscan nuns, who welcome visitors to see carpets, blankets and beautiful traditional embroidery being made from start to finish by local women. Girls learn techniques from as young as five years old (committing them to memory), and women who choose to continue after marriage, rather than focus on domestic duties, are paid for their work. Consequently, the women practise and pass on traditional skills and designs, and also contribute to their own domestic economies. Admittedly, this is not the cheapest place to buy a carpet (though there are also embroidered tablecloths and napkins, handkerchiefs and bags), but your money contributes directly to the local economy and the pieces are of high quality; all "*fait avec amour*", as the nuns put it.

Nôtre Dame de l'Atlas
The convent building itself, **Nôtre Dame de l'Atlas**, is home not to the nuns – who live in a house opposite – but to four elderly Trappist monks, part of the only monastery in North Africa; among their number is Frère Jean Pierre Flachaire, one of only two survivors of the massacre of seven Jesuit monks in Tibhirine, Algeria, in 1996. Visitors are welcome to join in the convent's Mass (times are posted on the metal gate at the entrance).

Cirque de Jaffar
The cirque loops 79km southwest of Midelt and takes a good half-day to complete • Guided tours cost 300dh (1–7 people) for a 3hr trip

The classic route around Midelt is the **Cirque de Jaffar**, a good *piste* that leaves the Midelt–Tattiouine road to edge its way through a hollow in the foothills of the Jebel Ayachi. The views of the High Atlas mountains are truly dramatic and the rugged road ensures an element of adventure – this is very different countryside to that immediately around Midelt, a place where eagles soar above the hills and mule tracks lead down to valleys dotted with the occasional kasbah. The route eventually loops back to the Midelt–Azrou road after 34km – turn right, onto the 3426, near the Maison Forestière de Mitkane.

El Ahouli and Mibladene
The S317 heads 15km northeast of Midelt to Mibladene, where the road (the 3419) deteriorates and the tarmac virtually disappears as you approach El Ahouli, 22km further on (4WD recommended for this stretch due to risk of flash floods); beyond El Ahouli, a rough track continues downstream to Ksabi from where you can complete the circuit to Midelt by the N15 and N13 • Grands taxis charge around 200dh for a return trip to El Ahouli, including a 2hr stopover at the mines (some refuse, though, due to the poor condition of the track); alternatively, 4WD and fossicking excursions cost between 200dh and 300dh per person, with 1hr 30min at the mine (see opposite)

Less than an hour's drive from Midelt, on the banks of the Oued Moulouya where it emerges from its spectacular gorge, lie the derelict mines of **El Ahouli**. From the turn of the twentieth century, and long before on a more modest scale, the locals extracted silver and lead from the rocky terrain here; in 1979, around three thousand people still worked the mines but all had gone by the mid-1980s. You don't have to be an industrial archeologist to be impressed by the ruins that lie strewn along both sides of the river: tunnels, aqueducts, aerial ropeways, barrack-like living quarters and, above all, the mine buildings themselves, pressed high against the cliff face like a Tibetan monastery. Tracks cut across the sides of the gorge – first used by mules, then a mineral-line railway passing through the tunnels – and everywhere there is rusting ironmongery.

CLIMBING JEBEL AYACHI

Seen from a distance, the long wave crest of **Jebel Ayachi** (3747m), 15km southwest of Midelt, appears to curve over the horizon, such is the scale of these dramatic mountains. A guide is recommended (see below), but to tackle Ayachi independently you can take a taxi to the springs 2km beyond Tattiouine, from where an easy ascent leads to the many summits of this huge range, long thought to be the highest in Morocco (at 4167m, Toubkal tops it by some 400m). The only information in English is in Des Clark's winter-walking *Mountaineering in the Moroccan High Atlas* and Michael Peyron's *Grand Atlas Traverse* guide, which details the whole zone between here and the Toubkal massif; EWP's 1:160,000 *Rich & Midelt* map covers the region.

Modest excavations are still being worked at **Mibladene** (appropriately, "Our Mother Earth" in Berber), around halfway to El Ahouli. In some respects, the desolate rust-red landscape around Mibladene, and the barren and tortuous route onwards from here, are reason enough to do the trip: the bleak plateau where Mibladene is located leads to a narrow and picturesque gorge, negotiated by frequent river crossings on rattling wooden bridges.

ARRIVAL AND DEPARTURE   MIDELT

By bus Midelt's *gare routière* is in the centre of town, though a new station on the road to Er Rachidia has been under construction for some time. Note that you can reach Imilchil on daily minibuses from Rich (see p.244).
Destinations Azrou (3 CTM & 1 Supratours daily, others every 30min; 1hr 45min–3hr 30min); Beni Mellal (3 daily; 4hr 30min); Er Rachidia (2 CTM daily, others every 30min; 3hr); Fez (1 CTM, 1 Supratours & 9 others daily; 5hr 40min–6hr 30min); Marrakesh (2 CTM & 3 others daily; 8hr); Meknes (3 CTM & 12 others daily; 4hr 40min); Merzouga (daily; 4hr); Ouarzazate (daily; 7hr); Rich (3 CTM & 1 Supratours daily, others every 30min; 1hr–1hr 30min);

Rissani (2 CTM daily, others every 30min; 4hr 30min).
By grand taxi Taxis depart regularly from the rank on Av Moulay Abdallah to Azrou (1hr 30min), Fez (3hr), Meknes (3hr 30min) and Er Rachidia (1hr 30min).
By car It's 120km from Azrou to Midelt (the R13/N13), along a magnificent stretch of the Middle Atlas; a possible break on the journey, 50km from Azrou, is the eerily beautiful Aguelmane Sidi Ali, the largest of the region's many mountain lakes (1km from the N13). A *piste* leads southwest from Midelt, beyond the Cirque de Jaffar, all the way to Imilchil, but with a standard car it's easier to push on to Rich, 75km to the south, and take the surfaced road west from there.

INFORMATION AND TOURS

Services Internet access is available at Cyber el Ayachi, 43 Av Tarik Souk Jamâa.
Tours *Ksar Timnay* specializes in 4WD excursions to the El Ahouli mines, Jebel Ayachi and around the Cirque de Jaffar as well as trekking (300dh per person per day, including guide, driver, lunch and insurance, plus homestay

accommodation where necessary), while *Hôtel Safari Weekend* arranges 4WD trips (a day-trip on a minibus costs from 1200dh for up to six people, including a driver and food). Otherwise, you could try Ouyahia Norolime, an unofficial mountain guide who hangs around *Hôtel Safari Weekend* (☎ 0677 742794, ✉ noro09@yahoo.fr).

ACCOMMODATION

Midelt has a reasonable spread of accommodation, but hotels are often full by mid-afternoon in peak season, so arrive early or make a reservation in advance. With your own transport, the *Ksar Timnay* is a better place to camp than the municipal campsite.

Atlas 3 Rue Mohammed Amraoui ☎ 0535 582938. Lovely *pension* run by a charming Berber family, their ten rooms spotless and cosy (hot showers 10dh). They also run their own little restaurant (see p.244). It's become very popular, and doesn't quite offer the same value as it once did. 120dh
Bougafer 7 Bd Mohammed V ☎ 0535 583099, ✪ bougaferweb.com. A friendly, modern place above a café, with rooms distributed over two floors, some fairly

newly renovated and en suite, others more basic with shared facilities (hot showers 10dh). There are great views from the roof terrace, which doubles as additional sleeping space. The in-house Moroccan restaurant has a reasonable 50dh menu. Terrace 80dh, double 150dh
Ksar Timnay On the N13, 19km northwest of Midelt ☎ 0535 583434, ✪ ksar-timnay.com. Very popular (and educational) spot, with friendly management and excellent facilities including a restaurant and swimming

pool (June–Oct; non-residents 50dh). Rooms are in either a motel-style block or a newer luxury faux-kasbah ("*Riad Mimouna*"), all with a/c, satellite TV and free wi-fi, and there's a pleasant camping area. There are plenty of cultural activities on offer, and treks and 4WD excursions can also be arranged (see p.243). Camping <u>60dh</u>, double BB <u>380dh</u>, riad BB <u>450dh</u>

Riad Villa Midelt 1 Pl Verte ☎ 0535 360851, ⓦ hotel-riad-villa-midelt.com. On the southern fringes of town, this traditional-style modern "villa" is comparatively pricey but is a cut above anything else in Midelt. The spacious

en-suite rooms enjoy a/c, and some also have a fireplace, while the Moroccan dishes served up in the restaurant are consistently good. The friendly owner can offer plenty of advice on onward routes. BB <u>500dh</u>

CAMPING

Municipal campsite Behind Hôtel el Ayachi ☎ 0670 180704. You won't be fighting others for pitch space at the town's campsite, which is rather bare and stony but does have clean (hot) showers, as well as a pool in summer. <u>30dh</u>

EATING

Hôtel Atlas 3 Rue Mohammed Amraoui. Delicious home-cooked Berber meals are prepared on the ground floor of this busy family-run *pension*, where the great-value menu (Berber tajine, sheesh kebab) is just 30dh. Daily 8am–9.30pm.

Fes Rue Lalla Aïcha. A few bare tables provide the setting for the indefatigable Fatima's generous *menus du jour*, simple but honest dishes including vegetarian tajines, and

quince stewed in sugar and cinnamon for afters (35–70dh). Daily noon–3pm & 6–9pm.

Le Pin Av Moulay Abdallah. Part of a tourist complex, with a hall-like dining room and a (more relaxing) bar and café in the gardens – a pleasant spot for breakfast or a light lunch of simple brochettes, chicken tajine or omelettes (menu 70dh). Daily: café 7am–midnight; restaurant noon–3pm.

SHOPPING

Maison Berbère 15 Rue Mohammed Amraoui. The friendly owners of this carpet boutiuqe (no link to the mini chain that has branches in the south) are happy to talk you through a variety of quality Berber rugs from the Middle

and High Atlas (their family is from Imilchil), unfurling plenty of geometrically patterned weaves but with less of the hard-sell than you might be used to at similar shops. Daily 8am–8pm.

South to Er Rachidia

The route **from Midelt to Er Rachidia**, 154km along the N13, is a striking one, marking the transition to the kasbahs and great palmeries of the south – and, beyond, the desert. The area was long notorious for raids upon caravans and travellers carried out by the **Aït Haddidou**, a nomadic Berber tribe, fear of whom led the main spring along this route to be known as *Aïn Khrob ou Hrob* – "Drink and Flee". The tribe were pacified with great difficulty by the French, with skirmishes only fizzling out as late as the 1930s, and as a result traditional *ksour* (fortified villages) are often shadowed by old Foreign Legion posts.

Around 30km south of Midelt, the road heaves up across one of the lower passes of the High Atlas, the **Tizi n'Talrhmeht** (Pass of the She-Camel), before descending onto a sparse desert plain. At **Aït Messaoud**, just beyond the pass, there's a distinctly *Beau Geste*-like Foreign Legion fort, and a few kilometres further down you come across the first southern *ksar*, **Aït Kherrou**, a river oasis at the entrance to a small gorge. After this, the *ksour* steadily begin to dot the landscape as the road follows the meanders of the great Oued Ziz.

Rich

The main settlement in these parts is **RICH**, a dusty, red-washed market town and administrative centre 75km from Midelt and spread out on a plain between mountains, the Atlas stretching off into the distance to the west. Enclosed by palms that are watered by the Oued Ziz, the town developed around a *ksar* and was an important fort during the Protectorate. There is a lively Monday **souk**, and a couple of hotels that serve as passable stopovers if you're heading across the Atlas to Imilchil (see p.230).

ARRIVAL AND DEPARTURE RICH

By bus The bus station is at the far western end of town, off the main road through Rich.

Departures Er Rachidia (2 CTM & 1 Supratours daily & others every 30min; 1–2hr); Fez (1 CTM & 1 Supratours daily; 6–7hr); Midelt (3 CTM & 1 Supratours daily, others every 30min; 1hr–1hr 30min).

INTO THE ATLAS

By car The R317 road west from Rich begins as the R706 and is surfaced all the way to Imilchil, though maintenance can vary; it's a wonderful 3hr trip that winds through great gorges and ever-more barren valleys.

By minibus taxi Minibuses ply the route to Imilchil daily (3hr), departing from a block east of the bus station, by the road sign to Imilchil, before heading to the bridge across the Oued Ziz (you can pick them up at either place).

By lorry You can travel the route in stages on Berber lorries (*camions*), which head for the Imilchil souk on Fridays or early Saturday morning.

ACCOMMODATION AND EATING

Isli Just off the main square ☎ 0535 368191. The best hotel in Rich – though that's not saying too much really – located above a café-restaurant and with clean rooms and free hot showers. **200dh**

El Massira Just off the main square ☎ 0535 589340. Just about covering the fundamentals, but still marginally preferable to the nearby *Hôtel Salama*, *El Massira* offers fairly basic rooms with hot showers, and meals in its own restaurant. **150dh**

The Ziz Gorges

The scenic highlight of the regular Midelt–Er Rachidia route is the dramatic **Ziz Gorges**, tremendous erosions of rock that carve a passage through the Atlas. The route follows the Ziz Valley from Aït Krojmane (7km from Rich) onwards, just past the Ziz petrol station.

About 20km from Rich, the road passes **Hammat Moulay Ali Shereef**, a small but well-known spa whose magnesium-rich hot springs are said to cure rheumatic disorders and kidney problems; you will probably see the afflicted hopefuls in steamy thickets nearby. A further 5km on, you enter the gorges proper, around 25km from Rich and shortly after the Tunnel de Foum Zabel, better known as the **Tunnel du Légionnaire**, which was built by the French in 1928 to open up the route to the south and is sometimes still guarded by drowsy soldiers. The gorges are truly majestic, especially in late afternoon, when they are lit by great slashes of sunlight and the mountain landscape reveals sudden vistas of brilliant green oases and red-brown *ksour*.

You emerge from the gorges near the vast **Barrage Hassan Addakhil**, constructed in 1971 to irrigate the far-reaching Tafilalt beyond, and to supply electricity for Er Rachidia. The dam also regulates the flow of the Oued Ziz, preventing the serious flooding that occurred frequently before it was built, as witnessed by the deserted *ksour* in the gorges above and below the lake.

The Atlantic coast: Rabat to Essaouira

HASSAN II MOSQUE, CASABLANCA

The Atlantic coast: Rabat to Essaouira

This five-hundred-kilometre stretch of Atlantic coastline takes in Morocco's urban heartland and accounts for close to a fifth of the country's total population. It's an astonishingly recent growth along what was, until the French Protectorate, a neglected strip of coast. The region is dominated by the country's elegant, orderly administrative capital, Rabat; and the dynamic commercial capital, Casablanca. Keep heading south, and you'll encounter some delightfully low-key coastal resorts, including El Jadida, Oualidia and Essaouira. This is the most Europeanized part of Morocco, where you'll see middle-class people in particular wearing Western-style clothes and leading what appear on the surface to be quite European lifestyles.

The fertile plains inland from Rabat (designated *Maroc Utile*, or "Useful Morocco", by the French) have been occupied and cultivated since Paleolithic times, with Neolithic settlements on the coast to the south, notably at present-day Temara and Skhirat, but today it is French and post-colonial influences that dominate in the main coastal cities. Don't go to Casa – as Casablanca is popularly known – expecting some exotic movie location; it's a modern city that looks very much like Marseilles, the French seaport on which it was modelled. Rabat, too, which the French developed as a capital in place of the old imperial centres of Fez and Marrakesh, looks markedly European, with its cafés and boulevards, though it also has some of Morocco's finest and oldest monuments, dating from the Almohad and Merenid dynasties. If you're on a first trip to Morocco, Rabat is an ideal place to get to grips with the country. Its Westernized streets make an easy cultural shift and it's an excellent transport hub, well connected by train with Tangier, Fez and Marrakesh. Casa is maybe more interesting after you've spent a while in the country, when you'll appreciate both its differences and its fundamentally Moroccan character.

Along the coast are a large number of beaches, but this being the Atlantic rather than the Mediterranean, tides and currents can be strong. Surfing is a popular sport along the coast and Essaouira is Morocco's prime resort for windsurfing.

The coast to Rabat

Although by no means an idyllic stretch of sand, the coast from **Kenitra to Rabat** still has a few decent beaches and a couple of attractions that are worthy stops along this very busy section of the national highway.

THE BEACH AT ESSAOUIRA

Highlights

❶ Hassan Mosque, Rabat Never completed, the minaret of this Almohad mosque is a masterpiece of Islamic architecture. **See p.259**

❷ Chellah, Rabat As beautiful a ruin as you could imagine, with Roman remains and royal tombs from the Merenids. **See p.261**

❸ Colonial architecture, Casablanca Downtown Casa is a living monument to French 1930s Art Deco styles. **See p.276**

❹ Hassan II Mosque, Casablanca Second in size only to Mecca, Hassan II's great mosque can (unusually for Morocco) be visited by non-Muslims. **See p.279**

❺ Cité Portugaise, El Jadida Walk round the ramparts of this unique UNESCO World Heritage Site, and check out the cistern where Orson Welles filmed *Othello*. **See p.288**

❻ Oualidia oysters North Africa's finest, best eaten fresh at one of this friendly coastal town's lagoonside restaurants. **See p.293**

❼ Essaouira Morocco's most relaxed seaside town, with a Medina that's easy to explore and a wide bay perfect for kite- and windsurfers. **See p.298**

HIGHLIGHTS ARE MARKED ON THE MAP ON P.250

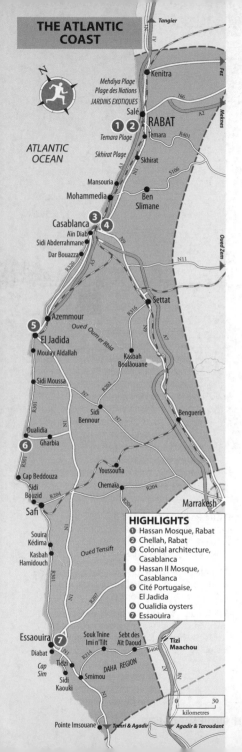

THE ATLANTIC COAST

Kenitra

KENITRA was established by the French as Port Lyautey – named after the Resident General – with the intention of channelling trade from Fez and Meknes. It never quite took off, however, losing out in industry and port activities to Casablanca, despite the rich farming areas of its hinterland. Today, it has a population of nearly 400,000, employed mainly in paper mills and a fish cannery. It's livelier than most Moroccan towns of its size, with a noticeably friendly atmosphere that goes some way to make up for the paucity of sights. There are also several **beaches** within easy reach.

Kenitra has two main streets: **Avenue Mohammed V**, the town's main artery, which runs east to west, and **Avenue Mohammed Diouri**, running north to south. The central square, dominated by the *baladiya* (town hall), is **Place de Municipalité**, two blocks north of Avenue Mohammed V and three blocks east of Avenue Mohammed Diouri.

ARRIVAL AND DEPARTURE   KENITRA

By train There are two train stations: Kenitra station, the most central, at the southern end of Av Mohammed Diouri; and Kenitra Medina, one stop north, off the eastern end of Av Mohammed V and near the bus station.

Destinations Asilah (8 direct & 1 connecting daily; 2hr 30min); Casa Port (over 20 daily; 1hr 30min); Casa Voyageurs (1–2 hourly; 1hr 35min); Fez (19 daily; 2hr); Marrakesh (9 daily; 5hr); Meknes (18 daily; 1hr 50min); Mohammedia (1–2 daily; 1hr); Oujda (3 direct & 2 connecting daily; 9hr); Rabat (1–2 hourly; 30min); Tangier (8 direct & 1 connecting daily; 3hr 15min).

By bus All companies, including CTM, operate from the main *gare routière*, 200m north of Av Mohammed V and three blocks east of Pl de Municipalité.

Destinations Casablanca (1 CTM and 10 others daily; 2hr 30min); Chefchaouen via Ouezzane (1 CTM and 5 others daily; 3hr); Larache (15 daily; 1hr 45min); Rabat (1 CTM daily and others hourly; 1hr); Souk el Arba du Rharb (1 CTM & 10 others daily; 1hr 15min); Tangier (8 daily; 3hr).

By grand taxi Grands taxis for Souk el Arba du Rharb (change here for Chefchaouen) operate from the *gare routière*, those for Rabat leave from Av Mohammed Diouri, one block north of Av Mohammed V.

Destinations Rabat (45min); Souk el Arba du Rharb (1hr).

HIGHLIGHTS
1. Hassan Mosque, Rabat
2. Chellah, Rabat
3. Colonial architecture, Casablanca
4. Hassan II Mosque, Casablanca
5. Cité Portugaise, El Jadida
6. Oualidia oysters
7. Essaouira

ACCOMMODATION

Ambassy 20 Av Hassan II ☎0537 379978, ☎0537 377420. Comfortable and central; each room has a little laundry room as well as a bathroom, and some have a/c. There are also two bars (one with a pool table) and a mediocre fish restaurant. BB **540dh**

Camping La Chenaie On the edge of town (approaching from Rabat, look for signs to the left for the Complexe Touristique) ☎0537 363001. Rather overgrown and run-down, although prices are pretty low and there's tennis, a pool and a football pitch. **55dh**

Jacaranda Pl Administrative ☎0537 373030, ⓦhoteljacaranda.net. The most upmarket place in town, with a swimming pool, restaurant, bar and separate nightclub. Spread out over a number of floors, the modern rooms are bright and spacious, with large windows, big beds and a small sitting area; ask for one at the (quieter) back, overlooking the pool. BB **681dh**

Mamora Pl Administrative ☎0537 371775, ⓦhotelmamora.com. Bland, business-class hotel with slightly small but modern rooms. There's a good swimming pool, popular nightclub, comfortable bar and reasonable restaurant, albeit with a limited menu. BB **647dh**

Marignan 185 Av Mohammed Diouri ☎0537 363424. This small and friendly old hotel is only 200m from Kenitra station, and offers large, high-ceilinged rooms that are airy and clean, though sparsely furnished. There's shared bathrooms with toilets and hand basins, but no showers. **120dh**

De la Poste 307 Av Mohammed V ☎0537 377769. The best of the town's cheapies, this friendly little place is about halfway up the avenue and close to a number of cafés. The tiled rooms are bright and well kept, and simply furnished with comfortable beds and antique wardrobes. Some rooms are en suite, while the shared bathrooms are clean and have hot water. **200dh**

La Rotonde 60 Av Mohammed Diouri ☎&☎0537 371401. A little gloomy inside but rooms are large and clean, if a bit basic. Hot water evenings only. The downstairs bar and reception area is popular with locals. BB **280dh**

EATING, DRINKING AND NIGHTLIFE

Café Metropole Cnr Av Mohammed V & Rue Sebta ☎0537 378206. Classy, comfortable establishment on the main street, with seating on a street-side wooden deck or inside the a/c interior, decorated with pictures of New York. The menu ranges from breakfast and light meals to pizza and pasta dishes (17–45dh). No alcohol. Daily 7am–11pm.

El Dorado 64 Av Mohammed Diouri. Clean and pleasant 1950s-style American diner, with a good range of meat dishes, plus couscous on Fridays, and chocolate mousse or pancakes for afters. Mains 25–48dh. Daily 11am–10pm.

DIRECTORY

Banks Banks can be found along avenues Mohammed V and Mohammed Diouri; Currency Exchange Point, Rue Al Mountanabi (opposite *Hôtel la Rotonde*).

Internet Acces Pro, 12 Rue Amira Aïcha; Téléboutique, Av Mohammed Diouri (next to Kenitra station).

Post office Av Hassan II, just off Pl Administrative.

Mehdiya

MEHDIYA, 9km west of Kenitra (take bus #15), is a dull **beach** with a ruined **kasbah**, overlooking the Oued Sebou estuary. Originally Portuguese but rebuilt under Moulay Ismail, the kasbah shelters the remains of a seventeenth-century governor's palace but has seen many residents, including the US Navy from the 1940s to 1970s. A couple of kilometres inland is the birdlife-rich **Lac Sidi Boughaba**, a narrow freshwater lake divided by a central causeway that gives access (daily 9am–5pm) to the lake's southern edge, where there are a number of shaded picnic sites. This is also where you'll find the National Centre for Environmental Education (CNEE; Sat & Sun: winter noon–4pm; summer noon–5pm; ☎0537 747209, Espana@spana.org.ma), focused mainly on environmental education for local schoolchildren but open to visitors on weekends and public holidays. The best viewing points for the lake's birdlife are from the causeway or the viewing deck at the education centre.

Plage des Nations

22km south of Kenitra

The **Plage des Nations** (also called Sidi Bouknadel) was named after the foreign diplomats and their families who started swimming here in the 1970s – and continue to do so.

Unlike Rabat's kasbah or Salé beaches, it has a very relaxed, friendly and cosmopolitan feel about it and is unusual in that young Moroccan women feel able to come out here for the day. The beach itself is relatively clean, with big, exciting waves – but dangerous currents, and is patrolled by lifeguards along the central strip. It's flanked by a couple of beach cafés, as well as the unsightly and ongoing construction of a large residential golf estate.

Museé Dar Belghazi

N1 Highway, directly opposite the turn-off for the beach • Daily 8am–5pm • 50dh for a simple tour, 100dh for a complete tour including the reserve collection • ☎ 0537 822178

The **Museé Dar Belghazi** is home to a wealth of manuscripts, nineteenth-century carpets and textiles, eighteenth- and nineteenth-century ceramics, and examples of woodwork, armour and jewellery. The more tightly packed reserve collection holds further treasures including a reproduction eighteenth-century cedarwood carriage, and the 1812 *minbar* from the Grand Mosque in Tangier, which was removed by the Ministry of Islamic Affairs (to the great outrage of many Tanjawis) and subsequently resurfaced here. There's not much by way of explanatory text in the museum other than a small booklet in French and Arabic, but if you have a particular interest in Moroccan or Islamic art, then the trip out here is worthwhile.

ARRIVAL AND DEPARTURE	MEHDIYA
By bus and grand taxi Bus #28 runs hourly from Av Moulay Hassan in Rabat and Plage des Nations and Bab	Khemis in Salé (8am–7pm; 50min); grands taxis operate from Salé during summer (30min).

ACCOMMODATION AND EATING	
Firdaous Plage des Nations ☎ 0537 822131, ☎ 0537 822143. A good place to stay – all rooms have a sea view, and you can get a suite for not much more than the price of	a room. There's a swimming pool (non-residents 70dh), plus a bar, restaurant and snack bar. BB **600dh**

Les Jardins Exotiques de Bouknadel

N1 Highway, 6km south of the Plage des Nations & 13km north of Rabat • Daily: winter 9am–5pm; summer 9am–7pm • 10dh • Bus #9 from Bab Chellah and Bab el Had in Rabat

The **Jardins Exotiques de Bouknadel** are a very pleasant and tranquil respite from the everyday traffic noise and commotion just metres from its walls. A compact botanical haven, the gardens were laid out by French horticulturalist Marcel François in the early 1950s, fell into decline in the 1980s and were rescued in 2003 by the king's "Fondation Pour la Protection de l'Environnement", being assiduously renovated before the grand reopening in November 2005.

Entering the gardens, colour-coded paths direct visitors across a series of precarious bamboo bridges and through a sequence of regional creations. There's a **Brazilian rainforest**, dense with water and orchids, a formal **Japanese garden**, a Mexican cactus garden, and a piece of **French Polynesia**, with rickety summerhouses set amid long pools, turtles paddling past, palm trees all round and flashes of bright-red flowers. The last of the series, returning to a more local level, is an **Andalusian garden** with a fine collection of Moroccan plants. There's also a **terrarium** (5dh) featuring a few snakes and tortoises.

Worth a visit at anytime of the year but particularly delightful in spring or early summer, the gardens are popular with school groups during the week and families at weekends.

Rabat

Capital of the nation since 1912, elegant and spacious **RABAT** is the very image of an orderly administrative and diplomatic centre. Lacking the frenetic pace of Morocco's other large cities, Rabat is sometimes harshly referred to as "provincial". Sure enough, there are times when it's hard to find a café open much past ten at night, but there's other times when the city comes out from its conservatism and even makes a little noise, such as the during the Festival of Rhythms each May. Befitting its regal status, Rabat – along with neighbouring **Salé** – has some of the most interesting historic and architectural monuments in the country, and the fact that the local economy does not depend on tourist money makes exploring these attractions a great deal more relaxed than cities like Fez and Marrakesh.

Brief history

The Phoenicians established a settlement at Sala, around the citadel known today as **Chellah**. This eventually formed the basis of an independent Berber state, which reached its peak of influence in the eighth century, developing a code of government inspired by the Koran but adapted to Berber customs and needs. It represented a challenge to the Islamic orthodoxy of the **Arab** rulers of the interior, however, and to stamp out the heresy, a *ribat* – the fortified monastery from which the city takes its name – was founded on the site of the present-day kasbah. The *ribat*'s presence led to Chellah's decline – a process hastened in the eleventh century by the founding of a new town, **Salé**, across the estuary.

The **Almohads** rebuilt the kasbah and, in the late twentieth century, **Yacoub el Mansour ("the Victorious")** created a new imperial capital here. His reign lasted almost thirty years, allowing El Mansour to leave a legacy that includes the superb **Oudaïa Gate** of the kasbah, **Bab er Rouah** at the southwest edge of town, and the early stages of the **Hassan Mosque**. He also erected over 5km of fortifications, though it is only in the last sixty years that the city has expanded to fill his circuit of *pisé* walls.

Notoriety and pirates

After Mansour's death, Rabat's significance was dwarfed by the imperial cities of Fez, Meknes and Marrakesh, and the city fell into neglect. Sacked by the Portuguese, it was little more than a village when, as New Salé, it was resettled by seventeenth-century Andalusian refugees. In this revived form, however, it entered into an extraordinary period of international piracy and local autonomy. Its corsair fleets, the **Sallee Rovers**, specialized in the plunder of merchant ships returning to Europe from West Africa and the Spanish Americas, but on occasion raided as far afield as Plymouth and the Irish coast – Daniel Defoe's Robinson Crusoe began his captivity "carry'd prisoner into Sallee, a Moorish port".

The Andalusians, owing no loyalty to the Moorish sultans and practically impregnable within their kasbah perched high on a rocky bluff above the river, established their own pirate state, the **Republic of the Bou Regreg**. They rebuilt the Medina below the kasbah in a style reminiscent of their homes in the Spanish city of Badajoz, dealt in arms with the English and French, and even accepted European consuls, before the town finally reverted to government control under Moulay Rachid, and his heavy-handed successor, Moulay Ismail.

A capital once again

Unofficial piracy continued until 1829 when Austria took revenge for the loss of a ship by shelling Rabat and other coastal towns. From then until the French made it their colonial capital, moving it from the more conservative and harder to defend Fez, Rabat-Salé was very much a backwater. Upon independence in 1956, and perhaps also concerned about the influence wielded by Fez, Mohammed V decided to keep Rabat as the country's capital. It's taken a few generations, but the city now seems comfortable with this weighty responsibility and, of late, has begun to promote itself as more than just a residence for the diplomatic and governmental corps. A number of large-scale developments, including a revamped riverside promenade and a new tramway system, were pushed through specifically to benefit the local people.

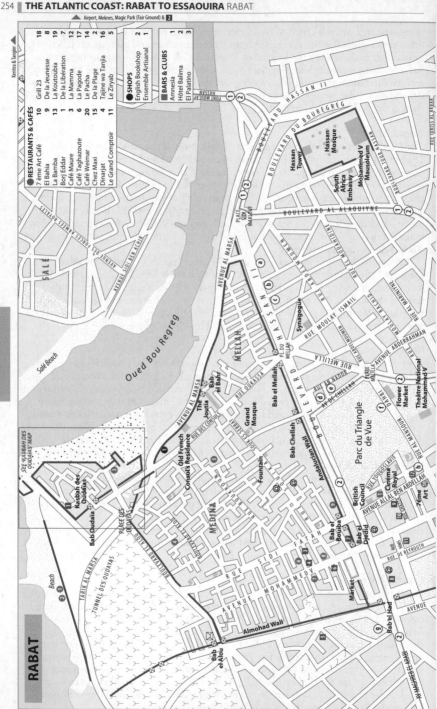

Airport, Meknes, Magic Park (Fair Ground) & 2

Kenitra & Tangier

RESTAURANTS & CAFÉS

7 ème Art Café	10
El Bahia	9
La Bamba	13
Borj Eddar	1
Café Maure	3
Café Taghazoute	6
Café Weimar	20
Chez Maxi	15
Dinarjat	4
Le Grand Comptoir	11
Grill 23	18
De la Jeunesse	8
La Koutoubia	19
De la Libération	7
La Mamma	12
La Pagode	17
Le Pacha	14
De la Plage	16
Tajine wa Tanjia	5
Le Ziryab	11

SHOPS
English Bookshop	2
Ensemble Artisanal	1

BARS & CLUBS
Amnesia	1
Hôtel Balima	2
El Palatino	3

RABAT

SALÉ

Oued Bou Regreg

Salé Beach

Beach

BOULEVARD DU BOUREGREG

BOULEVARD HASSAN II

Hassan Mosque

Hassan Tower

Mohammed V Mausoleum

South Africa Embassy

BOULEVARD AL ALAOUIYNE

AVENUE AL MARSA

MELLAH

Synagogue

RUE MOULAY ISMAIL

RUE MELILLA

Parc du Triangle de Vue

Flower Market

Théâtre National Mohammed V

AVENUE ABDERRAHMAN

Bab el Mellah

Bab Chellah

Bab el Bahr

The Joutia

Grand Mosque

Fountain

Andalucian Wall

Old French Consul's Residence

MEDINA

Kasbah des Oudaïas

Bab Oudaïa

SEE KASBAH DES OUDAÏAS MAP

British Council

Cinéma Royal

7ème Art

AVENUE ALLAL BEN ABDELLAH

Bab el Bouiba

Bab el Djedid

Market

RUE DE BEYROUTH

Bab el Had

Almohad Wall

Bab el Alou

AVENUE MOHAMMED V

RUE SIDI FATAH

TUNNEL DES OUDAÏAS

TARIK AL MARSA

BOULEVARD AL ALOU

PLACE DES OUDAÏAS

AVENUE

AN MACHICHE-MAHI

4

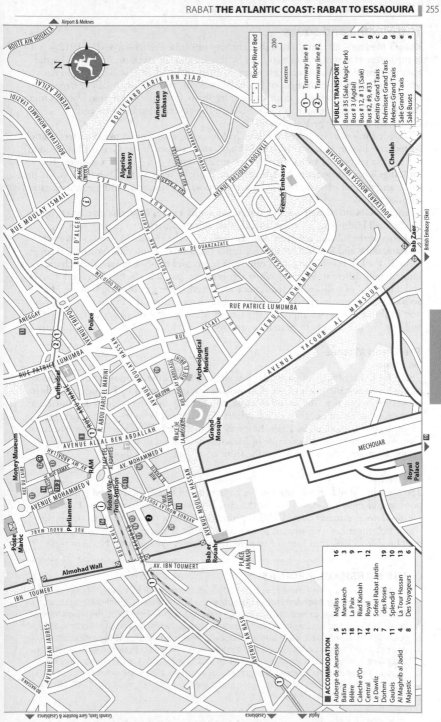

The Medina and souks

Rabat's **Medina** – all that there was of the city until the French arrived in 1912 – is a compact quarter, wedged on two sides by the sea and the river, on the others by the twelfth-century Almohad and seventeenth-century Andalusian walls. It's open and orderly in comparison to those of Fez or Marrakesh, and still essentially the town created by Muslim refugees from Badajoz in Spain, but with its external features intact, its way of life seems remarkably at odds with the government business and cosmopolitanism of the Ville Nouvelle.

The Medina's plan is typical of others in Morocco, with a main market street – **Rue Souika** and its continuation **Souk es Sebbat** – running beside the Grand Mosque, and behind it a residential area scattered with smaller souks and "parish" mosques. The buildings, characteristically Andalusian, like those of Tetouan or Chefchaouen, are part stone and part whitewash, with splashes of yellow and turquoise and great, dark-wood studded doors.

From **Boulevard Hassan II**, half a dozen gates and a series of streets give access to the Medina, all leading more or less directly through the quarter, to emerge near the kasbah and the hillside cemetery. On the west side, the two main streets – **Avenue Mohammed V** and **Rue Sidi Fatah** – are really continuations of Ville Nouvelle avenues, though, flanked by working-class café-restaurants and cell-like hotels, their character is immediately different. Entering along either street, past a lively, modern food market and a handful of stalls selling fruit, juice and snacks, you can turn right along **Rue Souika**, which is dominated by textiles and silverware along the initial stretch, giving way to shoe stalls as you approach the Grand Mosque. The shops are all fairly everyday, and not, for the most part, geared to tourists.

The Grand Mosque
Souk es Sebbat

There are few buildings of particular interest in the Medina, as most of the medieval city – which predated that of the Andalusians – was destroyed by Portuguese raids in the sixteenth century. The **Grand Mosque**, founded by the Merenids in the fourteenth century, is an exception, though it has been considerably rebuilt – its minaret, for example, was completed in 1939. Entry to the mosque is forbidden to non-Muslims. Opposite, there is a small example of Merenid decoration in the stone facade of a public **fountain**, which now forms the front of an Arabic bookshop.

The Mellah

The **Mellah**, the old Jewish quarter, lies to the east of Rue Oukassa, and remains the poorest and most run-down area of the city. It was only designated a Jewish quarter in 1808 – Jews previously owned several properties on Rue des Consuls, to the north – and no longer has a significant Jewish population. If you can find a local guide, you may be able to look into some of its seventeen former **synagogues**. None of these

---

THE MARSHAL'S MEDINAS

The existence of so many ancient, walled Medinas in Morocco – intact and still bustling with life – is largely due to **Marshal Hubert Lyautey**, the first of France's Resident Generals, and the most sympathetic to local culture. In colonizing Algeria, the French had destroyed most of the Arab towns, and Lyautey found this already under way when he arrived in Rabat in 1912, but, realizing the aesthetic loss – and the inappropriateness of wholesale Europeanization – he ordered demolition to be halted and had the Ville Nouvelle built outside the walls instead. His precedent was followed throughout the French and Spanish zones of the country, inevitably creating "native quarters", but preserving continuity with the past. Lyautey left Morocco in 1925 but when he died in 1934 he was returned and buried in a Moorish monument in Rabat until 1961, when his body was "repatriated" to Paris.

CARPETS IN RABAT

Rabat **carpets**, woven with very bright dyes (which, if vegetable-based, will fade), are a traditional cottage industry in the Medina, though they're now often made in workshops, one of which you can see on the kasbah's *plateforme* (see p.258). Some of the traditional carpets on sale, particularly in the shops, will have come from further afield. They are officially graded at a special centre just off Rue des Consuls – to the right as you climb towards the kasbah.

The upper, terraced end of Rue des Consuls, in Rabat's Medina, is a centre for **rug and carpet shops**. On Monday and Thursday mornings, a **souk** for carpets new and old takes place here, and on the adjoining street of Souk es Sebbat.

function: the only active synagogue in the city is a modern building, one block from here, at the northern end of Rue Moulay Ismail.

The Joutia

With its meat and produce markets, the Mellah looks a somewhat uninviting and impenetrable area, but it is worth wandering through towards the river. A **joutia**, or **flea market**, spreads out along the streets below Souk es Sebbat, down to Bab el Bahr. There are clothes, pieces of machinery, and general bric-a-brac, with the odd bargain occasionally to be found.

Rue des Consuls

Like the Mellah, **Rue des Consuls** used to be a reserved quarter – the only street of the nineteenth-century city where European consuls were permitted to live. Many of the residency buildings survive, as do a number of impressive merchants' *fondouks* – most in the alleys off to the west (the French consul's residence, now rather run-down, is at the end of an alley called Impasse du Consulat de France). Shopping is pleasantly hassle-free, and there are some good **jewellery shops**, with a mix of Middle Eastern and European designs at good prices.

4

The Kasbah des Oudaïas

The site of the original *ribat* and citadel of the Almohad, Merenid and Andalusian towns, the **Kasbah des Oudaïas** is an evocative, village-like quarter.

Bab Oudaïa

The kasbah's main gate, **Bab Oudaïa**, is Almohad, like so many of Morocco's great monuments. Built around 1195, it was inserted by Yacoub el Mansour into a line of walls already built by his grandfather, Abd el Moumen. The walls in fact extended well to its west, leading down to the sea at the edge of the Medina (excavations are now revealing some of these), and the gate cannot have been designed for any real defensive purpose – its function and importance must have been ceremonial. It became the heart of the kasbah, its chambers acting as a courthouse and staterooms,

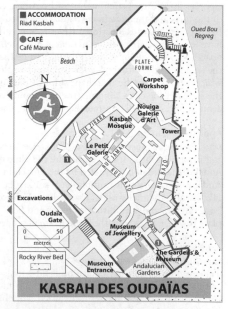

KASBAH DES OUDAÏAS

with everything of importance taking place nearby. The **Souk el Ghezel** – the main commercial centre of the medieval town, including its wool and slave markets – was located just outside the gate, while the original sultanate's palace stood immediately inside.

The gate impresses not so much by its size as by the strength and simplicity of its decoration, based on a typically Islamic rhythm, establishing a tension between the exuberant, outward expansion of the arches and the heavy, enclosing rectangle of the gate itself. Looking at the two for a few minutes, you begin to sense a kind of optical illusion – the shapes appear suspended by the great rush of movement from the centre of the arch. The basic feature is, of course, the arch, which here is a sequence of three, progressively more elaborate: first, the basic horseshoe; then, two "filled" or decorated ones, the latter with the distinctive Almohad *darj w ktaf* patterning (see p.579), a cheek-and-shoulder design somewhat like a fleur-de-lys. At the top, framing the design, is a band of geometric ornamentation, cut off in what seems to be an arbitrary manner but which again creates the impression of movement and continuation outside the gate. The dominant motifs (scallop-shell-looking palm fronds) are also characteristically Almohad, though without any symbolic importance.

Inside the kasbah

You can enter the **kasbah** through the small gateway to the right of Bab Oudaïa itself (which is sometimes used for exhibitions), or by a lower, horseshoe arch at the bottom of the stairway. This leads (straight ahead) through a door in the palace wall to Rue Bazo, where a right turn will take you down to the **Café Maure**, a fine place to retreat, high on a terrace overlooking the river (see p.265).

Inside Bab Oudaïa, **Rue Jamaa** (Street of the Mosque), runs straight down to a broad terrace commanding views of the river and sea. Along the way, you pass by the **Kasbah Mosque**, the city's oldest, founded in 1050, though rebuilt in the eighteenth century by an English renegade known as Ahmed el Inglisi – one of a number of European pirates who joined up with the Sallee Rovers.

El Inglisi was also responsible for several of the forts built below and round the seventeenth-century **plateforme**, originally a semaphore station, on which was built an eighteenth-century warehouse, now housing a carpet cooperative workshop. The guns of the forts and the *plateforme* regularly echoed across the estuary in Salé. The Bou Regreg ("Father of Reflection") River is quite open at this point and it would appear to have left the corsair fleets vulnerable, harboured a little downstream, where fishing boats today ferry people across to Salé. In fact, a long sandbank lies submerged across the mouth of the estuary – a feature much exploited by the shallow-keeled pirate ships, which would draw the merchant ships in pursuit, only to leave them stranded within the sights of the city's cannon. The sandbank proved a handicap in the early twentieth century and diverted commercial trade to the better-endowed Casablanca.

Andalusian Garden

Kasbah; access is via a small gateway facing Avenue al Marsa, or from Rue Bazo within the kasbah itself • Daily from sunrise to sunset • Free

In the kasbah's far southern corner are the old palace grounds, containing a formal **Andalusian Garden** constructed by the French in the twentieth century. True to Andalusian tradition, it features deep, sunken beds of shrubs and flowering annuals. Historical authenticity aside, it's a delightful place, full of the scent of tree daturas, bougainvillea and a multitude of herbs and flowers. It has a modern role too, as a meeting place for women, who gather here in small groups on a Friday or Sunday afternoon.

Jewellery Museum

Kasbah • Daily except Tues 9am–4pm • 10dh

The seventeenth-century **palace** built for Moulay Ismail now houses a **Museum of Jewellery**; explanations are in Arabic, French and Spanish. **Room 1** contains prehistoric jewellery, including some semi-fossilized ivory bracelets, as well as Phoenician gold, a scarab from Lixus (showing that it had trade with Egypt), and medieval jewellery, including a dinky little finger-ring in very fine filigree gold. From here you pass into the **central courtyard**, from which the rooms of the palace led off. Going round clockwise, **Room 2** contains daggers, guns and a wonderful nineteenth-century gold tiara from Fez with rubies and aquamarines. **Room 3** shows the jewellers' manufacturing process, including a traditional jeweller's furnace, and **Room 4** was the palace hammam. **Room 5**, once the palace mosque, displays jewellery typical of different Moroccan cities and regions, including some beautiful nineteenth-century pieces from Rabat.

The beach

Rabat's local **beach** is crowded throughout the summer, as is the Salé strip across the water, though neither is very inviting, and you'd be better off at the more relaxed (and less testosterone-charged) sands at the Plage des Nations or Temara Plage (see p.251 & p.270). There's often a fun wave for bodysurfers, although stand-up surfers also manage to get a few waves on most days. The beach is accessed from Avenue al Marsa or via a set of steep steps from the kasbah's *plateforme*.

The Hassan Mosque & Tower

Boulevard Tour Hassan

The most ambitious of all Almohad buildings, the **Hassan Mosque** was, in its time, the second largest mosque in the Islamic world, outflanked only by the one in Smarra, Iraq. Though little remains today apart from its vast tower, or minaret, its sheer size still seems a novelty.

The mosque was begun in 1195 – the same period as Marrakesh's Koutoubia and Seville's Giralda – and was designed to be the centrepiece of Yacoub el Mansour's new capital in celebration of his victory over the Spanish Christians at Alarcos, but construction seems to have been abandoned on El Mansour's death in 1199. Its extent must always have seemed an elaborate folly – Morocco's most important mosque, the Kairaouine in Fez, is less than half the Hassan's size, but served a much greater population. Rabat would have needed a population of well over 100,000 to make adequate use of the Hassan's capacity, but the city never really took off under the later Almohads and Merenids; when Leo Africanus came here in 1600, he found no more than a hundred households, gathered for security within the kasbah.

The mosque's hall, roofed in cedar, was used until the Great Earthquake of 1755 (which destroyed central Lisbon) brought down its central columns. Never rebuilt, some of the columns have been partially restored and at least offer some sense of the building's size. The imposing tower has remained standing, and dominates almost every view of the capital. It is unusually positioned at the centre rather than the northern corner of the rear of the mosque. Some 50m tall in its present state, it would probably have been around 80m if finished to normal proportions – a third again of the height of Marrakesh's Koutoubia. Despite its apparent simplicity, it is arguably the most complex of all Almohad structures. Each facade is different, with a distinct combination of patterning, yet the whole intricacy of blind arcades and interlacing curves is based on just two formal designs. On the south and west faces these are the same *darj w ktaf* motifs as on Bab Oudaïa (see p.257); on the north and east is the *shabka* (net) motif, an extremely popular form adapted by the Almohads from the lobed arches of the Cordoba Grand Mosque – and still in contemporary use.

Mausoleum of Mohammed V

Boulevard Tour Hassan • Daily 8.30am–6.30pm • Free

Facing the Hassan Tower – in an assertion of Morocco's historical independence and continuity – is the **Mausoleum of Mohammed V**, begun on the king's death in 1961 and inaugurated six years later. Hassan II and his brother, Moulay Abdellah, are buried here too, alongside their father.

The **mausoleum** was designed by Vietnamese architect Vo Toan. Its brilliantly surfaced marbles and spiralling designs seem to pay homage to traditional Moroccan techniques, but fail to capture their rhythms and unity. Visitors file past fabulously costumed royal guards to an interior balcony; the tomb of Mohammed V, carved from white onyx, lies below, an old man squatting beside it, reading from the Koran. If possible, plan a morning or afternoon visit as the mausoleum often closes on seemingly random days for midday prayers in the adjoining mosque.

The Ville Nouvelle

French in construction, style and feel, the **Ville Nouvelle** provides the main focus of Rabat's life, above all in the cafés and promenades of the broad, tree-lined Avenue Mohammed V. There's a certain grandeur, too, in some of the Mauresque colonial public buildings around the main boulevards, which were built with as much desire to impress as those of any earlier epoch.

Money Museum

Rue du Caire; entrance at the side of the Bank al Maghrib • Tues–Fri 9am–5.30pm, Sat 9am–noon, 3–5.30pm, Sun 9am–1pm • 30dh

Numismatists will enjoy the **Money Museum** (Musée de la Monnaie); it's quite plush and very well laidout, with coins dating back to the Phoenicians and the Berber kingdom of Mauretania, but the constant background musak starts to grate after a while.

The Almohad walls and gates

More or less complete sections of Yacoub el Mansour's **Almohad walls** run right down from the kasbah to the Royal Palace and beyond – an extraordinary monument to Yacoub el Mansour's vision. Along their course four of the original **gates** survive. Three – **Bab el Alou**, **Bab el Had** and **Bab Zaer** – are very modest. The fourth, **Bab er Rouah** (Gate of the Wind), is on an entirely different scale, recalling, and in many ways rivalling, the Oudaïa.

Contained within a massive stone bastion, **Bab er Rouah** again achieves the tension of movement – with its sun-like arches contained within a square of Koranic inscription – and a similar balance between simplicity and ornament. The west side, approached from outside the walls, is the main facade, and must have been designed as a monumental approach to the city; the shallow-cut, floral relief between arch and square is arguably the finest anywhere in Morocco. Inside, you can appreciate the gate's archetypal defensive structure – the three domed chambers aligned to force a sharp double turn. They're used for exhibitions and are usually open.

From Bab er Rouah, it's a fifteen-minute walk down towards the last Almohad gate, the much-restored **Bab Zaer**, and the entrance to **Chellah**. On the way, you pass a series of modern gates leading off to the vast enclosures of the **Royal Palace** – which is really more a collection of palaces, built mainly in the nineteenth century and decidedly off-limits to casual visitors.

Archeological Museum

Rue el Brihi • Daily except Tues 9am–4.30pm, but sometimes closed so call ahead • 10dh • ☎ 0537 701919

Rabat's **Archeological Museum** is the most important in Morocco. Although small – surprisingly so in a country which saw substantial Phoenician and Carthaginian settlement and three centuries of Roman rule – it houses an exceptional collection of Roman-era bronzes.

The bronzes are displayed in a special annexe with a separate entrance; although included in the entry fee, it's sometimes closed. If so, ask one of the attendants at the museum's entrance to open it up for you. The bronzes date from the first and second centuries AD and were found mainly at the provincial capital of Volubilis (near Meknes), together with a few pieces from Chellah and the colonies of Banasa and Thamusida. Highlights include superb figures of a guard dog and a rider, and two magnificent portrait heads, reputedly those of Cato the Younger (Caton d'Utique) and Juba II – the last significant ruler of the Romanized Berber kingdoms of Mauretania and Numidia before the assertion of direct imperial rule. Both of these busts were found in the House of Venus at Volubilis (see p.211).

Back in the main building, there are showcases on two floors; each contains finds from different digs, of little interest unless you have already visited the area – or plan to do so. Captions are in French and, if you ask, you may be provided with a guide to the museum – also in French.

Chellah

Cnr Avenue Yacoub Al Mansour & Boulevard Moussa Idn Nossair • Daily 8am–6pm • 10dh

The most beautiful of Moroccan ruins, **Chellah** is a startling sight as you emerge from the long avenues of the Ville Nouvelle. Walled and towered, it seems a much larger enclosure than the map suggests. The site has been uninhabited since 1154, when it was abandoned in favour of Salé across the Bou Regreg. But for almost a thousand years prior to that, Chellah (or Sala Colonia, as it was known) had been a thriving city and port, one of the last to sever links with the Roman Empire and the first to proclaim Moulay Idriss founder of Morocco's original Arab dynasty. An apocryphal local tradition maintains that the Prophet himself also prayed at a shrine here.

Under the Almohads, the site was already a royal burial ground, but most of what you see today, including the gates and enclosing wall, is the legacy of "The Black Sultan", **Abou el Hassan** (1331–51), the greatest of the Merenids. The **main gate** has turreted bastions creating an almost Gothic appearance. Its base is recognizably Almohad, but each element has become inflated, and the combination of simplicity and solidity has gone. An interesting technical innovation is the stalactite (or "honeycomb") corbels which form the transition from the bastion's semi-octagonal towers to their square platforms; these were to become a feature of Merenid building. The Kufic inscription above the gate is from the Koran and begins with the invocation: "I take refuge in Allah, against Satan."

To your left if coming from the entrance, signposted "Site Antique", are the main **Roman ruins**. They are of a small trading post dating from 200 BC onwards, are well signposted and include a forum, a triumphal arch, a Temple of Jupiter and a craftsmen's quarter.

The Sanctuary

From the main gate, the **Islamic ruins** are down to the right, within an inner sanctuary approached along a broad path through half-wild gardens. The most prominent feature is a tall stone-and-tile **minaret**, a ludicrously oversized stork's nest usually perched on its summit. Indeed, Chellah as a whole is a good spot for **birdwatching**, especially in nesting season.

The **sanctuary** itself appears as a confusing cluster of tombs and ruins, but it's essentially just two buildings: a mosque, commissioned by the second Merenid sultan, Abou Youssef (1258–86), and a *zaouia*, or mosque-monastery, added along with the enclosure walls by Abou el Hassan. You enter directly into the *sahn*, or courtyard, of **Abou Youssef's Mosque**, a small and presumably private structure built as a funerary dedication. It is now in ruins, though you can make out the colonnades of the inner prayer hall with its mihrab to indicate the direction of prayer. To the right is its minaret, now reduced to the level of the mosque's roof.

Behind, both in and outside the sanctuary enclosure, are scattered **royal tombs** – each aligned so that the dead may face Mecca to await the Call of Judgement. Abou Youssef's tomb has not been identified, but you can find those of both **Abou el Hassan**

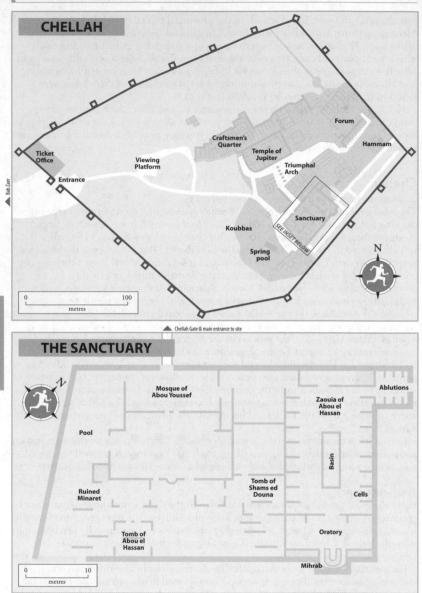

and his wife **Shams ed Douna**. El Hassan's is contained within a kind of pavilion whose external wall retains its decoration, the *darj w ktaf* motif set above three small arches in a design very similar to that of the Hassan Tower. Shams ed Douna (Morning Sun) has only a tombstone – a long, pointed rectangle covered in a mass of verses from the Koran. A convert from Christianity, Shams was the mother of Abou el Hassan's rebel son, Abou Inan, whose uprising led to the sultan's death as a fugitive in the High Atlas during the winter of 1352.

The Zaouia

The **Zaouia** is in a much better state of preservation, its structure, like Abou el Hassan's medersas, that of a long, central court enclosed by cells, with a smaller oratory or prayer hall at the end. There are fragments of zellij tilework on some of the colonnades and on the minaret, giving an idea of its original brightness, and there are traces, too, of the mihrab's elaborate stucco decoration. Five-sided, the **mihrab** has a narrow passageway (now blocked with brambles) leading to the rear – built so that pilgrims might make seven circuits round it. This was once believed to give the equivalent merit of the *hadj*, the trip to Mecca: a tradition, with that of Mohammed's visit, probably invented and propagated by the *zaouia*'s keepers to increase their revenue.

Off to the right and above the sanctuary enclosure are a group of **koubbas** – the domed tombs of local saints or *marabouts* – and beyond them a **spring pool**, enclosed by low, vaulted buildings. This is held sacred, along with the eels which swim in its waters, and women bring hard-boiled eggs for the fish to invoke assistance in fertility and childbirth. If you're here in spring, you'll get additional wildlife, with the storks nesting and the egrets roosting.

At the far end of the sanctuary, you can look down a side valley to the Bou Regreg estuary. From here, you can appreciate that this site was destined, from early times, to be settled and fortified. The site was easy to defend and the springs provided water in times of siege.

ARRIVAL AND DEPARTURE   RABAT

By plane Rabat–Salé airport is 7km northeast of the city, served by no public transport other than privately rented grands taxis. The current tariff for the ride is 150dh into the city centre (500dh to Casablanca – a sign in the terminal displays the official rates, and is worth checking before you approach a taxi), for up to six people. The modern terminal has three bureaux de change and three ATMs, plus car rental desks, which include Avis (☎ 0537 831677), Europcar (☎ 0537 724141), and local company First-Car (☎ 0537 835360, ✆ firstcar.ma). The airport serves only international flights, mainly to Brussels, Madrid and Paris. Royal Air Maroc has an office on the corner of avenues Mohammed V & Moulay Abdallah (☎ 0537 709710); Air France's office is at 281 Av Mohammed V, just north of *Hôtel Balima* (☎ 0537 707580).

By train Rabat Ville train station is right in the middle of the Ville Nouvelle, a few minutes' walk from many hotels. On street level are two bureaux de change with ATMs and Budget car rental (☎ 0537 705789). Business visitors and diplomats may have cause to alight at Rabat Agdal, which serves the southern suburbs and the Royal Palace.

Destinations Asilah (8 direct; 3hr & 1 connecting daily; 4hr 30min); Casablanca Port (6.30am–10pm 1–2 hourly; 1hr); Casa Voyageurs (over 20 direct & over 20 connecting daily; 1hr); Casablanca Mohammed V airport (over 30 connecting daily; 1hr 40min–2hr); Fez (19 daily; 3hr); Kenitra (1–2 hourly; 30min); Marrakesh (9 daily; 4hr 20min); Meknes

(18 daily; 2hr); Oujda (2 direct & 1 connecting daily; 9hr); Tangier (8 direct; 3hr 35min & 1 connecting daily; 5hr).

By bus Rabat's main bus station, Gare Routière Kamra is on Bd Hassan II (the N1 highway), 3km west of the centre. CTM operates from its own station 400m further southwest along Bd Hassan II. Local buses ply the route between the bus station and Bab el Had (bus #30 picks up right outside the terminal, buses #17 and #41 stop just behind it), or you can get a petit taxi (around 20dh).

Destinations Agadir (4 CTM & over 10 others daily; 10hr); Al Hoceima (1 CTM daily; 8hr 15min); Casablanca (over 20 CTM & very frequent others daily; 1hr 30min); Chefchaouen (1 CTM & 2 others daily; 5hr); Essaouira (over 10 daily; 8hr 30min); Fez (over 10 CTM daily & others hourly 5am–7pm; 3hr 30min); El Jadida (over 10 daily; 4hr); Marrakesh (4 CTM daily & others hourly; 4hr 30min); Meknes (8 CTM daily & others hourly; 2hr 30min); Nador (3 CTM & 10 others daily; 9hr); Ouarzazate (5 daily; 9hr 30min); Safi (8 daily; 6hr); Tangier (5 CTM and 22 others daily; 5hr); Tetouan (5 CTM & 20 others daily; 5–6hr).

By grand taxi Grands taxis between Rabat and Casablanca operate from just outside the main bus station. Those for Fez, Meknes and Salé congregate at the Shell petrol station on Bd Hassan II, next to *Hôtel Bou Regreg* and opposite Bab Chellah.

Destinations Casablanca (1hr 20min); Fez (2hr 30min); Meknes (1hr 50min); Salé (15min).

GETTING AROUND

By bus Local bus services can be very useful (see box, p.264), and some bus stops are clearly marked, with the numbers of the buses that stop at them posted up.

By tram A new, a/c tram system (daily 7am–10pm; ✆ tram-way.ma) links Rabat and Salé. Line 1 runs east to west via Agdal and both Rabat Ville and

USEFUL LOCAL BUS ROUTES

#2 from opposite Bab el Had to the intercity bus station.
#3 from just by Rabat Ville train station down Avenue Fal Ould Ouemir in Agdal to Avenue Atlas.
#9 from opposite Bab el Had to Salé, Jardins Exotiques, Museé Dar Belghazi and the Plage des Nations turn-off.
#12 and **#13** from just off Place Melilla to Salé.
#33 from opposite Bab el Had to Temara Plage.
#35 from Avenue Allal Ben Abdallah to Salé and Magic Park.

Salé train stations, while Line 2 runs northwest to southeast via Bd Hassan II and Salé bus station. Both cross the Oued Bou Regreg and stop near Rabat's Hassan Mosque and Salé's Bab Mrissa. Tickets cost 7dh per voyage and can be purchased from ticket vendors at each station or on-board conductors.

By taxi Petits and grands taxis can be found on Bd Hassan II and by the train station; petits taxis are not allowed to run between Rabat and Salé.

Car rental In addition to the offices at the airport and train station (see p.263), car rental companies in town include Avis, 7 Rue Abou Faris al Marini (☎0537 721818); Europcar, 25 bis Rue Patrice Lumumba (☎0537 722328); and Hertz, 467 Av Mohammed V (☎0537 707366).

INFORMATION

Tourist information Corner Rue Oued el Makhazine & Rue Zalaka, Agdal (Mon–Fri 8.30am–4.30pm; ☎0537 674013). The Conseil Regional du Tourisme have a website at ⓦ visitrabat.com.

ACCOMMODATION

Hotel space can be tight in midsummer, and especially in July, when budget-priced rooms in particular are at a premium, so it's a good idea to book in advance. A couple of cheapies aside, all of the better hotels are to be found in the Ville Nouvelle.

MEDINA AND KASBAH

Al Maghrib al Jadid 2 Rue Sebbahi ☎0537 732207. Basic and clean, though the decor is a garish combination of candy-pink and bright blue. Hot showers are available 8am–9.30pm (10dh). The owners also run the *Hôtel Marrakech*, down the street at no.10, with exactly the same prices and colour scheme. 120dh

Des Voyageurs 8 Souk Semarine, by Bab Djedid. Cheap, popular and often full, offering clean, airy rooms but no showers, and no public ones nearby. The same stretch of street has several similar places. 80dh

Dorhmi 313 Av Mohammed V ☎0537 723898. Refurbished to a decent standard, and nicely positioned, just inside Bab el Djedid above the *Café Salam*. Hot showers (7am–10pm) are external, and cost 10dh. Rooms cannot be reserved here in advance. 120dh

★ **Riad Kasbah** 39 Rue Zirara in the kasbah, on your left as you enter through Bab Oudaïas ☎0537 702392, ⓦ riadoudaya.com. This small riad oozes simplicity and authenticity. Pastel yellows, earthy pinks and sky blues abound in the six rooms of varying sizes, all nicely furnished and either facing the peaceful inner garden or up on the rooftop terrace with its glorious sea and Medina views. It's peaceful, well managed and the staff are overwhelmingly attentive. Minimum two-night stay and pre-booking required. BB 770dh

VILLE NOUVELLE

Auberge de Jeunesse 43 Rue Marrassa ☎0537 725769, ✉ info@aubergerabat.com. Conveniently sited just north of Bab el Had, this clean hostel has a nice courtyard, but the (segregated) dorms are a bit cramped and there are no self-catering facilities. Open 8am–11pm (till midnight in summer). H.I. membership required (100dh). 55dh

Balima Corner of Rue Jakarta and Av Mohammed V ☎0537 708625, ⓦ hotel-balima.net. This 1936 grand dame was once Rabat's top hotel but has long been overtaken by the competition. In desperate need of an overhaul, the whole hotel is looking very tired and reeks of cigarette smoke. Some of the rooms offer great views of parliament and the city, but you'll only stay here for the convenient, central location, and the never-failing warm welcome from the fez-topped concierge. BB 600dh

Bélère 33 Av Moulay Youssef ☎0537 203301, ⓦ belere-hotels.com. This is a comfortable, well -positioned hotel with impressive management and friendly staff. The rooms exude a touch of luxury with soft, neutral tones throughout, plush carpeted floors, spacious marble bathrooms, and heavy curtains to soften the outside street noise. The larger suites (3086dh) also have a small sitting area and balcony. There are also a couple of restaurants, a piano bar, as well as a nightclub. BB 1028dh

Caleche d'Or 11 Av Moulay Youssef, on Pl de la Gare ☎0537 701319. Close to Rabat Ville station, this is one of the city's better two-star options. Accessed from a steep marbled staircase, the tiled rooms are bright and clean with sparkling modern bathrooms. The lack of a/c is compensated by large windows, but ask for a room away from the busy street. 472dh

★ **Central** 2 Rue Al Basra ☎0537 707356, ✉hotel .central.rabat@gmail.com. Best of the cheapies, conveniently located for restaurants, banks and Rabat Ville station. Most rooms have patterned colonial floor tiles and some have showers (otherwise they're 10dh), with hot water mornings and evenings. 200dh

Gaulois Corner of Rue Hims and Av Mohammed V ☎0537 723022, ✉0537 738848. Friendly old hotel with a spacious grand entrance and both shared-shower and en-suite rooms, the former especially being pretty good value for money. 298dh

Majestic 121 Av Hassan II ☎0537 722997, ⓦhotelmajestic.ma. Long-established hotel, accessed only by a flight of stairs. The rather characterless rooms are bright and clean; some have showers. Sporadic hot water. 366dh

Majliss 6 Rue Zahla ☎0537 733726, ⓦmajlisshotel .ma. A modern four-star popular with Arabic-speaking tour groups and a good choice with friendly, efficient staff. Choose between two contrasting room styles, those with a distinct local flavour (heavily embroidered bedspreads, drapes and sofas, large carpets over tiled floors, and bright, garish furniture) and those with a softer, Western touch (carpeted floors, neutral colours, simple furnishings). BB 1100dh

La Paix 2 Rue Ghazza, on corner with Av Allal Ben Abdallah ☎0537 722926. Friendly staff and comfortable, if sombre, rooms with good en-suite bathrooms (hot water evenings only). The central location is its best attribute, with a couple of good cafés close by for breakfast. 250dh

Royal 1 Rue Amman, on corner with Av Allal Ben Abdallah ☎0537 721171, ⓦroyalhotelrabat.com. A long-standing mid-range hotel with comfortable and reasonable rooms – not huge, but refurbished, clean and well maintained. The best ones overlook the attractive Parc du Triangle de Vue. BB 698dh

Sofitel Rabat Jardin des Roses Junction of avenues Doustour & Imam Malik ☎0537 675656, ⓦsofitel.com. This deluxe five-star has had a major renovation and is looking very good; the rooms have been given a modern designer touch with all the mod cons you'd expect for the price and all have a balcony overlooking the vast gardens or the city. Located in the suburb of Souissi just beyond the royal palace, it's a 10min petit taxi drive from the Medina. 1936dh

Splendid 8 Rue Ghazza ☎0537 723283. The best rooms at this friendly old hotel overlook a pleasant courtyard with flowers and banana trees, and some have their own showers (hot water evenings only). 226dh

La Tour Hassan 26 Rue Chellah ☎0537 239000, ⓦlatourhassan.com. One of Rabat's plushest offerings, with exquisite, palatial decor in the public areas and several grades of rooms and suites (mostly priced according to the views available from them). The rooms, however, are not huge – comfort-wise, *Majliss* has the edge on it. The service is appropriately attentive but perhaps it's still not quite worth the splurge. 3622dh

EATING AND DRINKING

For a capital city, Rabat is pretty quiet, but it does have some excellent restaurants – many of them moderately priced or inexpensive – plus loads of good cafés. As ever, the cheapest places to eat are to be found in the Medina, just inside the walls on Av Mohammed V.

MEDINA AND KASBAH

El Bahia Bd Hassan II, built into the Andalusian wall, near the junction with Av Mohammed V. Tajines, kebabs and salads (25–65dh), in a pleasant courtyard, upstairs or on the pavement outside, though service can be slow. Daily noon–1opm. **Café Maure** Rue Bazo, Kasbah. Adjoining the kasbah's Andalusian Garden is this small shaded terrace-café. It's a great spot to take a break and look out over the river mouth and beyond to Salé. Non-alcoholic drinks (8–15dh) are on offer, and there's usually one or two biscuit salesmen selling their tasty wares. Daily 9am–5pm.

Café Taghazoute 7 Rue Sebbahi. This café serves simple dishes, including tasty fried fish, and also omelettes, which makes it a good option for breakfast. It tends to be busy with office workers at lunchtime. Mains 12–35dh. Daily 7am–10pm.

Dinarjat 6 Rue Belgnaoui, off Bd el Alou ☎0537 704239, ⓦdinarjat.com. This palatial restaurant with fine Moroccan dishes and musical entertainment, in a seventeenth-century mansion at the northern end of the Medina, makes a good choice if you wish to spoil yourself (menus 300–400dh). Licensed. Daily noon–3pm, 7.30–11pm.

De la Jeunesse 305 Av Mohammed V. One of the city's better budget restaurants, with generous portions of couscous, and decent tajines (10–25dh). Downstairs offers good people-watching while upstairs is quieter and has more seating. Daily noon–10pm.

Le Ziryab 10 Impasse Ennajar, off Rue des Consuls ☎0537 733636, ⓦrestaurantleziryab.com. Very popular among execs, diplomats and politicians, with good reason: the five-course menu (500dh) is first-class Moroccan fare.

4

Add the accompaniment of traditional music and the exquisite interior, and this is worth a special treat. Come hungry. Licensed. Mon–Sat 7–11pm.

VILLE NOUVELLE

7 ème Art Café Av Allal ben Abdallah. Next to the 7 ème Art cinema and within pleasant gardens, this is a great choice for a refreshment break or daytime meal. The menu includes daily specials, light dishes such as salads, burgers and panini, and more substantial tajines, pastas and *grillés* (20–68dh). Daily 7am–7pm.

La Bamba 3 Rue Tanta, a small side street behind the Hôtel Balima ☎0537 709839. European and Moroccan dishes, with good-value three-course set menus (80dh & 110dh), within a pleasant interior and accompanied by good service. Licensed. Mon–Sat noon–3pm & 8pm–midnight; Sun 8pm–midnight.

Café Weimar Goethe Institute, 7 Rue Sana'a ☎0537 428101. Well known among expats and local students, who enjoy the casual atmosphere and good-value menu, which includes a popular "half-half" (half pizza and half-size salad) for 45dh. Licensed. Daily 9am–10pm.

Chez Maxi 1 Rue Baghdad ☎0537 700180. A modern café-restaurant that attracts a young crowd who enjoy the large TVs showing Arabic pop and the free wi-fi. The menu offers mainly light options, though there are also brochette, pasta and pizza dishes available (29–75dh). Daily 7am–10pm.

Le Grand Comptoir 279 Bd Mohammed V ⓦ legrandcomptoir.ma. A classy brasserie with live easy-listening music in the evenings, serving excellent seafood as well as *grillés* and sushi (mains 85–280dh), and has a decent selection of wines. Daily 9am–1am.

Grill 23 386 Av Mohammed V. Near the station, so handy for carry-out food to take on a train journey, though there is a pleasant shaded seating area. The choices are mainly fast food, such as shawarma and burgers, and they also do big, crunchy salads. (15–35dh). Daily 7am–1am.

La Koutoubia 10 Rue Pierre Parent, off Rue Moulay Abdelaziz, and near the Helnan Chellah Hôtel ☎0537 701075. Home to an upmarket bar and, with a separate entrance through a quaint wood and glass extension, an old-style 1950s restaurant, serving excellent Moroccan food (75–140dh); try the honeyed lamb and almond tajine. The service is good, watched over by a patron who's been there from the beginning. Licensed. Daily noon–3.30pm & 7–10.30pm.

La Mamma 6 Rue Tanta ☎0537 707329. A typically dark and cosy pizzeria, with a varied menu of Italian classics including wood-fired pizza and char-grilled meats (45–95dh). *La Dolce Vita*, next door to *La Mamma*, is owned by the same patron and provides luscious Italian-style ice cream. Licensed. Daily noon–3pm & 7.30pm–midnight.

Le Pacha 4 Passage Hatim, Av Moulay Youssef ☎0537 767660. A popular café-restaurant with plenty of seating on two interior levels or on the shaded pavement. The varied menu covers all appetites, from light meals to steaks and tajines, or just a simple pastry or cake. The waitresses are often rushed but remain friendly. Mains 25–70dh. Daily 7am–10pm.

La Pagode 13 Rue Baghdad ☎0537 709381. Has been around for a while now and remains one of the more popular Asian restaurants in town, with a large menu of mainly Chinese and Vietnamese dishes (65–98dh). Recently refurbished, they also have a takeaway and delivery service. Licensed. Tues–Sun noon–3pm & 7.30–11pm.

★ **Tajine wa Tanjia** 9 Rue Baghdad ☎0537 729797. Great little restaurant with a nice atmosphere, accompanied most nights by live *oud* playing. The menu is mainly Moroccan food, well presented, with a range of tajines (including vegetarian), tanjia (jugged beef or lamb), and, on Fridays, couscous (76–120dh). Licensed. Mon–Sat noon–3pm & 7–11pm.

BEACH AREA

On the beachfront below the Kasbah des Oudaïas are two popular seafood restaurants, accessed via a path from the kasbah's *plateforme* (see p.258) or by a short side road off Av al Marsa. Both are licensed and offer great sea views from their large glass-fronted terraces.

Borj Eddar Plage de Rabat ☎0537 701500. The classy interior of this restaurant, set within seventeenth-century walls and popular with tour groups, belies a menu that is surprisingly good value. Besides the expected plethora of seafood dishes, there's also a good choice of meat tajines and couscous (95–230dh). Daily noon–10pm.

De la Plage Plage de Rabat ☎0537 707586. Perhaps the less fancy of the two beach restaurants, though the menu still offers a wide choice of fish and seafood dishes. House specialities include a salt-encrusted sea bass stuffed with fennel and served with a basil cream sauce (mains 85–150dh). Daily noon–10pm.

NIGHTLIFE AND ENTERTAINMENT

The city's nightlife is pretty sedate. Outside of the main hotels and restaurants, **bars** are few and far between, while many **nightclubs**, notably those around Pl de Melilla, are little more than pick-up joints, though they expect you to dress up in order to get in. For more culturally inclined pursuits, check out the monthly programme of events at the British Council, 11 Av Allal Ben Abdellah (☎0537 218130, ⓦ britishcouncil.org.ma). **The Théâtre National Mohammed V** on Rue du Caire (☎0537 208316, ⓦtnmv.ma) puts on a range of concerts (Arabic and Western classical music), opera, ballet and films.

Amnesia 18 Rue de Monastir ☎0537 701860. Consistently popular with Rabat's twenty-somethings, this American-themed club pumps out a mix of Euro and Arabic pop. There's also a diner-style restaurant at the rear. Cocktails 85–105dh, beer 65dh. Admission 100dh after 10pm. Daily 8pm–2am.

El Palatino 133 Av Allal Ben Abdallah ☎0537 708132. Very popular Spanish-style tapas bar. The in-house DJs know their stuff and there's nightly drink specials as well as regular themed parties. Good fun without too much pretentiousness. Tapas 45dh–65dh, beer 45dh. Daily 7pm–1.30am.

Hôtel Balima Corner of Rue Jakarta and Av Mohammed V ☎0537 708625, ⓦhotel-balima.net. The outdoor street-facing café is a popular spot for a coffee and some quality people watching, while the inside bar is a trifle seedy and smoky but has a terrace that attracts an interesting crowd of (mostly) male Moroccan drinkers. Spirits 75dh, beer 35dh. Daily 7am–10pm.

DIRECTORY

Banks & exchange Most are along avenues Allal ben Abdallah and Mohammed V. BMCE, 340 Av Mohammed V has a bureau de change (daily 8am–8pm), and two ATMs. Bureaux de change include Currency Exchange Point, Av Moulay Youssef between hotels *Bélère* and *Caleche d'Or* (Mon–Sat 9am–7pm) and Wafa Cash, cnr Av Mohammed V & Rue Ghaza (Mon–Fri 8am–7pm, Sat 8.30am–4pm). CIH bank, 4 Av Maghreb el Arabi (next door to Carrefour supermarket) has a foreign exchange ATM.

Bookshops There are several bookshops along Av Mohammed V – Kalila Wa Dimna (no. 344) and Éditions La Porte (just north of *Hôtel Balima*) both have a good selection of books on Morocco and phrasebooks.

Children Youngsters may appreciate a visit to the riverside Magic Park on Av du Bou Regreg, on the Salé side of the river ☎0537 885990 (bus #35 from Bd Al Alaouiyne in Rabat via Salé's Bab Mrisa). There are carousels and other gentle fairground rides, as well as bumper cars, and the park is open Wed 2–9pm, Sat & Sun 11am–9pm (Ramadan Mon–Fri 8pm–1am, Sat & Sun noon–1am); entry including all rides is 15dh for children and adolescents, 15dh for accompanying adults, and 35dh for adults with no children.

Dentist Dr Karim Yahyaouti, 5 Rue Tabaria (☎0537 702582).

Doctors and hospitals Dr Youssef Alaoui Belghiti, 6 Pl des Alaouites (☎0537 708029); Dr Mohammed el Kabbaj, 8 Rue Oued Zem (☎0537 764311). For emergencies call the Service Médical d'Urgence on ☎0537 737373. The US embassy maintains a list of useful medical contacts online at ⓦmorocco.usembassy .gov/service/professional-services/medical-information .html.

Embassies Algeria, 46 Bd Tariq Ibn Ziad (☎0537 661574); Canada, 13 bis Rue Jaâfar as Sadiq, Agdal (☎0537 687400, ⓦmorocco.gc.ca); Mauritania, 6 Rue Thami Lamdouar, Souissi (visa applications Mon–Fri 9–11am; ☎0537 656678, ⓔambarim-rabat@menara .com); South Africa, 34 Rue des Saadiens (☎0537 689159, ⓔsudaf@menara.ma); UK, 28 Av SAR Sidi Mohammed, Souissi (☎0537 633333, ⓦukinmorocco.fco.gov.uk); US,

2 Av Mohammed el Fassi (Av Marrakech) (☎0537 762265, ⓦmorocco.usembassy.gov). Australia is represented by the Canadian embassy and New Zealanders by their embassy in Madrid (☎00 34 91 523 0226), though they may get help from the Brits in cases of dire emergency. The nearest Irish representation is in Casablanca (see p.313).

Festivals Festival Mawazine ("Festival of Rhythms"; ⓦfestivalmawazine.ma) runs over 7 to 10 days each May in a number of venues around the city, including the Théâtre National Mohammed V, Rabat's riverside promenade, and Salé beach. The nightly performances usually cover a wide range of genres, from Classical and Andalusian to Arabic pop and Western rock. Jazz au Chellah (ⓦjazzauchellah.com), a joint effort between the EU and Morocco, takes place over 5 days in mid-June. Performances take place each evening at the Chellah (see p.261).

Golf The Dar es Salaam Royal Golf Club, 9km out of Rabat on Zaers Rd (☎0537 755864, ⓦroyalgolfdaressalam.com) is one of the country's finest, with two eighteen-hole and one nine-hole course designed by Robert Trent-Jones.

Internet access All cybercafés in Rabat typically open daily from 9am–11pm and charge around 5dh/hr. In the Medina are Cyber at 8 Impasse Bechkaoui (off Rue Souika) and Téléboutique Baghdad on Rue Souika opposite Impasse Bechkaoui. In the Ville Nouvelle are sacar@.net, 83 Av Hassan II; Phobos, 113 Bd Hassan II by *Hôtel Majestic*; and Téléboutique, Rue Tanta (next to *La Mamma*).

Pharmacies Rennaissance, 352 Av Mohammed V, just north of the post office.

Police The main station is on Av Tripoli, near the cathedral (☎0537 720231), with a police post at Bab Djedid and another at the northern end of Rue des Consuls, near the kasbah.

Post office Cnr avenues Mohammed V and Jean Jaurès, opposite the Bank Al Maghrib (Mon–Fri 8am–6pm, Sat 8am–noon).

Shopping For crafts, there's an Ensemble Artisanal on the west side of Avenue al Marsa.

4

Salé

Though now essentially a suburb of Rabat, **SALÉ** was the pre-eminent of the two right through the Middle Ages, from the decline of the Almohads to the pirate republic of Bou Regreg (see p.253). Under the Merenids, as a port of some stature, it was endowed with monuments such as its superb **Medersa Bou Inan**.

In the twentieth century, after the French made Rabat their capital and Casablanca their main port, Salé became a bit of a backwater. The original Ville Nouvelle was just a small area around the bus station and the northern gates, but recent developments have changed this, with a major project, Bou Regreg Marina, now taking shape on the riverbank. For the most part, Salé still looks and feels very different from Rabat, particularly within its medieval walls, where the souks and life remain surprisingly traditional.

The Medina

The most interesting point to enter Salé's Medina is through **Bab Mrisa**, near the grand taxi terminal. Its name – "of the small harbour" – recalls the marine arsenal that used to be sited within the walls, and explains the gate's unusual height. A channel running here from the Bou Regreg has long silted up, but in medieval times it allowed merchant ships to sail right into town. Robinson Crusoe was brought into captivity through this gate in Daniel Defoe's novel. The gate itself is a very early Merenid structure of the 1270s, its design and motifs (palmettes enclosed by floral decoration, bands of Kufic inscription and *darj w ktaf*) still inherently Almohad in tone.

The souks

Inside Bab Mrisa you'll find yourself in a small square, at the bottom of the old **Mellah** (Jewish quarter). Turning to the left and continuing close to the walls for around

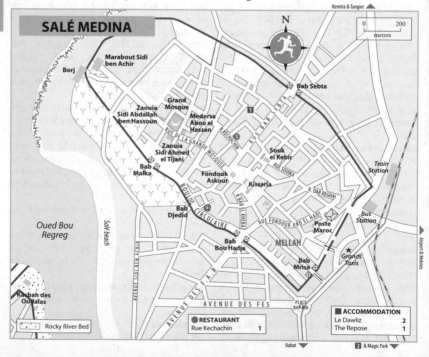

350m, you come to another gate, **Bab Bou Haja**, beside a small park. If you want to explore the souks – the route outlined below – veer right and take the road – Rue Bab el Khebaz – which runs along the left-hand side of the park. If not, continue on just inside the walls to a long open area; as this starts to narrow into a lane (about 40m further down) veer to your right into the town. This should bring you out more or less at the **Grand Mosque**, opposite which is the **Medersa of Abou el Hassan.**

The park-side street from Bab Bou Haja is **Rue Bab el Khebaz** (Street of the Bakers' Gate), a busy little lane that emerges at the heart of the **souks** by a small **kissaria** (covered market) devoted mainly to textiles. Most of the alleys here are grouped round specific crafts, a particular speciality being the pattern-weave mats produced for the sides and floors of mosques – to be found in the **Souk el Merzouk**. There is also a wool souk, the **Souk el Ghezel**, while wood, leather, ironware, carpets and household items are in the **Souk el Kebir** – the grand souk.

Close by the *kissaria* is a fourteenth-century hospice, the **Fondouk Askour**, with a notable gateway (built by Abou Inan), and beyond this the Medina's main street, **Rue de la Grande Mosquée**, leads uphill through the middle of town to the Grand Mosque. This is the simplest approach, but you can take in more of the souks by following **Rue Kechachin**, parallel. Along here are the carpenters and stone-carvers, as well as other craftsmen. In **Rue Haddadin**, a fairly major intersection which leads off to its right up towards Bab Sebta, you'll come upon gold- and coppersmiths.

Grand Mosque & Medersa

Rue de la Grand Mosquée • Medersa daily 8.30am–5pm, but sometimes closes early • 10dh

The area around the **Grand Mosque** is the most interesting part of town, with lanes fronting a concentration of aristocratic mansions and religious *zaouia* foundations. Almohad in origin, the mosque is one of the largest and earliest in Morocco. Unfortunately, non-Muslims can only see the gateway and minaret, which are recent additions, though Muslims can enter to see the prayer hall and mihrab, which are original.

ZAOUIAS, MOUSSEMS AND MARABOUTS

Round Salé's Grand Mosque, and over to the northwest, you can view (but only enter if you are Muslim) a trio of interesting buildings.

The first is the **Zaouia Sidi Ahmed el Tijani**, whose elaborate portal faces the Grand Mosque and Medersa. *Zaouias* are a mix of shrine and charitable establishment, maintained by their followers, who once or more each year hold a moussem, a pilgrimage festival, in the saint-founder's honour.

The most important of Salé's **moussems** is the "wax moussem" of its patron saint, Sidi Abdallah Ben Hassoun, whose **zaouia** stands at the end of the Rue de la Grande Mosquée, a few steps before the cemetery. The saint lived in Salé during the sixteenth century and plays a role like St Christopher for Muslim travellers. His moussem, held on the eve of Mouloud (the Prophet's birthday; see p.44), involves a spectacular procession through the streets of the town with local boatmen, dressed in corsair costumes, carrying huge and elaborate wax candles in the form of lanterns mounted on giant poles. The candle bearers (a hereditary position) are followed by various brotherhoods, dancing and playing music. The procession starts about 3pm and goes on into the early evening, culminating at the zaouia; the best place to see it is at Bab Bou Hadja, where the candles are presented to local dignitaries.

At the far end of a cemetery (again forbidden to non-Muslims), which spreads down to the river, is a third revered site, the white *koubba* and associated buildings of the **Marabout of Sidi Ben Achir**. Sometimes known as "Al Tabib" (The Doctor), Ben Achir was a fourteenth-century ascetic from Andalusia. His shrine, said to have the ability to attract ships onto the rocks and quell storms – good pirate virtues – reputedly also effects cures for blindness, paralysis and madness. Enclosed by nineteenth-century pilgrim lodgings, it, too, has a considerable annual moussem on the eve of Mouloud.

Everybody can visit the restored **Medersa**, opposite the mosque's monumental, stepped main entrance. The medersa was founded in 1341 by Sultan Abou el Hassan, and is thus more or less contemporary with the Bou Inania medersas in Meknes and Fez. Like them (though rather smaller), it is intensely decorated with carved wood, stucco and zellij, leaving hardly an inch of space that doesn't draw the eye into a web of intricacy.

The patterns, for the most part, derive from Almohad models, with their stylized geometric and floral motifs, but in the latter there is a much more naturalistic, less abstracted approach. There is also a new stress on calligraphy, with monumental inscriptions carved in great bands on the dark cedarwood and incorporated within the stucco and zellij. Almost invariably these are in the elaborate cursive script, and are generally passages from the Koran.

Close to its entrance there is a stairway up to the former cells of the students (now partially renovated to look almost liveable) and to the **roof**, where, looking out across the river to Rabat, you sense the enormity of the Hassan Tower.

ARRIVAL AND DEPARTURE
SALÉ

By train The train station is conveniently located just across the N1 highway from the Medina's eastern walls. Salé is connected to the national network via either Kenitra or Rabat.

Destinations Asilah (8 direct & 1 connecting daily; 2hr 30min); Casa Port (over 20 daily; 1hr 10min); Casa Voyageurs (1–2 hourly; 1hr 15min); Rabat (1–2 hourly; 30min); Tangier (8 direct & 1 connecting daily; 3hr 15min).

By tram The easiest way to travel between Salé and Rabat is by the new tramway (7dh; ⓦ tram-way.ma). Both lines cross the Oued Bou Regreg, stopping at the Hassan Mosque in Rabat and close to Bab Mrisa in Salé. Line 1 also calls at

both Rabat Ville and Salé train stations.

By bus The *gare routière* is 1km east of the Medina; however, most local buses from Rabat also stop outside Bab Mrisa. Regular buses – #12, #13, #14, #16, #34, #38 & #42 – run between the eastern end of Bd Hassan II in Rabat and Salé. Long-distance services are restricted to those listed below; CTM buses don't stop in Salé.

Destinations Casablanca (over 10 daily; 2hr); Kenitra (over 20 daily; 45min); Tangier (2 daily; 4hr 30min).

By grand taxi Grands taxis from the Shell petrol station on Bd Hassan II in Rabat, opposite Bab Chellah, will drop off at Bab Bou Hadja or Bab Mrisa.

ACCOMMODATION AND EATING

In the evenings, you can eat reasonably at one of the many snack cafés along Rue Kechachin, but the streets empty even earlier than in Rabat.

Le Dawliz Av du Bouregreg ☎ 0537 883277, ⓦ ledawlizrabat.com. To the east of the Medina and overlooking the river, this top-end hotel offers large rooms and suites with all mod cons, plus a complex of bars, restaurants and a nightclub. **1085dh**

★ **The Repose** 17 Zankat Talaa, Ras Chejra, Medina ☎ 0537 882958, ⓦ therepose.com. A luxurious yet relaxed riad within the Medina, with four individually decorated suites, some with a fireplace. The service and attention is impeccable, as are the in-house meals with locally sourced, often organic, ingredients. Traditional experiences can be arranged, such as a visit to the local hammam or henna hand painting. BB **850dh**

The coast from Rabat to Casa

Between Rabat and Casablanca lies a number of sandy beaches, popular with locals from both cities, especially during the summer holiday months. Apartment complexes are steadily taking over large tracts of the coastline here, supplying an increasing demand for city workers willing to commute.

Temara

Thirteen kilometres south of Rabat, the town of **Temara** is notable primarily for its small kasbah, which dates from Moulay Ismail's reign during the seventeenth and

---

COUP ON THE COAST

The **Royal Palace** at **Skhirat Plage**, between Rabat and Mohammedia, was the site of a coup attempt by Moroccan generals during King Hassan II's birthday celebrations in July 1971. The coup was mounted using a force of Berber cadets, who took over the palace, imprisoned the king and killed a number of his guests. It was thwarted by the apparently accidental shooting of the cadets' leader, General Mohammed Medbuh, and by the strength of personality of Hassan, who reasserted control over his captors. Among the guests who survived was Malcolm Forbes (see box, p.80). The palace still stands, though it has understandably fallen from royal favour.

---

eighteenth centuries. However, most visitors come here for it's beach, Temara Plage, 4km west of town. Packed in summer and deserted for the rest of the year, it's a pleasant if slightly wild stretch of golden sand; the sea here offers the odd wave for surfers but only confident swimmers should venture out past the breakers.

ARRIVAL AND DEPARTURE
TEMARA

By public transport Temara Plage is served by bus #17 from outside Bab el Had in Rabat, and in summer by grands taxis from Bd Hassan II. Temara Ville is on the Rabat–Casa Port train line, with twelve services stopping here daily. Petits taxis will take you from the train station to the beach for 5dh.

Mohammedia

Formerly known as Fedala, but renamed following the death of Mohammed V in 1961, the port of **MOHAMMEDIA** has a dual identity, as the site of Morocco's main oil refineries, and the base of its petrochemical industry, and as a holiday playground for Casablanca, with one of the best beaches on the Atlantic, a racecourse, and a royal golf club.

With its friendly, easy-going atmosphere, pleasant palm-lined streets and a fine selection of restaurants, Mohammedia makes a very pleasant stopover, or a base for Casablanca. Between the **train station** and the **Ville Nouvelle**, there is a small square **kasbah**, built during a period of Portuguese occupation and still preserving its original gateway.

ARRIVAL AND DEPARTURE
MOHAMMEDIA

By train The newly built train station is on the southeastern edge of the town, just under two kilometres (and a 5dh petit taxi fare) from the downtown hotels and restaurants Destinations Casa Port (6am–10pm 1–2 hourly; 20min); Casa Voyageurs (20 direct & 23 connecting daily; 20min); Rabat (1–3 hourly; 45min).

By bus Buses operate from Av Hassan II, just in front of the train station. Travelling to Casablanca, the best bus to take is #900.

By grand taxi Grands taxis to and from Casablanca operate from Av Hassan II, across the road from the train station.

ACCOMMODATION

L'Amphitrite Beach Bd Moulay Youssef ☎0523 306800, ⓦlamphitritehotels.com. Large top-end complex on the beachfront, with over 150 rooms and suites, all with balconies but not all with ocean views. There is a choice of restaurants and bars, as well as a decent-sized swimming pool, über-trendy nightclub and a pretty good spa that usually requires advance booking. **1122dh**

Camping l'Ocean Bleu 4km north of town on the R322 coast road towards Rabat ☎0660 911922. Friendly, family-run beachfront campsite with shaded pitches for tents and camper vans, as well as a few basic bungalows. Basic food provisions available all year and there's a restaurant in summer. **80dh**

La Falaise Rue Farhat Hachad ☎0523 324828. A basic but clean and friendly little place, with eight spotless rooms (only one is en suite but all have a hand basin) facing inwards to a tree-shaded central courtyard. There's a popular, at times noisy, bar next door. It's often full so worth trying to book ahead. **230dh**

Hager 3 Rue Farhat Hachad ☎0523 325921, ⓦhagerhotel.ma. Modest but modern hotel, with two well-established restaurants (one on the roof), and a bar. The tiled rooms are a bit spartan but clean and spacious; there's a few suites that also have a large sitting room. Spread out over three floors, there's a small but welcome lift. BB **520dh**

Riad Jnane Fedala 6 Av Abderrahmane Sarghini ☎0523 326900, ⊕jnane-fedala.com. A busy yet welcoming mid-range hotel across from the kasbah. The rooms are comfortable, despite suffering slightly from a garish over-the-top Moroccan theme, with lots of bright colour, intricate headboards and large, heavy drapes. There's a number of public areas, including a very pleasant rooftop bar and restaurant. <u>660dh</u>.

EATING AND DRINKING

For its size, Mohammedia's choice of **restaurants** is impressive, especially for fish. **Breakfast and snacks** are available from a number of cafés looking onto the pleasant, grassed Parc de Mohammedia or at the eastern end of the beachfront promenade.

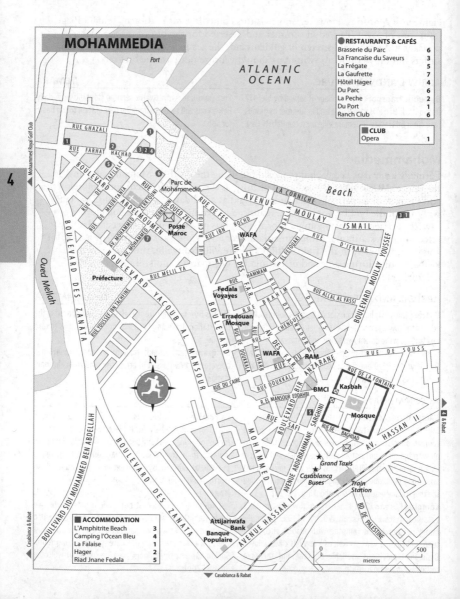

MOHAMMEDIA

RESTAURANTS & CAFÉS	
Brasserie du Parc	6
La Francaise du Saveurs	3
La Frégate	5
La Gaufrette	7
Hôtel Hager	4
Du Parc	6
La Peche	2
Du Port	1
Ranch Club	6

CLUB	
Opera	1

ACCOMMODATION	
L'Amphitrite Beach	3
Camping l'Ocean Bleu	4
La Falaise	1
Hager	2
Riad Jnane Fedala	5

La Francaise du Saveurs 1 Rue Farhat Hachad ☎ 0523 322062. Open since 1947 but looking sleek and modern from a recent facelift, this classy patisserie also doubles as the downtown bakery. Along with a good selection of breads and pastries (6–16dh), there's always a tempting display of chocolate creations (15dh/100g) that can be gift-boxed should you wish. Daily 7am–10.30pm.

La Frégate Rue Oued Zem, near the Hôtel Hager ☎ 0523 324447. Lobster, prawns and all manner of seafood in generous helpings, particularly with shellfish paella (mains 40–160dh). There's a takeaway and delivery service too. Licensed. Daily noon–10pm.

La Gaufrette Av Mohammed Zerktouni, facing Parc de Mohammedia. One of the better café-restaurants looking onto the park, with a pleasant and shaded pavement area along with more formal seating inside. A choice of breakfast options is accompanied by a snack menu offering sandwiches, pizza and pasta (mains 19–57dh). A good spot to while away a few hours of people-watching. Daily 7am–10pm.

Hôtel Hager 3 Rue Farhat Hachad ☎ 0523 325921, ⊛ hagerhotel.ma. This hotel's two restaurants are both worth a visit. The rooftop *Au Rejina* is the classier of the two, offering a varied menu that leans towards seafood, accompanied by ocean glimpses and a welcoming breeze during summer. The ground-floor *Le Coquillage* also offers a

pleasing menu of mainly seafood, and is something of an oasis during Ramadan. Licensed. Mains at both 65–145dh. Daily noon–11pm.

La Peche Rue Farhat Hachad. Unpretentious and popular seafood restaurant serving some of the best calamari, fish, oysters and cheap paella in town (30–90dh). There's also a few other options, including pizza. Can get very busy on Sundays with well-to-do Casablancans enjoying their weekly seafood feast. Daily 11am–11pm.

Du Parc Cnr Rue de Fez & Av Mohammed Zerktouni ☎ 0523 322211. Well-established, clean place with plenty of seating both inside and (shaded) outside. A varied seafood menu (90–190dh) includes the usual grilled and fried options, as well as a swordfish curry and good-value paella for two (150dh). Licensed. Daily 11am–11pm.

★ **Du Port** 1 Rue du Port ☎ 0523 325896, ⊛ restoport .ma. One of the classiest restaurants along the coast, with nautical decor inside and an outdoor upper deck sporting ocean views. Renowned for its charcoal grills, it isn't cheap but the dishes are inventive and accompanying sauces delicious (mains 130–240dh). Seafood is the obvious menu-filler, though meat-eaters and vegetarians are also accommodated. Licensed. Tues–Sun noon–4pm & 7.30–11pm.

DIRECTORY

Banks Attijariwafa Bank, Banque Populaire & SGMB are all on Av Hassan II, about 500m southwest of the train station. Attijariwafa Bank also has a couple of other branches along Av des FAR. The post office has an ATM.

Golf Mohammedia Royal Golf Club, Bd des Zanata (☎ 0523 324656, ⊛ rgam.ma).

Post office Av Mohammed Zerktouni, facing Parc de Mohammedia; Av Hassan II, opposite the train station.

Travel agency Fedala Voyages, 35 Av des FAR (☎ 0523 327390) is helpful for confirming flights and arranging car rental.

Casablanca

Morocco's biggest city and commercial capital, **CASABLANCA** (Dar el Baida in its literal Arabic form) is the Maghreb's largest port, and busier than Marseilles, on which it was modelled by the French. Its development, from a town of 20,000 in 1906, has been astonishing but it was ruthlessly deliberate. When the French landed their forces here in 1907, and established their Protectorate five years later, Fez was Morocco's commercial centre and Tangier its main port. Had Tangier not been in international hands, this probably would have remained the case. However, the demands of an independent colonial administration forced the French to seek an entirely new base. Casa, at the heart of *Maroc Utile*, the country's most fertile zone and centre of its mineral deposits, was a natural choice.

Superficially, with a population of over three million, Casa today is not unlike a large southern European city. Arriving here from the south, or even from Fez or Tangier, most of the preconceptions you've been travelling round with will be happily shattered by the city's cosmopolitan beach clubs or by the almost total absence of the veil. But these "European" images shield what is substantially a first-generation city – and one still attracting considerable immigration from the countryside – and perhaps inevitably some of Morocco's most intense social problems.

CASABLANCA

Hassan II
Mosque

Minaret

BOULEVARD SOUR DJEDID

BD DES ALMOHADES

MEDINA

Chleuh
Mosque

Grand
Mosque

Koubba
Sidi Belyout

Bab
Marrakesh

Carlson
Wagonlit

Clocktower

St John
Evangelist

Rialto
Cinema

PLACE DES
NATIONS
UNIES

PLACE 16
NOVEMBRE

Bus to
Ain Diab

PLACE OUED
EL MAKHAZNE

Synagogue

U.S. Consulate

LUSITANIA

Poste
Maroc

PLACE
MOHAMMED

Cathédrale du
Sacré Cœur

Law
Courts

Prefecture

French
Consul

Auto
Hall

Parc de la
Ligue Arabe

Administration
de Défense National

PLACE
SAINT-
EXUPÉRY

RUE ALLAL AL FASSI

BD RAHAL EL

Acima

Villa des
Arts

ONMT

MAARIF

BOULEVARD MOHAMMED ZERKTOUN

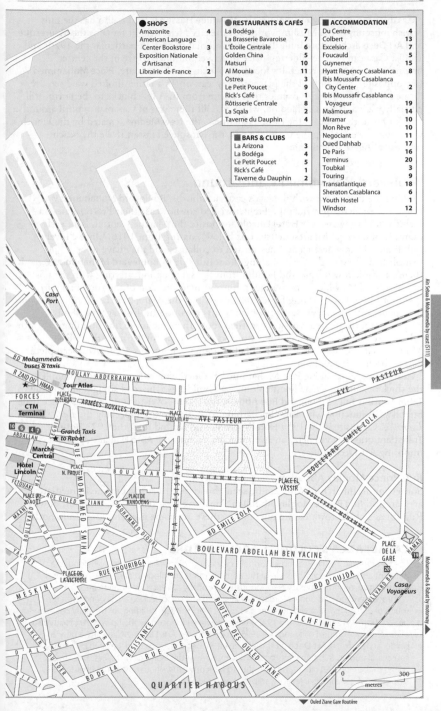

● SHOPS

Amazonite	4
American Language Center Bookstore	3
Exposition Nationale d'Artisanat	1
Librairie de France	2

● RESTAURANTS & CAFÉS

La Bodéga	7
La Brasserie Bavaroise	7
L'Étoile Centrale	6
Golden China	5
Matsuri	10
Al Mounia	11
Ostrea	3
Le Petit Poucet	9
Rick's Café	1
Rôtisserie Centrale	8
La Sqala	2
Taverne du Dauphin	4

■ BARS & CLUBS

La Arizona	3
La Bodéga	4
Le Petit Poucet	5
Rick's Café	1
Taverne du Dauphin	2

■ ACCOMMODATION

Du Centre	4
Colbert	13
Excelsior	7
Foucauld	5
Guynemer	15
Hyatt Regency Casablanca	8
Ibis Moussafir Casablanca City Center	2
Ibis Moussafir Casablanca Voyageur	19
Maâmoura	14
Miramar	10
Mon Rêve	10
Negociant	11
Oued Dahhab	17
De Paris	16
Terminus	20
Toubkal	3
Touring	9
Transatlantique	18
Sheraton Casablanca	6
Youth Hostel	1
Windsor	12

4

Ain Sebaa & Mohammedia by coast (S111)

Mohammedia & Rabat by motorway

Casa Port

BD Mohammedia buses & taxis

MOULAY ABDERRAHMAN

R ZAID OU HMAD

★ Tour Atlas

FORCES

CTM Terminal

PLACE ZELLACA

ARMÉES ROYALES (F.A.R.)

PLACE MIRABEAU

AVE PASTEUR

AVE PASTEUR

ABDALLAH

Grands Taxis to Rabat ★

Marché Central

Hôtel Lincoln

FETOUAKI

HASSAN

PLACE N. PAQUET

BOULEVARD MOHAMMED V

PLACE EL YASSIR

BOULEVARD EMILE ZOLA

BOULEVARD MOHAMMED V

PLACE DU 20 AOÛT

MAANI

YACOUT

RUE OULED ZIANE

SMIHA

PLACE DE BANDOENG

BD EMILE ZOLA

BOULEVARD ABDELLAH BEN YACINE

PLACE DE LA GARE

HMAD

RUE MOHAMMED DIOURI

PLACE DE LA VICTOIRE

RUE KHOURIBGA

BD

BD D'OUJDA

Casa Voyageurs

MESKINI

STRASBOURG

RESISTANCE

RUE DE LIBOURNE

ROUTE DES OULED ZIANE

BOULEVARD IBN TACHFINE

D'ALSACE

LANCER

RIFFI

BD DE LA

RUE

0   300

metres

QUARTIER HABOUS

▼ Ouled Ziane Gare Routière

Casablanca's most obvious sight is the **Mosquée Hassan II**, and it also has the only **Jewish museum** in the Muslim world, but the city's true delight remains the **Mauresque and Art Deco architecture** built during the colonial period, in particular the 1920s and 1930s. Casa can be a bewildering place to arrive, but once you're in the centre, orientation gets a little easier. It's focused on a large public square, **Place Mohammed V** (see opposite), and most of the places to stay, eat, or (in a rather limited way) see, are located in and around the avenues that radiate from it. A few blocks to the north, still partially walled, is the **Old Medina**, which was all there was of Casablanca until around 1907. Out to the south is the **Habous** quarter – the **New Medina**, created by the French, while to the west, along the Corniche past the Mosquée Hassan II, lie the beach suburbs of **Aïn Diab and Anfa**.

Boulevard Mohammed V and around

Linking the city centre with the city's eastern suburbs, **Boulevard Mohammed V** became the palette on which the French wished to showcase their Protectorate-era architectural prowess. The **Hôtel Lincoln**, opposite the Marché Central, is an early example of colonial Mauresque (see box below), dating from 1916. Once a lovely building, it is now derelict and has started to collapse, and may have to be demolished. West of the *Lincoln* along the south side of **Boulevard Mohammed V**, there's a whole row of splendid facades from the same period, starting with the post office at no. 116, which incorporates a Europeanized version of the Almohad *darj w ktaf* motif. The most striking facade on this strip is the *Maroc Soir/Le Matin du Sahara* newspaper office, one block west, which boasts a wonderful frontage based on a hexagram motif, topped with a green-tiled roof. There are more fine buildings on both sides of the boulevard for a couple of blocks east, but if you turn south up Rue Mohammed el Qorri, you'll see the **Rialto Cinema**, a gorgeous 1930s Art Deco picture palace, both inside and out.

Continuing south along Rue Mohammed el Qorri, you emerge at Place Aknoul, in the thick of some of Casa's finest colonial-era buildings. The road straight ahead, **Rue Tahar Sebti**, is full of them and **Rue Abdelkarim Diouri**, over to your left, has a nice little bunch at its junction with Rue Ibn Batouta (two blocks up), especially the *Bar Lyonnais*. Opposite is the 1919 **Hôtel Volubilis** and behind that, the 1922 **Hôtel Transtlantique**. Beyond here, on Avenue Lalla Yacout, the **Auto Hall** at no. 44 is a very imposing Art Deco edifice.

Rue Prince Moulay Abdallah

Some wonderful architecture can be seen above the street level in the immediate area around **Rue Prince Moulay Abdallah**. Heading west from Place Aknoul, down Rue Idriss Lahrizi towards the post office, there are some great facades along both

---

CASABLANCA'S COLONIAL ARCHITECTURE

The French-built city centre and its formal, colonial buildings already seem to belong to a different and distant age. The style of the administrative buildings in particular is known as **Mauresque**, or sometimes as "Neo-Moorish", essentially a French idealization and "improvement" on traditional Moroccan styles, with lots of horseshoe arches, and even the odd touch of *darj w ktaf*, originally an Almohad motif. Many private buildings of the early colonial period (from 1912 until the early 1920s) were heavily influenced by the flowery **Art Nouveau** of *fin-de-siècle* Europe. Following the 1925 Exposition des Arts Decoratifs in Paris, a new and bolder style, named **Art Deco** after the Exposition, began to take hold, inspired by many sources, including traditional Moroccan design. A meander along downtown Casa's streets, taking in the city's Deco heritage – be sure to look upwards, since most of the finer features stop short of ground-floor level – can prove very rewarding.

CHURCH OF ST JOHN THE EVANGELIST

The **Church of St John the Evangelist**, on the corner of Avenue Moulay Hassan I and Rue Félix et Max Guedj, stood in open fields when it was built in 1906. Within twelve months of its consecration, the church was involved in events that led to the **first French landings**. Some Europeans working on the port were murdered when Shaweea tribesmen from the interior invaded the town and sacked the church. Peace of a sort was restored by a French bombardment and subsequent occupation.

In 1942, during **World War II**, the church was filled with troops involved in Operation Torch. A member of the congregation at this time was General George Patton, who had led his troops ashore at Safi. He presented the oak pulpit, which still stands in the church, "in memory of the men of all nations who fell in the fighting around Casablanca".

sides of the street. It's worth making a detour to take the first street on the right, Rue Pergoud, where the **Hôtel Guynemer** (see p.282), at the first corner on the left, has some smashing Art Deco panels up on its cornerpiece. A right here brings you to the pedestrianized stretch of **Rue Prince Moulay Abdallah**, where there's a whole row of Mauresque and Art Deco facades on both sides, and some lovely little touches too: the Art Deco doorway at no. 48, for example, has a bird of paradise incorporated into the ironwork (as does 25 Rue Mouftakir Abdelkader, in the same block, just round the corner), while no. 72 is topped with some pretty Art Nouveau ironwork. At the northern end of the pedestrianized street is **Place 16 Novembre**, where no. 19 is the most handsome of a trio of charming Art Deco buildings, while at the southern end, Boulevard de Paris leads west to Place Mohammed V. On the way, check out the fine group of buildings around the junction with Rue Tata.

Place Mohammed V and around

Place Mohammed V is truly grand in scale. The public buildings around it served as models for administrative architecture throughout Morocco. The square stood at the centre of a network of boulevards drawn up by Resident General Lyautey's chief architect, **d'Henri Prost**, who made his plan based on a projected population of 150,000, considered far too high by many when he proposed it in 1914, but already exceeded by the time he left in 1923. Prost was keen to combine traditional Moroccan forms with current European town planning ideas, and was more than anyone else responsible for Casablanca's shape, and much of its architectural style.

The effect of the central ensemble in Place Mohammed V is very impressive indeed, the only feature out of place being a clock tower in the old **Préfecture**, on the south side of the square. The **law courts** on the east side of the square, and the **Bank al Maghrib** on the north are both solidly imposing too, and unlike much of the city's architecture, barely seem to have aged at all, probably because so many more recent buildings are modelled on them. On the west side of the square, the 1919 **post office** incorporates lots of surprisingly traditional features, in the tilework around the door for example, as well as the ceiling and brass chandelier within.

To the south of the square, at the junction of Avenue Hassan II with Rue d'Agadir and Rue Allal el Fassi, check out the building at 2 Pl Saint-Exupéry, an imposing edifice with an impressive semicircular facade. Opposite, across Avenue Hassan II, the Administration de Défense Nationale building, dating from 1916, represents an earlier and much simpler style of Mauresque, reminiscent of buildings in the Spanish zone of northern Morocco. Off Avenue Hassan II, you'll find some fine 1920s buildings along **Avenue Mers Sultan**, especially around *L'Entrecôte r*estaurant and the next main junction, Place Mers Sultan.

4

Cathedral of Sacré Cœur

Rue d'Alger

Casablanca's most classic piece of colonial architecture, the **Cathedral of Sacré Cœur**, sits at the western end of the **Parc de la Ligue Arabe**. More European in style, though adopting African forms, the cathedral was built to a wonderfully balanced and airy design, paying genuine homage to its Moroccan setting. Still in use for Sunday services (11am), most days you should be able to have a look around inside and if you're lucky, the *gardien* may escort you to the top of the tower for a brilliant view of the city and port.

Villa des Arts

30 Bd Brahim Roudani • Tues–Sun 9.30am–7pm, except Ramadan 10am–3pm & 8.30–10.30pm • Free • ☎ 0522 295087, ⓦ fondationona.ma

The **Villa des Arts**, set in a 1930s Art Deco villa, is part of the ONA Foundation, one of Morocco's eminent cultural and artistic organizations. Accessed through a peaceful garden and past a large fountain, the all-white villa has been lovingly restored by the foundation, and its grand high-ceilinged entrance leads to a number of galleries hosting both permanent and temporary exhibitions of contemporary art.

The Old Medina

Just to the west of both the port and Casa's downtown area, the **Old Medina** dates largely from the late nineteenth century. Before that, it was little more than a group of village huts, half-heartedly settled by local tribes after the site was abandoned by the Portuguese in 1755. Casa Branca, the town the Portuguese founded here in the

CASABLANCA'S SLUMS

Alongside its wealth and its prestige developments – notably the Hassan II Mosque – Casablanca has had a reputation for extreme poverty, prostitution, crime, social unrest and the **bidonvilles** (shanty towns) which you will see on both sides of the train track as you come into town. In fact, the French word *bidonville* – literally "tin-can town" – was coined in Casablanca in the 1920s, when construction workers on a building project in the Roches Noires district, east of the port area, knocked up some temporary accommodation next to their main quarry. Over the decades, other migrant workers followed suit, and the *bidonvilles* escalated, partly from the sheer number of migrants – over a million in the 1960s – and partly because few of them intended to stay permanently. Most sent back their earnings to their families in the country, meaning to rejoin them as soon as they had raised sufficient funds for a business at home.

The pattern is now much more towards permanent settlement, and this, together with a strict control of migration and a limited number of self-help programmes, has eased and cleared many of the worst slums. Also, *bidonville* dwellers have been accorded increasing respect during recent years. They cannot be evicted if they have lived in a property over two years, and after ten years they acquire title to the land and building, which can be used as collateral at the bank for loans. The dread of every *bidonville* family is to be evicted and put in a high-rise block, regarded as the lowest of the low on the housing ladder.

The problem of a concentrated urban poor, however, is more enduring and represents, as it did for the French, an intermittent threat to government stability. Through the 1940s and 1950s Casa was the main centre of anti-French rioting, and post-independence it was the city's working class that formed the base of Ben Barka's Socialist Party. There have been strikes here sporadically in subsequent decades, and on several occasions they precipitated rioting, most violently in the food strikes of 1982. More recently, the *bidonvilles* also proved a fertile recruiting ground for *jihadi* extremists – one *bidonville*, Sidi Moumen, was home to perpetrators of bomb attacks in Casablanca in 2003, and Madrid the following year, and also to a suicide bomber who blew himself up in a Casablanca internet café in 2007.

fifteenth century after the expulsion of the pirates, had been virtually levelled by the great earthquake of that year. Only its name ("White House": *Casablanca* in Spanish; *Dar el Baida* in Arabic) survives.

The Medina has a slightly disreputable air (it's said to be the place to go to look for any stolen goods you might want to buy back) but it isn't sinister, and it can be a good source for cheap snacks and general goods. A single main street, which starts from the top end of Boulevard Félix Houphouët Boigny, by a restored clocktower, as **Rue Chakib Arsalane**, becomes **Rue Jemaa Ach Chleuh** halfway along. A small eighteenth-century bastion, the **Skala**, has been restored, with some old cannons and an upmarket café-restaurant (see p.285).

Koubba of Sidi Belyout

Boulevard Félix Houphouët Boigny

Between the Medina and the port is the **Koubba of Sidi Belyout**. It's closed to non-Muslims, but the white-domed tomb can be seen through the door to the enclosure. Sidi Belyout is the patron saint of Casablanca and lent his name to the district southeast of the port. Legend has it that he despaired of mankind, blinded himself and went to live with animals that took care of him.

Quartier Habous – the New Medina

About a kilometre southeast of the city centre, at the end of Avenue Mers Sultan, is the **New Medina** – or **Quartier Habous** – which displays a somewhat bizarre extension of Mauresque. Built in the 1930s, it was intended as a model quarter, and it still has a kind of Legoland look, with its neat little rows of streets. What's most unreal, perhaps, is the neighbourhood mosque, flanked by a tidy stretch of green just as if it were a provincial French church.

South again from the New Medina, at the junction of avenues Mers Sultan and 2 Mars, alongside the Rond-point de l'Europe, the **Church of Notre-Dame de Lourdes** was completed in the 1950s. It's smaller than the Cathedral of Sacré Cœur and still in use. Its beautiful stained-glass windows, the work of Gabriel Loire, a master craftsman from Chartres, are its pride and joy.

Hassan II Mosque

Boulevard Sidi Mohamed Ben Abdallah • Accompanied visits Sat–Thurs 9am, 10am, 11am, & 2pm in winter, 2.30pm in summer, Fri 9am & 2pm/2.30pm • 120dh • 20min walk from the city centre along Boulevard Moulay Youssef; the mosque can also be reached by petit taxi (less than 10dh), or by bus #56 from Boulevard Félix Houphouët Boigny

Raised on a rocky platform reclaimed from the ocean, the **Hassan II Mosque** was inaugurated on August 30, 1993. Designed by French architect Michel Pinseau, it is open to non-Muslims on accompanied one-hour visits that also visit the mosque's huge and elaborate basement hammam.

From the city centre, the mosque's huge size tricks you into thinking it's nearer than it is. The minaret is 200m high, making it by far the tallest structure in the country, and the tallest minaret in the world. A laser on its summit projects a beam towards Mecca. It has space for 25,000 worshippers within, and 80,000 more in the courtyard. From the street, the mosque seems to float on the ocean below, a reminder of the Koran's statement (11:7), reiterated by Hassan II, that God's throne is upon the water. In order that the faithful can "contemplate God's sky", the enormous roof of the mosque rolls open on occasions. The mosque is second only to Mecca's in size, and St Peter's Basilica in Rome could fit comfortably inside it.

The facts of the mosque's construction are almost as startling as its size. During the early 1990s, when it was being readied for opening, 1400 men worked by day and a further 1100 by night. Most were master-craftsmen, working marble from Agadir, cedar from the Middle Atlas, granite from Tafraoute, and (the only import) glass from Murano in Venice. Its cost is reckoned to have exceeded £500m/US$750m, raised by not entirely voluntary public subscription.

Aïn Diab: the beach

3km east of the port and Old Medina • Bus #9 from Boulevard Félix Houphouët Boigny, petit taxi (about 20dh from Place des Nations Unies) or 30–45min walk

A beach within Casa may not sound alluring – and it's certainly not the cleanest and clearest stretch of the country's waters – but **Aïn Diab**'s big attraction is not so much the sea, in whose shallow waters Moroccans gather in phalanx formations, as the **beach clubs** along its front, each with one or more pools, usually of filtered sea water, a restaurant and a couple of snack bars. The prices and quality of the clubs vary – most locals have annual membership and for outsiders a day or weekend ticket can work out expensive (65–200dh) – so it's worth wandering round to check out what's available.

The Jewish Museum

81 Rue Chasseur Jules Gros, 5km south of town • Mon–Fri 10am–6pm • 25dh • ☎ 0522 994940, ⓦ casajewishmuseum.com • Petit taxi from the centre (about 20dh – ask your driver to wait as taxis locally are scarce), or a 15min walk from Oasis station

The **Museum of Moroccan Judaism**, in the southern suburb of Oasis, is Casablanca's one museum, and the only Jewish museum in any Muslim country. It is also an important resource of information on Morocco's massive Jewish heritage, one that rather dwarfs the country's 5000-strong Jewish population, of whom more than sixty percent live in Casablanca.

The museum, set up and run jointly by the Jewish-Moroccan Cultural Heritage Foundation and the Ministry of Culture, is housed in a bright, modern building. It exhibits photographs of synagogues, ancient cemeteries and Jewish holy sites nationwide, as well as reconstructed synagogue interiors, books and scrolls, traditional costumes, both full- and doll-size, and sacramental items, mostly made of silver and some hailing from Manchester, England. In fact, since silverwork was once the preserve of Morocco's Jews – even today, you'll find the jewellery souk in the Mellah (Jewish quarter) of many Moroccan towns – there are exhibits here of Jewish-made silver jewellery, and a reconstructed jeweller's workshop. There are also photos of ancient synagogues such as the Ibn Danan in Fez and others in Ifrane de l'Anti-Atlas and elsewhere.

ARRIVAL AND DEPARTURE

CASABLANCA

BY PLANE

Casablanca's Mohammed V Airport (☎ 0522 539040) is around 25km from downtown Casa. Trains run hourly between the airport and Casa Voyageurs via Aïn Sebaa from 6am to 10pm, with a further one or two services between midnight and 5am (35min; 40dh); for Casa Port station, change at Aïn Sebaa (16 daily; 1hr 10min). The official rate for a grand taxi between the airport and the city centre is 230dh for up to six people, but it often seems to depend on the number of passengers and time of day; taxis are located just outside the T1/T2 terminal building. Car rental companies with desks at the airport include Avis (☎ 0522 539072), Hertz (☎ 0522 539181) and local company First-Car (☎ 0522 300007, ⓦ firstcar.ma). There are bank ATMs and bureaux de change in the main terminal building.

Airlines Air France, 11 Av des FAR (☎ 0522 431818); British Airways, Centre Allal Ben Abdallah, 47 Rue Allal Ben Abdallah (☎ 0522 433300); Iberia, 17 Av des FAR (☎ 0522 439542); Royal Air Maroc, 44 Av des FAR (☎ 0522 314141). **Destinations** Agadir (4–7 daily; 1hr–1hr 20min); Dakhla (3 weekly; 2hr 15min); Fez (1–2 daily; 55min); Laayoune (5 weekly; 2hr 25min); Marrakesh (RAM 2–5 daily; 40min–55min); Ouarzazate (5–6 weekly; 55min–1hr 10min); Oujda (1–2 daily; 1hr 10min–1hr 30min); Tangier (1–2 daily; 1hr).

BY TRAIN
CASA PORT
The most convenient of Casablanca's train stations is Casa Port (*Gare du Port*), near the end of Bd Félix Houphouët

Boigny, 150m from Pl des Nations Unies. Unfortunately, only local trains from the surrounding region call here, as most intercity trains stop at the less convenient Casa Voyageurs (see below).

Destinations El Jadida (8 daily; 2hr 15min); Kenitra (over 20 daily; 1hr 30min); Mohammedia (1–2 hourly 6am–10pm; 20min); Rabat (1–2 hourly, 6.30am–10pm; 1hr).

CASA VOYAGEURS

Belying its status as one of the country's major rail hubs, the nondescript Casa Voyageurs (*Gare des Voyageurs*) station is tucked away some 2km from the city centre, at the far eastern end of Bd Mohammed V. Petits taxis are often waiting outside but are renowned for overcharging; hail one from the roadside and you'll pay about 10dh to get downtown. Otherwise catch the new tram or bus #2, both which travel along Bd Mohammed V between the station and Pl des Nations Unies, or you can walk (20min).

Destinations Aéroport Mohammed V (hourly 6am–10pm,1–2 daily midnight–5am; 33min); Asilah (8 direct & 1 connecting daily; 4hr–5hr 30min); Fez (1–2 hourly 5am–11pm; 4hr); Kenitra (1–2 hourly; 1hr 35min); Marrakesh (9 daily; 3hr 15min); Meknes (1–2 hourly 5am–11pm; 3hr 15min); Nador (1 direct & 2 connecting daily; 10hr 30min); Oujda (2 direct & 1 connecting daily; 10hr); Rabat (over 20 direct & over 20 connecting daily; 1hr); Tangier (8 direct; 4hr 45min & 1 connecting daily; 6hr 5min).

BY BUS

CTM buses operate from their conveniently located city-centre terminal on Rue Léon l'Africain. Both petits and grands taxis are usually parked directly outside. Most private bus firms operate out of the Ouled Ziane *gare routière*, 4km southeast of the city centre and best

reached by petit taxi; alternatively, bus #10 operates between Bd Mohammed V (opposite the Marché Central) and the busy Ouled Ziane road. For Mohammedia, local bus #900 (hourly 8am–7pm, daily) operates from Rue Ziad Ou Hmad, just west of Pl Zellaca and near Casa Port station.

Destinations Agadir (9 CTM and over 20 others daily; 8–9hr); Al Hoceima (1 CTM daily; 10hr); Beni Mellal (3 CTM daily & others roughly every half-hour; 4hr); Chefchaouen Casablanca (1 CTM & 1 other daily; 6hr 30min); El Jadida (4–7 CTM daily & others every 15min; 2hr); Er Rachidia (2 CTM & 2 others daily; 10hr); Essaouira (2 CTM & over 20 others daily; 8hr); Fez (10 CTM & 18 others daily; 5hr 30min); Laayoune (3 CTM daily; 20hr); Marrakesh (10 CTM daily & others half-hourly 4.30am–9pm; 4hr); Meknes (8 CTM & over 10 others daily; 4hr); Nador (3 CTM & 10 others daily; 11hr); Ouarzazate (3 CTM daily; 9hr); Oujda (2 CTM & over 5 others daily; 10hr); Rabat (over 20 CTM daily & very frequent private services; 1hr 30min); Tangier (5 CTM & over 20 others daily; 6hr); Tetouan (5 CTM & over 20 others daily; 7hr).

BY GRAND TAXI

Most grands taxis operate from the Ouled Ziane *gare routière*. The main exceptions include those for Rabat, which operate on Bd Hassan Seghir, very near the CTM terminal, Mohammedia, which operate from Rue Zaid ou Hmad, just west of Pl Zellaca and close to Casa Port train station, and El Jadida, Safi and Essaouira, which operate on Bd Brahim Roudani, by the junction with Bd Bir Anzarane in Maarif, 2km southeast of the city centre (served by local buses; see below).

Destinations El Jadida (2hr); Fez (3hr 30min); Mohammedia (30min); Rabat (1hr 20min); Safi (3hr 30min); Tangier (5hr).

GETTING AROUND

By bus The most useful bus routes are those that connect downtown with Casa Voyageurs (#2), Ouled Ziane *gare routière* (#10 or #11), and the Essaouira/El Jadida taxi stand in the suburb of Maarif (#7). The other useful services are #56 from Bd Félix Houphouët Boigny and Pl Oued el Makhzine to Mosquée Hassan II, and #9 from the same stops to Aïn Diab. Be warned that buses can get very crowded at rush hours.

By taxi Petits taxis are easy to find along the main avenues and are invariably metered – as long as the meter is switched on you will rarely pay more than 15dh/taxi for a trip round town. For Aïn Diab the fare is currently 20dh. There is a fifty-percent surcharge at night.

By tram Casa's new tramway network (w casatramway .ma) was nearing completion at the time of writing. The

intended routes will include almost fifty stops along some 30km of track, providing access between the city centre and the seaside suburb of Aïn Diab and the Casa Voyageurs train station.

By car Traffic is a nightmare in Casa, and frequently gridlocked: if you can avoid driving, try to do so. If you have a car, the larger hotels at Aïn Diab offer more security than those in the city centre. Car rental competition is stiff and it's worth phoning around. One of the best local firms is Afric Cars, 33 Rue Mohammed Radi Slaoui (T 0522 24 21 81), while others include: Ennasr Car, 18 Bd Anfa (T 0522 220813) and Goldcar, 5 Av des FAR (T 0522 202509). The international franchises are all grouped around the *Sheraton Hotel* on Av des Far, and include Budget (T 0522 313124) and Europcar (T 0522 313737).

OLD AND NEW STREET NAMES

The names of Casa's chief squares – **Place Mohammed V** and **Place des Nations Unies** - are a source of enduring confusion. In 1991, Hassan II declared that the old Place des Nations Unies (around which are grouped the city's main public buildings) be known as Place Mohammed V, while the old Place Mohammed V (the square beside the Medina) was renamed Place des Nations Unies.

As elsewhere in Morocco, many of the old French street names have been revised to bear Moroccan names, but many people use the old names – as do some street maps. In this edition, we have used the new Moroccan names. Significant conversions include:

Rue Branly – Rue Sharif Amziane
Rue Claude – Rue Mohammed el Qorri
Rue Colbert – Rue Chaouia
Rue Foucauld – Rue Araibi Jilali
Rue de l'Horloge – Rue Allal Ben Abdallah
Rue Jean Jaurès – Rue Mohammed Ben Ali
Rue Pegoud – Rue Mohammed Belloul
Rue Poincaré – Rue Tata

INFORMATION

Tourist information Syndicat d'Initiative, 98 Bd Mohammed V (Mon–Fri 8.30am–4.30pm, Sat 8.30am–noon; ☎0522 221524); central and offers free maps, but not much else. The Conseil Regional du Tourisme have a kiosk in the corner of Pl Mohammed V, and another next to the Mosquée Hassan II (both Mon–Sat 8.30am–12.30pm & 2.30–6.30pm; ⓦ visitcasablanca.ma) The ONMT

Délégation du Tourisme is south of the centre at 55 Rue Omar Slaoui (Mon–Fri 8.30am–4.30pm; ☎0522 271177).

Maps Editions Mauro (☎0522 440033) produce handy, detailed street maps of greater Casablanca, which are available for 10dh in bookshops at the airport or at Librairie de France (see p.286).

ACCOMMODATION

Although there are a large number of hotels in Casa, they operate at near capacity for much of the year and can fill up at short notice for conferences. If possible, phone ahead for a room, or at least arrive fairly early in the day. Even if you have a reservation, it's wise to phone ahead the day before to confirm.

DOWNTOWN

Du Centre 1 Rue Sidi Belyout, corner of Av des FAR ☎0522 446180, ☎0522 446178. Old-fashioned hotel with a creaky antique lift, but a well-located alternative should other cheapies be full. There's some nice Art Deco ironwork on the staircase, and though the rooms have seen better days, the clean en-suite bathrooms are a bonus. **200dh**

Colbert 38 Rue Chaouia ☎0522 314241. Conveniently located – one block from the CTM – and surprisingly large, with a handy lift. Rooms are a bit gloomy, but clean and friendly, some en suite. **210dh**

Excelsior 2 Rue el Amraoui Brahim, off Pl des Nations Unies ☎0522 200263, ☎0522 262281. A once-grand hotel, opened in 1915 and thus Casa's oldest surviving hotel. It's seen better days, and is a dusty old place, but it retains a certain faded elegance and has a central and very convenient location. BB **320dh**

Foucauld 52 Rue Araibi Jilali ☎0522 222666. A dependable cheapie with nice stuccowork in the lobby and a handy lift up to clean, if bare, salmon-pink rooms, some

en suite. Those facing outwards to the busy street can be a bit noisy. **180dh**

★ **Guynemer** 2 Rue Mohammed Belloul ☎0522 275764, ⓔ hotelguynemer@yahoo.com. Well-appointed, family-run hotel in the most architecturally interesting part of town, with great Art Deco touches on the exterior. Room sizes do vary – the singles and doubles are more modern whereas the older twins have larger bathrooms. It has a licensed restaurant and the staff are very friendly, helpful and speak good English. Airport (and sometimes bus & train) pick-ups if prearranged. BB **538dh**

Hyatt Regency Pl des Nations Unies ☎0522 431234, ⓦ casablanca.regency.hyatt.com. Casablanca's most prominent and perhaps best managed deluxe hotel, with a range of five-star facilities and three restaurants, as well as a bar and separate nightclub that are both popular with the after-work business crowd. Service is impeccable and the rooms are modern and spacious, including two adapted for wheelchair users. **2100dh**

Ibis Moussafir Casablanca City Center Cnr Rue Zaid Ou Hmad & Rue Sidi Belyout ☎0522 466560,

ⓦ ibishotel.com. This stock-standard offering from the Ibis chain holds no surprises. Located close to Casa Port, the rooms are comfortable, compact and with just enough modcons to justify the price; seven are wheelchair-adapted. There's a buffet breakfast and separate restaurant, and a 24hr bar. 900dh.

Ibis Moussafir Casablanca Voyageurs Bd Ba Hamad, Pl de la Gare ☎0522 401984, ⓦ ibishotel .com. As with most hotels in this popular chain, it's situated by the train station; in this case Casa Voyageurs, so it's hardly central, though very convenient for a late arrival (book in advance) or early departure. Rooms are small but functional, and there is a restaurant, (sometimes noisy) bar, and car park. 1090dh

Maâmoura 59 Rue Ibn Batouta ☎0522 452967, ⓦ hotelmaamoura.com. Owner managed and one of the city centre's better value options, located on a lively side street on the edge of the Art Deco neighbourhood. The modern, tiled rooms are very spacious if a little bland and soulless, neutral tones of beige and chocolate abound. Families can ask for interconnecting or may wish to upgrade an enormous suite, with its separate sitting room. There's a poky café for breakfast, and a grand restaurant. 480dh.

Miramar 22 Rue León l'Africain ☎0522 310308. Only 50m from the CTM, this is currently the cheapest of the little hotels in the city centre. It has an old-fashioned feel, and bathroom facilities are shared (shower 10dh), but the rooms are fine for the price. 140dh

Mon Rêve 7 Rue Chaouia ☎0522 311439. A friendly little place, and one that has long been a favourite with budget travellers. All rooms are accessed up a steep spiral staircase, and there's a choice of with or without bathroom, many of them recently renovated. 220dh

Negociant 116 Rue Allal Ben Abdallah ☎0522 314023. Opposite *Hôtel Touring* (see below), and very similar, though currently priced slightly higher, with clean, comfortable rooms (some en suite); it's a popular choice with Moroccan families. 220dh

Oued Dahhab 17 Rue Mohammed Belloul ☎0522 223866, ⓔ hotelguynemer@yahoo.com. Owned by the same family as the nearby *Hôtel Guynemer*, this is a rare budget option in this area of the city centre, offering basic but large, airy rooms, some en suite. Airport (and sometimes bus & train) pick-ups if prearranged. Good-value singles (120–150dh). 220dh

★ **De Paris** 2 Rue Sharif Amzian, on the corner with the pedestrianized length of Rue Prince Moulay Abdallah ☎0522 273871, ⓕ0522 298069. A popular lower end option in the centre of time; rooms facing the street are larger, and have balconies, but can also be noisy. There's a busy modern café at street level. It's often full, so book ahead or arrive early. 480dh

Sheraton Casablanca 100 Av des FAR ☎0522 439494,

ⓦ sheraton.com/casablanca. A very modern and central state-of-the-art five-star hotel with every conceivable facility, including a pool (summer only), three restaurants and a nightclub. The rooms (including one wheelchair-adapted) are comfortable but unexciting, and many of the staff speak English. 3700dh

Terminus 184 Bd Ba Hamad ☎0522 240025. Across from Casa Voyageurs, with clean, decent rooms – some sleeping up to four – with bathrooms on the corridor. It's not in the same league as the nearby *Ibis Moussafir* (see above) but then it's way cheaper. 180dh

Toubkal 9 Rue Sidi Belyout, off Av des FAR ☎0522 311414, ⓦ bestwestern.com/ma/hoteltoubkal. Part of the Best Western chain, this hotel's major attributes are its central location and safe parking. The rooms are comfortable enough but nothing very special for the price, though sizeable discounts are usually available, especially in the colder months. 1400dh

Touring 87 Rue Allal Ben Abdallah ☎0522 310216. A friendly old French hotel that's been refurbished and is in excellent value, with clean, comfortable rooms, some with their own shower, and hot water most of the day. It's even got its own little mosque. Definitely the first choice of the cheapies on this street. 200dh

Transatlantique 79 Rue Chaouia ☎0522 294551, ⓦ transatcasa.com. Founded in 1922 in a Lyautey colonial building and definitely under the "faded grandeur" category. The public areas are a great mix of colonial decor (including two big brass lions in the foyer) and traditional stucco, tilework and stained glass, but the rooms are a lottery; some have been renovated, some not. Those facing inwards to the courtyard are perhaps the best. The noisy in-house cabaret can last well into the night. 925dh

Windsor 93 Pl Oued el Makhazine ☎0522 200352. Regal looking hotel with spacious rooms with either a large bathroom or (cheaper) just a shower. There's also a decent bar, the staff are generally friendly and helpful, and there's a number of cafés close by. BB 300dh

Youth Hostel 6 Pl Ahmed el Biolaoui, previously Amiral Philibert ☎0522 22055, ⓔ lesauberges@ menara.ma. Just inside the Medina and within walking distance from Casa Port, this is not one of the country's better hostels, suffering from rising damp and indifferent management. There are (segregated) dorms and double rooms, but hot water can be nonexistent. Reservations are advisable though not always acknowledged. BB dorm 60dh, double 100dh

AÏN DIAB

The seaside suburb of Aïn Diab (about 20dh from the centre by petit taxi, 4dh on bus #9) provides an alternative base to the city. The options for tourists are all in the moderate to luxury price range, as the few cheaper hotels in the area cater exclusively for Moroccan guests.

4

YOU MUST REMEMBER THIS...

One of the best-known facts about Casablanca is that it wasn't the location for Michael Curtiz's movie, all of which was shot inside the Warner Bros studio in Hollywood. Banking on a major hit and upset by the Marx Brothers filming *A Night in Casablanca*, Warner Bros even wanted to copyright the very name Casablanca – which could have been inconvenient for the city.

The film of course owes its enduring success to the romantic tension between Humphrey Bogart and Ingrid Bergman, but at the time of its release it received a major publicity boost by the appearance of Casablanca and Morocco in the news. As the film was being completed, in November 1942, the Allies launched **Operation Torch**, landing 25,000 troops on the coast north and south of Casablanca, at Kenitra, Mohammedia and Safi. The troops, under General Eisenhower, consisted mainly of Americans, whom Roosevelt believed were less likely than the British to be fired on by the Vichy French colonial authorities. An even more fortunate coincidence took place in the week of the film's première in Los Angeles in January 1943, as Churchill and Roosevelt had arranged an Allied leaders' summit, and the newsreels revealed its location: the **Casablanca Conference**, held in Anfa, out beyond Aïn Diab. Such events – and the movie – are not, it has to be said, evoked by modern-day Casa, though the movie is commemorated in the city at the American-owned *Rick's Café* (see opposite).

Azur 41 Bd de la Corniche ☎0522 797493, ⓦazurhotelcasablanca.com. Across the road from the beach, equipped with a decent size swimming pool, an at times noisy bar, and a pretty good restaurant. The rooms, some sea-facing, are elegantly furnished with a few modern touches and good-sized bathrooms. BB **996dh**

Bellerive 38 Bd de la Corniche ☎0522 797504, ⓦbelleriv.com. An ageing but friendly family-run hotel overlooking the beach. Rooms are a bit small and dated; request a balcony with a sea view. There's a good pool, small playground, and a restaurant serving burgers, club sandwiches and kebabs. BB **750dh**

Le Littoral Bd de l'Ocean Atlantique ☎0522 797373, ☎0522 797374. Beachfront hotel with friendly management and staff, and large rooms with all the mod cons – most face seawards with a balcony. There's a very good restaurant, swimming pool and nightclub. BB **1290dh**.

CAMPING

Camping Oasis Dar Bouazza, 25km south of Casablanca on the coast road to Azemmour ☎0522 290767. Grassed and spacious, with modern, clean ablutions and facilities for camper vans. The beach and restaurants are nearby. **120dh**

EATING AND DRINKING

If you can afford the fancier restaurants, Casa has the best dining in Morocco. On a budget, your choice is more limited, but there are plenty of chicken rôtisseries and snack joints, so you won't starve. In addition to the places listed here, there are inexpensive hole-in-the-wall eateries in the Old Medina, and if you're putting together a picnic, the Marché Central (daily 6am–2pm) on Rue Chaouia groans under the weight of the freshest and best produce in Morocco.

DOWNTOWN

La Bodéga 127 Rue Allal Ben Abdallah ☎0522 541842, ⓦbodega.ma. Spanish and Tex-Mex cuisine in a lively, rustic taverna-style setting (tapas from 35dh, mains from 55dh). It can get very busy, and people come here for the vibe and alcohol (including sangría) more than for the food. Licensed. Mon–Sat noon–4pm & 7pm–1am, Sun 7pm–1am.

★ **La Brasserie Bavaroise** 129–131 Rue Allal Ben Abdallah ☎0522 311760, ⓦbavaroise.ma. Rough wooden floors and high ceilings hint at this French-style brasserie's previous life as a German ale house. Nowadays it's one of Casa's more intimate dining experiences, with an impressive menu of fish and meat dishes (70–195dh), exquisitely prepared and accompanied by an extensive wine list. Worth the splurge. Licensed. Mon–Fri noon–3pm & 7.30–11pm, Sat 7.30–11pm.

L'Étoile Centrale 107 Rue Allal Ben Abdallah ☎0661 637524. The most "local" of the restaurants on this street, with a traditional interior and good atmosphere. The menu concentrates on couscous, pastillas and tajines and is consistently good (mains 60–100dh). Daily 11.30am–3.30pm & 6.30–11pm.

Golden China 12 Rue Araibi Jilali ☎0522 273526. A welcome if trifle pricey diversion for those suffering from tajine fatigue. The large menu covers the whole gamut of Chinese-influenced Asian cuisine, with a few vegetarian options (mains 60–105dh). It's rarely full and service is usually attentive. Licensed (including Ramadan). Mon–Fri noon–3pm & 7.30–11pm, Sat 7.30–11pm.

Matsuri JM Suites Hotel, 161 Av Moulay Hassan I ☎0522 229874. More a sushi bar (complete with conveyor belt) than a restaurant, though it also serves dishes such as tempura, teriyaki, and beef in wasabi sauce. Sushi 25–55dh, mains 65–140dh. Licensed. Daily noon–3pm, 7–11pm.

Al Mounia 95 Rue du Prince Moulay Abdallah ☎0522 222669. Excellent traditional Moroccan cuisine served in a palatial salon or out in the shaded garden. Vegetarians will delight in the meze of filling salads, while the chicken tajine is a house speciality (120–150dh). Licensed. Mon–Sat 7.30–11pm.

★ **Ostrea** Port de Pêche ☎0522 441390. This place, tucked away in the port area, deserves to be better known, especially for its Oualidia oysters. Other fabulous fresh fish dishes include lobster or crayfish sold by weight, and even frogs' legs *à la provençale* (mains 75–240dh). For non-seafood eaters, there are *grillés* and pasta dishes. Licensed (including Ramadan). Daily noon–11pm.

Le Petit Poucet 86 Bd Mohammed V ☎0522 275420. A slice of old Casablanca, a French restaurant dressed up like a 1920s Parisian salon (which is what it was), where French aviator and writer Saint-Exupéry used to recuperate between his mail flights south to the Sahara; a couple of framed sketches by him grace the walls. You come for the decor rather than the food (mains 45–125dh), which is fine but nothing special, though the *soupe à l'oignon* is pretty good. Licensed. Daily 9am–10pm.

Rick's Café 248 Bd Sour Jdid, off Bd des Almohades ☎0522 274207, ⓦrickscafe.ma. A varied lunch and dinner menu offers a fusion of Moroccan, French and Californian cuisine – try the goat's cheese and fig salad (mains 130–160dh). The pianist (Issam rather than Sam) creates a Forties and Fifties musical ambience every night except Mon, and apparently never tires of playing the inevitable "As Time Goes By". Touristy, but not over the top. Mains 130–160dh. Licensed. Daily noon–3pm & 6.30pm–1am.

Rôtisserie Centrale 36 Rue Chaouia. The best of a bunch of cheap chicken-on-a-spit joints on this little stretch of road opposite the Marché Central. Chicken, chips and salad here won't set you back much more than 30dh. Daily 11am–11pm.

La Sqala Bd des Almohades ☎0661 820172, ⓦsqala .ma. An upmarket café-restaurant amid pleasant gardens in an eighteenth-century bastion of the Medina wall, complete with cannons. The menu is vast and inventive, with a tummy-expanding breakfast menu (80dh), a number of light and crunchy salads, as well as more substantial dishes such as tajines and grilled steaks. They also serve all-day juices, coffees, teas and cake. Mains 60–185dh. Mon noon–3pm & 7–11pm, Tues–Sun 8am–11pm.

Taverne du Dauphin 115 Bd Félix Houphouët Boigny ☎0522 221200, ⓦtaverne-du-dauphin.com. Long-established and very popular fish restaurant, with tables on the pavement as well as a more intimate, classier area at the rear, the two bisected by a lively, smoky bar serving seafood tapas. The menu is almost solely dedicated to the sea, with just a few *grillés* for non-seafood eaters. Reservations advisable. Licensed. 115dh 3-course set menu, mains 45–145dh. Mon–Sat noon–11pm.

ON THE COAST

Le 5 5 Rue de la Mer Adriatique, Aïn Diab ☎0522 797056. Opened in 2009, this large, contemporary bar-restaurant offers intimate dining inside or a more casual affair outside on the sunny terrace. The international menu offers something for everyone (seafood, pastas, *grillés*, sushi; from 85dh) and when accompanied by attentive service and smooth world music, makes for a surprisingly good evening. Licensed. Daily noon–3pm & 8–11pm. A

Ma Bretagne Bd de l'Océan Atlantique, 2km west of Aïn Diab ☎0522 397979, ⓦamabretagne.com. French gastronomes visit Casablanca purely to eat at this restaurant, run by *Maître Cuisinier* (master chef) André Halbert. Naturally, the menu is French-inspired and predominantly seafood (mains 180–320dh). The situation is delightful, close to the little island *marabout* of Sidi Abderrahmane, however, the restaurant itself suffers from a very high opinion of itself. Licensed. Mon–Sat noon–3.30pm & 7.30–11pm.

Le Poisson 59 Bd de la Corniche, Aïn Diab. A good place for fish and seafood, offering a whole range of different prawns (ordinary, king, Dublin Bay), not to mention bivalves (mussels, oysters, razor shells), a seafood hot pot, or cold plate. There's also a 150dh set menu. Mains 75–225dh. Licensed. Daily noon–11pm.

NIGHTLIFE

Casa has a surprisingly elusive nightlife in the city centre, where although **bars** are plentiful, they are almost exclusively the domain of men and prostitutes. This also goes for most of the clubs in town, which tend to be tacky cabaret joints at best. There are a few ultra-chic lounge bars out in the suburbs and Aïn Diab – self-conscious and full of self-importance, they don't usually charge admission but the drinks and meals are exorbitantly expensive.

BARS

Of ordinary bars around town, those attached to the restaurants *Le Petit Poucet* and *Taverne du Dauphin* (see above) are quite relaxed and there are also a few by the Rialto Cinema. If you want to check out some typical all-male hard-drinking dens, you'll find a row of them next to *La Bodéga*, along Rue Allal Ben Abdallah behind the Marché Central.

Le 5 5 Rue de la Mer Adriatique (off Bd de la Corniche), Aïn Diab ☎ 0522 797056. The lounge bar of this seaside restaurant can get quite busy on Sundays, when local and Paris-based DJs attract Casa's young and beautiful. All low-lighting and über cool, the drinks are expensive but it's a step up from most bars along the corniche. Beer 65dh, spirits 55dh. Daily 8–11pm.

La Bodéga 127 Rue Allal Ben Abdallah ☎ 0522 541842, ⦿ bodega.ma. Besides the atmospheric restaurant (see p.284), where it's OK to just have a drink, there's also a lively downstairs bar and dancefloor (salsa night Tues). Fun and not too pretentious. Mon–Sat noon–4pm & 7pm–1am, Sun 7pm–1am.

Rick's Café 248 Bd Sour Jdid, off Bd des Almohades ☎ 0522 274207, ⦿ rickscafe.ma. Although the ground floor is primarily a restaurant (see p.285), there's a 2nd floor cigar lounge just perfect for a gin & tonic while watching Bogey & Bergman's *Casablanca* on a big screen. There's also a less formal, tropical-themed rooftop terrace "bar'n'bbq". Daily noon–3pm & 6.30pm–1am.

T.G.I. Friday's Bd de la Corniche (opposite McDonalds), Aïn Diab ☎ 0522 150555. This Casablanca instalment of the American franchise is a two-storey diner-style outfit across from the corniche beach clubs. It's refreshingly low-key and friendly, attracting a mostly young crowd. The beer is cold and the comfort food menu is pretty good, but the service can be slow and it can get very smoky some nights. Karaoke or live music Tues–Sat from 8pm. Daily 11am–11pm.

CLUBS

There's a high concentration of clubs along Bd de la Corniche out in Aïn Diab. The term in general use for a dancefloor nightclub is "disco", while "nightclub" usually means a place with tables and a cabaret floorshow.

Armstrong Legend 41 Bd de la Corniche, Aïn Diab ☎ 0522 797758. A very popular, though small, club with live music and a great party atmosphere. It can get quite packed at the weekends, when it's worth reserving a table. Cocktails 130dh; admission 150dh. Tues–Sun 11pm–3am.

Le Bao Miami Beach Club, Bd de la Corniche, Aïn Diab ☎ 0679639280, ⦿ baonightclub.com. This newcomer to Casa's club scene is a refreshing change, thanks largely to its West African clientele who come to drink, dance and party. Cocktails 105dh; admission 100dh. Daily 11pm–4am.

DIRECTORY

Banks & exchange Most banks have main branches with ATMs along Av des FAR, between Pl des Nations Unies and Pl Zellaqa. Attijariwafa Bank, Av Hassan II (off Pl des Nations Unies) has an exchange ATM, and WafaCash bureau de change (Mon–Fri 8am–8pm, Sat 9am–4pm); BMCI, Bd Mohammed V (off Pl des Nations Unies) has an exchange ATM; Attika Bureau de Change, 22–24 Rue Allal Ben Abdellah (Mon–Sat 9am–1.30pm, 2–7.30pm; ☎ 0522 206020).

Books American Language Center Bookstore, 1 Pl de la Fraternité just off Bd Moulay Youssef (Mon, Tues, Thurs & Fri 9am–noon & 3–7pm, Wed & Sat 9am–noon); Librairie de France, 4 Rue Chenier (Mon–Fri 9am–noon & 2–7pm, Sat 9am–noon, Sun 2–7pm).

Consulates Algeria, 159 Bd Moulay Idriss I (☎ 0522 864175); Ireland (Honorary Consul), Résidence Al Hadi (entrance B, 5th floor), 57 Bd Abdelmoumen (☎ 0522 272721, ✉ irishconsulate@me.com); UK, 36 Rue de la Loire, Polo (☎ 0522 857400, ⦿ ukinmorocco.fco.gov.uk); US, 8 Bd Moulay Youssef (☎ 0522 264550, ⦿ morocco .usembassy.gov).

Dentists Dr Hassan Belkady, 305 Bd Bir Anzarane (☎ 0522 361039); Dr Hicham Benhayoun, 3 Bd Mohammed Abdou (☎ 0522 273314).

Festivals Jazzablanca (⦿ jazzablanca.com) brings together diverse international and Moroccan performers for five days of fusion Jazz, held each April or May at the Casa-Anfa Hippodrome.

Hospitals and doctors Dial ☎ 15 for emergency services or call SOS Médecin (☎ 0522 44 44 44) or SOS Médecins Maroc (☎ 0522 989898) for a doctor, or SAMU (☎ 0522 252525) for an ambulance. Clinics open round the clock for emergency treatment include: Clinique Badr, 35 Rue el Alloussi Bourgogne (☎ 0522 492380–84) and Clinique Yasmine, Bd Sidi Abderrahman Hay el Hana (☎ 0522 396960). English-speaking doctors include: Dr Mohammed Bennani, 45 Rue Atlas Maarif (☎ 0522 994799); Dr Alain Guidon, 4 Rue Mohammed Ben Ali (Rue Jean Jaurès), Gauthier (☎ 0522 267153).

Internet access Most internet cafés are open daily from 9am–10pm and cost 10dh/hr. Club Internet, Bd Mohammed V; Soukaina.net, 38 Rue Mouftaker Abdelkader, near *Guynemer* hotel; G@.net, 29 Rue Mouftaker Abdelkader; LG Net, 81 Bd Mohammed V, first floor.

Laundry Green Pressing, Rue Mohammed Belloul, opposite *Hôtel Oued Dahab* (Mon–Sat 8.30am–7.30pm; ☎ 0522 224343) will deliver to your hotel.

Pharmacies There's an all-night pharmacy (9pm–8am) in the Préfecture in Pl Mohammed V (☎ 0522 269491); details of other pharmacies open out of hours appear in the local press, or on lists displayed by all pharmacies.

Police Bd Brahim Roudani (☎ 0522 989865). For emergencies call ☎ 19.

Post office Pl Mohammed V (Mon–Fri 8am–6pm & Sat 8am–noon); 116 Bd Mohammed V, on the corner of Rue Chaouia (Mon–Fri 8am–4.15pm, Sat 9am–noon).

Shopping Beware of *trafika* (phoney fossils for example), and expect to pay higher prices for lower quality than elsewhere in Morocco. The Exposition

Nationale d'Artisanat at Av Hassan II with Rue Maarakat Ohoud (across from the *Hyatt Regency*), has crafts from around the country. Amazonite, 15 Rue Prince Moulay Abdallah has upmarket jewellery, objets d'art and antiques.

Sports Casa is the best place in Morocco to see football; the city's rivals, Raja and Wydad (also known as WAC) both play at the Complexe Mohammed V on Rue Socrate in Maarif; check the local press for fixtures. The complex also houses an Olympic-size indoor swimming pool, and has facilities open to the public (☎ 0522 362309). As well as the beach clubs on the Corniche, and the Complexe Mohammed V, you can swim in the open-air Piscine Océanique in Aïn Sebaa. The pool at the *Hyatt Regency* hotel costs 200dh for non-residents.

Travel agencies Carlson Wagonlit, 5 Av des FAR (☎ 0522 200039), and cnr Rue Allal Ben Abdellah & Rue Araibi Jilali (☎ 0522 203051).

South of Casablanca

The road and train line run side by side from Casablanca, firstly west past Azemmour to El Jadida, and then south across the plains to **Marrakesh**. To the east lies the desolae, dusty and largely unattractive phosphate-mining region, the Plateau des Phosphates.

Azemmour

Despite its strategic site at the mouth of the great Oum er Rbia River, **AZEMMOUR** has always been a backwater, and sees fewer tourists than any other Moroccan coastal town, making it a quiet, rather sedate place to visit, and perhaps stay in one of the riads in its whitewashed clifftop Medina.

Once in town, getting your bearings is pretty straightforward. The town lies between the N1 Casablanca–El Jadida highway and the El Jadida coastal road, and red petits taxis constantly ply the route between the two roads. The main thoroughfare is **Avenue Mohammed V**, which leads to a busy, grassed square, **Place du Souk**, with the **Medina** straight ahead.

The Medina

The Portuguese remained in Azemmour long enough to build a circuit of walls, directly above the banks of the river and dramatically extended by the white **Medina**. The best view of all this – and it is impressive – is from across the river, on the way out of town towards Casablanca.

To look round the Medina, make your way to Place du Souk, on the landward side of the ramparts, where you will see a sixteenth-century **gate** with an unusual, European-style, semicircular arch. Through it extends the old **kasbah** – largely in ruins but safe enough to visit. If you wait around, the local *gardien* will probably arrive, open things up and show you round; if he doesn't turn up, you might find him by asking at the cafés overlooking Place du Souk. Once inside the ruins, you can follow the parapet wall round the ramparts, with views of the river and the gardens, including henna orchards, along its edge. Also here is **Dar el Baroud** (The House of Powder), a large tower built over the ruins of an old gunpowder store; note also the ruined Gothic window.

The old **Mellah** – Azemmour had a substantial Jewish population until the 1960s – lies beyond the kasbah at the northern end of the Medina. Here, beside ramparts overlooking the Oum er Rbia, is the old town synagogue which is still well maintained and visited occasionally by practising Jews from Casablanca and El Jadida. It's cared for by a local family and you can – for a small donation – look inside to see the tomb of Rabbi Abrahim Moul Niss, a shrine for Jewish pilgrims and the focus of an August moussem.

Haouzia beach

The river currents at Azemmour are notoriously dangerous, but there's a nice stretch of **beach** half an hour's walk or a petit taxi ride (5dh) through the eucalyptus trees beyond the town. If you go by road, it's signposted to the "Balnéaire du Haouzia", a small complex of company holiday cabins occupying part of the sands.

For **birdwatchers**, the scrub dunes around the mouth of the river should prove rewarding territory.

ARRIVAL AND DEPARTURE   AZEMMOUR

By train The train station (Azemmour Halte) is inconveniently located 2km out of town, on the far side of the N1. You can usually catch a petit taxi (3dh) from the station, though sometimes demand outweighs supply. Aside from those listed below, services to all other major destinations connect through Casa Voyageurs.

Destinations Casa Port (8 connecting daily via Aïn Sebaa; 2hr); Casa Voyageurs (9 daily; 1hr 10min); El Jadida (9 daily; 20min).

By bus Local bus #101 operates between Azemmour's bus rank (Bd Boujdour, between the N1 and Av Mohammed V) and El Jadida (Pl de France, 200m south of the bus station). It departs hourly from 7am–8pm and the 25-minute journey costs 7dh.

By grand taxi Grands taxis operate all day between the bus rank (Bd Boujdour, between the N1 and Av Mohammed V) and El Jadida (Rue Abdelmoumen el Mouahidi, by the bus station).

ACCOMMODATION AND EATING

Accommodation and dining options are limited. Other than the in-house restaurants (open to non-residents) of the two excellent *maisons d'hôte* listed below, there are a few café-restaurants located around Pl du Souk.

★ **L'Oum Errebia** 25 Derb Chtouka, Medina ☎ 0523 347071, ⊛ azemmour-hotel.com. Once the kitchen and servant quarters for the town's *caid*, now renovated with a distinctly modern touch, with bright, abstract paintings adorning almost every spare bit of wall space. There's a choice of rooms and views; the river view from the terrace is unequalled. Dinner is a set menu (165dh) of traditional Moroccan food, sourced locally and often organic. BB <u>**1200dh**</u>

Riad Azama 17 Derb Ben Tahar ☎ 0523 347516. A nineteenth-century house tucked away in a residential area of the Medina, and restored with a more traditional feel. The rooms are all large and airy, and meals can be taken on the terrace overlooking the Medina or in the intricately decorated dining room. BB <u>980dh</u>

El Jadida and around

EL JADIDA is a stylish and beautiful town, retaining the lanes and ramparts of an old Portuguese Medina, now a UNESCO World Heritage Site. It was known as Mazagan under the Portuguese, who held it from 1506 until 1769. The city was taken from the Portuguese by Sultan Sidi Mohammed Ben Abdallah and then in the nineteenth century was renamed El Jadida – "The New" – after being resettled, partly with Jews from Azemmour, by Sultan Abd er Rahman. Under the French, it grew into a quite sizeable administrative centre and a popular beach resort.

Moroccans from Casablanca and Marrakesh, even Tangier or Fez, come down to the beach here in summer; when the bars are crowded, there's an almost frenetic evening promenade and – as in Casa – Moroccan women are visible and active participants.

The Cité Portugaise

El Jadida's **Medina** is the most European-looking in Morocco: a quiet, walled and bastioned seaside village, with a handful of churches. It was founded by the Portuguese in 1513, and retained by them until 1769, and it is still popularly known as the **Cité Portugaise**. As they withdrew, the Portuguese blew up several of the churches and other important buildings. The Moors who settled here after the Portuguese withdrawal tended to live outside the walls. Budgett Meakin, writing in the 1890s (see p.568), found an "extensive native settlement" spreading back from the harbour, while European merchants had re-established themselves in the "clean, prosperous and well-lighted streets" of the Medina. As in all the open ports on this coast, there was also

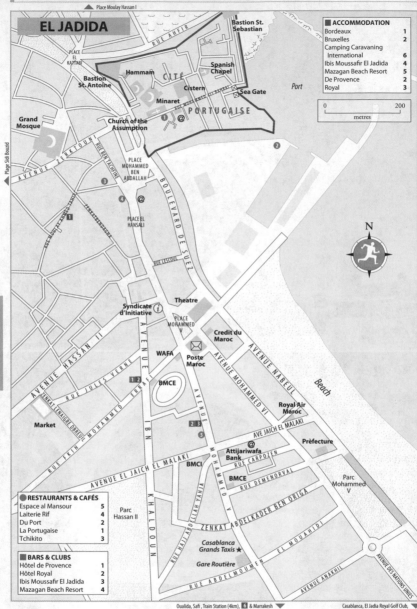

EL JADIDA

Place Moulay Hassan I

ACCOMMODATION
Bordeaux	1
Bruxelles	2
Camping Caravaning International	6
Ibis Moussafir El Jadida	4
Mazagan Beach Resort	5
De Provence	2
Royal	3

RESTAURANTS & CAFÉS
Espace al Mansour	5
Laiterie Rif	4
Du Port	2
La Portugaise	1
Tchikito	3

BARS & CLUBS
Hôtel de Provence	1
Hôtel Royal	2
Ibis Moussafir El Jadida	3
Mazagan Beach Resort	4

an important Jewish community handling the trade with Marrakesh; uniquely, old Mazagan had no separate Jewish Mellah.

Portuguese Cistern

Midway along Rue Mohammed Ali Bahbai • Daily 9am–1pm & 3–6pm, open until 7.30pm in summer • 10dh

The beautiful old **Portuguese Cistern** is a subterranean vault that mirrors its roof and pillars in a shallow film of water covering the floor. It was used to startling effect in Orson Welles's 1952 film of *Othello*; he staged a riot here and filmed it from within and above. It also featured in a Moroccan TV ad for Samar coffee and locals associate it with that, rather than Orson Welles.

The ramparts
Daily 9am–6.30pm • Free

From the original gate onto the port, Bab el Bahr (Sea Gate), you can climb onto the ramparts, and walk all the way round and onto all the bastions. By Bastion St Sebastian, the restored former **synagogue** has an interesting crescent and Star of David on its back wall.

Religious buildings

The Christian churches and chapels of the Portuguese City are generally closed; but worth seeking out for its shiny brass spire is the small **Spanish chapel**, located in the heart of the Medina to the north of Rue Mohammed Ali Bahbai and now bricked up bar a small section used as a shop. More impressive is the seventeenth-century Portuguese **Church of the Assumption** by the entrance to the Cité Portugaise, which was once restored and used as a cultural centre, but is now again empty. The minaret of the **Grand Mosque**, immediately north of the Church of Assumption, was once a five-sided watchtower or lighthouse, and is said to be the only pentagonal minaret in Islam.

4

The beaches

El Jadida's town **beach** spreads southeast from the *cité* and port, well beyond the length of the town. It's a popular strip, though from time to time polluted by the ships in port. Three kilometres further east along the coastal road, past the **Phare Sidi Ouafi** (lighthouse) and towards the Mazagan Beach Resort, is a broader strip of sand where Moroccan families set up tents for the summer. Good swimming is to be had and there are makeshift beach cafés in the summer.

   Plage Sidi Bouzid, 2km southwest, is more developed, with a seaside promenade flanked by some fancy villas and a few café-restaurants. Popular in summer but deserted at other times, especially during the week, the beach can be reached from El Jadida on bus #2 from alongside Place Mohammed Ben Abdallah, or by grand taxi.

ARRIVAL AND DEPARTURE   EL JADIDA

By train The train station is inconveniently located 4km south of town on the Marrakesh road (N1); petits taxis are usually available (about 15dh). Services to all major destinations, except Casa Port, connect through Casa Voyageurs.
Destinations Casa Port (8 connecting daily via Aïn Sebaa; 2hr 20in);. Casa Voyageurs (9 daily; 1hr 30min).
By bus All services including CTM call at the bus station on Av Mohammed V, at the southern end of town; from here it's a fifteen-minute walk to the Medina or to most hotels.

Petits taxis are usually available (10dh).
Destinations Casablanca (4–7 CTM daily & others every 15min; 2hr); Marrakesh (over 10 daily; 4hr); Oualidia (over 10 daily; 1hr 30min); Rabat (over 10 daily; 4hr); Safi (4 CTM & over 10 others daily; 2hr 30min).
By grand taxi Grands taxis from Casa drop you by the bus station, while those from Oualidia and Safi leave you by the lighthouse, about 1km up the Oualidia road from the city centre.
Destinations Casablanca (2hr); Oualidia (1hr); Safi (2hr).

INFORMATION

Tourist information There's a Délégation de Tourisme east of town at the Rond Point Marrakech roundabout (Mon–Fri 8.30am–4.30pm; ☎0523 344788) and the more accessible though no more useful Syndicat d'Initiative at 33 Pl Mohammed V (Mon, Tues, Thurs, Fri & Sat 9.30am–12.30pm & 3–6.30pm, Wed & Sun 9.30am–12.30pm; ☎0523 344788). There's also a useful website (in French) at ⊕eljadida.ma.

ACCOMMODATION

Rooms can be very hard to find in summer, so prices are higher and it's a good idea to book in advance.

Bordeaux 47 Rue Moulay Ahmed Tahiri, signposted from Rue Ben Tachfine, down a small side street ☎ 0523 373921, 📠 0523 340691. An old hotel – the oldest in town, so the patron claims – it is spotlessly clean and attractively refurbished, and some rooms are now en suite. The best of a number of cheapies in this neighbourhood. 230dh

Bruxelles 40 Av Ibn Khaldoun ☎ 0523 342072. Cheap and cheerful, this hotel is in a handy location just 10min walk from both the beach and Medina. The ageing but large, clean rooms are accessed by a steep stairway, some are en suite and others have balconies. Drivers will appreciate the undercover parking. 200dh

Camping Caravaning International 7 Av des Nations Unies ☎ 0523 342755. Campsite offering average facilities (including hot showers) with lots of shade and an on-site restaurant. Signposted from the beach, a couple of kilometres from town. 100dh

Ibis Moussafir El Jadida Pl Nour el Kamar ☎ 0523 379500, 🌐 ibishotel.com. In a prime location right on the beach. The rooms are the usual Ibis standard – compact, carpeted and with a couple of mod cons, many have sea views (no balconies), and two on the ground floor are wheelchair-friendly. The service is usually good,

and there is a restaurant, bar, swimming pool and secure parking. BB 520dh

Mazagan Beach Resort Plage Haouzia, 5km north of El Jadida ☎ 0523 388000, 🌐 mazaganbeachresort. com. Sprawling resort with hundreds of elegantly furnished rooms, all with French balconies offering sea (sometimes only partial) or pool views, and a choice of restaurants & bars, as well as a nightclub and casino. There's private beach access, an 18-hole golf course, a good spa and gym, and a free shuttle from Casablanca's Mohammed V Airport. Isolated and at times crowded with all-inclusive guests, it is nonetheless an impressive setup. BB 2900dh

De Provence 42 Av Fqih Mohammed Errafi ☎ 0523 342347, 📠 0523 352115. Getting a bit long in the tooth, but this grand old dame is still a decent mid-range choice, with a good restaurant, a garden for breakfast, and large rooms. Be sure to reserve ahead, particularly in the high season; in low season the price falls by almost half. 340dh

Royal 108 Av Mohammed V ☎ 0523 342839. An average hotel with large, airy rooms, some en suite with balcony, and erratic plumbing. Noise can be a problem, from both the busy street and the lively beer garden. Convenient for the bus station. 245dh

EATING AND DRINKING

El Jadida's dining scene leaves something to be desired, offering a plethora of snack fast food joints and just a few rare and worthy exceptions. Drinking is kept away from the public eye and consists mainly of hotel bars – try the *Hôtel de Provence*, *Hôtel Royal* or *Ibis Moussafir*.

Espace al Mansour 46 Av Mohammed V ☎ 0523 394105. A popular locals' restaurant between the bus station and town centre. Choose from pavement tables, shielded from the busy road by large windbreakers, or a colourful a/c interior. The menu offers fast, light fare such as pizzas, panini, pastas, shawarma and brochettes, as well as a great selection of fresh juices (mains 15–55dh). Daily 8am–11pm.

Laiterie Rif Rue Ben Tachfine. This small juice shop is perfect for a healthy breakfast. Order a bowl of fruit salad (15dh), accompanied by a fresh juice or smoothie (from 8dh), and enjoy at one of the simple pavement tables. Daily 8am–10pm.

Mazagan Beach Resort Plage Haouzia, 5km north of El Jadida ☎ 0523 388000, 🌐 mazaganbeachresort.com. If funds allow, head out to this resort, with its bars, casino and *Alias* nightclub, which has hosted big name "Eastern" live acts such as Cheb Mami. Bars daily 5pm–midnight;

Casino daily 9am–8am, Alias Fri–Sat 11.30pm–4.30am.

Du Port Northern end of the port ☎ 0523 342579. This first-floor restaurant in an unprepossessing building has a great view of the sea and serves good and plentiful seafood (from 80dh). Licensed. Mon–Sat 11am–3.30pm & 7–11pm, Sun 11am–3.30pm.

La Portugaise Rue Mohammed Ali Bahbai, Cité Portugaise ☎ 0523 371241. A very pleasant little restaurant with red-and-white-checked tablecloths, serving French rather than Portuguese dishes, including prawn bisque, sole *meunière* and chocolate mousse (mains 40–85dh). The food is good but the portions are not huge. Daily noon–3.30pm & 7–11pm.

Tchikito Rue Mohammed Smiha. A hole-in-the-wall fish restaurant that's been serving generous helpings at low prices since 1960. Try the mixed fish platter with chilli sauce for 35dh. Daily 11am–10pm.

DIRECTORY

Banks Located mostly south of the town centre between Pl Mohammed V and the bus station; exchange is available

from Currency Exchange Point, cnr Pl Mohammed V & Av Mohammed V (daily 8am–10pm).

Golf *Mazagan Beach Resort*, Plage Haouzia, 7km north of El Jadida (18 holes; ☎0523 388000, ⓦmazaganbeach resort.com); El Jadida Royal Golf Club, Plage Haouzia, 6km north of El Jadida (18 holes; 0523 352251, ⓦpullmanhotels.com).
Hammam There's one in the Cité Portugaise at 1 Rue No. 45 (enter the double gate, turn left along Rua do Arco and

it's 50m along on your right), open daily 7.30am–8pm, with separate entrances for women and men.
Internet access Cyber Téléboutique, Av Jaich el Malaki; Kiltec, 1st floor, 62 Pl el Hansali; Mellah Net, 11 Rue No. 11, off Rua Carreira, Cité Portugaise. All open daily 9am–10pm, 8dh/hr.
Post office Pl Mohammed V.

Moulay Abdallah

MOULAY ABDALLAH (also called Tit), 11km south of El Jadida on the R301 coast road, is a tiny fishing village, dominated by a large *zaouia* complex and partially enclosed by a circuit of ruined walls. An important **moussem** here in late August attracts thousands of devotees – and almost as many horses in the parades and *fantasias*.

Ribat Tit-n-Fitr

The village walls span the site of a twelfth-century **ribat**, or fortified monastery, known as **Ribat Tit-n-Fitr**, which was built as a base for Sufi mystics, and to defend the coast from a possible Norman invasion – a real threat at the time, the Normans having launched attacks on Tunisia. Today, there is little to see, though the minaret of the modern **zaouia** (prominent and whitewashed) is Almohad; behind it, through the graveyard, a second, isolated minaret is thought to be even older. If so, then it is the only one surviving from the Almoravid era – a claim considerably more impressive than its simple, block-like appearance might suggest.

4

ARRIVAL AND DEPARTURE   MOULAY ABDALLAH

By public transport Moulay Abdallah can be accessed by the buses and grands taxis plying the coastal road daily

between El Jadida (15–30min) and Oualidia(45min–1hr).

Oualidia

OUALIDIA, 78km south of El Jadida, is a stunningly picturesque little resort – a fishing port and lagoon beach, flanked by a kasbah and a royal villa. The **kasbah** is seventeenth-century, built under the Saadian sultan el Oualid (after whom the village is named) as a counterweight and alternative to Portuguese-held El Jadida. Until Sultan Sidi Mohammed took El Jadida, the lagoon made an excellent harbour and, as late as 1875, a French geographer thought that "by a little dredging the place would again become the safest shipping station on the whole Moroccan seaboard". The **royal villa**, now empty, was built for Mohammed V, who celebrated many birthdays and other family events here.

Today, most Moroccans know Oualidia for its **Japanese oysters**; Morocco's first oyster farm was launched here in 1957 and nowadays it harvests some two hundred tonnes a year, mostly sold locally. But the town really deserves to be better known as a resort: its beach is excellent for surfing and windsurfing, and swimming is safe and easy thanks to the shielded lagoon. The atmosphere for most of the year is very relaxed, aside from August when the place is jam-packed with Moroccan holidaymakers.

ARRIVAL AND DEPARTURE   OUALIDIA

Buses and grands taxis ply the route north to El Jadida (1hr–1hr 30min) and south to Safi (1hr) throughout the

day; both depart from Av Hassan II (the El Jadida–Safi highway).

ACCOMMODATION AND EATING

L'Hippocampe Cnr rues Palais Royal and 11 Janvier, Oualidia Lagoon ☎0523 366108. A delightful place, halfway up the slope between the lagoon and the

village. The simple, en-suite rooms are accessed off a flower-filled garden, while two suites overlook the lagoon. There are steps down to a "private" beach, as

---

BIRD HABITATS AROUND OUALIDIA

The 70km of coast between Sidi Moussa (36km south of El Jadida) and Cap Beddouza (34km south of Oualidia) is one of the richest **birdlife habitats** in Morocco. The coastal wetlands, sands and salt pans, the jagged reefs, and the lagoons of Sidi Moussa and Oualidia shelter a huge range of species – flamingos, avocets, stilts, godwits, storks, terns, egrets, warblers and many small waders. Numerous countryside species come in, too; golden oriole and hoopoe have been recorded, and flocks of shearwaters are often to be seen not far offshore. The best watching locations are the two **lagoons** and the rocky headland at **Cap Beddouza**.

---

well as a pool and a very good restaurant with an outdoor terrace bar. HB **1600dh**.

L'Initiale Oualidia Plage ☎ 0523 366246. A family-run place that's the last along the beach road, with six smallish rooms, two with a sea view (book ahead for these). The restaurant is without any views, despite its close proximity to the beach, but is still pleasant enough and has a leafy garden. Besides a wide choice of seafood, the menu also offers pizza and pastas and a few meat dishes. The

three-course set menus are good value (120–160dh). Licensed. BB **500dh**

Motel-Restaurant à l'Araignée Gourmande Oualidia Lagoon, opposite Bd Tariq Ibn Ziad ☎ 0523 366144. Standing alongside the lagoon beach, offering dated but well-kept rooms, some with lagoon views. There's also a suitably nautical yet unpretentious restaurant specializing in seafood. Set menus start at 135dh, with a lobster set menu for 300dh. BB **300dh**

Kasbah Gharbia

The Doukkala plains, inland from the El Jadida–Safi coast, have long been a fertile and fought-over region, and there are scattered forts and kasbahs at several villages. One of the most interesting and accessible is at **GHARBIA**, 20km from Oualidia on a road that takes you across an undulating limestone plateau. The **kasbah** here is a vast enclosure, four kilometres long on each side, bastioned at intervals, and with a gate at each point of the compass, giving onto roads to Oualidia, Safi, El Jadida and Marrakesh: a strategic site. Within, a few houses remain in use and there's a large white house in the centre, occupied by the *caid* in the days of the Protectorate.

Safi and around

The coastal port city of **SAFI**, halfway between El Jadida and Essaouira, with an old **Medina** in its centre, walled and turreted by the Portuguese, has a strong industrial-artisan tradition, with a whole quarter devoted to **pottery workshops**. These have a virtual monopoly on the green, heavily glazed roof tiles used on palaces and mosques, as well as providing Morocco's main pottery exports, in the form of bowls, plates and garden pots.

Safi has two main squares, **Place de l'Indépendance**, just south of the Medina, and **Place Mohammed V** on the higher ground in the Ville Nouvelle (also known as the *Plateau*).

Dar el Bahar

Place de l'Indépendance • Daily 8.30am–noon & 2.30–6pm • 10dh

The **Dar el Bahar**, or Château de la Mer, is the main remnant of Safi's 1508–41 Portuguese occupation. Built in the Manueline, or Portuguese late Gothic, style of the day as the governor's residence, it was later a fortress and a prison. Within, you can see the old prison cells at the foot of a spiral staircase to the ramparts, where a line of Dutch and Spanish cannon is ranged pointing out to sea.

The Kechla

Avenue Moulay Youssef • Museum Mon–Fri 8.30am–noon & 2.30–6pm, Sat & Sun 8.30am–6pm • 10dh • ☎ 0524 463895

The old Medina walls climb north, enclosing the Medina, to link with a large fortress known as the **Kechla**, Portuguese in origin, and entered from the east side, outside the Medina walls. Until 1990 it housed the town's prison, but is now the National Ceramics Museum with a not too exciting collection of local ceramics, plus cannons (British this time), garden courtyards and Portuguese coats of arms.

Cathédrale Portugaise

Off Rue du Socco • Daily 8.30am–noon & 2.30–6pm • 10dh

A visible relic of the Portuguese occupation is the **Cathédrale Portugaise** in the Medina, actually just the choir gallery of what was to be the cathedral, left uncompleted when the Portuguese withdrew, and adorned with sixteenth-century Manueline motifs. It's most easily found by heading northeast up the Rue du Socco – the Medina's main street – for about 100m, until it opens out a little; there on your right, by the entrance to the Grand Mosque, a sign painted on the wall points the way through a small doorway.

Sufi shrines

If you are Muslim, you can enter two important Sufi shrines in the Medina: the **Marabout Sidi Bou Dheb** (at the bottom end of Rue du Socco) and the **Zaouia of Hamidouch** (near the Kechla). Sidi Bou Dheb is perhaps the best-known Sufi saint in Morocco and both his *marabout* and the Hamdouchia *zaouia* host **moussems** (held in May in recent years) attended by their respective brotherhoods; these feature music, dervish-type dancing and, often, trance-induced self-mutilation with hatchets and knives.

Colline des Potiers

The **Colline des Potiers** (potters' quarter) sprawls above the Medina, with its dozens of whitewashed beehive-kilns and chimneys. The processes here remain traditional – electricity and gas have made scarcely an inroad on the tamarisk-fired kilns – and the quarter is worth at least the time it takes to wander up the new concrete steps and pathways. At the foot of the hillside is a street of showrooms. The products on display are of interest, but you are as likely to see U-bends for toilets being fired here as anything else. Unofficial guides may hustle you for business (they'll want you to buy stuff so that they can get a commission), and while the kilns are easily located without assistance, some guides may take you to more remote kilns and make it easier to take photographs and ask questions. If you do accept an offer of a guided "tour" make sure you agree a price beforehand (perhaps 10dh per person) and don't be intimidated into buying anything.

AND THE SARDINES?

Safi's famed **sardines** are caught in the deeper waters of the Atlantic, from Boujdour in the south to Safi in the north. There are around five hundred 18- to 20-metre wooden trawlers in the town fleet and you can still see them being made in the boatyards at Safi, Essaouira and Agadir. The fleet lands 350,000 tonnes of sardines annually (seventy percent of the country's total seafood catch) and most of them are canned in Safi. Increasingly, those caught further south are landed at the nearest port and brought to Safi in refrigerated trucks. Most of the tins get sold abroad – Morocco being the **world's largest exporter** of sardines.

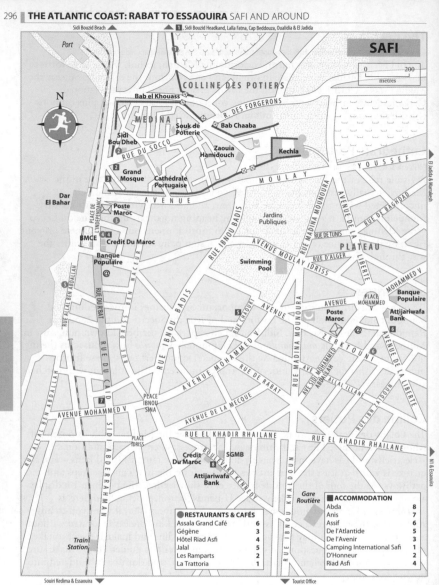

Sidi Bouzid beach

The road north of Safi first rises 2km up to the headland of Sidi Bouzid, where a glorious sweeping view looking back over the city awaits. Down below the headland is **Sidi Bouzid beach** – Safi's local strand – where on November 8, 1942, American troops under General Patton landed as the southernmost thrust of *Operation Torch* (see box, p.284), the Vichy French position offering little resistance. A pleasant 3km stretch of golden sand and accessed by walking through the port or driving down a hairpin road from Sidi Bouzid, the beach is jam-packed with Moroccan holidaymakers during summer, and virtually deserted for the rest of the year.

Lalla Fatna and Cap Beddouza

Local buses #10 and #15 run to **Lalla Fatna** and **Cap Beddouza** from Place de l'Indépendance

North of Safi, the rocky headland gives way intermittently to sandy beaches, sheltered by cliffs and with good waves for surfers as well as safe swimming conditions. The best of these cliff-sheltered beaches is **Lalla Fatna**, 15km north of Safi and a steep two-kilometre descent from the road, with a **koubba**, but little else, so bring provisions; if camping be sure to pitch your tent far enough back from the tides. 8km further on from Lalla Fatna (23km north of Safi) is the headland and lighthouse of **Cap Beddouza**, with another very pleasant sandy beach.

ARRIVAL AND DEPARTURE
SAFI

By train Safi's small train station is about 1.5km south of the Medina or about 15min walk. Petits taxis can usually be hailed from the street.

Destinations Benguerir (2 daily; 2hr); connecting at Benguerir for Casablanca (9 daily; 4hr 50min), Fez (8 daily; 8hr 40min), Marrakesh (9 daily; 4hr 15min) and Rabat (9 daily; 5hr 25min).

By bus All companies including CTM operate from the *gare routière*, around 1.5km and a confusing 20min walk south of the Medina. Petits taxis (7dh to the Medina) can be hailed from Bd Kennedy just outside the station's entrance.

Destinations Agadir (1 CTM & over 10 others daily; 6hr); Casablanca (5 CTM & over 20 others daily; 5hr); El Jadida (4 CTM & over 10 others daily; 2hr 30min); Essaouira (2 CTM, 1 Supratours & over 20 others daily; 2hr); Marrakesh (15 daily; 2hr); Oualidia (1 CTM & over 10 others daily; 1hr); Rabat (over 10 daily; 6hr).

By grand taxi Shared grands taxis operate from the bus station.

Destinations Casablanca (3hr 30min); Essaouira (2hr 30min); El Jadida (2hr); Marrakesh (2hr 30min); Oualidia (1hr).

INFORMATION

Tourist information 26 Rue Imam Malik (Mon–Fri 8.30am–4.30pm; ☎0524 624453, ⊛safi-ville.com).

ACCOMMODATION

Abda Bd Kennedy ☎0524 610202. A very good mid-range hotel in a good location, though on a busy street. Some of the compact rooms boast a balcony. There's also a ground-floor café and patisserie, and a separate restaurant. __402dh__

Anis Corner of Rue du R'bat and Rue de la Falaise ☎0524 463078. Cheerless but reasonably central place with a range of room types, some with en-suite facilities as well as a few good-value "apartment" suites. __270dh__

Assif Av de la Liberté ☎0524 622940, ⊛hotel-assif .ma. An average mid-range hotel, with functional but dated rooms, some (for not very much more) with a/c, heating and balcony, and there's an OK restaurant. __342dh__

De l'Atlantide Rue Chaouki ☎0524 462160, ⊛hotelatlantide-safi.ma. This old Art Deco dame is almost 100 years old and was once the centre of Safi society. She's well and truly lost her sparkle but still retains a certain old colonial charm, especially in the grand public rooms. The rooms are old and tired, but some offer a great view across to the Atlantic, and there is a swimming pool and restaurant. __350dh__

De l'Avenir 1 Impasse de la Mer ☎0524 131446. The best of a trio of cheap hotels tucked just inside the Medina (the *Essaouira* and *Paris* are tolerable fall-backs). Hot showers (7dh) on the first floor, grand views of the sea from some rooms and a busy café downstairs. __120dh__

Camping International Safi 2km north of town, signposted to the right of the road to Oualidia ☎0524 463816. Spacious and well shaded, with a shop and pool, as well as internet close by, it has some great views over the town and towards the sea and is 1km from the beach at Sidi Bouzid. __70dh__

D'Honneur (Foundouq esh Shraf) 56 Pl Douane ☎0660 577352. At the beginning of Rue du Socco, a homely little place with plain but clean rooms around a central patio (the top floor gets most light). Shared showers, and hot water if you're lucky. __100dh__

★ **Riad Asfi** 11 Pl de l'Indépendance ☎0524 464695, ⊛hotelriadsafi.com. Easily the best hotel in town, with large contemporary-style rooms, some with a fantastic view over the port and ocean. The fifth-floor restaurant offers the same great views. The management is spot-on and the young staff are refreshingly eager to please. Good-value singles (300dh). __450dh__.

EATING AND DRINKING

Assala Grand Café 19 Av Zerktouni ☎0524 622494. A large café-restaurant with a choice between pavement seating or tables inside spread out over two levels, where big-screen TVs show sport, music and news. A good spot for breakfast (23–26dh) and light dishes like panini and pizza (20dh–45dh). Daily 8am–10pm.

4

Gégène 8 Rue de la Marine, just off Pl de l'Indépendance ☎0524 463369. An old-style restaurant with a separate bar, and a good menu of both Mediterranean and Moroccan dishes (65–115dh). Licensed. Mon–Sat noon–3.30pm, 7–11pm.

Hôtel Riad Asfi 11 Pl de l'Indépendance ☎0524 464695, ⓦhotelriadsafi.com. Although lacking a little in ambience, this fifth-floor hotel restaurant is still one of the better dining options in town. The menu is mainly light, with a good choice of salads, pizza and pastas (25–60dh), although some heavier *grillés*, tajine and fish dishes (60–80dh) are also available. The recommended *couscous aux sept legumes* (couscous with seven vegetables) is available only on Fridays. Daily noon–3pm, 7–11pm.

Jalal Rue Allal ben Abdallah. A café with a large children's play area and a terrace overlooking the sea, serving tea, coffee and Moroccan staples (tajines and brochettes) as well as pizzas and burgers. Mains 35–85dh. Daily 9am–9pm.

Les Ramparts 1 Rue du Socco. Friendly café with a welcome shaded front porch looking out over the busy entrance to the Medina, as well as plenty of tables inside with large TV screens showing football. The reasonable menu offers pizza, pastas and tajines (mains 20–65dh), as well as a number of set breakfasts (23–28dh). Daily 8am–10pm.

La Trattoria 2 Route de l'Aouinate, near the Délégation des Pêches Maritime de Safi ☎0524 463176 or ☎620959. Upmarket and very pleasant restaurant with a good choice of Italian and seafood dishes, all reasonably priced (mains 65–185dh). The location isn't the best but it's comfortable inside. Licensed. Daily 7–11pm.

DIRECTORY

Banks Banque Populaire, BMCE, BMCI & Crédit du Maroc are all on or close to Pl de l'Indépendance. Attijariwafa Bank, Crédit du Maroc & SGMB are all on Bd Kennedy, next to *Hôtel Abda*.

Internet Club Internet, 29 Rue du R'bat; Lascala, Av Sidi Mohammed Abdallah, opposite the post office. Both open daily from 9am–11pm, and charge 8dh/hr.

Post office Av Sidi Mohammed Abdallah, off Pl Mohammed V; Pl de l'Indépendance.

Shopping For local pottery, head to the Souk de Poterie in the Medina – you're likely to find better pieces here than in the showrooms at the foot of the Colline des Potiers itself.

Essaouira (Mogador)

ESSAOUIRA is by popular acclaim Morocco's most likeable resort: an eighteenth-century town, enclosed by medieval-looking battlements. Its whitewashed and blue-shuttered houses and colonnades, wood workshops and art galleries, boat-builders and sardine fishermen and feathery Norfolk Island pines, which only thrive in a pollution-free atmosphere, all provide a colourful and very pleasant backdrop to the beach. Many of the foreign tourists making their own way to Essaouira are drawn by the wind, known locally as the *alizee*, which in spring and summer can be a bit remorseless for sunbathing but creates much-sought-after waves for **windsurfing** and, increasingly, **kitesurfing**. The same winds make Essaouira pretty terrible for **surfing** – those in the know head down the coast to Point Imsouane and Taghazout (see p.308 & p.463).

Brief history

A series of forts were built here from the fifteenth century but it was only in the 1760s that the town was established and the present circuit of walls constructed. It was known to Europeans as **Mogador**, possibly from the prominent *koubba* of Sidi Mgdoul, used for navigating entry to the bay. Less likely is the legend that the town's patron saint was a Scotsman named McDougal who was shipwrecked here in the fourteenth century. To Moroccans it was known as Seurah, from the Berber "little picture".

The walls were commissioned by sultan **Sidi Mohammed Ben Abdallah**, and carried out by a French military architect, Theodore Cornut, which explains the town's unique blend of Moroccan Medina and French grid layout. The original intention was to provide a military port, as Agadir was in revolt at the time and Sultan Mohammed Ben Abdallah needed a local base. Soon, however, commercial concerns gained pre-eminence. During the nineteenth century, Mogador was the only Moroccan port south of Tangier that was open to European trade, and it prospered greatly from the privilege. Drawn by protected trade status, and a harbour free from customs duties,

British merchants settled in the kasbah quarter, and a large Jewish community in the Mellah, within the northeast ramparts.

Decline set in during the French Protectorate, with Marshal Lyautey's promotion of Casablanca. Anecdote has it that he arrived in Essaouira on a Saturday when the Jewish community was at prayer; he cast a single glance at the deserted streets and decided to shift to the port of Casablanca further up the coast. The decline was accelerated after independence, by the exodus of the Jewish community. These days, however, the town is very much back on its feet, as a fishing port, market town and ever-more-popular resort. Orson Welles' 1952 film **Othello** was largely shot in Essaouira, and opens with a tremendous panning shot of the Essaouira ramparts, where Welles placed a scene-setting "punishment" of Iago, suspended above the sea and rocks in a metal cage.

The ramparts

The ramparts are the obvious place to start a tour of Essaouira. At the top of the **Skala de la Ville** (daily sunrise–sunset; free), the great sea bastion that runs along the northern cliffs, are a collection of European cannon, presented to Sultan Sidi Mohammed Ben Abdallah by nineteenth-century merchants. At its northern end is the circular **North Bastion**, with panoramic views across the Medina and out to sea.

Rue de Skala

Along the Rue de Skala, built into the ramparts, are a number of **marquetry and woodcarving workshops**, long established in Essaouira. Here – and in workshops around town – artisans produce amazingly painstaking and beautiful marquetry work from **thuya** (also spelt thuja; *arar* in Arabic), an aromatic mahogany-like hardwood from a local coniferous tree, from which they adapt both the trunk and the roots (or *loupe*). With total justice, they claim that their produce is the best in the country, and this is the best place to buy it. To gauge quality and prices before you come to make a purchase, visit Afalkay Art at 9 Pl Prince Moulay el Hassan (opposite the *Hôtel Beau Rivage*), a vast emporium where you can browse with no commitment to buy.

Musée Sidi Mohammed Ben Abdallah

Rue Laâlouj • Daily except Tues 8.30am–6.30pm • 10dh

The **Musée Sidi Mohammed Ben Abdallah** is set in a nineteenth-century mansion that served as the town hall during the Protectorate, and is now used to display a collection of traditional jewellery, coins, carpets, costumes and Gnaoua musical instruments decorated with marquetry, along with a gallery of pictures of old Essaouira.

The Mellah

In the northeast corner of the Medina, the Mellah is the former Jewish quarter. The **Jewish community** in the last quarter of the nineteenth century may have comprised as much as half of the town's population. **Sir Moses Montefiore**, the nineteenth-century leader of Britain's Jewish community, was born here. Largely businessmen, traders and jewellers, Essaouira's Jewish population built themselves large mansions within their quarter, some with up to twenty rooms. Alas, most of these residences are now derelict and the whole quarter lacks the vibe and energy of other parts of the Medina, reflecting the general trend in most of the country's Mellahs.

At the far northeast corner of the Medina, **Bab Doukkala** leads to a small Christian cemetery dating from colonial times (100m on the left). Some 400m beyond Bab Doukkala there is further evidence of the former Jewish community in the extensive Jewish cemetery – two vast grey lanes of tombstones, carefully tended and well ordered, in a site on both sides of the road. The principal entrance is on the right.

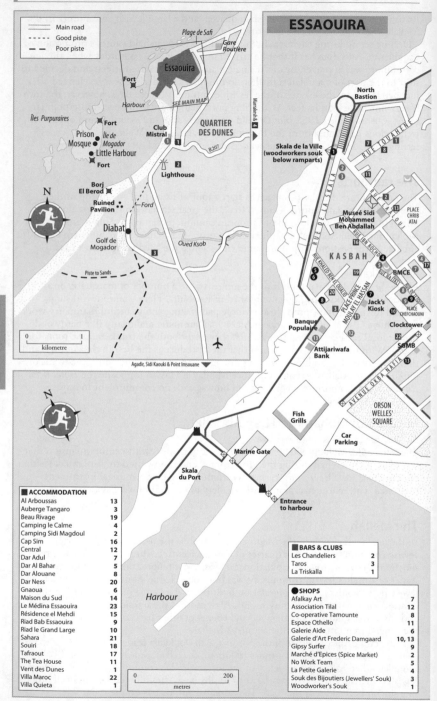

ESSAOUIRA

4

■ ACCOMMODATION

Al Arboussas	13
Auberge Tangaro	3
Beau Rivage	19
Camping le Calme	4
Camping Sidi Magdoul	2
Cap Sim	16
Central	12
Dar Adul	7
Dar Al Bahar	5
Dar Alouane	8
Dar Ness	20
Gnaoua	6
Maison du Sud	14
Le Médina Essaouira	23
Résidence el Mehdi	15
Riad Bab Essaouira	9
Riad le Grand Large	10
Sahara	21
Souiri	18
Tafraout	17
The Tea House	11
Vent des Dunes	1
Villa Maroc	22
Villa Quieta	1

■ BARS & CLUBS

Les Chandeliers	2
Taros	3
La Triskalla	1

● SHOPS

Afalkay Art	7
Association Tilal	12
Co-operative Tamounte	8
Espace Othello	11
Galerie Aide	6
Galerie d'Art Frederic Damgaard	10, 13
Gipsy Surfer	9
Marché d'Epices (Spice Market)	2
No Work Team	5
La Petite Galerie	4
Souk des Bijoutiers (Jewellers' Souk)	3
Woodworker's Souk	1

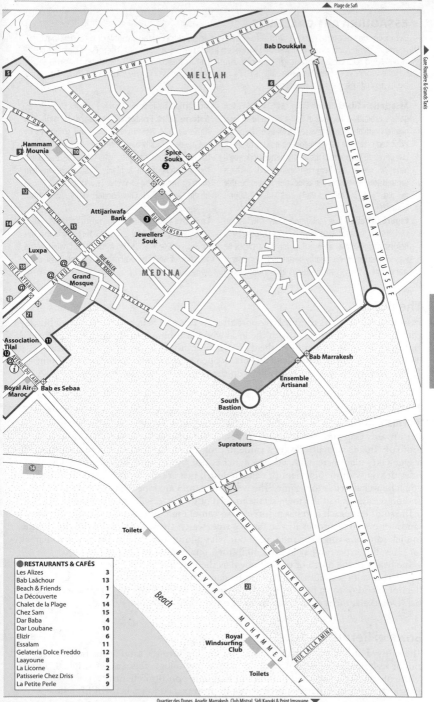

▶ Plage de Safi

Gare Routière & Grands Taxis

Bab Doukkala

MELLAH

RUE EL MELLAH

RUE DE KUWAIT

RUE OUIDA

RUE D'OUM RABIA

RUE SIDI MOHAMMED BEN ABDALLAH

RUE ABDELAZIZ EL FACHTALY

RUE MOHAMMED ZERKTOUNI

AVE MOHAMMED

Hammam
Mounia

Spice
Souks

RUE IBN KHALDOUN

Attijariwafa
Bank

RUE MOHAMMED EL QORRY

Jewellers'
Souk

RUE MENSRA

Luxpa

RUE DE L'ISTIQLAL

RUE SIDI ABDELSMIR

AVENUE DE

RUE MALEK BEN ROYAL

RUE D'AGADIR

MEDINA

RUE ATTARIN

Grand
Mosque

Association
Tilal

Bab Marrakesh

Ensemble
Artisanal

Royal Air
Maroc

Bab es Sebaa

AVENUE DU CAIRE

South
Bastion

BOULEVARD MOULAY YOUSSEF

4

Supratours

AVENUE LALLA AICHA

AVENUE EL MOUKAOUAMA

RUE LAGOUASS

Toilets

BOULEVARD MOHAMMED V

RUE LALLA AMINA

Beach

Royal
Windsurfing
Club

Toilets

⬤ RESTAURANTS & CAFÉS	
Les Alizes	3
Bab Laâchour	13
Beach & Friends	1
La Découverte	7
Chalet de la Plage	14
Chez Sam	15
Dar Baba	4
Dar Loubane	10
Elizir	6
Essalam	11
Gelateria Dolce Freddo	12
Laayoune	8
La Licorne	2
Patisserie Chez Driss	5
La Petite Perle	9

Quartier des Dunes, Agadir, Marrakesh, Club Mistral, Sidi Kaouki & Point Imsouane ▼

ESSAOUIRA ART GALLERIES

Essaouira has become quite a centre for painting and sculpture, and many of its artists have made a name for themselves in both Morocco and Europe. Artists with their own distinctive styles tend to have an entourage of second-rate imitators, so it's worth checking that the artist whose works you're looking at really is the one whose work you were interested in, as it should be in any of the galleries listed here.

Association Tilal 2 Rue du Caire ☎ 0524 475424. A gallery exhibiting the work of half a dozen or so local painters with quite distinctive styles. Many of the pieces exhibited here have been knocked up quickly to sell at low prices: to buy some of the artists' better work, you'll have to speak to them personally and perhaps commission something. The association should be able to put you in touch. Daily 8.30am–12.30pm, 2.30–7pm.

Espace Othello 9 Rue Mohammed Layachi, behind the Hôtel Sahara ☎ 0524 475095. Owned by a Belgian, originally as an overflow for the artwork he was exhibiting in his nearby restaurant; it's now a standalone gallery, with paintings and sculptures by

local artists. Daily 9am–1pm & 3–8pm.

Galerie d'Art Frederic Damgaard Av Okba Ibn Nafia ☎ 0524 784446. Paintings and sculptures by twenty or so locally based artists, in a gallery run by a Danish furniture designer, who uses the traditional thuya techniques in a highly imaginative, modern context. There's also an *atelier* (workshop) at 2 Rue el Hijalli, just off Pl Chefchaouni. Daily 9am–1pm, 3–7pm.

La Petite Galerie Just off the north end of Pl Prince Moulay el Hassan in the passage through to Rue Ibn Rochd, ☎ 0665 660630. A small but well-chosen selection of works by local painter Slimane Drissi. Daily 9am–9pm.

The port

Essaouira is Morocco's third fishing port after Agadir and Safi, and the port area bustles with life for most of the day, with the local wooden fishing boats being built or repaired, and the fishing fleet bringing in the day's catch. Some boats also offer rides. The sea bastion by the harbour, the **Skala du Port**, is open to the public (daily 9am–5.30pm; 10dh), and worth popping in to climb on the ramparts and enjoy the views.

The beaches

The main town beach, **south** of the Medina, extends for miles, often backed by dunes, out towards Cap Sim. On its early reaches, the main activity, as ever in Morocco, is football. There's virtually always a game in progress and at weekends a full-scale local league takes place here, with a dozen matches side by side and kick-offs timed by the tides. If you wish to join them (it's all barefoot), just ask alongside each "pitch" and you'll be welcomed into a game. The weekend games are especially fun just to watch, and on occasions half the town seems to turn out.

The southern beach also has a dozen or so **camel** men, offering rides up and down the sands, or out to the dunes. If you fancy a ride, watch the scene for a while and be sure to pick someone you feel confident about – it's a long way to fall. You'll need to bargain for rates, but expect to pay around 30dh for a ten-minute ride.

The beach to the north of town, known as the **Plage de Safi**, is good in hot weather and with a calm sea, but the water can be dangerous if the wind is up. It's reached from the north end of town by skirting left along scruffy side streets for 100m once outside Bab Doukkala, the reward being miles of often delightfully empty sand.

Bordj el Berod

The ruins of an old fort, Bordj el Berod, lie sinking into the sand at the far southern end of Essaouira's wide bay. According to local mythology, this was the original "Castle Made of Sand" that inspired the track of that name on Jimi Hendrix's *Axis Bold as Love* album, and it is said that Hendrix played impromptu concerts here for his fellow

THE ÎLE DE MOGADOR

Out across the bay from Essaouira lie the **Îles Purpuraires**, named from the dyes for purple imperial cloth that the Romans once produced on the islands from murex shellfish. Here also, Sir Francis Drake ate his Christmas lunch in 1577, commenting on the "verie ugly fish". The largest of the islands, known as the **Île de Mogador**, is flanked on each side by a fort which, together with the fort on the islet just off the town harbour and the Bord el Berod on the beach, covers all possible approaches to the bay. It also has a small harbour, a mosque, a few rusting cannons and a nineteenth-century prison used for political exiles but long closed. There was a Phoenician settlement on the landward side of the island in the late seventh century BC.

Nowadays the island is a nature reserve, and the only non-Mediterranean breeding site of **Eleonora's falcon**, Morocco's most dramatic bird, which is best seen with binoculars from the beach, in the early evening half-light. The falcons are summer visitors to Morocco, staying between May and October before heading south to Madagascar for the winter. They are often seen hunting over the dunes south of Oued Ksob. The nearby river course also has many **waders** and **egrets** and occasional rarities such as gull-billed tern and Mediterranean gull.

hippies back in the day. Nice though it would be to believe this, Hendrix stories in Essaouira want taking with a pinch or two of salt – *Axis Bold as Love*, for example, was released in January 1968, but Hendrix didn't visit Morocco until July 1969; he spent a week touring the country, of which a few days at most were in Essaouira. On the southern side of the Oued Ksob, which is impassable at high tide, the fort is an excellent viewing spot for the Îles Purpuraires, offshore, and their birdlife (see box above). Inland you can see the ruins of a royal summer pavilion.

4

ARRIVAL AND DEPARTURE ESSAOUIRA

By plane Essaouira–Mogador Airport (☏ 0524 476704) is 15km south of town on the Agadir road. Inside the modern terminal are a bureau de change and desks for the international car rental franchises Alamo/National (☏ 0524 431228), Avis (☏ 0524 474926) and Budget (☏ 0524 785692). The airport sees very little traffic, catering only to three flights a week from Paris, and while a few grands taxis are usually awaiting each flight, demand often exceeds supply and it's best to arrange a transfer through your accommodation in advance. Alternatively, local bus #2 travels past the airport turn-off, which is 1km from the airport itself (7dh; 8 daily; 30min). Royal Air Maroc, have an office at 15 Rue de Caire (☏ 0524 384385).

By train Although you can book train tickets to/from Essaouira, the Marrakesh–Essaouira sector is made by bus via the national rail carrier's road subsidiary, Supratours (see below).

By bus CTM and private buses arrive at the *gare routière*, about 500m north and 10-minute walk from Bab Doukkala. Especially at night, it's worth taking a petit taxi into town (no more than 7dh). Taxis cannot enter the Medina city walls, but you can hire one of the barrow boys who are usually on hand outside the Medina's *babs* (gates) to wheel

your luggage to a hotel for you – bargain for the price (about 20dh). Supratours (☏ 0524 475317) buses operate from their conveniently located office at the end of a short cul-de-sac by the Medina's south bastion (off Av Lalla Aïcha). Tickets for Essaouira to Marrakesh are best bought the day before, and you can also get connecting tickets for onward rail travel from Marrakesh.

Destinations Agadir (1 CTM, 1 Supratours & over 20 others daily; 3hr 30min); Casablanca (2 CTM & over 20 others daily; 8hr); Marrakesh (2 CTM, 6 Supratours & over 20 others daily; 3hr); Rabat (over 10 daily; 8hr 30min); Safi (2 CTM, 1 Supratours & over 20 others daily; 2hr).

By grand taxi Grands taxis operate from a yard by the *gare routière*. If arriving into Essaouira, request the driver to drop you off close to the Medina on the way to the *gare routière*.

Destinations Agadir (1hr 30min); Casablanca (5hr); Inezgane (2hr 30min); Marrakesh (2hr 30min); Safi (2hr 30min).

By car If you are driving, it's worth making use of the car park, guarded round the clock (40dh for first 24hr, 30dh thereafter), in front of the harbour offices, south of Pl Prince Moulay el Hassan.

GETTING AROUND

By taxi There is a petit taxi rank by the car park at the southern end of Av Okba Ibn Nafia, and taxis serving the

Medina also run to and from Bab es Sebaa and Bab Doukkala.

Car rental In addition to the firms at the airport (see p.303), Avis have a branch at 28 bis Av Oued el Makhazine (☎0524 475270); smaller, local firms include Dzira Location, 50 Bd Mohammed V (☎&☎0524 473716); and Isfaoun Rent-a-Car, 62 Bd Mohammed V (☎0524 474906, ⊛essaouiracar.com).

INFORMATION

Tourist information Av du Caire, opposite the police station (Mon–Fri 9am–4.30pm; ☎0524 783532). Alternatively there's Jack's Kiosk on Pl Prince Moulay el Hassan (daily 10am–10pm; ☎0524 475538), a newsagent and bookshop that has long served informally as an information booth and accommodation agency.

ACCOMMODATION

MEDINA

Al Arboussas 24 Rue Laâlouj, in a small alley opposite the museum ☎0524 472581, ☻arboussashotel@yahoo.fr. A nineteenth-century former Jewish residence that has been nicely converted, with soft shades of blue, green and yellow throughout, offering eight small but impeccably clean rooms, all en suite and decorated with local textiles and intricate zellij tiling, spread out over three floors. A delicious breakfast is served at wrought-iron tables on the discreet rooftop terrace, where there are also a few sun loungers. BB 410dh

Beau Rivage 4 Pl Prince Moulay el Hassan ☎0524 475925, ⊛beaurivage-essaouira.com. A prime location on this square, offering clean, modern rooms, each with its own balcony. Those overlooking the square, however, can be a bit noisy. There is a popular restaurant down below and a terrace up top with fantastic Medina and sea views. 350dh

Cap Sim 11 Rue Ibn Rochd ☎0524 785834, ☻hotelcapsim@menara.ma. Central, clean and popular, with small but comfortable rooms, some en suite and facing outwards to a busy street-level café-patisserie. The hotel's water is partly solar-heated. BB 225dh

Central 5 Rue Dar Dheb, off Av Mohammed Ben Abdallah ☎0524 783623, ☻si2007@live.fr. Cheap and cheerful basic rooms and friendly staff in a nice old house around a patio with a fig tree. Shared hot showers (8dh). 210dh

Dar Adul 63 Rue Touahene (near the Skala) ☎0524 473910, ⊛daradul.ma. Lashings of whitewash give this place a bright, airy feel, and help to keep it cool in summer. It's run by a French artist, with a selection of different-sized rooms, some split-level, and the largest with a fireplace to make it cosy in winter. BB 896dh

Dar Alouane (also called La Maison des Couleurs) 66 Rue Touahene ☎0524 476172, ⊛daralouane.com /home.html. Simple and stylish, done out in very original decor and beautiful colours, with a range of rooms (one single available) and suites at different prices, some with shared bathrooms but still excellent value. 652dh

Dar al Bahar 1 Rue Touahene ☎0524 476831, ⊛daralbahar.com. Wild sea views, especially from the terrace, cool whitewashed rooms, and paintings and window blinds by some of the best local artists make this an excellent choice, though it's a bit tucked away. BB 860dh

Dar Ness 1 Rue Khalid ben Oualid ☎0524 476804, ⊛darness-essaouira.com. A very well-located nineteenth-century house turned into an attractive place to stay by its French owner, with a variety of room sizes, some with ample and welcome natural light. There's also a great rooftop terrace. The staff are attentive yet not over friendly. BB 696dh

Gnaoua 89 Av Zerktouni ☎0524 475234, ☎0524 475236. Near Bab Doukkala and away from the more touristy parts of the Medina, spick and span but a little bit overpriced. All rooms are en suite but not all have outside windows. 330dh

Maison du Sud 29 Rue Sidi Mohammed Ben Abdallah ☎0524 474141, ⊛maisondusud.net. An eighteenth-century house built around a covered patio with a fountain. Most rooms are split-level with a sitting area and bathroom below the sleeping area; ask for one away from the noisy street. BB 632dh

Résidence el Mehdi 15 Rue Sidi Abdelsmih ☎0524 475943. A modernized old house with nice, airy rooms, two patios (one covered, one open), two terraces and a reliable kitchen, plus a couple of apartments and a suite. BB 425dh

★ **Riad Bab Essaouira** 35 bis, Bd Moulay Abderrahmane Eddakhil ☎0524 785508, ⊛riad-bab -essaouira.com. Small, stylish new riad decorated throughout in a subtle Afro-Gnaoua theme. Each suite occupies one floor, and includes a sitting room and separate bathroom with individual water heater. The rooftop suite also has its own small terrace. There's a communal salon and self-catering kitchen. Excellent management. BB 1166dh

Riad le Grand Large 2 Rue Oum Rabii ☎0524 472866, ⊛riadlegrandlarge.com. Despite its name, a small, cosy place with ten colourful yet smallish rooms, lovely staff, a restaurant and a roof terrace café. Good value, with reductions off-season. BB 525dh

Sahara Av Okba Ibn Nafia ☎0524 475292, ☎0524 476198. A large hotel in a very handy location. The spacious rooms are a quirky mix of bright colours, *faux*

European antiques and traditional Moroccan furnishings – all are en suite with central heating but some are smarter and brighter than others. Good value for the price. **285dh**

Souiri 37 Rue Attarine ☎ 0524 475339, ⓦ hotelsouiri .com. Very central and deservedly popular, with a range of rooms; the cheaper ones have shared bathroom facilities. Those at the front are larger and have outside windows, though the ones at the back are quieter. BB **360dh**

Tafraout 7 Rue de Marrakesh ☎ 0524 476276, ⓦ hoteltafraout.com. Friendly but characterless hotel with comfortable rooms, some en suite with rustic, brass sinks, others with outside windows. There's a spacious rooftop terrace and a bare, central courtyard. Slightly overpriced for what you get, but discounts available off-season. **400dh**

★ **The Tea House** 74 Rue Laâlouj, in an alley off the street ☎ 0524 783543, ⓦ theteahouse.net. Two self-contained and well-equipped apartments, each sleeping four, comprising two bedrooms, each with own shower, a sitting room, kitchen and bathroom, in an old house run by a British woman and her Marrakeshi husband. There is also a rooftop terrace with sea views. Among services offered are help with souvenir shopping, and a neighbour who'll come in and cook a Moroccan meal. BB **896dh**

Villa Maroc 10 Rue Abdallah Ben Yassin, just inside the Medina wall near the clock tower ☎ 0524 476147, ⓦ villa-maroc.com. Established long before riads became trendy, with two old houses converted into a score of rooms and suites, heated in winter and decorated with the finest Moroccan materials. It even has its own hammam. Most of the year you will need to book several months ahead, though it's always worth a call on the off-chance. Non-residents can dine here if they reserve before 4pm. Though accessible only on foot, they have porters on hand to carry your luggage from the car park. BB **1344dh**

NEAR THE BEACH

★ **Auberge Tangaro** Diabat village, 4km south of Essaouira and signposted from the main road ☎ 0524 784784, ⓦ auberge-tangaro.com. An Italian-owned place opened in 1920 that provides a quiet alternative to

staying in Essaouira. There's a main house with an excellent licensed restaurant and a communal lounge for an after dinner mint tea, flanked by two rows of rooms and suites, all simply furnished. While electricity arrived in 2011, the candles are still lit every night. It's peaceful, slightly rustic and full of charm. HB **700dh**

Le Médina Essaouira Hotel Bd Mohammed V ☎ 0525 072526, ⓦ accor.com. A sizeable resort located across the road from the beach, with large, contemporary styled rooms and suites that are nicely furnished and come with private balconies – there's also interconnecting rooms for families, and one adapted for wheelchair users. The facilities include bars, a large pool and a thalassotherapy spa centre, as well as two overpriced and underperforming restaurants. They also have a small, guests-only section on the beach, with umbrellas and sun loungers. **1815dh**

Vent des Dunes 20 Rue el Bakkay, Quartier des Dunes, ☎ 0524 475391, ⓦ ventdesdunes.com. Peaceful, well-managed villa-style hotel that offers a variety of different sized, great-value rooms, including a couple of larger ones for families. There's an in-house restaurant that also provides picnic baskets, or it's a 200m walk to the beach café-restaurants. BB **440dh**.

Villa Quieta 86 Bd Mohammed V, Quartier des Dunes ☎ 0524 785004, ⓦ villa-quieta.com. A luxurious mansion built in semi-traditional style by the current owner's father in the 1950s, some 2km south of town. The rooms are tasteful and comfortable, and the place retains the feel of an upscale guesthouse rather than a hotel. There's a sheltered pool and garden, and it's only 150m to the beach. BB **1662dh**

CAMPSITES

Camping le Calme Ida ou Gourd, 9km east of town, on the Marrakech road ☎ 0661 530413. Pleasant site located amongst the Aragn trees. Good ablutions, and there's an on-site restaurnt, as well as a shop selling basic provisions. Discounts for long stays. **70dh**

Camping Sidi Magdoul 3km south of town on the Agadir road, across from the lighthouse ☎ 0524 472196. Clean, friendly and well managed, with hot showers, and an area of soil and trees for pitching tents and parking vans. **34dh**

APARTMENTS FOR RENT

If you're looking for a little more space and privacy or plan to stay for more than a couple of nights, it can be worth **renting an apartment** or a suite within Essaouira's Medina. There are a surprising number available, all refurbished and modernized and especially affordable for families or small groups. The pioneer of this type of accommodation in Essaouira has been Jack's Apartments (ⓦ essaouiranet.com) whose office Jack's Kiosk is on Place Prince Moulay el Hassan. You may also be accosted by key-waving local residents either at the bus station or as you enter the town's southern fringe, but always check out what's on offer carefully, and be sure of the price and services you have agreed upon before accepting.

4

EATING AND DRINKING

For an informal lunch, or early evening meal, you can't do better than eat at the line of **grills** down at the port, an Essaouira institution, with fish as fresh as can be. You choose from the fish displayed in front of your stall, and have it grilled there and then. Prices are fixed and displayed, but unfortunately some of the stalls have been getting rather hassly of late, and also overcharging (needless to say, it's the same ones that hustle for business who try to pull a fast one), so check prices first, and choose a stall (*Chez Ali* at #33 is recommended) that doesn't try to accost you.

MEDINA

Les Alizes 26 Rue Skala ☎0524 476819. Quiet and intimate, this restaurant has built up a good reputation for Moroccan dishes, both traditional and inventive (three-course set menu 99dh). The place is spotless and the service always friendly. Book ahead if possible. Licensed. Closed Nov. Daily 7–11pm.

Bab Laâchour Bab Laâchour, by Pl Prince Moulay el Hassan ☎0524 473572. A café favoured by locals downstairs, with a more tourist-oriented restaurant on the floor above, overlooking the square. The menu includes fish and tajines (mains 35–80dh). Daily 8am–10pm.

Chez Sam in the harbour ☎0524 476513. An Essaouira institution – a wooden shack, built like a boat, set seductively right by the waterfront in the harbour. Service can be a bit hit-and-miss but the portions are generous, the fish is usually cooked pretty well, there's beer and wine available, and fishing boats to watch through the portholes. Moderate to expensive, with set menus at 85dh, or 250dh with lobster. Daily noon–3.30pm, 7 –10.30pm.

Dar Baba 1st floor, 2 Rue de Marrakech, on the corner with Rue Sidi Mohammed Ben Abdallah ☎0524 476809. Family-owned and-managed Italian restaurant. Simple and authentic, the pasta is handmade, the pizzas are thin-based, they use *real* cheese, and the wine list is pretty good (mains 25–75dh). Licensed. Daily noon–11pm.

Dar Loubane 24 Rue du Rif, a stone's throw from Pl Chefchaouni ☎0524 476296. Upmarket restaurant on the ground-floor patio of an attractive eighteenth-century riad, with tables placed among semi-kitsch decor and interesting exhibits. The mainly Moroccan menu attracts a loyal following of Essaouira expats, and live Gnaoua music takes place some evenings. Mains 45–95dh. Daily noon–3.30pm, 7 –10.30pm.

La Découverte 8 bis rue Houmane el Fetaouki ☎0524 473158, ⓦessaouira-ladecouverte.com. French-Moroccan cuisine is served at this little place run by a French couple (she does the cooking, he greets and serves the customers), with a short but sweet menu of excellent food including seafood pasta, vegetables stuffed with minced fish or meat, an excellent pastilla, and on Mondays, camel couscous. Mains 55–85dh. Sun–Fri 10am–10pm.

★ **Elizir** 1 Rue d'Agadir ☎0524 472103. A harmonious fusion of Italian and Moroccan cuisine using locally sourced ingredients is served up in this pioneering little owner-managed restaurant, with eclectic retro decor. The menu includes inventive inky black cuttlefish risotto, swordfish brochettes with ginger, or gnocchi with fromage frais and almond pesto (mains 65–110dh). Reservation recommended. Licensed. Daily 7.30–11pm.

Essalam 23 Pl Prince Moulay el Hassan. The cheapest set menus in town and certainly value for money, though the choice is limited to the usual soup–tajine–fruit combos (30–65dh). Good for breakfast too. Daily 8am–10pm.

Laayoune 4 bis Rue Hajjali ☎0524 474643. A popular place for Moroccan staples in a warm, relaxed setting with low-lying tables and friendly service. Tajine- and couscous-based menus for 68–88dh. Daily 11.30am–10.30pm.

La Licorne 26 Rue Skala ☎0524 473626, ⓦlalicorne-essaouira.com. An upmarket Moroccan restaurant serving some of the best traditional French and Moroccan food in town (mains 30–65dh). The tajine of saffron-infused chicken with roasted almonds is particularly recommended, and features on the 160dh set menu. Tues–Sun 7.30–11pm.

Patisserie Chez Driss 10 Rue Hajjali, just off Pl Prince Moulay el Hassan. One of the town's most popular meeting places, this long-established place serves up delicious fresh pastries and coffee in a quiet leafy courtyard. Ideal for a leisurely breakfast. Pastries 4–9dh, mains 18–25dh. Daily 8am–10pm.

La Petite Perle 2 Rue el Hajjalli ☎0524 475050. A small place with low divan seating, popular among travellers who come for the generous servings of good traditional Moroccan cooking. There's a number of three- and four-course set menus (60–95dh), all finishing off with a pot of freshly brewed mint tea. Daily noon–3pm, 7–10.30pm.

NEAR THE BEACH

Beach & Friends Bd Mohammed V, Quartier des Dunes ☎0524 474558. Worth the long walk for a lazy afternoon, this is one of a number of beachfront café-restaurants clustered together at the southern entrance to town. Partly shaded outside but still susceptible to the wind and sand, there's a choice of sun loungers, couches and comfy wicker chairs, or move inside onto one of the low lying lounges. The varied menu offers some great salads and pizzas, as well as heavier meals like a Thai beef curry (mains 45–100dh). Licensed. Daily 8am–10pm.

Chalet de la Plage Bd Mohammed V, on the seafront, just above the high-tide mark ☎0524 475972. Built entirely of wood by the Ferraud family in 1893, the building is now a little gloomy and barnacled with marine mementos, but the seafood and sea views are truly memorable (set menus for 150dh and 180dh). Avoid lunchtime when day-trippers overwhelm the place. Licensed. Mon 7–10pm, Tues–Sat noon–3pm and 7–10pm, Sun noon–3pm.

NIGHTLIFE

Essaouira doesn't have much by way of nightlife – it's a café more than a bar scene – with very few places where you can just have a drink. As well as those listed below, you can try the beachfront restaurants (see opposite) – you may need to buy a little food to do so.

Les Chandeliers 14 Rue Laâlouj ☎0524 475827. A well-established restaurant and wine bar run by a French family. While the food and service can be a little up and down, it's a cosy, intimate setting for a drink and tapas. Choose from tables on the ground floor, the mezzanine lounge or the rooftop terrace, sometimes accompanied by live acoustic music. Tapas 45dh, wines 65–135dh (bottle). Daily 6.30–11pm.

Taros 14 2 Rue de la Skala (overlooking Pl Prince Moulay el Hassan), ☎0524 476407, ⓦ taroscafe.com. Perhaps the best nightlife venue in town, on a rooftop terrace overlooking the main square. Ccome here for the happy vibe, great views, and drinks that aren't cheap but include cocktails and a good selection of wines and beer. There's live music some nights, especially during the Gnaoua Festival, and even the odd mingling musician. Beers from 35dh, cocktails from 95dh. Daily noon–3.30pm & 6.30–11pm.

★ **La Triskalla** 58 Rue Touahen ☎0524 476371. A friendly, chilled-out café-restaurant popular with a younger crowd of both locals and travellers; the dimly lit interior adds to the relaxed atmosphere. The menu offers healthy, light food, including some welcome vegetarian dishes, and there's a good selection of fresh juices and herbal teas. Occasionally there are art exhibitions, live music or film nights. Juices and teas 10–18dh. Daily noon–4pm & 6–10.30pm.

DIRECTORY

Banks Attijariwafa Bank and Banque Populaire, both Pl Prince Moulay el Hassan; BMCE, 8 Rue Hajjali (next to *Patisserie Chez Driss*); Société Générale, Av Okba Ibn Nafia; Attijariwafa Bank, 60 Av de l'Istiqlal.

Bookshops Galerie Aide, 2 Rue Skala, run by a former New Yorker, has a small and overpriced selection of secondhand English-language books. Jack's Kiosk on Pl Prince Moulay el Hassan offers a good range of English-language fiction and coffee table books.

Festivals A dozen or so local moussems, fairs and festivals are held between March and October. The main event is the Festival d'Essaouira (ⓦ festival-gnaoua.net) in late June, which focuses on a fusion of Gnaoua and world music.

Golf Golf de Mogador, Diabat (36 holes; ☎0524 479230, ⓦ golfdemogador.com).

Hammam Hammam Mounia, Rue d'Oum Rabia (near *Riad le Grand Large*; daily: women 3–8.30pm, men 5.30–8.30pm; ☎0524 334983). Luxpa, 12 Rue Drâa (off Rue el Attarin; daily 10am–10pm; ☎0524 476044, ⓦ luxpa -essaouira.com), offers massage and beauty treatments as well as a hammam.

Internet access There are numerous internet cafés on Av de L'Istiqlal, some open all day, every day. There is also Internet Club on Av du Caire, next to the tourist office (daily 9am–11pm; 10dh/hr).

Post office Rue Laâlouj, Medina; Av Lalla Aicha.

Shopping Despite its size, Essaouira rivals Marrakesh and Fez as a centre for attractive items, and it's relatively hassle-free. As usual, however, beware of tourist emporiums selling *trafika* (simulated antiques and fossils) – tiles with Hebrew lettering, supposedly old tiles from the Mellah, are a favourite scam here, and any shop selling them is probably worth avoiding. Hippy-style clothing is a good buy in Essaouira – a couple of shops on Rue el Hajjali are good for tunics and drawstring trousers. Thuya wood crafts are also good value (see p.299), and paintings by local artists are worth a look. Argan oil (see box, p.474) and its associated beauty products are widely sold but relatively pricey: Co-operative Tamounte at 6 Rue Souss is a good place for argan oil and thuya wood crafts, both made by local co-operatives. Of the souks, worth particular attention are the Marché d'Epices (spice market) and Souk des Bijoutiers (jewellers' market), on either side of Rue Mohammed Zerktouni.

South of Essaouira

The main road south from Essaouira offers some pleasant exploration, especially if you have your own transport. There are a number of hamlets and villages dotted along the coast, most of them the domain of wind-and wave surfers.

WATERSPORTS AROUND ESSAOUIRA

Essaouira and its nearby beaches are Morocco's prime **wind- and kitesurfing** destinations, drawing enthusiasts throughout the year. The trade wind at Essaouira is northwesterly and blows year-round; it's stronger in summer – if you're inexperienced try to get out early in the morning – but the swell is bigger in winter. The winds can be quite strong (sails required are 5.03.5) but the curved shape of Essaouira's bay, along with a gently sloping sandy bottom that creates a wide shallow area along the shoreline, makes it ideal for novices. Even during summer the water temperature rises only to 20ºC maximum, so a wet suit is required all year. There are numerous **surf shops** and schools in Essaouira, as well as one or two in Sidi Kaouiki and Point Imsouane (see below) further south. **Surfers** should be warned that for most of the year Essouaria's nonstop winds, though great for windsurfing, can be a disappointment for board surfing and you might be better off down at Point Imsouane with its easterly facing bay.

EQUIPMENT

Gipsy Surfer 14 Rue de Tetouan ☎0524 783268. Sells new and used surfing and windsurfing equipment, as well as a small range of accessories, surfwear and surfing DVDs.

Club Mistral Hotel Ocean Vagabond ☎0524 479222, ⌨oceanvagabond.com. Has a surf school at the far southern end of the beach where it also offers kitesurfing lessons and rents out kayaks, surfboards, kitesurfing and windsurfing equipment.

No Work Team 2 Rue Skala & 7 Rue Houmam el Fatouki ☎0524 475272. This British-owned place sells surfwear and surfing equipment from its two shops.

The Royal Windsurfing Club (Royal Club de Planche à Voile) Av Mohammed V ☎0670 577411. Offers windsurfing lessons.

Sidi Kaouki and around

The beach at **SIDI KAOUKI**, 20km south of Essaouira, attracts **windsurfers** virtually year-round, and wind generators have been installed to supply up to 95 percent of the village's electricity. For a village of only 120 or so inhabitants, it has an astonishing amount of **accommodation** (see opposite), though very little else including no banks.

Near the beach is the original **Marabout of Sidi Kaouki**, which has a reputation for curing female sterility, and beyond that is **Cap Sim**, backed by long expanses of dunes.

On towards Agadir

For off-road vehicles, the *pistes* south along the coast from Sidi Kaouki offer a mix of long strands, dunes and scenic headlands, with occasional blue-painted fishing boats. Eventually the main road (N1) is rejoined north of **Smimou**, a one-street town with a petrol station and a couple of café-restaurants. A few kilometres before Smimou, a metalled road which soon turns to *piste* leads west to **Ifrane**, one of the finest but most isolated beaches on this stretch of coast.

Inland, just south of Smimou, lies the forested whaleback of **Jebel Amsittene** (905m). A challenging *piste* climbs to traverse the crest of this grand viewpoint, and descends not far from **Imi n'Tilt**, a busy Monday souk, and a recommended venture if you have 4WD. A little further south of Smimou, another scenic *piste* leads westward to **Cap Tafelney**, below which lies a curious village and a bay full of fishing boats.

The coast is rockier if approached from **Tamanar**, a larger town with a few restaurants. Fifteen kilometres south, a surfaced road leads to **Pointe Imsouane**, which used to be a picturesque little harbour with a few fishermen's cottages, but is now overlooked by an increasing number of apartment blocks. No matter what swell, tide or wind condition prevails, its two bays should offer something for all surfers and windsurfers. Two **surf schools**, Kahina (⌨kahinasurfschool.com, lessons between 220–330dh/2hr session) and Planet Surf Morocco, and the Marok'n'Roll Surf Shop, which rents out secondhand surf gear, are all within fifty metres of each other down near the market.

ARRIVAL AND DEPARTURE

SIDI KAOUKI

By bus Bus #2 runs 9 times daily between Essaouira's Bab Doukkala and Sidi Kaouki (30min).

POINTE IMSOUANE

By public transport Buses and grands taxis running between Essaouira and Agadir can stop at Tamanar, from where there are irregular grands taxis down to Point Imsouane. A chartered grand taxi costs 200dh one way from Essaouira, and 150dh one way from Agadir.

ACCOMMODATION AND EATING

SIDI KAOUKI

There are a couple of restaurants at the village's entrance, as well as a few other café-restaurants scattered along the beachfront road. Light meals and cold beer are also available at the landmark Sidi Kaouki Surfclub (ⓦsidi -kaouki.com), which rents out gear for surfers, windsurfers and kitesurfers.

Camping Kaouki Beach ☎0612 223330. Barren but friendly site accessed from the beachfront road. There's a small ablution block and the secure site is fenced with the local limestone. 80dh

Résidence La Kaouki ☎0524 783206, ⓦsidikaouki .com. Rustic retreat that oozes simplicity and warmth. Electricity-free, the en-suite rooms are candlelit, the water is heated by gas and wood, and the meals are as authentic as they come. BB 330dh

★ **Villa Soleil** ☎0670 233097, ⓦhotelvillasoleil .com. Wonderful little place set back from the beachfront, with bungalows in a spacious garden as well as a larger villa. The Belgian owner-managers run a tight and happy ship, with spotless rooms and a very good in-house restaurant. BB 374dh

POINTE IMSOUANE

Around the village's small square and continuing for 100m down to the water's edge are a string of café-restaurants, as well as a small patisserie that does fresh juices and delicious crêpes.

Auberge Tasra Imsouane village, southern entrance ☎0528 820597. More a hostel than a hotel, offering rooms and dorms with shared bathrooms, a self-catering kitchen, and yoga, amid a laidback vibe. There's also a licensed restaurant open to non-residents. Dorm 70dh, double 160dh

Camping Imsouane Imsouane village, southern entrance, opposite Auberge Tasra ⓦmorocco-camping .com. Badly neglected until recently, this friendly site has been upgraded with modern ablutions, water access and trees planted for shade (but no electricity). Meals are available across the road at *Auberge Tasra*, and all sites have glorious, sweeping ocean views. 60dh

Kahina l'Auberge ☎0528 826032, ⓦkahinasurfschool.com. Home to Kahina Surf School with a prime site overlooking Imoucha, the east bay. The basic but comfortable rooms open onto a central grassed courtyard, showers are shared and there's constant hot water. There's also a restaurant with good seafood and great sea views from a shaded terrace, open to non-residents. Singles available (180dh). 330dh

4

Marrakesh

THE JEMAA EL FNA

5

Marrakesh

Marrakesh – "Morocco City", as early foreign travellers called it – has always been something of a marketplace where tribesmen and Berber villagers bring their goods, spend their money and find entertainment. At its heart is the Jemaa el Fna, an open space in the centre of the city, and the stage for a long-established ritual in which shifting circles of onlookers gather round groups of acrobats, drummers, pipe musicians, dancers, storytellers, comedians and fairground acts. The city's architectural attractions are no less compelling: the magnificent ruin of the El Badi Palace, the delicate carving of the Saadian Tombs and, above all, the Koutoubia Minaret, the most perfect Islamic monument in North Africa.

It won't take you long to see why Marrakesh is called the **Red City**. The natural red ochre pigment that bedecks its walls and buildings can at times seem dominant, but there's no shortage of other colours. Like all Moroccan cities, it's a town of two halves: the ancient walled **Medina**, founded by Sultan Youssef Ben Tachfine in the Middle Ages, and the colonial **Ville Nouvelle**, built by the French in the mid-twentieth century. Each has its own delights – the Medina with its ancient palaces and mansions, labyrinthine souks and deeply traditional way of life, and the Ville Nouvelle with its pavement cafés, trendy boutiques, gardens and boulevards.

Marrakesh has become Morocco's **capital of chic**, attracting the rich and famous from Europe and beyond. Though the vast majority of its residents are poor by any European standard, an increasing number of wealthy foreigners are taking up residence and their influence on the tourist experience is evident.

Marrakesh has **Berber** rather than Arab origins, having developed as the metropolis of Atlas tribes. Once upon a time, it was the entrepôt for goods – slaves, gold, ivory and even "Morocco" leather – brought by caravan from the ancient empires of Mali and Songhay via their great desert port of Timbuktu. All of these strands of commerce and population shaped the city's souks and its way of life, and even today, in the crowds and performers of the Jemaa el Fna, the nomadic and West African influence can still seem quite distinct.

Despite its size and the maze of its souks, Marrakesh is not too hard to **navigate**. The broad, open space of the **Jemaa el Fna** is at the heart of the Medina, with the main souks to its north, and most of the main sights within easy walking distance. Just west of the Jemaa el Fna is the unmistakable landmark of the **Koutoubia** Minaret, and from here, the city's main artery, **Avenue Mohammed V**, leads out through the Medina walls at Bab Nkob and up the length of **Guéliz**, the downtown area of the Ville Nouvelle. You might want to consider hiring a **guide** (see p.340) to explore the Medina, but given a decent map, it really isn't necessary.

MAJORELLE GARDEN

Highlights

❶ Jemaa el Fna The world's most amazing city square: an open-air circus of snake charmers, acrobats, musicians and storytellers. **See p.318**

❷ Koutoubia Mosque Simple but beautifully proportioned, its minaret is the most perfect in North Africa, and a classic piece of Almohad architecture. **See p.320**

❸ Almoravid koubba This tiny ablutions kiosk is the last remnant of the original city, and the only intact Almoravid building in Morocco. **See p.324**

❹ Ben Youssef Medersa Stucco, zellij tilework, and carved cedarwood mark this beautiful medersa. **See p.325**

❺ El Badi Palace The "Incomparable Palace", now an incomparable ruin. **See p.329**

❻ Bahia Palace The ideal of Arabic domestic architecture expressed in a nineteenth-century politician's mansion. **See p.332**

❼ Majorelle Garden A sublime garden, with cacti, lily ponds, and an Islamic Arts museum housed in a stunning pavilion. **See p.336**

❽ Riads One of the joys of Marrakesh is a stay in a well-chosen riad, a beautiful old house imprinted with the personality of its *patron*. **See p.343**

HIGHLIGHTS ARE MARKED ON THE MAP ON PP.314–315

5

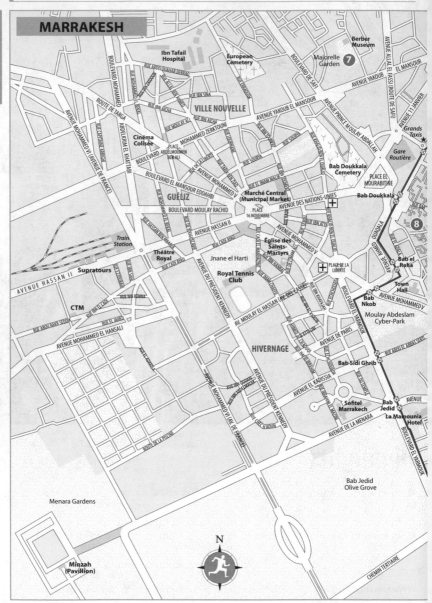

Brief history

Marrakesh was founded near the beginning of **Almoravid** rule, by the first Almoravid dynasty ruler, **Youssef Ben Tachfine**, around 1062–70. It must at first have taken the form of a camp and market with a *ksour*, or fortified town, gradually developing round it. The first seven-kilometre **circuit of walls** was raised in 1126–27, replacing an earlier stockade of thorn bushes. These, many times rebuilt, are essentially the city's present walls – made of *tabia*, the red mud of the plains, mixed and strengthened with lime.

5

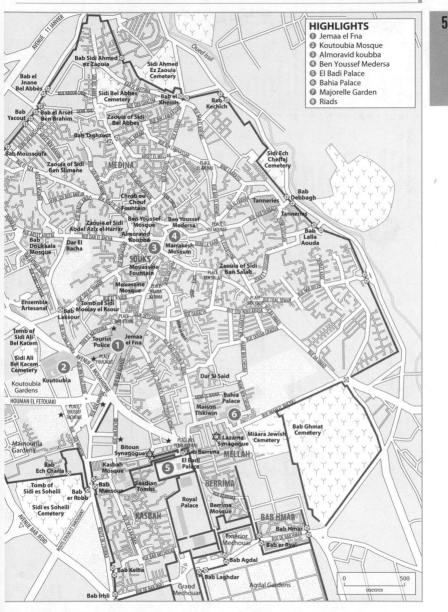

HIGHLIGHTS
1. Jemaa el Fna
2. Koutoubia Mosque
3. Almoravid koubba
4. Ben Youssef Medersa
5. El Badi Palace
6. Bahia Palace
7. Majorelle Garden
8. Riads

The golden age

Of the rest of the Almoravids' building works, hardly a trace remains. The dynasty that replaced them – the **Almohads** – sacked the city for three days after taking possession of it in 1147, but they kept it as their empire's capital.

With the 1184 accession to the throne of the third Almohad sultan, **Yacoub el Mansour**, the city entered its greatest period. *Kissarias* were constructed for the sale and storage of Italian and Oriental cloth, a new kasbah was begun, and a succession of

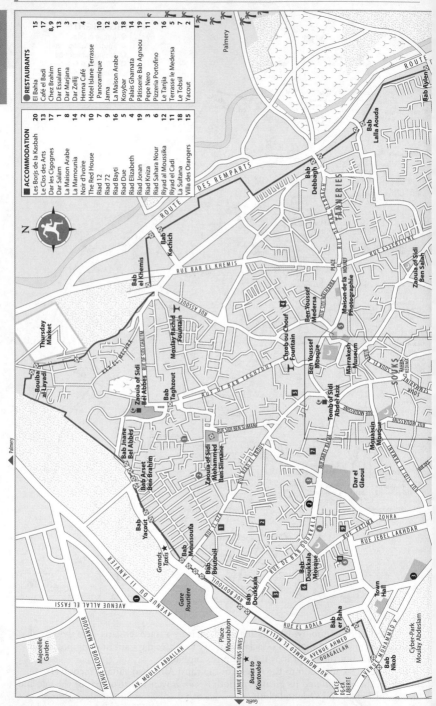

RESTAURANTS

El Bahia	15
Café el Badi	17
Chez Brahim	8,9
Dar Essalam	13
Dar Marjana	3
Dar Zellij	1
Henna Café	4
Hôtel Islane Terrasse	
Panoramique	10
Jama	12
La Maison Arabe	6
Kosybar	18
Pâtisserie Bab Agnaou	14
Pepe Nero	19
Pizzeria Portofino	9
Le Tanjia	16
Terrasse le Medersa	5
Le Tobsil	7
Yacout	2

ACCOMMODATION

Les Borjs de la Kasbah	20
Le Clos des Arts	13
Dar les Cigognes	17
Dar Salam	1
La Maison Arabe	8
La Mamounia	14
Noir d'Ivoire	2
The Red House	10
Riad 12	7
Riad 72	9
Riad Bayti	16
Riad Due	5
Riad Elizabeth	4
Riad Jonan	19
Riad Sahara Nour	6
Riyad al Moussika	12
Riyad el Cadi	11
La Sultana	18
Villa des Orangers	15

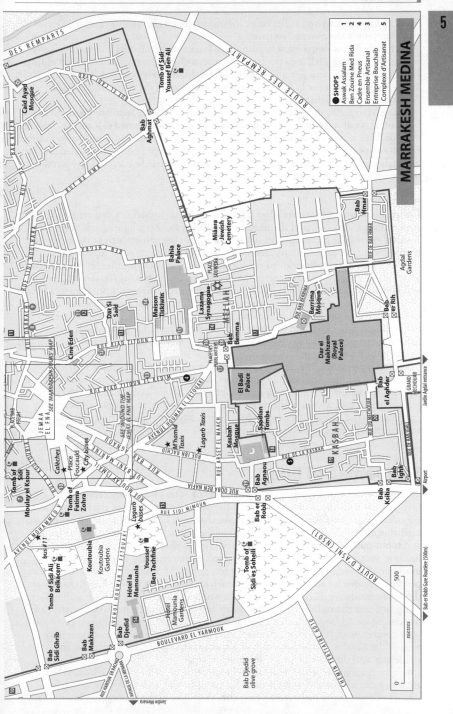

MARRAKESH MEDINA

● **SHOPS**
1 Aswak Assalam
2 Ben Zouine Med Rida
4 Cadre en Pneus
3 Ensemble Artisanal
Entreprise Bouchaib
5 Complexe d'Artisanat

DES REMPARTS

Caid Ayad Mosque

Tomb of Sidi Youssef Ben Ali

Bab Aghmat

ROUTE DES REMPARTS

Miäara Jewish Cemetery

Bahia Palace

Bab Hmar

PLACE SOUWEKA

Maison Tiskiwin

Dar Si Said

Lazama Synagogue

MELLAH

Bab Bemma

Berrima Mosque

RUE BAB BERRIMA

RUE DE BARTHMAR

Agdal Gardens

Bab er Rih

Cine Eden

RUE RIAD ZITOUN EL JEDID

El Badi Palace

Dar el Makhzem (Royal Palace)

PLACE DES FERBLANTIERS

RUE RIAD ZITOUN EL KEDIM

JEMAA EL FNA

SEE AROUND THE JEMAA EL FNA MAP

SEE MARRAKESH SOUKS MAP

Place Foucauld

Calèches

City buses

AVENUE HOUMAN EL FEETOUAKI

M'hamid Taxis

Lagarb Taxis

RUE BAB AGNAOU

RUE ASSEL EL MAACH

Kasbah Mosque

Saadian Tombs

KASBAH

Bab el Aghdar

GRAND MECHOUAR

Jardin Agdal entrance

Tomb of Sidi Moulay el Ksour

Tomb of Fatima Zohra

RUE DE LA KASBAH

Bab Ighli

Bab Agnaou

Bab Ksiba

RUE IBN RACHID

RUE OQBA BEN NAFIA

Lagarb buses

RUE SIDI MIMOUN

Bab el Robb

Airport

Koutoubia Gardens

Tomb of Sidi Ali Belkacem

Youssef Ben Tachfine

AVENUE HOUMAN EL FEETOUAKI

Koutoubia Gardens

Tomb of Sidi es Soheil

ROUTE D'ASNI (N501)

Hôtel la Mamounia

Bab Djedid

Bab Makhzen

Bab Sidi Ghrib

Hotel Mamounia Gardens

AVENUE HOUMAN EL FEETOUAKI

BOULEVARD EL YARMOUK

Bab Djedid olive grove

RUE HAROUN ER RACHID

MICHAEL DE LA MENARA

Jardin Menara

Bab er Robb Gare Routière (500m)

CHEMIN TERTIAIRE 6010

0   metres   500

AVENUE MOHAMMED V

5

poets and scholars arrived at the court. Mansour's reign also saw the construction of the great **Koutoubia Mosque** and minaret.

By the 1220s, the empire was beginning to fragment amid a series of factional civil wars, and Marrakesh fell into the familiar pattern of pillage, ruination and rebuilding. In 1269, it lost its status as capital when the Fez-based **Merenids** took power, though in 1374–86 it did form the basis of a breakaway state under the Merenid pretender Abderrahman Ibn Taflusin.

Taking Marrakesh, then devastated by famine, in 1521, the **Saadians** provided a last burst of imperial splendour. Their dynasty's greatest figure, **Ahmed el Mansour**, having invaded Mali and seized control of the most lucrative caravan routes in Africa, had the **El Badi Palace** – Marrakesh's largest and greatest building project – constructed from the proceeds of this new wealth, and the dynasty also of course bequeathed to Marrakesh their wonderful mausoleum, the **Saadian Tombs**.

Modern times

Under the **Alaouites** Marrakesh lost its status as capital to Meknes, but remained an important imperial city, and the need to maintain a southern base against the tribes ensured the regular presence of its sultans. But from the seventeenth to the nineteenth century, it shrank back from its medieval walls and lost much of its former trade.

During the last decades prior to the Protectorate, the city's fortunes revived somewhat as it enjoyed a return to favour with the Shereefian court. **Moulay Hassan** (1873–94) and **Moulay Abd el Aziz** (1894–1908) both ran their governments from here in a bizarre closing epoch of the old ways, accompanied by a final bout of frantic palace building. On the arrival of **the French**, Marrakesh gave rise to a short-lived pretender, the religious leader El Hiba, and for most of the colonial period it was run as a virtual fiefdom of its pasha, **T'hami el Glaoui** – the most powerful, autocratic and extraordinary character of his age (see p.327).

Since **independence**, the city has undergone considerable change, with rural emigration from the Atlas and beyond, new methods of cultivation on the Haouz plain and the development of a sizeable tourist industry. After Casablanca, it's Morocco's second largest city, with slightly over a million inhabitants, and its population continues to rise. It has a thriving industrial area and is the most important market and administrative centre of southern Morocco.

The Jemaa el Fna

There's nowhere in Morocco like the **Jemaa el Fna** – no place that so effortlessly involves you and keeps you coming back for more. By day, most of the square is just a big open space, in which a handful of **snake charmers** bewitch their cobras with flutes, **medicine men** (especially in the northeast of the square) display cures and nostrums, and **tooth-pullers**, wielding fearsome pliers, offer to pluck the pain from out of the heads of toothache sufferers, trays of extracted molars attesting to their skill. It isn't until late afternoon that the square really gets going. At dusk, as in France and Spain, people come out for an early evening promenade (especially in Rue Bab Agnaou), and the square gradually fills until it becomes a whole carnival of storytellers, acrobats, musicians and entertainers. Come on down and you'll soon be immersed in the ritual: wandering round, squatting amid the circles of onlookers, giving a dirham or two as your contribution. If you want a respite, you can move over to the rooftop terraces, such as the *Café du Grand Balcon*, for a vista over the square, its storytellers and musicians, and the crowds who come to see them.

As a foreigner in the Jemaa, you can feel something of an interloper. Most of the crowd are Moroccan of course (few foreigners, for example, will understand the storytellers' tales), but tourists also make a major contribution to both the atmosphere and the cash

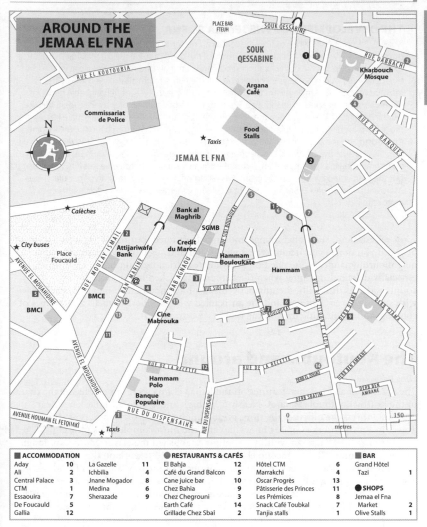

AROUND THE JEMAA EL FNA

■ ACCOMMODATION				● RESTAURANTS & CAFÉS				■ BAR	
Aday	10	La Gazelle	11	El Bahja	12	Hôtel CTM	6	Grand Hôtel	
Ali	2	Ichbilia	4	Café du Grand Balcon	5	Marrakchi	4	Tazi	1
Central Palace	3	Jnane Mogador	8	Cane juice bar	10	Oscar Progrès	13		
CTM	1	Medina	6	Chez Bahia	9	Pâtisserie des Princes	11	● SHOPS	
Essaouira	7	Sherazade	9	Chez Chegrouni	3	Les Prémices	8	Jemaa el Fna	
De Foucauld	5			Earth Café	14	Snack Café Toubkal	7	Market	2
Gallia	12			Grillade Chez Sbaï	2	Tanjia stalls	1	Olive Stalls	1

flow. Sometimes a storyteller or musician may pick on you to take part or contribute generously to the end-of-show collection and, entering into the spectacle, it's best to go denuded of the usual tourist trappings such as watches, money-belts or too much money; **pickpockets** and scam artists operate (giving a "present" and then demanding payment for it is an old scam to beware of, asking tourists to change counterfeit euro coins is a more recent one). The crowds around performers are sometimes used as an opportunity to grope female foreigners, and by male Moroccans and gay male tourists for cruising.

Sideshow attractions include games of hoop-the-bottle, **fortune-tellers** sitting under umbrellas with packs of fortune-telling cards at the ready and women with piping bags full of **henna** paste, ready to paint hands, feet or arms with "tattoos" that will last up to three months, though beware of synthetic "black henna", which contains a toxic chemical; only red henna is natural (the *Henna Café* guarantees to use only natural henna; see p.346).

5

THE DEVELOPMENT OF THE JEMAA EL FNA

Nobody is entirely sure when or how the Jemaa el Fna came into being – nor even what its **name** means. The usual translation is "assembly of the dead", a suitably epic title that may refer to the public display here of the heads of rebels and criminals (the Jemaa was a place of execution until well into the nineteenth century). The name might alternatively mean "the mosque of nothing" (Jemaa means both "mosque" and "assembly" – interchangeable terms in Islamic society), recalling an abandoned Saadian plan to build a new grand mosque on this site.

Either way, as an open area between the original kasbah and the souks, the square has probably played its present role since the city's earliest days. It has often been the focal point for **rioting** and the authorities have plotted before now to close it down and move its activities outside the city walls. This happened briefly after independence in 1956, when the government built a corn market on part of the square and tried to turn the rest into a car park, but the plan lasted barely a year. Tourism was falling off and it was clearly an unpopular move. As novelist Paul Bowles observed, without the Jemaa, Marrakesh would be just another Moroccan city.

For refreshment, stalls offer orange and grapefruit juice (but have it squeezed in front of you if you don't want it adulterated with water and sugar, or even squash), while neighbouring handcarts are piled high with dates, dried figs, almonds and walnuts, especially delicious in winter when they are freshly picked in the surrounding countryside. As dusk falls, the square becomes a huge open-air dining area, packed with stalls lit by gas lanterns, and the air is filled with wonderful smells and plumes of cooking smoke spiralling up into the night (see box, p.345).

The Koutoubia and around

Avenue Mohammed V

The absence of architectural features on the Jemaa el Fna serves to emphasize the drama of the nearby **Koutoubia Minaret**. Nearly 70m high and visible for miles on a clear morning, this is the oldest of the three great Almohad towers (the others are the Hassan Tower in Rabat and the Giralda in Seville) and the most complete. Its pleasing proportions – a 1:5 ratio of width to height – established the classic Moroccan design.

Completed under Sultan Yacoub el Mansour (1184–99), work on the minaret probably began shortly after the Almohad conquest of the city, around 1150. It displays many of the features that were to become widespread in Moroccan architecture – the wide band of ceramic inlay near the top, the pyramid-shaped, castellated *merlons* (battlements) rising above it, the use of *darj w ktaf* ("cheek and shoulder"; see p.579) and other motifs – and it also established the alternation of patterning on different faces. Here, the top floor is similar on each of the sides but the lower two are almost eccentric in their variety. The semicircle of small lobed arches on the middle niche of the southeast face was to become the dominant decorative feature of Almohad gates. The three great copper balls at the top are the subject of numerous legends, mostly of supernatural interventions to keep away thieves. They are thought to have originally been made of gold, the gift of the wife of Yacoub el Mansour, presented as penance for breaking her fast for three hours during Ramadan.

Close to the arches, the stones of the main body of the tower become slightly smaller, which seems odd today, but not originally, when the whole minaret was covered with plaster and painted, like that of the Kasbah Mosque (see p.328). There was talk about restoring this on the Koutoubia back in 2000, but the authorities settled for a straight clean-up – to stunning effect, especially when it's floodlit at night. At the same time, archeologists excavated the original mosque, which predates the tower, confirming that it had had to be rebuilt to correct its alignment with Mecca.

Tomb of Fatima Zohra

Alongside the mosque, and close to Avenue Mohammed V, is the **tomb of Fatima Zohra**, now in a white *koubba*. She was the daughter of a seventeenth-century religious leader and tradition has it that she was a woman by day and a white dove by night; women still dedicate their children to her in the belief that her blessing will protect them.

Koutoubia Gardens

To the south and west of the Koutoubia are the **Koutoubia Gardens**, attractively laid out with pools and fountains, roses, orange trees and palms, very handy for an afternoon stroll, and giving excellent views of the Koutoubia.

Hôtel la Mamounia

Avenue Bab Jdid • Non-guests Mon–Fri 11am–4pm, or daily 11am–midnight with 1500dh day pass, includes lunch and access to pool, spa, gardens • Dress code enforced: no jeans or trainers, and clothes must be deemed sufficiently "elegant" for entry

The luxurious **Hôtel la Mamounia**, has been rebuilt and enlarged since the days when Winston Churchill and Franklin Roosevelt stayed here, although the **Winston Churchill suite** (usually open only to hotel guests) is preserved as visited by its namesake. Decoratively, the hotel is of most interest for the 1920s Art Deco touches of **Jacques Majorelle** (see p.336), and their enhancements, in 1986, by King Hassan II's then favourite designer, André Paccard.

The *Mamounia's* **gardens** were once royal grounds, laid out by the Saadians with a succession of pavilions. Today they're slightly Europeanized in style but have retained the traditional elements of shrubs and walkways. Winston Churchill, who liked to paint in the gardens, described them to Franklin D. Roosevelt – when they were here together in 1943 – as the loveliest spot in the world.

The souks

It is spicy in the souks, and cool and colourful. The smell, always pleasant, changes gradually with the nature of the merchandise. There are no names or signs; there is no glass… You find everything – but you always find it many times over.

Elias Canetti: *The Voices of Marrakesh*

The **souks** north of the Jemaa el Fna seem vast the first time you venture in, and almost impossible to navigate, but in fact the area that they cover is pretty compact. A long, covered street, **Rue Souk Smarine**, runs for half their length and then splits into two lanes – **Souk el Attarin** and **Souk el Kebir**. Off these are virtually all the individual souks: alleys and small squares devoted to specific crafts, where you can often watch part of the production process.

If you are staying for some days, you'll probably return often to the souks – and this is a good way of taking them in, singling out a couple of specific crafts or products to see, rather than being swamped by the whole. To get to grips with the general layout, you might find it useful to walk round the whole area once with a **guide**, but it's certainly not essential: with a reasonable map, you can quite easily navigate the souks on your own, and besides, getting a little bit lost is all part of the fun.

The most interesting **times** to visit are in the early morning (6.30–8am) and late afternoon, at around 4 to 5pm, when some of the souks auction off goods to local traders. Later in the evening, most of the stalls are closed, but you can wander unharassed to take a look at the elaborate decoration of their doorways and arches; those stalls that stay open, until 7 or 8pm, are often more amenable to bargaining at the end of the day.

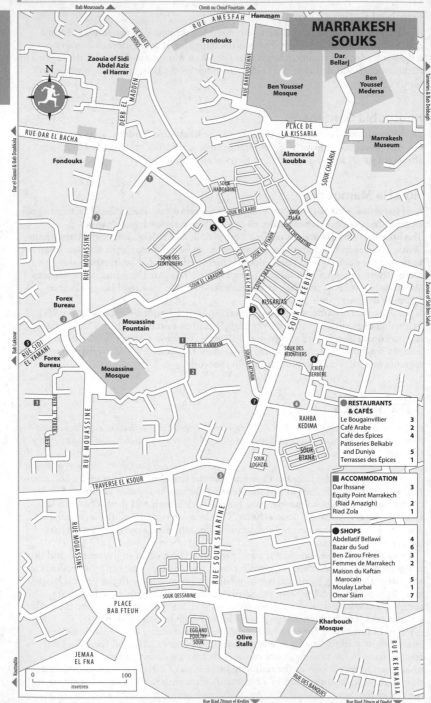

RUE AMESFAH

Hammam

MARRAKESH SOUKS

RUE KHAT EL ARROUS

DERB EL MADDEN

Fondouks

RUE BAROUDIENNE

Zaouia of Sidi Abdel Aziz el Harrar

Dar Bellarj

N

Ben Youssef Mosque

Ben Youssef Medersa

Tanneries & Bab Debbagh

Dar el Glaoui & Bab Doukkala

RUE DAR EL BACHA

PLACE DE LA KISSARIA

Fondouks

Almoravid koubba

SOUK CHAARIA

Marrakesh Museum

RUE MOUASSINE

①

②

SOUK HABDADINE

SOUK BELAARIF

①

②

SOUK TALAA

SOUK GHERBATINE

SOUK DES TEINTURIERS

SOUK EL LABADINE

SOUK KHACHBIA

SOUK EL ATTARIN

SOUK SMATA

SOUK EL KEBIR

Zaouia of Sidi Ben Salah

Forex Bureau

③

Mouassine Fountain

DERB EL HAMMAM

①

KISSARIAS

③

④

Bab Laksour

⑤

RUE SIDI EL YAMANI

Forex Bureau

Mouassine Mosque

②

SOUK EL ATTARIN

SOUK DES BIJOUTIERS

⑥

CRIÉE BERBÈRE

③

DERB CHORFA EL KEBIR

⑦

④

RAHBA KEDIMA

● **RESTAURANTS & CAFÉS**
Le Bougainvillier ... 3
Café Arabe ... 2
Café des Épices ... 4
Patisseries Belkabir and Duniya ... 5
Terrasses des Épices ... 1

RUE MOUASSINE

TRAVERSE EL KSOUR

⑤

SOUK LOGHZAL

SOUK BTANA

RUE SOUK SMARINE

■ **ACCOMMODATION**
Dar Ihssane ... 3
Equity Point Marrakech (Riad Amazigh) ... 2
Riad Zola ... 1

● **SHOPS**
Abdellatif Bellawi ... 4
Bazar du Sud ... 6
Ben Zarou Frères ... 3
Femmes de Marrakech ... 2
Maison du Kaftan Marocain ... 5
Moulay Larbai ... 1
Omar Siam ... 7

PLACE BAB FTEUH

SOUK QESSABINE

JEMAA EL FNA

EGG AND POULTRY SOUK

Olive Stalls

Kharbouch Mosque

RUE KENNARIA

Koutoubia

0 ——— 100
metres

The easiest approach to the main souks from the Jemaa el Fna is opposite Rue des Banques (see map, p.319), where a lane to the left of the *Terrasses de l'Alhambra* restaurant leads to Souk Ableuh, dominated by stalls selling olives. Continue through here and you will come out opposite the archway that marks the beginning of Rue Souk Smarine.

Souk Smarine

Busy and crowded, **Rue Souk Smarine** is an important thoroughfare, traditionally dominated by textiles and clothing. Today, tourist "bazaars" are moving in, but there are still dozens of shops in the arcades selling and tailoring traditional shirts and kaftans. The street is covered by an iron trellis with slats across it that restrict the sun to shafts of light; this replaces the old rush (*smar*) roofing, which along with many of the souks' more beautiful features was destroyed by a fire in the 1960s.

Rahba Kedima

To the east of Souk Smarine, **Rahba Kedima** is an open square with stalls set up in the middle selling baskets, hats and souvenirs. Around its southwestern corner, **Apothecary stalls** sell traditional cosmetics – earthenware saucers of cochineal (*kashiniah*) for lip-rouge, powdered *kohl* (traditionally made of stibnite, a mineral form of antimony trisulphide, but commonly substituted with cheaper lead sulphide – both are toxic) for darkening the edges of the eyes, henna (the only cosmetic unmarried women are supposed to use) and the sticks of *suak* (walnut root or bark) with which you see Moroccans cleaning their teeth. The same stalls also sell herbal and animal ingredients still in widespread use for spells and medicinal cures. As well as aphrodisiac roots and tablets, you'll see dried pieces of lizard and stork, fragments of beaks, talons and other bizarre animal products. Some shops (to be avoided) also sell gazelle skulls, leopard skins and other products from illegally poached endangered wild animals.

La Criée Berbère

On the north side of Rahba Kedima, a passageway leads through to a bustling, carpet-draped area known as **La Criée Berbère** (the Berber auction). **Slave auctions** used to be held here, until the French occupied the city in 1912, They were conducted, according to travel writer Budgett Meakin's 1900 account (see p.568), "precisely as those of cows and mules, often on the same spot by the same men…with the human chattels being personally examined in the most disgusting manner, and paraded in lots by the auctioneers, who shout their attractions and the bids". Most had been kidnapped and brought in with the caravans from Mali, travelling on foot – those too weak to make it were left to die en route.

These days, the souk specializes in **rugs and carpets**, and if you have the time and willpower you could spend the best part of a day here while endless (and often identical) stacks are unfolded and displayed before you. Some of the most interesting are the Berber rugs from the High Atlas – bright, geometric designs that look very different after being laid out on the roof and bleached by the sun. The dark, often black, backgrounds usually signify rugs from the Glaoui country, up towards Telouet; the reddish-backed carpets are from Chichaoua (see box, p.339).

Around the kissarias

The **kissarias**, lying between Souk el Attarin and Souk el Kebir, are the covered markets at the heart of the souks, mostly selling blankets, clothes and leather goods. To the east of Souk el Kebir, **Souk des Bijoutiers** is a modest jewellers' lane, less varied than the one established by Jewish craftsmen in the Mellah (see p.331).

5

At the northern end of Souk el Kebir is a convoluted web of alleys that comprise the **Souk Cherratine**, essentially a leather workers' souk, with dozens of purse-makers and sandal cobblers. If you bear left through this area and then turn right (or vice versa), you should arrive at Place de la Kissaria (see below).

The Dyers' Souk and around

West of the *kissarias*, **Souk el Attarin**, originally the spice and perfume souk, forks at its northern end. The street leading east, along the edge of the *kissarias* is **Souk Smata**, also called the **Souk des Babouches** (slipper market). Lined with shops selling Moroccan slippers, it eventually leads through to Souk Cherratine (see above).

The western fork from Souk el Attarin is **Souk Kchachbia**, which contains some interesting shops including Femmes de Marrakech (see p.353) and, directly behind it, Moulay Larbai's mirror shop. A right turn just past Femmes de Marrakech, by Moulay Larbai's shop, leads to **Souk Haddadine**, the blacksmiths' souk, whose banging and clanging you'll hear long before arriving. Before you get that far, the first and second left off Souk Kchachbia (if coming from Souk el Attarin) both lead through to **Souk des Teinturiers**, the dyers' souk, the area's main attraction, and always colourful, hung with bright skeins of wool or fabric drying in the sun. You can also usually catch some of the dyers at work, pounding cloth in their big vats of coloured liquid.

West of the dyers' souk, the street widens out into a square opposite an elaborate triple-bayed **fountain** adjoining the Mouassine Mosque. Built in the mid-sixteenth century under the prolific Saadian builder, Abdallah el Ghalib, it is one of many such fountains in Marrakesh with a basin for humans set next to two larger troughs for animals; its installation was a pious act, directly sanctioned by the Koran in its charitable provision of water for men and beasts.

Around Place de la Kissaria

Place de la Kissaria, an open space surrounded by important public buildings, sits at the northern end of the souks area. Its north side is dominated by the **Ben Youssef Mosque**, successor to an original put up by the city's Almoravid founders. The mosque was completely rebuilt under the Almohads, and several times since, so that the building you see today dates largely from the nineteenth century.

The Marrakesh Museum

East side of Place de la Kissaria • Daily 9am–6pm • 40dh; combined ticket with Ben Youssef Medersa and Almoravid *koubba* 60dh

The **Marrakesh Museum** is housed in a magnificent late nineteenth-century palace, **Dar Mnebbi**. The palace was built for Mehdi Mnebbi, defence minister of Moulay Abdelziz (1894–1908), who later became Moroccan ambassador in London. Nearly derelict after years of neglect, the palace was bought up and restored by local arts patron Omar Benjoullan, and opened as a museum in 1997. It houses exhibitions of Moroccan art and sculpture, both traditional (in the main hall and surrounding rooms), and contemporary (in what were the palace kitchens). It is the restoration itself, however, that is most remarkable, especially in what was the hammam, and in the now-covered inner courtyard with its huge brass lamp hung above a central fountain.

The Almoravid koubba

On the southern side of Place de la Kissaria • Daily 9am–6pm • 60dh combined ticket with Marrakesh Museum and Ben Youssef Medersa, available from those places (no separate entry tickets available for the *koubba* alone)

The **Almoravid koubba** (Koubba Ba'adiyn) is just a small, two-storey kiosk, but as the only Almoravid building to survive intact in Morocco (excepting possibly a minaret in Tit near El Jadida; see p.293), its style is at the root of all Moroccan architecture. Its motifs – such as pine cones, palms and acanthus leaves – appear again in later buildings such as the nearby Ben Youssef Medersa (see below). The windows on each of the different sides became the classic shapes of Almohad and Merenid design – as did the merlons, the complex "ribs" on the outside of the dome, and the square and star-shaped octagon on the inside, which is itself repeated at each of its corners. It was probably just a small ablutions annexe to the Ben Youssef Mosque, but its architecture gives us our only clue as to what that mosque might originally have looked like.

Excavated only in 1952, the *koubba* had previously been covered over amid the many rebuildings of the Ben Youssef Mosque. It is well below today's ground level, and you have to go down two flights of stairs to get to the level it was built at, now uncovered once again thanks to excavations. Once down there, you can also look around the attendant facilities, including a large water cistern, and remains of latrines and fountains for performing ablutions, much like those you will still find adjacent to many Moroccan mosques.

Ben Youssef Medersa

Derb Zaouiat Lahdar, 30m north of the Marrakesh Museum • Daily 9am–6pm • 50dh, combined ticket with Marrakesh Museum and Almoravid *koubba* 60dh

The **Ben Youssef Medersa** was a koranic school attached to the Ben Youssef Mosque, where students learned the Koran by rote, and is the most beautifully decorated building in Marrakesh, with lashings of classic Moroccan decor – zellij tiling, stucco plasterwork, carved cedarwood – all worked to the very highest standards.

Like most of its counterparts up in Fez, the Ben Youssef was a Merenid foundation, established by the "Black Sultan" Abou el Hassan (1331–49), but rebuilt in the 1560s, under the Saadians. As with the slightly later Saadian Tombs, no surface is left undecorated, and the overall quality of its craftsmanship, whether in carved wood, stuccowork or zellij tilework, is startling.

The **central courtyard**, its carved cedarwood lintels weathered almost flat on the most exposed side, is unusually large. Along two sides run wide, sturdy, columned arcades, which were probably used to supplement the space for teaching in the neighbouring mosque. Above them are some of the windows of the **dormitory quarters**, which are reached by stairs from the entry vestibule, and from which you can get an interesting perspective – and attempt to fathom how over eight hundred students were once housed in the building. One room is furnished as it would have been when in use.

At its far end, the court opens onto a **prayer hall**, where the decoration, mellowed on the outside with the city's familiar pink tone, is at its best preserved and most elaborate, with a predominance of pine cone and palm motifs.

Dar Bellarj

9 Derb Zaouiat Lahdar • Mon–Sat 9am–12.30pm & 2–5.30pm, Ramadan 9am–3pm • Free • Ⓦ darbellarj.org

Just across from the Ben Youssef Medersa, this 1930s mansion has been restored by its French owners, and now houses art exhibitions and sometimes concerts. Dar Bellarj was built on the site of a *fondouk* (merchants' inn) which had been converted into a bird hospital – hence its name, which means "House of the Storks".

East of Place de la Kissaria

The main route between the Ben Youssef Medersa and the city gate of Bab Debbagh is marked at its halfway point by **Place el Moukef**, more an intersection than a square, where

5

four routes meet. Eastward, Rue Souk des Fassis, the road to the Ben Youssef Medersa, is lined by *fondouks* (see box below), while in the opposite direction, Rue du Bab Debbagh passes through the rather smelly tanneries area on its way to Bab Debbagh. Northward, Rue Bab el Khemis leads to another city gate, Bab el Khemis (see opposite), while Rue Essebtiyne, leading south, forks after 200m. Bearing right here (if coming from Place el Moukef), you come to Place Ben Salah, where the **Zaouia of Sidi Ben Salah**, with its very fine and prominent minaret, was commissioned by a fourteenth-century Merenid sultan.

Maison de la Photographie

40 Rue Souk des Fassis • Daily 9.30am–7pm • 40dh • ⓦ maisondelaphotographie.ma

The **Maison de la Photographie** houses a reasonably interesting collection of early twentieth-century (and a few late nineteenth-century) photographs of Morocco, some made from glass negatives. The photographs are exhibited over three floors, with one room dedicated to pictures of the Jemaa el Fna, and the terrace gives good views over the Medina rooftops.

Bab Debbagh

Rue Bab Debbagh

Bab Debbagh is supposedly Almoravid in design, though over the years it must have been almost totally rebuilt. Passing through the gate, you become aware of its very real defensive purpose: three internal chicanes are placed in such a manner as to force anyone attempting to storm it to make several turns. Just before the gate, several shops on the left give good views over the quarter from their roofs, and shopkeepers will let you up (for a small fee – agree it first or you'll be mercilessly overcharged).

The tanneries

Marrakesh's **tanneries**, flanking Rue Bab Debbagh, are more scattered and thus less interesting to look at than those at Fez. They were built at the edge of the city not only because of the smell, but also for access to water: a stream, the Oued Issil, runs just outside the Medina walls. The smell comes largely from the first stage, where the hides are soaked in a vat of pigeon droppings. The natural dyes traditionally used to colour the leather have largely been replaced by chemicals, many of them carcinogenic – a fact to remember when you see people standing waist-deep in them.

FONDOUKS

One of the most characteristic types of building in the Medina is the **fondouk** or caravanserai. Originally inns used by visiting merchants when they were in Marrakesh to trade in its souks, *fondouks* have a courtyard in the middle surrounded by what were originally stables, while the upper level contained rooms for the merchants. Some date back to Saadian times (1520–1669), and some still have fine original woodcarving or stuccowork.

Today, Marrakesh's *fondouks* are in varying states of repair; some have become private residences, others commercial premises. Some have been converted to house tourist souvenir shops and welcome visitors, but even in others, the doors to the courtyards are often left open, and no one seems to mind if you wander in to have a look.

Interesting *fondouks* include: a group on Rue Dar el Bacha by the junction with Rue Mouassine, several of which welcome visitors; a couple just south of the junction on Rue Mouassine itself; a row on the south side of Rue Bab Debbagh, behind the Ben Youssef Medersa; a whole series along Rue Amesfah, north of the Ben Youssef Mosque; and one directly opposite the Chrob ou Chouf fountain. *Terrasse le Medersa* restaurant (see p.348) is on the terrace of a *fondouk*.

If you want to take a closer look at the tanning process, come in the morning, when the cooperatives are at work. One tannery that's easy to find is on the north side of the street about 200m before Bab Debbagh, opposite the blue-tiled stand-up fountain, with another one about 200m further west. Ignore hustlers trying to persuade you that you have to pay them for entry.

Bab el Khemis

Built at an angle in the walls near the Medina's northern end, **Bab el Khemis** is a reconstructed Almoravid gate surrounded by concentric rings of decoration and topped with Christmas-tree-like castellations. Its name means "Thursday Gate", a reference to the market held outside, 400m to the north, past a *marabout*'s tomb and a former cemetery, now landscaped as a little park. Although the main market is held on a Thursday morning, there are stalls out most days. It's really a local produce market, though handicraft items are also sold.

North of the Ben Youssef Mosque

The area immediately **north of the Ben Youssef Mosque** is cut by two main streets: Rue Assouel (which leads up to Bab el Khemis) and Rue Bab Taghzout, which runs up to Bab Taghzout and the Zaouia of Sidi Bel Abbes. These were, with Bab Doukkala, the principal approaches to the city until the twentieth century and along them you find many of the old **fondouks** used for lodging by merchants visiting the souks (see box opposite).

Chrob ou Chouf fountain

Marrakesh's most famous drinking fountain is a small sixteenth-century recessed fountain known as **Chrob ou Chouf** ("drink and look"), most notable for its finely carved cedarwood lintel. You can find it by following Rue Baroudienne north from its junction with Rue Amesfah, and turning right at the end.

The Zaouia of Sidi Bel Abbes
Rue Sidi Bel Abbes

The old city gate of **Bab Taghzout** marked the limits of the Medina from Almoravid times until the eighteenth century, when Sultan Mohammed Abdallah extended the walls to enclose the **Zaouia of Sidi Bel Abbes,** the most important of Marrakesh's seven saints – seven holy men whose tombs were established as a circuit for pilgrims under the Alaouite ruler Moulay Ismail in the seventeenth century to bring tourists into Marrakesh. The **zaouia**, as a cult centre, often wielded great influence and served as a refuge for political dissidents.

EL GLAOUI: THE PASHA OF MARRAKESH

T'hami el Glaoui, Pasha of Marrakesh during the French Protectorate, was the last great southern tribal leader, a shrewd supporter of colonial rule (see box, p.394) and personal friend of Winston Churchill. Cruel and magnificent in equal measure, he was a spectacular party-giver in an age where rivals were not lacking. At the extraordinary *difas* or banquets held at the Dar el Glaoui for his Western friends, "nothing", as Gavin Maxwell wrote, "was impossible." Hashish and opium were freely available, and "to his guests T'hami gave whatever they wanted, whether it might be a diamond ring, a present of money in gold, or a Berber girl or boy from the High Atlas".

As a despot, and agent of colonial rule, he was so hated that, on his death in 1956, a mob looted the palace, destroying its fittings and the cars in its garages, and lynching any of his henchmen that they found. However, passions have burnt out over the years, and the family has been rehabilitated. One of T'hami's sons, Glaoui Abdelssadak, rose to high rank in the Moroccan civil service and became vice president of Gulf Oil.

5

The present buildings date largely from the time of Moulay Ismail, who had them rebuilt, an act probably inspired more by politics than piety. Non-Muslims are not allowed to enter, but may see something of the complex and its activities from outside the official boundary, but they should not try to enter the main courtyard. The *zaouia* has always prospered and still owns much of the quarter to the north and continues its educational and charitable work, distributing food each evening to the blind.

Dar el Glaoui
Rue Dar el Bacha

The **Dar el Glaoui** was the palace of the pasha who ruled Marrakesh on behalf of the French during the colonial period, when he was feted by Europeans, and hated by Marrakshis (see box, p.327). His palace now houses the offices of the UMT trade union federation, and is unfortunately not open to the public.

The southern Medina

The area south of Jemaa el Fna is quite different from that to the north of it, generally more open and home to **Dar el Makhzen** (the royal palace), the **kasbah** (old inner citadel), and the **Mellah** (former Jewish quarter). The two obvious focal sights, not to be missed, are the **Saadian Tombs**, preserved in the shadow of the Kasbah Mosque, and **El Badi**, the ruined palace of Ahmed el Mansour. Also worth seeing are the **Bahia Palace** and the nearby Dar Si Said and Tiskiwin **museums**.

Bab Agnaou

From the Jemaa el Fna, **Rue Bab Agnaou** and its continuations lead to a square flanked by two gates. Directly ahead is **Bab er Robb**, leading out of the Medina towards the High Atlas mountains. To its left, somewhat battered and eroded, is **Bab Agnaou**, one of the two original entrances to the kasbah (citadel), though the magnificent blue granite gateway which stands here today was built in 1885. The name actually means "black people's gate", a reference to its use by swarthy commoners, while the fair-complexioned aristocracy had their own entrance into the kasbah (now long gone). The gate is surrounded by concentric arches of decoration and topped with an inscription in decorative script, which reads: "Enter with blessing, serene people." Notice how the semicircular frieze above the arch creates a three-dimensional effect without any actual depth of carving.

The Kasbah Mosque
On the east side of Bab Agnaou, also directly accessible from Rue Ibn Rachid

The **Kasbah Mosque**, was, as its name suggests, the main Friday mosque for the Kasbah. Its minaret looks gaudy and modern, but in fact it dates from 1190, making it contemporary with the Koutoubia (see p.320). It really was painted green and white back in the day, and was restored to its original state in the 1960s. The rest of the mosque is not original, however, as it was rebuilt after being destroyed when a gunpowder store blew up in 1569.

The Saadian Tombs
Off Place des Tombeaux Saadiens, accessed from a passage on the south side of the Kasbah Mosque • Daily 9am–4.45pm, Ramadan 9am–3pm • 10dh

The **Saadian Tombs** are the kasbah's main sight. Housed in a quiet, high-walled enclosure, shaded with shrubs and palms, they belong to the dynasty that ruled

BURIED IN HISTORY

There was probably a **burial ground** behind the royal palace before the Saadian period, but the earliest tomb here dates from 1557, and the main structures were built under Sultan Ahmed el Mansour, around the same time as the Ben Youssef Medersa and the El Badi Palace. A few prominent Marrakshis continued to be buried in the mausoleums after Saadian times: the last, in 1792, was the "mad sultan", Moulay Yazid, whose 22-month reign was one of the most violent and sadistic in the nation's history. Named as the successor to Sidi Mohammed, Moulay Yazid threw himself into a series of revolts against his father, waged an inconclusive war with Spain, and brutally suppressed a Marrakesh-based rebellion in support of his brother. A massacre followed his capture of the city, though he had little time to celebrate his victory – a bullet in the head during a rebel counterattack killed him soon after.

The tombs escaped plundering by the rapacious Alaouite sultan Moulay Ismail, probably because he feared bad luck if he desecrated them. Instead, he blocked all access bar an obscure entrance from the Kasbah Mosque. The tombs lay half-ruined and half-forgotten until they were rediscovered by a French aerial survey in 1917, and a passageway was built to give access to them.

Morocco from 1554 to 1669. The best time to see them is first thing in the morning, before the crowds arrive, or late in the afternoon when they, and the heat, have largely gone.

Ahmed el Mansour's mausoleum

There are two main **mausoleums** in the enclosure. The finest is on the left as you come in – a beautiful group of three rooms, built to house Ahmed el Mansour's own tomb and completed within his lifetime. Continuing round from the courtyard entrance, the first hall is a **prayer oratory**, a room probably not intended for burial, though now almost littered with the thin marble stones of Saadian princes. It is here that Moulay Yazid was laid out, perhaps in purposeful obscurity.

Architecturally, the most important feature of this mausoleum is the **mihrab**, its pointed horseshoe arch supported by an incredibly delicate arrangement of columns. Opposite this is another elaborate arch, leading to the domed **central chamber** and **Ahmed el Mansour's tomb**, which you can glimpse through the next door in the court. The tomb, slightly larger than those surrounding it, lies right in the middle, flanked on either side by those of the sultan's sons and successors. The room itself is spectacular; faint light filtering onto the tombs from an interior lantern in a tremendous vaulted roof, the zellij full of colour and motion and the undefined richness of a third chamber almost hidden from view.

The rest of the site

The **other mausoleum**, older and less impressive, was built by Ahmed in place of an existing pavilion above the tombs of his mother, Lalla Messaouda, and of Mohammed ech Sheikh, the founder of the Saadian dynasty. It is again a series of three rooms, though two are hardly more than *loggias*.

Outside, **round the garden and courtyard**, are scattered the tombs of over a hundred more Saadian princes and members of the royal household. Like the privileged 66 given space within the mausoleums, their gravestones are brilliantly tiled and often elaborately inscribed.

El Badi Palace

South of Place des Ferblantiers • Daily 9am–4.45pm; Ramadan 9am–3pm • 10dh; Koutoubia Minbar 10dh

Though substantially in ruins, and reduced throughout to its red *pisé* walls, enough remains of **El Badi** to suggest that its name – "The Incomparable" – was not entirely

5

immodest. The palace was originally commissioned by the Saadian sultan **Ahmed el Mansour** shortly after his accession in 1578. The money for it came from the enormous ransom paid by the Portuguese after the Battle of the Three Kings (see p.535). It took his seventeenth-century successor **Moulay Ismail** over ten years of systematic work to strip the palace of everything valuable, and there's still a lingering sense of luxury and grandeur. What you see today is essentially the ceremonial part of the **palace complex**, planned on a grand scale for the reception of ambassadors, and not meant for everyday living.

The scale of the palace, with its sunken gardens and vast, ninety-metre-long pool, is certainly unrivalled, and the odd traces of zellij and plaster still left evoke a decor that was probably as rich as that of the Saadian Tombs. The most enduring account of the palace concerns its state opening, a fabulous occasion attended by ambassadors from several European powers and by all the sheikhs and *caids* of the kingdom. Surveying the effect, Ahmed turned to his court jester for an opinion on the new palace. "Sidi," the man replied, "this will make a magnificent ruin".

The central court
The palace's **entrance** was originally in the southeast corner of the complex, but today you enter from the north, through the Green Pavilion, emerging into a vast **central court**, over 130m long and nearly as wide. In its northeast corner, you can climb up to get an overview from the ramparts, and a closer view of the **storks** that nest atop them.

Within the central court are four **sunken gardens**, two on the northern side and two on the southern side. **Pools** separate the two gardens on each side, and there are four smaller pools in the four corners of the court, which is constructed on a substructure of vaults in order to allow the circulation of water through the pools and gardens. When the pools are filled – as during the June folklore festival that takes place here – they are an incredibly majestic sight.

Summer pavilions
On each side of the courtyard were summer pavilions. Of the Crystal Pavilion, to the east, only the foundations survive. On the opposite side, a monumental hall that was used by the sultan on occasions of state was known as the **Koubba el Hamsiniya** (The Fifty Pavilion), after its size in cubits.

Stables and dungeons
South of the courtyard, accessed just to the right of the building housing the *minbar*, are ruins of the palace **stables**, and beyond them, leading towards the intriguing walls of the present royal palace, a series of **dungeons**, used into the last century as a state prison.

The Koutoubia Minbar
The original **minbar** (pulpit) from the Koutoubia Mosque (see p.320) is housed in a pavilion in the southwest corner of the main courtyard, and can be seen for an additional fee. It may not sound like much, but this *minbar* was in its day one of the most celebrated works of art in the Muslim world. Commissioned from the Andalusian capital Cordoba in 1137 by the last Almoravid sultan, Ali Ben Youssef, it took eight years to complete, and was covered with the most exquisite inlay work, of which, sadly, only patches remain. When the Almohads took power, they installed the *minbar* in their newly built Koutoubia Mosque, where it remained until it was removed for restoration in 1962, and eventually brought here. Unfortunately, members of the public are not usually allowed to walk all the way round it to inspect the surviving inlay work, but the *gardien* may relent if you show a particular interest. Photography is not usually allowed.

The Mellah

Marrakesh's **Mellah** (Jewish quarter) was created in 1558, though no record remains of why it was done at this particular time. It may have been to use the Jews as a buffer zone (and scapegoat) between the palace and the populace in times of social unrest, but more likely it was simply to make taxation easier. The Jews of Marrakesh were an important financial resource – they controlled most of the Saadian sugar trade, and comprised practically all of the city's bankers, metalworkers, jewellers and tailors. In the sixteenth century, at least, their quarter was almost a town in itself, supervised by rabbis, and with its own souks, gardens, fountains and synagogues.

The present-day Mellah, now known officially as **Hay Essalam**, is much smaller in extent and almost entirely Muslim – most Marrakshi Jews left long ago for Casablanca, France or Israel. The few who remain, outwardly distinguishable only by the men's small black skullcaps, are mostly poor, old or both. The quarter, however, is immediately distinct: its houses are taller than elsewhere, the streets are more enclosed, and even the shop cubicles are smaller. Until the Protectorate, Jews were not permitted to own land or property – nor even to ride or walk, except barefoot – outside the Mellah. Today, though not a sought-after neighbourhood, its air of neglect and poverty is probably less than at any time during the past three centuries.

The easiest approach to the Mellah is from **Place des Ferblantiers** – the tinsmiths' square. Formerly called Place du Mellah, this was itself part of the old Jewish souk, now prettied up into quite a pleasant little square, surrounded by the workshops of lantern makers. North of here, off the street leading up to Rue Riad Zitoun el Jedid, is a **jewellers' souk**, where one of the traditional Jewish trades has pretty much been taken over by Muslim craftsmen. The Mellah's main market, **Souk el Mellah**, just across the street, specializes in spices, but beware of hustlers trying to lead you to shops where they get a commission (and you pay double as a result).

Lazama Synagogue

36 Derb Ragraga (no sign, just knock on the door) • Sun–Thurs 9am–6pm, Fri 9am–1pm, closed Jewish hols • Free, but tip expected

The main road into the Mellah leads along the southern side of the Bahia Palace. Heading along it from Souk el Mellah (see above), the first left (under a low arch) takes you to **Place Souweka**, a small square at the centre of the Mellah, very much like the goal in a maze. If you ignore that turning, the main road does a twist, and the next left (Derb Ragraga) takes you after 100m to the unmarked **Lazama Synagogue**. Like all the Mellah's synagogues, it forms part of a private house, which you'll notice is decorated with Star of David zellij tiling. The synagogue is still in use, although the interior is modern and not tremendously interesting. Would-be guides may offer (for a tip, of course) to show you this, and some of the Mellah's other, smaller synagogues, now disused. Even when in use, these were as much private houses as places of worship.

Miâara cemetery

Avenue Taoulet el Miara • Sun–Thurs 7.30am–6pm, Fri 7.30am–3pm; closed Jewish holidays • Free, but tip expected for entry

The **Miâara**, the **Jewish cemetery**, is reckoned to date from the early seventeenth century. More sprawling than the cemetery in Fez (see p.183), it is well tended and boasts eleven shrines belonging to Jewish *marabouts* (*tsadikim* in Hebrew), illustrating an interesting parallel between the Moroccan varieties of Judaism and Islam.

Bitoun Synagogue

Rue Arset el Màach (Rue de l'Electricité)

Just outside the Mellah, the first-floor **Bitoun Synagogue** is out of use and its interior is not open to the public, but it has the most interesting and unusual exterior of any synagogue in Morocco, located above a herb shop and painted in mustard yellow with arcaded balconies, and of course a Star of David motif.

5

The Bahia Palace

Rue Riad Zitoun el Jedid • Daily 9am–4.30pm; Ramadan 9am–3.30pm • 10dh

The **Bahia Palace** was originally built in 1866–7 for **Si Moussa**, a former slave who had risen to become Moulay Hassan's chamberlain, and then grand vizier. His son, **Bou Ahmed**, who himself held the post of chamberlain under Moulay Hassan, became kingmaker in 1894 when Hassan died while returning home from a *harka* (tax-collecting expedition). Ahmed concealed news of the sultan's death until he was able to declare Hassan's fourteen-year-old son Moulay Abd el Aziz sultan in his place, with himself as grand vizier and regent (see p.538). He thus gained virtually complete control over the state, which he exercised until his death in 1900. He began enlarging the Bahia (meaning "brilliance") in the same year as his coup, adding a mosque, a hammam and even a vegetable garden. When he died, his servants ransacked the palace, but it was restored and, during the Protectorate, housed the French Resident General.

The small riad

Visitors enter the palace from the west, through an arcaded courtyard which leads to a **small riad** (enclosed garden), part of Bou Ahmed's extension. The riad is decorated with beautiful carved stucco and cedarwood, and salons lead off it on three sides. The eastern salon leads through to the **council room**, and thence through a vestibule – where it's worth pausing to look up at the lovely painted ceiling – to the **great courtyard** of Si Moussa's original palace. The rooms surrounding the courtyard are also all worth checking out for their painted wooden ceilings.

The large riad

South of the great courtyard is the **large riad**, the heart of Si Moussa's palace, fragrant with fruit trees and melodious with birdsong, approaching the very ideal of beauty in Arabic domestic architecture. To its east and west are halls decorated with fine zellij fireplaces and painted wooden ceilings. From here, you leave the palace via the **private apartment** built in 1898 for Ahmed's wife, Lalla Zinab, where again you should look up to check out the painted ceiling, carved stucco, and stained-glass windows.

Maison Tiskiwin

8 Rue de la Bahia • Daily 9.30am–12.30pm & 2.30–6pm • 20dh • 200m north of the Bahia Palace on Rue Riad Zitouan el Jedid, where the street opens out to the left, take a right turn (under an arch), and it's 100m ahead on the right (look for the yellow sign)

The **Maison Tiskiwin** is an early twentieth-century townhouse built in Spanish-Moroccan style. Within lies a unique collection of Moroccan and Saharan artefacts, billed as "a journey from Marrakesh to Timbuktu and back". They come from the collection of Dutch anthropologist Bert Flint, a Morocccan resident since 1957. Each room features carpets, fabrics, clothes and jewellery from a different region of the Sahara, and explanatory notes in French describe the exhibits room by room. The exhibition illustrates the long-standing cultural links across the desert, a result of the centuries of caravan trade between Morocco and Mali.

Dar Si Said

Derb Si Said • Daily except Tues 9am–4.45pm • 10dh

Dar Si Said, a smaller version of the Bahia Palace, was built in the late nineteenth century for a brother of Bou Ahmed, who, though something of a simpleton, nonetheless gained the post of royal chamberlain. It's a pleasurable building, with beautiful pooled courtyards, scented with lemons, palms and flowers, and it houses an impressive **Museum of Moroccan Arts** (though not all its exhibits will necessarily be on show at any one time).

5

The museum is particularly strong on its collection of eighteenth- and nineteenth-century **woodwork**, some of it from the Glaoui kasbahs and most of it in cedarwood. There are also (upstairs, but not always on display) a number of traditional **wedding palanquins** – once used for carrying the bride, veiled and hidden, to her new home. Today, such chairs are still made, and used symbolically, to carry the bride from her womenfolk in one room to the groom's menfolk in the next room. On the top floor, four **fairground ride seats** were part of a contraption like a small wooden Ferris wheel, in which children commonly rode at moussems until the early 1960s. A photograph shows the apparatus as it was when in use.

One of the museum's most important exhibits (at the end of the passage from the entrance) is a rectangular marble **basin**, dating from around 1005. Originally from the Andalusian capital, Cordoba, it is decorated along one side with what seem to be heraldic eagles and griffins. Although most Islamic artwork eschews images of plants and animals, the Andalusian Ummayad caliphs who commissioned it had few reservations about representational art. What is more surprising is that it was brought over to Morocco by the highly puritanical Almoravid sultan Ali Ben Youssef, placed in his mosque, and left untouched by the dynasty's equally iconoclastic successors, the Almohads.

Agdal gardens

Route d'Agdal • Fri & Sun 8am–5pm • Free • Bus #6 from Place Foucauld

The **Agdal gardens**, adjoining the Medina to the south, sprawl over four square kilometres. They were originally watered by a system of wells and underground channels, known as *khettera,* from the base of the Atlas in the Ourika Valley and dating, in part, from the earliest founding of the city. These fell into disrepair and the gardens were largely abandoned until the nineteenth century, when they were restored. At the heart of the gardens are a series of pools, the largest of which is the **Sahraj el Hana** (Tank of Health – now a green, algae-clogged rectangle of water), which was probably dug by the Almohads and is flanked by a ramshackle old *minzah*, or summer pavilion, where the last few pre-colonial sultans held picnics and boating parties.

The Ville Nouvelle

Marrakesh's **Ville Nouvelle** radiates out from **Guéliz**, its commercial centre. Though it's hardly chock-a-block with attractions, it does have one must-see: the **Majorelle Garden**. South of Guéliz, the **Hivernage** district, built as a garden suburb, is where most of the city's newer tourist hotels are located. Further afield, on the northeastern edge of town, is Marrakesh's **palmery**.

Guéliz

The heart of modern Marrakesh, Guéliz has a certain buzz that the sleepy old Medina rather lacks. Its main thoroughfare, **Avenue Mohammed V**, runs all the way down to the Koutoubia, and it's on and around this boulevard that you'll find the city's main concentration of upmarket shops, restaurants and smart pavement cafés. Its junctions form the Ville Nouvelle's main centres of activity: Place de la Liberté, with its modern fountain; Place 16 Novembre, by the main post office; and Place Abdelmoumen Ben Ali, epicentre of Marrakesh's modern shopping zone.

Looking back along Avenue Mohammed V from Guéliz to the Medina, on a clear day at least, you should see the Koutoubia rising in the distance, with the Atlas mountains behind.

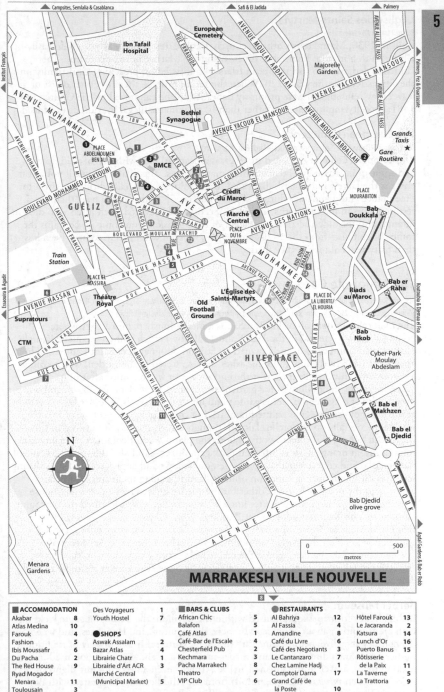

MARRAKESH VILLE NOUVELLE

■ ACCOMMODATION		Des Voyageurs	1	■ BARS & CLUBS		● RESTAURANTS		
Akabar	8	Youth Hostel	7	African Chic	5	Al Bahriya	12	Hôtel Farouk	13
Atlas Medina	10			Balafon	5	Al Fassia	4	Le Jacaranda	2
Farouk	4	● SHOPS		Café Atlas	1	Amandine	8	Katsura	14
Fashion	5	Aswak Assalam	2	Café-Bar de l'Escale	4	Café du Livre	6	Lunch d'Or	16
Ibis Moussafir	6	Bazar Atlas	4	Chesterfield Pub	3	Café des Negotiants	3	Puerto Banus	15
Du Pacha	2	Librairie Chatr	1	Kechmara	3	Le Cantanzaro	7	Rôtisserie	
The Red House	9	Librairie d'Art ACR	3	Pacha Marrakech	8	Chez Lamine Hadj	1	de la Paix	11
Ryad Mogador		Marché Central		Theatro	7	Comptoir Darna	17	La Taverne	5
Menara	11	(Municipal Market)	5	VIP Club	6	Grand Café de		La Trattoria	9
Toulousain	3					la Poste	10		

5

L'Église des Saints-Martyrs

Rue de l'Imam Ali • Free

Built in 1930, Marrakesh's Catholic church, **L'Église des Saints-Martyrs**, could easily be a little church in rural France but for its distinctly Marrakshi red-ochre hue. The church is dedicated to six Franciscan friars who insisted on preaching Christianity on the city's streets in the year 1220. When the sultan ordered them to either desist or leave, they refused, and were promptly beheaded, to be canonized by the Church in 1481. Proselytzing for religions other than Islam remains illegal in Morocco to this day.

The European Cemetery

Rue Erraouda • Daily: April–Sept 7am–7pm; Oct–March 8am–6pm • Free

The **European Cemetery**, opened in 1925, is a peaceful plot with lots of wild flowers, and some quite Poe-esque French family mausoleums. The first thing you'll notice on entry is the large white obelisk dedicated to the soldiers who fell fighting in Africa for Free France and democracy during World War II; 333 of these men have their last resting places in the cemetery's section H. Section B is devoted to children who died in infancy, and the oldest section, to the left of the obelisk as you come in, contains the tombs of colonists from the 1920s and 1930s, most of whom seem to have been less than forty years old when they died.

The Majorelle Garden

Rue Yves Saint Laurent (off Avenue Yacoub el Mansour) • Daily: Oct–April 8am–5.30pm; May–Sept 8am–6pm; Ramadan 9am–5pm • 50dh; Berber Museum 25dh • No picnics or unaccompanied children allowed • ⓦ jardinmajorelle.com

The **Majorelle Garden**, or Jardin Bou Saf, is a meticulously planned twelve-acre botanical garden, created in the 1920s and 1930s by French painter Jacques Majorelle (1886–1962), and subsequently owned by fashion designer Yves Saint Laurent. When Yves Saint Laurent died in 2008, his ashes were scattered in the garden, which contains a memorial to him, while the street the entrance is in was renamed after him.

The feeling of tranquillity in the garden is enhanced by verdant groves of bamboo, dwarf palm and agave, the cactus garden and lily-covered pools. The Art Deco pavilion at the heart of the garden is painted in a striking cobalt blue – the colour of French workmen's overalls, so Majorelle claimed, though it seems to have improved in the Moroccan light. This brilliantly offsets both the plants – multicoloured bougainvillea, rows of bright orange nasturtiums and pink geraniums – and also the strong colours of the pergolas and concrete paths – pinks, lemon yellows and apple greens. The enduring sound is the chatter of the common bulbuls, flitting among the leaves of the date palms, and the pools also attract other bird residents such as turtle doves and house buntings. The garden became better known abroad when it was featured by Yves Saint Laurent in a brilliant reproduction at London's 1997 Chelsea Flower Show. Pierre Bergé and Madison Cox's *Majorelle, A Moroccan Oasis* is a superbly photographed coffee table book on the garden, sometimes available at Librairie d'Art (see p.353).

When leaving the garden, ignore the taxi drivers waiting outside, who run a cartel and will not take you unless you pay well over the odds. The answer is simply to walk down to the main road and hail a cab there.

Berber Museum

In Majorelle's former studio, housed within the pavilion, the **Berber Museum** kicks off with an exhibition about Morocco's Berbers, their culture and languages, and where in the country they live, before launching (in the next room) into a display of traditional Berber crafts, including textiles and carpet-making, and showing the tools used in making them, as well as the finished articles. There's even a beautiful but slightly rickety wooden *minbar* (mosque pulpit) from the Middle Atlas, decorated with Berber designs. The next room is dedicated to jewellery, all of it silver, as gold is considered unlucky in Berber tradition. The last room contains a display of Berber costumes from different regions of the country.

The palmery

5km northeast of town, between the Route de Fès (N8) and the Route de Casablanca (N9) • The Route de Fès turn-off is served by bus #17 or #26, with plenty of taxis, but the Route de Casablanca end has no public transport, so it's best to take a cab up to that end to start, and finish at the Route de Fès

Marrakesh's **palmery**, or oasis, is far from being the most spectacular in the country, but it does make a change from the urban landscape if you're spending time in town. Supposedly, it sprang from stones spat out by the date-munching troops of Marrakesh's founder, Youssef Ben Tachfine, but in fact the dates produced by its fifty thousand-odd palms are not of eating quality. Dotted with the villas of prosperous Marrakshis, the palmery also boasts a golf course and a couple of luxury hotels. The clumps of date palms look rather windswept, but the palmery does have a certain tranquillity, and it's 5ºC cooler than the Medina, which could make it particularly appealing in summer.

The most popular route through the oasis is the **Circuit de la Palmeraie**, which meanders through the trees and villas from the Route de Fès to the Route de Casablanca. The classic way to see it is by *calèche* (see p.340), and the sightseeing bus, the Marrakech Bus Touristique (see box, p.341), travels round it too. It's also possible to ride around the palmery on a camel – men by the roadside offer rides – or you could even explore it on foot, though it's quite a long 5km stroll.

The Menara Gardens

Daily 7am–5pm • Free • Minzah daily 9am–2.45pm • 10dh • Bus #11 from Avenue Mohammed V (southbound) or Place Youssef Tachfine

Southwest of the Hivernage district, the **Menara Gardens** are a popular picnic spot for Marrakshi families, as well as tourists, centred on a rectangular pool providing a classic postcard image beneath a backdrop of the High Atlas mountains. Originally dating from the twelfth century, it was restored and its pavilions rebuilt in the mid-nineteenth century. The poolside *minzah* replaced an earlier Saadian structure. Aside from the pool, the garden is largely filled with olive trees. There's usually someone by the park entrance offering camel rides.

ARRIVAL AND DEPARTURE   MARRAKESH

BY PLANE

Menara airport Marrakesh's airport (☎0524 447910) is 4km southwest of town, and is connected with Pl Foucauld (by the Koutoubia) by bus #19 (30dh one-way, 50dh for a round trip within two weeks). The bus runs half-hourly (7am–9.30pm from the airport, 6.15am–9.15pm from Pl Foucauld) via Av Mohammed V and Bd Mohammed VI, and can be joined at any bus stop en route. Petits taxis (for up to three passengers) or grands taxis (for up to six) have fixed an artificially high fare for journeys between the airport and town (currently 80dh, half as much again at night). It's not advisable to walk to town from the airport (or vice versa), as people regularly get mugged on the road. If you really want to do it cheaply, you could exit the airport precincts, cross over the main road and take bus #11 or #18 (3.50dh), from in front of the first row of shops 200m to your left (the bus stop isn't marked, but buses will stop there), to Av Mohammed V, but these buses can be very slow, and also very crowded. From town to the airport, but not the other way, you can take a shared grand taxi for M'hamid from the north end of Rue Ibn Rachid (4dh) and ask to be put off at the airport turn-off, leaving you just 300m to walk. Arriving at the airport late at night, you won't always find the exchange kiosks open, but there are ATMs in the arrivals hall; taxis will in any case usually accept euros, and sometimes even dollars or sterling, at more or less the equivalent dirham rate, or you can have them call at an ATM en route (see p.354). Most international car rental firms have desks at the airport, or will meet arrivals by arrangement.

Airlines British Airways, Menara airport (☎0524 448951); Royal Air Maroc, 197 Av Mohammed V (☎0524 425500). Destinations Casablanca (3–5 daily; 40min).

BY TRAIN

The train station (☎0524 447768) is on Av Mohammed VI at Av Hassan II, a ten-minute walk west of

5

Guéliz. The taxi fare should be around 15dh to the Medina, less to hotels in Guéliz. Buses #8, #10, #14 and #66 connect the station with Pl Foucauld (by the Koutoubia); they can be picked up on Av Hassan II, opposite the old station exit (halfway down platform 1 – if it's closed, exit via the Supratours office). The most comfortable way to travel to Tangier is to take a couchette on the night train (350dh), preferably booking by the morning of your day of travel.

Destinations Casablanca Voyageurs (9 daily; 3hr 10min); Fez (8 daily; 7hr 10min); Kenitra (9 daily; 4hr 45min); Meknes (8 daily; 6hr 35min); Oujda (2 daily changing at Casa or Fez; 13–14hr); Rabat (9 daily; 4hr 15min); Safi (daily changing at Benguerir; 3hr); Settat (9 daily; 2hr 15min); Tangier (1 direct & 5 connecting daily; 9hr 30min).

BY BUS
GARE ROUTIÈRE
Long-distance buses, other than Supratours and most CTM services, depart from the *gare routière* just outside the walls of the Medina by Bab Doukkala, and has left-luggage facilities (daily 7am–8pm; 10dh/day). You can walk into the centre of Guéliz from the *gare routière* in around ten minutes by following Av des Nations Unies (to the right as you exit the bus station, then straight on bearing right). To the Pl Jemaa el Fna it's around 25 minutes: follow the Medina walls (to your left as you exit the bus station) down to Av Mohammed V, then turn left. A more direct route, but harder to follow, is to go through Bab Doukkala, head straight on down Rue Bab Doukkala and Rue Dar el Bacha, and take a right down Rue Mouassine – the tricky bits are bearing left before the Bab Doukkala Mosque, turning right down Rue Mouassine, and doing a dog-leg around the Mouassine Mosque; the route is easier to follow in the other direction. A petit taxi is about 10dh from the *gare routière* to the Jemaa el Fna, less to Guéliz. Alternatively, catch bus #16, from outside the bus station, which runs through the heart of Guéliz, or buses #3, #8, #10, #14, #16 and #66, which stop directly opposite Bab Doukkala itself (though the bus stop is not obvious), and head south to Pl Foucauld. Leaving town, it's worth buying tickets a day in advance for destinations with limited services, such as Tizi n'Test or Zagora.

Destinations Agadir (24 daily; 3hr 30min); Aoulouz via Tizi n'Test (2 daily; 9hr); Asni (10 daily; 1hr 30min); Azilal (3 daily; 3hr); Beni Mellal (13 daily; 4hr); Casablanca (roughly half-hourly 4am–midnight; 4hr); Demnate (12 daily; 1hr 30min); El Jadida (12 daily; 4hr); Essaouira (19 daily; 3hr); Fez (9 daily; 10hr); Laayoune (1 daily; 15hr); Meknes (7 daily; 9hr); Ouarzazate (8 daily; 5hr); Rabat (hourly; 4hr 30min–5hr 30min); Rissani (3 daily; 12hr); Safi (13–15 daily; 2hr); Tafraoute (4 daily; 10hr); Taliouine (1 daily;

10hr); Tangier (6–10 daily; 10hr); Taroudant (5 daily; 6hr 30min); Tetouan (3–7 daily; 10hr–11hr 30min); Tiznit (16 daily; 7hr); Zagora (3–5 daily; 9hr 30min).

SUPRATOURS
Supratours buses (✆ 0524 435525) terminate on Av Hassan II next to the train station (accessed via platform 1), though they only sell tickets if there is space after the allocation for train passengers from Casablanca/Rabat. Grands taxis are often on hand to pick up the overflow at these times, particularly for Agadir.

Destinations: Agadir (14 daily; 3–5hr); Dakhla (daily; 24hr 30min); Erfoud (daily: 11hr); Er Rachidia (daily; 10hr); Essaouira (6 daily; 3hr); Laayoune (6 daily; 16–18hr); Ouarzazate (4hr 30min–5hr 15min).

CTM
CTM buses terminate at the CTM office on Rue Aboubaker Sedik (✆ 0524 448328), west of Guéliz and two blocks south of Supratours (see above). They also have an office at the *gare routière*, where you can buy tickets and sometimes board the buses (or board a CTM bus which will take you to them). CTM tickets are best bought in advance.

Destinations: Agadir (14 daily; 3hr 30min); Beni Mellal (2 daily; 3hr 30min); Casablanca (14 daily; 3hr); Dakhla (daily; 24hr); Er Rachidia (daily; 10hr); Essaouira (2 daily; 3hr); Fez (4 daily; 8hr 30min); Laayoune (4 daily; 15hr); Meknes (2 daily; 7hr 30min); Ouarzazate (5 daily; 3hr 30min); Rabat (4 daily; 5hr); Tangier (daily; 9hr 15min); Taroudant (daily; 4hr 30min); Tetouan (daily; 10hr 30min); Tiznit (9 daily; 6hr); Zagora (2 daily; 7hr 30min).

BY GRAND TAXI
Collective grands taxis for most destinations terminate immediately behind the *gare routière* bus station, though they may drop you off in front of it on Pl Mourabiton. Bab er Robb taxi station – which is actually 1.5km southwest of Bab er Robb, near the junction of Av Mohammed VI and the Route d'Asni – is used by grands taxis for High Atlas destinations. It's about 15dh by petit taxi from the Jemaa el Fna, 20dh from Guéliz. Shared taxis to Oukaïmeden operate during the skiing season only, heading up in the morning and back in the evening, and you will have to pay for the round trip, even if staying the night, which may also leave you without any sure transport back. For Setti Fatma, although you may be lucky and find a shared taxi all the way from Bab er Robb taxi station, the best way is to take a shared grand taxi from the southern end of Rue Ibn Rachid (or a #24 bus from Pl Youssef Tachfine) to Lagarb (20min), where there are shared grands taxis on to Setti Fatma.

Destinations Asni (1hr); Azilal (2hr 30min); Casablanca (2hr 30min); Essaouira (2hr 30min); Inezgane (3hr); Moulay Brahim (1hr); Ouarzazate (3hr); Oukaïmeden (winter only; 2hr); Taroudant (4hr); Setti Fatma (infrequent; 1hr).

MARRAKESH TO AGADIR AND ESSAOUIRA

The new A7 toll **motorway** to Agadir supplements the old **N8** road over the Imi n'Tanoute or Tizi Maachou pass (see map, p.450), which was itself only built in the 1970s, and was something of a hot spot for accidents. Most buses and shared taxis now use the motorway, which cuts around an hour off the journey time, but the old road has its points of interest, and you'll be using the first part of it if heading for Essaouira.

CHICHAOUA

The road on **to Essaouira** (R207) branches off the N8 at **Chichaoaua**, a small town and administrative centre, known for its **carpets**. Brightly coloured, often with stylized animal forms, they are sold at the local Centre Coopératif and also at the town's Thursday market.

West of Chichaoua, the R207 extends across the drab Chiadma plains, passing **Sidi Mokhtar**, 25km from Chichaoua, which has a Wednesday souk with an attractive array of carpets.

KASBAH MTOUGGI

South from Sidi Mokhtar and west of the N8 and A7, roads lead to the **Kasbah Mtouggi**. This was the old tribal **kasbah of the Mtouggi** clan, and a ruin almost as impressive as Telouet (see p.393).

The Mtouggi were the third of the clans described by Gavin Maxwell (see p.569) as "Lords of the Atlas", alongside the Glaoui (see box, p.394) and the Goundafi (see p.382), and they dominated this western Atlas pass, just as the Goundafi and Glaoui did the eastern routes. Their kasbah, near the village of **Bouaboute**, looks, in its ruinous state, almost as large as Telouet. The site is not hard to reach, and you can gain access to the ruins and see something of their one-time splendour.

IMI N'TANOUTE AND TIZI MAACHOU

Heading for Agadir from Chichaoua, the N8 begins a slow climb towards **Imi n'Tanoute**, another administrative centre, with a **Monday souk**, before cutting through the westernmost edge of the High Atlas. A few kilometres further along the N8 from Imi n'Tanoute is the **Tizi Maachou pass** (1700m). The road south of the pass runs by the **dams of Tanizaourt** before descending into the fertile Souss Valley.

ALTERNATIVE ROUTES TO AGADIR

There is also a minor tarred road, the **R212**, which breaks off the N8 just west of a bridge over the Oued Nfis, 23km west of Marrakesh, and goes direct to Imi n'Tanoute. It's no faster than the N8, but pleasantly unbusy. And if you have 4WD transport, you might alternatively want to consider the **old Tizi Maachou road** (6404), a *piste* that runs east of the N8 and A7, which you can rejoin at **Argana**. As a more scenic alternative south of Argana, you can take the now surfaced road over the dramatic Tizi Iferd (Tizi Babaoun) pass, which descends into the Souss Valley nearer Taroudant.

GETTING AROUND

By bus There are a number of useful bus routes in the city (see box, p.340). The most important from a tourist point of view are buses #1 and #16 along Av Mohammed V between Guéliz and the Koutoubia.

By petit taxi It is a fairly long walk between Guéliz and the Medina, but there are plenty of petits taxis, which will take you between the two for around 10–15dh. There are taxi ranks at most major intersections in Guéliz, and in the Medina in the northwest corner of Pl Jemaa el Fna, outside the *Grand Hôtel Tazi*, and at the Pl des Ferblantiers at the end of Av Houman el Fetouaki. Petits taxis have meters, which they should use; most trips should cost around 10–20dh during the day, or 15–30dh at night, when there is a surcharge on the meter price. If a taxi driver doesn't want to use the meter, it is because they intend to overcharge you. To and from the airport, and from the Hivernage hotels, taxi drivers have agreed an artificially high fixed price among themselves, and won't use the meter. If taking a taxi far afield, such as to one of the campsites or golf courses, and the driver won't use the meter but specifies a price, confirm the price using the word "dirhams", or the driver may claim on arrival that the price he quoted was in euros. If you get a petit taxi out to somewhere on the periphery, such as the palmery or one of the golf courses, and especially if the driver doesn't try to pull any stunts over the fare, it's worth getting a phone number to call them for the return journey.

5

LOCAL BUS ROUTES

The following buses leave from Avenue el Mouahidine alongside Place Foucauld, opposite *Hôtel de Foucauld*:

#1 along Avenue Mohammed V to Guéliz, then up Avenue Mohammed Abdelkrim el Khattabi (Route de Casablanca) to Semlalia.

#8, #10, #14 & #66 all go to Bab Doukkala (for the bus station), then on down Avenue Hassan II past the train station.

#6 to Bab Ighli and the entrance to the Agdal gardens.

#16 to Guéliz via Bab Doukkala.

#17 and #26 to the Route de Fès for the palmery.

#19 circular route from the airport to Place Foucauld, then north up Avenue Mohammed V, south down Avenue Mohammed VI and back to the airport.

By grand taxi Grands taxis can also be chartered by the day for around 300dh – very reasonable if split between four people (the taxis take up to six passengers, but four is comfortable). Negotiate at the ranks in Jemaa el Fna or by the post office in Guéliz. By law grands taxis have to display prices for specified trips; these prices are per trip, not per person.

By calèche In addition to taxis, *calèches* (horse-drawn cabs) line up on Pl Foucauld near the Koutoubia, and at some of the fancier hotels. These can take up to five people and are not much more expensive than petits taxis, but be sure to fix the price in advance, especially for a tour of the town. If you are considering a *calèche* trip at any stage, the Menara and palmery, and also the Agdal Gardens (see p.334) are perfect destinations.

By bicycle, motorbike, moped or scooter You can rent bicycles on Pl de la Liberté and a number of roadside locations in Hivernage, but these are obviously rather fly-by-night operators, and mopeds or scooters from these places are

unlikely to be properly insured, so it is better to rent them from a reputable firm with a fixed address. Marrakech Roues, 3 Rue Bani Marine (☎ 0524 441011, ⍟ marrakech-roues.com) rent bicycles, scooters, mopeds and quad-bikes. Loc2Roues on the upper floor of Galerie Élite, 212 Av Mohammed V (☎ 0524 430294, ⍟ loc2roues.com) rents scooters, mopeds, quad-bikes and motorbikes. Expect to pay around 120dh a day for a bicycle, 250–300dh for a moped or scooter.

Car rental Concorde Cars, 154 Av Mohammed V (☎ 0524 431116) comes highly recommended. Other local firms include: First Car, 234 Av Mohammed V (☎ 0524 438764, ⍟ firstcar.ma); Najm Car, shop 9, Galerie Jakar, 61 Av Mohammed V (☎ 0524 437909, ⍟ najmcar.com). International franchises include: Budget, 66 Bd Mohammed Zerktouni (☎ 0524 431180); Europcar, 63 Bd Mohammed Zerktouni (☎ 0524 431228); Hertz, 154 Av Mohammed V (☎ 0524 439984). Many hotels can also arrange car rental, often at competitive rates.

INFORMATION

Tourist information The Délégation Regionale de Tourisme, on Pl Abdelmoumen Ben Ali in Guéliz (Mon–Fri 8.30am–4.30pm; ☎ 0524 436239), keeps a dossier of useful information with listings of hotels, campsites, car rental firms and other contacts, and staff are generally happy to answer any questions. The I Love Marrakesh website at ⍟ ilovemarrakesh.com has listings of upmarket hotels, riads and restaurants, plus write-ups and some photos of the main tourist sights. Marrakech Travel Guide at ⍟ travelmarrakech.co.uk has some good advice and recommendations, though it's a bit patchy.

Maps The Rough Guide map of Marrakesh is frankly the best

you'll get, but is unfortunately out of print, though you may still find a copy. The Villes en Couleurs map, available online or from good travel bookshops abroad, is a good second-best. Failing that, the *Marrakech Evasions* map (20dh), produced by Éditions Bab Sabaa, is available from Librairie Chatr, *Henna Café* and some shops around the Jemaa el Fna.

Guides The Délégation de Tourisme can put you onto a guide, with whom you'll need to negotiate a price. A 3hr Medina walking tour is available for €20 with tour guide Rachid Boussalem, who guarantees (unlike most guides) not to stop at any shops; for details call ☎ 0611 408244 or check ⍟ visit-marrakech-medina.com.

ACCOMMODATION

The Medina has the main concentration of small, budget hotels, especially in the area around the Jemaa el Fna. It is also where you'll find most of Marrakesh's **riads**, usually hidden away deep in its backstreets. Guéliz, whose hotels tend to be concentrated in the mid range, is handier for transport, especially for the train station. Hotels in Hivernage and Semlalia are upmarket, in modern buildings with swimming pools, but they're pretty soulless. **Advance bookings** are a wise idea, especially for the more popular places in the Medina. The busiest times are the Easter and Christmas/New Year holiday periods, when virtually every decent place can be full to capacity.

SIGHTSEEING BUS TOURS

If you don't have much time and you want to scoot around Marrakesh's major sights in a day or two, the **hop-on hop-off Marrakech Tour bus** (☎0663 527797, ⓦalsa.ma) could be for you. Using open-top double-deckers, with a commentary in several languages including English, the tour follows two circular routes: the first tours the Medina and Guéliz, calling at Place Foucauld (for the Jemaa and Koutoubia), Place des Ferblantiers (for the Bahia and El Badi Palaces, plus the Mellah), and the Menara Gardens; the second tours the palmery, following the Circuit de la Palmeraie. The Medina/Guéliz bus departs from outside *Boule de Neige* café in Place Abdelmoumen Ben Ali every 20–30min (April–Sept 9am–6.30pm, but winter times during Ramadan; Oct–March 9am–5.45pm); the palmery bus leaves from the same place five times a day (six times in summer; afternoons only). You can get on and off where you like, and tickets (145dh) can be bought on board, or at Place Abdelmoumen Ben Ali or Place Foucauld. They are valid for 24 hours, so even if you start your tour after lunch, you can finish it the following morning, but if you want to spread it out over two days, there are also 48-hour tickets (190dh). Disabled people get cheap rates of 30dh for 24hr, 50dh for 48hr.

MEDINA

Most of the Medina's budget hotel accommodation is concentrated in the small area south of the Jemaa el Fna. Riads and more deluxe hotels tend to be further afield.

HOTELS

★ **Aday** 111 Derb Sidi Bouloukat ☎0524 441920l; map p.319. This friendly budget hotel is well kept, clean and pleasantly decorated, though the rooms, grouped around a central patio, are small and most have only inward-facing windows. Shower facilities are shared, with hot water round the clock. Single rooms, though not always available, are half the price of doubles, making them a very good deal for lone travellers, and you can sleep on the roof for 30dh. __110dh__

Ali Rue Moulay Ismail ☎0524 444979, ⓦhotel-ali .com; map p.319. This busy hotel is used by groups heading to the High Atlas, so it's a good source of trekking (and other) information, and staff are always extremely helpful. They also change money, and can arrange car, minibus or 4WD rental, and the place has a general air of business and being right in the middle of things, though that won't appeal to everyone. Booking ahead is advisable; the rooms (all en suite with a/c) are being done up one by one, and it's worth asking for a refurbished one. There's also cheap dorm accommodation. BB Dorm __70dh__, double __360dh__.

Les Borjs de la Kasbah Rue du Mechouar, Kasbah ☎0524 381101, ⓦlesborjsdelakasbah.com; map pp.316–317. This cool boutique hotel, created out of seven old houses at the southern end of the kasbah, has much of the style of a riad along with the trappings of a luxury hotel. There are several patio spaces, a pool, a spa, and a classy restaurant, with a window on the kitchen so you can watch your meal being prepared. The rooms range from small, bargain-priced singles (1000dh) and doubles to full-sized deluxe rooms, still at good prices. BB __1500dh__

Central Palace 59 Derb Sidi Bouloukat ☎0524 440235, ⓦlecentralpalace.com; map p.319. The rooms here are a cut above those in the other budget hotels in the back alleys south of the Jemaa el Fna, and correspondingly slightly pricier, but what this place also has going for it is its easy-to-find location, just off Rue Bab Agnaou, a stone's throw from the Jemaa. __155dh__

CTM Pl Jemaa el Fna ☎0524 442325; map p.319. Situated above the old bus station (hence its name), now used as a car park, and handy if you're driving. There are three categories of rooms: old, unmodernized rooms with shared bathroom (no hot water); en-suite rooms, clean but drab, with hot-water showers; and modernized en-suite rooms with a/c in summer, heating in winter (300dh). The last category includes rooms 1–4, which overlook the square, though this does of course make them noisy. Breakfast is served on the roof terrace, which also overlooks the square. BB __175dh__

Dar les Cigognes 108 Rue de Berrima, Medina ☎0524 382740, ⓦlescigognes.com; map pp.316–317. A luxury boutique hotel run by a Swiss–American couple in two converted Medina houses that gets consistently good reports. It's done up in traditional fashion around the patio, but with modern decor in the rooms and suites. There's a library, a hammam, a jacuzzi, a salon and a terrace where you can see storks nesting on the walls of the royal palace opposite (hence the name, which means "house of the storks"). BB €258

Dar Salam 162 Derb Ben Fayda off Rue el Gza near Bab Doukkala, Medina ☎0524 383110, ⓦdar-salam.com; map pp.316–317. A Moroccan family home which takes in guests, this is a true *maison d'hôte* as opposed to a riad, a place to relax and put your feet up rather than admire the decor. The food is similarly unpretentious – tasty home-style Moroccan cooking, like your mum would make if she were Marrakshi. BB €32

Essaouira 3 Derb Sidi Bouloukat ☎0524 443805; map p.319. This is one of the most popular cheapies in

5

Marrakesh – and with good reason. It's a well-run, safe place, with thirty rooms, communal hot showers, a laundry service, baggage deposit and rooftop café. **100dh**.

De Foucauld Av el Mouahidine, facing Pl de Foucauld ☎0524 440806, ✉hoteldefoucauld@gmail.com; map p.319. Rooms are a little sombre and some are a bit on the small side, but they're decent enough, with a/c, heating and constant hot water (with a choice of tub or shower). There's a roof terrace with views of the Koutoubia, and a restaurant with buffet suppers. The staff can arrange tours, help with local information, and put you onto guides for High Atlas trekking. BB **192dh**.

★ **Gallia** 30 Rue de la Recette ☎0524 445913, ✉hotel.gallia@menara.ma; map p.319. This beautifully kept hotel, founded in 1929, claims to be the second-oldest in Marrakesh, after the *Mamounia*. It's housed in a restored Medina mansion with immaculate en-suite rooms off two tiled courtyards, one with a fountain, palm tree and caged birds. There's central heating in winter and a/c in summer. Book online, at least a month ahead if possible. It's not strictly wheelchair accessible, but staff are very helpful to chair users and there are rooms with more or less level access. **460dh**

La Gazelle 12 Rue Bani Marine ☎0524 441112, ✉hotel_lagazelle@hotmail.com; map map p.319. Well-kept if slightly dull hotel on a street with foodstalls and small grill cafés, with rooms around a covered patio – windows of downstairs rooms open onto the patio, those upstairs open to the outside. Some rooms have bathrooms, and there's a discount on the room price after three nights. **150dh**

Ichbilia 1 Rue Bani Marine ☎0524 381530; map p.319. Near the Mabrouka cinema, and well placed for shops, banks and cafés, with rooms off a covered gallery, some plain and simple (but still clean and comfortable), others with a/c and private bathroom (300dh). Sometimes referred to as *Hotel Sevilla* (*Ichbilia* is the Arabic for Seville). **160dh**

Jnane Mogador Derb Sidi Bouloukat by 116 Rue Riad Zitoun el Kedim ☎0524 426323, ⓦjnanemogador .com; map p.319. Run by the same management as the *Essaouira*, this more upmarket hostelry is just as homely, and a firm favourite among Marrakesh's mid-range accommodation options. Set in a beautifully restored old house, it boasts charming rooms, in warm tints with modern furnishings, around a lovely fountain patio, plus its own hammam and a roof terrace. **480dh**

★ **La Maison Arabe** 1 Derb Assebbe Bab Doukkala, behind the Doukkala mosque ☎0524 387010, ⓦlamaisonarabe.com; map pp.316–317. Though not as famous as the *Mamounia*, this is Marrakesh's classiest hotel, boasting high standards of service in a gorgeous nineteenth-century mansion restored with fine traditional workmanship. The furnishings are sumptuous,

as is the food (this was a restaurant before it was a hotel, and it offers cookery classes, at 600–800dh per person for small groups). There are two beautifully kept patios and a selection of rooms and suites, some with private terrace and jacuzzi. There is no pool on the premises, but a free shuttle bus can take you to the hotel's private pool nearby. **2000dh**

La Mamounia Av Bab Jdid ☎0524 388600, ⓦmamounia.com; map pp.316–317. Set in palatial grounds and renovated in 2010, this is Marrakesh's most famous, most expensive and most exclusive hotel (see p.321), though some would say it's more snooty than classy. Decoratively, it is of most interest for the 1920s Art Deco touches by Jacques Majorelle (of Majorelle Garden fame), and their enhancements, in 1986, by the then Moroccan king's favourite designer, André Paccard. The rooms are done out in warm reds and browns, with magnificent marble bathrooms, but some of the simple "classic" rooms can be a bit on the small side, so it's best to pay slightly more for a "superior" or "deluxe" room. **6000dh**

Medina 1 Derb Sidi Bouloukat ☎0524 44299; map p.321. Located in a street full of good budget hotels, the *Medina* is a perennial favourite among the cheapies, and often full. It's clean, friendly and pretty good value, and there's always hot water in the shared showers. The owner – who used to work in Britain as a circus acrobat – speaks good English. They have a small roof terrace where you can have breakfast (20dh), and in summer there's also the option of sleeping on the roof (30dh). **110dh**

Sherazade 3 Derb Jama, Rue Riad Zitoun el Kedim ☎0524 429305, ⓦhotelsherazade.com; map p.319. Before riads took off big time, this place was already on the scene, an old merchant's house, prettily done up, that gets rave reviews from our readers. Besides a lovely roof terrace, the hotel offers a wide variety of well-maintained rooms at different prices, not all en suite. Run very professionally by a German-Moroccan couple, it's extremely popular, so book well ahead. **320dh**

La Sultana 403 Rue de la Kasbah ☎0524 388008, ⓦlasultanamarrakech.com; map pp.316–317. For those who can't decide between a riad, a five-star or a boutique hotel, this is an extremely stylish blend of all three: riad style, boutique personal attention and five-star facilities. The whole place is done out in wonderful carved cedar wood, whose scent infuses the hotel, and liberally sprinkled with antiques and objets d'art; facilities include a hammam, pool, jacuzzi, spa, lounge bar, library, panoramic terraces and excellent dining – all just round the corner from Bab Agnaou and the Saadian Tombs. **4400dh**

Villa des Orangers 6 Rue Sidi Mimoun, off Pl Youssef Ben Tachfine ☎0524 384638, ⓦvilladesorangers.com; map pp.316–317. This gorgeous luxury establishment is officially a hotel, but it's a riad in the true sense of the word: an old house around a garden patio – three in fact – with orange trees and lots of lovely carved stucco. There's a range of rooms and suites, many with their own private terrace. Rates include breakfast and light lunch. **4000dh**.

RIADS

Marrakesh is where the riad craze started, and there are some sumptuous riads here, especially at the top end of the market, with some very friendly and homely places at the lower end of the market too, but some are overpriced and nothing special, so it's worth shopping around. Most places offer low rates in July and August. Though not officially classified as riads, *Les Borjs de la Kasbah* and *Dar les Cigognes* (see p.341), and *Hôtel Gallia, Jnane Mogador, Hôtel Sherazade* and *Villa des Orangers* (see opposite) are all worth considering too.

Le Clos des Arts 50 Derb Tbib, off Rue Riad Zitoun el Jedid ☎0524 375159, ⓦleclosdesarts.com; map pp.316–317. A beautiful riad, full of the works of one of the proprietors, who is a painter and sculptor as well as an interior designer. Each room has its own style and colour, and the whole effect is warm and delightful, as are the owners, who give it a real personal touch. Facilities include a rooftop pool and free wi-fi throughout. BB **€110**

Dar Ihssane 14 Derb Chorfa el Kebir, near Mouassine Mosque ☎0524 387826, ⓦriaddarihssane.com; map p.322. A good-value riad in an eighteenth-century mansion with many original features (some of which were only discovered during renovation). It's owned by the nephew of painter Georges Bretegnier, and decorated with some of Bretegnier's original paintings and drawings. BB **€35**

★ **Equity Point Marrakech (Riad Amazigh)** 80 Derb el Hammam Mouassine ☎0524 440793, ⓦequity-point .com; map p.322. A hostel in a riad, with all the architectural charm of any other riad, but a fun crowd and four- to eight-bed dorms (each with its own bathroom) instead of the usual flowers-on-the-pillow service. There's wi-fi, a pool, a bar and a restaurant, cool spaces to hang out in, and a friendly atmosphere rather than an exclusive one. The riad also has single rooms (€75) and one double, but they aren't such great value. BB dorm **€12**, double **€100**

★ **Noir d'Ivoire** 31 Derb Jedid, Bab Doukkala ☎0524 381653, ⓦnoir-d-ivoire.com; map pp.316–317. A magnificent riad, impressive from the moment you walk in, owned by an English interior designer, who's done it out in cream, brown and black (the name refers to the colour scheme), with a feel that manages to be classy yet cosy at the same time. There's a well-equipped gym, two pools and a bar, and service is punctilious, reflecting the fact that there's almost one staff member per guest. BB **€185**

Riad 72 72 Derb Arset Aouzal ☎0524 387629, ⓦriad72.com; map pp.316–317. A very sleek and stylish Italian-owned riad, with sparse but extremely tasteful modern decor, palms and banana trees in the courtyard and its own hammam (but no pool). The riad is part of a group called "Ouvo" (ⓦuovo.com) with two similarly stylish sister establishments (same phone number for bookings), *Riad 12* at 12 Derb Sraghnas (ⓦriad12.com; €198) and *Riad Due* at 2 Derb Chentouf (ⓦriaddue.com; €176). Rates include breakfast and afternoon tea. **€160**

Riad Bayti 35 Derb Saka, Bab el Mellah ☎0524 380180, ⓦriad-bayti.com; map pp.316–317. A great old house, formerly owned by a family of Jewish wine merchants in the Mellah, with that quarter's distinctive high ceilings and wide veranda, giving a spacious feel. Run by a dynamic young French couple, with warm modern decor that perfectly complements the classic architecture, and the smell of spices wafting in from the market below. Facilities include childcare and wi-fi. Rates include breakfast and afternoon tea. **€94**

Riad Elizabeth 33 Derb el Baroud, Hart Essoura ☎0524 383558, ⓦriadelizabeth.com; map pp.316–317. Elegant but homely, this good-value and very friendly riad is run by an English couple (she designed it, he built it), with a strong personal touch, lots of cool black-and-white decor, disco-style mirror-mosaic loos, quite a large patio pool, and a spacious roof terrace. There's also parking nearby. Each room is different, but all are modern and bright. BB **€115**

Riad Jonan 35 Derb Bzou, off Rue de la Kasbah ☎0524 386448, ⓦriadjonan.com; map pp.316–317. This British-run riad in the kasbah is laidback, reasonably priced and very friendly. It features lots of brick and terracotta tiles, stylish room decor, especially in the new wing, a/c in

---

RIAD-BOOKING AGENCIES

These agencies each manage a stable of riads, with a wide choice available.

Marrakech Médina 102 Rue Dar el Bacha, Northern Medina ☎0524 290707, ⓦmarrakech-medina.com. A firm that's actually in the business of doing up riads as well as renting them out, with a reasonable selection in all price ranges.

Marrakech Riads Dar Cherifa, 8 Derb Charfa Lakbir, Mouassine, Northern Medina ☎0524 426463, ⓦmarrakech-riads.net. A small agency with only eight riads (plus one in Fez), committed to keeping it chic and authentic.

Riads au Maroc 1 Rue Mahjoub Rmiza, Guéliz ☎0524 431900, ⓦriadomaroc.com. One of the first and biggest riad agencies with lots of choice in all price categories.

5

all but one room, a plunge pool, British TV, and a relaxed atmosphere, but for safety reasons children aren't allowed. BB £60

★ **Riad Kniza** 34 Derb l'Hotel, near Bab Doukkala ☎0524 376942, ⓦriadkniza.com; map pp.316–317. Owned by a top antique dealer and tour guide (whose clients have included US presidents and film stars), this is one classy riad, with beautiful rooms and a state-of-the-art pool, not to mention a sauna, hammam and massage room, genuine antiques for decoration, and solar panels for ecologically sound hot water, yet it still manages to feel like a real Moroccan family home. The family themselves (all English-speaking) are always on hand to make you feel welcome, the food is excellent and the service absolutely impeccable. BB €225

Riad Sahara Nour 118 Derb Dekkak ☎0524 376570, ⓦriadsaharanour-marrakech.com; map pp.316–317. More than just a riad, this is a centre for art, self-development and relaxation. Workshops in music, dance, painting and calligraphy are held here, and self-development programmes in meditation and relaxation techniques are available. Guests who wish to hold artistic happenings are encouraged, but you don't need to take part in these activities in order to stay here and enjoy the calm atmosphere on the patio, shaded by orange, loquat and pomegranate trees. BB €87

Riad Zolah 114–116 Derb el Hammam, near Mouassine Mosque ☎0524 387535, ⓦriadzolah.com; map p.322. An extremely well-run British-owned riad, with all sorts of little touches that make you feel like a special guest ("the most generous range of extras in Marrakesh", so they claim). Facilities include wi-fi, in-house hammam and massage room, tasteful decor with lots of white, generous splashes of colour, original features, and wonderful use of carpets and drapes. BB 2580dh

Riyad al Moussika 17 Derb Cherkaoui, off Rue Douar Graoua ☎0524 389067, ⓦriyad-al-moussika.ma; map pp.316–317. A gem of a riad, formerly owned by Thami el Glaoui (see box, p.327), with absolutely gorgeous decor, all designed to exact specifications in traditional Moroccan style by its Italian owner. The resulting combination of Moroccan tradition and Italian flair is harmonious and beautiful – like a traditional Marrakshi mansion, but better. The walls are decked with contemporary paintings by local artists, and the riad claims to have the finest cuisine in town (doubling as the *Pepe Nero* restaurant; see p.348). Rates include breakfast and afternoon tea. €235

Riyad el Cadi 86–87 Derb Moulay Abdelkader, off Rue Dabachi ☎0524 378098, ⓦriyadelcadi.com; map pp.316–317. The former home of a German diplomat who was ambassador to several Arab countries, embellished with his wonderful collection of rugs and antiques and incorporating five patios, three salons, a pool, a hammam, free wi-fi and excellent standards of service. As well as

ordinary guest rooms, there are two wonderful suites, and the "blue house", a patio with two double rooms, which is rented in its entirety (€260). BB €145

GUÉLIZ

Farouk 66 Av Hassan II ☎0524 431989, ⓔhotelfarouk@hotmail.com; map p.335. Owned by the same family as the *Ali* in the Medina, and housed in a rather eccentric building, with all sorts of branches and extensions, it offers a variety of rooms – check a few before choosing – all with hot showers, and some now under renovation. Staff are friendly and welcoming, and there's an excellent-value restaurant. 210dh

Fashion 45 Av Hassan II ☎0524 423707, ⓔfashionhotel@menara.ma; map p.335. Terracotta tiling, nicely carved black-painted wooden furnishings and large windows grace the rooms at this tastefully designed three-star, where the bathrooms feature reliable hot showers with a strong jet. There's also a rooftop pool and basement hammam. BB 584dh

Ibis Moussafir Marrakech Centre Gare Av Hassan II/ Pl de la Gare ☎0524 435929 to 33, ⓦibishotel.com; map p.335. This spick and span chain hotel located right by the train station is not the most exciting accommodation in town, but it's good value. It offers efficient service, a swimming pool, a restaurant and a bar in the lobby, and the buffet breakfasts are good. Lunch and dinner also available. BB 680d

Du Pacha 33 Rue de la Liberté ☎0524 431327, ⓦhotelpacha.net; map p.335. A 1930s-built hotel with large if rather drab rooms, most around a central courtyard, with a/c and satellite TV. There's a good restaurant, but no pool. BB 400dh

Toulousain 44 Rue Tariq Ben Ziad ☎0524 430033, ⓦhoteltoulousain.com; map p.335. This excellent budget hotel was originally owned by a Frenchman from Toulouse (hence the name). It has a secure car park, free wi-fi and a variety of rooms, plainly decorated but always spick and span, some with shower, some with shower and toilet, some with shared facilities, and some with ceiling fans. BB 190dh

Des Voyageurs 40 Bd Mohammed Zerktouni ☎0524 447218; map p.335. This long-established budget hotel has rather an old-fashioned feel, but it's well kept, with spacious if rather sombre rooms and a pleasant little garden. 144dh

HIVERNAGE

Hivernage's chain four- and five-stars are amateurish in comparison with their equivalents abroad, and far less attractive than similarly priced Medina riads, but they have wheelchair access, and are more child-friendly, with large pools.

Akabar Av Echouhada ☎0524 437799, ⓦhotelakabar .ma; map p.335. A modest hotel located between the

Medina and Guéliz, with a smallish pool and reasonably priced restaurant and bar (10am–11pm), all open to non-guests (the pool at 50dh). The rooms (equipped with a/c and satellite TV) are small but cool, and it's worth taking one at the back if you don't like noise. BB **490dh**

Atlas Medina Av Moulay el Hassan ☎0524 339999, ⓦhotelsatlas.com; map p.335. The Atlas chain's top offering in Marrakesh, set amid extensive gardens and best known for its spa facilities, but service is mediocre, and certainly not five-star. Three rooms are adapted for wheelchair users. BB **907dh**

The Red House Bd el Yarmouk opposite the city wall ☎0524 437040 or 41, ⓦtheredhouse-marrakech .com; map p.335. A beautiful nineteenth-century mansion (also called *Dar el Ahmar*) full of fine stucco and zellij work downstairs, where the restaurant offers gourmet Moroccan cuisine. Accommodation consists of eight luxurious suites – extremely chic and palatial – though European imperial rather than classic Moroccan in style. BB **3100dh**

Ryad Mogador Menara Av Mohammed VI (Av de France) ☎0524 339330, ⓦryadmogador.com; map p.335. Five-star (though really more like a four-star) whose facilities include a health club and three restaurants. The lobby is done out in classic style, with painted ceilings,

chandeliers and a very Moroccan feel. Rooms, on the other hand, are modern, light and airy. Four rooms are adapted for wheelchair users. **1900dh**

CAMPING AND YOUTH HOSTEL
Camping Caravanning Ferdaous 13km from the city centre on the Casablanca road (N9, formerly P7) ☎0524 304090, ⓦcamping-ferdaous.com. Good facilities and fine for an overnight stay if using a car or camper van, but not really convenient as a base for exploring Marrakesh on foot. **47dh**

Relais de Marrakech 10km from the city centre on the Casablanca road, opposite Grand Stade football ground ☎0664 717328, ⓦlerelaisdemarrakech.com. A large, quite upmarket campsite, with free hot showers, a pool and wi-fi, and also permanent tents and rooms as well as the option of pitching your own, or parking a camper van. Reduced rates for rooms and permanent tents often avilable. Pitch **€8.50**, permanent tent **€27**, double **€52**

Youth Hostel Rue el Jahid, Guéliz ☎0524 447713, ⓔaubergemarrakech@hotmail.fr; map p.335. Friendly, quiet and sparkling clean dorms, with a small garden. Very near to the train station, and even nearer to the CTM office. BB **73.50dh**

EATING AND DRINKING

Guéliz has most of the city's French-style cafés, bistros and restaurants, and most of the bars. In the Medina, there are the Jemaa el Fna food stalls, many inexpensive café-restaurants, and a number of upmarket palace-restaurants.

MEDINA
Recommendations for the Medina span the range: from a bench in the Jemaa el Fna to the most sumptuous palace setting. Only the more expensive places are licensed to sell alcohol. Among the posher eating places are

palace-restaurants in former mansions with beautiful traditional decor. Many of these are well hidden away, and can be difficult to find, especially at night; if in doubt, phone in advance and ask for directions – sometimes the restaurant will send someone to meet you.

JEMAA EL FNA FOOD STALLS

Even if you don't eat at them, at some stage you should at least wander down the makeshift lane of food stalls on the Jemaa el Fna, which look great in the evening, lit by lanterns. As well as couscous and pastilla, there are spicy merguez sausages, *harira* soup, salads, fried fish, or, for the more adventurous, stewed snails (over towards the eastern side of the square), and sheep's heads complete with eyes. To partake, just take a seat on one of the benches, ask the price of a plate of food and order all you like. It's probably worth avoiding places that try to hustle you, and it's always wise to check the price of a dish before you order, or you're likely to be overcharged. Stalls patronized by Moroccans are invariably better than those whose only customers are tourists. If you want a soft drink or mineral water with your meal, the stallholders will send a boy to get it for you. On the southern edge of the food stalls, a row of vendors sell a hot, spicy galangal drink (*khoudenjal*), said to be an aphrodisiac, and usually taken with a portion of nutty cake. Orange and grapefruit juice stalls line both sides of the food stall area at all hours of the day, but check the price first, and insist on having the juice pressed in front of you – if they pull out a bottle of ready-pressed juice, it'll most likely be watered down, and quite possibly mixed with squash.

5

THE CHEAPEST MEDINA EATS

Apart from the Jemaa itself (see box, p.345), there's a concentration of cheap and basic eateries on Rue Bani Marine, a narrow street that runs south from the post office and Bank al Maghrib on Jemaa el Fna, between and parallel to Rue Bab Agnaou and Rue Moulay Ismail. Another street of cheap eats, with grills on one side and fried fish on the other, is the small street that runs from Arset el Maach alongside Place des Ferblantiers to the entrance of the El Badi Palace (see map, p.316–317). There's also a row of places just outside the walls at Bab Doukkala, between the bus station and the grand taxi stand.

CAFÉS

Le Bougainvillier 33 Rue Mouassine ☎0524 441111; map p.322. An upmarket café and quiet retreat in the middle of the Medina: handy for a break after a hard morning's shopping in the souks. Set in a secluded patio, it tries hard to be stylish, and generally succeeds, the lack of actual bougainvillea flowers being made up for by bougainvillea-coloured paintwork and chairs. There are salads, sandwiches, cakes, juices, coffee and tea, even tajines (Berber beef tajine 85dh, Berber veg tajine 75dh), but most of all it's a pleasant space to relax in. Daily 10am–9.30pm (food served from noon).

Café el Badi by Bab Berrima ☎0524 389975; map pp.316–317. On a rooftop looking out over Pl des Ferblantiers and towards the Mellah, this is one place to get close to the storks nesting on the walls of the El Badi Palace. It serves a range of hot and cold (non-alcoholic) drinks, and set menus (80–120dh, including one vegetarian) featuring soup, salad, couscous, and Moroccan sweetmeats for afters. Daily noon–10pm.

Café des Épices Pl Rahba Kedima, north side ☎0524 391770; map p.322. A small café offering refuge from the hubbub, with orange juice, mint tea, coffee in various permutations, including spiced with cinnamon, plus sandwiches (30–45dh), salads (45–55dh) and views over the Rahba Kedima from the upper floor and the roof terrace. Daily 9.30am–9pm.

Café du Grand Balcon South side of Jemaa el Fna, next door to Hôtel CTM; map p.319. This place has the fullest view over the Jemaa, taking it all in from a perfect vantage point. You can come up for just a drink (tea, coffee or soda), but they also do food, including salads (30–35dh), brochettes (50dh) and tajines (meat 50dh, veg 45dh). Daily 8am–10pm.

Cane juice bar 38 Rue Bab Agnaou; map p.319. This may be a bog-standard coffee and juice bar at the back, but out front they sell wonderful freshly pressed sugar cane juice (from 10.30am; 6dh) – the only place in Marrakesh to sell it – along with bite-size pieces of coconut cake (2dh). They also have *msimmen* (pancake-like griddle bread), plain or with butter and/or honey. Look for the juice machine, as there's no sign. Daily 7am–1pm & 5–10pm.

Chez Chegrouni East side of Jemaa el Fna ☎0661 434133; map p.319. Come at a quiet time if you want to

bag one of the front seats on the upstairs terrace, as only these have a view over the square. Popular with tourists, this place does decent couscous and good tajines at moderate prices (chicken with raisins and almonds, 60dh), though the portions are on the small side. Daily 8am–11pm.

Henna Café 93 Rue Arset Azoual ☎0656 566374, ⓦhennacafemarrakech.com; map pp.316–317. As well as tea and coffee, this place offers salads and snacks that are slightly different from the Marrakesh norm (falafel and tahina, for example, at 40dh), and there's a quiet little terrace on the roof as well as the downstairs café area. They also have a henna menu, where you can choose a henna tattoo design (50–500dh, depending on the design), and all profits are ploughed back into the local community. Daily 11am–8pm.

Hôtel CTM South side of Jemaa el Fna ☎0524 442325; map p.319. The rooftop café here gives a view onto most of the square and does a very good-value continental breakfast (7.30–11am; 25dh), but otherwise serves only (non-alcoholic) drinks. Daily 7.30am–11pm.

Marrakchi 52 Rue des Banques ☎0524 443377, ⓦlemarrakchi.com; map p.319. High up above the square, with imperial but intimate decor, impeccable service and superb food, including delicious pastilla, and several couscous and tajine options (lamb tajines 150dh), including vegetarian. In the evenings there's a belly-dancer. Licensed. Daily noon–6pm & 7pm–midnight.

★ **Les Prémices** South side of Jemaa el Fna ☎0524 391970; map p.319. Good Moroccan and European food including tasty gazpacho (25dh), well-prepared tajines (chicken with lemon and olives 45dh), steaks, fish, pizzas and even crème brûlée (30dh). It's on the very southeastern corner of the square, but close enough for a view of the action. Daily noon–10.30pm.

PÂTISSERIES

Pâtisserie Bab Agnaou inside Bab Agnaou; map pp.316–317. Little more than a hole in the wall, actually in the gate (Bab Agnaou) itself, this little patisserie serves nothing fancy, just good, traditional Moroccan sticky delights, mostly involving nuts and filo pastry fried in syrup on the premises. Even if you don't want to buy a kilo of them, a triangular *briouat* (filo parcel, in this case with

CAFÉ ARGANA

One of the most popular café-restaurants overlooking the square, the **Argana**, was bombed in 2011, killing seventeen people, mostly tourists. One Adel Othmani, said to be an "al-Qaeda sympathizer", was convicted for the murders along with eight associates, but aside from hatred of non-Muslim foreigners, it is not clear what their motive was, nor what they aimed to achieve. The café is being rebuilt, and should open in the near future.

nuts), perfumed with orange blossom water, is irresistible, and a snip at just 3dh. Daily 9am–9pm.

Patisserie Belkabir and Patisserie Duniya 63–65 Souk Smarine, by the corner of Traverse el Ksour; map p.322. Two shops, side by side, specializing in traditional Moroccan sweetmeats, stuffed with nuts and drenched in syrup, and particularly popular during the holy month of Ramadan, when of course they are eaten at night. A kilo of assorted sticky delights costs 100dh. Daily 10am–7.30pm.

Pâtisserie des Princes 32 Rue Bab Agnaou ☎0524 443033; map p.319. A sparkling patisserie with mouthwatering pastries at prices that are a little high by local standards (typically 15–20dh) but worth the extra. They also have treats like almond milk and ice cream. The *salon de thé* at the back is a very civilized place to take breakfast, morning coffee or afternoon tea. Daily 6am–11pm.

DINERS AND SNACK BARS

El Bahja 24 Rue Bani Marine ☎0524 441351; map p.319. This place is popular with locals and tourists alike. It's good value, cheap and generally unexciting, though its *kofta* is highly rated, and don't miss the house yoghurt for afters. Set menus 60–70dh. Daily noon–11pm.

Chez Bahia 206 Rue Riad Zitoun el Kedim, 50m from Jemaa el Fna ☎0671 525224; map p.319. A café-diner offering pastilla, low-priced snacks and excellent set breakfasts with pancake-like *msimmen*. For the rest of the day, there are wonderful tajines bubbling away out front to tempt you (chicken 30dh). Daily 6am–midnight.

Grillade Chez Sbaï 91 Rue Kassabine; map p.319. The tables are upstairs but you order downstairs at this tiny hole-in-the-wall diner. It isn't much to look at, but the food is good, the portions are ample and the prices are low. Most customers go for the spit-roast chicken, but the best deal is a big plate of chicken brochettes with chips and salad, a snip at 25dh. Daily 8.30am–1am.

Oscar Progrès 20 Rue Bani Marine ☎0666 937147; map p.319. One of the best budget restaurants in town, with friendly service, excellent-value set menus, and large servings of couscous (go for that or the brochettes in preference to the tajines, which are rather bland). Lamb couscous costs 40dh, vegetarian couscous 30dh, or be a real pig and go for the 100dh set menu. Daily noon–11pm.

Snack Café Toubkal Southeast corner of Jemaa el Fna, by Rue Riad Zitoun el Kedim ☎0524 442262; map p.319. As well as fruit juices, home-made yoghurts

and pastries, they also offer a range of salads, tajines and couscous. It's also a great place for a breakfast of coffee with bread and jam or with *msimmen* (a chewy, flat griddle bread) and honey (19dh), and there are set menus for 45–50dh. Daily 24hr.

RESTAURANTS

Café Arabe 184 Rue Mouassine ☎0524 429728, ⓦ cafearabe.com; map p.322. A sophisticated bar-restaurant in the heart of the Medina, very handy for the souks, with excellent Moroccan and European cooking and snappy service, plus juices, teas, cocktails and mocktails, served on the terrace, on the patio or in the salon. A dish of roast lamb with thyme will set you back 160dh, brochettes 140dh. Daily 10am–midnight (food served noon–11pm).

Chez Brahim 38 & 86 Rue Dabbachi ☎0524 442029; map p.316–317. Two budget restaurants 100m apart, each offering rooftop dining with the usual range of Moroccan staples (brochettes at 45dh, for example, as well as tajines and couscous). *Chez Brahim #1*, at no. 38, has music in the evenings, and 75–120dh set menus, while *Chez Brahim #2*, at no. 86, has a patisserie downstairs, slightly less kitsch decor upstairs, and a 50dh daily set menu, Despite the waiters outside trying to hustle you in (usually a warning sign), both are good value and try hard to please. Daily noon–midnight.

Earth Café 1 Derb el Zouaq, off Rue Riad Zitoun el Kedim ☎0661 289402, ⓦ earthcafemarrakech.com; map p.319. Marrakesh's first vegetarian restaurant offers vegetarian and vegan dishes at 60–70dh a throw. Choices include veggie burgers, "warm salad" and filo pastry parcels containing various combinations of vegetables and sometimes cheese. The portions are generous, and the food is well prepared and delicious, enough to tempt any flesh-eating carnivore, and a nice change from the usual Moroccan fare. They also serve excellent juices and herbal infusions, and the atmosphere is intimate and relaxed. Daily 11am–10pm.

Hôtel Islane Terrasse Panoramique 279 Av Mohammed V ☎0524 440081; map pp.316–317. The main attraction at this rooftop restaurant is its unparalleled view of the Koutoubia rather than its not-very-good-value set menu (120dh). That said, its breakfast buffet (55dh) isn't bad. Daily 7am–midnight.

Jama 149 Rue Riad Zitoun el Jedid ☎0524 429872; map pp.316–317. A quiet little patio with a large palm

TANJIA

The dish for which Marrakesh is known throughout Morocco is **tanjia**, or jugged meat, usually beef but sometimes lamb. Strictly speaking, the tanjia is the jug itself, and the traditional way to make a tanjia is to go the butcher with your jug (or use one of the butcher's), buy the meat and spices to put in it, and then take it to a hammam and have it cooked slowly in the embers of the bathhouse furnace. When the urn emerges from the embers a few hours later, the meat is tender and ready to eat. Most reasonably upmarket Marrakesh restaurants offer tanjia, as do cheaper tanjia diners such as the **tanjia stalls** opposite the olive souk (see map p.319), where it is best ordered in advance.

tree growing out of it, lit up with candles in the evening, and serving a small selection of well-cooked and modestly priced traditional tajines, including beef with figs (60dh), or chicken with lemons and olives (50dh), followed by their own house yoghurt (20dh). Daily (occasionally closed Tues) noon–3pm & 7–10pm.

Kosybar 47 Pl des Ferblantiers ☎0524 380324, ⓦkosybar.com; map pp.316–317. A slick restaurant and bar with upstairs terraces, serving fusion food. There's sushi, snacks, sandwiches, pasta and salad at lunchtime, or a 150dh set menu, and for supper you can dine on the likes of duck-leg confit (175dh) or sea bass in shitake sauce (180dh). Restaurant daily 11am–3pm & 7pm–midnight; bar daily 11am–midnight.

La Maison Arabe 1 Derb Assebbe Bab Doukkala, behind the Doukkala mosque ☎0524 387010, ⓦlamaisonarabe.com; map pp.316–317. As well as being Marrakesh's best hotel (see p.342), *La Maison Arabe* is one of the city's top eating places, with two restaurants, of which the Moroccan one serves up a very fine 440dh menu including seasonal tajines and a pastilla of young pigeons (or a veg pastilla and veg tajine for non-carnivores). The *Three Flavours* restaurant offers Moroccan, European and Asian dishes including tandoori chicken kebabs with basmati rice (220dh) or spicy chicken with Thai basil (200dh). Licensed. Daily noon–3pm & 7–11pm.

Pepe Nero Riyad al Moussika, 17 Derb Cherkaoui (off Rue Douar Graoua) ☎0524 389067, ⓦpepenero-marrakech .com; map pp.316–317. The terrace and lounge of the *Riyad al Moussika* make an elegant venue for this classy restaurant, serving fine Moroccan and Italian food prepared by a Moroccan-Italian chef and accompanied by Moroccan and Italian wines. There's a Moroccan menu and an Italian one, and you can pick and mix, but the Italian dishes are generally the best. Starters include a wonderful salmon carpaccio (90dh), which you can follow with house pasta such as *pappardelle ai quattro formaggi* (120dh). Mains include an excellent tenderloin steak (150dh), and there's a gluttonous chocolate fondant pudding to finish (90dh). Daily noon–2.30pm & 7.30–11pm.

Pizzeria Portofino 279 Av Mohammed V ☎0524 391665; map pp.316–317. Quite a posh

ambience, tablecloths and all, and wood-oven pizzas (50–70dh) that are well cooked, but slightly bland, though this is easily remedied with a splash of the garlic-and-chilli olive oil they thoughtfully provide. Daily noon–11pm.

Le Tanjia 14 Derb Jedid, Hay Essalam/Mellah, near Pl des Ferblantiers ☎0524 383836; map pp.316–317. Stylish bar-restaurant billed as an "oriental brasserie" serving well-cooked Moroccan dishes, including vegetarian options, in an old mansion done out in modern decor, and not outrageously expensive. Try the Atlas lamb kebabs (180dh), the monkfish kebabs (190dh), or check out the tasting menu (780dh for two). Daily noon–3pm & 7.30–11pm.

Terrasse des Épices 15 Souk Cherifa ☎0524 375904, ⓦterrassedesepices.com; map p.322. Above the souks is this terrace restaurant run by the same people as *Café des Épices* (see p.346). It has separate bays for each table giving diners their own space and a bit of privacy – handy if you want to use the free wi-fi – while still allowing you to enjoy the great views. You can start with a trio of Moroccan salads (55dh), followed by *mechoui* (130dh), with crème brûlée for afters (55dh). There's also a 100dh lunctime set menu. Daily 10am–9.30pm.

Terrasse le Medersa Fondouk Lahbabi, 4 Rue de Souk des Fassis; map pp.316–317. On the terrace of a *fondouk* adjoining the roof of the Ben Youssef Medersa (hence its name), this unassuming little café-restaurant offers a variety of mocktails (30dh), juices and inexpensive Moroccan dishes (chicken tajine with lemon and olive, for example, at 45dh), served with a smile. On the downside, the seats could be larger and more comfortable. Daily 11am–9pm.

PALACE RESTAURANTS

El Bahia 1 Rue Riad Zitoun el Jedid, by the Bahia Palace ☎0524 378679. A proper palace restaurant, but with bargain-priced menus (150dh) in a beautifully restored mansion, all finely carved stucco and painted wooden ceilings, which used to offer meals with a floorshow at twice the price. Daily noon–3pm & 7–11pm.

Dar Essalam 170 Rue Riad Zitoun el Kedim ☎0524 443520, ⓦdaressalam.com; map pp.316–317. This seventeenth-century mansion has five different salons, all beautifully done out and dripping with zellij and stucco. Winston Churchill and Sean Connery are among the past diners here, and Doris Day and James Stewart also ate here in Hitchcock's *The Man Who Knew Too Much*. The food (lunchtime menus 200–250dh, evening 250–400dh, plus wine) is good, with pastilla or *harira* to start, followed by tajine, couscous or chicken *m'hammer* (with ginger and cumin), the ambience is superb, and in the evening there are musicians, belly-dancers and Moroccan Berber dancers. Daily noon–3pm & 8pm–midnight.

Dar Marjana 15 Derb Sidi Ali Tair, off Rue Arset Aouzal ☎0524 385110, ⓦdarmarjanamarrakech.com; map pp.316–317. This restaurant is housed in a beautiful early nineteenth-century palace. Look for the sign above the entrance to a passageway diagonally across the street from the corner of the Dar el Glaoui; take the passage and look for the green door facing you before a right turn. Among the tasty dishes they serve, two classics stand out: poultry pastilla and *couscous aux sept légumes*. The set menu costs 726dh including wine. Daily except Tues 8pm–midnight.

Dar Zellij 1 Kaa Essour, Sidi Ben Slimane ☎0524 382627, ⓦdarzellij.com; map pp.316–317. A seventeenth-century riad where you can take dinner (set menu 350–600dh, plus drinks) or weekend brunch (set menu 200–250dh) on the patio or in one of the lounges, all decked out in red and super-comfortable. Start with Moroccan salad and *briouats* (filo pastry parcels), followed by pastilla and then a tajine (vegetarian options are available), and round it off with sweet pastilla or orange in cinnamon. Mon, Wed & Thurs 7.30pm–midnight, Fri–Sun 11am–3pm & 7.30pm–midnight.

Palais Gharnata 5–6 Derb el Arsa, off Rue Riad Zitoun el Jedid ☎0524 389615, ⓦgharnata.com; map pp.316–317. Popular with foreign visitors, though unfortunately the food is merely so-so (the 750dh menu features pastilla, couscous, lamb tajine, and includes drinks), and individual diners play second-fiddle to groups. However, the decor is splendid, as the building is a magnificently decorated sixteenth-century mansion, with an Italian alabaster fountain at its centre; scenes from *The Return of the Pink Panther* were shot here. Past patrons have included Jacqueline Kennedy and the Aga Khan. Daily 8–11pm.

Le Tobsil 22 Derb Abdellah Ben Hessaien, near Bab Ksour ☎0524 444052; map pp.316–317. The Moroccan cuisine is sumptuous at this intimate riad, reached by heading south down a little alley just east of Bab Laksour. It's considered by many to be the finest restaurant in town, with delicious pastilla and the most aromatic couscous you could imagine, though the wine (included in the price) doesn't match the food in quality. Worth booking ahead. The set menu – which changes daily – is 625dh. Daily except Tues 7.30–11pm.

Yacout 79 Sidi Ahmed Soussi ☎0524 382929; map pp.316–317. Housed in a gorgeous old palace, the *Yacout* opened as a restaurant in 1987, with columns and fireplaces in super-smooth orange- and blue-striped *tadelakt* plaster, designed by acclaimed American interior designer Bill Willis, whose use of *tadelakt* here and elsewhere made it massively trendy in Moroccan interior design. The classic Moroccan tajine of chicken with preserved lemon and olive is a favourite here, but the fish tajine is also rated very highly. The cuisine has received Michelin plaudits in the past, though standards are beginning to slip as the tour groups move in. The menu costs 700dh per person including drinks. Tues–Sun 8pm–midnight.

GUÉLIZ

CAFÉS AND PÂTISSERIES

Amandine 177 Rue Mohammed el Bekal ☎0524 449612, ⓦamandinemarrakech.com; map p.335. If you're on a diet, look away now, because this is a double whammy: a café-patisserie, stuffed full of scrumptious almond-filled Moroccan pastries and French-style cream cakes, and right next door, a plush ice-cream parlour where you can sit and eat in comfort. You can have a coffee with your choice of sweetmeat in both halves, but the ice-cream section is more spacious. Daily 7am–9pm.

Café des Negotiants Pl Abdelmoumen Ben Ali ☎0524 435762; map p.335. Slap bang on the busiest corner in Guéliz, this grand café is the place to sit out on the pavement and really feel that you're in the heart of modern Marrakesh. It's also an excellent venue in which to spend the morning over a coffee, with a choice of set breakfasts (26.50–40.50dh), or an omelette or sandwich to accompany your caffeine fix. Daily 6am–midnight.

Café du Livre 44 Rue Tariq Ben Ziad, by Hôtel Toulousain ☎0524 432149, ⓦcafedulivre.com; map p.335. A very elegant space, serving tea and coffee, breakfasts, salads, sandwiches and brochettes, even tapas (25dh each, or a selection of three for 65dh) and cold cuts (100dh for a selection). There's also draught beer. The café has a library of secondhand English books to read or buy, and free wi-fi too. Mon–Sat 8am–midnight.

RESTAURANTS

Al Bahriya 69 Bd Moulay Rachid ☎0524 846186; map p.335. Very cheap and very popular fish restaurant, always crowded out at lunchtimes. For 30dh you get a big plate of fried squid and whiting, plus bread, olives and sauce, or for not much more there are swordfish brochettes, fish tajines, fried prawns and fish soup. Unbeatable value. Daily 11am–midnight.

★ **Al Fassia** Résidence Tayeb, 55 Bd Mohammed Zerktouni ☎0524 434060; map p.335. Truly Moroccan – both in decor and cuisine – specializing in dishes from

5

the country's culinary capital, Fez. Start with that great classic, pigeon pastilla (110dh), followed by a choice of five different lamb tajines (120dh), among other sumptuous Fassi offerings. The ambience and service are superb. Daily except Tues noon–2.30pm & 7.30–11pm.

Le Cantanzaro 50 Rue Tarik Ibn Ziad ☎0524 433731; map p.335. One of the city's most popular Italian restaurants, crowded at lunchtime with Marrakshis, expats and tourists. Specialities include *saltimbocca alla romana* (100dh) and rabbit in mustard sauce (90dh), and there's crème brûlée or tiramisu (both 30dh) to round it off with. You're strongly advised to book, but some people do just turn up and queue for a table. Licensed. Mon–Sat noon–2.30pm & 7.15–11pm.

Chez Lamine Hadj 19 Résidence Yasmine, Rue Ibn Aïcha, corner of Rue Mohammed Bekal ☎0524 431164; map p.335. Unpretentious, inexpensive restaurant, very poplar with Marrakshis for solid traditional meat dishes. A chicken tajine is only 30dh, or you can go all the way and get a sheep's head or half a kilo of tanjia for 70dh. Daily 9am–11pm.

Comptoir Darna Av Echouada, Hivernage ☎0524 437702, ⊛comptoirdarna.com; map p.335. Downstairs it's a restaurant serving reliably good Moroccan and international cuisine, with dishes like beef tajine with peas and artichokes (160dh) or weeping tiger (steak in ginger sauce; 220dh), as well as one or two vegetarian options, and there's cabaret entertainment starting at 10.30pm. Upstairs it's a chic lounge bar, very popular with Marrakesh's young and rich. Mon–Thurs 8pm–midnight, Fri–Sun 8pm–12.30am; bar daily 8pm–around 2am.

Grand Café de la Poste Rue el Imam Malik, just off Av Mohammed V behind the post office ☎0524 433038, ⊛grandcafedelaposte.com; map p.335. More grand than café, this is in fact quite a posh restaurant serving international cuisine. The menu changes regularly, but a typical dish might be tender roast beef and mashed potato (175dh) or sole meunière (270dh). Wash it down with a cup of Earl Grey, or a choice of rums, tequilas and fine brandies if you prefer something harder. Daily 8am–1am.

Hôtel Farouk 66 Av Hassan II ☎0524 431989; map p.335. From noon the hotel restaurant offers an excellent-value 50dh set menu with soup, salad, couscous, tajine or brochettes, followed by fruit, ice cream or home-made yogurt. Alternatively, tuck in to one of their excellent wood-oven pizzas (35–65dh). Daily 6am–11pm.

Le Jacaranda 32 Bd Mohammed Zerktouni, on Pl Abdelmoumen Ben Ali ☎0524 447215, ⊛lejacaranda .com; map p.335. Reliably good traditional French cuisine, starting with the likes of snails in garlic butter (90dh),

followed by duck confit with baked apples and wild mushrooms (160dh). There are lunchtime set menus for 100–120dh, and evening menus for 149–210dh. The restaurant doubles as an art gallery, with different exhibits on its walls each month. Licensed. Daily noon–3pm & 7.30–10.30pm.

Katsura 1 Rue Oum Errabia ☎0524 292544; map p.335. A Thai and Japanese restaurant, with the usual Thai standards including tom yum soup and green or red curries (curry and drink 70dh; set menu 115dh), plus Japanese snacks, mainly sushi. The food's fresh and tasty, and the service is pleasant and efficient. All in all, a nice change from the usual Moroccan dishes. Daily noon–2.30pm & 7.45–11.30pm.

Lunch d'Or Rue de l'Imam Ali, opposite the church; map p.335. It can be hard to find an honest-to-goodness cheap Moroccan eatery in the Ville Nouvelle, but this place serves tasty tajines at 25dh a shot, great value and very popular with workers on their lunch break. Daily 7.30am–8pm.

Puerto Banus Rue Ibn Hanbal (opposite the police headquarters and Royal Tennis Club) ☎0524 446534; map p.335. A good Spanish fish restaurant – though French-managed – with outdoor dining and specialities such as paella (200–300dh for two), or tapas at 24dh each, and a good-value midday menu with salad bar for 90dh. Daily noon–3pm & 7.30pm–midnight.

Rôtisserie de la Paix 68 Rue de Yougoslavie, alongside the former cinema Lux-Palace ☎0524 433118, ⊛restaurant-diaffa.ma/rotisserie; map p.335. An open-air grill, established in 1949, specializing in mixed grills (entrecôte steak 90dh, filet mignon 170dh) barbecued over wood, usually with a fish option available. It's all served either in a salon with a roaring fire in winter, or in the shaded garden in summer. Couscous served on Fridays only. Daily noon–5pm & 6.30–11pm.

La Taverne 22 Bd Mohammed Zerktouni ☎0524 446126; map p.335. As well as a drinking tavern, this is a pretty decent restaurant – in fact, it claims to be the oldest in town – where you can dine on French and Moroccan food indoors or in a lovely tree-shaded garden. Dishes include *steak au poivre* (85dh), and there's a good-value 130dh four-course set menu. Licensed. Daily 12.30–2pm & 7–10.30pm.

La Trattoria 179 Rue Mohammed el Bekal ☎0524 432641, ⊛latrattoriamarrakech.com; map p.335. The best Italian food in town, with impeccable service and excellent cooking, located in a 1920s house decorated by Bill Willis (as in *Yacout*; see p.349). As well as freshly made pasta, steaks and escalopes, there's the house speciality – beef medallions in parmesan (180dh) – plus a wonderful tiramisu (70dh) to squeeze in for dessert. Daily 7–11.30pm.

BARS AND NIGHTLIFE

Entertainment and nightlife in the **Medina** revolve around Jemaa el Fna. For a drink in the Medina, choices are limited; apart from the *Tazi* (see below), you can get a beer – or more likely a cocktail – in the *Café Arabe* (see p.347), *Kosybar* (see p.348) or *Le Tanjia* (see p.348), all of which double as upmarket bars. In the **Ville Nouvelle**, there's more variety; some of the bars are rather male, but women should be all right in the *Chesterfield* (see below) and also in the bars of hotels such as the *Akabar* (see p.345) and *Ibis* (see p.344), as well as the *Comptoir Darna* (see p.350), which is an upmarket bar as well as a restaurant. **Nightclubs** can be fun, though some at the top end of the market are a bit snooty, and may frown, for example, on jeans or trainers; most play a mix of Western and Arabic music, but it's the latter that really fills the dancefloor. None of them really gets going until around midnight (in fact, some don't open until then), and they usually stay open until 3 or 4am.

BARS

African Chic 5 Rue Oum Errabia ☏ 0524 431424, ⓦ african-chic.com; map p.335. One of Marrakesh's most congenial bars, informal and relaxed, with cocktails, wines and beers, tapas (five for 70dh, eight for 100dh), salads, pasta, or even meat or fish dishes, not to mention live Latin and Gnaoua music every night from 10pm. Daily 5pm–1.30am.

Café Atlas Pl Abdelmoumen Ben Ali ☏ 0524 448888; map p.335. A pavement café in the very centre of Guéliz, but wander inside, and hey presto, it is magically transformed into a bar, with bottled beer, spirits and plates of bar snacks on the counter. Taking your drink out on the pavement is considered rather indiscreet, so it's best to remain within, where respectable passers-by won't notice that you're partaking of alcoholic beverages. Daily 7am–11pm.

Café-Bar de l'Escale Rue Mauritanie, just off Av Mohammed V ☏ 0524 433447; map p.335. A down-at-heel, spit-and-sawdust kind of bar, this place has been going since 1947 and specializes in good bar snacks, such as fried fish or spicy merguez sausages – you could even come here for lunch or dinner (there's a dining area at the back). The interior isn't recommended for unaccompanied women, especially in the evening, but there's a family-friendly (no-booze) terrace out front by day (brochettes 32dh). Daily 7am–11pm.

Chesterfield Pub 119 Av Mohammed V ☏ 0524 446401; map p.335. Upstairs in the *Nassim Hôtel*, this supposedly English-style pub is one of Marrakesh's more sophisticated watering holes, with a comfortable if rather smoky bar area, all soft seats and muted lighting. There's also a more relaxed, open-air poolside terrace to lounge about on with your draught beer or cocktail of a summer evening. Daily 11am–midnight.

Grand Hôtel Tazi Corner of Rue Bab Agnaou and Rue el Mouahidine, Medina ☏ 0524 442787; map p.319. Once, this was the only place in the Medina where you could get a drink, and it's still the cheapest (beers from 30dh). There's nothing fancy about the bar area – squeezed in between the restaurant and the lobby, and frequently spilling over into the latter – but it manages to be neither rough nor pretentious (a rare feat among Marrakesh drinking dens). You can also drink on the roof

terrace, and women should have no worries about drinking here. Daily 7am–11pm.

Kechmara 3 Rue de la Liberté ☏ 0524 422532, ⓦ kechmara.com; map p.335. Downstairs, *Kechmara* is a cool bar-café with a slightly Japanese feel; upstairs there's an open-air terrace with a contemporary design. It's a hip place to hang out, with modern art exhibitions and music (mostly soul, jazz and blues) on the terrace Wed–Sat from 8pm. It also serves food including steaks, stir-fries and daily specials (90dh for the dish of the day, or tajine of the day). Daily noon–11pm.

NIGHTCLUBS

Balafon Rue Oum Errabia, behind Hôtel Marrakesh ☏ 0524 446391; map p.335. Look for the signpost on Av Mohammed V to find this lively dance club where Western pop and disco alternate with Algerian and Moroccan *raï* music. There are two bars, quite a sophisticated range of drinks, and a mainly young crowd, with a gay contingent. Entry (150dh) includes one drink. Daily 10pm–4am or later.

Pacha Marrakech Av Mohammed VI (southern extension), Nouvelle Zone Hôtelière de l'Aguedal ☏ 0524 388400, ⓦ pachamarrakech.com; map p.335. The Marrakesh branch of the famous Ibiza club claims to have the biggest and best sound system in Africa, and it's certainly the place to come if DJing skills, acoustics and visuals are important for your clubbing experience. Big-name DJs from abroad regularly play here – check the website for current line-ups. It also has two restaurants (one European, one Moroccan), a chill-out zone and a swimming pool. Entry 150dh Thurs & Fri, 200dh Sat, or more for special events such as big-name performers. Bar Tues–Sun 8pm–1am or 2am, club Thurs–Sat midnight–4am or 5am.

Theatro Hôtel es Saadi, Av el Kadassia (also spelt Qadassia), Hivernage ☏ 0524 448811, ⓦ theatromarrakech.com; map p.335. One of Marrakesh's more interesting nightclubs, located in, as its name suggests, an old theatre. Tuesday is ladies' night, and some other nights are themed. They play the usual mix of house, techno and r'n'b with Algerian *raï* and Middle Eastern pop (except on specific nights, such as Dutch house night, when the DJs are Dutch and the music's house), but the special

5

GAY MARRAKESH

For **gay men**, a certain amount of cruising goes on in the crowds of the Jemaa el Fna in the evening, and there's a gay presence at the *Diamant Noir* nightclub behind *Hôtel Marrakesh* (look for the sign on Av Mohammed V). The gay male tourist scene in Marrakesh is growing, and a number of riads are run by gay couples, but there is no easily perceptible **lesbian scene** in Marrakesh as yet. ⓦtravelmarrakech.co.uk has a small section on gay-friendly places.

effects and circus-style performers on stage make it a cut above most Marrakesh clubs. Entry 150dh. Daily midnight–6am.

VIP Club Pl de la Liberté ☎ 0524 434569; map p.335. The gullet-like entrance leads down to the first level, where there's an "oriental cabaret" (meaning a belly-dancing

floorshow), and then further down to the deepest level, where there's what the French call a *boîte*, meaning a sweaty little nightclub. It's got a circular dancefloor and a small bar area, but despite its diminutive size, the place rarely seems to be full. Entry 150dh. Daily midnight–4am.

SHOPPING

There are a massive number of shops in Marrakesh selling all kinds of crafts, but nothing you won't get cheaper elsewhere. Marrakesh's attraction is that you don't have to go elsewhere to get it, and if you're flying home out of Marrakesh, then buying your souvenirs here means you won't have to lug them round the country with you.

FIXED-PRICE CRAFTS

Ensemble Artisanal Av Mohammed V, 200m south of Bab Nkob; map pp.316–317. Before setting off into the souks, it's worth taking a look at this government-run complex of small arts and crafts shops, which holds a reasonable range of goods, notably leather, textiles and carpets. Shopping here is hassle-free, and the prices, which are supposedly fixed (though actually you can haggle here too), are a good gauge of the going rate if you intend to bargain elsewhere. At the back are a dozen or so workshops where you can watch young people learning a range of crafts including carpet-weaving. Mon–Sat 8.30am–7pm, Sun 9am–1pm.

Entreprise Bouchaib Complexe d'Artisanat 7 Derb Baissi Kasbah, near the Saadian Tombs ☎ 0524 381853; map pp.316–317. Another place with supposedly fixed prices, which are only slightly higher than what you might pay in the souks, and, though you won't be allowed to browse freely, the sales assistants who follow you round are generally quite charming and informative. In particular it's a good place to check out carpets and get an idea of the maximum prices you should be paying. Daily 8.30am–7pm.

CARPETS

Bazar du Sud 14 & 117 Souk des Tapis, off Pl Rahba Kedima, Medina ☎ 0524 443004; map p.322). A huge variety of carpets from all over the south of Morocco. Most claim to be old (if you prefer them spanking new, pop next door to Bazar Jouti at nos. 16 & 119), and are coloured with wonderful natural dyes such as saffron (yellow), cochineal (red) and indigo (blue). A large carpet could cost 4000dh, but you might be able to find a small kilim for around 500dh. Daily 8.30am–7.30pm.

JEWELLERY

Abdellatif Bellawi 56 & 103 Kissariat Lossta, between Souk el Kebir and Souk Attarine, Medina ☎ 0526 289304; map p.322. A great selection of beads and bangles, including Berber bracelets from the Atlas in chunky solid silver, traditional Berber necklaces from the Atlas and the Sahara, West African money beads, and necklaces from as far away as Yemen. There are also rings, earrings and woollen Berber belts, with some Cowrie-encrusted Gnaoua caps hanging up outside the door. Daily 9am–8pm.

Bazar Atlas 129 Av Mohammed V, Guéliz ☎ 0663 620103; map p.335. Some exquisite and interesting items grace this elegant little shop, mostly silver jewellery, but also ornaments for the home, including inkpots made from ram's horns, and colonial-era glass boxes. The selection is not huge, but it's well chosen. Daily 9am–8pm.

CLOTHES

Ben Zarou Frères 1 Kissariat Drouj (off Souk el Attarin by no.116), Medina ☎ 0524 443351; map p.322. This trio of shops in a little corner of the *kissaria* is the best place to come for pukka traditional Moroccan *babouches* (slippers), men's and women's, in various colours and traditional styles. Prices start at around 100dh, and there's no pressure or hard-sell here. Daily except Fri 9am–7pm.

Ben Zouine Med Rida 142 Rue Arset Azoual, Medina ☎ 0524 385056; map pp.316–317. A good place to get a tailor-made local-style shirt or blouse, be it in cotton, linen or wool, though opening hours can be a bit haphazard (morning is the best time to catch them). You choose your cloth, get measured up, specify what buttons or even embroidered design you want on it, and come back a day or two later to collect. Expect to pay around 300–500dh. Daily approximately 10am–noon & 5–8pm.

Femmes de Marrakech 67 Souk el Kchachbia, west of the Almoravid Koubba, Medina ☎ 0524 378308; map p.322. A dress shop run by a women's cooperative, creating their own garments, and also selling – on a fair-trade basis – clothes made at home by other women. The dresses are handmade from pure cotton and linen fabrics in a mix of Moroccan and Western styles. Colours range from sober pinks and greys to bright orange tie-dye, and there are some great *gandoras* (sleeveless kaftans) with hand-sewn multicoloured tassles. Daily 9.30am–1.30pm & 3.30–7pm.

Maison du Kaftan Marocain 65 Rue Sidi el Yamani, Medina ☎ 0524 44105; map p.322. Upmarket boutique selling robes, tunics and kaftans, from see-through glittery gowns and sequinned velvet tunics to lush embroidered silk kaftans that make sumptuous housecoats (except that they go for prices in excess of 2000dh). Most are for women, but there are also a few men's garments. Past customers include Jean-Paul Gautier, Mick Jagger and Samuel L. Jackson, as photos on the wall testify. Daily 9am–7.30pm.

BOOKS

Librairie Chatr 19 Av Mohammed V, Guéliz ☎ 0524 447997; map p.335. The best bookshop in town, selling mainly French titles, with lots of books on Morocco, sometimes including books on trekking and off-roading, plus a small selection of titles in English at the back. The front part of the shop supplies artists' materials, including paint and brushes, as well as a large and varied selection of pens. Mon–Thurs 8.30am–1pm & 3–8pm, Fri 8.30–11.30am & 3.30–8.30pm, Sat 8.30am–1pm & 4–8pm.

Librairie d'Art ACR Résidence Tayeb, 55 Bd Mohammed Zerktouni, Guéliz ☎ 0524 446792; map p.335. There are lots of full-colour coffee table books here, including several on Marrakesh and Moroccan interior design. There are also books on subjects such as architecture, textiles and jewellery, and cooking (though mostly in French) and even greetings cards. Mon–Sat 9am–12.30pm & 3–7pm.

FOOD

Aswak Assalam Av 11 Janvier at the junction with Av Prince Moulay Abdallah, Guéliz ☎ 0524 431004; map p.335. This is the most central supermarket, certainly not the most characterful shopping in town, but quick and easy. There's a good patisserie section, and serve-yourself grains and spices, so you can weigh out exactly as much or as little as you want. You'll also find a fuller (and probably fresher) range of commercial dairy products than you would at a grocery store, and there are even consumer items, including couscous steamers. Daily 10am–11pm.

Jemaa el Fna Market Jemaa el Fna (east side), Medina;map p.319. This little covered market is of most interest as a place to get fruit and veg just off the big square, though it also sells meat and even shoes. Daily 9am–9pm.

Marché Central (Municipal Market) Rue Ibn Toumert, Guéliz; map p.335. This is the Ville Nouvelle's main market, and it's a far cry from the markets in the Medina. It's where expats and better-off Marrakshis come for their fresh fish, meat, fruit and veg, and there are two butchers selling horsemeat, one selling pork, and shops specializing in pickled lemons, perfumed soaps, fossils, ceramics, booze, tourist tat, paintings and fresh flowers. Mon–Sat 7am–10pm, Sun 7am–noon, though shops within the market may keep shorter hours.

Olive stalls Souk Ableuh (just off Jemaa el Fna), Medina; map p.319. This souk consists of row of stalls piled up with olives. The wrinkled black ones are the typical Moroccan olive, delicious with bread but a bit salty on their own. Of the green olives, the ones flavoured with bits of lemon are among the tastiest. Other delicacies on sale here include the spicy red *harissa* sauce and bright yellow lemons preserved in brine, a favourite ingredient in Moroccan cooking. Daily 10am–8pm.

MISCELLANEOUS

Cadre en Pneus 97 Rue Riad Zitoun el Kedim, Medina; map pp.316–317. This is one of a group of small shops at the southern end of this street that recycle disused car tyres. Initially they made hammam supplies such as buckets and flip-flops, but they've since branched out into products such as picture frames and framed mirrors, odd rather than elegant, in black rubber, but certainly worth a look. Best buys are the *tuffets* (stools), which rather resemble giant liquorice allsorts. Sat–Thurs 9am–6.30pm, Fri 9am–1pm.

Moulay Larbai 96 Souk el Kchachbia, Medina; map p.322. Moulay Larbai's claim to fame is that it was he who first started making mirrors framed with small pieces of mirror or of coloured glass, and that he still makes the best ones in the souk, which indeed he does. His mirrors come in various shapes and sizes, and he uses proper Iraqi-style stained glass for the colours. Prices start at around 120dh. Daily 9am–7pm.

Omar Siam 39 Souk Nejjarine (part of Souk el Kebir), Medina; map p.322. It's not much more than a hole in the wall, but stop for a peek at Omar Siam's range of wooden spoons, handmade in all sizes, and really quite charming in their own small way. There are ladles for eating *harira*, smaller ones for measuring spices, spoons that you could stir your tea with, spoons with holes for fishing olives out of brine, and non-spoon items too: pastry moulds for making

5

FESTIVALS AND EVENTS

The two-week **Festival National des Arts Populaires** (ⓦ marrakechfestival.com), held in June or July each year, is the country's biggest and best folklore and music festival, with musicians and dancers coming in from across Morocco and beyond, spanning the range of Moroccan music; shows start around 9pm and are preceded by a fantasia at Bab Jedid, with Berber horsemen at full gallop firing guns into the air. Marrakesh also has an annual **Marathon**, run on the third or fourth Sunday in January (see ⓦ marathon-marrakech.com for details), and the **Marrakesh Film Festival** in November or early December (ⓦ festivalmarrakech.info), in which the featured movies are shown at cinemas across town, and on large screens in the El Badi Palace and the Jemaa el Fna.

Moroccan sweets, and even pairs of wooden scissors (for cutting fresh pasta, in case you wondered). Prices are fixed and the smallest items are just 5dh. Daily, no fixed hours but usually 2–7pm, and sometimes mornings.

ACTIVITIES

Golf Golf courses have proliferated around Marrakesh in recent years. The oldest is Marrakesh Royal Golf Club (☎ 0524 409828, ⓦ royalgolfmarrakech.com), 5km out of town on the old Ouarzazate road, once played on by Churchill and Eisenhower. Others include: Amelkis Golf Club, 12km out on the Route de Ouarzazate (☎ 0524 404414); Palmeraie Golf Club (☎ 0524 368704, ⓦ pgpmarrakech .com), attached to the *Palmeraie Golf Palace* hotel, off the Route de Casablanca, northeast of town; Samanah Golf Club, 14km south of town on the Route d'Amizmiz (☎ 0524 483200, ⓦ samanah.com); Atlas Golf Resort, 5km out on the Route de Fès (☎ 0801 009009, ⓦ atlasgolfresort .ma); Assoufid (☎ 0524 368368, ⓦ assoufid.com), 10km southwest of town on the road that goes past the airport; Al Maaden Golf Resort, 5km southeast of town off the P2012 (☎ 0524 401350, ⓦ almaaden.com).

Hammams There are plenty of hammams in the Medina. The three closest to the Jemaa el Fna are Hammam Polo on Rue de la Recette, Hammam Bouloukate on the same street as *Hôtel Afriquia*, and one at the northern end of Rue Riad Zitoun el Kedim (see map, p.319). All open simultaneously for men and women with separate entrances for each. Hammams for tourists include Hammam Ziani, 14 Rue Riad Zitoun el Jedid (☎ 0662 715571, ⓦ hammamziani.ma), open for both sexes (separate areas) daily 8am–10pm, costing 50dh for a simple steam bath, or 270dh for an all-in package with massage; even dearer is Les Bains de Marrakech, 2 Derb Sedra, down an alley by Bab Agnaou in the kasbah (☎ 0524 381428, ⓦ lesbainsdemarrakech.com), where prices start at 150dh; despite this, you won't (unless you're gay) be able to share a steam bath experience with your partner – if you want to do that, you'll have to stay at one of the many riads with their own in-house hammam.

Swimming pools Many hotels allow non-residents to use their pools if you have a meal, or for a fee. In the Medina, the *Grand Hôtel Tazi* (see p.351) charges 100dh. Also handy, especially if you're with kids, is Oasiria, at km4, Route du Barrage, on the Asni/Oumnass road (daily 10am–6pm; 210dh full day, 170dh half-day; ☎ 0524 380438, ⓦ oasiria .com); it even runs free shuttle buses from town in summer. The *Palmeraie Golf Palace* hotel in the palmery runs a similar place called Nikki Beach (daily 11.30am–sunset; 300dh; ☎ 0524 301010).

DIRECTORY

Banks and exchange The main area for banks in the Medina is off the south side of the Jemaa el Fna on Rue Moulay Ismail. In Guéliz, the main area is along Av Mohammed V between Pl Abdelmoumen Ben Ali and the market. Most major branches have ATMs. BMCE's branch in the Medina (Rue Moulay Ismail on Pl Foucauld) has a bureau de change (Mon–Fri 8am–8pm, Sat & Sun 9am–12.30pm & 3–6pm). The post office on Pl 16 du Novembre will also change cash, as will the post office at the train station, and the Jemaa el Fna post office has a bureau de change round the back, by the telephones (Mon–Fri 9am–8pm). There are also a growing number of private foreign exchange bureaux around town, including Global Cash at 13 Rue de la Liberté in Guéliz (daily 9am–8pm) and a couple around the Mouaisine Mosque in the Medina (similar hours; see map, p.322). Even outside these hours, the *Hotel Ali* (see p.341) and *Hotel Central Palace* (see p.341) will change money. The *Hotel Ali* often has the best rates in town in any case.

Cinemas The downmarket Cinéma Eden, off Rue Riad Zitoun el Jedid, dates from 1929 and is the oldest picture house in town. Watching a film here (typically a Bollywood/ Kung Fu double bill, known affectionately as "*L'histoire et la géographie*") is a real Moroccan experience. Other cinemas include the Colisée on Bd Mohammed Zerktouni, Guéliz, and Cinéma Mabrouka, Rue Bab Agnaou, Medina.

Consulates UK Honorary Consul: Mohammed Zkhiri, Résidence Taib (entrance A, mezzanine floor), 55 Bd Mohammed Zerktouni (☎ 0524 420846).

Dentist Dr Abdel Jouad Bennani, 112 Av Mohammed V (first floor), opposite the Délégation de Tourisme in Guéliz (☎0524 449136), speaks some English and has been recommended.

Doctors Dr Abdelmajid Ben Tbib, 171 Av Mohammed V, Guéliz (☎0524 431030), is recommended and speaks English. Dr Frédéric Reitzer, Immeuble Berdaï (entrance C, 2nd floor), 1 Av Moulay el Hassan (at Pl de la Liberté), Guéliz (☎0524 439562), also speaks some English. There's also an emergency call-out service, SOS Médecins (☎0524 404040), which charges around 400dh per consultation.

Hospitals Polyclinique du Sud, at the corner of Rue de Yougoslavie and Rue Ibn Aïcha, Guéliz (☎0524 447999), is a private clinic with a good reputation which is used to settling bills with insurance companies.

Internet access The best place to get online is at the Moulay Abdeslam Cyber-Park, on Av Mohammed V opposite the Ensemble Artisanal (daily 9.30am–6pm; 5dh/hr); there's a super-modern internet office with fast connections. Also, almost the entire park, especially the area near the fountain in the middle, is a free wi-fi zone. Internet cafés around the Jemaa el Fna include Cyber Café on the top floor at 24 Rue Ben Marine (daily 9am–midnight; 6dh/hr). In Guéliz, try Jawal, in a yard behind the old CTM office at 12 Bd Mohammed Zerktouni (daily 9am–10pm; 6dh/hr), or the Café Siraoua a block to the east (daily 8.30am–11.30pm; 7dh/hr).

Laundry Pressing Oasis, 44 Rue Tarik Ibn Zaid, Guéliz, two doors from *Hôtel Toulousain*.

Pharmacies Several along Av Mohammed V, including Pharmacie de la Liberté, just off Pl de la Liberté, which will call a doctor for you if necessary. In the Medina, try Pharmacie de la Place and Pharmacie du Progrès on Rue Bab Agnaou just by Pl Jemaa el Fna. There's an all-night pharmacy by the Commissariat de Police on Jemaa el Fna and another on Rue Khalid Ben Oualid near the fire station in Guéliz. Other all-night and weekend outlets are listed in pharmacy windows.

Police The tourist police (*brigade touristique*) are on the west side of the Jemaa el Fna (☎0524 384601).

Post office The main post office on Pl 16 du Novembre, midway down Av Mohammed V in Guéliz (Mon–Fri 8am–4.15pm for full services; Mon-Fri 8am–5.45pm & Sat 8am–noon for stamps) is undergoing reconstruction, but there's a temporray office round the side. This is where to go for poste restante. The Medina post office on Pl Jemaa el Fna is open similar hours, with a bureau de change round the back (Mon–Sat 8am–8pm, Sun 10am–8pm).

SPANA Visitors are welcome to come and see how animals are cared for at SPANA's clinic for *calèche* horses, mules and donkeys run by British animal welfare charity SPANA (see box, p.46) directly north of the Medina in Cité Mohammadi, Daoudiat (☎0524 303110).

The High Atlas

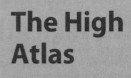

KASBAH IN THE HIGH ATLAS

The High Atlas

The High Atlas, North Africa's greatest mountain range, contains some of the most intriguing and beautiful regions of Morocco. A historical and physical barrier between the northern plains and the pre-Sahara, its Berber-populated valleys feel – and indeed are – very remote from the country's mainstream or urban life. The area is North Africa's premier trekking destination; casual day-hikers and serious mountaineers alike will find appealing routes in the region, offering both staggering peaks (*jebels*) and well-trodden passes (*tizis* or, in French, *cols*). Just a short distance from the hustle and bustle of Marrakesh is Tobkal National park, home to the impressive Jebel Toubkal (4167m) and numerous villages that appear locked in time. In addition to the highest peak, other worthy crests and hamlets can be reached with a trusted guide.

Mud-thatched Berber villages and remote pinnacles aren't the only draw here. The landscape varies from season to season: winter drops metres of snow that leads to gushing river valleys in spring; summer brings an unforgiving sun, while the autumnal sunlight brings the browns and reds of the peaks to life.

One of the benefits of trekking the region is being able to walk unencumbered: muleteers and their mules are available for hire, and mountain guides are an invaluable resource, particularly recommended if you are heading off the main routes. Other options include rock climbing and ski mountaineering, and mountain biking is increasingly popular on the dirt tracks (*pistes*) and mule paths.

The Ourika Valley

The **Ourika Valley** is a popular escape from the summer heat of Marrakesh. The village of **Setti Fatma** is a weekend resort for young Marrakshis, who ride out on their mopeds or BMWs to lie around and picnic beside the streams and waterfalls. The village lies at the end of the road, but a *piste* (to Timichi) and then a mule track continues up the valley to passes to **Tacheddirt** and **Oukaïmeden**, which has the best skiing in Morocco and interesting prehistoric rock carvings. The path also continues through to Imlil and Toubkal, making it a useful starting/finishing point for trekkers.

Marrakesh to Setti Fatma

Ourika Valley proper begins at **SOUK TNINE DE** (30km from Marrakesh), a small roadside village, which, as its name gives away, hosts a Monday **souk** – worthy of a

TREKKING NEAR IMLIL

Highlights

❶ Ourika Valley A cool escape from Marrakesh, the valley makes an easy day-trip for a walk around its waterfalls or lunch at a riverside café. **See p.358**

❷ Atlas Berbers The High Atlas is a stunning mountain range, populated mainly by Berbers who have a unique culture, dress and traditions. **See p.361**

❸ Skiing at Oukaïmeden Want to say you've skied in Morocco? Oukaïmeden is the spot; winter months bring snow and crowds enjoying the manageable peaks. **See p.363**

❹ Atlas flora and fauna Birds include bee-eaters, falcons, and other species unique to the region. Early summer sees acres of orchids. **See p.363**

❺ Jebel Toubkal North Africa's highest peak is a goal for most Atlas trekkers, offering summer walks and winter mountaineering. **See p.364**

❻ Imlil and Aroumd These Toubkal trailhead villages are remote enough to get a taste of Berber mountain life, even if you go no further. **See p.367** & **p.369**

❼ Ouirgane This region offers hidden walks and stunning panoramas in the cooler months and plenty of outdoor activities. **See p.377**

❽ Tin Mal This twelfth-century mosque in the heart of the Atlas can, uniquely, be visited by non-Muslims. **See p.382**

HIGHLIGHTS ARE MARKED ON THE MAP ON P.360

6

WEATHER AND AFFECTED ROUTES

The High Atlas is subject to **snow** from November to April, and even the major Tizi n'Tichka (road to Ouarzazate) and Tizi n'Test (road to Taroudant) can be closed for periods of a day or more. These passes are seldom blocked for long and **snow barriers** on the roads leading up into the mountains will be down if the passes are not open to the public. If blocked, the southern regions can be reached from Marrakesh via the Tizi Maachou pass (the N8, along with the newly finished A7 toll highway towards Agadir) followed by the N10 through Taroudant and Taliouine.

The **thaw** can present problems as well. When the snow melts in spring, swollen rivers are dangerous to cross. And the possibility of spring/summer **flash floods** must be taken seriously, as they can erupt suddenly and violently and are extremely dangerous. To keep safe, always camp on high ground while avoiding any spot where water might become a course for a torrent. This includes (even in summer) dried up and apparently terminally inactive riverbeds.

quick stop if you happen to be passing through. Just beyond, across the river, is **DAR CAID OURIKI**, with a picturesque *zaouia* set back in the rocks, near the ruins of an old *caidal* **kasbah**.

Beyond here, scattered at intervals over the next forty kilometres, are a series of tiny hamlets, interspersed with a few summer homes and the occasional hotel and café-restaurant. The only sizeable settlement of signficance along the route is **ARHBALOU** (50km southwest of Marrakesh), where most of the local people on the buses get off. Arhbalou sees smaller crowds in the summer months than Setti Fatma (see opposite) and offers riverside alfresco meals at slightly better prices.

Berber Museum

Tafza • Daily 9am–5pm • 20dh • ☎ 0524 385721

Located just past the town of Lagrab, 37km from Marrakesh, is the unimposing village of Tafza, where the kasbah has been restored and now houses the tasteful **Berber Museum**.

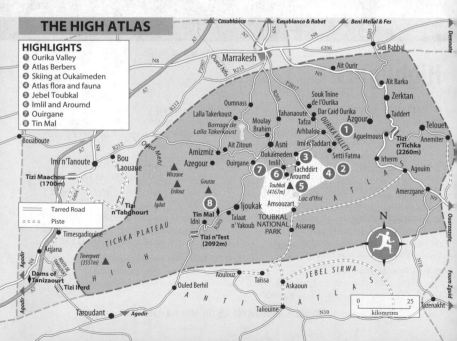

Exhibiting photographs, carpets, jewellery, agricultural tools and pottery, the museum is worth a visit to gain an understanding of Berber history and culture, especially helpful before setting out on any walk or trek in the region. Ask at reception about viewing a film by Daniel Chicault, which has stunning images of the mountains and of Berber life from decades past.

Setti Fatma

SETTI FATMA is a straggly riverside village, substantially rebuilt, expanded and made safer after its 1995 devastation by floods. The setting, with grassy terraces and High Atlas peaks rising to over 3600m, feels like a dreamscape after venturing from the dry plains that surround Marrakesh. In the rocky foothills above the village are a series of six (at times, seven) **waterfalls**.

The Ourika Valley cuts right into the **High Atlas**, whose peaks begin to dominate as soon as you leave Marrakesh. At Setti Fatma these mountains provide a startling backdrop that, to the southwest, include the main **trekking/climbing zone of Toubkal**. The usual approach to this is from Asni (see p.365) but it is possible to set out from Setti Fatma, or from Oukaïmeden (see p.363).

The waterfalls

To **reach the falls**, follow the road along the river southwest for five minutes, before crossing the river on the edge of town, over whichever makeshift bridge is currently

---

HIGH ATLAS BERBERS

Until recent decades, the High Atlas region – and its **Berber inhabitants** – was almost completely isolated. When the French began their "pacification" of Morocco in the 1920s, the way of life here was essentially feudal, based upon the control of the three main passes (*tizis*) by a trio of "clan" families, "the Lords of the Atlas". Even after the French negotiated the cooperation of these warrior chiefs, it was not until the spring of 1933 – just over two decades after the establishment of the Protectorate – that they were able to subdue them and control their tribal land. This occurred only with the cooperation of the main feudal chief, **T'hami el Glaoui**, who continued to control the region as pasha of Marrakesh (see box, p.327).

These days, the region is under official government control through a system of local *caids*, but in many villages the role of the state remains largely irrelevant, and if you go trekking you soon become aware of the mountains' highly distinctive culture and traditions. The longest established inhabitants of Morocco, the Atlas Berbers never adopted a totally orthodox version of Islam (see p.549) and the Arabic language has, even today, made little impression on their indigenous **Tachelhaït** dialects. Their **music** and **ahouache** dances (in which women and men both take part) are unique, as is the village **architecture**, with stone or clay houses tiered on the rocky slopes, craggy fortified **agadirs** (collective granaries), and **kasbahs**, which continued to serve as feudal castles for the community's defence right into the twentieth century.

Berber women in the Atlas go about unveiled and have a much higher profile than their rural counterparts in the plains and the north. They perform much of the heavy labour – working in the fields, herding and grazing cattle and goats and carrying vast loads of brushwood and provisions. Whether they have any greater status or power within the family and village, however, is questionable. The men retain the "important" tasks of buying and selling goods and the evening/night-time irrigation of the crops, ploughing and doing all the building and craftwork.

As an outsider, you'll be constantly surprised by the friendliness and openness of the Berbers, and by their amazing capacity for languages – there's scarcely a village where you won't find someone who speaks French or English, or both. The only areas where you may feel exploited – and pestered by kids – are the main trekking circuits around Jebel Toubkal, where tourism has become an all-important source of income. Given the harshness of life up here, its presence is hardly surprising.

SETTI FATMA MOUSSEM

The **Setti Fatma Moussem** – one of the three most important festivals in the country – takes place for four days around the middle of August, centred on the **Koubba of Setti Fatma**, some way upstream from the *Café des Cascades*. Entry to the *koubba* is forbidden to non-Muslims, but the festival itself is as much a fair and market as it is a religious festival and well worth trying to attend if your trip coincides with it.

there. After crossing the river, there are several cafés where you can order a tajine that should be ready by your return. It's here where the trail begins. The first waterfall is a fairly straightforward clamber over the rocks, and it is flanked by another café, the *Immouzer*. The higher waterfalls are a lot more strenuous to reach, and quite tricky when descending, requiring a head for heights and solid footwear.

ARRIVAL AND DEPARTURE — SETTI FATMA

By grand taxi Occasional shared grands taxis from Marrakesh run from Bab er Robb taxi station to Setti Fatma; it's generally easier, however, to take a shared grand taxi from the southern end of Rue Ibn Rachid (or a #24 bus from Pl Youssef Tachfine) to Lagarb (20min), and pick up a shared grand taxi from there. Taxis pick up and drop off across from *Café Azrrabzo* in Setti Fatma.

INFORMATION AND TREKKING PRACTICALITIES

Guides To hire a guide for the waterfalls of Setti Fatma, contact Hosain Izahan (T 0668 219784). Another good option for arranging a guide is to contact Mohamed Amarhoune (known as Bimou), the owner of the restaurant *Les Jardins de La Cascade* (also known as *Chez Bimou*; T 0670 107469, E amarhoune_bimo@yahoo.fr). For longer excursions to Oukaïmeden, Toubkal, and beyond, contact Omar Jellah (T 0670 414623, E omarjellah@yahoo.co.uk).

ACCOMMODATION

Setti Fatma has an ever-growing number of places to stay. The region is congested during summer weekends and at festival time (when there'll be nothing going – but a huge impromptu campsite along the terraced riverside). Outside these periods you should have little problem finding a room.

Asgaour Setti Fatma centre T 0666 416419 or T 0524 485294. Patron-chef Lahcen Chiboub runs a friendly, spic-and-span operation with superb prices. Rooms are simple, if slightly vacuous, yet well lit. Lunch and dinner set menu for 60dh. **200dh**

Le Jardin T 0666 454972, E sitifadma2@yahoo.fr This colourful and well-priced hotel has modern rooms overlooking the main thoroughfare or the back garden. Single, double and family rooms are available; most have their own bathroom. **200dh**

Kasbah Bab Ourika 25km south of Setti Fatma on the road east to Tnine Ourika and Aït Ourir T 0661 634234 or T 0661 252328, W kasbahbabourika.com. This stunning high-end, eco-friendly establishment is worth splurging on before or after any activities in the High Atlas and stands way above other hotels in the area. Picture-perfect panoramic views, first-class food and an on-site garden will entice a long stay. It's best to arrange a private transfer from Marrakesh to reach the kasbah. **2200dh**

★ **La Perle de l'Ourika** 3km north of Setti Fatma, if coming from Marrakesh T 0524 484477 or T 0624 857593. This little gem is both a famed restaurant and hotel, superbly run by Ammaria, an artist. There are five well-kept rooms, some of which overlook a garden, most with shared bathrooms, and there's a dorm-style room that sleeps six. The hotel has direct access to the river, and the restaurant (daily 11am–9pm) serves scrumptous couscous (80dh). Book well ahead on weekends and in the summer. Locals may say it's closed – don't believe them. Dorm **100dh**, double **200dh**

EATING

Azrou Setti Fatma centre T 0662 131359. This quaint restaurant has outdoor terraced seating shaded by willows near the river, and serves good portions of tasty tajines and kebabs (set menu 120dh). Daily 11am–9pm.

Les Jardins de La Cascade Across the river from the village T 0670 107469. Operated by unofficial waterfall guide, Mohamed Amarhoune (see above), this spotless little restaurant is a short stroll across the river. Clean, shady and comfortable, the restaurant's speciality is a superb chicken couscous (80dh). Basic apartments also available for rent (120dh per person). Daily 10am–10pm.

Oukaïmeden

The village and ski centre of **OUKAÏMEDEN** is a calmer and much easier trekking base when compared to Setti Fatma, especially in the summer and for those setting out towards Toubkal, and a good target in its own right. In summer, there are some attractive day hikes, and the chance to see prehistoric rock carvings (see box, p.364), while in winter, of course, there is the chance to **ski** – and it's hard to resist adding Africa to a list of places you have skied.

6

Skiing

The slopes of **Adrar-n-Oukaïmeden** offer the best **skiing** in Morocco and boasts the highest ski lift in North Africa (3273m). It gives access to good *piste* and off-*piste* skiing, while on the lower slopes a few basic drag lifts serve nursery and intermediate runs. For **cross-country skiers**, several crests and *cols* are accessible, and ski mountaineers often head south to Tacheddirt.

Snowfall and snow cover can be erratic but the **season** is regarded as February to April; the lifts close at the end of April (even if there are perfect skiing conditions). **Equipment** can be rented from several shops around the resort, at fairly modest rates but quality fluctuates so ask around. Ski passes are cheap (around US$8), and there are modest charges if you want to hire a **ski guide** or instructor – ask at any of the shops (or talk with the managers at *Chez Juju*).

Walks From Oukaïmeden

The **walking trails** from Oukaïmeden are strictly summer only: routes can be heavily snow-covered late into spring. However, weather conditions allowing, the **trail to Tacheddirt** (3hr) is pretty clear even in winter, being a *piste* as far as the pass, **Tizi n'ou Addi** (2928m), reached in about two hours. On the descent, the trail divides in two,

---

HIGH ATLAS WILDLIFE

The High Atlas has unique flora and fauna, which are accessible even to the most reluctant rambler if you base yourself at **Oukaïmeden**, **Imlil** or **Ouirgane**.

The spring bloom on the lower slopes comprises aromatic thyme and thorny caper, mingling with golden spreads of broom. Higher slopes are covered by more resilient species, such as the blue tussocks of hedgehog broom. The passes ring to the chorus of the painted frog and the North African race of the green toad during their spring breeding seasons, while some species of reptile, such as the **Moorish gecko**, have adapted to the stony walls of the area's towns and villages. **Butterflies** that brave these heights include the Moroccan copper and desert orange tip, and painted ladies heading from West Africa to western England. Other inhabitants include the almost invisible praying mantis, the scampering ground squirrel and the rare elephant shrew.

Birds to be found among the sparse vegetation include Moussier's redstart and the crimson-winged finch, which prefers the grassy slopes where it feeds in flocks; both birds are unique to North African ranges. The rocky outcrops provide shelter for both chough and alpine chough and the rivers are frequented by dippers who swim underwater in their search for food. Overhead, darting Lanner falcon or flocks of brilliantly coloured bee-eaters add to the feeling of abundance that permeates the slopes of the High Atlas. In the cultivated valleys, look out for the magpie, which, uniquely, has a sky-blue eye mark; there are also storks galore. Other High Atlas birds, as the snow melts, include shore larks, rock bunting, alpine accentor, redstarts and many species of wheatear.

Local flora is impressive, too. The wet meadows produce a fantastic spread of hooped-petticoat daffodils, *romulea* and other bulbs, and Oukaïmeden in May/June has acres of orchids in bloom.

6

PREHISTORIC ROCK CARVINGS IN THE ATLAS

Some of the Atlas's fascinating **prehistoric rock carvings**, depicting animals, weapons, battle scenes, an apparent game area, and various unknown symbols, can be found just before Oukaïmeden's ski area site – follow the sign pointing to "Gravures Rupestres." It's worth contacting local expert Hassan Hachouch (☎0678 551527, @eagle_atlas@hotmail .com) for a trip to the carvings. He speaks French well with limited English, but is a valuable resoure nonetheless to point out some of the lesser-known carvings; a modest tip of 50–100dh is sufficient.

A new eco-museum near the carvings displays photos of the flora and fauna of the national park and surroundings, as well as information about the carvings themselves.

A puzzling related feature of prehistoric rock sites in the Atlas and elsewhere are **cupmarks** – groups of small circular hollows (Peter Ustinov suggested they were egg-cups) with no apparent pattern carved into exposed rock surfaces at ground level. Unlike the usual rock art, they appear in granite (in the western Atlas) and conglomerate (at Tinerhir) as well as sandstone (in the Middle Atlas).

Most of the rock carvings are depicted in the indispensable guidebook, *Gravures Rupestres du Haut Atlas* (on sale in the Oukaïmeden Club Alpin Francais chalet and in some Marrakesh bookshops), though it is only available in French.

---

with both branches leading down into Tacheddirt. There are a number of routes on from Tacheddirt (see p.376).

If you want to get slightly more off the beaten path, it's possible to take the mule path from Tizi n'ou Addi southwest to the settlement of Ouanesekra, where a room (50dh) and meal (50dh) can be had for the night at the rustic *Gîte Ouanesekra* or *Gîte Gressafen* (☎0667 968617). From here, the options are endless. You can trek northeast via Tacheddirt towards the Ourika Valley, southwest to Imlil, or southeast towards Tizi Likemt and Azib Likemt.

ARRIVAL AND DEPARTURE   OUKAÏMEDEN

By grand taxi During the winter months, when snow is present on the mountains, grands taxis travel to Oukaïmeden from Bab er Robb in Marrakesh (1hr 30min). Alternatively, you can take the Alsa City bus #26 (from the Sidi Mimoun station in Marrakesh) to Lagrab, where you can then hire a grand taxi or a local minibus on to Oukaïmeden. If you're heading here for skiing, and travelling in a small group, the best option is to charter a whole taxi (350dh) from Marrakesh's Bab er Robb. There is little or no public transport to Oukaïmeden during the summer months; arranging a chartered taxi from Marrkaesh will prove difficult. The best bet is to travel first to Lagrab and then rent a grand taxi onward, which will cost around 200dh.

ACCOMMODATION

The hotels cater mainly for the ski season, but most stay open year-round.

Chez Juju On the main road, in the centre of Oukaïmeden ☎0524 319005, ⓦchezjuju.com. Recently restored and boasting a nice bar-restaurant with tables inside and out (mains from 120dh), *Chez Juju* also has first-rate rooms, making this a great base from which to ski or to walk. Request a room facing south towards the ski hill for the sun and the views. Private dorm-style rooms (for your own group or family members) are also available (200dh per person). **1400dh**

Club Alpine Chalet At the beginning of town just before the centre ☎0524 319036 (Oukaïmeden) or ☎0522 990141 (Casablanca Office), @cafmaroc@ menara.ma. Open for both members and non-members, this well-equipped lodge has six dormitories, along with a bar and restaurant, which serves substantial meals. **110dh**

The Toubkal Massif

The **Toubkal Massif**, enclosing the High Atlas's highest peaks, is the target destination of nearly everyone who goes trekking in Morocco. You can reach trailhead villages in just two hours from Marrakesh, and the main walking routes are easily followed. Walking just a short distance from the most common starting point – Imlil – you are transported to a very different world. Mountain villages offer a stark contrast to the previous roadside towns, with Berber houses, stacked one on top of another in apparently organic growth, appearing to sprout from the rocks. The local population is immediately distinct from their city compatriots; the women dress in brilliant attire even when working in the fields.

In summer, **Jebel Toubkal** (4167m), the highest peak in North Africa, is walkable right up to the summit; if you're pushed for time, you could climb it and be back in Marrakesh in three days – though at some risk of altitude sickness. Alternatively, if you feel unable to tackle an ascent of Toubkal, it's possible to have a genuine taste of the mountains by spending time exploring the lesser-visited valleys accessible from Imlil or Aroumd.

6

ARRIVAL AND DEPARTURE   THE TOUBKAL MASSIF

The Toubkal Massif can be reached easily from Marrakesh by driving, or by bus or taxi from Bab er Robb to Asni – just over an hour's journey – and then grabbing another taxi to Imlil where you can begin walking. The region can also be approached on various treks from Ouirgane or Ijoukak, a little further west, the Ourika Valley from the east, or the ski resort of Oukaïmeden. Some trekkers, with time to spend, also approach from the south, through the Tifnoute valley and Lac d'Ifni.

Asni

The end of the line for most buses and grands taxis, **ASNI** is little more than a roadside village and marketplace, from where you can head straight on to Imlil, though a night here is quite pleasant – at least once the touts have left off. The most interesting time to be here is for the **Saturday souk**, when the enclosure behind the row of shop cubicles is filled with local produce (this is a big fruit-growing region) and livestock stalls.

Treks around Asni

The forested slopes above Asni are dominated by rocky scarp. This forms the edge of the hidden limestone **Kik Plateau**. In spring, a walk up here is a delight, with a spread of alpine flowers and incomparable views. To get the best from it, set off early in the day and carry water; four hours' walking will bring you over the plateau if you take a bus or taxi up to the start.

From Asni, follow the Tizi n'Test road to where it swings out of sight (past the red conical hill). Just past a souvenir stall, a *piste* breaks off and can be seen rising up the hillside. Take this to reach the pass, then turn right again, through fields, to eventually join the plateau edge, which you can follow to **Moulay Brahim**; leave the crest to join a *piste* down to the left, which passes big marble quarries just before the village. You can also cut back down to Asni by a zigzag path that leaves the route midway along.

TREKKING IN TOUBKAL NATIONAL PARK

The valleys of Asni, Imlil (along the Mizane Valley), Tacheddirt (Imenane Valley) and Tizi Oussem/Ouirgane (Azzadene Valley) offer fine **walks**, which you might consider doing to **acclimatize** yourself before tackling Toubkal or other high peaks. They are all much easier if you walk them downhill.

From **late spring to late autumn** (see box, pp.370–371), the region's trails are accessible for any reasonably fit walker. **Mule tracks** that allow one to navigate around the mountain valleys are well contoured and are usually in excellent condition. Additionally, there's a network of village *gîtes*, houses and CAF refuges (small huts) for accommodation, which generally makes camping unnecessary unless you're traipsing far away from the villages.

6

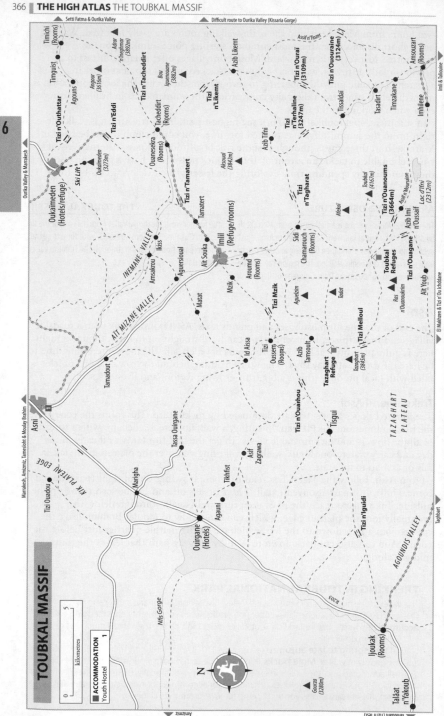

TOUBKAL MASSIF

ACCOMMODATION
Youth Hostel   1

0   kilometres   5

N

Setti Fatma & Ourika Valley

Difficult route to Ourika Valley (Kissaria Gorge)

Timichi
(Rooms)

Timguist

Aguns

Adrar
n'Imeghmar
(3892m)

Angour
(3616m)

Azib Likemt

Assif n'Tinzer

Tizi n'Ourai
(3109m)

Tizi n'Ououraine
(3124m)

Amsouzart
(Rooms)

Imil & Taliouine

Tizi n'Outhattar

Tizi n'Eddi

Bou
Iguenouane
(3882m)

Tizi n'Tacheddirt

Tizi
n'Likemt

Tissaldai

Tasadirt

Timzakane

Imihlene

Tacheddirt
(Rooms)

Tizi
n'Terhaline
(3247m)

Ouanesekra
(Rooms)

Oukaimeden
(3273m)

Azib Tifni

Tizi
n'Tamatert

Aksoual
(3842m)

Tizi
n'Tagharat

Toubkal
(4167m)

Tizi n'Ouanoums
(3664m)

Lac d'Ifni
(2312m)

Oukaimeden
(Hotels/refuge)

Ski Lift

Ourika Valley & Marrakesh

Tamatert

Ikiss

Aguersioual

Ait Souka

Imlil
(Refuge/rooms)

Aroumd
(Rooms)

Sidi
Chamarouch
(Rooms)

Afekoi

Asif n'Mouragene

Azib Imi
n'Oussaif

Toubkal
Refuges

Tizi n'Ouagane

Ait Youb

Amsakrou

Mzik

Aguelzim

Tizi Mzik

Todort

Ras
n'Ouanoudrim

El Makhzen & Tizi n'Ou Ichddane

INEMIANE VALLEY

AÏT MIZANE VALLEY

Matat

Tamadout

Tizi
Oussem
(Rooms)

Azib
Tamsoult

Id Aissa

Tazaghart
(3845m)

Tizi Melloul

Tazaghart
Refuge

TAZAGHART
PLATEAU

Marrakech, Amizmiz, Tameslolht & Moulay Brahim

Asni

KIK PLATEAU EDGE

Tassa Ouirgane

Marigha

Tizi Ouadou

Agauni

Tikhfist

Asif
Zagawa

Tizi n'Ouarhou

Tizi n'Iguidi

Tisgui

Taghbart

Nfis Gorge

Ourgane
(Hotels)

R203

AGOUNDIS VALLEY

Amizmiz

Gourza
(3280m)

Ijoukak
(Rooms)

Talaat
n'Yakoub

R203

Taroudant (Tizi n'Test)

Taroudant & Tizi n'Ou Ichddane

ARRIVAL AND DEPARTURE   ASNI

By bus Buses for Asni depart from Marrakesh's Bab er Robb at random intervals (50min), and stop on the main road near the taxi depot. Leaving Asni, buses depart from near the main market entrance (all destinations except Imlil) and from the roadside south of the petrol station for Imlil (45min) at random intervals. Buses from Asni run frequently throughout the day to Marrakesh, Moulay Brahim, Ijoukak and – at around 6am – over the Tizi n'Test for Taliouine (change at Ouled Berhil for Taroudant; see p.473), but check in advance as the service changes occasionally.

By grand taxi Grands taxis to Asni depart from Bab er Robb taxi station in Marrakesh (1hr) and arrive in the centre of town at the taxi depot. From here, you can travel 19km to Imlil where most treks begin, and also to Ouirgane (and onward to the Tizi n'Test) or to Amizmiz. Getting from Asni to Imlil by grand taxi is pretty straightforward, with minibuses and taxis shuttling back and forth along the 17km of road, with larger lorries on Saturdays for the souk. From Asni, a spot in a grand taxi can be negotiated to Marrakesh, Moulay Brahim or Ouirgane, and (in stages but unreliably) over the Tizi n'Test.

ACCOMMODATION AND EATING

Accommodation is limited in Asni, so it's worth considering moving straight on to Imlil or Ouirgane. For **meals**, most of the café-stalls by the souk will fix you a tajine or *harira*.

Auberge de Jeunesse At the south end of the village ☎ 0524 447713. Asni's youth hostel is open all year and to all-comers, with slightly higher charges for non-IYHF members. There are cold showers and you'll need your own sleeping bag, though blankets can be rented; the location by the river can be very cold in winter. Nonetheless, it is a friendly place and good meeting point. They will store luggage if you want to go off

trekking unencumbered. BB 70dh
Villa de l'Atlas Near the top end of the long straight road to Imlil, about 3km outside of town. ☎ 0524 484855 or ☎ 061 667736. A pleasant guesthouse, some way out of town, with decent rooms; the food served on the outdoor terrace is a highlight. Best reached by taxi if you don't have your own transport. 300dh

Imlil

IMLIL is currently the most frequented starting point for those going up to the top of Toubkal. Just past Asni, the road begins to climb; below it the valley of the Oued Rhirhaia unfolds, while above, small villages crowd onto the rocky slopes. Halfway up the valley, at a roadside café, there is a sudden good view of Toubkal. As you emerge at Imlil the air feels quite different – silent and rarefied at 1740m. Paths head off in all directions among the valleys, making this region a walker's paradise.

Imlil is little more than a roadside settlement, with shops and plenty of small guesthouses and hotels along the main thoroughfare. It's a good spot to get supplies, hire a guide, or spend the night to get your bearings in the region. It's not worth spending much more than one day here, however, given the much more appealing villages that are scattered just beyond it.

If you want to make an early start for the Toubkal refuges and the ascent of Toubkal, Imlil village makes a better trailhead than Asni, as is Aroumd (see p.369); it's possible to make it to the basecamp from Imlil in one day.

ARRIVAL AND DEPARTURE   IMLIL

The best and most straightforward method of arriving to Imlil is to hop in a shared grand taxi from Bab er Robb to Asni (50 min, 25dh). From Asni, you can take another grand taxi to Imlil (30 min, 15dh).

INFORMATION

TREKKING RESOURCES
Good sources of information include the Club Alpin Français (CAF) refuge and its *gardiens* (wardens), which has an office in Imlil with a list of qualified guides. They are located just near the first car park area.

TREKKING AND BIKING COMPANIES
A number of trekking companies have their offices or receptions in Imlil and are recommended for their qualifications, professionalism, language ability and overall quality.

6

Bike Adventures in Morocco (BAM) Reception in Morocco Adventure Holidays office ☎ 0666 238200, ⓦ bikeadventuresinmorocco.com. Owned by High Atlas biking expert Lahcen Jellah, BAM offers exclusive excursions into nearly every region of the country by bike. Itineraries include biking north to south in the Central High Atlas, riding from the High Atlas to the Atlantic, and a number of routes not offered by any others. High-quality bikes and equipment are available for rent. It's best to arrange trips prior to arrival.

Journey Beyond Travel Reception shared with Morocco Adventure Holidays ☎ 0610 414 573 Morocco; ☎ 0672 882 529; or ☎ 0661 283086, ⓦ journeybeyondtravel.com. A respected company arranging cultural tours throughout Morocco, they can arrange a variety of treks in the High Atlas,

Central Atlas and, Anti-Atlas, along with trips throughout the country. Outings are best arranged before your arrival. Other adventures include Sahara desert excursions, mountain biking, rafting (March through May) and more.

Morocco Adventure Holidays Located past the school and small hospital, near the Argan Cooperative ☎ 0670 414 623, ⓦ moroccoadventureholidays.com. Quality service and unique itineraries involving trekking, skiing, and desert expeditions for groups of all sizes can be arranged with this local team of experts.

Mountain Travel Morocco (MTM) In the centre of Imlil ☎ 0524 485784 ⓦ mountain-travel-morocco .com. Run by a handful of entrepreneurial, local guides, offering treks and walking excursions for all levels of expertise.

ACCOMMODATION AND EATING

Imlil has various accommodation options, ranging from hotels to refuges and *gîtes*. Small provisions shops line the main road through the village and affordable meals can be had at all of the local guesthouses.

CAF Refuge Located near the main car park lot ☎ 0524 485122 or ☎ 0677 307415. This long-established French Alpine Club refuge has been refurbished to a high standard and is now run by a French cook/guardian. Many French and Moroccan club members stay here throughout the year. Dormitory rooms are simple, clean and airy, though you're better opting for one of the more atmospheric local guesthouses. Meals can be self-prepared. 150dh

★ **Dar Adrar** Douar Achain, Imlil ☎ 0524 485024 or ☎ 0668 760165, ⓦ daradrar.com. Owned and operated by trekking guru Mohamed Aztat, *Dar Adrar* is a hidden gem. En-suite rooms, great food, nice sitting rooms, and even family rooms are offered in this cosy mountain guesthouse. Free wi-fi. Meals are prepared on site for 80dh per person. 220dh

Dar Assarou 400m from Imlil centre, on the road to Tacheddirt ☎ 0524 484853 or ☎ 0661 173549, ⓦ dar-assarou.com. A quality lodge with comfy rooms that are good for singles, doubles, triples and families; superb meals are also prepared. The ground-floor rooms have good wi-fi access, while terrace rooms all have their own bathrooms. 440dh

Imlil Lodge Guesthouse Tamatert ☎ 0671 157636, ⓦ imlil-lodge.com. Known locally as *Chez Jamal*, this slightly swanky lodge is located on the road connecting Asni to Tacheddirt in the village of Tamatert. It is within

the borders of the Toubkal National Park and makes an alternative base to access some of the remote outskirts of the region. Single, doubles and suites are available. 600dh

Riad Dar Imlil Imlil centre ☎ 0524 484917 or ☎ 0661 952619, ⓦ darimlil.com. For those longing for a touch of luxury, this little lodge competes with any sumptuous options in the area at better rates. The superior rooms offer the best deal, while the suites are tastefully decorated in a classic Moroccan style. 1400dh

Tamatert Guesthouse 1.8 km from Imlil on the road to Tacheddirt ☎ 0667 168906, ⓔ imerhane1973@hotmail.com. This little guesthouse has a prime location affording views of the surrounding valley and massif, offering several dormitory rooms and friendly staff. Mohammed and his family welcome both trekkers and those simply wanting to enjoy the serene village. 100dh

★ **Village du Toubkal & Spa** 15min walk between Imlil and Aroumd ☎ 0524 431 892 or ☎ 0661 242136, ⓦ levillagedutoubkal.com. Tucked in its own mini-valley and located between Imlil and Aroumd, this luxurious gem has splendid natural light, spacious rooms, an excellent on-site spa, and stands well above other luxury-type lodges in the area. There's only a handful or rooms, so book in advance. 1400dh

Climbing Toubkal

Most trekkers leaving Imlil are en route for the **ascent of Jebel Toubkal** – a walk rather than a climb after the snows have cleared, but serious business nonetheless. The route to the ascent trailhead, however, is fairly straightforward, and is enjoyable in its own right, following the Mizane Valley to the village of **Aroumd**, 4km from Imlil. From here, it's one and a half hours min to the pilgrimage site of **Sidi Chamarouch** followed by another four to five hours to the **Toubkal refuges** (3208m; 12km from Imlil; 5–7hr in all; 100dh), which lie at the foot of Toubkal's final slopes.

Most trekkers head to the refuges early to mid-morning in order to stay the night. Then, you'll have a fresh start at first light the next morning for the ascent of Toubkal, which will allow for the clearest panorama from the peak – afternoons can be cloudy. Arriving at the Toubkal refuge early in the day also gives you time to acclimatize to the altitude and rest: many people find the hardest part of the trek is the last hour before arriving at the refuges, so it's important to take it easy.

6

Imlil to Aroumd

The **walk from Imlil to Aroumd** (30–45min) follows the southward flank of the Mizane River and makes a nice excursion. On the west side there's a well-defined mule track that zigzags above the river for about 2km before dropping to the floor of the valley and heading up into the village; there is also a more circuitous *piste*, driveable in a reasonably hardy vehicle (although this should be avoided in the spring since you won't be able to cross the river on the edge of Aroumd). On the east bank, there's a rough path – much the same distance but slightly harder to follow.

Aroumd

AROUMD (also called Armed or Aremd) is the largest village of the Mizane Valley, an extraordinary looking place, built on a huge moraine spur above the valley at 1840m. Steep-tiered fields of potatoes, onions, barley and various kinds of fruit line the valley sides, their terraces edged with purple iris. The village is used as a base or overnight stop by a number of trekking companies, and several houses have been converted to well-equipped **gîtes**.

ARRIVAL AND DEPARTURE   AROUMD

By public transport To reach Aroumd from Marrakesh, you first need to get to Imlil (see p.367) by taking a grand taxi from Bab er Robb to Ansi and another onward to Imlil. From here, it's a relatively short walk to Aroumd (see above).

For those with a 4WD and accustomed to navigating along precarious mountainside roads, there is a *piste* connecting Imlil and Aroumd, but it is not advised (especially in the winter) and much better to park in Imlil and walk.

ACCOMMODATION AND EATING

There's only one small shop in Aroumd, so if you're cooking for yourself it's best to bring supplies with you. Otherwise, every guesthouse can provide meals at reasonable costs.

★ **Dar Warawte** Village centre ☎0670 414 623, ✉darwarawte@yahoo.co.uk. An impressive, yet affordable lodge located right in the centre of the village. With views of the surrounding valleys and Toubkal, it's a superb base from which to start or end your journey, and offers dormitory, budget and deluxe rooms, free wi-fi and a private hammam. The deluxe rooms on the upper floor have their own bathrooms with shower and a great terrace. Lunch and dinner also available to non-guests (ask ahead for *Rfeesa* – a wonderful lentil dish for 50dh). BB dorm 80dh, double 250dh

Gîte Roches Armed Village centre ☎0667 644915 or ☎0524 485751, ✉rochesarmed@yahoo.fr. A popular spot for local trekking companies, this lovely "lodge of rocks" has clean single, double and dorms, all with shared bathrooms. Meals can also be prepared on site. BB dorm 100dh, double 220dh

Gîte Touratine Village centre ☎0666 945661 or ☎0524 485879, ✉tadrart2@hotmail.com. This rustic lodge is well situated in the village and has simple rooms for the budget trekker. Meals on site are superb (60dh) and best ordered in the morning. Rooms on offer include single, double and dorms, all with shared bathrooms. Dorm 80dh, double 200dh

Aroumd to Sidi Chamarouch

From Aroumd, the **Toubkal trail** goes up the flood plain, with unavoidable river crossings, which are only sometimes problematic in the spring after periods of rain or

ATLAS TREKKING PRACTICALITIES

EQUIPMENT AND EXPERIENCE

Unless you're undertaking a particularly long or ambitious trek – or are here in winter conditions – there are no technical problems to hold anyone back from trekking in the Toubkal area, or climbing the peak itself. However, the mountain needs to be taken seriously. You must have decent **footwear and clothing** – it's possible to be caught out by summer storms as well as bad winter conditions – and you should be prepared to camp out if you are going on longer treks (or find the Toubkal refuges full). It's important to keep to a gentle pace until you are properly acclimatized as altitudes of 3000–4000m can be quite demanding, especially when combined with the midday heat and walking over long sections of rough boulders or loose scree.

SEASONS

Toubkal is usually under **snow** from November until June, and experienced mountaineers can enjoy some classic climbs, ski ascents and treks in winter, though be cautious of storms, which can last up to three days. In spring, the best trekking lies below the snow line, and less experienced trekkers should only aim for the summit when the snow has gone. In all cases, take local advice before you climb; ice axes and crampons can be rented in Imlil.

ALTITUDE

Toubkal is 4167m above sea level and much of the surrounding region is above 3000m, so it's possible that you might get **acute mountain sickness (AMS)**, also called altitude sickness. Aspirin can help, but just sucking on a sweet or swallowing is often effective, as is resting. Most people experience some symptoms of AMS, such as a mild headache, but serious cases are rare. Moving too hurriedly into higher altitudes is a major cause, so it's important to pace your ascent, allowing your body time to acclimatize. If you do develop a bad headache, dizziness, or more than slight breathlessness and really feel like vomiting, going down straight away just a few hundred metres can bring about immediate relief.

ACCOMMODATION

At most Atlas villages, it is usually possible to arrange a room in a local house; just turn up and ask. At some of the villages on more established routes, there are official *gîtes*, often the homes of mountain guides, who can provide mules and assistance – as well as food, showers, toilets and sometimes hammams. All *gîtes* are graded by the tourist authorities, who sometimes have lists of them available. Most charge 100–150dh per person for a night and for a further 60–80dh will provide meals.

There are also two CAF refuge **huts**, The Toubkal Refuge (formerly known as the *Neltner Basecamp*) and the Tazaghart Refuge (formerly known as *Lépiney*); they charge about 100dh for a bed (less for members of Alpine Clubs). The Toubkal Refuge. is the best appointed and often heavily booked; it's always crowded in March/April (ski-touring season) and July–September (trekking season). An independent refuge, *Les Mouflons* (☎0663 763713), offers one hundred beds in smaller rooms, with bathrooms, showers and a self-catering kitchen.

If you are planning to **camp**, there are designated areas. You will need a tent and warm sleeping bag – nights can be freezing, even in summer, and you must use the official water sources and toilet facilities.

GUIDES AND MULES

Guides can be engaged at Imlil and at a number of the larger villages in the Toubkal region; **mules**, too, can be hired, usually in association with a guide or porter. The level of expertise

snow melt (arrange a mule ride with your guesthouse over them if so). At the end of the flood plain the track zigzags up to make its way to the gorge high above. If you have been following the main mule trail on the west side of the valley from Imlil (see p.367), you can continue without going round into Aroumd.

The river is crossed once more by a bridge just before you arrive at the hamlet of **SIDI CHAMAROUCH** (1hr 30min–2hr from Aroumd). Set beside small waterfalls, this is a disordered row of houses, all built one into another. Its seasonal population of ten or

and quality among guides can vary greatly. Rates from Imlil start around 300dh a day, while more experienced guides may charge upwards of 400dh a day. A muleteer and a mule for baggage cost 150–200dh per day. One mule can usually be shared among two and sometimes three people – and if you're setting out from Imlil, say, for Lac d'Ifni, or the Toubkal or Tazaghart refuges, it can be a worthwhile investment. In addition, you will be expected to pay a small fee to the car park supervisor in Imlil if you have left your car and a tip to the muleteer at the end. (Payment to all parties, incidentally, is best made at the end of a trip.) Note that guides are more reluctant – and reasonably so – to work during the month of **Ramadan** (see p.43).

6

WATER

Sidi Ali, Aïn Saïs and Sidi Harazem bottled **waters** are spring sourced. If you are heading off main routes, a litre bottle of water is enough because you can refill it regularly. However, Giardiasis **bacteria** is present in many of the streams and rivers downriver from human habitation (including the Toubkal refuges huts), so purification tablets are highly advisable, as, of course, is boiling the water to make it safe.

CLOTHES

Even in the summer months you'll need a warm sweater or jacket and a wind-breaker. Hiking boots are ideal, although you can get by with a decent pair of trainers. The sun is very strong here, making a hat, sunblock and sunglasses essential.

OTHER THINGS TO BRING

You can buy **food** in Asni, Imlil and some of the other villages – or negotiate meals in the places you stay overnight – though it gets increasingly expensive the higher and the more remote you get. Water purification tablets or filtering systems are worthwhile on longer trips, as are stomach pills, insect repellent and wet wipes (which should be used on hands before meals).

Children constantly ask you for cigarettes, *bonbons* and *cadeaux* – but it's better for everyone if you don't give in; limit **gifts** to those who offer genuine assistance. A worthwhile contribution trekkers can make to the local economy is to trade or give away some of your gear – this is always welcomed by guides.

GUIDEBOOKS AND MAPS

There are limitless Atlas trekking routes, only a selection of which are detailed in these pages. For other ideas, either engage a professional guide or invest in one of the Atlas Mountain trekking guidebooks such as *Trekking in the Moroccan Atlas* by **Richard Knight** (Trailblazer) or *The Atlas Mountains: A Walking and Trekking Guide* by **Karl Smith** (Cicerone Press).

Large-scale survey **maps** are available for the region; most are 1:100,000, though Toubkal is also mapped at 1:50,000. These, like the guidebooks above, are best obtained in advance from specialist map/travel shops outside of Morocco, though occasionally guides or shops at Imlil or Oukaïmeden (or the *Hôtel Ali* in Marrakesh; see p.341) may have some maps to sell.

SKI-TOURING

The Toubkal Massif is popular with **ski-mountaineering** groups from February to April. Most of the *tizis* (*passes*), and Jebel Toubkal and other peaks, can be ascended, and there is an *Haute Route* linking the huts. The descent from Toubkal summit to Sidi Chamarouch must rank as fine as you'll find. The Toubkal refuges can get pretty crowded at these times. For those who are serious winter trekkers, the Tazaghart refuge can make a better base.

---

twelve run grocery shops for trekkers and Moroccan pilgrims, who come to the village's *marabout* shrine – a boulder sited across the river from the village and reached by a concrete bridge that non-Muslims are strictly forbidden to cross. The shrine is probably a survival of a very ancient nature cult – in these parts often thinly veiled by the trappings of Islam; on the approach to the village you may notice a tree, sacred to local tradition, where the Berbers hang strips of cloth and make piles of stones. Although it seems pristine, avoid drinking any untreated water here, or around the Toubkal huts.

Sidi Chamarouch to the Toubkal refuges

Beyond Sidi Chamarouch, the Toubkal trail climbs steeply in zigzags and then traverses the flank of the valley well above the Mizane. The trail is clear the whole way to the **Toubkal refuges**, which, at 3207m, is often the spring snow line. In winter, the snow line can drop to Sidi Chamarouch and mules have to be replaced by porters, which should be arranged before your trip in Imlil or Aroumd, if you want assistance to the Toubkal refuges.

6

ACCOMMODATION   SIDI CHAMAROUCH TO THE TOUBKAL REFUGES

After sunset, even in mid-August, it feels pretty cold at the two refuges, which sit at 3200m. Both refuges are open throughout the year, have hot showers, sitting rooms and kitchens, and meals can be ordered from the *gardiens*.

Les Mouflons ☎ 0663 763109. This nicely equipped lodge has a slightly larger community area than Toubkal Refuge, and has an open, alpine feel. However, it is slightly colder than the Toubkal Refuge and not as well kept. Meals are 80dh. <u>**190dh**</u>
Toubkal Refuge ☎ 0664 071838 or ☎ 0522 990141 (Casablanca). Formerly known as *Neltner*, this older

shelter has a bit more appeal than *Les Mouflons*. The sitting area is kept warm, and mobile phone coverage is reachable at the far wall. Eating areas are shared and chatting with other trekkers makes for a nice evening. Meals cost 80dh (expect spaghetti). <u>**180dh**</u>

The Toubkal refuges to the summit

At the Toubkal Refuge you're almost bound to meet people who have just come down from **Jebel Toubkal** – and you should certainly take advantage of talking to them and the refuge *gardiens* for an up-to-the-minute description of the routes and the state of the South Cirque (Ikhibi Sud) trail to the summit. If you don't feel too confident about going it alone, take a guide – they are usually available at the refuge – but don't let them try to rush you up the mountain. It's best to take your time allowing your body to acclimatize slowly to the altitude changes (see box, pp.370–371).

The **South Cirque** (Ikhibi Sud) gives the most popular and straightforward ascent of Toubkal and, depending on your fitness, should take between two and a half and three and a half hours (2–2hr 30min coming down). There is a worn path, which is easy enough to follow. More of a problem is finding the right track down through the upper slopes of loose scree. Take your time coming down since it can be rough on the knees.

The **trail** begins above the Toubkal Refuge, dropping down to cross the stream and then climbing again to reach the first of Toubkal's innumerable fields of boulders and scree. These are the most tiring (and memorable) features of the trek up, and gruelling for inexperienced walkers. The summit, a sloping plateau of stones marked by a tripod, is eventually reached after the serpentine path brings you to the spectacular southern cliffs. It should be stressed that **in winter** even this easiest of routes is a **snow climb** and best for experienced hikers or those climbing with a guide. Slips can and have had fatal consequences. If you are properly equipped, check out the start the night before, and set off early. Ice axes and crampons are essential in icy conditions and should be brought along with you. This is also a splendid ski route.

An alternate ascent – though longer (4hr 30min) and best for more experienced climbers – is the **North Cirque** (Ikhibi Nord). En route you will pass the remains of an aircraft that crashed while flying arms to Biafra, and the cairn of the small peak of Tibherine dominating the valley is actually one of its engines. The final ridge to the summit area calls for some scrambling. You should descend by the South Cirque back down to the refuges.

The Grand Toubkal Loop

The **Grand Toubkal Loop** takes four to five days and makes a satisfying (and very scenic) addition to the ascent of Toubkal. From the Toubkal refuges, the loop heads south to

6

scenic Lac d'Ifni, then north to Azib Likemt and Tacheddirt, before returning to Imlil. The walk isn't particularly strenuous and can be done by most fit walkers. For the first part of the walk, be sure to carry plenty of water and enough food for up to two to three days since there are no reliable facilities until you get past Lac d'Ifni. The walk is best done from June to mid-October; in the winter the passes of Tizi n'Ouanoums (3600m) and Tizi Likemt (3500m) can be closed with deep snow. Those with hefty mountaineering experience, proper equipment of crampons, ropes, ice axes (and satellite phone) can attempt the trek without much issue.

Day 1: Toubkal refuges to Azib Imi n'Ouassif

The **trail** begins at the Toubkal refuges, climbing up a rough, stony slope and then winding round to the head of the Mizane Valley towards the imposing **Tizi n'Ouanoums**. The path is reasonably easy to follow, zigzagging until you reach the pass (3664m), a narrow gap in the rocky wall, which takes around an hour to reach. The views from the *tizi* are superb, taking in the route that you've covered and, in the distance to the south, the outline of Lac d'Ifni (which disappears from view as you descend).

The path continues onward and downward to Azib Imi n'Oussaif (2800m) along the Assif n'Moursaine riverbed, which you'll cross back and forth several times. It's here at Azib Imi n'Ouassaif that a good camping spot can be had – it usually takes two to three hours to reach here from the refuges. This a good place to stop for the first night as camping around Lac d'Ifni is poor, especially in the summer – it's very hot and somewhat fly-ridden by day, and often has no drinking water (the lake waters are polluted and springs do exist but can run dry).

Day 2: Azib Imi n'Oussif to Amsouzert via Lac d'Ifni

At this point the hard work seems over – but this is a false impression. The path down the valley to Lac d'Ifni is steep, the scree apparently endless, and the lake doesn't come back into sight until you are almost there, enclosed as it is by the mountains, which look like heaps of rubble. When you do finally see it, Lac d'Ifni is a memorable sight, its only human habitations a few shepherds' huts (*azibs*), and the only sound that of water idly lapping on the shore; it is unusually deep (50m over much of its area) and stocked with trout. Incredibly there is a small café (closed in the winter) functioning by the lake, which offers minimal but welcome refreshments.

From the north side of the lake, follow the path east to the valley above Imhilene, and beyond it to the kasbah-like village of **Amsouzart**, reached in around three hours after the lake. This reasonably sized village has decent accommodation options, which all serve meals. *Gîte Himmi Omar* – to find it, ask at one of the local cafés or shops – has beds in a basic dorm for 50dh. Rooms are basic dormitories for 50dh per night. Note that Amsouzert is your last chance to fill up on any necessary provisions.

Day 3: Amsouzert to Azib Likemt

The walk from Amsouzert to Azib Likemt takes a solid seven to eight hours, so aim to depart early morning, with ample food and water supplies. From Amsouzart, the path continues north up the valley to reach Tagadirt in just over two hours. It's a steady climb and the scenery soon begins to open up to reveal some of the surrounding peaks.

From Tagadirt, the path heads northwest as the scenery begins to change impressively; you'll be treated to cliffs, pastureland and the river valley that snakes back and forth on your way towards Tizi n'Ououraine (3124m). Once you reach the river, known as the Assif n'Tinzer, bear north along the well-marked path heading along the majestic river gorge. You'll start out on the west side of the ridge before crossing onto the eastern side. By the time you reach Azib Likemt, you'll have crossed the river a handful of times. Some of the precipitous ridge walking isn't for the faint of heart, but the stunning views make it a worthwhile endeavour.

Continue along the path, eventually bearing east towards **Azib Likemt**, a region of intense cultivation and magnificent spring flowers. The friendly shepherds (using the area as summer feeding grounds in the summer) may invite you for tea and can show you a nice area to pitch your tent. In the winter, the area becomes windy, so pitch your tent along the rocky embankment. It was this spot from which Joseph Thomson noted Toubkal as the highest Atlas peak in 1888. Take care when camping as this upper valley is notorious for scorpions. The country east of Azib Likemt, the **Kissaria Gorges**, is wild in the extreme, and too hard even for mules.

6

Day 4: Azib Likemt to Tacheddirt
Leaving the lush pastureland of Azib Likemt will take some fortitude as you head off on one of the most boulder- and scree-ridden walks in the Atlas. The changing scenery, however, makes this six- to seven-hour walk fly by.

From Azib Likemt, the path heads along the west side of the Irhzer n'Likemt river gorge to the impressive **Tizi Likemt** (3555m) pass. The walk to the *tizi* takes about three hours.

From the pass, watch your step as the scree thickens for the following hour of walking. Continue heading along the well-worn path northwest – still along the river – towards **Tacheddirt** (2314m), which sits much lower than the pass and takes a further two to three hours to reach. In Tacheddirt, you can stay at the *Tigmi N' Tacheddirt* (see p.377). Alternatively, you could head on for a couple of kilometres to the lesser-visited village of Ouanesekra and spend the night in *Gîte Ouanesekra* or *Gîte Gressafen* (see p.364).

Day 5: Tacheddirt to Imlil
More a scenic walk of four to five hours than a trek, day five provides a well-merited respite after the previous, longer days. From Tacheddirt, a new road now connects straight to Imlil. This is the easiest path to follow, but not the most interesting. To take it, set out directly southwest and follow it through Tamatert where you'll eventually arrive in Imlil.

The more rewarding route (5–6hr) is to walk west from Tacheddirt to Ouanesekra, which shouldn't take you long to reach; the pleasant mountain hamlet has some small shops where you can stock up on food, snacks and water. From Ouanesekra, continue west to Tamguist and then head north to Tinerhourhine, in the direction of Ikkiss. Just before Ikiss, an easily spotted mule path heads west to Tizi n'Aguersioual (2050m), where you'll need to go southwest to Aguersioual and continue south along the Mizane Valley to Imlil.

West of Imlil: Tizi Oussem and the Tazaghart Refuge
The area west of Imlil offers a good acclimatization trek to **Tizi Oussem** village. A harder trek climbs to the **Tazaghart Refuge** (see p.376), accessible also from the Toubkal Refuge and Aroumd, and the possibility of one- or two-day treks out to **Ouirgane** or **Ijoukak** on the Tizi n'Test road, or back to the Asni–Imlil road at **Tamadout**.

Imlil to Tizi Oussem and the Ouirgane Valley
The village of **TIZI OUSSEM**, in the next valley west of Imlil, is reached in about four hours over the **Tizi Mzic**; the track is not that easy to find. Walk up from the taxi station on the main road in Imlil for 200m. When the road forks, turn right as if you are walking towards Aroumd. Once the road becomes quite steep, look to the right for a well-worn mule path that will take you up to Tizi Mzik. It's especially helpful here to have locals point you in the right direction in Imlil.

Once on the mule path, continue west initially; following this, for most of the journey you'll be heading southwest. At Tizi Mzik, the path forks. Take the path right (southwest) to approach Tizi Oussem from the south.

An alternative place to begin this walk is on the lesser-known yet slightly easier path to find, which begins two kilometres before Aguersioual (on the Asni–Imlil road). The trail begins on the west side and starts a slight ascent going towards Matate and taking you to **Tizi Oudite** (2219) before heading southwest to Aït Aïssi where a piste connects south to Tizi Oussem.

Once at Tizi Oussem, it's good to stay the night (at *Gîte Tizi Oussem*; 50dh, prepare your own meals) before continuing onward since the walk from here to Ouirgane is a long day's journey (6–7hr).

From Tizi Oussem, keep initially to the east bank and then drop onto the flood plain to cross to the west bank at a narrowing. The path keeps high then zigzags down to cross the river to gain height again on the east side, passing the walled farm of Azerfsane; a small village made up of one family inhabiting nine houses. Beyond here, the path swings west and drops to the river again, where a mule track on the left bank helps guide you to the top, with a commanding view to the rich Ouirgane Valley. From here, you can choose to follow a *piste* west to Ouirgane or northwest to Marigha. It's easier to get transport back to Marrakesh from Marigha and saves you about 45 minutes in walking. If you continue onward to Ouirgane, you'll end at the hotel, *Auberge Au Sanglier Qui Fume* where you can spend a night (☎0524 485709, ⓦausanglierquifume.com; 415dh) or head to Marrakesh.

Tazaghart Refuge and Toubkal Summit

To reach the Tazaghart Refuge (sometimes labelled as *Lépiney* on maps), follow the route to Tizi Mzik (see p.375). South of the pass, a path follows the hillside to Azib Tamsoult, and then on to the gorge, for the ascent to the refuge. From Aroumd, the refuge can be reached by following a mule path southwest to Tamsoult (summer only) over the Tizi n'Tizikert, north of Aguelzim. The **Tazaghart Refuge** (50dh) is essentially a climbing base for the fine cliffs of **Tazaghart**. To get access, you (or a porter) may have to go down to the village of Tizi Oussem to get the hut *gardien*, Omar Abdallah, to open it up. He is also a very good (and extremely pleasant) guide; he can arrange a room in the village, too.

From Tazaghart Refuge, there are three ways to access the Toubkal Refuge (sometimes labelled as *Neltner* on maps). Each route increases in difficulty the futher south you go.

The most common and easiest route (5hr) is to head east over the Tizi Aguelzim, where the well-worn trail continues south to the Toubkal refuges. Alternatively, you can continue southward from the Tazaghart Refuge and then bear east towards the Tizi n'Tadat. This trail eventually connects to and heads south on the trail leading to the Toubkal refuges (6hr).

The third and most difficult path, which should be reserved for experienced and well-geared trekkers (especially in winter) is via Tizi Melloul. It takes three to four hours to reach Tizi Melloul from the Tazaghart Refuge. Following this, the trail bears east and then north for two to three hours, bringing you to the south end of the Toubkal refuges.

West of Tizi Melloul is the extraordinary **Tazaghart Plateau** (3843m) with its fine vantage point of the entire region. This side trip takes up to five hours round trip and should also only be attempted by experienced trekkers, especially in winter.

The summit of Toubkal (see p.372) can be attempted once you've reached the refuges. This, however, should only be attempted in the early morning (for safety and the best weather), which takes on average two to three hours up and two hours return.

Tacheddirt

TACHEDDIRT (2000m), 8km east of Imlil, makes a great base from which to explore the surrounding mountains, of which the trek to Setti Fatma is one of the most scenic, satisfying, and challenging.

Tacheddirt to Setti Fatma

This is one of the best routes for anyone contemplating more than a simple day-trip into the hills; taken at a reasonable pace, the route takes two days. There is a well-defined mule track all the way, so no particular skills are needed beyond general fitness, though several sections of the trail are quite exposed and steep. You'll probably want to carry some food supplies with you, but meals are offered at the village of **Timichi**, so cooking gear and provisions are not essential.

Tacheddirt to Timichi is a superb day's walk. The first three hours or so are spent zigzagging up to the **Tizi n'Tacheddirt** (3616m), a route with ever more spectacular views. Green terraced fields give way to rough and craggy mountain slopes, before the path down crosses one of the more barren sections. As you approach Timichi the valley again becomes more cultivated and the area has several *gîtes* (60dh per person), making it a good overnight stop.

Continuing onward, Timichi to Setti Fatma is another stunning day-trek. At first you follow the river fairly closely, passing several villages before taking the *piste* up to avoid the gorge, with a great view from the last spur before it zigzags down to the flood plain of the Ourika Valley, which is about 2km north of Setti Fatma.

Tacheddirt to Asni

There is a long but straightforward *piste* (trail) from Tacheddirt down-valley to **Asni**, taking seven to nine hours. It's an enjoyable route through a fine valley – a good (and neglected) exit from the mountains. You could also do this route from Imlil, heading off down from the Tizi n'Tamatert (1hr from Imlil) to the bottom of the valley at Tinhourine. If you want to camp out at night, there are possible places to pitch a tent below Ikiss or Arg, and there are also **gîtes** at Ikiss and Amsakrou (60dh per person). A fine pass rises opposite Ikiss to cross a *tizi* to Aguersioual and so back to Imlil, an excellent round trip.

ARRIVAL AND DEPARTURE   TACHEDDIRT

You can walk to Tacheddirt from Imlil in three to four hours (see p.367). It's possible to self-drive the road from Asni to Tacheddirt, via Imlil, but the terrain is rough and steep in places.

By public transport To get to Tacheiddirt from Marrakesh, take a grand taxi to Asni from Bab er Robb; from Asni, local minibuses connect to Tacheddirt (1hr 30min), but only from 8am–noon, though sometimes it's possible to get one as late as 2pm, and they are especially frequent on Saturday (market day).

ACCOMMODATION

Tigmi N' Tacheddirt Village centre. This spacious and comfy lodge seated at the edge of the Imenane Valley offers the best accommodation in the region and was built by a local entrepreneur from Aroumd. The refuge has plenty of beds available for individuals and small groups and is often used by trekkers passing through on various circuits. HB dorm 180dh, double 220dh

Ouirgane

OUIRGANE is an up-and-coming destination due to its proximity to Marrakesh and its stunning greenery, red-earth hills and pine forests, all of which combine to make it worth an overnight stay (or longer). It's a wonderful spot to rest up after a few days of trekking around Toubkal and makes a pleasant base in itself for day walks into the surrounding foothills, mountain-bike forays or horseback riding. The village hosts a small Thursday souk.

Both Ouirgane and the lush Marigha town and region heat up in the summer due to their indented position among the peaks, which means that while it's cooler than Marrakesh, it's still best to visit (or plan activities) here from March to May and mid-September to December.

6

Trekking

Day treks in Ouirgane are best done with a guide (see opposite). One recommended walk that you can request from a local expert is to start in Marigha, head south to the village of Marigha Izdern (1200m) and on to Imareghan Noufla (1220m), which has some of its stone olive oil presses still in use. From here, you'll head onward to Tinzert; enjoy the view of the Takherkhourte Peak (2500m) in the distance. From Tinzert, continue to Tagadirt n'Ousni and the village of Tamgoussi and down to Asni for transport back to Ouirgane or to Marrakesh. The total walking time is four to five hours.

To Toubkal

At the time of writing, the National Park Office had nearly completed a five- to six-hour trail connecting Ouirgane to the Toubkal refuges (see p.372), which then gives access to the summit. The trail is rated as moderate, is easier than the current established route from Imlil, and is sure to become a main thoroughfare once it is open to the public. For up-to-date information, ask at local hotels.

To the Azzadene Valley and Imlil

Walking from Ouirgane to Imlil is an overnight treat full of stunning views and steady climbing. From Ouirgane (or easily followed on the road connecting Imarira and Tassa Ouirgane), head east towards Tassa Ouirgane, where the well-trodden path will take you along the edge of the beautiful Azzadene Valley. When you reach Azerfsane, head south along the major river valley, Assif n'Ouissadene, finally connecting to the town of Aït Aïssa (Id Aissa) after five to six hours, which has a couple of small *gîtes* offering basic accommodation (50dh) and meals (50dh).

From Aït Aïssa, continue south to Tizi Oussem where you'll change direction, heading east over Tizi Mzik, through Azib Mzikene, and finally into the Mizane Valley and on to Imlil. This second day's walk also takes about five to six hours.

Biking the Marigha Circuit

Exploring the area around Ouirgane by bike is a great way to see more of this rich region via the backroads. One of the best circuits is the Marigha Ciruit, an 18km route that should take about three hours to complete.

Head southwest out of Ouirgane on the paved road to Taroudant. At a sign for *Chez Momo II*, take the left turn. Further, the paved entry becomes a gravel road as it heads uphill. Keep right and at the crest of the hill, you'll have a superb view of the Ouirgane barrage.

The views of the Azaden Valley come into view as you continue uphill and the *piste* finally gives way to flat riding; continue along the same *piste* to the village of Agouni (which means hungry in the local dialect). The *piste* opens up at the edge of Agouni to an area once inhabited by a local Jewish population. The buildings are painted white (a rare feature, interpreted locally as holy ground), and the site comes to life every August for a private moussem celebration.

Behind the Jewish village, the *piste* splits – continue straight (slightly left) to stay on course. It's possible here to detour up to the stunning village of Tikhfirst, 4km away, by turning right and following the *piste* steeply uphill – sublime views over the countryside await. Local families are known for their tea-making (tip 10dh per person), so this makes a nice point to refresh before heading back downhill.

Continue on the road past the Jewish settlement; within a few minutes you'll reach the village of Anraz, where the *piste* becomes a smooth single-track trail. You'll bike for a short distance through shady homesteads as the trail becomes a road again after half a kilometre at the village of Torrort. From here, take the *piste* downhill (left) to cross the bridge over the Assif n'Ouissadene. Just after this point, there's an intersection where you'll see a sign for Takhrkhort National Park. Turn left here towards Tassa Ouirgane; a right turn will take you, a few minutes later, to some of the best views of the entire ride – from here, backtrack to take the parth to Tassa Ouirgane.

From the intersection, head north along the well-maintained road, which connects to the Taroudant and Marrakesh road after about five kilometres. Here, turn left to return back to Ouirgane.

ARRIVAL AND DEPARTURE   OUIRGANE

By grand taxi By far the best way to get to Ouirgane is by grand taxi from the Bab Doukkala station in Marrakesh (1hr).

Alternatively, you can travel to Asni (see p.365) and then take a grand taxi to Ouirgane, which is about 17km away.

INFORMATION

Bike hire Bikes can be rented from *Au Sanglier que Fume* or the *Hotel L'Oliveraie de Marigha* (see below); both hotels can arrange bike delivery to your starting point. You can also arrange guided biking excursions with Bike Adventures in Morocco (book at least a day in advance; ☎0666 238 200, ⓦbikeadventuresinmorocco.com).

Guides Hotels often have local guides on hand, otherwise, in advance you can contact Omar Jellah on ☎0670 414 623.

ACCOMMODATION AND EATING

All of the hotels listed below offer meals, which are usually available to both guests and non-guests. It's a good idea to book ahead, and to have a clean pair of clothes to change into if you've been trekking.

Chez Momo Located a few kilometres past Ouirgane on the main Taroudant road ☎0524 485704, ⓦaubergemomo.com. An attractive, quiet, garden-set hotel with a small pool, though slightly overpriced. Rooms are clean and offer minimum comforts. The restaurant serves classic Berber dishes. 1100dh

★ **Dar Tassa** Off the Ouirgane road – turn left towards Marigha; once in the village, turn right at the first mosque, left at the second, and follow the piste (OK for cars) 5km ☎0524 484312 or ☎0667 852768, ⓦdartassa.com. An eco-friendly guesthouse, offering a range of spacious and beautifully decorated rooms and suites. The food is top quaility, and they can arrange activities in the mountains. 400dh

★ **Domaine Malika** Located just before Ouirgane; in Maghira, turn right towards Amizmiz – it's situated 500m on the left ☎0661 493541, ⓦdomaine-malika .com. Claiming – and living up to – the "best service in Africa", this is a highly recommended luxury retreat. The affordable sumptuousness combines with freshly made gourmet meals to create a well-deserved respite after exploring the surrounding peaks and valleys. 1450dh

★ **L'Oliveraie de Marigha** Located at the intersection of the Amizmiz and Ouirgane roads, just before Ouirgane ☎0661 310482, ⓦoliveraie-de-marigha.com. Owned by famed photographer Gaetan and his wife Celine, *L'Oliveraie* makes a great spot for an retreat from Marrakesh. You can spend the day poolside, eating at their award-winning restaurant, and they can arrange pick-ups (both by car and – for the VIP experience – helicopter) from Marrakesh, plus helicopter rides around the Atlas Mountains (5000– 10,000dh/group). The rooms, suites and spacious bungalows are scattered through the lush gardens, and accessible rooms are also available. 900dh

Résidence de la Roseraie Located in the centre of Ouirgane ☎0524 432094, ⓦlaroseraiehotel.com. Once Ouirgane's most luxurious hotel, *Résidence de la Roseraie* has seen better days, but is still a gem in its own right. The 45 rooms are scattered around a rose garden, with a swimming pool, sauna, tennis, an equestrian centre (horseriding 150dh/ hr; book well in advance and bring your own helmet) and a renowned restaurant. It's worth considering half board as there are limited dining options in the area. 1200dh

Au Sanglier Qui Fume Located in the centre of Ouirgane ☎0524 485707, ⓦausanglierquifume.com. An attractive, long-established French-run *auberge*, with excellent food and a delightful garden and pool. Wellpriced for the amenities included; book well in advance during summer. 450dh

Amizmiz and Ait Zitoun

The small, dusty town of **AMIZMIZ**, 58km from Marrakesh, is the site of a long-established **Tuesday souk** – one of the largest Berber markets of the Atlas, and not a key destination for tourists. The town comprises several quite distinct quarters, including a *zaouia*, kasbah and former Mellah, separated by a small, usually dry, river. Amizmiz makes a good base for mountain biking in the High Atlas (see box, p.381).

From Amizmiz, the nearby village of **Ait Zitoun** is a lesser-known, yet much better place to start treks than Amizmiz, as you can arrange both mules and supplies here, along with a local guide. Ait Zitoun is a tricky place to find; it's located on a short *piste* veering left off the main road connecting Amizmiz to Ouirgane (look for a small sign stating *Gîte Ait Zitoun*). It's possible to arrange a walk to Ouirgane from here, which takes three to four days and is best done in the cooler months – a highly recommended guide is Omar Jellah (☏ 0670 414623, ✉ omarjellah@yahoo.co.uk; contact at least two to three days in advance), who specializes in this region. The walk is at a relatively low altitude for the mountains, and the surrounding hills are green in the spring months and roasted brown in the summer and fall. For the most part, it's a steady, easy foray into villages, valleys and foothills, but there are some slightly steep inclines approaching the ridges.

An alternative to both of these villages for an overnight stop is **Lalla Takerkoust**, 22km northeast of Amizmiz. Views from the lake of the surrounding mountains make for wonderful photo opportunities in the winter with the surrounding snowcapped peaks in clear view. A few villages dot the landscape and walking to some of the low-lying hills for views of the region makes a worthwhile day's venture.

ARRIVAL AND DEPARTURE

AMIZMIZ

By public transport Amizmiz is best reached by grand taxi or on the Alsa City Bus from the Bab er Robb station in Marrakesh (55min); alternatively, you could take a bus or grand taxi to Lalla Takerkoust, and pick up another to Amizmiz from there.

AIT ZITOUN

By public transport Public transport does not go directly to Ait Zitoun. The best way to get here is from Ouirgane or Amizmiz in a public or private-hired grand taxi. From Amizmiz, take a grand taxi from the centre of town in the direction of Ouirgane for 15km; look carefully for the sign

to the left. From Ouirgane, take a taxi in the direction of Amizmiz for 21km; look out for a sign to Ait Zitoun on the right. In both instances, ask the driver to stop at the Ait Zitoun sign.

LALLA TAKERKOUST

By public transport Getting to Lalla Takerhoust is most easily done by grand taxi from the Bab er Robb station in Marrakesh (40min); alternatively, you can take a grand taxi from Asni.

By car The road (P2024) via Moulay Brahim along the Kik Plateau with views of the High Atlas is splendid, especially in winter and spring.

ACCOMMODATION

AMIZMIZ

Dar Achorafa 3km from Amizmiz towards Imintanout ☏ 0672 026829 or ☏ 0670 215925, ⊛ achorafa.com. A comfy and affordable lodge set just on the edge of Amizmiz, *Dar Achorafa* is a peaceful escape dedicating both time and energy to local sustainable projects in the town and surrounding villages. Rooms are spacious and tidy, and the grounds well kept; the restaurant serves up affordable and tasty meals using produce grown on site. 500dh

Maroc Lodge (Berber Lodge) 1km from Amizmiz towards Tizguine ☏ 0524 454969 or ☏ 0661 202537, ⊛ berber-lodge.com. A splendid retreat at any time of year, *Maroc Lodge* has four small villas on site that are great for couples or families, an outdoor dining area, pool and heavenly gardens. It's a true escape into solitude after a day's trekking, and serves up first-rate meals. 1500dh

Le Source Bleu Irghagn, 4km from Amizmiz ☏ 0524 454595 or ☏ 0670 105714. A standard *auberge*, *Le Source Bleu* offers single, double and family rooms that are great for those on a budget. 160dh

AIT ZITOUN

Gîte Ait Zitoun 15km east from Amizmiz in the direction of Ouirgane; look for a very small sign on the left pointing

down a gravel road to the gîte ☏ 0667 236045 or ☏ 06667 06308. This rustic guesthouse is a good base for arranging treks, through owner Ibrahim Ouahmane, and trekkers are invited to turn up without reservation. Accommodation is in basic dorms with solid sponge mats serving as beds, and shared bathrooms. Good meals are available. HB 200dh

LALLA TAKERKOUST

Dar Zitoune On the road from Moulay Brahim, 18km before Lalla Takerkoust ☏ 0662 408380, ⊛ dar-zitoune .com. This affordable guesthouse is a diamond in the rough. With seven rooms (sleeping up to four), it's a solid middle-range place, and a great location to base yourself for paragliding and walking (in cooler months). There's a lovely small pool, a superbly manicured garden, and great food available. 300dh

Le Flouka Auberge On the northwest shore of Lalla Takerkoust; at the intersection of the Amizmiz and Asni road, continue towards Amizmiz (west) for 600m before turning left (southwest), then continue for 500m and turn left (southeast) towards the lake ☏ 0664 492660, ⊛ leflouka.com. *Le Flouka* (meaning "boat") has quite a few different accommodation options. A private apartment or villa is perfect for families or small groups, while the riad or regular

MOUNTAIN BIKING – AND SOME ROUTES FROM AMIZMIZ

Morocco offers some of the best adventure riding in the world with routes suitable for all abilities. The High Atlas has jeep and mule tracks that cover the countryside and several **adventure companies** offer mountain biking as a pursuit. Travelling independently, it's important to be aware of local sensibilities; ride slowly through villages, giving way to people where necessary, especially those on mules and children tending livestock. If **renting a bike**, negotiate essential extras like a pump, puncture repair kit and/or spare inner tube. A helmet is recommended, and carry plenty of water (see p.35 for more).

Of the **three routes** detailed below, the first two can be done by a novice with a rented bike, while the third is best left to the proficient, preferably on their own bike. All routes begin and end at *Restaurant Le Source Bleu* (see opposite) located in **Irghagn**, above Amizmiz. As few roads are signposted, the Amizmiz 1:100,000 **topographical map** is highly recommended, and best obtained from specialist map shops (see p.61) before you leave home.

ROUTE 1 THE OUED ANOUGAL CIRCUIT

From *Le Source Bleu*, descend to the *piste* road running from Amizmiz to Azegour and then head on uphill past the *Maison Forestière*. About 1.5km beyond, a narrow *piste* branches off left, taking you down the west side of the valley to pass through the village of Aït Ouskri, from where there are tremendous views up the valley, to Jebel Gourza and Jebel Imlit. The *piste* continues, passing the villages of Tizgui, Toug al Kheyr and, after 10km, Imi-n-Isli and Imi-n-Tala ("big spring"), before crossing the Anougal River below **Addouz** to the eastern side of the valley. Care should be taken **in spring**, when the river can become swollen from melted snow. Following the *piste* through Imzayn, and sticking to the lower track, leads to Igourdan and, after about 12km, uphill, to **Aït Hmad**.

Leaving Aït Hmad behind, the road widens to become a full-width *piste* jeep track allowing a fast but safe downhill back into Amizmiz.

ROUTE 2: JEBEL TIMERGHIT CIRCUIT

Follow the Route 1 description to Imi-n-Tala then take a *piste* westwards through the forest to reach the Oued Erdouz road from Azegour, with Jebel Timerghit towering above. Turn left and circuit the hill to Toulkine and on through the granite landscape towards Azegour. Five hundred metres before Azegour you come to a junction – turn left here, crossing a bridge over the Oued Wadakar, and continue past the remains of a mining site. The route then runs through forest and, after a gentle crest run, descends in numerous bends to Amizmiz, passing the *Maison Forestière*.

ROUTE 3: TOULKINE DESCENT

Begin the route in the same way as those above, but don't break off left as in Route 1. Keep on ahead for the long toil through the forest to gain the gentler crest before descending into the Erdouz-Wadakar valley where there are extensive ruins from the mining that once took place here. Cross the bridge and turn right to circuit round to Toulkine. A *piste* heads northwest from the village but instead follow the mule track that heads due north over the crest to circuit the valley heads with Adghous perched in the middle. This then wends through the Jebel Aborji forest before a rather brutal descent to the plains at Tiqlit. Note that it's advisable to check the route at Toulkine.

rooms are better for individuals and couples. Great pool, meals and a pirate ship's bar make it a fun place to stay. 600dh
Jnane Tihihit Douar Makhfamane, right on the edge of Lalla Takerkoust ☎ 0524 387352 or ☎ 0670 965970,

ⓦ riad-t.com. The former farm is now a rural guesthouse estate where travellers can truly escape to Morocco's countryside. Animals on site, a pool, and large grounds will make you want to stay. 800dh

Ijoukak and around

IJOUKAK is an important shopping centre where the Agoundis Valley joins the Nfis. Walking from Ijoukak, you can easily explore Tin Mal and Talaat n' Yakoub (see p.382) or try some more prolonged **trekking in the Nfis and Agoundis valleys**. The Agoundis can also be enjoyable just as a day's wandering, or you can take the winding forestry road up the hill dominating the village for its commanding view.

Tin Mal Mosque

8km from Ijoukak • Daily generally 10am–noon & 3–6pm; ask in town if you can't find the *gardien* • 10dh • You can walk from Ijoukak, passing the Goundafi Kasbah near Talaat n'Yakoub; you can return on the opposite side of the Nfis if a bridge (replaced seasonally) is in place – check before you set off from Ijoukak

The **Tin Mal Mosque**, quite apart from its historic and architectural importance, is a beautiful monument – isolated above a lush reach of river valley, with harsh mountains backing its buff-coloured walls. It has been partially restored and is a worthwhile stop.

The mosque is set a little way above the modern village of Tin Mal (or Ifouriren) and reached by wandering uphill from the road bridge. The site is kept locked but the *gardien* will soon spot you, open it up and let you look round undisturbed (tip is expected).

Brief history

The Tin Mal Mosque was finished by Abd el Moumen around 1153–54, partly as a memorial to Ibn Toumert who started constructing it in 1125 as a Koranic school (*tinmil* means "school" in ancient Berber), and also as his own family's mausoleum. Obviously fortified, it probably served also as a section of the town's defences, since in the early period of Almohad rule, Tin Mal was entrusted with the state treasury. Today, it is the only part of the fortifications – indeed, of the entire Almohad city – that you can make out with any clarity. The Almohad city had been home to twenty thousand Berbers before it was was largely destroyed in the Merenid conquest of 1276.

That Tin Mal remained standing for that long, and that its mosque was maintained, says a lot about the power Ibn Toumert's teaching must have continued to exercise over the local Berbers (see box, p.361). Even two centuries later the historian Ibn Khaldun found Koranic readers employed at the tombs, and when the French began restoration in the 1930s they found the site littered with the shrines of *marabouts*.

The interior

Architecturally, Tin Mal presents a unique opportunity for non-Muslims to take a look at the interior of a traditional Almohad mosque. It is roofless, for the most part, and two of the corner pavilion towers have disappeared, but the mihrab (or prayer niche) and the complex pattern of internal arches are substantially intact. The arrangement is in a classic Almohad design – the T-shaped plan with a central aisle leading towards the mihrab – and is virtually identical to that of the Koutoubia in Marrakesh (see p.320), more or less its contemporary. The one element of eccentricity is in the placing of the **minaret** over the mihrab: a weakness of engineering design that meant it could never have been much taller than it is today. In terms of decoration, the most striking feature is the variety and intricacy of the **arches** – above all those leading into the mihrab, which have been sculpted with a stalactite vaulting. In the **corner domes** and the **mihrab vault** this technique is extended with impressive effect. Elsewhere, and on the face of the mihrab, it is the slightly austere geometric patterns and familiar motifs (the palmette, rosette, scallop, etc) of Almohad decorative gates that are predominant.

The Goundafi kasbahs

6km from Ijoukak, 3km from Tin Mal, and clearly visible from the roadside at Talâat

The **Goundafi kasbahs** don't really compare historically with Tin Mal – nor with the Glaoui kasbah in Telouet (see p.393). But, as so often in Morocco, they provide an extraordinary assertion of just how recent the country's feudal past is. Despite their medieval appearance, the buildings are all nineteenth- or even twentieth-century creations.

Talaat n' Yakoub

The more important of the kasbahs is the former Goundafi stronghold known locally as Agadir n'Gouj, located on a hill overlooking the village of **TALAAT N'YAKOUB** (which

IBN TOUMERT AND THE ALMOHADS

Tin Mal's site seems now so remote that it is difficult to imagine a town ever existing in this valley. In some form, though, it did. It was here that **Ibn Toumert** and his lieutenant, **Abd el Moumen**, preached to the Berber tribes and welded them into the **Almohad** ("unitarian") movement; here that they set out on the campaigns which culminated in the conquest of all Morocco and southern Spain; and here, too, a century and a half later, that they made their last stand against the incoming Merenid dynasty.

Known to his followers as the *Mahdi* – "The Chosen One", whose coming is prophesied in the Hadith (Sayings of The Prophet) – Toumert was born in the High Atlas, a member of the Berber-speaking Masmouda tribe, who held the desert-born Almoravids, the ruling dynasty, in contempt. He was an accomplished theologian and studied at the centres of eastern Islam, a period in which he formulated the strict Almohad doctrines. For Toumert, Almoravid Morocco contained much to disapprove of and, returning from the East with a small group of disciples, he began to preach against all manifestations of luxury and against women mixing in male society.

After being exiled from the Almoravid capital, Marrakesh, in 1124, Ibn Toumert and Abd el Moumen set out to mould the Atlas Berbers into a religious and military force. They also stressed the significance of the "second coming" and Ibn Toumert's role as *Mahdi*. Hesitant tribes were branded "hypocrites" and massacred – most notoriously in the Forty-Day Purge of the mountains – and within eight years none remained outside Almohad control.

6

has an interesting mountain **souk** on Wed). Decaying and partially ruined, plans were afoot to restore the kasbah and turn it into a restaurant. However, those plans appear to have been halted and the kasbah is now locked and cannot be entered. The structure is well preserved – as indeed it should be, having been built only in 1907, mainly to stable the Goundafi horses.

It is difficult to establish the exact facts with these old tribal kasbahs, but it seems that it was constructed late in the nineteenth century for the next-to-last Goundafi chieftain. A feudal warrior in the old tradition, he was constantly at war with the sultan during the 1860s and 1870s, and a bitter rival of the neighbouring Glaoui clan. His son, Tayeb el Goundafi, also spent most of his life in tribal campaigning, though he finally threw in his lot with Sultan Moulay Hassan, and later with the French. At the turn of the twentieth century, he could still raise some five thousand armed tribesmen with a day or two's notice, but his power and fief eventually collapsed in 1924. The writer, Cunninghame Graham, was detained here by the Goundafi in the 1890s, and describes the medieval scene well in his book, *Mogreb el-Acksa*.

Aourir n'Tagoundaft

The crumbling remains of **Aourir n'Tagoundaft**, 18km south of Ikoukak, are best reached by car; at the village of Lbor n'Tgdast, an east turn down a *piste* after 500m will take you past a few villages before ending at the village of Arbalou. From here, you can walk up to the kasbah (10min). This is the most imposing but seldom visited of the Goundafi kasbahs. It retains its vast cistern, though the aqueduct that once served this has gone.

ARRIVAL AND DEPARTURE   **IJOUKAK**

By bus A daily bus to the centre of Ijoukak departs from Marrakesh's *gare routière* at 1pm and takes nearly two hours; returning to Marrakesh, a bus departs from Ijoukak daily at 7am taking two hours.

By grand taxi Grands taxis from Marrakesh do not usually stop in Ijoukak, but at nearby Talaat n' Yakoub, where you can take a local taxi for the five-minute journey to Ijoukak.

ACCOMMODATION

Ijoukak itself has limited accommodation options – the nearby village of Talaat n'Yakoub (4km away; see p.382), is a better option and connected to the town by local taxis.

Chez Imnir 800m from the centre, south of Talat n' Yakoub; ask directions at the corner café in town ☎ 0662 036364. This well-situated *gîte* has seven surprisingly comfortable rooms that sleep up to four people; not all the rooms have private bathrooms and cheaper dorms are also available. Free wi-fi, filling meals available, and the owner can help you set up treks. Dorm 80dh, double 120dh

6

The Agoundis Valley

To the East from Ijoukak winds the **Agoundis Valley**, which offers an alternative access to Toubkal; it takes two days of serious trekking from Ijoukak to reach the Toubkal Refuge. On foot, from Ijoukak head out on the Marrakesh road, cross the Oued Agoundis river bottom and turn right onto the up-valley road, passing several *gîtes*. The scenery opens up to distant peaks and there are a surprising number of villages. After an hour's walking you reach the wreck of an old mineral processing plant, a gondola still high in the air on a cable stretched across the valley to mines that closed decades ago. Continue walking to the village of **Taghbart** where there is a fork; take the right branch to cross the river, which makes an impressive ascent to the 2202-metre **Tizi-n-Ou-Ichddane** on the Atlas watershed. The Agoundis *piste* soon passes **El Makhzen** and a prominent house in wedding-cake style before becoming progressively narrower, exposed and rough, passing perched villages and ending at the village of **Aït Youl**. From Aït Youl, strong walkers can reach the Toubkal Refuge in a day, crossing the **Tizi n'Ougane** (risk of snow on the final slopes from November through May) passing through wild gorges and screes on the way.

ARRIVAL AND DEPATURE   THE AGOUNDIS VALLEY

It takes a long day's walk to reach Aït Youl; alternatively, enquire at *Chez Imnir* in Ijoukak (see above) about public transport up the valley.

ACCOMMODATION

Tigmmi n'Tmazirte (Chez Housseine) At the entrance to Ijoukak; turn east on the piste (OK for cars) before the bridge and continue for 3km ☎ 0612 199862 or ☎ 0668 253421, ✉ tamazirt.home@yahoo.fr, 🌐 tigmmi -ntmazirte.com. This tranquil, rustic lodge is the best spot to base yourself in the area, and would be a shame to miss. With great views, clean rooms, superb meals, large terraces and lots of activities on site, this is a trekker's dream escape. In addition, they run a nuvmber of workshops and classes (including pottery and essential oils), and offer various trekking and mountain biking opportunities. They offer a choice of double, triple and family rooms. 80dh

Tizi n'Test

Tizi n'Test (2092m) is an awe-inspiring pass that crosses the Atlas and connects to Taroudant and Taliouine. Cutting right through the heart of the Atlas, the road was blasted out of the mountains by the French from 1926 to 1932 – the first modern route to link Marrakesh with the Souss plain and the desert, an extraordinary feat of pioneer-spirit engineering. Until then, passage had been considered impracticable without local protection and knowledge: an important pass for trade and for the control and subjugation of the south, but one that few sultans were able to make their own.

The **Tizi n'Test** (2092m) itself becomes truly momentous 18km before it connects to the N10 – a rather torturous stretch filled with hairpin bends. A lovely, yet challenging drive, it's one of the more scenic jaunts in the whole country, giving way to unmatched panoramas that serve as a splendid gateway to the Souss region of the country.

TREKKING THE TICHKA PLATEAU

Exploring the **Tichka Plateau** and the **western fringes of the Atlas**, you move well away from established tour-group routes and pass through Berber villages that scarcely ever see a foreigner. You'll need to carry provisions, and be prepared to camp or possibly stay in a Berber village home if you get the invitation – as you almost certainly will. Sanitation is often poor in the villages and it's a good idea to bring water purification tablets (see box, pp.370–371). Eating and drinking in mountain village homes, though, is surprisingly safe, as the food (mainly tajines) is thoroughly cooked and the drink is invariably mint tea.

However you approach it, the **Tichka Plateau** is a delight. Grazing is controlled so the meadows, in spring, are a mass of early daffodils and flowers. **Imaradene** (3351m) and **Amendach** (3382m) are the highest summits, west and east, and are superlative viewpoints. The plateau is drained by the Oued Nfis, first through the Tiziatin oak forest, using or bypassing gorges, then undergoing a series of villages, one of which, another Imlil, has a shrine to Ibn Toumert, the founder of the Tin Mal/Almohad dynasty.

APPROACHING AND EXPLORING THE PLATEAU

There are approaches to the mountains from both north and south: **Imi n'Tanoute**, **Timesgadiouine** and **Argana**, on the main Marrakesh–Agadir bus route (north and west), and **Taroudant–Ouled Berhil** (south) or the Tizi n'Test road (east; see opposite). From the north and west approaches, taxis, or rides on trucks bound for mines or markets at trailheads, could be used; from the south, smaller pick-up trucks (*camionettes*) ply up daily to Imoulas, the Medlawa Valley and Tigouga. For eastern access by the Oued Nfis, take the *piste* down from the Tizi n'Test and follow up the south bank of the river.

If you can afford it, hiring **Land Rover transport** to take you, and possibly a **guide**, to meet prearranged mules and a muleteer is the most efficient procedure. El Aouad Ali in Taroudant (see box, p.468) is the recognized expert on the region and could make all arrangements. Or you could arrange a **small group trek** through the UK-based trekking company Walks Worldwide (🅦walksworldwide.com), who organize all levels of treks with El Aouad Ali. The IGN 1:100,000 maps for the area are *Tizi n'Test* and *Igli*.

Over the Tizi n'Test pass, the descent towards the **Taroudant–Taliouine road** is dramatic: a drop of some 1600m in little over 30km. Throughout, there are stark, fabulous vistas of the Tizi n'Test mountains jutting out around the Nfiss Valley with clusters of villages in view hundreds of feet below.

ARRIVAL AND DEPARTURE   TIZI N'TEST

The Tizi n'Test is not for the faint-hearted. From November to the end of April, the pass is occasionally blocked with snow. When this occurs, a sign is put up on the roadside at the point where the Asni–Test road leaves Marrakesh and on the roadside past Tahanaoute.

By bus Buses over the pass are erratic, though there is one service most days between Marrakesh and Taliouine (4hr 30min), with a change at Oulad Berhil if you are heading for Taroudant.

By grand taxi It's possible to travel by shared grand taxi to the pass, either from Marrakesh, Asni or (coming in the other direction) Taliouine or Taroudant.

By car If you are driving, some experience of mountain roads is advisable. The route is well contoured and paved, but between the pass and the intersection with the N10, the Taliouine–Taroudant road, it is extremely narrow (one and a half times a car's width) with almost continuous hairpin bends and blind corners. As you can see for some distance ahead, this isn't as dangerous as it sounds – but you still need a lot of confidence.

ACCOMMODATION

Dar El Mouahidines Located 8km past Ijoukak on the main road to Taroudant ☎ 0676 253452. The only hotel on the road between Tin Mal and the peak of the Tizi n' Test. Surprisingly nice rooms with a superb garden and outdoor dining area make it a nice base for day walks to see the protected mountain goat region of Adrar n'Iger. Buses from Bab er Robb station in Marrakesh will stop here on request. <u>**400dh**</u>

The southern oases routes

AÏT BENHADDOU

The southern oases routes

The Moroccan pre-Sahara begins as soon as you cross the Atlas to the south. It is not sand for the most part – more a wasteland of rock and scrub, which the Berbers call hammada – but it is powerfully impressive. There is, too, an irresistible sense of wonder as you catch a first glimpse of the great southern river valleys: the Drâa, Dadès, Todra and Ziz. Lush belts of date-palm oases, scattered with the fabulous mud architecture of kasbahs and fortified ksour villages, these are the old caravan routes that reached back to Marrakesh and Fez and out across the Sahara to Timbuktu, Niger and old Sudan, carrying gold, slaves and salt well into the nineteenth century.

7

Most travellers' first taste of the region is the **Tizi n'Tichka**, the dizzying pass up from Marrakesh, and the iconic kasbashs at **Telouet** and **Aït Benhaddou** – an introduction that is hard to beat. Benhaddou is less than an hour's drive from **Ouarzazate**, a modern town created by the French to "pacify" the south and one of the area's few urban centres of any significance, buoyed in recent years by its association with the film industry. From here, you can follow the old trading routes: south through the Drâa to **Zagora** and the fringes of the desert at **M'Hamid**; or east through the Dadès to the towering **Todra Gorge** and, ultimately, the dunes at **Erg Chebbi** near Merzouga. These are beautiful journeys, the roads rolling through crumbling mud-brick villages and past long ribbons of deep-green palmeries as they stretch out towards the Sahara.

The southern oases were long a mainstay of the pre-colonial economy. Their wealth, and the arrival of tribes from the desert, provided the impetus for two of the great royal dynasties: the Saadians (1554–1669) from the **Drâa Valley**, and the current ruling family, the Alaouites (1669–present) from the **Tafilalt**. By the nineteenth century, however, the advance of the Sahara and the uncertain upkeep of the channels that watered the oases had reduced life to bare subsistence, even in the most fertile strips. Under the French, with the creation of modern industry in the north and the exploitation of phosphates and minerals, they became less and less significant, while the old caravan routes were dealt a final death blow by the closure of the Algerian border in 1994.

Although the date harvests in October, centred on **Erfoud**, still give employment to the *ksour* communities, the rest of the year sees only the modest production of a

CAMEL TRIP IN THE ERG CHEBBI

Highlights

❶ Telouet The abandoned feudal kasbah of the "Lords of the Atlas" is hugely evocative. **See p.392**

❷ Aït Benhaddou The cream of the south's desert architecture, used as a striking location for numerous movies. **See p.395**

❸ Palmeries Fed by ancient water courses, the great palmeries of Morocco's southern oases form an astounding contrast with the desert. See p.412, p.424 & p.433

❹ Kasbah stays You should try and spend at least a night in one of these iconic buildings, hand-crafted with mud and straw and providing welcome respite from the desert heat. See p.414, p.425 & p.444

❺ Dadès Gorge Outlandish rock formations and ruined kasbahs at the head of a valley winding deep into the Atlas watershed. See p.418

❻ Todra Gorge This dramatic cleft in the High Atlas is one of the country's finest natural spectacles. **See p.426**

❼ Erg Chebbi Morocco's most impressive sand dunes, stretching out to the border with Algeria, are best explored on camel back. **See p.439**

HIGHLIGHTS ARE MARKED ON THE MAP ON PP.390–391

handful of crops – henna, barley, citrus fruits and, uniquely, roses, developed by the French around **El Kelâa M'Gouna** for the production of rose-water and perfume. Severe drought in the 1990s had a devastating effect on crops, including dates, and forced much of the male population to seek work further north, but since 2007 the water levels have greatly improved and the palmeries are returning to their picture-book lushness once more.

GETTING AROUND

The south is a vast region, stretching some 675km from Ouarzazate to Figuig, though the area can be broken down nicely into more manageable **circuits**. The simplest – Marrakesh to Zagora and back, or the return from Marrakesh to Tinghir – can be done in around five days, though to do them any degree of justice you'll need a lot longer. With ten days or more, the loop from Ouarzazate to Merzouga (via Tinghir), and thence southwest to Zagora and M'Hamid, becomes a possibility, stringing together the region's main highlights via good roads and dependable transport connections.

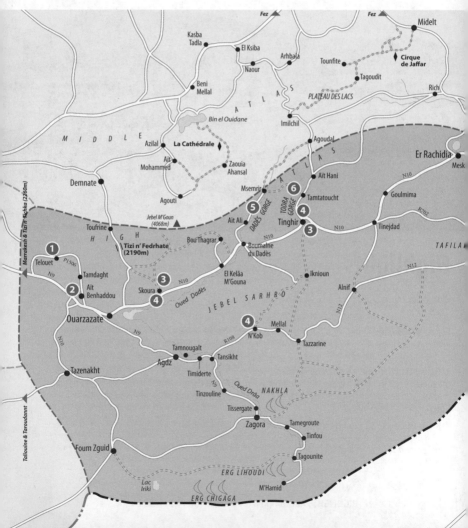

BY BUS

All the main routes in this chapter are covered by regular buses; the road from Ouarzazate to Tinghir and on to Erfoud (for Merzouga) is particularly well served. Travelling by bus in the desert in summer can be physically exhausting, though: most trips tend to begin at dawn to avoid the worst of the heat and, for the rest of the day, it can be difficult to summon up the energy to do anything.

BY CAR

If you can afford to rent a car, even for just two or three days, you'll be able to take in a lot more, with a lot less frustration, in a reasonably short period of time – there are numerous rental outlets in Ouarzazate (see p.400), some of which allow you to return their vehicles to Marrakesh, Fez, Agadir or Casablanca.

Services Petrol stations can be found along all the main routes. Local mechanics are generally excellent, and most minor problems can be quickly (and often cheaply) dealt with.

Equipment It's wise to carry water, in case of overheating, and, above all, be sure you've got a good spare tyre – punctures tend to be frequent on southern roads.

Driving on pistes Many of the *pistes* in the south are navigable in a rental car, but be aware that the insurance is invalid when you drive on them. In reality, 4WDs are a better bet for *pistes*, even more so in winter and early spring (they're essential for the Dadès route across the Atlas, for which you should also be able to do basic mechanical repairs).

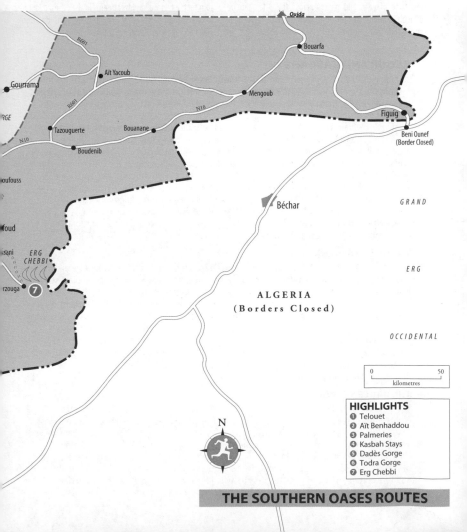

HIGHLIGHTS
1. Telouet
2. Aït Benhaddou
3. Palmeries
4. Kasbah Stays
5. Dadès Gorge
6. Todra Gorge
7. Erg Chebbi

THE SOUTHERN OASES ROUTES

Scams The practice known as "fake breakdowns" is prevalent throughout the south but particularly refined along the road from Ouarzazate to Zagora. People standing next to stationary cars will flag you down, ostensibly for help getting to a garage; but when you arrive at the next town, they'll insist on returning the favour by offering you a "special price" on items from their handicraft shop. As difficult as it may sound, don't stop to "help".

INFORMATION

When to visit Spring is by far the most enjoyable time to travel, particularly if you're heading for Zagora, reckoned to be the hottest town in the country, or Merzouga – though the Drâa, in particular, is subject to flash floods at this time of year, and passes across the Atlas can be difficult or impossible. Autumn, with the date harvests, is also good. Temperatures can climb well above 50°C in

BY TRUCK

On many of the minor routes, local Berber lorries (*camions*) or pick-ups (*camionettes*) run a bus-type service, charging standard fares for their trips, which are usually timed to coincide with the network of souks or markets in villages en route. The trucks cover a number of adventurous desert *pistes* as well as the very rough road over the Atlas from the Dadès Gorge.

midsummer, while in winter the days remain hot but it can get very cold at night.

Health Rivers in the south are reputed to contain bilharzia, a parasite that can enter your skin, including the soles of your feet; when walking by streams in the oases, take care to avoid contact with water. Travellers are advised to drink only bottled mineral water in southern Morocco.

KSOUR AND KASBAHS

Arguably *the* defining image of the south, **ksour** (**ksar** in the singular) and **kasbahs** are found throughout the region, peeking out of palmeries and edging the roads that cut through the great river valleys, most notably the Dadès, the so-called Route of a Thousand Kasbahs, and the Drâa.

A *ksar* (or *ighrem* in Berber) is essentially a fortified tribal village, while a kasbah (or *tighremt*) is a fortified home made for the ruling family. They are massive structures, built – in the absence of other available materials – out of the mud-clay **pisé** of the riverbanks. A unique and probably indigenous development of the Berber populations, they are often monumental in design and fabulously decorated, with bold geometric patterns incised into exterior walls and slanted towers. Seasonal rains wash off some of the mud, so the buildings require constant upkeep – once a kasbah has been left unmaintained, it declines very fast, with twenty years enough to produce a ruinous state if the walls are not renewed.

Agadirs, also variants of the *ksar* structure, used to serve as a combination of tribal fortress and communal granary or storehouse for the villages.

THE DRÂA KASBAHS

Few of the *ksour* and kasbahs that shadow **the Drâa** can be more than a hundred years old, though you frequently see the ruins and walls of earlier *ksour* abandoned just a short distance from their more modern counterparts. Most are populated by **Berbers**, but there are also Arab villages here, and even a few scattered communities of **Jews**, still living in their Mellahs. All of the southern valleys, too, have groups of **Haratin**, descendants of West African slaves brought into Morocco along the caravan routes. Inevitably, these populations have mixed to some extent – and the Jews here are almost certainly converted Berbers – though it is interesting to see just how distinct many of the *ksour* still appear, both in their architecture and customs. There is, for example, a great difference from one village in the Drâa to the next as regards women's costumes, above all in the wearing and extent of veils.

THE DADÈS KASBAHS

Though several of the Skoura kasbahs date, at least in part, from the seventeenth and eighteenth centuries, the majority of kasbahs in **the Dadès** oases are relatively modern. Most of the older fortifications were destroyed in a vicious tribal war in 1893, and many that survived were pulled down in the French pacification of the 1920s and 30s. The kasbah walls in the Dadès, higher and flatter than in the Drâa, often seem unscalable, but in the course of a siege or war there were always other methods of conquest – a favourite means of attack in the 1890s, according to the writer Walter Harris, who journeyed here in disguise, was to divert the water channels of the oasis round a kasbah and simply wait for its foundations to dissolve.

Telouet and the Tizi n'Tichka

The direct route between Marrakesh and Ouarzazate, the **Tizi n'Tichka** (N9) is a spectacular piece of engineering, its pulse-racing series of switchbacks providing evermore jaw-dropping views until it eventually crests the central High Atlas at its eponymous pass. It was built to replace the old caravan route to the Drâa and the south, which was controlled during the nineteenth century and much of the twentieth by the legendary **Glaoui family**, the greatest and most ambitious of all the Berber tribal leaders – their kasbah-headquarters, a vast complex of buildings abandoned only in 1956, still stands at **Telouet**, less than an hour from the main road.

Arrow-straight as it runs out from Marrakesh across the Haouz Plain, the Tizi n'Tichka soon contours forest slopes high above the Oued Ghdat valley, twisting past small villages and fields as it heads to **Taddert**, the last significant village on the north side of the pass – though most traffic now stops a kilometre on at busy **Upper Taddert**. The road thereafter climbs in an amazing array of hairpin bends to reach pastureland (*tichka* means "high pasture") before a final pull up to the **Tichka pass** itself (2260m), marked by cafés and the obligatory souvenir stall or two; not far down on the south side of the pass is the turning to Telouet and the Ounila Valley. The main road south winds down through **Igherm**, 10km further on and home to a well-restored *agadir* (to find someone to unlock it, ask at the roadside hotel, *Chez Mimi*), gradually flattening out until it reaches the turn-off to Aït Benhaddou (see p.395), just 19km before Ouarzazate.

Kasbah Telouet

Signed 500m down a track, north of Telouet village (the other side of the village if approaching from the Tizi n'Tichka) • Daily 9am–sunset • 20dh; optional guide 50dh

The bizarre **Kasbah Telouet** is one of the most extraordinary sights of the Atlas – fast crumbling into the dark red earth, but still offering, in parts, a peculiar glimpse of the style and melodrama of Moroccan political government and power still within living memory. There's little of aesthetic value – many of the rooms have fallen into complete ruin – but nevertheless, even after over a half-century of decay, there's still vast drama in this weird and remote site, and in the decorated salon walls, often roofless and open to the wind.

The main halls and reception rooms

The kasbah is an unbelievable labyrinth of locked doors and connecting passages – it is said that no single person ever fully knew their way around the entire complex – though these days you can only access the main halls and **reception rooms**. The latter, remarkably intact, given the crumbling exterior, at least give a sense of the quantity and style of the decoration, still in progress when the pasha died and the old regime came to a sudden halt. "The outward and visible signs of ultimate physical ambition", as Gavin Maxwell put it in *Lords of the Atlas* (see p.569), they have delicate iron window grilles and fine carved ceilings, though the overall result is once again the late nineteenth- and early twentieth-century combination of sensitive imitation of the past and out-and-out vulgarity.

The roof

There is a tremendous scale of affectation, too, perfectly demonstrated by the use of green Salé tiles for the **roof** – usually reserved for mosques and royal palaces. From up here, you can look down upon some of the courts and chambers, the bright zellij and stucco enclosing great gaping holes in the stone and plaster. The really enduring impression, though, is the wonder of how and why it ever came to be built at all.

7

THE GLAOUI

The extent and speed of **Madani** (1866–1918) and **T'hami el Glaoui**'s (1879–1956) rise to power is remarkable. In the mid-nineteenth century, their family were simply local clan leaders, controlling an important Atlas pass between Marrakesh and the south but lacking influence beyond it. Their entrance into national politics began dramatically in 1893. In that year's terrible winter, **Sultan Moulay Hassan**, on returning from a disastrous *harka* (subjugation or burning raid) of the Tafilalt, found himself at the mercy of the brothers for food, shelter and safe passage. With shrewd political judgement, they rode out to meet the sultan, feting him with every detail of protocol and, miraculously, producing enough food to feed the entire three-thousand-strong force for the duration of their stay.

The extravagance was well rewarded. By the time Moulay Hassan began his return to Marrakesh, he had given *caid*-ship of all the lands between the High Atlas and the Sahara to the Glaoui and, most important of all, was forced to abandon vast amounts of the royal armoury (including the first cannon to be seen in the Atlas) in Telouet. By 1901, the brothers had eliminated all opposition in the region, and when the **French** arrived in Morocco in 1912, the Glaoui were able to dictate the form of government for virtually all the south, putting down the attempted nationalist rebellion of El Hiba, pledging loyalty throughout World War I and having themselves appointed **pashas of Marrakesh**, with their family becoming *caids* in all the main Atlas and desert cities. The French were content to concur, arming them, as Gavin Maxwell wrote, "to rule as despots, [and] perpetuating the corruption and oppression that the Europeans had nominally come to purge". The Glaoui's controversial alliance with the Protectorate continued over the next few decades, and in 1953 T'hami again played an influential part in the dethroning of a sultan, conspiring with the French to **overthrow Mohammed V**. It was his last act of betrayal. Within a few months of Mohammed V's return to Morocco in 1955, T'hami was dead, his properties seized by the state and ultimately abandoned to the ravages of time.

ARRIVAL AND DEPARTURE

TELOUET AND THE TIZI N'TICHKA

By bus The daily bus from Marrakesh (bound for Anemiter, 12km beyond Telouet) departs from Bab Rhemat at 3pm (4hr), returning from Telouet at 7am; the daily bus from Ouarzazate leaves midday (3hr).

By grand taxi Grands taxis run from Marrakesh to Anemiter (see box opposite) via Telouet (3hr), and from Ouarzazate direct to Telouet (2hr).

By car It takes around 4hr to drive the Tizi n'Tichka from Marrakesh to Ouarzazate, with the pass itself roughly

half-way along the route. Like all High Atlas passes, the road is seasonal and can be snowbound in winter and early spring, when barriers at either end will block your way. The Kasbah Telouet is an easy but slow-going 20km drive (about 40min) from the main road, along the paved but potholed 6802; alternatively, it's 45km (around 1hr 15min) along the recently paved road from Tamdaght, just north of Aït Benhaddou (see box opposite), offering drivers a scenic short cut between two of the finest kasbahs in the south.

ACCOMMODATION

It's unlikely you'll need to stop on the way south to Ouarzazate, but there are a couple of places on the Tizi n'Tichka that are useful for drivers looking for a place to stay before hitting Marrakesh or heading to the airport – *I Rocha*, in particular, would make a very pleasant end to any Moroccan adventure.

THE TIZI N'TICHKA

★ **I Rocha** Tisselday, 145km from Marrakesh ☎0667 737002, ⓦirocha.com. Charming guesthouse up in the hills overlooking a quiet stretch of the Tizi n'Tichka, with lovely views from its terrace and a sheltered little pool. The homely rooms are on the cosy side but light-filled and thoughtfully decorated; good meals are served in the social salon – often accompanied by a roaring log fire – and there's a funky adjoining bar for afters. HB <u>920dh</u>

TELOUET

Auberge Telouet 500m north of the village, opposite

the turn-off to the Kasbah Telouet ☎0524 890717, ⓦtelouet.com. Accommdoation in an ersatz kasbah, with nicely kept rooms and views over Telouet from the panoramic terrace; the good food makes the half-board rates pretty decent value. There are a few cheaper rooms in an older inn across the road, and the owner can also arrange evening meals in a trio of village houses. HB <u>400dh</u>

Dar Aissa In the centre of the village ☎0670 222247, ⓦdaraissatelouet.onlc.eu. Sparsely decorated but good-value rooms in the home of Almodhik Aissa, with mix-and-match beds and a simple rug-strewn salon. Shower rooms with half-board are available for 400dh. <u>100dh</u>

THE OUNILA VALLEY: WALKING THE BACK ROAD TO AÏT BENHADDOU

As hard as it is to imagine today, the tranquil **Ounila Valley**, set amid high, parched hillsides and edged in by remarkably coloured scree slopes, served as the main route over the Atlas until the French constructed the Tizi n'Tichka to the west. Despite finally being paved in 2011, the road (the P1506) sees relatively little traffic and makes for a fine two-day **walk**, following the Oued Ounila as it snakes south to Aït Benhaddou.

The scattered communities here make abundant use of the narrow but fertile valley, which slowy unveils a wealth of dark red and crumbling **kasbahs** and **agadirs**, cliff dwellings, terraced orchards and olive trees – and everywhere children calling to each other from the fields, the river or the roadside. The first stop, after 12km, is **Anemiter** (2hr 30min walk from Telouet), one of the best-preserved fortified villages in Morocco and well worth a visit, even if you go no further. Leaving the village, the main track clings to the valley side, alternately climbing and descending, but with a general downhill trend as you make your way south. After 3km, you cross a sturdy bridge, beyond which the road follows the left bank of the river to the hamlet of **Assako** (2hr 30min from Anemiter), where it climbs to the left round some spectacular gorges before dropping steeply; walkers should aim to get beyond this exposed high ground before camping. The trail passes the little village of **Tourhat** (around 3hr 30min from Assako) before bringing you to **Tamdaght** (another 3hr), a scattered collection of buildings with a classic kasbah (see p.396). Just 6km from Tamdaght (1hr 15min), along a lush river valley, lies **Aït Benhaddou**.

INFORMATION

If you only wanted to walk part of the way, you could take a grand taxi from Telouet to Anemiter (the daily bus that runs between the two doesn't leave Telouet until 5pm). You'll need to take your own provisions, but mules can be hired in both Telouet and Anemiter.

ACCOMMODATION

Gîte d'étape de Tighza 10km from Anemiter ☎ 0524 885414, ⓦ telouet-anmiter.gitemaroc.net. A fine *gîte*, overlooking terraced fields in the village of Tighza and run by the Bouchahoud brothers, both mountain guides – they can arrange camping trips to turquoise Lake Tamda or walks into the mountains and on to Telouet, Tamdaght or Aït Benhaddou. The cheapest rooms are in the older section of the house. Dorm <u>70dh</u>, double <u>120dh</u>

Kasbah Tigmi N'Oufella Anguelz, 12.5km from Telouet. Just two en-suite rooms in a restored *pisé* home – one of which takes over the entire top floor – but both beautifully decorated, with carved trunks, black-and-white photos and semi-exposed Tatouine-style ceilings. Laoucine is a gracious host, who can cook a mean tajine. BB <u>450dh</u>

Aït Benhaddou and around

The first thing you hear from the guides on arrival at **AÏT BENHADDOU**, 190km from Marrakesh and just 34km from Ouarzazate, is a list of its film credits. Though this is a feature of much of the Moroccan south, the Benhaddou *ksar* has a definite edge over the competition. *Lawrence of Arabia* was filmed here, of course; Orson Welles used it as a location for *Sodom and Gomorrah*; and for *Jesus of Nazareth* the whole lower part of the village was rebuilt. In recent years, more controlled restoration has been carried out under UNESCO auspices, while film crews have been involved in some "re-modelling".

With its souvenir shops and constant stream of tour groups, Aït Benhaddou is not really the place to catch a glimpse of fading *ksar* life, but it is one of the most spectacular sights of the Atlas, piled upon a low hillock above a shallow, reed-strewn river. Its buildings are among the most elaborately decorated and best preserved in the south; they are less fortified than is usually the case along the Drâa or the Dadès, but, towered and crenellated, and with high, sheer walls of dark red *pisé*, they must have been near impregnable in this remote, hillside site.

The ksar

Entry to the *ksar* is free, although the gateways are "controlled" by people who may try to convince you otherwise – only pay the 10dh or so demanded if you want to see inside any of the kasbahs

As ever, it's impossible to determine exactly how old **the ksar** of Aït Benhaddou is, though there seem to have been buildings here since at least the eleventh century. The importance of the site, which commands the area for miles around, was its position on the trans-Saharan trade route from Marrakesh to Ouarzazate and the south. In the twentieth century, the significance of this route disappeared with the creation of the Tizi n'Tichka, which has led to severe depopulation – there are now only half a dozen families inhabiting the **kasbahs**, earning a sparse living from the valley's agriculture and rather more from the tourists who pass through.

Follow the network of lanes uphill and you'll eventually arrive at the ruins of a vast and imposing **agadir**, or fortified granary, from where there are great views over the surrounding desert.

7

Tamdaght

Spread across a platform above a bend in the river, its fringes hemmed in by canyon walls, **TAMDAGHT**, 6km further up the valley from Aït Benhaddou, has a more authentic Berber feel than its neighbour. The village, which formerly flourished with the caravan route over the Tizi n'Tichka, is dominated by the remnants of a **Glaoui kasbah**. Few of the day-trippers that pass through Aït Benhaddou make it this far, but the landscape en route is worth the journey in itself, road and river leading through some spectacular scenery, featured by Ridley Scott in *Gladiator* and Oliver Stone in *Alexander*; following the riverbank on foot (reached from below *Defat Kasbah*; 1hr 15min one-way), you've the added bonus of crossing the lush terraced gardens below the kasbah.

Beyond Tamdaght, the road leads 40km northwest to **Telouet** and the **Tizi n'Tichka** pass – a beautiful route, particularly on foot, the increasingly magnificent landscape punctuated at regular intervals by villages (see box, p.395).

Kasbah Tamdaght

Knock at the main door (facing the road) • 10dh

Quietly crumbling into the valley floor, the relatively little-visited **Kasbah Tamdaght** – its towers crowned by gigantic storks' nests – makes an interesting counterpoint to its more illustrious neighbour down the road. One or two wings are on the verge of collapse, but you can visit the only section of the building still inhabited – it was used as a set in the film *Gladiator* and still retains some of its Hollywood decor.

ARRIVAL AND INFORMATION   AÏT BENHADDOU AND AROUND

By public transport You can catch a bus or grand taxi from Ouarzazate to the turn-off to Benhaddou (20min), where you can pick up another taxi for the remaining leg to the village (10dh per place, or 120dh for the return journey plus waiting time). Leaving town at the end of the day can be tricky: local traffic tends to dry up by

4pm, allowing taxis to charge what they think they can get away with.

Guides Enthusiastic (but entirely unnecessary) guides hang around the parking area in the "new village", on the west bank of the river, hoping to escort visitors across the bridge to the *ksar*.

ACCOMMODATION AND EATING

Given how difficult it can sometimes be to find transport out of Aït Benhaddou, you may well end up deciding to **spend the night** here; if you do, get up at dawn to see the *ksar* at its best. There's no shortage of options (though note that the best places are actually outside of Aït Benhaddou itself), although **cafés** and **restaurants** are somewhat thinner on the ground, with most people opting to eat at their hotel or guesthouse. The places below are listed in the order you encounter them from the N10.

Riad Maktoub On the main road in the centre of Aït Benhaddou ☎ 0524 888694, ⓦ riadmaktoub.com. Attractive *pisé*-style building with small but cool rooms and a handful of more elaborate suites, enclosing a courtyard pool. Meals are served in the salon, around the pool or on either of the elegant terraces overlooking the kasbah. BB <u>450dh</u>

La Rose du Sable On the main road in the centre of Aït Benhaddou ☎ 0524 890022, ⓦ larosedusable.com. Arguably the best value in town, this family-run hotel has 18 comfy rooms (some sleeping up to 6), a decent restaurant, lovely terrace and a big pool, one end of which is perfect for toddlers. The cheapest rooms are in the basement, though bargain-hunters may prefer stargazing on the roof. Terrace <u>100dh</u>, double BB <u>280dh</u>

Riad Ksar Ighnda 2.5km north of Aït Benhaddou ☎ 0524 887644, ⓦ ksar.ighnda.net. Stylish hotel, oozing luxury chic and beautifully lit at night. Rooms offer the best of both worlds, where wonderful mattresses and DVD players meet smoothly traditional *tadelakt* bathrooms. Lounge about the immaculate gardens, take a dip in the sleek pool or unwind with an argan-oil treatment in the spa. The classy restaurant is top-notch, too. BB <u>1200dh</u>

★ **Auberge Ayouze** Asfalou, 3km north of Aït Benhaddou ☎ 0524 883757, ⓦ auberge-ayouze.com. This little mud-brick *auberge* is full of atmosphere and has fostered quite a loyal following thanks to its friendly French-Moroccan hosts and their likeable staff – with just five (attractive) rooms, you'll often need to book in advance. Good food, good music and a welcoming pool and bar complete the picture. <u>200dh</u>

Kasbah Ellouze On the southern edge of Tamdaght ☎ 0524 890459, ⓦ kasbahellouze.com. Stylish place run by a couple from Nîmes – modern, but following traditional lines, with a range of cavernous rooms that combine authentic Moroccan design with mod cons such as a/c, and heaters in winter. There's a petit heated swimming pool and plenty of roof areas for relaxing; beautifully cooked meals are served on a breezy rear terrace overlooking the village orchard (*ellouze* means "almond" in Arabic). Closed Ramadan and early Jan. HB <u>946dh</u>

Ouarzazate

At some stage, you're almost bound to spend a night in **OUARZAZATE**, the main access point and crossroads of the south, and it can be a useful if functional base from which to visit the *ksour* and kasbahs of Aït Benhaddou or Skoura. Although lacking the architectural charm of other settlements down here, the town nevertheless has a buzzy, almost cosmopolitan feel, which contrasts sharply with the sleepier places found elsewhere in the region.

Like most of the new Saharan towns, Ouarzazate was created as a Foreign Legion garrison and administrative centre by the French in the late 1920s. During the 1980s, it became something of a boom town, as the tourist industry embarked on a wildly optimistic building programme of luxury hotels, based on Ouarzazate's marketability as a staging point for the "Saharan Adventure", and the town was given an additional boost from the attentions of **filmmakers** (see box below).

Ouarzazate holds a mystic attraction for Moroccans, too – similar to the resonance of Timbuktu for Europeans – and recent years have seen renewed **expansion**. Vast residential complexes are springing up in response to the growing demand from young people unwilling to live with their parents, as well as an influx from rural areas. An ill-fated golf course development to the north of the city was, unsurprisingly, abandoned, but there are

LIGHTS, CAMERA, ACTION! OUARZAZATE ON THE SILVER SCREEN

Ever since David Lean shot **Lawrence of Arabia** at nearby Aït Benhaddou in 1962, film directors have been drawn to Ouarzazate, and the area has, over the years, stood in for Jerusalem, Persia, Somalia, Ancient Egypt and even Tibet. Bernardo Bertolucci came here in 1990 to film Paul Bowles's novel, **The Sheltering Sky**, while Martin Scorsese based much of **The Last Temptation of Christ** (1998) and **Kundun** (1996) in the surrounding *hammada* – as a tottering Tibetan temple at the Atlas Corporation Studios just outside of town (see p.398) can testify to. Oliver Stone shot **Alexander** here in 2004, while Ridley Scott can't seem to get enough of the place, choosing the region for **Gladiator** (1999), **Black Hawk Down** (2001), **Kingdom of Heaven** (2005) and – proving that Ouarzazate has still got what it takes – **Prometheus** (2012).

7

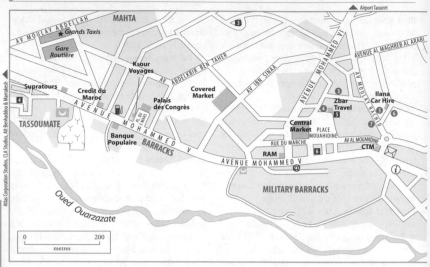

plans to build yet more five-star hotels and a slew of casinos. Whether the region will attract enough visitors in the future to sustain all this development remains to be seen.

Kasbah Taourirt

Off Avenue Mohammed V, at the eastern (Tinghir) end of town; it's a dusty, 20min walk from the centre • Daily 8am–6pm • 20dh

Although built by the Glaoui, the **Kasbah Taourirt** was never an actual residence of its chiefs, though its location, at this strategic junction of the southern trading routes, meant that it was always controlled by a close relative. In the 1930s, when the Glaoui were the undisputed masters of the south, it was perhaps the largest of all Moroccan kasbahs – an enormous family domain housing numerous sons and cousins of the dynasty, along with several hundred of their servants and labourers, builders and craftsmen, including Jewish tailors, jewellers and moneylenders.

After being taken over by the government following independence, the kasbah fell into drastic decline. Work carried out in the 1990s was only partially successful, with parts of the structure washed away by heavy rains. What you can see – the main reception courtyard and a handful of principal rooms – are lavishly decorated but not especially significant or representative of the old order of things. A small section of the original, a kind of village within the kasbah, remains occupied today, though, and makes for interesting wandering.

Musée de Cinema

Avenue Mohammed V, opposite Kasbah Taourirt • Daily 8.30am–12.30pm & 2.30–6.30pm, Fri from 3pm • 30dh

Housed in a former studio, the **Musée de Cinema** is a neat introduction to Ouarzazate's movie-making history and worth a nose around if you're unable to get out to the bigger studios on the edge of town: you can wander among dusty props and sets used in international films such as *Asterix and Obelix: Mission Cleopatra*, as well as an interesting collection of cinematic paraphernalia.

Atlas Corporation Studios

Just off Avenue Mohammed V, on the western outskirts of town • Guided visits in English every 20min from 8.30am to 5pm • 50dh • Catch the regular yellow bus from Avenue Mohammed V, or take a petit taxi from the centre of town (10dh)

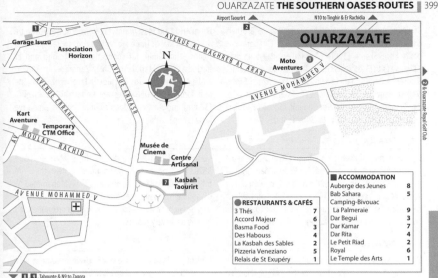

Established in 1983 for the production of *The Jewel in the Nile*, the **Atlas Corporation Studios** put Ouarzazate on the movie map. Blockbusters such as *Gladiator* were shot here, while Timothy Dalton's James Bond bounded about a Moroccan "Afghanistan" in *The Living Daylights* at Atlas. It's still a popular studio with the TV networks, and film crews are often on site, in an endless cycle of constructing sets and taking them down again.

Several of the bigger pieces have been kept for posterity, and a few minutes' wandering will take you from a Buddhist temple (Martin Scorsese's *Kundun*) to the pyramids (ABC's *Cleopatra*), via a biblical Middle Eastern street scene or two. Many are on the brink of collapse, though, and look like a strong gust could finish them off at any moment – which is strangely part of their appeal.

CLA Studios

Just off Avenue Mohammed V, on the western outskirts of town • Daily 9am–5pm • 40dh • ☎ 0544 882053, ⓦ www.cla-studios.com • A petit taxi from the centre of town costs around 10dh

The gated **CLA Studios**, just along the road from the Atlas Corporation Studios, is slicker than its predecessor, but not necessarily more enjoyable. A small museum displays various props from various films, including *Body of Lies* and *Prince of Persia*, and there are a couple of large sets some 2km from the studios and visited by car – the settlement you can see in the distance served as Ridley Scott's "Jerusalem" in *Kingdom of Heaven*.

ARRIVAL AND DEPARTURE   OUARZAZATE

By plane Aéroport Taourirt (☎ 0524 899150) is 2km north of Ouarzazate, and served by flights from Casablanca (5 weekly; 1hr 10min); petits taxis make the short run into town (30dh). RAM has an office at 1 Av Mohammed V (☎ 0524 885102, ✉ 024 886893).

By bus There's a temporary CTM office on Av Moulay Rachid, while their bus station on Av Mohammed V is being refurbished. The Supratours office is at the far western end of Av Mohammed V. Private long-distance buses operate from the *gare routière* at Mahta, 1km from the centre; it's a

15min walk, or take a petit taxi (5dh). If possible, book your ticket at least one day in advance.

Destinations Agadir (1 CTM & 14 others daily; 7hr 30min); Agdz (3 CTM daily; 1hr); Boumalne du Dadès (1 CTM, 2 Supratours & 4 others daily; 1hr 45min–2hr 15min); Casablanca (3 CTM & 13 others daily; 8hr 15min); El Kelâa M'Gouna (1 CTM & 4 others daily; 1hr 35min); Er Rachidia (1 CTM, 1 Supratours & 5 others daily; 4hr 50min–5hr 30min); Erfoud (1 Supratours & 4 others daily; 6hr 30min); Foum Zguid (2 daily; 2hr 30min); M'Hamid (1 CTM daily;

4hr 40min); Marrakesh (5 CTM, 2 Supratours & 8 others daily; 3hr 30min–5hr 15min); Merzouga (1 Supratours daily; 8hr); Skoura (1 CTM & 4 others daily; 45min); Taliouine (1 CTM & 5 others daily; 3hr); Taroudant (1 CTM & 5 others daily; 5hr); Tata (2 daily; 5hr); Tazenakht (1 CTM & 5 others daily; 1hr 30min); Tinghir (1 CTM & 11 others daily; 3hr 20min); Tiznit (daily; 9hr 30min); Zagora (2 CTM, 2 Supratours & 6 others daily; 2hr 30min–4hr).

By grand taxi Most grands taxis arrive outside the *gare routière* in Maha. There are regular runs to Boumalne du Dadès (1hr 30min; for connections to Tinghir and Er Rachidia) and Marrakesh (3hr), Zagora (2hr 30min) and points westwards (including Tazenakht, Taliouine and Taroudant). Depatures are negotiable for Skoura (30min) and Aït Benhaddou (45min, but an expensive private trip).

GETTING AROUND

By car Dozens of agencies operate in Ouarzazate, most from offices on Av Mohammed V or Pl du 3 Mars. Best of the local firms is Ilana, down the road behind *Restaurant Accord Majeur* (☎ 0524 884142, 🖥 ilana-car.com), which has helpful staff and new cars. International companies are more expensive: National, Pl du 3 Mars

(☎ 0524 888000); Europcar, Pl du 3 Mars (☎ 0524 882035); Budget, 4 Av Mohammed V, near the RAM office (☎ 0524 884202); Hertz, 33 Av Mohammed V, diagonally opposite the RAM office (☎ 0524 882084). Garage Isuzu on Av Al Maghreb al Arabi is recommended for any necessary repairs.

INFORMATION

Tourist office The region's principal tourist office, on Av Mohammed V, just across from the post office (Mon–Fri

8.30am–4.30pm; ☎ 0524 882485, 📧 atouarzazate@yahoo.fr), has a few brochures, but you're better off asking advice from your (or any other) hotel.

TOURS

Désert et Montagne Maroc Kasbah Dar Daif Talmasla, signed 3km off Route de Zagora ☎ 0524 854949, 🖥 desert-montagne.ma. Run by French-qualified mountain guides Jean-Pierre and Zineb Datcharry, and the best option for arranging tailor-made adventure trips into the High Atlas, including trekking and mountaineering, as well as multi-day trips into the Erg Chebbi.

Kart Aventure Av Moulay Rachid ☎ 0524 886374, 🖥 kart-aventure.com. Runs buggy and 4WD trips and circuits to the desert, gorges and mountains, from a few

hours to a week-long adventure (from 1300dh for a half-day excursion).

Ksour Voyages Pl du 3 Mars ☎ 0524 882840, 🖥 ksour-voyages.com. Bespoke tours of repute, which range from overnighting in the desert near Zagora or Merzouga (from 1750dh) to two-week treks in the Jebel Saghro.

Zbar Travel Pl Mouahidine ☎ 0524 885610, 🖥 zbartravel.com. Recommended agency offering tours to the dunes near M'Hamid, where they have another office (see p.410). A two-day fully inclusive 4WD trip to the desert with camel rides and sandboarding costs 875dh per person.

ACCOMMODATION

Most of the cheaper and unclassified places in Ouarzazate are grouped in the centre of town; the more upmarket chain **hotels** are mainly set back on the plateau to the north. A more picturesque alternative would be to stay out at Aït Benhaddou (see p.395).

Auberge des Jeunes Inzbiaten, Tarmigt, 3km south of the city centre ☎ 0526 511564, 📧 aubergedesjeunes .ouarzazate@gmail.com; the #1 bus stops on the main road, 50m north of the hostel. Friendly and efficient HI hostel but not the most covenient of locations, some way out of town. The rooms (doubles and 3- to 6-bed dorms) have personality, and the four-bed bunks in particular are fairly spacious, though some "doubles" are little more than a mattress on the floor. There's a small Berber tent on the terrace, where you can lay out your laundry. BB Dorm 70dh, double 150dh

Bab Sahara Pl Mouahidine ☎ 0524 884722, 📠 0524 884465. Central place on a quiet square, well located for the market and the restaurants along Av Mohammed V.

Rooms are available with showers, and those that face the square have small balconies. Breakfast and other meals are available in the sunny café. BB 220dh

⭐ **Dar Begui** Sidi H'ssain Ben Nacer ☎ 0524 887727, 🖥 villakerdabo.com. Hard to find but heavenly when you do. Run by a delightful French couple, *Dar Begui* (formerly *Villa Kerdaboo*) has six airy *pisé* rooms set around a tremendous pool, and a lovely terrace with stunning Atlas views. Non-guests can enjoy the fine Berber cuisine on offer, too (guests 135dh, non-guests 165dh). BB 660dh

Dar Kamar Kasbah Taourirt ☎ 0524 888733, 🖥 darkamar.com. Wonderfully romantic hotel hidden in the heart of the kasbah, with plush rooms, wall-to-wall candles, a deluxe hammam and a dreamy terrace. It's quite pricey, though. Tailor-made excursions can be arranged to the desert and beyond. BB 1200dh

★**Dar Rita** 39 Rue de la Mosquée, Tassoumate ☎0654 164726, ⓦdarrita.com. A great find, tucked down the back alleys of one of Ouarzazate's oldest neighbourhoods and run with pride by its charming Portuguese owner, Rita, and her indefatiguable brother. Seven brightly painted rooms are spread across two floors and decorated with lanterns, clay pots and carved wooden doors that the owners have picked up during their time in Morocco. Dinner is a social affair, and a good forum for honest local sightseeing advice. BB 660dh

Le Petit Riad Av Moulay Abdellah, Hay Al Wahda ☎0524 885950, ⓦlepetitriad.com. A charming and tranquil *maison d'hôte* run on the eastern outskirts of town, looking out towards the snowcapped Atlas mountains. Chic rooms, a small pool and fabulous meals cooked by owner Fatima Agoujil, the first officially trained female guide in the region – you can help her out in the kitchen and learn some authentic recipes as well as valuable local information. BB 590dh

Royal 24 Av Mohammed V ☎0524 882258. Clean, well maintained and decent value, fronted by its own pizzeria and with a variety of rooms, priced accordingly; it's central but can be noisy. 90dh

Le Temple des Arts 173–174 Hay Al Wahda ☎0524 888831, ⓦtempledesarts-ouarzazate.com. Lavish five-star just north of the city centre, bedecked in marble, scattered with sculptures and dedicated to the city's movie industry, with most of the grand public areas looking like they're straight off a movie set themselves. Ouarzazate's film credentials are put into good use in the themed rooms, with Lawrence of Arabia, Gladiator, Kundun and the "Royal Suite", Cleopatra reflecting their blockbuster names. BB 2100dh

CAMPING

Camping-Bivouac La Palmeraie Route de Zagora, 3km south of town ☎0524 854237, ⓦcamping-ouarzazate .com. Pitch your tent amid fruit trees in a palmery just outside of town. All the usual facilities (hot showers 10dh), plus a few simple en-suite rooms and a wonderfully camp pink dining room where produce from the garden is served and music is occasionally laid on. Camping 34dh, double 250dh

EATING AND DRINKING

Ouarzazate is one of the few places in the south where you can eat well outside your hotel, with several very good **restaurants** indeed. The best bets for cheap eats are the **café-grills** grouped around the central market at Pl Mouahidine, Av Al Mouahidine and along nearby Rue du Marché. For **breakfast**, the sunnier north side of Av Mohammed V is the area to head for, with a row of terrace cafés serving French baguettes, pastries and coffee.

3 Thés Av Moulay Rachid ☎0524 886363. Generous portions of classic Moroccan dishes – follow one of eight salads (from 20dh) with a tasty tajine (a week's worth to choose from; starting at 40dh) – as well as lighter snacks available all day. Popular with locals and expats alike. Daily 8am–10pm.

Accord Majeur Av Moulay Rachid ☎0524 882473. Mingle with the film stars and lap up *tarte tatin* (50dh), duck confit (155dh) and "mountain" rabbit (85dh) in this chic French-run restaurant with a pretty roadside terrace. A treat if you're bored of tajines and have a burgeoning wallet. Mon–Sat noon–3pm & 6.30–11pm.

★**Basma Food** Hay El Hassani. Perhaps the best deal in town, but just far enough back from Av Mohammed V to remain off the radar of most visitors. The brochette and chips is great value at 30dh, but try and drop by here on a Tuesday or a Saturday (fresh-fish days in Ouarzazate), when you can tuck into fish tajine or a fried-fish meal for just 25dh. Mon–Sat 11am–10pm.

Des Habouss Pl Mouahidine. Ouarzazate's top spot for a coffee stop, serving several kinds of delicious Moroccan bread, in addition to crusty baguettes, croissants and pains au chocolat; they also do the full gamut of sticky local patisserie (sold by weight). The lengthy menu of the adjoining grill features pasta, pizza and various steaks (from 69dh). Daily 7am–10pm.

★**La Kasbah des Sables** 195 Hay Aït Kasif ☎0524 885428, ⓦlakasbahdessables.com. Arguably the finest dining in Ouarzazate, in a rambling refurbished kasbah on the eastern fringes of the city. The half-dozen salons leading off the sprawling central courtyard are full of paintings, sculptures and antiques, making a rather grand setting for dishes that include confit of rabbit with peach nectar and fillet of sea bass with fig *en papillote* (mains from 190dh). No wonder film crews celebrate here after wrapping up. Daily 11am–2pm & 7–11pm.

Pizzeria Veneziano Av Moulay Rachid ☎0524 887676. Unexpectedly smart little pizza joint serving a wide range of European dishes and tajines, in addition to filling, tasty pizzas (from 39dh). They also offer plenty of veggie options. Takeaway available. Daily 10.30am–10pm.

Relais de St Exupéry 13 Av Moulay Abadallah, just off the main Tinghir road ☎0524 887779, ⓦrelais-ouarzazate.com. Excellent Moroccan and French cuisine cooked by Jean-Pierre, the indomitable Bordelais chef-proprietor. Memorabilia from the *Aéropostale* days of *Little Prince* author Antoine de

7

Saint-Exupéry adorns the walls, but the food is the real attraction: try the wonderful pigeon pastilla (part of a mouthwatering 268dh six-course feast), camel with "Mali" sauce or saffron ice cream. Menus start at 125dh. Daily 11.30am–2pm & 6.30am–10pm.

SHOPPING

The **central market** on Rue du Marché is great for spices and souvenir trinkets. Head to the **covered market** on Av Ibn Sinaa for fruit and veg, or to the **supermarket** at 73 Av Mohammed V (daily 8am–10pm), which also sells beer and wine. **Souk days** are Saturday, in Tabounte, and Sunday, out by the Zone Industrielle.

Association Horizon Av Ammasr ☎0524 886938, ⓦassociation-horizon.org. Self-help scheme whose less able-bodied workers craft attractive pottery, weaving and metalwork. You can also visit workshops to watch them in action. Mon–Thurs 8.30am–12.30pm & 2.30–6pm, Fri 8.30–11.30am & 3–6pm.

Centre Artisanal Opposite the Kasbah Taourirt. Undergoing expansion at the time of writing to include fifteen shops selling stone carvings, pottery and a couple of local specialities worth looking out for: geometrically patterned, silky woollen carpets and silver necklaces and earrings incorporating *tazras* (chunky orange copal beads). Daily 9am–6pm.

DIRECTORY

Banks Banks and ATMs are plentiful, with a Banque Populaire and a Crédit du Maroc, among others, along Av Mohammed V.
Golf Ouarzazate Royal Golf Club, 10km east of town (☎0524 882218). Has a 9-hole, par-36 course, with plans to develop it into an eighteen-holer; green fees start at 150dh.

Internet There are numerous cybercafés on Rue du Marché and Av Mohammed V; the one above Hertz is 24hr.
Medical services Hôpital Bougafer, Av Mohammed V (☎0524 882444), between the tourist office and Kasbah Taourirt.
Post office The post office on Av Mohammed V has poste restante facilities.

The Drâa

South of Ouarzazate, on the other side of a tremendous ridge of the Anti-Atlas, begins the **Drâa Valley** – a 125km belt of date-palm oases that eventually merges into the Sahara near the village of **M'Hamid**. It is possible to complete a circuit through and out from the Drâa, heading from the valley's main town, **Zagora**, west through Foum Zguid and Tata to the Anti-Atlas, or east to the Jebel Saghro or Rissani and Merzouga. However, most visitors content themselves with a return trip along the N9 between Ouarzazate and Zagora: a great route, taking you well south of anywhere in the Tafilalt, and flanked by an amazing series of turreted and creamy pink *ksour* and kasbahs (see box, p.392); most of the larger and older ones are grouped a little way from the road, up above the terraces of date palms.

GETTING AROUND

THE DRÂA

By car The road from Ouarzazate to Zagora is well maintained and, for the most part, broad enough for two vehicles, though it narrows beyond Tamegroute, south of Zagora. Be wary of "fake breakdowns", a scam prevalent throughout the south but refined along this road (see p.392).

BIRDING AT THE EL MANSOUR EDDAHBI BARRAGE

Some 15km of bleak, stony *hammada* from Ouarzazate, a side road leads 11km down to the **El Mansour Eddahbi Barrage**, an essential stop on any birdwatcher's itinerary. Throughout the year (especially March–May & late July to Nov), the area attracts a variety of migrants, waterfowl and waders. There have also been sightings of various desert-dwelling species such as blackbellied sandgrouse, thick-billed lark and raptors including lanner falcon. Over the last few decades, freak rains have occasionally flooded the reservoir, and the Drâa has, for the first time in recent memory, run its course to the sea beyond Tan Tan.

LIFE IN THE PALMERIES

The vast **palmeries** that carpet the Drâa, Dadès and Ziz valleys are the historical lifeblood of the Moroccan south – indeed, oases down here are traditionally measured by the number of their palms, rather than in terms of area or population – and they still play a vital role for their communities. Families continue to toil over individual plots that have been handed down through the generations, growing apricots, pomegranates, figs and almonds among the palms, and tomatoes, carrots, barley and mint in the shaded earth below.

Irrigation methods have barely changed in centuries, either. The fields are watered by a combination of communal wells and *khettara*, underground channels that can run for large distances across the *hammada*. Water is funnelled off to each plot in turn, with every family receiving the same amount of time to replenish its crop.

The greatest threat to this traditional way of life is **Bayoud disease**, a fungus that attacks the roots of palms, killing them off within a year and leaving a gap in the protective wedge of trees through which the wind (and destructive sand) blows through. First detected in the Drâa in the second half of the nineteenth century, Bayoud disease is reckoned to have infected two-thirds of Moroccan palmeries, wiping out nearly 12 million trees over the last century or so. Recent years, however, have seen the successful introduction of disease-resistant hybrids, which, together with increased rainfall, has led to much-improved health in the majority of the region's palmeries – in addition to the palmery at Agdz, there are fine examples at Skoura (see p.412), Tinghir (see p.424) and in the Ziz Valley (see p.433).

By public transport If you're taking the bus south from Ouarzazate, get yourself a seat on the left-hand side for the most spectacular views. You could hire a grand taxi for the day from Ouarzazate, stopping to explore some of the kasbahs en route; be very clear to the driver about your plans and agree on a fee before setting off.

Agdz and the road to Zagora

You descend into the Drâa Valley at **AGDZ** (pronounced "Ag-dèz"), 70km from Ouarzazate and a minor administrative centre for the region. *Agdz* means "Place of Rest", and it's certainly worth taking a break here: there are several well-preserved **kasbahs** in the original town (reached by turning north from the main square), including the seventeenth-century former home of Agdz's *caïd*, or chieftain. Just to the north of the village begins a beautiful **palmery**, and if the river here is low enough (take care to avoid the bilharzia-infested water), you can get across to view a few kasbahs on the far side, in the shadow of Jebel Kissane.

Tamnougalt

A first, magnificent sign of the architecture to come, the *ksar* at **TAMNOUGALT**, perched on a hill 6km south of Agdz, is one of the oldest in Morocco and perhaps the most dramatic and extravagant of any in the locality. The village was once the capital of the region, and its assembly of families (the *jemaa*) administered what was virtually an independent republic. Today, it's a wild cluster of buildings, each fabulously decorated with pockmarked walls and tapering towers, and populated by Mezguita Berbers.

Timiderte

Some 15km south of Tamnougalt, on the opposite side of the river, is the Glaoui kasbah of **TIMIDERTE**, now operating as a guesthouse (see p.404) but also giving travellers the chance to poke around a refurbished mud-brick palace for the price of a lunchtime tajine.

You'll have to ford the river again, this time on foot – ideally with some local assistance as the best crossing place isn't all that obvious – to reach another superb kasbah, the **Aït Hammou-Sa'd**.

Tinzouline

Beyond Timiderte, and after the junction with the R108 to Rissani and Merzouga, a striking group of *ksour*, dominated by a beautiful and imposing *caïd*'s kasbah, stands back from the road at **TINZOULINE**. The village hosts a large Monday souk, and with some guidance you can follow a *piste* 7km west of the village to see a group of three-thousand-year-old **rock carvings** at Foum Chenna.

ARRIVAL AND INFORMATION   AGDZ AND THE ROAD TO ZAGORA

By public transport Buses from Ouarzazate (1hr) and Zagora (1hr 55min–3hr) call in at the Grande Place in Agdz; the CTM office is on the northeast corner of the square. The back-country road from Rissani and N'Kob meets the N9 south of Timiderte, where grands taxis hang around in the shade.

Services There's a Banque Populaire on the western side of Agdz's Grande Place. The post office is 100m along the road that leads north off the square.

ACCOMMODATION AND EATING

If you stop in Agdz, travelling on public transport in either direction, you'll probably have to stay overnight to get a place on the Zagora/Ouarzazate bus; having your own vehicle brings Tamnougalt and Timiderte into play. As befits the *ksar*-studded Drâa, many of the best choices around here are converted historical kasbahs.

AGDZ

Café Restaurant Sables d'Or On the northern side of the Grande Place. Nice little place on the edge of the square, airy inside and with a few tables set back on the outside pavement. Simple menu of turkey kebabs (35dh) and chicken (30dh), slowly roasting on a spit by the entrance. Daily 7am–9pm.

Casbah Caïd Ali 2km along the road north of the Grande Place ☎0524 843640, ⓦcasbah-caidali.net. In a great location, nestled in the palmery north of town and in the shadow of meringue-topped Jebel Kissane, this one-hundred-year-old kasbah has been restored by descendants of the local *caïd*. Rooms are simple but traditional, and there's a sizeable spring-fed pool. You'd be hard-pushed to find a more authentic kasbah experience for less. 190dh

★ **Dar Qamar** 1.8km along the road north of the Grande Place ☎0524 843784, ⓦlocsudmaroc.com. One of the nicest hotels in the region, run by a charming French couple. Carefully restored rooms feature *tataoui* ceilings and *tadelakt* baths (some come with charming four-posters) and are clustered around a pretty garden with a small pool. Relax in the hammam, the library or in the cosy firelit salon, and tuck into delicious Moroccan/Mediterranean dishes served under stars on the terrace. BB 770dh

TAMNOUGALT

Bab el Oued 1km off the N9 ☎0524 885395, ⓦbabelouedmaroc.com. Set at the foot of Tamnougalt *ksar* and not far from the gurgling Drâa, this French-Morrocan-run place is a veritable oasis – hiding behind the walls are several stylish mud-brick "huts", dotted around a serene garden full of colour. Friendly hosts and an inviting pool complete the picture. BB 825dh

Chez Yacob 2km off the N9 ☎0524 843394, ⓦlavalleedudraa.com. Perenially popular place offering eight simple but gorgeously cool rooms in a refurbished kasbah, and a large roof terrace where you can bed down for the night. Mohammed, the manager, speaks good English and will give you the lowdown on the area. HB terrace 150dh, double 250dh

TIMIDERTE

Kasbah Timidarte 800m from the N9 ☎0668 680047, ⓦkasbahtimidarte.com. Restored by local craftsmen, *Kasbah Timidarte* is the first fruits of a community association intent on breathing new life into the *ksar*. Accommodation is simple, even sparse in parts, but the rooms look good in a minimalist sort of way, and the friendly staff can help you meet locals keen to share their experiences of life in Timiderte. BB 240dh

Zagora

ZAGORA seems unpromising at first sight: a drawn-out modern market town with a big crop of hotels and government buildings and few sights of specific interest. Even the famous Timbuktu road sign that once adorned the edge of town has been removed in an overzealous bout of city-council tidying. As the region's main staging post for trips to the fringes of the Sahara, it attracts more tourist attention than it deserves in itself, yet still manages to make a pretty agreeable rest stop, particularly if you're staying in the **Amazrou palmery** south of town.

Aside from its relative proximity to the desert, another draw are Zagora's festivals. The Drâa's big event, the **Moussem of Moulay Abdelkader Jilali**, is celebrated here during the Mouloud, and like other national festivals in the town, such as the **Fête du Trône** in July, is always entertaining.

Amazrou

Across the river to the southeast, the hamlet and palmery of **Amazrou** is a great place to spend the afternoon, wandering amid the shade of its gardens and *ksour*. The village is, inevitably, wise to the ways of tourism – children try to drag you into their houses for tea and will hassle you to adopt them as guides – but, for all that, the traditional ways of oasis life remain largely unaffected.

The local sight, which any of the kids will lead you to, is the old Jewish kasbah, **La Kasbah des Juifs**. The Jewish community here was active in the silver jewellery trade – a craft continued by Muslim Berbers after their exodus, as a visit to the workshops lining the road to Tamegroute will testify.

Jebel Zagora

Turn left at the roundabout just beyond the river in Amazrou and, after 2km, take the rough track opposite *Camping de la Montagne*; on foot, you can climb the mountain more directly on an old zigzag footpath up from near the Palais Asmâa

Watching the sunset from the slopes of **Jebel Zagora**, the bulkier of the two mountains southeast of town, is something of a tradition. Strictly speaking, Zagora is the one with a military post on top, though the name is also used for the smaller, sugarloaf hill nearby.

The track up the mountain leads to a pass between the two peaks, then curves back, rising across the hillside to a popular viewpoint; unless you've got a 4WD, you'll need to walk the last few hundred metres. Just below the track are the remnants of a colossal eleventh-century **Almoravid fort**, built as an outpost against the powerful rulers of the Tafilalt and later used to protect the Timbuktu-bound caravans passing below. The track subsequently goes on to the military fort on the summit (entry forbidden) but

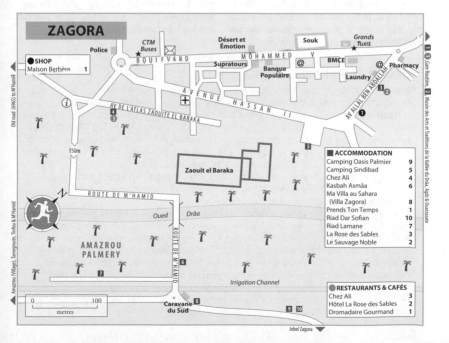

the view gains little; from the viewpoint, a footpath runs across the hillside and can be followed back down to the road.

Musée des Arts et Traditions de la Vallée du Drâa

Hidden down a covered alleyway in the Ksar Tissergate, abutting the palmery 5km north of Zagora • Daily 8.30am–7pm • 20dh • ☎ 0661 348388

The excellent **Museé des Arts et Traditions de la Vallée du Drâa** is a dusty old museum in the nicest of senses. Housed in a mud-brick kasbah, its three well-worn floors offer a charming insight into life in the Drâa, from a motley ensemble of agricultural implements to collections of colourful marriage costumes and the forty of so medicinal herbs used by a *fakir*, or Islamic holy man. The proud guardian is on hand to answer questions (in French), though all the displays are (refreshingly) labelled in English.

ARRIVAL AND DEPARTURE ZAGORA

By bus CTM buses depart from the company's office on Bd Mohammed V; Supratours is further north along Mohammed V, near the Banque Populaire. Private buses leave from the *gare routière* on the northern outskirts of town.

Destinations Agadir (1 CTM & 2 others daily; 11hr); Agdz (3 CTM & 3 others daily; 1hr 55min–3hr); Casablanca (2 CTM & 6 others daily; 12hr); Foum Zguid (2 daily; 3–4hr); M'Hamid (1 CTM & others hourly; 1hr 40min–2hr); Marrakesh (2 CTM & 3 others daily; 7hr 30min–9hr 30min); Ouarzazate (2 CTM, 2 Supratours & 6 others daily; 2hr 30min–4hr); Taliouine (1 CTM & 1 other daily; 5hr 10min–6hr); Tamegroute (1 CTM daily & others hourly; 25min); Taradount (2 CTM & 2 others daily; 7hr 40min); Tazenakht (2 CTM & 2 others daily; 3–4hr).

By grand taxi Grands taxis run regularly to Tamegroute (20min), M'Hamid (1hr 30min) and Ouarzazate (3hr), from the rank on Bd Mohammed V.

By truck Lorries make the daily haul to Rissani (10hr) in the other direction, along the rough road to Foum Zguid (5hr), with more leaving on Mondays (souk day in Foum Zguid, and also a good day for onward travel).

INFORMATION

Tourist information Zagora's Provincial Tourist Office is in a rather grand-looking building on the roudabout at the far western end of Av Atlas Zaouit el Baraka (Mon–Fri 9am–4.30pm; ☎0524 848686). The town and regional map they provide is pretty simplistic, but the staff themselves are a friendly source of information.

Services BMCE and Banque Populaire on Bd Mohammed V have ATMs and will advance cash against Visa cards; the post office is near the CTM on the same road. Of the many internet cafés, Cyber Café Al Ahbass, on Av Allal Ben Abdallah, is perhaps the most reliable.

DESERT TRIPS FROM ZAGORA

Nearly every tourist in town is here for the Sahara, and yet Zagora is still some way from the desert proper, so make sure you know exactly where your trip is headed. The closest dunes are at **Nakhla**, northeast of town, and **Tinfou**, about 25km south along the N9 (see p.409), which are easy to get to but not particularly impressive. Closer to M'Hamid lie the **Erg Lihoudi** (see p.409) and the **Erg Ezahar**, though the latter – also known as the Screaming Dunes due to the incredible sound they make (the noise is actually caused by vibrating sand grains) – are usually only offered on trips out of M'Hamid (see p.410). Finally, around 60km southwest of M'Hamid (and a good 3hr from Zagora), is the unforgettable **Erg Chigaga** (see p.409), the real deal, offering relative isolation and a sea of golden sand ebbing out into the distance; though getting here involves a much longer (and expensive) journey.

Virtually all the hotels and campsites in Zagora have tie-ins with camel-riding outfits, and there are numerous agencies just itching to get you onto the back of a dromedary. **Rates**, as ever, are negotiable, so it pays to shop around, but you can expect to pay in the region of 400dh for a trip to Nakhla and closer to 2000dh for the Erg Chigaga, including 4WD transfers, camel rides, guide and all meals, less if you can get to M'Hamid under your own steam and pick up the 4WD from there. Recommended **agencies** include Caravane du Sud, on the roundabout just over the Oued Drâa in Amazrou (☎0524 847569, ☾caravanedusud.com), and Désert et Émotion, a Moroccan-French setup opposite the Supratours office on Bd Mohammed V (☎0524 846206, ☾desert-emotion.com).

ACCOMMODATION

There's a wide range of hotels – in both Zagora and Amazrou, an excellent, fast-growing alternative base – and some nicely located campsites, especially for those with transport. Travellers on tight budgets should also note that many mid-scale hotels will let you bed down on roof terraces or in nomad tents; most hotels are also happy for non-residents to use their pools, bars and restaurants.

★ **Chez Ali** Av Atlas Zaouit el Baraka ☎ 0524 846258, ⓦ chezali.net. A haven of greenery on the edge of town, offering clean, secure and relaxing accommodation in a dozen comfortable rooms (most en suite), the plushest being in the middle of the back garden. The owner, Ali, is genuinely hospitable and has, over two decades, created a lovely space filled with flowers, fruit trees and peacocks; a pool was being added in late 2012. Altogether the nicest option in Zagora itself (and with a recommended restaurant to boot: see p.408), but far from a secret, so book ahead. BB 140dh

Kasbah Asmâa Near the Oued Drâa, Amazrou ☎ 0524 847599, ⓦ asmaa-zagora.com. Large kasbah-style hotel, faced with traditional *pisé* and set in a beautiful garden overlooking the palmery, with a shaded swimming pool and a good restaurant – take dinner in a *menzah*, Berber tents or on the poolside patio. The best of the thirty or so rooms are those in the new (and more expensive) block. BB 500dh

Ma Villa au Sahara (Villa Zagora) Route de Nakhla, Amazrou; 100m north of the roundabout ☎ 0524 846093, ⓦ mavillaausahara.com. A lovely little place south of the Drâa, with understated *pisé*-pastel rooms, some with balconies; the luxuriant garden is drenched in bougainvillea and cut through by lantern-lit walkways. The chunky fireplace will keep you warm in the colder months, and there's a petit pool for hotter days. BB Berber tent 225dh, double 720dh

Prends Ton Temps Signed off Bd Mohammed V 1km north of the junction with Av Allal Ben Abdellah ☎ 0524 846543, ⓦ prendstontemps.com. "Take Your Time" pretty much sums up this laidback and slightly eccentric joint: a courtyard ringed by funkily decorated little cabins (most with shared bathrooms), a couple of salons and room to pitch a tent. The irrepressible owner Belaid comes from a nomadic tribe and is an accomplished player of the Arabian lute, so expect long evenings of music and folk stories. Camping 60dh, cabin 150dh

★ **Riad Dar Sofian** Route de Nakhla, Amazrou; 700m north of the roundabout ☎ 0524 847319, ⓦ riaddarsofian.com. Stunning family home on the fringes of the palmery, built for the owner's son (pictures of Sofian dot the walls) and converted into arguably the most stylish guesthouse in Zagora. Constructed in traditional *pisé*, the interior is much more contemporary, with a sleek lounge, lightly decorated rooms with embroidered linen and rain showers, and a striking set-piece fountain that cuts through the floors. The charming manager can help arrange tours, though most guests are happy to lounge by the lovely swimming pool, edged with towering palms. Superb food, too. BB 800dh

Riad Lamane Route M'Hamid, Amazrou ☎ 0524 848388, ⓦ riadlamane.com. Swish hotel hidden behind high walls in the heart of the palmery. The rooms are beautifully appointed, with decor looking towards sub-Saharan Africa, tiled en-suite bathrooms and private balconies; deceptively grand villas frame the garden, or you can bed down in cosy Berber tents. A library, pool and well-stocked bar add to the charm. BB 1200dh

La Rose des Sables Av Allal Ben Abdellah ☎ 0524 847274, ⓔ hotel_larose@hotmail.fr. This deceptively large budget hotel has a range of clean and comfortable rooms – some with shared bathrooms, others with balconies – and a very friendly owner. The ground-floor restaurant is simple but has some of the best food in town (see p.408). 90dh

Le Sauvage Noble Near Ksar Tissergate, 7km north of Zagora ☎ 0524 838072, ⓦ sauvage-noble.org. Some way out of town, but a little gem, with traditional decor by local craftsmen (the *tadelakt* bathrooms are particularly fine), sumptuous bedrooms and a very good kitchen. A Moroccan-German collaboration, it also encompasses La Renard Bleu Touareg (ⓦ renard-bleu-touareg.org), running recommended social, ecological and tourism projects with local desert tribes. BB 570dh

CAMPING

Camping Oasis Palmier Route de Nakhla, Amazrou; 400m north of the roundabout ☎ 0666 569750, ⓔ pixameharee@hotmail.com. Set at the foot of Jebel Zagora, on the far side of the river, this simple campsite has a pleasant mix of well-shaded pitches and Berber tents, with clean toilet blocks (showers 10dh), a relaxing café and friendly management. 45dh

Camping Sindibad Av Hassan II ☎ 0673 208844. Small, friendly site, with adequate shade, a tiny swimming pool (not always in use), and clusters of middle-aged French campers playing *boules*; it's in the centre of town but far enough off Av Hassan II to retain its tranquillity. Free (hot) showers. 30dh

EATING AND DRINKING

Most people eat in their hotels, particularly if they're based in the Amazrou palmery, with many offering competitive half- or full-board deals, though the cafés clustered around the intersection of Bd Mohammed V and Av Allal Ben Abdallah are a good bet for cheaper eats.

A DATE TO REMEMBER

The **dates** of the Zagora oasis are reputedly some of the finest in the country, a claim you can put to the test at the twice-weekly souk (Wed & Sun), where stallholders sell several dozen of Morocco's 220 or so different date varieties – look out for **mejhoul**, **bouskri**, **jihel** and, particularly, the sweet **boufeggous**, which will last for up to four years if stored properly. If you're not in town for the market, never fear: you can't get too far along the Drâa's roads before being accosted by kids brandishing boxes of the sugary snacks, often encouraging you to make a purchase by leaping out in front of your car.

Chez Ali Av Atlas Zaouit el Baraka ☎0524 846258, ⓦchezali.net. For a delightful evening meal, it's hard to beat the restaurant at Ali's: dining is communal, at candle-lit tables in the lush grounds, and most of the food – *chakchouka* salad, *makfoul* tajine – comes straight from his walled vegetable garden. Menus 80dh. Daily 7–10pm.

Hôtel La Rose des Sables Av Allal Ben Abdellah ☎0524 847274, ⓔhotel_larose@hotmail.fr. Good-value Moroccan staples attract locals and tourists alike to this popular hotel restaurant. Chose from eleven tajines (from 45dh) or push the boat out for a comparatively keenly priced pastilla or *mechoui* (both 125dh); there's a filling 70dh menu, too. Daily noon–10pm.

Dromadaire Gourmand Bd Mohammed V, 2km north of the junction with Av Allal Ben Abdallah ☎0661 348394. It's quite a way along the Agdz road from the centre of Zagora, but the "Gourmet Camel" is one of the better places to eat in town, with a pleasant traditional salon and pavement tables. The menu is classic Moroccan, including a "Marriage" tajine (80dh); you can ask in advance for *mechoui* (200dh) and, of course, camel. Daily 8am–9.30pm.

SHOPPING

Maison Berbère Av Hassan II ☎0524 847233, ⓦmaisonberbere.com. The Zagora branch of the Alaoui family chain, which has a reputation for its rugs, is one of the best-quality outlets in the south, fairly hassle-free and likely to draw you in for an hour or so's mint tea-assisted browsing. Daily 8am–8pm.

South to M'Hamid and the Erg Chigaga

The Zagora oasis stretches for some 30km south of town, where the Drâa dries up for a while, to resurface in a final fertile belt before the desert. With a car, it's a fine journey, with the interesting village of **Tamegroute** a worthwhile stop on the way down to **M'Hamid**, the climax of this trip and the gateway to the towering dunes of the **Erg Chigaga**.

Tamegroute

Despite appearances, **TAMEGROUTE**, 18km from Zagora, was once the most important settlement in the Drâa Valley. It's an unusual place, a group of *ksour* and kasbahs wedged tightly together and linked by low, covered passageways. Here, uniquely, the narrow alleys extend beneath the village (locals refer to it as the "**underground kasbah**"), though you'll need a guide to venture into the darkness.

Tamegroute's standout sight is the **Zaouia Naciri**, but the village is also known for its pottery, which bears the green glaze reminiscent of ceramics from Fez. Wanting to develop Tamegroute, the founders of the Naciri Brotherhood invited merchants and craftsmen from Fez to settle in the village – two families still working in the small **potters' cooperative** (Mon–Fri 8am–6pm), on the left as you leave Tamegroute travelling towards Tinfou, claim Fez forebears.

Zaouia Naciri

Faux guides will try to show you the way, but it's easy enough to find unaided: look for the tall white minaret through the archway at the back of the main square (the library is through the other archway, on the square's northeast corner) • Daily 9am–noon & 3–6pm; tomb closed to non-Muslims • Donations expected • No photography allowed in the library

Tamegroute owes its importance to its ancient and highly prestigious **Zaouia Naciri**, which was a seat of learning from the eleventh century and, from the seventeenth century, the base of the Naciri Brotherhood. Founded by Abou Abdallah Mohammed Ben Naceur (an inveterate traveller and revered scholar), the *zaouia* exercised great influence over the Drâa tribes until recent decades. Its sheikhs (or holy leaders) were known as the "peacemakers of the desert", and it was they who settled disputes among the *ksour* and between the caravan traders converging on Zagora from the Sudan. They were missionaries, too, and as late as the 1750s sent envoys to convert the wilder, animist-minded Berber tribes of the Atlas and Rif.

As in centuries past, the *zaouia* is today a refuge for the sick and mentally ill, whom you'll see sitting around the courtyard; they come in the hope of miraculous cures and/or to be supported by the charity of the brotherhood and other benevolent visitors. The complex consists of a **marabout** (the tomb of Naceur), a **medersa** (still used by up to eighty students, preparing for university) and, in a nearby building, a small but very interesting **library** that was once the richest in Morocco, containing forty thousand volumes on history, languages, mathematics, astronomy and, above all, Islam. Most of these have now been stolen or dispersed to Koranic schools round the country, but Tamegroute preserves a number of very early editions of the Koran printed on gazelle hide – the English-speaking curator can point out one dating from 1063 – and some rare ancient books, including a thirteenth-century algebra primer featuring Western Arabic numerals, which, although subsequently dropped in the Arab world, formed the basis of the West's numbers, through the influence of the universities of Moorish Spain.

Tinfou

You'll get your first glimpse of the Sahara at **TINFOU**, 7km on from Tamegroute – though, in reality, it is little more than that. Abruptly rising from the blackened *hammada*, the dunes ("dune" would be a more accurate description) are a national monument; it is thought that they cover the ruins of the kasbah of Tiguida, which was once used as a bank for the trans-Saharan nomad traders, and rumour has it that there is still gold hidden beneath the sand.

M'Hamid and the dunes

A small administrative centre built around a café-lined square, **M'HAMID** (also known as M'Hamid el Ghizlane) was once an important marketplace for nomadic and trans-Saharan trade, but of this role only a rather mundane Monday souk remains. Although M'Hamid is still more low-key than Zagora, you might be forgiven for thinking the village's main *raison d'être* these days is getting tourists onto camels – there are any number of operators, official and unofficial, who offer **camel trips** into the desert proper.

Erg Lehoudi

The most easily accessible of the dunes around M'Hamid are those at **Erg Lehoudi** ("Dunes of the Jews"), 8km north of town, which can be reached, with guidance, in a normal car via a *piste* just outside the village. They see more than their share of day-trippers (and their rubbish) and hustlers, and despite reaching a height of over a hundred metres, somehow feel rather mundane.

Erg Chigaga

The most dramatic dunes in the entire Zagora region lie some 60km southwest of M'Hamid, where the 300m-high crescents of the **Erg Chigaga** ripple away into the horizon. The expense and time involved in getting here – a return trip by camel takes around five days; by costly 4WD, you can get there in less than two hours – is well worth it, and with quieter dunes and more spaced-out camps, the desert experience is much more akin to how you might imagine it.

ARRIVAL AND DEPARTURE

By bus The timing of the daily CTM bus from Zagora to Tamegroute and M'Hamid is inconvenient (it leaves Zagora at 7pm, arriving in Tamegroute 15min later and in M'Hamid after a further 1hr 25min), though local minibuses leave every hour or so. The daily CTM service to Casablanca (13hr 30min) leaves M'Hamid's main square at 6am, stopping en route at Zagora (1hr 20min), Agdz (3hr 30min), Ouarzazate (4hr 45min) and Marrakesh (9hr 45min); private services run twice daily on the same route.

By grand taxi Taxis leave throughout the day from Zagora to Tamegroute (20min) and M'Hamid (1hr 30min),

SOUTH TO M'HAMID AND THE ERG CHIGAGA

depending on demand; alternatively, chartering one for an early morning trip to Tamegroute and the sand dunes near Tinfou costs around 250dh.

By car The road is surfaced over the full 94km to M'Hamid. Beyond Tamegroute, though, it narrows to a single (and at times, potholed) lane, where the *hammada* has eaten into the edges; it's slow going, as you'll have to pull onto the gravel shoulder every time you meet an oncoming vehicle. Note that the old road south of Zagora to Anagam, on the south bank of the Drâa (the 6965, still marked on some maps), is now out of use.

TOURS

A lot of travellers organize their desert trips from Zagora, but there's no shortage of opportunities in M'Hamid to arrange a (usually cheaper) camel safari – including at most of the hotels. Prices are pretty standard, at around 350dh per person per day (600dh for Erg Chigaga), which should include a guide, camel, all meals and a tent; if you want a longer trip, the day-rate quoted may rise dramatically.

Iguidi Tours Near the car park just beyond the end of the tarmac, M'Hamid ☎0672 385395, ⚲iguiditours .com. Run by a local Saharwi nomad family, offering trekking as well as overnights in the Erg Lihouda and multi-day trips into the Erg Chigaga.

Sahara Services Opposite the Hotel Kasbah Sahara, M'Hamid ☎0661 776766, ⚲saharaservices.info. Overnight camel trips to a variety of desert camps, from

mobile tents to luxury setups, plus Arabic and cooking courses. They can arrange trips around M'Hamid's Nomad Festival in mid-March.

Zbar Travel On the village square in M'Hamid ☎0668 517280, ⚲zbartravel.com. Camel and 4WD excursions, including trips to Erg Ezahar (Screaming Dunes), the nearest big dunes to M'Hamid; Zbar's trips usually include sandboarding.

ACCOMMODATION

TAMEGROUTE

Jnane-Dar Diafa Opposite the Zaouia Naciri ☎0524 840622, ⚲jnanedar.ch. Homely and run by a good-humoured Moroccan-Swiss couple, with accommodation spread between the kasbah-style main house (nine rooms, some with shared bathrooms) and the well-tended garden (Berber tents). Traditional meals are around 50dh. All in all, one of the best-value options in the region. BB tent 140dh, double 170dh

TINFOU

Kasbah Hotel SaharaSky Tinfou ☎0667 351943, ⚲hotel-sahara.com. Five hundred metres from Tinfou's large dune, this specialist hotel, run by a German astronomer, is the first private observatory in North Africa, the small astro-observatory on its roof attracting astrophotographers and astronomers from all over the world. Guests can gaze at the immense desert sky through one of eight telescopes – one with enough power to view galaxies ten billion light years away – and read up about their discoveries in the astronomy library; non-guests can enjoy dinner with guided stargazing (250dh per person; book in advance). The rooms themselves are very comfortable, with fantastic sunset views, and the traditional Berber food is good. Closed during Ramadan. HB 490dh

M'HAMID

Dar Azawad Near Oulad Driss, 4km north of M'Hamid ☎0524 848730, ⚲darazawad.com. The most upmarket digs in town: opt for one of the "Saharan" rooms or a slightly bigger and more attractively furnished "Sultan" room – both are in the shady garden and share the same careful craftsmanship, particularly in their Tataouine-style ceilings. Guests can enjoy a heated pool and a swanky hammam and spa, and tuck into dinners created with produce from the hotel's vegetable garden. Their range of desert bivouacs includes the most luxurious option in M'Hamid, a private camp with king-size beds in a tent with its own bathroom (3500dh per person). BB 700dh

★ **Dar Sidi Bounou** Bounou, 4km north of M'Hamid ☎0524 846330, ⚲darsidibounou.com. This is a real find. Run by a wonderful Canadian-British artist and her Moroccan musician partner, *Sidi Bounou* has just four comfortable rooms in the main house, as well as magical Berber tents and *nwala* huts in the garden. Guests are treated as part of the family, meaning excellent food, local gossip and impromptu music sessions most nights. HB tent or hut 600dh, double 800dh

Hamada du Drâa 500m south of M'Hamid, on the opposite side of the riverbed ☎0524 848086,

ⓦhamada-sahara.com. Pitching a tent on the orange earth at *Hamada* is by far the cheapest option in M'Hamid, though they also have box-shaped mud-brick "nomad tents", and a/c standard rooms inside the main building. The pool and restaurant are open to everyone. Camping **80dh**, nomad tent **400dh**, double **600dh**

West of the Drâa

There's little to detain you in **Foum Zguid** or **Tazenakht**, the two main towns lying west of the Drâa, though the latter can be a fruitful hunting ground for carpets. They are, however, useful stopovers on the way to the Anti-Atlas or the coast.

Foum Zguid

A rough road (recently upgraded from a *piste* but still in poor condition) heads west from Zagora to tiny **FOUM ZGUID**, where it joins up with the R111 to Tazenakht and the N12 to Tissint and Tata. The journey itself is rather monotonous, though the onward roads are quite scenic in parts, the latter charting a wide river valley through some startlingly barren backdrops. The town itself is slowly becoming a base for (much-touted) tours to **Lac Iriki**, a saltpan 65km south of Foum Zguid.

Tazenakht

North of Foum Zguid, the carpet-weaving town of **TAZENAKHT** stands at the junction of the Agadir and Ouarzazate roads, at the centre of a wonderfully remote route. If you're going to buy a rug, this is probably the best place to do so – there are numerous shops and a good cooperative, the **Espace Zoukini**, on Avenue Hassan II (ⓞ0524 841028), whose attractive weaves are made by women from nearby villages.

ARRIVAL AND INFORMATION
WEST OF THE DRÂA

FOUM ZGUID

By bus In addition to the Tazenakht service, buses run from the centre of Foum Zguid to Tata and Zagora, among others.
Destinations Tata (2 daily; 2hr 30min); Tazenakht (3 daily; 1hr 30min); Zagora (2 daily; 3–4hr).
By truck Pick-ups serve Zagora (5hr), with more on Mondays (souk day in Foum Zguid) and Wednesdays and Sundays (souk days in Zagora).

TAZENAKHT

By bus Tazenakht is quite a transport hub, with buses heading off in all directions.
Destinations Agadir (1 CTM & 3 others daily; 6hr); Foum Zguid (3 daily; 1hr 30min); Marrakesh (3 daily; 6hr 30min); Ouarzazate (1 CTM & 10 others daily; 1hr 35min); Taliouine (1 CTM & 5 others daily: 25min–1hr).
By grand taxi There are regular grands taxis to Ouarzazate (1hr) and (less so) Taliouine (1hr).
Services Tazenakht has a Banque Populaire with an ATM, and a couple of petrol stations.

THE MARATHON DES SABLES

A gruelling slog across 250km of barren *hammada* and scorching desert, the **Marathon des Sables** is generally acknowledged as the toughest foot race in the world. Runners are required to carry all their own equipment, including GPS (in 1994, Italian runner Mauro Prosperi spent nine days lost in the desert after getting caught in a sandstorm – he survived by drinking bats' blood and was eventually found in Algeria, 300km off track) and the dozen litres of water they'll consume during each of the six days it takes to complete the course.

Founded by a Frenchman, Patrick Bauer, in 1986, the race takes place in March or April, and today attracts around 900 runners each year, 250 or so from the UK, from a surprisingly broad range of demographics; in 2012, the French runner Joseph Le Louarn completed his sixth Marathon des Sables at the ripe old age of eighty. The constantly changing route has recently included places such as Foum Zguid and Merzouga. For further information, see ⓦdarbaroud.com; UK runners interested in competing should contact Running Sahara (ⓦrunningsahara.com).

ACCOMMODATION AND EATING

You're unlikely to need to **spend the night** in Tazenakht – and some people find the late evening atmosphere in town can be a little edgy – though stopping off in Foum Zguid can be useful if you're taking a trip out to Lac Iriki. For cheap **meals** in Tazenakht, the cafés opposite the bus station turn out grilled kebabs and lentil stews.

FOUM ZGUID

Auberge Iriki Hay Alhalawane ☎0528 806568, ⓦ auberge-iriki.com. Candy-striped building at the far end of Foum Zguid (on the way out to Tata), with simple but clean and bright rooms and views over Jebel Bani. A pool was being added at the time of writing. HB 400dh

The Dadès and Todra

Stretching northeast from Ouarzazate, the **Dadès Valley** is at times harsh and desolate, but there is a bleak beauty on the plain between the parallel ranges of the High Atlas and the Jebel Saghro. Along much of its length, the river is barely visible above ground, making the sudden appearance of its vast oases all the more astonishing. Littered with half-hidden mud-brick houses – the Dadès is also known as the **Route of a Thousand Kasbahs**, for obvious reasons – the palmeries lie along the N10 from Ouarzazate to Erfoud, offering an excellent and easy opportunity for a close look at a working oasis and, in **Skoura**, a startling range of imposing kasbahs.

Impressive though these are, however, it is the two gorges that cut from the valley into the High Atlas that steal the show: the **Dadès Gorge** itself, carving up a fertile strip of land behind **Boumalne du Dadès**, and, to the east, the **Todra Gorge**, a narrowing cleft in high rock walls north of **Tinghir**. Beyond both, roads run into the heart of the Atlas, a wonderful (and, from Tinghir, fairly easy) trip that emerges near Beni Mellal in the Middle Atlas.

To the south of the Dadès, the volcanic rock and limestone pinnacles of the **Jebel Saghro** offers exciting options, either on foot or on its network of rough *piste* roads in a 4WD.

Skoura oasis

The **Skoura oasis** begins quite suddenly, around 30km east of Ouarzazate, along a tributary of the Drâa, the Oued Ameridil. It is an extraordinary sight even from the road, which for the most part follows its southern edge – a very extensive, very dense palmery, with an incredibly confusing network of tracks winding across fords and through palms to scattered groups of *ksour* and kasbahs.

Kasbah Ameridil

Follow the footpath behind Kasbah Aït Ben Moro, across the (usually dry) Oued Ameridil; the kasbah can also be reached along a short but bumpy "road" (actually the riverbed) from a turning off the main road 700m west of Skoura • Daily 9am–sunset • 10dh; 50dh with guided tour • ☎0616 101604

The grandest and most extravagantly decorated kasbah in the oasis, **Kasbah Ameridil** may well look familiar: it's eminently photogenic and features in travel brochures and coffee-table books – and on the front of the current fifty-dirham note.

Ameridil was built in the seventeenth century for the *caïd* of Skoura, and various implements from the original building line one wall of the courtyard, including some ingenious little locks whose keys doubled as toothbrushes. You can poke around a variety of rooms that once served as kitchens – one still retains the ovens used to cook *tafarnoute* (bread baked over stones on the ground) and *tanourte* (bread baked on the the side of the oven) – a Koranic school and a mosque, and bedrooms used by the chief and his four wives.

Dar Aït Sous, Dar Lahsoune and Kasbah Aït Abou

Follow signs (green triangles painted on trees) to Dar Lorkham up the main *piste* at the eastern end of Skoura village, crossing the (dry) riverbed en route; you can also reach Aït Abou by turning left off the road to Toundant

THE R307: TRANS ATLAS TO DEMNATE

The spectacular **R307** is an attractive alternative to the Tizi n'Tichka, serving as an adventurous short cut through the heart of the Atlas for drivers bound for Fez. Paved but severely deteriorated in parts, it is passable in a normal car but more comfortable in a 4WD – mudslicks and rockslides are not uncommon, and in several stretches the runoff from rivers has eaten away at large chunks of the tarmac.

About 15km east of Ouarzazate and 26km west of Skoura, the road heads north from the N10 towards the mountains, making a dramatic ascent through extremely barren country to reach the **Tizi n'Fedrhate** (2191m). The road loses this height in the descent to the **Valleé de Tessaout** and the village of **Toufrine**, after which there is a long climb, with some tremendous views all round, before the road heads down to **Demnate** (see p.240), some 135km (around 3hr 30min) after leaving the N10 behind.

There are several impressive kasbahs in the palmery to the north of Skoura village. After about 4km, you'll come to a pair of kasbahs, **Dar Aït Sous** and **Dar Lahsoune**; the former, small but once very grand, is in a ruinous state, used only for animals; the latter, once a Glaoui residence, is state-owned, and private. A further 2km drive takes you to the magnificent **Kasbah Aït Abou**, the tallest in the palmery and second in Skoura only to Kasbah Ameridil. It lies on well-farmed land and is still inhabited; you can pop in for a drink (it's now a restaurant but the food isn't recommended) and soak up the views from its terrace.

Marabout Sidi M'Barek

Beyond Kasbah Aït Abou, on the edge of the palmery, you can follow a trail to the imposing **Marabout Sidi M'Barek**, one of seven in the Skoura oasis. A high wall, broken only by a door, encloses the *marabout*, which doubles as a grain store – a powerful twofold protection on both spiritual and military levels.

ARRIVAL AND INFORMATION   SKOURA OASIS

By bus Buses stop in tiny Skoura village, which lies off the main road, at the eastern end of the oasis, with services from Ouarzazate (1 CTM & 4 others daily; 45min), Boumalne du Dadès (1 CTM & 6 others daily; 1hr 15min), El Kelâa M'Gouna (hourly; 35min) and Tinghir (1 CTM & 11 others daily; 2hr 35min); *Restaurant La Kasbah*, at the junction where the main street peels off the N10, doubles as the CTM office.

Services There's a post office and a branch of the Al Barid bank on Skoura's single main street.

Guides Navigating the tiny palmery roads can be confusing, so hiring a guide (around 50dh/hr) is definitely worth considering, particularly for the kasbahs north of Skoura, which can otherwise be hard to find; most hotels provide their own guides and run their own excursions.

ACCOMMODATION AND EATING

Accommodation around Skoura runs the full gamut, from basic *auberges* to luxurious hideaways; many places rent bikes for exploring the palmery (from 80dh for a half-day). Most people dine at their hotels, though the no-frills **restaurants** ranged around the main junction in Skoura village are handy for a bite to eat if you're passing through, serving cheap omelettes, salads, tajines and brochettes.

Chez Slimani Signed off the N10, 700m west of the village; follow the orange-painted rocks along a piste for 1.5km ☎ 0661 746882. Hidden in the palmery beyond Kasbah Ameridil, this is the best budget option: a handful of basic rooms and (clean) shared washrooms surrounding a dusty courtyard, with a sunny roof terrace overlooking the palmery and a pleasant garden. You'll have livestock for neighbours, but what *Slimani* lacks in comforts it more than makes up for with atmosphere. HB **240dh**

Dar Ahlam ☎ 0524 852239, ⊛ darahlam.com. Set amid an oasis that was once the local ruler's private falconry ground, this beautiful Relais & Châteaux property – so exclusive that there aren't any signs to it – is as well appointed as you'd expect for the (extortionate) price, which includes as many Moroccan clay scrubs and Thai massages as your body can handle. BB & HB available in low season only. Rates are fully inclusive. **11500dh**

Dar Lorkam 7km up the main piste at the eastern end of Skoura village; follow the green triangles painted on trees ☎0524 852240, ⊛dar-lorkam.com. Tucked away deep in the palmery, *Dar Lorkam* has six lovely double rooms around a courtyard with a child-friendly swimming pool at its centre. The restaurant serves a fusion of French and Moroccan cuisines. Closed Jan & July. HB **800dh**

★ **Les Jardins de Skoura** Signed off the N10, 700m west of Skoura village; follow the orange arrows along a piste for 4km ☎0524 852324, ⊛lesjardinsdeskoura .com. A real oasis within the oasis. The lovely bedrooms at this beautifully renovated farmhouse show great attention to detail, the staff are friendly yet attentive, and the tranquil gardens that give the guesthouse its name are the perfect place to unwind, ending in an inviting little pool. Compulsory dinner on the first night (200dh), but the food is superb. Guided walks in the palmery, on *Les Jardins'* own

donkeys if you choose. BB **1000dh**

Kasbah Aït Ben Moro On the N10, 1.5km west of Skoura village ☎0524 852116, ⊛aitbenmoro.com. An eighteenth-century kasbah beautifully renovated by its Spanish expat owner (the family he bought it off have since set up their own low-key operation next door) and comprising a dozen or so doubles (plus several triples), furnished and decorated in traditional style. The swimming pool, set in a stone terrace at the back, affords good views over the palmery, and the food is top-notch, too. HB **600dh**

Kasbah Les Nomades 600m up the main piste at the eastern end of Skoura village ☎0661 896329, ⊛skoura-nomades.com. Rather grand for the price, this family affair has colourful a/c rooms in turrets that overlook the palmery; en-suite showers available. BB **150dh**

El Kelâa M'Gouna and around

Travelling through the Dadès in spring, you'll find the fields around **EL KELÂA M'GOUNA**, 45km east of Skoura, laced with the bloom of thousands of small pink **roses**, cultivated into hedgerows dividing the plots. The roses – *Rosa damascena*, probably brought here from Persia by the Phoenicians – are harvested by local women, who start very early in the morning before the heat dries the bloom. Trucks ferry the petals to Kelâa's two factories, where they're distilled into the rose oil that forms the basis of all the moisturisers, hand creams and other rose-related products that you'll see in the region's shops. The size of the factories reflects the task at hand: there are an estimated 4200km of rose hedges around Kelâa, with each metre yielding around a kilogram of petals, and ten tonnes of petals are needed to produce just two or three litres of rose oil.

In late May (sometimes early June), a **rose festival** is held in the village to celebrate the new year's crops – a good time to visit, with villagers coming down from the mountains for the market, music and dancing.

Cooperative Artisanale des Poignards Azlag

On the N10 on the eastern edge of town • Daily 8am–9pm

Kelâa's tradition of dagger-making is still going strong at the **Cooperative Artisanale des Poignards Azlag**, a one-stop knife shop that provides work for seventy artisans and their families. There's usually someone working away at the exposition by the entrance, hammering intricate designs into curved (synonymous with the Berber town of Azlag) and straight (Taureg) blades in pretty much the same way that Berber crafstman have for the last seven hundred years. You can pick up a small dagger for 250dh, though a huge customs-risking one will set you back 1500dh.

Vallée des Roses

North of El Kelâa M'Gouna begins one of the most scenic but least explored regions of the central High Atlas. Tourist literature likes to refer to it as the "**Vallée des Roses**", but in fact the famous roses are grown not so much in a single valley as a tangle of different ones. A spectacular 35km road runs here from El Kelâa, weaving up the Hdida Valley and traversing the Imi n'Louh plateau (where Berber nomads still pass the winter in little caves) to cross the Jebel Ta'Louit. From the pass (2084m), you can survey the full glory of the M'Goun massif to the north; turn back here unless you have a 4WD, in which case you can drop steeply via some hair-raising switchbacks to **Bou Thaghrar** (pronounced "Boot-Ag-*ra*"), a trio of villages on the valley floor that hold some impressive ruined kasbahs.

RIGHT DADÈS GORGE (P.418)>

TREKKING IN THE VALLÉE DES ROSES

Beyond Bou Thaghrar, the *pistes* degenerate or disappear altogether, making this prime **trekking territory**, which for the most part remains blissfully beyond the reach of most 4WDs. Depending on the amount of time you have, a typical route in the region could range from a day hike through the **satellite villages of Bou Thaghrar** to a ten-day trek north through the magnificent **Gorges du M'Goun**, a real adventure involving hours of wading waist-deep through meltwater. With three days to spare, the varied (and mostly dry) walk to **Ameskar**, via Alemdoun and Amejgag – the conventional approach route for mountaineers bound for M'Goun – would be an ideal sampler, passing through a series of pretty villages and some superb gorges.

PRACTICALITIES

April and May, while the roses are being harvested, are the **best months** to walk here, but the routes are practicable in all but the height of summer. **Guides** (around 300dh/day) are essential, not just to show the way but also to help relate to local Berber people, few of whom see many trekkers; contact *Kasbah Itran* (see below), whose trips around the region are highly recommended, or El Kelâa's Bureau des Guides, 500m west of town (☎ 0661 796101).

7

ARRIVAL AND INFORMATION   EL KELÂA M'GOUNA

By public transport Buses and grands taxis pull into a strip at the centre of El Kelâa, with buses running to and from Ouarzazate (1 CTM & 4 others daily; 1hr 35min), Skoura (hourly; 35min), Boumalne du Dadès (1 CTM daily & others hourly; 35min) and Tinghir (1 CTM daily & others hourly; 1hr 30min–1hr 55min) among others.

Regular minibuses run to Bou Thaghrar for the Vallée des Roses (30min).
Services Banque Populaire and Crédit Agricole, in the centre of town, both have ATMs. The small supermarket next to the Banque Populaire has a good stock (daily 8am–8pm).

ACCOMMODATION

Du Grand Atlas On the main road, opposite the grand taxi rank ☎ 0524 836838. The cheapest option, a nondescript but serviceable little place with mix-and-match furniture, a hammam out the back and a simple café-restaurant on the ground floor – the "terrace" leaves a lot to be desired, though. Its cheerful owners can put you in touch with guides for trekking in the Vallée des Roses, Jebel Saghro and up Jebel M'Goun. 120dh

Kasbah Assafar 1km off the road that runs to Bou Thaghrar, 5km north of El Kelâa ☎ 0524 836577, ⓦ kasbahassafar.com. Restored *pisé* kasbah in the village of Ait Khyar, with a terrace that makes the most of its lofty position – there are eight rooms (two en suite) but make sure you ask for one with valley views. Cooking centres round honest Berber food

(cooking classes are available). They also organize walking and mountain biking in the Vallée des Roses. BB 250dh

★ **Kasbah Itran** 3.5km north up the road to Bou Thaghrar ☎ 0524 837103, ⓦ kasbahitran.com. Run by the hospitable Taghda brothers (all seven of them), the enchanting *Kasbah Itran* is set high on an escarpment overlooking the mouth of the M'Goun river valley, with its spectacular ruined kasbah, *ksour* and irrigated gardens. The stylishly decorated rooms make the most of the views, which extend across the Dadès to the distant Jebel Saghro and snow-covered Jebel M'Goun. Breakfasts are served on a magnificent terrace, dinner indoors in a candlelit Moroccan salon. They also run excellent walking trips in the Vallée des Roses and into the M'Goun massif. BB 410dh

Boumalne du Dadès

The perfunctory town of **BOUMALNE DU DADÈS**, 50km east of El Kelâa M'Gouna, holds little of interest – it's not much more than a straggle of shops and cafés and a large market square where farmers trade their livestock on busy Sunday mornings. But there's a likeable commercial buzz about the place, and as the main gateway to the Dadès Gorge, which starts just a few kilometres to the northwest of town, and the Jebel Saghro, it can serve as a useful base. Boumalne also offers some exceptional wildlife-watching possibilities, particularly in the bird-rich **Vallée des Oiseaux**.

BOUMALNE DU DADÈS

ARRIVAL AND DEPARTURE

BOUMALNE DU DADÈS

By bus Buses from Ouarzazate (1 CTM, 2 Supratours & 4 others daily; 1hr 45min–2hr 15min), Skoura (1 CTM & 6 others daily; 1hr 15min), El Kelâa M'Gouna (1 CTM daily & others hourly; 35min) and Tinghir (1 CTM daily & others hourly; 45min) pull up outside the covered market; the CTM office operates out of *Hôtel Tamazirte*. Minibuses head off throughout the day to the Dadès Gorge and Msemrir (2hr), departing from a stop just in front of the covered market.

By grand taxi Taxis make regular runs from the rank outside the covered market to Ouarzazate (1hr 20min) and Tinghir (40min), with several daily services to Msemrir (1hr 30min).

INFORMATION

Services There's a Banque Populaire on the main street, but the post office is a little harder to find, hidden down a bumpy track at the top end of town. Petrol stations bookend Boumalne.

Guides El Houssaine Ed-Dahby (☎0610 631368, ✉berbero1986@hotmail.com) is an official guide who can take you on hikes through the Dadès Gorge, birdwatching in the Vallée des Oiseaux or on multi-day trekking trips in the nearby Jebel Saghro (all 600dh per person/day, 400dh if 2 or more people, including transport, meals, tents and, where necessary, mules); you can normally find him at the *Hôtel Tamazirte* (see p.418). Hamou Ait Lhou, at the Bureau des Guides near the western end of town (☎0667 593292, ✉hamou57@voila.fr), runs similar trips.

ACCOMMODATION

Bougafer Near the market square, just off the main road ☎0612 212278. Best of a mediocre bunch of cheapies, though still with a general sense of structural neglect. Small rooms with decent beds are set off a bare-bones salon, but it's clean enough – and breakfast (18dh) on the little terrace overlooking central Boumalne is a good start to any day. There's also a popular café on the ground floor. **100dh**

La Perle du Dadès 500m down a piste off the N10 (crossing the Oued Dadès en route), 6.5km west of

7

WILDLIFE-WATCHING NEAR BOUMALNE

There's a surprising variety of habitats within easy reach of Boumalne. The expanse of **hammada**, or desert fringe, to the south of town is an austere environment, whose dry, sunny conditions are ideal for reptiles and are frequented by Montpelier snake, Atlas agama and fringe-toed lizard. The **grassy plains** beyond this provide food for small herds of Edmi gazelle and Addax antelope and shelter for a variety of bird species such as red-rumped wheatear, lanner falcon and the elusive Houbara bustard.

The most rewarding birding trip in the region, though, is to the aptly named **Vallée des Oiseaux**, which heads off the R6907 from Boumalne to Iknioun in the Jebel Saghro. The Tagdilt track – marked by a line of green shading on the Michelin map and well known to birdwatchers – is home to Temmink's horned lark, eagle owl and several species of sandgrouse.

Boumalne; if the river's too deep, follow blue markers for 6km along a piste signed off the main road at the top of Boumalne itself ☎0524 850548, ⊛perledudades .com. A little out of town, but hugely popular with families, as it's big on room size and even bigger on things to do, including ping pong, billiards, table football and watching films on their mini cinema. There are a variety of rooms at a variety of prices (including some troglodyte cave rooms for 1050dh), all decorated with mementoes from the French owners' time in West Africa. **550dh**

Riad Soleil Bleu At the end of a piste, 500m beyond the Xaluca Dadès ☎0524 830163, ⊛hotelsoleilbleu .com. Appealing place, with sweeping views of the valley, psychedelic decor and two kinds of room: "standard" on the ground floor and more luxurious ones upstairs. There's space for camping (showers 15dh), and budget travellers are welcome to sleep on the terrace. Delicious, inventive meals also. Camping **30dh**, terrace **60dh**, double **700dh**

Xaluca Dadès Signed off the N10, near the Shell station ☎0524 830060, ⊛xaluca.com. Popular tourgroup hotel with the personal touch of a much smaller operation, thanks to nicely designed rooms and great staff. There's a gym, tennis court and a funky bar, and a varied (and tasty) buffet spread each night (210dh). Nonresidents are welcome to lounge around the beautiful pool drinking beer and enjoying the fine views. BB **990dh**

EATING AND DRINKING

Atlas Dadès Bd Mohammed V ☎0524 831904. Agreeable café covering the seasonal bases with two terraces, a small garden and a fire-heated salon for winter. Grab a coffee or an orange juice, or tuck into grilled sausages (45dh) or a vegetable tajine (60dh). Daily 7.30am–9pm.

Hôtel Tamazirte Bd Mohammed V ☎0668 886564. Friendly staff and a sunny roof terrace make this one of the better places in Boumalne to grab a bite to eat. Tajines are good value at 40dh, but they are better known for their great brochettes (45dh). Daily 7am–9.30pm.

Oussikis On the eastern side of the market square ☎0666 641421. An established spot for people-watching over lunch, with a well-kept kitchen and an 80dh menu of traditional Moroccan dishes that changes regularly. Simple but smart-looking rooms were being added upstairs at the time of writing. Daily 6am–9pm.

Dadès Gorge

The **Dadès Gorge**, with its high cliffs of limestone and weirdly shaped erosions, begins almost immediately north of Boumalne du Dadès. A mixture of modern houses and older *ksour* edge the road, with fields fronting gentle slopes at first but giving way to increasingly precipitous drop-offs as the road nears Msemrir. Most travellers get as far as Aït Oufi, 25km or so into the gorge, before turning back. It's a fine day-trip, but it would be a shame not to explore the area further – pushing on, the gorge closes to its narrowest point just 9km further along, while a couple of days' walking in and around the gorge from one of its many hotels will reward you with superb scenery, with plenty of kasbahs and *pisé* architecture to admire.

Boumalne to Aït Oudinar

About 8km along the road into the gorge, you pass the old, rust-red Glaoui kasbah of **Aït Youl**, shortly after which the road climbs over a little pass, flanked by the *Hotel-Restaurant Meguirne*, a fine place to stop for lunch (see p.420); its owner takes a proprietary interest in a hidden side-valley nearby, organizing enjoyable half-day hikes.

The most impressive rock formations in this area lie another few kilometres along the road at **Tamlalt**, just after the *Hôtel Tamlalte*, where an extraordinary cliff known as the "**Monkey's Fingers**" rises from the far side of the valley. The rock, a weathered conglomerate of pebbles thought to have lay where a huge river entered a primordial sea, is a startling sight, looming over the villagers who toil in the fields below; a gorge, in places only a few feet wide, can be followed right through the rocks (ask locally).

Beyond Tamlalt, the valley floor is less fertile and the hills gentler. The road continues through the hamlet of Aït Ali to **Aït Oudinar** (around 23km from Boumalne), where a bridge spans the river and the gorge narrows quite dramatically.

Aït Oudinar to Msemrir

After passing *Les Vieux Chateaux*, the road climbs by a coil of hairpin bends before squeezing through the tight, narrow mouth of the gorge to reach **Taghia n'Dadès**. From here, you can scramble east up the hill to a cave with stalactites, or walk north to a small but impressive gorge (the "Petit Gorge"), with views down over the Dadès Valley.

For a distance beyond Taghia, the east side of the gorge is dominated by the **Isk n'Isladene** cliffs. Emerging from their shadow, the road follows a canyon to **Tidrit** where it snakes up and crosses the face of one of the huge canyon loops before the final run to Msemrir; the rock face all along this route is run through with incredible swirling patterns. Two kilometres before Msemrir, the **Oussikis valley** can be visited by an even rougher *piste* that runs off to the left, accessing a scenic walk along the Barrage d'Oussikis (2hr return).

Msemrir

Little more than a scattering of dusty government buildings and cafés, **Msemrir**, 60km from Boumalne, has a desultory, frontier feel to it. The lively Saturday souk provides the only real incentive to stop, but you may want to use the village as a staging post in a longer journey across the mountains – north of Msemrir, *pistes* run east to join the Todra Gorge at Tamtatoucht and north across the High Atlas.

ARRIVAL AND DEPARTURE
DADÈS GORGE

By public transport Grands taxis, minibuses and Berber pick-ups leave regularly from outside the covered market in Boumalne du Dadès for Aït Ali and Msemrir (1hr 30min by grand taxi, 2hr by minibus).

By car The road up the Dadès Gorge is surfaced all the way to Msemrir and is accessible – spring floods permitting – throughout the year.

much easier (and quicker) to backtrack down the Dadès and access the Todra Gorge/Tamtatoucht via Tinghir.

On a tour El Houssaine Ed-Dahby, in Boumalne, is one of several guides who runs two-day treks along the *piste* (see p.417); he can also organize 4WDs, though at 1500dh for the 7hr trip, it's prohibitively expensive unless you can get a group together.

TO THE TODRA GORGE

By car With a 4WD, you could tackle the *piste* that runs from Msemrir to Tamtatoucht, north of the Todra Gorge (see map, p.231). The route (passable May–Sept) runs northeast off the Msemrir–Agoudal *piste* (which starts at Tilmi, 15km north of Msemrir) to the Tizi n'Uguent Zegsaoun (2639m), before dropping down through a long valley and across wobbly limestone strata to emerge just north of Tamtatoucht. In reality, though, few people drive this route: it's a long, uphill haul from the Dadès, and the seventy-odd kilometres of *piste*, often in a shocking state, can take a full day to travel. It's

ACROSS THE ATLAS

By truck Pick-up trucks run daily up the *piste* from Msemrir to Agoudal, where you can connect with trucks to Imilchil (see p.230).

By car With a 4WD, you can drive to Agoudal yourself (passable May–Sept), picking up the *piste* at Tilmi: allow 4hr to Agoudal – it's 60km or so of very rough driving, cresting the Tizi n'Ouano (2750m) along the way – and a further 2hr 30min along the paved road to Imilchil. Most people, however, cross the Atlas on the recently paved road from Tamtatoucht (see p.426).

TOURS

Guides Most of the hotels within the gorge offer guided walks, either within the gorge itself, to the Petit Gorge or to other hidden canyons (200–300dh/day); alternatively,

several guides in Boumalne run trips in and around the gorge (see p.417).

ACCOMMODATION

The first 10km of the route is speckled with *auberges* and restaurants, though the gorge's largest concentration of hotels lies 27km from Boumalne, hemmed in by slabs of cliff. In winter, temperatures in the gorge plummet at night, so check what sort of heating your hotel has if visiting at this time of year. The accommodation below is listed here in the order you encounter it from Boumalne du Dadès.

Riad des Vieilles Charrues 24km from Boumalne ☎0670 634176, ⓦriadvieillescharrues.com. Skilfully restored riad in the village of Aït Oudinar, run by the welcoming Naïm family. The spacious rooms have a homely touch, a feeling emphasized by Aziza's cooking. Relax on the suntrap of a terrace or head off into the hills on guided walks. BB **300dh**

★ **Auberge Chez Pierre** 25km from Boumalne ☎0524 830267, ⓦchezpierre.org. The eponymous Pierre might no longer be in charge, but the new owners of this hospitable *auberge* have kept the family feel. Eight tastefully decorated rooms occupy a traditional-style *pisé* building, with its own pool and well-kept gardens, but the main event here is the tremendous food: duck and lamb feature regularly on a locally sourced menu that combines the best of Moroccan and French cooking. Organized activities include walks to the Gorge of Sidi Boubker. BB **550dh**

Auberge Tissadrine 27km from Boumalne ☎0524 831745, ⓔaguondize@yahoo.fr. Light and airy hotel, whose rooms have been nicely refurbished in authentic style; some come with balconies. Take dinner in the attractive salon or out on the riverside terrace. Varied guided walks explore a nearby canyon. HB **200dh**

Source de Dadès 33km from Boumalne ☎0524 831258. A traditional building that catches the sun in winter, the friendly *Source de Dadès* comprises only four rooms, all impeccably clean; charm is derived from its striking location, just before the gorge narrows, and hospitable service. The owners organize numerous walks in the area, including gorge-top hikes and trips to nearby caves. HB **400dh**

Berbère de la Montagne 34km from Boulmane ☎0524 830228, ⓦberbere-montagne.ift.fr. One of the best-value mid-scale places in the area – with six tastefully furnished, immaculately clean rooms (some en suite) that have the feel of a Mediterranean villa about them, and carefully prepared Berber meals served on a lovely streamside terrace. The hotel also has a campsite (with electricity) and makes a good base for short walks in and around the gorge. Camping **75dh**, HB double **340dh**

Agdal Msemrir, 60km from Boumalne ☎0671 532052. This simple hotel-cum-café on Msemrir's main drag is only of interest if you're looking for somewhere to stop on a longer journey across the Atlas. It's the best choice in town, though, thanks to its gregarious owner, who oversees eight en-suite rooms set around a small Berber salon. BB **60dh**

EATING AND DRINKING

Hotel-Restaurant Meguirne 14km from Boumalne ☎0668 763804. The views make this a fine place to stop for lunch (as tour groups do); the food, such as brochette and chips (50dh), is prepared by Ali, the unfailingly cheerful owner. In summer, the breakfast terrace is the first in the valley to catch the sun. Daily 6.30am–11pm.

Hôtel Café Timzzillite 29km from Boumalne ☎0524 830533. Worth a coffee stop at least, with stupendous views from a blustery terrace down over the Dadès' much-photographed section of switchback turns – though they also do vegetable kebabs (50dh) and an unusual spagetti-based menu for just 45dh. Daily 6am–7pm.

The Jebel Saghro

The brooding mountain range looming to the south of the N9 is the **Jebel Saghro**, a starkly beautiful jumble of volcanic peaks and weirdly eroded tabletop mesas. Dramatically barren ("*jebel saghro*" means "dry mountain" in Berber), it is quite unlike the High Atlas or Anti-Atlas, and is increasingly attracting trekkers keen to explore its gorges, ruined kasbahs and occasional villages. The austere landscape is punctuated by the black tents of the semi-nomadic Aït Atta tribe – fiercely independent through the centuries, and never subdued by any sultan, the Aït Atta were the last bulwark of resistance against the French, making their final stand on the slopes of Jebel Bou Gafer (see box, p.422).

The traverse

The classic Saghro trek cuts through the heart of the range, from **Tagdilt to N'Kob**, on the other side of the mountains (3 days). Following the *piste* south out of Tagdilt, you can pick up a path that wends past the **Isk n'Alla** (2569m) and then up towards

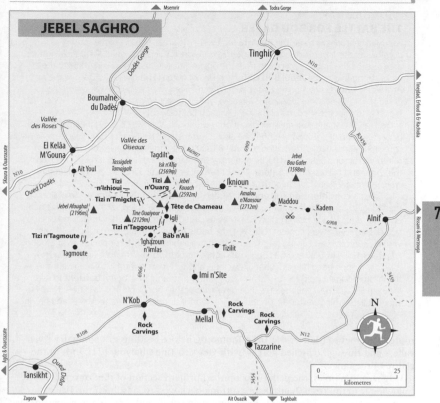

the **Tizi n'Ouarg**, an area of high meadows and a good spot to camp. A side trip up **Jebel Kouaouch** (2592m) is rewarded with fine views back towards snowcapped M'Goun and south towards N'Kob; or you can push on, past some extraordinary rock formations: the spires of **Tassigdelt Tamajgalt** and the **Tête de Chameau**, near Igli, a striking conglomerate that, in the right light, doesn't look too unlike a camel's head. From Igli, you can then either follow a path south over the **Tizi n'Taggourt** or divert east to take in **Bab n'Ali**, the Saghro's most notable feature and a spectacular sight at dawn or dusk. The routes converge near the village of **Ighazoun n'Imlas**, from where a *piste* heads south down a remarkably green valley before climbing out to wander a barren waste to N'Kob (see p.443).

An alternative **route from Iknioun** (5 days) heads east, under the shadow of **Amalou n'Mansour** – at 2712m, the highest summit in the Saghro – to Maddou, from where you can make a side-trip north to **Jebel Bou Gafer** (see box, p.422); you'll probably need to camp here overnight to make the most of a visit to the battlefield. Backtracking to Maddou, the route continues via **Tizilit** and **Imi n'Site** to emerge near some rock carvings at the R108, 8km east of N'Kob.

The circuit

The much longer anticlockwise **loop from El Kelâa M'Gouna** and back (10 days) follows part of the traverse but also takes in the more diverse scenery of the Saghro's northern and southern foothills. From El Kelâa (you could also hike a similar circuit to and from Boumalne), the path crosses a plain to the villages of **Aït Youl** (also reachable in a taxi) and, much further on, **Afoughal**, at the foot of **Jebel Afoughal** (2196m). The

7

THE BATTLE FOR BOU GAFER

For three centuries or more, the **Aït Atta** tribe were the great warriors of the south, dominating the Jebel Saghro and its eastern extension, the Jebel Ougnat. As guerrilla fighters, they resisted the French occupation from the outset, finally retreating in early 1933 to the rocky stronghold of the **Jebel Bou Gafer**, a chaos of gorges and pinnacles. Despite the Aït Atta being vastly outnumbered by superior French forces, what followed was, according to David Hart in *The Aït 'Atta of Southern Morocco*, "the hardest single battle which the French had ever had to fight in the course of their 'pacification' of Morocco".

The French first attacked the stronghold on February 21, after which they launched almost daily attacks on the ground and from the air – the French are believed to have used four air squadrons at the battle, in addition to some 83,000 troops (the Aït Atta, in comparison, numbered around a thousand fighting men). Many died on both sides, but the Aït Atta, under the command of **Hassou Ba Salem**, did not surrender for over a month, by which time they were reduced to half their strength and had run short of ammunition.

Ba Salem's **conditions on surrender** included a promise that the Aït Atta could maintain their tribal structures and customs, and that they would not be "ruled" by the infamous T'hami el Glaoui, the pasha of Marrakesh, whom they regarded as a traitor to their homeland (see box, p.327). The French were content to accept, the battle meaning that their "pacification" was virtually complete, and giving them access to the valuable silver and copper mines at Moudou.

Ba Salem died in 1960 and was buried at Taghia, his birthplace, 5km from Tinghir (see p.424). Ali, his son, succeeded him as leader of the tribe, and took part in the 1975 Green March into the Western Sahara; he died in 1992 and is also buried at Taghia. As for the **battlefield** itself, local guides will show you the sites, including ruins of the stronghold. It is still littered with spent bullets, which are covered in spring by colourful clumps of thyme, rockroses and broom.

---

route continues south over the **Tizi n'Tagmoute** before heading east along dry river valleys and through chiselled gorges, with views to **Tine Ouaiyour** (2129m), in the centre of the range.

At Ighazoun n'Imlas, the path picks up the northern section of the "traverse" route, following it to the **Tizi n'Ouarg** before turning back west to crest both the **Tizi n'Tmighcht** and the **Tizi n'Irhioui**, steep mountain passes with breathtaking views as far as the High Atlas. From here on, it's a downwards hike back to Aït Youl and, ultimately, El Kelâa again.

INFORMATION   JEBEL SAGHRO

When **planning a trek** in the Saghro, bear in mind the harshness of the terrain and the considerable distances involved. With the exception of the Vallée des Oiseaux, off the Boumalne–Iknioun road, which is a feasible destination for day-trips (see box, p.418), this is not an area for short treks, nor does it have much infrastructure; accommodation is normally a mix of camping, *gîtes* and *chez l'habitant* (village homes).

When to visit The Jebel Saghro is a popular trekking destination between October and April, when the High Atlas is too cold and snow-covered for walking; in the summer, it's too hot and exposed and water, always scarce, is impossible to find.

Guides Hiring a guide is highly recommended both for trekking and for exploring the area in your own (4WD) vehicle – road signs are rare and navigating your way around isn't easy, while flash floods often lead to diversions or worse. There are *bureau des guides* and/or independent guides in Boumalne du Dadès (see p.417), Tinghir (see p.424), El Kelâa M'Gouna (see box, p.416) and, to the south, N'Kob (see p.443); you can also sometimes hire guides and muleteers in the villages at the northern base of the mountains.

Tours Treks can be arranged through AMIS (see p.46) or adventure tour companies abroad, including Explore (w explore.co.uk), Walks Worldwide (w walksworldwide .com) and Sherpa Expeditions (w sherpa-walking -holidays.co.uk); prices start at around £495 (6150dh) for a two-week trip that includes nine days trekking in Jebel Saghro.

Transport There's a daily pick-up truck from Boumalne du Dadès to Tagdilt, off the R6907, and taxis run most days from Tinghir and Boumalne to Iknioun, further along the road. The N'Kob souk is on a Sunday, so you may also be able to pick up a ride south on the Saturday. You can also access Iknioun on a *piste* from Tinghir, a very beautiful road but one that's only passable in a 4WD.

Tinghir

Despite serving largely as a base for the trip up into the Todra Gorge, **TINGHIR** is a more interesting place than other administrative centres along the N10: overlooked by a ruinous but ornamental Glaoui kasbah and flanked by extensive **palmeries** that feel a world apart, with their groups of *ksour* built at intervals into the rocky hills above. Tinghir's own *ksar* has been extensively restored in parts (one of its mosques has even been rebuilt in pink concrete), but the Aït el Haj Ali district, in the south, retains an appealing air of authenticity. The Monday **souk**, just west of town, is one of the largest in the south and a good place to pick up pottery from the palmery village of El Hart.

The lushness of Tinghir's palmeries seems all the more special after the journey from Boumalne, a bleak 53km drive across desolate plains with only the hazy **Jebel Saghro**

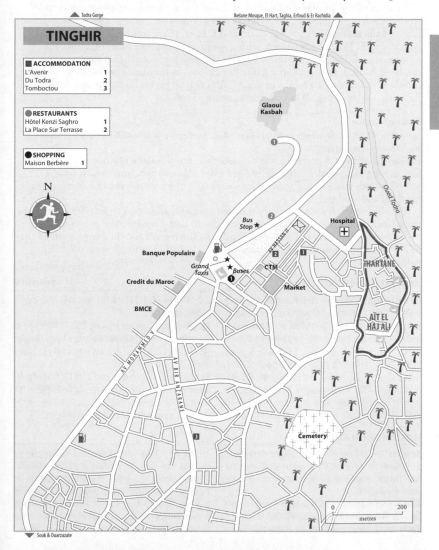

7

TINGHIR

■ ACCOMMODATION
L'Avenir	1
Du Todra	2
Tomboctou	3

● RESTAURANTS
| Hôtel Kenzi Saghro | 1 |
| La Place Sur Terrasse | 2 |

● SHOPPING
| Maison Berbère | 1 |

Todra Gorge

Ikelane Mosque, El Hart, Taghia, Erfoud & Er Rachidia

Glaoui Kasbah

Oued Todra

Bus Stop

Hospital

THARTANE

Banque Populaire

Grand Taxis

Buses

CTM

Credit du Maroc

Market

AÏT EL HAJ ALI

BMCE

AV MOHAMMED V

AV BIR ANZARANE

Cemetery

0   200
metres

Souk & Ouarzazate

for company, the barren outlines of its mountains looming to the south like something from the steppes of Central Asia.

Tinghir and Todra palmeries

You can access the Tinghir palmery through the town's *ksar*, or by heading east (right) off the N10 just beyond the Todra Gorge turning; for the Todra palmery, catch a taxi to the entrance to the Todra Gorge and head south into the palmery on foot from there

Lining both sides of the Oued Todra to the north of town, the **Tinghir and Todra palmeries** are major attractions in themselves, dotted with picturesque villages whose *ksour* and kasbahs are incised with extraordinarily complex patterns. Walk or ride on the west side of the valley for the best panoramas of the Todra palmery, a blanket of palms shielding olives, figs, almonds and alfalfa; the *Hôtel Kenzi Saghro* (see opposite) enjoys fine views of the Tinghir palmery from its terrace bar.

The small village of **Afanour** makes a pleasant destination for an afternoon ramble around the Tinghir palmery, with its restored *pisé* mosque, though a longer walk could take in **Souk el Khemis** (Thursday souk) and **El Hart**, 15km southeast of Tinghir and comprising El Hart n'Igourramen, with a *marabout* that is the focus of a June/July moussem, and the larger El Hart n'Iaamine, famous for its earthen pottery; the potters can be difficult to find without a guide (see below), as they work out of their (unmarked) homes. The tombs of the Aït Atta chief, Hassou Ba Salam, and his son, Ali Ba Salam (see box, p.422) can be seen at nearby **Taghia**.

Ikelane Mosque

Signed off the N10, just north of the turning to the Todra Gorge; follow the white arrows for 300m • Daily 8am–noon & 3pm–sunset • 20dh • If no one's around, call ☏ 0659 907518

Despite its ancient appearance, the nineteenth-century **Ikelane Mosque** was a fully functioning focus of the community until a decade or so ago, until which time it served as both mosque and *medersa* for the people of Afanour – the *ksar* itself was only finally abandoned in 2002.

The whole complex was lovingly restored in 2007, and you can wander around the mud-brick ablutions room (complete with well) and peek into the prayer hall, with its characterfully cockeyed supporting pillars. The reward for climbing up on to the roof – once the Koranic school's "classroom" – is far-reaching views across the palmery.

ARRIVAL AND DEPARTURE   TINGHIR

By bus Local buses leave from the Pl Principale, near which you'll find the CTM office. Long-distance buses passing through Tinghir stop either here or on Av Mohammed V, opposite the municipal gardens that mark the centre of town. Destinations Boumalne du Dadès (1 CTM daily & others hourly; 45min); Er Rachidia (1 CTM & 8 others daily; 2–3hr); Erfoud (2 daily; 3hr 30min); Fez (3 daily; 8hr 30min); Marrakesh (1 CTM, 1 Supratours & 8 others daily; 7hr 30min); Meknes (4 daily; 9hr); Merzouga (1 Supratours daily; 5hr); Ouarzazate (5 daily; 2hr 30min); Rissani (2 daily; 4hr); Tinejdad (1 CTM & 10 others daily; 1hr); Zagora (1 daily; 6hr 15min).

By grand taxi Taxis run regularly from Pl Principale to Boumalne du Dadès (40min), Ouarzazate (2hr), Tinejdad (45min) and Er Rachidia (2hr), and occasionally to Erfoud (2hr) and Rissani (2hr 15min).

By truck Berber lorries also leave from the Pl Principale, bound for villages in the Todra Gorge and beyond; after the Monday souk, numerous lorries set out for villages in the High Atlas, passing Imilchil on their way to Aghbala.

INFORMATION AND TOURS

Services There's a Banque Populaire opposite Pl Principale, and a Crédit du Maroc and BMCE further south along the N10. The post office is on the northeastern corner of the municipal gardens.

Bike rental You can rent bikes to explore the palmeries from *Hôtel L'Avenir* and *Kasbah Lamrani* (250dh/day).

Tours *Hôtel Tomboctou* runs a variety of local trips, from a 4hr trek in the Todra Gorge (220dh) to a full-day palmery excursion that visits the potteries at El Hart n'Iaamine (250dh); contact the highly recommended Suprateam Travel agency, which operates out of the hotel, for multi-day packages in the High Atlas or the desert (daily 8am–noon & 2–6pm; ☏ 0524 888901, ⊚ supratravel.com). You can also arrange trips for the gorge (or beyond) at *Camping Ourti*.

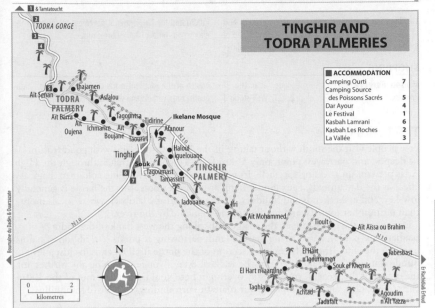

TINGHIR AND
TODRA PALMERIES

■ ACCOMMODATION	
Camping Ourti	7
Camping Source des Poissons Sacrés	5
Dar Ayour	4
Le Festival	1
Kasbah Lamrani	6
Kasbah Les Roches	2
La Vallée	3

ACCOMMODATION

L'Avenir In the pedestrian zone near the central market ☏ 0672 521389; see box, p.423. A very decent little budget hotel above a cluster of shops, with good-value rooms and a great roof terrace – its very central location means it can get noisy, though. An excellent source of information on climbing in the gorge, too. Terrace 30dh, double 90dh

Camping Ourti On the N10, near the Shell station, just over 1km west of the centre ☏ 0524 833205; map above. Enthusiastically managed by a young crowd and with a range of facilities, including hot showers, a small pool (30dh; June–Sept) and a restaurant. You can bed down in the salon or on the terrace, while a few bungalows (sleeping up to three) provide more substantial accommodation. They can also arrange 4WD transport, drivers and guides for the gorge, or other expeditions. Salon/terrace 20dh, camping 40dh, bungalow 150dh

Kasbah Lamrani On the N10, 1km west of the centre ☏ 0524 835017, ⓦ kasbahlamrani.com; map above. A large upscale hotel in ersatz kasbah style, though the

well-equipped rooms have been smartly done and there are plenty of facilities, including a big pool, huge terraces, a bar and two decent restaurants. 560dh

Du Todra Av Hassan II ☏ 0524 834249; map p.423. Open since 1935, this cheery place is lifted above the norm thanks to its penchant for eccentric design, from the retro lobby to the unusual ceiling decorations – at some point, covering wardrobe doors in padded cushion fabric must have been the height of fashion in Tinghir. There's also a pleasant terrace and bar. 95dh

★ **Tombouctou** Av Bir Anzarane ☏ 0524 835191, ⓦ hoteltomboctou.com; map p.423. A kasbah built for Sheikh Bassou in 1944, tastefully converted by Moroccophile Spaniard Roger Mimó, *Tombouctou* is one of the country's memorable small hotels. There's a range of tasteful and cosy rooms (all cool in summer and heated in winter) and friendly staff on hand to help with exploring the local area (see opposite). There's also a pool in the courtyard, a good restaurant and a small bar. BB 550dh

EATING AND DRINKING

Tinghir isn't a place for fancy dining, though you can get tasty meals at the *Hôtel Tombouctou*. There are plenty of cheap cafés and grills around the centre, where you can fill up at any time of day; stock up at the market on trekking and picnic food for trips up the gorge.

Hôtel Kenzi Saghro On the hill north of the centre ☏ 0524 834181, ⓦ bougafer-saghro.com/saghro.htm; map p.423. It's worth venturing up to the *Kenzi Saghro* to

enjoy a drink at the bar, or more accurately the bar's panoramic *terrasse*, which enjoys superb views across the Tinghir palmery. Daily 10am–10pm.

La Place Sur Terrasse On the N10, at the eastern end of the municipal gardens; map p.423. A good blend of tourists and locals, all tucking into above-average tajines (50dh) and the like, either at pavement tables or on the eponymous terrace. Daily 7am–9pm.

SHOPPING

Maison Berbère Next to the mosque, near the Pl Principale ☏0524 834359; map p.423. Well-stocked branch of the excellent crafts chain, heaving with high-quality rugs, carpets and silver. Daily 8am–8pm.

The Todra Gorge

Few people visit the south without taking in the **Todra Gorge**, and with good reason. At its deepest and narrowest point, only 15km from Tinghir, this trench through the High Atlas presents an arresting spectacle, its gigantic rock walls changing colour to magical effect as the day unfolds. Faux guides hang around the gorge, but the hassle is generally low-key, and at weekends and holidays, there's a cheerfully laidback vibe – locals more than outnumber tourists, and families come to picnic by the river.

En route to the gorge proper, the road climbs along the west flank of the **Todra palmery** (see p.424), a last, fertile shaft of land, narrowing at points to a ribbon of palms between the cliffs. The really enclosed section of the **gorge** itself extends for just a few hundred metres and should certainly be walked, even if you're not going any further, for the drama of the scenery; you can stay overnight here, too, right at the foot of the 300m cliffs (see p.428), and contemplate your majestic surroundings in relative tranquillity.

Tamtatoucht and beyond

The road up the Todra Gorge grows gradually less spectacular as you progress uphill, but with your own vehicle it's worth pressing on to **TAMTATOUCHT**, 18km beyond the gorge, for a taste of the high mountains. A sizeable sprawl with a growing number of attractive hotels and cafés, the village is situated beneath a ring of beautiful peaks, and with local guidance you can head off for rewarding day-walks in the area.

Just beyond Tamtatoucht, a rough *piste* heads west to the **Dadès Gorge**, scaling huge slabs of unstable limestone (this is 4WD-only territory) on its way (see p.419). Staying on the main route will bring you to **Aït Hani**, 15km further on and set in a high and barren landscape. From here, surfaced roads lead east to Rich (for Midelt) and north **across the High Atlas** to Imilchil and Aghbala – a superb journey, offering a real experience of Berber mountain life and some of the most exciting scenery in Morocco, in a succession of passes, mountains, rivers and gorges.

ARRIVAL AND INFORMATION   THE TODRA GORGE

By bus Minibuses run regularly from Tinghir to Tamtatoucht (45min), beyond the gorge itself, and on to Aït Hani, 35km north of Tinghir.

By petit taxi Taxis ferry back and forth between Tinghir and the group of hotels just before the narrowing of the gorge, as well as further on to Tamtatoucht.

WALKING IN THE TODRA GORGE

Most of the guides hanging around the gorge try to lead visitors on walks, but the following **route** (1hr 30min–2hr) can be hiked without assistance. Once through the cliffs that mark the narrowest section of the gorge, look for a side valley leading quite steeply left (south) from the roadside to a pronounced saddle between two peaks – you'll be able to make out the path climbing on the left flank of the hillside. An easy ascent takes you to the pass (around 45min), from where you could head for the peaks for splendid views over the gorge, or follow the path dropping downhill to your left, keeping to a line of silvery-grey rocks that fringe a dry riverbed. After around thirty minutes, the path then climbs briefly to a second pass, from where it descends to Tizgui, a well-preserved *ksar* on the edge of the Todra palmery.

FROM TOP PALMERY NEAR TINGHIR (P.424); TODRA GORGE >

7

ACROSS THE ATLAS

By car The road north from Aït Hani (see map, p.231) was paved in 2011, shortening the journey to Agoudal dramatically and opening up the route to normal tourist cars. At Agoudal (see p.231), you can join the surfaced road to Imilchil and Aghbala, which eventually see-saws down to Kasba Tadla and the N8 (the Beni Mellal–Fez road).

By grand taxi Grands taxis run from Tinghir to Imilchil (2hr 30min), where you can connect with other taxis heading further north.

By truck Not so long ago, travelling on a succession of Berber lorries was the only real way of negotiating this stretch of the Atlas, and without your own transport they can still provide a useful (and memorable) service. The lorries are timed to coincide with local village souks: promising days to start out are Wednesday (for Aït Hani's Thursday souk) and Friday (for Imilchil's Saturday souk), but there's usually at least one lorry heading north each day. Setting out from Todra, the managers of the hotels at the mouth of the gorge usually have an idea of when the next one will pass through – and will help arrange your first ride.

INFORMATION

Money There are no banks between Tinghir and Kasba Tadla, so you'll need to carry enough money for the journey. Don't underestimate the expense of buying food in the mountains (up to twice the normal rate), nor the prices charged for rides in Berber lorries.

Police There are police stations at Aït Hani and Imilchil if you need serious help or advice on the state of the area's *pistes*.

ACCOMMODATION

Given the traffic and crowds of tourists and hustlers who mill around them through the day, the cluster of small hotels at the foot of the cliffs are far from peaceful, and in winter can be very cold as the sun only reaches them at midday. However, things calm down considerably in the evening after the day-trippers have left, and their rooftops make ideal vantage points from which to admire the escarpments. The accommodation below is listed in the order you encounter it from Tinghir.

EN ROUTE TO THE GORGE

Camping Source des Poissons Sacrés 9km from Tinghir ☏0668 255309; map p.425. Flanking a particularly luxuriant stretch of the palmery, this is the best choice of a string of well-established campsites, with simple rooms and the option of rooftop sleeping or shady camping. It also boasts a spring flowing into a pool where a shoal of sacred fish swim, a dip in which is said to cure infertility. Terrace 25dh, camping 60dh, double 140dh

★ **Dar Ayour** 15km from Tinghir ☏0524 895271, ⓦdarayour.com; map p.425. A little gem, this brightly furnished guesthouse in the village of Tizgui has a range of individually designed rooms (it's worth looking at a couple first, as they are very different), some with lovely little balconies. The cushion-strewn lounge is a great place to relax, as is the garden that runs down to the Oued Todra. Breakfast and dinner (Moroccan/French) are served on a gorgeous terrace. HB 500dh

La Vallée 15.5km from Tinghir ☏0524 895126; map p.425. Pick of the budget places just before the entrance to the gorge, offering simple en-suite rooms (and a few cheaper ones with shared facilities) that are generally cleaner than the competition. Popular with climbers, thanks to its logbook with useful route descriptions (climbing gear also available to rent). 120dh

IN THE GORGE

Kasbah Les Roches 16.5km from Tinghir ☏0661 743617, ⓦles-roches.mezgarne.com; map p.425. One of two mid-range hotels inside the most dramatic section of the gorge, set on the opposite bank of the

---

CLIMBING IN THE TODRA GORGE

Climbers have been scaling the Todra Gorge's craggy cliffs since 1977, when a group of Frenchmen opened the West Pillar way, and there are now over three hundred **routes** spread across thirty different sectors. The routes are fairly technical, with most ranging from French Grade 5 to 8 and varying in length from 25m to 300m, so tend to suit experienced climbers more – though the fairly newly developed Kilimanjaro section offers several routes for beginners.

A number of hotels and guides in town rent equipment and run climbing **trips**: try *Hôtel L'Avenir* (see p.425) or look out for Hassan Mouhajir, a vastly experienced climber who can normally be contacted through the *Hôtel La Vallée* near the start of the gorge (see above). If you're climbing on your own, it's worth consulting the **logbooks** at various hotels in the gorge first, which will alert you to any problems on the rock – over the past few years, kids have been known to tamper with several access bolts, and even fixtures for top ropes.

Oued Todra and beneath vast overhanging cliffs, *Les Roches* is a smart family-run affair, with comfy beds topped by thick Berber blankets (essential in winter). You can set off into the gorge on horseback (400dh/half-day) or by bike (100dh/day). HB **500dh**

⭐ **Le Festival** 5km from the mouth of the gorge, 22km from Tinghir ☎0661 267251, ⓦauberge-lefestival.com; map p.425. This intimate solar-powered hotel, the only accommodation between the mouth of the gorge and Tamtatoucht, has a truly rustic feel and provides an excellent base for climbers and trekkers. Apart from the simple, comfortable rooms on the first floor of the hotel, there are "tower" rooms in a castle-like building and five inventive en-suite "cave rooms" built into the rock below. A refreshingly different and atmospheric place to spend the night. Double **230dh**, tower room BB **500dh**, cave room HB **700dh**

TAMTATOUCHT

Les Amis At the entrance to the village ☎0670 234374, ⓦamistamtt.wg.vu. The nicest of the group of hotels that has sprung up at the entrance to town, with an ever-burgeoning number of rooms, hearty food and impromptu music sessions. Ali, one of the seven charming brothers who run the place, has over twenty years' experience climbing in these parts and runs excellent climbs and treks. He has full climbing kit to rent – but note that he does not recommend this area for beginners. Camping **20dh**, HB double **200dh**

Auberge Baddou Near the entrance to the village ☎0672 521389, ⓦaubergebaddou.com. Just up the road from *Les Amis*, this friendly, brightly painted place has low-slung beds, hot showers and a sunny terrace with kidney-shaped pool. The owner is one of the most experienced guides in the region. Camping **35dh**, HB double **250dh**

East to the Tafilalt

After the comparatively populous area around the gorges, the run east to Er Rachidia, Erfoud and the great palmeries of the Tafilalt is a desolate one. The **N10 to Er Rachidia** (for Midelt and the road to Fez) is a fast but dull highway through barren country that's broken only by the oasis of **Goulmima**. The more attractive **R702 to Erfoud** (for Merzouga) is, in parts, eerily impressive, with sections of the road occasionally submerged in sand.

The R702 branches off the N10 3km east of **Tinejdad**, from where it follows a course of lush oases – populated by the Aït Atta tribe, traditional warriors of the south who once controlled land and exacted tribute as far afield as the Drâa (see box, p.422). After leaving the oasis at **Mellab**, which has a fine *ksar*, it is more or less continuous desert *hammada* until the beginning of the vast palmery of **El Jorf**, the Tafilalt's largest *ksar*, on the approach to Erfoud. Over much of the journey from Mellab to Erfoud, the land is pockmarked by parallel lines of strange, volcanic-shaped humps – actually man-made entries to the old underground **irrigation channels** or *khettara* (see box, p.403).

Tinejdad

TINEJDAD itself is one long street, but the town is distinguished by having two of the best **museums** in the region just a few kilometres to the west along the N10. There are further impressive kasbahs and *ksour* in the Ferkla oasis, which spreads to the north and west of Tinejdad: ask directions to **Ksar Asrir**, the one-time capital of the oasis, in the palmery north of the main road; or head to **El Khorbat**, an immaculate nineteenth-century *ksar* further towards Tinghir that is also home to the Musée des Oasis.

Musée Sources Lalla Mimouna

9km west of Tinejdad • Daily 8am–6pm • 50dh • ☎ 0535 786798, ⓦ sourcesmimouna.com

The extraordinary **Musée Sources Lalla Mimouna** achieves that rare combination of inspirational setting and absorbing content. Its owner, Zaid, has spent the last thirty years

---

> #### BERBER CEMETERIES
> The long fields of pointed stones that you'll see thrust into the ground, both here and elsewhere along the oasis routes, are **Berber cemeteries**. Otherwise unidentified, they are usually walled off from the desert at the edge of the *ksour*: a wholly practical measure to prevent jackals from unearthing bodies – and in so doing, frustrating the dead's entry to paradise.

collecting artefacts including eighteenth- and nineteenth-century agricultural tools, pottery from Fez and Tamegroute, Berber jewellery and textiles, all displayed here in a beautiful complex of *pisé* buildings set around exposed underground springs. Don't miss the wooden Koran tablets in the last room, or Zaid's demonstration of a *tanassa*, an ancient Berber water clock that ensured every plot within the palmery received its equal share.

Musée des Oasis

800m off the N10, 2km west of Tinejdad • Daily 9am–9pm; pick up the key from the restaurant at the *Gîte El Khorbat* (see below) • Guided tour 20dh • ⊛ museedesoasis.com

Spread over three beautifully restored buildings in the heart of El Khorbat, the informative **Musée des Oasis** houses a collection of artefacts and photos showcasing rural life, from local festivals to the economy of the Salt Road. It's all been thoughtfully put together by Spanish writer and architectural conservationist Roger Mimó, though the displays on the tribal system and the *pisé* construction underlying the region's many kasbahs and *ksour* are particularly pertinent for travelling in the south.

Goulmima

Located roughly halfway along the N10 from Tinejdad to Er Rachidia, **GOULMIMA** is a long, straggling palmery, made up of some twenty or so scattered *ksour*. Its modern part, beside the highway, is signalled by the usual "triumphal" entrance and exit arches of the south but has little more within. If you're interested in exploring the older half of town, ask directions along the complex network of tracks to the *ksar* of **Gheris de Charis** – Saïd Hansali, contactable through *Les Palmiers* (see below), is an excellent English-speaking guide who can show you around the labyrinthine *ksar* and its adjacent palmery.

ARRIVAL AND INFORMATION   EAST TO THE TAFILALT

By public transport Most buses heading east from Tinghir stop in the centre of Tinejdad (1hr); buses bound for Er Rachidia also run via Goulmima (1hr 30min). Grands taxis pull into the eastern end of Tinejdad.

Services There are banks in both Tinejdad and Goulmima; the former also has a post office, the latter a tiny internet café at the *Gheris* hotel on Bd Hassan II (daily 8.30am–9pm).

ACCOMMODATION AND EATING

TINEJDAD

★ **Gîte El Khorbat** 800m off the N10, 2km west of Tinejdad ☎ 0535 880355, ⊛ elkhorbat.com. A handful of rooms stylishly converted, with en-suite bathrooms and Berber textiles. You can also eat here at a swish little restaurant, with tasty local (including camel tajine) and Mediterranean dishes, as well as vegetarian options. The owner, Spanish writer and hotelier Roger Mimó, restored the adjacent kasbah that houses the Musée des Oasis. BB **550dh**

Reda On the Tinghir road on the western outskirts of town ☎ 0535 880284. Clean café with a wicker-shaded roadside terrace, offering half a dozen inexpensive rooms upstairs; breakfast is also cheap at 20dh. **120dh**

GOULMIMA

Gheris 101 Bd Hassan II ☎ 0535 783167. Small, dusty hotel with standard rooms on the first floor and a ground-floor café whose pavement seating is much the best place in town to tuck into breakfast (25dh). **150dh**

Maison d'Hôte Les Palmiers Turn right at the roundabout at the northern end of town and follow the signs ☎ 0535 784004, ⊛ palmiersgoulmima.com. Five homely rooms in the suburban house of a welcoming French-Moroccan couple, which opens out onto a large walled garden where you can camp. The owner organizes a variety of unique 4WD excursions and treks, including camping in the Gorges du Gheris and fossil-finding day-trips. Camping **100dh**, double **210dh**

The Ziz and the Tafilalt

The great date-palm oases of the **Oued Ziz** and the **Tafilalt** come as near as anywhere in Morocco to fulfilling Western fantasies about the Sahara. They do so by occupying the last desert stretches of the **Ziz Valley**: a route shot through with lush and amazingly

THE TALE OF THE TAFILALT

The **Tafilalt** was for centuries the main Moroccan terminus of the **caravan routes** – the famous **Salt Road** across the Sahara to West Africa, by way of Timbuktu. Merchants travelling south carried weapons, cloth and spices, part of which they traded en route at Taghaza (in modern-day Mali) for local **salt**, the most sought-after commodity in West Africa. They would continue south, and then make the return trip from the old Kingdom of Ghana, to the west of Timbuktu, loaded with **gold** (one ounce of gold was exchanged for one pound of salt at the beginning of the nineteenth century) and, until European colonists brought an end to the trade, **slaves**.

These were long journeys: Taghaza was twenty days by camel from the Tafilalt, Timbuktu sixty, and merchants might be away for more than a year if they made a circuit via southern Libya (where slaves were still sold up until the Italian occupation in 1911). They also, of course, brought an unusual degree of contact with other cultures, which ensured the Tafilalt a reputation as one of the most unstable parts of the Moroccan empire, frequently riven by religious dissent and separatism.

Dissent began when the *Filalis*, as the Tafilalt's predominantly Berber population is known, adopted the **Kharijite heresy**, a movement that used a Berber version of the Koran (orthodox Islam forbids any translation of God's direct Arabic revelation to Mohammed). Separatist tendencies date back much further though, to the eighth century, when the region prospered as the independent kingdom of **Sijilmassa** (see box, p.438).

In the fifteenth century, the region again emerged as a centre of trouble, fostering the *marabout* uprising that toppled the Wattasid dynasty, but it is with the establishment of the **Alaouite** (or, after their birthplace, *Filali*) dynasty that the Tafilalt is most closely associated. Mounted from a *zaouia* in Rissani by Moulay Rachid (see p.437), and secured by his successor Moulay Ismail, this is the dynasty that still holds power in Morocco, through Mohammed VI. The Tafilalt also proved a major centre of resistance to the French, who were limited to their garrison at Erfoud and an outpost of the Foreign Legion at Ouled Zohra until 1931.

THE TAFILALT TODAY

Deprived of its contacts to the south, the Tafilalt today is something of a backwater, with a population estimated at around eighty thousand and declining, as the effects of drought and **Bayoud disease** have taken hold on the palms (see box, p.403). Most of the population are smallholding farmers, with thirty or so palms for each family, from which they could hope to produce around a thousand kilos of dates in a reasonable year – with the market price of hybrid dates around 15dh a kilo, there are certainly no fortunes to be made.

cinematic scenes, from the river's fertile beginnings at the **Source Bleue**, the springwater pool that is the oasis meeting point of **Meski**, to a climax amid the rolling sand dunes of **Merzouga**. Along the way, once again, are an impressive succession of *ksour*, and an extraordinarily rich palmery – historically the most important territory this side of the Atlas.

Strictly speaking, the **Tafilalt** (or Tafilalet) comprises the oases south of **Erfoud**, its principal town and gateway. Nowadays, however, the provincial capital is the French-built garrison town and administrative centre of **Er Rachidia**, a convenient pit stop heading north, through the great canyon of the Ziz Gorges, to Midelt and Fez, or east, on a much less-travelled route, to **Figuig** – an important crossing point into Algeria when the frontier was open.

Er Rachidia and around

ER RACHIDIA was established by the French as a regional capital – when it was known as Ksar es Souk, after their Foreign Legion fort. Today, it represents more than anywhere else the new face of the Moroccan south: a shift away from the old desert markets and trading routes to a modern, urban centre. The town's role as a military outpost, originally against tribal dissidence, particularly from the **Aït Atta** (see box, p.422), was

maintained after independence by the threat of territorial claims from Algeria, and there is still a significant garrison here – not that you'd ever really know that from the relaxed air that pervades its orderly grid of tidy streets.

Meski and the Source Bleue

Signed off the N13, 17km south of Er Rachidia • 5dh • Coming by bus, ask to get out by the turn-off, a 400m walk down to the pool (note, though, that going on to Erfoud or back to Er Rachidia can be tricky, since most of the buses pass by full and don't stop); a petit taxi from Er Rachidia costs 7dh

The small palm grove of **Meski** is watered by a natural springwater pool: the famous **Source Bleue**, extended by the French Foreign Legion and long a postcard image and favourite campsite for travellers (see opposite). It's set on the riverbank, below a huge ruined *ksar* on the opposite bank and with several of the springs channelled into a naturally heated **swimming pool**. The fish-frequented pool is perfectly safe to swim in, though as it's a popular hangout for local boys, women bathers may feel self-conscious; be warned, though, that the river is likely infected with bilharzia (see p.392).

Outside midsummer, you might also consider walking part of the way downstream in the valley bottom, southeast of Meski. The superb four-hour **trek** along the Oued Ziz will bring you to **Oulad Aïssa**, a *ksar* with fabulous views over the upper Tafilalt.

ARRIVAL AND DEPARTURE

ER RACHIDIA AND AROUND

By bus The bus station is on Pl Principale, just south of Av Moulay Ali Cherif, the main street (highway) that runs all the way through town.

Destinations Casablanca (2 CTM & 2 others daily; 10hr); Erfoud (1 CTM, 2 Supratours & 12 others daily; 1hr–1hr 30min); Fez (2 CTM, 1 Supratours & 10 others daily; 7hr

15min–8hr); Figuig (2 daily, via Bouarfa; 7hr); Marrakesh (1 CTM & 1 Supratours daily; 10hr); Meknes (3 CTM & 5 others daily; 5hr 30min); Midelt (3 CTM, 1 Supratours & 7 others daily; 2hr); Ouarzazate (1 CTM, 1 Supratours & 5 others daily; 4hr 50min–5hr 30min); Rich (8 daily; 1hr 15min); Rissani (1 CTM & 5 others daily; 2hr); Tinejdad (2 daily; 1hr 30min); Tinghir (1 CTM & 8 others daily; 2–3hr).

By grand taxi There's a large rank southeast of the bus station, from where grands taxis make fairly frequent runs to Erfoud (1hr; you can get dropped off at the Meski turning, for the same price) and to Tinejdad (1hr 30min).

INFORMATION

Tourist office There's a rather unhelpful Délégation Provinciale du Tourisme at 44 Av Prince Moulay Abdallah (Mon–Fri: summer 7am–2pm; winter 8.30am–noon & 2.30–6.30pm; ☎0535 570944), found by leaving town on the N10 to Tinejdad and turning right at the sign opposite the (smaller) post office.

Services There are plenty of banks and numerous internet cafés around the centre, including one in the basement of the *Hôtel Le France* on Av Cheikh El Islam (daily 9am–midnight). The post office on Av Mohammed V has all the usual services; there's a smaller branch out on the N10 to Tinejdad.

ACCOMMODATION AND EATING

Despite its size, Er Rachidia has a limited choice of decent **hotels** within the city centre and if you want to camp, the *Source Bleue* at Meski is the nearest possibility. A couple of the hotels listed below host decent **restaurants**, and there are also many good grills and cafés clustered around the centre. The **covered market** is a reliable source of fresh fruit and vegetables.

Auberge Tinit 3km west of the city centre on the N10 to Tinejdad ☎0535 791759, ⓦauberge-tinit.info. Squat kasbah-style complex with spotless en-suite rooms, an on-site restaurant (*menus* from 95dh) and a nice central swimming pool. **500dh**

Café-Restaurant Merzouga Av Moulay Ali Cherif. Dinky restaurant in a pleasant setting diagonally opposite the covered market, attracting savvy travellers with its delicious brochettes (40dh with chips) and bargain omelettes (15dh). Daily 6am–9.30pm.

M'Daghra 92 Rue M'Daghra ☎0535 574047, ☎0535 574049. Much the best deal in this category, with larger-than-average en-suite rooms (avoid the ones at the front of the building, which can get noisy) and a café. **174dh**

Le Riad 4km west of the city centre on the N10 to Tinejdad ☎0535 791006, ⓦhotelleriad.com. The most upscale option in town (or at least near it), with comfortable enough rooms – each with a small sitting area and fitted with all mod cons – facing into a courtyard with a huge swimming pool and bar. It's pricey for what you get, though: service can be half-hearted, and you're best off driving into town to eat. **700dh**

CAMPING

Source Bleue Meski, 17km south of Er Rachidia ☎0671 560144, ⓔmomobleue@hotmail.com. Shaded by bamboo, palms and tamarisks, the famous *Source Bleue* campsite is well maintained by the local commune of M'Daghra, with a pool, a decent shower block, a couple of friendly little café-restaurants and the inevitable souvenir shops. **30dh**

SHOPPING

Ensemble Artisanal Av Moulay Ali Cherif, just before the bridge. Impressive from the outside, Er Rachidia's Ensemble Artisanal seems to have fallen on hard times, with just a small art exhibition in the lobby and nothing you can actually buy. But should the good days return, expect to see displays of local crafts: pottery, brass, wood and (truly indigenous) basketware made of palm leaves. Mon–Fri 8.30am–6.30pm.

The Ziz palmery

Trailing the final section of the **Oued Ziz**, the road south of Er Rachidia (the N13) is one of the most pleasing of all the southern routes – a dry red belt of desert just beyond Meski, it suddenly drops into the valley and the great **Ziz palmery**, a prelude of the Tafilalt, leading into Erfoud. Away from the road, *ksour* are almost continuous, glimpsed through the trees and high walls enclosing gardens and plots of cultivated land.

If you want to stop and take a closer look, the *ksar* at **Aoufouss**, 40km from Er Rachidia and the site of a Thursday souk, is perhaps the most accessible, though **Maadid**, off to the left of the road as you approach Erfoud, is also interesting – a really massive *ksar*, which is considered to be the start of the Tafilalt proper.

Gîte dans la Palmerie On the main road at Aoufous ☎ 0661 769804, ⓦ danslapalmeraie.com. Simple rooms with patchwork quilts, plus a four-person apartment with its own (large) terrace (750dh). Laze in hammocks or relax in the shady garden. You can sleep on the terrace if you can take your eyes off the palmery views for long enough. Terrace **90dh**, double **300dh**

Maison d'Hôte Zouala 2km off the main road at Aoufouss; follow the arrows painted on the palms ☎ 0535 578182, ⓔ zouala2000@yahoo.fr. Pleasant little guesthouse in a Berber farmhouse with traditional en-suite rooms and hot showers – and delicious evening meals served in a vast salon. Trickier to find than the *Gîte dans la Palmerie*, but worth seeking out for the warm welcome and tranquil location. **300dh**

Erfoud

ERFOUD, like Er Rachidia, is largely a French-built administrative centre, and its desultory frontier-town atmosphere fulfils little of the promise of the Tafilalt. Arriving from Er Rachidia, however, you get a first, powerful sense of proximity to the desert, with frequent sandblasts ripping through the streets, and total darkness in the event of a (not uncommon) electrical blackout. Erfoud once functioned as a launchpad for trips to the dunes at Merzouga, but has been left high and dry with the surfacing of the Rissani–Merzouga road. Now, unless they're here for the **date festival** (see box opposite), it tends to be bypassed by travellers who arrive early enough in the day to pick up onward transport.

Manar Marbre

On the R702 to Tinghir • Daily 8am–6.30pm • Free • ☎ 0535 578126

Erfoud's only point of (minor) interest is the local marble industry, which produces the attractive black marble that adorns every bar top and reception desk in town.

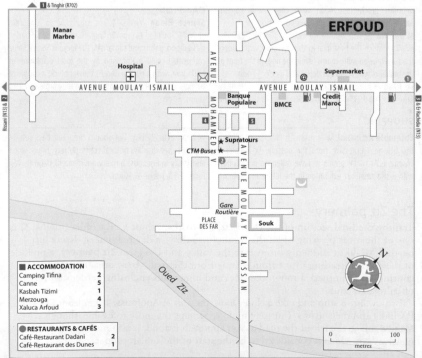

ACCOMMODATION
Camping Tifina	2
Canne	5
Kasbah Tizimi	1
Merzouga	4
Xaluca Arfoud	3

RESTAURANTS & CAFÉS
| Café-Restaurant Dadani | 2 |
| Café-Restaurant des Dunes | 1 |

THE FESTIVAL OF DATES

As with all such events, Erfoud's lively **Festival of Dates**, held over three days in early October, is a mixture of symbolism, sacred rites and entertainment – traditionally, dates bring good luck, whether tied to a baby's arm (to ensure a sweet nature), thrown at a bride (to encourage fertility) or offered to strangers (to signify friendship).

On the first morning of the festival, prayers are said at the *zaouia* of Moulay Ali Shereef at Rissani (see p.437), followed in the evening by a fashion show of traditional costumes: a pride of embroidered silk, silver and gold headdresses, sequins and elaborate jewellery. Then there are processions, camel races and, on the last night, traditional music and spiritual songs.

Uniquely, the high-quality stone contains hundreds of little fossils – mostly nautilus and cone-shaped orthoceras – which you can see being slowly revealed in 3D at the **Manar Marbre** just west of town. It takes an hour for hefty-looking saws to cut the huge blocks into workable chunks, which are then carved, and polished up at smaller hand-held machines.

7

ARRIVAL AND INFORMATION   ERFOUD

By bus CTM and Supratours buses depart from their offices on Av Mohammed V; others, including local buses and minibuses for Merzouga (you may have to change at Rissani), leave from the *gare routière* on Pl des FAR.
Destinations Er Rachidia (1 CTM, 2 Supratours & 12 others daily; 1hr–1hr 30min); Fez (1 CTM & 1 Supratours daily; 8hr 35min–9hr 45min); Marrakesh (1 Supratours daily; 11hr); Meknes (1 CTM & 1 Supratours daily; 7hr 20min–8hr); Merzouga (2 Supratours & 4 others daily; 1hr–1hr 30min); Midelt (1 CTM & 1 Supratours daily; 3hr–3hr 20min);

Ouarzazate (1 Supratours & 4 others daily; 6hr 30min); Rissani (1 CTM, 1 Supratours & 5 others daily; 30min–1hr); Tinghir (2 daily; 3hr 30min).
By grand taxi Grands taxis leave from Pl des FAR, making fairly frequent runs to Er Rachidia (1hr 30min), Rissani (30min) and Merzouga (1hr).
Services Most of what you may need – banks, internet, post office, the hospital and a little supermarket (daily 8am–8pm) – can be found along Av Moulay Ismail.

ACCOMMODATION

There are a surprising number of hotels – a legacy of the days when the town served as a staging post for dune trips – but budget choices are limited. Erfoud's municipal campsite is very shabby; best to head for *Camping Tifina*.

Canne 85 Av Moulay Hassan ☎0535 578696. Good value, if noisy, and run by a team of efficient women, the dated *Canne* has spotlessly clean a/c rooms with a lively café below. **180dh**
Kasbah Tizimi 2km west of town on the R702 to Tinghir ☎0535 576179, ⓦ kasbahtizimi.com. A modern *pisé* building featuring traditional wood beams, ironwork and immaculate tiling. The rooms are attractively decorated and ranged around patios and a flower-filled garden, and there's a large pool, bar and spacious terrace. **400dh**
Merzouga 114 Av Mohammed V ☎0535 576532. Best of the rock-bottom options, this hotel has reasonably clean en-suite rooms with hot showers; or you can sleep on the terrace for next to nothing. Breakfast is decent value at just 20dh. Terrace **25dh**, double **80dh**
Xaluca Arfoud 7km north of town on the N13 to Er

Rachidia ☎0535 578450, ⓦ xaluca.com. Smart *pisé* hotel complex, part of a small Spanish-owned chain, offering good value at this level. Swish rooms, opening onto small courtyards, are dominated by pastel colours, and the furniture, decor and fittings make use of regional arts and crafts – all the bathrooms are made from the local fossil-filled marble. The poolside bar is open to non-residents. BB **540dh**

CAMPING

Camping Tifina 8km south of town, on the N13 to Rissani ☎0610 231415, ⓦ tifina-maroc.com. Very well-appointed complex spread across several acres, with camping, Berber tents or West African-style bungalows, all with access to a variety of facilities, including a nice pool, ping pong, a BBQ area and bar. Camping **80dh**, Berber tent **220dh**, bungalow **280dh**

EATING AND DRINKING

Most cafés and restaurants are found on Av Mohammed V and around Pl des FAR. Try to sample the local specialities: *khalia*, a spicy stew of mutton or kid, flavoured with over forty spices and served in a tajine with vegetables, egg and parsley; or *madfouna*, a wheat-flour base topped with onions, tomatoes, olives, minced lamb and cheese that is southern Morocco's answer to pizza.

7

★ **Café-Restaurant Dadani** Av Mohammed V ☎ 0535 577958. Grab a drink and some patisserie at this congenial corner café with a large terrace, or head to the upstairs restaurant for Moroccan staples (including *khalia*) prepared with fresh ingredients and served in huge portions. Good coffee, too. Mains from around 45dh. Daily 8am–9pm.

Café-Restaurant des Dunes Av Moulay Ismaïl

☎ 0535 576793, ⊛ restaurantdesdunes.com. Smart little restaurant with a welcome greeting: the mouthwatering waft of pizza freshly baked in a wood-fired oven. Moroccan is also on the menu, but it's difficult to look past their speciality, with nine varieties to choose from – though given the surroundings you should probably go for heart of palm (60dh). Daily 9am–10pm.

Rissani

RISSANI stands at the last visible point of the Oued Ziz; beyond it, steadily encroaching on the present town and its ancient **ksour ruins**, begins the desert. From the eighth to the fourteenth centuries, this was the site of the first independent kingdom of the south, **Sijilmassa**, traces of which survive to the west of town. Much later, it became the first capital of the Tafilalt, and served for centuries as the last stop on the great caravan routes – the British journalist Walter Harris reported thriving gold and slave auctions in Rissani as late as the 1890s.

A quarter of today's population still live in a large seventeenth-century **ksar**, in addition to which there is just Place al Massira and a single street, lined by the usual administrative buildings. It's a quiet town, coming to life only for its famous **souk** (Tues, Thurs & Sun), which can often turn up a fine selection of Berber jewellery, including the crude, almost iconographic designs of the desert.

Centre Etudes et de Recherches Alaouites
On the main road (N13) through town • ☎ 0535 770305

Operating out of an eighteenth-century kasbah at the middle of town, the **Centre Etudes et de Recherches Alaouites** (CERA) is mainly concerned with the study and restoration of the Tafilalt's many significant kasbahs and *ksour*. It does, however, house a comprehensive **library** of some five thousand books and a small **museum** containing archeological finds from Sijilmassa, including ceramics (pots from Nigeria were uncovered here) and coins – a useful introduction given the scant remains at the site itself.

Sijilmassa

Clearly visible at the beginning of the last century, the ruins of **Sijilmassa** have all but vanished, its crumbling buildings methodically worn away by the relentless shifting of the sands. The most accessible and visible remains of this once-powerful kingdom (see box, p.438) are to be found a little to the west of Rissani, on the east bank of the Oued Ziz, and within the right angle formed by the N13 as it turns east to run into town – here you can trace the walls of a **mosque** with an early mihrab facing south, an adjoining **medersa** and the waffle-like walls of the citadel, topped by towers on the length by the river.

Just south of El Mansouriya, again on the east bank of the Oued Ziz, you can still see the gate that marked the ancient city's northern extremity. Known locally as the **Bab er Rih**, it is thought to date from the Merenid period but has certainly undergone restoration since then.

The Circuit Touristique
The circuit is signed off the N13 1.5km west of Rissani but is better driven in a clockwise direction, starting at Ksar Akbar and the Zaouia of Moulay Ali Shereef; from Pl al Massira, head towards Merzouga and turn right at the first roundabout (about 1.5km from the square)

The local tourist office has strung together a number of well-preserved medieval *ksour* to the south of Rissani on a waymarked 21km "**Circuit Touristique**" through the palmeries. While no longer the bustling communities they once were, the *ksour* make an interesting and thought-provoking excursion, especially beautiful in the golden light of sunset.

Ksar Akbar

Heading clockwise around the circuit, the first *ksar* you'll encounter, about 2.5km southeast of Rissani, is the nineteenth-century **Ksar Akbar**, an awesomely grandiose ruin that was once a palace in exile, housing the unwanted members of the Alaouite family and the wives of the dead sultans. Most of the structure, which still bears considerable traces of its former decoration, dates from the beginning of the nineteenth century.

Zaouia of Moulay Ali Shereef

Daily 8am–7pm; mosque and tomb closed to non-Muslims • Free

Standing proud beside Ksar Akbar is the popular but peaceful **Zaouia of Moulay Ali Shereef**, the original Alaouite stronghold and mausoleum of the dynasty's founder. It was from this *zaouia* (which is still an important national shrine) that the ruling Alaouite dynasty launched its bid for power, conquering first the oases of the south,

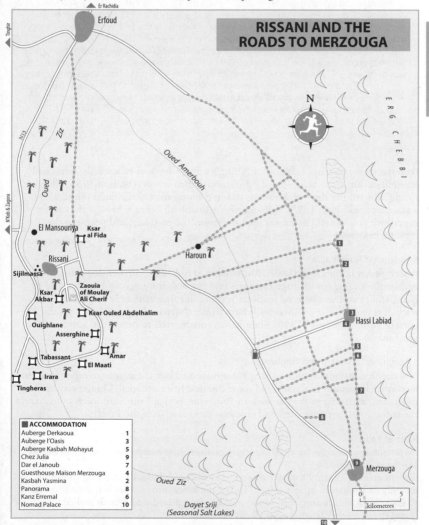

RISSANI AND THE ROADS TO MERZOUGA

7

ACCOMMODATION	
Auberge Derkaoua	1
Auberge l'Oasis	3
Auberge Kasbah Mohayut	5
Chez Julia	9
Dar el Janoub	7
Guesthouse Maison Merzouga	4
Kasbah Yasmina	2
Panorama	8
Kanz Erremal	6
Nomad Palace	10

THE BERBER KINGDOM

Sijilmassa was founded in 757 AD by Berber dissidents, who had broken away from orthodox Islam, and for five centuries, until its collapse under civil unrest in 1393, it dominated southern Morocco. The kingdom's wealth was built on the fertility of the **oases** south of Erfoud, a string of lush palmeries that are watered by the Oued Gheris and Oued Ziz, which led to Sijilmassa's description as the "Mesopotamia of Morocco". Harvests were further improved by diverting the Ziz, just south of modern-day Erfoud, to the west of its natural channel, thus bringing it closer to the Gheris and raising the water table. Such natural wealth was reinforced by Sijilmassa's trading role on the **Salt Road** to West Africa (see box, p.431), which persisted until the coast was opened up to sea trade, particularly by the Portuguese, in the fifteenth century – coins from Sijilmassa in this period have been found as far afield as Aqaba in Jordan.

Most historians agree that the ancient city of Sijilmassa stretched for 14km, from just south of El Mansouriya to a point near the *ksar* of Gaouz, on the "Circuit Touristique" (see p.436), though opinion is still divided over its plan: some see it as a fragmented city, comprising several dispersed *ksour*, much as it was after the civil war at the end of the fourteenth century, others as a single, elongated city, spread along the banks of the rivers.

The garrison underwent a major restoration by the Alaouites, who brought Sijilmassa to renewed prominence as the provincial capital of the Tafilalt in the seventeenth century, but it was destroyed – this time for good – by the Aït Atta in the early part of the nineteenth century.

In the mid-1990s, the ruins were on the radar of the World Monuments Fund as an endangered site in need of urgent attention. But despite a decade of excavation (finds of which can be seen at the Alaouite research centre in town), no further preservation work has been carried out since 1998, and the ruins continue to slowly recede into the dry earth of the Tafilalt.

With thanks to Dr Ron Messier

then the vital Taza Gap, before triumphing finally in Fez and Marrakesh. It has had several face-lifts in its time – most significantly when it was rebuilt in 1965 following the flooding of the Ziz – and owes its modern appearance to the latest round of aesthetic tweaking, in 1997. Although you're unable to venture beyond the central courtyard, you can still make out the tomb from the entrance, and peer into the mosque next door.

Ksar Oualed Abdelhalim

A second royal *ksar*, **Ksar Oualed Abdelhalim**, stands 2km further down the road. Although notable for its huge ramparts and the elaborate decorative effects of its blind arches and unplastered brick patterning, it's unfortunately in a pretty poor state of repair. A *ksar* was first built here in the fourteenth century, though the current ruins date from 1846, when it was constructed to house the governor of the Tafilalt.

Asserghine, Tabassant and Tingheras

The circuit continues round, passing Asserghine and half a dozen or so other *ksour* on its way to Tabassant, to the left and some distance from the road. On the way back up to Rissani, a turning to the left leads to **Tingheras**, perhaps the most interesting *ksar* on the entire route, set on a knoll and enjoying fine views over the Tafilalt.

Ksar al Fida

2km northeast of town; follow signs from the N13 towards Mezguida • Closed for renovation at the time of writing but normally daily 8am–7pm • Donation expected

The nineteenth-century **Ksar al Fida** served as the *caïd*'s palace until 1965 and more recently as a museum of archeology. Today, the welcoming owner is normally on hand to give you a whistle-stop tour of the building in a mixture of French and Arabic; even if you speak neither language, you'll get his drift.

ARRIVAL AND DEPARTURE   RISSANI

By bus CTM services run from their offices in busy Pl al Massira; private buses pull into the bus station 500m to the north. Minibus vans leave for Merzouga hourly from the square.
Destinations Er Rachidia (1 CTM, 2 Supratours & 5 others daily; 1hr 45min–2hr); Erfoud (1 CTM, 1 Supratours & 4 others daily; 30min–1hr); Fez (1 CTM & 1 Supratours daily; 9hr 15min–10hr); Marrakesh (1 Supratours & 3 others daily; 12hr); Meknes (1 CTM & 1 Supratours daily; 8–9hr);

Merzouga (2 Supratours daily; 30min); Midelt (1 CTM & 1 Supratours daily; 4hr); Ouarzazate (1 Supratours & 3 others daily; 7hr 30min); Tinghir (1 Supratours daily; 4hr 30min); Zagora (1 daily; 6hr).
By grand taxi Taxis to and from Erfoud (30min) use a rank opposite *Hôtel Sijilmassa*, just north of Pl al Massira; taxis for Merzouga (30min) leave from opposite the pharmacy on the corner of the square.

INFORMATION AND TOURS

Services Both the Banque Populaire and Crédit Agricole on Pl al Massira have ATMs (the last chance to get money out before the Sahara, as there are no ATMs in Merzouga).
Guides You can explore the Circuit Touristique outside

town with the help of the knowledgeable Driss Youssoufi Alaui (1hr; 50dh) or take in the wider area on a half-day tour (4hr; 100dh); he can usually be found at the Zaouia of Moulay Ali Shereef or ring in advance on ☎ 0661 872975.

7

ACCOMMODATION AND EATING

With the dunes just down the road, few travellers **spend the night** in Rissani, instead visiting on a day-trip from Merzouga (or Erfoud) or taking in the *ksour* en route elsewhere. Those that do stop over tend to stay at places just outside of town, on the N13 to Erfoud – the small hotels in the centre are generally grubby and overpriced. Eating options are equally limited: head for the area around the souk for standard **café** food.

El Filalia Next to the CTM office on Pl al Massira ☎ 0672 314193. The best of the central budget options, with adequate rooms and a street-side café that doubles as a breakfast spot (20dh). <u>100dh</u>
Kasbah Ennasra Next to the Ziz petrol station 3km north of town, on the N13 to Erfoud ☎ 0535 774403,

ⓦ kasbahennasra.net. Rissani's best luxury option: highlights include four-poster beds (in spacious rooms), an attractive patio and swimming pool, and a first-class restaurant. Non-residents can drop by for lunch or dinner (90–120dh menu, depending on the season) and a dip in the pool. BB <u>850dh</u>

Merzouga and the Erg Chebbi

"No one who has stayed in the Sahara for awhile is quite the same as when he came… Once a man has been under the spell of the vast, luminous, silent country, no other place is quite strong enough for him, no other surroundings can provide the supremely satisfying sensation of existing in the midst of something that is absolute."
Their Heads are Green and their Hands are Blue, Paul Bowles

The Erg Chebbi dunes at **MERZOUGA** are indisputably one of the great sights of Morocco. Rising to 150m in places, these giant sand hills lining the Algerian border may not be as imposing nor as extensive as some in North Africa, but they come closer than anywhere else in the country (at least, anywhere else that's relatively accessible) to fulfilling most people's expectations of what a true desert should be. The result, though, is that Merzouga can sometimes feel less like the *désert profond* than a Saharan circus, with groups of luxuriously turbaned tourists posing for photographs with *hommes bleus* under the acacia trees or astride camels.

To stand any chance of experiencing the scenery in its essential state, you should aim to come here out of season (Jan & Feb are the quietest months) and choose your spot very carefully. At the height of summer, the few visitors who brave the fierce heat to reach Merzouga are mostly Moroccans, attracted by the reputed power of the sands to cure rheumatism. Sufferers are buried up to the neck for a few minutes in the afternoon – any longer (and earlier) than that can be fatal.

The dunes

Rising dramatically from a plain of blackened *hammada*, the dunes of the **Erg Chebbi** stretch 28km from north to south and are 7km across at their widest point – a

CAMEL RIDES AROUND MERZOUGA

Having crossed Morocco to stand at the edge of the Sahara, you can hardly leave without hopping onto a **camel** and heading off into the dunes. **Rides** range from a two-hour lollop over the crescents to catch the sunset (100dh) to a fifteen-night expedition deep into the desert (4500dh); most people opt for an overnight stay at a Berber camp (300–400dh), where you'll enjoy the clearest of night skies and a memorable sunrise the following day. A cameleer, meals, tea and blankets are included in the price, but it's advisable to bring extra clothes and a sleeping bag, as nights can get excruciatingly cold. If you've never been to the desert before, think about starting with a short trip before signing up for longer journeys – the feeling of pure isolation, surrounded by a seemingly never-ending sea of sand, is an incredible experience (described as a "baptism of solitude" by Paul Bowles), but it's not to everyone's taste. Trips can be arranged through your hotel or at one of the other *auberges* around Merzouga (see opposite); *Kasbah Mohayut* and *Nomad Palace* are particularly recommended, or you could contact Best of Merzouga (☎0661 144620, ⊕bestofmerzouga.com), who specialize in longer trips and tours from Marrakesh and Fez. Each outfit works its own jealously guarded routes and **camps** – the smaller, more expensive setups (usually no more than six people) are more atmospheric but less comfortable than the permanent camps – but it can be a matter of luck whether you hit a crowded section of the dunes or not. Generally, the further from the main group of *auberges* you go, the more chance you have of avoiding other camel trains and (even more importantly) 4WD drivers and quad bikers, though their noisy antics have been more limited in recent years. Note, too, that the longer multi-day trips stop operating after February, after which time it just gets too hot.

relatively modest sea of sand compared with the great Erg Occidental of southern Algeria but still an impressive taste of the Sahara's grandeur. The highest dunes are those near, or just south of, Merzouga itself, peaking with the aptly named **Grand Dune de Merzouga**, a golden mountain recognizable – in addition to being the tallest dune around – by the distinctive tamarisk tree at its base. The dunes are spectacular at any time of day, but early morning and late afternoon are the best times to view them; to find a relatively peaceful ridge free of footprints, however, you'll have to be prepared to walk for an hour, or else arrange a camel trip (see box above).

ARRIVAL AND DEPARTURE   MERZOUGA

Thanks to the paved road from Rissani, getting to Merzouga is easy these days, though getting to your hotel isn't quite so smooth. *Pistes* – marked with posts – peel east off the main road at regular intervals (at junctions flagged by signboards); if you're **driving** in a standard rental car, don't be tempted to improvise, as there are many patches of soft sand where you might easily get stuck. To avoid the **faux guides** who greet buses and grands taxis, book your accommodation in advance and try to get your hotel to meet you on arrival.

By bus Supratours make the long journey down from Fez and across the south from Ouarzazate, via Tinghir, Erfoud and Rissani, but there are also local buses from Erfoud and Rissani as well as hourly minibus vans from the latter.
Destinations Erfoud (2 Supratours & 4 others daily; 1hr–1hr 30min); Fez (1 Supratours daily; 10hr 45min); Ouarzazate (1 Supratours daily; 8hr); Rissani (2 Supratours daily; 30–45min); Tinghir (1 Supratours daily; 5hr).
By grand taxi Grands taxis regularly ply the route from Rissani to Merzouga village (30min), leaving from the corner of Pl al Massira.

INFORMATION AND ACTIVITIES

Services There's a post office at the northern end of Merzouga village, just beyond the turn-off to *Nomad Palace*, and internet cafés in Merzouga and Hassi Labiad. Note, though, that there are no ATMs, so you'll need to get cash out in Rissani if necessary.
Activities Camel rides are the most popular excursion in Merzouga (see box above), but several hotels also run guided tours of the oasis at the end of Hassi Labiad or to nearby villages to listen to Gnaoua music. Alternatively, you can go sandboarding on the dunes south of the village; Le Grand Dépôt de Merzouga, 300m down the street from *Café des Amis*, on the corner of the main road through Merzouga village, rents boards (and skis) for 100dh a day (☎0535 576605, ⊕ammar_karraoui@hotmail.com).

7

DESERT WILDLIFE

At first glance, the desert seems harsh and inhospitable, a scorched habitat devoid of life bar the occasional scarab beetle leaving tiny tracks across the sand. But there are acacias, tamarisk and calotropis here, and lichens and algae that survive on the dew that clings to the undersides of rocks and stones.

Such modest pickings provide sustenance for the many **birds** that pass through on their spring and autumn migrations, as well as native desert-dwelling species. Spotted sandgrouse, white-crowned wheatears, Egyptian nightjars, eagle owls and Houbara bustards are just a few of the magnificent species that can be seen, while, incredibly, greater flamingos can sometimes be found at Dayet Sriji and other lakes near Merzouga – but bear in mind that these can disappear to nothing in dry years.

The desert and *hammada* also house **reptiles** such as Berber skink, Montpellier snake and fringe-toed lizard, whose feet are perfectly adapted for their desert environment, as well as nocturnal **mammals**; you're less likely to see them, but jerboa, desert hedgehogs and fennec (desert fox) make their presence felt by leaving footprints in the morning sand.

7

ACCOMMODATION AND EATING

Accommodation in Merzouga (see map, p.437) is strung out over a wide area, nestled at the foot of the dunes in a straggling line; much of it is actually around Hassi Labiad, the small village north of Merzouga proper. It helps to know where your chosen hotel actually is before you arrive, as the final leg off the N13 from Rissani is across rough *hammada* and can be a long one if you stay at the northernmost group of hotels, some of which lie a considerable way from the tarmac. Outside high season, rates are surprisingly low, mainly because most places make their real money on camel trips. With just a few unremarkable **café-restaurants** to choose from, you'll get a much better deal if you eat at your hotel, paying an inclusive half- or full-board rate. The accommodation below is listed in the order you encounter it from Rissani.

★ **Auberge Derkaoua** 23km north of Merzouga village; 5km from the main road ☎ 0535 577140, ⓦ aubergederkaoua.com. Beautiful *pisé* complex in traditional style, set amid olive, almond and fruit orchards on the northern fringes of Erg Chebbi. The traditionally decorated en-suite rooms are very comfortable, but you'll probably want to spend more time lazing in the lovely garden, which has a pool and a pretty terrace restaurant. Closed Jan, July & Aug. BB 700dh

Kasbah Yasmina 18km north of Merzouga village; 11km from the main road ☎ 0535 576783, ⓦ hotelyasminamerzouga.com. Established budget *auberge* right on the dunes, beside a seasonal lake where you might see flamingos – the situation is spectacular and the views from the sunny rear terrace superb. The rooms, mostly en suite, are cool, and there is a large grouping of Berber tents at the edge of the sand. Nice pool also, but the food is so-so. HB Berber tent 400dh, double 550dh

Auberge l'Oasis 6.5km north of Merzouga village, at Hassi Labiad; 2.5km from the main road ☎ 0535 577321, ⓦ aubergeoasismerzouga.com. Jolly little setup with simple en-suite rooms around a central garden, and the option of bunking down on the roof terrace or pitching a tent (with light, water and power). Bargain dinner menu for 30–60dh. Terrace 30dh, camping 60dh, double 300dh

Guesthouse Maison Merzouga 6.5km north of Merzouga village; at Hassi Labiad, 2.5km from the main road ☎ 0535 577299, ⓦ merzouga-guesthouse .com. Six doubles in the *pisé* guesthouse of the Seggaoui family, set back from the dunes but with cosy rooms, a keyhole pool and plenty of good old-fashioned hospitality. Courses in Berber and Berber cooking available. HB 600dh

Auberge Kasbah Mohayut 4.5km north of Merzouga village; 2km from the main road ☎ 0666 039185, ⓦ mohayut.com. Welcoming duneside kasbah, run with a smile by Moha and his cousin, whose cheerily decorated rooms flank shady corridors or are dotted around a pleasant pool. You can tuck into tasty meals in an attractive tree-dappled courtyard; there's a good buffet breakfast, too. Organizes a variety of camel rides as well as more unusual trips, such as a mule-back tour of the Hassi Labiad oasis. BB 700dh

★ **Kanz Erremal** 4km north of Merzouga village; 2km from the main road ☎ 0535 578482, ⓦ kanzerremal.com. Stylish kasbah with a variety of lantern-lit rooms adorned with a variety of hand-crafted local knick-knacks – some come with private terraces, all have swish little bathrooms. The large public areas leading off the central atrium make a pleasant retreat from the sun, though the highlights lie outside: a chic terrace at the edge of the sand and a superb infinity pool that gives the impression you're actually taking a dip in the Sahara. BB 580dh

7

Dar el Janoub 3.5km north of Merzouga village; 2km from the main road ☏ 0535 577852, ⓦ dareljanoub.com. The best of the top-end places, with large, minimalist rooms, a shady courtyard, a lovely pool that's softly lit at night, and a perfect terrace for sundowners, right by the desert's edge. If you really want to push the boat out, take one of the two suites that enjoy their own lounge and private terrace overlooking the dunes (1600dh). HB **1160dh**

Panorama 2km north of Merzouga village; 1km from the main road ☏ 0662 085573, ⓦ kasbahpanorama.c.la. Run by the hospitable Aït Bahaddou family, this budget *auberge* stands further from the sand than most, at the top of a hill outside Merzouga, but the views are stupendous: the sunset terrace enjoys arguably the best panorama this side of the Atlas. The rooms are well aired and the restaurant serves tasty tajines and *madfouna* ("pizza Berber"). They run various tours including visits to hear Gnaoua music at a nearby village. HB **450dh**

★ **Chez Julia** 100m behind the mosque in Merzouga village ☏ 0535 573182, ⓦ chez-julia.com. In a traditional desert house in Merzouga itself, this perennial favourite is defined by an appealing combination of comfort and authenticity. Owned and run by Austrian painter, Julia Günther, the *auberge* has half a dozen uniquely decorated colour-themed rooms, sharing three bathrooms between them. When it's available, the good menu features a combination of Moroccan and Austrian dishes (from Schnitzel to pastilla), all freshly prepared at reasonable prices. **500dh**

Nomad Palace 7km south of Merzouga village, at Ksar Mezguida ☏ 0535 882089, ⓦ hotelnomadpalace .com. The dunes aren't as high at this far southern end of the Erg Chebbi, but the area's much more peaceful as a result. The *auberge* boasts a huge Moroccan salon with an open fire, and well-furnished rooms opening onto a quiet courtyard garden. The owner also runs excellent camel trips to a less frequented area on the far, east side of Erg Chebbi, via a more varied route than normal. HB **500dh**

West to the Drâa

Around 3km north of Rissani, the N12 branches west off the main Erfoud road **towards Alnif**, **Tazzarine**, **N'Kob** and, ultimately, **Zagora**. The route sees little tourist traffic but provides a scenic link between the Tafilalt and the Drâa Valley, with the barren majesty of the Jebel Saghro shadowing the road for much of its length. Aside

---

PRECIOUS STONES? BUYING ROCKS AND FOSSILS IN THE SOUTH

Throughout the south, boys bound into the paths of oncoming cars to offer crystalline mementoes of Morocco, and **rocks** and **fossils** are staples of most tourist shops across the region. But before you part with your hard-earned dirhams, it's worth knowing what to look out for: tennis-ball-sized crystals in a hollow **geode** can often cost more on the Moroccan hard-shoulder than they would in Britain or the US, while brilliant orange and red geodes and slices of rock crystal (quartz) look attractive but are unknown to natural science, as are the quartz geodes given an iridescent metal coating by vendors.

Attractive spirals of **ammonites** (from Carboniferous to Jurassic) are common in the limestone areas of Britain, but in Morocco they can be bought sliced and polished as well as "raw". Do not rely on the names you're given by the shopkeeper – look at the centre of the spiral of the ammonite and at the ridge around its shell to check how far natural features have been "enhanced" by a chisel.

Slightly older than ammonites, **trilobites** often appear in shops as identical beige-coloured fossils on grey slate. In nature, they are rarely so perfect – beware plaster casts. The early trilobite *Paradoxides* is about the size of a hand, with long whisker-like spines. A deep-sea inhabitant, it is often found looking rather squashed sideways, where the silts on which it lived have been sheared by pressure. The *Calymene* and *Phacops* types of trilobites are about 200 million years younger than *Paradoxides*, and measure about two inches long, with a crab-like outer skeleton. The half-rounded shield-like skull, often found separated from the exo-skeleton, can appear in a shop with the rest of the skeleton carved around it as a tribute to modern Moroccan craftsmanship.

In the black limestone regions near Erfoud, the white crystalline shapes of **nautilus** and **orthoceras** are cross-sectioned and polished to emphasize their internal structure before being formed into ashtrays and even coffee tables (see p.434), a striking souvenir that can of course be transported for you at a cost – though they never quite seem to look so good back home.

from the landscape, **fossils** are this region's main attraction – the stretch between Alnif and Tazzarine, in particular, has become the centre of a low-scale mining industry whose principal export is large trilobites (see box opposite), sold from dozens of roadside stalls.

Alnif

Trilobites and potatoes are the stock in trade of **ALNIF**, 90km west of Rissani – the former scraped from ancient canyon walls around the town, the latter grown in the palmery winding northwards into the hills. It's along the line of this old watercourse that a well-frequented *piste* cuts across a saddle dividing the Jebel Saghro and Jebel Ougnat ranges to join the N10, the main Dadès highway, 21km southeast of Tinghir.

Tazzarine

Beyond Alnif, the scenery grows wilder as you approach **TAZZARINE**, 66km to the west and set in a grassy oasis surrounded by bare mountains. There's a straggling row of shops but little you'd really want to stop for in town. Further afield, though, at Tiouririne (7km away) and Aït Ouazik (26km), you can find some vivid **prehistoric rock carvings** (*gravures rupestres*), the six-thousand-year-old drawings depicting giraffes, ostriches, buffalo, antelope and other animals from a time when the surrounding area was grassy steppe – ask at *Camping Amasttou*, 800m down a track to the left at the Taghbalte/N'Kob junction just west of town.

N'Kob

The rambling *ksar* of **N'KOB**, 190km west of Rissani and only 40km from the junction with the Drâa Valley road, dominates the most spectacular stretch of the N12, its kasbah-studded old quarter looking north from the rim of an escarpment across a large palmery to the peaks of the Jebel Saghro. The number of grand houses in N'Kob testify to its former prominence as a market hub for the region, but today the town is a refreshingly off-track destination – other than a couple of **prehistoric rock-carving** sites across the valley (which you'll need help from your hotel or guesthouse to find), there's nothing much to see, but the traditional *pisé* architecture and fine views from the roof terraces tempt many visitors into staying longer than they intended.

Into the Jebel Saghro

For trekkers, N'Kob serves as an important staging post for trips across the **Jebel Saghro** (see p.420), though you can also explore the mountains from a spectacular *piste* that heads north of town to crest the Saghro via the **Tazi n' Tazazert**, eventually dropping into the Dadès Valley at Iknioun, near Boumalne du Dadès. Winding through dramatic rock formations and gorges, the route rivals the crossing of the High Atlas, with superb views from the pass. An added incentive is the spectacular pinnacles of **Bab n'Ali**, which you can reach in a half-day's walk from a pleasant, conveniently situated *gîte*, 8km along the road from N'Kob.

| ARRIVAL AND INFORMATION | WEST TO THE DRÂA |

By public transport Buses cover the route between Rissani and Zagora (1 daily; 6hr), leaving Rissani's *gare routière* at 10am; grands taxis depart from the rank near *Hôtel Sijilmassa* (1hr) for Alnif, where you can pick up another taxi for the next onwards leg.

By car It's a long haul to the Drâa (295km from Rissani to Zagora), but the road is good; there are petrol stations in Mecissi, Alnif and Tazzarine. Leaving Tazzarine, make sure you turn right to stay on the N12/R108 for Zagora – the road that heads straight on, to Zagora via Taghbalte, is a rough *piste* that, despite being much shorter, will actually take you a lot longer.

Guides Mohammed at the Bureau des Guides in N'Kob (☎0667 487509) speaks very good English and runs various treks into the Jebel Saghro, including a reverse of the classic three-day Tagdilt–N'Kob crossing (see p.420); alternatively any of the hotels in N'Kob can arrange excursions into the range.

7

ACCOMMODATION AND EATING

Most people cover the road between Rissani and the Drâa in one go, but given the distance, you may want to break the journey in two; if so, it's worth pushing on to **N'Kob**, by far the most appealing place to stay along this route, with a good choice of accommodation.

ALNIF

Etoile du Sud In the centre of town, on the left as you head towards Tazzarine. The best place for a quick meal if you're just passing through, this simple café has friendly staff and reasonably priced traditional food – the menu includes brochette and good chips, made from Alnif's staple staple (60dh). Daily 8am–9pm.

La Gazelle du Sud At the top end of town ☎0670 233942, ✉ lagazeldesud@yahoo.fr. There's no denying this place is bright: done out in pink, with the handful of small and simple rooms (three en suite) a contrasting shade of mint green. The clean bathrooms are spiked with incense, and there's also an on-site restaurant (half-board rates at 150dh are a decent deal). 100dh

N'KOB

Auberge-Camping Ouadjou 500m west of town ☎0524 839314, ⓦ ouadjou.com. The best camping option in the area, with very welcoming staff, though you can also sleep in Berber tents or in compact but clean rooms in a pisé kasbah complex. There's a swimming pool and a basic but cheerful café. Camping 100dh, Berber tent 180dh, double 280dh

Kasbah Baha Baha The old quarter ☎0524 307801, ⓦ kasbahabaha.com. This splendidly renovated kasbah is owned by an ethnographer from Marrakesh, with a library of interesting academic papers, a small museum and some lovely rooms in the square towers on the upper floors, decorated with plush Moroccan textiles and carpets. Outside, the garden features a couple of mock-Berber encampments flanking a pool, and the whole site enjoys a wonderful panorama over the valley. Mule trips into the Jebel Saghro and camel rides into the hammada can be arranged. BB Berber tent 190dh, double 370dh

Ksar Jenna 2km west of town ☎0524 839790, ⓦ ksarjenna.com. Owned and run by an Italian-Moroccan couple, this self-consciously chic place has just seven rooms, all stylishly furnished with ceramics and expensive textiles – though the highlight is a lush garden filled with flowers, fruit trees and water features. Lunch and dinner (open to non-residents) is a daily-changing affair. HB 900dh

Figuig

Hard up against the Algerian border, in the far southeast of the country, the charming oasis town of **FIGUIG** (pronounced "F'geeg") is literally the end of the road. The border has been closed since 1994, and so the long slog to get here from Er Rachidia is a somewhat perverse route to take – a lot of travelling in order to complete a loop **via Bouarfa** to Oujda in northern Morocco. For those that do make the trip (and not many do), the journey is half the fun: spectacular in its isolation and scenically extraordinary, dominated by huge empty landscapes, blank red mountains, mining settlements and military garrisons.

The other half is the town itself. Figuig is notable for the strange, archaic shape of its pink-tinged *ksour*, their watchtowers having evolved as much from internal tension within the *ksour* as from any need to protect themselves from the nomadic tribes of the desert. It's a laidback place, where life ticks by at an addictively slower rhythm, and the simple pleasure of wandering its shady alleys never seems to fade.

Ksar Zenega

Figuig sprawls along an escarpment (essentially the new town), dropping down into the palmery and **Ksar Zenega**, the oldest of what were once seven distinct *ksour* but now, with their defensive walls largely crumbled away, more like a collection of neighbourhoods. Head for the *platforme*, a man-made lookout poised above the *ksar*; the view from here spans a large part of the palmery (allegedly home to some two hundred thousand trees, making it one of the largest in the south), and you can gaze at the weird, multicoloured layers of the enclosing mountains. Descending into the covered alleyways of Ksar Zenega itself, head to your left to reach its centre, more developed than most in this area, with a couple of shops and a café in addition to its mosque.

ARRIVAL AND DEPARTURE   FIGUIG

By bus Most buses use the CTM office on Bd Hassan II, the main road that runs through the new town (tickets are sold in advance), with services to Oujda (1 CTM & 2 others daily; 6hr) via Bouarfa (2hr), where you can pick up buses to Er Rachidia (2 daily; 5hr).

By car It's a very long journey from both Er Rachidia (378km) and Oujda (386km) but easy enough in a normal tourist car, the only diversion being the roadside *gendarmerie* who pass the time collecting car numbers and your mother's maiden name (the "undefined boundary" with Algeria runs parallel to the road).

INFORMATION

Guides It can be worth hiring a guide through your hotel to help you navigate the confusing network of alleyways that make up Figuig's various *ksour* – try English-speaking Youseff Jebbari (☎051 659473, ✉survivor.afiguig@hotmail.com), who is also contactable through *Hotel Figuig*.

Services There are a couple of internet cafés, and a Banque Populaire on Bd Hassan II in the new town.

ACCOMMODATION AND EATING

Auberge Oasis Rue Jamaa, Ksar Zenaga ☎0536 899220, ⓦauberge-oasis.com. A proper guesthouse, set in a restored traditional house deep in Ksar Zenaga, with comfy beds weighed down by Berber blankets and communal dining that's centred around honest home-cooked local dishes. **170dh**

Figuig Bd Hassan II ☎0536 899309, ⓦfiguig-hotel .com. Well-maintained, mid-range place in the modern part of town, with stunning views down the valley to the closed border, and Algeria beyond. There's also a secure area for camping and a café that benefits from the same memorable vista, though the pool can sometimes lack its essential ingredient. Camping **70dh**, double **220dh**

Maison Nana Rue Ouled Sellam, Ksar Zenaga ☎0536 897 570, ⓦmaison-dhote-nanna-figuig.com. The hotch-potch of modern en suites may lack character, but the warmth of hosts Sylvie and Mostapha more than makes up for it, as does the food, made with vegetables from their own garden. Great views and stargazing are to be had on the panoramic terrace. BB **370dh**

7

Agadir, the Souss and Anti-Atlas

PAINTED ROCKS, AMELN VALLEY

Agadir, the Souss and Anti-Atlas

Southern Morocco's major tourist destination is Agadir, a winter beach resort for Europeans, rebuilt after its destruction by an earthquake in 1960. Inland and to the south of Agadir are the Souss and the Anti-Atlas, easy-going regions whose Tashelhaït (Chleuh) Berber populations share the distinction of having together cornered the country's grocery trade. Taroudant, capital of the wide and fertile Souss valley, has massive walls, animated souks and good hotels. Further south, into the Anti-Atlas mountains, Tafraoute and its valley are even more compelling – the stone-built villages and villas set amid a stunning landscape of pink granite and vast rock formations. On the coast north of Agadir is a series of less developed beaches, including Taghazout, Morocco's number-one surfing resort. A short way inland is Paradise Valley, a beautiful and exotic palm gorge, from which a mountain road trails up to the seasonal waterfalls of Immouzer des Ida Outanane. To the south of Agadir, the beaches are scarcely developed, ranging from solitary campsites at Sidi Rbat – one of Morocco's best locations for birdwatching – and Sidi Moussa d'Aglou, down to the old port of Sidi Ifni – only relinquished by Spain in 1969 and full of splendid Art Deco colonial architecture.

Agadir

AGADIR was, by all accounts, a characterful port, prior to the terrible earthquake of 1960 that completely destroyed it. Just four years into independence, the earthquake was an especially traumatic event, but its reconstruction showed modern Morocco at its best, and half a century on, the result is quite impressive. Swathes of park and garden break up the hotel and residential zones, and the magnificent beach is untrammelled by Spanish Costa-style high-rise building. It sometimes feels that the city is a little souless, but the lack of bustle has novelty value coming from any other Moroccan town. Despite the air of calm, Agadir is nonetheless the core of Morocco's fifth-biggest urban conglomeration, with a population of some 700,000. Its main industry, as will be immediately apparent to even a casual visitor, is tourism.

Downtown Agadir is centred on the junction of Boulevard Hassan II and Avenue Prince Moulay Abdallah with Avenue du Prince Sidi Mohammed. Rebuilt in 1960s "modernist" style, it has all the trappings of a town centre, with office blocks, a post office, town hall (Hôtel de Ville), municipal market and banks. Just to the northeast is an area known as **Talborjt**, with a concentration of budget hotels and small café-restaurants.

AGADIR BEACH

Highlights

❶ Agadir beach Golden sand, top-class hotels and sun pretty much all year round make this the country's number one seaside resort. **See p.451**

❷ Surfing at Taghazout Morocco's top surfing spot, a village beach resort with a whole series of excellent right breaks attracting tubehounds both local and foreign. **See p.466**

❸ Taroudant Once the capital, this delightful walled town with two markets and bags of character is nowadays being dubbed "mini Marrakesh" by the tourist industry. **See p.467**

❹ Ancient rock carvings Across the whole region between Tafraoute and Tata, these prehistoric artworks attest to a time when elephants and giraffes roamed this neck of the woods. **See p.480**

❺ Tafraoute Tucked away in the Anti-Atlas mountains amid a landscape of strange rock formations, this friendly little town makes a great base to explore them from. **See p.488**

❻ Sidi Ifni A former Spanish enclave built from scratch in the 1930s with an Art Deco town hall, an Art Deco mosque and even an Art Deco lighthouse. **See p.497**

HIGHLIGHTS ARE MARKED ON THE MAP ON P.450

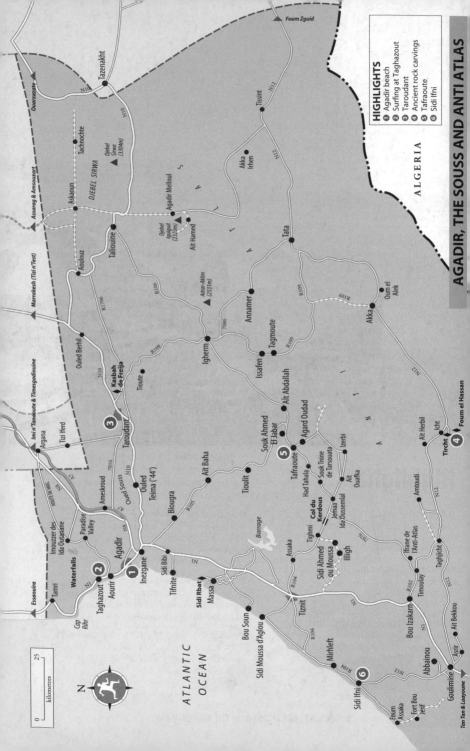

AGADIR, THE SOUSS AND ANTI ATLAS

HIGHLIGHTS
1. Agadir beach
2. Surfing at Taghazout
3. Taroudant
4. Ancient rock carvings
5. Tafraoute
6. Sidi Ifni

ALGERIA

ATLANTIC OCEAN

N

0 — 25 kilometres

Foum Zguid

Tazenakht

Tachnochte

Djebel Sirwa (3304m)

DJEBEL SIRWA

Askaoun

Aoulouz

Tissint

Akka Irhen

Agadir Melloul

Djebel Izuguil (2323m)

Ait Hamed

Tata

Taliouine

Adrar-Aklim (2531m)

Annamer

Oum el Alek

Akka

Ighern

Tagmoute

Issafen

Oued Berhil

Tioute

Kasbah de Freija

Ait Abdallah

Foum el Hassan

Taroudant

Souk Ahmed El Jabat

Agard Oudad

Ait Herbil

Tircht

Icht

Ameskroud

Ouled Teima ('44')

Ait Baha

Tioulit

Tafraoute

Souk Tnine de Tarsouata

Izerbi

Argana

Tizi Iferd

Paradise Valley

Biougra

Had Tahala

Ait Ouafka

Imouzzer des Ida Outanane

Waterfalls

Tamri

Agadir

Inezgane

Sidi Bibi

R105

Barrage

Col du Kerdous

Jemaa Ida Oussemlal

Amtoudi

Cap Rihr

Taghazout

Aourir

Tifnite

Sidi Rbat

Massa

Assaka

Tighmi

Sidi Ahmed ou Moussa

Illigh

Iffrane de l'Anti-Atlas

Taghjicht

Bou Soun

Tiznit

Abbainou

Asrir

Sidi Moussa d'Aglou

Bou Izakarn

Timoulay

Ait Bekkou

Mirhleft

Goulimine

Abbainou

Sidi Ifni

Foum Assaka

Fort Bou Jerif

Essaouira

Ouarzazate

Assarag & Amsouzart

Marrakesh (Tizi n'Test)

Imi n'Tanoute & Timesgadiouine

Tan Tan & Laayoune

Brief history

Agadir's **history** closely parallels that of Morocco's other Atlantic ports. It was colonized first by the Portuguese in the fifteenth century, then, recaptured by the Saadians in the sixteenth, carried on its trading with intermittent prosperity, overshadowed, more often than not, by the activities of Mogador (Essaouira) and Mazagan (El Jadida).

Abroad, Agadir's name was known mainly for the **Agadir Crisis** of 1911, when, during the run-up to World War I, Germany sent a warship to Agadir bay to support Moroccan independence against French designs. Germany's real motive – to undermine a Franco-British alliance by using Britain and France's conficting interests in Morocco – failed when Britain cut a deal with France, allowing the French to split Morocco with Spain while the British got a free hand in Egypt and Cyprus.

The really big event in Agadir's history was the devastating **earthquake** of February 29, 1960: a tremor that killed 15,000 and left most of the remaining 50,000 population homeless. In the aftermath, the whole place had to be rebuilt from scratch.

The beach

Agadir's **beach** is as good as they come: a wide expanse of fine sand, which extends an impressive distance to the south of the town, is swept each morning and patrolled by mounted police. Along its course are a number of cafés which rent out sunbeds and umbrellas. The ocean – it should be stressed – has a **very strong Atlantic undertow** and is definitely not suitable for children unless closely supervised. Even adults are advised not to go out swimming alone. The northern end of the beach has lifeguards on duty from June 15 to September 15 8am to 7pm daily, and a system of flags to tell you how dangerous it is to swim.

Jetskiing (wet-biking; 300dh for 20min) is available at the northern end of the beach at Club Royale de Jet-Ski. Surfboards and windsurfing equipment can be rented nearby.

There are **guarded sections** at the northern end of the beach, mostly run by neighbouring restaurants, where you can rent a sunbed with a parasol. The big beach hotels also have guarded sections for their residents. Toilets can be found behind the beach restaurants just east of the *Jour et Nuit*, and (including a disabled one, though there's a step to get up to it) just north of *Agadir Beach Club*.

8

The Valley of the Birds

Between Boulevard Hassan II and Boulevard du 20 Août • Daily 11am–6pm • Free

As a break from the beach, and especially if you have kids to amuse, you might wander into the **Valley of the Birds**, a narrow strip of parkland, with a little aviary of exotic birds, a small herd of Barbary sheep and some other mammals, a waterfall and a children's playground. It's all very pleasant, and the lush vegetation draws a rich variety of birds throughout the year, but inevitably, some of the animal enclosures are distressingly small.

Children may also enjoy a ride on the "**tourist train**", which does a 35-minute run around town, starting from Boulevard du 20 Août at the bottom of the Valley of the Birds (every 40min; 9.15am–5pm; 18dh, child 12dh).

The Amazigh Heritage Museum

Rue de la Foire • Mon–Sat 9am–1pm & 1.30–5.15pm • 20dh

Towards the southern end of the city centre is an outdoor theatre – built along Roman odeon lines – and a pedestrian precinct of tourist shops and restaurants, where the small **Amazigh Heritage Museum** has a collection of Berber cultural artefacts, including a few old mansucripts (in Arabic, not Berber), some wooden doors and bowls, and

8

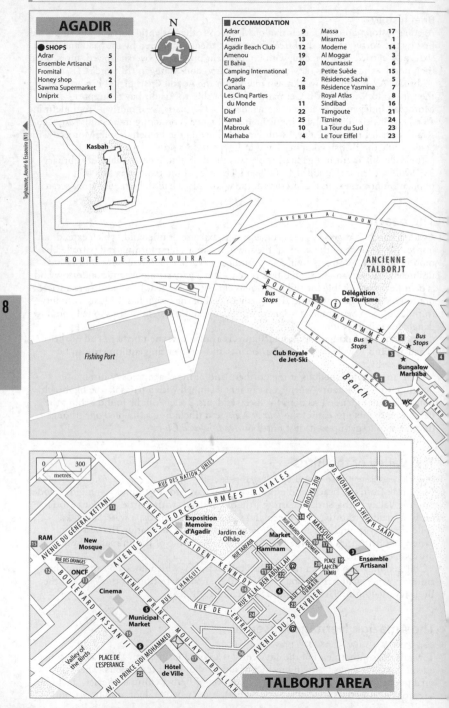

AGADIR

N

● SHOPS

Adrar	5
Ensemble Artisanal	3
Fromital	4
Honey shop	2
Sawma Supermarket	1
Uniprix	6

■ ACCOMMODATION

Adrar	9	Massa	17
Aferni	13	Miramar	1
Agadir Beach Club	12	Moderne	14
Amenou	19	Al Moggar	3
El Bahia	20	Mountassir	6
Camping International		Petite Suède	15
Agadir	2	Résidence Sacha	5
Canaria	18	Résidence Yasmina	7
Les Cinq Parties		Royal Atlas	8
du Monde	11	Sindibad	16
Diaf	22	Tamgoute	21
Kamal	25	Tiznine	24
Mabrouk	10	La Tour du Sud	23
Marhaba	4	Le Tour Eiffel	23

Taghazoute, Aourir & Essaouira (N1)

Kasbah

AVENUE AL MOUN

ROUTE DE ESSAOUIRA

ANCIENNE TALBORJT

BOULEVARD MOHAMMED

Bus Stops

Délégation de Tourisme

Fishing Port

Club Royale de Jet-Ski

RUE LA PLACE

Bus Stops

Bus Stops

Beach

Bungalow Marhaba

WC

BOULEVARD

0   300
metrès

RUE DES NATIONS UNIES

AVENUE DES FORCES ARMÉES ROYALES

B.D. MOHAMMED SHEIKH SAADI

RUE YACOUB

EL MANSOUR

Exposition Memoire d'Agadir

Jardim de Olhão

Market

RUE MAHDI IBN TOUMERT

RAM

AVENUE DU GENERAL KETTANI

AVENUE DU PRESIDENT KENNEDY

Hammam

RUE TARFAYA

PLACE LAHCEN TAMRI

Ensemble Artisanal

New Mosque

RUE DES ORANGES

ONCF

RUE CHANGUIT

RUE ALLAL BEN ABDALLAH

RUE EL HACHTOUK OUMAR

BOULEVARD HASSAN II

AVENUE PRINCE MOULAY ABDALLAH

Cinema

RUE DE L'ENTRAIDE

AVENUE DU 29 FEVRIER

Municipal Market

Valley of the Birds

PLACE DE L'ESPERANCE

AV. DU PRINCE SIDI MOHAMMED

Hôtel de Ville

TALBORJT AREA

■ **BARS & CLUBS**

Actor's	3
Disco Tan Tan	5
English Pub	4
Flamingo	7
Jour et Nuit	1, 2
Papagayo	8
Red Lion Dance Bar	6
So Night Lounge	9

● **RESTAURANTS & CAFÉS**

Des Arcades	14
Daffy	13
L'Étoile de Marrakech	7
Fishing port stalls	1
Ibtissam	10
Jour et Nuit	4, 5
Mezzo Mezzo	8
Le Miramar	2
Patisserie Tafarnout	6
La Scala	9
Select	11
SOS Poulet	17
Tour de Paris	12
Via Veneto	15
Yacht Club Restaurant du Port	3
Yacout	16

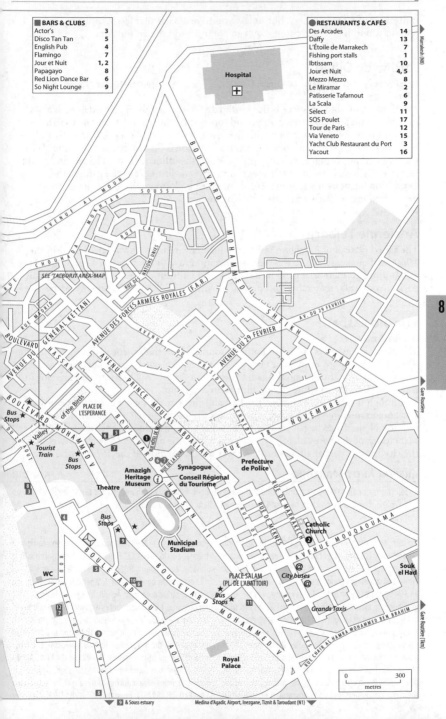

quite a lot of silver jewellery, but unless you have a particular fascination for Berber jewellery, nothing very exciting. You can see the lot in fifteen minutes.

Jardim de Olhão

Avenue Kennedy, just south of Avenue des FAR • **Jardim de Olhão** daily 2–6pm • Free • **Exposition Mémoire d'Agadir** Tues–Sat 9.30am–12.30pm & 3–6pm • 20dh

A very pleasant outdoor space is the **Jardim de Olhão**, a landscaped garden with a café-restaurant and children's playground, opened in 2003 to celebrate the fourth anniversary of Agadir's twinning with the town of Olhão in Portugal. The walls and buildings in the garden are constructed in a traditional Berber style which some claim was inspired by Portuguese architecture, though the influence is hard to see, and could just as easily have been the other way round anyway. Just next to the garden, the **Exposition Mémoire d'Agadir** has some interesting photographs of Agadir as it was before and immediately after the 1960 earthquake.

Ancienne Talborjt

The raised plateau of **Ancienne Talborjt**, which entombs the town demolished in the 1960 earthquake, stands to the west of the city centre. It's marked by a small mosque and unfinished memorial garden. Relatives of the fifteen thousand dead come to this park area to walk, remember and pray: a moving sight, even after so many years.

The old kasbah

On the hill north of the port

The city's old **kasbah** is an eight-kilometre round trip from the centre, but worth making if you have transport, or by petit taxi, for a marvellous view of Agadir and the coast. You can see the kasbah from central Agadir, with a vast Arabic "Allah–King–Nation" slogan on the slope below, in white stones, illuminated at night.

Although it survived the quake, the kasbah is little more than a bare outline of walls and an entrance arch – the latter with an inscription in Dutch and Arabic recording that the Netherlands began trading here in 1746 (capitalizing on the rich sugar plantations of the Souss plain). It's not much, but it is one of the few reminders that the city has any past at all, so complete was the destruction of the 1960 earthquake.

ARRIVAL AND DEPARTURE	AGADIR

Agadir is a reasonable transport terminal, but for many services, especially in shared grands taxis, you'll need to go to Inezgane. This can be reached by grand taxi from Pl Salam (4dh, 6dh at night), or on bus #21 or #23 from Av Mohammed V.

By air Al Massira Airport (☏ 0528 839112, ⊛ agadir -airport.com) is 25km east of Agadir. At least one bank is generally open all the time, but taxis will usually accept euros, and sometimes pounds or dollars, or will take you to an ATM en route to your hotel. Holiday companies run their own buses to meet flights and shuttle passengers to their hotels, and if you've bought a flight-only deal you could try tagging along with fellow passengers. Otherwise, grands taxis waiting outside charge a standard 200dh fare (250dh at night) to Agadir, or 150dh (200dh at night) to Inezgane (13km southeast of Agadir; see p.461), for up to six passengers. If you plan to share a fare, arrange this inside the terminal. There is no bus to downtown Agadir, but if you don't want to shell out for a grand taxi, you can get to Inezgane on local bus #37 from outside the airport building (hourly; 7am–7pm; 5dh), and from there take bus #21 or #23 or shared grand taxi (4dh) to Agadir. If you are planning to move straight on from Agadir, it's best to head straight for Inezgane, from where there's a greater choice of onward transport, especially if you intend to travel by grand taxi. The #37 drops you off right next to the grand taxi station in Inezgane; for the bus station, just walk across to the other side of the grand taxi stands; the #21 and #23 to Agadir stop around the corner on the Agadir road. Several car rental agencies have branches at the airprt, including First Car (☏ 0528 839297), Budget (☏ 0528 839101), Europcar

(☎0528 840337), Hertz (☎0528 83907) and Avis (☎0528 829244). Royal Air Maroc have an office on Av Général Kettani, opposite the junction with Bd Hassan II (☎0528 829120). In the past, airport staff at Agadir have been known to tell passengers – falsely – that valuables (such as cameras) are not allowed as hand baggage and must be carried in the hold. This is not true, and any such items are likely to disappear if not securely locked away.

Destinations Casablanca (4–5 daily; 1hr 10min); Dakhla (2 weekly; 1hr 40min).

By bus All buses serving Agadir now operate from the bleak new concrete *gare routière* at the eastern edge of town on Rue Chair el Hamra (aka Bd Abderrahim Bouabid) at the junction with Av Qadi Ayyad (☎0528 822077) 3km from Talborjt. It's around 10–12dh by petit taxi, or 4dh on bus #04, or #413 from Av Mohammed V, where the stop just east of Av Prince Sidi Mohammed is the most convenient for Talborjt. The best and most convenient bus services from Agadir (though not the cheapest) are operated by Supratours (10 Rue des Oranges ☎0528 841207) and CTM (Rue Yacoub el Mansour ☎0528 822077), and can be booked at their offices in town. Many buses will take you to **Inezgane** rather than to Agadir itself, but since Agadir's *gare routière* is so far out of the centre anyway, it doesn't actually make much difference. From Inezgane you can take local bus #21 or #23 to Bd Mohammed V, where the stop just before Av Prince Sidi Mohammed (by an "In Barbecue" fast food sign) is the most convenient for Talborjt.

Destinations Beni Mellal (1 CTM & 3 others daily; 8hr); Casablanca (10 CTM daily & others roughly hourly during the day; 8–9hr); Dakhla (3 CTM, 3 Supratours & 3 others daily; 19hr 30min); Essaouira (1 CTM & others roughly hourly during the day; 3hr 30min); Fez (3 CTM & 5 others daily; 12hr); Goulimine (9 CTM, 8 Supratours & 18 others daily; 4hr 30min); Laayoune (6 CTM, 4 Supratours & 3 others daily; 11hr); Marrakesh (13 CTM, 19 Supratours & 24 others daily; 4hr); Meknes (2 CTM & 5 others daily; 12hr); Ouarzazate (1 CTM & 2 others daily; 7hr 30min); Rabat (4 CTM & 8–10 others daily; 10–11hr); Safi (1 CTM & others roughly hourly during the day; 5–6hr); Tafraoute (1 CTM & 6 others daily; 5hr); Tangier (1 CTM & 1–2 others daily; 14–16hr); Tan Tan (8 CTM, 6 Supratours & 18 others daily; 6hr); Taroudant (1 CTM & 2 others daily; 1hr 30min); Tata (6 daily; 7hr); Tiznit (11 CTM, 8 Supratours & 17 others daily; 2hr).

By grand taxi Grands taxis use a rank a block south of the local bus station at Pl Salam (aka Pl de l'Abattoir), a longish walk or short taxi ride from Talborjt. Shared grands taxis serve Aourir (15min), Inezgane (15min), Taghazout (20min), Taroudant (1hr 15min) and Tiznit (1hr 15min). They sometimes serve other destinations, but otherwise you'll have to take one to Inezgane and get a connection there, which may be easier even for Taroudant and Tiznit, especially since drivers at Agadir have started trying to charge tourists (not Moroccans, of course) extra for their baggage. The fare in a shared taxi to Inezgane is 4dh, and grands taxis for points beyond will cost 4dh less from Inezgane than direct from Agadir, so you lose nothing by going there, and you could well get a faster connection, with no nonsense about baggage charges. As with buses, shared grands taxis from elsewhere in Morocco may leave you at **Inezgane**, from where local bus #21 or #23 runs along Bd Mohammed V, with the stop just east of Av du Prince Sidi Mohammed being the most convenient for Talborjt.

8

GETTING AROUND

Agadir is for the most part a walkable city, though you may want to use petits taxis for transport between the bus or taxi stations and Talborjt or the beach hotels. Alternatively, you can rent mopeds or motorbikes, which would also allow you to explore the beaches north and south of town.

By bus The main bus terminal is at Place Salam (Place de l'Abattoir), a couple of blocks north of the grand taxi station, but the most useful routes (see box, p.456) run along Bd Mohammed V.

Bicycle and motorbike rental Various operators rent out motorbikes, scooters and bicycles along Bd du 20 Août south of Route de l'Oued Souss, but many are cowboys. A reliable firm will rent for 24hr rather than just until nightfall, and will show full paperwork (rather than just a receipt) proving that the insurance, minimal though it might be, covers you (and passenger if necessary) and detailing help in the event of a breakdown. You can also rent from the Quick Service supermarket in the Souk Tafoukt shopping area next to the *Royal Atlas* hotel. Typically, motorbikes are 400dh/day, scooters 250dh, bicycles 120dh.

Car rental Bungalow Marhaba on Bd Mohammed V houses Budget (☎0525 060981), Europcar (☎0528 845024), Hertz (☎0528 840939), Lotus Cars (☎0528 840588), Weekend Cars (☎0528 840667), and local operator Youness Cars (☎0528 840750, ✉youness-cars @hotmail.com), of whom we've had good reports in the past. The main agencies also have branches at the airport (see opposite). Other companies include: First Car, Immeuble Oumlil, 17 Bd Hassan II, at the corner of Rue de l'Hôtel de Ville (☎0528 826796); and recommended local firm Amoudou Cars on Bd Hassan II, at the corner of Av Mouqaouama (☎0528 825010, ✉amadou.car@laposte.net), who offer a ten percent discount to Rough Guide readers renting cars for three days or more, and may do special deals in combination with accommodation at the *Petite Suède* hotel.

USEFUL BUS ROUTES

#04, #413 Anza – Avenue Mohammed V – Avenue Mouqaouama – Gare Routière
#13 Place Salam – Inezgane
#21, #23 Port – Avenue Mohammed V – Inezgane
#31 Place Salam – Avenue Mohammed V – Aourir – Imi Miki
#32 Place Salam – Avenue Mohammed V – Aourir – Taghazout
#33 Place Salam – Avenue Mohammed V – Aourir – Taghazout – Tamri
#37 Inezgane (ALSA bus station) – Agadir airport
#42 Inezgane (Agadir road) – Massa

INFORMATION

Tourist information The Délégation de Tourisme (Mon–Fri 8.30am–4.30pm; ☎0528 846377) is in Immeuble Iguenwane, on Bd Mohammed V, northwest of town towards the port; staff are helpful and generally happy to answer questions. There is also a Conseil Régional du Tourisme (Mon–Fri 8.30am–noon & 2.30–6.30pm; ☎0528 842629) in the Chamber of Commerce building on Av Hassan II near the Amazigh Heritage Museum, which is not strictly speaking a tourist information office, but staff are usually happy to give out information.

ACCOMMODATION

Most of the budget hotels are in Talborjt, which has the advantage of good shops, cafés and street life. More upmarket places are worth booking ahead in high season – Christmas/New Year, Easter, July and August – but may offer large discounts off-season. If you plan to move on more or less immediately, you might be better off staying at **Inezgane** (see p.461), where budget hotels are cheaper, and where you have a greater number of long-distance buses and grands taxis.

TALBORJT/CITY CENTRE

Aferni Av Général Kettani ☎0528 840730, ✉hotelaferni@wanadoopro.ma. It's worth asking for a room with a bathtub and balcony in this three-star hotel with a pool (heated in winter) and terrace, plus TVs and safes in each room. There's wi-fi too, but only in the lobby area. The hotel also lacks a bar, which you may consider a plus or a minus. **510dh**

Amenou 1 Rue Yacoub el Mansour ☎0528 841556. A plain and simple hotel with showers in some of the rooms, hot water round the clock, and a roof terrace in case you fancy a spot of sunbathing. On the downside, some of the beds are soft and springy, so check yours before taking the room. **90dh**

El Bahia Rue el Mahdi Ibn Toumert ☎0528 822724, ☎0528 824515. A fine little two-star hotel, beautifully modernized with three categories of room (with shower and toilet, with shower only, and with shared bathroom facilities), all with satellite TV, but not all with outside windows. The breakfast terrace is beautifully sunny, with an interestingly kitsch fountain. **200dh**

Canaria 2 Pl Lahcen Tamri ☎0528 846727. A slightly disreputable hotel, and getting rather shabby, but a reasonable fall-back if the other cheap places are full. Some rooms have en-suite showers, but there's only one shower shared between the rest. The rooms are arranged around a sunny central courtyard, so it doesn't matter that most have windows facing inwards only (exceptions are rooms 6 and 10, which have outside windows). **100dh**

Diaf Rue Allal Ben Abdallah ☎0528 825852, ☎0528 821311. The rooms here are small but everything's neat and clean, and some rooms have en-suite bathrooms. Rooms on the first floor are a lot nicer than those on the roof, however, which are a bit poky. Reservations are only accepted if taken up before 2pm, and staff may be scarce if you turn up at lunchtime. There's a handy café downstairs. **100dh**

★ **Kamal** Bd Hassan II ☎0528 842817, ⊕hotel-kamal .com. Centrally located three-star with quite large, cool rooms set round a small swimming pool. Of all the hotels in town, this one gets consistently good reports for the courtesy and efficiency of its staff. They also offer discounts for longer stays, and there are often promotional rates on offer. **465dh**

Massa Pl Lahcen Tamri ☎0528 826362. Simple rooms but clean and well looked after, around an upstairs courtyard decorated with murals, plus some drearier rooms downstairs, with shared bathroom facilities but 24hr hot water. At last check (though this can change from one year to the next), this was the cheapest option for lone travellers (60dh). **100dh**

Moderne Rue el Mahdi Ibn Toumert ☎0528 840473. Tucked away in a quiet location, and quite prim and proper. Rooms are done out in salmon pink and blue, and have showers but not toilets en suite. **160dh**

Mountassir Rue de la Jeunesse ☎0528 843228, ✉h.almountassir@menara.ma. A city-centre block that offers good value for money – the rooms are plain but decent enough, with balconies, and there's a small pool and garden. **340dh**

★ **Petite Suède** Bd Hassan II ☎0528 840779, ⊕petitesuede.com. One of the first hotels built after the earthquake, and not too far from the beach. The manager is extremely friendly and helpful, and all rooms have en-suite showers, though most have shared toilets. Some also have a balcony, and there's a sun terrace, wi-fi, and a ten percent discount for Rough Guide readers. BB **320dh**

Résidence Sacha Pl de la Jeunesse ☎0528 841167, ⓦagadir-maroc.com. Just off the town centre in a quiet square. French-managed, with a range of good-sized self-catering studios and apartments (some with private gardens), free wi-fi in public areas (and some rooms), and a small swimming pool. **490dh**

Résidence Yasmina Rue de la Jeunesse ☎0528 842660, ⓦresidence-yasmina.com. Self-catering apartments with small bedrooms but large sitting rooms and decent-sized kitchens, plus a lobby and salon done out in traditional zellij tilework, and a swimming pool and children's pool. There's often a discounted rate of one sort or another available. **566dh**

Sindibad Pl Lahcen Tamri ☎0528 823477, ⓔsinhot @menara.ma. A deservedly popular two-star hotel with a restaurant and bar, spotless a/c rooms, and a plunge pool on the roof. They normally offer discounts if you're staying three nights or more. **396dh**.

Tamgoute 38 Av Allal ben Abdallah ☎0528 847866. Located above the *Restaurant Select*, with the entrance round the back, this quiet little place has en-suite rooms that are a touch more comfortable than those in the ultra-cheapies, and only a bit more expensive. **150dh**

Tiznine 3 Rue Drarga ☎&ⓕ0528 843925. Tucked away up a side street, this little hotel is bright and gleaming, with pleasant if plain rooms, some en suite. It's slightly pricier than the other Talborjt cheapies, but worth the difference. **140dh**

La Tour du Sud Av Kennedy ☎0528 822694, ⓕ0528 824846. A small but immaculate hotel whose en-suite rooms have smoked-glass windows and little balconies, built around two courtyards with large trees growing out of them. It's worth avoiding the ground-floor rooms, however, especially on the side facing the street. **240dh**

Le Tour Eiffel 25 Av du 29 Février ☎0528 823712. This little hotel with small, simple rooms has a café-restaurant downstairs which is handy for breakfast. The bathroom facilities are shared, and the hot water supply is a bit iffy, but in theory it's on round the clock. **100dh**

MAIN BOULEVARDS – TOWARDS THE BEACH

Adrar Bd Mohammed V ☎0528 840417, ⓦhoteladrar .com. Not a very imposing building but it has charming staff and a good reputation for service, as well as a full range of facilities including pool and restaurant. The room decor is unconvincingly pseudo-Berber, but strangely pleasing nonetheless. BB **600dh**

Agadir Beach Club Route de l'Oued Souss ☎0528 844343, ⓦagadir-beach-club.net. A very grand

four-star at the southern end of the beach, with no less than seven restaurants, four bars, a nightclub, a very large pool, and loads of sports facilities. Rooms are not huge but have a/c, satellite TV and a mini-bar, and there are ramps for wheelchairs (whose users often stay here), but no specifically adapted rooms. **1235dh**

Les Cinq Parties du Monde Bd Hassan II ☎0528 845481, ⓕ0528 842504. Handy for the Pl Salam bus and grand taxi station, in a busy part of town not much frequented by tourists. The third-floor rooms are done out in red, orange and fuchsia, which is very jolly, but maybe a bit garish for some people's tastes. The first- and second-floor rooms are in a more subued shade of cream. There's wi-fi in the lobby, but not in the rooms. **320dh**

Mabrouk Bd du 20 Août ☎0528 828701/2, ⓦhmabrouk.ma. A small, friendly three-star hotel, with an attractive garden and large pool. The rooms are smartly done out in red, black, orange and cream. There's also quite a lively bar, the Red Lion (see p.459). BB **490dh**

Marhaba Bd Hassan II ☎0528 840670, ⓔhotel .marhaba125@menara.ma. An excellent-value three-star hotel with spacious rooms, wi-fi, a nice pool and gardens, and promotional deals out of season. The beach isn't too far away, but it's across a busy main road. BB **400dh**

Miramar Bd Mohammed V ☎0528 840770. The only hotel to survive the earthquake, a homely, twelve-room place, elegantly redesigned by André Paccard, doyen of the *Hôtel La Mamounia* in Marrakesh and several of King Hassan II's palaces, with a good restaurant (see p.458), but no pool. **414dh**

Al Moggar Bd Mohammed V ☎0528 842270, ⓦhotelalmoggar.com. A large, well-equipped beach-package-hotel complex, with a nightclub, a large pool, tennis courts, extensive gardens, and concrete bungalow-style rooms that are ugly without but spacious within and have balconies facing the beach. Big discounts are often available off-season; in high season (mid-June to mid-Sept), you have to take half-board. HB **1133dh**

Royal Atlas Bd du 20 Août ☎0528 294040, ⓦhotelsatlas.com. A five-star hotel which actually tries quite hard to meet that standard. It's very grand, with well-appointed rooms, friendly but laidback staff, three restaurants, three bars, and a spa. It claims to be wheelchair accessible, although it doesn't have any specially adapted rooms. Promotional rates are often available. BB **2600dh**

CAMPING

Camping International Agadir Bd Mohammed V ☎0528 841054. Reasonably well located, within easy walking distance of the centre and beach, open all year and fairly secure, with a snack bar and other facilities but there's limited shade, camper vans dominate, prices are relatively high and it's usually pretty crowded. **60dh**

8

EATING

For an international resort, Agadir has few bars, clubs or discos, outside of the large hotels. There are plenty of **cafés** and **restaurants**, for all budgets, but most of those lining the beach and the boulevards are tourist traps, with waiters outside trying to hustle in any passing foreigner who shows an interest. If your hotel doesn't provide **breakfast**, several places in Talborjt will do so (the *Ibtissam* and the *Select* for example), while many cafés around Pl Salam bus station – and the café of the *Hôtel Massa*, and its neighbour on Pl Lahcen Tamri – have stalls outside selling *harsha* and *msimmen* (Moroccan breads) to eat with a coffee and croissant.

RESTAURANTS

Inexpensive café-restaurants are concentrated in Talborjt, some with bargain set menus. There's also a scattering of cafés and mid-price restaurants on or near the beach, including two that stay open 24 hours, along with a fair range of more sophisticated places.

TALBORJT/CITY CENTRE

Des Arcades Rue Allal Ben Abdallah. The combination of a traditional-style painted stucco ceiling with glass chandeliers and seaside-blue-and-white-striped walls is a bit jarring, but the food, which includes fried fish as well as tajines and couscous, isn't bad for the price, with a good-value 50dh set menu, and snacks such as omelettes. Daily 7am–11pm.

L'Étoile de Marrakech Studiotel Afoud, Rue de la Foire ☎0528 843999. Renowned for its traditional Moroccan dishes (such as lamb tajine with prunes and almonds, 75dh), the restaurant out front is open all day, serving snacks between mealtimes, while the dinner cabaret, at the back of the hotel (with the same food at the same prices), opens at 6pm, gets going with live music at 10pm and continues until around 1am. Daily 7.30am–1am (food 7.30–10.30am, noon–3pm & 7.30–11pm).

Daffy 2 Rue des Oranges ☎0656 158516. A long-time favourite offering pavement dining, or couches around the tables inside, and reasonable set menus (55dh), plus dishes like pastilla, *mechoui* or tanjia for two if ordered in advance. Daily 9am–10pm.

Ibtissam Pl Lahcen Tamri ☎0670 128435. The best of a trio of cheapies all next to each other, handy for breakfast as well as for lunch and dinner. Serves Moroccan and international staples, with a bargain set menu (40–45dh), and vegetarian options if requested. Daily 11am–11pm.

Select 38 Rue Allal Ben Abdallah ☎0528 821116. The food here varies from mediocre to delicious, but it's always good value for the price. The set menu (45dh) is a great deal, or there are steaks, escalopes, and also juices. Daily 7.30am–10pm.

SOS Poulet (Allo Pizza) Av Moulay Abdallah, near the post office ☎0528 843047. Although at first glance it looks like two separate fast food joints, this is in fact a single establishment, where you can get chicken meals (brochettes, sandwiches, or roast – 25dh for a quarter of a roast chicken with rice or chips), as well as pizzas and pasta, to eat in or take away. They also deliver. Daily noon–midnight.

Tour de Paris 40 Bd Hassan II ☎0528 840901. Quite a high-quality restaurant, offering classic Moroccan dishes like pastilla, couscous and several tasty tajines, as well as French dishes such as duck confit (95dh) or beef noisette with prawns (120dh). Daily noon–midnight.

Via Veneto Bd Hassan II ☎0528 841467. This place used to serve the best Italian food in town; it's now been overtaken by new outfits such as *Mezzo Mezzo*, but it still rustles up decent wood-oven pizzas (35–60dh), and other Italian dishes such as *osso bucco* (120dh). Daily 11am–4pm & 5pm–midnight.

MAIN BOULEVARDS/TOWARDS THE BEACH

Fishing port stalls Outside Port d'Agadir. Not on a par with their equivalents in Essaouira, but the gathering of stalls here will do you a freshly caught fish grilled over charcoal for not very much money – 34dh for shrimp, squid or whiting, 300dh for lobster, crawfish or king prawns. Daily winter noon–7pm, summer noon–11pm.

Jour et Nuit Bd Tawada (on the beach off Rue de la Plage) ☎0528 840248. International-style dishes such as lamb chops (70dh), steaks (70dh) and roast chicken (50dh), and snacks including assorted sandwiches and a range of salads, plus a bar. There's a slightly posher branch (without a bar) in a 1930s-style building just 50m to the north. Daily 24hr.

Mezzo Mezzo 19 Bd Hassan II ☎0528 848819. Agadir's poshest pizzeria, with a wide selection of wood-oven pizzas (50–110dh), and dishes made with their own fresh pasta, such as spinach and ricotta ravioli (90dh), all served in cosy modern surroundings. Daily 7.30pm–midnight.

★ **Le Miramar** Hôtel Miramar, Bd Mohammed V ☎0528 840770. The city's most chic restaurant – a beautifully decorated place overlooking the fishing port. Fine international cuisine, particularly fish and seafood, including lobster bisque (120dh) and grilled sole (180dh). Daily noon–2pm & 7.30–10pm.

La Scala Bd de l'Oued Souss ☎0528 846773. This well-regarded upmarket restaurant specializes in Mediterranean cuisine, including modern dishes such as duck with ginger and orange (320dh for two people), or salmon *paupiette* (rolled up and stuffed with dill; 150dh), all served on a large terrace surrounded by trees. Daily noon–3pm & 7pm–midnight.

Yacht Club Restaurant du Port Port d'Agadir ☎0528 843708. An excellent place for fresh fish and seafood – as you'd expect from the location inside the fishing port. Specialities include fillet of John Dory with orange sauce (90dh), or fish brochettes (80dh). For some reason their alcohol licence has been revoked, so the only drinks available are water, juice or soda pops. Take your passport, as you have to go through customs. Daily noon–3pm & 7–10pm.

PATISSERIES

Patisserie Tafarnout Bd Hassan II at Rue de la Foire ☎ 0528 844450, ⓦ tafarnout.com. Agadir's poshest patisserie, the place to indulge yourself with utterly sinful pastries such as raspberry mousse on a sponge base

(15dh), or just a common or garden coffee and croissant. Daily 7am–10.15pm.

Yacout Av du 29 Février between Rue de l'Entraide and Rue Prince Moulay Abdallah ☎ 0528 847588. Patisserie selling excellent almond-stuffed Moroccan favourites such as corne de gazelle (130dh/kg). It also has a café and garden, great for a tea and pastry, but don't bother with the set menu (65dh). Daily 7am–10pm.

BARS AND NIGHTLIFE

The Jour et Nuit restaurant (see opposite) has a **bar** open 24 hours. **Nightclubs** get going around 11pm or midnight, and stay open till 3 or 4am, or later, depending on how many people are still there; entry tends to be 100dh, but some clubs charge 200dh; this may include your first drink, but otherwise expect to pay as much as 80–100dh for a beer. The club scene in Agadir can be quite sleazy, and it's a good idea in the more popular clubs to pay for your drinks as you buy them rather than running up a tab to pay at the end of the evening, when you may be too drunk to notice the addition of extraneous items. Prostitution is rife (at the Flamingo and the Papagayo, for example) but it's illegal, to the extent that girls and punters travel in separate taxis to avoid police attention (if they travel together, the cab driver may flash police en route to alert them), and clampdowns are not unknown.

Actor's Hôtel Royal Atlas, Bd du 20 Août ☎ 0661 268900. One of Agadir's top nightclubs, with guest DJs, a variety of sounds and a mixed crowd; Fri & Sat 150dh including one drink, Sun–Thurs 100dh; entry may reach 200–250dh for special occasions or top-name DJs. Nightly 11pm–3am.

Disco Tan Tan Hôtel Almohades, Bd du 20 Août ☎ 0528 840233. Long-established hotel disco, and generally a safe bet. Not one of the "in" clubs in Agadir, but it has the advantage of being nearer to town than most of the others, and usually charges for drinks rather than entry. Nightly 11pm–3am.

English Pub Bd du 20 Août ☎ 0528 847390, ⓦ english-pub-agadir-morocco.com. Full English breakfast served all day (75dh), live English footie on the telly, karaoke every night, free wi-fi and a range of lagers (no bitter, however) make this a home from home for English tourists determined not to go native. It also doubles up as the local British consulate. Daily 7am–1.30pm.

Flamingo in the Agadir Beach Club, Bd du 20 Août, ☎ 0528 844343. Lively if rather seedy nightclub attached

to one of the bigger beach package hotels, and very popular with Moroccans as well as foreigners. Entry 100dh. Nightly 11pm–3am.

Papagayo Tikida Beach Hotel, Bd du 20 Août, ☎ 0528 845400. Very lively with a mix of Western and a few Arabic pop sounds, and they put on a decent light show. It's known for prostitution, and entry is a bit steep at 200dh, though that includes one drink. Nightly 11pm–3am.

Red Lion Dance Bar Mabrouk Hôtel, Bd du 20 Août ☎ 0528 828701. Not a discotheque, but a bar with an Arabic band – it opens early, around 8pm, but you won't find anyone dancing much before midnight. Entry 100dh, including one drink. Nightly 8pm–2am.

So Night Lounge Sofitel Hotel, Baie des Palmiers, Founty, ☎ 0528 82008. Agadir's coolest nightclub, the furthest from town and with the highest entry fee, featuring a live band until around 1.30am, and DJs thereafter. Sun–Thurs 300dh, Fri & Sat 500dh. Nightly 11pm–3am.

DIRECTORY

Banks and exchange There are many banks with ATMs on Av Général Kettani between Bd Hassan II and Bd Mohammed V, plus BMCE and Banque Populaire on Av Kennedy near the junction of Av du 29 Février in Talborjt. Forex bureaux include Change Err, 31 Av Kennedy (Mon–Sat 8.30am–9pm, Sun 10am–9pm), and Currency Exchange Point, on the beach 100m north of Jour et Nuit restaurant (supposedly daily 10am–10pm, but often closed).

Cinema Cine Sahara on Pl Lahcen Tamri in Talborjt is very cheap and specializes in Bollywood epics and martial arts action films.

Consulates Ireland (honorary consul), Hôtel Kenzi Europa, Bd du 20 Août (☎ 0528 821212, ⓔ mahfoud @kenzi-hotles.com); UK (honorary consul), English Pub, Bd 20 Août ☎ 0528 841219.

Dentist Dr Noureddine Touhami, Immeuble M2, Apt 4, second floor (behind SOS Pêcheurs), Av Prince Moulay Abdallah (☎ 0528 846320), by appointment only

Doctors and clinics Most of the big hotels can provide addresses for English-speaking doctors. Current recommendations include Dr Mustapha Benjelloun, Immeuble Tinmal, Rue des FAR (☎ 0528 843737). Clinique al Massira, on Av Prince Moulay Abdallah at the junction of Av du 29 Février (☎ 0528 843238) has 24hr emergency service.

Festival July's Timitar Festival (ⓦ festival-timitar-agadir .blogspot.com), dedicated to nomadic music, is not on a par with Essaouira's (see p.307), but draws musicians from all over southern Morocco, as well as North and West Africa, France, Spain and even Latin America. Agadir also has a small film festival in February (ⓦ festivalagadir.com), at

8

SHOPPING IN AGADIR

CRAFTS AND SOUVENIRS

Prices for crafts and souvenirs in Agadir are generally high. Good first stops are **Adrar**, 30 Av Prince Moulay Abdallah (daily 8am–8pm), which has fixed, marked prices, although some of its "Moroccan" souvenirs actually come from India, and **Uniprix**, at the corner of Boulevard Hassan II and Avenue Prince Sidi Mohammed (daily 8.15am–1pm & 2.15–8.15pm), which sell goods at fixed prices, as does the chaotic **Ensemble Artisanal** (Mon–Fri 9am–7pm, though individual shops may open later, close for lunch or shut earlier) on Avenue du 29 Février, just north of Place Lahcen Tamri. There are stalls selling crafts in the Souk el Had (see below).

FOOD AND DRINK

For food and drink, **Sawma Supermarket**, 1 Rue Hôtel de Ville, just off Boulevard Hassan II near Rue de la Foire, has a good selection, and **Uniprix** (see above) also sells the cheapest booze, along with general provisions, hidden away at the back behind the clothes and tourist tat. The biggest supermarket is **Marjane**, just out of town on the Inezgane road. The Souk el Had and the market in Talborjt (see below) are good for fresh produce. The **honey shop** at 129 Rue Marrakech, by the junction with Avenue Mouqaouama, sells various kinds of honey, and olive and argan oil. In Talborjt, **Fromital** at 6 Rue Fal Ould Omair (daily 8am–6pm; ❿fromital.com) purveys its own excellent, locally produced cheeses (also available at big supermarkets elsewhere in the country).

MARKETS

The **Municipal Market** (daily 9am–8pm) is a two-storey concrete block in the centre of town between Avenue des FAR and Avenue Prince Sidi Mohammed, with a display of wet fish downstairs cheek by jowl with fossils and handicrafts. Upstairs, it's mostly souvenir shops with rather high prices. **Talborjt** has a plain and simple little food market (daily 8am–6pm) on Rue Mahdi Ibn Toumert just northwest of Place Lahcen Tamri, selling mostly fruit and veg.

Agadir's most impressive market is the **Souk el Had**, in a massive walled enclosure on Rue Chair al Hamra (Tues–Sun 8am–6pm), selling fruit, vegetables, household goods and clothes, with a few tourist stalls thrown in. Sunday is the big day, when it spreads out over the neighbouring streets, as people come from all over the region to buy and sell their wares.

the Rialto cinema behind the municipal market, which otherwise appears to be out of action.

Golf Agadir has four golf clubs, all southeast of town. Agadir Royal Golf, 12km out on the Route d'Aït Melloul (❿0528 248551), is the oldest-established, and generally considered the finest course, now eighteen-hole. The others are off the Inezgane road at km7: Golf des Dunes (❿0528 834690), with three nine-hole courses; Golf du Soleil (❿0528 337329, ❿golfdusoleil.com), also with three nine-hole courses; and Golf de l'Ocean (❿0528 824146), the newest, with an ocean view, and 27 holes amid dunes and trees.

Hammam To sweat out the grime in Talborjt, the Bain Maure Essalama, on Rue Mahdi Ibn Toumert, is open daily for women 6am–6pm, and for men 6pm–midnight.

Internet access In Talborjt, there's Streamjet at 19 Rue Allal Ben Abdallah (Mon–Fri 10.30am–1pm & 2–10pm, Sun 2–10pm, Sat closed; 5dh/hr), and Futurnet on the first floor of a building on Av Kennedy opposite the mosque at the junction of Av du 29 Février (daily 9am–11pm; 7dh/hr). There are also a few places on Rue de Meknes by Pl Salam bus station.

Pharmacies There's a night pharmacy at the town hall behind the main post office, and a list of *pharmacies de garde* (chemists open all night) posted in the windows of most town pharmacies.

Post offices The main post office is right at the top of Av Sidi Mohammed (Mon–Fri 8am–4.15pm, stamps and some other services until 6pm; Sat 9am–1pm; Ramadan 9am–3pm). There's a branch post office on Av du 29 Février in Talborjt, opposite the Ensemble Artisanal, with similar hours, and a very small one on Bd du 20 Août near the junction of Chemin de Oued Souss (Mon–Fri 9am–12.30pm).

Around Agadir

Aside from Inezgane, which is mainly of interest for its transport connections, there are a few places within easy day-trip reach of Agadir, although many of the places to its north in particular are worth an overnight stay at least.

Inezgane

INEZGANE, on the north bank of the Oued Souss, is almost a suburb of Agadir, just 13km distant. The two could hardly be more different, though, for Inezgane is wholly Moroccan, and is a major transport hub for the region – much more so than Agadir – with buses and grands taxis going to most southern destinations. Across Avenue Mokhtar Soussi from the *gare routière*, through the arcades, is a wonderful city **market**, full of fruit, veg, spices, knick-knacks and traditional cosmetics.

ARRIVAL AND DEPARTURE   INEZGANE

By bus Local buses #21 and #23 (very frequent, both running along Av Mohammed V) and frequent grands taxis (from Pl Salam; 4dh a place) connect Agadir with Inezgane, and #42 runs to Massa. The buses will drop you on the Agadir road in the centre of Inezgane. Other local buses, such as #37 to the airport, use the local bus station by the *gare routière*. The *gare routière* is off Av Mokhtar Soussi, a wide street with arcades on both sides, which runs from the Agadir road to the central Pl al Massira. Intercity buses serving destinations across the country use the *gare routière*, with the exception of CTM and Supratours buses, which stop just outside it, by their offices on Av Mokhtar Soussi.

Destinations Agadir (very frequent local buses; 15min); Casablanca (12 CTM and 23 others daily; 9hr); Fez (4 CTM and 8 others daily; 12hr); Er Rachidia (daily; 12hr); Goulimine (11 CTM, 7 Supratours and 10 others daily; 4hr 30min); Laayoune (10 CTM, 5 Supratours and 4 others daily; 11hr); Marrakesh (16 CTM, 16 Supratours and 18 others daily; 3hr 30min); Meknes (4 CTM and 6 others daily; 11hr); Ouarzazate (1 CTM and 5 others daily; 7hr); Rabat (6 CTM and 7 others daily; 10hr 30min); Sidi Ifni (2 daily; 3hr 30min); Tafraoute (1 CTM & 6 others daily; 5hr); Tangier (1 CTM and 5 others daily; 15hr), Tan Tan (10 CTM, 6 Supratours and 7 others daily; 6hr); Taroudant (1 CTM and 3 others daily; 1hr 15min) and Tiznit (13 CTM, 7 Supratours and 16 others daily; 2hr).

Grands taxis Depart from the *gare routière*, off Av Mokhtar Soussi.

Destinations: Agadir (15min); Essaouira (2hr 30min); Goulimine (4hr 30min); Laayoune (9hr); Marrakesh (3hr); Massa (45min); Ouled Teima (40min); Ouled Berhil (2hr); Sidi Ifni (3hr 30min); Tan Tan (6hr 15min); Taroudant (1hr 15min) and Tiznit (2hr).

ACCOMMODATION AND EATING

If you arrive late at Agadir airport, and want to head straight on, you could do a lot worse than stay here, rather than Agadir.

IN TOWN

Hagounia 9 Av Mokhtar Soussi ☎0528 832783. Right by the bus station at the junction with the Inezgane–Agadir road, this place is very well located, and its rooms are reasonable enough, with en-suite showers and 24hr hot water, and the choice of a balcony overlooking the main road or a quieter room at the back. **170dh**

De Paris 30 Bd Mohammed V ☎0808 375508. Pictures and maps of Paris decorate this ultra-cheap and very simple hotel, where the rooms have windows looking inward only (so you may want to opt for the top floor, which gets more direct daylight), but some have their own bathrooms and there's hot water 5pm–10am. The restaurant (daily 11am–3pm & 5.30–10pm) is also very inexpensive, with 27dh couscous, among other dishes. **70dh**

THE SOUSS ESTUARY

If the Oued Souss is flowing (it often dries out), the **estuary** is of interest to **birdwatchers**. The northern banks of the river have good views of a variety of waders and wildfowl including greater flamingo (most evident in Aug and Sept), spoonbill, ruddy shelduck, avocet, greenshank and curlew, while the surrounding scrubby banks also have large numbers of migrant warblers and Barbary partridge. The **Royal Palace**, built in the 1980s in an imaginative blend of traditional and modern forms, can be glimpsed from the riverbank, but is not open to visitors.

To reach the estuary by road, take the Inezgane road out of Agadir (bus #21 or #23 from Avenue Mohammed V), to the junction 7km out of town, where a sign announces the beginning of Inezgane's city limits; turn right here, opposite a military base, but be warned if wandering around the woods here that there have been reports of robberies, sometimes at knifepoint, so leave your valuables behind, and don't go alone.

This is also the location of three golf courses (see opposite), and **Souss Park** (daily: Nov–Feb 9am–5pm; March–May & Sept–Oct 9am–6pm; June–Aug 9am–7pm; 220dh; free shuttle bus from town; ☎0546 153579), where you can harness up and swing through the treetops like Tarzan.

8

Al Qods 50 Pl al Massira ☏0528 836322. Friendly, reasonably clean (though some rooms are a bit musty), and handy for the market and bus station. Some rooms have an en-suite shower but the cheapest have shared bathroom facilities, though there's hot water round the clock. It's worth checking the mattresses before you take a room, as some of them are a bit lumpy. **110dh**

ON THE AGADIR ROAD

La Pergola Inezgane–Agadir road (east side, 4km from Inezgane, 8km from Agadir) ☏0528 271801, ⓦlapergola.ma. Charming little French-run hotel, formerly a colonial villa, with parking facilities and

well-appointed rooms. It's very handy for visiting the Souss estuary (see box, p.461). It's also worth coming here for the restaurant (daily noon–3pm & 7.30–10pm; expensive but with a 145dh set menu, and deals for full- or half-board), which serves classic French cuisine and, when on form, is memorable – the menu changes daily, depending on what they select in the market. **264dh**

Le Provençal Inezgane–Agadir road, on the edge of Inezgane (west side, 2km from Inezgane, 10km from Agadir) ☏0528 832612, ⓦleprovencaleagadir.com. A French-style *auberge*, with bungalow-like rooms arranged around a medium-sized swimming pool and a well-kept garden with flowers and banana trees, and also a bar. **242dh**

The Massa lagoon

The **Massa lagoon**, on the coast around 40km south of Agadir, is part of the Souss–Massa National Park, and is one of Morocco's most important **bird habitats** (see box opposite), attracting unusual desert visitors and often packed with flamingos, avocets and ducks. The best times to visit are March to April or October to November. Most transport takes you to Massa village, from which you can walk along the oued, an area rich in birdlife, and to the beach at **Sidi Rbat**. It was here in 682 AD, according to legend, that the Arab general Okba Ibn Nafi (see p.531), after sweeping westward with his armies to take North Africa for Islam, famously rode his horse into the ocean, declaring before God that only the sea prevented him from going further. The beach itself is often misty and overcast – even when Agadir is basking in the sun – but on a clear day, it's as good as anywhere else and the walks are enjoyable.

ARRIVAL AND DEPARTURE   MASSA

Transport of your own is a considerable advantage for getting to and exploring the lagoon area. Otherwise, you could charter a **taxi** in Agadir or Inezgane for the day, or

take **bus** #42 (every 30min till 7pm) or a grand taxi to Massa from Inezgane.

ACCOMMODATION

Ksar Massa ☏0661 280319, ⓦksarmassa.com. A gorgeous and isolated kasbah-style resort with a swimming pool, hammam, restaurant and beach, not to mention sumptuous rooms done out with different colours

and materials in each, mostly inspired by different parts of Morocco, and the option of sleeping in a deluxe *caidal* (Bedouin-style tent) instead. BB tent **1100dh**, double **1900dh**

North of Agadir

The coast road north from Agadir passes first through the industrial suburb of **Anza**. Beyond that is a great swathe of **beach**, interrupted here and there by headlands and for the most part deserted.

Aourir and Tamraght

Eleven kilometres north of Agadir, the road reaches **AOURIR**, where it branches inland to Paradise Valley and Immouzer des Ida Outanane (see p.466). Aourir and its sister village of **TAMRAGHT**, a kilometre beyond, are jointly known as "Banana Village" after the banana groves that divide them; the roadside stalls sell local bananas in season.

Aourir and Tamraght share "**Banana Beach**", a sandy strip, broken by the Oued Tamraght, the dividing line between the two villages. Banana Beach is used by surfers, and is especially good for the less experienced, with slower, fatter breaks than those at points to the north.

Around 2km north of Tamraght, a prominent rocky headland, **Les Roches du Diable**,

---

THE MASSA LAGOON: BIRDWATCHING

Oued Massa has a rich mix of habitats and draws a fabulous array of birds. The **sandbars** are visited in the early morning by flocks of sandgrouse (black-bellied and spotted) and often shelter large numbers of cranes; the **ponds** and **reedbed** margins conceal various waders, such as black-tailed godwit, turnstone, dunlin and snipe, as well as the black-headed bush shrike (*tschagra*) and little crake; the deeper **open waters** provide feeding grounds for greater flamingo, spoonbill, white stork and black-winged stilt; and overhead the skies are patrolled by marsh harrier and osprey. The surrounding **scrubby areas** also hold black-headed bush shrike and a variety of nocturnal mammals such as Egyptian mongoose, cape hare and jackal, while **Sidi Rbat** has a local population of Mauritanian toads.

Twenty kilometres inland, the **Barrage Youssef Ben Tachfine** is an enormous freshwater reservoir where possible sightings include black wheatear and rock dove.

---

is flanked by further good beaches, including **Cro Cro Beach** to its north, where surfboards can be rented. Also just north of Tamraght, Amodou Cheval (☎ 0662 200474, ⊚ amodoucheval.com) offer **horse treks** into the mountains behind the coast.

ARRIVAL AND DEPARTURE — AOURIR AND TAMRAGHT

By bus and grand taxi Buses #32 and #33 stop here on their way between Taghazout and Agadir. Aourir is also served by #31, and by shared grands taxis. Shared taxis and minivans serve Paradise Valley and Immouzer, particularly quite early in the day, with usually none at lunchtime and few in the afternoon.

ACCOMMODATION

8

Camping Atlantica Km14 ☎ 0528 315592, ⊚ atlanticaparc.com. A huge new campsite, full of retired Europeans in large camper vans, on little plots divided by hedges, giving it the air of a prim small-town suburb on the Continent – there are even prefab bungalows. It has a large pool and direct access to Cro Cro Beach, and there isn't much shade as yet, but trees planted between the plots mean there should be in a year or two. Camping 90dh, bungalow 800dh
Littoral Km 12 (in the centre of Aourir) ☎ 0528 314726, ⊚ hotellittoral.com. This two-star is Aourir's best hotel, just north of the Immouzer turn-off, on the inland side of

the road, with spotless rooms, tiled floors, self-catering suites, a restaurant and a pool. It's an amazing bargain compared to Agadir's hostelries. 310dh
Riad Imourane Km15 ☎ 0670 052839, ⊚ riadimourane@gmail.com. This lovely little place is 2km north of Tamraght, a block off the main road on the landward side, and not visible from it. It's a lovely villa, and even more of a bargain than the *Littoral*, with immaculate and prettily decorated rooms set around a small pool, with beautiful tiled floors, carpets and tasteful traditional decor throughout. BB 350dh

EATING

Baraka Aourir, 200m north of the Immouzer turn-off, opposite the Afriquia petrol station ☎ 0528 314074. Particularly at weekends, people come up from Agadir to eat at the row of roadside café-restaurants here, of which this is the best. You can have delicious chicken, beef, lamb or goat tajines, or *mechoui* (all at

160dh/kg – a quarter kilo is fine for one person), served on an upstairs terrace. Daily noon–11pm.
Hôtel Littoral ☎ 0528 314726. The restaurant at the *Hôtel Littoral* offers a variety of fish and pasta dishes, including pesto (40dh) or Napolitana (35dh) for vegetarians, and has an 80dh set menu. Daily 11.30am–3pm & 6.30–10pm.

Taghazout

Eighteen kilometres from Agadir is the fishing village of **TAGHAZOUT** (Tarhazoute, or even Taghagant). At one time Morocco's hippy resort *par excellence*, it is now the country's main surfing resort instead, but the laidback vibe and friendly relationship between villagers and tourists remains. Several surf shops rent out, sell or repair boards, and sell surfing accoutrements (the longest established is Free Surf on Rue Sidi Said Ouhmed, just opposite the main square).

The main movers and shakers on the surfing scene are British firm Surf Maroc (see p.464), who rent out equipment from their office at *Taghazout Villa*, and offer surf guiding and tuition along with accommodation in Taghazout. They also rent out apartments at surfing spots further north.

ARRIVAL AND DEPARTURE TAGHAZOUT

By bus and grand taxi Taghazout is served by local buses #32 (half-hourly) and #33 (approximately hourly) from Pl Salam in Agadir via Bd Mohammed V. There are also frequent intercity buses in each direction between Agadir and Essaouira (and beyond), most of which will stop here, and shared grands taxis to Pl Salam, which will drop you off on Bd Mohammed V on their way through Agadir if you ask them to.

ACCOMMODATION

Local firms rent out apartments, typically at around 250dh a night for a one-bedroom apartment, 350dh for a two-bedroom place, but you may be able to find a cheaper deal by renting a room from a local family – you'll need to haggle, but two people should be able to get a room for 150–200dh a night or less, especially if staying for a week or more. Surf Maroc's two places, listed here, will give you a room if you just turn up, so long as they aren't booked up – it's wiser to book ahead.

L'Auberge Taghazout main beach ☎ 0528 200272, bookings from UK ☎ 01794 322 709, ⊛ surfmaroc .co.uk/auberge. Once a guesthouse for hippies on the beach, this place just grows and grows, with new facilities all the time, but it still manages to be easy-going, informal and friendly, and a delightful place to stay, with small but pleasant rooms, hot-water showers, a roof terrace, wi-fi, a movie room (often as not showing surfing films) and a restaurant downstairs (see below). BB **500dh**

Taghazout Villa Hash Point ☎ 0528 200368, bookings from UK ☎ 01794 322 709, ⊛ surfmaroc.co.uk/ taghazoutvilla. Larger rooms than the *Auberge*, with the option of a dorm bed too, and they serve dinner. There's free tea and (instant) coffee all day, and they even have yoga classes on the terrace, which has great views over Anchor Point. The ground floor has a communal lounge and wi-fi. All in all, it's fun and well run. BB dorm **350dh**, double **700dh**

EATING AND DRINKING

Small restaurants in the village serve up grilled fresh fish and fish tajines as well as the usual Moroccan fare, and typical tourist breakfasts. Prices nowadays are higher than at equivalent places in Agadir.

Aftas Just next to l'Auberge. A juice bar serving juices and smoothies at 15dh for a quarter-litre, 25dh for half a litre, although most of the juices are actually just orange juice with a few morsels of other fruit added and whizzed in a blender. They also have breakfasts for 30dh. Daily 8.30am–10pm.

L'Auberge ☎ 0528 200272. Dishes on offer at the restaurant here include a number of vegetarian options such as falafel in pitta bread with all the trimmings (45dh) or chickpea and vegetable curry with couscous (45dh). Indeed, the food here makes a nice change from the standard dishes

sold at all the other restaurants in town. There's also a set menu for 80dh. Daily 8am–10pm.

Café Restaurant Tenerife ☎ 0673 325568. This is one of several very similar restaurants on the main road just north of the bus stop. Among the offerings are breakfasts at 20–30dh, and dishes such as squid tajine (50dh). Daily 7am–10pm.

Panorama ☎ 0602 179675. A simple restaurant overlooking the beach at the south end of the village. Dishes include fish kebabs (50dh) or fried pawns (50dh), or there's a set menu for 95dh. Daily 8am–9pm.

North of Taghazout

North of Taghazout, **25km Plage** (its distance from Agadir) is an attractive beach by a rocky headland, with good surfing. From here on to Cap Rhir, a stretch also known as **Paradis Plage**, are many little beaches, with caves on the rocky outcrops, including a really superb strand at Amesnaz, 33km from Agadir.

Cap Rhir (41km from Agadir) is distinguished by its 1926 French-built lighthouse and a **surfing** spot called **Boilers**, a powerful right break named after the relic of a shipwreck that's perched on an island: the paddle-out between the wreck and the shore demands good duckdiving or immaculate timing to avoid being washed up by sets. **Draculas**, a fast, shallow right named after its pincushion of sea urchins, breaks just inshore of Boilers. The whole area, together with **TAMRI** village and **lagoon**, 3km north, is good for **birdwatching** – including the rare bald ibis, Madeiran and Bulwer's petrels, Cory's and Manx

RIGHT ROCK ARCH, LEGZIRA BEACH, TAGHAZOUT (P.496) >

SURFING AROUND TAGHAZOUT

For right-footed surfers, the points just north of Taghazout are an absolute paradise, with a cluster of excellent right-hand breaks. Six kilometres north of the village, **Killers**, named after the killer whales which are often seen here, has one of the most consistent breaks, a powerful, perfectly peeling charger which breaks over a cliff shelf. **Source**, just south of Killers, is so called for the fresh water bubbling up underneath it. **Anchor Point**, just north of Taghazout, has long waves and big breaks, while at the north end of the village beach itself, **Hash Point** is supposedly used by those too stoned to make it to the others. A number of places in Taghazout, such as Almugar Surf Shop by the bus stop, rent and repair surfing equipment.

There are also good surf spots north and south of Taghazout, notably at **Banana Beach** between Aourir and Tamraght (see p.462), and **Cro Cro Beach** just north of Tamraght (see p.463), and at **Cap Rhir** near Tamri (see p.464). Further information about surf spots around Taghazout can be found on the Surf Maroc website at ⓦsurfmaroc.co.uk.

---

shearwaters, gannets, common scoter and Audouin's gulls – but we've heard of birdwatchers being menaced here by youths, so it's best not to come alone. Tamri's excellent bananas are sold at roadside stalls, and there are cafés for other sorts of sustenance.

The continuation of this route along the N1 is covered in Chapter four, in a north–south direction from Essaouira (see pp.307–309). For much of the way the road runs inland, with just the occasional *piste* leading down to the sea.

ARRIVAL AND DEPARTURE   TAMRI

By bus Tamri is at the end of local bus route #33 from Agadir and Taghazoute, which runs approximately hourly.

Frequent intercity buses run south to Agadir, and north to Essaouira, Casablanca and beyond, but may not always stop.

Inland to Paradise Valley and Immouzer

The trip up to **Immouzer des Ida Outanane** – via **Paradise Valley**, a beautiful palm-lined gorge – is a superb excursion from Agadir. It is feasible in a day (Immouzer is 62km from Agadir) but it is more enjoyable to stay at one of the *auberges* or camp in the valley.

The 7002 road to Immouzer leaves the N1 coast road at Aourir, 12km north of Agadir (make sure you take the right-hand fork in the village – the left-hand one is a dead-end). A scenic surfaced road connects Immouzer with the N8 Agadir–Marrakesh road, allowing easy access from Ameskroud, Taroudant or Marrakesh.

Paradise Valley

Paradise Valley begins around 10km east of Aourir, a deep, palm-lined gorge, with a river snaking along the base. There's a well-marked 2.7-kilometre walking trail at around 28km from Aourir, or you can hire a mule to explore the valley's Berber villages, and it's a glorious place to camp, though pitch your tent well away from the riverbed in case of flash floods.

ARRIVAL AND DEPARTURE   PARADISE VALLEY

By public transport Trucks, minibuses and shared taxis between Aourir and Immouzer will set you down at

Paradise Valley on request, and will pick you up if not full.

ACCOMMODATION

Auberge Bab Immouzer 2.5km above Paradise Valley ☎0528 216395, ⓦaubergebabimmouzer .com. Not quite such good value as the other *auberges*, nor as well kept, though it benefits from a large swimming pool surrounded by a spacious sun terrace, well hidden away from the road. There are good views

from the restaurant (daily 8am–8pm; tajines 50–60dh), but the small windows in the rooms mean that they don't share it, and the cheaper rooms don't really have a view at all. 250dh

Auberge la Bonne Franquette Aqseri (5km above Paradise Valley) ☎0528 823191. A couple of kilometres further up the road than the other *auberges*, this French-farmhouse-style *auberge* has five very charming split-level bungalows (sleeping area upstairs, sitting area downstairs), a pool and a French restaurant. BB **550dh**

★ **Auberge le Panoramic** 3.5km above Paradise Valley ☎0528 216709, ⓦhotelpanoramic.e-monsite .com. This *auberge* certainly lives up to its name, with impressive views down the valley, and a panoramic terrace where you can take lunch. There's another panoramic terrace on the roof of its accommodation wing, which is just across the road, boasting a swimming pool and its own little fruit orchard. It's run by a charming family, and has recently been refurbished – of the new rooms, room 1

boasts the best view. It's worth taking half-board here, unless you plan to eat at one of the other *auberges*. The restaurant is open 8am–midnight (tajines 50dh). **200dh**

Tifrit 3km above Paradise Valley (500m below Auberge le Panoramic) ☎0528 216708, ⓦhotel-tifrit.com. Run by the same family as the *Panoramic*, and set among palms and olives, this small *auberge* has cool rooms, a swimming pool, and fine Moroccan meals on its terrace (restaurant daily 7am–midnight; tajines 55dh); they also sell locally made honey and argan oil. Like its sister *auberge*, this one was undergoing an upgrade at time of research, which will result in the rooms being larger, en suite, and probably around 100dh more expensive. **200dh**

Immouzer des Ida Outanane

From Paradise Valley, a further 20km of winding mountain road takes you to the village of **IMMOUZER DES IDA OUTANANE**, a small regional and market centre (of the Ida Outanane tribe, as its full name suggests) tucked away in a westerly outcrop of the Atlas. The **waterfall**, for which the village was renowned, is nearby, and was best seen at its foot, 4km downhill to the northwest. Unfortunately the falls have been very adversely affected by drought over the last few years; tight control of irrigation now reduces the cascade on most occasions to a trickle, with the villagers "turning on" the falls for special events only. However, the petrified canopy of the falls is of interest in its own right, and there's a full **plunge pool**.

The whole area is perfect for walkers. A four-kilometre surfaced road twists down to the foot of the falls, with cafés and souvenir stalls on both sides of the riverbed. A path from the lowest point in the garden of the *Hôtel des Cascades* follows a water channel across cliffs (it's then possible to scramble down into the olive groves, but it isn't a route for the timid or unfit, and ascending again is harder still). Several of the staff at the hotel can help you spot local birdlife, including golden eagles and crag martins.

In Immouzer village, there's a **souk** every Thursday. The local speciality is honey, made by bees that browse on wild thyme, lavender and other mountain herbs. There's also a five-day honey moussem in late July or early to mid-August. Note if you are considering buying honey here that it may well be illegal for you to import it into your home country.

ARRIVAL AND DEPARTURE IMMOUZER DES IDA OUTANANE

By public transport From Agadir, take a grand taxi or city bus to Aourir, from where there are shared grands taxis and minibuses to Immouzer, though mostly on Thursday for the weekly souk (other days you may have a long wait, though you should be able to get a paid lift on the way down).

ACCOMMODATION

★ **Des Cascades** Signposted from the main square ☎0528 826016, ⓦcascades-hotel.net. *Hôtel des Cascades* is delightful, set amid gardens of vines, apple and olive trees, roses and hollyhocks, with a panorama of the mountains rolling down to the coast (all rooms have a balcony and a share of the view), and a spectacular path down to the foot of the falls. The food, too, is memorable and there's a swimming pool (summer only) and tennis court. The hotel can organize trekking on foot or by donkey, maintains *gîtes* to overnight in, and has arrangements with families further afield to put up guests. **572dh**

Taroudant

With its majestic, tawny-brown and honey-gold circuit of walls, **TAROUDANT** is one of the most elegant towns in Morocco. Its position at the heart of the fertile Souss valley has always given it a commercial and political importance, and the Saadians briefly made it their capital in the sixteenth century before moving on to Marrakesh. Taroudant is a friendly, laidback sort of place, with a population of around 70,000 and the good-natured bustle of a Berber market town. It's a good base for trekking into the Western High Atlas or the Jebel Sirwa as well as for two superb road routes – north over the **Tizi n'Test** to Marrakesh (see p.384), and south to **Tata** (see p.477), Foum el Hassan (see p.480) and beyond.

Despite its extensive ramparts and large tracts of open space, the town is quite compact. Within the walled "inner city" there are just two main squares – **Place Assarag** (officially renamed Place Alaouyine) and **Place Talmoklate** (officially Place en Nasr)– and these mark the centre of town, with the main **souk** area between them to the north. The pedestrianized area of Place Assarag is the centre of activity, and comes alive in late afternoon as the sun's heat eases off and people come out to promenade. Lately it has seen the return of performers such as storytellers, snake charmers and musicians – as in Marrakesh's Jemaa el Fna, but on a smaller scale, of course.

The souks

Aside from its ramparts, Taroudant's main attractions are its two daily souks: the **Souk Arab**, immediately east of Place Assarag (and north of Place Talmoklate), and the **Marché Berbère**, south of Place Talmoklate.

The **"Arab" souk** – easiest approached along the lane by the BMCE bank (you will probably emerge in Place Talmoklate; it's a tiny area) – is good for rugs, carpets, leather goods and other traditional crafts, but especially jewellery. This comes mainly from the Anti-Atlas villages (little of it is as "antique" as the sellers would have you believe), though until the 1960s there was an artisan quarter here of predominantly Jewish craftsmen. For good-quality wares, the Antiquaire Haut Atlas, run by Licher el Houcine at 61 Souk el Kebir, is recommended (to find him, if entering the souk from Pl Assarag by the BMCE bank, continue roughly straight ahead, and his shop is on the right after 200m).

The **Marché Berbère** is a more everyday souk, with spices and vegetables, as well as clothing and pottery, and again jewellery and carpets. It is most easily entered from Place Talmoklate.

On Thursdays and Sundays there is a **souk** by the northeast gate, **Bab el Khemis**, where Berbers from the villages sell farm produce and sometimes craftwork. For something more offbeat, check out the distinctive **sandstone sculptures** sold by eccentric local artist Avolay Moulay Rachid from his shop at 52 Av Moulay Rachid.

The tanneries

The leather **tanneries** are outside the town walls on account of their smell – leather is cured in cattle urine and pigeon droppings – and for the proximity to a ready supply of

---

TREKKING FROM TAROUDANT

From Taroudant's rooftop terraces, the fang-like **peaks** of Awlim (3482m) and Tinerghwet (3551m) look temptingly close on the rugged northern skyline. The area is easily reached from Taroudant, as is the Tichka Plateau (see box, p.385). The Jebel Sirwa (see p.475) is also within practical reach of the town; you should really allow at least a week for a cursory visit, more if possible. One of the very best **trekking routes** in Morocco, nicknamed "The Wonder Walk", is a two-week trip up to the plateau and on to Jebel Toubkal (see p.364), Morocco's highest peak.

If you are interested in a **guided trek**, contact El Aouad Ali (BP127, Taroudant 83000, Morocco ☎0666 637972; or through the *Hôtel Roudani* or *Hôtel Taroudant*). He is a highly knowledgeable, English-speaking mountain expert, and can organize treks at short notice if need be. It is best to avoid other agencies as there have been some unpleasant rip-offs by cowboy operators.

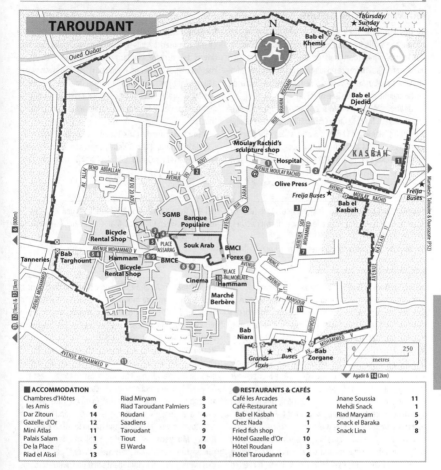

■ ACCOMMODATION					RESTAURANTS & CAFÉS			
Chambres d'Hôtes		Riad Miryam	8		Café les Arcades	4	Jnane Soussia	11
les Amis	6	Riad Taroudant Palmiers	3		Café-Restaurant		Mehdi Snack	1
Dar Zitoun	14	Roudani	4		Bab el Kasbah	2	Riad Maryam	5
Gazelle d'Or	12	Saadiens	2		Chez Nada	1	Snack el Baraka	9
Mini Atlas	11	Taroudant	9		Fried fish shop	7	Snack Lina	8
Palais Salam	1	Tiout	7		Hôtel Gazelle d'Or	10		
De la Place	5	El Warda	10		Hôtel Roudani	3		
Riad el Aïssi	13				Hôtel Taroudannt	6		

water. Compared with those in Marrakesh or Fez, they are small, but tidy. Sheep, cow and goat leather articles are all on sale, but don't buy skins of rare or endangered species, also unfortunately on sale: their importation is banned in most Western countries, and buying them, or indeed patronizing shops which sell them, encourages illegal poaching of rare animals. To visit the tanneries, follow the continuation of the main street past *Hôtel Taroudant* to Bab Targhount, turn left outside, and right after 100m.

The walls and kasbah

The town's **walls and bastions**, now restored in many places, make an enjoyable five-kilometre circuit, with stairs up onto them in a couple of spots, most notably at **Bab el Kasbah** (also called Bab Essalsla). Some people walk round the outside, but it's easier to rent a bicycle (see p.470) and cycle round, or take a *calèche* from just inside Bab el Kasbah. The finest stretch runs south from there to Bab Zorgane.

Just to the north of Bab el Kasbah, the **kasbah**, now a kind of village within the town, was originally a Saadian winter palace complex, and contains the ruins of a fortress built by Moulay Ismail.

ARRIVAL AND DEPARTURE

TAROUDANT

By bus Buses use the *gare routière*, which is a yard just outside the walls by Bab Zorgane. Buses to Freija use a stop outside the town hall at the beginning of the Ouarzazate road. There are no longer any bus services from Taroudant to Marrakesh via Tizi n'Test, but two daily buses can be caught in Aoulouz (see p.473).
Destinations: Agadir (1 CTM & 2 others daily; 1hr 30min); Casablanca (1 CTM & 12 others daily; 10hr); Igherm (3 daily; 2hr 30min); Marrakesh (1 CTM & 5 others daily; 6hr 30min); Ouarzazate (1 CTM & 5 others daily; 5hr); Rabat (3 daily; 13hr); Taliouine (1 CTM & 5 others daily; 2hr); Tata (3 daily; 4hr 30min); Tazenakht (1 CTM & 5 others daily; 3hr).

By grand taxi Grands taxis use a yard immediately west of the one used by buses. If heading to Agadir and the drivers try to give you any nonsense about baggage charges (which Moroccans do not pay), you can always take a taxi to Inezgane and another one on from there. To Tata, there are rarely direct shared grands taxis, and you risk getting stranded at Igherm if you take one that's only going that far.
Destinations: Agadir (1hr 15min); Aoulouz (1hr); Freija (20min); Igherm (1hr 30min); Inezgane (1hr 15min); Marrakesh (4hr); Ouled Berhil (40min); Taliouine (1hr 30min).

GETTING AROUND

By petit taxi and calèche There are petits taxis (usually to be found in Pl Assarag) and a few horse-drawn *calèches*, with similar tariffs.
By bicycle You can rent bicycles by the hour, half- or full-day from a little shop on Av Mohammed V just off Pl Assarag between Crédit du Maroc and Bank Attijaraiwafa (10dh/hr, 60dh/day).

ACCOMMODATION

★ **Chambres d'Hôtes Les Amis** 800m west of Bab Targhount ☎ 0667 601686, ⓦ chambreslesamis.com. A stay at this guesthouse is more like being in a Moroccan family home than a hotel, with clean and pleasant rooms, constant hot water, a roof terrace, and use of the kitchen. BB **160dh**
Dar Zitoun 2km west of town, on the Agadir road ☎ 0528 551141, ⓦ darzitoune.com. With fourteen a/c bungalows and eight suites, all set in a magnificent garden, with traditional-style decor and a big pool, this is a good upmarket choice, though some way out of town. BB **€120**
Gazelle d'Or 1km southwest of town, on the Ameskroud road ☎ 0528 852039, ⓦ gazelledor.com. An extraordinary place: a hunting lodge created by a French baron in the 1920s, in a Morocco-meets-Provence style. It was converted to a hotel after World War II, and guests (mostly super-rich Brits) stay in bungalows in the lush gardens. Rates are among the highest in North Africa, and one dresses for dinner. They usually like you to take half board, though this may be negotiable off-season; facilities include horseriding and croquet. Advance reservation is compulsory; you won't be allowed past the gate if you don't have one. HB **6400dh**
Mini Atlas Av el Mansour Eddahbi ☎ 0528 551880, ☎ 0528 851739. The staff here are very friendly and the rooms are small but sparkling, with en-suite showers, though there's hot water 6–10am & 6–11pm only. **130dh**
Palais Salam ☎ 0528 852501, ⓔ palsalam@menara .ma. A package hotel in a nineteenth-century palace, just inside the ramparts of the kasbah (entrance outside the walls). It's worth asking for a room or suite in the towers or garden pavilions, rather than on the new modern floor. Facilities include two swimming pools, a cocktail bar and three restaurants. BB **934dh**

De la Place Pl Assarag. Though it's located on the main square, the rooms are grubby and very basic, with shared bathroom facilities and no hot water. If you can negotiate a reduced rate, however, its low price might make it worthwhile for tight budgets. **80dh**
Riad el Aïssi Nouayl el Homr, on the Ameskroud road ☎ 0661 173089, ⓦ riadelaissi.com. A beautifully restful place in a little village 3km southeast of town (past the *Gazelle d'Or*), set amid nineteen hectares of orange, lemon and banana trees in a 1930 pasha's mansion. The rooms are enormous, though the decor is sparse, and there's a restaurant serving Moroccan and Italian food. BB **€48**
Riad Maryam 40 Derb Maalem Mohammed, signposted off Av Mohammed V ☎ 0528 551112, ⓦ riadmaryam.com. Taroudant's first riad, with six rooms and a suite around a lovely patio garden. The decor isn't exactly tasteful, nor really even kitsch, but it has a certain charm, as do the family who run the place, and the food is wonderful. BB **€80**
Riad Taroudant Palmiers Av Prince Héritier Sidi Mohammed ☎ 0528 854507, ⓦ riadtaroudantpalmiers .com. Not what you'd normally call a riad, though it does have a patio garden, this is a colonial-era convent converted into a hotel. It's very peaceful, but decorated quite simply, with ironwork furniture and the odd rug, rather than being heavy with stucco and zellij. Some rooms are en suite, and profits go to help the neighbouring abandoned children's home. **200dh**
Roudani overlooking Pl Assarag ☎ 0528 852219. A one-time backpackers' cheapie, located on a prime spot slap-bang in the middle of town, this place is now a little bit overpriced considering that its rooms are pretty basic, with bathrooms but no hot water. There's also a

restaurant on the square, and a nice rooftop terrace for breakfast. **100dh**

Saadiens Bordj Oumansour ☎ 0528 852473, ✉ hotsaadi@iam.net.ma. A quiet hotel, north of the two main squares, with a rooftop restaurant, a patisserie and a swimming pool, but its rooms could do with a revamp, and there's hot water mornings and evenings only. BB **280dh**

Taroudant Pl Assarag ☎ 0528 852416, ☎ 0528 851553. A Taroudant institution and the oldest hotel in town, this was run by a grand old French *patronne* up until her death in 1988, and retains her influence (and some of her old poster collection). Very good value, with a patio

garden, a generally good restaurant, and a noisy bar that closes at 11pm. **200dh**

Tiout Av Prince Héritier Sidi Mohammed ☎ 0528 850341, ✉ hoteltiout.com. Spotless, airy and prettily decorated rooms, all with en-suite showers, some with baths, and most with a balcony, plus a restaurant, car park, wi-fi, and a pleasant roof terrace with a fountain. BB **414dh**

⭐ **El Warda** 8 Pl Talmoklate ☎ 0528 852763. By far the best deal among the cheapies, offering clean, cosy rooms with en-suite toilets and shared hot showers. Rooms at the front have balconies overlooking the square; those at the back are quieter but get less light. **100dh**

EATING AND DRINKING

Juice shops around town sell all kinds of concoctions including creamy avocado with almond milk, but for freshly pressed orange and grapefruit juice you can't beat the stalls on Pl Talmoklate. The town's main bar is in the *Hôtel Taroudant* (daily 10am–11pm; see above).

Café les Arcades Pl Assarag. A restaurant on the square serving tajines, at 60dh a go, as well as breakfasts at 18dh. The location's good, with outside tables, but you can get similar tajines for half the price elsewhere in town. Daily 6.30am–11pm.

Café-Restaurant Bab el Kasbah Av Moulay Rachid, opposite the oil press ☎ 0528 551330. A 24hr café with a rather incongruous revolving door. The 40dh set menu is good value, and they also do decent tajines (30–40dh) and 13dh breakfasts. Daily 24hr.

Chez Nada Av Moulay Rachid. Excellent tajines, an 80dh set menu, and even pastilla (90–95dh), though you have to order it two hours in advance, and they don't have a phone. The food is served upstairs and on the roof terrace, as the downstairs is a café (daily 7am–11pm). Daily noon–3pm & 7–11pm.

Fried fish shop Av Prince Héritier Sidi Mohammed. The best of a handful of shops selling fried fish of different varieties, including prawns and squid rings, sold by weight, to eat in or take out. Always busy, so the fish is freshly cooked. A quarter kilo will set you back the princely sum of 12.50dh. Daily 11am–10pm.

Hôtel Gazelle d'Or Route d'Agadir, 1km west of town ☎ 0528 852039. The tented dining room here is quite a sight, especially at dinner (menu 650dh), when men are required to wear jackets and ties. Lunch by the pool is less costly (450dh). Reservations compulsory. Daily 1–3pm & 8–9.30pm.

Hôtel Roudani Pl Assarag ☎ 0528 852219. Simple Moroccan dishes, such as tajines and couscous, but all tasty, fresh and well prepared, with vegetarian options available, served on the *place*, a great place to take in the evening atmosphere or daytime bustle. Meals (set menu 60dh) are served noon–8.30pm, with breakfasts served 9–11am, and coffee or tea all day. Daily 9am–10.30pm.

Hôtel Taroudant Pl Assarag ☎ 0528 852416. An old-school colonial-style restaurant serving French and

Moroccan food, along with wine, beer or pastis. The cooking is variable, but good if you strike lucky, with set menus at 70dh and 90dh. Daily noon–2.30pm & 7–10pm.

⭐ **Jnane Soussia** Av Mohammed V, outside the walls, south of town ☎ 0528 854980. Very traditional Moroccan cuisine served in a relaxed, open-air restaurant around a pool with orange trees and music, and a tented area. There's veal tajine with prunes (75dh), chicken tajine with lemon and olives (65dh) or, if ordered in advance, *mechoui* or pigeon tajine with raisins (110dh). As tradition dictates, couscous is served on Fridays only. You can also drop in for a mint tea. Daily 8am–9.30pm or later.

Mehdi Snack Av Moulay Rachid. Directly behind *Chez Nada* (see above) and run by the same family, this is a low-priced fast food joint, offering salads, burgers, fried fish, and set menus (30–50dh) based around those dishes. They also do fast food-style pizzas (30–60dh). Daily 11am–11pm.

Snack Lina Av Sidi Mohammed, just east of Pl Assarag. Shiny tiles and fluorescent lighting make this basic diner rather stark. The shawarma and spit-roast chicken are all right, but make sure they're today's. The tajines are good though, and rather cheaper than the ones on the square, at 20–33dh for one, with family-sized versions also available. Daily 10am–midnight.

Riad Maryam 40 Derb Maalem Mohammed, signposted off Av Mohammed V ☎ 0528 551112. The Moroccan home cooking here is so good that it has featured more than once in the French gourmet magazine *Saveurs*. Non-residents can eat here for 200dh, but must book at least two hours ahead. Daily noon–3pm & 7–10pm.

Snack el Baraka (Chez Moustapha) Av Sidi Mohammed, between the two squares. A small restaurant serving a variety of kebabs (lamb, chicken, liver, *kefta*), spit-roast chicken and sandwiches. A kebab with chips and salad costs 30dh. Daily noon–midnight.

8

DIRECTORY

Banks and exchange Several banks on and around Pl Assarag have ATMs and exchange facilities, as do a trio east of Bab el Kasbah on Av Hassan II. There's a forex bureau in Pl Talmoklate, on the corner of Av Bir Zaran (summer daily 8.30am–noon & 2.30–7pm; winter Mon–Fri 8.30am–noon & 2.30–7pm, Sat & Sun 8.30am–1pm).

Car repairs There are garages and spares shops just inside and outside Bab Targhount, and inside Bab Zorgane.

Hammams Hammam Tunsi, 30 Av Mohammed V, 30m along from the *Hôtel Taroudant* (daily: men 4–11am & 6pm–midnight; women 11am–6pm; 10dh; massage

extra). There's also a hammam with an entrance for men just next to the *Hôtel el Warda*, and an entrance for women round the back in an alley between 177 and 162 Av Mohammed V (daily 6am–11pm; men 9dh, women 10dh).

Internet Internet surfing is cheap in Taroudant – usually only 3dh an hour. Current locales include Club Roudana on Av Bir Zaran (daily 9am–11pm or later), the back of a *tabac* on Av Moulay Rachid, opposite Moulay Rachid's sculpture shop (daily 9am–midnight), and an unnamed place off Av Prince Héritier, two doors from the entrance to the *Hôtel Tiout* (daily 9am–11pm).

Around Taroudant

East of Taroudant, the oases and kasbahs of Freija and Tioute are close enough to explore in a half-day's trip by car (or an energetic day by rented bike). The Oued Souss, which passes Freija, is a key Moroccan bird habitat, with a rich array of winter residents, and a huge range of migrants in the spring.

Freija

Eleven kilometres east of Taroudant, on the south bank of the Oued Souss, the ancient, fortified village **Freija** stands atop a hill rising above the Oued Souss. The *oued* is quite wide here, and usually dry, but when it does flood, the hill keeps the *pisé* (mud-brick) houses safely high and dry. As well as being quite picturesque, and a good spot for birdwatching, Freija affords sweeping views of the river, the fertile plains beyond, and the High Atlas.

ARRIVAL AND DEPARTURE   FREIJA

By bus or grand taxi Hourly local buses leave for Freija from in front of Taroudant's town hall (Hôtel de Ville) on the

Ouarzazate Road, and there are shared grands taxis from the *gare routière* at Bab Zorgane.

ACCOMMODATION

Riad Freija Just south of Freija, alongside the access road from the R1706 ☎ 0528 216638, ✿ riadfreija.ma. Freija's old *pisé* (mud and gravel) kasbah has been converted into a great little hotel, owned by the same

proprietor as the *Hôtel Tiout* in Taroudant (see p.471). The decor in the bedrooms isn't as posh as in some riads, but all are en suite with a/c in summer and heating in winter, and the location is superb. BB **450dh**

Tioute

The stone-built Glaoui kasbah at **TIOUTE**, 25km southeast of Taroudant, is one of the grandest in the south, and is still owned by the local *caid*. Profiled against the first foothills of the Anti-Atlas, it is a wonderfully romantic sight, and was used as a location in Jacques Becker's 1954 French film *Ali Baba and the Forty Thieves*. Equally impressive are its fabulous views over the luxuriant palmery, with the High Atlas peaks beyond. If you want to avoid sharing it with the tour groups (who arrive around lunchtime), get here early.

Just by the *auberge* (see opposite), at the Taitmatine all-women's argan oil producers' cooperative, you can see argan oil being made, and of course buy some if you wish. El Aouad Ali (see box, p.468) can organize day walks in the hills above Tioute.

ARRIVAL AND DEPARTURE   TIOUTE

By grand taxi Shared grands taxis from Taroudant serve   Tioute infrequently (mainly mornings and late afternoons).

ACCOMMODATION

Auberge Tigmmi By the main road below the kasbah ☎0528 850555, ⓦaubergetigmmi.com. Good food and a great location are on offer in this villa set amid orange groves and just by the palmery, with stylishly understated cool white decor, a good restaurant and a pool. **315dh**

From Taroudant to Taliouine

The roads east from Taroudant to Taliouine follow the Souss valley, with the Atlas mountains to the north and the Anti-Atlas to the south. The new R1706, along the south side of the valley, is the fastest route, and the one followed by direct shared taxis, while buses take the older N10 road, via Ouled Berhil and Aoulouz, both of which are staging posts for shorter shared taxi routes.

Ouled Berhil

OULED BERHIL, 43km east of Taroudant, is largely of note for its old kasbah, 800m south of the main road (signposted from the centre of the village), which has been turned into a sumptuous **hotel-restaurant**, the *Riad Hida*.

ARRIVAL AND DEPARTURE   OULED BERHIL

By bus Buses along the N10 stop at Ouled Berhil, and there are shared taxis to Taroudant and Aoulouz.

ACCOMMODATION AND EATING

★ Riad Hida ☎0528 531044, ⓦriadhida.com. This nineteenth-century palace, constructed for local pasha Hida Oumiss, was bought in the 1950s by Danish millionaire Börg Kastberg, who spent thirty years restoring it to its former glory. On his death in 1989, his former employee, Mohammed Laafissi, opened it to the public as a deluxe hotel and restaurant, with rooms, suites, spacious grounds and a magnificent garden. The restaurant is open 11.30am–3pm & 7.30–10pm, with a 120dh set menu, and it's wise to reserve in advance. BB **€69**

Aoulouz and around

AOULOUZ, 34km east of Ouled Berhil, is the starting point for the early bus to Marrakesh via Tizi n'Test (see p.384), and has quite a lively little market, at its busiest on Wednesdays and Sundays. **Aoulouz Gorge**, north of town, is a prime birdwatching locale. Spring migrants include everything from booted eagle and black kite to white stork; Barbary falcon, Moussier's and black redstart, blue rock thrush and rock bunting all winter here.

East of Aoulouz, a *piste* leads to **Taïssa**, at the southern end of the **Assif n'Tifnout** valley, with a rough *piste* to Amsouzart (see p.374). It is possible to drive this in a sturdy vehicle and you can make a two-day tour, returning to Taliouine (or doing it in the opposite direction). Alternatively, you could walk it (four to five days). From Aoulouz there are minibuses to Assarag, where you'll find rooms, and from where a few hours' walk north will take you to Amsouzart.

ARRIVAL AND DEPARTURE   AOULOUZ

By grand taxi There are shared taxis from the centre of the village to Taroudant (1hr), Inezgane (2hr 15min), Ouled Berhil (30min) and Taliouine (40min).

To Tizi n'Test The most important bus connection is the service to Marrakesh via Tizi n'Test, one of the most exciting mountain roads in Morocco: a series of hairpin bends cutting across the High Atlas (see p.384). There are two buses, one at 2pm (in practice usually more like 3pm), which starts here, and one at 5pm (in practice more like 6pm), which starts in Taliouine. Tickets are on sale outside the *Café Restaurant Oued Souss*, on the main road in the centre of town. Unless you are travelling in summer, it will be too dark to catch the spectacular scenery if you take the 5pm bus, so you are best off taking the earlier one. With your own transport, you can drive the route, but be aware that the road is pretty hairy going, and in winter it can

8

ARGAN TREES

One of the stranger sights of the Souss and surrounding coastal region is goats browsing among the branches of spiny, knotted **argan** trees, a species similar to the olive that is found only in this region. Though some younger goatherds seem to have a sideline in charging tourists to take photographs, the actual object of the exercise is to let the goats eat the outer, fleshy part of the argan fruit. The hard, inner nut is then cracked open and the kernel crushed to extract the expensive oil.

Argan **oil** is sweet and rich, and is used in many Moroccan dishes and in salads, or for dunking bread. It is also used to make **amalou**, a delicious dip of honey and almond paste.

An expensive delicacy, argan oil is not easily extracted: while one olive tree provides around five litres of olive oil, it takes the nuts from thirty argan trees to make just one litre of argan oil. Plastic **bottles** of argan oil are occasionally sold at the roadside in the Oued Souss area, but are very often adulterated with cheaper oils. It is therefore better to buy argan oil or amalou from a trustworthy source such as the cooperative at Tioute (see p.472), the honey shop in Agadir (see box, p.460), *Hôtel Tifrit* in Paradise Valley (see p.467), or specialist shops in Marrakesh or Essaouira. Argan oil is also sometimes sold in larger supermarkets.

---

occasionally get snowed up. An alternative is to charter a grand taxi to Talaat n' Yakoub, where there is onward transport to Asni and thence Marrakesh, with basic accommodation nearby at Ijoukak (see p.381).

ACCOMMODATION

Café Restaurant Sa'ada 300m south of the main road, by the market ☎0662 221067. This very male upstairs café, with pool, pinball and table football, has just a handful of single rooms on the top floor, with a toilet but no showers. Most women won't want to stay here, but the rooms are clean enough, and very cheap, and especially on souk days, they may be the only ones in town that are available. Single <u>25dh</u>

Sahara on the main drag ☎0672 674948. The best accommodation in town, with nice, fresh rooms and shared but clean bathroom facilities. If there's no one about, try the *téléboutique* next door. If it's full, the nearby *Café Restaurant Oued Souss* (100dh) is a reasonable fall-back. <u>80dh</u>

Taliouine and around

More a village than a town, **TALIOUINE** makes a good day-trip from Taroudant, or a stop en route to Ouarzazate. Its magnificent **kasbah** (east of the village) was built by the Glaoui after the French evicted the original landowners to make way for it, but they regained the land after independence, and although large parts of the kasbah are derelict, one member of the family, together with his French wife, has restored part of it and opened a *maison d'hôte* in it (see opposite). There are more kasbahs in the hills round the village, if you have time to explore them.

Taliouine is a centre for **saffron**, harvested in September and October. This is the only area in Morocco in which it is grown. It can be bought in one-gram packets from the Cooperative Souktana de Safran (⊛souktanadusafran.org) at their office on the eastern edge of town, where their small **museum** (daily 9am–6pm; free) is under renovation until at least mid-2013. Saffron is also sold at shops in town, such as L'Or Rouge, opposite the bus stop, where you may be offered a cup of saffron tea if you call by at the right time. Note that saffron is damaged by light, so it's best not to buy if it has been left out in glass jars for any length of time.

Taliouine has a Monday **souk**, held across the valley behind the kasbah.

Jebel Iguiguil

South of Taliouine, **Jebel Iguiguil** is an isolated peak reaching 2323 metres in height and offering a good day's excursion. The road from the N10 (signposted to Agadir Melloul), once it has hauled up the first pass from Taliouine, is surfaced right through to the N12 Tata–Foum Zguid road just west of Tissint, a spectacular drive. From just below **Agadir Melloul**, a *piste* heads west to pass the village of **Aït Hamed**, whose old *agadir* is worth a visit, before curling up to the lower slopes of the highest peak between Jebel Aklim (the highest peak in the Anti-Atlas, reaching 2531m) and the Saghro. Detailed information on this area can be obtained from AMIS in Scotland (see p.46).

ARRIVAL AND DEPARTURE

By bus The main bus stop is in the centre of the village; they can be picked up outside the *Souktana*, for example, but they won't stop there if they are full.
Destinations: Agadir (1 CTM & 4 others daily; 3hr 30min); Casablanca (2 daily; 13hr 30min); Er Rachidia (daily; 11hr); Marrakesh (daily via Tizi n'Test; 10hr); Ouarzazate (1 CTM &

TALIOUINE AND AROUND

5 others daily; 3hr); Taroudant (1 CTM & 5 others daily; 2hr); Tazenakht (1 CTM & 5 others daily; 1hr 30 min); Rabat (daily; 15hr 30min); Tinerhir (daily; 8hr); Zagora (daily; 6hr).
By grand taxi Grands taxis leave just along from the bus stop, serving Aoulouz (40min), Taroudant (1hr 30min) and (less frequently) Tazenakht (1hr).

ACCOMMODATION AND EATING

Atlas Bordeaux By the bus stop ☎0666 752292. The best of the handful of ultra-cheapies on the main drag in the centre of the village. The rooms are simple, but clean and fresh, with hot showers at 10dh a go. The neighbouring small hotels may be slightly cheaper, they are also correspondingly dirtier. 100dh
Auberge Askaoun Just east of town ☎0528 534017, ⓦ askaoun.voila.net. Friendly staff, good food (the set menus all involve saffron somewhere along the line) and nice big rooms with private bathrooms make this a decent alternative if the *Souktana* is full. 200dh
Auberge Camping Toubkal 3.5km east of town ☎0528 534343. Run by the same proprietor as the *Auberge Askaoun*, this campsite with a cheap restaurant also has bungalow rooms, including some a/c and two adapted for wheelchair users, as well as wi-fi (near the reception only), a small grocery store, and a swimming pool. Camping 60dh, bungalow 150dh
★ **Auberge Souktana** Opposite the kasbah, 2km east of town ☎0528 534075, ⓔ souktana@menara.ma. A

wonderful little place, run by Ahmed Jadid and his French wife, Michelle (Ahmed is an excellent mountain guide; see below), offering good meals and a choice of accommodation: en-suite rooms in the main building, or bungalows outside. They have a separate campsite just up the Askaoun road (*Zagmouzen Bivouac Camping Restaurant*), to which they direct campers, and where they have tent bungalows available. BB bungalow 166dh, double 226dh
Escale Rando Taliouine In the kasbah ☎0528 534600, ⓦ escalerando.fr. A member of the family who owned the land before the kasbah was built has now established this *maison d'hôte* in part of it which has been restored from its ruinous state. At present the bathroom facilities are shared, though some rooms will be en suite in the near future. BB 300dh
Grand Hôtel Ibn Toumert Right next to the kasbah ☎0528 534125, ⓦ hotelibntoumert.com. The most comfortable place in town, though rather impersonal, with a pool, a bar, a restaurant, wi-fi and views of the kasbah from some rooms. BB 486dh

Jebel Sirwa (Djebel Siroua)

The **Jebel Sirwa** (or Siroua) is an isolated volcanic peak, rising from a high area (3000m-plus, so take it easy) to the south of the High Atlas. It offers trekking as good as you can find anywhere – rewarded by magnificent views, a cliff village and dramatic gorges. It is best in spring; winter is extremely cold. For those with 4WD, one of the great scenic *pistes* of Morocco circles north of Sirwa, a two- to three-day trip from Taliouine via **Askaoun** and **Tachnocht**, rejoining the N10 north of Tazenakht.

A week-long walking circuit taking in Jebel Sirwa is outlined on our map (see p.476), the numbers being the overnight halts. Mules to carry gear, as well as tent rental, can be arranged by **Ahmed Jadid** at the *Auberge Souktana* (see above) in Taliouine or by **El Aouad Ali** in Taroudant (see box, p.468), both good cooks who speak fluent English, though they don't operate in the Sirwa in winter. Mules are a worthwhile investment, but having Ali or Ahmed along is the best guarantee of success. If you are going it alone, the relevant survey maps are the 1:100,000 Taliwine and 1:50,000 Sirwa. Ahmed Jadid can show you these, and dispenses advice whether or not you engage his guiding services.

8

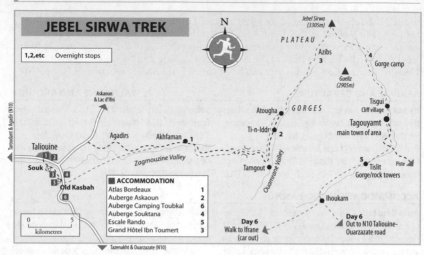

The circuit

The initial day is a gentle valley ascent along a *piste* from Taliouine to **AKHFAMAN** where there are rooms and a kasbah. The *piste* actually reaches west of here as far as Atougha but, souk days apart, transport is nonexistent and the walk is a pleasant introduction to the trek. Beyond Akhfaman the *piste* climbs over a pass to another valley at **TAMGOUT** and up it to **ATOUGHA**, before contouring round into the upper valley, where you can stay at *azibs* (goat shelters) or bivouacs.

Jebel Sirwa (3304m) can be climbed from **Atougha** in five to six hours: a pull up from the southern cirque onto a plateau, crowned with rock towers; the nervous may want to be roped for one section of the final scramble. The sub-peak of **Guliz** is worth ascending, too, and a bivouac in the gorge below is recommended.

Beyond Guliz, you should keep to the lower paths to reach **TISGUI**, where there are rooms available. In Tisgui, don't fail to visit the unique **cliff village**, whose houses, ranked like swallows' nests on a 300-metre precipice, are now used as grain stores. Continuing the circuit, past fields of saffron, you reach **TAGOUYAMT**, the biggest village of the Sirwa area, where rooms are available, and which is connected by *piste* to the Taliouine road. Trails leave it to pass through a couple of villages before reaching the river, which is followed to the extraordinary conglomerate features of the **Tislit gorges**. This natural sculpture park is amazing; you can camp or get rooms at the village.

On the last day, you can follow the valley to **IHOUKARN** and then to **IFRANE**, where it's possible to get a vehicle out; alternatively, a three-hour trek to the southeast leads to the Taliouine–Ouarzazate road, near its highest point, from where transport back to Taliouine is easier. Ahmed Jadid (see p.475) can arrange transport at Ihoukarn or Ifrane to meet unaccompanied parties.

The Tata circuit

Heading **south** across the **Anti-Atlas** from Taroudant, or east from Tiznit, you can drive, or travel by bus, or a combination of grands taxis and trucks, to the desert oases of **Tata**, **Akka** and **Foum el Hassan** to the west, or **Foum Zguid** to the east. This is one of the great Moroccan routes, still very much a world apart, with its camel herds and lonely, weatherbeaten villages. As throughout southern Morocco, **bilharzia** is prevalent in the oases, so avoid contact with pool and river water.

TRAVELLING FROM TAROUDANT TO TATA

Leaving the N10 Taroudant–Taliouine road after 8km at Aït Iazza, the R109 Tata road passes **Freija** and the turning to **Tioute** (see p.472), before winding its way up into the stark Anti-Atlas mountains. Transport is scarce – only four buses a day in each direction, three of which leave Taroudant early in the morning (4.30–6.30am), with just one evening departure (currently at 5pm).

Direct shared grands taxis between Taroudant and Tata are rare: most shared taxis from Taroudant terminate at **IGHERM** (also spelt Irherm; 93km from Taroudant), where there's a **Wednesday souk**. The region was once known for its silver daggers and inlaid rifle butts. If you get stranded here, basic rooms are available at a couple of café-restaurants, including the *Hôtel Restaurant Anzal* by the bus stop (☎0661 846478; 100dh).

Igherm is also a crossroads, with scenic, surfaced roads to Taliouine (see p.474) and Tafraoute (see p.488), as well as the old R109 road to Tata via Issafen. Though buses still continue south on the R109, it has now been superseded by a spectacular new road, climbing over the ragged mountain strata before dropping down into a valley, which it follows to Tata. On this road, at **Annamer** – a blaze of almond blossom in March – you can visit one of the best-preserved *agadirs* in Morocco, a huge walled courtyard with tiers of minute storerooms reached by ladders made of notched tree trunks. If you want to see inside, ask around for the *gardien*, who will of course expect a tip for his trouble.

If you want to enquire about trucks from Igherm to Taliouine or Tafraoute, try asking around the petrol station in the middle of town, or the cafés around it, where the truck drivers hang out and play cards. Market day (Wednesday in Igherm, Sunday or Thursday in Tata) sees more transport between Tata and Igherm; on other days, you face a long wait and risk getting stuck. There may be transport of some kind to Issafen on the R109, where it should be possible to get transport to Tata (especially on a Thursday, Issafen's souk day). Issafen doesn't have any accommodation, and after 8.30am the next regular transport south is the 7pm bus to Tata.

8

GETTING AROUND   THE TATA CIRCUIT

By public transport Transport can be sparse, which means you'll have to think ahead if you want to stop off at various places en route and be somewhere with a reasonable hotel by the time transport dries up. The other problem is that smaller places like Oum el Alek and Aït Herbil have nowhere for visitors to stay and are not served by grands taxis – they'll drop you off, but are unlikely to be passing with a free space and pick you up. Buses are more frequent than they were, but it can be a long wait. Hitching is possible but not advisable – we've heard of hitchhikers being robbed by motorists who've picked them up on the N12 road west of Tata. One way to solve these problems if you have the money is to rent a car.

Tata

TATA is a small administrative and garrison town with colonnaded streets, flanking a large oasis, below a steep-sided hill known as **La Montagne** (largely occupied by the military). It's a leisurely place with a friendly (if early-to-bed) air, and distinct desert influences in the dark complexion of the people, the black turbans of the men and the colourful sari-like coverings of the women.

There's a Sunday market in town and a very lively Thursday **souk** held at an enclosure – or, more accurately, a series of *pisé* courtyards known as El Khemis, 6km out on the Akka road (N12); the mainstay is dates.

ARRIVAL AND DEPARTURE   TATA

By bus Buses terminating at Tata will drop you in a yard at the eastern end of Zenkat el Warda, about 200m from Pl Marche Verte, where they park up, but they depart from Pl Marche Verte itself. The best time to catch them is in the morning; transport dries up quickly in the afternoon, buses can be fully booked, and they may not let foreigners travel without a seat (it's illegal, and though Moroccan passengers may tip the *gendarmes* to do it, foreigners are out of the *baksheesh* loop).

Destinations: Agadir (6 daily; 7hr); Akka (8 daily; 1hr); Bou Izakarn (8 daily; 4hr); Casablanca (3 daily; 16hr); Foum el Hassan (8 daily; 2hr); Foum Zguid (2 daily; 2hr 30min); Goulimine (2 daily; 5hr); Igherm (4 daily; 2hr 30min); Marrakesh (4 daily; 10hr); Ouarzazate (2 daily; 5hr); Rabat

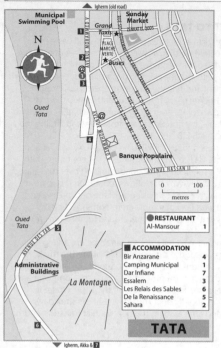

(daily; 17hr); Tan Tan (2 daily; 8hr); Taroudant (4 daily; 4hr 30min); Tiznit (6 daily; 5hr).

By grand taxi Collective grands taxis leave from just north of Pl Marche Verte, and sometimes from the square itself. It can take some time for them to get together enough passengers to set off, and services are extremely sparse, but there are occasional departures, especially in the morning, and depending on demand, to Akka (1hr), Foum el Hassan (2hr), Bou Izakarn (3hr 30min), Issafen (2hr), Tissint (1hr) and Foum Zguid (2hr 30min), as well as taxi-trucks to Foum Zguid (especially on Sunday night and Monday morning for Foum Zguid's Monday souk).

By car It's always a good idea to fill your tank before leaving Tata. If driving westward, the only fuel stop before Bou Izakarn is the Ziz station at Aït Herbil (see p.480).

INFORMATION

Tourist information The Délégation de Tourisme (Mon–Fri 8.30am–4.30pm; ☎ 0528 802075) is on the old Igherm road, 500m north of the campsite.

Bicycles can be rented from the campsite (see below) at 60dh/day.

Services There's a Banque Populaire with ATM on Av Mohammed V; the post office is also on Av Mohammed V. Internet access is available at Cyber de Luxe, 38 Av Mohammed V (daily 8.30am–1pm & 3–10pm).

ACCOMMODATION

Bir Anzarane off Av Mohammed V by the market ☎ 0667 099842. This bare-bones ultra-cheapy is at least cleaner, and also slightly cheaper, than the others on Av Mohammed V (the *Essalam* at no. 41 and the *Sahara* at no. 81), and unlike those, this one at least has a shower, albeit in the toilet. **80dh**

Camping Municipal Av Mohammed V, overlooking the oued. A small and very basic campsite, whose facilities seem to diminish year by year, though it still has clean showers, and a certain amount of shade. It did have a swimming pool, but that has now been separated off. **30dh**

Dar Infiane off the Akka road, in the palmery ☎ 0661 610170, ⊕ darinfiane.com. Upmarket boutique hotel with six rooms and several terraces and patios, in a 500-year-old converted kasbah with palm-frond furnishings and traditional palm-wood ceilings. BB **€60**

Les Relais des Sables Av des FAR ☎ 0528 802301, ⊕ 0528 802300. A three-star hotel with a bar, restaurant and small swimming pool. The rooms are small but comfortable with en-suite showers and toilets, or there are mini-suites with a/c, sitting area and a complete bathroom. To eat in the restaurant (noon–3pm & 6.30–10pm; set menu 90dh), you need to order two or three hours ahead. **268dh**

★ **De la Renaissance** 9 Av des FAR ☎ 0528 802225, ⊕ htl.larenaissance.tata@gmail.com. The best-value choice in town, welcoming you with large, gleaming, a/c suites or small, gleaming rooms, the latter at very reasonable prices. The restaurant is good, and licensed (the bar is in principle open noon–midnight), though meals (set menu 90dh) have to be ordered two hours in advance, and there's a pool too. **210dh**

EATING AND DRINKING

The only alternatives to *Al Mansour* are the restaurants at the *Relais des Sables* and *Renaissance* hotels (see above), which have the advantage of being licensed, though you have to order meals at both of them in advance.

Al Mansour 43 Av Mohammed V. The best of the small restaurants on the main street, they can at least usually whip up a tajine for you (meat 40dh, chicken 30dh). Daily 8am–10pm.

Akka

Fifty kilometres west of Tata, the N12 passes through **AKKA**, a flyblown roadside town with a large palmery, and a weekly **souk** on Thursdays, where the oasis dates

(Akka means "dates" in Teshalhit) are much in evidence. There's a smaller souk on Sundays.

The oasis

It's worth taking a morning to explore Akka's oasis. You will probably need to do so on foot, as most of the oasis *pistes* are impossible in a two-wheel-drive vehicle. Local sights include a **kasbah** and **agadir** (granary) southeast of the village of Aït Rahal, and **Les Cascades** – a series of shallow, dammed irrigation pools, enclosed by palms. Local people bathe in these pools, but they are reputed to harbour **bilharzia**, so avoid contact with the water – both here and in the irrigation canals. To reach them on foot, you leave Akka by crossing the dry riverbed by a concrete barrage and then follow a path through the almost continuous palmery villages of Aït Aäntar, Tagadiret and Taouriret.

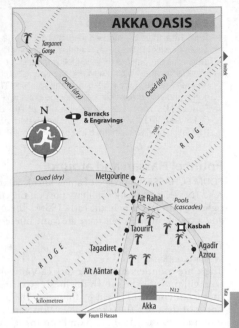

Targannt Gorge

A three-hour scorching trek to the northwest of Aït Rahal (don't forget to carry plenty of water) is the **Targannt Gorge**, in which a cluster of oases are tucked between the cliffs. There are ruins of houses, though the place is deserted nowadays, save for the occasional nomadic camel herder. The route is across desert, passable to Land Rover-type vehicles, though the track is poorly defined. En route (and an aid to navigation) is a small hill on which the French built a barracks. There are **rock engravings** of oxen at the eastern end of the hill – some modern, others perhaps up to two thousand years old. Approaching the gorge, a lone palm tempts you to its mouth. A guide from the village would be helpful, while bringing food and a tent would reward you with a gorgeous camping spot.

Oum el Alek

There are more **rock carvings**, said to be prehistoric, near the village of **OUM EL ALEK** (or Oum el Aälague), 7km southeast of Akka, off the Tata road. Anyone with a particular interest is best advised to get in touch with the *gardien* – the *Café-Hôtel Tamdoult* in Akka should be able to put you in touch.

ARRIVAL AND DEPARTURE   AKKA

By bus Nine buses a day go to Tata (two continuing to Ouarzazate, and one all the way to Meknes and Fez, via Taroudant and Marrakesh), with eight the other way to Bou Izakarn (two continuing to Goulimine and Tan Tan, the others to Tiznit and Agadir, and three all the way to Casa), running to and from the main road in the middle of the village.

By grand taxi There are shared grands taxis to Tata and Bou Izakarn, but sparse. Don't leave it too late if you want onward transport – as at Tata, it dries up early, and given the dearth of accommodation, this is not a place you'll want to get stuck in.

ACCOMMODATION AND EATING

Café-Restaurant Tamdoult On the main road (N12) in the middle of the village ☏ 0528 808030. This is the only place to stay in Akka, and pretty much the only place to eat as well. The rooms are very basic, though they'll do if you have to overnight here, and the food's decent enough, though nothing spectacular. **80dh**

8

EAST TO FOUM ZGUID

From **Tata**, there is a surfaced road, two daily buses, and occasional grands taxis to Foum Zguid (see p.411), the buses continue to Tazenakht (see p.411) and Ouarzazate (see p.397). The route runs through a wide valley, following the course of a seasonal river, amid an extremely bleak landscape, which is now and then punctuated by the occasional oasis and *ksar*, with the wave-like range of the Jebel Bani to the south. At **Tissint**, halfway to Foum Zguid, there's a gorge and waterfall, whose best vantage point is 2km before town on the road from Tata. Tissint is also a good base for scenic walks into the desert. A surfaced road from Akka-Irhen (25km east of Tata, with a Thurs souk) heads north via Agadir Melloul (see p.475) to join the N10 Taliouine–Tazenakht road just east of Taliouine.

Foum el Hassan and around

FOUM EL HASSAN (also spelt Fam el Hisn), 90km west of Akka, and 4km off the main road (N12), is basically a military post on the edge of an oasis where there was some fighting with Polisario in the early 1980s. There isn't much here aside from a few shops and a couple of cafés, but there are some interesting rock carvings nearby.

Tircht
5km from Foum el Hassan

There are countless **prehistoric rock carvings** in this region, and engaging a guide you will probably be shown the local favourites. Those at **Tircht** can be reached by foot from Foum el Hassan by following the *oued* through the "V" in the mountains north of the town (bear right after 2km where it splits). Tircht is a peaked mountain to the left about 5km from town, but neither it nor the carvings are easy to find: you are best advised to employ someone from town as a guide (they probably won't ask for more than 30dh, but you may well feel they deserve more than that). The best carvings require a little climbing to get to, but they are among the finest in Morocco – elephants and rhinoceroses, 15cm to 30cm high, dating roughly from 2000–500 BC, a time when the Sahara was full of lakes and swamps. Camping is possible here in the valley.

ARRIVAL AND DEPARTURE   FOUM EL HASSAN

By bus Buses between Tata and Bou Izakarn make the four-kilometre detour to stop at Foum el Hassan.

By grand taxi If you're lucky, you may find a shared grand taxi to Bou Izakarn or Tata.

ACCOMMODATION AND EATING

Borj Biramane Icht ☎ 0610 469933, ⊕ borj-biramane .com. The nearest accommodation to Foum el Hassan is *Borj Biramane*, just off the main road at Icht, which has shared Berber tents, rooms and camping facilities as well as food. Camping **80dh**, Berber tent **100dh**, double **420dh**

Aït Herbil

Less renowned than those at Tircht are the rock carvings at the village of **AÏT HERBIL**, 2km off the N12, 15km northwest of Foum el Hassan. The junction is easy to recognize, as it's right opposite a Ziz filling station. You can get there by grand taxi from Foum el Hassan, Akka, Tata or Bou Izakarn. For onward travel, however, you'll be lucky to find a passing grand taxi with places free, so short of hitching you'll have to depend on buses, of which there are just eight daily in each direction. There are two series of rock carvings, marked as "A" and "B" on our map (on p.482), both easily accessible on foot.

"A", overlooking Oued Tamanart, consists of as many as a hundred small carvings, depicting gazelles, bison, a giraffe and a bird or two, in a steep rock fall, and to the

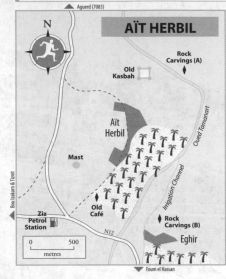

right of a patch of distinctively lighter grey rocks (indicating several deep and dangerous wells). The rock fall looks recent but clearly, with the carvings all in the same place, it has not shifted for centuries, even millennia. "**B**" north of the partly deserted village of Eghir, can be found by following the irrigation channel for 800m from the main road, where a signpost points the way. There are fewer carvings here but they are larger and more impressive.

Amtoudi (Id Aïssa)

If you have transport, it's worth making an excursion from the N12 Bou Izakarn–Tata road to visit **AMTOUDI** (or Id Aïssa, as it appears on most maps). Its **agadir** (fortified granary), with formidable towers and ramparts, sits on an eyrie-like setting atop the spur of a hill, reached up a steep zigzag path. A *gardien* shows visitors round. There is a small museum, and parts of the walls and towers have been restored. Make sure the *gardien* is available before tackling the climb, as the *agadir* is kept locked. You should allow around three hours for the visit.

Both Amtoudi's *auberges* (see belowq) can organize excursions in the area's susbtantial gorges. A walk up the gorge at the end of the village leads to another *agadir*, with huge curtain walls, perched high above a cliff, and, 3km on, a spring and waterfall. You can climb (or ride a mule) up a winding track and walk around the site, providing the *gardien* is there. If by chance you find the place overrun by visitors, you can escape the crowds with a walk down the palm-filled **gorge**; here another imposing but decaying *agadir* is perched on top of the cliff and, after about 3km, you'll come to a spring and waterfall.

ARRIVAL AND DEPARTURE
AMTOUDI

By car Amtoudi can be reached on a *piste* which leaves the N12 at the village of Taghicht, or on a surfaced road (signposted to Amtoudi) which leaves the N12 14km east of Taghicht. The two roads join at Souk Tnine D'Adaï, a village known for its decorative doors.

ACCOMMODATION
AMTOUDI

Amtoudi ☏ 0528 216540, ⊛ amtoudi.villesaumaroc .com/hotel-amtoudi. A friendly *auberge* with simple rooms, hot water, a restaurant and a camping area, at the end of the approach road into the village. As well as food and accommodation, they offer three- or four-hour walking tours. Camping <u>100dh</u>, BB double <u>150dh</u>

Ondiraitlesud ☏ 0528 218569, ⊛ ondiraitlesud .ma.free.fr. At the north end of the village, at the mouth of a gorge, this French-created *auberge* promotes eco-tourism in the area, and offers dorms and shared tents as well as a variety of rooms. They also organize treks and can point you in the direction of rock carvings or birdwatching sites. Dorm/shared tent <u>53dh</u>, double <u>366dh</u>

Ifrane de l'Anti-Atlas

IFRANE DE L'ANTI-ATLAS is one of the most rewarding oasis detours on the Tata loop, but you would have to do it as a day-trip (from Bou Izakarne, for example) because there is nowhere to stay. The junction for it on the N12 is at **Timoulay**, 26km west of Taghjicht.

A small Berber settlement in a long oasis, Ifrane comprises three surrounding *douar* (villages), each with its own kasbah and endless walls, together with **Souk Ifrane**, an administrative and market centre (Saturday souk), with a pink, fort-like barracks. Visitors exploring the oasis can expect to be the object of attention, especially from children, but it's worth braving them: there are beautiful walks among the *douar*, springs, and ingenious water channels.

The Ifrane oasis is the centre of one of the oldest settled regions in Morocco – and was one of the last places in the south to convert to Islam. Across the dry riverbed stand the ruins of the old **Jewish kasbah**, or **Mellah**. Legend holds that Ifrane's Jews settled here in the sixth century BC, and certainly the Jewish community goes back to pre-Islamic days. It endured up until the 1950s,

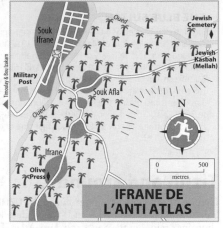

when, as elsewhere in the south, there was a mass exodus to Israel and, to an extent, Casablanca and Rabat. Thanks to a joint initiative by the Ministry of Culture and the Moroccan Jewish community's Heritage Foundation, the synagogue has now been restored, and if you can find the *gardien*, you should be able to have a look inside.

Around the next bend in the stony riverbed, and up the hill on the right, lies the Jewish **cemetery**. Broken tombstones, inscribed in Hebrew, lie strewn about. Relatives still come here to visit the graves and burn candles in memory of the deceased. Ifrane's Muslim past is also evident, with white-domed tombs of saints and *marabouts* dotting the surrounding countryside.

ARRIVAL AND DEPARTURE   IFRANE DE L'ANTI-ATLAS

There is a sealed road north to Tafraoute, but no public transport.

By grand taxi There are shared grands taxis to Ifrane from Timoulay and Bou Izakarn. Even if you can't find a shared one, it won't break the bank to charter one.

Bou Izakarn

The village of **BOU IZAKARN** – set where the roads from Tata, Tiznit and Goulimine meet, and strung out to a certain extent along all three of them – is mostly of interest to people needing to change buses or shared taxis here, but it's also a useful base for visiting Ifrane (see opposite). It's a lazy kind of place, where not much happens, but it has a Friday **souk**, a post office, Banque Populaire, post office and municipal swimming pool (summer only).

ARRIVAL AND DEPARTURE   BOU IZAKARN

By bus Buses pass through Bou Izakarn between Tiznit and Goulimine (18 daily each way), Tiznit and Tata (six a day each way), and Tata and Goulimine (two a day each way). All stop in the centre of the village, usually at the start of the road they'll be taking.

By grand taxi Shared grand taxis leave from the Tiznit road by the main roundabout in the centre of town for Tiznit (1hr) and Inezgane (2hr). Across the square, at the start of the Tata road, they run to Timoulay (10min), Ifrane de l'Anti-Atlas (20min) and occasionally Foum el Hassan (1he 30min). For Goulimine (30min), they leave from a rank on the Goulimine road at the south end of the village, 500m off the main square.

ACCOMMODATION

Anti-Atlas Tiznit road by the main roundabout ☎ 0528 788134. So far as cheapies go, this is a much better place to make for than the grubby offerings at the same price in Akka and Tata. The rooms are decent enough, grouped around a little courtyard with flowers and citrus trees, and there are shared bathroom facilities. **<u>80dh</u>**

THE BLUE SULTAN

Tiznit itself was used as a base by **El Hiba**, the ruler of Smara in the Western Sahara, who declared himself sultan of Morocco here in 1912 after learning of Moulay Hafid's surrender to the French under the Treaty of Fez. El Hiba (also known as Ma el Aïnin) was known as the Blue Sultan on account of his blue desert robes. El Hiba led a considerable force of Berbers to Marrakesh, which acknowledged his authority, before advancing on Fez in the spring of 1913. Here his forces were defeated, but El Hiba continued his resistance. Basing himself at Taroudant, and then in the Anti-Atlas mountains, he fought on until his death, near Tafraoute, in 1919. Despite his defeat, the Berbers of the Anti-Atlas mountains still remained outside of French control, and only suffered their first true occupation with the bitter French "pacification" of the early 1930s.

Tiznit and around

Despite its solid circuit of huge *pisé* walls, **TIZNIT** was only founded in 1882, when Sultan Moulay Hassan (Hassan I) was undertaking a *harka* – a subjugation or (literally) "burning" raid – in the Souss and Anti-Atlas. Tiznit is clean, neat and tidy, and a good staging point en route to Tafraoute, Sidi Ifni or Tata, but perhaps because of its relatively recent origin, it somehow lacks the atmosphere of Morocco's other walled cities.

The Medina

Tiznit has five kilometres of **walls** and eight major **gates**, the most important of which are **Bab Ouled Jarrar** and **Bab Jedid**. The second of these was a French addition, as its name ("New Gate") indicates; it is also called Les Trois Portes ("the three gates"), though in fact it consists of four gateways. The Medina also contains a number of *ksour* which were there before the walls were built.

The walled town's main square, the **Mechouar**, was once a military parade ground. The **Great Mosque** in the centre of the Medina has an unusual minaret, punctuated by a series of perches, which are said to be an aid to the dead in climbing up to paradise, and are more commonly found south of the Sahara in Mali and Niger. Alongside the mosque is the **Source Bleue**, a spring dedicated to the town's patroness, Lalla Tiznit, a saint and former prostitute martyred on this spot, whereupon water miraculously appeared (though nowadays it's usually dry).

Souks

The **jewellery souk** (Souk des Bijoutiers) is still an active crafts centre despite the loss to Israel of the town's large number of Jewish craftsmen. The jewellers occupy the northern part of the **main souk**, which can be entered from the Mechouar. Over to the south, outside the walls, off Avenue du 20 Août, there's a **municipal market** selling meat, fruit, veg and household goods. The town's main weekly souk (Thursday) is held out on the Tafraoute road.

Sidi Moussa d'Aglou (Aglou Plage)

The beach at **SIDI MOUSSA D'AGLOU** (Aglou Plage) is 17km from Tiznit, along a barren, scrub-lined road. It's an isolated expanse of sand with body-breaking Atlantic surf. It has a dangerous undertow, and is watched over in summer by military police coastguards, who only allow swimming if conditions are safe. **Surfing** can be good but you have to pick the right spots. Quite a few Moroccans (including migrant workers from France) come down in summer, with a trickle of Europeans in winter. Between times, the place is very quiet.

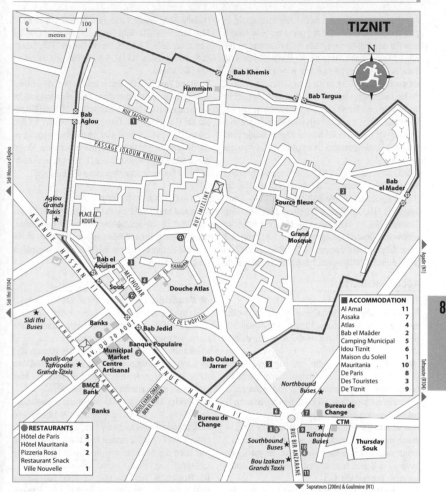

There are a couple of *marabout* tombs on the beach and, about 1.5km to the north, a tiny (and rather pretty) **troglodyte fishing village**, with a hundred or so primitive cave huts dug into the rocks.

ARRIVAL AND DEPARTURE

TIZNIT AND AROUND

TIZNIT

By bus Most buses stop near the main roundabout where the Tafraoute road meets the Goulimine road (Rue Bir Anzarane), with several hotels close by. CTM buses stop outside their office on Rue Mohammed Hafidi, less than 100m east of the main roundabout (☎ 0528 866693). Many pass through during the night, and the office is open 24/7. Supratours buses stop outside their office on Rue Bir Anzarane, about 300m south of the main roundabout (☎ 0528 602865). Private buses heading north tend to pick up passengers on the Route d'Agadir, just north of the main roundabout and the *Hôtel Assaka*, but they may also drop off passengers south of the roundabout. Buses for Bou Izakarn and points south will tend to pick up passengers by the Bou Izakarn taxi stand, just south of the main roundabout. Buses for Mirleft and Sidi Ifni (of which there are now only two a day, since local bus #26 stopped running), will pick up passengers on the corner of Av Mohammed V and the Sidi Ifni road. Buses to Tafraoute stop on Rue Mohammed Hafidi, just east of the main roundabout. Because it is so hard to find out when exactly buses will be leaving, and even to be sure where they will stop, most foreigners prefer to use shared grands taxis. Thus it is much easier, for example, to get a taxi collectif to Inezgane and catch a bus to Marrakesh from the *gare routière* there, than to stand around on the Route d'Agadir hoping that a bus for Marrakesh may stop there at some point. One solution is to ask at the bus company offices (SATAS is by the *Hôtel Assaka,* others are in the Mechouar, where buses used to stop), or at the cafés by the *Hôtel Assaka,* but of course information that you get from these sources may not be very reliable. The most useful local bus was the #26 to Sidi Moussa d'Aglou, Mirhleft and Sidi Ifni, currently suspended, though it may be reinstated in some form.

Destinations: Agadir (11 CTM, 12 Supratours & 17 others daily; 2hr); Bou Izakarn (9 CTM & 24 others daily; 1hr–1hr 30min); Casablanca (8 CTM &10 others daily; 10–11hr); Dakhlka (3 CTM, 3 Supratours & 3 others daily; 17–18hr); Goulimine (9 CTM, 11 Supratours & 18 others daily; 1hr 30min–2hr 30min); Laayoune (6 CTM, 7 Supratours & 3 others daily; 9–10hr); Marrakesh (9 CTM, 8 Supratours & 16 others daily; 5–8hr); Mirhleft (2 daily; 45min); Ouarzazate

(1 daily; 9hr 30min); Rabat (3 CTM & 5 others daily; 11–13hr); Sidi Ifni (2 daily; 1hr 30min); Smara (1 CTM & 2 Supratours daily; 7–8hr); Tafraoute (5 daily; 3hr); Tata (6 daily; 7hr); Tan Tan (8 CTM, 9 Supratours and 18 others daily; 4hr 30min).

By Grand Taxi Collective grands taxis for most destinations use a yard opposite the post office, were you'll find vehicles serving Agadir (1hr 15min), Inezgane (1hr), Mirhleft (45min), Sidi Ifni (1hr 30min) and Tafraoute (2hr). Vehicles for Bou Izakarn (1hr) and Goulimine (1hr 30min) have a station on Rue Bir Anzarane, just south of the main roundabout. Shared grands taxis for Sidi Moussa d'Aglou (15min) can be found on Av Hassan II by the southwestern corner of the city wall.

SIDI MOUSSA D'AGLOU

By grand taxi Shared grands taxis leave from Av Hassan II in Tiznit by the southwestern corner of the Medina, though some only go to Aglou village, 3km short of the beach, so be sure to take one that goes all the way, unless you fancy the walk.

ACCOMMODATION

8

TIZNIT

Hotels in the Medina cannot all guarantee hot water, but there's a public showerhouse, Douche Atlas (men and women 7am–9pm; 9dh) in a cul-de-sac off Rue du Bain Maure.

★ **Assaka** Rue Bir Anzarane, on main roundabout ☎0528 602286, ⓦassakahotel.com. The best bargain in town, effectively a three-star hotel at backpacker prices. The rooms are impeccable, with a/c, heating, balcony, TV and good en-suite bathrooms. **165dh**

Bab el Maâder 132 Rue el Haj Ali ☎0673 907314, ⓦbab-el-maader.com. A small *maison d'hôte* run by a French couple who've lived in Morocco for years, very homely and located in an interesting area of the Medina just inside Bab el Mader. **€33**

Camping Municipal Right up against the walls by Bab Ouled Jarrar ☎0528 601354. Tiznit's campsite is secure but doesn't have much shade. It's popular with retired Europeans in camper vans, especially in winter. **42dh**

Idou Tiznit Av Hassan II ☎0528 600333, ⓦidoutiznit .com. Tiznit's poshest option, a four-star that's part of a small nationwide chain, with spacious rooms, a/c, satellite TV, wi-fi, a pool, very professional staff, and usually some kind of promotional rate on offer, but it's a little bit soulless. Claims to be wheelchair accessible, though no adapted rooms, and your chair will have to fit in the lift. BB **633dh**

Maison du Soleil 470 Rue Tafoukt ☎0676 360387, ⓦmaison-du-soleil.com. A small, prettily done out little *maison d'hôte* in a residential area of the Medina, near Bab Aglou and away from the main tourist zone, with just five rooms (two en suite) and a sunny patio, not to mention very reasonably priced home-cooked meals. BB **€30**

★ **Mauritania** Rue Bir Anzarane ☎0528 863632, ⓔhoteltiznitmauritania@gmail.com. Best of the cheapies: a well-kept hotel with lovely little en-suite rooms, very cosy and beautifully turned out, on top of which there are parking facilities and free (though iffy) wi-fi, and the staff are charming, too. A far better deal than the equivalently priced Medina hotels; the nearby *El Amal* (100dh) is a reasonable fall-back if it's full. **80dh**

De Paris Av Hassan II, by main roundabout ☎0528 862865, ⓦhoteldeparis.ma. A friendly and modestly priced hotel, with cosy rooms (en suite, with a/c, heating and TV) and a popular restaurant. However, the only thing this hotel has over the *Assaka* (currently the same price) is its free wi-fi access. **164dh**

De Tiznit Rue Bir Anzarane, on main roundabout ☎0528 862411, ⓔtiznit-hotel@menara.ma. Formerly the poshest hotel in town, though looking a bit down at heel since the *Idou* opened opposite and upstaged it. Nonetheless, it's a decent enough three-star, with a bar and swimming pool, though the rooms are nothing special. **336dh**

Des Touristes 80 Mechouar ☎0528 862018. A deservedly popular backpacker hotel, with hot showers, friendly staff and old-fashioned iron bedsteads. The communal areas are decorated with pictures of Paris in the 1950s and an impressive collection of banknotes. *The Atlas* (100dh), a few doors away, is a reasonable fall-back if it's full. **100dh**

SIDI MOUSSA D'AGLOU

Aglou Beach By the beach ☎0528 613034, ⓦagloubeach.com. It's wise to book ahead at this friendly hotel with fresh, spacious rooms, and a restaurant (daily 11am–3pm & 6.30–9pm) offering fish tajines (45dh) and other tasty grub. A room with a sea view costs 40dh extra. **250dh**

Camping Aglou Plage On the main road ☎0528 613234, ⓦcampingaglou.com. This popular municipal campsite with grocery stores and a pool is about 500m up from the beach, on the right if coming from Tiznit. **45dh**

EATING AND DRINKING

Hôtel de Paris Av Hassan II ☎0528 862865. This is one of the more upmarket spots to eat in town, though that admittedly isn't saying very much. More to the point, it's licensed, so you can have beer or wine with your meal. Lamb chops are 42dh, prawn pili-pili 40dh. Daily 10am–10pm.

Hôtel Mauritania Rue Bir Anzarane ☎0528 863632. Like the *Hôtel de Paris*, the modest restaurant here – unusually – has the advantage of being licensed. The food is nothing special (brochettes with chips and salads for 30dh), and tends to be better at lunchtime than in the evening, but being able to wash it down with a cold beer is a major bonus. Daily 8am–11pm.

Pizzeria Rosa Av Hassan II ☎0528 860011. The pizzas here (30–55dh) are not going to satisfy any serious

cognoscenti, but they're reasonable enough as Moroccan pizzas go, and the venue is clean and pleasant, though the service is not very good. If you don't want a pizza, they also do a reasonable seafood gratinée (40dh) among other dishes, but you'll be waiting a while for it. Daily noon–10pm.

Restaurant Snack Ville Nouvelle Av du 20 Août ☎0528 600963. A good place for bargain breakfasts (13dh), and the top floor has a "panoramic terrace" (with a huge TV screen but not much of a panorama), with a non-smoking saloon on the middle floor. Food on offer includes spaghetti, steaks, brochettes and tajines. There's also free wi-fi. Spagbol goes for 30dh, chicken tajine 25dh. Daily 7am–9pm.

DIRECTORY

Banks and exchange There are plenty of banks in town, as well as a couple of bureaux de change. The one just east of the main roundabout seems to open at random hours, but Chaoli Change Money off Av Hassan II by the Medina's southern corner is open Mon–Sat 8.30am–6pm.

Hammam There's a traditional hammam just inside the

walls at Bab el Khemis, open for men and women (adjacent entrances; daily 8am–11pm; 9dh).

Internet Internet access is available at a number of places including Venmar on the corner of Rue el Hammam and Rue Imizline (daily 9am–midnight; 4dh/hr), or Cyber el Mechouar on the Mechouar (daily 9am–6pm; 5dh/hr).

Tiznit to Tafraoute

The Tiznit–Tafraoute road (R104, previously numbered 7074) passes a succession of villages, most named after their souk day (see p.575). In winter and spring the road is sometimes crossed by streams but it is generally passable enough; the drive takes around two hours, but leave plenty of time to see (and navigate) the mountains before dusk.

At **ASSAKA** (20km from Tiznit), a bridge has been built over Oued Tazerouait – the river that causes most difficulty in winter and spring. Nineteen kilometres further on, a side road heads 10km south to the *zaouia* of **Sidi Ahmed ou Moussa**, which in the seventeenth century controlled its own state, the Tazeroualt, its capital at nearby (and now deserted) **Illigh**. The *zaouia* hosts a **moussem** in the second or third week of August, which is worth trying to attend. Sidi Ahmed is the patron saint of Morocco's acrobats, most of whom come from this region – and return to perform.

Just beyond **Tighmi**, 42km from Tiznit, the road begins its ascent of the **Col du Kerdous** (1100m), with the kasbah-like *Hôtel Kerdous* (p.488) marking the top of the pass. The area is good for paragliding, though there isn't much activity these days.

At the end of the descent, entering the village of **JEMAA IDA OUSSEMLAL** (64km from Tiznit), the road divides. The left fork, which runs downhill through the village, is the direct road to Tafraoute, a picturesque route that drops into the Ameln Valley at Tahala, once a Jewish village. The right fork, a newer road, which skirts round Jemaa Ida Oussemlal, is longer but well surfaced, flatter and faster going, arriving in Tafraoute through a grand spectacle of mountains and the lunar landscape around Agard Oudad (see p. 494). Just after Aït Ouafka, it splits again – take the right-hand fork for **IZERBI**, where an ex-housing minister has built a Disney-style chateau.

Kerdous At the top of the Col du Kerdous pass ☏ 0663 141492, ⊕ hotel-kerdous.com. This old fort with well-turned-out a/c rooms and a pool, deserves at least a stop for a tea and breathtaking views. If you're staying, it's worth taking half-board: the food's good, there's nowhere else to eat within walking distance, and it doesn't cost much more than bed and breakfast anyway. BB **600dh**

Agadir to Tafraoute

The R105 road from Agadir to Tafraoute (three daily buses each way) is a bit drab until you reach the village of **Aït Baha**, which is a lively shopping centre on Wednesday, its souk day. From Aït Baha, the road south to Tafraoute is a highly scenic, though slow and winding mountain ride past a series of fortified kasbah-villages.

The most spectacular fortified village in the region, **TIOULIT**, is to the west of the road, around 35km south of Aït Baha, with the best views of it from the south (so looking back, if you're coming from Agadir). If heading south, another 25km brings you to a junction of roads, with the left fork heading off to Igherm on the R109 Taroudant–Tata road. Around 5km south of this junction is the village of **SIDI ABDALLAH EL JABAR**, scene of a small, but lively moussem around its *zaouia* (Oct 20–22).

Al Adarissa Aït Baha ☏ 0528 254462, ✉ h.eladarissa@menara.ma. This good-value three-star hotel is a handy resting place on the road. Rooms are cool and en suite, arranged round an atrium court, but have outside windows too, and there's a good restaurant. **250dh**

Kasbah de Tizourgan R105, 48km south of Aït Baha ☏ 0661 941350, ✉ tizourganekasbah@yahoo.fr. Almost exactly halfway between Aït Baha and Tafraoute, this guesthouse, located in a thirteenth-century kasbah, makes a great spot to spend your last night in Morocco if you're flying home from Agadir (though it helps if you have your own transport, as there are only three buses a day). Rooms are small but immaculate, with shared bathroom facilities, and there's a very good restaurant – indeed you have to take half-board. HB **480dh**

Tafraoute

TAFRAOUTE is worth all the effort and time it takes to reach, approached by scenic roads through the Anti-Atlas from Tiznit (see p.484) or Agadir (see p.448) – both are beautiful, but the Tiznit approach has the edge, winding through a succession of gorges and a grand mountain valley. With your own transport, you can also get here from Ifrane de l'Anti-Atlas, Igherm or (with 4WD) Aït Herbil. Tafraoute is a centre for villages built among a wind-eroded, jagged panorama of granite tors – "like the badlands of South Dakota", as Paul Bowles put it, "writ on a grand scale". The best time to visit is early spring, when the almond trees are in full blossom, or in autumn, after the intense heat has subdued; in midsummer, it can be debilitatingly hot.

GROUND SQUIRRELS

Along the road from Tiznit to Tafraoute, you may occasionally see children holding little furry animals for sale – live, on a piece of string – by the roadside. These are **ground squirrels**, which are known locally as *anzid* or *sibsib*, and are destined for the **tajine** dish, in which they are considered quite a delicacy, their flesh being sweet since they subsist mainly on a diet of almonds and argan nuts. Recognizable by the prominent stripes down their backs, and by their long tails, ground squirrels are common in the tropics, and have long been ascribed medicinal properties in Morocco. You will not get *anzid* tajine in any restaurant, however, unless perhaps you provide the squirrels yourself.

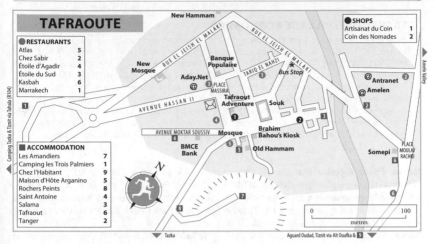

Created as an administrative centre by the French, and little expanded since, Tafraoute is one of the most relaxed destinations in Morocco, though a few *faux guides* may still make a nuisance of themselves, claiming to be the guides mentioned in this and other books, and spinning all sorts of yarns to coax the unwary into carpet shops where they can be subjected to the old hard-sell routine.

ARRIVAL AND DEPARTURE   TAFRAOUTE

By bus The only CTM service (daily to Casablanca via Tiznit, Inezgane and Agadir) starts from the CTM office, just south of Pl Moulay Rachid (☎ 0528 801798). Most other services start from Rue el Jeish el Malaki, with departures to Agadir (6 daily; 5hr); Aït Baha (3 daily; 2hr); Casablanca (5 daily; 14hr); Inezgane (7 daily; 4hr 30min); Marrakesh (4 daily; 10hr); Rabat (2 daily; 16hr); Tiznit (5 daily; 3hr).

By grand taxi Shared grands taxis for Tiznit leave from Rue el Jeish el Malaki. For the Ameln Valley they leave

from the Route d'Amelne by the alley to *Chez Sabir* restaurant.

By minibus Minibuses to Tiouada leave from Pl Moulay Rachid Mon–Sat at around 11.30am, returning at 5.30am the next morning.

Bicycle rental Maison de Vacances, opposite *Kasbah* restaurant has well-kept bicycles (☎ 0528 800197; 80dh/day); *Maison d'Hôtes Arganino* (☎ 0670 661105; 40–70dh/day); Said, Route de Tazka, opposite Maison Tuareg (☎ 0670 409384; 40–80dh/day).

ACCOMMODATION

The hotels in Tafraoute are generally pretty good value. At the top end, the arrival of competition has made prices even more negotiable than usual, and it's worth shopping around to see who'll give you the best deal (all frequently offer promotional rates). Further accommodation options can be found 4km north in the Ameln Valley (see p.491).

Les Amandiers On the hill above town ☎ 0528 800008, ⓦ hotel-lesamandiers.com. Tafraoute's top hotel, which displays photos of Mohammed V laying a foundation stone here and overlooks the whole of Tafraoute, has to a certain extent been upstaged by the new kids in town, but it still has a lot of old-fashioned charm, with a wood-panelled lobby, great views, and large, airy rooms (wi-fi too). There's also a cosy little bar, for residents only. BB 496dh
Camping les Trois Palmiers Off the Tiznit road ☎ 0662 405870. The most central campsite, ten minutes' walk from the centre, is a small, secure enclosure with hot showers, and three small rooms. It tends to overflow out of

its enclosure and spread onto the surrounding land in winter and spring, when Tafraoute plays host to a swarm of camper vans driven by sun-seeking retired Europeans. Camping 30dh, double 80dh
Chez l'Habitant Route d'Aguard Oudad, 1km south of town, on the road to Napoleon's Hat ☎ 0662 029305. Rustic accommodation in a Berber house with views of the Napoleon's Hat and Lion's Face rock formations. You can take a room, rent the whole house, camp out, sleep in a Bedouin-style tent, or on the terrace. Toilets and showers are in a separate block outside. Dorm or tent bed 80dh, double 200dh

8

TAFRAOUTE: VILLAGE ECONOMICS

Among Tafraoute villagers, **emigration** to work in the grocery and hotel trade – all over Morocco and France – is a determining aspect of life. The men return home to retire, however, building European-looking villas amid the rocks, and most of the younger ones manage to come back for a month's holiday each year – whether it be from Casablanca, Tangier, Paris or Marseille.

But for much of the year, it is the women who run things in the valley, and the only men to be found are the old, the family-supported or the affluent. It is a system that seems to work well enough: enormously industrious, and very community-minded, the Tafraoutis have managed to maintain their villages in spite of adverse economic conditions, importing all their foodstuffs except for a little barley, the famed Tafraoute almonds and the sweet oil of the argan tree.

Maison d'Hôte Arganino Near the old mosque ☎ 0670 661105, ✉ arganino@hotmail.fr. This delightful little *pension*-style guesthouse is run by the family who used to live in it, and it still very much has a family atmosphere. It also has its own little hammam. BB 130dh

Rochers Peints Route de Tazka ☎ 0528 800032, ⓦ hotelrocherspeints-tafraoute.com. A very impressive hotel, tastefully done out. The first-floor rooms are more attractive than those on the second floor, with straw-and-*pisé*-covered walls, coloured glass windows, and carved wooden doors from Mali. All rooms have a/c and satellite TV. 300dh

Saint Antoine Av Moktar Soussi ☎ 0528 801497, ⓦ hotelsaintantoine-tafraout.com. A slick, modern hotel, with efficient, English-speaking staff, cool, spacious rooms, a bar and a nice big swimming pool. There's also a decent restaurant and 24hr room service. BB 460dh

Salama By the river ☎ 0528 800026, ⓦ hotelsalama .com. A good-value hotel, originally dating from 1966, but refurbished, with quite large rooms in warm, earthy colours, en-suite bathrooms, free wi-fi throughout, a roof terrace, a fire in winter, and a reputable restaurant. 256dh

★ **Tafraout** Pl Moulay Rachid, by the petrol station ☎ 0528 800060. This is the best of the budget hotels, offering a warm welcome, hot showers and very helpful staff. It isn't quite as cheap as the *Tanger*, but it's quieter, and has larger and more comfortable rooms. 100dh

Tanger Rue el Jeish el Malaki, by the oued ☎ 0546 233966. A cheap and cheerful hotel, cheaper and better than its competitor, the *Redouane* over the road, with friendly staff, and a good restaurant where you can eat outside. The rooms are quite small, but decent enough; the ones on the roof are best. 80dh

EATING AND DRINKING

In addition to the hotels (of which the *Tanger* and the *Salama* both have good restaurants), there are a few reasonable restaurants in town. The only bar open to the public is in the *Hôtel Saint Antoine*.

Atlas Route de Tazka ☎ 0667 120793. Basic but well-presented Moroccan nosh – chicken or lamb brochettes, liver, steak, sandwiches and breakfasts – in spotlessly bright café surroundings complete with blaring TV. Dishes include chicken brochettes (35dh) or veal brochettes (45dh). Daily 7am–8pm.

Chez Sabir 41 Route d'Amelne (100m from Pl Moulay Rachid, then left down a little alley, signposted) ☎ 0528 800636. A small, intimate place with a good 75dh Moroccan or 90dh French set menu, including vegetarian couscous, but best ordered an hour ahead. It's also possible to eat on the roof terrace. On the downside, tables are at the same level as the seats, making eating a rather backbreaking experience. Daily 8am–10.30pm.

Étoile d'Agadir off Pl Massira ☎ 0663 229250. A great little place, serving classic tajines (lamb with prunes and almonds, or chicken with lemon and olives, both 40dh) and other Moroccan dishes, all delicious and beautifully presented. There's also an 80dh set menu. Daily 7am–9pm.

Étoile du Sud Av Hassan II ☎ 0528 800038. A set-menu restaurant (90dh) serving delicious Moroccan food, either indoors or outside in a Bedouin-style tent, with an occasional cabaret and floor show for tour groups. Daily 11am–9pm.

Kasbah Route d'Aguard Oudad ☎ 0660 954269. A large salon, where the 90dh set menu includes a handful of vegetarian options as well as tajines and couscous, with Moroccan wine available, not to mention saffron tea. Daily 11am–9pm.

★ **Marrakech** Tariq el Nahzi ☎ 0663 229250. An unpretentious family-run place with excellent-value meals (60dh set menu) and friendly service. The couscous here (35dh) is particularly good. Daily 9am–9pm.

DIRECTORY

Banks The Banque Populaire on Pl Massira and the BMCE on Av Moktar Soussi have ATMs.

Car repairs You'll find a few mechanics and tyre repair shops north of the bus stop in the crook where the main road does a sharp bend, and also down towards the Afriquia filling station.

Festival A moussem is held in the second week of February to celebrate the almond harvest.

Guides One guide highly recommended for trekking or four-wheel-driving around the region is Mohammed Ouhammou Sahnoun, who lives in the village of Tiouadou and can be contacted by phone or email (☎ 0667 095376, ✉ m_sahnoun@hotmail.com), or via either the *Hôtel Tafraout* or Houssine Laroussi, who runs the Coin des Nomades shop (☎ 0661 627921, ✉ sahara.44@hotmail .com). Brahim Bahou (☎ 0661 822677, ✉ brahim -izanzaren@hotmail.com) offers tourist information from his kiosk by the souk mosque and two-day treks to Jebel el Kest. Beware, however, of touts falsely claiming to know or to be these people – if someone who accosts you in the street claims to be them, ask to see their state-issued ID cards. For excursions further afield, a recommended firm is Tafraout Adventure on Pl Massira (☎ 0528 801368, ⌨ tafraout -aventure.com).

Hammam The old hammam is down a side street by the central mosque. There's another near the bend in the main street (behind the bakery, turn left and it's 100m further, under the arch), and a new one, off Pl Moulay Rachid (50m down the Ameln Valley road, then right and right again after another 50m). All the hammams have entrances for men and women, open from around 5am, but the women's side closes at around 5pm, the men's stays open till about 7.30pm (10–12dh).

Internet access Antranet in the same little street as *Chez Sabir* restaurant (daily 8am–midnight; 5dh/hr); Amelen, behind *Hôtel Tanger* (daily 8am–9pm; 5dh/hr); Aday.Net, Av Hassan II by Pl Massira (daily 9am–11pm; 4dh/hr).

Post office The post office on Place Massira is open Mon– Fri 8.30am–4.15pm (Ramadan 9am–3pm).

Shopping There's a Wednesday souk, held in the centre of town. Worthwhile permanent craft shops include the Coin des Nomades (also called Meeting Place of Nomads; daily 8am–9pm) and Artisanat du Coin (daily 9am–8.30pm), both unpressurized. Tafraoute is well known for its *babouches*, and a narrow street of *cordonniers* sells quality slipperwear just north of the Coin des Nomades.

8

Around Tafraoute

Tafraoute's biggest appeal lies in exploring the surrounding area – north to the beautiful villages of the Ameln Valley, nestled under an awesome escarpment, or south to gorges, palmeries, and curious rock formations such as Napoleon's Hat.

The Ameln Valley

You could spend days, if not weeks, wandering round the 26 villages of the **Ameln Valley**, north of Tafraoute. Set against the backdrop of the Jebel el Kest's rock face, they are all beautiful both from afar and close up – with springs, irrigation systems, brightly painted houses and mosques. On no account, either, should you miss out on a walk to see the **painted rocks** in their, albeit faded, glory.

The **Ameln villages** are built on the lower slopes of the Jebel el Kest, between the "spring line" and the valley floor, allowing gravity to take the water through the village and on to the arable land below. Many have basic shops where you can buy drinks, if little else. Getting around them, you can use a combination of taxis and walking, or rent bicycles.

Even a casual walker could stroll along the valley from village to village: Oumesnat to Anemeur, for example, is around 12km. More serious walkers might consider making the ascent of the **Jebel el Kest** (2359m) or, best of all, **Adrar Mkorn** (2344m), an isolated peak to the southeast with spectacular twin tops (this involves some hard scrambling). A striking feature on it is the **Lion's Face** at Asgaour – a rock formation which really does look like the face of a lion in the afternoon light when seen from Tafraoute. The area around it (and many other areas scattered on both the southern and northern slopes of the Jebel el Kest) offers excellent rock climbing on sound quartzite.

Oumesnat

OUMESNAT, like most Ameln settlements, emerges out of a startling green and purple rockscape, crouched against the steep rock walls of the valley. From a distance, its houses,

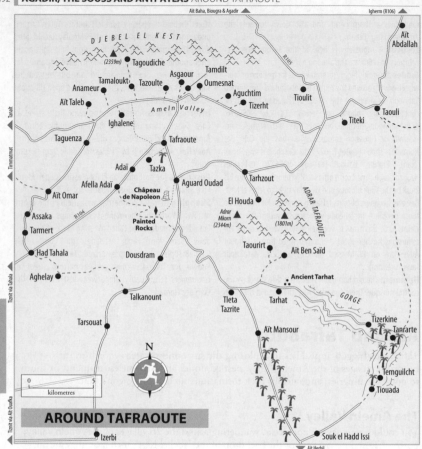

8

perched on the rocks, seem to have a solidity to them – sensible blocks of stone, often three storeys high, with parallel sets of windows. Close up, they reveal themselves as bizarre constructions, often built on top of older houses deserted when they had become too small or decrepit; a few of them, with rooms jutting out over the cliffs, are held up by enormous stilts and have raised doorways entered by short (and retractable) ladders.

La Maison Traditionelle

⊠⊠⊠⊠⊠ ⊠⊠⊠ ⊠⊠⊠⊠⊠

One of Oumesnat's houses, known as **La Maison Traditionelle**, is owned by a blind Berber and his family, who show visitors round. They give an interesting tour, explaining the domestic equipment – grindstones, water-holders, cooking equipment – and the layout of the house with its guest room with separate entrance, animals' quarters, and summer terrace for sleeping out. To get the most from a visit, you may need to engage an interpreter, such as one of the guides recommended in Tafraoute (see p.488).

Anameur

From Oumesnat, you can walk through or above a series of villages to **ANAMEUR**, where there is a *source bleue*, or natural springwater pool, a meandering hike of around three hours. Along the way is **Tazoulte**, one of four local villages with Jewish cemeteries, remnants of a community now completely departed, though Jewish symbols are still inscribed on the region's silverware, which was traditionally made by Jews.

Tagoudiche

The Ameln's highest village, **TAGOUDICHE** (Tagdichte on the road sign), where the trail up the **Jebel el Kest** (or Lekst) begins, is accessible by Land Rover along a rough *piste*. There is a shop and a *gîte* (see p.494) here. The Jebel el Kest is a rough and rocky scramble – there's no actual climbing involved – over a mountain of amethyst quartzite. There is a black igneous dyke below the summit pyramid, and the summit, being a pilgrimage site, has shelters on the top, as well as hooped petticoat daffodils blooming in spring. The easiest route is not obvious and a guide is advisable.

A loop back to Tafraoute

Returning to Tafraoute from the Ameln Valley, you can walk over a pass back from the R104 road near Ighalene in around three hours. The path isn't particularly easy to find but it's a lovely walk, taking you past flocks of sheep and goats tended by their child-shepherds. The route begins as a *piste* (east of the one to Tagoudiche), then you follow a dry riverbed off to the right, up a side valley, where the zigzags of an old track can be seen. Cross to go up here – not straight on – and, once over the pass, keep circling left till you can see Tafraoute below.

Tirnmatmat

The road west along the Ameln Valley crosses an almost imperceptible watershed, beyond which, at Aït Omar (see map opposite), a *piste* heads north to **TIRNMATMAT**, a partly abandoned village. Around 200m further, on the north bank of the river, are numerous **carvings** in the rocks, depicting hunters and animals (some of these may be prehistoric), along with more modern graffiti (including a VW Beetle).

The **ridge walk** to the south of this village is taken by some trekking parties and is really special, with Bonelli's eagles circling below, goats climbing the argan trees, and wild boar snuffling round the bushes.

8

ARRIVAL AND DEPARTURE
AMELN VALLEY

Shared grands taxis run between the Route d'Amelne in Agadir (by the alley to *Chez Sabir* restaurant) and the junction of the Ameln Valley road with the road from Tafraoute, but at only 4km, it's also quite a pleasant walk, or you could rent a bicycle.

INFORMATION

Rock climbing If you intend doing any rock climbing in the region, two invaluable sources of information are *Climbing in the Moroccan Anti-Atlas* by Claude Davies (Cicerone, 2004), and *Moroccan Anti-Atlas North* by Steve Broadbent, both of which detail each site they cover, showing the ascents on photographs of the rock face. Houssine Laroussi at the Coin des Nomades (see p.491) also keeps and dispenses information on rock climbing, and has copies of both books (but not for sale).

ACCOMMODATION

AMELN VALLEY ROAD

L'Argannier d'Ammelne 500m east of the junction with the road from Tafraoute, where the piste for Tamdilt and Asgaour branches off ☎0528 800020, ⓦ arganierammelne.com. Small but sweet rooms, with smooth, polished walls, each in a different colour, set around a small garden, plus camping facilities, and dorm beds. There's also wi-fi. Camping 65dh, BB dorm 50dh, BB double 260dh

Auberge la Tête du Lion 500m east of the junction with the road from Tafraoute, where the piste for Tamdilt and Asgaour branches off ☎0528 801165, ⓦ latetedulion.com. A scenic spot, located directly opposite the Lion's Face (hence the name). The spacious rooms with a/c and wi-fi are arranged around a lush garden, and there's a panoramic roof terrace and a restaurant. 300dh

Chez Amaliya By the junction with the road from Tafraoute ☎0528 800065, ⓦ chezamaliya.com. A cool hotel with quite a cavernous lobby and a pool, surrounded by small but comfortable rooms, plus four larger ones dubbed "junior suites", and more rooms planned for the roof, all run by an enthusiastic Dutch woman. There's wi-fi in the lobby area, but not in the rooms, to encourage the guests to come out and socialize. BB **500dh**

Maison d'Hôte Yamina 1km up the road to Tamdilt ☎ 0670 523883, ⓦ yamina-tafraout.com. A nickel-clean little *auberge* professionally run by a French-Moroccan couple in a traditional Berber house, upgraded with hot running water, a/c, heating, pretty little rooms and en-suite bathrooms. HB **440dh**

Municipal campsite By the junction with the road from Tafraoute. This small campsite is surprisingly empty compared to the sites on the edge of town, but it's just as good, and in summer it even has a swimming pool. **20dh**

OUMESNAT

Gîte Lkst ☎ 0666 556274, ⓔ benabbou12@hotmail .com. A tranquil setting and beautiful scenery are the plus points here, with hard mattresses and darkish rooms the minus points. It isn't the most traditional Berber experience ever, but it's a decent place to stay, at a very decent price. **120dh**.

Maison Traditionelle ☎ 0666 917768, ⓔ maisonhote @gmail.com. The owners of the *Maison Traditionelle* (see p.492) also offer bed and breakfast or half-board in a nearby village house, with a/c rooms (heated in winter) and a little garden. BB **300dh**

TAGOUDICHE

Gîte de Tagoudiche C/o Abed at the village shop ☎ 0667 029484. Very simple village accommodation in a small house with dorm beds mainly aimed at climbers wanting to stay overnight in the village for an early morning ascent. Transport can usually be arranged from Tafraoute for people staying at the *gîte*. **50dh**

Agard Oudad

A short but enjoyable walk from Tafraoute is to head south to **AGARD OUDAD** (3km from Tafraoute), a dramatic-looking village built under a particularly bizarre outcrop of granite. Like many of the rocks in this region, this has been given a name. Most of the others are named after animals – people will point out their shapes to you – but this one is known (in good French-colonial tradition) as **Le Chapeau de Napoléon** (Napoleon's Hat).

The painted rocks

The **Painted Rocks** (Pierres Bleues or Pierres Peints), 1.5km to the southwest of Agard Oudad, were executed in 1984 by Belgian artist **Jean Verame** and a team of Moroccan firemen, who hosed some eighteen tons of paint over a large area of rocks; Verame had previously executed a similar project in Sinai. The rocks had lost some of their colour over the years so a local man decided to refresh them in 2010, to mixed reactions from local people, many of whom disliked the project, especially after pieces of the paint started washing off into the local streams.

To reach the rock on foot, walk through the village and follow the flat *piste* round to the right, behind the Chapeau de Napoléon; you'll see the rocks on your left after a couple of kilometres. You should be able to engage a young guide in the village to help you find them. By car, a smooth *piste* breaks off the Tiznit road 5km further on and wends its way up towards the rocks, leaving a ten-minute walk at the end, but unless you prefer this longer route, don't follow the road sign if you are on foot.

Tazka

Another easy walk from Tafraoute is to **TAZKA**, about 2km southwest, where there is a prehistoric carving of a gazelle. To get there, follow a path through the palmery, arrowed off at the bottom of our Tafraoute map (p.489). When you emerge, past the remains of an old kasbah, you will see on your left the houses of Tazka at the foot of a high granite bluff. Take the lesser path to the right of the bluff and the carvings – a modern one on the rock face and an old one on the tilted surface of a fallen rock – are on your left after around 200m.

The Souk el Hadd Issi loop

A beautiful day-trip from Tafraoute is to drive southeast towards **Souk el Hadd Issi**, a route that takes in some of the most beautiful country of the Anti-Atlas, including some fabulous gorges and palmeries. Most of it is now surfaced, though about 10km are still *piste*, and if you have a sturdy enough vehicle to handle that, you can make a loop of it, travelling down via Aït Mansour and returning via Tizerkine, or vice versa.

Tleta Tazrite

Leaving Tafraoute, follow the road out past Agard Oudad, turning left around 3km south of the village. This road climbs over the hills, with superb panoramas back across Tafraoute and the Ameln Valley, to reach **TLETA TAZRITE** (15km from Tafraoute), which has a souk on Friday – not Tuesday as its name implies, Tleta ("three") being Arabic for Tuesday, which is considered the third day of the week.

Aït Mansour

From Tleta Tazrite, the road heads south to **Aït Mansour**, where many people like to park up and stroll through the massive palmery, which is beautifully cool in the heat of the day. The palmery stretches a good 6km along the floor of a valley, while the road itself rises above it, giving amazingly beautiful vistas, before descending, past largely abandoned villages, back to the level of the palm trees.

Souk el Hadd Issi

At the southern end of the Aït Mansour palmery, the road passes a fine *agadir* (fortified granary). Just south of this, at **SOUK EL HADD ISSI**, the palmery ends. To the south, a *piste* (for which really you need 4WD) heads off to Aït Herbil (see p.480), passing a number of ancient **rock carvings**, though they are not easy to find and a guide would be advisable. The first and least difficult group of carvings to find are some 700m east of the road, about 6.4km south of the junction, and feature long-horned cattle and elephants, which lived in this part of Africa when the carvings were made.

The village of Souk el Hadd Issi itself (Souk el Had Arfallah Ihrir on the Michelin map) is east of the junction with the Aït Herbil *piste*, and as its name suggests ("Hadd" or "one" meaning Sunday), it has a Sunday souk. The road through and beyond the village is now surfaced most of the way to **TIOUADA**, where there's accommodation (see below).

Tiouada to Tarhat

From just south of Tiouada to **TIZERKINE**, all semblance of paved road comes to an end, and a passable *piste* takes you through a lovely oasis snaking along a canyon. The first village you pass if heading north along the canyon is **TEMGUILCHT**, dominated by the very large and impressive **Zaouia Sidi Ahmed ou Mohammed** (no entrance to non-Muslims), where there is a moussem in honour of the saint every August.

At Tizerkine, the oasis peters out, but you regain the tarmac to take you through the northern section of the gorge. If you are heading south rather than north, you'll need to bear right where the road forks, 5km beyond Tizerkine.

At the northern end of the canyon is the modern village of **TARHAT** (Taghaout), but just to its east, high above the north side of the road, are the twelfth-century remains of **ancient Tarhat**, a fortified village and *agadir* perched on the lip of a sheer rock wall. A footpath leads up to it from the modern village.

ARRIVAL AND DEPARTURE   TIOUADA

By minibus Minibuses leave for Tiouada and Souk el Hadd	Issi around 11.30am–noon, returning at 5.30am.

ACCOMMODATION

★ **Auberge Sahnoun** Tiouada ☎0528 216609 or ☎0667 095376, ✉m_sahnoun@hotmail.com. The accommodation's simple but homely, and the setting is lovely, on the edge of Tiouada's palmery. There are hot showers, home cooking, and traditional music by the fire available, but space is limited (you may have to share a room, depending on how full they are), so it's best to call or email ahead. Mohammed can also arrange mule treks in the region, and help locate rock carvings. HB **150dh**

Tiznit to Goulimine via Sidi Ifni

Heading **south from Tiznit to Goulimine**, you have a choice of routes: the N1, a fast inland road across scrubby desert via **Bou Izakarn**, where the road to Tata heads off east; or a more circuitous journey along the coast, by way of the splendid former Spanish enclave of **Sidi Ifni**.

Mirhleft

MIRHLEFT is a friendly, bustling village, about halfway between Tiznit and Sidi Ifni, set a kilometre back from a series of good beaches with crashing waves and strong currents, which particularly attract **surfers**. A 1935 **French military fort** overlooks the village from the hill above, which you can climb for beautiful views over the surrounding countryside. The village hosts a Monday **souk**, devoted mainly to secondhand items.

ARRIVAL AND DEPARTURE   MIRHLEFT

By grand taxi Mirhleft is served by grands taxis from Sidi Ifni and Tiznit, but they can be sparse, especially around lunchtime – they run from the main road in the middle of the village.
By bus The bus between Tiznit and Sidi Ifni, currently

suspended, would serve Mirhleft if reinstated. Otherwise there are only two daily buses running north to Tiznit in the morning, and south to Sidi Ifni in the evening; they stop in the centre of the village.

ACCOMMODATION

★ **Abertih** On the corner of the main street with the Tiznit–Ifni road ☎0528 719304, ⓦabertih.com. The best hotel in the the village, well run and tastefully decorated, with a good restaurant and free wi-fi, constant hot water and some en-suite rooms. Also a good place to get paragliding information. **200dh**

Aftas Beach House Aftas beach ☎0675 164271, ⓦaftasmirleft.com. A small guesthouse run by an English woman, in a great location, right on its own little beach, with almost nothing else there. The rooms are small, and some (slightly pricier) have ocean views; food is available (for guests only) and the *Café Aftas* next door (☎0670 729583, ⓦcafeaftas.com) offers surfing lessons. **382dh**

Atlas Opposite the souk ☎0528 719309, ⓦatlas-mirleft.com. A bog-standard Moroccan hotel revamped for tourists. The rooms are but small and simple, some en suite, but most without outside windows. There's a roof terrace giving views of the fort, the showers and toilets are impressively clean, and they supply towels, soap and shampoo. It's not a bad place, but overpriced. **240dh**

★ **Auberge des Trois Chameaux** On the hill above town, just below the fort ☎0528 719187, ⓦ3chameaux.com. Classy *maison d'hôte* housed in what used to be the officers' quarters of the French army fort. There's a choice of rooms (which are actually more

like junior suites) and, for not much more money, suites with private terraces and wonderful views. There's also a heated swimming pool, parking facilities, an in-house hammam, good food and great vistas over the countryside. **900dh**

Dar Najmat Plage Sidi Mohammed Ben Abdallah, 2km south of town ☎0528 719056, ⓦdarnajmat.com. A beautiful *auberge* with bright modern a/c rooms and a scenic pool, standing on its own at the end of a small, picturesque beach dominated by an impressively large rock and overlooked by a mosque and a row of small shops, with just one beach café. The beach is not suitable for surfing, which keeps most of the Mirhleft crowd away. HB **€107**

Du Sud opposite the souk ☎0528 719407, ⓦhoteldusud.fr. Fresh white rooms, hot-water showers (shared) and a splash of paint have turned what was a basic Moroccan hotel into somewhere quite nice to stay, and there's a good restaurant too. **170dh**

Tafoukt Next to the souk ☎0528 719077. This simple, no-nonsense hotel charges ordinary Moroccan rates, and makes no particular concessions to tourists, but it's clean and decent, and frankly just as good as the *Atlas* and the *du Sud* opposite, which are over twice the price. Most of the rooms have windows facing inward, and those at the top get a lot more light than those on the first floor. **80dh**

EATING AND DRINKING

À la Bonne Franquette Hôtel du Sud ☎0528 719407. The *Hôtel du Sud*'s restaurant cooks up some tasty grub, including grilled fish (75dh) and camel tajine (50dh), and it's also licensed. Daily noon–9pm.

Café Snack Centre On the street opposite the taxi stand

☎0611 601322. In principle this is a Moroccan rather than tourist-oriented restaurant, but it still serves up quite posh dishes such as stuffed tomato (35dh) and *steak au poivre* (45dh), along with the usual couscous, tajines, salads and sandwiches, not to mention coffee and mint tea. Daily 7am–10pm.

Hôtel Abertih ☎ 0528 719304. The menu changes daily here, but the food is always good, and you can have beer or wine with your meal. There's usually fish cooked *a la plancha* (70–80dh) and couscous (60dh) on offer. Daily 7pm–midnight.

DIRECTORY

Bank There's an Attijariwafa Bank with an ATM on the main road.

Internet Cyber Tzarzit (daily 9am–midnight; 5dh/hr)

and Cyber@Farah (daily 8am–past midnight; 5dh/hr), both in the middle of the village on the road opposite the taxi stand.

Legzira Beach

This fine **beach**, with natural sea-worn rock archways, 10km north of Sidi Ifni, is overlooked by an old Spanish fort from the hills above, whose thermal currents attract hang-gliding and paragliding enthusiasts. A rather horrible vacation village is unfortunately now being built directly above the beach.

ARRIVAL AND DEPARTURE   LEGZIRA

By public transport Apart from two evening buses to Sidi Ifni and two in the morning to Tiznit, there is pretty much no public transport here unless you can flag down a passing grand taxi with a spare place.

On foot You can walk here along the coast from Sidi Ifni, a two-and-a-half-hour hike along beach and cliffs, coming into Legzira under the rock archways.

ACCOMMODATION AND EATING

There are four *auberges* on the beach, each with a restaurant and generator (evenings only). These will probably survive the arrival of the vacation village, but the beach may become less attractive as a result, especially at weekends.

Auberge Sables d'Or On the beach ☎ 0661 302495. Good rooms, some with bathrooms and terraces, plus a decent restaurant downstairs make this a good choice among the *auberges*, currently with lower prices than the neighbouring *Beach Club*. BB **200dh**

Ocean Lagzira On the beach ☎ 0670 970321. This is the newest and, at present anyway, the best value of the *auberges*. The rooms are large, all en suite, and each with its own terrace and seating area. BB **250dh**

Sidi Ifni

SIDI IFNI is uniquely interesting: an enclave relinquished by Spain only in 1969, after the Moroccan government closed off landward access. Built in the 1930s, on a clifftop site, it is surely the finest and most romantic Art Deco military town ever built. Many of its 1930s buildings have been the victims of neglect, but with a realization by the authorities that they attract tourists, steps are now being taken to conserve the town's heritage, and many are also being bought up by foreigners.

The site, then known as Santa Cruz del Mar Pequeño ("Holy Cross of the Small Sea"), was held by the Spanish from 1476 to 1524, when the Saadians threw them out. In 1860, the Treaty of Tetouan (see p.537) gave it back to them, though they didn't reoccupy it until 1934, after they (or rather, the French) had "pacified" the interior.

Sidi Ifni's main attractions are its Spanish feel and **Art Deco architecture**. The beach, with a *marabout* tomb at its northern end, is not that great (the beaches at Legzira and Mirhleft are better; see p.497 & p.496) and is prone to long sea mists. On Sundays a large **souk** takes place just east of the abandoned airfield.

Plaza de España

The heart of the town is **Plaza de España** (officially renamed Place Hassan II), its centrepiece an Andalusian garden with Spanish tiled benches and a Moroccan tiled fountain. A plinth in the middle once bore the statue of General Capaz, who took Ifni for Spain in 1934. At the northern end of the square, the now empty **Spanish**

8

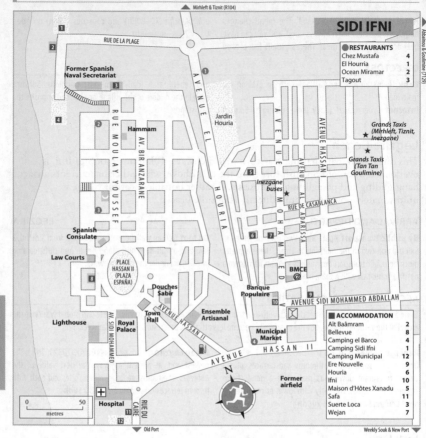

consulate, a building straight out of García Márquez, stands next to a Moorish Art Deco building, which used to be the **church**, and is now the law court. At the other end of the plaza, the blue-and-white-striped **town hall**, complete with its town clock, stands next to the former governor-general's residence, now the **royal palace**. Behind it, there's a magnificent Art Deco **lighthouse**.

Rue Moulay Youssef

Rue Moulay Youssef boasts, halfway along it, what must be the world's only **Art Deco mosque**, small and rather pretty, with blue piping up the sides of the minaret. At the street's northern end is the *Hôtel Suerte Loca*, and next to it, a building in the shape of a ship, which once housed the **naval secretariat**. It was the first building to go up in Sidi Ifni, and its two forward portholes were the windows of cells where miscreant sailors were held.

Avenue Mohammed V

Old Spanish street signs on **Avenue Mohammed V** still identify it as Calle Seis de Abril, and several of its buildings are original Ifni Art Deco. The **post office** was much more splendid before the top storey was demolished, and under Spanish rule it used to issue its own stamps, featuring wildlife, traditional costumes and even the town's buildings. Across the street, the **Banque Populaire**, like the Naval Secretariat, is built in the form of a ship.

SURFING AND PARAGLIDING

In recent years, Sidi Ifni has become something of a base for **surfing and paragliding**. Favourite surfing spots are the main beach, just in front of the tennis courts, and another beach 100m south of the new port. *Hotel Suerte Loca* runs a small surfing supplies shop. Favourite paragliding spots are the hills behind Ifni, and at Legzira (see p.497).

The ports

Two kilometres south of town, the **old port**, built by the Spanish, has an odd little concrete island where ships used to dock. It was connected to the mainland by a unique cable car, which hauled goods as well as passengers. The **new port**, just south of the old one, has big new sardine- and anchovy-processing factories. On the way is the former Spanish prison, now disused, and an airfield, also disused, whose last landing was an American locust-spraying plane, forced down here on one engine after being shot at by Polisario guerrillas in 1988. The airport building is now a meteorological station.

ARRIVAL AND DEPARTURE   SIDI IFNI

By bus Sidi Ifni has two early morning buses to Inezgane (3hr 30min), one continuing to Marrakesh (8hr 30min); both stop on Av Mohammed V. The AGB bus #26 which served Tiznit via Mirhleft used to run every two hours 7am–7pm (and hourly in summer) but the service is currently suspended. There are, however, moves afoot to reinstate it in some form, so it may be up and running again by the time you read this.

By grand taxi Grands taxis leave four blocks east of Av Mohammed V, serving Goulimine (1hr), Mirhleft (45min), Tiznit (1hr 30min) and sometimes Inezgane (3hr 30min).

ACCOMMODATION

HOTELS

Aït Baâmram Rue de la Plage – at the bottom of the steps ☎0528 780217. By the beach, and with a restaurant and bar, this hotel has immaculate tiled walls and floors in its public areas, but the rooms are a bit chipped and scuffed, though all are en suite. <u>180dh</u>

Bellevue Pl Hassan II (Plaza de España) ☎0528 875072, ☎0528 780499. Housed in an original Ifni Art Deco building, right on Plaza de España, and next to the law courts, this well-kept hotel has sweeping views over the beach, wi-fi and a good restaurant. Some rooms are en suite, but the shared bathroom facilities for those that aren't have hot water from 7–11am only. <u>130dh</u>

Ere Nouvelle Av Sidi Mohammed Abdallah ☎0528 875298. The best of the four cheap hotels in the main part of town, with friendly staff and clean rooms, though not all have outside windows. There's also a good-value restaurant. The big problem with this hotel is that the showers are currently out of action, but there are public showers at Douches Sabir, off Av Hassan II (both sexes daily 8am–1pm & 2–8pm; 12dh). <u>70dh</u>

Houria (aka Liberté) 9 Rue Mohammed el Kauzir, off Av Mohammed V; **Hotel Ifni** Av Mohammed V; **Hotel Wejan** 119 Rue Mohammed el Kauzir. A trio of small, basic hotels very close to each other, and all catering mainly for a Moroccan clientele. Prices are similar to those at the *Ere Nouvelle*, for which these can be considered as fall-back alternative options. Only the *Ifni* currently has working hot showers. <u>70dh</u>

★ **Suerte Loca** Rue Moulay Youssef ☎0528 875350, ☎suerteloca-ifni.com. A characterful place – the name ("Crazy Luck") and a bodega-style bar (not licensed) reveal its small-town Spanish origins – run by a very welcoming English-speaking family. It has cheap rooms in the old Spanish wing, slightly pricier en-suite ones (200dh) in a new wing, and is deservedly popular. It also has a good café-restaurant and a terrace overlooking the town and sea. <u>125dh</u>

Maison d'Hôtes Xanadu 5 Rue el Jadida (look for the Ψ symbol on the door) ☎0528 876718, ☎maisonxanadu.com. Bright, cheerful *maison d'hôte* with lots of jolly pastel colours, and breezy, modern, en-suite rooms, plus wi-fi and great views from the roof terrace. BB <u>550dh</u>

Safa (aka Ifni Marina Hôtel) Rue du Caire ☎0528 780790, ☎ifnimarina.com. This modern hotel, built to accompany a marina development, is generic and totally lacking in character, but it's fresh and bright, with yellow-and terracotta-painted rooms, all with balconies and a/c. It claims to be wheelchair accessible, but has no specially adapted rooms. BB <u>300dh</u>

CAMPSITES

Camping el Barco Rue de la Plage ☎0528 780707, ☎complexe-elbarco.com. Right by the beach, and, like the other two campsites, unshaded, this one also has some

8

slightly weatherbeaten rooms (dubbed "bungalows") with sea-facing balconies and kitchenettes. Discounts for long stays. Camping **40dh**, bungalow **300dh**

Camping Municipal Rue du Caire (no phone). Located in the centre of town, so handy for the market and the Art Deco buildings, but not for the beach. **55dh**

Camping Sidi Ifni Rue de la Plage ☎ 0528 876734. The best of the three campsites, run by the proprietors of the *Hôtel Bellevue*. It has absolutely no shade at all, but it does have free wi-fi, a swimming pool in summer (open to all, 20dh), high walls for security, and sunshine most of the day. Rooms are also available. Camping **35dh**, double **70dh**

EATING AND DRINKING

Chez Mustafa By the market ☎ 0633 812958. Best of a bunch of hole-in-the-wall eateries on the western side of the municipal market (it's the one nearest Av Hassan II), serving good fish tajines, as well as fried squid, sole, prawns or whiting (34dh), though actually these all come down from Agadir daily rather than being caught locally. Daily 10am–11pm.

El Hourria Av el Houria ☎ 0528 816343. Eat inside or out in the garden at this attractive restaurant in a valley between the two sides of town, with options such as fried squid (45dh) or prawn pili-pili (36dh). On Fridays there's also couscous. Daily 9am–11pm.

Ocean Miramar 3 Av Moulay Abdellah ☎ 0528 876637. Immaculate restaurant with a scenic terrace specializing in fish and seafood, including fish tajines (60dh) and paella (50dh), and chocolate mousse (15dh) or banana split (20dh) for afters. Also does breakfasts. Daily 7am–10pm.

Tagout 2 Av Moulay Abdellah ☎ 0672 769520. A pleasant and good-value little place offering a good array of tajines and fish dishes, though it may not have everything that's on the menu. Options include fish or octopus tajine (35dh), or octopus with chips and salad (40dh). Daily 9am–10pm.

DIRECTORY

Banks BMCE and Bankque Populaire on Av Mohammed V, both with ATMs.

Festival Annual celebration on June 30 to celebrate Ifni's 1969 reincorporation into Morocco.

Internet IfniWeb behind BMCE bank (9.30am–1pm & 3–11pm; 5dh/hr).

Swimming Pool *Camping Sidi Ifni* (summer only; 20dh).

Goulimine

Surrounded by some impressively bleak scenery, **GOULIMINE** (also spelt Guelmim or Gulimime) is an administrative town with a distinctly frontier feel and a couple of small, fairly animated souks. The nearest thing it has to a tourist sight is the remains of **Caid Dahman Takni's palace**, in the backstreets behind the *Hôtel la Jeunesse*, ruined now but barely a hundred years old. One or two local hustlers indulge in theatrical cons, usually involving invitations to see "genuine *hommes bleus*" (supposedly desert nomads, clad in blue) in tents outside town, inevitably just an excuse to relieve tourists of some money.

Goulimine's Saturday souk, known as the **camel market**, is rather a sham. It has the usual Moroccan goods (grain, vegetables, meat, clothes, silver, jewellery, sheep and goats), but what it doesn't have many of is camels, which have fallen from favour over the years in the wake of lorries and transit vehicles, and the caravan routes are more or less extinct. The few you do see have been brought in for show or to be sold for meat. The market is held a kilometre out of town on the road to Tan Tan; it starts around 6am, and a couple of hours later the first tour buses arrive. There are a couple of quite animated **evening markets**, one off the Route d'Agadir (now officially renamed Boulevard Mohammed VI), mainly selling food, and one off Avenue des FAR, mainly selling clothes.

ARRIVAL AND DEPARTURE
GOULIMINE

By plane The airport (☎ 0528 872230) is 5km out of town, off the Sidi Ifni road; there's no public transport so you'll have to charter a grand taxi to get there (20dh); arriving by air, you may need to call your hotel to send a taxi. Royal Air Maroc, represented by 3S Travel at 177 Bd Mohammed VI (Route d'Agadir; ☎ 0528 771269), run flights to Casablanca (3 weekly; 1hr 30min) and to Tan Tan (3 weekly; 30min).

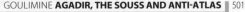

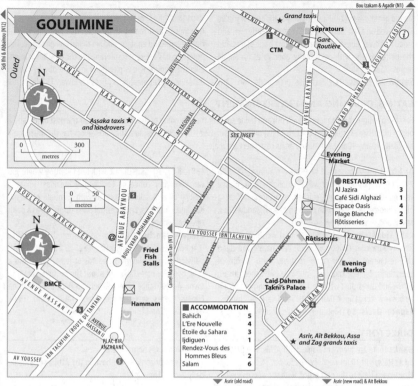

By bus Private buses use the *gare routière* on the Bou Izakarn road. The CTM office is just across the street on Av Ibn Battouta (☎0528 871135), and Supratours buses are at the other side of the *gare routière* on Av Abaynou (☎0528 871503).

Destinations: Agadir (9 CTM, 14 Supratours & 18 others daily; 4hr 30min); Casablanca (6 CTM & 12 others daily; 14hr); Dakhla (3 CTM, 3 Supratours & 3 others daily; 16hr); Laayoune (6 CTM, 9 Supratours & 3 others daily; 7hr); Marrakesh (7 CTM, 8 Supratours & 14 others daily; 9hr 30min); Ouarzazate (2 daily; 15hr) via Tata (9hr 30min), Foum el Hassan (6hr) & Akka (8hr); Rabat (2

CTM & 7 others daily; 16hr); Smara (1 CTM, 2 Supratours & 1 other daily; 6hr); Tan Tan (8 CTM, 11 Supratours & 20 others daily; 3hr); Tiznit (9 CTM, 14 Supratours & 18 others daily; 2hr 30min).

By grand taxi Grands taxis leave from next to the *gare routière* for Agadir (4hr 45min), Bou Izakarn (1hr), Inezgane (4hr 30min), Laayoune (5hr), Sidi Ifni (1hr), Tiznit (2hr 30min) and Tan Tan (2hr 30min). For Assaka (1hr), they leave from a station on Av Hassan II at the junction of Av el Moukouama, where Land Rover taxis can also be found. For Aït Bekou (30min), Asrir (15min) and Assa-Zag (2hr), they use a station southeast of the centre, on the new Asrir road.

INFORMATION

Tourist information Délégation de Tourisme, 209 Bd   Mohammed VI (Mon–Fri 8.30am–4.30pm; ☎0528 872911).

ACCOMMODATION

Bahich 31 Av Abaynou ☎0528 772178, ✉bahich -hotel@hotmail.com. A nice little place, centrally located, with cool rooms, if a bit plain and functional, some with en-suite showers. The distinctive 3-D paintings in the lobby are by local artist, Hamid Kahlaoui. **180dh**

l'Ere Nouvelle 115 Bd Mohammed V ☎0662 020817.

This is the best of Goulimine's ultra-cheapies (some of which are very grotty indeed). It's basic but it's clean, the staff are friendly and welcoming, and there are hot showers (10dh) on request. **60dh**

★ **Ijdiguen** 194 Av Ibn Battouta ☎&✉0528 771453. Bright, clean, and right opposite the *gare routière*, with shared hot showers (7dh) and friendly staff; great if you've just arrived on a late bus, or need to catch an early one, and a good halfway house between the most basic places and the better hotels, with particularly good rates for single rooms (75dh). **150dh**

Salam Av Youssef Ibn Tachfine (Route de Tan Tan)

☏ 0528 872057, ✉ hotelsalamguelmim@hotmail.com. Goulimine's best rooms, though not its most expensive – they're large and en suite, and set round an open patio. The hotel also has a decent restaurant and the only bar in town. Like the *Bahich*, it has paintings in the lobby by Hamid Kahlaoui, and at present its prices are lower. **153dh**

EATING, DRINKING AND ENTERTAINMENT

For cheap eating, there's a row of fried fish and tajine spots at the beginning of the Agadir road near the post office, and a bunch of *rôtisseries* (spit-roast chicken joints) on Av Mohammed V by Pl Bir Anzarane. The *Hôtel Salam* has the town's only bar (daily 10am–10pm), but nearly all its customers are male.

Al Jazira Bd Mohammed VI (Route d'Agadir) ☏ 0528 772818. A popular diner with striplights and plastic seating, selling spit-roast chicken, shawarma (40dh a plate), brochettes (35dh with chips and salad), sandwiches, salads and snacks. Daily noon–4am.

Café Sidi Alghazi at the junction of Av Ibn Battouta and Av Abaynou ☏ 0661 479855. Very handy and clean café-restaurant by the *gare routière*, with a bit of everything: tajines, couscous, pizzas, sandwiches, juices, coffee and cakes, Just what you need if arriving or leaving by bus at a stupid hour. Daily 24hr; food 8am–midnight.

Espace Oasis Bd Mohammed VI (Route d'Agadir)

☏ 0528 877303. Kitsch café with lurid lighting where you can take your coffee or Continental breakfast under a canopy or in a salon decorated with a couple of Hamid Kahlaoui paintings, and a central pillar disguised as a palm tree. Daily 6am–10pm.

Plage Blanche 143 Bd Mohammed VI (Route d'Agadir), by Ziz filling station ☏ 0528 871020. A posh patisserie (by Goulimine standards at least) that's also a café, good for breakfast, and about the best restaurant in town. A beef tajine here will set you back 35dh, and on Fridays there's seven-veg couscous (also 35dh). Daily 6am–2am; food from noon.

DIRECTORY

Banks There are plenty of banks with ATMs. The BMCE is on Av Hassan II, 100m west of *Hôtel Salam*.

Hammam Next to the post office, with showers as well as steam; men's and women's entrances are either side of a café, (both sexes 6am–8pm).

Internet Horizons, 4 Av Abaynou (by Attijariwafa Bank; daily 9am–11pm; 4dh/hr).

Around Goulimine

A large **moussem** is held yearly in early June at **Asrir**, 10km southeast of Goulimine, with lots of camels (it was traditionally a camel traders' fair) and the chance to see **Guedra dancing**, a seductive women's dance of the desert, performed from a kneeling position (developed for the low tents) to a slow, repetitive rhythm.

Abbainou

ABBAINOU (Abeïno) is a tiny oasis, 15km northeast of Goulimine, and an easy excursion if you have transport (head up the Sidi Ifni road for a kilometre and it's signposted to the right). If you don't have a vehicle, you could negotiate a grand taxi (from the main rank by the souk). There are hot springs, which have been tapped, and on cool mornings the irrigation channels through the palmery can be seen steaming. There's a basic **campsite**, and a café and bakery in the village centre, but the main interest is the *station thermale* at the immaculate *Hôtel Abaynou* (☏0528 872892; BB 300dh), where two indoor pools have been created, one for women at 28°C, the other for men, at a scalding 38°C.

Aït Bekkou

The largest and most spectacular oasis in the Goulimine area is **AÏT BEKKOU** (or Aït

Boukka), 10km southeast along the Asrir road, then 7km on *piste*. It can be reached by shared grand taxi from Goulimine (station on the Asrir road). Aït Bekkou is a thriving agricultural community, with an especially lush strip of cultivation along a canal, irrigated from the old riverbed and emerging from a flat expanse of sand. You might even see the odd herd of camels being grazed out here. To reach the canal, head for the thicket of palms about 2km behind the oasis (or pick up a guide on the way).

Fort Bou-Jerif

Fort Bou-Jerif is a truly romantic spot, set beside the Oued Assaka, 13km from the sea, with a wonderful **auberge-campsite** in an old French Foreign Legion camp in the middle of nowhere. From here, you can go on some superb four-wheel-drive excursions in the area, including trips to the **Plage Blanche** – the "White Beach" that stretches for sixty or so kilometres along the coast southwest of Goulimine. Travellers heading for Mauritania and Senegal should also be able to pick up information here as a lot of overlanders stop over at the fort on their way down.

ARRIVAL AND DEPARTURE   FORT BOU-JERIF

By car and chartered transport The easiest route to the fort from Goulimine is via a paved road to Tisséguemane which branches left off the Sidi Ifni road a kilometre outside Goulimine, then 20km of *piste*, which you could probably persuade a grand taxi driver to take you along for a small fee, and which can be negotiated, with care, in a car or camper van. The fort can alternatively be approached on a paved road down the coast from Sidi Ifni to Foum Assaka, which leaves only 6km of *piste*. Failing that, you should be able to charter a Land Rover taxi in Goulimine from the junction of Av Hassan II with Av el Moukaouama.

ACCOMMODATION

Fort Bou-Jerif auberge-campsite ☎ 0672 130017, ⒲ fortboujerif.com. This wonderful place offers accommodation in a "motel", a "little hotel" and a "hotel" or you can camp, with a nomadic tent on offer if you don't have your own. Most people take half-board, which is a good idea as the food is good (camel tajine the speciality) and there is nowhere else nearby to eat. Camping **95dh**, nomadic tent (per person) **70dh**, double **470dh**

8

The Tarfaya Strip and Western Sahara

DUNES NEAR LAAYOUNE

9

The Tarfaya Strip and Western Sahara

Few travellers venture south of Goulimine unless bound for Mauritania or Senegal. Certainly, the dead-end administrative town of Tan Tan has few attractions, though surfers in particular may want to check out the rather more appetizing beach resort of Tan Tan Plage. The last town in Morocco proper, Tarfaya, is really just a sleepy little fishing village that sometimes gives the impression of having been all but forgotten, but it has a charmingly lazy air about it. Once over the demarcation line into the Western Sahara, things change, and the towns of Laayoune, Boujdour and Dakhla, are bright, modern places by comparison, settled by pioneering Moroccans enticed with state subsidies. Smara is the only really historical site in the territory.

Of more interest to many travellers than the towns of the region is the surrounding **landscape**, and you are sure spend much of your time here travelling across vast, bleak tracts of *hammada* (stony desert); there's certainly no mistaking that you've reached the Sahara proper. Returning, if you don't fancy a repeat of the journey, there are flights from Dakhla and Laayoune to Agadir or the Canary Islands. And once you've reached Dakhla, Dakkar and Banjul are actually as close as Marrakesh and Casablanca.

Although the area covered by this chapter was all formerly under Spanish rather than French colonial rule, French has now almost entirely replaced Spanish as the dominant **second language** throughout the region.

The region's **economic importance** was long thought to centre on the phosphate mines at Boukra, southeast of Laayoune. However, these have not been very productive in recent years, and the deposits are not especially rich by the standards of the Plateau des Phosphates east of Casablanca. In the long term, the rich deep-water fishing grounds offshore are likely to prove a much better earner. This potential is gradually being realized with the development of fishing ports at Laayoune, Dakhla and Boujdour, together with industrial plants for fish storage and processing.

Tan Tan and around

The approach from Goulimine to **Tan Tan** runs along 125km of straight desert road, across a bleak area of scrub and *hammada*. There are few features to speak of en route: a café and petrol station (55km from Goulimine); a small pass (85km); and finally a crossing of the **Oued Drâa** (109km), invariably dry at this point, where you may be asked to show your passport (as you also may coming into Tan Tan). A *piste* from here heads west to a last French **fort** at the mouth of the oued.

Parallels and demarcation lines p.509
Travelling in the Western Sahara p.512
Western Saharan history pp.522–523
Simmering tensions in Dakhla p.525
The road to Mauritania p.527

Highlights

❶ Smara This red-ochre desert town was once the seat of local ruler the Blue Sultan, whose palace and great mosque constitute the town's main sights. **See p.511**

❷ Tarfaya A sleepy fishing village with an offshore fort, which you can walk over to at low tide, and a museum dedicated to Antoine de Saint-Exupéry. **See p.515**

❸ Laayoune A pioneering boom town built on subsidies and determination, with excellent fish and seafood, and just a ghost, in its oldest quarters, of a Spanish colonial past. **See p.516**

❹ Fish Laayoune and Dakhla in particular have some really fabulous fish and seafood on offer, locally caught, fresh as can be, and – especially in Dakhla – often served up in the form of Spanish dishes such as *paella or pulpo alla gallega*. **See pp.520 & 526.**

❺ Dakhla The furthest south you can go by land from Europe without a visa – 22km from the tropics, sun all year round, a laidback vibe, and some lovely beaches within spitting distance of town. **See p.525**

HIGHLIGHTS ARE MARKED ON THE MAP ON P.508

9

Tan Tan is a drab administrative centre of around 70,000 inhabitants. Because it's part of a duty-free zone, along with the rest of the Tarfaya Strip and Western Sahara, a lot of shops sell goods such as radios, computers and electric razors. Aside from its moussem (see p.511), Tan Tan's one claim to fame is that it was a departure point for Hassan II's famous **Green March** to occupy the Western Sahara (*La Marche Verte*, or *el Massira el Khadra*; see p.543).

Tan Tan Plage (El Ouatia)

TAN TAN PLAGE (also called El Ouatia), 26km from town, and just off the coastal route to Laayoune, is a fishing port, responsible for a large percentage of Morocco's sardine exports. It has a shadeless and often windswept **beach** that gets quite crowded in summer, and is increasingly popular with surfers, though not very good for casual bathing due to its large breakers and strong currents. With a large number of small hotels and restaurants, however, it's a lot more attractive as a place to stay than Tan Tan itself.

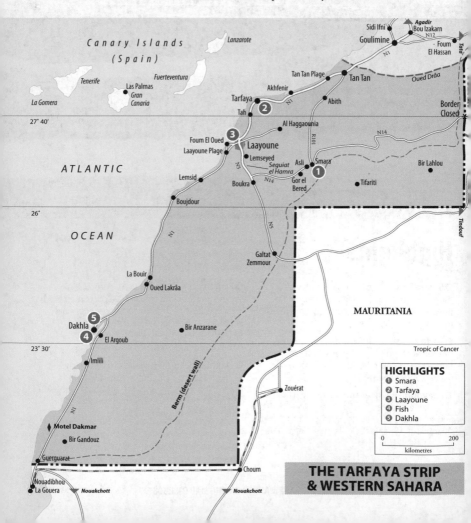

9

PARALLELS AND DEMARCATION LINES

In colonial times, the Oued Drâa was the border between the French and Spanish protectorates. The land to the south, the **Tarfaya strip**, was part of the Spanish Protectorate in Morocco, along with the area around Tetouan and Al Hoceima in the north. It was not considered part of Spain's two Saharan colonies (together known as the **Spanish Sahara**), of which the northernmost, **Seguiat el Hamra**, began at the 27°40´ N line just south of Tarfaya, while the southern one, **Rio de Oro**, began at the 26th parallel, just south of Boujdour. In 1958, two years after the rest of Morocco gained independence, the Spanish gave back the Tarfaya strip, but they kept the Spanish Sahara until November 1975 (see box, pp.522–523).

ARRIVAL AND DEPARTURE

TAN TAN AND AROUND

TAN TAN

By plane The airport (☎ 0528 877043) is 7km out of town on the road to Laayoune and Smara, 20dh by shared grand taxi; arriving by air, however, you may find no taxis at the airport, in which case you'll have to walk 1km down to the main road, where buses, and any shared grands taxis with space should pick you up. Flights serve Casablanca (3 weekly; 1hr 55min) and Goulimine (2 weekly; 30min).

By bus All buses except Supratours and CTM leave from Pl de la Marche Verte. Supratours buses stop outside their office at 118 Bd Hassan II (☎ 0528 877795). Southbound services are often full by the time they get to Tan Tan so you may not get a seat – it's advisable to book in advance. CTM buses stop at their office (☎ 0528 765886), 300m down the Laayoune road from the main post office. Southbound services all pass through in the wee hours; none stop at Tarfaya, nor will even let you off at the *croisement*.

Destinations: Agadir (8 CTM, 12 Supratours & 18 others daily; 6hr); Casablanca (5 CTM & 10 others daily; 14–16hr); Dakhla (3 CTM, 3 Supratours & 3 others daily; 13hr 30min–14hr); Goulimine (8 CTM, 12 Supratours & 20 others daily; 1hr 30min–2hr); Laayoune (6 CTM, 9 Supratours & 4 others daily; 4hr 30min–6hr 30min); Marrakesh (6 CTM, 7 Supratours & 12 others daily; 9–12hr); Ouarzazate (2 daily; 17hr 30min); Rabat (2 CTM & 4 others daily; 16hr–17hr 30min); Smara (1 CTM, 2 Supratours & 1 other daily; 3–4hr); Tarfaya (5 Supratours & 1 other daily; 3hr–4hr 30min); Tata (2 daily; 12hr 30 min); Tiznit (8 CTM, 12 Supratours and 18 others daily; 4hr 30min).

By grand taxi Most shared grands taxis leave from Place de la Marche Verte. Regular runs include Dakhla (12hr), Goulimine (2hr 30 min), Inezgane (6hr), Smara (3hr) and Laayoune (3hr 30min). If you strike lucky, you may also find direct taxis for Tarfaya (2hr 30min) and Tiznit (5hr), especially early in the morning (Inezgane-bound grands taxis should drop you in Tiznit anyway). Shared taxis for Tan Tan Plage (20min) run from just north of La Poste de la Police, usually extremely frequently.

TAN TAN PLAGE

By grand taxi and bus Grands taxis for Tan Tan (20min) arrive in and leave from the town centre by *El Firdaous* café. You may be able to pick up buses for Akhfenir, Tarfaya (or the Tarfaya *croisement*) and Laayoune at the junction (Rond Point des Poissons) with the Laayoune road, 1km from the beach, but don't count on them stopping for you.

ACCOMMODATION

TAN TAN

There are a large number of unclassified hotels on and around Pl de la Marche Verte and La Poste de la Police, most of them very grotty but very cheap. Grubby and insalubrious as they are, many of these places will balk at letting unmarried couples share a room.

Aoubour Junction of Av Mohammed V and Bd Hassan II ☎ 0617 150654. The upstairs rooms, with outside windows, are a lot nicer than the dingy downstairs ones, but they're all reasonably well kept, and the location is handy for Supratours bus departures. It's not good value for double rooms compared to the *Bir Anzarane* down the road, but it's a bit cheaper for singles (50dh). **100dh**

★ **Bir Anzarane** 154 Bd Hassan II ☎&☎ 0528 877834. The best deal in town, carpeted throughout, with shared bathrooms and very reasonable prices, though not all rooms have outside windows, and it's a bit of a haul from Pl de la Marche Verte. **100dh**

El Hagounia 1 Rue Sidi Ahmed Rguibi ☎ 0528 878561. A cut above the other hotels in this part of town, with bare but large and generally clean rooms, and shared hot showers. As in a lot of very cheap hotels here, it charges per person, so the cost of a single is exactly half the price of a double. **60dh**

Sable d'Or Bd Hassan II ☎ 0528 878069. This is the best hotel in town, a two-star with large and immaculate en-suite rooms, some of which have a balcony. It has a restaurant, but only serves food if you order it in advance. **200dh**.

TAN TAN PLAGE

Belle Vue Av Mohammed V, by the beach ☎ 0528 879133. This beachside hotel is newly redecorated, and hung with paintings by local artist Abdallah, not exactly

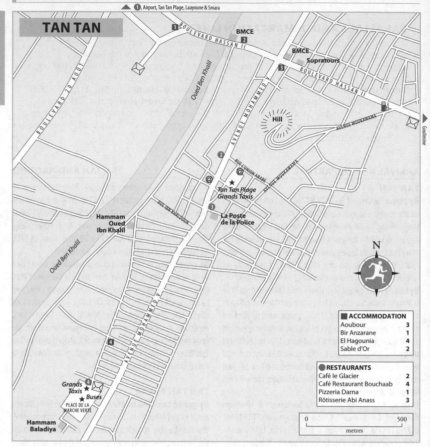

tasteful, but with a certain naive charm. Not all double rooms have windows, so be sure to ask for one that does, or better still, go for a sea-facing suite (300dh), with a balcony overlooking the beach. The restaurant (daily 10am–1pm) specializes in fried fish (50dh), but the grilled fish (70dh) is better, or there's squid tajine (40dh). BB **200dh**

Camping Auberge des 2 Chameaux Rond Point des Poissons (junction of Tan Tan and Laayoune roads) ☎ 0618 490681, ⓦ aaubergecampingdes2chameaux .com/. A popular stopoff for overlanders heading to West Africa, with space for tents and camper vans, or in their own Bedouin tent, as well as pleasant rooms and plenty of hot shower facilities. The restaurant (Mon–Sat 8am–10pm) has a good selection of dishes including fish tajine (75dh) and camel ribs (140dh). Camping **70dh**, Bedouin tent **70dh**, dorm **90dh**, double **200dh**

Marin Av Sid el Garne ☎ 0528 879146, ✉ hotel-lemarin @hotmail.fr. A block inland from the *Belle Vue*, longer-established but more rustic and weatherbeaten, the *Marin* is a bargain, though its rose-pink rooms (all en suite) are a little bit scuffed. **100dh**

EATING AND DRINKING

TAN TAN

Food is not one of Tan Tan's high points, and most eating places are grubby and unappetizing. If you have your own transport, it may be worth popping down to Tan Tan Plage (see p.508), where they are a lot nicer. Expect cafés to fill up whenever there's a big Spanish or European football game on, especially if it involves Barça or Real Madrid. As for bars, forget it: Tan Tan is dry.

Café le Glacier By the (defunct) Renaissance cinema, off Av Mohammed V. The name means "ice-cream shop", but don't expect any ice creams here now, nor indeed anything above bog-standard in the way of tea or coffee (*café au lait* 7dh). What you do get with this place, however, is a terrace with a nice view over the oued. Daily 6am–9pm.

Café Restaurant Bouchaab 111 Av Chaab, by Pl de la Marche Verte ☎ 0528 878416. This bright three-floor café with free wi-fi and a restaurant on the ground floor claims to serve tajines (30dh) and harira (5dh) at any time of the day or night. This claim is of course not to be relied on, but you can at least hold there for a coffee or juice at any time. Women may find the upper floors a bit all-male for their liking, especially on match days, but downstairs is fine. Daily 24hr.

Pizzeria Darna Laayoune road, about 300m west of the post office ☎ 0528 766464. Small and cosy, done out in orange and black, this is about the nicest place to eat in Tan Tan, and it also has free wi-fi. Pizzas cost 30–70dh depending on size and ingredients, and they have other dishes too (*spaghetti aux fruits de mer* for 25dh), and even

claim to offer *mahalabia* (Arabic blancmange) for afters (12dh), though they failed on this one when we actually asked for it. Daily 10am–11pm.

Rôtisserie Abi Anass Poste de Police square, north side. About the most pleasant and salubrious of the little eating places around the Poste de Police square. A plate of spit-roast chicken with chips and salad here will set you back the princely sum of 21dh. Daily noon–11pm.

TAN TAN PLAGE

Korea House Rond Point des Poissons (next door to Auberge des 2 Chameaux) ☎ 0661 479789. Run by a Korean family, this restaurant serves a small selection of Korean, Moroccan and Spanish dishes. You can get a Korean version of won ton ("ravioli") soup for 70dh, sautéed octopus for 80dh, or beef *jjim* (marinaded and steamed stew) for 160dh, but you need to order three hours in advance. Daily 10am–10pm.

DIRECTORY

Banks There are a few banks on Bd Hassan II (including two branches of BMCE within 100m of each other), as well as the Banque Populaire down near La Poste de la Police, all with ATMs.

Car repairs There are plenty of mechanics around Pl de la Marche Verte, and a few around the Tan Tan Plage taxi stand.

Festival The moussem of Sidi Mohammed Ma el Aïnin, a tribal gathering featuring a camel fair and the sacrifice of a female camel, was traditionally held in June, but the provincial government keeps moving it (most recently it was in March), so the date cannot currently be predicted from year to year.

Hammam Hammam Baladiya, just behind the southern end of Pl de la Marche Verte (both sexes 8am–10pm; 8dh); Hammam Oued Ibn Khalil, northern end of Av Chaab (both sexes 7am–11pm; 8dh).

Internet Places open and close at a dizzying pace, but current internet cafés include: Anzinet, Rue Chellah, off Pl de la Poste de Police (daily 9am–noon & 3pm–midnight; 3dh/hr); Internet Abdelmajid, Rue l'Union Arabe, near Tan Tan Plage taxi stand (supposedly daily 9am–11pm, but often closed; 3dh/hr).

Post office The main post office is off the Laayoune road, with a branch office on Pl de la Marche Verte.

A loop through Smara

It's possible to make a **loop** from Tan Tan along the R101, to Smara, returning by way of the N1 to Laayoune, and from there across to Tan Tan via Tarfaya – a circuit of some 800km. There are **buses** along each section, but they aren't very frequent. If driving, be sure to carry water supplies.

The R101 between Tan Tan and Smara is almost devoid of habitation and features, though you will see some hills and valleys on either side of the road, starting around 20km out of Tan Tan. After 91km more, you enter the Saharan Provinces and a gaggle of petrol stations allow you to take advantage of the lower fuel prices.

Smara (Es Semara)

SMARA (also written as Es Semara), once an important caravan stop, is today a garrison town, occupied by the Moroccan army (so be careful where you point your camera). Otherwise, it's a small, sleepy old place, with not a lot going on, though there's a **souk** every Thursday, and a **festival** every April featuring musical and other entertainments. Because accommodation options are so dire, it's wise to avoid spending the night here, by making an early start from Tan Tan or Laayoune to get here, and heading off before transport dries up.

9

TRAVELLING IN THE WESTERN SAHARA

Tourists can travel freely in most Moroccan-controlled parts of what are called the **Saharan Provinces** (an administrative area created to include the **former Spanish Sahara**, while not coinciding with its boundaries), but do check first on the political situation. 2010 and 2011 saw violent clashes between Saharawis and Moroccan settlers and police in Laayoune, Smara and Dakhla, among other places, and you should be aware that protests often involve violence, and should be avoided. Government advisories (see p.64) will have up-to-date information if any problems have arisen. Apart from this, the only obstacle would be for visitors who admit to being a writer or journalist: a profession not welcome in the region, unless under the aegis of an official press tour.

Otherwise, visiting Laayoune, Smara, Boujdour and Dakhla is now pretty routine, though it does involve answering a series of questions (name, age, profession, parents' names, passport number and date of issue etc) at numerous **police checkpoints** along the way. This is all usually very amicable, but time-consuming (you'll be asked for these details four times, for example, between Laayoune and Dakhla). To save time it is a good idea to print out and/or photocopy several copies of a sheet with the following information listed, preferably in French (as given here in brackets): family name (*nom*), given names (*prénoms*), date of birth (*date de naissance*), place of birth (*lieu de naissance*), marital status (*situation familiale*), father's name (*nom de père*), mother's name (*nom de mère*), nationality (*nationalité*), occupation (*profession*), address (*addresse* – which should be given in full), passport number (*numéro de passeport*), date of issue (*date de délivrance*), place of issue (*lieu de délivrance*), expiry date (*date d'expiration*), purpose of visit (*motif du voyage* – *tourisme*, for example), make of vehicle (*marque du véhicule* – you may of course have to leave this one blank), vehicle registration number (*matriculation* – ditto), date of entry into Morocco (*date d'entrée en Maroc*), place of entry (*ville d'entrée*) and police number (*numéro de police* – this is the number stamped in your passport alongside your first entry stamp into Morocco, typically six digits and two letters). For marital status, you could be single (*célibataire*), married (*marié* if male, *mariée* if female), divorced (*divorcé/divorcée*) or widowed (*veuf/veuve*). Armed with this, you can then give your details to police at every checkpoint, which will save them having to ask you for the information point by point.

Petrol and diesel are subsidized in the Saharan provinces (basically the Western Sahara), and cost about a third less than in Morocco proper.

The palace and Great Mosque

Smara's only link with its past is the remains of the palace and Great Mosque of **Ma el Aïnin**, the "Blue Sultan", a local ruler who tried to oust the French colonialists at the beginning of the twentieth century (see box, p.484). The **palace**, near the oued, contains the residences of Ma el Aïnin's four main wives, one of them now occupied by the *gardien* and his family. The attached **zaouia** is well maintained, but usually closed, except on Fridays. If you knock on the door, however, someone should open up and show you around, usually for a fee. Though plastered over, the *zaouia* is, like the rest of the palace, built of black basalt from the local hills. What's left of the **Great Mosque**, a separate building further away from the river, is less well preserved, but you can still see the mihrab, and rows of basalt arches.

The town centre

The part of town built under Spanish rule lies between Rue de l'Hôpital, Avenue Hassan II and the oued. The **old mosque** on the corner of Avenue Mohammed V and Rue de l'Hôpital is made of local basalt, with a rather pretty stone minaret, as is the **El Hajra Mosque** to its southwest, which is the main mosque actually used for worship nowadays. A distinctive aspect of the houses here (and elsewhere in the Western Sahara) is the **eggshell-like dome** that serves as a roof. The domes are said to keep the interior cooler by means of convection currents, but a more likely story is that the Spanish built them like this to prevent build-ups of wind-blown sand on the roofs; the domes are certainly not traditional Saharawi structures, as the Saharawis were always nomads and their traditional homes were tents.

ARRIVAL AND DEPARTURE SMARA

By bus All buses leave from the *gare routière*, a yard on Bd de Stade near the stadium, where you'll find the offices of Supratours, SATAS and CTM, the only firms that serve Smara. Supratours run the only daily service to Laayoune (3hr – check ⓦ oncf.ma for current timings). Destinations: Agadir (4 daily; 8hr); Goulimine (4hr 30min); Marrakesh (2 daily; 13hr 15min); Tan Tan (4 daily; 3hr); Tiznit (6hr).

By grand taxi Shared grands taxis leave from the *gare routière*, serving Goulimine (4hr 30min), Laayoune (3hr) and Tan Tan (2hr).

INFORMATION

Tourist information An Ensemble Artisanal is being built southwest of the El Hajra Mosque to sell crafts, and should incorporate a tourist information point when completed.

ACCOMMODATION AND EATING

Smara has a dismal array of hotels and eating places. There are around a dozen small and very cheap hotels, and the only place with anything approaching comfort is hardly a bargain. There isn't much in the way of **restaurants** either, though a trio of places along Av Hassan II serve basic snacks, and there are open-air grills and fried fish stalls around the souk and on Bd de Stade.

Amine 97 Av Ribat el Khair ☎ 0528 887368. The only decent place to stay in town, with clean rooms and satellite TV, but pretty run-down. Some rooms are en suite, but only two of those had hot water at last check. There are no shared shower facilities, so if you take a room without its own bathroom, you'll have to shower elsewhere – there was a communal shower round the back, but that was also out of action at last check, though supposedly due to reopen shortly. **200dh**

De Paris 156 Av Hassan II ☎ 0610 780988. Marginally better than the rock-bottom options – and so it should be at four times the price. The rooms are cell-like but clean, though most lack windows, and there are working hot showers, at 7dh a go. **160dh**

Hilal el Jenoub 64 Bd du Stade ☎ 0653 113743. This is the newest of the little ultra-cheap hotels, and along with the *Hôtel les Fleurs* next door at no. 66 (☎ 0672 970689), which is the same price, it has small and very basic rooms, but with an acceptable level of cleanliness. Although neither of the two have showers, there are public ones across the street and a hammam just round the corner. **40dh**

9

Maghrib el Arbi 15 Av Hassan II ☎0528 899151. Before the *Amine* opened this was Smara's top offering, which isn't saying much. There's no hot water, and no rooms are en suite, but they're a bit bigger and brighter than the ones in the other ultra-cheap places. <u>50dh</u>

DIRECTORY

Banks The BMCE and Banque Populaire on Av Hassan II both have ATMs.

Hammam The town hammam is just off Bd de Stade, with the left-hand entrance for women (daily 7am–7pm; 10dh) and the right-hand one for men (daily 7am–9pm; 10dh).

Internet There are a few internet offices on Av Hassan II, on the south side, including one east of Rue de l'Hôpital (daily 10am–1am; 4dh/hr), and one to its west (daily 9am–11pm; 4dh/hr).

Post office The post office is by the local Province (county hall), at the eastern end of Av Mohammed V.

Smara to Laayoune

Heading towards Laayoune, the desert is blackish from basalt for the first 5km, before resuming a lighter hue. At **Asli**, 15km out of Smara, there are prehistoric rock carvings, and a visitors' centre has now been installed to help those wishing to see them, but it is not as yet open.

South of the new road, 30km from Smara, stands a large brown flat-topped hill called **Gor el Bered** (Hill of the Wind). At the foot of its west side, just north of the road, a small brown cupola-domed building resembling a *marabout* is in fact a structure built by the Spanish in the 1930s to extract chalk from the calcium-rich rock of the hill. A genuine *marabout* is to be found at **Sidi Khatari**, south of the road some 90km from Smara.

After around 220km, you reach the turn-off to **Boukra**, a phosphate mining town with a large garrison 25km to the southeast. The café at the junction serves bowlfuls of sweetened camel's milk. Boukra and the vast region to its south is a restricted military zone, and inaccessible to casual visitors, but continuing north from the junction, you'll see the **Boukra–Laayoune conveyor belt** snaking its way south of the road, bearing phosphates seaward for export.

The Seguiat el Hamra

For the last 50km before Laayoune, the canyon of the **Seguiat el Hamra** comes into view on the western side of the road. Seguiat el Hamra means "Red River" and, though there is no water in it for most of the year, the local clay turns it red when it does flow. The canyon is pretty impressive, but if you stop to take a snapshot be sure you are out of range of anything military. The oasis of **Lemseyed**, 12km before Laayoune, offers fine views over the canyon. Across the oued from the road, **Fort Dchira**, built by the Spanish in the very early days of their rule, is now occupied by the Moroccan army.

Tan Tan to Laayoune

The N1 road from Tan Tan to Laayoune hugs the coast, passing over dramatic oued mouths and through sand dunes as it rolls down through the southernmost slice of Morocco. The only towns of note are Akhfenir and, 3km off the road, Tarfaya. The Western Sahara starts at the village of **Tah**, where a red granite monument flanking the road commemorates the 1975 Green March (see p.543). Once south of the border, you begin to traverse real sand desert – the **Erg Lakhbayta** – before crossing the Seguiat al-Hamra (a wide and usually dry river) to enter Laayoune.

Akhfenir

AKHFENIR (140km south of Tan Tan, and served by buses between Tan Tan and Laayoune) is little more than a flyblown roadside settlement with a couple of 24-hour petrol stations and a handful of cafés serving fried fish or tajines. **Flamingos** and migratory birds can sometimes be seen in the lagoons and saltpans along the coast to the south, or in the oued mouths to the north.

ACCOMMODATION AND EATING   **AKHFENIR**

Akhfenir On the main road, in the centre of the village ☎ 0672 591004. A small, no-frills, Moroccan hotel, friendly and clean, with quite large, fresh rooms, shared showers with hot water round the clock, and a kitchen. **100dh**

Centre de Pêche et de Loisirs At the eastern end of the village, south of the main road ☎ 0528 765560, ⓦ peche.sudmaroc.free.fr. A French-run *auberge* offering good meals and fishing expeditions. The rooms are small

and homely, but not en suite. BB **€20**

La Courbine d'Argent N1, 1km west of the village ☎ 0671 422377, ⓦ lacourbinedargent.com. Mostly a centre for sports fishing, the *Courbine* also offers good accommodation, birdwatching excursions, and arranges jaunts into the desert on 4WDs, bikes and quad bikes in conjunction with Laayoune Off-Road (ⓦ laayoune-offroad .com). HB **€40**

Tarfaya

TARFAYA is a quiet little fishing town (population 6000) that's probably not far different from its years as a staging post for the Aéropostale Service – when aviators such as **Antoine de Saint-Exupéry** (author of *Night Flight* and *The Little Prince*) used to rest up here on their way down to West Africa.

Oddly enough, Tarfaya was actually founded, at the end of the nineteenth century, by a Scottish trader named Donald Mackenzie, and was originally called Port Victoria after Britain's queen. Mackenzie had a fort built, now known as **Casa Mar**, which is just offshore – a few metres' swim at low tide. The Spanish called the town Villa Bens. These days Tarfaya is a lazy, do-nothing place. The main street, Boulevard Ahmed el Hayar, running roughly east–west through the town centre, has two banks (with ATMs), a handful of cafés, and a couple of internet offices (one next to Attijariawafa Bank).

The Aéropostale air service is commemorated annually in October by a "**Rallye Aérien**", with small planes stopping here on their way south from Toulouse to Dakar. A **monument to Saint-Exupéry** in the form of a plane stands at the northern end of the beach. Nearby, a **Musée Antoine de Saint-Exupéry** (Mon–Fri 8.30am–12.30pm & 2.30–5pm; 10dh) has exhibits on the air mail service that Saint-Exupéry pioneered, but (despite being in the formerly Spanish zone of an Arabic-speaking country) with explanations in French only.

ARRIVAL AND DEPARTURE   **TARFAYA**

Transport can be tricky getting to and from Tarfaya, you may have to wait a few hours before anything turns up, or you may even have to resort to walking to the junction on the N1 (3km out of town) and hitchhiking, or at least trying to flag down passing buses and shared taxis.

By bus Only two daily buses in each direction stop here (on Bd Ahmed el Hayar): one Supratours service between Dakhla and Agadir, and Noujoum al Sahara's service between Tan Tan and Laayoune. Other Supratours buses (7 daily), as well as SATAS and SAT (1 daily each) will set down passengers at the junction (*croisement*) for Tarfaya on the

N1, 3km out of town, but they won't usually pick passengers up there. Officially at any rate, CTM won't even set you down.

By grand taxi Shared grands taxis make the run from both Tan Tan and Laayoune if they can find the passengers – as always, mornings are best.

ACCOMMODATION AND EATING

The hotels all serve meals, and the cafés along the north side of Av Ahmed el Hayar have excellent and very cheap fresh fried fish, or fish tajines.

Aoudate Eastern end of Bd Ahmed el Hayar ☎ 0528 895868, ⓦ hoteltarfaya.ma. A choice of very large rooms, or smaller but still ample ones, all en suite with balconies on two sides and free wi-fi, located at the entrance into

town from the main road. **200dh**

El Bahja Bd Bir Anzarane, 300m north of Bd Ahmed el Hayar ☎ 0528 895506. This small and very welcoming hotel offers poky rooms and a terrace with a view over the

9

town, plus a self-catering apartment in a house just up the street (200dh). 100dh

Casamar By the port entrance at the western end of Bd Ahmed el Hayar ☎0528 895326, ⓦappart-casamar .com. Both the rooms and the apartments here are an amazing bargain at current prices, all bright and modern, with wi-fi throughout. The apartments (with bedroom, sitting room, bathroom and kitchen; 200dh), which are supposed to be self-catering, don't have stoves in their kitchens, but this may be negotiable. 100dh

Laayoune and around

With a population of around 200,000, **LAAYOUNE** (Al Ayoun, sometimes spelt Aaiun in the Spanish colonial period) is the largest and most interesting town in the Western Sahara, though it was only founded in 1940. The city has the highest per capita government spending in Morocco, and soldiers, billeted here for the conflict with Polisario (see box, pp.522–523), have been employed in many construction projects. The old **lower town**, built by the Spanish, lies on the southern slope of the steep-sided valley of the **Seguiat el Hamra**, with the new **upper town**, developed since the Green March, on the high plateau beyond.

The population growth – from little more than a village when the Moroccans took over – has been aided by massive subsidies, which apply throughout the Western Sahara, and by an agreement that settlers should initially pay no taxes. The fact that most of Laayoune's residents are here by choice – only a minority of current residents were actually born here – gives the place a dynamism and pioneering feel that contrasts quite sharply with the weight of tradition that hangs heavy on cities like Fez and Marrakesh. The result is that, although Laayoune has little in the way of obvious sights, its atmosphere is quite a change from that of towns in Morocco proper.

The main square

The old **cathedral**, on the city's original main square, Plaza de Africa – is open for Sunday morning Mass, and the priest will normally let you have a look inside if you ring on his bell at a reasonable hour. Across the main square, on the east side, the **town hall** was formerly used by the Spanish administration, and is now largely occupied by the Moroccan military (so don't try to photograph it).

Souk ej Jaj

The district stretching east from the main square, **Souk ej Jaj** (Glass Market), is the oldest part of Laayoune, and many of its residents have been here since Spanish days. It's very run-down, but it's undoubtedly Laayoune's most atmospheric quarter. There's a smattering of cheap hotels, and many of the houses still have the eggshell-domed roofs typical of the Western Sahara (see p.512). One that doesn't any more is **Laayoune's oldest house**, at 16 Rue 28 du Février (on the corner of Rue No.18, and opposite the end of Bd Mohammed V), originally constructed in 1934.

Ejercito

East of Souk ej Jaj, the district of **Ejercito** (Spanish for army) houses Moroccan troops as it did their Spanish predecessors. South of Avenue Bahariya, some of the tubular barracks are now private houses, hemmed in by more modern, box-like, blocks of flats.

Colomina

The other district left from Spanish times is **Colomina**, to the south of Avenue Mecka al Mokarrama. It is nicknamed Colomina Tarduss ("Kick") because, when the Spanish left, Moroccan settlers kicked in the doors to squat their houses. Nowadays, most of the quarter has

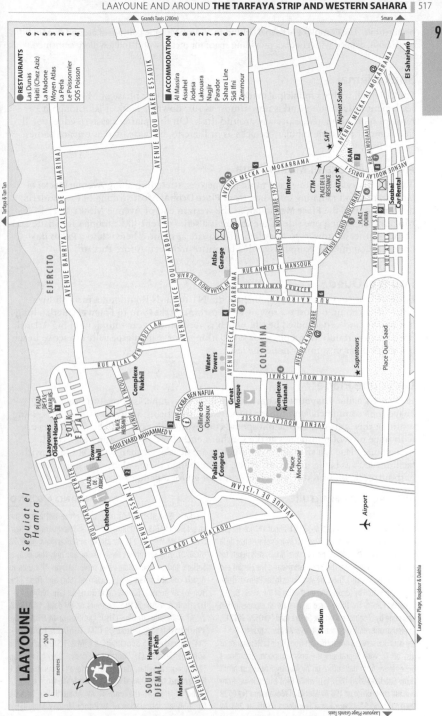

LAAYOUNE

0   200
metres

Grands Taxis (200m)

Smara

● RESTAURANTS
Las Dunas   6
Haiti (Chez Aziz) 7
La Madone   5
Moyen Atlas   3
La Perla   2
Le Poissonnier   1
SOS Poisson   4

■ ACCOMMODATION
Al Massira   4
Assahel   8
Jodesa   5
Lakouara   2
Nagjir   7
Parador   3
Sahara Line   6
Sidl Ifni   1
Zemmour   9

El Sahariano

Tarfaya & Tan Tan

EJERCITO

AVENUE ABOU BAKER ESSADIK

AVENUE BAHRIYA (CALLE DE LA MARINA)

AVENUE MECCA AL MOKARRAMA

AVENUE PRINCE MOULAY ABDALLAH

RUE ALLAL BEN ABDULLAH

Complexe
Nakhil

Atlas
Garage

AVENUE 29 NOVEMBRE 1975

Binter

SAT

AVENUE MECCA AL MOKARRAMA

Nejmat Sahara

RAM

RUE ALMOUAALA

AVENUE MOULAY IDRISSI

CTM
PLACE DE LA
RÉSISTANCE
SATAS

Soubni
Car Rental

AVENUE OUM SAAD

RUE AIT LA

AVENUE CHAHID BOUCHRAYA

PLACE
DCHIRA

RUE AHMED EL MANSOUR

NATAIHA BNOU ZOUBAIR

RUE BRAHMAN ENNACER

RUE KAIROUAN

AVENUE MECCA AL MOKARRAMA

Place Oum Saad

COLOMINA

Supratours

AVENUE 24 NOVEMBRE

AVENUE MOULAY ISMAIL

Water
Towers

Great
Mosque

Complexe
Artisanal

AVENUE OCKBA BEN NAFUA

PLAZA
DE CASA
CANARIAS

SOUK
ELJTA

RUE ELLA YACOUT

PLACE
HASSANI

Complexe

Laayounes
Oldest House

Town
Hall

Colline des
Oiseaux

BOULEVARD MOHAMMED V

AVENUE HASSAN I

PLAZA
DE ARGEN

Cathedral

BOULEVARD 28 FÉVRIER

RUE CADI EL GHALAOUI

AVENUE MOULAY YOUSSEF

Palais des
Congrès

Place
Mechouar

AVENUE DE L'ISLAM

Airport

Seguiat el
Hamra

SOUK
DJEMAL

Hammam
el Fath

Market

AVENUE SALEM BILA

Stadium

N

Laayoune Plage, Boujdour & Dakhla

Laayoune Plage Grands Taxis

9

been rebuilt. The **Complexe Artisanal** behind the Great Mosque consists of around twenty little workshops, capped with cupolas, providing space for metal, wood and jewellery craftsmen.

Souk Djemal

Souk Djemal, with its **municipal market**, represents the first phase of Moroccan settlement in Laayoune, and is now almost as run-down as Souk ej Jaj, though it remains quite animated, especially around dusk. On the quarter's eastern edge, you'll find some of the same tubular barracks as in Ejercito, likewise used as private homes.

Avenue Mecka el Mokarrama

The newer areas of the town are more prosperous, stretching along **Avenue Mecka el Mokarrama**, and radiating outwards from **Place Dchira**. Most striking of the modern developments is the **Place Mechouar**, at the western end of Avenue Mecka al Mokarrama. Lining one side of the square is a series of tent-like canopies for shade and at each corner are towers to floodlight the square at night. There is also a **Palais des Congrès**, designed by King Hassan II's favourite architect, André Paccard.

Foum el Oued

Fifteen kilometres south of Laayoune on the N1 towards Boujdour, a turn-off by a police checkpoint, opposite a row of wind turbines, takes you to **Foum el Oued**, a long but narrow and very exposed beach, which is very windy, year-round, with big Atlantic breakers. It certainly isn't a place for safe bathing, nor is it an especially attractive beach, but it's popular in summer none the less.

Laayoune Plage

Despite its name, **Laayoune Plage**, 20km out of Laayoune, isn't really a beach, but Laayoune's commercial and fishing port. Aside from being a huge centre for processing sardines, this is also where the phosphate conveyor from Boukra (see p.514) ends up, with huge piles of phosphates at the southern end of the port, waiting for export.

Laayoune Plage is a sizeable town, much more developed than Foum el Oued, with facilities such as banks and a post office, but although there's plenty of sand, it's in a harbour, and you wouldn't want to sit on it or go for a paddle.

ARRIVAL AND DEPARTURE   LAAYOUNE AND AROUND

LAAYOUNE

By plane The airport (☎ 0528 893791) is about a kilometre out of town, south of Pl Mechouar. Royal Air Maroc's office on Pl de la Résistance (☎ 0528 894077), next to *Hôtel Nagjir*, sells tickets for flights to Agadir (weekly; 1hr), Casablanca (daily; 1hr 25min) and Dakhla (2 weekly; 1hr). There are also flights to Las Palmas (daily; 45min) operated by (depending on the day of the week) Binter, Islas and Canary Fly. These three airlines are all represented in Laayoune by El Sahariano on the Smara road (☎ 0528 981212, ⓦ elsahariano.com), who also sell Royal Air Maroc tickets.

By bus Bus services mostly depart from Pl de la Résistance or just off it, with Supratours the only exception. Supratours buses leave from their office on Av Moulay Ismail just off Pl Oum Saad (☎ 0528 893245), while CTM buses leave from outside their office at 198 Av Mecka al Mokarrama (☎ 0528 990763), and SATAS are just a few doors south, at 208 Av

Mecka al Mokarrama. SAT have their office just across the street from SATAS (☎ 0528 893773), and Noujoum al Sahara are by *Café Ibiza* at 237 Av Mecka al Mokarrama (☎ 0528 892070). Only Supratours serve Smara, and only Noujoum al Sahara and one Supratours bus serve Tarfaya. All buses to Agadir call at Tan Tan (4hr), Goulimine (6hr) and Tiznit (8hr 30min). All buses to Dakhla call at Boujdour (3hr 30min).

Destinations: Agadir (9 Supratours, 6 CTM daily, 1 SATAS & 2 SAT daily; 9hr 30min–11hr); Casablanca (4 CTM daily; 19hr); Dakhla (5 Supratours, 3 CTM, 1 SATAS & 1 SAT daily; 8hr); Marrakesh (5 Supratours, 4 CTM & 1 SAT daily; 14hr 30min); Smara (1 Supratours daily; 3hr); Tan Tan (1 Noujoum al Sahara daily; 5hr); Tarfaya (1 Supratours & 1

By grand taxi Shared grands taxis leave from a single stand located at the end of Av Abou Baker Essadik (roughly a continuation of Av Prince Moulay Abdallah), about 2km east of the town centre. The only shared grands taxis which don't use this station are those to Foum el Oued (15min) and Laayoune Plage ("Playa"; 20min), which use a station at the far western end of town, right at the end of the road past the stadium.

Destinations: Dakhla (9hr); Goulimine (5hr); Inezgane (9hr); Smara (3hr); Tan Tan (3hr 30min); Tarfaya (1hr).

Car rental The longest-established car rental firm is Soubai, on Rue Afila just behind *Hôtel Zemmour* (☎0528 893199, ✉soubaimed@yahoo.es).

FOUM EL OUED & LAAYOUNE PLAGE

By grand taxi Grands taxis ply the route from Laayoune to Laayoune Plage and, less frequently, Foum el Oued, leaving from a station 2km west of town, out past the stadium.

By car You'll usually see a lot of camels on the road between Foum el Oued and Laayoune Plage. Picturesque they may be, but they're also a hazard to motorists, especially at night.

INFORMATION

LAAYOUNE

Tourist information Délégation de Tourisme, Av de l'Islam, in a compound opposite the *Hotel Parador* (Mon–Fri 8.30am–4.30pm; ☎0528 891694).

ACCOMMODATION

LAAYOUNE

Unclassified hotels are concentrated in the Souk ej Jaj and Souk Djemal districts, but they can be very basic indeed, and none too clean.

Assahel Av Moulay Idriss I ☎0528 890170. A good-value choice among the small group of ultra-cheapies off Pl Dchira. The upstairs café, where you can get a freshly squeezed orange juice, overlooks Pl Dchira. Hot showers are available but cost 10dh a go. **50dh**

Jodesa 223 Av Mecka al Mokarrama ☎0528 992064, ☎0528 893784. Somewhat better value than the neighbouring *Hôtel Mekka*, the *Jodesa* offers decent-sized, airy rooms, a roof terrace and a car rental service as well as free wi-fi. It's worth paying the tiny amount extra to get an en-suite room (155dh). **144dh**

Lakouara Av Hassan II ☎0528 893378. A comfortable, if old-fashioned, two-star with large rooms, en-suite bathrooms, satellite TV and 24hr hot water, just south of the old main square. A lot of it is block-booked by the UN, but they also set some rooms aside for tourists. **420dh**

Al Massira 12 Av Mecka al Mokarrama ☎0528 894225, ✉sahara_hospitality@yahoo.fr. This four-star hotel has had a much needed revamp. The small rooms have been spruced up, and an extension added. The hotel is partly block-booked by the UN, but keeps a number of rooms free. **736dh**

Nagjir 6 Pl Bir Anzarane ☎0528 894168, ⊕hotel-nagjir.com. A modern four-star with a good restaurant, and a new wing with spacious suites. Though most rooms are taken by the UN, they keep thirty odd for casual visitors and generally have promotional rates off-season. **786dh**

Parador Av de l'Islam ☎0528 890000, ✉sahara_hospitality@yahoo.fr. This was the old Spanish grand hotel, and is now run by the same management as the *Al Massira*, but it's rather more traditional in style, with larger rooms, and also undergoing a revamp. The corridors are decorated with photos of the 1975 Green March. **1436dh**

★ **Sahara Line** Av 24 Novembre at Rue Kairouan ☎0528 995454, ✉sahara_line@menara.ma. This is

officially a four-star, though it doesn't have a bar or a pool, but it does have efficient management and carpeted rooms, not huge, but equipped with satellite TV and a/c, as well as suites, and even a presidential suite if you need something more spacious. They usually have a promotional discount of around thirty percent, which they offer on a permanent basis to anyone presenting this guidebook at reception. **750dh**

Sidi Ifni 12 Rue Sanhaja, Souk ej Jaj, off Av Bahariya ☎0659 082729. This place has to its credit the fact that it's at the heart of the oldest part of town, and of Laayoune's original community, with rooms that are decent enough for the price. It's also been spruced up of late, and has hot showers, making it the best rock-bottom choice. **50dh**

★ **Zemmour** 1 Av Oum Saad, just off Pl Dchira ☎0528 892323. Better, cleaner and brighter than any of the other budget options by a long way; great value with pretty little apple-green and cream rooms, some with a balcony. Bathroom facilities are shared but spotless, and showers are hot. It costs slightly more than the rock-bottom options, but it's well worth the difference. **150dh**

FOUM EL OUED & LAAYOUNE PLAGE

Josefina By the port entrance Laayoune Plage ☎0528 998478, ⊕hotel-restaurant_josefina.com. A hotel with a bar and restaurant, right by the port. The rooms are pretty and homely, equipped with TV and fridge, and the restaurant (daily noon–4.30pm & 6–11pm) specializes, unsurprisingly, in fish, with seafood soup at 25dh and grilled octopus at 90dh. There's also a bar, making this a good place to pop down to for lunch. **355dh**

Nagjir Plage At the north end of the beach, Foum el Oued ☎0528 991018, ⊕hotel-nagjir.com. This cavernous four-star, run by the same firm as the *Nagjir* in Laayoune, is almost empty out of season (price remains the same), and even in summers it usually has rooms. Those in the hotel itself are very 1970s, and could do with a revamp, but they're spacious enough. More popular are the bungalows around the large pool area, some of which have their own little kitchens. Bungalow **400dh**, double **496dh**

9

EATING AND DRINKING

LAAYOUNE

Cafés around the market in Souk Djemal serve cheap evening meals of tajine or fried fish, and also breakfasts, with *melaoui* and *harsha*.

Las Dunas Middle of Pl Dchira ☎0528. You can get anything from a coffee and a croissant to a burger (20dh) or a chicken tajine (25dh) here, served in a pleasant a/c saloon or outside around a fountain in the square. Very civilized. Daily 11am–8pm.

Haiti (Chez Aziz) 16 Rue Almouaala ☎0528 994442. A small but pleasant pizzeria-restaurant behind the *Hôtel Nagjir*, with pizza, pasta, fish kebabs, fried squid and roast chicken. The pizzas themselves (30–60dh) aren't very good, but their fish dishes (such as cheese stuffed squid 40dh) aren't bad. Daily noon–12.30am.

La Madone Av 24 du Novembre ☎0528 993252. A small pizzeria whose pasta dishes are pretty good (try the *spaghetti aux fruits de mer*; 40dh), and they also do reasonable fish dishes and pizzas (50–60dh). Daily noon–midnight.

Moyen Atlas 50 Av Mecka al Mokarrama, opposite *Hôtel al Massira* ☎0528 996223. Laayoune's top patisserie, where you can sit in or out and have your pastry with tea, coffee or orange juice. Daily 24hr.

La Perla 185 Av Mecka al Mokarrama ☎0528 991191. The menu looks great, with prawn bisque (25dh), chocolate mousse (15dh) and a fine selection of fabulous-sounding fish dishes (such as squid pili-pili at 40dh), but unfortunately it fails to live up to its promise, though it isn't bad for the price. Daily noon–3pm & 6.30pm–midnight.

★ **Le Poissonnier** 183 Av Mecka al Mokarrama ☎0528 893241. It looks like *La Perla* next door, and the prices are similar, but the ambience is a bit slicker and the food is far superior, with excellent fish soup (20dh) and wonderful grilled giant sea bass (70dh), though the service can be a bit iffy. Daily 11am–3.30pm & 7.30pm–midnight.

SOS Poisson Av Moulay Ismail ☎0528 894048. Great fish dishes, including good fish soup (20dh), fried cuttlefish (35dh) and sometimes fish brochettes (45dh), though availability depends on what's in the market on a given day. Daily noon–3pm & 6–11pm.

DIRECTORY

Banks and exchange There are plenty of banks in town with ATMs and exchange facilities, with one group at the foot of Bd Mohammed V, near Pl Hassan II, and another in Pl Dchira. There's a bureau de change at 83 Av 24 du Novembre, near *Hotel Sahara Line* (Mon–Fri 9am–1pm & 4–8pm, Sat & Sun 10am–1pm & 5–8pm).

Festival The Rawafid Azawan festival in October hosts musicians from across the Arab world, and beyond.

Hammams The very modern Complexe Nakhil, at the eastern end of Av Lalla Yacout, has hammams or showers for both sexes (7am–10pm; 10dh). In Souk Djemal, there's Hammam El Fath off Av Salem Bila (north side) by no. 123 (7.30am–11pm; 10dh).

Internet access Baraka Allah Net, 65 Av 24 Novembre (daily 9am–1am; 5dh/hr); Google Cyber Café, 331 Av Mecka al Mokarrama (daily 9am–6am; 4dh/hr); Téléboutique Friouato, 142 Av Mecka al Mokarrama (daily 9.30am–midnight; 5dh/hr).

Post office The main office is on Pl Dchira (Mon–Fri 8am–6pm Sat 8am–noon), with branch offices on Av Mecka al Mokarrama and Pl Hassan II (Mon–Fri 8am–4.15pm).

Laayoune to Dakhla

Shared grands taxis and nine daily buses do the run from Laayoune to Dakhla. The road is reasonably good, with cliffs plunging down to the sea on the western side of the road, and plain desert on the inland side. Drivers should beware of occasional sand-drifts, and camels grazing by or on the road. Foreigners will need to form-fill at checkpoints along the way, unless they already have the details printed out (see box, p.512).

Boujdour

The sea is guarded by cliffs most of the way to the fishing port of **BOUJDOUR**, 188km southwest of Laayoune. The beach is dirty with dangerous rocks – the nearest beaches suitable for swimming (if you have the transport to reach them) are 20km south, below the cliffs, and 40km north, just beyond a military checkpoint and fishing settlement. The nearest thing to a sight in town is the lighthouse, though it's not open to the public, and the soldiers guarding it won't be happy if you try to photograph it. If you need a bank, the BMCE and Banque Populaire both have branches with ATMs.

9

WESTERN SAHARAN HISTORY

The **Saharawi people** who live in the Western Sahara are largely descended from Arab tribes who moved into the area in the fifteenth century, and established themselves definitively with victory over the indigenous Sanhaja Berbers in the 1644–74 Char Bouba war. They speak an Arabic dialect called Hassania, which is much the same as that spoken in Mauritania, and somewhat different from the dialect spoken in most of Morocco. Their food and music are also more like those of Mauritania than of Morocco. However, Hassania-speaking Saharawis are not confined to the Western Sahara, and many live in southern Morocco too.

SPANISH COLONIAL RULE

Spain held part of the Saharan coast in the early sixteenth century, but the **Saadians** drove them out in 1524, establishing **Moroccan control** over the coastline. In 1884, while European powers, such as Britain, France and Portugal, were carving up the rest of Africa, **Spain** got in on the act and declared the coast between Boujdour and the Nouadibhou peninsula to be a Spanish "**protectorate**", gradually extending its boundaries inland and northward by agreement with other European powers. The Spanish didn't actually have much control over the area in practice, but built ports at La Gouera and Villa Cisneros (Dakhla), with occasional forays into the interior to "pacify" the Saharawi tribes. Full colonial rule was only introduced after the Spanish Civil War, when the territory was split into two colonies: **Rio de Oro**, with its capital at Villa Cisneros, and **Seguiat el Hamra**, with a new, purpose-built capital at Laayoune.

Following Moroccan independence and the 1958 return of the Tarfaya strip (see box, p.509), Spain merged its two colonies to form the **Spanish Sahara**, which was considered a province of Spain itself, much like Ifni, Ceuta and Melilla. But it was only in the 1960s, after the discovery of **phosphates at Boukra**, that Spain actually started to develop the territory.

By that time colonialism was out of fashion. Britain and France had pulled out of most of Africa, and only the Fascist-ruled Iberian states of Spain and Portugal still held onto their African colonies, with international pressure mounting on them to quit. In 1966 for example, the **UN** passed a resolution calling on Spain to organize a referendum on independence in the Sahara. Meanwhile, as education became more widespread, the Spaniards were confronted with the same problem that they and the French had faced in Morocco thirty years earlier – the rise of nationalism. **The Movement for the Liberation of the Sahara** was formed in 1967, and in 1970 organized a protest in Laayoune against Spanish rule. This was brutally put down, and the Movement was banned, but Spanish repression only succeeded in radicalizing opposition. In 1973, a group of militants formed the Frente para la Liberación de Seguiat el Hamra y Rio de Oro (**Polisario**), and began a guerrilla campaign for independence.

THE GREEN MARCH, AND WAR

Under pressure from Polisario, and with its dictator General Franco on his last legs, Spain began to consider pulling out of the Sahara, but Morocco's King **Hassan II** now claimed sovereignty over the territory on the basis that it had been under Moroccan rule before Spanish colonization. The case went to the **International Court of Justice** in the Hague, which ruled that, though some Saharawi tribes had indeed paid allegiance to the Moroccan sultan, the territory had not been substantially Moroccan before colonization, and its people were entitled to self-determination. In accordance with this ruling, Spain reluctantly agreed to hold a referendum on independence. Under pressure at home over domestic issues, however (see p.542), Hassan saw advantages in waving the nationalist flag as a distraction, and the next month led a "**Green March**" (*Massira el Khadra*) of 350,000 Moroccan civilians (subsequently

---

ARRIVAL AND DEPARTURE   BOUJDOUR

By public transport Buses between Laayoune and Dakhla pass through Boujdour, and shared taxis run to and from both destinations.

ACCOMMODATION AND EATING

Av Mohammed V, which runs from the grand taxi stand down to the campsite comes alive in the evening with restaurants frying up freshly caught fish, and stalls selling charcoal-grilled brochettes and sausages. There are also

replaced by soldiers) across the border to claim the territory. At the same time a secret agreement was hatched in Madrid to divide the territory between Morocco and Mauritania as soon as Spanish troops had withdrawn.

The Madrid signatories had, however, underestimated the Saharawis' determination to fight for their independence. In February 1976, when Spanish forces left, Polisario proclaimed the **Saharawi Arab Democratic Republic (SADR)**, and fought back against Moroccan and Mauritanian occupation, backed by Algeria, and sometimes Libya, who saw the Sahara as a stick with which to beat their regional rival. Thousands of refugees fled into Algeria, where they settled into increasingly unhygienic Polisario-run refugee camps rather than submit to Moroccan or Mauritanian rule. Algeria ceded the territory around the camps to the SADR; 200,000 people still live in them today.

Polisario's early military successes were impressive, and Mauritania in particular did not have the resources to beat them. In 1978, the war's destabilization of the Mauritanian economy brought down the government. The new regime made peace with Polisario and pulled out of the Sahara (apart from La Gouera and the western side of the Nouadibhou peninsula, which Mauritania still occupies). The Moroccans moved in to replace them, but by the early 1980s they had been pushed into a small area around Laayoune and Dakhla, and the phosphate mines lay idle. Polisario guerillas even managed to infiltrate into Morocco itself. But the Moroccans fought back and, beginning in 1981, built a series of heavily defended **desert walls** (berm) that excluded Polisario forces from successively larger areas. The sixth wall, built in 1987, established Moroccan control over two-thirds of the territory, including all its economically important parts and the whole of the coastline. Polisario, now confined to areas behind the berm, particularly the region around Bir Lahlou and Tifariti, increasingly turned to diplomacy to gather support, with some success. In 1985, the OAU (now the African Union) admitted the SADR to full membership; Morocco left the organization in protest.

CEASEFIRE AND FUTURE PROSPECTS

In 1988 a UN plan for a **referendum**, to choose between incorporation or independence, was accepted in principle by both sides, and 1991 saw a ceasefire, with the deployment of a UN peacekeeping force called MINURSO, but the years since have seen the UN aims frustrated, with arguments over the voting list leading to repeated postponement of the referendum; Morocco in particular has brought in large numbers of supporters to vote its way should the promised referendum ever be held. In theory, it will still take place, but observers are sceptical. Having invested so much in the territory – not only in military terms, as subsidies, tax concessions and infrastructure building have all been a heavy drain on the Moroccan economy – it seems inconceivable that Morocco will relinquish its claims. In 2002, Morocco's King Mohammed VI stated that he would never give up any part of the territory, but the king has tried to be conciliatory, granting a royal pardon to hundreds of Saharawi political prisoners, and inviting refugees to come home. In 2007 he proposed a new settlement based on limited autonomy under Moroccan sovereignty, which Polisario inevitably rejected. In 2010, Saharawi residents set up a protest camp at **Gdim Izik** near Laayoune, at first to protest against discrimination, but with calls for independence soon added; Moroccan police dispersed the camp by force, killing a number of people and sparking riots across the territory. Protests continued into 2011, and in Dakhla, Moroccan settlers and Saharawis came to blows. Meanwhile Morocco has started building little villages along the coast to establish "facts on the ground", and, as an important strategic ally of the West, is unlikely to face much international pressure on the issue. Truth is, prospects for independence are bleak, and limited autonomy is probably the best the Saharawis can hope for.

café-restaurants on the main road, especially around the SATAS and Supratours offices.

Camping Sahara Line Av Mohammed V ☎0528 896893, ✉ campingsaharaline@menara.ma. Laayoue's *Hotel Sahara Line* runs this bleak and shadeless but well-equipped campsite, 200m from the shore, with cheerful rooms and quite deluxe bungalows, as well as

car wash facilities. Camping <u>65dh</u>, double <u>200dh</u>, bungalow <u>400dh</u>

Al Qods Av Hassan II ☎0528 896573. One of a handful of small hotels in town, this little place on the main drag is neat, tidy and cheap. Bathroom facilities are shared but clean, and there's constant hot water. <u>100dh</u>

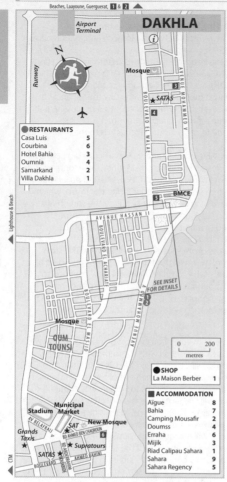

Dakhla

Some 544km from Laayoune, on a long spit of land, **DAKHLA** (formerly Villa Cisneros, capital of Spain's Rio de Oro colony), is just 22km north of the Tropic of Cancer. Under Spanish rule, only the colonists and people working for them were allowed into town – the Saharawi nomads who lived in the desert were excluded. In 1975, the Spanish left and the Mauritanians moved in, to be replaced four years later by the Moroccans. Since then, Dakhla has grown somewhat, but it retains a lazy, sun-bleached atmosphere, with whitewashed, low-rise buildings and an easy-going feel. Europeans in camper vans head down in winter, drawn by the deserted beaches and year-round sunshine – even in January it's hot, and this is the furthest south you can get by land without needing a visa. Dakhla has also been developing a small **surfing** scene, with windsurfing and kitesurfing increasingly popular pursuits at the northern end of the lagoon, and there are a couple of surfing supply shops in town.

The town centre

In the centre of town, the 1953 **Church of Nuestra Señora del Carmen** is about the only thing surviving from Spanish times. Across Avenue Hassan II, a large **statue of the Dakhla peninsula** is reflected in the paving stones of the large, open square.

Avenue Sidi Ahmed Laroussi, which is really more a square than an avenue, comes into its own in the evenings, when it is transformed into an open-air market for anything from Senegalese woodcarvings to secondhand electronic equipment.

Beaches

Three kilometres west of town, a pencil-like, black-and-white-striped **lighthouse** stands next to an old **Spanish fort**. The fort is inside the lighthouse compound, and neither are open to the public. Directly to their north, however, is a wide sweep of Atlantic **beach**. Strong

SIMMERING TENSIONS IN DAKHLA

While Dakhla is generally quiet and peaceful, deep tensions underlie this apparent tranquillity, and occasionally they surface. The Saharawi neighbourhood of **Oum Tounsi** hit the news in February 2011 when it came under attack by Moroccan settlers during the now-abolished annual Dakhla festival. One factor behind the attacks was the resentment of settlers at the subsidies given to returnees from the Polisario camps in Algeria if they accept Moroccan citizenship, but the continued opposition of Saharawis to the Moroccan occupation remains the most serious issue. Further clashes between settlers and Saharawis erupted after a football match in September 2011, leaving eight dead. The Moroccan news agency Morocco World News, calling Oum Tounsi "a stronghold of smugglers", blamed "ex-convicts" for the trouble, adding that unnamed foreigners had taken advantage of the violence to carry out "activities of subversion". For all that, Dakhla is generally peaceful, but the periodic appearance of SADR flags in Saharawi neighbourhoods invariably leads to raids by Moroccan forces, and the tension between settlers and Saharawis does not look like going away any time soon.

currents make it dangerous to swim, but the beach is beautiful, and all but deserted.

For bathing, the beaches north of town on the east side of the peninsula are more suitable, starting with a small one by the campsite (see below), but with others further north, though you'd need your own transport to reach them. The beach at the very northern end of the lagoon, at **Trouk**, 26km north of Dakhla, is very popular with kitesurfers.

ARRIVAL AND DEPARTURE   DAKHLA

By plane Dakhla's airport terminal (☎ 0528 897256) is 1km to the north of the town centre, off Bd de Walae. Royal Air Maroc, with an office two doors along from the post office (Mon–Fri mornings only; ☎ 0528 897049), have flights to Agadir (2 weekly; 1hr 30min), Laayoune (2 weekly; 1hr) and Casablanca (daily; 1hr 55min). Canary Fly, represented by Rio de Oro Voyages on Bd 4 Mars (☎ 0528 930974), fly to Las Palmas (3 weekly; 1hr 15min).

By bus Arriving by bus, you'll be dropped off by the bus companies' offices at the southern end of town: CTM, at the western end of Bd Ahmed Bahnini (☎ 0528 930318); Supratours, Bd Abderrahim Bouabide (☎ 0528 930085); ATAS, Bd Abderrahim Bouabide (opposite Supratours; ☎ 0528 930333); SAT, Bd Ahmed Ben Chaqroun (☎ 0528 931123). When leaving town, you can pick up CTM and Supratours

buses at their town-centre branch offices on Bd 4 Mars and Av Mohammed V respectively, and SATAS buses at their branch office 500m north of the centre on Bd de Walae near *Hôtel Doumss*; buses do not call at these offices when arriving in Dakhla. All northbound buses from Dakhla stop at Boujdour (3hr 30min).

Destinations: Agadir (3 CTM, 4 Supratours, 1 ATAS & 1 SAT daily; 19hr–20hr); Casablanca (1 CTM daily; 28hr); Guerguarat (1 Supratours daily; 5hr); Laayoune (3 CTM, 4 Supratours daily; 8hr); Marrakesh (1 CTM, 1 Supratours daily; 22hr 30min–23hr 30min); Tarfaya (1 Supratours daily; 9hr 30min).

By grand taxi The grand taxi station is at the southern end of town, southwest of the market and the stadium.

Destinations: Boujdour (3hr 30min); Laayoune (8hr); Tan Tan (12hr).

INFORMATION

Tourist information Délégation de Tourisme, Immeuble al Baraka, Bd de Walae, 700m north of Av Hassan II

(Mon–Fri 8.30am–4.30pm; ☎ 0528 898388).

ACCOMMODATION

Aigue Rue Laroussiyine, corner of Av Sidi Ahmed Laroussi ☎ 0528 897395. Clean and friendly, with pleasant rooms, shared showers and 24hr hot water. It's the best choice among the budget hotels on Av Sidi Ahmed Laroussi, especially for lone travellers, although single rooms (50dh) fill up quickly. **80dh**

Bahia 12 Av Mohammed V, corner of Rue Essaouira ☎ 0667 719310. Dakhla's oldest hotel, and not its most comfortable, but it's been given a lick of paint and is quite presentable. It only has one shower, however, and that's down by reception. **60dh**

Camping Mousafir Bd Walae, 6km north of town, ☎ 0528 898279. Located right by the beach, but far from town amenities, this campsite, run by the *Hôtel Doumss*, is friendly and popular with overlanders heading for Mauritania. It has some bare but reasonably large rooms, as well as hot showers (10dh), and is fun and easy-going compared with sites in Morocco proper. The only way into town without your own transport, however, is to walk, hitch, or wait for a petit taxi to turn up (which should charge 15dh to run you into town). Camping **60dh**, double **80dh**

9

Doumss Bd Walae, 500m north of Av Hassan II ☎ 0528 898046, ✉ hoteldoumss@hotmail.com. A comfortable two-star, not very central but handy for SATAS bus departures, and a good mid-market choice, with large en-suite rooms, wi-fi and a bar. BB <u>542dh</u>

Erraha Av Ahmed Belafrij, at the southern end of town, opposite the new mosque ☎ 0528 898811. For those seeking good value but not necessarily the cheapest place in town, this is a step up from the budget hotels around Av Sidi Ahmed Laroussi. The rooms are large and en suite, and even have kitchenettes, though without stoves (which rather defeats the purpose). It's away from the town centre but handy for SAT, SATAS, Supratours and the grand taxi stand, as well as the municipal market. <u>350dh</u>

Mijik on the seafront, behind the Hôtel Doumss ☎ 0655 421112, ✉ hotelmijik@hotmail.com. Quieter and more seaside-like than most of Dakhla's hotels, this budget place has small but well-kept rooms and a restaurant, overlooking a rocky and rather rubbish-strewn shore. En-suite rooms have a sea view, and the single rooms are the cheapest in town (40dh). <u>80dh</u>

Riad Calipau Sahara 13 Bd Walae, 5km north of town ☎ 0528 898886, ✉ info@calipau-resort.com. A deluxe five-star done out like a Moroccan riad, with lots of *tadelakt*, a hammam, jacuzzi, scenic pool and private beach, and even a suite with its own pool. It's lazy and sun-baked, but perhaps not quite as well kept as it might be considering the price. BB <u>1030dh</u>

Sahara Av Sidi Ahmed Laroussi ☎ 0528 897773. Not to be confused with the *Sahara Regency*, this budget hotel is friendly and central, and can arrange transport to Mauritania at competitive prices, but it isn't as clean as it once was, and the shared showers have hot water 6–9pm only (though en-suite rooms have it round the clock). <u>80dh</u>

Sahara Regency Bd Walae, at the junction with Av Hassan II ☎ 0528 931666, ⓦ sahararegency.com. Slap-bang in the centre of town, this is an efficient four-star with large rooms, separate bathrooms and toilets, and balconies. There are three bars, a rooftop restaurant and a pool. The hotel also organizes jetskiing, kitesurfing, 4WD rental and visits to an oyster farm, but none of them cheaply. Wi-fi in the lobby area only. <u>826dh</u>

EATING AND DRINKING

In addition to the places listed below, you'll find a handful of cheap places to eat at the southern end of town on Bd Ahmed Ben Chaqroun around the junction with Bd Abderrahim Bouabide.

★ **Casa Luis** 14 Av Mohammed V by Hôtel Bahia ☎ 0528 898193. Good Spanish food including omelettes and a paella (180dh for two; order 45min in advance) that makes up in flavour, fish and octopus what it lacks in molluscs and crustaceans. Also does a reasonable *pulpo alla gallega* (fresh boiled octopus drizzled with olive oil and sprinkled with paprika; 80dh). Licensed. Daily 8am–10.30pm.

Courbina Bd el Achariate. A no-nonsense Moroccan café-diner, where you can start the day with a bowl of *bisara* (5dh), then fill up at lunchtime or suppertime with one of the chicken or lamb tajines they keep simmering on the stove (25dh). Daily 5am–1am.

Hotel Bahia 12 Av Mohammed V, corner of Rue Essaouira ☎ 0667 719310. Good Moroccan food and local fish dishes, including paella (150dh for two; order 45min in advance) and giant sea bass steak (60dh). Slightly cheaper than the *Casa Luis* next door, but no alcohol. Daily noon–4pm & 7.30pm–midnight.

Oumnia Rue Twarta. This is basically a café, but it also serves soups, sandwiches, tajines and even fried squid. Nothing fancy, but decent enough, and very cheap. A plate of pan-fried giant sea bass and salad will set you back 25dh, as will a tajine. On Fridays there's couscous (30dh). Daily 11am–2pm & 6pm–midnight.

Samarkand Bd de la Achariate. ☎ 0528 898316. A beautiful terrace by the sea; the downstairs area is a café, pizzeria and ice-cream and juice bar. Upstairs it's a more sophisticated Moroccan restaurant, serving tajines (40–60dh) but also fish brochettes (50dh) and other international dishes. Daily 7am–midnight; food noon–3pm & 7pm–midnight.

Villa Dakhla ☎ 0648 315818, ⓦ villa-dakhla.com. A sleek and rather posh restaurant, with stylish decor, a carpeted salon and a sea terrace. The menu changes daily, but typical dishes might include half a dozen local oysters (60dh) followed by pan-fried swordfish steak (100dh). Daily noon–3pm & 7–11pm.

SHOPPING

The municipal market on Bd el Masjid, as well as a smaller market just south of the post office, are good places to stock up on supplies before heading off on the long journey south (or indeed north).

La Maison Berber Rue Mansour Ali Jabar (the alley opposite Hotel Riad) ☎ 0662 543905. The name's a bit incongruous, and some of the stuff on sale here is just Moroccan tat, but there are also some interesting local goods, from Saharawi camel saddles, tobacco pouches and camelskin water bags to prehistoric stone blades and meteorites found in the desert, as well as local and Moroccan fossils. Daily 10am–1pm & 3–11pm.

DIRECTORY

Banks Banks with ATMs include the BMCE off Av Hassan II by the *Hôtel Sahara Regency*, and the Banque Populaire, a block south of the post office. There are also a couple opposite the new mosque at the southern end of town.

Internet Cyber Yehdi Net, Bd Imlili (daily 10am–1am; 5dh/hr); Cyber @ Net, Rue Twarta. (daily 9am–2am; 5dh/hr).

Post office The main post office (Mon–Fri 8am–4pm, Sat 8am–noon) is on Bd des PTT, by Bd el Moukouama.

THE ROAD TO MAURITANIA

In order to travel south from **Dakhla to Mauritania**, you'll have to arrange transport, unless you have your own. Supratours run an overnight bus to the border for 150dh, but once there you're on your own, and you'll have to hitch a ride onward; Mauritanian vehicles will charge around €15–20 to take you from the border to Nouadibhou, but of course all vehicles heading south will have to stop at the border, so you may be able to find a better deal by waiting to see who turns up. None the less, it's generally better to arrange transport in Dakhla straight to Nouadibhou or Nouakchott. The *Hôtel Sahara* can arrange a ride for good rates (opening bids are currently 350dh/€35 to Nouadibhou, or 600dh/€60 to Nouakchott, but you should be able to bargain them down to 300dh/€30 to Nouadibhou, 500dh/€50 to Nouakchott). Otherwise, touts around town can put you in contact with Mauritanian drivers (try asking at the *Café Jazira* at the corner of Avenue Sidi Ahmed Laroussi with Avenue Mohammed V), but you'll need to bargain hard to get a good price – try to find out the current rate from *Hôtel Sahara* in advance. Alternatively, try asking around the campsite, a favourite staging post for Europeans doing the run. Many of these will be bypassing Nouadibhou and heading straight for Nouakchott, which you may or may not see as an advantage (Nouakchott will get you to Senegal quicker, but Nouadibhou is where you need to go for the ore train to Choum). The number of European drivers heading in that direction has diminished somewhat since Senegal slapped a massive duty on the import of cars over five years old, thus putting the kibosh on an established trade in secondhand Peugeots from Europe, though these can still be sold in Mauritania, or beyond Senegal in Mali. It should be possible to obtain a **Mauritanian visa** at the border, for the same price as you would pay at the embassy in Rabat (see p.267).

DAKHLA TO THE BORDER

The road south is now surfaced all the way from Dakhla to the border, 370km from Dakhla. The Mauritanian border post closes at 5.30pm, so set off early if you don't want to spend the night en route. The Moroccans are building settlements along the road, little villages with identikit pretty houses and a mosque. The first is 5km after the military post at **El Argoub**, opposite Dakhla, across the lagoon enclosed by the spit; the next is at **Imlili**, some 50km further (124km from Dakhla). From there, it's 256km to the border post at **Guerguarat**, open daily 8am–7pm on the Moroccan side, 9am–5.30pm on the Mauritanian side (if you arrive after 5pm, you can camp for the night on the Moroccan side).

The last stop for **fuel and proper accommodation** in Moroccan-held territory is the **Motel Barbas**, approximately 300km south of Dakhla and 80km north of Guerguarat (☎0528 897961; 150dh), and a welcome sight on the long road.

CROSSING THE BORDER

Five kilometres beyond Guerguarat, the tarmac ends and you enter Mauritanian-held territory. **Guides** are on hand just beyond the frontier to lead you to the **Mauritanian border post**, and you should accept their assistance, as the area is heavily mined. The western side of the Nouadibhou peninsula is part of the Western Sahara, but occupied by Mauritania. Its main town, La Gouera (Lagwira), is used by the Mauritanian military and is off-limits to foreigners. The Mauritanian border post is on the eastern side of the peninsula, in Mauritania proper. Formalities completed, you can continue to "**Quarante-Six**", where the road crosses the railway 46km out of Nouadibhou. If your lift is continuing across the desert to Nouakchott and you want to go to Nouadibhou, get off here to wait for a vehicle, but be warned that you may be charged heavily for the journey (see above), especially if it is getting late.

Coming from Mauritania, if you have a vehicle, you will need to get a permit from the Moroccan embassy in Nouakchott (see p.57); you cannot get it from the consulate in Nouadibhou. If you don't have a vehicle, arrange transport at the *auberges* and campsites in Nouadibhou, or in Nouakchott.

ARGAN-TREE GOAT

Contexts

History

Morocco's emergence as a nation-state is astonishingly recent, dating from the occupation of the country by the French and Spanish at the turn of the twentieth century, and its independence in 1956. Prior to this, it is best seen as a kind of patchwork of tribal groups, whose shifting alliances and sporadic bids for power defined the nature of government. With a handful of exceptions, the country's ruling sultans controlled only the plains, the coastal ports and the regions around the imperial capitals of Fez, Marrakesh, Rabat and Meknes. These were known as Bled el Makhzen – the governed lands, or, more literally, "Lands of the Storehouse". The rest of the Moroccan territories – the Rif, the three Atlas ranges and the outlying deserts – comprised Bled es Siba, "Lands of the Dissidents". Populated almost exclusively by Berbers, the region's original (pre-Arab) inhabitants, they were rarely recognized as being under anything more than local tribal authority.

The balance between government control and tribal independence is one of the two enduring themes of Moroccan history. The other is the emergence, expansion and eventual replacement of the various **sultanate dynasties**. These at first seem dauntingly complicated – a succession of short-lived tribal movements and confusingly similar-named sultans – but there are actually just seven main groups. The first of them, the **Idrissids**, became the model by founding the city of Fez towards the end of the eighth century and bringing a coalition of Berber and Arab forces under a central *makhzen* (government) authority. The last, the **Alaouites**, emerged in the mid-seventeenth century from the great palm oasis of Tafilalt and, continuing with the current king, Mohammed VI, still hold constitutional power.

Prehistory

Morocco is part of the **Maghreb**, an island of fertile land between the Sahara and the Mediterranean that also includes Algeria and Tunisia. Until around 3000 BC, the Sahara was savannah, fertile enough to support elephants, zebras and a whole range of other wildlife. It seems likely that there were groups of hunter-and-gatherer hominids here as early as a million years ago. Around 15,000 BC there seem to have been **Paleolithic** settlements, and before the Sahara became desert, primitive pastoral and agricultural systems had begun to develop. It is possible also to trace the arrival of two independent Stone Age cultures in the Maghreb: the **Oranian** or **Mouillian Culture** (from around 12,000 BC), and **Capsian Culture** (from around 8000 BC). These are the people who made the cave and rock drawings of the pre-Sahara and High Atlas, Morocco's oldest archeological sites.

c.15,000 BC	c.3000 BC	c.1100 BC
First Paleolithic settlements	Desertification of the Sahara	Arrival of Phoenicians

Phoenicians and Carthaginians

Morocco's recorded history begins around 1100 BC with the arrival of the **Phoenicians**, a seafaring people from what is now Lebanon. By the seventh century BC, they had established settlements along the coast, inlcuding Rusadir (Melilla), Tingis (Tangier), Zila (Asilah), Lixis (Larache), Chellah (Rabat), and even Mogador (Essaouira) – of all their colonies, the furthest from their homeland – where they maintained a dye factory on the Îles Purpuraires (see p.303). The settlements were small, isolated colonies, most built on defensible headlands round the coast, and there was probably little initial contact between them and the inhabitants of the interior (known by their Greek name, *Barbaroi*, or **Berbers)**. By the fifth century BC, one Phoenician colony, **Carthage** (in Tunisia), had become pre-eminent and gained dominance over the rest. Under Carthaginian leadership, some of the Moroccan colonies grew into considerable cities, exporting grain and grapes, and minting their own coins.

Following Carthage's defeat and destruction by Rome in 146 BC, Morocco's Punic colonies grew in prosperity, taking in hundreds of Carthaginian refugees. Even after Rome had annexed and then abandoned the country, Phoenician was still widely spoken along the coast.

Berber kingdoms and Roman rule

Before Rome imposed direct imperial rule in 40 AD, the "civilized" Moroccan territories for a while formed the Berber **Kingdom of Mauretania**, probably little more than a confederation of local tribes, centred round **Volubilis** (near Meknes) and **Tangier**, which gained a certain influence through alliance and occasional joint rule with the adjoining Berber state of **Numidia** (essentially modern Algeria).

The kingdom's most important rulers, and the only ones of which any substantial records survive, were **Juba II** (25 BC–23 AD) and his son **Ptolemy** (23–40 AD). Juba, an Algerian Berber by birth, was brought up and educated in Rome, where he married the daughter of Antony and Cleopatra. His reign, if limited in its extent, seems to have been orderly and prosperous, and the pattern might have continued under his son, but in 40 AD, Emperor Caligula summoned Ptolemy to an audience in Lyons and had him assassinated – so the story goes, for appearing in a more brilliant cloak than his own. Four years later, the new emperor Claudius imposed direct rule, dividing Rome's North African domains into two provinces: Mauritania Caesarensis (the old Numidia) and **Mauritania Tingitana** (essentially, Morocco). Tingis (Tangier) was the capital of Tingitana, while Volubilis became the seat of the provincial governor.

Roman rule

The early years of Rome's new imperial province were taken up with near-constant **rebellions** – the first one alone needing three years and over twenty thousand troops to subdue.

Perhaps discouraged by this unexpected resistance, the **Romans** never attempted to colonize Morocco–Mauretania beyond its old limits, and the Rif and Atlas mountains were left unpenetrated, establishing an enduring precedent. But Tingitana had a considerable Roman presence: the second-century AD geographer Ptolemy listed more than thirty Roman cities in the province, which provided exotic animals for Roman games, as well as grains, wines, fish sauce (*garum*), olive oil, copper and purple murex

146 BC	44 AD	429 AD
Fall of Carthage marks start of Roman domination	Claudius imposes direct Roman rule	Vandals occupy Morocco

dye. **Volubilis**, the most extensive surviving Roman site in Morocco, was a significant city, at the heart of the north's fertile vineyards and grain fields.

However, as Roman power waned, and Berber uprisings became more frequent, administration was moved from Volubilis to Tingis. Meanwhile, as the Roman Empire crumbled, Germanic tribes from the east moved in to take over its territories. One of these tribes, the Vandals under King Gaiseric, invaded Roman Mauretania in 429 AD, and remained its rulers until 533, when the Byzantine general **Belisarius** defeated them and laid claim to the Maghreb for Byzantium's Emperor Justinian. Since the Byzantine Empire was a continuation of the Roman Empire in the east, this marked a kind of return to Roman rule.

The arrival of Islam

Within thirty years of its foundation (in 622 AD, when the Prophet Mohammed moved with his followers from Mecca to Medina), **Islam** had established itself in the Maghreb at Kairouan in present-day Tunisia, but westward expansion was slowed by Algeria's Berbers – mainly pagans but including communities of Christians and Jews – who put up a strong and unusually unified resistance to Arab control. It was only in 680 that the governor of Kairouan, **Oqba Ibn Nafi**, made an initial foray into Morocco, taking in the process the territory's last Byzantine stronghold at Ceuta. The story goes that Oqba then embarked on a 5000km march through Morocco, all the way to the Atlantic Ocean, but whether this expedition had any real Islamicizing influence on the Moroccan Berbers is questionable. Oqba left no garrison forces and was himself killed in Algeria on his way back to Kairouan.

Islam may, however, have taken root among some of the tribes. In the early part of the eighth century the new Arab governor of the west, **Moussa Ibn Noussar**, returned to Morocco and managed to establish Arab control (and carry out mass conversions to Islam) in both the northern plains and the pre-Sahara, but his main thrust was towards **Spain**. In 711, the first Muslim forces crossed over from Tangier to Tarifa and defeated the Visigoths in a single battle; within a decade the Moors had taken control of all but the remote Spanish mountains in northern Asturias; and their advance into Europe was only halted at the Pyrenees by the victory of Charles Martel at Poitiers in 732.

The bulk of this invading and occupying force were almost certainly **Berber converts** to Islam, and the sheer scale of their military success must have had enormous influence in turning Morocco itself into a largely Muslim nation. It was not at this stage, however, in any way an Arab one. The extent of the Islamic Empire – from Persia to Morocco, and ancient Ghana to Spain – was simply too great for Arab numbers. Early attempts to impose taxes on the Moroccan Berbers led to a rebellion and, once again outside the political mainstream, the Maghreb fragmented into a series of small, independent **principalities**.

The Idrissids (eighth–eleventh century)

Meanwhile the Muslim world was split by the schism between **Sunnis** and **Shi'ites**; when the Islamic empire came under the control of Sunni caliphs, the Shi'ites dispersed, seeking refuge both east and west. One of them, arriving in Morocco around 787, was **Moulay Idriss**, an evidently charismatic leader and a great-grandson of the

533 AD	622 AD	680 AD
Belisarius takes Morocco for the Byzantines	Mohammed's flight to Medina marks start of Islamic era	Oqba Ibn Nafi brings Islam to Morocco

Prophet (see box, p.216). He seems to have been adopted almost at once by the citizens of Volubilis – then still a vaguely Romanized city – and by the Aouraba Berber tribe. He was poisoned two years later, possibly by order of caliph Harun al-Rashid (of *Arabian Nights* fame), but had managed to set up the infrastructure of an essentially Arab court and kingdom – the basis of what was to become the Moroccan nation – and his successors, the **Idrissids**, became the first recognizable Moroccan dynasty. His son **Moulay Idriss II**, born posthumously to a Berber woman, was declared sultan in 807, after an apparently orderly regency, and ruled for just over twenty years – something of a golden age for the emerging Moroccan state, with the extension of a central authority throughout the north and even to the oases beyond the Atlas.

Moulay Idriss II's most important achievement was the development of the city planned (and possibly actually started) by his father: **Fez**. Here, he set up the apparatus of court government, and here he also welcomed large contingents of Shi'ite **refugees**, particularly from Western Islam's two great cities, Cordoba and Kairouan. In incorporating them, Fez (and, by extension, Morocco) became increasingly Arabized, and was transformed into a major Arab centre in its own right. The **Kairaouine University** was established, becoming one of the three most important in Islam (and far ahead of those in Europe), and Fez became a vital link in the trade between Spain and the East, and between the Maghreb and Africa south of the Sahara.

After Moulay Idriss's death, the kingdom split into nine different **principalities**. In the ninth century, the dissident Kharijite sect (a movement to the left of Shi'ism) gained the support of many Berbers because it denied any need for the leader of Islam to be an Arab. The desert caravan port of **Sijilmassa** (see p.438) became an important Kharijite stronghold, and remained so until it was attacked in 909 AD by the Shi'ite Fatimids, whose leader the Sijilmassans had imprisoned. The Fatimids went on to conquer Egypt, leaving Morocco in the hands of their Berber allies, the Zirids, but when the Zirids declared their allegiance to the Sunni caliphs in Baghdad, the Fatimids invited an Arabian tribe, the Banu Hilal, to invade and plunder the Maghreb.

The Almoravids (1062–1145)

The Banu Hilal did most of their plundering in Tunisia, and by the time they reached Morocco (where they settled in some of the southern oases), the worst effects of their invasion was over, but they shattered the infrastructure and created a power vacuum, which was filled by the two great Berber dynasties of the Middle Ages – the **Almoravids** and the **Almohads**. Both emerged from the south, and in each case their motivating force was religious: a purifying zeal to **reform** or destroy the decadent ways that had reached Morocco from the wealthy Andalusian Muslims of Spain. The two dynasties together lasted only a century and a half, but in this period Morocco was the pre-eminent power of western Islam, maintaining an **empire** that at its peak reached Spain, Libya, Senegal and ancient Ghana.

The **Almoravids** began as a reforming movement among the Sanhaja Berbers of what is now Mauritania. A nomadic desert tribe like today's Touaregs, they converted to Islam in the ninth century, but the founders of the Almoravid movement, a local sheikh who had returned from the pilgrimage to Mecca and a *fakir* from the Souss plain, found widespread abuse of orthodox practice. In particular, they preached against drinking palm wine, playing licentious music and taking more than four wives,

711 AD	732 AD	787 AD
Muslims under Tariq Ibn Ziad invade Spain	Battle of Poitiers marks furthest Islamic expansion	Moulay Idriss I arrives in Morocco

and their movement rapidly took hold among this already ascetic, tent-dwelling people.

Founding a *ribat* – a kind of warrior monastery similar to the Templar castles of Europe – the Almoravids soon became a considerable military force. In 1054, they set out from the *ribat* (from which the word Almoravids derives) to spread the message through a *jihad* (holy war), and within four years they had destroyed the empire of ancient Ghana (mostly in what is now Mali) and captured its capital Koumbi Saleh (now in Mauritania). Turning towards Morocco, they founded a new capital at Marrakesh in 1062, and under the leadership of **Youssef Ben Tachfine** went on to extend their rule throughout the north of Morocco and, to the east, as far as Algiers.

Spanish expeditions

In 1085, Youssef undertook his first expedition to **Spain**, invited by the princes of Muslim Spain (Andalusia) after the fall of Toledo to the Christians. He crossed over the Straits again in 1090, this time to take control of Spain himself. Before his death in 1107, he restored Muslim control to Valencia and other territories lost in the first wave of the Christian Reconquest. The new Spanish territories reoriented Moroccan culture towards the far more affluent and sophisticated Andalusian civilization, and also stretched the Almoravid forces too thinly. Youssef, disgusted by Andalusian decadence, had ruled largely from **Marrakesh**, leaving governors in Seville and other cities. After his death, the Andalusians proved disinclined to accept these foreign overlords, while the Moroccans themselves became vulnerable to charges of being corrupt and departing from their puritan ideals.

Youssef's son **Ali** was not interested in ceaseless military activity, and in Spain used Christian mercenaries to maintain control. His reign, and that of the Almoravids, was supplanted in the early 1140s by a new movement, the Almohads.

The Almohads (1145–1248)

Ironically, the **Almohads** shared much in common with their predecessors. Again, they were forged from the Berber tribes – this time in the High Atlas – and again, they based their bid for power on an intense Puritanism. Their founder **Ibn Toumert** attacked the Almoravids for allowing their women to ride horses (a tradition in the desert), for wearing extravagant clothes, and for being subject to what may have been Andalusian corruptions – the revived use of music and wine. He also claimed that the Almoravids did not recognize the unitary nature of God, the basis of Almohad belief, and the source of their name – the "unitarians". Banished from Marrakesh by Ali, Ibn Toumert set up a *ribat* in the Atlas at **Tin Mal** in 1124, waging war on local tribes until they accepted his authority, and he eventually claimed to be the Mahdi, the final prophet promised in the Koran.

Ibn Toumert was aided by a shrewd assistant and brilliant military leader, **Abd el Moumen**, who took over the movement after his death. In 1145, he was strong enough to displace the Almoravids from Fez, and two years later he drove them from their capital, Marrakesh, making him effectively sultan.

The third Almohad sultan, **Yacoub el Mansour** (The Victorious), defeated the Christians at Alarcos in Spain in 1195 and pushed the frontiers of the empire east to Tripoli. For the first time, there was one single rule across the entire Maghreb and most

808 AD	828 AD	909 AD
Moulay Idriss II orders construction of Fez	Death of Moulay Idriss II and fragmentation of Morocco	Fatimids take Sijilmassa

of Spain, though it did not stretch as far south as under the Almoravids. With the ensuing wealth and prestige, El Mansour launched a great building programme, including a new capital in **Rabat** and magnificent gateways and minarets in Marrakesh and Seville.

Once more though, imperial expansion precipitated disintegration. In 1212, Yacoub's successor, **Mohammed en Nasr**, attempting to drive the Spanish Christians back to the Pyrenees, was decisively defeated at the Battle of **Las Navas de Tolosa**; the balance of power in Spain was changing, and within four decades only the kingdom of Granada remained in Muslim hands. In the Maghreb, the eastern provinces declared independence from Almohad rule and Morocco itself was returning to the authority of local tribes. In 1248, one of these, the **Merenids** (or Beni Merin), took the northern capital of Fez and turned towards Marrakesh.

Merenids and Wattasids (1248–1554)

The last three centuries of Berber rule in Morocco were marked by increasing domestic **instability** and economic stagnation. The last Andalusian kingdom, Granada, fell to Ferdinand and Isabella la in 1492. The Portuguese established footholds on Morocco's Atlantic and Mediterranean coasts, while, to the east, the rest of the Maghreb fell under the domination of the Ottoman Empire. The Portuguese ability to navigate beyond the Western Sahara also meant the eventual end of the trans-Sahara caravan route.

In Morocco, the main development was a centralized administrative system – the **Makhzen** – maintained without tribal support by standing armies of Arab and Christian mercenaries. It is to this age that the real distinction of Bled el Makhzen and Bled es Siba belongs – the latter coming to mean everything outside the immediate vicinities of the imperial cities.

The Merenids

Perhaps with this background it is not surprising that few of the 21 **Merenid sultans** – or their cousins and successors, the Wattasids – made any great impression. The early sultans were occupied mainly with Spain, at first in trying to regain a foothold on the coast, later in shoring up the kingdom of Granada. There were minor successes in the fourteenth century under the "Black Sultan", **Abou el Hassan**, who for a time occupied Tunis, but he was to die before being able to launch a planned major invasion of Al-Andalus, and his son, **Abou Inan**, himself fell victim to the power struggles within the mercenary army.

The thirteenth and fourteenth centuries, however, did leave a considerable **legacy of building**, perhaps in defiance of the lack of political progress (and certainly a product of the move towards government by forced taxation). In 1279, the garrison town of **Fez el Jedid** was established, to be followed by a series of brilliantly endowed colleges, or **medersas**, which are among the finest surviving Moorish monuments. Culture, too, saw a final flourish. The historians **Ibn Khaldun** and **Leo Africanus**, and the travelling chronicler **Ibn Battuta**, all studied in Fez under Merenid patronage.

The Wattasids

The **Wattasids**, who usurped Merenid power in 1465, had ruled in effect for 45 years previously as a line of hereditary viziers. After their coup, they maintained a semblance

1062	1124	1147
Marrakesh founded by the Almoravids	Ibn Tumert founds Amohad *ribat* at Tin Mal	Almohads take Marrakesh

of control for a little under a century, though the extent of the Makhzen lands was by now minimal.

The **Portuguese** had annexed and colonized the seaports of Ceuta, Tangier, Asilah, Agadir and Safi, while large tracts of the interior lay in the hands of religious warrior brotherhoods, or **marabouts**, on whose alliances the sultans had increasingly to depend.

The Saadians and civil war (1554–1669)

The Saadians, the first **Arab dynasty** since the Idrissids, were the most important of the *marabouts* to emerge in the early years of the sixteenth century, rising to power on the strength of their religious positions (they were Shereefs – descendants of the Prophet). They began by setting up a small principality in the **Souss**, where they established their first capital at Tagmadert in the Draa Valley (exact location uncertain) before moving it to **Taroudant**. Normally, this would have formed a regular part of Bled el Makhzen, but the absence of government in the south allowed them to extend their power to **Marrakesh** around 1524, with the Wattasids for a time retaining Fez and ruling the north.

In the following decades the Saadians made breakthroughs along the coast, capturing Agadir in 1541 and driving the Portuguese from Safi and Essaouira. When the Wattasids fell into bankruptcy and invited the Turks into Fez, the Saadians were ready to consolidate their power. This proved harder, and more confusing, than anyone might have expected. **Mohammed esh Sheikh**, the first Saadian sultan to control both the southern and northern kingdoms, was himself soon using Turkish troops, and was subsequently assassinated by a group of them in 1557. His death unleashed an incredibly convoluted sequence of factional murder and power politics, which was only resolved, somewhat fortuitously, by a battle with the Portuguese twenty years later.

The Battle of the Three Kings

This event, the 1578 **Battle of the Three Kings**, was essentially a Portuguese crusade, led by the youthful King Sebastião on the nominal behalf of a deposed Saadian king against his uncle and rival. At the end of the day all three were to perish on the battlefield, the Portuguese having suffered one of the most disastrous defeats in Christian medieval history, and a little-known Saadian prince emerged as the sole acknowledged ruler of Morocco.

His name was **Ahmed "El Mansour"** (The Victorious, following this momentous victory), and he was easily the most impressive sultan of the dynasty. Not only did he begin his reign clear of the intrigue and rivalry that had dogged his predecessors, but he was immensely wealthy as well. Ransoms paid for the remnants of their nobility after the battle reduced Portugal to bankruptcy, and the country, with its Moroccan enclaves, even fell, for a time under the control of Habsburg Spain.

Breaking with tradition, Ahmed himself became actively involved in European politics, generally supporting the Protestant north against the Spanish and encouraging Dutch and British trade. Within Morocco he was able to maintain a reasonable level of order and peace, and diverted criticism of his use of Turkish troops (and his own Turkish-educated ways) by embarking on an **invasion of Mali**. This secured control of the Saharan salt mines and the gold and slave routes from Senegal, all sources of phenomenal wealth, which won him the additional epithet of El Dhahabi (The Golden One) and reduced his need to tax Moroccans, making him a popular man. His reign

1195	1212	1248
Yacoub el Mansour defeats Castilians at Battle of Alarcos	Christians defeat Muslims at Battle of Las Navas de Tolosa	Merenids take Fez

was the most prosperous period in the country's history since the time of the Almohads – a cultural and political renaissance reflected in the coining of a new title, the Shereefian Empire, the country's official name until independence in 1956.

Civil war and piracy

Ahmed's death in 1603 caused abrupt and lasting chaos. He left three sons, none of whom could gain authority, and, split by **civil war**, the country once again broke into a number of principalities. A succession of **Saadian rulers** retained power in the Souss and in Marrakesh (where their tombs remain testimony to the opulence and turbulence of the age); another *marabout* force, the **Jila**, gained control of Fez; while around Salé and Rabat arose the pirate **Republic of the Bou Regreg** (see p.253).

Moulay Ismail and the early Alaouites (1665–1822)

Like the Saadians, the **Alaouites** were Shereefs, first establishing themselves as religious leaders – this time in Rissani in the **Tafilalt**. Their struggle to establish power also followed a similar pattern, spreading first to Taza and Fez and finally, under Sultan **Moulay Rachid**, reaching Marrakesh in 1669. Rashid, however, was unable to enjoy the fruits of his labour, since he was assassinated in a particularly bloody palace coup in 1672. It was only with Moulay Ismail, the ablest of his rival sons, that an Alaouite leader gained real control over the country.

Moulay Ismail

The 55-year reign of **Moulay Ismail** (see box, p.201) was the country's last stab at imperial glory. In Morocco, where his shrine in Meknes is still a place of pilgrimage, he is remembered as a great and just, if unusually ruthless, ruler; to contemporary Europeans – and in subsequent historical accounts – he is noted for extravagant cruelty (though he was not much worse than the European rulers of his day). He stands out for the grandness of the scale on which he acted. At **Meknes**, his new imperial capital, he garrisoned a permanent army of some 140,000 African troops, a legendary guard he had built up personally through slaving expeditions in Mauritania and Mali, as well as by starting a human breeding programme. The army kept order throughout the kingdom – Morocco is today still littered with their kasbah garrisons – and were able to raise taxes as required. The Bou Regreg pirates were brought under the control of the state in 1668, along with their increasingly lucrative revenues.

With all this, Ismail was able to build a palace in Meknes that was the rival of its contemporary, Versailles, and he negotiated on equal terms with European rulers. Indeed, it was probably the reputation he established for Morocco that allowed the country to remain free for another century and a half before the European colonial powers began carving it up.

Mohammed III and Moulay Slimane

Like all the great, long-reigning Moroccan sultans, Moulay Ismail left innumerable sons and a terminal dispute for the throne, with the powerful standing army supporting and dropping heirs at will.

Remarkably, a capable ruler emerged fairly soon – Sultan **Mohammed III** – and for a while it appeared that the Shereefian Empire was moving back into the mainstream of

1415	1471	1492
Portuguese take Ceuta	Portuguese take Tangier	Fall of Granada: end of Muslim Andalusia

European and world events. Mohammed recaptured El Jadida from the Portuguese, founded the port of Essaouira, traded and conducted treaties with the Europeans, and was the first ruler to recognize the **United States of America**.

At his death in 1790, the state collapsed once more into civil war, Fez and Marrakesh in turn promoting claimants to the throne. When this period drew to some kind of a close, with **Moulay Slimane** (1792–1822) asserting his authority in both cities, there was little left to govern. The army had dispersed; the Bled es Siba reasserted its old limits; and in Europe, with the ending of the Napoleonic Wars, Britain, France, Spain and Germany were all looking to establish themselves in Africa.

Moulay Slimane's rule was increasingly isolated from the new realities outside Morocco. An intensely orthodox Muslim, he concentrated the efforts of government on eliminating the power and influence of the **Sufi brotherhoods** – a power he underestimated. In 1818 Berber tribes loyal to the Derakaoui brotherhood rebelled and, temporarily, captured the sultan. Subsequently, the sultans had no choice but to govern with the cooperation of local sheikhs and brotherhood leaders.

Even more serious, at least in its long-term effects, was Moulay Slimane's isolationist attitude towards **Europe**, and in particular to Napoleonic France. Exports were banned; European consuls banished to Tangier; and contacts that might have helped maintain Moroccan independence were lost.

European domination

European powers had from time to time occupied Moroccan ports such as Ceuta, Tangier, El Jadida and Essaouira, but European encroachment in earnest got under way in the nineteenth century. The Moroccan state, still medieval in form, virtually bankrupt and with armies press-ganged from the tribes to secure taxes, was unable to do much about it.

When the **French** occupied Algiers after a victory over the Ottomans in 1830, Sultan **Abd Er Rahman** (1822–59) mustered a force to defend his fellow Muslims but was severely defeated at Isly in 1843. In 1859, the **Spanish** occupied Tetouan, restored to Morocco only after payment of massive indemnities using money borrowed from Britain (for which the sultan had to surrender control of customs administration). The sultan also had to provide Spain with an Atlantic port, which the Spanish later claimed in Sidi Ifni.

Moulay Hassan

By the end of the nineteenth century, both France and Spain had learned to use every opportunity to step in and "protect" their nationals in Morocco. Complaints by **Moulay Hassan** (Hassan I), the last pre-colonial sultan to have any real power, actually led to a debate on this issue at the 1880 **Madrid Conference**, but the effect was only to regularize the practice on a wider scale, beginning with the setting up of an "international administration" in Tangier.

Moulay Hassan could, in other circumstances, have proved an effective and possibly inspired sultan. Acceding to the throne in 1873, he embarked on an ambitious series of modernizing **reforms**, including attempts to stabilize the currency by minting the rial in Paris, to bring in more rational forms of taxation, and to retrain the army under the instruction of Turkish and Egyptian officers. But his social and monetary reforms were

1465	1506	1509
Wattasid viziers seize power from Merenids	Portuguese take Mogador (Essaouira)	Foundation of Saadian kingdom at Tagmadert

obstructed by foreign merchants and local *caids*, while the European powers forced him to abandon plans for other Muslim states' involvement in the army.

Moulay Hassan played off the Europeans as best he could, employing a British military chief of staff, **Caid MacClean**, a French military mission and German arms manufacturers. On the frontiers, he built kasbahs to strengthen the defences at Tiznit, Saïdia and Selouane. But the government had few modern means of raising money to pay for these developments. Moulay Hassan was thrown back on the traditional means of taxation, the *harka*, setting out across the country to subdue the tribes and to collect tribute. In 1894, returning across the Atlas on just such a campaign, he died.

The last sultans

Hassan's son **Abd el Aziz** (1894–1907) was a boy of fourteen at his accession, but for the first six years of his rule the country was kept in at least a semblance of order by his father's chamberlain, **Bou Ahmed**. In 1900, however, Bou Ahmed died, and Abd el Aziz was left to govern alone – surrounded by an assembly of Europeans, preying on the remaining wealth of the court. In the Atlas mountains, the tribal chiefs asserted their freedom from government control, and in the Rif, a pretender to the throne, **Bou Hamra**, led a five-year revolt.

European manipulation during this period was remorselessly cynical. In 1904, the French negotiated agreements on "spheres of influence" with the British (who were to hold Egypt and Cyprus), and with the Italians (who got Tripolitania, or Libya). The following year saw the German kaiser Wilhelm visiting Tangier and swearing to protect Morocco's integrity, but he was later bought off with the chance to "develop" the Congo. France and Spain, meanwhile, reached a secret arrangement on dividing Morocco and simply awaited a pretext to execute it.

In 1907, the French moved troops into **Oujda**, on the Algerian border, and, after a mob attack on French construction workers, into Casablanca. Abd el Aziz was deposed by his brother, **Moulay Hafid** (1907–12), in a last attempt to resist the European advance. His reign began with a coalition with the principal Atlas chieftain, **Madani el Glaoui**, and intentions to take military action against the French, but the new sultan first had to put down the revolt of Bou Hamra – who was finally captured in 1909. Meanwhile, supposedly to protect their nationals in Rif mineral mines, the Spanish brought over ninety thousand troops to Melilla. Colonial occupation, in effect, had begun.

The Treaty of Fez

Dissidence at home finally drove Moulay Hafid into the hands of the Europeans. With Berber tribesmen at the walls of his capital in Fez supporting a pretender to the throne (one of a number who arose at the time), the sultan went for help to the French, and was forced to accept their terms.

These were ratified and signed as the **Treaty of Fez** in 1912, which gave the French the right to defend Morocco, represent it abroad and conquer the Bled es Siba. A similar document was also signed with the Spanish, who were to take control of a strip of territory along the northern coast, with its capital in Tetouan and another thinner strip of land in the south, running eastwards from Tarfaya. In between, with the exception of a small Spanish enclave in Sidi Ifni, was to be French Morocco. A separate agreement gave Spain colonial rights to the Sahara, stretching south from Tarfaya to the borders of French Mauritania.

1524	1541	1554
Saadians take Marrakesh	Saadians expel Portuguese from Agadir, Safi and Mogador	Saadians take Fez

The French and Spanish Protectorates (1912–56)

The fates of **Spanish and French Morocco** under colonial rule were to be very different. When **France** signed its Protectorate agreement with the sultan in 1912, its sense of **colonial mission** was running high. The colonial lobby in France argued that the colonies were vital not only as markets for French goods but because they fulfilled France's *mission civilisatrice* – to bring the benefits of French culture and language to all corners of the globe. The Spanish saw themselves more as conquerors than colonists and did little to develop their sector, whose government was described by one contemporary as a mixture of "battlefield, tavern and brothel".

Lyautey and "Pacification"

France's first resident-general in Morocco was **General Hubert Lyautey**, often held up as the ideal of French colonialism with his stated policy: "Do not offend a single tradition, do not change a single habit". Lyautey recommended respect for the terms of the Protectorate agreement, which placed strict limits on French interference in Moroccan affairs. He recognized the existence of a functioning Moroccan bureaucracy based on the sultan's court with which the French could cooperate – a hierarchy of officials, with diplomatic representation abroad, and with its own social institutions.

But there were other forces at work: French soldiers were busy unifying the country, ending tribal rebellion; in their wake came a system of roads and railways that opened the country to further colonial exploitation. For the first time in Moroccan history, the central government exerted permanent control over the mountain regions. The "**pacification**" of the country brought a flood of French settlers and administrators.

In France, these developments were presented as echoing the history of the opening up of the American Wild West. Innumerable articles celebrated "the transformation taking place, the stupendous development of Casablanca port, the birth of new towns, the construction of roads and dams…The image of the virgin lands in Morocco is contrasted often with metropolitan France, wrapped up in its history and its routines…".

Naturally, the interests of the natives were submerged in this rapid economic development, and the restrictions of the Protectorate agreement were increasingly ignored.

Spain and revolt in the Rif

The early history of the **Spanish zone** was strikingly different. Before 1920, Spanish influence outside the main cities of Ceuta, Melilla and Tetouan was minimal. When the Spanish tried to extend their control into the Rif mountains of the interior, they ran into the fiercely independent Berber tribes of the region.

Normally, the various tribes remained divided, but faced with the Spanish troops they united under the leadership of **Abd el Krim**. In the summer of 1921, he inflicted a series of crushing defeats on the Spanish army, culminating in the massacre of at least thirteen thousand soldiers at **Annoual**. The scale of the defeat, at the hands of tribal fighters armed only with rifles, outraged the Spanish public and worried the French, who had Berber tribes of their own to deal with in the Atlas mountains. As the war began to spread into the French zone, the two colonial powers combined to crush the rebellion. It took a combined force of around 360,000 colonial troops to do so.

1578	**1603**	**1627**
Battle of the Three Kings puts Ahmed el Mansour on throne	Ahmed el Mansour's death leads to political fragmentation	Republic of Bou Regreg founded at Salé

It was the last of the great tribal rebellions. Abd el Krim had fought for an independent **Rifian state**. An educated man, he had seen the potential wealth that could result from exploiting the mineral deposits of the Rif. After the rebellion was crushed, the route to Moroccan independence changed from armed revolt to middle-class campaigning.

French colonial strategies backfire

The French tried but failed to cultivate support from groups within the Moroccan population. Initially they hoped that by educating a middle-class elite, they would find native allies who would favour binding Morocco permanently to France. In fact, the opposite happened: the educated classes of Rabat and Fez were the first to demand reforms from the French that would give greater rights to the Moroccans. When the government failed to respond, the demand for reforms escalated into demands for total independence.

The other French tactic for heading off opposition to their rule was to try and play off Berbers against Arabs. It was a classic attempt to "divide and rule", but it failed dismally. The French hoped that by spreading Christianity and setting up French schools in Berber areas, the Berbers would become more Europeanized, and thus allies for them against the Muslim Arabs, but the Berber–Arab division they tried to encourage was largely of their own creation, and had little resonance among Moroccans. Nor were the Berbers especially interested in becoming Christian or European. In 1930, the French tried to bring in a **Berber dahir** – a law setting up a separate legal system for the Berber areas. This was an obvious breach of the Protectorate agreement, which prevented the French from changing the Islamic nature of government, and the depth of feeling against it took the French by surprise and forced them to back down.

The rise and decline of the Istiqlal Party

Until World War II, Morocco's **nationalists** were weak and their demands were for reform of the existing system, not independence. After riots in 1937, the government was able to round up and arrest the entire executive committee of the small nationalist party. But with French capitulation in the war, the climate changed. In 1943, the party took the name of **Istiqlal** (Independence); the call for complete separation from France grew more insistent.

The loyal performance of Moroccan troops during the war had raised hopes of a fairer treatment for nationalist demands, but postwar France continued to ignore Istiqlal, exiling its leaders and banning its publications. During the postwar period, it steadily developed into a mass party – growing from 10,000 members in 1947 to 100,000 by 1951.

To some extent, the developments of the 1950s, culminating in Moroccan independence in 1956, resemble events in Algeria and Tunisia. The French first underestimated the strength of local independence movements, then tried to resist them and finally had to concede defeat. In Algeria and Tunisia, the independence parties gained power and consolidated their positions once the French had left. But in Morocco, Istiqlal was never uncontested after 1956 and the party soon began to fragment – becoming, by the 1970s, a marginal force in politics.

Mohammed V leads Morocco to independence

The decline and fall of Istiqlal was due mainly to the astute way in which Sultan (later King) **Mohammed V** associated himself with the independence movement. Despite

1661	1666	1672
British occupy Tangier, introduce tea to Morocco	Moulay Rashid takes Fez for Alaouites	Moulay Ismail becomes sultan, makes Meknes his capital

threats from the French government, Mohammed became more and more outspoken in his support for independence, paralysing government operations by refusing to sign legislation. Serious rioting in 1951 persuaded the French to act: after a period of house arrest, the sultan was sent into exile in 1953 and a puppet, **Ben Arfa**, installed in his place.

This only increased Mohammed V's popularity. Seeing no way out of the spiralling violence of nationalist guerrillas and French settlers, and unable to simultaneously defend three North African colonies (with economic interests dictating that they concentrate on holding Algeria), France let Mohammed V return in 1955, and the following year, 1956, Morocco gained **independence**. Mohammed V then changed his title from sultan to king.

Morocco under Mohammed V

Unlike his ancestor sultans, **Mohammed V** had inherited a united country with a well-developed industrial sector, an extensive system of irrigation and a network of roads and railways. But years of French administration had left little legacy of trained Moroccan administrators. As leader of the Muslim faith in Morocco and the figurehead of independence, the king commanded huge support and influence. Istiqlal party members held key posts in his first **government**, which established schools and universities, introduced a level of regional government, and launched ambitious public works schemes. There were moves against the Sufi brotherhoods, and also against European "decadence", with a wholesale clean-up of Tangier. But the king did not perceive the Istiqlal as natural allies and instead built links with the army – with the help of Crown Prince Hassan, whose period as commander-in-chief was a defining moment in his political development – and with the police.

Mohammed's influence on the army would prove a decisive factor in the Moroccan state withstanding a series of **rebellions** against its authority. The most serious of these were in the Rif, in 1958–59, but there were challenges, too, in the Middle Atlas and Sahara. The king's standing and the army's efficiency stood the test. In party politics, Mohammed's principal act was to lend his support to the **Mouvement Populaire** (MP), a moderate party set up to represent the Berbers, and for the king a useful counterweight to Istiqlal. In 1959, the strategy paid its first dividend. Istiqlal was seriously weakened by a split which hived off the more left-wing members into a separate party, the **Union Nationale des Forces Populaires** (UNFP) under Mehdi Ben Barka. There had always been a certain tension within Istiqlal between the moderates and those favouring a more radical policy, in association with the unions. A tendency towards parties dividing within and among themselves has been apparent in Moroccan politics ever since, helping to maintain the palace's leading role in the political arena.

Hassan II (1961–99)

Mohammed V's death in 1961 brought his son **Hassan II** to the throne, whose **autocratic rule** had a very thin veneer of parliamentary politics. But by the time he died, in July 1999, the monarchy, although still by far the most powerful political institution in Morocco, had begun to engage with other political and social forces – and had established the roots of a more open political culture.

1727	1757	1792
Moulay Ismail's death leads to political fragmentation	Mohammed III becomes sultan	Moulay Slimane becomes sultan

Despite the poverty still apparent in large areas of the country, much was done during Hassan's reign to bring the kingdom into the modern world. It was an achievement in the face of a huge **population explosion** in the 1970s and 1980s, which saw the population rise from eight million at independence to more than thirty million today.

Elections and coup attempts

In many respects Hassan was a very modern monarch, regularly pictured playing golf, flying a jet fighter, or meeting fellow heads of state. As a power politician he had few peers. But he was also careful to maintain his status as a traditional ruler. **Domestic politics** since independence has centred on a battle of wills between the dominant political forces in the kingdom: the palace and its allies; a legalized opposition which has at times formed a part of the government; and underground movements such as the Marxist-Leninist Ilal Amam (which has all but disappeared) and, more recently, groups of Islamist radicals.

Even before independence, in a 1955 speech, Mohammed V had promised to set up "democratic institutions resulting from the holding of free elections". The country's first constitution was not ready until after his death, and it was only in 1962, under Hassan II, that it was put to, and approved by, a popular referendum. The constitution was drafted in such a way as to favour the pro-monarchy parties of the centre – setting the pattern that was to prevail up until the end of Hassan's reign.

The 1960s were marked by the fragility of Morocco's political party structure and the authorities' greater enthusiasm for using the bullet and torture chamber rather than the ballot box to handle opposition. This mood was reflected in the **Ben Barka affair**, a notorious incident whose political ramifications endured for the next two decades, when Mehdi Ben Barka, leader of the opposition UNFP party, was assassinated in Paris, with apparent connivance between the governments of Morocco and France.

The opposition subsequently split, with the largest element of the UNFP going on to form the USFP, led by Abderrahim Bouabid until his death in 1992. These parties were largely ineffectual, especially after Hassan announced a new constitution in 1970, following a period of emergency rule. However, the events of 1971–72 showed the real nature of the threat to the monarchy.

In July 1971, a group of soldiers broke into the royal palace in Skhirat in an attempt to stage a **coup**; more than one hundred people were killed, but in the confusion Hassan escaped. The following year another attempt was launched, as the king's private jet was attacked by fighters of the Moroccan Air Force. Again, Hassan had a very narrow escape – his pilot was able to convince the attacking aircraft by radio that the king had already died. The former interior minister, General Mohamed Oufkir disappeared (apparently murdered in custody) soon after and the armed forces were restructured.

The Saharan conflict and the UMA

Hassan's great challenge was to give a sense of destiny to the country, a cause similar to the struggle for independence that had brought such prestige to his father. That cause was provided in 1975, when the Spanish finally decided to pull out of their colony in the **Western Sahara** (see box, pp.522–523).

In the 1950s the nationalist Istiqlal party had laid claim to the Spanish Sahara, as well as to Mauritania and parts of Algeria and Mali, as part of its quest for a "Greater Morocco". By 1975, Hassan had patched up the border dispute with Algeria and

1859	**1873**	**1880**
Spanish occupy Tetouan	Moulay Hassan (Hassan I) becomes sultan	Madrid Conference confirms Europeans' "protection" rights

recognized the independent government in Mauritania, but he retained a more realistic design – Moroccan control of the Spanish Sahara.

Spanish withdrawal from the Western Sahara in 1975 coincided with General Franco's final illness and Hassan timed his move perfectly, sending some 350,000 Moroccan civilians southwards on **El Massira** – the "**Green March**" – to the Sahara. Spain could either go to war with Morocco by attacking the advancing Moroccans or withdraw without holding a referendum on independence, which they had agreed to call after UN pressure. Hassan's bluff worked, and the popular unrest of the 1960s and the coup attempts of 1971–72 were forgotten under a wave of patriotism. Without shedding any blood, Morocco had "recaptured" part of its former empire. But the Polisario guerrillas who had led the fight against Spanish rule (see box, pp.522–523) now began a campaign against Moroccan occupation. Despite early Polisario successes, the Moroccans managed to assert control over most of the territory, and all of its economically important areas, but in 1988 the two sides agreed a ceasefire under UN auspices, on the principle that a **referendum** would be held on the territory's future.

That promised referendum has yet to take place, but the dispute has damaged Morocco diplomatically; in particular it has left her isolated in African politics since the African Union recognized the Polisario-declared Saharawi Arab Democratic Republic, prompting Morocco to leave. A resolution is also essential if Morocco is to have normal relations with its neighbours, particularly Algeria, which strongly backed Polisario; friction between Morocco and Algeria has hampered efforts towards regional unity.

In February 1989 Algerian, Libyan, Mauritanian, Moroccan and Tunisian leaders, meeting in Marrakesh, had agreed to form the long-awaited regional grouping, the **Arab Maghreb Union**, known by its evocative acronym UMA (from the French Union du Maghreb Arabe but sounding like the Arabic word *'umma*, or community). However, the UMA has been stalled by disputes hinging on long-standing rivalries between the North African states. Chief among the UMA's problems has been Moroccan–Algerian hostility arising largely from the Saharan question. This led in 1994 to the closure of the Algerian–Moroccan border, which has not reopened since.

Economic and social problems

The Saharan war proved to be only a temporary distraction from discontent in Morocco itself. Moreover, the occupation of the Western Sahara and its demands on the economy added to the very problems it was designed to divert attention from. By 1981, an estimated sixty percent of the population were living below the poverty level, unemployment ran at approximately twenty percent (forty percent among the young) and perhaps twenty percent of the urban population lived in shantytowns, or *bidonvilles*.

Popular unrest erupted in the 1984 "**bread riots**" in cities across the country, most notably in Marrakesh, Oujda, Nador and Tetouan. The riots were triggered when the government raised the prices of staple foods following pressure from the International Monetary Fund (IMF) to repay its **burgeoning debt** while phosphate prices were depressed and the country was suffering one of its regular **droughts**. King Hassan had to intervene personally to reverse the decision and, in the opinion of many analysts, save his monarchy from a populist rising.

Dissatisfaction with Hassan's regime in the 1980s and 1990s surfaced in the form of protests by unemployed graduates (despite the dangers of political protest in Hassan's

1900	1907	1912
Death of Bou Ahmed leaves Morocco without effective ruler	French occupy Oujda	Treaty of Fez splits Morocco between France and Spain

police state), and sometimes violent incidents in the kingdom's universities. In 1990, a general strike called by the CDT trade union federation led to riots in Fez and Tangier. On campus, the student movement linked to Morocco's biggest opposition party, the **Union Socialiste des Forces Populaires** (USFP), went into retreat as a growing Islamist movement took control of student unions.

In the 1990s, Morocco embarked on one of Africa's biggest **privatization** drives as King Hassan firmly nailed his colours to the mast of economic liberalization. New efforts were made to encourage foreign investment in technologically advanced manufacturing industries, **textiles** and, an increasingly important earner, **tourism**. Modern management skills began to take hold with the emergence of a new managerial class independent of the old social loyalties. The decade ended with the Medi Telecom consortium bidding over US$1 billion for a licence to install a GSM mobile telephone system, and privately financed power plants helping to raise energy capacity.

A 1980s application to join the **European Union** was rejected, but in 1996 Morocco's joined the EU's **Euro-Mediterranean Partnership** agreement, intended to create a free trade zone around the Mediterranean, and closer ties with the EU, including preferential trade deals, have followed.

Change and elections

The opposition, which had been quiet through much of the 1980s, started to reassert itself in the 1990s, as traditional opposition parties showed revived enthusiasm for challenging the government – though not the king. The mid-1990s saw Morocco cleaning up its previously appalling **human rights** record. In 1992, a leading dissident, Abraham Serfaty, was one of many well-known figures in a **release of political prisoners** that included many soldiers held, since the 1972 failed coup, in a dungeon prison at Tazmamart in the High Atlas. Several former student radicals who survived imprisonment and torture in the 1960s, '70s and '80s went on to hold positions of responsibility in the local press, universities and even government departments.

In 1996, Hassan judged there to be sufficient consensus on the direction of Moroccan politics to hold a referendum on constitutional reforms, opening the way for a new bicameral parliamentary system. Local and national elections were held in 1997 and for the first time there seemed the prospect of bringing the opposition into government, with genuine power. Disappointingly, the elections produced a lacklustre campaign and much voter apathy, as a three-way split gave right-wing, centrist and left-wing/nationalist groupings a similar number of seats in the lower house of parliament. Hassan appointed as prime minister the USFP leader **Abderrahmane Youssoufi** at the head of a coalition government that included both USFP and Istiqlal ministers.

One notable factor in the 1997 general election was that Islamist deputies were voted into parliament for the first time, under the Mouvement Populaire Constitutionnel et Démocratique (**MPCD**) banner. This parliamentary debut for the Islamists came at a time when their calls for a change in views on public morality and private sector development were gaining appeal among those most alienated by increasing social tensions and allegations of corruption, but many have seen the administration's acceptance of the **MPCD**, who stand at the moderate end of the Islamist spectrum, as a classic piece of Moroccan divide-and-rule, aimed at splitting the Islamist movement.

1921	**1943**	**1956**
Abd el Krim launches Rif revolt against colonial rule	Istiqlal Party founded	Morocco gains independence under Mohammed V

Mohammed VI (1999–)

On Hassan's death in 1999, his son **Mohammed VI** quickly emerged from his father's shadow, ushering in a **new style** of rule with widespread popular support. From the very start he made clear his more inclusive agenda by visiting the **troubled north** (long ignored by Hassan), restoring **civil rights** to those remaining political prisoners not covered by previous amnesties (with over eight thousand released in first-year amnesties), and promising a more **relaxed and consensual** form of rule. He sacked Hassan's powerful but unpopular right-hand man, Minister of State for the Interior **Driss Basri**, and allowed a number of high-profile dissidents to return to Morocco, most notably leftist **Abraham Serfaty**, whom he appointed as a personal adviser. In May 2000, he made headlines by freeing his father's most implacable critic, **Abdessalam Yassine**, leader of the banned **Al-Adl wal Ihsane** (Justice and Charity) movement. Dissent is not always tolerated, however, and the king's forces have on occasion clamped down rather harshly on street protests, notably a protest by unemployed graduates in Rabat in June 2000, while newspapers are still prosecuted under laws against "undermining" the monarchy or Morocco's "territorial integrity". Nonetheless, the tenor of Mohammed's reign has been to extend democracy, human rights and free speech, albeit in a cautious fashion.

Legal reforms

In March 2000, the king announced a **National Action Plan**, whose main feature was a Family Law that radically improved the **position of women** under Moroccan law, banning polygamy and introducing more equal family rights. The proposal sparked a backlash by Islamists, who mustered around a quarter of a million supporters at a march in Casablanca to protest the proposals, and the government responded by setting up a consultative commission to consider the question more carefully. After due consideration, parliament decided to go ahead with the proposals, which came into force in 2004, giving women greater legal rights in Morocco than anywhere else in the Muslim world, and more on a par with those of women in Europe.

The birth of a son and heir, Prince Moulay Hassan, in 2003, gave the king an excuse to release some nine thousand prisoners and remit the sentences of thousands more. The same year also saw a major extension of **rights for Berber speakers**, whose languages were taught for the first time in schools in the 2003–4 academic year. Programmes in Berber are also now broadcast on TV.

Terrorism

The Moroccan government was swift to condemn the September 2001 **attacks by al-Qaeda** on the Pentagon and the New York World Trade Center, but the apparent involvement of pro-Islamist Moroccans in those attacks and in the train bombs that killed over two hundred people in Madrid in March 2004 severely embarrassed the Moroccan authorities. In Morocco itself, May 2003 saw attacks on Jewish and Western targets by suicide bombers in Casablanca, which resulted in the deaths of 33 people (plus the bombers). The attack severely dented fundamentalist appeal, but a hardcore of support for such actions continues to exist. The authorities reacted to the bombings by rounding up over 1500 people suspected of involvement with militant groups, of whom several hundred were given prison sentences ranging from three months to thirty years. 2011 saw another bomb attack, this time on the *Argana Café* in

1961	1975	1984
Hassan II becomes king	Green March: occupation of Western Sahara	Bread riots break out

Marrakesh, in which seventeen people were killed. The Moroccan government blamed al-Qaeda, and nine people described as "admirers of al-Qaeda" were convicted of the murders, but no organization claimed responsibility and the bombers' motives remain unclear, though they were obviously targeting tourists, who were the *Argana*'s main customers.

Elections

In the **2002 elections**, the moderate Islamist MPCD, now renamed the PJD (Parti de la Justice et du Développement), took thirteen percent of the vote and emerged as Morocco's third biggest political party after the USFP and Istiqlal, which formed an administration together with representatives of four other parties, all essentially organizations for the distribution of patronage, whose ministries were largely staffed by their own people. The same pattern continued after the **2007 elections**, in which Istiqlal regained its position as the largest party in parliament – the fact that it could do so with just over a tenth of the vote shows just how fragmented the party system was. Istiqlal leader Abbas el Fassi took over as PM at the head of a four-party coalition that included the USFP.

In 2011, the **Arab Spring**, which sprang out of revolutions in Tunisia and Egypt, sparked large demonstrations for jobs and democracy across Morocco. On 20 February, a large pro-democracy **demonstration** in Rabat quickly spread nationwide, with protests in all major cities and many minor ones. The king responded on 9 March by announcing a commission on the constitution, which swiftly reported in June, proposing that elections should be binding, with the king obliged to appoint as prime minister the leader of the largest party. Women's rights were also entrenched in the constitution, and Beber joined Arabic as an official language. The constitution was approved by referendum in July, despite scepticism on the part of the largely student-run pro-democracy **20 February Movement**, which grew out of the wave of protests. When **elections under the new constitution** were held in November 2011, the 20 February Movement called for a boycott, despite which, turnout rose from 37 percent to 45 percent, on an admittedly smaller electoral register. The victors were the PJD, who took 107 of the 395 seats in parliament.

Prospects

To the outside world, the king seems to have done just enough to head off a movement for radical change, but many issues remain unresolved. The king still has huge powers which he has not surrendered to elected politicians: he still runs the army, the security forces and the religious establishment, and control of the economy and the country's wealth remains in the hands of a small elite strongly linked to the palace. Meanwhile, in the Western Sahara, even before the Arab Spring spread to Morocco proper, protest camps calling for independence were broken up by force in late 2010, and in Morocco itself many people failed to register for the 2011 elections, while of those who did, less than half bothered to vote. While the democracy movement has apparently been contained, for the present at any rate, many Moroccans remain disgruntled, and there are still massive problems of poverty, unemployment and unequal wealth distribution to deal with, not to mention the need for a resolution in the Western Sahara, and the spectre of radical Islam lurking in the background. What the king and the politicians will do about these questions remains to be seen.

1989	1999	2004	2011
Arab Maghreb Union founded	Mohammed VI becomes king	Family Law extends women's legal rights	PJD wins election

Moroccan street names

Moroccan streets are often named after well-known historical figures, events and dates. Transliteration from Arabic into the Roman alphabet means that there are often many variations of the same name.

Abd el krim el Kattabi Leader of the 1921–27 Rif war against the Spanish (see box, p.130).

Al Jamia Al Arabi The Arab League, founded in Egypt in 1945.

Allal Ben Abdallah House-painter from Guercif shot down in 1953 after driving an open-topped car into a royal procession and attacking France's puppet sultan Ben Arfa with a kitchen knife.

Al Massira al Khadra/La Marche Verte The Green March of November 1975 to occupy the Western Sahara (see p.543).

Bir Anzarane Town in the Western Sahara and site of fierce 1979 battle between Morocco and the Polisario.

El Farabi Islamic philosopher (870–950) from Farab in Uzbekistan who tried to harmonize Greek philosophy with Islamic thinking.

El Houria Freedom.

El Mansour Eddahbi Saadian sultan 1578–1603.

F.A.R. (Forces Armées Royales) The armed forces.

Ferhat Hachad Tunisian trade union leader and Arab nationalist murdered in 1952 by extremist French settlers.

Hassan II King 1975–99.

Ibn Batouta Fourteenth-century Tanjawi traveller who visited China, India and most of the Islamic world.

Ibn Khaldoun Tunisian historian (1332–1406), who first proposed a cyclical view of history.

Ibn Rochd One of Islam's greatest philosophers (1126–98), also known as Averroes, who was based in Marrakesh and doctor to Yacoub el Mansour.

Ibn Toumert/Mehdi Ibn Toumert Founder of the Almohads (see box, p.383).

Ibn Zaidoun Eleventh-century Andalusian poet.

Istiqlal Independence; also the name of Morocco's first political party (see p.540).

Mohammed Ben Abdallah/Sidi Mohammed Ben Abdallah Grandson of Moulay Ismail, sultan 1757–90.

Mohammed V Sultan and subsequently king 1927–53 and 1955–61 (see p.541).

Mohammed VI King since 1999.

Mohammed Zerktouni Armed resistance leader, accused of killing twenty people in a 1953 bomb attack on Casablanca's central market, who took cyanide to avoid giving information under torture.

Mokhtar Soussi Poet and intellectual who inspired the nationalist movement during the French occupation.

Moulay Abdallah/Prince Moulay Abdallah Younger son of Mohammed V, brother of Hassan II.

Moulay el Cherif/Moulay Rachid First Alaouite sultan, ruled 1666–72 (see p.536).

Moulay Hassan/Hassan I Sultan 1873–94 (see p.537).

Moulay Idriss Moulay Idriss I (788–91) or Moulay Idriss II (804–28), Morocco's first Arab rulers (see p.531).

Moulay Ismail Second Alaouite sultan (1672–1727; see p.531).

Moulay Youssef French-appointed sultan (1912–27), brother of Moulay Hafid, father of Mohammed V and great-grandfather of Mohammed VI.

Moussa Ibn Noussar General who consolidated the Arab conquest of Morocco in the eighth century (see p.531).

Oqba Ibn Nafi Arab general who brought Islam to Morocco (see p.535).

Oued el Makhazine Site of the Battle of the Three Kings (see p.533).

Salah Eddine el Ayoubi Kurdish-born Islamic leader, known in English as Saladin, who ruled Egypt and Syria 1171–93, and recaptured Jerusalem from the Crusaders in 1187.

Tarik Ibn Ziad Berber chieftain who led the 711 Islamic invasion of Spain and gave his name to Gibraltar – Jebel (mount) Tarik.

Yacoub el Mansour Third Almohad sultan (1184–99; see p.451).

Youssef Ben Tachfine First Almoravid sultan (1062–1106; see p.543).

DATES

January 11, 1944 The Istiqlal party issued a manifesto demanding independence.

February 29, 1960 The Agadir earthquake (see p.451).

March 2, 1956 French recognition of Moroccan independence.

August 16, 1953 Anti-French riots in Casablanca, Rabat, Marrakesh and Oujda.

August 20, 1953 Mohammed V was deposed by the French and exiled on the eve of Aïd el Kebir.

November 6, 1975 The Green March (see p.543).

November 16, 1955 Mohammed V's return from exile.

November 18, 1927 Mohammed V's accession to the throne.

November 18, 1955 Officially considered independence day (though full independence was achieved the following year).

Islam in Morocco

It's difficult to get any grasp of Morocco, and even more so of Moroccan history, without first knowing something of Islam. What follows is a very basic background: some theory, some history and an idea of Morocco's place in the modern Islamic world.

Practice and belief

Islam was founded by **Mohammed** (also spelt Muhammad), a merchant from the wealthy city of Mecca, now in Saudi Arabia. In about 609 AD, he began to receive divine messages, and continued to do so for the rest of his life. After his death, these were collated, and form the **Koran** (*Qur'an*). Muslims consider Mohammed to be the final prophet of the same God who is worshipped by Jews and Christians, and Islam recognizes all the prophets of the biblical Old Testament as his predecessors, and also regards Jesus (*Aïssa* in Arabic) as a prophet, but not as the Son of God.

The distinctive feature of Islam is its directness – there is no intermediary between man and God in the form of an institutionalized priesthood or complicated liturgy, as in Christianity; and worship, in the form of prayer, is a direct and personal communication with God.

The Pillars of Faith

Islam has five essential requirements, called "**Pillars of faith**": prayer (*salat*); the pilgrimage to Mecca (*hadj*); the Ramadan fast (*sanm*); almsgiving (*zakat*); and, most fundamental of all, the acceptance that "There is no God but God and Mohammed is His Prophet" (*shahada*). The Pillars of Faith are central to Muslim life, articulating and informing daily existence. **Prayers** are performed five times daily, at sunset (when the Islamic day begins), nightfall, dawn, noon and afternoon, and can be performed anywhere, but preferably in a mosque (*jemaa* in Arabic). In the past, and even today in some places, a *muezzin* would climb his minaret each time and summon the faithful. Nowadays, the call is likely to be pre-recorded, but this most distinctive of Islamic sounds has a beauty all its own, especially when neighbouring *muezzins* are audible simultaneously. Their message is simplicity itself: "God is most great (*Allah o Akhbar*). I testify that there is no God but Allah. I testify that Mohammed is His Prophet. Come to prayer, come to security. God is most great." Another phrase is added in the morning: "Prayer is better than sleep".

Prayers are preceded by ritual washing. The worshipper then removes their shoes and, facing Mecca (the direction indicated in a mosque by the mihrab), recites the Fatina, the first chapter of the Koran: "Praise be to God, Lord of the worlds, the Compassionate, the Merciful, King of the Day of Judgement. We worship you and seek your aid. Guide us on the straight path, the path of those on whom you have bestowed your Grace, not the path of those who incur your anger nor of those who go astray." The same words are then repeated twice in the prostrate position, with some interjections of *Allah o Akhbar*. The prostrate position symbolizes the worshipper's submission to God (Islam literally means "submission"), and the sight of thousands of people going through the same motions simultaneously in a mosque is a powerful one. On Friday, believers try to attend prayers in their local grand mosque, where the whole community comes together in worship, led by an *imam* (much like a Protestant pastor), who may also deliver the *khutba*, or sermon.

Ramadan is the name of the ninth month in the lunar Islamic calendar, during which believers must fast between sunrise and sundown, abstaining from food, drink, cigarettes and sex. Only children, pregnant women and warriors engaged in a *jihad* (holy war) are exempt. Though the day is thus hard, nights are a time of celebration. The pilgrimage, or **hadj**, to Mecca is an annual event, with millions flocking to

Mohammed's birthplace from all over the world. Here they go through several days of rituals, the central one being a sevenfold circumambulation of the Kaba, before kissing a black stone set in its wall. Islam requires that all believers go on a *hadj* as often as is practically possible, but for the poor it may be a once-in-a-lifetime occasion, and is sometimes replaced by a series of visits to lesser, local shrines – in Morocco, for instance, to Fez and Moulay Idriss.

Islam's development in Morocco

Morocco was virtually untouched by the Sunni–Shia conflict that split the Muslim world – but the country's unusual geographical and social circumstances have conspired to tip the balance away from official orthodoxy. In the eighth century, many Berbers were attracted to the dissident Kharijite strain of Islam, which rejected the Sunni and Shi'te argument that the leader of the faithful had to be an Arab, and Sijilmasa (Rissani) became the capital of a powerful Kharijite kingdom. Subsequently, Moroccans have in principle been almost universally Sunni, but Sufism and maraboutism became very strong within the religion.

Marabouts

Sufism is the idea that, in addition to following religious rules, people can personally get closer to God by leading a spiritual rather than a materialistic lifestyle, and even by chanting and meditating to achieve a trance-like state. Everywhere in Morocco, as well as elsewhere in North Africa, the countryside is dotted with small domed **koubbas** – the tombs of **marabouts** Sufi holy men (though the term is also used for the *koubba*) – which became centres of worship and pilgrimage. This elevation of individuals goes against strict Islamic teaching, but probably derives from the Berbers' pre-Islamic tendency to focus worship round individual holy men.

More prosperous cults would also endow educational institutions attached to the *koubba*, known as **zaouias**, which provided an alternative to the official education given in urban medersas (Koranic schools). These inevitably posed a threat to the authority of the urban hierarchy, and as rural cults extended their influence, some became so popular that they endowed their saints with genealogies traced back to the Prophet. The title accorded to these men and their descendants was Shereef, and many grew into strong political forces. The classic example in Morocco is the tomb of Moulay Idriss – in the eighth century just a local *marabout*, but eventually, the base of the Idrissid clan, a centre of enormous influence that reached far beyond its rural origins.

The most influential *marabouts* spawned Sufi **brotherhoods**, whose members meet to chant, play music, meditate, and thus seek personal union with God. This is particularly an important part of the **moussem**, an annual festival associated with each *marabout*. The most famous and flamboyant Moroccan Sufi brotherhood is that of **Sidi Mohammed Ben Aïssa**. Born in Souss in the fifteenth century, he travelled in northern Morocco before settling down as a teacher in Meknes and founding a *zaouia*. His powers of mystical healing became famous there, and he provoked enough official suspicion to be exiled briefly to the desert – where he again revealed his exceptional powers by proving himself immune to scorpions, snakes, live flames and other hostile manifestations. His followers tried to achieve the same state of grace. The Aissaoua brotherhood made itself notorious with displays of eating scorpions, walking on hot coals and other ecstatic practices designed to bring union with God.

Towards crisis

With all its different forms, Islam permeated every aspect of the country's pre-twentieth-century life. Unlike Christianity, at least Protestant Christianity, which to some extent has accepted the separation of church and state, Islam sees no such distinction. **Civil law** was provided by the *sharia*, the religious law contained in the Koran, and **intellectual life** by the *msids* (Koranic primary schools where the 6200 verses were learned by heart) and by the great medieval mosque universities, of which the Kairaouine in Fez (together with the Zitoura in Tunis and the Al Azhar in Cairo) was the most important in the Arab world.

At first, Islam brought a great scientific revolution, uniting the traditions of Greece and Rome with those of India and Iran, and then developing them while Christian Europe rejected the sciences of pagan philosophers. As Europe went through its Renaissance, however, it was Islam that started to atrophy, as the religious authorities became increasingly suspicious of any challenge to established belief, and actively discouraged innovation. At first this did not matter in political terms, but as the Islamic world fell behind in science and learning, Europe was able to take advantage of its now superior technology. Napoleon's expedition to Egypt in 1798 marked the beginning of a century in which virtually every Islamic country came under the control of a **European power**. Because East–West rivalry had always been viewed in religious terms, the nineteenth and twentieth centuries saw something of a **crisis in religious confidence**. Why had Islam's former power now passed to infidel foreigners?

Fundamentalism

Reactions and answers veered between those who felt that Islam should try to incorporate some of the West's materialism, and those who held that Islam should turn its back on the West, purify itself of all corrupt additions and thus rediscover its former power. As colonies of European powers, Muslim nations had little chance of putting any such ideas into effective practice. But **decolonization**, and the discovery of oil in the Middle East, brought the Islamic world face to face with the question of its own spiritual identity. How should it deal with Western values and influence, now that it could afford – both politically and economically – almost total rejection? A return to the totality of Islam – **fundamentalism** – is one option. It has a reactionary side, harking back to an imagined time of perfection under the Prophet and the early caliphs, but it is also radical in its rejection of colonialism and materialism, and its most vehement adherents tend to be young rather than old.

Islam in Modern Morocco

In Morocco today, Islam is the official state religion, and King Mohammed's secular status is interwoven with his role as "commander of the faithful". Internationally too, he plays a leading role. Meetings of the Islamic Conference Organization are frequently held in Morocco and students from as far afield as Central Asia come to study Islam at Fez University. For all these indications of Islamic solidarity, though, **state policy** remains distinctly moderate – sometimes in the face of fundamentalist pressure. The 2004 law on the status of women is a good example of this: 100,000 people marched in Rabat to support the new law, and over 200,000 marched in Casablanca against it, a sign of increasing **polarization** on religious questions, not unlike that in the United States.

In the cities, there has long been tension between those for and against secularization, as well as a large body of urban poor, for whom Islamic fundamentalism can seem to offer solutions. In some circles, Islam is becoming very relaxed; in Casablanca, Rabat, El Jadida and Marrakesh, young people of both sexes can be seen socializing together, young women no longer wear the veil, and have exchanged their frumpy cover-alls for flattering, and even sexy clothes, while young couples go to nightclubs and even drink socially. But against this, the number of people going to pray at mosques is on the up, and among the poor especially, Islam is becoming a mark of pride and respectability. That this is reflected in politics is not surprising, and the moderate Islamist PJD (founded in 1998) has gradually developed into a mainstream party, winning the 2011 election, although any programme involving enforcement of religious strictures would be strongly resented by secular Moroccans.

In the **countryside**, religious attitudes have changed less over the past two generations. Religious brotherhoods such as the Aissaoua have declined since the beginning of the century, when they were still very powerful, and the influence of mystics generally has fallen. As the official histories put it, popular credulity in Morocco provided an ideal setting for charlatans as well as saviours, and much of this has now passed. All the same, the rhythms of rural life still revolve around local *marabouts*, and the annual moussems, or festivals-cum-pilgrimages, are still vital and impressive displays.

Moroccan architecture

As befits a Muslim country, Morocco's architecture is dominated by Islamic religious buildings, most particularly **mosques**, but also **zaouias** (the shrines of local saints) and **medersas** (religious schools). Many features of Moroccan architecture – such as the familiar pointed horseshoe arches of doorways and city gates – come from the Middle East and arrived with the **Arabs**. Though the style has been refined, and decorative details added over the centuries, the country's architectural traditions have changed little since then. The **colonial period** did, however, make its mark, and there are some particularly fine examples of Art Deco and Art Nouveau styles to be found, though they are confined to the French-built Villes Nouvelles, leaving the traditional Medinas often remarkably untouched.

Brief history

As far as we can tell from their only surviving building of note – the Koubba Ba'adiyn in Marrakesh – it was the **Almoravids** who first used many of the decorative elements that have become so typical of the country's architecture, including merlons (battlement-like castellations), a ribbed dome, and stylized plant-inspired designs resembling pine cones and palm fronds. The **Almohads** introduced the classic Moroccan square minaret, as seen in the Koutoubia at Marrakesh, the Hassan Tower in Rabat, and the Giralda at Seville in Spain. Architectural styles were refined but not radically altered under the **Merenids** and the **Saadians**, who brought in techniques of zellij tilework and carved stucco and cedarwood.

The next big change came with the **colonial period**, when European styles – and the Europeanized North African style known as **Mauresque** – began to appear in the Villes Nouvelles of larger cities, most notably in Casablanca. **Art Nouveau** made a major impact on the Spanish enclave of Melilla, and **Art Deco** similarly dominates the former Spanish enclave of Sidi Ifni, as well as having had a major impact on downtown Casa.

Concrete-and-glass modern architecture has not made many inroads in Morocco, though you'll see it on the outskirts of Casablanca if you're coming in from the south. Nor has post-World War II European architecture especially impressed Moroccans – one of Le Corbusier's brutalist blocks was demolished in the centre of Meknes in 2004 without much comment. Morocco's most impressive modern building, the Mosquée Hassan II in Casablanca, was built using completely traditional styles and techniques.

Mosques

Mosques follow the same basic plan regardless of their age or size. All mosques face Mecca, the birthplace of Islam and the direction in which all Muslims pray. This direction is indicated by an alcove called the **mihrab**, set in the Mecca-facing *qibla* wall. Next to the mihrab in larger mosques is a pulpit, usually wooden, called the **minbar**. Larger mosques will also have a **courtyard**, often with a fountain for ablutions, but the *qibla* end is taken up by a covered **prayer hall**. The **minaret** is a tower from which, back in the day, the *muezzin* would climb to call the faithful to prayer. Moroccan mosques invariably have only one minaret, and since the days of the Almohads in the twelfth century, almost all Moroccan minarets have been square in shape, with a ratio of 5:1 height to width.

A **zaouia** is a shrine or Sufi retreat built around the tomb of a *marabout*, or Islamic saint. It is typically a small whitewashed building with a small dome or *koubba*, often found among the ordinary tombs in a graveyard. A larger *zaouia* may have a prayer hall attached, and function like a mosque. It will certainly have a mihrab, though not usually a minaret.

Morocco's most important mosque architecture includes the Koutoubia in Marrakesh, the Kairaouine Mosque and the Zaouia of Moulay Idriss in Fez, the Hassan Tower in Rabat, and the Mosquée Hassan II in Casablanca. Non-Muslims, unfortunately, are not allowed inside most mosques.

Medersas

A **medersa** (or madrasa) is a religious school where students come to study Islam, and unlike mosques, medersas are open to non-Muslims. Typically they consist of a large courtyard, with rooms around it for teaching, and rooms upstairs where the students sleep. The medersas of Fez in particular, such as Bou Inania and the Attarin, are richly decorated with carved stucco and cedarwood, and zellij mosaic tilework. Because Islam is suspicious of representational art (lest it lead to idol worship), religious buildings such as medersas are decorated with geometric designs and calligraphy, the latter almost always consisting of quotations from the Koran. Other architecturally interesting medersas include the Abou el Hassan in Salé, and the Ben Youssef in Marrakesh.

Traditional homes

People's **houses** in Morocco do not look outward, like a Western home, but rather inward, to an enclosed patio, an arrangement that guards privacy, particularly for women, who traditionally observed purdah and did not allow men outside the family to see them. Rooms are arranged around the **patio**, usually on two floors with a roof terrace. At one time, most homes would have had a well in the middle of the patio to supply drinking water. A grand house or mansion might have a whole garden in the patio, typically with orange trees, and sometimes a second patio too. The ceilings would be wooden and often beautifully painted.

The very best way to take in Moroccan domestic architecture is to stay in an old riad, particularly in a city such as Marrakesh or Fez. Second best is to visit one of the palatial restaurants in those two cities. In Marrakesh, the Bahia Palace and Dar el Glaoui are also worth a visit.

Kasbahs

A **kasbah** can be a walled residential district (as in Fez), or the citadel of a walled city (as in Tangier and Marrakesh), but in southern Morocco, most impressively in Telouet, Tamdaght and the Skoura Oasis, a kasbah is a fortified citadel, something like a castle, where everyone in a village could take refuge in times of trouble (see box, p.392). Built of mud-bricks, these kasbahs are rectangular structures with turrets at each corner, usually decorated with Berber motifs.

Wildlife and the environment

Few countries in the Mediterranean region can match the variety and quality of the wildlife habitats to be found in Morocco. The three bands of mountains – Rif, Middle Atlas and High Atlas – with the Mediterranean coastal strip to the north, and the desert to the south, provide a wide variety of habitat types, from coastal cliffs, sand dunes and estuarine marshlands to subalpine forests and grasslands, to the semi-arid Sahel and true desert areas of the south. The climate is similarly diverse: warm and humid along the coastal zones, relatively cooler at altitude within the Atlas ranges and distinctly hotter and drier south of the High Atlas. Not surprisingly, the plant and animal life in Morocco is accordingly parochial, species distributions being closely related to the habitat and climate types to which they are adapted.

Birds

In addition to a unique range of **resident bird species**, distributed throughout the country on the basis of vegetation and climatic zonation, the periods of late March/April and September/October provide the additional sight of vast **bird migrations**.

Large numbers of birds which have overwintered south of the Sahara migrate northwards in the spring to breed in Europe, completing their return passage through Morocco in the autumn, and some north European species choose Morocco to avoid the harshness of the northern winter. These movements can form a dramatic spectacle in the skies, dense flocks of birds moving in procession through bottleneck areas such as Tangier and Ceuta where sea crossings are at their shortest.

Among **field guides** to Moroccan birdlife, the definitive tome is Michael Thévenot, Rae Vernon and Patrick Bergier's *The Birds of Morocco* (British Ornithologists' Union, UK), while Patrick and Fédora Bergier's *Prion Birdwatcher's Guide to Morocco* (Prion Press, UK) is an excellent practical guidebook that includes site maps and species lists. Pete Combridge and Alan Snook's similarly titled *A Birdwatching Guide to Morocco* (Arlequin Press, UK) covers seventeen sites, with maps, directions and a species checklist.

Resident species

Coastal and marine species include the familiar moorhen and less familiar crested coot, an incongruous bird which, when breeding, resembles its northern European relation but with an additional pair of bright red knobs on either side of its white facial shield. Other species include the diminutive little ringed plover and rock dove.

South of the High Atlas are **desert species**, such as the sandgrouse (spotted, crowned, pin-tailed and black-bellied varieties), stone curlew, cream-coloured courser and Houbara bustard – the latter standing over two feet in height. Other well-represented groups include wheatears (four varieties), larks (seven varieties) and finches, buntings, warblers, corvids, jays, magpies, choughs and ravens (crow family), tits (primarily blue, great and coal) and owls (barn, eagle, tawny and little).

Raptors (birds of prey) provide an enticing roll call of resident species, including red- and black-shouldered kite, long-legged buzzard, Bonelli's, golden and tawny eagles, Barbary, lanner and peregrine falcons and the more familiar kestrel.

Migrant species

Summer visitors include, among marine and coastal types, Manx shearwater, Eleonora's falcon and the bald ibis – for whom Tamri (see p.464) has one of its few remaining breeding colonies in the world. Mountain species include the small Egyptian vulture and several of the hirundines (swallows and martins) and their close relatives, the swifts, such as little swift, red-rumped swallow and the more familiar house martin. A particularly colourful summer visitor in the Sahel regions is the blue-cheeked bee-eater, a vibrant blend of red, yellow, blue and green, unmistakeable if seen close up.

The list of **winter visitors** is more extensive but composed primarily of marine or coastal species. The most common of the truly marine (*pelagic*) flocks include Cory's shearwater, storm petrel, gannet, razorbill and puffin. These are often found congregated on the sea surface, along with any combination of skuas (great, arctic and pomarine varieties), terns (predominantly sandwich) and gulls (including black-headed, Mediterranean, little, herring and the rarer Audouin's) flying overhead. A variety of coastal and estuarine species also arrive during this period, forming large mixed flocks of grebes (great-crested, little and black-necked), avocet, cattle egret, spoonbill, greater flamingo, and wildfowl such as shelduck, wigeon, teal, pintail, shoveler, tufted duck, pochard and coot. Migrant birds of prey during the winter months include the common buzzard (actually a rarity in Morocco), dashing merlin and both marsh and hen harriers.

Many **passage migrants** pass through Morocco en route to other areas. Well-represented groups include petrels (five varieties) and terns (six varieties) along coastal areas, and herons (four varieties), bitterns, cranes, white and black stork and crake (spotted, little, Baillon's and corncrake) in the marshland/estuarine habitats. Further inland, flocks of multicoloured roller, bee-eater and hoopoe mix with various larks, wagtails and warblers (thirteen varieties), forming large "windfall" flocks when climatic conditions worsen abruptly. Individual species of note include the aptly named black-winged stilt, an elegant black and white wader, with long, vibrant red legs, often found among the disused saltpans; and the nocturnal nightjars (both common and red-necked), which are most easily seen by the reflection of their eyes in the headlamps of passing cars. Birds of prey can also form dense passage flocks, often mixed and including large numbers of black kite, short-toed eagle and honey buzzard. Over open water spaces, the majestic osprey may be seen demonstrating its mastery of the art of fishing.

Finally, Morocco has its share of occasional or **"vagrant" species**, so classified on the unusual or rare nature of their appearances, including such exotic varieties as glossy ibis, pale-chanting goshawk, Arabian bustard and lappet-faced vulture, but they provide few, if any, opportunities for viewing.

Amphibians and reptiles

Morocco's few remaining **amphibians** are restricted to scarce watery havens, and more apparent by sound than sight. One of the more common is the green frog, typically immersed up to its eyes in water, releasing the odd giveaway croak. Toads are represented by the Berber toad, another nocturnal baritone, and the Mauritanian toad whose large size and characteristic yellow-and-brown-spotted coloration make it quite unmistakeable. The painted frog is a common participant in the chorus that emanates from the *oueds* (riverbeds) of the High Atlas, while the wide-ranging whistle of the North African race of the green toad, famed for its ability to change its colour with the surrounding environment, can be heard at altitudes in excess of 2000m.

Reptiles extend from the Mediterranean to the desert. Tortoises are now sadly depleted through "craft items" sold to the tourist trade. The blue and green-eyed lizard and the chameleon frequent the **Middle Atlas**, while the Spanish wall lizard is a common basker on the stony **walls** of towns and villages, as is the Moorish gecko.

Further south, the drier, scrub-covered slopes form an ideal habitat for the horseshoe snake (which can exceed 2m in length) and the Montpelier snake, which feeds on birds and rats, as well as the Atlas agama and fringe-toed lizard.

Desert species include the Algerian sand lizard and the Berber skink, also known as the "sand fish", which inhabits the *ergs* and appears to "swim" through the sand. Morocco's one really poisonous reptile is the horned viper, only half a metre in length, which spends the days buried just below the surface of the sand and feeds by night on jerboas and lizards.

Mammals

Larger animal life in Morocco is dominated by the extensive nomadic herds of goats, sheep and camels which use the most inaccessible and barren patches of wilderness as seasonal grazing areas. One of the most impressive of the wild mammals, however, is the **Barbary ape** – in fact not a true ape but a Macaque monkey. These frequent the cedar forests south of Azrou in the Middle Atlas and can be seen on the ground foraging for food in the glades. Other inhabitants of the cedar forest include **wild boar** and **red fox**. A speciality of the Oued Souss, outside Agadir, is the **common otter**; this is now a rare species in Morocco and can only be seen with considerable patience and some fortune.

The majority of the smaller mammals in Morocco live south of the Atlas ranges in the *hammada*, where the ever-present problem of water conservation plays a major role in the lifestyle of its inhabitants. Larger herbivores include the **Edmi gazelle** and the smaller, and rarer, **Addax antelope,** which graze the thorn bushes and dried grasses to obtain their moisture. Many of the desert varieties reduce the problems of body temperature regulation by adopting a nocturnal lifestyle. Typical exponents of this strategy are the **desert hedgehog** and numerous small rodents such as the **jerboa**. A common predator of the jerboa is the **fennec** (desert fox), whose characteristic large ears are used for both directional hearing (invaluable as a nocturnal hunter) and heat radiation to aid body cooling.

An oddity, found in the Jebel Toubkal area of the High Atlas, is the African **elephant shrew** – a fascinating, mouse-like creature with an elephantine trunk.

Insects and arachnids

Over a hundred species of **butterflies** have been recorded, predominantly in the Middle and High Atlas ranges and are seen from April until September. The Atlas also witnesses one of the world's most extraordinary butterfly migrations in spring, when waves of painted ladies and Bath whites pass through, having crossed the Sahara from West Africa, en route across the Bay of Biscay to the west of England. Other common groups include grasshoppers, crickets and locusts. In the High Atlas, praying mantis may be seen.

There are three main groups of **arachnids** in Morocco – scorpions, camel spiders and spiders. Scorpions are nocturnal, hiding under suitable covered depressions during the day such as rocks and boulders (or rucksacks and shoes). Some Moroccan species are poisonous (see p.58) but most are harmless and unlikely to sting unless provoked. Camel spiders (or wind-scorpions) lack a poisonous tail but possess huge jaws with which they catch their main source of prey – scorpions. In the Atlas it is possible to see several small species of tarantula (not the hairy South American variety) and the white orb-web spider *Argiope lobata*.

Flora

Morocco's flora is remarkably diverse. Plant species have adapted strategies to cope with the Moroccan climate, becoming either specifically adapted to one particular part of the environment (a habitat type), or evolving multiple structural and/or biochemical means of surviving the more demanding seasons. Others have adopted the proverbial "ostrich" philosophy of burying their heads (or rather their seeds in this case) in the sand and waiting for climatic conditions to become favourable – often an extremely patient process. Oleg Polunin and Anthony Huxley's *Flowers of the Mediterranean* (Chatto & Windus, UK; out of print, but easy to find secondhand) is the leading field guide.

The type of flowers that you see will obviously depend entirely on where and when you decide to visit. Some parts of the country have very short flowering seasons because of high temperatures or lack of available water, but generally the best times of year for flowering plants are either just before or just after the main temperature extremes of the North African summer.

The very best time to visit is **spring** (late March to mid-May), when most flowers are in bloom. Typical spring flowers include purple barbary nut iris, deep blue germander and the aromatic claret thyme, all of which frequent the slopes of the Atlas ranges. Among the woodland flora at this time of year are the red pheasant's eye, pink viburnum, violet calamint and purple campanula, which form a resplendent carpet beneath the cedar forests. By late spring, huge tracts of the High Atlas slopes are aglow with the golden hues of broom and, secluded among the lowland cereal crops, splashes of magenta reveal the presence of wild gladioli.

By **midsummer** the climate is at its most extreme and the main concern of plants is to avoid desiccation in the hot, arid conditions. Two areas of exception to these conditions are the **Atlantic coastal zones**, where sea mists produce a slightly more humid environment, and the upper reaches of the **Atlas ranges**, which remain cool and moist at altitude throughout the year. Spring comes later in these loftier places and one can find many of the more familiar garden rock plants, such as the saxifrages and anemones, in flower well into late July and August. Once the hottest part of the summer is past (September onwards), a second, autumn bloom begins with later varieties such as cyclamens and autumn crocus.

The plants you will see in Morocco also vary enormously with the type of habitat, which ranges from Mediterranean lowlands through to mountains and desert.

Seashores

Seashores have a variety of sand-tolerant species, with their adaptations for coping with water loss, such as sea holly and sea stocks. The dune areas contrast starkly with the Salicornia-dominated salt marshes – monotonous landscapes broken only by the occasional dead tamarisk tree.

Farmland

Arable land is often dominated by cereal crops – particularly in the more humid Atlantic and Mediterranean coastal belts – or olive and eucalyptus groves, which extend over large areas. On the coast around Essaouira and Agadir the indigenous argan tree (see box, p.474) is common. The general lack of use of herbicides allows the coexistence of many "wild flowers", especially in the fallow hay meadows which are ablaze with the colours of wild poppy, ox-eye daisy, muscali (borage) and various yellow composites.

Lowland hills

Lowland hills form a fascinating mosaic of dense, shrubby species, known as *maquis*, lower-lying, more grazed areas, known as *garrigue*, and more open areas with abundant aromatic herbs and shrubs. *Maquis* vegetation is dominated by cistaceae (rockroses) and the endemic argan tree. The lower-lying *garrigue* is more typically composed of aromatic herbs such as rosemary, thyme and golden milfoil. Among these shrubs, within the more open areas, you may find an abundance of other species such as anemones, grape hyacinths and orchids. The orchids are particularly outstanding, including several of the *Ophrys* group, which use the strategy of insect imitation to entice pollinators and as such have an intricate arrangement of flowers.

Mountains

Flowering later in the year, the slopes of the **Atlas ranges** are dominated by the blue-mauve pitch trefoil and golden drifts of broom. As you travel south through the **Middle Atlas**, the verdant ash, oak, Atlantic cedar and juniper forest dominates the landscape. Watered by the depressions that sweep across from the Atlantic, these slopes form a luxurious spectacle, ablaze with colour in spring. Among the glades beneath the giant cedars of the Middle Atlas, a unique flora may be found, dominated by the vibrant pink peony. Other plants which form this spectacular carpet include geranium, anchusa, pink virburnum, saffron mulleins, mauve cupidanes, violet calamint, purple campanula, the diminutive scarlet dianthus and a wealth of golden composites and orchids.

Further south, in the **High Atlas**, the Toubkal National Park boasts its own varieties and spring bloom; the thyme and thorny caper are interspersed with the blue-mauve

KEY WILDLIFE SITES

Features on key Moroccan wildlife, and especially bird habitats are to be found throughout the guide. They include:

Agadir/Oued Souss Riverbank that attracts waders and wildfowl, migrant warblers and Barbary partridge. See box, p.461.

Aguelmane Azigza Middle Atlas occasional inland lake and forest: hawfinch, diving duck and marbled teal in autumn/winter. See p.228.

Boumalne: Desert Hammada Atlas agama and fringe-toed lizard; specialist bird species such as cream-coloured courser, red-rumped wheatear and thick-billed lark; houbara bustard. See box, p.418.

Cedar forests south of Azrou Species include green-eyed lizard and chameleon; butterflies from April onwards; Barbary apes; Moroccan woodpecker and booted eagle. See p.227

Dayet Aaoua Another Middle Atlas occasional lake: flocks of grebes, crested coot, grey heron and cattle egret; migrant birds of prey include red kite. See p.221

Essaouira Coastal dunes, river and offshore islands attract waders and egrets; also Eleanora's falcon between May and October. See p.298

Fez Evening roost of egret and alpine swift; white stork on rooftop nests of walls. See p.162

Jebel Tazzeka National Park Where the Rif merges with the Middle Atlas: slopes covered in cork oak and woodland; butterflies from late May/early June, and birds such as the hoopoe. See p.153

Jebel Toubkal National Park High Atlas mountains: sights include Moorish gecko, rare butterflies; Moussier's redstart and crimson-winged finch, both unique to North African mountains; hooped-petticoat daffodils, *romulea* and various other bulbs in spring. See p.364

Merja Zerga Large wetland area that guarantees good bird numbers at all times of year, especially gulls and terns (including the Caspian tern). See box, p.441

Merzouga Sandy (or "true") desert: all-too-brief spring bloom of pink asphodels and mauve statice; Algerian sand lizard and Berber skink; birds include fulvous babbler, blue-cheeked bee-eater, the rare desert sparrow and even Arabian bustard. See box, p.143

Nador/Kariet Arkmane/Ras el Ma Salt marshes and coastal sand dunes, good for waders and gulls. See box, p.294

Oualidia Mix of ragged, rocky coast, sands, lagoon, marshes and saltpans. Good for small waders. See box, p.463

Oued Massa Important inland lagoon and reserve that is perhaps the country's number one bird habitat. See box, p.143

Oued Moulouya Lagoons and sand spits, with outstanding birds. See p.426

Todra Gorge Marsh frog and green toad; ground squirrel; common bulbul, black wheatear, blue rock thrush and rock dove. Bonelli's eagles nest in the gorge. See p.426

pit trefoil, pink convulvulus, the silver-blue and pinks of everlasting flowers of cupidane and phagnalon and golden spreads of broom. At the highest altitudes, the limestone Atlas slopes form a bleak environment, either covered by winter snows or scorched by the summer sun. However, some species are capable of surviving even under these conditions, the most conspicuous of these being the widespread purple tussocks of the hedgehog broom.

Steppe
In the **steppeland** south of the Atlas, temperatures rise sharply and the effect on flora is dramatic; the extensive cedar forests and their multicoloured carpets are replaced by sparse grass plains where the horizon is broken only by the occasional stunted holm oak, juniper or acacia. Commonly known as wattle trees, the acacia were introduced into North Africa from Australia and their large yellow flowers add a welcome splash of colour to this barren landscape. One of the few crop plants grown in this area is the date palm, which is particularly resistant to drought. The steppeland is characterized by the presence of esparto (halfa) grass, which exudes toxins to prevent the growth of competing species. These halfa grass plains are only broken by the flowering of broom in May. Within rocky outcrops, this spring bloom can become a mini-explosion of colour, blending the hues of cistus and chrysanthemum with the pink of rockrose, yellow of milfoil and mauve of rosemary.

Desert
Even **desert areas** provide short-lived blooms of colour during the infrequent spring showers; dwarf varieties such as pink asphodels, yellow daisies and mauve statice thrive briefly while conditions are favourable. Under the flat stones of the *hammada* (stony desert), colonies of lichens and microscopic algae eke out an existence; their shade tolerance and ability to obtain sufficient water from the occasional condensation which takes place under these stones allows them to survive in this harshest of environments. No matter how inhospitable the environment or extreme the climate, somewhere, somehow, there are plants surviving – if you take time to look for them.

Moroccan music

Traditional music, both folk and classical, remains very much a part of life in Morocco, evident at every celebration. Every popular or religious festival involves musicians, and the larger moussems (see p.45) are always good. Keep an eye out for cultural festivals, too, in particular the summer Asilah Festival (p.91), the Essaouira Gnaoua Festival (p.307), the Marrakesh Festival of Popular Arts (box, p354), and the Festival of World Sacred Music in Fez (p.196).

Berber music

Berber music predates the arrival of the Arabs in Morocco, and comes in three main categories: village music, ritual music and the music of professional musicians.

Village music is performed when men and women of a village assemble on festive occasions to dance and sing together. The best-known dances are the **ahouache**, in the western High Atlas, and the **ahidus**, performed by Chleuh Berbers in the eastern High Atlas. In each, drums (*bendirs*) and flute (*nai*) are the only instruments used. The dance begins with a chanted prayer, to which the dancers respond in chorus, the men and women gathered in a large ring in the open air, round the musicians. The *ahouache* is normally performed at night in the patio of the kasbah; the dance is so complicated that the musicians meet to prepare for it in a group called a *laamt* set up specially for the purpose. In the **bumzdi**, a variation on the *ahouache*, one or more soloists perform a series of poetic improvisations. Some of these soloists, such as **Raïs Ajmaa Lahcen** and **Raïs Ihya**, have a national reputation.

Ritual music is rarely absent from celebrations such as moussems or marriages. It may also be called upon to help deal with *jinn*, or evil spirits, or to encourage rainfall. Flutes and drums are usually the sole instruments, along with much rhythmic hand-clapping, although people may engage professional musicians for certain events.

The **professional musicians**, or *imdyazn*, of the Atlas mountains are itinerant, travelling during the summer, usually in groups of four. The leader of the group is called the *amydaz* or poet. He presents his poems, which are usually improvised and give news of national or world affairs, in the village square. The poet may be accompanied by one or two members of the group on drums and *rabab*, a single-string fiddle, and by a fourth player, known as the *bou oughanim*. This latter is the reed player, throwing out melodies on a double clarinet, and also acting as the group's clown. *Imdyazn* are found in many weekly souks in the Atlas.

Rwais

Groups of **Chleuh Berber** musicians, from the Souss Valley, are known as **rwais**. A *rwai* worthy of the name will not only know all the music for any particular celebration, but have its own repertoire of songs – commenting on current events – and be able to improvise. A *rwai* ensemble can be made up of a single-string *rabab*, one or two *lotars* (lutes) and sometimes *nakous* (cymbals), together with a number of singers. The leader of the group, the **raïs**, is in charge of the poetry, music and choreography of the performance. Fine clothes, jewels and elaborate gestures also have an important part to play in this ancient rural form of musical theatre.

A **rwai performance** will start with the *astara*, an instrumental prelude, played on *rabab*, giving the basic notes of the melodies that follow (this also makes it possible for the other instruments to tune to the *rabab*). Then comes the *amarg*, the sung poetry which forms the heart of the piece. This is followed by the *ammussu*, which is a sort of choreographed overture; the *tamssust*, a lively song; the *aberdag*, or dance; and finally the *tabbayt*, a finale characterized by an acceleration in rhythm and an abrupt end. Apart from the *astara* and *tabbayt*, the elements of a performance may appear in a different order.

Andalous music

Morocco's classical music evolved in Muslim Spain (Andalusia) though its invention is usually credited to an outstanding musician from Baghdad called **Zyriab**. One of his greatest innovations was the founding of the classical suite called **nuba**, which forms what is now known as **Andalous music**, or **al-âla**. There are, in addition, two other classical traditions, **milhûn** and **gharnati**, each with a distinctive style and form. Andalous music is very popular and greatly loved; during Ramadan, nightly programmes of Andalous classics are broadcast on TV, and people without their own sets gather in cafés to watch them.

The nuba

Originally there were twenty-four **nuba** linked with the hours in the day, but only four full and seven fragmentary *nuba* have been preserved in the Moroccan tradition. Complete *nuba* last between six and seven hours and so are rarely performed in one sitting. Each *nuba* is divided into five main parts, or *mizan*, of differing durations. These five parts correspond to the five different rhythms used within a suite. If a whole *nuba* were being performed then these five rhythms would be used in order: the *basît* rhythm (6/4); *qaum wa nusf* rhythm (8/4); *darj* rhythm (4/4); *btâyhi* rhythm (8/4); and *quddâm* rhythm (3/4 or 6/8).

Traditionally each *mizan* begins with instrumental preludes – *bughya*, *m'shaliya* and *tuashia* – followed by a number of songs, the *sana'a*. There can be as many as twenty *sana'a* within a given *mizan*, although for shorter performances an orchestra may only play three or four before going on to the next rhythm.

The words to many *sana'a* deal, though often obliquely, with subjects generally considered taboo in Islamic society like alcohol and sex – perhaps signifying archaic, pre-Islamic and nomadic roots – although others are religious, glorifying the Prophet and divine laws.

When the Arabs were driven out of Spain, the different Andalusian musical schools were dispersed across Morocco. The school of Valencia was re-established in Fez, that of Granada in Toua and Chefchaouen. Today, the most famous **orchestras** are those of **Fez** (led by **Mohammed Briouel**), **Rabat** (led by **Haj Mohamed Toud**) and **Tetouan**. Many fans of Andalous music mourn the passing of the "golden age" in the 1970s and 1980s, when a trio of much lamented masters – **Abdelkrim Rais**, **Abdesadak Chekara** and **Moulay Ahmed Loukili** – led the Fez, Tetouan and Rabat orchestras.

A typical Andalous orchestra uses the following instruments: *rabab* (fiddle), *oud* (lute), *kamenjah* (violin-style instrument played vertically on the knee), *kanun* (zither), *darabouka* (metal or pottery goblet drums), and *taarija* (tambourine). Each orchestra has featured unusual instruments from time to time. Clarinets, flutes, banjos and pianos have all been used with varying degrees of success.

Milhûn

Milhûn is a semi-classical form of sung poetry. Musically it has many links with Andalous music, having adopted the same modes as *al-âla* orchestras, and, like them, it uses string instruments and percussion, though the result can be quite wild and danceable. Unlike Andalous music, which has always been the province of an educated elite, *milhûn* was originally the poetic expression of artisans and traders. Indeed, many of the great *milhûn* singers of the twentieth century began their lives as cobblers, tanners, bakers or doughnut sellers. The greatest *milhûn* composer was **Al-Thami Lamdaghri**, who died in 1856.

The *milhûn* suite comprises two parts: the *taqsim* (overture) and the *qassida* (sung poems). The *taqsim* is played on the *oud* or violin in free rhythm, and introduces the mode in which the piece is set. The *qassida* is divided into three parts: *al-aqsâm*, verses sung solo; *al-harba*, refrains sung by the chorus; and *al-drîdka*, a chorus where the rhythm gathers speed and eventually announces the end of the piece. The words of the *qassida* can be taken from anywhere – folk poetry, mystical poems or nonsense lines used for rhythm.

A **milhûn orchestra** generally consists of *oud, kamenjah, swisen* (a small, high-pitched folk lute related to the *gimbri*), the *hadjouj* (a bass version of the *swisen*), *taarija, darabouka* and *handqa* (small brass cymbals), plus a number of **singers**. The most renowned *milhûn* singer of recent times was **Hadj Lhocine Toulali**, who dominated the vibrant *milhûn* scene in Meknes for many decades before his death in 1999. Contemporary singers of note include **Abdelkrim and Saïd Guennoun** of Fez, **Haj Husseïn** and **Abdallah Ramdani** of Meknes, **Muhammad Berrahal** and **Muhammad Bensaïd** of Salé, and the brothers **Mohammed and Ahmed Amenzou** from Marrakesh. In the past ten or so years, some female singers have become stars, including Touria Hadraoui (who is also a novelist) and Sanaa Marahati, whom many consider the future of *milhûn*.

Gharnati

Gharnati, the third music of Arab–Andalusian tradition, derives from the Arabic name of the Andaluisan city of Granada. It is mainly played in Algeria, but Rabat and Oujda are centres for it in Morocco. As with *al-âla*, it is arranged in suites or *nuba*, of which there are twelve complete and four unfinished suites. The *gharnati* orchestra consists of plucked and bowed instruments together with percussion: the usual *ouds* and *kamenjahs* supplemented by the addition of banjo, mandolin and Algerian lute or *kwîtra*.

Sufi music

Among the **Sufi brotherhoods**, music is seen as a means of getting closer to Allah by reaching a trance-like state of mystical ecstasy. In a private nocturnal ceremony called the *hadra*, Sufis may attain this by chanting the name of Allah or dancing in a ring holding hands. The songs and music are irregular in rhythm, and quicken to an abrupt end. Some brotherhoods play for alms in households that want to gain the favour of their patron saint.

The best known Moroccan brotherhood is the **Gnaoua** – whose members are descendants of slaves from across the Sahara. They claim spiritual descent from **Sidi Bilal**, an Ethiopian who was the Prophet's first *muezzin*. Gnaoua ceremonies are often held to placate spirits, good and evil, who are inhabiting a person or place. They are often called in cases of mental disturbance or to help treat someone stung by a scorpion. These rites have their origins in sub-Saharan Africa, and African influence is evident in the music. The main instrument, the *ginbri* or *sentir*, is a long-necked lute almost identical to instruments from West Africa. The other characteristic sound of Gnaoua music is the *garagab*, a pair of metal castanets. Each Gnaoua troupe is lead by a *ma'alem*, or "master", who plays the *ginbri* and sings the lead vocal parts. The ceremonial part of the proceedings is usually led by a female *mogadema*, or "medium", who is mistress of the arcane spiritual knowledge and huge gallery of saints and spirits, both good and evil, that underpin and influence Gnaoui ritual. In recent decades Gnaoua music has been blended with jazz, rock, funk, hip-hop and even drum 'n' bass. Essaouira holds an annual festival dedicated to Gnaoua music (see p.307).

Jilala are another brotherhood – the devotees of **Moulay Abdelkader Jilal**. Their music is perhaps even more hypnotic and mysterious than that of the Gnaoua and sometimes seems to come from a different plane of existence. The plaintive cycling flute (*qsbah*) and mesmeric beats of the *bendir* (frame drums) carry you forward unconsciously. While in a trance, Jilala devotees can withstand the touch of burning coals or the deep slashes of a Moroccan dagger, afterwards showing no injury or pain.

Other Sufi brotherhoods still practising their own brand of psychic-musical healing in various parts of Morocco include the **Hamadja**, followers of Sidi Ben Ali Hamduj and Sidi Ahmed Dghughi, two saints who lived at the end of the eighteenth century, and the **Aissaoua** from Meknes, who venerate the sixteenth-century holy man Sidi Mohamed Ben Aïssa. The boundaries between these different brotherhoods are often quite blurred, and they tend to hold a common veneration for many saints and spirits, prominent among whom is the fiendish female *jinn* Aisha Kandisha.

FOLK INSTRUMENTS

The most common **stringed instrument** is the **ginbri**, an African lute whose soundbox is covered in front by a piece of hide. The rounded, fretless stem has two or three strings. The body of the smaller treble *ginbri* is pear-shaped, that of the bass *ginbri* (*hadjuj* or *sentir*) rectangular. The Gnaoui often put a resonator at the end of the stem to produce the buzz typical of Black African music. The **lotar** is another type of lute, used by Chleuh Berbers. It has a circular body, also closed with a piece of skin, and three or four strings which are plucked with a plectrum. The classic Arab lute, the **oud**, is used in classical orchestras and the traditional Arab orchestras known as *takhts*. Its pear-shaped body is covered by a piece of wood with two or three rosette-shaped openings. It has a short, fretless stem and six strings, five double and one single. The most popular stringed instruments played with a bow are the **kamanjeh** and the **rabab**. The former is an Iranian violin which was adopted by the Arabs. Its present Moroccan character owes a lot to the Western violin, though it is held vertically, supported on the knees. The *rabab* is a spike fiddle, rather like a viol. The bottom half of its long, curved body is covered in hide, the top in wood with a rosette-shaped opening. It has two strings. The Chleuh Berbers use an archaic single-stringed *rabab* with a square stem and soundbox covered entirely in skin. Lastly, there is the **kanum**, a trapezoidal Arab zither with over seventy strings, grouped in threes and plucked with plectra attached to the fingernails. It is used almost exclusively in classical music.

Rapid hand clapping and the clashes of bells and cymbals are only part of the vast repertoire of Moroccan **percussion**. Like most Moroccan drums the **darbuka** is made of clay, shaped into a cylinder swelling out slightly at the top. The single skin is beaten with both hands. It is used in both folk and classical music. The **taarija**, a smaller version of the *darbuka*, is held in one hand and beaten with the other. Then there are treble and bass **tan-tan** bongos, and the Moorish **guedra**, a large drum that rests on the ground. There is also a round wooden drum with skins on both sides called a **tabl**, which is beaten with a stick on one side and by hand on the other. This is used only in folk music. As for **tambourines**, the ever-popular **bendir** is round and wooden, 40 or 50cm across, with two strings stretched under its single skin to produce a buzzing sound. The **tar** is smaller, with two rings of metal discs round the frame and no strings under its skin. The **duff** is a double-sided tambourine, often square in shape, which has to be supported so that it can be beaten with both hands. Only two percussion instruments are made of metal: **karkabat**, also known as *krakesh* or *karakab*, double castanets used by the Gnaoui, and the **nakous**, a small cymbal played with two rods.

The **Arab flute**, known by different tribes as the *nai*, *talawat*, *nira* or *gasba*, is made of a straight piece of cane open at both ends, with no mouthpiece and between five and seven holes, one at the back. It requires a great deal of skill to play it properly, by blowing at a slight angle. The **ghaita** or *rhaita*, a type of oboe popular under various names throughout the Muslim world, is a conical pipe made of hardwood, ending in a bell often made of metal. Its double-reeded mouthpiece is encircled by a broad ring on which the player rests his lips in order to produce the circular breathing needed to obtain a continuous note. It has between seven and nine holes, one at the back. The **aghanin** is a double clarinet, identical to the Arab *arghoul*. It consists of two parallel pipes of wood or cane, each with a single-reed mouthpiece, five holes and a horn at the end for amplification.

Chaabi – Morocco's pop music

Chaabi simply means "popular" music – which covers a huge mix of styles, just as it does in the West. More or less since the advent of radio, the whole Arab world has listened to **Egyptian popular songs**. The tradition is epitomized by Umm Kulthum (Oum Khalsoum) and Mohammed Abdalwahab, but Morocco has added names of its own to the tradition, in particular **Houcine Slaoui** (in the 1940s), and in the following decades, **Ahmed Bidaoui**, **Abdelhadi Belkhayat** and **Abdelwahab Doukkali**. These stars tended to record in Cairo or Beirut, and their music – and language – is essentially Egyptian.

Al'aïta

The oldest of Morocco's own *chaabi* styles is **al'aïta**, the music of the Arabic-speaking rural populations of Morocco's Atlantic coast. It is performed at private and public celebrations, as well as in concert, and is usually sung in Darija (Moroccan colloquial Arabic). Its songs tell of love, loss, lust and the realities of daily life. They begin with a *lafrash*, a slow instrumental prelude (usually played on the violin), then move into free rhythm verses before shifting gear for the finale or *leseb*, which is often twice the speed of the song and forms a background for syncopated clapping, shouting and dancing. An *al'aïta* ensemble usually consists of a male or female vocalist, a violinist, and several percussionists and backing singers, though some groups add a *lotar*. Stars over the years have included the singers **Bouchaïb el Bidaoui** and **Fatna bent Lhoucine**, and the (literally) six-fingered violinist, **Abdelaziz Staati**. In the 1990s, an electric style of *al'aïta* developed, adding keyboards, electric guitars and drum machines. This is still very popular and is the music you most often hear blasting out of stalls in Casablanca or Rabat. Top artists include **Orchestre Jedouane**, **Orchestre Senhaji**, **Khalid Bennani** and **Moustapha Bourgogne**.

Chaabi groups

During the 1970s, a more sophisticated Moroccan *chaabi* began to emerge, using *hadjuj* (bass *ginbri*), lute and *bendir* percussion, along with bouzoukis and electric guitars, to combine Berber music with elements of Arab *milhûn*, Sufi and Gnaoua ritual music, Western rock, reggae and, more recently, rap. The songs were often political, carrying messages that got their authors into trouble with the authorities – even jailed. The leading lights in this movement were **Nass el Ghiwane**, **Jil Jilala** and **Lemchaheb**. The music was hugely influential in the development of **raï music** in neighbouring Algeria, where *raï* singers like Khaled, Cheb Mami, Chaba Fadela and Chaba Sahraoui emerged in the 1980s.

In the 1980s, another wave of *chaabi* groups emerged, based in Marrakesh and employing Gnaoua rhythms. One of the most successful of these has been **Muluk el Hwa** (Demon of Love), a group of Berbers who used to play in Marrakesh's Jemaa el Fna. By far the most popular of the Berber *chaabi* singers, however, is singer **Najat Aatabou**, whose sensational debut, *J'en ai marre* ("I am sick of it"), sold 450,000 copies – many of them in France.

Moroccan raï

Raï – meaning "opinion", "outlook" or "point of view" – originated in the western Algerian region around the port of Oran. It has traditional roots in Bedouin music, with its distinctive refrain (*ha-ya-rai*), but as a modern phenomenon has more in common with Western music. The backing is now solidly electric, with rhythm guitars, synthesizers and usually a rock drum kit as well as traditional drums. Its lyrics reflect highly contemporary concerns – cars, sex, sometimes alcohol – which have created some friction with the authorities.

Moroccans have taken easily to the music, especially in the northeastern part of the country around the towns of Oujda and Al Hoceima, an area that shares the same

SEPHARDIC MUSIC

Moroccan Jews, many of whom have now emigrated to Israel, left an important legacy in the north of the country, where their songs and ballads continued to be sung in Ladino, the medieval Spanish spoken at the time of their expulsion from Spain five centuries ago. Apart from the narrative ballads, these were mainly songs of courtly love, as well as lullabies and biblical songs, usually accompanied on a tar. Rounder Records released *Sacred Music of the Moroccan Jews*, a two-CD set of Paul Bowles' 1959 recordings of Moroccan Jewish liturgy, which transport you into the heart of what was once a vibrant subculture but is now, sadly, almost extinct in Morocco.

Moroccan Jewry also produced a great classical Arabic singer, **Samy el Maghribi**, who was born in Safi in 1922. Inspired by the Algerian singer Say el Hilali, he was one of the most appreciated Arabic singers of the 1950s. In 1960 he moved to Canada and in later years devoted himself to a liturgical repertoire. Moroccan Sephardic traditions and music continue to thrive in Israel, the best-known names including Albert Bouhadanna and Rabat-born Emil Zrihan, whose music mixes Arab and Andalusian influences with the Hebrew liturgy.

cultural roots as the province of Oran over the border in Algeria, where *raï* was born. Home-grown *raï* stars include **Cheb Khader, Cheb Mimoun** and the superb **Cheb Jellal**, a pop-*raï* legend from Oujda whose recordings are well worth seeking out. *Raï* influence can also be heard in the sound of folk artists like **Rachid Briha** and **Hamid M'Rabati**, from the Oujda region.

Fusion and Moroccan hip-hop

Morocco was the starting point for all kinds of fusion experiments, with such disparate figures as Brian Jones, Ornette Coleman, Jimi Hendrix, Robin Williamson, John Renbourn and Pharaoh Sanders attracted by its rhythms. One of the earliest attempts to combine Moroccan music with European electronic sounds was made by the German group **Dissidenten** in the 1980s, and since then all manner of Moroccan sounds have been successfully blended with reggae, funk, hip-hop, house and drum 'n' bass.

Hip-hop in particular has become immensely popular in Morocco, as throughout Africa, and accounts for some of the most dynamic Moroccan music of the twenty-first century so far, having taken over from rai in the 1990s as Morocco's popular musical genre. Breaking out of a largely localized underground scene, bands like **Fnaïre** from Marrakesh, **H-Kayne** from Meknes and **Fez City Clan** from Fez have galvanized the Moroccan pop scene, singing about social and political issues with a hard-edged lyric that is actually more daring than foreigners might realize: musicians are not as free in Morocco as they are in the West, a fact brought home in 2003, when the authorities imprisoned members of the heavy metal bands **Nekros**, **Infected Brain** and **Reborn**, along with five of their fans, on charges of moral depravity and playing "anti-Islamic" music.

Rock nonetheless continues to exercise a strong influence on the Moroccan pop scene. Casa band **Hoba Hoba Spirit**, who owe more to punk than to heavy metal, despite their track "El Caïd Mötorhead", put themselves in the forefront of the pro-democracy movement, with their 2011 single "La Volonté de Vivre", and reacted to the 2003 Casablanca bomb attacks with "Ma Tkich Bladi" ("Don't touch my country"), a play on the French anti-racist slogan "touche pas mon pot".

Discography

Most music shops in Britain and the US with a decent world music section should yield at least a few discs of ethnic, folk and Andalous music, or fusion with European groups. In Morocco itself, cassettes are still dominant.

COMPILATIONS

Various *Morocco: Crossroads of Time* (Ellipsis Arts, US). An excellent introduction to Moroccan music that comes with a well-designed and informative book. The disc includes everything from ambient sounds in the Fez Medina, to powerful Jilala and Gnaoua music, Andalous, *rwai*, Berber, and some good contemporary pop from Nouamane Lahlou.

★ **Various** *The Rough Guide to the Music of Morocco* (World Music Network, UK). This Rough Guide's release focuses on contemporary Moroccan sounds, featuring selections from the Amenzou Ensemble, Nass el Ghiwane, Nass Marrakech, Jil Jilala, Mustapha Bourgogne, Bnet Marrakech and U-cef. It is backed up by fulsome liner notes.

Various *Anthologie de la Musique Marocaine* (Ministère de la Culture, Morocco). These four boxed sets (with a total of 31 CDs) cover most bases in Moroccan folk and traditional music. All include liner notes in French and Arabic and can be purchased at the Ministry of Culture in Rabat.

BERBER MUSIC

Compagnies musicales du Tafilalet *The Call of the Oasis* (Institut du Monde Arabe, France). Sublime recordings from the edge of the Sahara, showcasing four groups recorded live at a festival in Erfoud.

Hmaoui Abd El-Hamid *La Flûte de l'Atlas* (Arion, France). Hypnotic and haunting flute-like *ney*, backed by percussion, oud and zither.

Les Imazighen *Chants du Moyen-Atlas* (Institut du Monde Arabe, France). A fantastic live recording of musicians from the Middle Atlas, full of power and extravagant emotion.

CLASSICAL/ANDALOUS

Ensemble Amenzou *Le Malhûn à Marrakech* (Institut du Monde Arabe, France). The Amenzou brothers belong to a revered dynasty of *milhûn* singers and their energetic, youthful approach to the genre is much admired.

El Hadj Houcine Toulali *Le Milhûn de Meknes* (Institut du Monde Arabe, France). A fine live recording of the great *milhûn* master on top form.

Ustad Massano Tazi *Musique Classique Andalouse de Fès* (Ocora, France). Again, beautifully recorded and presented. Includes Nuba Hijaz Al-Kabir and Nuba Istihilal.

Various *Maroc: Anthologie d'Al-Melhûn* (Maison des Cultures du Monde, France). A three-CD set containing performances from many of Morocco's finest *milhûn* singers. An excellent introduction.

SUFI MUSIC

Les Aissawa de Fès *Trance Ritual* (L'Institut du Monde Arabe, France). Entrancing and intricate music from the Aissawa brotherhood of Fez.

Ihsan Rmiki *Al-Samâa: Ecstatic Spiritual Audition* (Institut du Monde Arabe, France). Rmiki is the new voice of Andalous music – and this is a moving set, her voice leading a six-person ensemble.

The Master Musicians of Jajouka *Apocalypse Across the Sky* (Axiom, UK). The power and clarity of these remarkable performers stands out on this Bill Laswell production.

★ **Various** *Gnawa Night – Music of the Marrakesh Spirit Masters* (Axiom, UK). Gnaoua music at its evocative best, again recorded by Bill Laswell.

JEWISH MOROCCAN MUSIC

Samy ElMaghribi *Samy el Maghribi* (Club du Disque Arabe, France) A collection of old recordings by this legendary Jewish musician whose pride of place in the annals of Moroccan music proves what a big influence Jews once had on urban music.

CHAABI

Najat Aatabou *The Voice of the Atlas* (GlobeStyle, UK). A superb collection of some of Najat's best-loved songs, including "Shouffi Rhirou" which has been covered brilliantly by the 3Mustaphas3.

Jil Jilala *Chama'a* (Blue Silver, France). A classic early recording of the seminal *chaabi* rockers. The title track "Chama'a" ("Candle") is an old *milhûn* song which is given a very moody and edgy modern makeover.

Nass el Ghiwane *Maroc: Chants d'Espoir* (Créon Music, France). Many recordings by the "Rolling Stones of North Africa" are marred by atrocious sound quality, however, this set captures them razor-sharp and passionate.

FUSION

★ **Aisha Kandisha's Jarring Effects** *El Buya* (Barbarity, Switzerland). An intoxicating mix of Moroccan melodies and traditional string instruments with scratching reverb and rushes of industrial noise.

Hoba Hoba Spirit *Blad Skizo* (Platinum Music, UK). Hoba Hoba's second album, released in 2005, contains some of their strongest Morocc'n-roll tunes, most notably the title track ("Schizophrenic Country") and the more Gnaoua-flavoured "Ma Ajebtinich".

MoMo *The Birth Of Dar* (Apartment 22, UK).

House-flavoured Moroccan madness with a heavy dance beat. *Dar* means "house" in Arabic. . . you get the picture.

U-cef *Halalium* (Apartment 22, UK). A Moroccan producer based in London who fuses the roughneck sounds of the English capital with traditional *chaabi* and Gnaoua, often to wondrous effect.

MOROCCAN HIP-HOP

Fnaire *Yed el Henna*. Fnaire's amazing mix of hip-hop with a wide assortment of traditional Moroccan music makes a richly sweet combination. Tunes like the title track and the percussive "Lalla Mennana" are a truly masterful combination of rap and trad.

Fez City Clan *Fès*. Slicker, more tuneful and more electronic than Morocco's other hip-hop bands, the Clan have taken their very underground Fassi sound nationwide and beyond. This is their first album, and like all really worthwhile pleasures, it leaves you craving for more.

H-Kayne *HK 1426*. The Meknes rappers' sound is deeper, darker and purer than most Moroccan hip-hop. This album, named after the Islamic year in which it was recorded (2005), contains their biggest hit, "Issawa Style".

Books

There is a wealth of books about Morocco, set in Morocco, or by Moroccans, and you won't regret having one or two along on a trip. The main internet book shops are likely to yield the highest returns on the more esoteric recommendations below. Otherwise, you might want to try the UK-based Maghreb Bookshop, 45 Burton St, London WC1 (☎020 7388 1840, ⓦmaghrebbookshop.com), which supplies current, out-of-print and rare books on all aspects of North Africa, and will ship worldwide.

GENERAL AND TRAVEL

Paul Bowles *Points in Time, Their Heads Are Green.* Novelist, poet and composer Paul Bowles (1910–99) lived in Tangier for half a century and, more or less single-handedly, brought translations of local writers to Western attention (see p.570). These two books of his own are superb. *Points* is a series of tales and short pieces inspired by episodes and sources from earliest times to the present day. *Heads* includes a couple of travel essays on Morocco and a terrific piece on the psychology of desert travel.

★ **Hamish Brown** *The Mountains Look On Marrakech: A Trek Along the Atlas Mountains.* Hamish Brown has been to Morocco every year since 1965 to visit his beloved Atlas mountains, and his love for the country, its people, its landscapes and its wildlife shines through in this inspirational account of a 900-mile trek right across the High Atlas range.

Hamish Brown *The High Atlas: Treks and Climbs on Morocco's Biggest and Best Mountains.* The best and most important trekking guide to the High Atlas mountains, where to go and how to get there. This is as much about the people as the landscapes, and is as insightful as it's practical.

Elias Canetti *The Voices of Marrakesh.* A small, compelling volume of impressions of Marrakesh in the last years of French rule, by the Nobel Prize-winning author. The atmosphere of many pieces still holds.

★ **Walter Harris** *Morocco That Was.* Harris, *Times* correspondent in Tangier from the 1890s until his death in 1933, saw the country at probably the strangest ever stage in its history – the last years of "Old Morocco" in its feudal isolation and the first of French occupation. *Morocco That Was*, first published in 1921, is a masterpiece – alternately sharp, melodramatic and very funny. It incorporates, to some extent, the anecdotes in his earlier *Land of an African Sultan* (1889) and *Tafilet* (1895, o/p).

Orin Hargraves *Culture Shock! Morocco.* Hargraves worked in Morocco in the 1980s as a Peace Corps volunteer and this valuable paperback, revised in 2007, is a

distillation of his experience, supported by an impressive range of research and, clearly, a lot of conversations throughout the country. He offers perceptive accounts of almost every aspect of contemporary Moroccan life, along with a good overview of history and religion, and an instructive section of dos and don'ts.

John Hopkins *Tangier Journals 1962–79.* Highly entertaining journals of Tangier life – and travels across Morocco – from an American novelist, resident in Tangier during the Beat years. Paul and Jane Bowles and William Burroughs all figure large in the diary entries.

Peter Mayne *A Year in Marrakesh.* Mayne went to Marrakesh in the early 1950s, found a house in an ordinary district of the Medina, and tried to live like a Moroccan. He couldn't, but wrote an unusually perceptive account explaining why.

★ **Budgett Meakin** *The Land of the Moors* (ⓦarchive .org/details/landofmoorscompr00meak), *The Moors: A Comprehensive Description* (1902). Out of print but available online, these wonderful encyclopedic volumes were the first really detailed books on Morocco and Moroccan life.

Barnaby Rogerson (ed.) *Marrakech Through Writers' Eyes.* A feast of an anthology, ranging from the earliest accounts, through eighteenth- and nineteenth-century explorers and envoys, to contemporary writers such as Esther Freud and Juan Goytisolo.

Tahir Shah *The Caliph's House.* This is a terrific read: a funny, eccentric and insightful look at Casablanca, and Morocco as a whole, through the narrative of buying and restoring a house in the city.

Jeffrey Tayler *Valley of the Casbahs.* Tayler set out, in 2001, on a journey to trace the Drâa Valley from source to sea, on foot and by camel. His chief objective was to try to meet and understand the "Ruhhal" – the remaining desert nomads. The journey – one of the most compelling of modern accounts – left him by turns appalled and inspired.

HISTORY

J.M. Abun-Nasr *History of the Maghreb in the Islamic Period*. Morocco in the wider context of North Africa by a distinguished Arab historian.

Marvine Howe *Morocco: The Islamist Awakening and Other Challenges*. A former *New York Times* correspondent who had known the country since the 1950s, returns to live there in 1999. Her return coincides with the new king, Mohammed VI, and the rise of Islamic radicalism in the Arab world. She takes the story through to 2005.

★ **Gavin Maxwell** *Lords of the Atlas*. Drawing heavily on Walter Harris's accounts of the Moorish court (see opposite), this is the story of the Glaoui family – literally the "Lords" of the High Atlas, where they exercised almost complete control from the turn of the nineteenth century right through to Moroccan independence in 1956. Not an attractive tale but a compelling one, and superbly told. Originally published in 1966, it was republished in a superbly illustrated edition in 2000.

C.R. Pennell *Morocco from Empire to Independence*. This is the first general history of modern Morocco. It covers the

major strands of power but also the social and cultural life of ordinary Moroccans and is strong on the country's pressing contemporary concerns of poverty, drought and worsening agricultural land.

Douglas Porch *The Conquest of Morocco*. Accessible and fascinating account of the extraordinary manoeuvrings and characters in Morocco at the turn of the twentieth century.

Susan Raven *Rome in Africa*. A well-illustrated survey of Roman (and Carthaginian) North Africa.

Barnaby Rogerson *A Traveller's History of North Africa*. A good, up-to-date, general history, authoritative but very readable, covering not just Morocco, but also Tunisia, Algeria and Libya, which Rogerson sees as a kind of island, isolated by sea and desert, and thus set apart from Europe and sub-Saharan Africa.

David Woolman *Rebels in the Rif*. An academic but fascinating study of the Riffian war in the 1920s and of the tribes' uprising against the Moroccan government in 1956, unfortunately no longer in print.

ANTHROPOLOGY

Michael Brett and Elizabeth Fentress *The Berbers*. An overview of the Berber peoples of Morocco, Algeria and beyond, ranging through anthropology, history and literature.

Elizabeth Fernea *A Street in Marrakech*. A nicely written account of a woman anthropologist's study of and experiences in Marrakesh in the 1980s.

David Hart *Tribe and Society in Rural Morocco*. A collection of essays, dating from 1985 to 2000, around the

themes of tribalism and Berber identity in Morocco. More accessible than it sounds, with titles such as *Scratch a Moroccan, Find a Berber*.

Fatima Mernissi *Doing Daily Battle: Interviews with Moroccan Women*. Eleven women – carpet weavers, rural and factory workers, teachers – talk about all aspects of their lives, from work and housing to marriage. A fascinating insight into a normally very private world.

ISLAM

The Koran (translated by Arthur J. Arberry, Oxford University Press; translated by J.M Rodwell, o/p but on-line at ⓦ gutenberg.org/etext/2800). The word of God as proclaimed by Mohammed is notoriously untranslatable. Arberry's version attempts to preserve its poetic beauty and retains the traditional arrangement of suras (according to their length). Rodwell's 1861 translation is a little dated, but provides analytical footnotes, and was originally arranged, as far as possible,

in the order in which the suras were composed, making it easier to follow the development of ideas; unfortunately most modern editions of Rodwell's translation revert to the traditional order.

Seyyed Hossein Nasr *Ideals and Realities of Islam*. A good general introduction to the Islamic faith by an Iranian-born American academic, told from the point of view of a believer explaining his faith for the benefit of non-Muslim Westerners.

ART, ARCHITECTURE AND CRAFTS

James F. Jereb *Arts and Crafts of Morocco*. A fine introduction, with over 150 colour photographs.

Lisa Lovatt-Smith *Moroccan Interiors*. A coffee-table tome aimed at the interior design market, but goes beyond that in its coverage of traditional crafts, and traditional and modern architecture, with lots of gorgeous colour photographs.

Brooke Pickering et al *Moroccan Carpets*. Edited by a New York collector and dealer, this is the best book on

Moroccan carpets – a large format, fully illustrated guide, showing examples region by region.

Herbert Ypma *Morocco Modern*. A superbly illustrated book that traces the origins of the great artisan traditions of Morocco (weavers, woodworkers, potters, zellij-makers) and looks at the way contemporary designers and architects reinterpret these influences to create surprisingly modern work.

FOOD

Paula Wolfert *The Food of Morocco*. This is rather lavishly illustrated for a cookbook, but its rich mix of recipes, photographs and general discussion on the basics, principles and defining ingredients of Moroccan cooking, make it an excellent all-round primer. Wolfert's earlier and simpler *Couscous and Other Good Food from Morocco*, originally published in 1973, was the first Moroccan cookbook available in English, and remains among the best, with an emphasis on ordinary, rural cooking.

MOROCCAN FICTION/BIOGRAPHY

TRANSLATIONS BY PAUL BOWLES

By far the largest (and finest) body of Moroccan fiction published in English are the translations by the American writer Paul Bowles, who lived in Tangier from the 1940s until his death in 1999, and also translated the first part of Mohammed Choukri's autobiography (see below). The short stories share a common fixation with intrigue and unexpected narrative twists, and are often punctuated by episodes of violence. None have particular characterization, though this hardly seems relevant as they have such a strong, vigorous narrative style – brilliantly matched by Bowles' sharp, economic language.

Driss Ben Hamed Charhadi *A Life Full of Holes*. Bowles' first Moroccan translation – in 1964 – a direct narrative of street life in Tangier. It was published under a pseudonym, the author being Larbi Layachi who, two decades later, published *Yesterday and Today*, a kind of sequel, describing in semi-fictionalized (and not very sympathetic) form his time with Paul and Jane Bowles.

★ **Mohammed Mrabet** *Love with a Few Hairs; The Boy Who Set the Fire & Other Stories; The Lemon; M'Hashish; The Chest; Marriage With Papers; The Big Mirror; Harmless Poisons, Blameless Sins; The Beach Café and The Voice; Look and Move On: An Autobiography*. Mohammed Mrabet's stories – *The Beach Café* is perhaps his best – are often *kif*-inspired, which gives them a slightly paranoid quality, as Mrabet himself explained: "Give me twenty or thirty pipes…and an empty room can fill up with wonderful things, or terrible things. And the stories come from these things."

OTHER TRANSLATIONS

Abdelkader Benali *Wedding by the Sea*. Moroccan magic realism, and an impressive debut novel by a Moroccan-born author living in the Netherlands since childhood. The story is about a young man who returns (from Holland) to his seaside village in Morocco for his sister's wedding, and during the festivities finds the bridegroom has made off to the local brothel. Sweet revenge lies in store from his sister.

Mahi Binebine *Welcome to Paradise*. Binebine grew up in Morocco, lived in America and has now settled in France. This is his first book to be published in English and it is utterly engaging: a tale of life in the poorest areas of contemporary Morocco and the motivations that drive people to hand over all their savings to a trafficker to cross the Straits of Gibraltar and take their chances as illegals in Europe. Superbly translated and hugely evocative.

★ **Mohamed Choukri** *For Bread Alone* and *Streetwise*. Choukri's two-part autobiography (the first volume translated by Paul Bowles, the second by Ed Emery) ranks among the best works of contemporary Arabic literature. Born in the Rif, he moved with his family to Tangier at a time of great famine, spending his childhood in abject poverty. During his adolescence he worked for a time for a French family. He then returned to Tangier, where he experienced the violence of the 1952 independence riots. Throughout his adversities, two things shine through: Choukri's determination to use literacy to surmount his desperate circumstances; and his compassion for the normally despised human beings who share this life of "the lowest of the low".

Driss Chraibi *Heirs to the Past*. A benchmark novel, which takes the crisis of Moroccans' post-colonial identity as its theme. It is semi-autobiographical as the author-narrator (who has lived in France since the war) returns to Morocco for the funeral of his father. A number of other Chraibi novels are also available in translation.

Tahar Ben Jelloun *The Sand Child* and *Corruption*. The best of around a dozen books by Ben Jelloun that have been translated into English. *The Sand Child*, which won the prestigious Prix Goncourt, is the tale of a girl brought up in southern Morocco as a boy in order to thwart Morocco's inheritance laws. *Corruption*, as its title suggests, explores the endemic corruption in contemporary Morocco, through the story of Mourad, the last honest man in the country, who attempts to stay clear of brown envelopes in Casablanca and Tangier.

Fatima Mernissi *Dreams of Trespass: Tales of a Harem Girlhood*. Part fairy tale, part feminist manifesto, a mix of biographical narrative, stories and fantasies by a renowned Moroccan sociologist (author of *Doing Daily Battle*; see p.569), who was born in a Fez harem in 1940.

Brick Ousaïd *Mountains Forgotten by God*. Autobiographical narrative of an Atlas Berber family, which gives an impressive sense of the harshness of mountain life. As the author describes it, it is "not an exercise in literary style [but] a cry from the bottom of my heart, of despair and revolt".

FOREIGN FICTION & BIOGRAPHY SET IN MOROCCO

Once again, Paul Bowles is the outstanding figure in American and European fiction set in Morocco.

PAUL BOWLES

★ **NOVELS**: *The Sheltering Sky*; *Let It Come Down*; *The Spider's House*. **STORIES**: *Collected Stories of Paul Bowles 1939–76* gathers together work from numerous editions, as does the more selective *Collected Stories*. Post-1976 collections include *Midnight Mass* and *Unwelcome Words*. Bowles is the most interesting and the most prolific foreign writer using North African themes, and many of his stories are similar in vein to those of Mohammed Mrabet (see opposite), employing the same sparse forms, bizarre twists and interjections of violence. The novels are something different, exploring both Morocco and the ways in which Westerners react to it. If you read nothing else on the country, at least get hold of *The Spider's House* – one of the best political novels ever written, its backdrop the traditional daily life of Fez, its theme the conflicts and transformation at the last stages of the French occupation of the country.

The best of the biographies and memoirs of Bowles and his literary friends and acquaintances in Tangier are:

Michelle Green *The Dream at the End of the World: Paul Bowles and the Literary Renegades of Tangier*. A strong narrative, compulsively peopled: the best read if you're looking for one book on Tangier literary life.

Paul Bowles *Without Stopping*. Bowles' autobiography is of interest for its Moroccan episodes (though William Burroughs wryly dubbed it "Without Telling"), as is his *Two Years Beside the Strait* (published in US as *Days: A Tangier Journal, 1987–89*).

OTHER FICTION

William Burroughs *Naked Lunch*. This iconic Beat novel written in a Tangier hotel room in 1954–57 consists of a series of nightmarish sex-and-drugs-obsessed tableaux dreamed up by Burroughs while withdrawing from a heroin habit. It isn't especially about Morocco, but Tangier features as "Interzone", and is undoubtedly the place to read it.

Rafael Chirbes *Mimoun*. Compelling tale of a Spanish teacher, based south of Fez, adrift amid sexual adventures and bizarre local life and antagonisms.

Esther Freud *Hideous Kinky*. An English hippy takes her two daughters to Marrakesh, where they live simply, as locals. The narrative – funny, sad, and full of informed insights – is narrated by the 5-year-old.

John Haylock *Body of Contention*. An enjoyable romp set amid the expat community of Tangier in the months following Independence in 1957.

John Hopkins *All I Wanted Was Company*. A gossipy tale about an American in Tangier and his lovers, one of whom disappears to the Sahara. The author's *Tangier Diaries 1962–1979* document his time as an expat in Morocco's seediest city.

Jane Kramer *Honor to the Bride*. A fictional narrative based on a true story about a bride-to-be who is kidnapped, and her family's desperate struggle to get her respectably married off after such a disgrace.

Umberto Pasti *Age of Flowers*. An Italian novel set in Tangier at the end of the 1990s, with a decadent scene of writers and artists counterposed by the growing influence of Islamists in the streets.

Moroccan Arabic

Few people who come to Morocco learn to speak any Arabic, let alone anything of the country's three Berber languages, but you'll be treated very differently if you make even a small effort to master basic phrases. If you can speak French, you'll be able to get by almost anywhere. Spanish is also useful, especially among older people in the former Spanish colonial zones around Tetouan and the Rif, and in Ifni, Tarfaya and the Western Sahara. People who have significant dealings with tourists will know some English, but that is still a small minority.

Moroccan Arabic

Moroccan Arabic, the country's official language, is substantially different from classical Arabic, or from the modern Arabic spoken in Egypt or the Gulf. If you speak any form of Arabic, however, you should be able to make yourself understood. Egyptian Arabic, in particular, is familiar to most Moroccans from TV soaps. If you want to **learn Arabic** in Morocco, ALIF in Fez (see p.197) offer classes.

ARABIC/BERBER PHRASEBOOKS & LEARNING MATERIALS

ARABIC PHRASEBOOKS AND DICTIONARIES
Richard S. Harrell, Harvey Sobelman and Thomas Fox *A Dictionary of Moroccan Arabic* (Georgetown UP). Two-way Arabic–English dictionary.

ARABIC COURSEBOOKS
Abdellah Chekayri, *An Introduction to Moroccan Arabic and Culture* (Georgetown UP). A textbook and multimedia DVD which does pretty much what it says on the cover. It teaches you not only to speak, but also to read and write Arabic.
Aaron Sakulich, *Moroccan Arabic* (Collaborative Media International). Witty and engaging introduction to Moroccan Arabic with an emphasis on making learning fun.

BERBER COURSEBOOKS
Ernest T. Abdel Massih, *A Course in Spoken Tamazight* (Michigan UP). A coursebook with seven cassettes, out of print but can be found at a price. The same author's *A Reference Grammar of Tamazight* provides backup.

PRONUNCIATION

There are no silent letters – you pronounce everything that's written including double vowels. Letters and syllables in bold should be stressed. Here are some keys to follow:

kh	like the "ch" in Scottish lo*ch*	ou/oua	w/wa (Essaouria is pronounced Essa-weera)
gh	like the French "r" (a slight gargling sound)	q	like "k" but further back in throat
ai	as in *"eye"*	j	like "s" in pleasure
ay	as in "*say*"		

ARABIC AND FRENCH GLOSSARY

English	Arabic	French

BASICS AND EVERYDAY PHRASES

English	Arabic	French
yes	*eyeh, naam*	oui
no	*la*	non
I	*ena*	moi
you (m/f)	*enta/entee*	vous

he	*hoowa*	lui
she	*heeya*	elle
we	*nehnoo*	nous
they	*hoom*	ils/elles
(very) good	mezyen (*bzef*)	(très) bon
big	*kebeer*	grand
small	*segheer*	petit
old	*kedeem*	vieux
new	*jedeed*	nouveau
a little	*shweeya*	un peu
a lot	*bzef*	beaucoup
open	*mahlul*	ouvert
closed	*masdud*	fermé
hello/how's it going?	*le bes?*	ça va?
good morning	*sbah l'kheer*	bonjour
good evening	*msa l'kheer*	bon soir
good night	*leila saeeda*	bonne nuit
goodbye	*biselama*	au revoir
who...?	*shkoon...?*	qui...?
when...?	*imta...?*	quand...?
why...?	*alash...?*	pourquoi...?
how...?	*kifesh...?*	comment...?
which/what...?	*shnoo...?*	quel...?
is there...?	*kayn...?*	est-ce qu'il y a...?
do you have...?	*andak...?/kayn...*	avez-vous...?
please	*afak/minfadlak* to a man or *afik* */minfadlik* to a woman	s'il vous plaît
thank you	*shukran*	merci
ok/agreed	*wakha*	d'accord
that's enough/that's all	*safee*	ça suffit
excuse me	*ismahlee*	excusez-moi
sorry/ I'm very sorry	*ismahlee/ana asif*	pardon/je suis désolé
let's go	*nimsheeyoo*	on y va
go away	*imshee*	va t'en
I (m/f) don't understand	*mafahemsh/mafahmash*	je ne comprends pas
do you (m/f) speak English?	*takelem/takelmna ingleesi?*	parlez-vous anglais?

DIRECTIONS

where's...?	*fayn...?*	où est...?
the airport	*el matar*	l'aeroport
the train station	*mahattat el tren*	la gare de train
bus station	*mahattat el car*	la gare routière
the bank	*el bank*	le banque
the hospital	*el mostashfa*	l'hôpital
near/far (from here)	*qurayab/baeed (min huna)*	près/loin (d'ici)
left	*liseer*	à gauche
right	*limeen*	à droit
straight ahead	*neeshan*	tout droit
here	*hina*	ici
there	*hinak*	là

ACCOMMODATION

hotel	*funduq*	hôtel
do you have a room?	*kayn beet?*	avez-vous une chambre?
two beds	*jooj tlik*	deux lits
one big bed	*wahad tlik kebir*	un grand lit
shower	*doosh*	douche
hot water	*maa skhoona*	eau chaud
can I see?	*Mumkin ashoofha?*	je peux le voir?
key	*sarut*	clé

SHOPPING

I (don't) want...	*ena (mish) bgheet...*	je (ne) veux (pas)...
how much (money)?	*shahal (flooss)?*	combien (d'argent)?
(that's) expensive	*(hada) ghalee*	(c'est) cher

NUMBERS

0	*sifr*	zéro
1	*wahad*	un
2	*jooj*	deux
3	*tlata*	trois
4	*arbaa*	quatre
5	*khamsa*	cinq
6	*sitta*	six
7	*sebaa*	sept
8	*temanya*	huit
9	*tisaoud*	neuf
10	*ashra*	dix
11	*hadashar*	onze
12	*etnashar*	douze
13	*talatashar*	treize
14	*arbatashar*	quatorze
15	*khamstashar*	quinze
16	*sittashar*	seize
17	*sebatashar*	dix-sept
18	*tamantashar*	dix-huit
19	*tisatashar*	dix-neuf
20	*ashreen*	vingt
21	*wahad wa ashreen*	vingt-et-un
22	*jooj wa ashreen*	vingt-deux
30	*talateen*	trente
40	*arbaeen*	quarante
50	*khamseen*	cinqante
60	*sitteen*	soixante
70	*abaeen*	soixante-dix
80	*tamaneen*	quatre vingts
90	*tisaeen*	quatre-vingt-dix
100	*mia*	cent
121	*mia wa wahad wa ashreen*	cent vingt-et-un
200	*miateen*	deux cents
300	*tolta mia*	trois cents
1000	*alf*	mille

a half	nuss	demi
a quarter	roba	quart

DAYS AND TIMES

Monday	nahar el it neen	lundi
Tuesday	nahar et telat	mardi
Wednesday	nahar el arbaa	mercredi
Thursday	nahar el khemis	jeudi
Friday	nahar el jemaa	vendredi
Saturday	nahar es sabt	samedi
Sunday	nahar el had	dimanche
yesterday	imbarih	hier
today	el yoom	aujourd'hui
tomorrow	gheda	demain
what time is it?	shahal fisa'a?	quelle heure est-il?
one o'clock	sa'a wahda	une heure
2.15	jooj wa roba	deux heures et quart
3.30	tlata wa nuss	trois heures et demi
4.45	arbaa ila roba	quatre heures moins quart

FOOD AND DRINK

BASICS

restaurant	mataam	restaurant
breakfast	iftar	petit déjeuner
egg	beyd	ouef
butter	zibda	beurre
jam	marmalad	confiture
cheese	jibna	fromage
yoghurt	rayeb	yaourt
salad	salata	salade
olives	zitoun	olives
oil	zit	huile
bread	khobz	pain
salt	melha	sel
pepper	haroor	piment
without	bilesh	sans
sugar	sukkar	sucre
the bill	el hisaab	l'addition
fork	forshaat	fourchette
knife	mooss	couteau
spoon	malka	cuillère
plate	tabseel	assiete
glass	kess	verre
What do you have …	Ashnoo kane…	Qu'est ce que vous avez…
…to eat?	…f'l-makla?	…pour manger?
…to drink?	…f'l-mucharoubat?	…pour boire?
What is this?	Shnoo hada?	Qu'est ce que c'est?

I (m/f) am a vegetarian	*ana nabati/nabatiya wa la akulu lehoum wala hout*	Je suis vegetarien /vegetarienne
This is not what I asked for!	*Hedee meshee heea li tlubt!*	Ceci n'est pas ce que j'ai demandé
The bill, please.	*El hisaab, minfadlik*	L'addition s'il vous plaît
Please write it down.	*Minfadlik, k'tib'h*	Est-ce que vous pouvez l'écrite s'il vous plaît?

MEAT, POULTRY AND FISH

meat	*lahem*	viande
beef	*baqri*	boeuf
chicken	*jaj*	poulet
lamb	*houli*	mouton
liver	*kibda*	foie
pigeon	*hamam*	pigeon
fish	*hout*	poisson
prawns	*qambri*	crevettes

VEGETABLES

vegetables	*khadrawat*	légumes
artichoke	*qoq*	artichaut
aubergine	*badinjan*	aubergine
beans	*loobia*	haricots
onions	*basal*	oignons
potatoes	*batata*	patates
tomatoes	*mateesha*	tomates

FRUITS AND NUTS

almonds	*looz*	amandes
apple	*tufah*	pomme
banana	*banan*	banane
dates	*tmer*	dattes
figs	*kermooss*	figues
grapes	*ainab*	raisins
lemon	*limoon*	limon
melon	*battikh*	melon
orange	*limoon*	orange
pomegranate	*rooman*	granade
prickly pear (cactus fruit)	*hendiya*	figues de Barbarie
strawberry	*frowla*	fraise
watermelon	*dellah*	pastèque

BEVERAGES

water	*maa*	de l'eau
mineral water	*Sidi Ali/Sidi Harazem* (brand names)	eau minérale
ice	*jeleedi*	glace
ice cream	*glace*	glace
milk	*haleeb*	lait
coffee	*qahwa*	café
coffee with a little milk	*nuss nuss*	café cassé
coffee with plenty of milk	*qahwa bi haleeb*	café au lait/café crème

tea (with mint/with wormwood)	*atay (bi nana bi sheeba)*	thé (à la menthe/ à l'absinthe)
juice	*aseer*	jus
beer	*birra*	bière
wine	*sharab*	vin
almond milk	*aseer looz*	jus d'amande
apple milk shake	*aseer tufah*	jus de pomme
banana milk shake	*aseer banan*	jus des bananes
orange juice	*aseer limoon*	jus d'orange
mixed fruit milk shake		jus panaché

COMMON DISHES AND FOODS

bisara	thick pea soup, usually served with olive oil and cumin	pastilla	sweet pigeon or chicken pie with cinnamon and filo pastry; a speciality of Fez
chakchouka	a vegetable stew not unlike ratatouille, though some times containing meat or eggs	(pommes) frites	French fries
		salade Marocaine	salad of tomato and cucumber, finely chopped
couscous aux sept légumes	seven-vegetable couscous (sometimes vegetarian, though often made with meat stock)	tajine	a Moroccan casserole cooked over charcoal in a thick ceramic bowl (which is what the word really refers to) with a conical lid
harira	bean soup, usually also containing pasta and meat	tajine aux olives et citron	tajine of chicken with olive and preserved lemon
kefta	minced meat (usually lamb)	tanjia	a Marrakshi speciality, jugged beef – the term in fact refers to the jug
loobia	bean stew		
mechoui	roast lamb		
merguez	small, spicy dark red sausages – typically lamb, though sometimes beef – usually grilled over charcoal		

BREADS AND PASTRIES

briouats/doits de Fatima	sweet filo pastry with a savoury filling, a bit like a miniature pastilla	m'hencha	almond-filled pastry coils, often covered in honey or syrup
briouats au miel	sweet filo pastry envelopes filed with nuts and honey	millefeuille	custard slice
cornes de gazelles (Fr.)/ kab l-ghzal (Ar.)	marzipan-filled, banana-shaped pastry horns	msammen	flat griddle bread made from dough sprinkled with oil, rolled out and folded over several times, rather like an Indian paratha
harsha	flat, leavened griddle bread with a gritty crust, served at cafés for breakast		

Berber words and phrases in Tashelhaït

There are three Berber languages, which encompass roughly geographical areas. They are known by several names, of which these are the most common:
Tarfit, Riffi – The Rif mountains (Northern Morocco)
Tamazight, Zaian – The Middle and High Atlas (Central Morocco)
Tashelhaït, Soussi, Chleuh – The Anti-Atlas and Souss Valley (southern Morocco)
As the most popular Berber areas for visitors are the High Atlas and South, the following is a very brief guide to **Tashelhaït words and phrases**.

BASICS

Yes, no	Eyeh, Oho	Tomorrow	Sbah
Thank you, please	Barakalaufik	Yesterday	Eegdam
Good	Eefulkee/Eeshwa	Excuse me	Semhee
Bad	Khaib	Berbers	Shleuh
Today	Ghasad		

GREETINGS AND FAREWELLS (ALL ARABIC GREETINGS UNDERSTOOD)

Hello	La bes darik (man); La bes darim (woman) (response – la bes)	See you later	Akrawes dah inshallah
		Goodbye	Akayaoon Arbee
		Say hello to your family	Sellum flfamilenik
How are you?	Meneek antgeet? (response – la bes lmamdulah)		

DIRECTIONS AND NAMES ON MAPS

Where is…?	Mani heela…?
…the road to…	…aghares s…
…the village…	…doowar…
…the river…	…aseet…
…the mountain…	…adrar…
…the pass…	…tizee…
…your house	…teegimeenik
Is it far/close?	Ees yagoog/eeqareb?
Straight	Neeshan
To the right/left	Fofaseenik/fozelmad
Where are you going?	Manee treet? (s.)/Manee drem? (pl.)
I want to go to…	Reeh…(literally, "I want")

ON SURVEY MAPS YOU'LL FIND THESE NAMES:

Mountain	Adrar, Jebel
River	Assif, Oued
Pass (of)	Tizi (n.)
Shepherd's hut	Azib
Hill, small mountain	Aourir
Ravine	Talat
Rock	Azrou

("n" between words indicates the possessive," of")

BUYING AND NUMBERS

1	yen
2	seen
3	krad
4	koz
5	smoos
6	sddes
7	sa
8	tem
9	tza
10	mrawet
11	yen d mrawet
12	seen d mrawet
20	ashreent
21	ashreent d yen d mrawet
22	ashreent d seen d mrawet
30	ashreent d mrawet
40	snet id ashreent
50	snet id ashreent d mrawet
100	smoost id ashreent/meeya
How much is it?	Minshk aysker?
No good	Oor eefulkee

Too expensive	Eeghula bzef
Come down a little (in price)	Nuqs emeek
Give me…	Feeyee…
I want …	Reeh…
Big/Small	Mqorn/Eemzee
A lot/little	Bzef/eemeek
Do you have…?	Ees daroon…?
Is there…?	Ees eela…?
…food	…teeremt
…a mule	…aserdon
…a place to sleep	…kra lblast mahengwen
…water	…amen

IMPERATIVES YOU MAY HEAR

Gawer, Skoos	Sit
Soo	Drink
Shta	Eat
Rede	(when handing something to someone) Here

Glossary

Adhan The call to prayer

Agadir Fortified granary, where grain, dates, gunpowder and other valuables were kept safe during times of inter-clan conflict

Agdal Garden or park containing a pool

Aguelmane Lake

Aïn Spring

Aït Tribe (literally, "sons of")

Alaouite Ruling Moroccan dynasty from the seventeenth century to the present king, Mohammed VI

Almohad The greatest of the medieval dynasties, ruled Morocco (and much of Spain) from c.1147 until the rise to power of the Merenids c.1224

Almoravids Dynasty that preceded the Almohads, from c.1060 to c.1147

Amazigh Berber

Andalous Muslim Spain (a territory that centred on modern Andalusia)

Arabesque Geometrical decoration or calligraphy

Assif River (often seasonal) in Berber

Bab Gate or door

Babouches Slippers

Baladiya Town hall or local council

Bali Old

Baraka Sanctity or blessing, obtained through saints or *marabouts*

Barbary European term for North Africa in the sixteenth to nineteenth centuries

Beni Tribe (literally, "sons of")

Berbers Original inhabitants of Morocco and their descendants, particularly those whose first language is Berber (though most Moroccans claim to be at least partly Berber)

Bildi Country-style (of the *bled*)

Bled Countryside, or, literally "land"; **Bled es Makhzen** – governed lands; **Bled es Siba** – land outside government control

Borj Fort

Cadi is an Islamic judge

Caid District administrator

Chleuh Tashelhaït-speaking Atlas and Souss Valley Berbers

Col Mountain pass (French)

Dar House or palace; **Dar el Makhzen**, royal palace

Darj W Ktaf Literally "cheek and shoulder", an Almohad architectural motif resembling a fleur-de-lis

Daya, Deyet Lake

Erg Sand dune

Fakir Koranic schoolteacher or lawyer, or just an educated man

Fantasia Display of horsemanship performed at larger festivals or moussems

Fassi Inhabitant of Fez

Filali Alternative name for the Alaouite dynasty – from the southern Tafilalt region

Firdaous Paradise

Fondouk Inn and storehouse, known as a caravanserai in the eastern part of the Arab world

Gandoura Man's cotton garment (male equivalent of a kaftan); also known as a *fokia*

Gharb Coastal plain between Larache and Kenitra

Gnaoua Itinerant musician belonging to a brotherhood of West African origin (the name is from the same root as "Guinea")

Habbous Religious foundation or bequest of property for religious charities

Hadj Pilgrimage to Mecca

Hammada Stony desert of the sub-Sahara

Hammam Turkish-style steam bath

Harka "Burning" raid undertaken by sultans in order to raise taxes and assert authority

Idrissid First Arab dynasty of Morocco – named after its founder, Moulay Idriss

Imam Prayer leader and elder of mosque

Istiqlal Nationalist party founded during the struggle for independence

Jebel Mountain peak or ridge; a **Jebali** is someone from the mountains; the **Jebala** are the main tribe of the Western Rif

Jedid New

Jellaba Wool or cotton hooded outer garment

Jemaa, Jamaa Mosque, or Friday (the main day of worship)

Jinn Nature spirits (genies)

Joutia Flea market

Kasbah Palace centre and/or fortress of an Arab town; also used to mean a walled residential quarter around the Medina (eg Fez), or the citadel (eg Tangier and in Tunisia), or the whole Medina (eg Algiers). In the south of Morocco, it is a feudal family castle – and it's the root of the Spanish *alcazar*

Kedim Old

Khettara Underground irrigation canal

Kif Marijuana, cannabis

Koubba Dome; small *marabout* tomb

Ksar, Ksour (pl.) Village or tribal stronghold in the south

Lalla "Madam", also a saint

Litham Veil

Maghreb "West" in Arabic, used for Morocco and the North African countries

Maison d'hôte Guesthouse, usually upmarket

Makhzen Government

Marabout Holy man, and by extension his place of burial. These tombs, usually whitewashed domes, play an important (and heterodox) role in the religion of country areas

Mechouar Assembly place, court of judgment

Medersa Student residence and, in part, a teaching annexe, for the old mosque universities

Medina Literally, "city", now used for the original Arab part of any Moroccan town

Mellah Jewish quarter

Merenids Dynasty from eastern plains who ruled from the thirteenth to fifteenth century

Mihrab Niche indicating the direction of Mecca (and for prayer)

Minaret Tower attached to a mosque, used for call to prayer

Minbar The pulpit, usually placed next to the mihrab, from which the imam delivers his sermon at the midday Friday service in the mosque

Minzah Pavilion in a (usually palace) garden

Moulay Descendant of the Prophet Mohammed, a claim and title adopted by most Moroccan sultans

Mouloud Festival and birthday of the Prophet

Moussem Pilgrimage festival

Msalla Prayer area

Muezzin, Mueddin Singer who calls the faithful to prayer

Nazarene, Nsrani Christian, or, more loosely, a European

Oued (**wadi** in its anglicized form) River, but particularly a seasonal river or creek

Pisé Mud and rubble building material

Piste Unsurfaced road or track

PJD (Parti de la Justice et du Développement) Moderate Islamist political party, the largest party in Parliament

Protectorate period of French and Spanish colonial occupation (1912– 56)

Qahouaji Café *patron*

Qahwa Coffee or café

Ramadan Month of fasting (see p.43)

Ras Source or head

Ras el Ma Water source

Riad Patio garden, and by extension a house built around a patio garden; now also used to signify an upmarket guesthouse

Ribat Monastic fortress

Romi Urban, sophisticated – the opposite of *bildi* (see p.579)

Saadian Southern dynasty from Drâa Valley, who ruled Morocco during the fifteenth century

Sebgha Lake or lagoon

Sebsi Pipe for smoking *kif*

Seguia Irrigation canal

Sheikh Leader of religious brotherhood

Shereef Descendant of the Prophet

Sidi, Si Respectful title used for any man, like "Sir" or "Mister"; also a saint

Souk Market, or market quarter

Sufi Religious mystic; philosophy behind most of the religious brotherhoods

Tabia Mud building material, as *pisé*

Tighremt Similar to an agadir – fortified Berber home and storage place

Tizi Mountain pass

Touareg Nomadic Berber tribesmen of the disputed Western Sahara, fancifully known as "Blue Men" because of the blue dye of their cloaks (which gives a slight tinge to their skin)

UMA (Union du Maghreb Arabe) Regional association whose members are Morocco, Algeria, Tunisia, Libya and Mauritania

Wattasid Fifteenth-century dynasty who replaced their cousins, the Merenids

Zaouia Sanctuary established around a *marabout* tomb; seminary-type base for religious brotherhood

Zellij Geometrical mosaic tilework

Small print and index

A ROUGH GUIDE TO ROUGH GUIDES

Published in 1982, the first Rough Guide – to Greece – was a student scheme that became a publishing phenomenon. Mark Ellingham, a recent graduate in English from Bristol University, had been travelling in Greece the previous summer and couldn't find the right guidebook. With a small group of friends he wrote his own guide, combining a highly contemporary, journalistic style with a thoroughly practical approach to travellers' needs.

The immediate success of the book spawned a series that rapidly covered dozens of destinations. And, in addition to impecunious backpackers, Rough Guides soon acquired a much broader readership that relished the guides' wit and inquisitiveness as much as their enthusiastic, critical approach and value-for-money ethos.

These days, Rough Guides include recommendations from budget to luxury and cover more than 200 destinations around the globe, as well as producing an ever-growing range of eBooks and apps.

Visit **roughguides.com** to see our latest publications.

Rough Guide credits

Editor: Emma Gibbs
Layout: Ankur Guha
Cartography: Ashutosh Bharti
Picture editor: Mark Thomas
Proofreader: Karen Parker
Managing editor: Keith Drew
Assistant editor: Jalpreen Kaur Chhatwal
Photographer: Suzanne Porter
Production: Charlotte Cade
Cover design: Wilf Matos & Ankur Guha

Editorial assistant: Olivia Rawes
Senior pre-press designer: Dan May
Design director: Scott Stickland
Travel publisher: Joanna Kirby
Digital travel publisher: Peter Buckley
Reference director: Andrew Lockett
Operations coordinator: Becky Doyle
Publishing director (Travel): Clare Currie
Commercial manager: Gino Magnotta
Managing director: John Duhigg

Publishing information

This tenth edition published April 2013 by
Rough Guides Ltd,
80 Strand, London WC2R 0RL
11, Community Centre, Panchsheel Park,
New Delhi 110017, India
Distributed by the Penguin Group
Penguin Books Ltd,
80 Strand, London WC2R 0RL
Penguin Group (USA)
375 Hudson Street, NY 10014, USA
Penguin Group (Australia)
250 Camberwell Road, Camberwell,
Victoria 3124, Australia
Penguin Group (NZ)
67 Apollo Drive, Mairangi Bay, Auckland 1310,
New Zealand
Penguin Group (South Africa)
Block D, Rosebank Office Park, 181 Jan Smuts Avenue,
Parktown North, Gauteng, South Africa 2193
Rough Guides is represented in Canada by Tourmaline
Editions Inc. 662 King Street West, Suite 304, Toronto,
Ontario M5V 1M7
Printed in Singapore by Toppan Security Printing Pte. Ltd.

Help us update

We've gone to a lot of effort to ensure that the tenth
edition of **The Rough Guide to Morocco** is accurate and
up-to-date. However, things change – places get "discovered", opening hours are notoriously fickle, restaurants
and rooms raise prices or lower standards. If you feel we've
got it wrong or left something out, we'd like to know, and
if you can remember the address, the price, the hours, the
phone number, so much the better.

Please send your comments with the subject
line "**Rough Guide Morocco Update**" to ⊜mail
@uk.roughguides.com.
We'll credit all contributions and send a copy of the next
edition (or any other Rough Guide if you prefer) for the
very best emails.
Find more travel information, connect with fellow
travellers and book your trip on ⊛roughguides.com

Acknowledgements

Keith Drew would like to thank: Lionel Westerski;
Abdelfettah Seffar; Robert Johnstone; Kamal & Beatrice
Chaoui; Christine el Halaissi; Amine el Moumni; Hicham;
Boris Chabanis; Caroline Lecomte; Francoise & Jean Michel
Kurc; Roger Mimó; Moha Oubadi; Claire & Moulay Slimane
Tayebi; Rita Leitão; Michel & Colette Guillen; Catherine &
Ahmed Ayour; and everyone else who helped along the
way. Thanks, too, to the excellent team at Rough Guides,
especially to Kathryn, for giving me the gig; Ankur, for tight
typesetting; Ashutosh & Deshpal, for map magic; MT, for
sourcing some superb images; and to Emma, for erudite
editing and for keeping the whole show on the road. Most
of all, though, a huge and heartfelt thanks to my wife, Kate,
for her incredible support during a roller coaster of a trip

– and beyond; and to Maisie and Joe, for not being fazed
by Fez, and for charming the locals in every desert town
and mountain village we stopped off at along the way.

Daniel Jacobs: Thanks to the Délégation de Tourisme,
Agadir; Fatima and Hassan at the Hôtel Aday in Marrakesh;
Ahmed at the Hôtel Petite Suède in Agadir; Houssine
Laroussi at Coin des Nomades in Tafraoute; Haj Lahcen
Ben Abbou; Hmad Ouardarass of Tafraoute Aventure;
Mohammed Ouhammou Sahnoun; Mohammed Ameskal
and Hôtel Tioute in Taroudant.

Thomas Hollowell would like to thank Omer Jellah, Fazia
Farrook and Bob Diforio.

ABOUT THE AUTHORS

Daniel Jacobs is a Londoner who misspent his youth seeing the world (or as much if it as he could) before joining Rough Guides, who packed him off to places like Tunisia, Egypt, India and Mexico. Years down the line, he's still checking out hotels, restaurants and tourist sights across the globe, but spends his summer holidays in London.

Keith Drew has travelled in nearly sixty countries but has yet to visit another city quite as bewitching as Fez, or drive on mountain roads quite as hairy as the High Atlas's. Managing Editor at Rough Guides, he is also co-author of the *Rough Guide to Costa Rica* and, slightly closer to home, the *Rough Guide to Bath, Bristol & Somerset*.

Readers' letters

Thanks to all the readers who have taken the time to write in with comments and suggestions (and apologies if we've inadvertently omitted or misspelt anyone's name):

Jacqueline Bell, Richard Blagg, Eoin Brody, David Jazay, Francois Liegey, Patrick Mattison, Rowlie McBeath, Giovanni Robazza and Keith Ryan.

Photo credits

All photos © Rough Guides except the following:
(Key: t-top; c-centre; b-bottom; l-left; r-right)

p.1 Getty Images, Karen Su
p.2 Getty Images, Doug Pearson
p.4 Getty Images
p.8 Getty Images, Jed Share
p.9 Getty Images, Eric Nathan (br); Doug Pearson (bl)
p.11 Alamy, Hemis (b); Corbis, Alan Keohane (c)
p.12 Getty Images, David Sutherland
p.13 Alamy, Imagebroker (b)
p.14 Alamy, Focusphotographic
p.15 Alamy, WILDLIFE GmbH; PhotoPulp (br); Getty Images, Julian Love (bl)
p.16 Alamy, Rob Crandall (t)
p.17 Alamy, LOOK Die Bildagentur der Fotografen GmbH (t); Alamy, Barry Turner (cl); Alamy, Valerie Landrin (b)
p.18 Corbis, Jose Fuste Raga (c); Getty Images, Matthew Scholey (b); Terry Williams (t)
p.19 Alamy, Ian Dagnall
p.20 Alamy, Hemis (tl); Alamy, Tim Mossford (tr); Getty Images, Julian Love (b)
p.21 Alamy, Findlay
p.22 Alamy, The Photolibrary Wales
p.66 SuperStock, Photononstop
p.69 Alamy, Marek Zuk
p.89 Alamy, Peter Forsberg (t); Getty Images, Bruno Morandi (b)
p.119 Getty Images, Michele Falzone (t); Getty Images, Caroline von Tuempling (b)
p.124 Alamy, Chris Hellier

p.127 Alamy, Emanuele Ciccomartino
p.147 Corbis, Image Source
p.163 Alamy, Prisma Bildagentur
p.229 Alamy, Imagbroker
p.249 Alamy, Yadid Levy
p.289 Alamy, Danita Delimont (t)
p.313 Getty Images, Peter Phipp
p.356 Alamy, Kevin Foy
p.359 Alamy, LOOK Die Bildagentur der Fotografen GmbH
p.373 Alamy, PhotoAlto (t); Getty Images, Peter Phipp (b)
p.389 Keith Drew
p.415 Alamy: John Elk III
p.446 Alamy, Imagebroker
p.449 Alamy, Nicholas Pitt
p.465 Alamy, Aurora Photos
p.481 Alamy, Ian Dagnall (t); Alamy, Paul Thompson Images (b)
p.504 Alamy, Hemis
p.507 SuperStock, Photononstop
p.521 Alamy, Geoff Wiggins
p.528 Getty Images, Steve Casimiro

Front cover Sahara Desert © SuperStock/Axiom Photo Agency
Back cover Kasbah in desert oasis © Getty Images/Michele Falzone (t); Carpets © Axiom Photographic Agency/Chris Caldicott (bl); Detail of door, Mohamed V Mausoleum, Rabat © Getty Images/JD Dallet (br).

Index

Maps are marked in grey

Map symbols

The symbols below are used on maps throughout the book

✈	Airport	⌒	Arch	〰	Waterfall	♀	Church (regional maps)
★	Bus/taxi stop	🏰🏰	Fort/fortress	🌴	Oasis	⊡	Church (town maps)
P	Parking	⊠-⊠	Gate	⚓	Viewpoint	⌄	Mosque
⊃⊂	Bridge	⌢⌢	Mountain range	🕯	Lighthouse	□	Market
♦	Point of interest	▲	Peak	▮	Tower	◯	Stadium
@	Internet access	⌇	Rocks	⊏⊐	Ksar	▨	Building
ⓘ	Tourist office	⌇	Gorge	✕	Battle site	⬚	Park
✉	Post office	◖	Dune	✡	Synagogue	□	Beach
✚	Hospital	◠	Cave	⚰	Tomb	⬚	Christian cemetery
⊥	Gardens/fountain	∴	Ruins	⚟	Campsite	⬚	Jewish cemetery
⛽	Fuel station	⌂	Refuge hut	━━	Wall	⬚	Muslim cemetery
🏊	Swimming pool	//	Mountain pass	- - -	Ferry route	⬚	Saltpan

Listings key

- ■ Accommodation
- ● Restaurant/café
- ■ Bar/club
- ● Shop

Skala de la Ville
(woodworkers souk
below ramparts)

Museé Sidi
Mohammed
Ben Abdallah

Riad Alkantara

Riad Alkantara is an exceptional location within the walls of the medieval city of Fès; it is a hidden enchantment in the heart of a shaded area surrounded by 5 riads of different periods and architectural styles

The garden has a vast swimming pool surrounded by greenery and supplied with pure spring water, there are many fountains and patios, where you can relax and listen to the birds soothing singing.

At nightfall the delicate light breeze from the Atlas Mountains highlights the assorted fragrances of musk, jasmine and honeysuckle. The oriental sweetness and delicacy is revealed. In the vein of Italian theatre, the esplanades located at various levels are very well adapted to all types of events, whether cultural, artistic or just for amusement.

Riad Alkantara also has its lounge bar and smoking area on a shaded terrace, a restaurant where cuisine inspired from all over the world is served, traditional Moroccan cuisine which is served in the guest dining room, a shop selling traditional Moroccan clothes and decorative items, an exhibition area and creative workshops.

24, OUED SOUAFFINE • DOUH FES MEDINA • MAROC
TEL: 00 212 (0) 535 74 02 92 • FAX: 00 212 (0) 535 63 77 62 • CELL: 00 212 (0) 663 28 01 90
E-MAIL: FESRIADALKANTARA@GMAIL.COM • WWW.RIADALKANTARA.COM